Ideas in the News

Brought to you by **Houghton Mifflin**
In cooperation with MeansBusiness

W9-BZL-195

Houghton Mifflin and MeansBusiness bring you this FREE, biweekly **e-mail** newsletter in conjunction with your purchase of ***Management,*** Seventh Edition, by Ricky Griffin. In every issue we'll bring you instant access to new ideas from leading business thinkers and experts to help you define, evaluate, and improve your management learning.

MeansBusiness editors scan some 100 prominent magazines, newspapers, journals, and web sites in search of these top ideas, which are chosen for their originality, cogency, and relevance to today's rapidly changing economy.

Read on for a sample of the latest top ten business **ideas in the news** . . .

1 U.S. Economy Remains Largely Independent
— Robert M. Dunn, *The Washington Quarterly*

2 Friction-*Ful* Capitalism
— Gary Hamel, *Fortune*

3 Social Responsibility Indicates Good Management
— Frank Dixon and Karen M. Kroll, *Industry Week*

4 The Slow Burn of the Technology Market
— Vinod Khosla and Carleen Hawn, *Forbes*

5 Content Ownership Facilitates Knowledge Innovation
— Ranjit Singh, *Knowledge@Wharton*

6 When Layoffs Hurt Productivity
— Jon E. Hilsenrath and Jeff Bennett, *Wall Street Journal*

7 Stock Options: Cost or Benefit?
— Peter Coy, Brian J. Hall, and Kevin J. Murphy, *Business Week*

8 Gauging Online Communities Accurately
— Joseph Cothrel and Carolyn M. Brown, *Executive Edge*

9 Managing a Heterogeneous Workforce
— Lawrence A. West, Jr. and Walter A. Bogumil, Jr., *The Academy of Management: Executive*

10 Pay Attention to Gender for Effective Training
— Elisabeth Hayes and Ruth Palombo Weiss, *Training & Development*

To register
please see the URL under
the pull-off tab on the
cover of your new text.

Management

SEVENTH EDITION

Management

Ricky W. Griffin

Texas A & M University

Houghton Mifflin Company

Boston   New York

*As always, this is for Glenda—my constant source
of inspiration and the singularity of my life.*

Executive Editor: George T. Hoffman
Associate Editor: Damaris R. Curran
Senior Project Editor: Fred Burns
Senior Manufacturing Coordinator: Sally Culler
Marketing Manager: Steven W. Mikels

Cover illustration © Nicholas Wilton.

Photo credits may be found on page 729.

Printed in the U.S.A.

Library of Congress Control Number: 2001131500

ISBN: 0-618-11360-6

123456789—VH—05 04 03 02 01

Brief Contents

Contents

PART TWO

The Environmental Context of Management   66

3 The Environment of Organizations and Managers   68

4 The Ethical and Social Environment   100

8 Managing Strategy and Strategic Planning *226*

9 Managing Decision Making and Problem Solving *258*

PART FOUR

The Organizing Process 322

11 Basic Elements of Organizing 324

12 Managing Organization Design 354

13 Managing Organization Change and Innovation *384*

PART FIVE

The Leading Process *452*

19 Managing Work Groups and Teams   582

PART SIX

The Controlling Process   612

20 Basic Elements of Control   614

22 Managing Information and Information Technology *678*

APPENDIX

Tools for Planning and Decision Making *708*

Preface

Since the publication of its first edition in 1984, almost a million students have used *Management* in preparation for their careers in business. *Management* continues to be used in hundreds of universities, graduate programs, community colleges, and management development programs throughout the world. Indeed, the last edition of the book was used in over forty countries and translated into several foreign languages.

In this edition, I retained all the elements that have contributed to the book's success in the past while also taking a clear look toward the future—the future of business, of management, and of textbooks.

Writing a survey book poses a number of challenges. First, because it is a survey, it has to be comprehensive. Second, it has to be accurate and objective. Third, because management is a real activity, the book has to be relevant. Fourth, it has to be timely and up-to-date. And fifth, it needs to be as interesting and as engaging as possible. Feedback on previous editions of my text has always suggested that I have done an effective job of meeting these goals. In this edition, I think these goals have been met even more effectively.

I believe that previous users of *Management* will be pleased with how we retained the essential ingredients of a comprehensive management textbook while adding a variety of new elements and perspectives. I also believe that those new to this edition will be drawn to the solid foundations of management theory and practice, combined with new and exciting material.

Improvements in the Seventh Edition

The seventh edition of *Management* is a significant revision of the earlier work. Rather than simply adding the "hot topics" of the moment, I continued to thoroughly revise this book with the long-term view in mind. There are significant revisions of key chapters; an increased emphasis on the service sector, ethics, global management, and information technology; and a more integrated organization of chapters. These changes reflect what I, together with reviewers and employers, believe students will need to know as they enter a brand new world of management. In addition, several new pedagogical features such as "Managing in an E-business World" will also prove to be invaluable.

Integrated Coverage

Many books, including early editions of this text, set certain material off from the rest of the text. A separate section is often created at the end of the book called "emerging trends," "special challenges," or something similar. New and emerging topics, along with other material that doesn't easily fit anywhere else, are covered in that section. Unfortunately, by setting those topics apart in this way, the material often gets ignored or receives low-priority treatment.

I have chosen, however, to eliminate this material as a separate section. I decided that if this material was really worth having in the book at all, it needed to be fully integrated with the core material. Thus, all material has been integrated throughout the text in order to provide a more unified coverage of the entire field of management. This organization also helps to streamline the book's overall organization into six parsimonious and symmetrical parts. Because reviewers and students responded so favorably to this approach, it has been retained in the seventh edition. Further, more cross-referencing strengthens the integrated coverage throughout the text.

Improved Chapter Organization

This integrated approach to management also results in very effective chapter organization. Part One introduces the field of management, while Part Two focuses on the environment of management. The remaining four parts cover the basic managerial functions of planning and decision making, organizing, leading, and controlling.

New Material for a Brand New World of Management

A variety of topics are new to this edition, and coverage of other areas has been increased. In addition, new research and new examples have been integrated throughout the book. A few of the highlights are noted below:

Chapter 1, Managing and the Manager's Job An expanded managerial skills framework incorporates technical, interpersonal, conceptual, diagnostic, communication, decision-making, and time management skills.

Chapter 2, Traditional and Contemporary Issues and Challenges An expanded discussion of contemporary applied perspectives introduces the work of Senge, Covey, Peters, Porter, Kotter, and Adams. The section on contemporary management challenges was revamped. It introduces today's labor shortages, diversity, demography, change, technology, alternative models of organization, globalization, ethics and social responsibility, quality, and the service economy.

Chapter 4, The Ethical and Social Environment The section on individual ethics has been streamlined. New coverage of triggers for unethical behavior has been added. A new model for assessing ethical decisions was also added. A discussion of organizational constituents was reframed to reflect contemporary models of organizational stakeholders. And new terminology used to describe different approaches to social responsibility is now included.

Chapter 5, The Global Environment The discussion of developing economies was revised and recast as high potential/high growth economies. All data and statistics were updated. Coverage of cultural issues in international business was expanded.

Chapter 6, The Cultural and Multicultural Environment All data, statistics, and trends were updated.

Chapter 10, *Managing New Venture Formation and Entrepreneurship* Coverage of entrepreneurship and international management was expanded.

Chapter 12, *Managing Organization Design* Coverage of the team organization, the virtual organization, and the learning organization is included.

Chapter 14, *Managing Human Resources In Organizations* Coverage of change and human resource management was revamped. There is new coverage of the ADA and issues in managing high-skill workers.

Chapter 15, *Basic Elements of Individual Behavior In Organizations* Coverage of the "big five" model of personality is included. New coverage of affect and mood in organizations was added, as well as individual creativity in organizations.

Chapter 16, *Managing Employee Motivation and Performance* Coverage of the goal-setting theory of motivation is included. Coverage of new forms of working arrangements is also included.

Chapter 17, *Managing Leadership and Influence Processes* Coverage of impression management was added. There is also new coverage of the latest version of Vroom's decision-making model.

Chapter 18, *Managing Interpersonal Relations and Communication* Coverage of communication in teams was revised and reframed. Coverage of electronic communication is now included.

Chapter 21, *Managing Operations, Quality, and Productivity* The organization was improved by using operations management as a framework for introducing quality and productivity.

Chapter 22, *Managing Information and Information Technology* This chapter has been thoroughly revised, including new and expanded coverage of the Internet and corporate intranets.

In addition to these content revisions and additions, all in-text examples have been carefully reviewed and most have been replaced and/or updated.

Features of the Book

Basic Themes

Several key themes are prominent in this edition of *Management*. One theme is the global character of the field of management. It is reinforced throughout the book by examples and cases. Another key theme is information technology. While information technology is covered in detail in Chapter 22, it is also highlighted in boxed inserts in other chapters and is integrated into the text itself throughout the book. Still another theme is the balance of theory and practice. Managers need to have a sound basis for their decisions, but the theories that provide that basis must be grounded in reality. Throughout the book I explain the theoretical frameworks that guide managerial activities, and then I provide illustrations and examples of how and when those theories do and do not work. A fourth theme is that management is a generic activity not confined to large businesses. I use examples and discuss management in both small and large businesses as well as in not-for-profit organizations.

A Pedagogical System That Works

The pedagogical elements built into *Management*, Seventh Edition, continue to be effective learning and teaching aids for students and instructors.

- *Learning objectives and a chapter outline* serve to preview key themes at the start of every chapter as in the previous edition. *Key terms and concepts* are highlighted in boldface type, and many terms are defined in the margin next to where they are discussed. Effective *figures, tables,* and *photographs* with their own detailed captions help bring the material to life.

- Another exciting feature is called *Management Implications*. Each major section in every chapter concludes with a highlighted paragraph that clearly and succinctly reminds the reader of the specific application value of the preceding discussion.

- Three kinds of questions are found at the end of every chapter, designed to test different levels of student understanding. *Questions for Review* ask students to recall specific information; *Questions for Analysis* ask students to integrate and synthesize material; and *Questions for Application* ask students to apply what they've learned to their own experiences.

- Each chapter also concludes with three useful *skill-development exercises.* These exercises give students insights into how they approach various management situations and how they can work to improve their management skills in the future. The exercises are derived from the overall managerial skills framework developed in Chapter 1.

Applications That Keep Students Engaged

To fully appreciate the role and scope of management in contemporary society, it is important to see examples and illustrations of how concepts apply in the real world. I rely heavily on fully researched examples to illustrate real-world applications. They vary in length, and all were carefully reviewed for their timeliness. To give the broadest view possible, I vary examples of traditional management roles with nontraditional roles; profit-seeking businesses with nonprofits; large corporations with small businesses; manufacturers with services; and international examples with U.S. examples. Other applications include:

- *Opening incidents at the beginning of every chapter.* These brief vignettes draw the student into the chapter with a real-world scenario that introduces a particular management theme. Most opening incidents were revised for this edition.

■ Each chapter also includes three or four boxed features. These boxes are intended to briefly depart from the flow of the chapter to highlight or extend especially interesting or emerging points and issues. Altogether there are five different featured boxes represented throughout the text:

 "Managing in an E-business World"
(the increasing role of E-commerce)

 "Management InfoTech"
(new technology and its role in management)

 "Today's Management Issues"
(current controversies, challenges, and dilemmas facing managers)

 "Working with Diversity"
(the role of diversity in organizations)

 "The World of Management"
(global issues in management)

■ *End-of-chapter cases.* Each chapter concludes with a detailed case study. Virtually all the cases in the seventh edition are new and have been especially written for this book.

An Effective Teaching and Learning Package

■ *Instructor's Resource Manual* (Margaret Hill, Texas A&M University). This resource includes suggested class schedules and detailed teaching notes for every chapter. These notes include chapter summaries; learning objectives; detailed chapter lecture outlines, including opening incident summaries, highlighted key terms, teaching tips, group exercise ideas, and references to the transparencies; responses to review, analysis, and case questions; and information to help facilitate the skills development exercises. Teaching guides to accompany the video cases are also included.

■ *Test Bank* (Betty M. Pritchett and Thomas K. Pritchett, Kennesaw State University). Well over 4,000 test items have been carefully and substantially revised for the seventh edition. The *Test Bank* includes true/false, multiple-choice, completion, matching, and essay questions. Each type of question is identified as a definition or fact (DEF), a concept or term relating to real-life incidences (APP), or a denotative understanding of a term or concept (COMP).

■ *HMTesting.* This electronic version of the printed *Test Bank* allows instructors to generate and change tests easily. The program includes an on-line testing feature by which instructors can administer tests via their local area network or over the Web. It also has a gradebook feature that lets users set up classes, record and track grades from tests or assignments, analyze grades, and produce class and individual statistics.

■ *HM ClassPrep™ CD-ROM* is designed to assist the instructor with in-class lectures. The CD includes Lecture Outlines, Chapter Outlines, Learning Objectives, PowerPoint slides, including text art, and the Student CD's Knowledgebank.

■ *Color Transparencies.* There are 130 full-color transparencies that illustrate every major topic in the text. The package consists of several key figures from the book as well as new materials that can be used to enrich classroom discussions. Four types of transparencies are included. *Chapter Text* transparencies reproduce key chapter figures. *Chapter Enrichment* transparencies provide images not in the text that will enhance chapter material. *Text Transition* transparencies introduce material in each of the six parts. *Supplemental Resource* transparencies provide general information that can be used when and as the instructor chooses.

■ *Video Package.* An expanded, professionally developed video case collection is available with the Seventh Edition, and supplementary video case material can be found in the Instructor's Resource Manual. These videos explore various aspects of the management process.

■ *Blackboard Course Cartridges.* This online course allows flexible, efficient, and creative ways to present learning materials and opportunities. In addition to course management benefits, instructors may make use of an electronic grade book, receive papers from students enrolled in the course via the Internet, and track student use of the communication and collaboration functions.

■ *WebCT e-Packs.* This on-line course provides instructors with a flexible, Internet-based education platform. These Internet-based e-Packs provide multiple ways to present learning materials. The WebCT e-Packs come with a full array of features to enrich the on-line learning experience.

■ *Web Site.* This site offers valuable information for both students and instructors. For students, the site includes ACE, management skills assessments, ready notes, flash cards, term paper help, related web resources, learning objectives, outlines, and company links. For instructors, PowerPoint slides, lecture outlines, and the instructor resources for Exercises in Management are available.

■ *Study Guide* (Joseph Thomas, Middle Tennessee State University). The *Study Guide* has been revised to optimize student comprehension of definitions, concepts, and relationships presented in the text. Each chapter contains an expanded chapter outline to facilitate note taking, multiple-choice and true/false questions, and targeted questions that ask students to integrate material from lectures and the text. Annotated answers appear at the end of the *Study Guide*.

■ *Student CD-ROM.* This CD has been carefully tailored to supplement and enhance the content of the text. The Knowledgebank, a feature new to the Seventh Edition, offers more information about various topics in the text. It can be used to gain additional management knowledge or for a research project, and it can be found only on the Student CD. In addition, the CD also includes Chapter Outlines, Company Web Links, a Glossary, Learning Objectives, Ready Notes, Self-Assessment exercises, and Chapter Summaries.

■ *Real Deal Upgrade CD-ROM.* This CD will replace the Student CD in December 2001. It will contain the material found on the Student CD, as well as additional Knowledgebank information and selected videos.

■ *Exercises in Management.* This student manual provides experiential exercises for every chapter. The overall purpose of each exercise is given, along with the time required for each step, the materials needed, the procedure to be followed, and questions for discussion.

■ *Manager: A Simulation,* Third Edition. This business simulation, developed by the successful team of Jerald R. Smith and Peggy Golden (Florida Atlantic University), allows student players to make business decisions through simulated real-world experiences. It presents cross-functional decisions about the operation of an organization in the home stereo industry. Acting as management teams, students encounter many factors as they tackle each phase of the business. Ongoing decisions include areas of pricing, advertising, quality control, cash flow, market research, and inventory management. Support materials are provided for instructors.

■ *The Ultimate Job Hunter's Guidebook,* Third Edition. This practical, how-to handbook by Susan Greene (Greene Marketing and Advertising) and Melanie Martel (New Hampshire Technical Institute) is a concise manual containing abundant examples, practical advice, and exercises related to each of the job hunter's major tasks: conducting self-assessment, preparing resumés and cover letters, targeting potential employers, obtaining letters of recommendation, filling out job applications, interviewing, and starting a new job. The guide also covers current topics of interest such as online job hunting, handling rejection, networking, evaluating job offers, negotiating salary, and looking ahead to future opportunities. It also includes numerous success stories to inspire students.

I would also like to invite your feedback on this book. If you have any questions, suggestions, or issues to discuss, please feel free to contact me. The most efficient way to reach me is through e-mail. My address is rgriffin@tamu.edu.

R.W.G.

Acknowledgments

I am frequently asked by my colleagues why I write textbooks, and my answer is always, "Because I enjoy it." I've never enjoyed writing a book more than this one. For me, writing a textbook is a challenging and stimulating activity that brings with it a variety of rewards. My greatest reward continues to be the feedback I get from students and instructors about how much they like this book.

I owe an enormous debt to many different people for helping me create *Management*. My colleagues at Texas A&M have helped create a wonderful academic climate. The rich and varied culture at Texas A&M makes it a pleasure to go to the office every day. My assistant, Phyllis Washburn, deserves special recognition for putting up with me and making me look good.

The fine team of professionals at Houghton Mifflin has also been instrumental in the success of this book. Sponsoring editor George Hoffman and associate editor Damaris Curran each had a major role in the development and creation of this edition of *Management*. Fred Burns and Marcy Kagan were also instrumental in the production of this edition.

Many reviewers have played a critical role in the evolution of this project. They reviewed my work with a critical eye and in detail. I would like to tip my hat to the following reviewers, whose imprint can be found throughout this text:

Ramon J. Aldag
University of Wisconsin

Dr. Raymond E. Alie
Western Michigan University

William P. Anthony
Florida State University

Jeanne Aurelio
Stonehill College

Jay B. Barney
Ohio State University

Richard Bartlett
Muskigum Area Technical College

John D. Bigelow
Boise State University

Allen Bluedorn
University of Missouri

Henry C. Bohleke
Tarrant County College

Marv Borglett
University of Maryland

Gunther S. Boroschek
University of Massachusetts— Harbor Campus

Gerald E. Calvasina
University of North Carolina, Charlotte

Joseph Cantrell
DeAnza College

George R. Carnahan
Northern Michigan University

Ron Cheek
University of New Orleans

Thomas G. Christoph
Clemson University

Charles W. Cole
University of Oregon

Elizabeth Cooper
University of Rhode Island

Carol Cumber
South Dakota State University

Joan Dahl
California State University, Northridge

Carol Danehower
University of Memphis

Satish Deshpande
Western Michigan University

Gregory G. Dess
University of Kentucky

Gary N. Dicer
University of Tennessee

Nicholas Dietz
State University of New York— Farmingdale

Thomas J. Dougherty
University of Missouri

Shad Dowlatshahi
University of Wisconsin—Platteville

John Drexler, Jr.
Oregon State University

Stan Elsea
Kansas State University

Douglas A. Elvers
University of South Carolina

Jim Fairbank
West Virginia University

Dan Farrell
Western Michigan University

Gerald L. Finch
Universidad Internacional del Ecuador and Universidad San Francisco de Quito

Charles Flaherty
University of Minnesota

Ari Ginsberg
New York University Graduate School of Business

Norma N. Givens
Fort Valley State University

Carl Gooding
Georgia Southern College

George J. Gore
University of Cincinnati

Jonathan Gueverra
Lesley College

Stanley D. Guzell, Jr.
Youngstown State University

John Hall
University of Florida

Mark A. Hammer
Washington State University

Barry Hand
Indiana State University

Paul Harmon
University of Utah

John Hughes
Texas Tech University

J. G. Hunt
Texas Tech University

John H. Jackson
University of Wyoming

Neil W. Jacobs
University of Denver

Arthur G. Jago
University of Missouri

Madge Jenkins
Lima Technical College

Gopol Joshi
Central Missouri State University

Norman F. Kallaus
University of Iowa

Ben L. Kedia
University of Memphis

Thomas L. Keon
University of Central Florida

Charles C. Kitzmiller
Indian River Community College

William R. LaFollete
Ball State University

Kenneth Lawrence
New Jersey Institute of Technology

Clayton G. Lifto
Kirkwood Community College

John E. Mack
Salem State University

Myrna P. Mandell, Ph.D.
California State University, Northridge

Patricia M. Manninen
North Shore Community College

Thomas Martin
University of Nebraska—Omaha

Barbara J. Marting
University of Southern Indiana

Wayne A. Meinhart
Oklahoma State University

Melvin McKnight
Northern Arizona University

Aratchige Molligoda
Drexel University

Linda L. Neider
University of Miami

Mary Lippitt Nichols
University of Minnesota

Winston Oberg
Michigan State University

Michael Olivette
Syracuse University

Eugene Owens
Western Washington University

Sheila Pechinski
University of Maine

Monique Pelletier
San Francisco State University

E. Leroy Plumlee
Western Washington University

Raymond F. Polchow
Muskigum Area Technical College

Paul Preston
University of Texas—San Antonio

John M. Purcell
State University of New York— Farmingdale

James C. Quick
University of Texas—Arlington

Ralph Roberts
University of West Florida

Nick Sarantakas
Austin Community College

Gene Schneider
Austin Community College

H. Schollhammer
University of California— Los Angeles

Diane R. Scott
Wichita State University

Harvey Shore
University of Connecticut

Marc Siegall
California State University

Nicholas Siropolis
Cuyahoga Community College

Michael J. Stahl
University of Tennessee

Charlotte D. Sutton
Auburn University

Robert L. Taylor
University of Louisville

Mary Thibodeaux
University of North Texas

Joe Thomas
Middle Tennessee State University

Robert D. Van Auken
University of Oklahoma

Fred Williams
University of North Texas

James Wilson
University of Texas—Pan American

Carl P. Zeithaml
University of Virginia

I would also like to make a few personal acknowledgments. The fine work of Elton John, Phil Collins, Lyle Lovett, Johnny Rivers, and the Nylons helped me make it through many late evenings and early mornings of work on the manuscript that became the book you hold in your hands. And Stephen King, Tom Clancy, James Lee Burke, Peter Straub, and Carl Barks provided me with a respite from my writings with their own.

Finally, there is the most important acknowledgment of all—my feelings for and gratitude to my family. My wife, Glenda, and our children, Dustin and Ashley, are the foundation of my professional and personal life. They help me keep work and play in perspective and give meaning to everything I do. It is with all my love that I dedicate this book to them.

R.W.G.

Management

An Introduction to Management

CHAPTER 1

Managing and the Manager's Job

CHAPTER 2

Traditional and Contemporary Issues and Challenges

1 Managing and the Manager's Job

Motorola can trace its roots back to 1928, when Paul Galvin started a small business making electronic products and parts. The firm grew rapidly in the 1940s when it first began making automobile radios and then televisions. In 1947 Galvin renamed the company Motorola after the brand name it was using on its car radios. As time passed, and under the leadership of Robert Galvin, the founder's son, Motorola branched out into increasingly diverse product areas and by the 1980s had become one of the world's largest and most successful electronic enterprises.

In the early 1990s, with a new leadership team at the helm, Motorola was a leader in semiconductors, data communications, and cellular telephone technology. It was also renowned for its quality, winning the first Malcolm Baldrige U.S. National Quality Award in 1988. By the mid-1990s, however, Motorola was on a downward spiral that seemed irreversible. A series of managerial blunders, poorly conceived plans, and plain old bad luck had cost the firm dearly—it had lost its preeminence in the marketplace, had lost touch with its customers, and was taking heat for shoddy product and service quality.

For one thing, Motorola fell behind in digital telephone technology and lost crucial market leadership to Finland's Nokia Group. The semiconductor market also shifted, leaving the firm's semiconductor business poorly positioned for new technologies and areas of new growth potential. Moreover, because the firm did about 24 percent of its business in Asia, the currency crisis that wracked that continent also hit Motorola hard. And a $6 billion iridium communications satellite system that the company invented, financed, and helped build missed its launch date, failed to attract customers, and eventually had to file for bankruptcy protection.

Finally, in 1997 Motorola's board had seen enough. It fired the company's CEO and installed Christopher Galvin, the founder's grandson, in the top spot. Galvin, meanwhile, knew the firm was in dire straits but was a bit unsure where even to begin to start to rebuild the firm. In late 1997 and 1998, the company really hit rock bottom and analysts were writing it off as an also-ran, and a few were quietly already questioning whether or not Galvin had the same managerial skills as his father and grandfather. By that time, though, Galvin had figured out what to do and reconciled both himself and other top managers to the hard realities they faced.

> *"This is a journey, not a destination."*
>
> —Christopher Galvin, CEO of Motorola and chief architect of the firm's amazing turnaround.

After studying this chapter, you should be able to:

◼ Describe the nature of management, define management and managers, and characterize their importance to organizations.

◻ Identify and briefly explain the four basic management functions in organizations.

◼ Describe the kinds of managers found at different levels and in different areas of the organization.

◼ Identify the basic managerial roles that managers may play and the skills they need to be successful.

◼ Discuss the science and the art of management and describe how people become managers.

◼ Summarize the scope of management in organizations.

Over a period of the next several months Galvin refocused the business on its core strengths, selling off numerous underperforming and peripheral operations. He also renewed Motorola's commitment to innovation and new product development and made marketing a much higher priority than at any time in the firm's history. As part of these changes, Galvin also revamped how the firm was organized, eliminating managerial in-fighting and fiefdoms that had built up over decades. He also played a key inspirational role as well, rallying employees behind the firm's revitalization efforts and encouraging them to develop bold new ideas and to think in different ways. But he also made tough decisions when he had to, cutting 15,000 jobs at one point.

And the result? Motorola has indeed turned itself around and is once again at the forefront of its industry. For example, quality has again become a watchword at Motorola, analysts are promoting Motorola stock, and the company's products are again market leaders.

But Galvin isn't finished yet. In his own words, "This is a journey, not a destination." He plans to continue refining and developing the company to make it even more effective. He has grand visions for the future, visions filled with amazing new products, technologies, and services. And Galvin sees the name "Motorola" emblazoned across this future technology landscape.[1]

5

Christopher Galvin is clearly a manager. So, too, are Philip Knight (CEO of Nike), Carly Fiorina (CEO of Hewlett-Packard), Mikio Sasaki (president of Mitsubishi Corp.), Sir David Wilson (director of the British Museum), Debbie Fields (president of Mrs. Fields Inc. cookie stores), Joe Torre (coach of the New York Yankees), George W. Bush (President of the United States), Jeff Bezos (CEO of Amazon.com), John Paul II (pope of the Roman Catholic Church), and Marilyn Ferguson (owner of the Garden District Gift Shop in Bryan, Texas). As diverse as they and as their organizations are, all of these managers are confronted by many of the same challenges, they strive to achieve many of the same goals, and they apply many of the same concepts of effective management in their work.

For better or worse, our society is strongly influenced by managers and their organizations. Most people in the United States are born in a hospital (an organization), educated by public or private schools (all organizations), and buy almost all their consumable products and services from businesses (organizations). And much of our behavior is influenced by various government agencies (also organizations). We define an **organization** as a group of people working together in a structured and coordinated fashion to achieve a set of goals. The goals may include such things as profit (Starbucks Corporation), the discovery of knowledge (Iowa State University), national defense (the U.S. Army), coordination of various local charities (United Way of America), or social satisfaction (a sorority). Because they play such a major role in our lives, understanding how organizations operate and how they are managed is important.

organization A group of people working together in a structured and coordinated fashion to achieve a set of goals

This book is about managers and the work they do. In Chapter 1, we examine the general nature of management, its dimensions, and its challenges. We explain the concepts of management and managers, discuss the management process and present an overview of the book, and identify various kinds of managers. We describe the different roles and skills of managers, discuss the nature of managerial work, and examine the scope of management in contemporary organizations. In Chapter 2 we describe how both the practice and theory of management have evolved. As a unit, then, these first two chapters provide an introduction to the field with both contemporary and historical perspectives on management.

An Introduction to Management

While defining "organization" is relatively simple, the concept of "management" is a bit more elusive. It is perhaps best understood from a resource-based perspective. As we discuss more completely in Chapter 2, all organizations use four basic kinds of resources from their environment: human, financial, physical, and information. Human resources include managerial talent and labor. Financial resources are the capital used by the organization to finance both ongoing and long-term operations. Physical resources include raw materials, office and production facilities, and equipment. Information resources are usable data needed to make effective decisions. Examples of resources used in four very different kinds of organizations are shown in Table 1.1.

Table 1.1

Examples of Resources Used by Organizations

All organizations, regardless of whether they are large or small, profit-seeking or not-for-profit, domestic or multinational, use some combination of human, financial, physical, and information resources to achieve their goals. These resources are generally obtained from the organization's environment.

Organization	Human Resources	Financial Resources	Physical Resources	Information Resources
Shell Oil	Drilling platform workers Corporate executives	Profits Stockholder investments	Refineries Office buildings	Sales forecasts OPEC proclamations
Iowa State University	Faculty Administrative staff	Alumni contributions Government grants	Computers Campus facilities	Research reports Government publications
New York City	Police officers Municipal employees	Tax revenue Government grants	Sanitation equipment Municipal buildings	Economic forecasts Crime statistics
Susan's Corner Grocery Store	Grocery clerks Bookkeeper	Profits Owner investment	Building Display shelving	Price lists from suppliers Newspaper ads for competitors

Managers are responsible for combining and coordinating these various resources to achieve the organization's goals. A manager at Royal Dutch/Shell Group, for example, uses the talents of executives and drilling platform workers, profits earmarked for reinvestment, existing refineries and office facilities, and sales forecasts to make decisions regarding the amount of petroleum to be refined and distributed during the next quarter. Similarly, the mayor (manager) of New York City might use police officers, a government grant (perhaps supplemented with surplus tax revenues), existing police stations, and detailed crime statistics to launch a major crime prevention program in the city.

How do these and other managers combine and coordinate the various kinds of resources? They do so by carrying out four basic managerial functions or activities: planning and decision making, organizing, leading, and controlling. **Management**, then, as illustrated in Figure 1.1, can be defined as a set of activities (including planning and decision making, organizing, leading, and controlling) directed at an organization's resources (human, financial, physical, and information) with the aim of achieving organizational goals in an efficient and effective manner.

Management is a complex, challenging, and exciting process. Rapid changes in today's business environment make it imperative that managers stay abreast of business opportunities and trends. Catherine Rodriguez, for example, is the training manager at Cisco System's plant in San Jose. Key components of her job include knowing the latest technology, designing instructional content, and assisting others in using advanced training methods to improve their own job performance. She is shown here helping an assembler master electronic learning. About 90 percent of all of Cisco's training is handled through electronic media.

Figure 1.1

Management in Organizations

Basic managerial activities include planning and decision making, organizing, leading, and controlling. Managers engage in these activities to combine human, financial, physical, and information resources efficiently and effectively and to work toward achieving the goals of the organization.

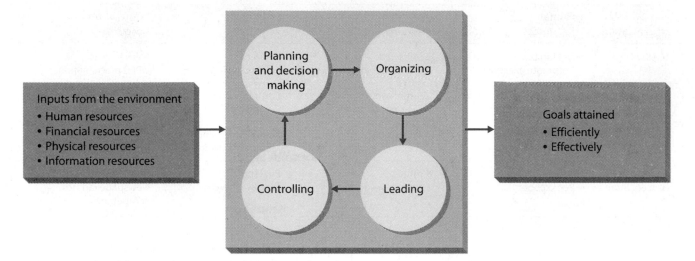

management A set of activities (including planning and decision making, organizing, leading, and controlling) directed at an organization's resources (human, financial, physical, and information) with the aim of achieving organizational goals in an efficient and effective manner

efficient Using resources wisely and in a cost-effective way

effective Making the right decisions and successfully implementing them

manager Someone whose primary responsibility is to carry out the management process

The last phrase in our definition is especially important because it highlights the basic purpose of management—to ensure that an organization's goals are achieved in an efficient and effective manner. By **efficient**, we mean using resources wisely and in a cost-effective way. For example, a firm like Toyota Motor Corp. that produces high-quality products at relatively low costs is efficient. By **effective**, we mean making the right decisions and successfully implementing them. Toyota also makes cars with the styling and quality to inspire consumer interest and confidence. A firm could produce black-and-white console televisions very efficiently but still not succeed because black-and-white televisions are no longer popular. A firm that produces products that no one wants is therefore not effective. In general, successful organizations are both efficient and effective.[2]

With this basic understanding of management, defining the term *manager* becomes relatively simple—a **manager** is someone whose primary responsibility is to carry out the management process. In particular, a manager is someone who plans and makes decisions, organizes, leads, and controls human, financial, physical, and information resources. Today's managers face a variety of interesting and challenging situations. The average executive works sixty hours a week, has enormous demands placed on his or her time, and faces increased complexities posed by globalization, domestic competition, government regulation, shareholder pressure, and Internet-related uncertainties. The job is complicated even more by rapid changes, unexpected disruptions, and both minor and major crises. The manager's job is unpredictable and fraught with challenges, but it is also filled with opportunities to make a meaningful difference.

Many of the characteristics that contribute to the complexity and uncertainty of management stem from the environment in which their organizations function. For example, as shown in Figure 1.1, the resources used by organizations to create products and services all come from the environment. Thus, it is critical that managers understand this environment. Part II of the text discusses the environmental context of management in detail. Chapter 3 provides a general overview and discussion of the organization's environment, and Chapters 4 through 6 address specific aspects of the environment more fully. In particular, Chapter 4 discusses the ethical and social context of management. Chapter 5 explores the global context of management. Chapter 6 describes the cultural and multicultural environment of management. After reading these chapters, you will be better prepared to study the essential activities that comprise the management process.

The Management Process

We noted earlier that management involves the four basic functions of planning and decision making, organizing, leading, and controlling. Because these functions represent the framework around which this book is organized, we introduce them here and note where they are discussed more fully. Their basic definitions and interrelationships are shown in Figure 1.2. (Note that Figure 1.2 is an expanded version of the central part of Figure 1.1.)

Recall the details of Motorola's turnaround discussed earlier. Christopher Galvin first created a clear set of goals and plans that articulated what he wanted the company to become. He also created a more effective organization to help make those goals and plans a reality. Galvin also pays close attention to the people who work for Motorola. And he keeps a close eye on how well the company is performing. Each of these activities represents one of the four basic managerial functions illustrated in the figure—setting goals is part of planning, setting up the organization is part of organizing, managing people is part of leading, and monitoring performance is part of control. *Managing in an E-business World* summarizes how managers at one company, United Parcel Service, are also using these same functions as they move the company more and more into the world of electronic commerce.

It is important to note, however, that the functions of management do not usually occur in a tidy, step-by-step fashion. Managers do not plan on Monday, make

Figure 1.2

The Management Process

Management involves four basic activities—planning and decision making, organizing, leading, and controlling. Although there is a basic logic for describing these activities in this sequence (as indicated by the solid arrows), most managers engage in more than one activity at a time and often move back and forth between the activities in unpredictable ways (as shown by the dotted arrows).

MANAGING IN AN *e*-BUSINESS WORLD

MANAGING E-COMMERCE DELIVERIES

When a consumer clicks to make a purchase on-line, United Parcel Service (UPS) wants to deliver the package. Because other shippers are also jockeying for position in e-commerce delivery, UPS's managers will need skillful planning, organizing, leading, and controlling to stay ahead of the pack.

UPS ships more than half of all consumer e-commerce purchases, while the U.S. Postal Service ships about one-third and FedEx ships just one-tenth. But all three companies want more of this fast-growing market, which could top 4.2 million packages daily within a few years.

Knowing that the stakes are high, UPS CEO James Kelly starts the planning process by setting strategic goals. A top priority is building UPS into the leading shipper of on-line purchases to any destination. From there, other management decisions—such as investing in sophisticated technology to track packages—are designed to bring UPS closer to its goals.

Organizing to implement these decisions, UPS has combined its air express and ground shipping businesses so customers can arrange for any delivery with one phone call. Kelly, like nearly every top manager, started his career driving a UPS truck, so he has firsthand knowledge of what employees can and should be doing to stay ahead of competitors.

As Kelly and his top managers rose through the ranks, they forged connections with other managers and employees and learned what works (and doesn't work) when leading and motivating the UPS workforce. Profit-sharing is a powerful incentive, for example, as is the opportunity to own company stock now that UPS has gone public.

Controlling is vital in the shipping business, where customers demand on-time delivery. UPS managers use technology to track every shipment and to analyze the productivity of personnel and other resources. The system runs so smoothly that UPS now offers a money-back guarantee for ground shipments. By monitoring progress and making corrections as needed, Kelly and his managers are keeping UPS on course to remain the leader in e-commerce delivery.

> *We are going to involve ourselves in global commerce more deeply and more extensively than ever.*
>
> —*James Kelly, CEO, United Parcel Service**

References: Brian O'Reilly, "They've Got Mail!" *Fortune,* February 7, 2000, pp. 100–112 (*quote on p. 103); David Rocks, "Going Nowhere Fast in Cyberspace," *Business Week,* January 31, 2000, pp. 58–59.

---

decisions on Tuesday, organize on Wednesday, lead on Thursday, and control on Friday. At any given time, as illustrated in the cartoon, for example, a manager is likely to be engaged in several different activities simultaneously. Indeed, from one setting to another, managerial work is as different as it is similar. The similarities that pervade most settings are the phases in the management process. Important differences include the emphasis, sequencing, and implications of each phase.[3] Thus, the solid lines in Figure 1.2 indicate how, in theory, the functions of management are performed. The dotted lines, however, represent the true reality of management. In the sections that follow, we explore each of these activities.

Planning and Decision Making: Determining Courses of Action

In its simplest form, **planning** means setting an organization's goals and deciding how best to achieve them. **Decision making**, a part of the planning process, involves selecting a course of action from a set of alternatives. Planning and decision making help maintain managerial effectiveness by serving as guides for future activities. That is, the organization's goals and plans clearly help managers know how to allocate their time and resources. Carly Fiorina was appointed as CEO of Hewlett-Packard in 1999 and given a mandate to get the struggling firm back on track. Her first actions, in turn, included developing a new set of corporate goals refocusing the company on its core competencies and outlining a new business strategy to energize the company and integrate Internet technology throughout all its operations.[4]

Four chapters making up Part III of this text are devoted to planning and decision making. Chapter 7 examines the basic elements of planning and decision making, including the role and importance of organizational goals. Chapter 8 looks at strategy and strategic planning, which provide overall direction and focus for the organization. Chapter 9 explores managerial decision making and problem solving in detail. Finally, Chapter 10 addresses planning and decision making as they relate to the management of new ventures and entrepreneurial activities, increasingly important parts of managerial work.

Organizing: Coordinating Activities and Resources

Once a manager has set goals and developed a workable plan, the next management function is to organize people and the other resources necessary to carry out the plan. Specifically, **organizing** involves determining how activities and resources are to be grouped. One of the immediate obstacles facing Carly Fiorina at Hewlett-Packard was a rigid and bureaucratic hierarchy that promoted insular thinking and limited innovation. She swept this structure aside, creating a much more organic and flexible organization that, in turn, quickly became much more responsive and forward looking.

Organizing is the subject of Part IV. Chapter 11 introduces the basic elements of organizing, such as job design, departmentalization, authority relationships, span of control, and line and staff roles. Chapter 12 explains how managers fit these elements and concepts together to form an overall organization design. Organization change and innovation are the focus of Chapter 13. Finally, processes associated with hiring and assigning people to carry out organizational roles are described in Chapter 14.

"*Do you mind? I happen to be on the phone!*"

Drawing by S. Gross

Managers are constantly engaged in many different activities. The types and sequences of activities are often difficult to predict from one day to the next, however, and managers often do their work in impromptu settings or on airplanes, in taxis, over meals, or even when walking down the street. The manager shown here, for example, may be helping a colleague develop goals for the next quarter (planning), discussing a proposed company restructuring (organizing), praising a subordinate for outstanding performance (leading), or checking on last month's sales information (controlling). The pace of this work may be stressful for some people, and exhilarating for others.

planning Setting an organization's goals and deciding how best to achieve them

decision making Part of the planning process that involves selecting a course of action from a set of alternatives

organizing Determining how activities and resources are to be grouped

Leading: Motivating and Managing People

leading The set of processes used to get members of the organization to work together to advance the interests of the organization

The third basic managerial function is leading. Some people consider leading to be both the most important and the most challenging of all managerial activities. **Leading** is the set of processes used to get members of the organization to work together to advance the interests of the organization. Carly Fiorina came to Hewlett-Packard with a reputation for being a trustworthy and honest manager, but also one who would make tough decisions and hard choices. Her personality blended perfectly with other top managers at the company and they were soon working together as a cohesive and effective team.

Leading involves several different processes and activities, which are discussed in Part V. The starting point is understanding basic individual and interpersonal processes, which we focus on in Chapter 15. Motivating employees is discussed in Chapter 16, and leadership itself and the leader's efforts to influence others are covered in Chapter 17. Managing interpersonal relations and communication is the subject of Chapter 18. Finally, managing work groups and teams, another important part of leading, is addressed in Chapter 19.

Controlling: Monitoring and Evaluating Activities

controlling Monitoring the organization's progress toward its goals

The final phase of the management process is **controlling**, or monitoring the organization's progress toward its goals. As the organization moves toward its goals, managers must monitor progress to ensure that it is performing so that it arrives at its "destination" at the appointed time. A good analogy is that of a space mission to Mars. NASA does not simply shoot a rocket in the general direction of the planet and then look again in four months to see whether the rocket hit its mark. NASA monitors the spacecraft almost continuously and makes whatever course corrections are needed to keep it on track. Controlling helps ensure the effectiveness and efficiency needed for successful management. While Carly Fiorina is off to a great start at Hewlett-Packard, the firm still has a long way to go to regain its technological leadership. Thus, she has set in place numerous benchmarks that will be used to assess the firm's progress over the next few years as it evolves toward her model of strategic competitiveness.

The control function is explored in Part VI. First, Chapter 20 explores the basic elements of the control process, including the increasing importance of strategic control. Managing operations, quality, and productivity is explored in Chapter 21, along with productivity and operations management. Finally, Chapter 22 addresses the management of information and information technology, still other critical areas of organizational control.

MANAGEMENT IMPLICATIONS Managers should thoroughly understand each of the basic functions—planning and decision making, organizing, leading, and controlling—that comprise their jobs. They should also recognize that while each is important in its own right, effective managers are skilled in performing each function, must be capable of moving back and forth among the functions as circumstances warrant, and must often juggle multiple functions and activities simultaneously. Managers cannot afford to be effective in or to enjoy performing only some of the functions because all are important.

Kinds of Managers

Earlier in this chapter we identified as managers people from a variety of organizations. Clearly, there are many kinds of managers. One point of differentiation is among organizations, as those earlier examples imply. Another point occurs within an organization. Figure 1.3 shows how managers within an organization can be differentiated by level and area.

Managing at Different Levels of the Organization

Managers can be differentiated according to their level in the organization. Although large organizations typically have several **levels of management**, the most common view considers three basic levels: top, middle, and first-line managers.

levels of management The differentiation of managers into three basic levels—top, middle, and first-line

Top Managers Top managers make up the relatively small group of executives who manage the overall organization. Titles found in this group include president,

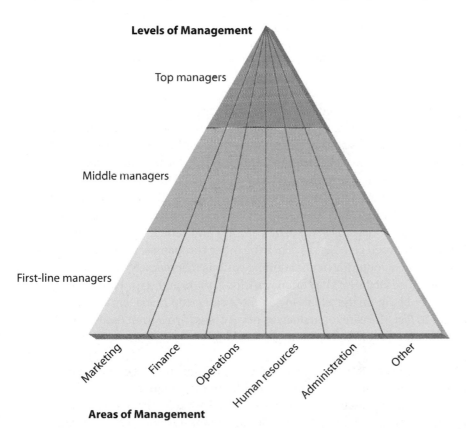

Figure 1.3

Kinds of Managers by Level and Area
Organizations generally have three levels of management, represented by top managers, middle managers, and first-line managers. Regardless of level, managers are also usually associated with a specific area within the organization, such as marketing, finance, operations, human resources, administration, or some other area.

Businesses have many different kinds of managers. Top managers are the small group of executives who manage the overall organization. Matt Massengill (left) is president and CEO of Western Digital; Carly Fiorina (center) is the president and CEO of Hewlett-Packard; and Michael Capellas (right) is president and CEO of Compaq Computer. Each is a top manager. The three are shown here at a news conference where Ms. Fiorina is explaining a new venture between twelve high-tech companies, including Western, HP, and Compaq, that will create an Internet exchange to serve the needs of its member companies. Top managers are instrumental in developing concepts for such new enterprises, are responsible for committing resources for them, and are ultimately accountable for their success or failure.

vice president, and chief executive officer (CEO). Top managers create the organization's goals, overall strategy, and operating policies. They also officially represent the organization to the external environment by meeting with government officials, executives of other organizations, and so forth. *Today's Management Issues* explores the question of how involved a CEO should be in day-to-day operations versus "bigger picture" kinds of issues. Howard Schultz, CEO of Starbucks, is a top manager, as is Deidra Wager, the firm's Senior Vice President for Retail Operations. The job of a top manager is likely to be complex and varied. Top managers make decisions about such activities as acquiring other companies, investing in research and development, entering or abandoning various markets, and building new plants and office facilities. They often work long hours and spend much of their time in meetings or on the telephone. In most cases, top managers are also very well paid. In fact, the elite top managers of very large firms sometimes make several million dollars a year in salary, bonuses, and stock.[5]

Middle Managers   Middle management is probably the largest group of managers in most organizations. Common middle-management titles include plant manager, operations manager, and division head. Middle managers are primarily responsible for implementing the policies and plans developed by top managers and for supervising and coordinating the activities of lower-level managers.[6] Plant

TODAY'S MANAGEMENT ISSUES

NO DETAIL TOO SMALL FOR TOP MANAGEMENT ATTENTION?

How should top executives spend their time? Walt Disney CEO Michael Eisner believes his time is best spent delving into minute details of his company's operations. Bill Gates of Microsoft and Steve Case of AOL Time Warner, on the other hand, believe their time is better spent on strategic issues. Which way is most effective?

Eisner enjoys getting deeply involved in everyday decisions. After naming Robert A. Iger as Disney's president and chief operating officer, Eisner could have turned his attention to the big picture. After all, Disney is a multifaceted organization, with movie studios, television stations, theme parks, retail stores, Internet sites, and other businesses. Instead, Eisner began reading movie scripts and discussing new park rides, while delegating long-range planning to the head of strategic planning and the chief financial officer. He's especially interested in cost-cutting measures. Paging through one script, for example, he made a note about a change that could save the company several million dollars during filming.

In contrast, after Microsoft's Bill Gates promoted Steve Ballmer into the CEO position, he named himself chief software architect. Given the regulatory and competitive challenges that Microsoft is facing, this role enables Gates to think through major issues about the company's future. Similarly, AOL's founder, Steve Case, decided to become chairman of the board after his company acquired Time Warner. He named Gerald Levin as CEO and then stepped back from day-to-day operations to make long-term plans for new technology and global expansion.

Should top managers follow Eisner's example and make nitty-gritty decisions about operational details? Or should they follow the example of Gates and Case and concentrate on strategy, letting other executives make daily decisions? There is no correct answer, of course, especially since all three of these managers are acknowledged as being very effective. But each manager needs to assess carefully both her or his personal preferences and the needs of the organization and work to ensure that they align effectively.

> *In the entertainment business, it's about the details.*
>
> *—Michael Eisner, CEO, Walt Disney**

References: Bruce Orwall, "Michael Eisner's New Agenda: Details, Details," *Wall Street Journal*, January 26, 2000, pp. B1, B4 (*quote on p. B1); Joseph Nocera, "The Men Who Would Be King," *Fortune*, February 7, 2000, pp. 66–69.

---

managers, for example, handle inventory management, quality control, equipment failures, and minor union problems. They also coordinate the work of supervisors within the plant. Jason Hernandez, a regional manager at Starbucks responsible for the firm's operations in three eastern states, is a middle manager.

In recent years, many organizations have thinned the ranks of middle managers to lower costs and eliminate excess bureaucracy. Still, middle managers are necessary to bridge the upper and lower levels of the organization and to implement the strategies developed at the top. Although many organizations have found that they can indeed survive with fewer middle managers, those who remain play an even more important role in determining how successful the organization will be.[7]

First-Line Managers First-line managers supervise and coordinate the activities of operating employees. Common titles for first-line managers are supervisor, coordinator, and office manager. Positions such as these are often the first held by employees who enter management from the ranks of operating personnel. Wayne Maxwell and Jenny Wagner, managers of Starbucks coffee shops in Texas, are first-line managers. They oversee the day-to-day operations of their respective stores, hire operating employees to staff them, and handle other routine administrative duties required of them by the parent corporation. In contrast to top and middle managers, first-line managers typically spend a large proportion of their time supervising the work of subordinates.

Managing in Different Areas of the Organization

Regardless of their level, managers may work in various areas within an organization. In any given firm, for example, **areas of management** may include marketing, financial, operations, human resource, administrative, and other areas.

areas of management Managers can be differentiated into marketing, financial, operating, human resource, administration, and other areas

Marketing Managers Marketing managers work in areas related to the marketing function—getting consumers and clients to buy the organization's products or services (be they Motorola digital cell phones, Ford automobiles, *Newsweek* magazines, Associated Press news reports, flights on Southwest Airlines, or cups of latte at Starbucks). These areas include new product development, promotion, and distribution. Given the importance of marketing for virtually all organizations, developing good managers in this area can be critical.

Financial Managers Financial managers deal primarily with an organization's financial resources. They are responsible for activities such as accounting, cash management, and investments. In some businesses, such as banking and insurance, financial managers are found in especially large numbers. Jacques Nasser, CEO of Ford Motor Co., started his career with the company more than thirty years ago as a financial analyst.

Operations Managers Operations managers are concerned with creating and managing the systems that create an organization's products and services. Typical responsibilities of operations managers include production control, inventory control, quality control, plant layout, and site selection.

Human Resource Managers Human resource managers are responsible for hiring and developing employees. They are typically involved in human resource planning, recruiting and selecting employees, training and development, designing compensation and benefit systems, formulating performance appraisal systems, and discharging low-performing and problem employees.

Administrative Managers Administrative, or general, managers are not associated with any particular management specialty. Probably the best example of an administrative management position is that of a hospital or clinic administrator. Administrative managers tend to be generalists; they have some basic familiarity with all functional areas of management rather than specialized training in any one area.[8]

Other Kinds of Managers Many organizations have specialized management positions in addition to those already described. Public relations managers, for example, deal with the public and media for firms like Philip Morris Companies, Inc., and The Dow Chemical Co. to protect and enhance the image of the organization. Research and development (R&D) managers coordinate the activities of scientists and engineers working on scientific projects in organizations such as Monsanto Company, NASA, and Merck & Co. Internal consultants are used in organizations such as The Prudential Insurance Co. of America to provide specialized expert advice to operating managers. International operations are often coordinated by specialized managers in organizations like Eli Lilly and Rockwell International Corp. The number, nature, and importance of these specialized managers vary tremendously from one organization to another. As contemporary organizations continue to grow in complexity and size, the number and importance of such managers are also likely to increase.

MANAGEMENT IMPLICATIONS Managers can be found at all levels and in all areas of an organization. A career path up the organizational ladder might be primarily within a single area, or might span several areas. Thus, managers should try to understand where their current position fits into the organization, and what path they may want to pursue to advance their career goals. Cutbacks in the ranks of middle managers also mean that lower level managers in major corporations may have to wait longer for a promotion, since there are fewer jobs at the higher levels for them to enter.[9]

Basic Managerial Roles and Skills

Regardless of their level or area within an organization, all managers must play certain roles and exhibit certain skills if they are to be successful. The concept of a role, in this sense, is similar to the role an actor plays in a theatrical production. A person does certain things, meets certain needs in the organization, and has certain responsibilities. In the sections that follow, we first highlight the basic roles managers play and then discuss the skills they need to be effective.

Managerial Roles

Henry Mintzberg offers a number of interesting insights into the nature of managerial roles.[10] He closely observed the day-to-day activities of a group of CEOs by literally following them around and taking notes on what they did. From his observations, Mintzberg concluded that managers play ten different roles, as summarized in Table 1.2, and that these roles fall into three basic categories: interpersonal, informational, and decisional.

Interpersonal Roles There are three **interpersonal roles** inherent in the manager's job. First, the manager is often asked to serve as a *figurehead*—taking visitors to dinner, attending ribbon-cutting ceremonies, and the like. These activities are

interpersonal roles The roles of figurehead, leader, and liaison, all of which involve dealing with other people

Table 1.2

Ten Basic Managerial Roles

Research by Henry Mintzberg suggests that managers play ten basic managerial roles.

Category	Role	Sample Activities
Interpersonal	Figurehead	Attending ribbon-cutting ceremony for new plant
	Leader	Encouraging employees to improve productivity
	Liaison	Coordinating activities of two project groups
Informational	Monitor	Scanning industry reports to stay abreast of developments
	Disseminator	Sending memos outlining new organizational initiatives
	Spokesperson	Making a speech to discuss growth plans
Decisional	Entrepreneur	Developing new ideas for innovation
	Disturbance handler	Resolving conflict between two subordinates
	Resource allocator	Reviewing and revising budget requests
	Negotiator	Reaching agreement with a key supplier or labor union

typically more ceremonial and symbolic than substantive. The manager is also asked to serve as a *leader*—hiring, training, and motivating employees. A manager who formally or informally shows subordinates how to complete tasks and how to perform under pressure is leading. Finally, managers can have a *liaison* role. This role often involves serving as a coordinator or link between people, groups, or organizations. For example, companies in the computer industry may use liaisons to keep other companies informed about their plans. This enables Microsoft, for example, to create software for interfacing with new Hewlett-Packard printers while those printers are being developed. And, at the same time, managers at Hewlett-Packard can also incorporate new Microsoft features into the printers they introduce.

Informational Roles   The three **informational roles** flow naturally from the interpersonal roles just discussed. The process of carrying out these roles places the manager at a strategic point to gather and disseminate information. The first informational role is that of *monitor*, one who actively seeks information that may be of value. The manager questions subordinates, is receptive to unsolicited information, and attempts to be as well informed as possible. The manager is also a *disseminator* of information, transmitting relevant information back to others in the workplace. When the roles of monitor and disseminator are viewed together, the manager emerges as a vital link in the organization's chain of

Managers play several basic roles in organizations. Consider, for example, the case of Charlie Woo. Mr. Woo, an immigrant from Hong Kong, started a new toy company in downtown Los Angeles called ABC Toys. He imports cheap but sturdy toys from Asia and then sells them in the United States and Mexico. ABC Toys are generally cheaper than those offered by big multinationals like Mattel but of higher quality than most cheap knock-offs offered by other small toy importers. By effectively playing the various interpersonal, information, and decisional roles, Woo has made his firm one of the most profitable in the industry.

communication. The third informational role focuses on external communication. The *spokesperson* formally relays information to people outside the unit or outside the organization. For example, a plant manager at Union Carbide Corp. may transmit information to top-level managers so that they will be better informed about the plant's activities. The manager may also represent the organization before a chamber of commerce or consumer group. Although the roles of spokesperson and figurehead are similar, there is one basic difference between them. When a manager acts as a figurehead, the manager's presence as a symbol of the organization is what is of interest. In the spokesperson role, however, the manager carries information and communicates it to others in a formal sense.

informational roles The roles of monitor, disseminator, and spokesperson, all of which involve the processing of information

Decisional Roles   The manager's informational roles typically lead to the **decisional roles**. The information acquired by the manager as a result of performing the informational roles has a major bearing on important decisions that he or she makes. Mintzberg identified four decisional roles. First, the manager has the role of *entrepreneur*, the voluntary initiator of change. A manager at 3M Company developed the idea for the Post-it Note Pad but had to "sell" it to other skeptical managers inside the company. A second decisional role is initiated not by the manager but by some other individual or group. The manager responds to her role as *disturbance handler* by handling such problems as strikes, copyright infringements, or problems in public relations or corporate image.

decisional roles The roles of entrepreneur, disturbance handler, resource allocator, and negotiator, all of which relate primarily to making decisions

The third decisional role is that of *resource allocator*. As resource allocator, the manager decides how resources are distributed, and with whom he or she will work most closely. For example, a manager typically allocates the funds in the unit's operating budget among the unit's members and projects. A fourth decisional role is that of *negotiator*. In this role the manager enters into negotiations with other groups or organizations as a representative of the company. For example, managers may negotiate a union contract, an agreement with a consultant, or a long-term relationship with a supplier. Negotiations may also be internal to the organization. The manager may, for instance, mediate a dispute between two subordinates or negotiate with another department for additional support.

Managerial Skills

In addition to fulfilling numerous roles, managers also need a number of specific skills if they are to succeed. The most fundamental management skills are technical, interpersonal, conceptual, diagnostic, communication, decision-making, and time-management skills.[11]

Technical Skills   **Technical skills** are the skills necessary to accomplish or understand the specific kind of work being done in an organization. Technical skills are especially important for first-line managers. These managers spend much of their time training subordinates and answering questions about work-related problems. They must know how to perform the tasks assigned to those they supervise if they are to be effective managers. Horst Schulze, CEO of Ritz-Carlton, got his start washing dishes and waiting tables at hotels in Germany. Over the next several

technical skills The skills necessary to accomplish or understand the specific kind of work being done in an organization years he also worked as a bellhop, a front-desk clerk, and a concierge. These experiences gave him keen insight into the inner workings of a quality hotel operation, insights he has used to take Ritz-Carlton to the top of its industry.[12]

interpersonal skills The ability to communicate with, understand, and motivate both individuals and groups

Interpersonal Skills   Managers spend considerable time interacting with people both inside and outside the organization. For obvious reasons, then, the manager also needs **interpersonal skills**—the ability to communicate with, understand, and motivate both individuals and groups. As a manager climbs the organizational ladder, she must be able to get along with subordinates, peers, and those at higher levels of the organization. Because of the multitude of roles managers must fulfill, a manager must also be able to work with suppliers, customers, investors, and others outside the organization. Although some managers have succeeded with poor interpersonal skills, a manager who has good interpersonal skills is likely to be more successful. When A. G. Lafley was recently appointed CEO of Procter & Gamble, observers were quick to praise him for his strong interpersonal skills. As one colleague put it, "A. G. has a reputation for both people skills and strategic thinking."[13]

conceptual skills The manager's ability to think in the abstract

Conceptual Skills   **Conceptual skills** depend on the manager's ability to think in the abstract. Managers need the mental capacity to understand the overall workings of the organization and its environment, to grasp how all the parts of the organization fit together, and to view the organization in a holistic manner. These conceptual skills allow them to think strategically, to see the "big picture," and to make broad-based decisions that serve the overall organization.

diagnostic skills The manager's ability to visualize the most appropriate response to a situation

Diagnostic Skills   Successful managers also possess **diagnostic skills**, or skills that enable a manager to visualize the most appropriate response to a situation. A physician diagnoses a patient's illness by analyzing symptoms and determining their probable cause. Similarly, a manager can diagnose and analyze a problem in the organization by studying its symptoms and then developing a solution. According to one source, Eckhard Pfeiffer ultimately failed as CEO of Compaq Computer because he did not have strong diagnostic skills.[14]

communication skills The manager's abilities both to convey ideas and information effectively to others and to receive ideas and information effectively from others

Communication Skills   **Communication skills** refer to the manager's abilities both to convey ideas and information effectively to others and to receive ideas and information effectively from others. These skills enable a manager to transmit ideas to subordinates so that they know what is expected, to coordinate work with peers and colleagues so that they work well together properly, and to keep higher-level managers informed about what is going on. In addition, they help the manager listen to what others say and to understand the real meaning behind letters, reports, and other written communication.

decision-making skills The manager's ability to recognize and define problems and opportunities correctly and then to select an appropriate course of action to solve problems and capitalize on opportunities

Decision-Making Skills   Effective managers also have good decision-making skills. **Decision-making skills** refer to the manager's ability to recognize and define problems and opportunities correctly and then to select an appropriate course of action to solve problems and capitalize on opportunities. No manager makes the right decision all the time. However, effective managers make good decisions most of the time. And when they do make a bad decision, they usually recognize their mistake quickly and then make good decisions to recover with as little cost or damage to their organization as possible.

Time-Management Skills Finally, effective managers usually have good time-management skills. **Time-management skills** refer to the manager's ability to prioritize work, to work efficiently, and to delegate appropriately. As already noted, managers face many different pressures and challenges. It is too easy for a manager to get bogged down doing work that can easily be postponed or delegated to others. When this happens, unfortunately, more pressing and higher-priority work may get neglected.[15] Jeff Bezos, CEO of Amazon.com, schedules all his meetings on three days a week, but insists on keeping the other two days clear so that he can pursue his own ideas and maintain the flexibility to interact with his employees informally.[16]

time-management skills The manager's ability to prioritize work, to work efficiently, and to delegate appropriately

MANAGEMENT IMPLICATIONS Effective managers recognize both the multiplicity of roles inherent in their jobs and the array of skills they need to perform those jobs. Few managers have equally strong skills in all areas. However, it is very useful for managers to understand their own strengths and weaknesses and to use this understanding to capitalize on their strengths while also working to overcome their weaknesses. For example, a manager with weak time-management skills might be sure to hire an especially effective assistant to help maintain an efficient schedule, while a manager with weak decision-making skills can use group decision making whenever possible to help utilize the skills of others.

The Nature of Managerial Work

We have already noted that managerial work does not follow an orderly, systematic progression through the workweek. Indeed, the manager's job is fraught with uncertainty, change, interruption, and fragmented activities. Mintzberg's study, mentioned earlier, found that in a typical day, CEOs were likely to spend 59 percent of their time in scheduled meetings, 22 percent doing "desk work," 10 percent in unscheduled meetings, 6 percent on the telephone, and the remaining 3 percent on tours of company facilities. (These proportions, of course, are different for managers at lower levels.) Moreover, the nature of managerial work continues to change in complex and often unpredictable ways.[17]

In addition, managers also perform a wide variety of tasks. In the course of a single day, for example, a manager might have to make a decision about the design of a new product, settle a complaint between two subordinates, hire a new assistant, write a report for the boss, coordinate a joint venture with an overseas colleague, form a task force to investigate a problem, search for information on the Internet, and deal with a labor grievance. Moreover, the pace of the manager's job can be relentless. She may feel bombarded by mail, telephone calls, and people waiting to see her. Decisions may have to be made quickly and plans formulated with little time for reflection.[18] But in many ways, these same characteristics of managerial work also contribute to its richness and meaningfulness. Making critical decisions under intense pressure, and making them well, can be a major source of intrinsic satisfaction. And managers are usually well paid for the pressures they bear.

The Science and the Art of Management

Given the complexity inherent in the manager's job, a reasonable question relates to whether management is a science or an art. In fact, effective management is a blend of both science and art. And successful executives recognize the importance of combining both the science and the art of management as they practice their craft.[19] *Management InfoTech* details how electronic commerce is making it even more important for top managers to recognize the roles of science and art in the way they perform their jobs.

The Science of Management   Many management problems and issues can be approached in ways that are rational, logical, objective, and systematic. Managers

---

MANAGEMENT INFOTECH

MAKING DECISIONS AT THE SPEED OF TECHNOLOGY

As technology picks up the pace of change in the business world, managers have to move faster than ever before and make decisions on the fly. In addition to Internet technology, managers are also dealing with challenges and opportunities brought on by advances in computing power and software. The result is full-speed-ahead management, where every second counts in the race to attract customers and beat the competition.

In the past, managers had more time to analyze and debate key decisions such as acquisitions. Today, the luxury of time is almost a memory. For example, Halsey Minor, chairman of CNET, an on-line publisher of technology news and reviews, acquired three companies in three weeks after learning that a rival was about to sell stock to the public. Minor knew that if he didn't act quickly, the competitor would soon have the financing to buy those companies and pose a stronger threat to CNET.

Technology helps managers stay connected with employees as well as with outside sources of information so they can get up to speed quickly. Even when they're out of the office, managers are never more than a click, chime, or buzz away, using wireless Internet access devices, mobile phones, laptop computers, and pagers.

Despite these tools, managers still have to make quick decisions that are all too often based on insufficient or incomplete data, as Bill Harris well knows. Harris is CEO of Intuit, the software company that produces Quicken and other finance programs. Competing against Microsoft and others, Harris uses his long-range vision of where the industry and the technology are headed to fuel lightning-fast decisions—even when the immediate future is unclear. For Harris, Minor, and other managers making decisions in today's technology-rich environment, management is clearly as much an art as it is a science.

> *You have to be deadly, brutally honest with yourself and others because if you let a problem fester a day or two, you'll see someone in your rear-view mirror coming after you.*
>
> —*Roger Siboni, CEO, Epiphany**

Reference: Geoffrey Colvin, "How to Be a Great E-CEO," *Fortune,* May 24, 1999, pp. 104–110 (*quote on p. 105).

can gather data, facts, and objective information. They can use quantitative models and decision-making techniques to arrive at "correct" decisions. And they need to take such a scientific approach to solving problems whenever possible, especially when they are dealing with relatively routine and straightforward issues. When Starbucks considers entering a new market, its managers look closely at a wide variety of objective details as they formulate their plans. Technical, diagnostic, and decision-making skills are especially important when practicing the science of management.

The Art of Management   Even though managers may try to be scientific as much as possible, they must often make decisions and solve problems on the basis of intuition, experience, instinct, and personal insights. Relying heavily on conceptual, communication, interpersonal, and time-management skills, for example, a manager may have to decide between multiple courses of action that look equally attractive. And even "objective facts" may prove to be wrong. When Starbucks was planning its first store in New York, market research clearly showed that New Yorkers preferred drip coffee to more exotic espresso-style coffees. After first installing more drip coffee makers and fewer espresso makers than in their other stores, managers had to backtrack when New Yorkers lined up clamoring for espresso. Starbucks now introduces a standard menu and layout in all its stores, regardless of presumed market differences, and then makes necessary adjustments later. Thus, managers must blend an element of intuition and personal insight with hard data and objective facts.[20]

Becoming a Manager

How does one acquire the skills necessary to blend the science and the art of management and thus become a successful manager? Although there are as many variations as there are managers, the most common path involves a combination of education and experience.[21] Figure 1.4 illustrates how this generally happens.

The Role of Education   Many of you reading this book right now are doing so because you are enrolled in a management course at a college or university. Thus, you are acquiring management skills in an educational setting. When you complete the course (and this book), you will have a foundation for developing your management skills in more advanced courses. A college degree has become almost a requirement for career advancement in business, and virtually all CEOs in the United States have a college degree. MBA degrees are also common among successful executives today. More and more foreign universities, especially in Europe, are also beginning to offer academic programs in management.

Figure 1.4

Sources of Management Skills
Most managers acquire their skills as a result of education and experience. Though a few CEOs today do not hold college degrees, most students preparing for management careers earn college degrees and go on to enroll in MBA programs.

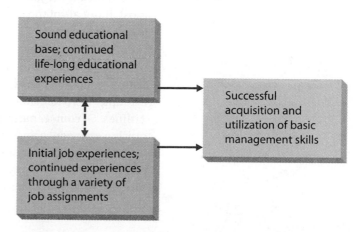

Even after obtaining a degree, most prospective managers have not seen the end of their management education. Many middle and top managers periodically return to campus to participate in executive or management development programs ranging in duration from a few days to several weeks. First-line managers also take advantage of extension and continuing education programs offered by institutions of higher education. A recent innovation in extended management education is the Executive MBA program offered by many top business schools, in which middle and top managers with several years of experience complete an accelerated program of study on weekends.[22] Finally, many large companies have in-house training programs for furthering managers' education. Regardless of the type of training, there is also a distinct trend toward educational development for managers conducted online.[23]

The primary advantage of education as a source of management skills is that, as a student, a person can follow a well-developed program of study, becoming familiar with current research and thinking on management. And many college students can devote full-time energy and attention to learning. On the negative side, management education is often very general to meet the needs of a wide variety of students, and specific know-how may be hard to obtain. Further, many aspects of the manager's job can be discussed in a book but cannot really be appreciated and understood until they are experienced.

The Role of Experience   This book will help provide you with a solid foundation for enhancing your management skills. Even if you were to memorize every word in every management book ever written, however, you could not then step into a top-management position and be effective. The reason? Management skills must also be learned through experience. Most managers advanced to their present position from other jobs. Only by experiencing the day-to-day pressures a manager faces and by meeting a variety of managerial challenges can an individual develop insights into the real nature and character of managerial work.

For this reason most large companies, and many smaller ones as well, have developed management training programs for their prospective managers. People are hired from college campuses, from other organizations, or from the ranks of the organization's first-line managers and operating employees. These people are systematically assigned to a variety of jobs. Over time, the individual is exposed to most, if not all, of the major aspects of the organization. In this way the manager learns by experience. The training programs at some companies, such as Procter & Gamble, General Mills, and Shell Oil, are so good that other companies try to hire people who have gone through their training.[24] Even without formal training programs, managers can achieve success as they profit from varied experiences. For example, Herb Kelleher was a practicing attorney before he took over at Southwest Airlines. Of course, natural ability, drive, and self-motivation also play roles in acquiring experience and developing management skills.

Most effective managers learn their skills through a combination of education and experience. Some type of college degree, even if it is not in business administration, usually provides a foundation for a management career. The individual then gets his or her first job and subsequently progresses through a variety of management situations. During the manager's rise in the organization, occasional education "updates," such as management development programs, may supplement on-the-job experience. And increasingly, managers need to acquire international expertise as part of their personal development. As with general managerial skills, international expertise can also be acquired through a combination of education and experience.

MANAGEMENT IMPLICATIONS Students should recognize that even if certain material in a course does not seem relevant, they are still building an intellectual foundation for future growth. They should also recognize, however, that knowledge alone is usually not sufficient for success in the business world. Finally, students should also understand that just because they walk across the stage and get a diploma, their education is far from complete. People already in the business world, meanwhile, should not forget the importance of continuing to learn, regardless of how or where this learning occurs.

The Scope of Management

When most people think of managers and management, they think of profit-seeking organizations. Throughout this chapter we have used people like Christopher Galvin of Motorola, Howard Schultz of Starbucks, and Carly Fiorina of Hewlett-Packard as examples. But we also mentioned examples from sports, religion, and other fields in which management is essential. Indeed, any group of two or more persons working together to achieve a goal and having human, material, financial, or informational resources at its disposal requires the practice of management.

Managing in Profit-Seeking Organizations

Large Businesses Most of what we know about management comes from large profit-seeking organizations because their survival has long depended on efficiency and effectiveness. Examples of large businesses include industrial firms like Tenneco, BP Amoco, Toyota, Xerox, Unilever, and Levi Strauss; commercial banks like Citicorp, The Fuji Bank, and Wells Fargo; insurance companies like Prudential, State Farm, and Metropolitan Life; retailers like Sears, Safeway, and Kmart; transportation companies like Delta Air Lines and Consolidated Freightways; utilities like Pacific Gas & Electric and Consolidated Edison of New York; communication companies like CBS and The New York Times Company; and service organizations like Kelly Services, Kinder-Care Learning Centers, and Century 21 Real Estate.

Small and Start-Up Businesses Although many people associate management primarily with large businesses, effective management is also essential for small businesses, which play an important role in the country's economy. In fact, most of this nation's businesses are small. In some respects, effective management is more important in a small business than in a large one. A large firm such as Texaco or

Management is an important part of any organization, regardless of its size or mission. Luke Davis combines his business acumen with technical skills as he reaches out to a wide array of different kinds of organizations and offers his services as a web site designer. Here, for instance, he is demonstrating the new web site he designed for the Tyburn Convent in London. Davis has become quite successful by focusing on diverse kinds of religious, civic, and social organizations.

Monsanto can easily recover from losing several thousand dollars on an incorrect decision; even losses of millions of dollars would not threaten their long-term survival. But a small business may ill afford even a much smaller loss. Of course, some small businesses become big ones. Compaq Computer Corporation, for example, was started by three men in 1982. By 1999 it had become one of the largest businesses in the United States, with annual sales of over $31 billion.

International Management In recent years, the importance of international management has increased dramatically. The list of U.S. firms doing business in other countries is staggering. Exxon Mobil, for example, derives almost 75 percent of its revenues from foreign markets, and Coca-Cola derives more than 80 percent of its sales from foreign markets. Other major U.S. exporters include General Motors, General Electric, Boeing, and Caterpillar. And even numbers like Ford's are deceptive. For example, the automaker has large subsidiaries based in many European countries whose sales are not included as foreign revenue. Moreover, a number of major firms that do business in the United States have their headquarters in other countries. Firms in this category include the Royal Dutch/Shell Group (the Netherlands), Fiat S.P.A. (Italy), Nestlé SA (Switzerland), and Massey-Ferguson Inc. (Canada). International management is not confined, however, to profit-seeking organizations. Several international sports federations (such as Little League Baseball), branches (embassies) of the federal government, and the Roman Catholic Church are established in most countries as well. In some respects, the military was one of the first multinational organizations. International management is covered in depth in Chapter 5.

Managing in Not-for-Profit Organizations

Intangible goals such as education, social services, public protection, and recreation are often the primary aim of not-for-profit organizations. Examples include United Way of America, the U.S. Postal Service, Girl Scouts of the United States of America, the International Olympic Committee, art galleries, museums, and the Public Broadcasting System. Although these and similar organizations may not have to be profitable to attract investors, they must still employ sound management practices if they are to survive and work toward their goals.[25] And they must handle money in an efficient and effective way. If the United Way were to begin to spend large portions of its contributions on administration, contributors would lose confidence in the organization and make their charitable donations elsewhere.

Government Organizations   The management of government organizations and agencies is often regarded as a separate specialty: public administration. Government organizations include the Federal Trade Commission, the Environmental Protection Agency, the National Science Foundation, all branches of the military, state highway departments, and federal and state prison systems. Tax dollars support government organizations, and politicians and citizens' groups are acutely sensitive to the need for efficiency and effectiveness.

Educational Organizations   Public and private schools, colleges, and universities all stand to benefit from the efficient use of resources. Taxpayer "revolts" in states such as California and Massachusetts have drastically cut back the tax money available for education, forcing administrators to make tough decisions about allocating remaining resources.

Healthcare Facilities   Managing healthcare facilities such as clinics, hospitals, and HMOs (health maintenance organizations) is now considered a separate field of management. Here, as in other organizations, scarce resources dictate an efficient and effective approach. In recent years many universities have established healthcare administration programs to train managers as specialists in this field.

Management in Nontraditional Settings   Good management is also required in nontraditional settings to meet established goals. To one extent or another, management is practiced in religious organizations, terrorist groups, fraternities and sororities, organized crime, street gangs, neighborhood associations, and households. In short, as we noted at the beginning of this chapter, management and managers have a profound influence on all of us.

MANAGEMENT IMPLICATIONS   Management is applicable to all organizations. Thus, when a manager leaves work and goes to a weekly meeting of a civic or church group, to an organizing meeting for a child's youth soccer league, or to do volunteer work in a political campaign, he or she should keep in mind that many of the same functions used in a business can also be used in these other organizations as well. And while each organization has its own unique goals and mission, effective management can help every organization better accomplish those goals and more successfully realize its mission.

Summary of Key Points

Management is a set of activities (including planning and decision making, organizing, leading, and controlling) directed at an organization's resources (human, financial, physical, and information) with the aim of achieving organizational goals in an efficient and effective manner. A manager is someone whose primary responsibility is to carry out the management process within an organization.

The basic activities that comprise the management process are planning and decision making (determining courses of action), organizing (coordinating activities and resources), leading (motivating and managing people), and controlling (monitoring and evaluating activities). These activities are not performed on a systematic and predictable schedule.

Managers can be differentiated by level and by area. By level, we can identify top, middle, and first-line managers. Managers differentiated by area include marketing, financial, operations, human resource, administrative, and specialized managers.

Managers have ten basic roles to play: three interpersonal roles (figurehead, leader, and liaison), three informational roles (monitor, disseminator, and spokesperson), and four decisional roles (entrepreneur, disturbance handler, resource allocator, and negotiator). Effective managers also tend to have technical, interpersonal, conceptual, diagnostic, communication, decision-making, and time-management skills. The manager's job is characterized by varied, unpredictable, nonroutine, and fragmented work, often performed at a relentless pace. Managers also receive a variety of intrinsic and extrinsic rewards.

The effective practice of management requires a synthesis of science and art, that is, a blend of rational objectivity and intuitive insight. Most managers attain their skills and positions through a combination of education and experience.

Management processes are applicable in a wide variety of settings, including profit-seeking organizations (large, small, and start-up businesses and international businesses) and not-for-profit organizations (government organizations, educational organizations, healthcare facilities, and nontraditional organizations).

Discussion Questions

Questions for Review

1. What are the four basic activities that comprise the management process? How are they related to one another?
2. Identify different kinds of managers by both level and area in the organization.
3. Briefly describe the ten managerial roles identified by Mintzberg. Give an example of each.
4. Identify the different important skills that help managers succeed. Give an example of each.

Questions for Analysis

5. The text notes that management is both a science and an art. Is one of these more important than the other? Under what circumstances might one characteristic be more important than the other?
6. Recall a recent group project or task in which you have participated. Explain how each of the four basic management functions was performed.
7. Some people argue that CEOs in the United States are paid too much. Find out the pay

for a CEO and discuss whether you think he or she is overpaid.

Questions for Application

8. Interview a manager from a local organization. Learn about how he or she performs each of the functions of management, the roles he or she plays, and the skills necessary to do the job.
9. Locate a recent business management publication like *Fortune, Business Week*, or *Forbes*. Read an article in the magazine that profiles a specific manager or executive. Identify as many examples in the article as you can that illustrate management functions, roles, and/or skills.
10. Watch a television program that involves an organization of some type. Good choices include *N.Y.P.D. Blue, The West Wing, Spin City*, or *E.R.* Identify as many management functions, skills, and roles as you can.

BUILDING EFFECTIVE *technical* SKILLS

Exercise Overview

Technical skills refer to the manager's abilities to accomplish or understand work done in an organization. More and more managers today are realizing that having the technical ability to use the Internet is an important part of communication, decision making, and other facets of their work. This exercise helps you see the link between the Internet and management.

Exercise Background

The so-called information highway, or the Internet, is an interconnected network of information and information-based resources accessed by computers, computer systems, and other devices. While electronic mail was perhaps the first widespread application of the Internet, increasingly popular applications are based on home pages and search engines.

A home page is a file (or set of files) created by an individual, business, or other entity. It contains whatever information its creator chooses to include. For example, a company might create a home page for itself that includes its logo, its address and telephone number, information about its products and services, and so forth. An individual seeking employment might create a home page that includes a résumé and a statement of career interests. Home pages are indexed by key words chosen by their creators.

A search engine is a system through which an Internet user can search for home pages according to their indexed key words. Suppose an individual is interested in knowing more about art collecting. Key words that might logically be linked to home pages related to this interest include *art, artists, galleries*, and *framing*. A search engine will take these key words and provide a listing of all home pages that are indexed to them. The user can then browse each page to see what information it contains. Popular search engines include Yahoo, Google, and Webcrawler.

Exercise Task

1. Review the content of this chapter and identify three or four general management-related terms (i.e., *management, organization, business*).
2. Using whichever search engine you prefer, conduct a search for these terms.
3. Now select a more specific management topic and search for two or three specific terms (if you cannot think of any terms, scan the margin notes in this book).
4. Finally, select three or four companies and search for their home pages.
5. Comment on the relative ease and value of each of these searches from the standpoint of a practicing manager.

BUILDING EFFECTIVE *diagnostic* SKILLS

Exercise Overview

Diagnostic skills are those that enable a manager to visualize the most appropriate response to a situation. This exercise will encourage you to apply your diagnostic skills to a real business problem and to assess the possible consequences of different courses of action.

Exercise Background

For some time now college textbook publishers have been struggling with a significant problem. The subject matter that comprises a particular field, such as management, chemistry, or history, continues to increase in size, scope, and complexity. Thus, authors feel compelled to add more and more information to new editions of their textbooks. Publishers have also sought to increase the visual sophistication of their texts by adding more color and photographs. At the same time, some instructors find it increasingly difficult to cover the material in longer textbooks. Moreover, longer and more attractive textbooks cost more money to produce, resulting in higher selling prices to students.

Publishers have considered a variety of options to confront this situation. One option is to work with authors to produce shorter and more economical books (such as this one). Another option is to cut back on the complimentary supplements that publishers provide to instructors (such as videos and color transparencies) as a way of lowering the overall cost of producing a book. Another option is to eliminate traditional publishing altogether and provide educational resources via CD-ROM, the Internet, or other new media.

Confounding this situation, of course, is cost. Profit margins in the industry are such that managers feel the need to be cautious and conservative. That is, they cannot do everything and must not risk alienating their users by taking too radical a step. Remember, too, that publishers must consider the concerns of three different sets of customers: the instructors who make adoption decisions, the bookstores that buy educational materials for resale (at a retail markup), and students who buy the books for classroom use and then often resell them back to the bookstore.

Exercise Task

With this background in mind, respond to the following:
1. Discuss the pros and cons of each option currently being considered by textbook publishers.
2. Identify the likely consequences of each option.
3. Can you think of other alternatives that publishers in the industry should consider?
4. What specific recommendations would you make to an executive in a publishing company regarding this set of issues?

BUILDING EFFECTIVE *conceptual* SKILLS

Exercise Overview

Conceptual skills form the manager's ability to think in the abstract. This exercise will help you extend your conceptual skills by identifying potential generalizations of management functions, roles, and skills for different kinds of organizations.

Exercise Background

This introductory chapter discusses four basic management functions, ten common managerial roles, and seven vital management skills. The chapter also stresses that management is applicable across many of different kinds of organizations.

Identify one large business, one small business, one educational organization, one health-care organization, and one government organization. These might be organizations about which you have some personal knowledge or simply organizations that you recognize. Now imagine yourself in the position of a top manager in each organization.

Write the names of the five organizations across the top of a sheet of paper. List the four functions, ten roles, and seven skills down the left side of the paper. Now think of a situation, problem, or opportunity relevant to the intersection of each row and column on the paper. For example, how might a manager in a govern-

ment organization engage in planning and need diagnostic skills? Similarly, how might a manager in a small business carry out the organizing function and play the role of negotiator?

Exercise Task

1. What meaningful similarities can you identify across the five columns?
2. What meaningful differences can you identify across the five columns?
3. Based on your assessment of the similarities and differences as identified in Exercise Tasks 1 and 2, how easy or difficult do you think it might be for a manager to move from one type of organization to another?

CHAPTER CLOSING CASE

MANAGING IN A WIRED WORLD

Although Amazon.com is not yet a decade old, it's already a case study in Internet success. Founded by Jeff Bezos in 1995 as an on-line bookstore, Seattle-based Amazon rings up more than $1.6 billion in e-commerce sales every year. First books, then music and videos, and now software, screwdrivers, and sofas—Amazon has grown into a virtual department store for its 17 million on-line customers worldwide. Even as successful chains such as Barnes and Noble and Wal-Mart try to grab a larger piece of the on-line retailing pie, CEO Bezos has maintained Amazon's market leadership and customer base through constant innovation.

Nothing like Amazon existed when Bezos was researching software and the Internet for a New York City firm in 1994. He became intrigued by the business possibilities of selling books on the World Wide Web in much the same way that mail-order firms sell books by mail. This idea proved so compelling that Bezos quickly quit his job, raised money from family and friends, wrote a business plan, and moved to Seattle to be located near a major book wholesaler. One year later, Amazon.com was open for business. In its first month, without advertising or public relations, the site attracted customers from every U.S. state and more than forty other countries.

In those early days, the giant bookstore chains paid little attention to Amazon. Within two years, however, Amazon's discount prices, free e-mail book reviews, and easy search capabilities had attracted so many shoppers and so much media coverage that competitors started scrambling to open their own Internet book stores. But Amazon's established reputation and loyal customer following were major hurdles for rivals to overcome. In fact, despite aggressive promotions and pricing, Barnesandnoble.com is still trying to catch up to Amazon's on-line sales and sizable customer base.

Meanwhile, Bezos has expanded into all kinds of products by buying stakes in e-commerce companies such as drugstore.com and pets.com. He's also set up an auction section on Amazon to tap the excitement generated by the success of eBay, the first Internet auction site. In addition, he made room on the Amazon site for zShops, an area where smaller businesses can, for a fee, sell products.

One reason for Amazon's success is founder Bezos's action-oriented management style. Although he carefully plans his company's future moves, he also wants to avoid the paralysis that can come from endless analysis and deliberation. As an e-commerce pioneer,

Bezos is accustomed to making speedy decisions to take advantage of unexpected or fleeting opportunities. He encourages everyone at Amazon to do the same, even if that means an occasional misstep. Working on Internet time, Bezos would rather lead his troops into the unknown, and fix problems later, than slow down now.

To continue growing and innovating, Amazon must keep recruiting, training, and motivating good managers and employees. Bezos gets personally involved in hiring decisions about top managers, who he trusts to hire the people who will work under them. Because he knows that a skilled workforce is critical to Amazon's success, Bezos asks probing questions about hiring techniques when he interviews top management candidates.

Still, Bezos carves out precious time from his hectic management schedule to surf the Web, click around the Amazon site, and, on occasion, wander through shopping malls in search of new ideas. To stay in touch, he goes out of his way to thank specific employees for their efforts, and he reads e-mail messages from customers to find out what they like and don't like. About one-third of the CEO's time is devoted to visiting Amazon's national network of distribution centers, where he answers employee questions and reinforces the company's six "core values": customer obsession, ownership, bias for action, frugality, high hiring bar, and innovation.

Every December, Bezos and his entire management team pitch in to meet the holiday rush. By wrapping packages for customer shipments or answering customer service phone calls, they all get a better sense of what Amazon's first-line managers and employees face—and what their customers want. This yearly tradition of hands-on experience also rekindles the managers' sense of purpose, no small consideration in an industry where change is the only constant.

Case Questions

1. Which managerial skills does Jeff Bezos appear to be emphasizing at Amazon?

2. How does Bezos carry out his interpersonal, informational, and decisional roles at Amazon?

3. Why are communication skills particularly vital for managers at a fast-growing firm such as Amazon?

Case References

"Can Amazon Make It?" *Business Week*, July 11, 2000, pp. 38+; Miguel Helft, "Poster Boy Grows Up," *thestandard.com*, April 24, 2000, http://www.thestandard.com/article/display/0,1151,14264,00.html (June 2, 2000); George Anders, "Taming the Out-of-Control In-Box," *Wall Street Journal*, February 4, 2000, pp. B1, B4; Michael Krantz, "Cruising Inside Amazon," *Time*, December 27, 1999, pp. 68+; Joshua Cooper Ramo, "Jeffrey Preston Bezos: 1999 Person of the Year," *Time*, December 27, 1999, pp. 50+; Joshua Quittner, "An Eye on the Future: Jeff Bezos Merely Wants Amazon.com to Be Earth's Biggest Seller of Everything," *Time*, December 27, 1999, pp. 56+.

CHAPTER NOTES

1. "Luck, Pain, and Perseverance," *USA Today*, January 27, 2000, pp. 1B, 2B (quote on p. 1B); "A New Company Called Motorola," *Business Week*, April 17, 2000, pp. 86–92; *Hoover's Handbook of American Business 2000* (Austin: Hoover's Business Press, 2000), pp. 996–997.

2. Fred Luthans, "Successful vs. Effective Real Managers," *The Academy of Management Executive*, May 1988, pp. 127–132.

3. Sumantsa Ghospal and Christopher A. Bartlett, "Changing the Role of Top Management: Beyond Structure to Process," *Harvard Business Review*, January–February 1995, pp. 86–96.

4. Patricia Sellters, "These Women Rule," *Fortune*, October 25, 1999, pp. 94–96.

5. See "The Age of the $100 Million CEO," *Forbes*, April 3, 2000, pp. 122–129; "Homes, Cars, Jets Among Perks Piling Up For CEOs," *USA Today*, May 22, 2000, pp. 1B, 2B.

6. Rosemary Stewart, "Middle Managers: Their Jobs and Behaviors," in Jay W. Lorsch (ed.), *Handbook of Organizational Behavior* (Englewood Cliffs, N.J.: Prentice-Hall, 1987), pp. 385–391.

7. Anne Fisher, "Six Ways to Supercharge Your Career," *Fortune*, January 13, 1997, pp. 46–48.

8. John P. Kotter, "What Effective General Managers Really Do," *Harvard Business Review*, March–April 1999, pp. 145–155.

9. Brent B. Allred, Charles C. Snow, and Raymond E. Miles, "Characteristics of Managerial Careers in the 21st Century," *The Academy of Management Executive*, November 1996, pp. 17–27.

10. Henry Mintzberg, *The Nature of Managerial Work* (New York: Harper & Row, 1973).

11. See Robert L. Katz, "The Skills of an Effective Administrator," *Harvard Business Review*, September–October 1974, pp. 90–102, for a classic discussion of several of these skills.

12. "Ritz-Carlton Opens with Training Tradition," *USA Today*, June 29, 2000, p. 3B.

13. "New P&G Chief Is Tough, Praised for People Skills," *The Wall Street Journal*, June 6, 2000, pp. B1, B4.

14. Ram Charan and Geoffrey Colvin, "Why CEOs Fail," *Fortune*, June 21, 1999, pp. 68–78.

15. For a recent discussion of the importance of time-management skills, see David Barry, Catherine Durnell Cramton, and Stephen J. Carroll, "Navigating the Garbage Can: How Agendas Help Managers Cope with Job Realities," *The Academy of Management Executive*, May 1997, pp. 26–42.

16. "Taming the Out-of-Control In-Box," *The Wall Street Journal*, February 4, 2000, pp. B1, B4.

17. See Michael A. Hitt, "Transformation of Management for the New Millennium," *Organizational Dynamics*, Winter 2000, pp. 7–17.

18. James H. Davis, F. David Schoorman, and Lex Donaldson, "Toward a Stewardship Theory of Management," *Academy of Management Review*, January 1997, pp. 20–47.

19. Gary Hamel and C. K. Prahalad, "Competing for the Future," *Harvard Business Review*, July–August 1994, pp. 122–128.

20. James Waldroop and Timothy Butler, "The Executive as Coach," *Harvard Business Review*, November–December 1996, pp. 111–117.

21. Walter Kiechel III, "A Manager's Career in the New Economy," *Fortune*, April 4, 1994, pp. 68–72.

22. "The Executive MBA Your Way," *Business Week*, October 18, 1999, pp. 88–92.

23. "Turning B-School into E-School," *Business Week*, October 18, 1999, p. 94.

24. See "Reunion at P&G University," *The Wall Street Journal*, June 7, 2000, pp. B1, B4, for a discussing of Procter & Gamble's training programs.

25. James L. Perry and Hal G. Rainey, "The Public-Private Distinction in Organization Theory: A Critique and Research Strategy," *Academy of Management Review*, April 1988, pp. 182–201; see also Ran Lachman, "Public and Private Sector Differences: CEOs' Perceptions of Their Role Environments," *Academy of Management Journal*, September 1985, pp. 671–680.

2

Traditional and Contemporary Issues and Challenges

When Leslie Wexner opened the first Limited clothing store in an Ohio shopping mall in 1963, he had no idea that his fledgling business would grow to include thousands of specialty stores comprised of such well-known brands as Express, Abercrombie & Fitch, and Victoria's Secret. But by 1993 his firm was running out of steam and rivals like Gap and J. Crew were attracting more and more attention. Now, though, Limited seems to have righted itself and is again moving toward the forefront of the specialty retailing industry. The reasons for the decline and rebirth of Limited underscore the importance of maintaining compatibility between a manager's style and the organization's situation.

When Wexner started Limited, he was clearly an entrepreneur and his focus was primarily on business growth and expansion. He pursued this growth in two ways. First, he continually looked for ways to branch out and systematically launched several different chains. Second, he grew each chain rapidly by opening new stores at a breakneck pace. Part of Wexner's strategy was to place his stores adjacent to one another in large shopping malls. Thus, customers might walk from The Limited to Express to Lerner, buying clothes at each without realizing that they were actually buying from the same company.

Wexner created or bought several major chains, including The Limited, Express, Lerner New York, Lane Bryant, Henri Bendel, Victoria's Secret, Bath & Body Works, Structure, and Abercrombie & Fitch. Wexner himself also jumped from business to business, leaving the day-to-day operations in the hands of others. His focus, meanwhile, continued to be on growth and expansion as he continued to buy other chains, retool his existing chains, and build more and more stores. In some malls, for instance, Limited stores might comprise as much as 25 percent of total square footage.

But in the early 1990s troubles began to surface. Sales declined in some markets, for example, and costs and operating expenses began to creep up. Moreover, competitors such as Gap and Old Navy started attracting more customers and were increasingly the store of choice for hip young consumers. Investors also began to get nervous and the company's stock price plummeted. And some experts openly questioned whether or not Limited could be turned around.

Wexner recognized that he had a problem, but he also didn't know quite how to define it. So, starting in the mid-1990s, he began to visit several of the very best managers in the United States, including such lumi-

> *"I was an entrepreneur. . . .*
> *I think what went wrong was*
> *the . . . entrepreneurial style*
> *wasn't working."*
>
> —*Leslie Wexner, founder and*
> *CEO of Limited*

naries as Sam Walton (founder of Wal-Mart), Jack Welch (CEO of General Electric), and Wayne Calloway (former CEO of PepsiCo). And he gradually began to recognize the problem: Limited had stopped being an entrepreneurial start-up operation and had evolved into a mature major business operation, yet he was still trying to run it using the same managerial style he had used when he had only a few dozen stores. Clearly, he realized, running a global company with more than five thousand stores, generating annual revenues of $9.3 billion, and employing 127,000 people required a different approach than he had been using.

So Wexner immersed himself in a crash-course on how to manage a mature business. He learned about operations and financial control, revamped the firm's organization design, and implemented a more professional approach to human resource management. He also began to focus more on profit margins and acknowledged that sometimes you have to close or sell underperforming stores and businesses. And he learned the difference between competitive strategy and growth strategy.

By the end of the decade, signs were clearly pointing to a resurgence at Limited. For example, same-store sales are again increasing and the firm's stock price reached a record high in mid-2000. But Wexner is quick to point out that, even though he has helped reinvent his company, that he doesn't want to make the same mistake again. Hence, he has committed himself to staying abreast of modern management techniques and contemporary management thought.[1]

One lesson managers can learn from Leslie Wexner is that as circumstances change, so too must they be prepared to change their approach to running their business. It is critically important that all managers focus on today's competitive environment and how that environment will change tomorrow. But it is also important that they use the past as context. Managers in a wide array of organizations can learn both effective and less effective practices and strategies by understanding what managers have done in the past. Indeed, history plays an important role in many businesses today, and more and more managers are recognizing that the lessons of the past are important ingredients of future success.

This chapter provides an overview of traditional management thought so that you, too, can better appreciate the importance of history in today's business world. We set the stage by establishing the historical context of management. We then discuss the three traditional management perspectives—classical, behavioral, and quantitative. Next we describe the systems and contingency perspectives as approaches that help integrate the three traditional perspectives. Finally, we introduce and discuss a variety of contemporary management issues and challenges.

The Role of Theory and History in Management

Practicing managers are increasingly seeing the value of theory and history in their work. In this section we first explain why theory and history are important and then identify important precursors to management theory.

The Importance of Theory and History

Some people question the value of history and theory. Their arguments are usually based on the assumptions that history has no relevance to contemporary society

No one knows the origins of Stonehenge, a mysterious circle of huge stones rising from Salisbury Plain in England. But one fact that is known is that whoever built the ancient monument must have relied heavily on a variety of management tools and techniques. For example, the stones were probably cut over 300 miles away, in Wales, and transported to Salisbury Plain. This enormous feat alone would have required careful planning and coordination and the united efforts of hundreds of laborers.

and that theory is abstract and of no practical use. In reality, however, both theory and history are important to all managers today.

Why Theory? A theory is simply a conceptual framework for organizing knowledge and providing a blueprint for action. Although some theories seem abstract and irrelevant, others appear very simple and practical. Management theories, used to build organizations and guide them toward their goals, are grounded in reality.[2] Practically any organization that uses assembly lines (such as Emerson Electric, Black & Decker, and Fiat) is drawing on what we describe later in this chapter as scientific management. Many organizations, including Monsanto, Texas Instruments, and Seiko, use the behavioral perspective (also introduced later) to improve employee satisfaction and motivation. And naming a large company that does not use one or more techniques from the quantitative management perspective would be difficult. For example, retailers like Kroger and Target Stores routinely use operations management to determine how many check-out stands they need. In addition, most managers develop and refine their own theories of how they should run their organizations and manage the behavior of their employees.

For example, Andrew Grove, CEO of Intel Corp., has developed his own operating theory of organizations. The basis of his theory is that organizations need to focus on continually becoming more agile and responsive to their environment. By implementing his theory, Grove has transformed Intel into just such a company. As a direct result of Grove's keen understanding of his business and his ability to implement his operating theory, Intel has become the world's largest manufacturer of semiconductors.[3]

Why History? An awareness and understanding of important historical developments are also important to contemporary managers.[4] Understanding the historical context of management provides a sense of heritage and can help managers avoid the mistakes of others. Most courses in U.S. history devote time to business and economic developments in this country, including the Industrial Revolution, the early labor movement, and the Great Depression, and to captains of U.S. industry such as Cornelius Vanderbilt (railroads), John D. Rockefeller (oil), and Andrew Carnegie (steel). The contributions of those and other industrialists left a profound imprint on contemporary culture.[5]

Many managers are also realizing that they can benefit from a greater understanding of history in general. For example, Ian M. Ross of AT&T Bell Laboratories cites *The Second World War* by Winston Churchill as a major influence on his approach to leadership. Other books often mentioned by managers for their relevance to today's business problems include such classics as Plato's *Republic*, Homer's *Iliad*, and Machiavelli's *The Prince*.[6] And in recent years, new business history books have appeared that are directed more at women managers and the lessons they can learn from the past.[7]

Managers at Wells Fargo & Company clearly recognize the value of history. For example, the company maintains an extensive archival library of its old banking documents and records and even employs a full-time corporate historian. As part of their orientation and training, new managers at Wells Fargo take courses to become acquainted with the bank's history.[8] Similarly, Polaroid, Shell Oil, Levi Strauss, Ford, Lloyd's of London, Disney, Honda, and Unilever all maintain significant archives about their past and frequently evoke images from that past in their orientation and training programs, advertising campaigns, and other public relations activities.

Precursors to Management Theory

Even though large businesses have been around for only a few hundred years, management has been practiced for thousands of years. By examining management in antiquity and identifying some of the first management pioneers, we set the stage for a more detailed look at the emergence of management theory and practice over the last one hundred years.

Management in Antiquity   The practice of management can be traced back thousands of years. The Egyptians used the management functions of planning, organizing, and controlling when they constructed the great pyramids. Alexander the Great employed a staff organization to coordinate activities during his military campaigns. The Roman Empire developed a well-defined organizational structure that greatly facilitated communication and control. Management practices and concepts were discussed by Socrates in 400 B.C.; Plato described job specialization in 350 B.C., and Alfarabi listed several leadership traits in A.D. 900.[9] Figure 2.1 is a simple time line showing a few of the most important management breakthroughs and practices over the last four thousand years.

Figure 2.1

Management in Antiquity
Management has been practiced for thousands of years. For example, the ancient Babylonians used management in governing their empire, and the ancient Romans used management to facilitate communication and control throughout their far-flung territories. The Egyptians used planning and controlling techniques in the construction of their pyramids.

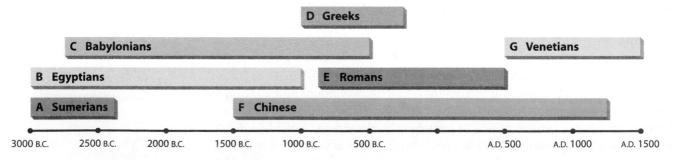

A   Used written rules and regulations for governance

B   Used management practices to construct pyramids

C   Used extensive set of laws and policies for governance

D   Used different governing systems for cities and state

E   Used organized structure for communication and control

F   Used extensive organization structure for government agencies and the arts

G   Used organization design and planning concepts to control the seas

Early Management Pioneers In spite of this history, however, management per se was not given serious attention for several centuries. Indeed, the study of management did not begin until the nineteenth century. Robert Owen (1771–1858), a British industrialist and reformer, was one of the first managers to recognize the importance of an organization's human resources. Until his era, factory workers were generally viewed in much the same way that machinery and equipment were. A factory owner himself, Owen believed that workers deserved respect and dignity. He implemented better working conditions, a higher minimum working age for children, meals for employees, and reduced work hours. He assumed that giving more attention to workers would pay off in increased output.

Whereas Owen was primarily interested in employee welfare, Charles Babbage (1792–1871), an English mathematician, focused his attention on efficiencies of production. His primary contribution was his book, *On the Economy of Machinery and Manufactures*.[10] Babbage placed great faith in division of labor and advocated the application of mathematics to problems such as the efficient use of facilities and materials. In a sense, his work was a forerunner to both the classical and quantitative management perspectives. Nor did he overlook the human element. He understood that a harmonious relationship between management and labor could serve to benefit both, and he favored such devices as profit-sharing plans. In many ways, Babbage was an originator of modern management theory and practice.

MANAGEMENT IMPLICATIONS While all managers should obviously focus their attention on present-day and future issues, they should also remember the lessons from the past. An understanding of business history in general and the history of their own company in particular can help them better understand why contemporary circumstances have developed as they have, and also provide useful ideas for enhancing the effectiveness of their organization.[11] In addition, managers should recognize the value of theory as a way of organizing and thinking about information and ideas.[12]

The Classical Management Perspective

At the dawn of the twentieth century, the preliminary ideas and writings of these and other managers and theorists converged with the emergence and evolution of large-scale businesses and management practices to create interest and focus attention on how businesses should be operated. The first important ideas to emerge are now called the **classical management perspective**. This perspective actually includes two different viewpoints: scientific management and administrative management.

classical management perspective Consists of two distinct branches—scientific management and administrative management

Scientific Management

Productivity emerged as a serious business problem during the first few years of the twentieth century. Business was expanding and capital was readily available,

Frederick W. Taylor was a pioneer in the field of labor efficiency. He introduced numerous innovations in how jobs were designed and how workers were trained to perform them. These innovations resulted in higher-quality products and improved employee morale. Taylor also formulated the basic ideas of scientific management.

scientific management Concerned with improving the performance of individual workers

soldiering Employees deliberately working at a pace slower than their capabilities

but labor was in short supply. Hence, managers began to search for ways to use existing labor more efficiently. In response to this need, experts began to focus on ways to improve the performance of individual workers. Their work led to the development of **scientific management**. Some of the earliest advocates of scientific management included Frederick W. Taylor (1856–1915), Frank Gilbreth (1868–1924), Lillian Gilbreth (1878–1972), Henry Gantt (1861–1919), and Harrington Emerson (1853–1931).[13] Taylor played the dominant role.

One of Taylor's first jobs was as a foreman at the Midvale Steel Company in Philadelphia. There he observed what he called **soldiering**—employees deliberately working at a pace slower than their capabilities. Taylor studied and timed each element of the steelworkers' jobs. He determined what each worker should be producing, and then he designed the most efficient way of doing each part of the overall task. Next he implemented a piecework pay system. Rather than paying all employees the same wage, he began increasing the pay of each worker who met and exceeded the target level of output set for his or her job.

After Taylor left Midvale, he worked as a consultant for several companies, including Simonds Rolling Machine Company and Bethlehem Steel. At Simonds he studied and redesigned jobs, introduced rest periods to reduce fatigue, and implemented a piecework pay system. The results were higher quality and quantity of output and improved morale. At Bethlehem Steel, Taylor studied efficient ways of loading and unloading rail cars and applied his conclusions with equally impressive results. During these experiences, he formulated the basic ideas that he called scientific management. Figure 2.2 illustrates the basic steps Taylor suggested. He believed that managers who followed his guidelines would improve the efficiency of their workers.[14]

Taylor's work had a major impact on U.S. industry. By applying his principles, many organizations achieved major gains in efficiency. Taylor was not without his detractors, however. Labor argued that scientific management was just a device to

Figure 2.2

Steps in Scientific Management

Frederick Taylor developed this system of scientific management, which he believed would lead to a more efficient and productive workforce. Bethlehem Steel was among the first organizations to profit from scientific management and still practices some parts of it today.

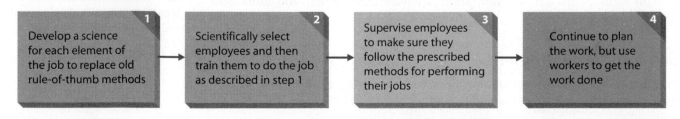

1. Develop a science for each element of the job to replace old rule-of-thumb methods
2. Scientifically select employees and then train them to do the job as described in step 1
3. Supervise employees to make sure they follow the prescribed methods for performing their jobs
4. Continue to plan the work, but use workers to get the work done

get more work from each employee and to reduce the total number of workers needed by a firm. There was a congressional investigation into Taylor's ideas, and evidence suggests that he falsified some of his findings.[15] Nevertheless, Taylor's work left a lasting imprint on business.[16]

Frank and Lillian Gilbreth, contemporaries of Taylor, were a husband-and-wife team of industrial engineers. One of Frank Gilbreth's most interesting contributions was to the craft of bricklaying. After studying bricklayers at work, he developed several procedures for doing the job more efficiently. For example, he specified standard materials and techniques, including the positioning of the bricklayer, the bricks, and the mortar at different levels. The results of these changes were a reduction from eighteen separate physical movements to five and an increase in output of about 200 percent. Lillian Gilbreth made equally important contributions to several different areas of work, helped shape the field of industrial psychology, and made substantive contributions to the field of personnel management. Working individually and together, the Gilbreths developed numerous techniques and strategies for eliminating inefficiency. They applied many of their ideas to their family and documented their experiences raising twelve children in the book and movie *Cheaper by the Dozen*. Of course, as illustrated in the cartoon, concerns for efficiency can be carried too far!

Henry Gantt, another contributor to scientific management, was an associate of Taylor at Midvale, Simonds, and Bethlehem Steel. Later, working alone, he developed other techniques for improving worker output. One, called the Gantt chart, is still used today. A Gantt chart is essentially a means of scheduling work and can be generated for each worker or for a complex project as a whole. Gantt also refined Taylor's ideas about piecework pay systems.

Like Taylor, the Gilbreths, and Gantt, Harrington Emerson was also a management consultant. He made quite a stir in 1910 when he appeared before the Interstate Commerce Commission to testify about a rate increase requested by the railroads. As an expert witness, Emerson asserted that the railroads could save $1 million a day by using scientific management. He was also a strong advocate of specialized management roles in organizations, believing that job specialization was as relevant to managerial work as it was to operating jobs.

Harley Schwadron

All organizations, of course, should be concerned about efficiency and productivity. But as this cartoon illustrates, they might sometimes go a bit too far! While there are no organizations that are likely to go as far as this one, there are work sites today that forbid talking among employees at work, prohibit any personal telephone calls, and require employees to have permission to take a restroom break. Managers responsible for such practices would most likely argue that employees should be doing nothing but work when they are being paid and that they can't be trusted to exercise self-control about work, and so they must be tightly supervised and strictly controlled.

Administrative Management

Whereas scientific management deals with the jobs of individual employees, **administrative management** focuses on managing the total organization. The primary contributors to administrative management were Henri Fayol (1841–1925), Lyndall Urwick (1891–1983), Max Weber (1864–1920), and Chester Barnard (1886–1961).

administrative management
Focuses on managing the total organization

Henri Fayol was administrative management's most articulate spokesperson. A French industrialist, Fayol was unknown to U.S. managers and scholars until his most important work, *General and Industrial Management*, was translated into English in 1930.[17] Drawing on his own managerial experience, he attempted to systematize the practice of management to provide guidance and direction to other managers. Fayol also was the first to identify the specific managerial functions of planning, organizing, leading, and controlling. He believed that these functions accurately reflect the core of the management process. Most contemporary management books (including this one) still use this framework, and practicing managers agree that these functions are critical parts of their jobs.

After a career as a British army officer, Lyndall Urwick became a noted management theorist and consultant. He integrated scientific management with the work of Fayol and other administrative management theorists. He also advanced modern thinking about the functions of planning, organizing, and controlling. Like Fayol, he developed a list of guidelines for improving managerial effective-

---

MANAGING IN AN *e*-BUSINESS WORLD

B2B SITES BRING ORGANIZATIONAL CHANGES

Max Weber developed his ideas about bureaucracy many decades before computers became commonplace business tools. Yet he would have been pleased at the way business-to-business (B2B) Web sites are improving organizational efficiency through more productive purchasing.

Traditionally, the purchasing department was considered a backwater compared with line positions in production or other departments. Today, however, purchasing agents are at the forefront of an Internet-driven revolution. E-purchasing—buying goods and services via B2B Web sites—is helping companies slash costs and streamline their organizations.

Here's one example. When Norfolk Southern Railway needed contractors to handle repair work, employees would spend days calling construction companies to solicit bids. These days, the railroad posts simple requests for bids on Rail-Net-USA.com, a B2B site for rail contractors. With e-purchasing, the railroad receives more bids and more competitive pricing in far less time, which frees employees to work on other tasks.

The potential savings are enormous. John Deere, a leading farm-equipment manufacturer, will shave 5 percent off the cost of supplies and components through e-purchasing—a savings of $1 billion within five years. United Technologies has already sliced its supplier bills by more than $700 million. In some industries, e-purchasing could reduce supply costs as much as 20 percent.

Just as important, e-purchasing through B2B sites is shaking up the organizational pyramid. Processing a single transaction, from the initial requisition to the final payment, used to require a stream of paperwork handled as many as nine times. Now e-purchasing is trimming the paperwork and reducing the handling to as few as three steps. General Electric says that getting rid of so much paperwork will reduce transaction costs by at least $49 per purchase. And, with a simpler, speedier process, companies will need fewer employees in purchasing. Once John Deere completes its move to e-purchasing, its purchasing department will drop from 1,200 to 900 or fewer employees. Max Weber would have applauded such bottom-line savings.

Collectively, [e-purchasing agents] will drive efficiency across industries and geographies.

—*Leah Knight, e-business analyst**

References: Laura Cohn, "B2B: The Hottest Net Bet Yet?" *Business Week*, January 17, 2000, pp. 36–37; Del Jones, "E-purchasing Saves Businesses Billions," *USA Today*, February 7, 2000, pp. 1B–2B (*quote on p. 2B).

Table 2.1

The Classical Management Perspective

General Summary	The classical management perspective had two primary thrusts. Scientific management focused on employees within organizations and on ways to improve their productivity. Noted pioneers of scientific management were Frederick Taylor, Frank and Lillian Gilbreth, Henry Gantt, and Harrington Emerson. Administrative management focused on the total organization and on ways to make it more efficient and effective. Prominent administrative management theorists were Henri Fayol, Lyndall Urwick, Max Weber, and Chester Barnard.
Contributions	Laid the foundation for later developments in management theory. Identified important management processes, functions, and skills that are still recognized today. Focused attention on management as a valid subject of scientific inquiry.
Limitations	More appropriate for stable and simple organizations than for today's dynamic and complex organizations. Often prescribed universal procedures that are not appropriate in some settings. Even though some writers (such as Lillian Gilbreth and Chester Barnard) were concerned with the human element, many viewed employees as tools rather than resources.

ness. Urwick is noted not so much for his own contributions as for his synthesis and integration of the work of others.

Although Max Weber lived and worked at the same time as Fayol and Taylor, his contributions were not recognized until some years had passed. Weber was a German sociologist, and his most important work was not translated into English until 1947.[18] Weber's work on bureaucracy laid the foundation for contemporary organization theory, discussed in detail in Chapter 12. The concept of bureaucracy, as we discuss later, is based on a rational set of guidelines for structuring organizations in the most efficient manner.

Chester Barnard, former president of New Jersey Bell Telephone Company, made notable contributions to management in his book *The Functions of the Executive*.[19] The book proposes a major theory about the acceptance of authority. The theory suggests that subordinates weigh the legitimacy of a supervisor's directives and then decide whether to accept them. An order is accepted if the subordinate understands it, is able to comply with it, and views it as appropriate. The importance of Barnard's work is enhanced by his experience as a top manager.

The Classical Management Perspective Today

The contributions and limitations of the classical management perspective are summarized in Table 2.1. The classical perspective is the framework from which later theories evolved, and many of its insights still hold true today. For example, many of the job specialization techniques and scientific methods espoused by Taylor and his contemporaries are still reflected in the way that many industrial jobs are designed today.[20] Moreover, many contemporary organizations still use some of the bureaucratic procedures suggested by Weber. Also, these early theorists were the first to focus attention on management as a meaningful field of study. Several aspects of the classical perspective are also relevant to our later discussions of planning, organizing, and controlling. And, as described more fully in *Managing in an E-business World*, recent advances in areas such as business-to-business (B2B) commerce also have efficiency as their primary goal.

The limitations of the classical perspective, however, should not be overlooked. These early writers dealt with stable, simple organizations; many organizations today, in contrast, are changing and complex. They also proposed universal guidelines that we now recognize do not fit every organization. A third limitation of the classical management perspective is that it slighted the role of the individual in organizations. This role was much more fully developed by advocates of the behavioral management perspective.

MANAGEMENT IMPLICATIONS   The classical management perspective provides many techniques and approaches to management that are still relevant today. For example, thoroughly understanding the nature of the work being performed, selecting the right people for that work, and approaching decisions rationally are all useful ideas—and each was developed during this period. Similarly, some of the core concepts from the bureaucratic model can still be used in the design of modern organizations as long as their limitations are recognized.[21] Managers should also recognize that efficiency and productivity can indeed be measured and controlled in many situations. On the other hand, managers must also recognize the limitations of the classical perspective and avoid its narrow focus on efficiency to the exclusion of other important perspectives.

The Behavioral Management Perspective

behavioral management perspective Emphasizes individual attitudes and behaviors and group processes and recognizes the importance of behavioral processes in the workplace.

Early advocates of the classical management perspective essentially viewed organizations and jobs from a mechanistic point of view; that is, they essentially sought to conceptualize organizations as machines and workers as cogs within those machines. Even though many early writers recognized the role of individuals, their focus tended to be on how managers could control and standardize the behavior of their employees. In contrast, the **behavioral management perspective** emphasizes individual attitudes and behaviors and group processes and recognized the importance of behavioral processes in the workplace.

The behavioral management perspective was stimulated by a number of writers and theoretical movements. One of those movements was industrial psychology, the practice of applying psychological concepts to industrial settings. Hugo Munsterberg (1863–1916), a noted German psychologist, is recognized as the father of industrial psychology. He established a psychological laboratory at Harvard in 1892, and his pioneering book, *Psychology and Industrial Efficiency,* was translated into English in 1913.[22] Munsterberg suggested that psychologists could make valuable contributions to managers in the areas of employee selection and motivation. Industrial psychology is still a major course of study at many colleges and universities. Another early advocate of the behavioral approach to management was Mary Parker Follett.[23] Follett worked during the scientific management era but quickly came to recognize the human element in the workplace. Indeed, her work clearly anticipated the behavioral management perspective and she appreciated the need to understand the role of behavior in organizations.

The Hawthorne Studies

Although Munsterberg and Follett made major contributions to the development of the behavioral approach to management, its primary catalyst was a series of studies conducted near Chicago at Western Electric's Hawthorne plant between 1927 and 1932. The research, originally sponsored by General Electric, was conducted by Elton Mayo and his associates.[24] Mayo was a faculty member and consultant at Harvard. The first study involved manipulating illumination for one group of workers and comparing their subsequent productivity with the productivity of another group whose illumination was not changed. Surprisingly, when illumination was increased for the experimental group, productivity went up in both groups. Productivity continued to increase in both groups, even when the lighting for the experimental group was decreased. Not until the lighting was reduced to the level of moonlight did productivity begin to decline (and General Electric withdrew its sponsorship).

Another experiment established a piecework incentive pay plan for a group of nine men assembling terminal banks for telephone exchanges. Scientific management would have predicted that each man would try to maximize his pay by producing as many units as possible. Mayo and his associates, however, found that the group itself informally established an acceptable level of output for its members. Workers who overproduced were branded "rate busters," and underproducers were labeled "chiselers." To be accepted by the group, workers produced at the accepted level. As they approached this acceptable level of output, workers slacked off to avoid overproducing.

Other studies, including an interview program involving several thousand workers, led Mayo and his associates to conclude that human behavior was much more important in the workplace than had been previously believed. In the lighting experiment, for example, the results were attributed to the fact that both groups received special attention and sympathetic supervision for perhaps the first time. The incentive pay plans did not work because wage incentives were less important to the individual workers than was social acceptance in determining output. In short, individual and social processes played a major role in shaping worker attitudes and behavior.

The Hawthorne studies were a series of early experiments that focused on behavior in the workplace. In one experiment involving this group of workers, for example, researchers monitored how productivity changed as a result of changes in working conditions. The Hawthorne studies and subsequent experiments led scientists to the conclusion that the human element is very important in the workplace.

The Human Relations Movement

The **human relations movement**, which grew from the Hawthorne studies and was a popular approach to management for many years, proposed that workers respond primarily to the social context of the workplace, including social conditioning,

human relations movement Proposed that workers respond primarily to the social context of the workplace, including social conditioning, group norms, and interpersonal dynamics

group norms, and interpersonal dynamics. A basic assumption of the human relations movement was that the manager's concern for workers would lead to increased satisfaction, which would in turn result in improved performance. Two writers who helped advance the human relations movement were Abraham Maslow and Douglas McGregor.

In 1943, Maslow advanced a theory suggesting that people are motivated by a hierarchy of needs, including monetary incentives and social acceptance.[25] Maslow's hierarchy, perhaps the best known human relations theory, is described in detail in Chapter 16. Meanwhile, Douglas McGregor's, Theory X and Theory Y model best represents the essence of the human relations movement (see Table 2.2).[26] According to McGregor, Theory X and Theory Y reflect two extreme belief sets that different managers have about their workers. **Theory X** is a relatively negative view of workers and is consistent with the views of scientific management. **Theory Y** is more positive and represents the assumptions that human relations advocates make. In McGregor's view, Theory Y was a more appropriate philosophy for managers to adhere to. Both Maslow and McGregor notably influenced the thinking of many practicing managers.

Theory X A relatively negative view of workers consistent with the views of scientific management

Theory Y A positive view of workers; it represents the assumptions that human relations advocates make

The Emergence of Organizational Behavior

Munsterberg, Mayo, Maslow, McGregor, and others have made valuable contributions to management. Contemporary theorists, however, have noted that many assertions of the human relationists were simplistic and inadequate descriptions of work behavior. For example, the assumption that worker satisfaction leads to improved performance has been shown to have little, if any, validity. If anything, satisfaction follows good performance rather than precedes it. (These issues are addressed in Chapters 15 and 16.)

Table 2.2

Theory X and Theory Y

Douglas McGregor developed Theory X and Theory Y. He argued that Theory X best represented the views of scientific management and Theory Y represented the human relations approach. McGregor believed that Theory Y was the best philosophy for all managers.

Theory X Assumptions	1. People do not like work and try to avoid it. 2. People do not like work, so managers have to control, direct, coerce, and threaten employees to get them to work toward organizational goals. 3. People prefer to be directed, to avoid responsibility, and to want security; they have little ambition.
Theory Y Assumptions	1. People do not naturally dislike work; work is a natural part of their lives. 2. People are internally motivated to reach objectives to which they are committed. 3. People are committed to goals to the degree that they receive personal rewards when they reach their objectives. 4. People will both seek and accept responsibility under favorable conditions. 5. People have the capacity to be innovative in solving organizational problems. 6. People are bright, but under most organizational conditions their potentials are underutilized.

Source: Douglas McGregor, "Theory X and Theory Y" from *The Human Side of Enterprise*, Copyright © 1960 by McGraw-Hill. Reprinted by permission of The McGraw-Hill Companies, Inc.

Current behavioral perspectives on management, known as **organizational behavior**, acknowledge that human behavior in organizations is much more complex than the human relationists realized. The field of organizational behavior draws from a broad, interdisciplinary base of psychology, sociology, anthropology, economics, and medicine. Organizational behavior takes a holistic view of behavior and addresses individual, group, and organization processes. These processes are major elements in contemporary management theory.[27] Important topics in this field include job satisfaction, stress, motivation, leadership, group dynamics, organizational politics, interpersonal conflict, and the structure and design of organizations.[28] A contingency orientation also characterizes the field (discussed more fully later in this chapter). Our discussions of organizing (Chapters 11–14) and leading (Chapters 15–19) are heavily influenced by organizational behavior. And finally, as noted in *Working with Diversity*, managers need a solid understanding of human behavior as they address such diversity-related issues as religion in the workplace.

organizational behavior Contemporary field focusing on behavioral perspectives on management

WORKING WITH DIVERSITY

RELIGION AND THE WORKPLACE

Globalization and an increasingly diverse workforce has brought more employees of varying religious beliefs together in the workplace. What can companies do about managing on the job conflicts that can arise from different religious customs?

Some companies, such as Jeepers, a theme-park operator, have eased restrictions on facial hair to accommodate men who wear beards for religious or medical reasons. Others, including Royal Caribbean Cruises, have rehired Muslim women who were fired for wearing head scarves while working. But other workplace issues raised by religious practices can be more difficult to resolve, as Whirlpool has learned.

At Whirlpool's appliance factory in LaVergne, Tennessee, Muslims comprise about 10 percent of the workforce during the peak production months of January to June. Initially, the assembly line for air conditioners and refrigerators was disrupted when Muslim employees stopped working to pray during work hours. Another problem was arranging the work schedule so Muslim employees could attend a midday congregational prayer session every Friday. Ultimately, plant managers found a way to handle scheduling better. Now some Muslim employees start working earlier on Fridays so they can take an extended break for the noontime prayer session.

Clothing is another area where religious customs can conflict with workplace requirements. For safety reasons, Whirlpool's plant managers decided that women employees could not wear head scarves near assembly lines and similar equipment. After discussing the issue with the Muslim women on staff, however, the managers agreed to allow scarves tied close to the head.

A more complex issue is differing attitudes toward women in positions of authority. Some Muslim men have left Whirlpool rather than remain in positions where they were supervised by women managers. Yet other Muslim men have learned to adapt to such workplace situations. In the end, managing diversity means finding creative ways to resolve these kinds of conflicts so both employees and the organization are satisfied.

> *We've had conflicts and confrontations over any number of things. I'm just happy things didn't erupt into a religious war.*
>
> *— William J. Chickering, director of employee relations, Whirlpool**

Reference: Timothy D. Schellhardt, "In a Factory Schedule, Where Does Religion Fit In?" *Wall Street Journal*, March 4, 1999, pp. B1, B12 (*quote on p. B1).

Table 2.3

The Behavioral Management Perspective

General Summary	The behavioral management perspective focuses on employee behavior in an organizational context. Stimulated by the birth of industrial psychology, the human relations movement supplanted scientific management as the dominant approach to management in the 1930s and 1940s. Prominent contributors to this movement were Elton Mayo, Abraham Maslow, and Douglas McGregor. Organizational behavior, the contemporary outgrowth of the behavioral management perspective, draws from an interdisciplinary base and recognizes the complexities of human behavior in organizational settings.
Contributions	Provided important insights into motivation, group dynamics, and other interpersonal processes in organizations. Focused managerial attention on these same processes. Challenged the view that employees are tools and furthered the belief that employees are valuable resources.
Limitations	The complexity of individual behavior makes prediction of that behavior difficult. Many behavioral concepts have not yet been put to use because some managers are reluctant to adopt them. Contemporary research findings by behavioral scientists are often not communicated to practicing managers in an understandable form.

The Behavioral Management Perspective Today

Table 2.3 summarizes the behavioral management perspective and lists its contributions and limitations. The primary contributions relate to ways in which this approach has changed managerial thinking. Managers are now more likely to recognize the importance of behavioral processes and to view employees as valuable resources instead of mere tools. On the other hand, organizational behavior is still imprecise in its ability to predict behavior. It is not always accepted or understood by practicing managers. Hence, the contributions of the behavioral school have yet to be fully realized.

MANAGEMENT IMPLICATIONS   Managers should remember that people are not machines and should not focus so much on the technical side of things that they ignore behavioral forces and processes in their organizations. People and their behaviors represent a powerful force that can enhance—or diminish—the effectiveness of any organization.[29] At the same time, managers should also not fall prey to the commonsense fallacy that improving employee satisfaction will result in increased performance. Further, while employee morale and satisfaction are indeed important, managers should not stress these and other behavioral forces to the detriment of productivity and operating systems.

The Quantitative Management Perspective

The third major school of management thought began to emerge during World War II. During the war, government officials and scientists in England and the United States worked to help the military deploy its resources more efficiently and effectively. These groups took some of the mathematical approaches to management developed decades earlier by Taylor and Gantt and applied them to logistical problems during the war.[30] They learned that problems regarding troop, equipment, and submarine deployment, for example, could all be solved through mathematical analysis. After the war, companies such as Du Pont and General Electric began to use the same techniques for deploying employees, choosing plant locations, and planning warehouses. Basically, then, this perspective is concerned with applying quantitative techniques to management. More specifically, the **quantitative management perspective** focuses on decision making, economic effectiveness, mathematical models, and the use of computers. There are two branches of the quantitative approach: management science and operations management.

quantitative management perspective Applies quantitative techniques to management

Management Science

Unfortunately, the term *management science* appears to be related to scientific management, the approach developed by Taylor and others early in this century. But the two have little in common and should not be confused. **Management science** focuses specifically on the development of mathematical models. A mathematical model is a simplified representation of a system, process, or relationship.

management science Focuses specifically on the development of mathematical models

At its most basic level, management science focuses on models, equations, and similar representations of reality. For example, managers at Detroit Edison use mathematical models to determine how best to route repair crews during blackouts. The Bank of New England uses models to figure out how many tellers need to be on duty at each location at various times throughout the day. In recent years, paralleling the advent of the personal computer, management science techniques have become increasingly sophisticated. For example, automobile manufacturers Daimler Chrysler and Ford use realistic computer simulations to study collision damage to cars. These simulations give them precise information and avoid the costs of "crashing" so many test cars.

Operations Management

Operations management is somewhat less mathematical and statistically sophisticated than management science and can be applied more directly to managerial situations. Indeed, we can think of **operations management** as a form of applied management science. Operations management techniques are generally concerned with helping the organization produce its products or services more efficiently and can be applied to a wide range of problems.

operations management Concerned with helping the organization produce its products or services more efficiently

For example, Rubbermaid and The Home Depot each use operations management techniques to manage their inventories. (Inventory management is concerned with specific inventory problems such as balancing carrying costs and ordering costs and determining the optimal order quantity.) Linear programming (which involves computing simultaneous solutions to a set of linear equations) helps United Air Lines plan its flight schedules, Consolidated Freightways develop its shipping routes, and General Instrument Corporation plan what instruments to produce at various times. Other operations management techniques include queuing theory, breakeven analysis, and simulation. All of these techniques and procedures apply directly to operations, but they are also helpful in such areas as finance, marketing, and human resource management.

Table 2.4

The Quantitative Management Perspective

General Summary	The quantitative management perspective focuses on applying mathematical models and processes to management situations. Management science specifically deals with the development of mathematical models to aid in decision making and problem solving. Operations management focuses more directly on the application of management science to organizations. Management information systems are developed to provide information to managers.
Contributions	Developed sophisticated quantitative techniques to assist in decision making. Application of models has increased our awareness and understanding of complex organizational processes and situations. Has been very useful in the planning and controlling processes.
Limitations	Cannot fully explain or predict the behavior of people in organizations. Mathematical sophistication may come at the expense of other important skills. Models may require unrealistic or unfounded assumptions.

The Quantitative Management Perspective Today

Like the other management perspectives, the quantitative management perspective has made important contributions and has certain limitations. Both are summarized in Table 2.4. It has provided managers with an abundance of decision-making tools and techniques and has increased understanding of overall organizational processes. It has been particularly useful in the areas of planning and controlling. On the other hand, mathematical models cannot fully account for individual behaviors and attitudes. Some believe that the time needed to develop competence in quantitative techniques retards the development of other managerial skills. Finally, mathematical models typically require a set of assumptions that may not be realistic.

MANAGEMENT IMPLICATIONS It is important for managers to learn and understand the basic mathematical techniques and procedures that have been developed within management science. They should also know when to use these techniques and when to recognize their limitations. Further, managers should also avoid placing so much reliance on quantitative results that they ignore their own experience and intuition.

Integrating Perspectives for Managers

Recognizing that the classical, behavioral, and quantitative approaches to management are not necessarily contradictory or mutually exclusive is important. Even though very different assumptions and predictions are made by each of the three perspectives, each can also complement the others. Indeed, a complete understanding of management requires an appreciation of all three perspectives. The systems and contingency perspectives can help us integrate the earlier approaches and enlarge our understanding of all three.

The Systems Perspective

We briefly introduced the systems perspective in Chapter 1 in our definition of management. A **system** is an interrelated set of elements functioning as a whole.[31] As shown in Figure 2.3, by viewing an organization as a system, we can identify four basic elements: inputs, transformation processes, outputs, and feedback. First, inputs are the material, human, financial, and information resources the organization gets from its environment. Next, through technological and managerial processes, inputs are transformed into outputs. Outputs include products, services, or both (tangible and intangible); profits, losses, or both (even not-for-profit organizations must operate within their budgets); employee behaviors; and information. Finally, the environment reacts to these outputs and provides feedback to the system.

> **system** An interrelated set of elements functioning as a whole

Thinking of organizations as systems provides us with a variety of important viewpoints on organizations, such as the concepts of open systems, subsystems, synergy, and entropy. **Open systems** are systems that interact with their environment, whereas **closed systems** do not interact with their environment. Although organizations are open systems, some make the mistake of ignoring their environment and behaving as though their environment is not important.

> **open system** An organizational system that interacts with its environment
>
> **closed system** An organizational system that does not interact with its environment
>
> **subsystem** A system within a broader system

The systems perspective also stresses the importance of **subsystems**—systems within a broader system. For example, the marketing, production, and finance functions within Mattel are systems in their own right but are also subsystems within the overall organization. Because they are interdependent, a change in one subsystem can affect other subsystems as well. If the production department at Mattel lowers the quality of the toys being made (by buying lower-quality materials, for example), the effects are felt in finance (improved cash flow in the short run owing to lower costs) and marketing (decreased sales in the long run because of customer dissatisfaction). Managers must therefore remember that, although organizational subsystems can be managed with some degree of autonomy, their interdependence should not be overlooked.

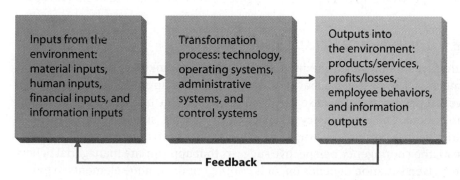

Figure 2.3

The Systems Perspective of Organizations

By viewing organizations as systems, managers can better understand the importance of their environment and the level of interdependence among subsystems within the organization. Managers must also understand how their decisions affect and are affected by other subsystems within the organization.

Open systems are those that interact with their environment. In an age of increasing globalization and diversity, an open systems perspective is becoming increasingly important to all businesses. For example, this food service center in Singapore was created to serve Chinese, Indian, and Malay dishes. Not only does the station provide a variety of foods, but it must also offer different varieties of cutlery and other dining accoutrements as well as use signage in different languages.

synergy Two or more subsystems working together may often be more successful than when working alone

Synergy suggests that organizational units (or subsystems) may often be more successful working together than working alone. The Walt Disney Company, for example, benefits greatly from synergy. The company's movies, theme parks, television programs, and merchandise licensing programs all benefit one another. Children who enjoy a Disney movie like Tarzan want to go to Disney World and see the Tarzan show there and buy stuffed animals of the film's characters. Music from the film generates additional revenues for the firm, as do computer games and other licensing arrangements for lunch boxes, clothing, and so forth. Synergy was also the major objective in the first megamerger of 2000 between America Online and Time Warner.[32] Synergy is an important concept for managers because it emphasizes the importance of working together in a cooperative and coordinated fashion.[33]

entropy A normal process leading to system decline

Finally, **entropy** is a normal process that leads to system decline. When an organization does not monitor feedback from its environment and make appropriate adjustments, it may fail. For example, witness the problems of Studebaker (an automobile manufacturer) and Montgomery Ward (a major retailer). Each of these organizations went bankrupt because it failed to revitalize itself and keep pace with changes in its environment. A primary objective of management, from a systems perspective, is to re-energize the organization continually to avoid entropy.

The Contingency Perspective

universal perspective An attempt to identify the one best way to do something

contingency perspective Suggests that appropriate managerial behavior in a given situation depends on, or is contingent on, unique elements in that situation

Another recent noteworthy addition to management thinking is the contingency perspective. The classical, behavioral, and quantitative approaches are considered **universal perspectives** because they tried to identify the "one best way" to manage organizations. The **contingency perspective**, in contrast, suggests that universal theories cannot be applied to organizations because each organization is unique. Instead, the contingency perspective suggests that appropriate managerial behavior in a given situation depends on, or is contingent on, unique elements in that situation.[34]

Stated differently, effective managerial behavior in one situation cannot always be generalized to other situations. Recall, for example, that Frederick Taylor assumed that all workers would generate the highest possible level of output to maximize their own personal economic gain. We can imagine some people being motivated primarily by money—but we can just as easily imagine other people being motivated by the desire for leisure time, status, social acceptance, or any combination of these (as Mayo found at the Hawthorne plant). This perspective relates perfectly to Leslie Wexner and Limited, featured in the chapter opening incident. His managerial style worked perfectly when his firm was small and rapidly growing, but it did not match as well when Limited became a huge, mature enterprise. Thus, he had to alter his style at that point to match the changing needs of his business.

An Integrating Framework

We noted earlier that the classical, behavioral, and quantitative management perspectives can be complementary and that the systems and contingency perspectives can help integrate them. Our framework for integrating the various approaches to management is shown in Figure 2.4. The initial premise of the framework is that before attempting to apply any specific concepts or ideas from the three major perspectives, managers must recognize the interdependence of units within the organization, the effect of environmental influences, and the need to respond to the unique characteristics of each situation. The ideas of subsystem interdependencies and environmental influences are given to us by systems theory, and the situational view of management is derived from a contingency perspective.

With these ideas as basic assumptions, the manager can use valid tools, techniques, concepts, and theories of the classical, behavioral, and quantitative

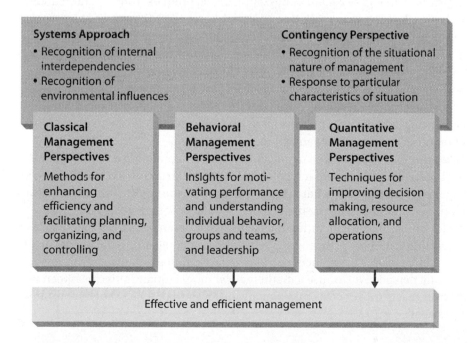

Systems Approach
- Recognition of internal interdependencies
- Recognition of environmental influences

Contingency Perspective
- Recognition of the situational nature of management
- Response to particular characteristics of situation

Classical Management Perspectives

Methods for enhancing efficiency and facilitating planning, organizing, and controlling

Behavioral Management Perspectives

Insights for motivating performance and understanding individual behavior, groups and teams, and leadership

Quantitative Management Perspectives

Techniques for improving decision making, resource allocation, and operations

Effective and efficient management

Figure 2.4

An Integrative Framework of Management Perspectives
Each of the major perspectives on management can be useful to modern managers. Before using any of them, however, the manager should recognize the situational context within which they operate. The systems and contingency perspectives serve to integrate the classical, behavioral, and quantitative management perspectives.

management perspectives. For example, managers can still use many of the basic techniques from scientific management. In many contemporary settings, the scientific study of jobs and production techniques can enhance productivity. But managers should not rely solely on these techniques, nor should they ignore the human element. The behavioral perspective is also of use to managers today. By drawing on contemporary ideas of organizational behavior, the manager can better appreciate the role of employee needs and behaviors in the workplace. Motivation, leadership, communication, and group processes are especially important. The quantitative perspective provides the manager with a set of useful tools and techniques. The development and use of management science models and the application of operations management methods can help managers increase their efficiency and effectiveness.

Consider the new distribution manager of a large wholesale firm whose job is to manage one hundred truck drivers and to coordinate standard truck routes in the most efficient fashion. This new manager, with little relevant experience, might attempt to increase productivity by employing strict work specialization and close supervision (as suggested by scientific management). But doing so may decrease employee satisfaction and morale and increase turnover (as predicted by organizational behavior). The manager might also develop a statistical formula to use route driver time more efficiently (from management science), but this new system could disrupt existing work groups and social patterns (from organizational behavior). The manager might create even more problems by trying to impose programs and practices derived from her previous job. An incentive program welcomed by retail clerks, for example, might not work for truck drivers.

The manager should soon realize that a broader perspective is needed. Systems and contingency perspectives help provide broader solutions. Also, as the integrative framework in Figure 2.4 illustrates, applying techniques from several schools works better than trying to make one approach solve all problems. To solve a problem of declining productivity, the manager might look to scientific management (perhaps jobs are inefficiently designed or workers improperly trained), organizational behavior (worker motivation may be low or group norms may be limiting output), or operations management (facilities may be improperly laid out or materials shortages may be resulting from poor inventory management). And before implementing any plans for improvement, the manager should try to assess their effect on other areas of the organization.

Now suppose that the same manager is involved in planning a new warehouse. She will probably consider what type of management structure to create (classical management perspective), what kinds of leaders and work-group arrangements to develop (behavioral management perspective), and how to develop a network model for designing and operating the facility itself (quantitative perspective). As a final example, if employee turnover is too high, the manager might consider an incentive system (classical perspective), plan a motivational enhancement program (behavioral perspective), or use a mathematical model (quantitative perspective) to discover that turnover costs may actually be lower than the cost of making any changes at all.

MANAGEMENT   Managers should always remember that there are no universal
IMPLICATIONS   solutions to problems or standard responses to situations. Just as
a carpenter selects certain tools for certain jobs, so too should a manager carefully
evaluate each situation and then select from the broad array of management techniques, models, and theories that best suit each situation. Managers should also keep
in mind that any given situation may require multiple perspectives and viewpoints.

Contemporary Management Issues and Challenges

Interest in management theory and practice has heightened in recent years as
new issues and challenges have emerged. No new paradigm has been formulated
that replaces the traditional views, but managers continue to strive toward a better understanding of how they can better compete and lead their organizations
toward improved effectiveness. Figure 2.5 summarizes the historical development
of the major models of management, described in the preceding sections, and

Figure 2.5

The Emergence of Modern Management Perspectives

Most contemporary management perspectives have emerged and evolved over the last one hundred years or so. Beginning with the
classical management perspective, first developed toward the end of the nineteenth century, and on through contemporary applied
perspectives, managers have an array of useful techniques, methods, and approaches for solving problems and enhancing the effectiveness of their organizations. Of course, managers also need to recognize that not every idea set forth is valid, and that even those
that are useful are not applicable in all settings. And new methods and approaches will continue to be developed in the future.

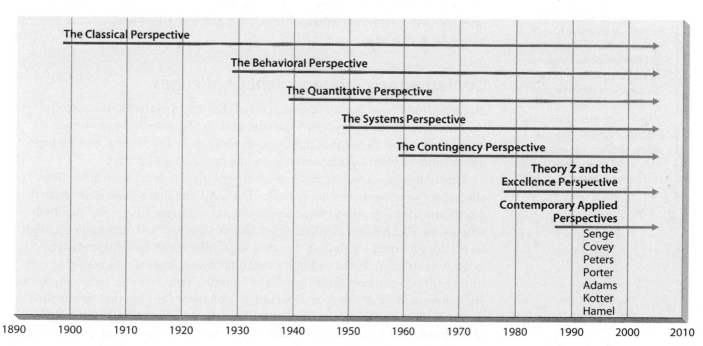

One of the biggest issues facing businesses today is how to integrate most effectively traditional operations with e-business opportunities. Consider, for example, the approach taken by Sephora Dimensions, the leading chain of perfume and cosmetics stores in France and the second-largest in Europe. Sephora builds traditional "brick-and-mortar" stores in key fashion centers. But each store also has computer terminals, such as the one shown here, that allow customers to browse for other products and place on-line orders. Sephora has recently transferred this business model to U.S. and Asian markets and now has over 200 stores around the world.

puts into historical context the contemporary applied perspectives discussed in the next section.

Contemporary Applied Perspectives

In recent years, books written for the so-called popular press have also had a major impact on both the field of organizational behavior and the practice of management. This trend first became noticeable in the early 1980s with the success of books such as William Ouchi's *Theory Z* and Thomas Peters and Robert Waterman's *In Search of Excellence*. Each of these books spent time on the *New York Times* best-seller list and was virtually required reading for any manager wanting at least to appear informed. Biographies of executives like Lee Iacocca and Donald Trump also received widespread attention. And bidding for the publishing rights to Jack Welch's memoirs, to be published when he retires as CEO from General Electric in 2001, exceeded $7 million.[35]

In recent years other applied authors have had a major impact on management theory and practice. Among the most popular applied authors today are Peter Senge, Stephen Covey, Tom Peters, Michael Porter, John Kotter, and Gary Hamel. These books highlight the management practices of successful firms like Shell, Ford, IBM, and others or outline conceptual or theoretical models or frameworks to guide managers as they formulate strategy or motivate their employees. The impact of their work is discussed in more depth in *Today's Management Issues*. Scott Adams, creator of the popular comic strip *Dilbert*, is also immensely popular today. Adams himself is a former communications industry worker who developed his strip to illustrate some of the absurdities that occasionally afflict contemporary organizational life. The daily strip is routinely posted outside office doors, above copy machines, and beside water coolers in hundreds of offices.

Contemporary Management Challenges

Managers today also face an imposing set of challenges as they guide and direct the fortunes of their companies. Coverage of each of these challenges is thoroughly integrated throughout this book. In addition, many of them are also highlighted and/or given focused coverage in one or more special ways.

One of the most critical challenges facing managers today is an acute labor shortage. The booming economy has combined with rapid advances in technology to provide more jobs in some employment sectors than there are qualified employees. This pattern manifests itself in several ways. First, companies in high-technology markets are finding that they must offer lavish benefits and high salaries to attract talented and motivated employees. And even though they continue to provide an ever-growing array of benefits, many of these same employees still move on to other—and more lucrative—jobs more quickly than at any time in recent memory. This trend has also trickled down to lower-skill jobs as well. Many hotels and restaurants, for example, are having difficulties in maintaining

TODAY'S MANAGEMENT ISSUES

CAN GURUS HELP COMPANIES COPE?

Contemporary management perspectives have been shaped and advanced by the ideas of a number of high-powered gurus. Michael Porter's groundbreaking analyses of competitive forces affecting businesses and nations have attracted AT&T and other companies as clients for his consulting firm, Monitor. Gary Hamel's work on corporate strategy has brought to *Strategos*, his consulting firm, clients such as General Motors. Like nearly every other well-known guru, both Porter and Hamel have written best-selling books that spread their ideas throughout the corporate world. But can gurus really help companies cope with thorny business issues and challenges?

Sam Hill, a marketing consultant based in Connecticut, observes that some gurus may be good at counseling—offering broad, general advice—but not at consulting—which requires in-depth research and analysis of a specific problem to find a specific solution. In Hill's view, few consultants are equipped to solve complicated business problems off the cuff. He also says that digging down to the nitty-gritty of a problem and weighing possible solutions requires any number of "constructive arguments." Yet clients rarely debate with gurus; most of the time, they simply listen and make notes as gurus speak.

For their part, clients who hire a guru may have unrealistic expectations. Because they are paying thousands of dollars per day for the guru's time, clients may want the expert to offer solutions too quickly. Gurus realize that complex management problems cannot be solved with simplistic, one-solution-fits-all answers. Nonetheless, some clients believe that gurus should have the expertise and background to go to the heart of the matter and suggest answers without a great deal of analysis.

Some gurus have built large consulting firms to help clients apply their ideas and tackle major business challenges. Others disseminate their insights through books, articles, and speeches. In general, gurus can be a rich source of new ideas and a spark for creative problem-solving—if managers are careful to analyze critically how concepts apply to their particular organizations and situations.

> *Companies that bring in gurus as consultants tend to think that if they're paying $20 a minute, the guru should bypass the analysis and get straight to the answer.*
>
> —*Sam Hill, co-founder of Helios Consulting Group**

Reference: Stuart Crainer and Des Dearlove, "Gurus Inc.," *Across the Board,* October 1999, pp. 17–22 (*quote on p. 18).

---

an adequate staff of house cleaners and dishwashers because of the abundance of more attractive jobs available today.[36]

A second important challenge today is the management of diversity. Diversity refers to differences among people. While diversity may be reflected along numerous dimensions, most managers tend to focus on age, gender, ethnicity, and physical abilities/disabilities. The internationalization of businesses has also increased diversity in many organizations, carrying with it additional challenges as well as new opportunities. We cover diversity in detail in Chapter 6 and in several boxed features called *Working with Diversity*, which appaer throughout the text.

Aside from demographic composition, the workforce today is also changing in other ways. It seems like the values, goals, and ideals of each succeeding generation differ from those of their parents. Today's young workers, for example, are sometimes stereotyped as being less devoted to long-term career prospects and are less willing to conform to a corporate mind-set that stresses conformity and uniformity. Thus, managers are increasingly faced with the challenge of first creating an environment that will be attractive to today's worker. And they must address the challenge of providing new and different incentives to keep people motivated and interested in their work. And finally, they must incorporate sufficient flexibility in the organization to accommodate an ever-changing set of lifestyles and preferences.

Another management challenge that managers must be prepared to address is change. While organizations have always had to be concerned with managing change, the rapid and constant environmental change faced by businesses today has made change management even more critical. Simply put, an organization that fails to monitor its environment and to keep pace with that environment is doomed to failure. But more and more managers are seeing change as an opportunity, not a cause for alarm. Indeed, some managers think that if things get too calm in an organization and people start to become complacent, managers should shake things up to get everyone energized. We discuss the management of organizational change in more detail in Chapter 13.

New technology, especially as it relates to information, also poses an increasingly important management challenge. The Internet and the increased use of e-mail and voice-mail systems are among the most recent technological changes in this area. Among the key issues associated with information technology are employee privacy, decision-making quality, and optimizing a firm's investments in new forms of technology as they continue to emerge. A related issue confronting managers has to do with the increased capabilities this technology provides for people to work at places other than their offices. Finally, the appropriate role of the Internet in business strategy is also a complex arena for managers. We cover information technology in Chapter 22, as well as in several boxed features called *Management InfoTech*. We also provide numerous illustrations of Internet-related business issues in other boxes called *Managing in an E-business World*.

Another important management challenge today is the complex array of new ways of organizing that managers can consider. Recall from our earlier discussion that early organization theorists like Max Weber advocated "one best way" of organizing. These organizational prototypes generally resembled pyramids—tall structures with power controlled at the top and rigid policies and procedures governing most activities. Now, however, many organizations are seeking greater flexibility and the ability to respond more quickly to their environment by adopting flat structures. These flat structures are characterized by few levels of management, wide spans of management, and fewer rules and regulations. The increased use of work teams also goes hand in hand with this new approach to organizing. These issues are given considerable attention in Chapters 12 and 19.

Globalization is yet another significant contemporary challenge for managers. Managing in a global economy poses many different challenges and opportunities. For example, at a macro level, property ownership arrangements vary widely. So does the availability of natural resources and components of the infrastructure, as well as the role of government in business. But for our purposes, a very important consideration is how behavioral processes vary widely across cultural and national boundaries. For example, values, symbols, and beliefs differ sharply among cultures. Different work norms and the role work plays in a person's life, for example, influence patterns of both work-related behavior and attitudes toward work. They also affect the nature of supervisory relationships, decision-making styles and processes, and organizational configurations. Group and intergroup processes, responses to stress, and the nature of political behaviors also differ from culture to culture. Chapter 5 is devoted to global issues, as are numerous boxed features called *The World of Management.*

Another management challenge that has taken on renewed importance is ethics and social responsibility. Unfortunately, business scandals have become almost commonplace today. From the view of social responsibility, increasing attention has been focused on pollution and business's obligation to help clean our environment, business contributions to social causes, and so forth. Chapter 4 covers ethics and social responsibility in more detail, as do several boxed features called *Today's Management Issues.*

Quality also continues to pose an important management challenge today. Quality is an important issue for several reasons. First, more and more organizations are using quality as a basis for competition. Continental Airlines, for example, stresses its high rankings in the J.D. Powers survey of customer satisfaction in its print advertising. Second, improving quality tends to increase productivity because making higher-quality products generally results in less waste and rework. Third, enhancing quality lowers costs. Whistler Corporation once found that it was using one hundred of its 250 employees to repair defective radar detectors that were built incorrectly the first time. Quality is also important because of its relationship to productivity. Quality is highlighted in Chapter 21.

Finally, the shift toward a service economy also continues to be important. Traditionally, most businesses were manufacturers—they used tangible resources like raw materials and machinery to create tangible products like automobiles and steel. In the last few decades, however, the service sector of the economy has become much more important. Indeed, services now account for well over half of the gross domestic product in the United States and play a similarly important role in many other industrialized nations as well. Service technology involves the use of both tangible resources (such as machinery) and intangible resources (such as intellectual property) to create intangible services (such as a haircut, insurance protection, or transportation between two cities). While there are obviously many similarities between managing in a manufacturing and a service organization, there are also many fundamental differences.

MANAGEMENT Staying abreast of contemporary management issues and chal-
IMPLICATIONS lenges is a bit of a juggling act for managers. On the one hand, they need to keep up with current developments in their field by reading current literature. On the other hand, some of the popular press material about business and management is simply fad or, worse, an incomplete or inaccurate "recipe" for success.[37] Similarly, new challenges and issues often arise with little or no advance warning. Some of these remain significant and enduring, while others fall by the wayside very quickly. Thus, the astute manager will learn to take an open-minded but critical view toward new ideas and issues.

Summary of Key Points

Theories are important as organizers of knowledge and as road maps for action. Understanding the historical context and precursors of management and organizations provides a sense of heritage and can also help managers to avoid repeating the mistakes of others. Evidence suggests that interest in management dates back thousands of years, but a scientific approach to management has emerged only in the last one hundred years. During the first few decades of the twentieth century, three primary perspectives on management emerged: the classical perspective, the behavioral perspective, and the quantitative perspective.

The classical management perspective had two major branches: scientific management and administrative management. Scientific management was concerned with improving efficiency and work methods for individual workers. Administrative management was more concerned with how organizations themselves should be structured and arranged for efficient operations. Both branches paid little attention to the role of the worker.

The behavioral management perspective, characterized by a concern for individual and group behavior, emerged primarily as a result of the Hawthorne studies. The human relations movement recognized the importance and potential of behavioral processes in organizations but made many overly simplistic assumptions about those processes. Organizational behavior, a more realistic outgrowth of the behavioral perspective, is of interest to many contemporary managers.

The quantitative management perspective and its two components, management science and operations management, attempt to apply quantitative techniques to decision making and problem solving. These areas are also of considerable importance to contemporary managers. Their contributions have been facilitated by the tremendous increase in the use of personal computers and integrated information networks.

The three major perspectives should be viewed in a complementary, not a contradictory, light. Each has something of value to offer. The key is understanding how to use them effectively. Two relatively recent additions to management theory, the systems and contingency perspectives, appear to have great potential both as approaches to management and as frameworks for integrating the other perspectives.

A variety of popular applied perspectives influence management practice today. Important issues and challenges facing managers include employee retention, diversity, the new workforce, organization change, ethics and social responsibility, the importance of quality, and the continued shift toward a service economy.

Discussion Questions

Questions for Review

1. Briefly summarize the classical management perspective and identify the most important contributors to each of its two branches.
2. Briefly summarize the Hawthorne studies. What are the primary conclusions reached following their completion?
3. Describe the contingency perspective and outline its usefulness to the study and practice of management.
4. What are some contemporary issues and challenges that managers must confront?

Questions for Analysis

5. In what ways do you think management in other countries evolved in the same ways as in the United States, and in what ways do you think it may have evolved differently?
6. Explain how a manager can use tools and techniques from each of the major management perspectives in a complementary fashion.
7. What recently published popular business books have been especially successful? Who are the prominent business leaders today whose ideas are widely accepted?

Questions for Application

8. Go to the library and locate material on Confucius. Outline his major ideas. Which seem to be applicable to management in the United States today?
9. Identify a local firm that has been in existence for a long time. Interview the current owner about the history of the firm and see if you can gain a better understanding of its current practices by learning about its past.
10. Read about or study the history of a company in which you are interested. Prepare for the class a brief report that stresses the impact of the firm's history on its current practices.

BUILDING EFFECTIVE *decision-making* SKILLS

Exercise Overview

As defined in Chapter 1, decision-making skills refer to a manager's ability to recognize and define problems and opportunities correctly and then to select an appropriate course of action to solve those problems and capitalize on the opportunities. This exercise will help you develop your own decision-making skills while also helping you to understand better the importance of subsystem interdependencies in organizations.

Exercise Background

Assume you are the vice president of operations for a large manufacturing company. Your firm makes home office furniture and cabinets for home theater systems. Because of the growth in each product line, the firm has also grown substantially in recent years. At the same time, this growth has not gone unnoticed, and several competitors have entered the market in the last two years. Your CEO has just instructed you to determine how to cut costs by 10 percent so prices can be cut by that same amount. She feels that this tactic is necessary to retain your market share in the face of new competition.

You have looked closely at the situation and have decided that there are three different ways you can accomplish this cost reduction. One option is to begin buying slightly lower-grade materials, such as wood, glue, and stain. Another option is to lay off a portion of your workforce and then pressure the remaining workers to work harder. As part of this same option, employees hired in the future will be selected from a lower-skilled labor pool and thus be paid a lower wage. The third option is to replace your existing equipment with newer, more efficient equipment. While this will require a substantial up-front investment, you are certain that lower production costs can be achieved.

Exercise Task

With this background in mind, respond to the following:

1. Carefully examine each of the three alternatives under consideration. In what ways might each alternative affect other parts of the organization?
2. Which is the most costly option (in terms of impact on other parts of the organization, not absolute dollars)? Which is the least costly?
3. What are the primary obstacles that you might face regarding each of the three alternatives?
4. Can you think of other alternatives that might accomplish the cost-reduction goal?

BUILDING EFFECTIVE *communication and interpersonal* SKILLS

Exercise Overview

As defined in Chapter 1, communication skills refer to the manager's abilities both to convey ideas and information to others effectively and to receive ideas and information effectively from others, and interpersonal skills refer to the ability to communicate with, understand, and motivate individuals and groups. This exercise applies these skills from a contingency perspective in selecting modes of communication to convey various kinds of news.

Exercise Background

You are the regional branch manager for a large insurance company. For the last week you have been so tied up in meetings that you have had little opportunity to communicate with any of your subordinates. You are now caught up, however, and have a lot of information to convey. Specifically, here is what people need to know and/or what you need to do:

1. Three people need to be told that they are getting a pay raise of 10 percent.
2. One person needs to be told that she has been placed on probation and will lose her job if her excessive absenteeism isn't corrected.
3. One person needs to be congratulated for receiving his master's degree.

4. Everyone needs to be informed about the schedule for the next cycle of performance reviews.
5. Two people need to be informed that their requests for transfers have been approved, while a third was denied. In addition, one other person is being transferred, even though she did not submit a transfer request. You know that she will be unhappy.

You can convey this information via telephone calls during regular office hours, a cell phone call as you're driving home this evening, a formal written letter, a handwritten memo, a face-to-face meeting, or e-mail.

Exercise Task

With this background in mind, respond to the following:

1. Choose a communication mode for each message you need to convey.
2. What factors went into your decision about each situation?
3. What would be the least appropriate communication mode for each message?
4. What would be the likely consequences for each inappropriate choice?

BUILDING EFFECTIVE *diagnostic and conceptual* SKILLS

Exercise Overview

Diagnostic skills are the skills that enable a manager to visualize the most appropriate response to a situation. Conceptual skills refer to the manager's ability to think in the abstract. This exercise will enable you to apply your diagnostic and conceptual skills to extrapolate from the past to the present to the future.

Exercise Background

While some basic consumer products have been around for decades, others have only recently come into being. Likewise, a variety of products were once commonplace but are now no longer available. Examples of such products include the automobile crank (once used to start car engines manually before electric starters were invented) and the wooden slide rule (once used to perform calculations before electronic calculators were invented).

Working alone, identify ten products or services currently available that might not exist in the next few years. Next, form small groups of four or five. Compare your individual lists and create a single group list that contains the ten best examples of products or services that may not exist in the future.

Exercise Task

Using the group list, respond to the questions that follow (your instructor will tell whether to do this individually or as a group):

1. Why might each product or service disappear?
2. Can you think of ways to prolong the existence of each product or service?
3. What advice might you give to the owner or top manager of a firm in these industries?
4. How easy or difficult was it to identify the ten requested examples? What factors made it easy or difficult?

CHAPTER CLOSING CASE

CONAGRA SEARCHES FOR SYNERGY

What do Hunt's ketchup, Orville Redenbacher's popcorn, Healthy Choice frozen meals, and Slim Jim jerky have in common? All are part of ConAgra's empire of food brands. With $25 billion in annual sales, ConAgra is the number-two U.S. food products company behind Kraft Foods. Aggressive acquisitions during the 1980s brought ninety different operating companies into the ConAgra family. Now CEO Bruce Rohde is working to lower systemwide costs and boost overall profits by improving coordination and cooperation among these diverse operations.

The corporate buying spree took place under Charles M. Harper, ConAgra's CEO before Rohde. Harper snapped up well-known food brands such as Butterball (turkeys), Swift Premium (cold cuts), and Hunt-Wesson (salad oils and tomato-based foods). Once under the ConAgra banner, these different companies were encouraged to continue operating as independent divisions. ConAgra had no corporate computer system; instead, the divisions used their own systems for accounting. In addition, each division continued to sell through its own sales force, forcing supermarket chains to arrange separate purchases with each division. Harper also started the Healthy Choice line of low-fat foods after suffering a heart attack and changing his diet to emphasize healthier fare.

ConAgra's highly decentralized structure worked well as long as sales and profits were growing at a strong pace. By the time Rohde was named to the top slot in 1996, however, consumers were spending more on restaurant meals, which meant they weren't spending as much on groceries for home-cooked meals. At the same time, the supermarket chains were consolidating through mergers and acquisitions, which gave the stores even more bargaining power when dealing with ConAgra and other suppliers. Meanwhile, competitors Kraft and Quaker Oats stepped up their trade promotions, offering special displays and other inducements to solidify relationships with major food chains. The road ahead looked extremely challenging for ConAgra.

As CEO, Rohde has cooked up a new recipe for synergy, reorganizing ConAgra's diverse collection of companies into three divisions. The food-service division sells ConAgra products such as chicken to restaurant chains such as Wendy's and Arby's. This division already accounts for half of the corporation's sales revenues and could potentially contribute even more to the bottom line. The retail division sells ConAgra products such as

Parkay margarine and Peter Pan peanut butter to grocery stores and supermarkets. The agricultural products division sells fertilizer and other products to farm producers. As part of this reorganization, ConAgra is closing more than a dozen inefficient factories and laying off 7,000 workers. So far, this reorganization has helped the company cut its costs by $100 million, a figure that could soon rise to $600 million in annual cost savings as reorganization continues.

ConAgra is also preparing a coordinated program to cross-sell brands inside supermarkets. For example, the company is considering offering a supermarket chain like Kroger's a special display featuring various foods for backyard barbecues. The display might hold bottles of Hunt's ketchup, cans of Van Camp's baked beans, and packages of Healthy choice bread—plus a sign reminding shoppers to pick up a package of Armour hot dogs in the refrigerated meats section. This enterprising cross-sell approach is designed to help ConAgra's powerful brands sell each other while giving supermarkets an attractive tool for sales building.

Today, ConAgra is continuing to acquire food-related businesses such as Seaboard poultry. It is also readying a counterattack on rivals with a fatter advertising budget for consumer campaigns to support its brands. But the environment remains challenging, and competitors are not letting up. Can Rohde's recipe successfully combine such disparate units as Marie Callender frozen foods, Egg Beaters egg substitutes, and Monfort beef products into one highly profitable corporate entity?

Case Questions

1. What management actions seem to have contributed to inefficient operation of ConAgra's subsystems?

2. What signs of entropy should ConAgra's management be alert for—and why?

3. What other kinds of programs might ConAgra develop to improve synergy among its brand-name food products?

Case References

Brandon Copple, "Synergy in Ketchup?" *Forbes*, February 7, 2000, pp. 68–69; "Food Giant ConAgra to Buy Company," Associated Press news story published in *The Bryan-College Station Eagle*, June 24, 2000, p. C6.

CHAPTER NOTES

1. "A Makeover That Began at the Top," *The Wall Street Journal*, May 25, 2000, pp. B1, B4 (quote on p. B1); Hoover's *Handbook of American Business 2000* (Austin: Hoover's Business Press, 2000), pp. 872–873.

2. Peter F. Drucker, "The Theory of the Business," *Harvard Business Review*, September–October 1994, pp. 95–104.

3. David Kirkpatrick, "Intel's Amazing Profit Machine," *Fortune*, February 17, 1997, pp. 60–72.

4. "Why Business History?" *Audacity*, Fall 1992, pp. 7–15. See also Alan L. Wilkins and Nigel J. Bristow, "For Successful Organization Culture, Honor Your Past," *The Academy of Management Executive*, August 1987, pp. 221–227.

5. Daniel Wren, *The Evolution of Management Thought*, 4th ed. (New York: Wiley, 1994); and Page Smith, *The Rise of Industrial America* (New York: McGraw-Hill, 1984).

6. Martha I. Finney, "Books That Changed Carreers," *HRMagazine*, June 1997, 141–145.

7. See Harriet Rubin, *The Princessa: Machiavelli for Women* (New York: Doubleday/Currency, 1997). See also Nanette Fondas, "Feminization Unveiled: Management Qualities in Contemporary Writings," *Academy of Management Review*, January 1997, pp.257–282.

8. Alan M. Kantrow (Ed.), "Why History Matters to Managers," *Harvard Business Review*, January–February 1986,pp. 81–88.

9. Wren, *The Evolution of Management Thought*.

10. Charles Babbage, *On the Economy of Machinery and Manufactures* (London: Charles Knight, 1832).

11. See Marina v. N. Whitman, *New World, New Rules* (Boston: Harvard Business School Press, 1999) for a recent discussion that reinforces this recommendation

12. Moshe F. Rubenstein and Iris R. Firstenberg, *The Minding Organization* (New York: John Wiley & Sons, 1999).

13. Wren, *The Evolution of Management Thought*.

14. Frederick W. Taylor, *Principles of Scientific Management* (New York: Harper and Brothers, 1911).

15. Charles D. Wrege and Amedeo G. Perroni, "Taylor's Pig-Tale: A Historical Analysis of Frederick W. Taylor's Pig-Iron Experiment," *Academy of Management Journal*, March 1974, pp. 6–27; and Charles D. Wrege and Ann Marie Stoka, "Cooke Creates a Classic: The Story Behind Taylor's Principles of Scientific Management," *Academy of Management Review*, October 1978, pp. 736–749.

16. Robert Kanigel, *The One Best Way* (New York: Viking, 1997); Oliver E. Allen, "'This Great Mental Revolution,'" *Audacity*, Summer 1996, pp. 52–61.

17. Henri Fayol, *General and Industrial Management*, trans. J. A. Coubrough (Geneva: International Management Institute, 1930).

18. Max Weber, *Theory of Social and Economic Organizations*, trans. T. Parsons (New York: Free Press, 1947); and Richard M. Weis, "Weber on Bureaucracy: Management Consultant or Political Theorist?" *Academy of Management Review*, April 1983, pp. 242–248.

19. Chester Barnard, *The Functions of the Executive* (Cambridge, Mass.: Harvard University Press, 1938).

20. "The Line Starts Here," *The Wall Street Journal*, January 11, 1999, pp. R1, R25.

21. See, for example, David A. Nadler and Michael L. Tushman, *Competing by Design—The Power of Organizational Architecture* (New York: Oxford University Press, 1997).

22. Hugo Munsterberg, *Psychology and Industrial Efficiency* (Boston: Houghton Mifflin, 1913).

23. Wren, *The Evolution of Management Thought*, pp. 255–264.

24. Elton Mayo, *The Human Problems of an Industrial Civilization* (New York: Macmillan, 1933); and Fritz J. Roethlisberger and William J. Dickson, *Management and the Worker* (Cambridge, Mass.: Harvard University Press, 1939).

25. Abraham Maslow, "A Theory of Human Motivation," *Psychological Review*, July 1943, pp. 370–396.

26. Douglas McGregor, *The Human Side of Enterprise* (New York: McGraw-Hill, 1960).

27. Sara L. Rynes and Christine Quinn Trank, "Behavioral Science in the Business School Curriculum: Teaching in a Changing Institutional Environment," *Academy of Management Review*, 1999, Vol. 24, No. 4, pp. 808–824.

28. See Gregory Moorhead and Ricky W. Griffin, *Organizational Behavior*, 6th ed. (Boston: Houghton Mifflin, 2001) for a review of current developments in the field of organizational behavior.

29. Jeffrey Pfeffer, *The Human Equation* (Boston: Harvard Business School Press, 1998); Sumantra Ghoshal and Christopher A. Bartlett, "Rebuilding Behavioral Context: A Blueprint for Corporate Renewal," *Sloan Management Review*, Winter 1996, pp. 23–36.

30. Wren, *The Evolution of Management Thought*, Chapter 21.

31. For more information on systems theory in general, see Ludwig von Bertalanffy, C. G. Hempel, R. E. Bass, and H. Jonas, "General Systems Theory: A New Approach to Unity of Science," I–VI *Human Biology*, Vol. 23, 1951, pp. 302–361. For systems theory as applied to organizations, see Fremont E. Kast and James E. Rosenzweig, "General Systems Theory: Applications for Organizations and Management," *Academy of Management Journal*, December 1972, pp. 447–465. For a recent update, see Donde P. Ashmos and George P. Huber, "The Systems Paradigm in Organization Theory: Correcting the Record and Suggesting the Future," *Academy of Management Review*, October 1987, pp. 607–621.

32. "Morning After," *Forbes*, February 7, 2000, pp. 54–56.

33. Kathleen M. Eisenhardt and D. Charles Galunic, "Coevolving—At last, a Way to Make Synergies Work," *Harvard Business Review*, January–February 2000, pp. 91–103.

34. Fremont E. Kast and James E. Rosenzweig, *Contingency Views of Organization and Management* (Chicago: Science Research Associates, 1973).

35. "Welch Memoirs Fetch $7.1M," *USA Today*, July 14, 2000, p. 1B.

36. See Angelo S. DeNisi and Ricky W. Griffin, *Human Resource Management* (Boston: Houghton Mifflin, 2001), Chapter 17.

37. "A Way Too Short History of Fads," *Forbes ASAP*, April 7, 1997, p. 72; "Management Theory—Or Fad of the Month?" *Business Week*, June 23, 1997, p. 47.

PART TWO

The Environmental Context of Management

The Environment
of Organizations
and Managers

67

3

The Environment of Organizations and Managers

Most organizations operate within a complex network of environmental markets. A market is simply a mechanism for exchange between the buyers and sellers of a particular good or service. In earlier times, markets were actual physical settings where buyers and sellers would gather. While such market settings are still used for things like fish, fruits and vegetables, and antiques and collectibles, many commercial markets today are fundamentally different because buyers and sellers are not at the same place—they arrange their exchange via mail orders, telephones, fax machines, and so forth. And the growth of the Internet is serving to transform some markets and thus make it even easier for buyers and sellers to transact their business at a distance.

A good example of this trend is the recently announced partnership among some of the world's largest automobile manufacturers. It all

started when various individual automobile makers began to create their own global purchasing web sites. Ford, for instance, was creating a site called Auto-Xchange. The company intended to post all of its global procurement needs on the site, while also requesting that its suppliers post availability and prices for the parts and equipment they had to offer.

Concerns began to arise, however, when it quickly became apparent that other automobile companies were planning to do the same thing. Major suppliers to the auto industry, meanwhile, began to realize that they might soon be facing an unwieldy array of separate web sites for each car company, potentially driving their own costs up. So a coalition of the largest suppliers approached Ford and General Motors with a novel proposal—why not team up and create a single site both firms could use?

Ford and GM executives quickly saw the wisdom of this idea and then convinced DaimlerChrysler to join them. Their plan is to create a single web site that will serve as a marketplace for all interested automobile manufacturers, suppliers, and dealers—essentially creating a global virtual market for all firms in the industry. Almost immediately, France's Renault and Japan's Nissan, which is controlled by Renault, indicated they would join. Toyota also

"We brought in DaimlerChrysler to prevent Europe from creating a separate standard. We think we'll have the industry standard, and we see value in having that."

—Harold Kutner, General Motors vice president responsible for purchasing

After studying this chapter, you should be able to:

- Discuss the nature of the organizational environment and identify the environments of interest to most organizations.

- Describe the components of the general and task environments and discuss their impact on organizations.

- Identify the components of the internal environment and discuss their impact on organizations.

- Identify and describe how the environment affects organizations and how organizations adapt to their environment.

- Discuss the meaning of and approaches to assessing organizational effectiveness.

showed strong interest. In addition, both Ford and GM said that they would encourage their foreign affiliates and strategic partners to join as well. The three partners creating the web site also intend to establish it as a self-contained organization that will eventually offer shares to the public.

Experts also believe that the impact of this global electronic market will be tremendous. For example, it currently costs GM about $100 per transaction in ordering costs to buy parts or supplies the traditional way—with paper, over the telephone, etc. But the firm estimates that its or-

dering costs will drop to less than $10 per transaction under the new system. Clearly, then, the automobile makers will realize substantial cost savings. The suppliers, too, will benefit in various ways. Besides having more information about what different companies need, they will be able to buy and sell among themselves.[1]

The Internet has become a major business tool for managers. On-line auctions are just one of the myriad applications that managers can leverage for competitive advantage. And sometimes, as illustrated in the chapter opening incident, it pays for competitors to work together. Indeed, the catalyst for cooperation among Ford, General Motors, and other competitors was their own suppliers, many of whom also compete with one another. Clearly, then, the environmental context of business today is changing in unprecedented ways.

As we noted in Chapter 1, managers must have a deep understanding and appreciation of the environment in which they and their organizations function. Without this understanding they are like a rudderless ship—moving along but with no way of maneuvering or changing direction. This chapter is the first of four devoted to the environmental context of management. After introducing the nature of the organization's environment, we describe first the general and then the task environments in detail. We then discuss key parts of the internal environment of an organization. We then address organization-environment relationships and, finally, how these relationships determine the effectiveness of the organization.

The Organization's Environments

To illustrate the importance of the environment to an organization, consider the analogy of a swimmer crossing a wide stream. The swimmer must assess the current, obstacles, and distance before setting out. If these elements are properly evaluated, the swimmer will arrive at the expected point on the far bank of the stream. But if they are not properly understood, the swimmer might end up too far upstream or downstream. The organization is like a swimmer, and the environment is like the stream. Thus, just as the swimmer needs to understand conditions in the water, the organization must understand the basic elements of its environment to maneuver among them properly.[2] More specifically, a key element in the effective management of an organization is determining the ideal alignment between the environment and the organization and then working to achieve and maintain that alignment. To do these things, however, the manager must first thoroughly understand the nature of the organization's environments.[3]

external environment Everything outside an organization's boundaries that might affect it

internal environment The conditions and forces within an organization

The **external environment** is everything outside an organization's boundaries that might affect it. As shown in Figure 3.1, there are actually two separate external environments: the general environment and the task environment. An organization's **internal environment** consists of conditions and forces within the organization. Of course, not all parts of these environments are equally important for all organizations. A small two-person partnership does not have a board of directors, for example, whereas a large public corporation is required by law to have one. A private university with a large endowment (like Harvard) may be less concerned about general economic conditions than might a state university (like the University of Missouri) that is dependent on state funding from tax revenues. Still, organizations need to understand fully which environmental forces are important and how the importance of others might increase.

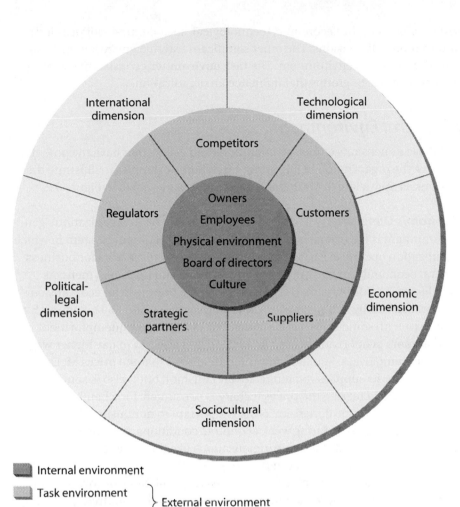

Figure 3.1

The Organization and Its Environments

Organizations have both an external and an internal environment. The external environment consists of two layers: the general environment and the task environment.

MANAGEMENT
IMPLICATIONS Managers should always be aware of the environments in which they and their organizations function. Indeed, maintaining an effective alignment between the organization and the environment is a key part of the manager's job. And managers themselves must also be cognizant of the environment in which they as individuals and as members of groups carry out their responsibilities.

The External Environment

As just noted, an organization's external environment consists of two parts. The **general environment** of an organization is the set of broad dimensions and forces in its surroundings that create its overall context. These dimensions and forces are not necessarily associated with other specific organizations. The general environment

general environment The set of broad dimensions and forces in an organization's surroundings that create its overall context

task environment Specific external organizations or groups that influence an organization

economic dimension The overall health and vitality of the economic system in which the organization operates

The technological dimension of the general environment continues to evolve at breakneck speed. The pace of change and complexity involving computers and information technology is especially pronounced. Take this marketplace in Kampala, Uganda, for example. Buyers and sellers of fruits and vegetables have gathered here for centuries. But the presence of an Internet Service Provider is a new feature at the market, and one that has the potential to revolutionize how the citizens of Africa live, work, and interact with the rest of the world.

of most organizations has economic, technological, sociocultural, political-legal, and international dimensions. The other significant external environment for an organization is its task environment. The **task environment** consists of specific external organizations or groups that influence an organization.

The General Environment

Each of these dimensions embodies conditions and events that have the potential to influence the organization in important ways. Some examples to illustrate these dimensions as they relate to McDonald's Corporation are shown in Figure 3.2.

The Economic Dimension   The **economic dimension** of an organization's general environment is the overall health and vitality of the economic system in which the organization operates.[4] Particularly important economic factors for business are general economic growth, inflation, interest rates, and unemployment. As noted in Figure 3.2, McDonald's U.S. operation is functioning in an economy currently characterized by strong growth, low unemployment, and low inflation.[5] But economic strength sometimes has two sides. For example, low unemployment means that more people can eat out, but McDonald's also has to pay higher wages to attract new employees. Similarly, low inflation means that the prices McDonald's must pay for its supplies remain relatively constant, but it also is somewhat constrained from increasing the prices it charges consumers for a hamburger or a milk shake. The economic dimension is also important to nonbusiness organizations as well. For example, during weak economic conditions, funding for state universities may drop and charitable organizations like the Salvation Army are asked to provide greater assistance at the same time their own incoming contributions dwindle. Similarly, hospitals are affected by the availability of government grants and the number of low-income patients they must treat for free.

The Technological Dimension   The **technological dimension** of the general environment refers to the methods available for converting resources into products or services. Although technology is applied within the organization, the forms and availability of that technology come from the general environment. Computer-assisted manufacturing and design techniques, for example, allow Boeing to simulate the more than three miles of hydraulic tubing that run through a 777 aircraft. The results include decreased warehouse needs, higher-quality tube fittings, fewer employees, and major time savings. While some people associate technology with manufacturing firms, it is also relevant in the

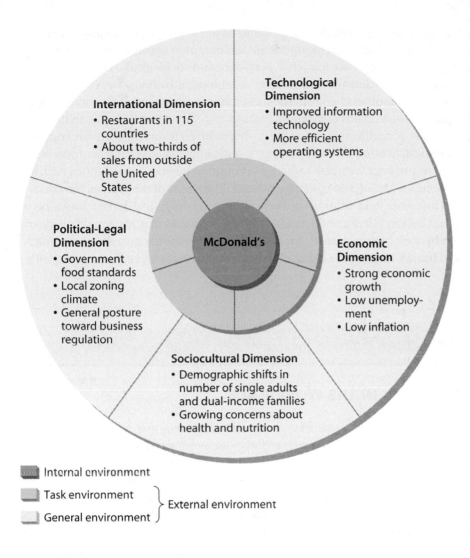

Figure 3.2

McDonald's General Environment

The general environment of an organization consists of technological, economic, sociocultural, political-legal, and international dimensions. This figure clearly illustrates how these dimensions are relevant to managers at McDonald's.

International Dimension
• Restaurants in 115 countries
• About two-thirds of sales from outside the United States

Technological Dimension
• Improved information technology
• More efficient operating systems

McDonald's

Political-Legal Dimension
• Government food standards
• Local zoning climate
• General posture toward business regulation

Economic Dimension
• Strong economic growth
• Low unemployment
• Low inflation

Sociocultural Dimension
• Demographic shifts in number of single adults and dual-income families
• Growing concerns about health and nutrition

■ Internal environment
■ Task environment   } External environment
□ General environment   }

service sector. For example, just as an automobile follows a predetermined pathway along an assembly line as it is built, a hamburger at McDonald's similarly follows a predefined path as the meat is cooked, the burger is assembled, and then it is wrapped and bagged for a customer. The rapid advancement of the Internet into all areas of business is also a reflection of the technological dimension.

The Sociocultural Dimension   The **sociocultural dimension** of the general environment includes the customs, mores, values, and demographic characteristics of the society in which the organization functions. Sociocultural processes are important because they determine the products, services, and standards of conduct that the society is likely to value. In some countries, for example, consumers are willing to pay premium prices for designer clothes. But the same clothes have virtually no market in other countries. Consumer tastes also change over time. Preferences for

technological dimension The methods available for converting resources into products or services

sociocultural dimension The customs, mores, values, and demographic characteristics of the society in which the organization functions

color, style, taste, and so forth, change from season to season, for example. Drinking hard liquor and smoking cigarettes are less common activities in the United States today than they were just a few years ago. And sociocultural factors influence how workers in a society feel about their jobs and organizations. *Working with Diversity* explores another change in the sociocultural dimension of the environment.

Appropriate standards of business conduct also vary across cultures. In the United States, accepting bribes and bestowing political favors in return are considered unethical. In other countries, however, payments to local politicians may be expected in return for a favorable response to common business transactions such as applications for zoning and operating permits. The shape of the market, the ethics of political influence, and attitudes in the workforce are only a few of the many ways in which culture can affect an organization. Figure 3.2 shows that McDonald's is clearly affected by sociocultural factors. For example, in response to concerns about nutrition and health, McDonald's has added salads to its menus and experimented with

WORKING WITH DIVERSITY

FEMININITY IN THE WORKPLACE

How the workplace has changed. A few decades ago, working women felt like outsiders in a man's world, so they donned suits and floppy ties and tried to blend in. Today, women are in nearly every career and work position, even cracking the glass ceiling to assume top-management posts at Hewlett-Packard and other companies. The working women of this generation are more comfortable with their roles in the workplace—and more willing to show their softer sides.

Just as tailored suits have given way to casual dress in many job settings, a growing number of women are becoming less formal in the way they look and act at work. Instead of wearing buttoned-down shirts, some women are wearing t-shirts—and a few even wear tank tops. Behavior is also changing as more women choose to emphasize their feminine qualities. One woman says that she smoothes the way in her mostly male office by offering a smile and being enthusiastic. Another, an Internet entrepreneur, talks about capturing the attention of male business contacts because she is attractive.

Is this flirting behavior—and is it appropriate? Jill Ireland, the president of the National Organization for Women, argues that flirting is a short-term strategy that can confuse male coworkers and invite unwanted attention. But Brian Bogosian, CEO of Valens Information Systems, says that good-natured banter makes the workplace fun and more interesting. Leonard Brown, an engineer, has yet another perspective: he says that men get angry because they believe attractive women have an edge that they shouldn't be allowed to use in business.

Times have definitely changed. Now that fewer working women are dressing and acting much like their male colleagues, men and women are negotiating new adjustments to clarify the fine line between appropriate and inappropriate behavior.

> *Men are more comfortable with you if you're able to banter with them and engage in that way as opposed to being very stiff.*
>
> —*Michelle Kramer, consultant, McKinsey & Co.* *

Reference: Ellen Joan Pollock, "In Today's Workplace, Women Feel Freer to Be, Well, Women," *Wall Street Journal*, February 7, 2000, pp. A1, A20 (*quote on p. A1).

other low-fat foods. And the firm was the first fast-food chain to provide customers with information about the ingredients used in its products.

The Political-Legal Dimension   The **political-legal dimension** of the general environment refers to the government regulation of business and the general relationship between business and government. It is important for three basic reasons. First, the legal system partially defines what an organization can and cannot do. Although the United States is basically a free market economy, there is still major regulation of business activity. McDonald's, for example, is subject to a variety of political and legal forces, including food preparation standards and local zoning requirements.

Second, pro- or antibusiness sentiment in government influences business activity. For example, during periods of probusiness sentiment, firms find it easier to compete and have fewer concerns about antitrust issues. On the other hand, during a period of antibusiness sentiment, firms may find their competitive strategies more restricted and have fewer opportunities for mergers and acquisitions because of antitrust concerns. Among the most recent examples of the effects of the political-legal dimension were the court-order breakup of Microsoft in 2000 and the Justice Department's efforts to block a proposed merger between WorldCom and Sprint that same year.[6]

Finally, political stability has ramifications for planning. No business wants to set up shop in another country unless trade relationships with that country are relatively well defined and stable. Hence, U.S. firms are more likely to do business with England, Mexico, and Canada than with Haiti and El Salvador. Similar issues are also relevant to assessments of local and state governments. A new mayor or governor can affect many organizations, especially small firms that do business in only one location and are susceptible to deed and zoning restrictions, property and school taxes, and the like.

The International Dimension   Yet another component of the general environment for many organizations is the **international dimension**, or the extent to which an organization is involved in or affected by business in other countries.[7] As we discuss more fully in Chapter 5, multinational firms such as General Electric, Boeing, Nestlé, Sony, Siemens, and Hyundai clearly affect and are affected by international conditions and markets. For example, as noted in Figure 3.2, McDonald's operates restaurants in 115 countries and derives about two-thirds of its total sales outside the United States. More information about McDonald's international experiences are documented in *The World of Management*. Even firms that do business in only one country may face foreign competition at home, and they may use materials or production equipment imported from abroad. The international dimension also has implications for not-for-profit organizations. For example, the Peace Corps sends representatives to underdeveloped countries. As a result of advances in transportation and information technology in the past century, almost no part of the world is cut off from the rest. As a result, virtually every organization is affected by the international dimension of its general environment.

political-legal dimension The government regulation of business and the general relationship between business and government

international dimension The extent to which an organization is involved in or affected by business in other countries

WORLD OF MANAGEMENT

MEXICAN FIRMS GO GLOBAL

For Mexico's Grupo Industrial Bimbo SA, the drive to sell internationally began the day a buyer for McDonald's tried and rejected the company's hamburger buns. Sensing future opportunity despite this setback, the company chairman, Roberto Servitje, invested $30 million to make improvements that ultimately allowed Bimbo to win over the McDonald's buyer. Now Bimbo is McDonald's only bun supplier in Mexico, Peru, Colombia, and Venezuela. The company also exports snacks, candy, cakes, and other foods to more than a dozen countries. This aggressive international expansion has helped Bimbo increase sales fivefold during the past ten years.

Bimbo, like other leading Mexican firms, started thinking about global markets when the North American Free Trade Agreement (NAFTA) paved the way for nontariff trade throughout the continent. U.S. companies quickly stormed into Mexico in search of suppliers, partners, and customers. Managers of local companies were exposed to new management and production techniques—which they adapted to compete more effectively within Mexico as well as in other countries.

Grupo Mabe SA has taken a slightly different route to international success. As the top Mexican appliance manufacturer, Mabe was chosen by U.S.-based General Electric to make kitchen appliances for the North American market un-der the GE brand. This arrangement worked so well that GE contracted with Mabe to produce appliances for Latin American countries. Meanwhile, Mabe decided that NAFTA was making the U.S. market too crowded. Instead of exporting to the north, the company took advantage of other regional trade agreements to expand south into Brazil, Venezuela, Colombia, and Argentina.

> *We put our ranges and washing machines in Manizales, Colombia, and our refrigerators in Maracaibo, Venezuela.*
>
> —Luis Berrondo, director, Grupo Mabe*

Thanks to NAFTA and nimble management, Mexican companies have catapulted the country onto the list of the world's top ten exporting nations. Its export levels are still one-quarter of Japan's levels. However, with more Mexican firms going global, the country will soon move ahead of South Korea and Hong Kong on the list.

Reference: Joel Millman, "Trade Wins: The World's New Tiger on the Export Scene Isn't Asia; It's Mexico," *Wall Street Journal*, May 9, 2000, pp. A1, A10 (*quote on p. A10).

The Task Environment

Because the impact of the general environment is often vague, imprecise, and long-term, most organizations tend to focus their attention on their task environment. This environment includes competitors, customers, suppliers, regulators, and strategic allies. Although the task environment is also quite complex, it provides useful information more readily than does the general environment because the manager can identify environmental factors of specific interest to the organization rather than having to deal with the more abstract dimensions of the general environment.[8] Figure 3.3 depicts the task environment of McDonald's.

competitor An organization that competes with other organizations for resources

Competitors   An organization's **competitors** are other organizations that compete with it for resources. The most obvious resources that competitors vie for are customer dollars. Reebok, Adidas, and Nike are competitors, as are Albertson's,

Figure 3.3

McDonald's Task Environment
An organization's task environment includes its competitors, customers, suppliers, strategic partners, and regulators. This figure clearly highlights how managers at McDonald's can use this framework to identify and understand their key constituents.

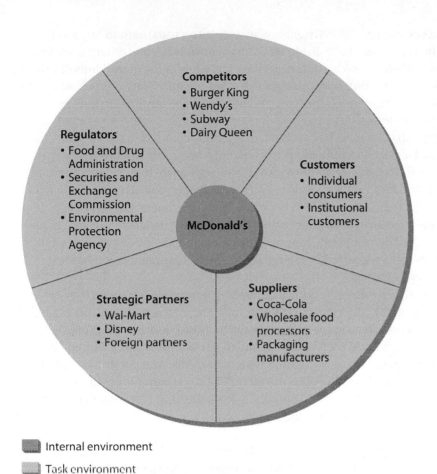

Competitors
- Burger King
- Wendy's
- Subway
- Dairy Queen

Regulators
- Food and Drug Administration
- Securities and Exchange Commission
- Environmental Protection Agency

McDonald's

Customers
- Individual consumers
- Institutional customers

Strategic Partners
- Wal-Mart
- Disney
- Foreign partners

Suppliers
- Coca-Cola
- Wholesale food processors
- Packaging manufacturers

Internal environment

Task environment

Safeway, and Kroger. McDonald's competes with other fast-food operations like Burger King, Wendy's, Subway, and Dairy Queen. But competition also occurs between substitute products. Thus, Ford competes with Yamaha (motorcycles) and Schwinn (bicycles) for your transportation dollars, and Walt Disney World, Club Med, and Carnival Cruise Lines compete for your vacation dollars. Nor is competition limited to business firms. Universities compete with trade schools, the military, other universities, and the external labor market to attract good students, and art galleries compete with each other to attract the best exhibits.

Organizations may also compete for different kinds of resources besides consumer dollars. For example, two totally unrelated organizations may compete to acquire a loan from a bank that has only limited funds to lend. Two retailers might compete for the right to purchase a prime piece of real estate in a growing community. In a large city, the police and fire departments may compete for the same tax dollars. And businesses also compete for quality labor, technological breakthroughs and patents, and scarce raw materials.

Customers A second dimension of the task environment is **customers**, or whoever pays money to acquire an organization's products or services. Most of

customer Whoever pays money to acquire an organization's products or services

McDonald's customers are individuals who walk into a restaurant to buy food. But customers need not be individuals. Schools, hospitals, government agencies, wholesalers, retailers, and manufacturers are just a few of the many kinds of organizations that may be major customers of other organizations. Some institutional customers like schools, prisons, and hospitals also buy food in bulk from restaurants like McDonald's.

Dealing with customers has become increasingly complex in recent years. New products and services, new methods of marketing, and more discriminating customers have all added uncertainty to how businesses relate to their customers, as has lower brand loyalty. A few years ago McDonald's introduced a new sandwich called the Arch Deluxe, intended to appeal to adult customers. Unfortunately, the product failed because most adult customers preferred existing menu choices like the Quarter Pounder. Similarly, Tommy Hilfiger, a popular clothing designer, has fallen from favor in recent years in large part because his organization has lost touch with its customers.[9]

Companies face especially critical differences among customers as they expand internationally. McDonald's sells beer in its German restaurants, for example, and wine in its French restaurants. Customers in those countries see those particular beverages as normal parts of a meal, much as customers in the United States routinely drink water, tea, or soft drinks with their meals. And the firm has even opened restaurants with no beef on the menu! Those restaurants are in India, where beef is not a popular menu option. Instead, the local McDonald's restaurants in that country use lamb in their sandwiches.

supplier An organization that provides resources for other organizations

Suppliers   **Suppliers** are organizations that provide resources for other organizations. McDonald's buys soft-drink products from Coca-Cola; individually packaged servings of ketchup from Heinz; ingredients from wholesale food processors; and napkins, sacks, and wrappers from packaging manufacturers. Common wisdom in the United States used to be that a business should try to avoid depending exclusively on particular suppliers. A firm that buys all of a certain resource from one supplier may be crippled if the supplier goes out of business or is faced with a strike. This practice can also help maintain a competitive relationship among suppliers, keeping costs down. But firms eager to emulate successful Japanese firms have recently tried to change their approach. Japanese firms have a history of building major ties with only one or two major suppliers. This enables them to work together more smoothly for their mutual benefit and makes the supplier more responsive to the customer's needs.

Honda picked Donnelly Corp. to make all the mirrors for its U.S.-manufactured cars. Honda chose Donnelly because it learned enough about the firm to know it did high-quality work and that its corporate culture and values were consistent with those endorsed by Honda. Recognizing the value of Honda as a customer, Donnelly built an entirely new plant to make the mirrors. And all this was accomplished with only a handshake. Motorola goes even further, providing its principal suppliers with access to its own renowned quality training program and evaluating the performance of each supplier as a way of helping that firm boost its own quality.

Regulators   **Regulators** are elements of the task environment that have the potential to control, legislate, or influence an organization's policies and practices. There are two important kinds of regulators. The first, **regulatory agencies**, are created by the government to protect the public from certain business practices or to protect organizations from one another. Powerful federal regulatory agencies include the Environmental Protection Agency (EPA), the Securities and Exchange Commission (SEC), the Food and Drug Administration (FDA), and the Equal Employment Opportunity Commission (EEOC).

Many of these agencies play important roles in protecting the rights of individuals. The FDA, for example, helps ensure that the food we eat is free from contaminants and thus is an important regulator for McDonald's. At the same time, many managers complain that there is too much government regulation. Most large companies must devote thousands of labor hours and hundreds of thousands of dollars a year to comply with government regulations. To complicate the lives of managers even more, different regulatory agencies sometimes provide inconsistent—or even contradictory—mandates.

For example, several years ago the *Exxon Valdez* tanker ran aground, spilling 11 million gallons of crude oil off the coast of Alaska. The Environmental Protection Agency (EPA) forced Exxon to cover the costs of the ensuing cleanup. Since many observers thought that the ship's captain was drunk at the time, the EPA also mandated that Exxon impose stricter hiring standards for employees in high-risk jobs. To comply with this mandate, Exxon adopted a policy of not assigning anyone with a history of alcohol or substance abuse to certain jobs like tanker captain. However, another regulatory agency, the Equal Employment Opportunity Commission (EEOC), then sued Exxon on the grounds that restricting people who have been

regulator A unit that has the potential to control, legislate, or influence an organization's policies and practices

regulatory agency An agency created by the government to protect the public from certain business practices or to protect organizations from one another

Danny Shanahan

"I've been speaking to my attorneys, Larson, and this time we think we've got you fired."

The regulatory environment of business imposes numerous constraints on organizations. Laws regarding employment practices have become particularly complicated in recent years. For example, a firm that uses discriminatory practices can be sued for not hiring someone or for firing a current employee. But the firm can also be penalized if it should reject or fire someone but fails to do so! Not surprisingly, then, many employment decisions today are routinely reviewed by attorneys. And the opinions of these attorneys often determine whether or not someone will be hired or fired.

rehabilitated from alcohol abuse from any job violates their rights under the Americans with Disabilities Act. Exxon was thus forced to change its policy, but was then again criticized by the EPA. The cartoon provides another take on this type of issue.

The regulatory environment in other countries, however, is even more stringent. When U.S. retailer Wal-Mart wants to open a new store, its regulatory requirements are actually quite low and the procedures it must follow are clearly spelled out. In a sense, within reason and general basic ground rules, the firm can open a store just about anywhere it wants and operate it in just about any manner it wants. But conditions in Germany are quite different. That country's largest retailer, Allkauf, tried to open a store in one town—on land that it already owned—for over fifteen years. But the city government did not allow it because it feared that local competitors would suffer. And by German law Allkauf's existing stores can be open only 68.5 hours a week; they must close no later than 6:30 P.M. on weekdays and 2:00 P.M. on Saturday, and must remain closed on Sunday. And they can only hold large sales twice a year and can never discount food items.

interest group A group organized by its members to attempt to influence organizations

The other basic form of regulator is the interest group. An **interest group** is organized by its members to attempt to influence organizations. Prominent interest groups include the National Organization for Women (NOW), Mothers Against Drunk Driving (MADD), the National Rifle Association (NRA), the League of Women Voters, the Sierra Club, Ralph Nader's Center for the Study of Responsive Law, the Consumers Union, and industry self-regulation groups like the Council of Better Business Bureaus. Although interest groups lack the official power of government agencies, they can exert considerable influence by using the media to call attention to their positions. MADD, for example, puts considerable pressure on alcoholic-beverage producers (to put warning labels on their products), automobile companies (to make it more difficult for intoxicated people to start their cars), local governments (to stiffen drinking ordinances), and bars and restaurants (to refuse to sell alcohol to people who are drinking too much).

strategic partner or **ally** An organization working together with one or more other organizations in a joint venture or other partnership

Strategic Partners   A final dimension of the task environment is **strategic partners** (also called **strategic allies**)—two or more organizations that work together in joint ventures or other partnerships.[10] As shown in Figure 3.3, McDonald's has several strategic partners. For example, it has one arrangement with Wal-Mart whereby small McDonald's restaurants are built in many Wal-Mart stores. The firm also has a long-term deal with Disney; McDonald's will promote Disney movies in its stores, and Disney will build McDonald's restaurants or kiosks in its theme parks. And many of the firm's foreign stores are built in collaboration with local investors. Strategic partnerships help companies get from other companies the expertise they lack. They also help spread risk and open new market opportunities. Indeed, most strategic partnerships are actually among international firms. For example, Ford has strategic partnerships with Volkswagen (sharing a distribution and service center in South America) and Nissan (building minivans in the United States).

MANAGEMENT IMPLICATIONS   The external environment of an organization can appear complex and ambiguous. Managers can help bring order to this complexity and ambiguity by realizing that some parts of the external environment are of a more general character (the general environment), while others are more concrete and definable (the task environment). This understanding allows managers to monitor all parts of the environment while focusing more attention on and being more responsive to those dimensions most relevant to the organization itself.

The Internal Environment

As shown earlier in Figure 3.1, organizations also have an internal environment that consists of their owners, board of directors, employees, and the physical work environment. (Another especially important part of the internal environment is the organization's culture, discussed separately in Chapter 6.)

Owners

The **owners** of a business are, of course, the people who have legal property rights to that business. Owners can be a single individual who establishes and runs a small business, partners who jointly own the business, individual investors who buy stock in a corporation, or other organizations. McDonald's has 700 million shares of stock, each of which represents one unit of ownership of the firm. The family of McDonald's founder Ray Kroc stills owns a large block of this stock, as do several large institutional investors. In addition, there are thousands of individuals who own just a few shares each. McDonald's, in turn, also owns other businesses. For example, it owns several large regional bakeries that supply its restaurants with buns. These are each incorporated as separate legal entities and managed as wholly-owned subsidiaries by the parent company. McDonald's has also recently bought partial ownership of Chipotle Mexican Grill and Donatos Pizza chain.

owner Someone who has legal property rights to a business

Board of Directors

A corporate **board of directors** is elected by the stockholders and is charged with overseeing the general management of the firm to ensure that it is being run in a way that best serves the stockholders' interests. Some boards are relatively passive. They perform a general oversight function but seldom get actively involved in how the company is really being run. But this trend is changing, however, as more and more boards are more carefully scrutinizing the firms they oversee and exerting more influence over how they are being managed.

board of directors Governing body elected by a corporation's stockholders and charged with overseeing the general management of the firm to ensure that it is being run in a way that best serves the stockholders' interests

Employees

An organization's employees are also a major element of its internal environment. *Managing in an E-business World* discusses what can happen when a firm's own employees disagree over business strategy. Of particular interest to managers

Employees are a critical part of an organization's internal environment. Ann Bamesberger is director of workplace effectiveness for Sun Microsystems. Her primary responsibilities are to insure that employees and workplaces are appropriately aligned so that the goals of individual employees and the goals of the company are all met. Ms. Bamesberger is very creative when it comes to workplace design. She gives employees a big say in how their workplace is designed and is very open to letting them work at home and/or design their offices in whatever way they think works best for them.

today is the changing nature of the workforce as it becomes increasingly more diverse in terms of gender, ethnicity, age, and other dimensions. Workers are also calling for more job ownership—either partial ownership in the company or at least more say in how they perform their jobs.[11] Another trend in many firms is the increased reliance on temporary workers—individuals hired for short periods of time with no expectation of permanent employment. Employers often prefer to use "temps" because they provide greater flexibility, earn lower wages, and often do not participate in benefits programs. But these managers also have to deal with what often amounts to a two-class workforce and with a growing number of employees who have no loyalty to the organization where they work because they may be working for a different one tomorrow.[12]

The permanent employees of many organizations are organized into labor unions, representing yet another layer of complexity for managers. The National Labor Relations Act of 1935 requires organizations to recognize and bargain with a union if that union has been legally established by the organization's employees. Presently, around 23 percent of the U.S. labor force is represented by unions. Some large firms such as Ford, Exxon, and General Motors have several different unions. Even when an organization's labor force is not unionized, its managers do not ignore unions. For example, Kmart, J. P. Stevens, Honda of America, and Delta Air Lines all actively work to avoid unionization. And even though people think primarily of blue-collar workers as union members, many white-collar workers such as government employees and teachers are also represented by unions.

Physical Work Environment

A final part of the internal environment is the actual physical environment of the organization and the work that people do. Some firms have their facilities in downtown skyscrapers, usually spread across several floors. Others locate in suburban or rural settings and may have facilities more closely resembling a college campus. Some facilities have long halls lined with traditional offices. Others have modular cubicles with partial walls and no doors. The top one hundred managers at Mars, makers of Snickers and Milky Way, all work in a single large room. Two co-presidents are located in the very center of the room, while others are arrayed in concentric circles around them. Increasingly, newer facilities have an even more open arrangement where people work in large rooms, moving between different tables to interact with different people on different projects. Free-standing computer workstations are available for those who need them, and a few small rooms might be off to the side for private business.[13]

MANAGING IN AN *e*-BUSINESS WORLD

SEEKING A HARMONIOUS E-BUSINESS STRATEGY

The e-business revolution has brought innovation—and dissension—to the music industry. Sony, a leader in consumer electronics, pioneered the Walkman and other devices for recording and listening to music. Sony has also been a major force in the recording side of the music business, distributing songs by Celine Dion, Savage Garden, and other artists. Even as Web-based technology was reshaping the way people obtain songs, managers at the two Sony music divisions were unable to agree on one consistent strategy.

Both divisions were eyeing the rising popularity of MP3 and similar software used to digitize songs for downloading from the Internet. Managers at Sony's record labels worried that this type of technology would lead to illegal copying of songs and thus hurt CD sales. They wanted to go slow and wait for an industry test of on-line music sales. Sony's electronics division already had some intriguing music technology in the works. Its managers saw how the Internet was changing consumer behavior, and they believed the public would soon be ready to buy portable players for listening to downloaded music.

The two divisions argued about an overall direction for more than a year. The stakes are high: nearly one billion CDs were being sold every year, and Sony's music revenues topped $6 billion. Meanwhile, Sony's top management began investing in Internet music companies and negotiating agreements for digital-music and copyright-protection technologies. Customer habits were changing so rapidly that the company could not afford to ignore the digital music movement—especially with over thirteen million consumers using the Napster web site to download and trade digital music files for free.

Sony's president finally intervened, establishing a committee to resolve the issues so the company could move forward with a suitable strategy. Within months, the company was showing prototypes of new devices to store and play digital music downloaded from web sites. Although the U.S. music industry was not yet prepared for full-scale digital downloading, Sony was selling copyright-protected downloadable songs in Japan by the end of 1999. Now Sony was fully committed to an e-business music strategy.

> *People didn't want to go too fast. It could have had a lot of repercussions.*
>
> *—Masao Morita, head of Sony Music Entertainment Japan's international business**

References: Robert A. Guth, "Inside Sony, A Clash Over Web Music," *Wall Street Journal*, January 26, 2000, pp. B1, B4 (*quote on p. B1); Alex Berenson and Matt Richtel, "Heartbreakers, Dream Makers," *New York Times*, June 25, 2000, sec. 3, pp. 1, 6.

MANAGEMENT While managers strive to align their organizations with the ex-
IMPLICATIONS ternal environment, they must also remember that their own work is carried out within the internal environment of their organizations. Owners, a corporate board of directors, employees, the physical environment, and the organization's culture interact to define the environment of managers.

■ *Organization-Environment Relationships*

Our discussion to this point has identified and described the various dimensions of organizational environments. Because organizations are open systems, they interact with these various dimensions in many different ways. Hence, we will now examine those interactions. First we discuss how environments affect organizations and then note several ways in which organizations adapt to their environments.

How Environments Affect Organizations

Three basic perspectives can be used to describe how environments affect organizations: environmental change and complexity, competitive forces, and environmental turbulence.[14]

Environmental Change and Complexity   James D. Thompson was one of the first people to recognize the importance of the organization's environment.[15] Thompson suggests that the environment can be described along two dimensions: its degree of change and its degree of homogeneity. The degree of change is the extent to which the environment is relatively stable or relatively dynamic. The degree of homogeneity is the extent to which the environment is relatively simple (few elements, little segmentation) or relatively complex (many elements, much segmentation). These two dimensions interact to determine the level of uncertainty faced by the organization. **Uncertainty**, in turn, is a driving force that influences many organizational decisions. Figure 3.4 illustrates a simple view of the four levels of uncertainty defined by different levels of homogeneity and change.

The least environmental uncertainty is faced by organizations with stable and simple environments. Although no environment is totally without uncertainty, some entrenched franchised food operations (such as Subway and Taco Bell) and many container manufacturers (like Ball Corporation and Federal Paper Board) have relatively low levels of uncertainty to contend with. Subway, for example, focuses on a certain segment of the consumer market, produces a limited product line, has a constant source of suppliers, and faces relatively consistent competition.

Organizations with dynamic but simple environments generally face a moderate degree of uncertainty. Examples of organizations functioning in such environments include clothing manufacturers (targeting a certain kind of clothing buyer but sensitive to fashion-induced changes) and compact disc (CD) producers (catering to certain kinds of music buyers but alert to changing tastes in music). Levi Strauss faces relatively few competitors (Wrangler and Lee), has few suppliers and few regulators, and uses limited distribution channels. This relatively simple task environment, however, also changes quite rapidly as competitors adjust prices and styles, consumer tastes change, and new fabrics become available.

Another combination of factors is one of stability and complexity. Again, a moderate amount of uncer-

uncertainty A driving force caused by change and complexity that influences many organizational decisions

Figure 3.4

Environmental Change, Complexity, and Uncertainty

The degree of homogeneity and the degree of change combine to create uncertainty for organizations. For example, a simple and stable environment creates the least uncertainty, and a complex and dynamic environment creates the most uncertainty.

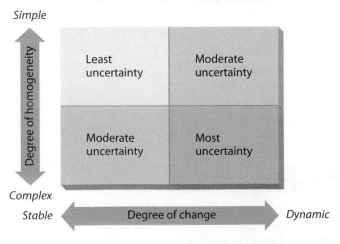

Source: Adapted from J. D. Thompson, *Organizations in Action.* Copyright © 1967 by McGraw-Hill. Reprinted by permission of The McGraw-Hill Companies.

tainty results. Ford, DaimlerChrysler, and General Motors face these basic conditions. Overall, they must interact with a myriad of suppliers, regulators, consumer groups, and competitors. Change, however, occurs quite slowly in the automobile industry. Despite many stylistic changes, cars of today still have four wheels, a steering wheel, an internal combustion engine, a glass windshield, and many of the other basic features that have characterized cars for decades.

Finally, very dynamic and complex environmental conditions yield a high degree of uncertainty. The environment has a large number of elements, and the nature of those elements is constantly changing. Intel, Compaq, IBM, Sony, and other firms in the electronics field face these conditions because of the rapid rate of technological innovation and change in consumer markets that characterize their industry, their suppliers, and their competitors. Likewise, Internet-based firms like eBay and Amazon.com face similar high levels of uncertainty.

Organizations and their environments affect each other in a variety of ways. For example, gasoline prices in Europe are considerably higher than they are in the United States—recent prices for a gallon of gasoline were $4.29 in London, $3.64 in Italy, and $3.58 in Belgium. In each case well over half the price is tax. To protest high prices, these truckers in Belgium worked together to blockade a major highway for several hours. In this one instance, oil companies, government agencies, and transportation firms all affect one another in a variety of ways.

Competitive Forces   Although Thompson's general classifications are useful and provide some basic insights into organization-environment interactions, in many ways they lack the precision and specificity needed by managers who must deal with their environments on a day-to-day basis. Michael E. Porter, a Harvard professor and expert in strategic management, has proposed a more refined way to assess environments. In particular, he suggests that managers view the environment of their organizations in terms of **five competitive forces**.[16]

five competitive forces The threat of new entrants, competitive rivalry, the threat of substitute products, the power of buyers, and the power of suppliers

The *threat of new entrants* is the extent to which new competitors can easily enter a market or market segment. It takes a relatively small amount of capital to open a dry-cleaning service or a pizza parlor, but it takes a tremendous investment in plant, equipment, and distribution systems to enter the automobile business. Thus, the threat of new entrants is fairly high for a local hamburger restaurant but fairly low for Ford and Toyota. The arrival of the Internet has reduced the costs and other barriers of entry in many market segments, however, so the threat of new entrants has increased for many firms in recent years.

Competitive rivalry is the nature of the competitive relationship between dominant firms in the industry. In the soft-drink industry, Coca-Cola and Pepsi often engage in intense price wars, comparative advertising, and new-product introductions. Other firms that have intense rivalries include American Express and Visa, and Fuji and Kodak. And U.S. auto companies continually try to outmaneuver each other with warranty improvements and rebates. Xerox also faces extreme competition from a variety of firms.[17] Local car-washing establishments, in contrast, seldom engage in such practices.

The *threat of substitute products* is the extent to which alternative products or services may supplant or diminish the need for existing products or services. The electronic calculator eliminated the need for slide rules. The advent of personal computers, in turn, has reduced the demand for calculators as well as for typewriters and large mainframe computers. Nutra-Sweet is a viable substitute product threatening the sugar industry. And DVD players may render VCRs obsolete in the next few years.

The *power of buyers* is the extent to which buyers of the products or services in an industry have the ability to influence the suppliers. For example, a Boeing 747 has relatively few potential buyers. Only companies such as Delta, Northwest, and KLM Royal Dutch Airlines can purchase them. Hence, these buyers have considerable influence over the price they are willing to pay, the delivery date for the order, and so forth. On the other hand, some DaimlerChrysler dealerships charged premium prices for the company's PT Cruiser, introduced to high demand in mid-2000. They could charge these prices because if the first buyer wouldn't pay the price, two more customers were waiting in line who would. In this case, buyers had virtually no power.

The *power of suppliers* is the extent to which suppliers have the ability to influence potential buyers. The local electric company is the only source of electricity in your community. Subject to local or state regulation (or both), it can therefore charge what it wants for its product, provide service at its convenience, and so forth. Likewise, even though Boeing has few potential customers, those same customers have only two suppliers that can sell them a 300-passenger jet (Boeing and Airbus, a European firm). So Boeing, too, has power. Indeed, the firm recently exercised its power by entering into long-term, sole supplier agreements with three major U.S. airlines.[18] On the other hand, a small vegetable wholesaler has little power in selling to restaurants because if they don't like the produce, they can easily find an alternative supplier.

Environmental Turbulence   Although always subject to unexpected changes and upheavals, the five competitive forces can nevertheless be studied and assessed systematically and plans developed for dealing with them. At the same time, though, organizations also face the possibility of environmental change or turbulence, occasionally with no warning at all. The most common form of organizational turbulence is a crisis of some sort.

For example, in mid-1999 reports surfaced in Belgium that several dozen local schoolchildren had become nauseous after drinking Coca-Cola. Similar reports subsequently started coming from France, Luxembourg, and the Netherlands. France quickly ordered Coke to cease production in its Dunkirk bottling plant; other countries in the region started banning all Coca-Cola products. The firm eventually traced its problems to defective carbon dioxide in one plant and to wood preservative leaking onto cans in another. While no truly serious health problems resulted, Coke nevertheless lost considerable income and suffered a blow to its public image as a result of all the bad publicity it received.[19]

Other notable examples of crises include the crash of the space shuttle *Challenger* in 1986, which essentially paralyzed the U.S. space program for almost three years; product tampering aimed at Tylenol in 1982, which cost Johnson & Johnson $750 million in product recalls and changes in packaging and product design; and the 2000 crash of an Alaska Airlines plane that killed everyone on board. Another type of crisis that has captured the attention of managers in recent years is workplace violence—situations in which disgruntled workers or former workers assault other employees, often resulting in injury and sometimes in death. Finally, yet another kind of crisis that can affect business today, as detailed more fully in *Management InfoTech*, is the rapid spread of computer viruses such as the so-called love bug, which shut down businesses around the world in early 2000.

Such crises affect organizations in different ways, and many organizations are developing crisis plans and teams.[20] When a Delta Air Lines plane crashed at the

MANAGEMENT INFOTECH

VIRUSES ADD TO ENVIRONMENTAL UNCERTAINTY

Who could resist opening an e-mail love letter?

When computer users opened an e-mail with the subject line, "I love you," they unleashed a computer virus that clogged electronic systems around the world in a matter of hours. Dubbed the "love bug," this virus infected computer networks at Ford, the U.S. Congress, the British Parliament, Nomura Securities in Japan, and nearly everywhere in between.

The virus lay hidden in an e-mail disguised as a love letter. Once a computer user opened the e-mail attachment, the virus launched itself and looked for the user's Microsoft Outlook mail program. Then it sent copies of its nasty attachment to every name in the user's on-line address book. These copies looked as though they actually came from the user, which is why recipients were tempted to open them. Some recipients maintained extensive on-line address books, so the virus spread quickly from user to user and organization to organization. The huge volume of messages crippled some corporate e-mail systems. Adding insult to injury, once the love bug was launched, it also damaged sound and graphics files on the recipient's hard drive.

The love bug virus demonstrated how computer problems are adding to the uncertainty of the organizational environment. First, no two viruses are exactly the same, so new viruses mean more change—and more scrambling to cope with the

change. Second, managers never know what form a virus will take or when it will strike, yet they must plan in advance to prevent disasters.

The less destructive Melissa virus, which circulated a year before the love bug, was regarded as a wake-up call for organizations to strengthen their antivirus safeguards. However, months without any major virus attacks may have lulled computer users into a false sense of complacency. By the time the love bug emerged, people opened it without worrying about potential viruses. Now, while computer security firms develop new ways of detecting and disabling viruses, hackers are working on new types of viruses. The best antidote to this uncertainty remains prevention—training employees to leave suspicious e-mails (even love letters) unopened.

All the technology in the world and they can't stop it from happening because people won't act responsibly.

—*Richard Power, Computer Security Institute.* *

Reference: Kevin Maney, "Tainted Love," *Wall Street Journal,* May 5, 2000, pp. 1B–2B (*quote on p. 2B).

Dallas–Fort Worth airport a few years ago, for example, fire-fighting equipment was at the scene in minutes. Only a few flights were delayed, and none had to be canceled. Similarly, a grocery store in Boston once received a threat that someone had poisoned cans of its Campbell's tomato juice. Within six hours, a crisis team from Campbell Soup Co. removed two truckloads of juice from all eighty-four stores in the grocery chain. Still, far too few companies in the United States have a plan for dealing with major crises.

How Organizations Adapt to Their Environments

Given the myriad issues, problems, and opportunities in an organization's environments, how should the organization adapt? Obviously, each organization must assess its own unique situation and then adapt according to the wisdom of its senior management. Figure 3.5 illustrates the six basic mechanisms through which organizations adapt to their environment. One of these, social responsibility, is given special consideration in Chapter 4.

Information Management   One way organizations adapt to their environment is through information management. Information management is especially important when forming an initial understanding of the environment and when monitoring the environment for signs of change. One technique for managing information is relying on boundary spanners. A *boundary spanner* is an employee, such as a sales representative or a purchasing agent, who spends much of his or

Figure 3.5

How Organizations Respond to Their Environments

Organizations attempt to influence their environments. The most common methods are through information management, strategic response, mergers, takeovers, acquisitions, alliances, organization design and flexibility, and direct influence.

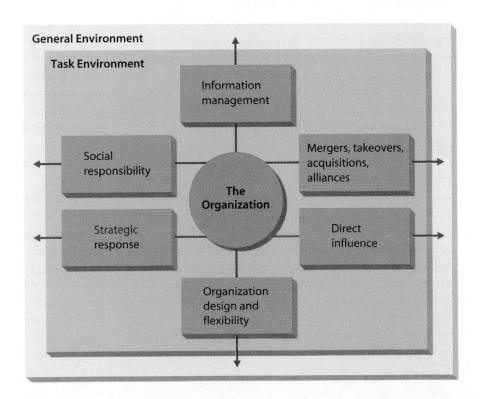

her time in contact with others outside the organization. Such people are in a good position to learn what other organizations are doing. All effective managers engage in *environmental scanning*, the process of actively monitoring the environment through activities such as observation and reading. Within the organization, most firms have also established computer-based *information systems* to gather and organize relevant information for managers and to assist in summarizing that information in the form most pertinent to each manager's needs. (Information systems are covered more fully in Chapter 22.)

Strategic Response   Another way that an organization adapts to its environment is through a strategic response. Options include maintaining the status quo (for example, if an organization's management believes that it is doing very well with its current approach), altering strategy a bit, or adopting an entirely new strategy. If the market that a company currently serves is growing rapidly, the firm might decide to invest even more heavily in products and services for that market. Likewise, if a market is shrinking or does not provide reasonable possibilities for growth, the company may decide to cut back. For example, during the late 1990s managers at Starbucks realized that the firm's growth opportunities in the United States were slowing simply because there already were so many Starbucks coffee shops. Accordingly, they devised a new plan to expand aggressively into international markets, thus providing an avenue for continued rapid growth.

Mergers, Acquisitions, and Alliances   A related strategic approach that some organizations use to adapt to their environment involves mergers, acquisitions, and partnerships. A *merger* occurs when two or more firms combine to form a new firm. For example, DaimlerChrysler was created as a result of a merger between Daimler-Benz (a German firm) and Chrysler (a U.S. company). An *acquisition* occurs when one firm buys another, sometimes against its will (usually called a hostile takeover). The firm taken over may cease to exist and becomes part of the other company. For example, as part of its international expansion Starbucks bought a British coffee shop chain called the Seattle Coffee Company. Starbucks then systematically changed each Seattle Coffee outlet into a Starbucks coffee shop.

In other cases, the acquired firm often continues to operate as a subsidiary of the acquiring company. Royal Caribbean Cruise Lines bought controlling interest in Celebrity Cruise Lines but maintains it as a separate cruise line. And as already

Organizations attempt to adapt to their environments in a variety of different ways. PJM Interconnection manages the entire electrical grid for the Middle Atlantic region of the United States. This means that PJM managers must remain continually on top of power supplies and power usage to maintain the optimum balance of electric power across the entire grid. Information management, then, is a key element in how PJM operates. Charts such as this one are updated constantly so as to provide decision makers with the information they need to keep the power flowing properly.

discussed, in a *partnership* or *alliance* the firm undertakes a new venture with another firm. A company engages in these kinds of strategies for a variety of reasons, such as easing entry into new markets or expanding its presence in a current market.

Organization Design and Flexibility

An organization may also adapt to environmental conditions by incorporating flexibility in its structural design. For example, a firm that operates in an environment with relatively low levels of uncertainty might choose to use a design with many basic rules, regulations, and standard operating procedures. Alternatively, a firm that faces a great deal of uncertainty might choose a design with relatively few standard operating procedures, instead allowing managers considerable discretion and flexibility over decisions. The former type, sometimes called a mechanistic organization design, is characterized by formal and rigid rules and relationships. The latter, sometimes called an organic design, is considerably more flexible and permits the organization to respond quickly to environmental change. We learn much more about these and related issues in Chapter 12.

Direct Influence of the Environment

Organizations are not necessarily helpless in the face of their environments. Indeed, many organizations are able to influence their environment directly in many different ways. For example, firms can influence their suppliers by signing long-term contracts with fixed prices as a hedge against inflation. Or a firm might become its own supplier. Sears, for example, owns some of the firms that produce the goods it sells, and Campbell Soup Company makes its own soup cans. Similarly, almost any major activity a firm engages in affects its competitors. When Mitsubishi lowers the prices of its DVD players, Sony may be forced to follow suit. Organizations also influence their customers by creating new uses for a product, finding entirely new customers, and taking customers away from competitors. Organizations also influence their customers by convincing them that they need something new. Automobile manufacturers use this strategy in their advertising to convince people that they need a new car every two or three years.

Organizations influence their regulators through lobbying and bargaining. Lobbying involves sending a company or industry representative to Washington in an effort to influence relevant agencies, groups, and committees. For example, the U.S. Chamber of Commerce lobby, the nation's largest business lobby, has an annual budget of more than $100 million. The automobile companies have been successful on several occasions in bargaining with the EPA to extend deadlines for compliance with pollution control and mileage standards. Continental Airlines routinely criticizes what it considers an antiquated air traffic control system in an effort to get the U.S. government to upgrade its technology and systems.

MANAGEMENT IMPLICATIONS   Managers should remember that their organization is influenced by a wide array of forces and elements in the external environment. Some of these forces and elements are relatively easy to recognize and anticipate, while others are more unpredictable or even impossible to antici-pate. Fortunately, managers can adopt one or more strategies to adapt to their en-vironment. While some events are, of course, uncontrollable, managers can at least buffer their organizations to some extent through the astute use of these strategies.

■ The Environment and Organizational Effectiveness

Earlier in this chapter we noted the vital importance of maintaining proper align-ment between the organization and its environments. The various mechanisms through which environments and organizations influence one another can cause this alignment to shift, however, and even well-managed organizations sometimes slip from their preferred environmental position. But well-managed companies recognize when this happens and take corrective action to get back on track. In Chapter 1 we said that effectiveness involved doing the right things. Given the in-teractions between organizations and their environments, it follows that effective-ness is ultimately related to how well an organization understands, reacts to, and influences its environment.[21]

Models of Organizational Effectiveness

Unfortunately, there is no consensus about how to measure effectiveness. For ex-ample, an organization can make itself look extremely effective in the short term by ignoring research and development (R&D), buying cheap materials, ignoring quality control, and skimping on wages. Over time, though, the firm will no doubt falter. On the other hand, taking action consistent with a long-term view, such as making appropriate investments in R&D, may displease investors who have a short-term outlook. Little wonder, then, that there are many different models of organizational effectiveness.

The *systems resource* approach to organizational effectiveness focuses on the extent to which the organization can acquire the resources it needs.[22] A firm that can get raw materials during a shortage is effective from this perspective. The *in-ternal processes approach* deals with the internal mechanisms of the organization and focuses on minimizing strain, integrating individuals and the organization, and conducting smooth and efficient operations.[23] An organization that focuses primarily on maintaining employee satisfaction and morale and being efficient subscribes to this view. The *goal approach* focuses on the degree to which an or-ganization obtains its goals.[24] When a firm establishes a goal of increasing sales by 10 percent and then achieves that increase, the goal approach maintains that the organization is effective. Finally, the *strategic constituencies approach* focuses on the groups that have a stake in the organization.[25] In this view, effectiveness is the extent to which the organization satisfies the demands and expectations of all these groups.

Although these four basic models of effectiveness are not necessarily contradictory, they do focus on different things. The systems resource approach focuses on inputs, the internal processes approach focuses on transformation processes, the goal approach focuses on outputs, and the strategic constituencies approach focuses on feedback. Thus, rather than adopting a single approach, organizational effectiveness can best be understood by an integrated perspective, such as the one illustrated in Figure 3.6. At the core of this unifying model is the organizational system, with its inputs, transformations, outputs, and feedback. Surrounding this core are the four basic approaches to effectiveness as well as a combined approach, which incorporates each of the other four. The basic argument is that an organization must essentially satisfy the requirements imposed on it by each of the effectiveness perspectives.

Achieving organizational effectiveness is not an easy task. The key to doing so is understanding the environment in which the organization functions. With this understanding as a foundation, managers can then chart the "correct" path for the

Figure 3.6
A Model of Organizational Effectiveness
The systems resource, internal processes, goal, and strategic constituencies each focuses on a different aspect of organizational effectiveness. Thus, they can be combined to create an overall integrative perspective on effectiveness.

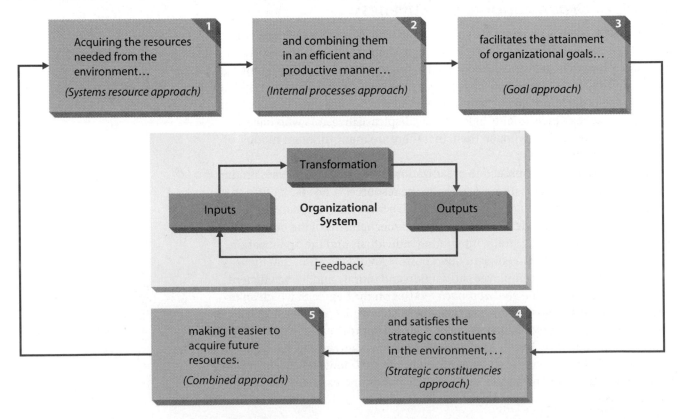

organization as it positions itself in that environment. If managers can identify where they want the organization to be relative to other parts of their environment, and how best to get there, they stand a good chance of achieving effectiveness. On the other hand, if they pick the wrong target to aim for, or if they go about achieving their goals in the wrong way, they are likely to be less effective.

Examples of Organizational Effectiveness

Given the various models and perspectives on organizational effectiveness, it's not surprising that even the experts do not always agree on which companies are most effective. For example, for years *Fortune* has compiled an annual list of the "most admired" companies in the United States. Based on a large survey of leading executives, the rankings presumably reflect the organizations' innovativeness; quality of management; value as a long-term investment; community and environmental responsibility; quality of products and services; financial soundness; use of corporate assets; and ability to attract, develop, and keep talented people. The 2000 list of *Fortune's* ten most admired firms is shown in Table 3.1.

Also illustrated in the table is a list published in *Business Week*, also in 2000. This list represents the ten best performing companies in the United States as determined by revenue and profit growth, return on investment, net profit margins, and return on equity over periods of one and three years. Interestingly, there are more differences than similarities between the lists. Given that "admiration" and "performance" would each seem to be highly related to effectiveness, a stronger correspondence between the two lists might have been expected. It is important to note, of course, that different variables and methods are used to develop the two lists, and every firm included on one list but not the other is still a very well-managed company. But the disparities in the lists also underscores the difficulties and judgment calls that are involved when trying to evaluate the effectiveness of any given company or organization.

MANAGEMENT IMPLICATIONS Managers need to remember that the performance of their organization is best evaluated from a multifaceted and dynamic point of view. No one single measure or calculation can be used to judge effectiveness. Instead, effectiveness must be approached from several perspectives. Moreover, managers should also keep in mind that even experts may disagree about what constitutes effectiveness and how different organizations compare to one another.

Table 3.1

Examples of Admired and High-Performing Firms

Fortune's Most Admired Companies (2000)	*Business Week's* Best Performing Companies (2000)
1. General Electric	1. Microsoft
2. Microsoft	2. Time Warner
3. Dell Computer	3. Cisco Systems
4. Cisco Systems	4. Oracle
5. Wal-Mart	5. EMC
6. Southwest Airlines	6. Citrix Systems
7. Berkshire Hathaway	7. Morgan Stanley Dean Witter
8. Intel	8. Gap
9. Home Depot	9. Warner-Lambert
10. Lucent Technologies	10. Lucent Technologies

Source: "America's Most Admired Companies," *Fortune*, February 21, 2000, pp. 108–110; "The Business Week 50," *Business Week*, March 27, 2000, pp. 123–125.

Summary of Key Points

Environmental factors play a major role in determining an organization's success or failure. Managers should strive to maintain the proper alignment between their organization and its environment. All organizations have both external and internal environments.

The external environment is composed of general and task environment layers. The general environment is composed of the nonspecific elements of the organization's surroundings that might affect its activities. It consists of five dimensions: economic, technological, sociocultural, political-legal, and international. The effects of these dimensions on the organization are broad and gradual. The task environment consists of specific dimensions of the organization's surroundings that are very likely to influence the organization. It also consists of five elements: competitors, customers, suppliers, regulators, and strategic partners. Because these dimensions are associated with specific organizations in the environment, their effects are likely to be more direct and immediate.

The internal environment consists of the organization's owners, board of directors, employees, physical work environment, and culture (discussed separately in Chapter 6). Owners are those who have property rights claims on the organization. The board of directors, elected by stockholders, is responsible for overseeing a firm's top managers. Individual employees and the labor unions they sometimes join are other important parts of the internal environment. The physical environment, yet another part of the internal environment, varies greatly across organizations.

Organizations and their environments affect each other in several ways. Environmental influences on the organization can occur through uncertainty, competitive forces, and turbulence. Organizations, in turn, use information management; strategic response; mergers, acquisitions, and alliances; organization design and flexibility; direct influence; and social responsibility to adapt to their task environments.

One important indicator of how well an organization deals with its environment is its level of effectiveness. Organizational effectiveness requires that the organization do a good job of procuring resources, managing them properly, achieving its goals, and satisfying its constituencies. Because of the complexities associated with meeting these requirements, however, experts may disagree about the effectiveness of any given organization at any given point in time.

Discussion Questions

Questions for Review

1. Why is an organization's environment so important? Identify and discuss each of the major dimensions of the general environment.
2. What is an organization's task environment? What are the major dimensions of that environment?
3. What are the major forces that affect organization-environment relationships? Describe those forces.
4. What is organizational effectiveness? How is it studied and assessed?

Questions for Analysis

5. Can you think of dimensions of the task environment that are not discussed in the text? Indicate their linkage to those that are discussed.
6. Some organizations become part-owners of other firms through mergers and acquisitions. How does the nature of partial ownership complicate the organization-environment relationship?
7. How would each dimension of an organization's task environment and internal envi-

ronment assess the organization's effectiveness? Can an organization be equally effective to each of these different groups? Why or why not?

Questions for Application

8. Go to the library and research a company. Characterize its level of effectiveness according to each of the four basic models. Share your results with the class.

9. Interview a manager from a local organization about his or her organization's environments—general, task, and internal. In the course of the interview, are all of the major dimensions identified? Why or why not?

10. Outline the several environments of your college or university. Be detailed about the dimensions, and provide specific examples to illustrate how each dimension affects your institution.

BUILDING EFFECTIVE *time management* SKILLS

Exercise Overview

Time-management skills refer to the manager's ability to prioritize work, to work efficiently, and to delegate appropriately. This exercise will provide you with an opportunity to relate time-management issues to environment pressures and opportunities.

Exercise Background

As discussed in this chapter, managers and organizations must be sensitive to a variety of environment dimensions and forces reflected in the general, task, and internal environments. The general environment consists of the economic, technological, political-legal, sociocultural, and international dimensions. The task environment includes competitors, customers, suppliers, regulators, and strategic partners. The internal environment consists of owners, board of directors, employees, and the physical work environment.

The problem faced by managers is that time is a finite resource. There are only so many hours in a day and only so many tasks that can be accomplished in a given period of time. Thus, managers must constantly make choices about how they spend their time. Clearly, of course, they should try to use their time wisely and direct it at the more important challenges and opportunities they face. Spending time on a trivial issue while neglecting an important issue is a mistake.

Time-management experts often suggest that managers begin each day by listing what they need to accomplish that day. After the list is compiled, the manager is then advised to sort these daily tasks into three groups: those that must be addressed that day, those that should be addressed that day but could be postponed if necessary, and those that can easily be postponed. The manager is then advised to perform the tasks in order of priority.

Exercise Task

With the background information above as context, do the following:

1. Write across the top of a sheet of paper the three priority levels noted above.
2. Write down the left side of the same sheet of paper the various elements and dimensions of the task and internal environment of business.
3. At the intersection of each row and column, think of an appropriate example that a manager might face; That is, think of a higher priority, a moderate priority, and a low-priority situation involving a customer.
4. Form a small group with two or three classmates and share the examples you each developed. Focus on whether or not there is agreement about the prioritization of each example.

BUILDING EFFECTIVE *diagnostic* SKILLS

Exercise Overview

Diagnostic skills are the skills that enable a manager to visualize the most appropriate response to a situation. These skills are especially important as managers try to achieve effective environmental alignment. In some ways the various elements of the environment are like a chess board—taking action with respect to one part of the environment may also affect other parts of the environment. Diagnostic skills can help a manager anticipate these second-level influences.

Exercise Background

Assume that you are the top manager at a relatively young retailing company specializing in children's clothes and accessories. The firm (today) is healthy, has almost 1,000 stores, and is growing rapidly. To fuel new growth, however, you want to implement some new plans. One option you are considering is launching a new chain of stores targeted at older consumers. Another option is to expand your existing stores to include nonclothing products like compact disks, videos, DVDs, books, and magazines also geared to younger consumers. The logic behind this strategy is to provide one-stop shopping for your existing customers.

Exercise Task

With the background information above as context, do the following:

1. On a sheet of paper list the elements that comprise an organization's task environment.
2. Beside each element write down how the first strategy above might affect your relationship with that part of the task environment. For example, how might strategy one affect your relationship with your existing suppliers?
3. Repeat this activity for the second strategy.

BUILDING EFFECTIVE *communication* SKILLS

Exercise Overview

Communication skills refer to the manager's abilities both to convey ideas and information to others effectively and to receive ideas and information effectively from others. Communication skills are very important when a manager is attempting to respond to or influence some element from the organization's external environment. This exercise will help you develop your communication skills as they relate to this situation.

Exercise Background

Assume that you work for a large manufacturing firm. Nine years ago a factory owned by your company was involved in a major environmental disaster involving toxic waste disposal. The managers involved in the disaster, clearly your company's fault, were all fired. New procedures for dealing with waste disposal were also developed, and since that earlier situation, no further problems have occurred.

The state where the factory is located is currently under fire from the Environmental Protection Agency to impose tighter environmental protection regulations on a variety of industries. The state, however, has a very tight budget and cannot afford to impose these regulations out of its existing budget. A plan recently introduced in the state legislature calls for the imposition of a new tax on all businesses found guilty of improper waste disposal, as well as other forms of pollution, any time during the last ten years. This tax will be used to enforce the new regulations.

At the present time it is unclear whether the tax would apply to your firm for a single year, or if it will be imposed indefinitely on any firm that initially qualifies. Your boss has told you—off the record—that the firm can live with a one-time tax. But if the tax will remain in place for your company indefinitely, the company will close the plant. A plant closure would also have a serious negative impact on the state's economy. Your boss has also placed you in charge of media relations regarding this situation.

Exercise Task

With the background information above as context, do the following:

1. Draft a press release stating your company's position on the potential tax.
2. Imagine that you are going to be interviewed by a reporter known to be "friendly" to your company. The reporter has agreed that you can submit potential interview questions in advance. Draft three such questions and your answers to them.
3. Imagine that a reporter known to be "hostile" to your company has requested an interview. List three questions that might be asked and draft your answers to them.

ENRON POWERS UP THE ENERGY WORLD

Enron is putting new power into the energy industry. Until fairly recently, U.S. power companies enjoyed highly regulated, stable environments. Houston-based Enron, like other companies operating interstate pipelines, was forced to follow complex government rules for buying and selling natural gas. Although the regulations simplified the company's planning process in many ways, it also prevented Enron from adjusting its pricing, regardless of actual supply and demand.

That inflexibility became a liability when, in the mid-1980s, oil prices dropped lower than gas prices. Many utilities saw a chance to lower their costs by switching from gas to oil for their generating plants, creating a two-pronged problem for the pipelines. First, Enron was locked into multiyear contracts that forced it to buy from gas producers at specified prices. And second, the company could not deviate from federal pricing rules, so it was unable to lower prices to retain its utility customers.

CEO Kenneth Lay quickly realized that the industry was headed for trouble. He tried, without success, to persuade government regulators to change the rules.

Eventually, to avoid financial ruin, Enron and many other pipeline companies abandoned their purchasing contracts, which led to years of legal battles. Meanwhile, the regulators finally changed the rules. Now the pipeline companies are free to buy and sell gas supplies in the marketplace.

In deregulation, Enron's managers saw enormous opportunity where competitors saw dangerous, uncharted waters. Up to that point, nobody had thought of buying and selling gas and electricity as if they were commodities such as pork bellies. However, Lay and his team knew that utility companies were unsettled by the unaccustomed up-and-down movement of deregulated gas prices. So they customized their offerings to balance each utility's specific requirements for gas supply and pricing. Whether a utility was interested in steady prices over a certain period or needed uninterrupted gas supplies for peak times, Enron was ready to help—at a profit.

Gas deregulation was just the beginning. Within a few years, the U.S. electric power industry was also deregulated. Once again, Enron's management recognized the potential for new, profitable activities. Building on its experience in buying and selling natural gas, Enron was able to outmaneuver competitors by forging highly sophisticated deals to buy and sell electric power across a sprawling network of suppliers and customers. This head start allowed the company to start and keep trading power supplies at volumes that are 25 percent higher than its rivals.

As deregulation spread to other countries, Enron began to widen its reach as well. Country by country, it became the largest energy trading company in Europe, which allowed management to monitor issues affecting future energy prices closely, such as regional weather patterns. The company also entered the Indian market by building a giant generating plant in Dabhol, south of Bombay. Enron managers became so skilled at navigating India's legal structure that the contracts they negotiated led the country to change its laws on business arbitration, currency controls, and insurance.

One of Enron's latest ventures is buying and selling excess bandwidth on the fiber-optic networks that carry Internet connections. Telecommunications firms traditionally offered only long-term, fixed-rate contracts for connections to such networks—the kinds of deals that were once all too common in the energy industry. Sensing opportunity, Enron acquired a specialized software company to help develop a system for switching surplus bandwidth with only fifteen minutes of lead time. The company then partnered with Sun Microsystems to create a gigantic distribution network for fiber-optic bandwidth. Now Enron is buying and selling bandwidth, energy, pulp and paper products, coal, and plastics. What industry will Enron energize next?

Case Questions

1. Identify how dimensions of the task environment created new opportunities for Enron.

2. Describe how elements of Enron's general environment affected its ability to exploit new opportunities.

3. Discuss the various ways in which Enron adapted to its environment. What other adaptations would allow Enron to maintain its market leadership in the power industry?

Case References

Brian O'Reilly, "The Power Merchant," *Fortune,* April 17, 2000, pp. 148–160; *Hoover's Handbook of American Business 2000* (Austin: Hoover's Business Press), pp. 558–559.

CHAPTER NOTES

1. "Three Carmakers Create Link," *USA Today,* February 28, 2000, p. 8B; "Big Three Car Makers Plan Net Exchange," *Wall Street Journal,* February 28, 2000, pp. A3, A16 (quote on p. A16); Shawn Tully, "The B2B Tool That Really *Is* Changing the World," *Fortune,* March 20, 2000, pp. 132–145.

2. Arie de Geus, *The Living Company—Habits for Surviving in a Turbulent Business Environment* (Boston: Harvard Business School Press, 1997). See also John G. Sifonis and Beverly Goldberg, *Corporation on a Tightrope* (New York: Oxford University Press, 1996), for an interesting discussion of how organizations must navigate through the environment.

3. Eric D. Beinhocker, "Robust Adaptive Strategies," *Sloan Management Review,* Spring 1999, pp. 95–105.

4. See Jay B. Barney and William G. Ouchi (Eds.), *Organizational Economics* (San Francisco: Jossey-Bass, 1986), for a detailed analysis of links between economics and organizations.

5. "How Prosperity Is Reshaping the American Economy," *Business Week,* February 14, 2000, pp. 100–110.

6. "A Breakup Primer for Microsoft?" *The Wall Street Journal,* June 6, 2000, pp. B1, B4; "WorldCom Takeover of Sprint Looks Dead as U.S. Sues to Halt It," *The Wall Street Journal,* June 28, 2000, pp. A1, A6.

7. See Ricky Griffin and Michael Pustay, *International Business: A Managerial Perspective,* 3rd Edition (Upper Saddle River, NJ: Prentice Hall, 2002), for an overview.

8. For example, see Susanne G. Scott and Vicki R. Lane, "A Stakeholder Approach to Organizational Identity," *The Academy of Management Review,* 2000, Vol. 25, No. 1, pp. 43–62.

9. "Why Tommy Hilfiger Is So Like, Um, 1998," *Business Week,* April 24, 2000, p. 55.

10. Richard N. Osborn and John Hagedoorn, "The Institutionalization and Evolutionary Dynamics of Interorganizational Alliances and Networks," *Academy of Management Journal,* April 1997, pp. 261–278; see also "More Companies Cut Risk by Collaborating with Their 'Enemies,'" *The Wall Street Journal,* January 31, 2000, pp. A1, A10.

11. "The Wild New Workforce," *Business Week,* December 6, 1999, pp. 38–44.

12. "Temporary Workers Getting Short Shrift," *USA Today,* April 11, 1997, pp. 1B, 2B.

13. "Curves Ahead," *The Wall Street Journal,* March 10, 1999, pp. B1, B10.

14. For a recent review, see Allen C. Bluedorn, "Pilgrim's Progress: Trends and Convergence in Research on Organizational Size and Environments," *Journal of Management*, Vol. 19, No. 2, 1993, pp. 163–191.

15. James D. Thompson, *Organizations in Action* (New York: McGraw-Hill, 1967).

16. Michael E. Porter, *Competitive Strategy: Techniques for Analyzing Industries and Competitors* (New York: Free Press, 1980); see also Joel A. C. Baum and Helaine J. Korn, "Competitive Dynamics of Intefirm Rivalry," *Academy of Management Journal*, April 1996, pp. 255–291.

17. See "Xerox Faces Mounting Challenge to Copier Business," *The Wall Street Journal*, December 17, 1999, p. B4.

18. "Plane Maker May Not Seek More 'Sole Supplier' Deals," *USA Today*, June 26, 1997, p. 3B.

19. "Coke Scrambles to Contain a Scare in Europe," *The Wall Street Journal*, June 17, 1999, pp. B1, B4.

20. Bala Chakravarthy, "A New Strategy Framework for Coping with Turbulence," *Sloan Management Review*, Winter 1997, pp. 69–82.

21. Gareth Jones, *Organizational Theory and Design*, 3rd Edition (Upper Saddle River, NJ: Prentice Hall, 2001).

22. E. Yuchtman and S. Seashore, "A Systems Resource Approach to Organizational Effectiveness," *American Sociological Review*, Vol. 32, 1967, pp. 891–903.

23. B. S. Georgopoules and A. S. Tannenbaum, "The Study of Organizational Effectiveness," *American Sociological Review*, Vol. 22, 1957, pp. 534–540.

24. Jones, *Organizational Theory and Design*.

25. Anthony A. Atkinson, John H. Waterhouse, and Robert B. Wells, "A Stakeholder Approach to Strategic Performance Measurement," *Sloan Management Review*, Spring 1997, pp. 25–37.

CHAPTER

4

The Ethical and Social Environment

Businesses exist for one fundamental purpose—to earn profits for their owners. But the manner in which they work to fulfill this purpose and the uses to which they put those profits can vary dramatically. Consider, for example, the case of Patagonia, Inc., a small, privately held, outdoor apparel business. Patagonia was founded in 1973 by a group of surfers in Ventura, California, and was led by Yvon Chouinard. Chouinard still runs the business today.

The founders enjoyed spending part of their time hiking and mountain climbing but felt that the equipment available for such activities was often of poor quality and/or was overpriced. Their objective, then, was to become a provider of high-quality, reasonably priced outdoor equipment. But they expressed this in the form of an unusual goal—

to do the right thing. Indeed, in Chouinard's words, "Business[people] who focus on profits wind up in the hole. For me, profit is what happens when you do everything else right."

At first, this meant making the most useful, durable, and environmentally friendly products possible. For instance, for years mountain climbers had embedded steel "chocks" into rocks for attaching their ropes and creating hand- and foot-holds. But Patagonia began selling aluminum chocks because they were less damaging to the rocks. Once the firm started making outdoor adult clothing, it quickly added a line of children's clothing as well, not because there was a known market for such products but because they wanted to find a use for the scraps that were cut from sheets of fabric in making the larger pieces.

Patagonia also markets a line of shirts made of fibers from recycled plastic bottles and shirts made from hemp, which is easy to grow organically.

As the firm grew, its environmental concerns also became more and more tangible. For example, in 1996 it decided to use only organic cotton (grown without fertilizers or chemical insecticides) in its clothing. This created a problem, however, because most cotton grown and sold in the United States doesn't meet one or the other of the requirements for being organic. Thus, the firm had to start dealing directly with farmers, instructing them about what they wanted to buy and guaranteeing them competitive

> *"Business[people] who focus on profits wind up in the hole. For me, profit is what happens when you do everything else right."*
>
> *—Yvon Chouinard, founder and CEO of Patagonia*

After studying this chapter, you should be able to:

■ Discuss managerial ethics, three areas of special ethical concern for managers, and how organizations manage ethical behavior.

□ Discuss the concept of social responsibility, specify to whom or what an organization might be considered responsible, and describe four types of organizational approaches to social responsibility.

■ Explain the relationship between the government and organizations regarding social responsibility.

■ Describe some of the activities organizations may engage in to manage social responsibility.

prices to reduce their risk. In a few cases, Patagonia even had to co-sign loans for farmers so that they could buy new equipment and technology to meet the company's stringent requirements.

More recently Chouinard has mandated that henceforth 1 percent of Patagonia's revenues would be given to environmental groups each year. (Because the firm is private, its financial records are not disclosed. However, estimates suggest that the firm generates about $180 million in revenues each year.) And Chouinard himself has been actively involved in efforts aimed at removing dams from rivers to return the rivers to their natural states.

Patagonia always seems to put its social agenda at the forefront of everything it does. For example, in early 2000 the firm set up a major new operation on the Internet to sell its products more efficiently to consumers. One of the more interesting twists, though, is a section called "Rants & Raves." Customers can use this section to post on-line reviews and comments about Patagonia products—both positive and negative. But even a firm as socially active as Patagonia is not always above criticism. For instance, some people criticize the fact that part of its social giving goes to such radical groups as Earth First.[1]

usinesses everywhere need to earn profits to remain in existence. But there are disparate views about how a firm can legitimately pursue and then use those profits. Some companies aggressively seek to maximize their profits, to grow at any cost, and focus on nothing but what's best for the company. Others, like Patagonia, take a much different approach to business and actively work for the betterment of society, even when it means less profit for the owners. Most businesses, however, adopt a position somewhere between these extremes. Decisions about which of these approaches to take, in turn, are affected by managerial ethics and social responsibility.

This chapter explores the basic issues of ethics and social responsibility in detail. We look first at individual ethics and their organizational context. Next, we expand our discussion to the more general subject of social responsibility. After we explore the relationships among businesses and the government regarding socially responsible behavior, we examine the activities organizations sometimes undertake to be more socially responsible.

Individual Ethics in Organizations

ethics An individual's personal beliefs about whether a behavior, action, or decision is right or wrong

ethical behavior Behavior that conforms to generally accepted social norms

unethical behavior Behavior that does not conform to generally accepted social norms

We define **ethics** as an individual's personal beliefs about whether a behavior, action, or decision is right or wrong.[2] Note that we define ethics in the context of the individual—people have ethics, organizations do not. Likewise, what constitutes ethical behavior varies from one person to another. For example, one person who finds a twenty-dollar bill on the floor believes that it is okay to stick it in his pocket, whereas another feels compelled to turn it in to the lost-and-found department. Further, although **ethical behavior** is in the eye of the beholder, it usually refers to behavior that conforms to generally accepted social norms. **Unethical behavior**, then, is behavior that does not conform to generally accepted social norms.

A society generally adopts formal laws that reflect the prevailing ethical standards—the social norms—of its citizens. For example, because most people consider theft to be unethical, laws have been passed to make such behaviors illegal and to prescribe ways of punishing those who do steal. But while laws attempt to be clear and unambiguous, their application and interpretation still lead to ethical ambiguities. For example, virtually everyone would agree that forcing employees to work excessive hours, especially for no extra compensation, is unethical. Accordingly, laws have been passed to define work and pay standards. But applying that law to organizational settings can still result in ambiguous situations that can be interpreted in different ways.

An individual's ethics are determined by a combination of factors. People start to form ethical standards as children in response to their perceptions of the behavior of their parents and/or other adults and the behaviors they are allowed to choose. As children grow and enter school, they are also influenced by peers with whom they interact every day. Dozens of important individual events also shape people's lives and contribute to their ethical beliefs and behavior as they grow into adulthood. Values and morals also contribute to ethical standards. People who place financial gain and personal advancement at the top of their list of priorities, for example, will adopt personal codes of ethics that promote the pursuit of wealth. Thus, they may be ruthless in efforts to gain these rewards, regardless of the costs to others. In contrast, people who clearly establish their family and/or friends as their top priority will adopt different ethical standards.

Managerial Ethics

Managerial ethics are the standards of behavior that guide individual managers in their work.[3] Although ethics can affect managerial work in any number of ways, three areas of special concern for managers are shown in Figure 4.1.

managerial ethics Standards of behavior that guide individual managers in their work

How an Organization Treats Its Employees   One important area of managerial ethics is the treatment of employees by the organization. This area includes things such as hiring and firing, wages and working conditions, and employee privacy and respect. For example, both ethical and legal guidelines suggest that hiring

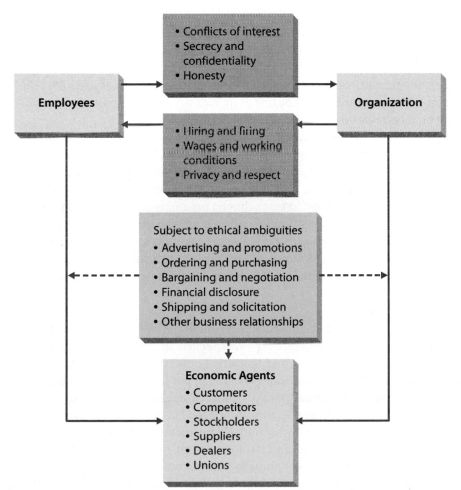

Figure 4.1

Managerial Ethics

The three basic areas of concern for managerial ethics are the relationships of the firm to the employee, the employee to the firm, and the firm to other economic agents. Managers need to approach each set of relationships from an ethical and moral perspective.

The Container Store is consistently ranked as one of the best companies to work for in the United States. One key factor in this recognition is the manner in which management treats the firm's employees. For example, the company allows all employees to have access to all its financial information. The company also provides extensive training for its employees and works to insure that its compensation and benefits packages are the best in the industry. And all employees from top management on down are treated as equals.

and firing decisions should be based solely on an individual's ability to perform the job. A manager who discriminates against African Americans in hiring is exhibiting both unethical and illegal behavior. But consider the case of a manager who does not discriminate in general, but occasionally hires a close friend or relative when other applicants might be just as qualified. While these hiring decisions may not be illegal, they may be objectionable on ethical grounds.

Wages and working conditions, while also tightly regulated, are also areas for potential controversy. For example, the fact that a manager is paying an employee less than he deserves, simply because the manager knows the employee cannot afford to quit or risk losing his job by complaining, might be considered unethical. Finally, most observers also would agree that an organization is obligated to protect the privacy of its employees. A manager's spreading a rumor that an employee has AIDS or is having an affair with a coworker is generally seen as an unethical breach of privacy. Likewise, the manner in which an organization responds to and addresses issues associated with sexual harassment also involves employee privacy and related rights.

How Employees Treat the Organization   Numerous ethical issues also stem from how employees treat the organization, especially in regard to conflicts of interest, secrecy and confidentiality, and honesty. A conflict of interest occurs when a decision potentially benefits the individual to the possible detriment of the organization. To guard against such practices, most companies have policies that forbid their buyers from accepting gifts from suppliers. Divulging company secrets is also clearly unethical. Employees who work for businesses in highly competitive industries—electronics, software, and fashion apparel, for example—might be tempted to sell information about company plans to competitors. A third area of concern is honesty in general. Relatively common problems in this area include using a business telephone to make personal long-distance calls, stealing supplies, and padding expense accounts. While most employees are inherently honest, organizations must nevertheless be vigilant to avoid problems from behaviors such as these.

How Employees and the Organization Treat Other Economic Agents   Managerial ethics also come into play in the relationship between the firm and its employees and other economic agents. As listed previously in Figure 4.1, the primary agents of interest include customers, competitors, stockholders, suppliers, dealers, and unions. The behaviors between the organization and these agents that may be subject to ethical ambiguity include advertising and promotions, financial disclosures, ordering and purchasing, shipping and solicitations, bargaining and negotiation, and other business relationships.

For example, businesses in the pharmaceuticals industry have been under growing fire because of the rapid escalation of the prices they are charging for many of their drugs. These firms counter that they need to invest more heavily in research and development programs to develop new drugs, and that higher prices are needed to cover these costs. The key in situations like this, then, is to find the right balance between reasonable pricing and price gouging. And like so many questions involving ethics, there are significant differences of opinion.[4] Another area of concern in recent years involves financial reporting by various e-commerce firms. Because of the complexities inherent in these firms, some of them have been very aggressive in presenting their financial positions in a very positive light. And in at least a few cases, some firms have substantially overstated their earnings projections to entice more investment.[5]

Additional complexities faced by many firms today are the variations in ethical business practices in different countries. In many countries bribes and side payments are a normal and customary part of doing business. However, U.S. laws forbid these practices, even if a firm's rivals from other countries are paying them. For example, a U.S. power-generating company lost a $320 million contract in the Middle East because government officials demanded a $3 million bribe. A Japanese firm paid the bribe and won the contract. Enron Company had a big project in India cancelled because newly elected officials demanded bribes. While these kinds of cases are illegal under U.S. law, other situations are more ambiguous. In China, for example, local journalists expect their cabfare to be paid if they are to cover a business-sponsored news conference. In Indonesia the normal time to get a driver's license for a foreigner is over a year, but it can be "expedited" for an extra $100. And in Romania, building inspectors routinely expect a "tip" for a favorable review.[6] *The World of Management* summarizes a recent incident of international price fixing.

Ethics in an Organizational Context

It is also important to note that while ethics are an individual phenomenon, ethical or unethical actions by particular managers do not occur in a vacuum. Indeed, they most often occur in an organizational context that is conducive to them.

WORLD OF MANAGEMENT

DEALING WITH INTERNATIONAL PRICE FIXING

When managerial ethics collide with profits, customers pay the price. That's what happened in a recent case of global pricing collusion. Switzerland's F. Hoffmann-LaRoche, France's Rhone-Poulenc, and Germany's BASF all cooperated in a sophisticated conspiracy to control international pricing of vitamins and vitamin ingredients for cereals and other foods.

During the course of their inquiry, U.S. Department of Justice investigators learned that the firms got together every year to set prices and track progress. In effect, the three acted more like a single company than a set of rivals, setting specific agendas and budgets for their meetings and activities. Investigators found that top managers initiated and directed the price-fixing arrangement, middle managers implemented the prices, and first-line managers confirmed that the prices were set as agreed.

Hoffmann-LaRoche paid $500 million to settle this price-fixing case, one of the highest fines levied by the Justice Department for antitrust violations. In addition, Hoffmann-LaRoche's former director of worldwide marketing was ordered to pay a $100,000 fine and serve four months in prison. This was not the pharmaceutical company's first brush with antitrust proceedings. Only two years earlier, it had been fined for its part in a price-fixing case involving citric acid.

BASF paid a $225 million fine to settle the vitamin price-fixing case. Rhone-Poulenc was able to avoid prosecution because it cooperated with the Department of Justice's investigation. Even after the antitrust case was settled, the legal maneuvering continued as distributors and food processors who purchased vitamins from the three firms filed suit for restitution. Despite the settlement, experts doubted that consumers would see any drop in vitamin prices. So although the negative publicity and heavy fines hurt the conspirators, customers ultimately paid the price for this global price-fixing scandal.

> *The criminal conduct of these companies hurt the pocketbook of virtually every American consumer—anyone who took a vitamin, drank a glass of milk, or had a bowl of cereal.*
>
> —*Joel Klein, Assistant Attorney General**

Reference: Jayne O'Donnell, "U.S. Fines Drug Companies $725M for Price Fixing," *USA Today,* May 21, 1999, p. 1B (*quote on p. 1B).

Actions of peer managers and top managers, as well as the organization's culture, all contribute to the ethical context of the organization.[7]

The starting point in understanding the ethical context of management is, of course, the individual's own ethical standards. Some people, for example, will risk personal embarrassment or lose their job before they would do something unethical. Other people are much more easily swayed by the unethical behavior they see around them and other situational factors, and they may be willing to commit major crimes to further their own careers or for financial gain. Organizational practices may strongly influence the ethical standards of employees. Some organizations openly permit unethical business practices as long as they are in the best interests of the firm.

If managers become aware of unethical practices and allow them to continue, they have contributed to an organization culture that says such activity is permitted. For example, a few years ago Lars Bildman was fired from his post as CEO of Astra USA, a subsidiary of a large Swedish drug manufacturer, Astra AB. During his

tenure with the firm, he allegedly sexually harassed dozens of Astra employees, used company funds to remodel his home, and took frequent company-paid private cruises with other company executives and prostitutes. While only Bildman was formally charged with criminal wrongdoing, dozens of senior managers apparently knew of the problems at Astra and either ignored them or began to participate in similar activities themselves. Thus, their collective behaviors served first to create and then to reinforce an environment that appeared to sanction those behaviors.[8]

The organization's environment also contributes to the context for ethical behavior. In a highly competitive or regulated industry, for example, a manager may feel more pressure to achieve high performance. When managers feel pressure to meet goals or lower costs, they may explore a variety of alternatives to help achieve these ends. And in some cases, the alternative they adopt may be unethical or even illegal. The cartoon illustrates one way this can happen—if a manager feels pressure to get more work done, she or he may apply similar pressure on others to work extra hours, stay later in the evenings, and so forth.

Managers should strive to be ethical in all their dealings with their employees. Sometimes the pressures and stresses they experience cause them to apply those same pressures and stresses to employees, often in inappropriate ways. For example, as illustrated here, managers sometimes go too far in their efforts to entice employees to work harder or to spend more time on the job. The result can be disgruntled employees and low morale.

Managing Ethical Behavior

Spurred partially by increased awareness of ethical scandals in business and partially from a sense of enhanced corporate consciousness about the importance of ethical and unethical behaviors, many organizations have reemphasized ethical behavior on the part of employees. This emphasis takes many forms, but any effort to enhance ethical behavior must begin with top management. Top managers, for example, establish the organization's culture and define what will and will not be acceptable behavior. Some companies have also started offering employees training in how to cope with ethical dilemmas. At Boeing, for example, line managers lead training sessions for other employees, and the company also has an ethics committee that reports directly to the board of directors. The training sessions involve discussions of different ethical dilemmas that employees might face and how managers might handle those dilemmas. Chemical Bank and Xerox also have ethics training programs for their managers.

Organizations are also going to greater lengths to formalize their ethical standards. Some, such as General Mills and Johnson & Johnson, have prepared

code of ethics A formal, written statement of the values and ethical standards that guide a firm's actions

guidelines that detail how employees are to treat suppliers, customers, competitors, and other constituents. Others, such as Whirlpool and Hewlett-Packard, have developed formal **codes of ethics**—formal, written statements of the values and ethical standards that guide a firm's actions.

Of course, no code, guideline, or training program can truly make up for the quality of an individual's personal judgment about what is right behavior and what is wrong behavior in a particular situation. Such devices may prescribe what people should do, but they often fail to help people understand and live with the consequences of their choices. Making ethical choices may lead to very unpleasant outcomes—firing, rejection by colleagues, and the forfeiture of monetary gain, to name a few. Thus managers must be prepared to confront their own consciences and weigh the options available when making difficult ethical decisions. *Today's Management Issues* highlights an increasingly important issue that relates to this point, privacy and the Internet.

Unfortunately, what distinguishes ethical from unethical behavior is often subject to differences of opinion. So how does one go about deciding whether or not a

---

TODAY'S MANAGEMENT ISSUES

PRIVACY ON THE INTERNET

Who's watching when people surf the Internet? On-line privacy has become a hot issue as companies sort out the ethical and management issues. DoubleClick, an on-line advertising network, is one of the firms at the eye of the privacy storm. The company has collected data on the habits of millions of web surfers, recording which sites they visit and which ads they click on. DoubleClick insists the profiles are anonymous and are used to match surfers better with appropriate ads. After the company announced a plan to add names and addresses to its database, however, it was forced to back down because of public concerns over invasion of on-line privacy.

DoubleClick isn't the only firm gathering personal data about people's Internet activities. People who register at Yahoo! are asked to list date of birth, among other details. Amazon.com, eBay, and other sites also ask for personal information. As Internet use increases, however, surveys show that people are troubled by the amount of information being collected and who sees it.

One way management can address these concerns is to post a privacy policy on the web site. The policy should explain exactly what data the company collects and who sees the data. It should also allow people a choice about having their information shared with others and indicate how people can opt

out of data collection. Walt Disney, IBM, and other companies support this position by refusing to advertise on web sites that have no posted privacy policies.

In addition, companies can offer web surfers the opportunity to review and correct information that has been collected, especially medical and financial data. In the off-line world, consumers are legally allowed to inspect credit and medical records. In the on-line world, this kind of access can be costly and cumbersome because data are often spread

> *I am troubled, very troubled, by leaders who have failed to recognize our responsibility in the transformation of the new economy.*
>
> *—Louis Gerstner, chairman, IBM**

across several computer systems. Despite the technical difficulties, government agencies are already working on Internet privacy guidelines, which means companies will need internal guidelines, training, and leadership to ensure compliance.

Reference: Heather Green, Mike France, Marcia Stepanek, and Amy Borrus, "Online Privacy: It's Time for Rules in Wonderland," *Business Week,* March 20, 2000, pp. 83–96 (*quote on p. 85).

particular action or decision is ethical? Traditionally, experts have suggested a three-step model for applying ethical judgments to situations that may arise during the course of business activities. These steps are (1) gather the relevant factual information, (2) determine the most appropriate moral values, and (3) make an ethical judgment based on the rightness or wrongness of the proposed activity or policy.

But this analysis is seldom as simple as these few steps might imply. For instance, what if the facts are not clear-cut? What if there are no agreed-upon moral values? Nevertheless, a judgment and a decision must be made. Experts point out that, otherwise, trust is impossible; and trust, they add, is indispensable to any business transaction. Thus, to assess more completely the ethics of a particular behavior, a more complex perspective is necessary. To illustrate this perspective, consider a common dilemma faced by managers involving their expense accounts.[9]

Companies routinely provide their managers with an account to cover their work-related expenses when they are traveling on company business and/or entertaining clients for business purposes. Common examples of such expenses include hotel bills, meals, rental cars or taxis, and so forth. But employees, of course, are expected to claim only expenses that are accurate and work-related. For example, if a manager takes a client out to dinner while in another city on business and spends $100 for dinner, submitting a receipt for that dinner to be reimbursed for $100 is clearly accurate and appropriate. Suppose, however, that the manager then has a $100 dinner the next night in that same city with a good friend for purely social purposes. Submitting that receipt for full reimbursement would be unethical. A few managers, however, might rationalize that it would be okay to submit a receipt for dinner with a friend. They might argue, for example, that they are underpaid and this is just a way for them to increase their income.

Other principles that come into play in a case like this include various ethical norms. Four such norms involve utility, rights, justice, and caring. By utility, we mean deciding whether a particular act optimizes what is best for its constituencies. By rights, we mean deciding whether a particular act respects the rights of the individuals involved. By justice, we mean deciding whether it is consistent with what we would see as being fair. And by caring, we mean deciding whether it is consistent with people's responsibilities to each other. Figure 4.2 illustrates a model that incorporates these ethical norms.

Now, reconsider the case of the inflated expense account. While the utility norm would acknowledge that the manager benefits from padding an expense account, others, such as coworkers and owners, do not. Similarly, most experts would agree that it does not respect the rights of others. Moreover, it is clearly unfair and compromises responsibilities to others. Thus, this particular act appears to be clearly unethical. However, the figure also provides mechanisms for considering unique circumstances that might fit certain limited situations. For example, suppose the manager loses the receipt for the legitimate dinner but has the receipt for the same amount for the social dinner. Some people would now argue that it is okay to submit the social dinner receipt because the manager is doing so only to get what he or she is entitled to. Others, however, would still argue that submitting the social dinner receipt is wrong under any circumstances. The point, simply, is that changes in the situation can make the issue more or less clear-cut.

Figure 4.2

A Guide for Ethical Decision Making

Managers should attempt to apply ethical judgment to the decisions they make. For example, this useful framework for guiding ethical decision making suggests that managers apply a set of four criteria based on utility, rights, justice, and caring when assessing decision options options. The resulting analysis allows a manager to make a clear assessment of whether or not a decision or policy is ethical.

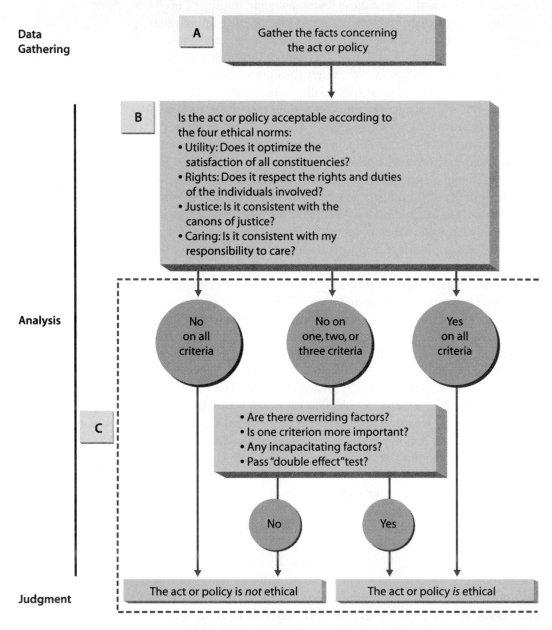

Source: Adapted from Gerald F. Cavanagh, Dennis J. Moberg, and Manuel Velasquez, "Making Business Ethics Practical," *Business Ethics Quarterly* (July 1995); and Manuel Velasquez, Gerald F. Cavanagh, and Dennis Moberg, "Organizational Statesmenship and Dirty Politics," *Organizational Dynamics* (Autumn, 1983). p. 84. Copyright 1983, with permission from Elesevier Science. Reprinted from Gerald F. Cavanagh, *American Business Values*, 4th Edition (Upper Saddle River, N.J.: Prentice-Hall, 1998). Reprinted by permission of Prentice-Hall, Inc.

MANAGEMENT Managers need to understand the basic meanings of ethical
IMPLICATIONS and unethical behaviors. They also need to understand fully
the various ethical links among the organization, its employees, and other economic agents and to ensure, to the extent possible, that these links are maintained
according to the proper ethical standards. Managers should also acknowledge the
organizational context of individual ethics and be prepared to interpret ethical
problems from an organizational perspective. And finally, managers should take
various measures to maintain ethical behavior by those in their organizations,
while also recognizing that any individual's personal actions may offset the best
organizational strategies for promoting ethical conduct. The key, then, is to make a
thorough attempt to apply reasonable judgment to ethical situations.

Social Responsibility and Organizations

As we have seen, ethics relate to individuals and their decisions and behaviors.
Organizations themselves do not have ethics, but they do relate to their environment in ways that often involve ethical dilemmas and decisions. These situations
are generally referred to within the context of the organization's social responsibility. Specifically, **social responsibility** is the set of obligations an organization has
to protect and enhance the society in which it functions.

social responsibility The set of
obligations an organization has to
protect and enhance the society in
which it functions

Areas of Social Responsibility

Organizations may exercise social responsibility
toward their stakeholders, toward the natural environment, and toward general social welfare. Some
organizations acknowledge their responsibilities in all
three areas and strive diligently to meet each of them,
while others emphasize only one or two areas of social
responsibility. And a few acknowledge no social responsibility at all.

Organizational Stakeholders In Chapter 3 we described the task environment as comprising those elements in an organization's external environment that
directly affect the organization in one or more ways.
Another way to describe these same elements is from
the perspective of **organizational stakeholders**, or
those people and organizations who are directly affected by the behaviors of an organization and that
have a stake in its performance.[10] Major stakeholders
are depicted in Figure 4.3.

Most companies that strive to be responsible to
their stakeholders concentrate first and foremost on

Businesses face an array of stakeholders when addressing issues
of social responsibility. For example, consider the problems faced
by McDonald's. The firm contracted with a Chinese manufacturer
to make toys for its Happy Meals and various promotional ventures. The Chinese firm, in turn, allegedly used child labor in its factory. As a result, these protestors are calling on consumers in Hong
Kong to boycott McDonald's. They also demanded that the firm
provide additional compensation to the families of the underage
children.

Figure 4.3

Organizational Stakeholders

All organizations have a variety of stakeholders that are directly affected by the organization and that have a stake in its performance. These are people and organizations to whom an organization should be responsible.

organizational stakeholders
People and organizations who are directly affected by the behaviors of an organization and that have a stake in its performance

three main groups: customers, employees, and investors. They then select other stakeholders that are particularly relevant or important to the organization and then attempt to address their needs and expectations as well.

Organizations that are responsible to their customers strive to treat them fairly and honestly. They also seek to charge fair prices, to honor warranties, to meet delivery commitments, and to stand behind the quality of the products they sell. Companies that have established excellent reputations in this area include L.L.Bean, Land's End, Dell Computer, and Johnson & Johnson.

Organizations that are socially responsible in their dealings with employees treat their workers fairly, make them part of the team, and respect their dignity and basic human needs. Organizations such as 3M Company, Hoescht Celanese, SAS Institute, and Southwest Airlines have all established strong reputations in this area. In addition, they also go to great lengths to find, hire, train, and promote qualified minorities. *Working with Diversity* also explains how some organizations today are helping their employees prepare for and compete in the Olympic Games.

To maintain a socially responsible stance toward investors, managers should follow proper accounting procedures, provide appropriate information to shareholders about the financial performance of the firm, and manage the organization to protect shareholder rights and investments. Moreover, they should be accurate and candid in their assessment of future growth and profitability and avoid even

WORKING WITH DIVERSITY

SUPPORTING OLYMPIC ATHLETES

Summer and winter Olympic games take place every four years, which leaves plenty of time between for athletes to climb the career ladder while funding their dreams. Although training for the Olympics takes time and costs money, some U.S. athletes have a new source of support: their employers. Companies such as U.S. West, UPS, and Home Depot, which have paid millions of dollars for Olympic sponsorship, are also demonstrating their social responsibility by supporting employees who are training for slots on U.S. Olympic teams.

Telecommunications giant U.S. West pays training costs—as much as $100,000—for eight employees who are Olympic-level athletes, including Anthony Washington, a market analyst who competes in the discus throw. U.S. West, like other sponsors, proudly lets the world know about its employees' achievements. After Washington won the World Track and Field Championships, U.S. West offered public congratulations in a special advertisement.

UPS, the global delivery firm, is another strong supporter of Olympic athletes on staff. Tongula Givens, who competes in the triple jump event, is one of several UPS employees whose training and travel expenses are paid by the company. UPS also adjusts work schedules to accommodate its employees' training

needs, allowing time off with full pay for intensive training just before Olympic events. The UPS athletes have become in-house celebrities, giving motivational talks to employees and appearing in UPS ads and on shipping materials.

Home Depot has become a magnet for Olympic hopefuls. Over the past five years, nearly 100 top athletes have worked for the home improvement retailer. Each works a flexible part-time schedule at full-time pay while in training. Like UPS, Home Depot touts its sponsorship of Olympic athletes through advertising and other promotions.

> *It's good for marketing purposes. But it's also a good thing to do for athletes who might otherwise give up competing.*
>
> —Anthony Washington, market analyst and discus thrower, U.S. West*

After the Olympics, employees who have won medals appear at corporate meetings and new store openings. Then it's back to work and back to training until the next Olympic games.

Reference: Bruce Horovitz, "Employers Back Olympic Hopefuls," *USA Today*, February 7, 2000, p. 1B (*quote on p. 1B).

---

the appearance of improprieties involving such sensitive areas as insider trading, stock price manipulation, and the withholding of financial data.[11]

The Natural Environment A second critical area of social responsibility relates to the natural environment.[12] Not long ago, many organizations indiscriminately dumped sewage, waste products from production, and trash into streams and rivers, into the air and on vacant land. When Shell Oil first explored the Amazon River Basin for potential drilling sites in the late 1980s, its crews ripped down trees and left a trail of garbage in their wake. Now, however, many laws regulate the disposal of waste materials. In many instances, companies themselves have also become more socially responsible in their release of pollutants and general treatment of the environment. For example, when Shell launched its most recent exploration expedition into another area of the Amazon Basin, the group included a biologist to oversee environmental protection and an anthropologist to help the team interact more effectively with native tribes.[13]

Still, much remains to be done. Companies need to develop economically feasible ways to avoid contributing to acid rain and global warming; to avoid depleting the ozone layer; and to develop alternative methods of handling sewage, hazardous wastes, and ordinary garbage. Procter & Gamble, for example, is an industry leader in using recycled materials for containers. Hyatt Corporation established a new company to help recycle waste products from its hotels. Monsanto is launching an entirely new product line aimed at improving the environment with genetically engineered crops.[14] Ford has also announced its intention to create a new brand to cover the development and marketing of low-pollution and electric powered vehicles.[15] The Internet is also seen as potentially playing an important role in resource conservation because many e-commerce businesses and transactions reduce both energy costs and pollution.[16]

Companies also need to develop safety policies that cut down on accidents with potentially disastrous environmental results. When one of Ashland Oil's storage tanks ruptured several years ago, spilling more than five hundred thousand gallons of diesel fuel into Pennsylvania's Monongahela River, the company moved quickly to clean up the spill but was still indicted for violating U.S. environmental laws.[17] After the Exxon oil tanker *Valdez* spilled millions of gallons of oil off the coast of Alaska, it adopted new and more stringent procedures to keep another disaster from happening.

General Social Welfare Some people believe that in addition to treating constituents and the environment responsibly, business organizations should also promote the general welfare of society. Examples include making contributions to charities, philanthropic organizations, and not-for-profit foundations and associations; supporting museums, symphonies, and public radio and television; and taking a role in improving public health and education. Some people also believe that organizations should act even more broadly to correct the political inequities that exist in the world. For example, these observers would argue that businesses should not conduct operations in countries with a record of human rights violations. Thus, they stand in opposition to companies doing business in China and Vietnam.

Arguments For and Against Social Responsibility

On the surface, there seems to be little disagreement about the need for organizations to be socially responsible. In truth, though, those who oppose wide interpretations of social responsibility use several convincing arguments.[18] Some of the more salient arguments on both sides of this contemporary debate are summarized in Figure 4.4 and are further explained in the following sections.

Arguments for Social Responsibility People who argue in favor of social responsibility claim that because organizations create many of the problems that need to be addressed, such as air and water pollution and resource depletion, they should play a major role in solving them. They also argue that because corporations are legally defined entities with most of the same privileges as private citizens, businesses should not try to avoid their obligations as citizens. Advocates of social responsibility point out that while governmental organizations have

Figure 4.4

Arguments For and Against Social Responsibility

While many people want everyone to see social responsibility as a desirable aim, there are in fact several strong arguments that can be used both for and against social responsibility. Hence, organizations and their managers should carefully assess their own values, beliefs, and priorities when deciding which stance and approach to take regarding social responsibility.

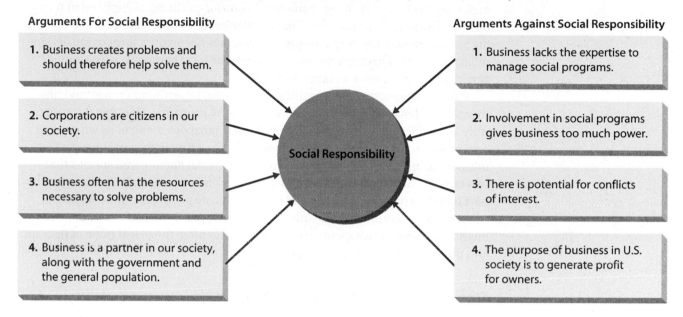

Arguments For Social Responsibility

1. Business creates problems and should therefore help solve them.

2. Corporations are citizens in our society.

3. Business often has the resources necessary to solve problems.

4. Business is a partner in our society, along with the government and the general population.

Social Responsibility

Arguments Against Social Responsibility

1. Business lacks the expertise to manage social programs.

2. Involvement in social programs gives business too much power.

3. There is potential for conflicts of interest.

4. The purpose of business in U.S. society is to generate profit for owners.

stretched their budgets to the limit, many large businesses often have surplus revenues that could potentially be used to help solve social problems. For example, IBM routinely donates surplus computers to schools and many restaurants give leftover food to homeless shelters.

Although each of the arguments just summarized is a distinct justification for socially responsible behaviors on the part of organizations, another more general reason for social responsibility is profit itself. For example, organizations that make clear and visible contributions to society can achieve enhanced reputations and garner greater market share for their products. Although claims of socially responsible activities can haunt a company if they are exaggerated or untrue, they can also work to the benefit of both the organization and society if the advertised benefits are true and accurate.

Arguments Against Social Responsibility   Some people, however, including the famous economist Milton Friedman, argue that widening the interpretation of social responsibility will undermine the U.S. economy by detracting from the basic mission of business: to earn profits for owners. For example, money that Chevron or General Electric contributes to social causes or charities is money that could otherwise be distributed to owners as a dividend. Ben & Jerry's Homemade Inc. has a very ambitious and widely touted social agenda. But some shareholders recently criticized the firm when it refused to accept a lucrative exporting deal to Japan simply because the Japanese distributor did not have a similar social agenda.[19]

Another objection to deepening the social responsibility of businesses points out that corporations already wield enormous power and that their activity in social programs gives them even more power. Another argument focuses on the potential for conflict of interest. Suppose, for example, that one manager is in charge of deciding which local social program or charity will receive a large grant from her business. The local civic opera company (a not-for-profit organization that relies on contributions for its existence) might offer her front-row tickets for the upcoming season in exchange for her support. If opera is her favorite form of music, she might be tempted to direct the money toward the local company, when it might actually be needed more in other areas.[20]

Finally, critics argue that organizations lack the expertise to understand how to assess and make decisions about worthy social programs. How can a company truly know, they ask, which cause or program is most deserving of its support, or how money might best be spent? For example, Exxon recently announced a commitment to spend $5 million to help save the tiger, an endangered species that serves as the firm's corporate symbol. Exxon committed most of the money to support breeding programs in zoos and to help educate people about the tiger. But conservationists criticized the firm and its plan, arguing instead that the money might have been better spent on eliminating poaching, the illegal trade of tiger fur, and the destruction of the tiger's natural habitat.[21]

Organizational Approaches to Social Responsibility

As we have seen, some people advocate a larger social role for organizations, and others argue that the role is already too large. Not surprisingly, organizations themselves adopt a wide range of positions on social responsibility. As Figure 4.5 illustrates, the four stances that an organization can take concerning its obligations to society fall along a continuum ranging from the lowest to the highest degree of socially responsible practices.

obstructionist stance An approach to social responsibility in which firms do as little as possible to solve social or environmental problems

Obstructionist Stance The few organizations that take what might be called an **obstructionist stance** to social responsibility usually do as little as possible to solve social or environmental problems. When they cross the ethical or legal line that separates acceptable from unacceptable practices, their typical response is to deny or avoid accepting responsibility for their actions. For example, when the various problems at Astra USA, noted earlier in the chapter, first began to surface, top officials at both that firm and its Swedish parent company all denied any wrongdoing.

Another more recent case of a firm taking this approach involves IBP, a major Iowa-based meat-processing firm with a truly checkered history. In the

Figure 4.5

Approaches to Social Responsibility

Organizations can adopt a variety of approaches to social responsibility. For example, a firm that never considers the consequences of its decisions and tries to hide its transgressions is taking an obstructionist stance. At the other extreme, a firm that actively seeks to identify areas where it can help society is pursuing a proactive stance toward social responsibility.

Degree of Social Responsibility

| Obstructionist stance | Defensive stance | Accommodative stance | Proactive stance |

Lowest   *Highest*

early 1970s one of the firm's founders was found guilty of paying a mob-related meat broker $1 million to ensure that unions wouldn't interfere with the firm's New York City distribution plans. In the late 1970s the company was investigated for anticompetitive practices, although this inquiry was subsequently dropped. In the 1980s, IBP was fined $2.6 million and penalized by OSHA for not reporting workers' hand injuries caused by its meat-cutting equipment. The firm also has a long history of abysmal labor relations with its employees.

In January 2000 the U.S. Justice Department, acting on behalf of the Environmental Protection Agency, filed a lawsuit accusing IBP of violating numerous federal air, water, and hazardous waste laws at the company's flagship plant and former headquarters in Dakota City, Nebraska. Among the charges in this case are that the firm emitted up to 1,800 pounds of hydrogen sulfide per day from the Dakota City plant without informing federal regulators (disclosure is required if total emissions exceed 100 pounds per day) and that IBP violated the federal Clean Water Act by dumping excessive ammonia into the Missouri River. Moreover, the suit charges IBP with either failing to file or else filing incorrectly federal toxic-air reports at several of its plants in Iowa, Nebraska, and Kansas. In addition, various state agencies where IBP has operations are investigating numerous allegations against the company regarding pollution. Idaho's State Division of Environmental Quality has charged the firm with exceeding its state wastewater guidelines by as much as 1,200 percent. Illinois's state attorney general is seeking fines against IBP for violating the state's odor law. And officials in Nebraska are closely watching the federal investigation to see if there have been violations that fall under state regulation.[22]

Organizations can take a number of different approaches to questions of social responsibility. Consider, for example, the situation when charges emerged that Firestone tires mounted on Ford vehicles experienced systematic tread separation such that passengers were endangered. Both firms indicated that they wanted to do the right thing, but each was also cautious about accepting too much of the blame. As a result of what they saw as an overly conservative response, Venezuelan officials have filed lawsuits against both firms. In the United States, in contrast, Ford in particular has generally been praised for its quick and thorough response.

Defensive Stance   One step removed from the obstructionist stance is the **defensive stance**, whereby the organization does everything that is required of it legally but nothing more. This approach is most consistent with the arguments used against social responsibility just described. Managers in organizations that take a defensive stance insist that their job is to generate profits. For example, such a firm would install pollution-control equipment dictated by law but would not install higher-quality equipment even though it might limit pollution further. Tobacco companies such as Philip Morris take this position in their marketing efforts. In the United States, they are legally required to include warnings to smokers on their products and to limit their advertising to prescribed media. Domestically they follow these rules to the letter of the law but use broader marketing methods in countries that have no such rules. In many African countries, for

defensive stance A social responsibility stance in which an organization does everything that is required of it legally but nothing more

example, cigarettes are heavily promoted, contain higher levels of tar and nicotine than those sold in the United States, and carry few or no health warning labels.[23] Firms that take this position are also unlikely to cover up wrongdoing and will generally admit their mistakes and take appropriate corrective actions.

accommodative stance A social responsibility stance in which an organization meets its legal and ethical obligations and also goes beyond these requirements in selected cases

Accommodative Stance   A firm that adopts an **accommodative stance** meets its legal and ethical obligations and also goes beyond these requirements in selected cases. Such firms voluntarily agree to participate in social programs, but solicitors have to convince the organization that the programs are worthy of their support. Both Exxon and IBM, for example, will match contributions made by their employees to selected charitable causes. And many organizations will respond to requests for donations to Little League, Girl Scouts, youth soccer programs, and so forth. The point, though, is that someone has to knock on the door and ask—the organizations do not proactively seek such avenues for contributing.

proactive stance A social responsibility stance in which an organization views itself as a citizen in a society and proactively seeks opportunities to contribute to that society

Proactive Stance   The highest degree of social responsibility that a firm can exhibit is the **proactive stance**. Firms that adopt this approach take to heart the arguments in favor of social responsibility. They view themselves as citizens in a society and proactively seek opportunities to contribute to that society. An excellent example of a proactive stance is the Ronald McDonald House program undertaken by McDonald's Corp. These houses, located close to major medical centers, can be used by families for minimal cost while their sick children are receiving medical treatment nearby. Sears offers fellowships that support promising young performers while they develop their talents. Target has stopped selling guns in its stores, while some national toy retailers such as KayBee and Toys "R" Us have voluntarily stopped selling realistic toy guns. These and related activities and programs exceed the accommodative stance—they indicate a sincere and potent commitment to improving the general social welfare in this country and thus represent a proactive stance to social responsibility.

Remember that these categories are not discrete but merely define stages along a continuum of approach. Organizations do not always fit neatly into one category. The Ronald McDonald House program has been widely applauded, for example, but McDonald's also came under fire a few years ago for allegedly misleading consumers about the nutritional value of its food products. And even though Astra and IBF took an obstructionist stance in the cases we cited, many individual employees and managers at both firms have no doubt made substantial contributions to society in several different ways.

MANAGEMENT IMPLICATIONS   Managers need to be aware of their key and relevant stakeholders and to ensure that their organization's interactions with those stakeholders, as well as their interactions with the natural environment and society in general, are handled with the appropriate level of social responsibility. Managers should also carefully weigh the various arguments for and against social responsibility and use these arguments in developing a coherent and consistent stance that their organization can take to social responsibility.

The Government and Social Responsibility

An especially important element of social responsibility is the relationship between business and government. For example, in planned economies the government heavily regulates business activities, ostensibly to ensure that business supports some overarching set of social ideals. And even in market economies there is still considerable government control of business, much of it again directed at making sure that social interests are not damaged by business interests. On the other side of the coin, however, business also attempts to influence the government. Such influence attempts are usually undertaken in an effort to offset or reverse government restrictions. As Figure 4.6 shows, organizations and the government use several methods in their attempts to influence each other.

How Government Influences Organizations

The government attempts to shape social responsibility practices through both direct and indirect channels. Direct influence is most frequently manifested through regulation, whereas indirect influence can take a number of forms, most notably taxation policies.

Direct Regulation   The government most often directly influences organizations through **regulation**, or the establishment of laws and rules that dictate what organizations can and cannot do. As noted earlier in the chapter, this regulation usually evolves from societal beliefs about what businesses should or should not be allowed to do. To implement legislation, the government generally creates special agencies to monitor and control certain aspects of business activity. For example, the Environmental Protection Agency handles environmental issues; the

regulation Government's attempts to influence business by establishing laws and rules that dictate what businesses can and cannot do in prescribed areas

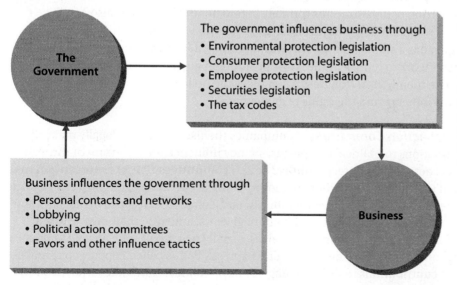

The Government

The government influences business through
- Environmental protection legislation
- Consumer protection legislation
- Employee protection legislation
- Securities legislation
- The tax codes

Business

Business influences the government through
- Personal contacts and networks
- Lobbying
- Political action committees
- Favors and other influence tactics

Figure 4.6

How Business and the Government Influence Each Other
Business and the government influence each other in a variety of ways. Government influence can be direct or indirect. Business influence relies on personal contacts, lobbying, political action committees (PACs), and favors. Federal Express, for example, has a very active PAC.

Federal Trade Commission and the Food and Drug Administration focus on consumer-related concerns; the Equal Employee Opportunity Commission, the National Labor Relations Board, and the Department of Labor help protect employees; and the Securities and Exchange Commission handles investor-related issues. These agencies have the power to levy fines or bring charges against organizations that violate regulations.

Indirect Regulation   Other forms of regulation are indirect. For example, the government can indirectly influence the social responsibility of organizations through its tax codes. In effect, the government can influence how organizations spend their social responsibility dollars by providing greater or lesser tax incentives. For instance, suppose that the government wanted organizations to spend more on training the hard-core unemployed. Congress could then pass laws that provide tax incentives to companies that opened new training facilities. As a result, more businesses would probably do so. Of course, some critics argue that regulation is already excessive. They maintain that a free market system would eventually accomplish the same goals as regulation with lower costs to both organizations and the government.

How Organizations Influence Government

As we mentioned in Chapter 3, organizations can influence their environment in many different ways. In particular, businesses have four main methods of addressing governmental pressures for more social responsibility.

Personal Contacts   Because many corporate executives and political leaders travel in the same social circles, personal contacts and networks offer one method of influence. A business executive, for example, may be able to contact a politician directly and present his or her case regarding a piece of legislation being considered.

lobbying The use of persons or groups to represent an organization or group of organizations formally before political bodies to influence legislation

Lobbying   **Lobbying**, or the use of persons or groups to represent an organization or group of organizations formally before political bodies, is also an effective way to influence the government. The National Rifle Association (NRA), for example, has a staff of lobbyists in Washington with a large annual budget. These lobbyists work to represent the NRA's position on gun control and potentially to influence members of Congress when they vote on legislation that affects the firearms industry and the rights of gun owners.

political action committee (PAC) An organization created to solicit and distribute money to political candidates

Political Action Committees   Companies themselves cannot legally make direct donations to political campaigns, so they influence the government through political action committees. **Political action committees (PACs)** are organizations created to solicit and distribute money to political candidates. Employees of a firm may be encouraged to make donations to particular PACs because managers know that it will support candidates with political views similar to their own. PACs, in turn, make the contributions themselves, usually to a broad slate of state and national candidates. For example, Federal Express's PAC is called Fepac. Fepac makes regular contributions to the campaign funds of political candidates who are most likely to work in the firm's best interests.

Favors Finally, organizations sometimes rely on favors and other influence tactics to gain support. Although these favors may be legal, they are still subject to criticism. A few years back, for example, two influential members of a House committee attending a fund-raising function in Miami were needed in Washington to finish work on a piece of legislation that Federal Express wanted passed. The law being drafted would allow the company and its competitors to give their employees standby seats on airlines as a tax-free benefit. As a favor, Federal Express provided one of its corporate jets to fly the committee members back to Washington. The company was eventually reimbursed for its expenses, so its assistance was not illegal, but some people argue that such actions are dangerous because of how they might be perceived. Similarly, in 1997 there were congressional hearings into allegations that certain foreign interests had attempted to influence political elections in the United States through illegal campaign contributions.[24]

MANAGEMENT IMPLICATIONS Managers should understand fully the various ways in which business and the government influence one another. Further, while recognizing that under certain conditions it may be both legal and appropriate to endeavor to influence the government, managers should also be careful to avoid crossing legal or ethical boundaries.

Managing Social Responsibility

The demands for social responsibility placed on contemporary organizations by an increasingly sophisticated and educated public are probably stronger than ever. As we have seen, there are pitfalls for managers who fail to adhere to high ethical standards and for companies that try to circumvent their legal obligations. Organizations therefore need to fashion an approach to social responsibility the same way that they develop any other business strategy; that is, they should view social responsibility as a major challenge that requires careful planning, decision making, consideration, and evaluation. They may accomplish their approach through both formal and informal dimensions of managing social responsibility.

The effective management of social responsibility requires care and thought. For example, Hyatt Corporation is recognized as an excellent employer for minorities. The firm donated a state-of-the-art kitchen to predominantly Hispanic Robert Clemente High School in Chicago. These students are exploring their passion for cooking and may one day be head chefs at a leading hotel or restaurant.

Formal Organizational Dimensions

Some dimensions of managing social responsibility are formal and planned activities on the part of the organization. Formal organizational dimensions that can help manage social responsibility are legal compliance, ethical compliance, and philanthropic giving.

legal compliance The extent to which an organization complies with local, state, federal, and international laws

Legal Compliance   **Legal compliance** is the extent to which the organization complies with local, state, federal, and international laws. The task of managing legal compliance is generally assigned to the appropriate functional managers. For example, the organization's top human resource executive is responsible for ensuring compliance with regulations concerning hiring, pay, and workplace safety and health. Likewise, the top finance executive generally oversees compliance with securities and banking regulations. The organization's legal department is also likely to contribute to this effort by providing general oversight and answering queries from managers about the appropriate interpretation of laws and regulations.

ethical compliance The extent to which an organization and its members follow basic ethical (and legal) standards of behavior

Ethical Compliance   **Ethical compliance** is the extent to which an organization and its members follow basic ethical (and legal) standards of behavior. We noted earlier that organizations have increased their efforts in this area—providing training in ethics and developing guidelines and codes of conduct, for example. These activities serve as vehicles for enhancing ethical compliance. Many organizations also establish formal ethics committees, which may be asked to review proposals for new projects, help evaluate new hiring strategies, or assess a new environmental protection plan. They might also serve as a peer review panel to evaluate alleged ethical misconduct by an employee.[25]

philanthropic giving The awarding of funds or gifts to charities or other social programs

Philanthropic Giving   Finally, **philanthropic giving** is the awarding of funds or gifts to charities or other social programs. Dayton-Hudson Corp. routinely gives 5 percent of its taxable income to charity and social programs. Giving across national boundaries is also becoming more common. For example, Alcoa gave $112,000 to a small town in Brazil to build a sewage treatment plant. And Japanese firms like Sony and Mitsubishi make contributions to a number of social programs in the United States. Unfortunately, in this age of cutbacks, many corporations have also had to limit their charitable gifts over the past several years as they continue to trim their own budgets. And many firms that continue to make contributions are increasingly targeting them to programs or areas where the firm will get something in return. For example, firms today are more likely to give money to job training programs than to the arts, which wasn't the case just a few years ago. The logic is that they get more direct payoff from the former type of contribution—in this instance, a better trained workforce from which to hire new employees.[26]

Informal Organizational Dimensions

In addition to these formal dimensions for managing social responsibility, there are also informal ones. Leadership, organization culture, and how the organization responds to whistle blowers each helps shape and define people's perceptions of the organization's stance on social responsibility.

Organization Leadership and Culture   Leadership practices and organization culture can go a long way toward defining the social responsibility stance an organization and its members will adopt.[27] For example, Johnson & Johnson executives for years provided a consistent message to employees that customers, employees, communities where the company did business, and shareholders were all important—and primarily in that order. Thus, when packages of poisoned Tylenol showed up on store shelves in the 1980s, Johnson & Johnson employees didn't need to wait for orders from headquarters to know what to do: they immediately pulled all the packages from shelves before any other customers could buy them.[28] By contrast, the message sent to Astra USA employees by the actions of their top managers communicates much less regard for social responsibility.

Whistle-Blowing **Whistle-blowing** is the disclosure by an employee of illegal or unethical conduct on the part of others within the organization.[29] How an organization responds to this practice often indicates its stance toward social responsibility. Whistle blowers may have to proceed through a number of channels to be heard, and they may even get fired for their efforts. Many organizations, however, welcome their contributions. A person who observes questionable behavior typically first reports the incident to his or her boss. If nothing is done, the whistle blower may then inform higher level managers or an ethics committee if one exists. Eventually, the person may have to go to a regulatory agency or even the media to be heard. For example, Charles W. Robinson Jr. once worked as a director of a SmithKline lab in San Antonio. One day he noticed a suspicious billing pattern the firm was using to collect lab fees from Medicare that were considerably higher than the firm's normal charges for those same tests. He pointed out the problem to higher level managers, but his concerns were ignored. He subsequently took his findings to the U.S. government, which sued SmithKline and eventually reached a settlement of $325 million.[30]

Evaluating Social Responsibility

Any organization that is serious about social responsibility must ensure that its efforts are producing the desired benefits. Essentially this assurance requires applying the concept of control to social responsibility. Many organizations now require current and new employees to read their guidelines or code of ethics and then sign a statement agreeing to abide by it. An organization should also evaluate how it responds to instances of questionable legal or ethical conduct. Does it follow up immediately? Does it punish those involved? Or does it use delay and cover-up tactics? Answers to these questions can help an organization form a picture of its approach to social responsibility.

More formally, an organization may evaluate the effectiveness of its social responsibility efforts. For example, when Amoco recently established a job training program in Chicago, it allocated additional funds to evaluate how well the program was meeting its goals. Some organizations occasionally conduct corporate social audits. A **corporate social audit** is a formal and thorough analysis of the effectiveness of the firm's social performance. The audit is usually conducted by a task force of high-level managers from within the firm. It requires that the organization clearly define all its social goals, analyze the resources it devotes to each goal, determine how well it is achieving the various goals, and make recommendations about which areas need additional attention.

whistle-blowing The disclosure by an employee of illegal or unethical conduct on the part of others within the organization

corporate social audit A formal and thorough analysis of the effectiveness of a firm's social performance

Ben & Jerry's conducts a formal audit of its social responsibility programs each year and publishes the results—favorable or otherwise—in its annual report. For example, one recent audit found that the firm was using a misleading label on one of its ice cream products. This criticism was published in the firm's next annual report, along with a promise both to correct the error and to strive to avoid similar problems in the future.[31] Unfortunately, such audits are not conducted often because they are expensive and time consuming. Indeed, most organizations probably could do much more to evaluate the extent of their social responsibility than they do.[32]

MANAGEMENT IMPLICATIONS Managers should understand that social responsibility is not something that just "happens." Instead, like other organizational activities, it must be actively managed. Recognizing and using both formal and informal dimensions can help manage the social responsibility process, as can actually evaluating the firm's social responsibility efforts and strategies.

Summary of Key Points

Ethics are an individual's personal beliefs about what constitutes right and wrong behavior. Important areas of ethical concern for managers are how the organization treats its employees, how employees treat the organization, and how the organization and its employees treat other economic agents. The ethical context of organizations consists of each manager's individual ethics and messages sent by organizational practices. Organizations use leadership, culture, training, codes, and guidelines to help them manage ethical behavior.

Social responsibility is the set of obligations an organization has to protect and enhance the society in which it functions. Organizations may be considered responsible to their stakeholders, to the natural environment, and to the general social welfare. Even so, organizations present strong arguments both for and against social responsibility. The approach an organization adopts toward social responsibility falls along a continuum of lesser to greater commitment: the obstructionist stance, the defensive stance, the accommodative stance, and the proactive stance.

Government influences organizations through regulation, which is the establishment of laws and rules that dictate what businesses can and cannot do in prescribed areas. Organizations, in turn, rely on personal contacts, lobbying, political action committees, and favors to influence the government.

Organizations use three types of activities to manage social responsibility formally: legal compliance, ethical compliance, and philanthropic giving. Leadership, culture, and whistle-blowing are informal means for managing social responsibility. Organizations should evaluate the effectiveness of their socially responsible practices as they would any other strategy.

Discussion Questions

Questions for Review

1. Do organizations have ethics? Why or why not?
2. Summarize the basic stances that an organization can take regarding social responsibility.
3. What are the arguments for and against social responsibility?
4. How does the government influence organizations? How do organizations influence the government?

Questions for Analysis

5. What is the relationship between the law and ethical behavior? Can illegal behavior possibly be ethical?
6. How are the ethics of an organization's CEO related to social responsibility?
7. How do you feel about whistle-blowing? If you were aware of a criminal activity taking place in your organization, and if reporting it might cost you your job, would you report it?

Questions for Application

8. Refresh your memory about the Exxon *Valdez* oil spill. Evaluate the social responsibility dilemmas facing the company. For example, if Exxon had pledged unlimited resources to the cleanup, would this action have been fair to the company's stockholders?
9. Assume that you own a large and highly profitable business. What stance would you take toward social responsibility? List five specific programs or causes that you might be inclined to support.
10. Review the arguments for and against social responsibility. On a scale of one to ten, rate the validity and importance of each point. Use these ratings to develop a position regarding how socially responsible an organization should be. Now compare your ratings and position with those of two of your classmates. Discuss your respective positions, focusing primarily on disagreements.

BUILDING EFFECTIVE *decision-making* SKILLS

Exercise Overview

Decision-making skills refer to the manager's ability to recognize and define problems and opportunities correctly and then to select an appropriate course of action to solve problems and capitalize on opportunities. Many decisions made by managers have an ethical component. This exercise will help you better appreciate the potential role of ethics in making decisions.

Exercise Background

Read and reflect on each of the following scenarios:

1. You are the top manager of a major international oil company. Because of a recent oil spill by another firm, all the companies in the industry have been subjected to close scrutiny regarding the safety of various work practices. Your safety manager has completed a review and informed you that your firm has one potential problem area. The manager estimates the probability of a problem within the next five years as being about 3 percent. The costs of fixing things now would be about $1.5 million. Should you do nothing and a problem develop, however, the costs will be $10 million, plus your firm will receive a lot of bad publicity.

2. You manage a small fast-food restaurant. The owner has just informed you that you need to cut your payroll by twenty hours per week. There are two obvious choices. One is a retired woman who works part-time for

you. She lives on a fixed income, is raising three grandchildren, and really needs the money she earns from this job. The other is a college student who also works part-time. He is one year away from getting his degree and must work to pay his tuition and fees.

3. You have decided to donate $1,000 to a worthy cause in your neighborhood on behalf of the small business you own. Based on your own research, you have learned that the groups and charities most in need of funds are a local homeless shelter, a youth soccer league, an abortion clinic, and a tutoring program for illiterate adults.

Exercise Task

With the background information above as context, do the following:

1. Make a decision between the two courses of action for scenario one.
2. Decide which of the two employees to terminate in scenario two.
3. Decide where to donate your money in scenario three.
4. What role did your own personal ethics play in making each of these decisions?
5. Compare your decisions with those of a classmate and discuss why any differences arose.

BUILDING EFFECTIVE *interpersonal* SKILLS

Exercise Overview

Interpersonal skills refer to the ability to communicate with, understand, and motivate individuals and groups. Interpersonal skills may be especially important in a situation in which ethics and social responsibility issues are involved. This exercise will help you better relate interpersonal skills to ethical situations.

Exercise Background

Assume that you are a department manager in a large retail store. Your work group recently had a problem with sexual harassment. Specifically, one of your female employees reported to you that a male employee was telling off-color jokes and making mildly suggestive comments. When you asked him about the charges, he did not deny them but instead attributed them to a misunderstanding.

He was subsequently suspended with pay while the situation was investigated. The human resource manager who interviewed both parties, as well as other employees, concluded that the male employee should not be fired but should instead be placed on six months' probation. During this period, any further substantiated charges against him will result in immediate dismissal.

The basis for this decision included the following: (1) the male has worked in the store for over ten years, has a good performance record, and has had no earlier problems; (2) the female indicated that she did not believe that he was directly targeting her for harassment but instead was guilty of general insensitivity; and (3) the female did not think that his actions were sufficiently blatant as to warrant dismissal but simply wanted him to stop those behaviors.

Tomorrow will be his first day back at work. You are a bit worried about tensions in the group when he returns. You intend to meet with the female today and with the male tomorrow morning and attempt to minimize this tension.

Exercise Task

With the background information above as context, do the following:

1. Write general notes about what you will say to the female.
2. Write general notes about what you will say to the male.
3. What are the ethical issues in this situation?
4. If you have the option of having them work closely together or keeping them separated, which would you do? Why?

BUILDING EFFECTIVE *communication* SKILLS

Exercise Overview

Communication skills refer to the manager's abilities both to convey ideas and information effectively to others and to receive ideas and information effectively from others. Communication, ethics, and social responsibility are closely intertwined in certain situations. This exercise will help you relate these concepts to one another.

Exercise Background

You are the public relations manager for a large chemical company. One of your foreign plants has just suffered an explosion. While no one was killed, several dozen employees were injured. In addition, toxic chemical compounds were discharged into a nearby river and will undoubtedly cause major environmental damage. It is also clear that your company's managers at the plant are responsible for the explosion. You have learned, for example, that they took shortcuts when safety equipment was installed, used inferior materials, and failed to train key employees adequately in basic safety procedures.

Your experts' best estimates now are that it will take at least six months to clean up the river. There are also reports that the injured employees are already preparing lawsuits against the company. The local press at the plant site is also calling for an immediate and public apology and a commitment by the firm to make full restitution for all damages caused by the explosion.

A press conference has been called for one hour from now. You will be making a prepared statement about the situation and then answering questions from the reporters. Your boss, however, has given you some directions. For one thing, he says that acknowledging that six months will be needed to clean up the river will be disastrous. Instead, he wants you to indicate that cleanup will be completed in two months. He also wants you to recognize the pain caused to your injured employees and to wish them a speedy recovery, but not to acknowledge any guilt or liability on the part of your company.

Exercise Task

With the background information above as context, do the following:

1. Write a press statement that meets your boss's mandate.
2. Write a press statement that is completely accurate.
3. What are the likely short- and long-term ethical implications of each statement?
4. Could you personally deliver the first statement?

CHAPTER CLOSING CASE

ETHICAL CHARGES ROCK PRUDENTIAL

In recent years, Prudential Insurance Company of America has been rocked by charges of unethical behavior. Soon after the company settled one class-action lawsuit over questionable sales tactics, it became embroiled in a second round of legal battles over charges related to the first lawsuit.

The trouble started in the mid-1990s, when thousands of customers complained about the way Prudential salespeople were selling insurance policies. Some customers were told they were buying retirement programs when, in actuality, they were buying insurance. Others were told, incorrectly, that the dividends on their insurance policies would build up enough to cover the premium payments within as little as seven years. Still others said they were tricked into turning in older insurance policies and buying new, more costly policies.

More than six hundred thousand Prudential customers banded together in a class-action lawsuit over these sales abuses. The suit was settled in 1997 for $2.7 billion, but the terms of the settlement were controversial: Prudential was given the task of reviewing customers' claims to determine the level of restitution for each. Because of the pervasiveness of the sales abuses, observers believed that many customers would receive large restitution awards. After Prudential reviewed the cases, however, it awarded the top level of restitution to only one in four customers.

The second round of lawsuits stemmed from the way Prudential handled its review of customer claims in the wake of the class-action suit. The company had to hire thousands of new workers to investigate these claims and recommend appropriate compensation on a case-by-case basis. Although the new employees received fast but intensive training, they had difficulty getting clear direction from their managers as they worked to unravel the complexities of individual claims.

When insurance regulators who were hoping to get quicker restitution for customers protested the slow pace of the reviews, Prudential management decided to put more emphasis on productivity. The company promised employees money, gift certificates, candy, and gifts to reward speedier processing of claims reviews. As the process speeded up, reviewers began to complain that managers were ordering them to overlook documents that might support the customer's side. They also said some managers balked when reviewers tried to recommend the top level of restitution for some customers.

Prudential admitted seeking higher productivity but said it was still keeping a close eye on quality. The company also stressed that customers could appeal to independent arbitrators (at Prudential's expense) if they believed they were due higher levels of restitution. Only about one in ten customers who were eligible wound up appealing, perhaps because few knew how the appeals process operated.

Meanwhile, some of the employees reviewing claims became upset at the situation and filed suit. One said the insurer retaliated against him by demoting him for attempting to obtain top-level restitution for customers. Another said he was pressured to hurry through the review process by setting aside some types of documentation, rather than examining all the information for each case. In all, dozens of employees went to court against Prudential.

This second round of lawsuits drew the attention of the federal judge who handled the original class-action suit. He ordered Prudential and the class-action attorneys for its customers to investigate the employees' charges. As the probe progressed, Prudential said that it had safeguards in place to protect customers and to correct errors that might have been made during the review process. The insurer was eager to close this troubled chapter in its history.

Case Questions

1. Do you think the court was right to leave Prudential in charge of reviewing its customers' claims after the class-action lawsuit? Should someone outside the company have been given this responsibility instead? Why?

2. Within which of the three areas of concern for managerial ethics did Prudential appear to be experiencing problems?

3. If you headed Prudential, what standards would you include in a code of ethics to guide managers in making ethical decisions when dealing with customers and employees?

Case Reference

Deborah Lohse, "Worker Suits Are Latest Woes for Prudential," *Wall Street Journal*, January 20, 2000, p. C1.

CHAPTER NOTES

1. *Hoover's Handbook of American Business 2000* (Austin, Texas: Hoover's Business Press, 2000), pp. 750–751; Roger Rosenblatt, "Reaching the Top by Doing the Right Thing," *Time*, October 18, 1999, pp. 89–91 (quote on p. 90).
2. See Norman Barry, *Business Ethics* (West Lafayette, Indiana: Purdue University Press, 1999).
3. Thomas Donaldson and Thomas W. Dunfee, "Toward a Unified Conception of Business Ethics: An Integrative Social Contracts Theory," *Academy of Management Review*, Vol. 19, No. 2, 1994, pp. 252–284.
4. "Drug Companies Face Assault on Prices," *The Wall Street Journal*, May 11, 2000, pp. B1, B4.
5. Jeremy Kahn, "Presto Chango! Sales are Huge," *Fortune*, March 20, 2000, pp. 90–96; "More Firms Falsify Revenue to Boost Stocks," *USA Today*, March 29, 2000, p. 1B.

6. "How U.S. Concerns Compete in Countries Where Bribes Flourish," *The Wall Street Journal*, September 29, 1995, pp. A1, A14; Patricia Digh, "Shades of Gray in the Global Marketplace," *HRMagazine*, April 1997, pp. 90–98.

7. Patricia H. Werhane, *Moral Imagination and Management Decision-Making* (New York: Oxford University Press, 1999).

8. "Sex, Lies, and Home Improvements?" *Business Week*, March 31, 1997, p. 40; Abuse of Power," *Business Week*, May 13, 1996, pp. 86–98.

9. Gerald F. Cavanagh, *American Business Values*, 2nd Edition (Upper Saddle River, N.J.: Prentice-Hall, 1998).

10. Thomas Donaldson and Lee E. Preston, "The Stakeholder Theory of the Corporation: Concepts, Evidence, and Implications," *Academy of Management Review*, 1995, Vol. 20, No. 1, pp. 65–91; see also Jeffrey S. Harrison and R. Edward Freeman, "Stakeholders, Social Responsibility, and Performance: Empirical Evidence and Theoretical Perspectives," *Academy of Management Journal*, 1999, Vol. 42, No. 5, pp. 479–495.

11. See "Tyco: Aggressive or Out of Line?" *Business Week*, November 1, 1999, pp. 160–165.

12 Aseem Prakash, *Greening the Firm* (Cambridge: The Cambridge University Press, 2000); Forest L. Reinhardt, *Down to Earth* (Boston: Harvard Business School Press, 2000).

13. "Oil Companies Strive to Turn a New Leaf to Save Rain Forest," *The Wall Street Journal*, July 17, 1997, pp. A1, A8.

14. Linda Grant, "There's Gold in Going Green," *Fortune*, April 14, 1997, pp. 116–118.

15. "Ford to Reveal Plans for Think Brand," *USA Today*, January 10, 2000, p. 1B.

16. Christine Y. Chen and Greg Lindsay, "Will Amazon(.com) Save the Amazon?" *Fortune*, March 20, 2000, pp. 224–226.

17. "Ashland Just Can't Seem to Leave Its Checkered Past Behind," *Business Week*, October 31, 1988, pp. 122–126.

18. For discussions of this debate, see Jean B. McGuire, Alison Sundgren, and Thomas Schneeweis, "Corporate Social Responsibility and Firm Financial Performance," *Academy of Management Journal*, December 1988, pp. 854–872, and Margaret A. Stroup, Ralph L. Neubert, and Jerry W. Anderson, Jr., "Doing Good, Doing Better: Two Views of Social Responsibility," *Business Horizons*, March–April 1987, pp. 22–25.

19. "Is It Rainforest Crunch Time?" *Business Week*, July 15, 1996, pp. 70–71; "Yo, Ben! Yo, Jerry! It's Just Ice Cream," *Fortune*, April 28, 1997, p. 374.

20. Andrew Singer, "Can a Company Be Too Ethical?" *Across the Board*, April 1993, pp. 17–22.

21. "Help or Hype From Exxon?" *Business Week*, August 28, 1995, p. 36.

22. *Hoover's Handbook of American Business 2000* (Austin, Texas: Hoover's Business Press, 2000), pp. 750–751; "Stench Chokes Nebraska Meatpacking Towns," *USA Today*, February 14, 2000, pp. 1B, 2B.

23. "Inside America's Most Reviled Company," *Business Week*, November 29, 1999, pp. 176–192.

24. "1st Evidence of Foreign Campaign Money Found," *USA Today*, July 16, 1997, pp. 1A, 4A.

25. Lynn Sharp Paine, "Managing for Organizational Integrity," *Harvard Business Review*, March–April 1994, pp. 106–115.

26. "A New Way of Giving," *Time*, July 24, 2000, pp. 48–51.

27. David M. Messick and Max H. Bazerman, "Ethical Leadership and the Psychology of Decision Making," *Sloan Management Review*, Winter 1996, pp. 9–22.

28. "Unfuzzing Ethics for Managers," *Fortune*, November 23, 1987, pp. 229–234.

29. See Janet P. Near and Marcia P. Miceli, "Whistle-Blowing: Myth and Reality," *Journal of Management*, 1996, Vol. 22, No. 3, pp. 507–526, for a recent review of the literature on whistle-blowing.

30. "Whistle-Blowers on Trial," *Business Week*, March 24, 1997, pp. 172–178; see also "How a Whistle-Blower Spurred Pricing Case Involving Drug Makers," *The Wall Street Journal*, May 12, 2000, pp. A1, A8.

31. "Ben & Jerry Tell on Themselves," *Business Week*, June 26, 1995, p. 8.

32. See Michael V. Russo and Paul A. Fouts, "A Resource-Based Perspective on Corporate Environmental Performance and Profitability," *Academy of Management Journal*, June 1997, pp. 534–559.

5 The Global Environment

Mickey Mouse's famed silhouette is no doubt just as recognizable in Brazil, India, Italy, or Nigeria as is the shape of a Coca-Cola bottle or the golden arches of McDonald's. But the Walt Disney Company has done a surprisingly poor job of capitalizing on the global potential for its various products. In 1999, for instance, 80 percent of Disney's $23.4 billion in revenues came from the United States, a country with only 5 percent of the world's population. This statistic contrasts markedly with Coca-Cola and McDonald's, who each derive about two-thirds of their revenue from other countries.

Disney's most visible global efforts have involved theme parks. Its first foreign venture, Tokyo Disneyland, opened in 1984. To limit its risk, the firm did not directly invest in the park. Instead, a Japanese investment group financed and owns Tokyo Disneyland. Disney oversaw construction and manages the park but receives only royalty income.

Tokyo Disneyland has been an enormous success. For example, it greeted its one hundred millionth visitor after only eight years, a milestone that Disneyland in California took twice as long to reach. Indeed, in retrospect, Disney managers acknowledge that they were overly cautious when they chose not to risk equity ownership in the park.

Disney subsequently decided to build a theme park in Europe just outside Paris. This time, though, Disney decided to participate more fully in the park and retained 49 percent ownership for itself. The French government also provided numerous economic incentives by selling the land for the park to Disney at bargain-basement prices and extending the Parisian rail system to the park's front gate. But as Euro Disney opened its doors to the public on April 12, 1992, amid widespread hoopla, problems started to arise.

For example, the French cultural elite lambasted Euro Disney as an af-

front to the country's cultural heritage, and farmers picketed aside the main gates protesting the manner in which their land had been taken. Disney also severely misjudged the spending and lodging habits of its visitors. Disney planners had presumed hotel guests would stay an average of three days, as they do in Orlando. But Euro Disney visitors typically stayed two days or less. A recession also led to weak attendance and even lower spending. At this point, Euro Disney seemed to be burning money, and it even came close to being shut down. Eventually, a complex and costly financial restructuring plan implemented in 1994 barely saved the park, and it has only been within the last few years

> *"Disney is in the ironic position of being one of the best-known brands on the planet, but with too little of its income being generated outside of the United States."*
>
> *—Michael Eisner, CEO of The Walt Disney Company*

After studying this chapter, you should be able to:

■ Describe the nature of international business, including its meaning, recent trends, the management of globalization, and competition in a global environment.

☐ Discuss the structure of the global economy and how it affects international management.

■ Identify and discuss the environmental challenges inherent in international management.

■ Describe the basic issues involved in competing in a global economy, including organization size and the management challenges in a global economy.

that Disneyland Paris, as the park was renamed, has begun earning profits.

Fortunately, Disney seems to be getting its act together regarding international theme park operations. For example, in 2001 it opened Tokyo DisneySea adjacent to Tokyo Disneyland. Both attendance and spending have improved at Disneyland Paris, and a new park will also open there in 2002. Disney's biggest news, though, was its recent announcement that it would build a new park in Hong Kong. The company gets a 43 percent equity stake in the $3.6 billion project in exchange for an investment of only $314 million. The local government, in turn, will invest over $2.9 billion in low-interest loans, land, and infrastructure improvements for the remaining 57 percent share.

But Disney continues to struggle in other areas of its international operations. For example, there are only 11 million subscribers to the Disney Channel cable television network outside the United States; this contrasts with 54 million foreign subscribers to Time Warner's Cartoon Network.

And the company has experienced a $159 million decline in worldwide licensing revenues in recent years. Indeed, things have gotten so bad that Disney is overhauling its business and has created a separate unit called Walt Disney International. Its goal? Obviously, to increase international revenues. For example, managers have calculated that if they can increase per capita consumer spending on Disney-related products in just five countries—England, Italy, Germany, France, and Japan—to 80 percent of the level in the United States, the firm would generate an additional $2 billion in annual revenues.[1]

While every business is unique, the challenges and opportunities facing The Walt Disney Company are increasingly common among today's multinational corporations. Specifically, such businesses must make critical decisions regarding how they will allocate their resources in different markets and how they will strive to gain a competitive advantage in those markets. Indeed, to be successful today, managers have to understand the global context within which they function. And this fact holds true regardless of whether the manager runs a *Fortune* 500 firm or a small independent company.

This chapter explores the global context of management. We start by describing the nature of international business. We then discuss the structure of the global market in terms of different economies and economic systems. The basic environmental challenges of management are introduced and discussed next. We then focus on issues of competition in a global economy. We conclude by characterizing the managerial functions of planning, organizing, leading, and controlling as management challenges in a global economy.

The Nature of International Business

As you prepared breakfast this morning, you may have plugged in a coffee pot manufactured in Asia and perhaps ironed a shirt or blouse made in Taiwan with an iron made in Mexico. The coffee you drank was probably made from beans grown in South America. To get to school, you may have driven a Japanese car. Even if you drive a Ford or Chevrolet, some of its parts were engineered or manufactured abroad. Perhaps you didn't drive a car to school but rather rode a bus (manufactured by DaimlerChrysler, a German company, or by Volvo, a Swedish company) or a motorcycle (manufactured by Honda, Kawasaki, Suzuki, or Yamaha—all Japanese firms).

Our daily lives are strongly influenced by businesses from around the world. But no country is unique in this respect. For instance, people drive Fords in Germany, use Dell computers in China, eat McDonald's hamburgers in France, and snack on Mars candy bars in England. They drink Pepsi and wear Levi Strauss jeans in China. The Japanese buy Kodak film and use American Express credit cards. People around the world fly on American Airlines in planes made by Boeing. Their buildings are constructed with Caterpillar machinery, their factories are powered by General Electric engines, and they buy Chevron oil.

In truth, we have become part of a global village and have a global economy where no organization is insulated from the effects of foreign markets and competition.[2] Indeed, more and more firms are reshaping themselves for international competition and are discovering new ways to exploit markets in every corner of the world. Failure to take a global perspective is one of the biggest mistakes managers can make.[3] Thus, we start laying the foundation of our discussion by introducing and describing the basics of international business.

Lowest ← Level of International Activity → Highest

Domestic business

International business

Multinational business

Global business

Figure 5.1

Levels of International Business Activity

The Meaning of International Business

There are many different forms and levels of international business. While the lines that distinguish one from another are perhaps arbitrary, we can identify four general levels of international activity that differentiate organizations.[4] These levels are illustrated in Figure 5.1. A **domestic business** acquires essentially all its resources and sells all its products or services within a single country. Most small businesses are essentially domestic in nature, as are many banks, retailers, agricultural enterprises, and service firms. However, there are very few large domestic businesses left in the world today.

Indeed, most large firms today are either international or multinational companies. An **international business** is one that is primarily based in a single country but acquires some meaningful share of its resources or revenues (or both) from other countries. Sears fits this description. Most of its stores are in the United States, for example, and the retailer earns around 90 percent of its revenues from its U.S. operations, with the remaining 10 percent coming from Sears stores in Canada. At the same time, however, many of the products it sells, such as tools and clothing, are made abroad.[5]

A **multinational business** has a worldwide marketplace from which it buys raw materials, borrows money, and manufactures its products and to which it subsequently sells its products. Ford Motor Company is an excellent example of a multinational company. It has design and production facilities around the world. The Ford Focus, for instance, was jointly designed by European and U.S. teams and is sold with only minor variations in dozens of foreign markets. Ford makes and sells other cars in Europe that are never seen in the United States. Ford cars are designed, produced, and sold for individual markets, wherever they are and without regard for national boundaries. Multinational businesses are often called *multinational corporations* or *MNCs*.[6]

The final form of international business is the global business. A **global business** is one that transcends national boundaries and is not committed to a single home country. Although no business has truly achieved this level of international involvement, a few are edging closer and closer. For example, Hoechst AG, a large German chemical company, portrays itself as a "non-national company." Similarly, Unocal Corporation is legally headquartered in California. But in its company literature, Unocal says it "no longer considers itself as a U.S. company," but is, instead, a "global energy company."[7]

domestic business A business that acquires all its resources and sells all its products or services within a single country

international business A business that is primarily based in a single country but acquires some meaningful share of its resources or revenues (or both) from other countries

multinational business One that has a worldwide marketplace from which it buys raw materials, borrows money, and manufactures its products and to which it subsequently sells its products

global business A business that transcends national boundaries and is not committed to a single home country

Trends in International Business

To understand why and how these different levels of international business have emerged, we must briefly look to the past. Most of the industrialized countries in Europe had been devastated during the last world war. Many Asian countries, especially Japan, had fared no better. There were few passable roads, few standing bridges, and even fewer factories dedicated to the manufacture of peacetime products. And those regions less affected by wartime destruction—Canada, Latin America, and Africa—had not yet developed the economic muscle to threaten the economic pre-eminence of the United States.

Businesses in war-torn countries like Germany and Japan had no choice but to rebuild from scratch. Because of this position, they essentially had to rethink every facet of their operations, including technology, production, finance, and marketing. Although it took many years for these countries to recover, they eventually did so, and their economic systems were subsequently poised for growth. During the same era, U.S. companies grew complacent. Their customer base was growing rapidly. Increased population spurred by the baby boom and increased affluence resulting from the postwar economic boom greatly raised the average person's standard of living and expectations. The U.S. public continually wanted new and better products and services. Many U.S. companies profited greatly from this pattern, but most were also perhaps guilty of taking it for granted.

But U.S. firms are no longer isolated from global competition or the global market. A few simple numbers help tell the full story of international trade and industry. First of all, the volume of international trade increased more than 3,000 percent from 1960 to 2000. Further, while 162 of the world's largest corporations are headquartered in the United States, there are also 126 in Japan, 42 in France, 41 in Germany, and 34 in Britain.[8] Within certain industries, the pre-eminence of non-U.S. firms is even more striking. For example, only one each of the world's ten largest banks and ten largest electronics companies is based in the United States. Only two of the ten largest chemical companies are U.S. firms. On the other hand, U.S. firms comprise six of the eight largest aerospace companies, four of the seven largest airlines, six of the nine largest computer companies, four of the five largest diversified financial companies, and six of the ten largest retailers.[9]

U.S. firms are also finding that international operations are an increasingly important element of their sales and profits. For example, in 1999 Exxon Corporation realized 82 percent of its revenues and 68 percent of its profits abroad. For Avon, these percentages were 66 percent and 70 percent, respectively.[10] From any perspective, then, it is clear that we live in a truly global economy. Virtually all businesses today must be concerned with the competitive situations they face in lands far from home and with how companies from distant lands are competing in their homeland.

Managing the Process of Globalization

Managers should also recognize that their global context dictates two related but distinct sets of challenges. One set of challenges must be confronted when an organization chooses to change its level of international involvement. For example, a firm that wants to move from being an international to a multinational business has to manage that transition.[11] The other set of challenges occurs when the organization has achieved its desired level of international involvement and must then function effectively within that environment. This section highlights the first set of challenges, and the next section introduces the second set of challenges. When an organization makes the decision to increase its level of international activity, there are several alternative strategies that can be adopted.

Importing and Exporting Importing or exporting (or both) is usually the first type of international business in which a firm gets involved. **Exporting**, or making the product in the firm's domestic marketplace and selling it in another country, can involve both merchandise and services. **Importing** is bringing a good, service, or capital into the home country from abroad. For example, automobiles (Mazda, Ford, Volkswagen, Mercedes-Benz, Ferrari) and stereo equipment (Sony, Bang and Olufsen, Sanyo) are routinely exported by their manufacturers to other countries. Likewise, many wine distributors buy products from vineyards in France, Italy, and/or California and import them into their own countries for resale.

An import/export operation has several advantages. For example, it is the easiest way of entering a market with a small outlay of capital. Because the products are sold as is, there is no need to adapt the product to the local conditions, and little risk is involved. Nevertheless, there are also disadvantages. For example, imports and exports are subject to taxes, tariffs, and higher transportation expenses. Furthermore, because the products are not adapted to local conditions, they may miss the needs of a large segment of the market. Finally, some products may be restricted and thus can be neither imported nor exported.

Licensing A company may prefer to arrange for a foreign company to manufacture or market its products under a licensing agreement. Factors that may lead to this decision include excessive transportation costs, government regulations, and home production costs. **Licensing** is an arrangement whereby a firm allows another company to use its brand name, trademark, technology, patent, copyright, or other assets. In return, the licensee pays a royalty, usually based on sales. For example, Kirin Brewery, Japan's largest producer of beer, wanted to expand its international operations but feared that the time involved in shipping beer from Japan would cause it to lose its freshness. Thus, it has entered into a number of licensing arrangements with breweries in other markets. These brewers make beer according to strict guidelines provided by

exporting Making a product in the firm's domestic marketplace and selling it in another country

importing Bringing a good, service, or capital into the home country from abroad

Licensing is an increasingly popular method for entering foreign markets. Franchising, a form of licensing, is especially popular these days. Pizza Hut, for example, is rapidly expanding into new markets around the world via franchising agreements with local investors and managers. The popular restaurants can now be found in over 100 different countries. St. Petersburg, Russia, is one of the more recent markets where Pizza Hut has set up shop.

licensing An arrangement whereby a firm allows another company to use its brand name, trademark, technology, patent, copyright, or other assets in exchange for a royalty based on sales

the Japanese firm, and then package and market it as Kirin Beer. They then pay a royalty to Kirin for each case sold. Molson produces Kirin in Canada under such an agreement, while the Charles Wells brewery does the same in England.[12]

Two advantages of licensing are increased profitability and extended profitability. This strategy is frequently used for entry into less developed countries where older technology is still acceptable and, in fact, may be state of the art. A primary disadvantage of licensing is inflexibility. A firm can tie up control of its product or expertise for a long period of time. And if the licensee does not develop the market effectively, the licensing firm can lose profits. A second disadvantage is that licensees can take the knowledge and skill that they have been given access to for a foreign market and exploit them in the licensing firm's home market. When this happens, what used to be a business partner becomes a business competitor.

strategic alliance A cooperative arrangement between two or more firms for mutual gain

Strategic Alliances   In a **strategic alliance**, two or more firms jointly cooperate for mutual gain.[13] For example, Kodak and Fuji, along with three major Japanese camera manufacturers, collaborated on the development of a new film cartridge. This collaboration allowed Kodak and Fuji to share development costs, prevented an advertising war if the two firms had developed different cartridges, and made it easier for new cameras to be introduced at the same time as the new film cartridges. A

joint venture A special type of strategic alliance in which the partners share ownership of a new enterprise

joint venture is a special type of strategic alliance in which the partners share ownership of a new enterprise. General Mills and Nestlé formed a new company called Cereal Partners Worldwide (CPW). The purpose of CPW is to produce and market cereals. General Mills supplies the technology and proven formulas, while Nestlé provides its international distribution network. The two partners share equally in the new enterprise. Strategic alliances have enjoyed a tremendous upsurge in the past few years. In most cases, each party provides a portion of the equity or the equivalent in physical plant, raw materials, cash, or other assets. The proportion of the investment then determines the percentage of ownership in the venture.[14]

Strategic alliances have both advantages and disadvantages. For example, they can allow quick entry into a market by taking advantage of the existing strengths of participants. Japanese automobile manufacturers employed this strategy to their advantage to enter the U.S. market by using the already established distribution systems of U.S. automobile manufacturers. Strategic alliances are also an effective way of gaining access to technology or raw materials. And they allow the firms to share the risk and cost of the new venture. One major disadvantage of this approach lies with the shared ownership of joint ventures. Although it reduces the risk for each participant, it also limits the control and the return that each firm can enjoy.[15]

direct investment When a firm headquartered in one country builds or purchases operating facilities or subsidiaries in a foreign country

Direct Investment   Another level of commitment to internationalization is direct investment. **Direct investment** occurs when a firm headquartered in one country builds or purchases operating facilities or subsidiaries in a foreign country. The foreign operations then become wholly owned subsidiaries of the firm. Ford's acquisitions of Jaguar, Volvo, and Kia and British Petroleum's acquisition of Amoco were each major forms of direct investment. Similarly, Dell Computer's new factory in China is also a direct investment.

A major reason many firms make direct investments is to capitalize on lower labor costs; that is, the goal is often to transfer production to locations where labor is cheap. Japanese businesses have moved much of their production to Thailand because labor costs are much lower there than in Japan. Many U.S. firms are using maquiladoras for the same purpose. **Maquiladoras** are light assembly plants built in northern Mexico close to the U.S. border. The plants are given special tax breaks by the Mexican government, and the area is populated with workers willing to work for very low wages. More than one thousand plants in the region employ three hundred thousand workers, and more are planned. The plants are owned by major corporations, primarily from the United States, Japan, South Korea, and major European industrial countries. This concentrated form of direct investment benefits the country of Mexico, the companies themselves, and workers who might otherwise be without jobs. Some critics argue, however, that the low wages paid by the maquiladoras amount to little more than slave labor.[16]

maquiladoras Light assembly plants built in northern Mexico close to the U.S. border that are given special tax breaks by the Mexican government

Like the other approaches for increasing a firm's level of internationalization, direct investment carries with it a number of benefits and liabilities. Managerial control is more complete, and profits do not have to be shared as they do in joint ventures. Purchasing an existing organization provides additional benefits because the human resources, plant, and organizational infrastructure are already in place. Acquisition is also a way to purchase the brand-name identification of a product. This could be particularly important if the cost of introducing a new brand is high. When Nestlé bought the U.S. firm Carnation Company several years ago, it retained the firm's brand names for all its products sold in the United States. Notwithstanding these advantages, the company is now operating part of its business entirely within the borders of a foreign country. The additional complexity in the decision making, the economic and political risks, and so forth, may outweigh the advantages that can be obtained by international expansion.

Of course, we should also note that these approaches to internationalization are not mutually exclusive. Indeed, most large firms use all of them simultaneously. MNCs have a global orientation and worldwide approach to foreign markets and production. They search for opportunities all over the world and select the best strategy to serve each market. In some settings, they may use direct investment; in others, licensing; in others, strategic alliances; in still others they might limit their involvement to exporting and importing. The advantages and disadvantages of each approach are summarized in Table 5.1.

Competing in a Global Environment

Even when a firm is not actively seeking to increase its desired level of internationalization, its managers are still responsible for seeing that it functions effectively within whatever level of international involvement the organization has achieved. In one sense, the job of a manager in an international business may not be that much different from the job of a manager in a domestic business. Each may be responsible for acquiring resources and materials, making products, providing services, developing human resources, advertising, or monitoring cash flow.

In another sense, however, the complexity associated with each of these activities may be much greater for managers in international firms. Rather than buying

Table 5.1

Advantages and Disadvantages of Different Approaches to Internationalization

When organizations decide to increase their level of internationalization, they can adopt several strategies. Each strategy is a matter of degree, as opposed to being a discrete and mutually exclusive category. And each has unique advantages and disadvantages that must be considered.

Approaches to Internationalization	Advantages	Disadvantages
Importing or Exporting	1. Small cash outlay 2. Little risk 3. No adaptation necessary	1. Tariffs and taxes 2. High transportation costs 3. Government restrictions
Licensing	1. Increased profitability 2. Extended profitability	1. Inflexibility 2. Helps competitors
Strategic Alliance/ Joint Ventures	1. Quick market entry 2. Access to materials and technology	1. Shared ownership (limits control and profits)
Direct investment	1. Enhances control 2. Existing infrastructure	1. Complexity 2. Greater economic and political risk 3. Greater uncertainty

raw materials from sources in California, Texas, and Missouri, an international purchasing manager may buy materials from sources in Peru, India, and Spain. Rather than train managers for new plants in Michigan, Florida, and Oregon, the international human resources executive may be training new plant managers for facilities in China, Mexico, and Scotland. And instead of developing a single marketing campaign for the United States, an advertising director may be working on promotional efforts in France, Brazil, and Japan. *Managing in an E-world* illustrates some of the complexity associated with e-commerce in Latin America.

The key question that must be addressed by any manager trying to be effective in an international market is whether to focus on globalization or regionalism. A global thrust requires that activities be managed from an overall global perspective as part of an integrated system. Regionalism, on the other hand, involves managing within each region with less regard for the overall organization. In reality, most larger MNCs manage some activities globally (for example, finance and manufacturing) and others locally (such as human resources management and advertising). We explore these approaches more fully later in this chapter.

MANAGEMENT IMPLICATIONS   All managers need to understand the global environment in which they function. For managers in large multinational corporations, the global context is obvious. But even smaller domestic companies are affected by international forces. It is also important to understand the different methods for entering a foreign market and the strengths and weaknesses of each. Managers should also recognize the distinctions between the processes of internationalization and the management issues inherent in running a company with an existing international context.

MANAGING IN AN *e*-BUSINESS WORLD

E-COMMERCE GROWTH IN LATIN AMERICA

Problems with old computer systems, unwieldy distribution channels, and credit card fraud are keeping many Latin American businesses from jumping on the e-commerce bandwagon. Other barriers to growth in Latin American e-commerce include government policies that lag behind the Internet revolution and a scarcity of venture capital to fund entrepreneurial web start-ups.

Despite this slow start, e-commerce in the region is on the brink of a major growth spurt. Experts say that nearly seven million people will be logging onto the Internet from Latin America by 2004. Not surprisingly, this fast-growing market is drawing the interest of visionary local companies as well as MNCs based in other countries.

For example, America Online is offering Internet access in Brazil and Mexico, and Telefonos de Mexico SA has partnered with Microsoft to create a Spanish language portal. Grupo Televisa, Mexico's leading television network, is expanding into online media with its own web portal. Eyeing cross-border sales potential, U.S.-based e-commerce veterans such as Dell and Compaq are mounting campaigns to sell computers on-line in Latin America.

While some Latin American companies are reluctant to be on-line pioneers, others are moving full speed ahead. Consider the experience of Infosel in Mexico. Owned by Madrid-based Terra Networks SA, Infosel serves as an Internet service provider (ISP), sells on-line subscriptions to financial data, and hosts a well-trafficked consumer portal. The company is also launching a web retail site to sell a variety of high- and low-tech items within Mexico. Still, the head of Infosel has had difficulty convincing Mexican retail chains, mutual fund companies, and other businesses to give e-commerce a try.

As the external environment for Mexican e-commerce becomes friendlier, however, more companies— local and global—will take advantage of the opportunities. Infosel is helping things along by developing the technology for secure digital signatures, a legal innovation that will accelerate the growth of business-to-business e-commerce in Mexico. Day by day, business by business, innovation by innovation, Latin America is becoming a major on-line market.

> *If the Mexican businesses lose, I'm going to lose. Mexicans will end up buying products on Yahoo!*
>
> —*Arturo Galvan, head of the Mexican unit of Terra Networks SA**

References: Andrea Petersen, "Opening a Portal: E-Commerce Apostles Target Latin America, But It's a Tough Sell," *Wall Street Journal*, January 25, 2000, pp. A1, A8 (*quote on p. A8); Jim Hu, "Lycos Bought In First Foreign Portal Deal," *CNET News.com*, May 16, 2000, http://news.cnet.com/news/0-1005-200-1877185.html?tag=st (July 10, 2000).

The Structure of the Global Economy

One thing that can be helpful to managers seeking to operate in a global environment is to understand the structure of the global economy better. Although each country, and indeed each region within any given country, is unique, we can still note some basic similarities and differences. We describe three different elements of the global economy: mature market economies and systems, high potential/high growth economies, and other economies.[17]

Mature Market Economies and Systems

market economy An economy based on the private ownership of business and allows market factors such as supply and demand to determine business strategy

A **market economy** is based on the private ownership of business and allows market factors such as supply and demand to determine business strategy. Mature market economies include the United States, Japan, the United Kingdom, France, Germany, and Sweden. These countries have several traits in common. For example, they tend to employ market forces in the allocation of resources. They also tend to be characterized by private ownership of property, although there is some variance along this dimension. France, for example, has a relatively high level of government ownership among the market economies.

U.S. managers have relatively few problems operating in market economies. Many of the business "rules of the game" that apply in the United States, for example, also apply in Germany or England. And consumers there often tend to buy the same kinds of products. For these reasons it is not unusual for U.S. firms seeking to expand geographically to begin operations in another market economy. Although the task of managing an international business in an industrial market country is somewhat less complicated than operating in some other type of economy, it still poses some challenges. Perhaps foremost among them is that the markets in these economies are typically quite mature. Many industries, for example, are already dominated by large and successful companies. Thus, competing in these economies poses a major challenge.

market systems Clusters of countries that engage in high levels of trade with each other

The map in Figure 5.2 highlights three relatively mature market systems. **Market systems** are clusters of countries that engage in high levels of trade with

Figure 5.2

The Global Economy

The global economy is dominated by three relatively mature market systems. As illustrated here, these market systems consist of North America, Europe (especially those nations in the European Union), and Pacific Asia (parts of which are high potential/high growth economies). Other areas of Asia, as well as Africa and South America, have the potential for future growth but currently play only a relatively small role in the global economy.

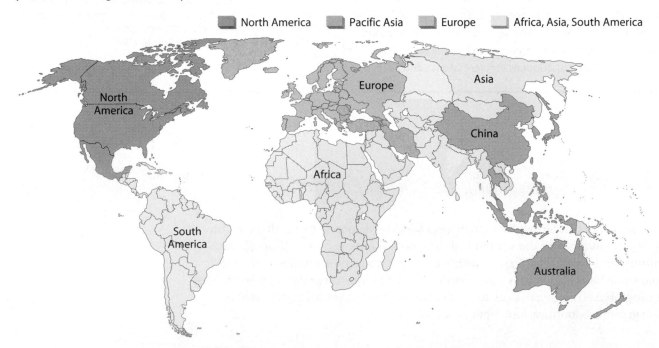

each other. One mature market system is North America. The United States, Canada, and Mexico are major trading partners with one another; more than 70 percent of Mexico's exports go to the United States, and more than 65 percent of what Mexico imports comes from the United States. During the last several years these countries have negotiated a variety of agreements to make trade even easier. The most important of these, the **North American Free Trade Agreement**, or **NAFTA**, eliminates many of the trade barriers—quotas and tariffs, for example— that existed previously.[18]

Another mature market system is Europe. Until recently, Europe was two distinct economic areas. The eastern region consisted of communist countries such as Poland, Czechoslovakia, and Romania. These countries relied on government ownership of business and greatly restricted trade. In contrast, western European countries with traditional market economies have been working together to promote international trade for decades. In particular, the **European Union** (or **EU** as it is often called) has long been a formidable market system. The formal members of the EU are Denmark, the United Kingdom, Portugal, the Netherlands, Belgium, Spain, Ireland, Luxembourg, France, Germany, Italy, and Greece. For years these countries followed a basic plan that led to the elimination of most trade barriers in 1992.

The European situation has recently grown more complex, however. Communism has collapsed in most eastern countries, and they are trying to develop market economies. They also want greater participation in trade with the western European countries. In some ways the emergence of the east has slowed and complicated business activities in the west. In the long-term, however, the new markets in the east are likely to make Europe an even more important part of the world economy. For example, Poland is increasingly becoming a significant market for many MNCs.

Yet another mature market system is **Pacific Asia**. As shown in Figure 5.2, this market system includes Japan, China, Thailand, Malaysia, Singapore, Indonesia,

North American Free Trade Agreement (NAFTA) An agreement among the United States, Canada, and Mexico to promote trade with one another

European Union (EU) The first and most important international market system

Pacific Asia A market system located in Southeast Asia

Most international business managers see the People's Republic of China as the most important emerging marketplace in the world. Its vast population and growing interest in consumerism combine to offer tremendous potential for a wide array of products and services. For example, even farmers in China's most remote regions hunger for new technology like the satellite dish shown here. Products like televisions, cellular telephones, computers, and automobiles are also experiencing strong demand as the citizens of China take their place alongside consumers from Japan, Europe, the United States, and the rest of the world.

South Korea, Taiwan, the Philippines, and Australia. Indeed, Japan, Taiwan, Singapore, Thailand, and South Korea were major economic powerhouses until a regional currency crisis slowed their growth in the 1990s. That crisis appears to be coming to an end, however; trade among these nations is on the rise, and talk has started about an Asian economic community much like the EU.[19]

High Potential/High Growth Economies

In contrast to the highly developed and mature market economies just described, other countries have what is termed *high potential/high growth economies*. These economies have been relatively underdeveloped and immature and, until recently, were characterized by weak industry, weak currency, and relatively poor consumers.[20] The governments in these countries, however, have been actively working to strengthen their economies by opening their doors to foreign investment and by promoting international trade. Some of these countries have only recently adopted market economies, while others still use a command economy.

Even though it is technically part of Pacific Asia, the People's Republic of China is largely underdeveloped. The transfer of control of Hong Kong from Great Britain to China in 1997 focused even more attention on the market potential in the world's most populous country.[21] India is also showing signs of becoming a major market in the future.[22] Vietnam has become a potentially important market, and Brazil is becoming more important as well.[23] Likewise, Russia and the other states and republics that previously made up the Commonwealth of Independent States are being closely watched by many companies for emerging market opportunities.[24]

The primary challenges presented by the developing economies to those interested in conducting international business there are the lack of wealth on the part of potential consumers and the underdeveloped infrastructure. Developing economies have enormous economic potential, but much of it remains untapped. Thus, international firms entering these markets often have to invest heavily in distribution systems, in training consumers how to use their products, and even in providing living facilities for their workers. They also run the risk of major policy changes that can greatly distort the value of their investments.[25]

Other Economies

There are some economic systems around the world that defy classification as either mature markets or high potential/high growth economies. One major area that falls outside these categories is the oil-exporting region generally called the Middle East. The oil-exporting countries present mixed models of resource allocation, property ownership, and the development of infrastructure. These countries all have access to major amounts of crude oil, however, and thus are important players in the global economy.

The oil-exporting countries include Iran, Iraq, Kuwait, Saudi Arabia, Libya, Syria, and the United Arab Emirates. High oil prices in the 1970s and 1980s created enormous wealth in these countries. Many of them invested heavily in their infrastructures. Whole new cities were built, airports were constructed, and the population was educated. As oil prices have fallen, many of the oil-producing countries have been forced to cut back on these activities. Nevertheless, they are still quite wealthy. The per capita incomes of the United Arab Emirates and Qatar, for example, are among the highest in the world. Although there is great wealth in the oil-producing nations, they provide great challenges to managers. Political instability (as evidenced by the Persian Gulf War in 1991) and tremendous cultural differences, for example, combine to make doing business in many parts of the Middle East both very risky and very difficult.

Other countries pose risks to business of a different sort. Politically and ethnically motivated violence, for example, still characterizes some countries. Foremost among these are Peru, El Salvador, Turkey, Colombia, and Northern Ireland. Cuba presents special challenges because it is so insulated from the outside world. With the fall of communism, some experts believe that Cuba will eventually join the ranks of the market economies. If so, its strategic location will quickly make it an important business center.

MANAGEMENT IMPLICATIONS International managers need to have a fundamental understanding of the structure of the global economy. They should also recognize the advantages and disadvantages of competing in mature market economies and systems, high potential/high growth economies, and other economies.

Environmental Challenges of International Management

We noted earlier that managing in a global context both poses and creates additional challenges for the manager. As illustrated in Figure 5.3, three environmental challenges in particular warrant additional exploration at this point—the economic environment, the political/legal environment, and the cultural environment of international management.[26]

The Economic Environment

Every country is unique and creates a unique set of challenges for managers trying to do business there. However, there are three aspects of the economic environment that in particular can help managers anticipate the kinds of economic challenges they are likely to face when working abroad.

Economic System The first of these is the economic system used in the country. As we described earlier, most countries today are moving toward market economies. In a mature market economy, the key element for managers is freedom of choice. Consumers are free to make decisions about which products they prefer to purchase, and firms are free to decide what products and services to provide. As long as both

Figure 5.3

Environmental Challenges of International Management

Managers functioning in a global context must be aware of several environmental challenges. Three of the most important include economic, political/legal, and cultural challenges.

the consumer and the firm are free to decide to be members in the market, then supply and demand determine which firms and which products will be available.

A related characteristic of market economies that is relevant to managers concerns the nature of property ownership. There are two pure types—complete private ownership and complete public ownership. In systems with private ownership, individuals and organizations—not the government—own and operate the companies that conduct business. In systems with public ownership, the government directly owns the companies that manufacture and sell products. Few countries have pure systems of private ownership or pure systems of public ownership. Most countries tend toward one extreme or the other, but usually a mix of public and private ownership exists.

Natural Resources   Another important aspect of the economic environment in different countries is the availability of natural resources. A very broad range of resources are available in different countries. Some countries, like Japan, have few resources of their own. Japan is thus forced to import all of the oil, iron ore, and other natural resources it needs to manufacture products for its domestic and overseas markets. The United States, in contrast, has enormous natural resources and is a major producer of oil, natural gas, coal, iron ore, copper, uranium, and other metals and materials that are vital to the development of a modern economy.

One natural resource that is particularly important in the modern global economy is oil. As we noted earlier, a small set of countries in the Middle East, including Saudi Arabia, Iraq, Iran, and Kuwait, controls a very large percentage of the world's total known reserves of crude oil. Access to this single natural resource has given these oil-producing countries enormous clout in the international economy. One of the more controversial global issues involving natural resources today is the South American rain forest. Developers and farmers in Brazil, Peru, and other countries are clearing vast areas of rain forest, arguing that it is their land and they can do what they want with it. Many environmentalists, however, fear that defor-estation is wiping out entire species of animals and may so alter the environment that it will affect weather patterns around the world.[27]

Infrastructure   Yet another important aspect of the economic environment of relevance to international management is infrastructure. A country's **infrastructure** is composed of its schools, hospitals, power plants, railroads, highways, ports, com-munication systems, air fields, commercial distribution systems, and so forth. The United States has a highly developed infrastructure. For example, its educational system is modern, roads and bridges are well developed, and most people have ac-cess to medical care. Overall, the United States has a relatively complete infrastruc-ture sufficient to support most forms of economic development and activity.

> **infrastructure** The schools, hospi-tals, power plants, railroads, high-ways, ports, communication sys-tems, air fields, and commercial distribution systems of a country

Some countries, on the other hand, lack a well-developed infrastructure. Some countries do not have enough electrical generating capacity to meet demand. Such countries —Kenya, for example—often schedule periods of time during which power is turned off. These planned power failures reduce power demands but can be an enormous inconvenience to business. In the extreme, when a coun-try's infrastructure is greatly underdeveloped, firms interested in beginning busi-ness may have to build an entire township, including housing, schools, hospitals, and perhaps even recreation facilities, to attract a sufficient overseas workforce.

The Political/Legal Environment

A second environmental challenge facing the international manager is the politi-cal/legal environment in which he or she will do business. *Today's Management Issues* describes how the political/legal environment affects immigration policies. Four other especially im-portant aspects of the political/legal environment of international management are government stability, incentives for multinational trade, controls on interna-tional trade, and the influence of economic communi-ties on international trade.

Government Stability   Stability can be viewed in two ways—as the ability of a given government to stay in power against other opposing factions in the country and as the permanence of government policies toward business. A country that is stable in both respects is preferable because managers have a higher probability of successfully predicting how government will affect their business. Civil war in countries such as Lebanon has made it virtually impossible for international man-agers to predict what government policies are likely to be and whether the government will be able to guaran-tee the safety of international workers. Consequently, international firms have been very reluctant to invest in Lebanon.

Government stability is of keen interest to managers looking for international opportunities. No business wants to set up shop in a foreign market only to see its investment disappear in the face of government nationalization or civil unrest. Continued clashes in the Middle East, for example, have made many managers wary of making new investments or seeking to expand their operations in that troubled part of the world.

TODAY'S MANAGEMENT ISSUES

CHANGING POLICIES ON IMMIGRATION

During the heyday of the Industrial Revolution, immigration helped the United States build its infrastructure, laying a solid foundation for future economic growth. Over the years, however, government policy on immigration changed, allowing fewer immigrants to enter the United States. Now U.S. companies eager to tap the global labor pool are clamoring for government changes that will ease immigration restrictions.

In a low-unemployment economy, both low-skilled and high-skilled workers are in great demand. All kinds of companies are turning to immigrants to keep their operations humming. Service businesses such as hotels and restaurants need a constant stream of job applicants to keep up with the high turnover in employees. High-tech companies are also suffering a labor shortage. The Information Technology Association of America estimates that more than eight hundred thousand high-tech job openings will remain unfilled if immigration laws are not changed. This shortfall is hurting businesses that need to hire more employees if they want to expand.

The seven hundred thousand immigrants legally admitted to the United States every year are helping to ease the labor shortage and keep the economy moving ahead. Coming from Mexico, India, China, the Philippines, Vietnam, Canada, and many other countries, these immigrants have a range of educational and work backgrounds. In addition, illegal immigration brings as many as six hundred thousand people into the United States every year.

Although some legislators and labor leaders are concerned about how many immigrants the country can absorb, many managers and company owners believe that the U.S. government must significantly increase the number of immigrants who are granted permanent residency status. Otherwise, U.S. businesses may not have the personnel power to keep growing and competing effectively in the global economy.

> *An increase in the number of immigrants is fundamental to us keeping a competitive position in the New Economy.*
>
> —*Jack Mollen, senior vice president of human resources, EMC Corporation**

Reference: Wendy Zellner, "Keeping the Hive Humming," *Business Week*, April 24, 2000, pp. 50–52 (*quote on p. 51).

In many countries—the United States, Great Britain, and Japan, for example— changes in government occur with very little disruption. In other countries—India, Argentina, and Greece, for example—changes are likely to be somewhat chaotic. Even if a country's government remains stable, the risk remains that the policies adopted by that government might change. In some countries foreign businesses may be **nationalized** (taken over by the government) with little or no warning. The government of Peru once nationalized Perulac, a domestic milk producer owned by Nestlé, because of a local milk shortage.

nationalized Taken over by the government

Incentives for International Trade   Another facet of the political environment is incentives to attract foreign business. For example, the state of Alabama offered Mercedes-Benz huge tax breaks and other incentives to entice the German firm to select a location in that state for a new factory. In like fashion, as noted earlier, the French government sold land to The Walt Disney Company far below its market value and agreed to build a connecting freeway in exchange for the company's agreement to build its European theme park outside Paris.

Such incentives can take a variety of forms. Some of the most common include reduced interest rates on loans, construction subsidies, and tax incentives. Less developed countries tend to offer different packages of incentives. In addition to lucrative tax breaks, for example, they can also attract investors with duty-fee entry of raw materials and equipment, market protection through limitations on other importers, and the right to take profits out of the country. They may also have to correct deficiencies in their infrastructures, as noted above, to satisfy the requirements of foreign firms.

Controls on International Trade A third element of the political environment that managers need to consider is the extent to which there are controls on international trade. In some instances, the government of a country may decide that foreign competition is hurting domestic trade. To protect domestic business, such governments may enact barriers to international trade. These barriers include tariffs, quotas, export restraint agreements, and "buy national" laws.

A **tariff** is a tax collected on goods shipped across national boundaries. Tariffs can be collected by the exporting country, countries through which goods pass, and the importing country. Import tariffs, which are the most common, can be levied to protect domestic companies by increasing the cost of foreign goods. Japan charges U.S. tobacco producers a tariff on cigarettes imported into Japan as a way to keep their prices higher than the prices charged by domestic firms. Tariffs can also be levied, usually by less developed countries, to raise money for the government.

Quotas are the most common form of trade restriction. A **quota** is a limit on the number or value of goods that can be traded. The quota amount is typically designed to ensure that domestic competitors will be able to maintain a certain market share. Honda is allowed to import 425,000 autos each year into the United States. This quota is one reason Honda opened manufacturing facilities here. The quota applies to cars imported into the United States, but the company can produce as many other cars within our borders as it wants because they are not considered imports. **Export restraint agreements** are designed to convince other governments to limit voluntarily the volume or value of goods exported to a particular country. They are, in effect, export quotas. Japanese steel producers voluntarily limit the amount of steel they send to the United States each year.

"Buy national" legislation gives preference to domestic producers through content or price restrictions. Several countries have this type of legislation. Brazil requires that Brazilian companies purchase only Brazilian-made computers. The United States requires that the Department of Defense purchase only military uniforms manufactured in the United States, even though the price of foreign uniforms would be half as much. Mexico requires that 50 percent of the parts of cars sold in Mexico be manufactured in Mexico.

Economic Communities Just as government policies can either increase or decrease the political risk facing international managers, trade relations between

tariff A tax collected on goods shipped across national boundaries

quota A limit on the number or value of goods that can be traded

export restraint agreements Accords reached by governments in which countries voluntarily limit the volume or value of goods they export and import from one another

countries can either help or hinder international business. Relations dictated by quotas, tariffs, and so forth, can hurt international trade. There is currently a strong movement around the world to reduce many of these barriers. This movement takes its most obvious form in international economic communities.

economic community A set of countries that agree to reduce or eliminate trade barriers markedly among its member nations (a formalized market system)

An international **economic community** is a set of countries that agree to reduce or eliminate trade barriers markedly among its member nations. The first, and in many ways still the most important, of these economic communities is the European Union (EU), discussed earlier. The passage of NAFTA, as also noted earlier, represents perhaps the first step toward the formation of a North American economic community. Other important economic communities include the Latin American Integration Association (Bolivia, Brazil, Colombia, Chile, Argentina, and other South American countries) and the Caribbean Common Market (the Bahamas, Belize, Jamaica, Antigua, Barbados, and twelve other countries).

The Cultural Environment

Another environmental challenge for the international manager is the cultural environment and how it affects business. A country's culture includes all the values, symbols, beliefs, and language that guide behavior. *The World of Management* provides an interesting illustration of cultural dynamics at work!

Values, Symbols, Beliefs, and Language   Cultural values and beliefs are often unspoken; they may even be taken for granted by those who live in a particular country. Cultural factors do not necessarily cause problems for managers when the cultures of two countries are similar. Difficulties can arise, however, when there is little overlap between the home culture of a manager and the culture of the country in which business is to be conducted. For example, most U.S. managers find the culture and traditions of England familiar. The people of both countries speak the same language and share strong historical roots, and there is a history of strong commerce between the two countries. When U.S. managers begin operations in Japan or the People's Republic of China, however, most of those commonalities disappear.

In Japanese the word *hai* (pronounced "hi") means "yes." In conversation, however, this word is used much like people in the United States use "uh-huh"; it moves a conversation along or shows the person you are talking to that you are paying attention. So when does "hai" mean "yes" and when does it mean "uh-huh"? This question turns out to be relatively difficult to answer. If a U.S. manager asks a Japanese manager if he agrees to some trade arrangement, the Japanese manager is likely to say "hai"—which may mean "yes, I agree," or "yes, I understand," or "yes, I am listening." Many U.S. managers become frustrated in negotiations with the Japanese because they believe that the Japanese continue to raise issues that have already been settled (the Japanese managers said "yes"). What many of these managers fail to recognize is that "yes" does not always mean "yes" in Japan.

Cultural differences between countries can have a direct impact on business practice. For example, the religion of Islam teaches that people should not make a living by exploiting the misfortune of others and that making interest payments is immoral. This means that in Saudi Arabia there are few businesses that provide auto-wrecking services to tow stalled cars to the garage (because that would be

WORLD OF MANAGEMENT

FRENCH LANGUAGE SPECIALISTS COIN NEW WEB WORDS

As the Internet revolution sweeps the world, the Academie Française in France is fighting to maintain the language by coining uniquely French words and phrases for well-known Internet buzzwords. The World Wide Web, which hip Parisian netizens call "le Web," is officially known as *la toile*, which translates into "the spider web." Similarly, the academy's official phrase for e-mail is *message électronique*.

Subtle differences, perhaps, but the writers who serve on the academy are determined to keep foreign words out of the language by providing French substitutes for use in government documents and schools. Ordinary citizens are not required to use the terms offered by the academy, although officials hope they will adopt suggested French phrases such as *causette* instead of chattering on about on-line chat sessions.

Sometimes the drive to use French words makes for unusual designations. The academy calls hackers—programmers who break into computer systems and web sites—*les fouineurs*, meaning "the nosy people." Other substitutes are fairly close, such as *localisateur universal*, which translates into "universal locator," the official French term for URL (universal resource locator), a web address.

Since the Academie Française was founded by Cardinal Richelieu in 1635, it has made considerable headway in persuading the French to adopt its substitutes for non-French words. Nobody talks about a computer in France; instead, they talk about an *ordinateur*, a word the academy proposed. On the other hand, many Internet entrepreneurs resist the official French phrases. They prefer to say "le start-up" instead of *la jeune pousse*, which means "young sapling." Although the popular press continues to mix French and web terms with headlines such as "Surfez le Web," the academy is pressing on with its mission to keep non-French buzzwords out of the language.

> **In a few years, no one in France will use le Web.**
>
> —*Serge Petillot-Niemetz, director of external affairs, Academie Française**

Reference: Vivienne Walt, "E-Words Are Tough for France to Swallow," *USA Today,* May 1, 2000, pp. 1A, 2A (*quote on p. 2A).

---

capitalizing on misfortune), and in the Sudan banks cannot pay or charge interest. Given these cultural and religious constraints, those two businesses—automobile towing and banking—don't seem to hold great promise for international managers in those particular countries!

Some cultural differences between countries can be even more subtle and yet have a major impact on business activities. For example, in the United States most managers clearly agree about the value of time. Most U.S. managers schedule their activities very tightly and then adhere to their schedules. Other cultures don't put such a premium on time. In the Middle East, managers do not like to set appointments, and they rarely keep appointments set too far into the future. U.S. managers interacting with managers from the Middle East might misinterpret the late arrival of a potential business partner as a negotiation ploy or an insult, when it is rather a simple reflection of different views of time and its value.[28]

Language itself can be an important factor. Beyond the obvious and clear barriers posed by people who speak different languages, subtle differences in meaning

DILBERT by Scott Adams

DILBERT by Scott Adams reprinted by permission of United Feature Syndicate.

Dealing with people from other cultures can be a rewarding experience, and it can also be a challenge. Language barriers, for example, pose major obstacles. Interestingly, some people believe that if they talk slower or louder, people who do not speak their language will somehow have a better understanding of what is being said. As illustrated in this cartoon, this flawed logic can even extend to electronic communication!

can also play a major role. For example, Imperial Oil of Canada markets gasoline under the brand name Esso. When the firm tried to sell its gasoline in Japan, it learned that Esso means "stalled car" in Japanese. The Chevrolet Nova was not selling well in Latin America, and General Motors executives couldn't understand why until it was brought to their attention that, in Spanish, *no va* means "it doesn't go." The color green is used extensively in Moslem countries, but it signifies death in some other countries. The color associated with femininity in the United States is pink, but in many other countries yellow is the most feminine color.

Individual Behaviors Across Cultures   From another perspective, there also appear to be clear differences in individual behaviors and attitudes across different cultures. For example, Geert Hofstede, a Dutch researcher, studied 116,000 people working in dozens of different countries and found several interesting differences.[29] Hofstede's initial work identified four important dimensions along which people seem to differ across cultures. More recently, he has added a fifth dimension. These dimensions are illustrated in Figure 5.4.

social orientation A person's beliefs about the relative importance of the individual versus groups to which that person belongs

The first dimension identified by Hofstede is social orientation.[30] **Social orientation** is a person's beliefs about the relative importance of the individual versus groups to which that person belongs. The two extremes of social orientation are individualism and collectivism. *Individualism* is the cultural belief that the person comes first. Hofstede's research suggested that people in the United States, the United Kingdom, Australia, Canada, New Zealand, and the Netherlands tend to be relatively individualistic. *Collectivism,* the opposite of individualism, is the belief that the group comes first. Hofstede found that people from Mexico, Greece, Hong Kong, Taiwan, Peru, Singapore, Colombia, and Pakistan tend to be relatively collectivistic in their values. In countries with higher levels of individualism, many workers may prefer reward systems that link pay with the performance of individual employees. In a more collectivistic culture, such a reward system may, in fact, be counterproductive.

power orientation The beliefs that people in a culture hold about the appropriateness of power and authority differences in hierarchies such as business organizations

A second important dimension is **power orientation**, the beliefs that people in a culture hold about the appropriateness of power and authority differences in hierarchies such as business organizations. Some cultures are characterized by *power respect.* This means that people tend to accept the power and authority of

Figure 5.4

Individual Differences Across Cultures

Hofstede identified five fundamental differences that can be used to characterize people in different cultures. These dimensions are social orientation, power orientation, uncertainty orientation, goal orientation, and time orientation. Different levels of each dimension affect the perceptions, attitudes, values, motivation, and behaviors of people in different cultures.

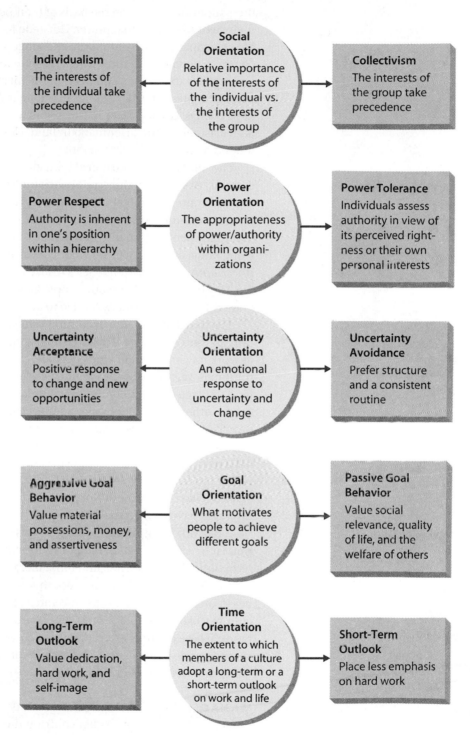

Social Orientation
Relative importance of the interests of the individual vs. the interests of the group

Individualism
The interests of the individual take precedence

Collectivism
The interests of the group take precedence

Power Orientation
The appropriateness of power/authority within organizations

Power Respect
Authority is inherent in one's position within a hierarchy

Power Tolerance
Individuals assess authority in view of its perceived rightness or their own personal interests

Uncertainty Orientation
An emotional response to uncertainty and change

Uncertainty Acceptance
Positive response to change and new opportunities

Uncertainty Avoidance
Prefer structure and a consistent routine

Goal Orientation
What motivates people to achieve different goals

Aggressive Goal Behavior
Value material possessions, money, and assertiveness

Passive Goal Behavior
Value social relevance, quality of life, and the welfare of others

Time Orientation
The extent to which members of a culture adopt a long-term or a short-term outlook on work and life

Long-Term Outlook
Value dedication, hard work, and self-image

Short-Term Outlook
Place less emphasis on hard work

Source: R. W. Griffin/M. Pustay, *International Business* © 1996. Reprinted by permission of Pearson Education, Inc. Upper Saddle River, NJ 07458.

their superiors simply on the basis of their position in the hierarchy and to respect their right to control that power. Hofstede found that people in France, Spain, Mexico, Japan, Brazil, Indonesia, and Singapore were relatively power accepting. In contrast, people in cultures with a *power tolerance* orientation attach much less significance to a person's position in the hierarchy. These individuals are more willing to question a decision or mandate from someone at a higher level or perhaps even refuse to accept it. Hofstede's work suggested that people in the United States, Israel, Austria, Denmark, Ireland, Norway, Germany, and New Zealand tended to be more power tolerant.

uncertainty orientation The feeling individuals have regarding uncertain and ambiguous situations

The third basic dimension of individual differences studied by Hofstede was uncertainty orientation. **Uncertainty orientation** is the feeling individuals have regarding uncertain and ambiguous situations. People in cultures with *uncertainty acceptance* are stimulated by change and thrive on new opportunities. Hofstede suggested that many people from the United States, Denmark, Sweden, Canada, Singapore, Hong Kong, and Australia are among those in this category. In contrast, people with *uncertainty avoidance* tendencies dislike and will avoid ambiguity whenever possible. Hofstede found that many people in Israel, Austria, Japan, Italy, Colombia, France, Peru, and Germany tended to avoid uncertainty whenever possible.

goal orientation The manner in which people are motivated to work toward different kinds of goals

The fourth dimension of cultural values measured by Hofstede is goal orientation. In this context, **goal orientation** is the manner in which people are motivated to work toward different kinds of goals. One extreme on the goal orientation continuum is *aggressive goal behavior*. People who exhibit aggressive goal behaviors tend to place a high premium on material possessions, money, and assertiveness. On the other hand, people who adopt *passive goal behavior* place a higher value on social relationships, quality of life, and concern for others. According to Hofstede's research, many people in Japan tend to exhibit relatively aggressive goal behaviors, whereas many people in Germany, Mexico, Italy, and the United States reflect moderately aggressive goal behaviors. People from the Netherlands and the Scandinavian countries of Norway, Sweden, Denmark, and Finland all tend to exhibit relatively passive goal behaviors.

time orientation The extent to which members of a culture adopt a long-term versus a short-term outlook on work, life, and other elements of society

A recently identified fifth dimension is called Time orientation.[31] **Time orientation** is the extent to which members of a culture adopt a long-term versus a short-term outlook on work, life, and other elements of society. Some cultures, such as Japan, Hong Kong, Taiwan, and South Korea, have a long-term orientation that values dedication, hard work, perseverance, and the importance of self-image. Other cultures, like Pakistan and West Africa, are more likely to have a short-term orientation. These cultures, in contrast, put considerably less emphasis on work, perseverance, and similar values. Hofstede's work suggests that people in the United States and Germany tend to have an intermediate time orientation.

MANAGEMENT IMPLICATIONS   Managers need to understand the basic environmental challenges that confront them as they do business in international settings. These basic challenges involve political/legal differences in different countries, differences in the economic environments of different countries, and variations in the cultural environment. Each difference adds to the complexities that international managers must address.

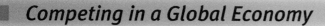

Competing in a Global Economy

Competing in a global economy is both a major challenge and an opportunity for businesses today. The nature of these challenges depends on a variety of factors, including the size of the organization. In addition, international management also has implications for the basic functions of planning, organizing, leading, and controlling.

Globalization and Organization Size

Although organizations of any size may compete in international markets, there are some basic differences in the challenges and opportunities faced by MNCs, medium-size organizations, and small organizations.

Multinational Corporations   The large MNCs have long since made the choice to compete in a global marketplace. In general, these firms take a global perspective. They transfer capital, technology, human resources, inventory, and information from one market to another. They actively seek new expansion opportunities wherever feasible. MNCs tend to allow local managers a great deal of discretion in addressing local and regional issues. At the same time, each operation is ultimately accountable to a central authority. Managers at this central authority (headquarters, a central office, etc.) are responsible for setting the overall strategic direction for the firm, making major policy decisions, and so forth. MNCs need senior managers who understand the global economy and who are comfortable dealing with executives and government officials from a variety of cultures. Table 5.2 lists the world's largest multinational enterprises.

Medium-Size Organizations   Many medium-size businesses remain primarily domestic organizations. But they still may buy and sell products made abroad and compete with businesses from other countries in their own domestic market. Increasingly, however, medium-size organizations are expanding into foreign markets as well. For example, Gold's Gym, a U.S. fitness chain, has opened a very successful facility in Moscow.[32] In contrast to MNCs, medium-size organizations doing business abroad are much more selective about the markets they enter. They also depend more on a few international specialists to help them manage their foreign operations.

Small Organizations   More and more small organizations are also finding that they can benefit from the global economy. Some, for example, serve as local suppliers for MNCs. A dairy farmer who sells milk to Carnation Company, for example, is actually transacting business with Nestlé. Local parts suppliers have also been successfully selling products to the Toyota and Honda plants in the United States. Beyond serving as local suppliers, some small businesses also buy and sell products and services abroad. For example, the Collin Street Bakery, based in Corsicana, Texas, ships fruitcakes around the world. In 1999, the firm shipped over 150,000 pounds of fruitcake to Japan. Most small businesses rely on simple

Table 5.2
The World's Largest MNCs: Industrial Corporations

Rank 1999	Company	Country	Revenues $ million	Profits $ million	Assets $ million	Employees Number
1	General Motors	U.S.	176,558.0	6,002.0	273,921.0	388,000
2	Wal-Mart Stores	U.S.	166,809.0	5,377.0	70,245.0	1,140,000
3	Exxon Mobil	U.S.	163,881.0	7,910.0	144,521.0	106,000
4	Ford Motor	U.S.	162,558.0	7,237.0	276,229.0	364,550
5	DaimlerChrysler	Germany	159,985.7	6,129.1	175,068.8	466,938
6	Mitsui	Japan	118,555.2	320.5	62,360.0	38,454
7	Mitsubishi	Japan	117,765.6	233.7	78,949.2	42,050
8	Toyota Motor	Japan	115,670.9	3,653.4	160,571.6	214,631
9	General Electric	U.S.	111,630.0	10,717.0	405,200.0	340,000
10	Itochu	Japan	109,068.9	(792.8)	59,153.9	5,306
11	Royal Dutch/Shell Group	Brit./Neth.	105,366.0	8,584.0	113,883.0	96,000
12	Sumitomo	Japan	95,701.6	314.9	47,819.8	33,057
13	Nippon Telegraph & Telephone	Japan	93,591.7	(609.0)	179,512.2	223,954
14	Marubeni	Japan	91,807.4	18.5	54,446.9	32,000
15	Axa	France	87,645.7	2,155.8	508,647.3	92,008
16	International Business Machines	U.S.	87,548.0	7,712.0	87,495.0	307,401
17	BP Amoco	Britain	83,566.0	5,008.0	89,561.0	80,400
18	Citigroup	U.S.	82,005.0	9,867.0	716,900.0	176,900
19	Volkswagen	Germany	80,072.7	874.7	67,275.9	306,275
20	Nippon Life Insurance	Japan	78,515.1	3,405.4	423,281.5	71,434
21	Siemens	Germany	75,337.0	1,773.7	65,488.8	443,000
22	Allianz	Germany	74,178.2	2,382.1	383,686.9	113,584
23	Hitachi	Japan	71,858.5	152.0	95,911.7	398,348
24	Matsushita Electric Industrial	Japan	65,555.6	895.5	74,946.3	290,448
25	Nissho Iwai	Japan	65,393.2	91.8	39,762.9	18,446

Source: Adapted from *Fortune*, July 24, 2000; p. F-1. Used with permission from Fortune, Inc.

importing or exporting operations (or both) for their international sales. Thus, only a few specialized management positions are needed. Collin Street Bakery, for example, has one local manager who handles international activities. Mail-order activities within each country are subcontracted to local firms in each market.

Management Challenges in a Global Economy

The management functions that constitute the framework for this book—planning, organizing, leading, and controlling—are just as relevant to international managers as to domestic managers. International managers need to have a clear view of where they want their firm to be in the future, they have to organize to implement their plans, they have to motivate those who work for them, and they have to develop appropriate control mechanisms.[33]

Planning in a Global Economy To plan effectively in a global economy, managers must have a broad-based understanding of both environmental issues and competitive issues. They need to understand local market conditions and technological factors that will affect their operations. At the corporate level, executives need a great deal of information to function effectively. What markets are growing? What markets are shrinking? What are our domestic and foreign competitors doing in each market? They must also make a variety of strategic decisions about their organization. For example, if a firm wishes to enter the market in France, should it buy a local firm there, build a plant, or seek a strategic alliance? Critical issues include understanding environmental circumstances, the role of goals and planning in a global organization, and how decision making affects the global organization. We note special implications for global managers as we discuss planning in Chapters 7 through 10.

Most large businesses have already faced the challenges of entering major foreign markets and now focus their energies on competing with other companies in those markets. Take Vodafone, for example, the world's largest cell phone operator. Vodafone has over 65 million subscribers in 25 countries, including the Netherlands. But as successful as the firm has become, it must still compete with such other global telecommunications giants as Sprint PCS, NTT, and AT&T.

Organizing in a Global Economy Managers in international businesses must also attend to various organizing issues. For example, General Electric has operations scattered around the globe. The firm has made the decision to give local managers a great deal of responsibility for how they run their business. In contrast, many Japanese firms give managers of their foreign operations relatively little responsibility. As a result, those managers must frequently travel back to Japan to present problems or get decisions approved. Managers in an international business must address the basic issues of organization structure and design, managing change, and dealing with human resources. We address the special issues of organizing the international organization in Chapters 11 through 14.

Leading in a Global Economy We noted earlier some of the cultural factors that affect international organizations. Individual managers must be prepared to deal with these and other factors as they interact with people from different cultural backgrounds. Supervising a group of five managers, each of whom is from a different state in the United States, is likely to be much simpler than supervising a group of five managers, each of whom is from a different culture. Managers must understand how cultural factors affect individuals, how motivational processes vary across cultures, the role of leadership in different cultures, how communication varies across cultures, and the nature of interpersonal and group processes in different cultures. In Chapters 15 through 19 we note special implications for international managers that relate to leading and interacting with others.

Controlling in a Global Economy   Finally, managers in international organizations must also be concerned with control. Distances, time zone differences, and cultural factors all play a role in control. For example, in some cultures close supervision is seen as being appropriate, and in other cultures it is not. Likewise, executives in the United States and Japan may find it difficult to communicate vital information to one another because of the time zone differences. Basic control issues for the international manager revolve around operations management, productivity, quality, technology, and information systems. These issues are integrated throughout our discussion of control in Chapters 20 through 22.

MANAGEMENT IMPLICATIONS   The international challenges and opportunities facing managers in large multinational corporations, medium-size businesses, and small companies are subtly different. Similarly, the basic management functions of planning, organizing, leading, and controlling are also affected by the degree of internationalization of the organization. Thus, managers need to appreciate both the size of their organization and the relevant functional activities as they carry out their work in a global environment.

Summary of Key Points

International business has become one of the most important features of the world's economy. Learning to operate in a global economy is an important challenge facing many managers today. Businesses can be primarily domestic, international, multinational, or global in scope. Managers need to understand both the process of internationalization as well as how to manage within a given level of international activity.

To compete in the global economy, managers must understand its structure. Mature market economies and systems dominate the global economy today. North America, the European Union, and Pacific Asia are especially important. High potential/high growth economies in eastern Europe, Latin America, the People's Republic of China, India, and Vietnam are increasingly important to managers. The oil-exporting economies in the Middle East are also important.

Many of the challenges of management in a global context are unique issues associated with the international environmental context. These challenges reflect the economic, political/legal, and cultural environments of international management.

Basic issues of competing in a global economy vary according to whether the organization is an MNC, a medium-size organization, or a small organization. In addition, the basic managerial functions of planning, organizing, leading, and controlling must all be addressed in international organizations.

Discussion Questions

Questions for Review

1. Describe the four basic levels of international business activity. Do you think any organization will achieve the fourth level? Why or why not?
2. Summarize the basic structure of the global economy. What are the major changes today occurring within that structure?
3. Briefly note some of the basic environmental challenges of international management.
4. What are the basic cultural differences identified by Hofstede?

Questions for Analysis

5. An organization seeking to expand its international operations must monitor several different environments. Which aspect of each environment is likely to have the greatest impact on decisions involved in such a strategic move? Why?
6. What industries do you think will have the greatest impact on international business? Are there any industries that might not be affected by the trend toward international business? If so, what are they? If there are none, why are there none?
7. You are the CEO of an up-and-coming toy company and have plans to go international soon. What steps would you take to carry out that strategy? What areas would you stress in your decision-making process? How would you organize your company?

Questions for Application

8. Identify a local company that does business abroad. Interview an executive in that company. Why did the company go international? What major obstacles did it face? How successful has that decision been? Share your findings with the class.
9. Go to the library and find some information about the European Union's continued move toward a relaxation of trade barriers. What will be the effect of that relaxation? What will be some of the difficulties? Do you think that it is a good idea? Why or why not?
10. Many organizations fail to allow for cultural and language differences when they do business with other countries. For example, Pepsi was introduced into Asia with the slogan "Come alive with Pepsi." The slogan, however, was translated as "Bring your ancestors back from the dead with Pepsi." Go to the library and locate mistakes made by other companies entering foreign markets. What did they do wrong? How could they have prevented their mistakes?

BUILDING EFFECTIVE *interpersonal* SKILLS

Exercise Overview

Interpersonal skills refer to the manager's ability to communicate with, understand, and motivate individuals and groups. Managers in international organizations must understand how culture and other factors affect how they communicate with other people in different parts of the organization. This exercise will enable you to learn more about your current levels of cultural understanding and to develop insights into areas where you may need additional cultural awareness.

Exercise Task

The task that follows consists of ten statements. Indicate your level of agreement with each statement as described in the instructions below.

Instructions: You will agree with some of the following statements and disagree with others. In some cases, you may find it difficult to make a decision, but you should force a choice. Record your answers next to each statement according to the following scale:

4 Strongly agree   **2** Somewhat disagree

3 Somewhat agree   **1** Strongly disagree

_____ 1. Some areas of Switzerland are very much like Italy.

_____ 2. Although aspects of behavior such as motivation and attitudes within organizational settings remain quite diverse across cultures, organizations themselves appear to be increasingly similar in terms of design and technology.

_____ 3. Spain, France, Japan, Singapore, Mexico, Brazil, and Indonesia have cultures with a strong orientation toward authority.

_____ 4. Japan and Austria define male-female roles more rigidly and value qualities like forcefulness and achievement more than Norway, Sweden, Denmark, and Finland.

_____ 5. Some areas of Switzerland are very much like France.

_____ 6. Australia, Great Britain, the Netherlands, Canada, and New Zealand have cultures that view people first as individuals and place a priority on their own interests and values, whereas Colombia, Pakistan, Taiwan, Peru, Singapore, Mexico, Greece, and Hong Kong have cultures in which the good of the group or society is considered the priority.

_____ 7. The United States, Israel, Austria, Denmark, Ireland, Norway, and New Zealand have cultures with a low orientation toward authority.

_____ 8. The same manager may behave differently in different cultural settings.

_____ 9. Denmark, Canada, Norway, Singapore, Hong Kong, and Australia have cultures in which employees tolerate a high degree of uncertainty, but such levels of uncertainty are not well tolerated in Israel, Austria, Japan, Italy, Argentina, Peru, France, and Belgium.

_____10. Some areas of Switzerland are very much like Germany.

BUILDING EFFECTIVE *technical* SKILLS

Exercise Overview

Technical skills are the skills necessary to accomplish or understand the specific kind of work being done in an organization. Some managers in international businesses must pay attention to fluctuations in currency exchange rates in the countries where the firm does business. These fluctuations affect the financial impact of many different kinds of decisions. This exercise will help you better understand the impact of exchange rates.

Exercise Background

The exchange rates of most major currencies relative to the others are published regularly in newspapers such as the *Wall Street Journal, USA Today,* and the *New York Times.* Locate a recent edition of such a newspaper and determine the exchange rate on that day for U.S. dollars relative to British pounds. (Note that the pound is one of the few currencies that has a value greater than the dollar.)

Next, assume that six months has passed from the date of the exchange rate you have located. Major economic shifts have caused the exchange rate to fluctuate to a level such that one pound is worth one dollar; that is, the exchange rate six months hence will be 1 to 1.

Exercise Task

Using the information gathered above, do the following:

1. Determine the impact of this exchange rate shift on a U.S. tourist visiting England.

2. Determine the impact of the shift on an English tourist visiting the United States.
3. Determine the impact of this shift on a U.S. business that exports its products to England, where they compete with locally made products.
4. Determine the impact of this shift on an English business that exports its products to the United States, where they compete with locally made products.
5. Determine the impact of this shift on a U.S. business that buys raw materials in England, imports them into the United States, and makes products for shipment to Japan.

BUILDING EFFECTIVE *communication* SKILLS

Exercise Overview

Communication skills refer to the manager's ability both to convey ideas and information effectively to others and to receive ideas and information effectively from others. International managers have additional communication complexities due to differences in language, time zones, and so forth. This exercise will enable you to enhance your communication skills by better understanding the impact of different time zones.

Exercise Background

Assume that you are a manager in a large multinational firm. Your office is located in San Francisco. You need to arrange a conference call with several other managers to discuss an upcoming strategic change by your firm. The other man-

agers are located in New York, London, Rome, Moscow, Tokyo, Singapore, and Sydney.

Exercise Task

Using the information above, do the following:
1. Determine the time-zone differences in each of these cities.
2. Assuming that people in each city have a "normal" workday of 8 A.M. to 5 P.M., determine the "optimal" time for your conference call; that is, what time can you place the call and thus minimize the number of people who are inconvenienced?
3. Now assume that you need to visit each office in person. You need to spend one full day in each city. Using the Internet, review airline schedules, account for differences in time zones, and develop an itinerary.

CHAPTER CLOSING CASE

WAL-MART COURTS EUROPEAN SHOPPERS

With a beachhead of stores spread across England and Germany, Wal-Mart is bringing American-style retailing to European shoppers. Already the world's largest retail chain, with $165 billion in global sales, Wal-Mart entered the United Kingdom by buying the Asda chain, which operates more than 230 stores across the country. Wal-Mart

wants its non–U.S. sales to bring in a larger chunk of its overall sales revenue, and Europe is an attractive region for a retailer that knows its business.

The Arkansas-based Wal-Mart began shaking up British retailing by cutting prices, highlighting selection, and promoting friendly service. Because British retailers are accustomed to higher profit margins, the Wal-Mart formula of low markup pricing has put pressure on rival chains such as Tesco and given smaller stores even bigger headaches. Wal-Mart has touched off price wars in food products and other categories, sending competitors scrambling to meet or beat its price tags. Through Asda@Home, the chain's first European Internet shopping site, Wal-Mart is expanding its brand of low-price retailing to reach shoppers in other countries.

In Germany, however, giant discounters are commonplace, so Wal-Mart is basing its competitive strategy there on service and selection. Many German stores have a much narrower merchandise selection than Wal-Mart. Small wonder that shoppers gawk at the huge quantities of food items, from fresh fruits and vegetables to specialty meats and cheeses in Wal-Mart outlets in Dortmund and other cities. As in the United States, the Wal-Mart stores in Germany also carry all sorts of toys, clothing, appliances, and assorted products for household and personal use. Customer service is as much a draw as selection, because service in German stores is much less friendly and personalized. The twin weaknesses of poor selection and poor service leave German retailing open to aggressive competitive attacks from Internet retailers as well as from Wal-Mart.

To enter the German market, Wal-Mart bought ninety-five stores from two struggling local chains and hung an American flag outside each to herald the change in management. Then it began a massive renovation project to enlarge and modernize each outlet. Renovations have proceeded slowly, however. Within three years of the acquisition, fewer than one-third of the stores had been renovated. The renovated stores are definitely more spacious and inviting, with wider aisles, brighter lights, and more accessible shelving loaded with merchandise—all of which is helping to boost sales. Few German stores allow credit payments, so Wal-Mart is successfully attracting shoppers by accepting major credit cards. German shoppers are also pleased at not having to bag their own purchases or pay for the plastic bags at Wal-Mart, amenities that U.S. shoppers take for granted.

Just as visible as the physical changes are the managerial changes. The managers in each Wal-Mart store hold a daily staff meeting to extol new products and motivate store personnel. For example, the comanager of the store in Dortmund, Germany, dressed in a sailor suit when announcing the introduction of a new line of nautical gifts. Knowing that customer service is spotlighted in the chain's television commercials, managers in the German stores encourage good service by praising good performance and keeping communication lines open. Still, even the best service will not make up for cramped stores, so Wal-Mart will have to speed up its renovations if it wants German shoppers to come back and buy—again and again.

Case Questions

1. On which of Hofstede's five dimensions are Wal-Mart's American roots and German operations fairly similar? How do these similarities affect the company's ability to manage its German stores?

2. Why would Wal-Mart choose to operate in Germany and Great Britain on the basis of direct investment rather than through a joint venture or strategic alliance?

3. If you were a retailer in Great Britain or Germany, what would you do to blunt Wal-Mart's competitive advantages?

Case References

Steven Komarow, "Wal-Mart Takes Slow Road in Germany," *USA Today*, May 9, 2000, p. 3B; Kerry Capell and Heidi Dawley, "Wal-Mart's Not-So-Secret British Weapon," *Business Week*, January 24, 2000, http://www.businessweek.com/2000/00_04/b3665095.htm (July 10, 2000).

CHAPTER NOTES

1. "Mickey Stumbles at the Border," *Forbes*, June 12, 2000, p. 58; *The Walt Disney Company Annual Report 1999* (quote on p. 6).
2. See Ricky W. Griffin and Michael Pustay, *International Business*, 3rd Edition (Upper Saddle River, N.J.: Prentice-Hall, 2002) for an overview of international business.
3. Raymond Saner, Lichia Yiu, and Mikael Sondergaard, "Business Diplomacy Management: A Core Competency for Global Companies," *Academy of Management Executive*, 2000, Vol. 14, No. 1, pp. 80–90.
4. For a more complete discussion of forms of international business, see Griffin and Pustay, *International Business*.
5. *Hoover's Handbook of American Business 2000* (Austin, Texas: Hoover's Business Press, 2000), pp. 1266–1267.
6. John H. Dunning, *Multinational Enterprises and the Global Economy* (Wokingham, England: Addison-Wesley, 1993); and Christopher Bartlett and Sumantra Ghoshal, *Transnational Management* (Homewood, Illinois: Irwin, 1992).
7. "A Company Without a Country?" *Business Week*, May 5, 1997, p. 40.
8. "The *Fortune* Global 5 Hundred—The World's Largest Corporations," *Fortune*, July 24, 2000, p. F-1.
9. "The *Fortune* Global 5 Hundred," *Fortune*, July 24, 2000, p. F-1.
10. *Hoover's Handbook of American Business 2000* (Austin, Texas: Hoover's Business Press, 2000), pp. 198–199; 574–575.
11. Christopher A. Bartlett and Sumantra Ghoshal, "Going Global—Lessons from Late Movers," *Harvard Business Review*, March–April 2000, pp. 132–141.
12. "Creating a Worldwide Yen for Japanese Beer," *Financial Times*, October 7, 1994, p. 20.
13. Kenichi Ohmae, "The Global Logic of Strategic Alliances," *Harvard Business Review*, March–April 1989, pp. 143–154.
14. Jeremy Main, "Making Global Alliances Work," *Fortune*, December 17, 1990, pp. 121–126.
15. Hans Mjoen and Stephen Tallman, "Control and Performance in International Joint Ventures," *Organization Science*, May–June 1997, pp. 257–274.
16. "The Border," *Business Week*, May 12, 1997, pp. 64–74.
17. Griffin and Pustay, *International Business*.
18. For an excellent discussion of the effects of NAFTA, see "In the Wake of NAFTA, a Family Firms Sees Business Go South," *The Wall Street Journal*, February 23, 1999, pp. A1, A10.
19. Griffin and Pustay, *International Business*. See also "Overseas Economies Rally, Giving the U.S. a Very Mixed Blessing," *The Wall Street Journal*, August 19, 1999, pp. A1, A8.
20. Eileen P. Gunn, "Emerging Markets," *Fortune*, August 18, 1997, pp. 168–173.
21. "In Many Ways, Return of Hong Kong to China Has Already Happened," *The Wall Street Journal*, June 9, 1997, pp. A1, A2; "How You Can Win in China," *Business Week*, May 26, 1997, pp. 66–68.
22. "Investing in India: Not for the Fainthearted," *Business Week*, August 11, 1997, pp. 46–47.
23. "Argentina Cries Foul as Choice Employers Beat a Path Next Door," *The Wall Street Journal*, May 2, 2000, pp. A1, A8.
24. "GM Is Building Plants in Developing Nations to Woo New Markets," *The Wall Street Journal*, August 4, 1997, pp. A1, A4.
25. For example, see "China Weighs Lifting Curbs on Foreign Firms," *The Wall Street Journal*, January 1, 2000, p. A17.
26. Griffin and Pustay, *International Business*.
27. "Oil Companies Strive to Turn a New Leaf to Save Rain Forest," *The Wall Street Journal*, July 17, 1997, pp. A1, A8.
28. "What If There Weren't Any Clocks to Watch?" *Newsweek*, June 30, 1997, p. 14.
29. Geert Hofstede, *Culture's Consequences: International Differences in Work Related Values* (Beverly Hills, California: Sage, 1980).
30. I have taken the liberty of changing the actual labels applied to each dimension for several reasons. The terms I have chosen to use are more descriptive, simpler, and more self-evident in their meaning.
31. Geert Hofstede, "The Business of International Business Is Culture," *International Business Review*, Vol. 3, No. 1, 1994, pp. 1–14.
32. "Crazy for Crunchies," *Newsweek*, April 28, 1997, p. 49.
33. Stratford Sherman, "Are You as Good as the Best in the World?" *Fortune*, December 13, 1993, pp. 95–96.

CHAPTER 6

The Cultural and Multicultural Environment

Old Navy is clearly one of the funkiest retailers around. Where else, for example, can young consumers buy today's hottest fashions stacked in old freezers, surrounded by old advertising signs, and in the shadows of a vintage Chevrolet at bargain-basement prices? Indeed, Old Navy is growing at the rate of over 100 stores per year and is the current favorite among the budget-minded younger set. And observers give much of the credit for the firm's success to its president, Jenny Ming. For her part, Ming brings to the table a keen understanding of the importance of corporate culture and a sense of fashion tastes that are in tune with a diverse population of younger consumers.

For Ming, the starting point in building a successful business is having a strong foundation built on people. Thus, she populates Old Navy stores with high-energy, fashion-conscious people just like the firm's target consumers. She also encourages everyone to lead a well-balanced life; she herself, for example, doesn't work on weekends and she doesn't expect her staff to, either. Ming also puts a lot of emphasis on teamwork in Old Navy stores and is always on the alert for new ways to get people to work together as a team rather than individually. In short, she wants Old Navy to become *the* place to work among those interested in a retailing job.

Ming also works hard to stay ahead of the game in terms of fashion trends and fads. For example, she was one of the first in the industry to spot the emergence of both baggy cotton cargo pants and fleece pullovers as fashion staples. By relying on her own intuition, she was able to order these and other products in massive quantities before other retailers caught on and then get a head start by establishing a reputation as the first and best place to buy them. Indeed, it seems like Old Navy is the first retailer to pick up on one fashion trend after another.

So, how does Ming do it? She relies on several tactics to learn about and spot emerging fashion trends. For one thing, she watches and talks to her own teen-age daughters and their friends. One daughter, she says, latches on to things just as they are on the verge of becoming a trend, while another picks up on things just as they've peaked. So, Ming might be willing to bet on trends she sees in the first daughter's clothing. But she knows that if it's the other daughter who tries something new that it may be too late.

> *"One thing I know best is when to maximize something. If I believe in something, I'll push it bigger and harder."*
>
> —*Jenny Ming, president of Old Navy*

After studying this chapter, you should be able to:

- Describe the nature of organization and social culture.

- Discuss the importance and determinants of an organization's culture and how the culture can be managed.

- Identify and describe the major trends and dimensions of diversity and multiculturalism in organizations.

- Discuss the primary effects of diversity and multiculturalism in organizations.

- Describe individual and organizational strategies and approaches to managing diversity and multiculturalism.

- Discuss the six characteristics of the fully multicultural organization.

Ming also travels extensively to keep abreast of trends in other parts of the world. For example, she makes regular trips to London, Paris, and New York to observe firsthand what people are wearing in the street cafés and other student hangouts. In addition, she reads fashion magazines voraciously and contracts with various market-research firms to ensure that she has the very latest information about what's going on. And as a result, while Old Navy stores pull in the hip young consumers Ming sees as the firm's bread-and-butter, they also attract older consumers who want to look fashionable, as well as others who are simply looking for good value.

With an eye on the future, Old Navy and Jenny Ming are currently riding a crest of popularity. Old Navy itself is one division of The Gap, a long-time darling of the retailing trade; and Ming, hand-picked by the CEO of The Gap to lead the charge at Old Navy, is widely recognized as one of the industry's rising stars. For her, of course, the trick will be to stay ahead of the pack. And for Old Navy, the trick will be to maintain its popularity and growth rate while avoiding major mistakes. The culture that Ming has created at the firm and her understanding of diverse fashion tastes may not guarantee continued success, but they certainly give the company a great chance to ride the crest of popularity for a while longer yet.[1]

Like many other organizations in the world today, Old Navy faces a variety of challenges, opportunities, and issues in its quest to grow and become an increasingly vital part of the retailing landscape. One key ingredient to the firm's success is the strong and focused culture that president Jenny Ming has created. Another is her keen understanding of diverse consumer tastes and how those cultural tastes translate into fashion trends and fads.

This chapter is about these two broad forms of culture—organization and social. After establishing the similarities and differences between the two, we discuss organization culture first. We then turn to diversity and multiculturalism, in organizations. We begin by describing trends in diversity and multiculturalism, and identify and discuss several common dimensions of diversity. The effects of diversity and multiculturalism on organizations are then explored. We next address individual strategies and organizational approaches for managing diversity and multiculturalism. Finally, we characterize and describe the fully multicultural organization.

The Nature of Organization and Social Culture

organization culture The set of values, beliefs, behaviors, customs, and attitudes that help the members of the organization understand what it stands for, how it does things, and what it considers important.

At its most general level, *culture* refers to the collection of values, beliefs, behaviors, customs, and attitudes that characterize a community of people. Such a community can range from a small group of individuals to an entire nation. Our interests here start with culture at the organizational level. Thus, since the members of an organization can be viewed as a community, the organization they comprise will have its own unique community. **Organization culture**, therefore, is the set of values, beliefs, behaviors, customs, and attitudes that help the members of the organization understand what it stands for, how it does things, and what it considers important.[2]

At a much broader level, culture can also be used to characterize the community of people who comprise an entire society. Some of the basic managerial issues associated with doing business across cultures were introduced and explored in Chapter. 5. But a different set of issues involving social culture also arises within the boundaries of an organization. That is, when the people comprising an organization represent different cultures, their differences in values, beliefs, behaviors, customs, and attitudes pose unique opportunities and challenges for managers. These broad issues are generally referred to as **multiculturalism**.

multiculturalism The broad issues associated with differences in values, beliefs, behaviors, customs, and attitudes held by people in different cultures.

diversity Exists in a group or organization when its members differ from one another along one or more important dimensions such as age, gender, or ethnicity

A related area of interest is diversity. **Diversity** exists in a community of people when its members differ from one another along one or more important dimensions. These differences can obviously reflect the multicultural composition of a community. In the business world, however, the term *diversity* per se is more generally used to refer to demographic differences among people within a culture—differences in gender, age, and so forth. Diversity is not an absolute phenomenon, of course, wherein a group or organization is or is not diverse. Instead, diversity can be conceptualized as a continuum. If everyone in the community is exactly

An organization's culture plays a vital and fundamental role in its successes and failures. Khai Minh Phan is the founder and CEO of Easy PlaNet, an Internet start-up firm that is constructing a new kind of web portal intended to compete with Yahoo! and other existing portals. Mr. Phan is shown here leading a discussion about strategic issues with his managers at his home in California. Even if PlaNet succeeds and grows to become a major corporation with dozens of foreign subsidiaries, each employing thousands of people, its culture will have been largely formed from these early intense and exciting brainstorming sessions.

like everyone else, there is no diversity whatsoever. If everyone is different along every imaginable dimension, total diversity exists. In reality, of course, these extremes are more hypothetical than real. Most settings are characterized by a level of diversity somewhere between these extremes. Therefore, diversity should be thought of in terms of degree or level along relevant dimensions.

Organization culture, multiculturalism, and diversity are all closely related to one another. For example, the culture of an organization will affect the levels of diversity and multiculturalism that exist within its boundaries. Old Navy, for example, has an open culture that promotes diversity throughout its business. And similarities and differences arising from diversity and multicultural forces will also influence the culture of an organization. Social culture and diversity are also interrelated. For example, the norms reflected in a social culture will partially determine how that culture values demographic differences among people of that culture.

Each of these levels of culture represents important opportunities and challenges for managers. As we will see, if managers effectively understand, appreciate, and manage their organization's culture, diversity, and multiculturalism, their organization is more likely to be effective. But if managers ignore cultural forces or, even worse, attempt to circumvent or control them, then their organization is almost certain to experience serious problems.

MANAGEMENT IMPLICATIONS Managers need to have a clear understanding of organizational culture, multiculturalism, and the relationship between the two.

The Organization's Culture

Culture is an amorphous concept that defies objective measurement or observation. Nevertheless, because it is the foundation of the organization's internal environment, it plays a major role in shaping managerial behavior.

The Importance of Organization Culture

Executives at Ford Motor Company recently decided to move the firm's Lincoln Mercury division from Detroit to southern California. Interestingly, though, this move had little to do with costs or any of the other reasons most business relocations occur. Instead, they wanted to move Lincoln Mercury out from the corporate shadow of its dominating bigger corporate cousin, Ford itself. For years, Lincoln Mercury managers had complained that their business was always given short shrift and that most of Detroit's attention was focused on Ford. At least partially as a result, Mercury products all tended to look like clones of Ford products, and the division consistently failed to meet its goals or live up to its expectations. Finally, the company decided that the only way to turn the division around was to give it its own identity. And where better to start than by moving the whole operation—lock, stock, and barrel—to car-centric southern California, where its managers could be freer to hire new creative talent and start carving out a new and unique business niche for themselves.[3] In short, they wanted to create a new culture.

While all organizations have a culture, each one is also unique. Take the Peter Morgan Band, for instance. Morgan and some of his amateur musician co-workers at Intel composed a little number called "The Cubicle Blues," poking fun at their Intel workspaces. After they started playing it at corporate parties, it quickly embedded itself into Intel's culture. And today, Intel flies the band all over the world to perform at company meetings and charity events.

Culture determines the "feel" of the organization. The stereotypic image of Microsoft, for example, is a workplace where people dress very casually and work very long hours. In contrast, the image of Bank of America, for some observers, is a formal setting with rigid work rules and people dressed in conservative business attire. And Texas Instruments likes to talk about its "shirt-sleeve" culture, in which ties are avoided and few managers ever wear jackets. Southwest Airlines maintains a culture that stresses fun and excitement. The firm's CEO, Herb Kelleher, explains the company's emphasis on fun in an orientation video set to rap music.

Of course, the same culture is not necessarily found throughout an entire organization. For example, the sales and marketing department may have a culture quite different from that of the operations and manufacturing department. Regardless of its nature, however, culture is a powerful force in organizations, one that can shape the firm's overall effectiveness and long-term success. Companies that can develop and maintain a strong culture, such as Hewlett-Packard and Procter & Gamble, tend to be more effective than companies that have trouble developing and maintaining a strong culture, such as Kmart.[4]

Determinants of Organization Culture

Where does an organization's culture come from? Typically it develops and blossoms over a long period of time. Its starting point is often the organization's founder. For example, James Cash Penney believed in treating employees and customers with respect and dignity. Employees at J.C. Penney are still called associates rather than employees (to reflect partnership), and customer satisfaction is of paramount importance. The impact of Sam Walton, Ross Perot, and Walt Disney is still felt in the organizations they founded.[5] As an organization grows, its culture is modified, shaped, and refined by symbols, stories, heroes, slogans, and ceremonies. For example, an important value at Hewlett-Packard (HP) is the avoidance of bank debt. A popular story still told at the company involves a new project being considered for several years. All objective criteria indicated that HP should borrow money from a bank to finance it, yet Bill Hewlett and David Packard rejected it out of hand simply because "HP avoids bank debt." This story, involving two corporate heroes and based on a slogan, dictates corporate culture today. And many decisions at Walt Disney Company today are still framed by asking, "What would Walt have done?"

"I don't know how it started, either. All I know is that it's part of our corporate culture."

Corporate success and shared experiences also shape culture. For example, Hallmark Cards has a strong culture derived from its years of success in the greeting cards industry. Employees speak of the Hallmark family and care deeply about the company; many of them have worked at the company for years. At Kmart, in contrast, the culture is quite weak, the management team changes rapidly, and few people sense any direction or purpose in the company. The differences in culture at Hallmark and Kmart are in part attributable to past successes and shared experiences.

An organization's culture can be determined in a variety of ways. Symbols, stories, heroes, slogans, and ceremonies, for example, all play a role in defining and continuing culture. Sometimes, however, the meaning of some element of culture can become blurred or even forgotten over time. As illustrated here, some organizations do things simply because they "always have," even to the point where these things become institutionalized standard practices. And occasionally, some of these things may even border on the absurd!

Managing Organization Culture

How can managers deal with culture, given its clear importance but intangible nature? Essentially, the manager must understand the current culture and then decide if it should be maintained or changed. By understanding the organization's current culture, managers can take appropriate actions. At Hewlett-Packard, the values represented by "the HP way" still exist and guide most important activities undertaken by the firm. Indeed, the firm's CEO, Carly Fiorina, launched her tenure at the firm with a series of television commercials focusing on the firm's Silicon Valley roots and the garage where it started. Culture can also be maintained by rewarding and promoting people whose behaviors are consistent with the existing culture and by articulating the culture through slogans, ceremonies, and so forth. *The World of Management* describes how Merrill Lynch has extended its famed organizational culture into its foreign offices.

But managers must walk a fine line between maintaining a culture that still works effectively versus changing a culture that has become dysfunctional. For example, many of the firms already noted, as well as numerous others, take pride in perpetuating their cultures. Shell Oil Company, for example, has an elaborate display in the lobby of its Houston headquarters building that tells the story of the firm's past. But other companies may face situations in which their culture is no longer a strength. For example, some critics feel that the organization culture at General Motors places too much emphasis on product development and internal competition among divisions and not enough on marketing and competition with other firms.

WORLD OF MANAGEMENT

SPREADING THE MERRILL LYNCH CULTURE

Merrill Lynch & Co. is the largest brokerage operation in the United States. Ever since Charles Merrill and Edmund Lynch formed the company in 1914, the firm has focused its attention on individual investors and has based its operations on customer service. A manager who has been totally immersed in the company's culture heads each local Merrill Lynch office. These managers start as assistants in existing offices to learn the ropes and then go through an extended series of training programs at the firm's training center in Princeton, New Jersey. One ongoing component of this training focuses on the firm's culture—where it started and how it is to be perpetuated.

In the last several years Merrill Lynch has been undergoing a major expansion into international markets. Fueled in part by opening new offices and in part by buying existing brokerage firms, Merrill Lynch has become one of the largest retail brokerage companies in the world. When this expansion started, many of the firm's competitors doubted that it would be able to transfer its culture abroad. But, so far at least, these skeptics are wrong.

Merrill Lynch knew from the beginning of its internationalization efforts that sustaining its culture would be both important and difficult. Therefore, the company made the same commitment to global training as it makes to training its local managers—each and every Merrill Lynch office manager from foreign offices receives the same level of training as the firm's domestic managers receive. And like domestic managers, international managers receive continued exposure to the firm's heritage and culture. As a result, company executives say, the organization culture of any Merrill Lynch office, regardless of where it is, remains true to the spirit of the company's founders.

> *Visit our offices, whether it be Thailand, Malaysia, South Africa, or Germany, and you will see the same plaques on the wall with those same Merrill Principles in the local language.*
>
> —David H. Komansky, Merrill Lynch CEO*

References: "In a Matter of Months, Merrill Sets Itself Up as a Force in Japan," *The Wall Street Journal*, April 8, 1998, pp. A1, A10; "Merrillizing the World," *Forbes*, February 10, 1997, pp. 146–151 (*quote on p. 147); Shawn Tully, "Merrill Lynch Takes Over," *Fortune*, April 27, 1999, pp. 138–144.

Culture problems sometimes arise from mergers or the growth of rival factions within an organization. For example, Wells Fargo and Company, which relies heavily on snazzy technology and automated banking services, acquired another large bank, First Interstate, which had focused more attention on personal services and customer satisfaction. Blending the two disparate organization cultures was difficult for the firm as managers have argued over how best to serve customers and operate the new enterprise.[6]

To change culture, managers must have a clear idea of what they want to create. Schwinn has tried to redefine itself to be more competitive and to break free of its old approaches to doing business. The firm's new motto—"Established 1895. Re-established 1994."—represents an effort to create a new culture that better reflects today's competitive environment in the bicycle market. Likewise, when Continental Airlines "re-invented" itself a few years ago, employees were taken outside the corporate headquarters building in Houston to watch the firm's old policies and procedures manuals set afire. The firm's new strategic direction is known throughout Continental as the "Go Forward" plan, intentionally named to avoid reminding people about the firm's troubled past and to focus instead on the future.

One major way to shape culture is by bringing outsiders into important managerial positions. The choice of a new CEO from outside the organization is often a clear signal that things will be changing. Indeed, new CEOs were the catalyst for the changes at Schwinn and Continental noted above. Adopting new slogans, telling new stories, staging new ceremonies, and breaking with tradition can also alter culture. Culture can also be changed by methods discussed in Chapter 13.[7] We now turn our attention to other related parts of the cultural environment of management: diversity and multiculturalism.

MANAGEMENT Managers need to have a clear understanding and apprecia-
IMPLICATIONS tion of the importance of organization culture. In addition, they need to know how culture is determined. They should also understand how to manage organization culture.

Diversity and Multiculturalism in Organizations

As introduced and defined earlier in this chapter, diversity and multiculturalism essentially relate to differences among people. Because organizations today are becoming more diverse and multicultural, it is important that all managers understand the major trends and dimensions of diversity and multiculturalism.

Trends in Diversity and Multiculturalism

The most fundamental trend in diversity and multiculturalism is that virtually all organizations, simply put, are becoming more diverse and multicultural. The

Figure 6.1

Reasons for Increasing Diversity and Multiculturalism

Diversity and multiculturalism are increasing in most organizations today for four basic reasons. These reasons promise to make diversity even greater in the future.

composition of their workforces is changing in many different ways. The basic reasons for this trend are illustrated in Figure 6.1.

One factor contributing specifically to increased diversity is changing demographics in the labor force. As more women and minorities enter the labor force, for example, the available pool of talent from which organizations hire employees has changed in both size and composition. If talent within each segment of the labor pool is evenly distributed (for example, if the number of very talented men in the workforce as a percentage of all men in the workforce is the same as the number of very talented women in the labor force as a percentage of all women in the workforce), it follows logically that, over time, proportionately more women and proportionately fewer men will be hired by an organization.

A related factor contributing to diversity is the increased awareness by organizations that they can improve the overall quality of their workforce by hiring and promoting the most talented people available. By casting a broader net in recruiting and looking beyond traditional sources for new employees, organizations are finding more broadly qualified and better qualified employees from many different segments of society. Thus, these organizations are finding that diversity can be a source of competitive advantage.[8]

Another reason for the increase in diversity is that legislation and legal actions have forced organizations to hire more broadly. In earlier times, organizations in the United States were essentially free to discriminate against women, blacks, and other minorities. While not all organizations consciously and/or openly engaged in these practices, many firms nevertheless came to be dominated by white males. But starting with the passage of the Civil Rights Act in 1964, numerous laws have outlawed discrimination against African Americans and most other groups. As we detail in Chapter 14, organizations must hire and promote people today solely on the basis of their qualifications.

A final factor contributing to increased multiculturalism in particular is the globalization movement. Organizations that have opened offices and related facilities in other countries have had to learn to deal with different customs, social norms, and mores. Strategic alliances and foreign ownership also contribute because managers today are more likely to have job assignments in other countries and/or to work with foreign managers within their own countries. As employees and managers move from assignment to assignment across national boundaries, organizations and their subsidiaries within each country thus become more diverse and multicultural.

Dimensions of Diversity and Multiculturalism

As we indicated earlier, many different dimensions of diversity and multiculturalism can characterize an organization. In this section we discuss age, gender, ethnicity, and other dimensions of diversity.

Age Distributions   One important dimension of diversity in any organization is the age distribution of its workers. The average age of the U.S. workforce is gradually increasing and will continue to do so for the next several years. Figure 6.2 presents age distributions for U.S. workers in 1999 and projected age distributions through the year 2025; over that span the median age is expected to rise from 35.5 years to 38 years.

Several factors are contributing to this pattern. For one, the baby-boom generation (a term used to describe the unusually large number of people who were born in the twenty-year period after World War II) continues to age. Declining birth rates among the post-baby-boom generations simultaneously account for smaller percentages of new entrants into the labor force. Another factor that contributes to the aging workforce is improved health and medical care. As a result of these improvements, people are able to remain productive and active for longer periods of time. Combined with higher legal limits for mandatory retirement, more and more people are working beyond the age at which they might have retired just a few years ago.

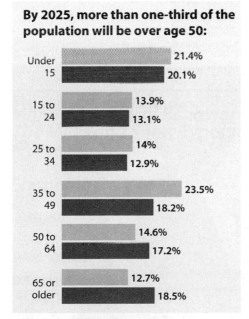

By 2025, more than one-third of the population will be over age 50:

Age	1999	2025
Under 15	21.4%	20.1%
15 to 24	13.9%	13.1%
25 to 34	14%	12.9%
35 to 49	23.5%	18.2%
50 to 64	14.6%	17.2%
65 or older	12.7%	18.5%

■ 1999 ■ 2025

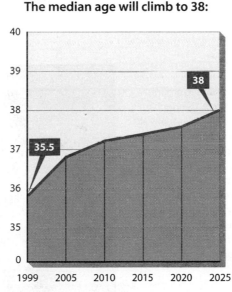

The median age will climb to 38:

35.5 → 38 (1999, 2005, 2010, 2015, 2020, 2025)

Figure 6.2

Age Distribution Trends in the United States

The U.S. population is gradually growing older. For example, in 1999 the median age in the United States was 35.5 years; by 2025, however, this figure will rise to 38 years. By that same year, more than one-third of the entire U.S. population will be over age 50.

Source: U.S. Census Bureau as reported in *USA Today,* September 7, 1999, p. 13A. Copyright 1999, *USA Today.* Reprinted with permission.

How does this trend affect organizations? Older workers tend to have more experience, to be more stable, and to make greater contributions to productivity than younger workers. On the other hand, despite the improvements in health and medical care, older workers are nevertheless likely to require higher levels of insurance coverage and medical benefits. And the declining labor pool of younger workers will continue to pose problems for organizations as they find fewer potential new entrants into the labor force.[9]

Gender   As more and more women have entered the workforce, organizations have subsequently experienced changes in the relative proportions of male and female employees. In the United States, for example, the workforce in 1964 was 66 percent male and 34 percent female. In 1994 the relative proportions had changed to 54 percent male and 46 percent female. By the year 2000 the proportions were around 52 percent male and 48 percent female.

glass ceiling A barrier that keeps women from advancing to top management positions in many organizations

These trends aside, a major gender-related problem that many organizations face today is the so-called glass ceiling. The **glass ceiling** describes a barrier that keeps women from advancing to top management positions in many organizations.[10] This ceiling is a real barrier that is difficult to break, but it is also so subtle that it is hard to discern. Indeed, whereas women comprise almost 45 percent of all managers, there are very few female CEOs among the one thousand largest businesses in the United States. Similarly, the average pay of women in organizations is lower than that of men. Although the pay gap is gradually shrinking, inequalities are present nonetheless. *Management InfoTech* explains how the gender gap is an especially big problem in some high-tech firms.

Many different dimensions of diversity are relevant in organizations today. Gender is among the most significant. Gender barriers are being broken almost every day at all levels in virtually all organizations as women and men increasingly move into positions that have traditionally been dominated by one gender or the other. One area where it has been particularly difficult for women to advance has been the wine industry, traditionally a tightly controlled male bastion. However, Michaela Rodeno has made it to the top spot in France's St. Supery U.S. subsidiary. Indeed, she and several other women have recently assumed executive positions in leading wine producing and distributing firms, both in the United States and in Europe.

MANAGEMENT INFOTECH

THE MALE NERD CULTURE OF SILICON VALLEY

In the work-hard, play-hard environment of California's Silicon Valley, eligible single women are almost as scarce as snow. As a result, too many engineering or programming nerds in dot-coms or software start-ups have hot cars and stock options but few dates. Why? In most areas of the United States, unmarried women outnumber unmarried men. However, the situation is reversed in Santa Clara County. Attracted by the infotech opportunities, this area contains sixty-eight thousand more single men than women.

Given the long hours and dedication that infotech careers demand, many men and women have very little free time for romance. When two people do manage to connect, the intense competition among area firms complicates matters even further. To protect themselves and their employers, the two may ask each other to sign nondisclosure agreements—forbidding any outside discussion of company secrets—before they start to date.

Not surprisingly, dating services, singles mixers, and matchmakers in the area are doing a booming business as men go on the hunt for potential partners. Silicon Valley is so lopsidedly male that some recruiters are concerned about being able to attract a steady influx of talented single men for local high-tech jobs. In fact, some men have already switched jobs, moving to Boston and other infotech zones in search of a better ratio of unattached women to unattached men. For their part, women in Silicon Valley are enjoying their after-hours popularity—working in the male nerd culture is not a problem for them.

> *This is the best time in history to be a woman in Northern California.*
>
> —*Nicole Lorenzo, Stanford Graduate School of Business student**

References: Michelle Conlin, "Valley of No Dolls," *Business Week,* March 6, 2000, pp. 126, 129 (*quote on p. 126); Joel Dreyfuss, "Valley of Denial," *Fortune,* July 19, 1999, pp. 60–61.

Why does the glass ceiling still seem to exist? One reason may be that real obstacles to advancement for women, such as subtle discrimination, may still exist in some organizations.[11] Another is that many talented women choose to leave their jobs in large organizations and start their own businesses. Still another factor is that some women choose to suspend or slow their career progression to have children. But there are also many talented women continuing to work their way up the corporate ladder and getting closer and closer to a corporate "top spot."[12]

Ethnicity   A third major dimension of cultural diversity in organizations is enthnicity. **Ethnicity** refers to the ethnic composition of a group or organization. Within the United States, most organizations reflect varying degrees of ethnicity comprising whites, African Americans, Hispanics, and Asians. Figure 6.3 shows the ethnic composition of the U.S. workforce in 1999 and projections for the year 2025 in terms of these ethnic groups.[13]

The biggest projected changes involve whites and Hispanics. In particular, the percentage of whites in the workforce is expected to drop from 72 percent to 62.4 percent. At the same time, the percentage of Hispanics is expected to climb from 11.5 percent to 17.6 percent. The percentages of African Americans, Asians, and

ethnicity The ethnic composition of a group or organization

Figure 6.3

Ethnicity Distribution Trends in the United States

Ethnic diversity in the United States is also increasing. For example, while 72 percent of the U.S. population was white in 1999, this will drop to 62.4 percent by 2025. Hispanics will reflect the largest percentage increase, moving from 11.5 percent in 1999 to 17.6 percent of the U.S. population by 2025.

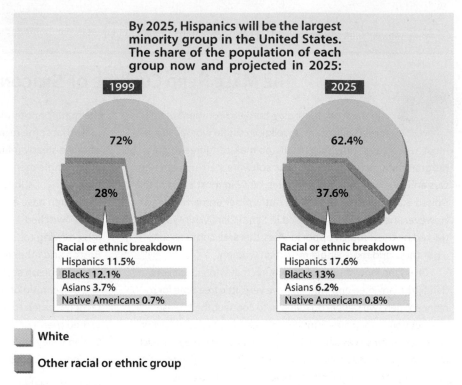

By 2025, Hispanics will be the largest minority group in the United States. The share of the population of each group now and projected in 2025:

1999

72%

28%

Racial or ethnic breakdown
Hispanics **11.5%**
Blacks **12.1%**
Asians **3.7%**
Native Americans **0.7%**

2025

62.4%

37.6%

Racial or ethnic breakdown
Hispanics **17.6%**
Blacks **13%**
Asians **6.2%**
Native Americans **0.8%**

■ **White**

■ **Other racial or ethnic group**

Source: U.S. Census Bureau as reported in *USA Today,* September 7, 1999, p. 13A. Copyright 1999, *USA Today.* Reprinted with permission.

others are also expected to climb, but at lower rates. As with women, members of the African American, Hispanic, and Asian groups are generally underrepresented in the executive ranks of most organizations today. And their pay is similarly lower than might be expected. But as is the case for women, the differences are gradually disappearing as organizations fully embrace equal employment opportunity and recognize the higher overall level of talent available to them.[14]

Other Dimensions of Diversity   In addition to age, gender, and ethnicity, organizations are also confronting other dimensions of diversity. Handicapped and physically challenged employees are increasingly important in many organizations, especially since the recent passage of the Americans with Disabilities Act. Different religious beliefs also constitute an important dimension of diversity.[15] And single parents, dual-career couples, gays and lesbians, people with special dietary preferences (e.g., vegetarians), and people with different political ideologies and viewpoints also represent major dimensions of diversity in today's organizations.[16]

Multicultural Differences   In addition to these various diversity-related dimensions, organizations are increasingly being characterized by multicultural differences as well. Some organizations, especially international businesses, are actively seeking to enhance the multiculturalism of their workforce. But even organizations that are more passive in this regard may still become more multicultural because of changes in the external labor market. Immigration into the United States is at its highest rate since 1910, for example. Over five million people from Asia, Mexico, Europe, and other parts of the world entered the United States between 1991 and 1995.[17]

MANAGEMENT
IMPLICATIONS
Managers should be thoroughly familiar with recent trends in diversity and multiculturalism. In addition, they should understand the basic dimensions of diversity and multiculturalism in organizations.

■ Effects of Diversity and Multiculturalism in Organizations

There is no question that organizations are becoming ever more diverse and multicultural. But how does this affect organizations? As we see, diversity and management provide both opportunities and challenges for organizations. They also play a number of important roles in organizations today.

Multiculturalism and Competitive Advantage

Many organizations are finding that diversity and multiculturalism can be sources of competitive advantage in the marketplace. In general, six arguments have been proposed for how they contribute to competitiveness.[18] These arguments are illustrated in Figure 6.4.

The *cost argument* suggests that organizations that learn to manage diversity and multiculturalism generally have higher levels of productivity and lower levels of turnover and absenteeism. Those organizations that do a poor job of managing diversity and multiculturalism, on the other hand, suffer from problems of lower productivity and higher levels of turnover and absenteeism. Because each of these factors has a direct impact on costs, the former organization remains more competitive than does the latter. Ortho Pharmaceutical Corporation estimates that it has saved $500,000 by lowering turnover among women and ethnic minorities.[19]

The *resource acquisition argument* suggests that organizations who manage diversity and multiculturalism effectively become known among women and minorities as good places to work. These organizations are thus better able to attract qualified employees from among these groups. Given the increased importance of these groups in the overall labor force, organizations that can attract talented employees from all segments of society

Figure 6.4

How Diversity and Multiculturalism Promote Competitive Advantage

Many organizations today are finding that diversity and multiculturalism can be sources of competitive advantage. Various arguments have been developed to support this viewpoint. For example, an African-American sales representative for Revlon helped that firm improve its packaging and promotion for its line of darker skin-tone cosmetics.

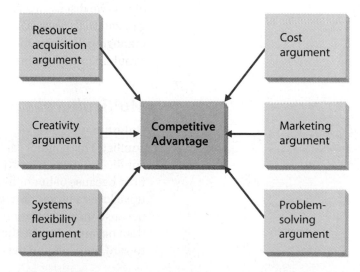

are likely to be more competitive. Table 6.1 lists companies that have an especially good reputation for minorities to work.

The *marketing argument* suggests that organizations with diverse and multicultural workforces are better able to understand different market segments than are less diverse organizations. For example, a cosmetics firm like Avon that wants to sell its products to women and African Americans can better understand how to create such products and effectively market them if women and African-American managers are available to provide input into product development, design, packaging, advertising, and so forth.[20] Both Sears and Target have profited by focusing part of their marketing efforts on building consumer awareness among Hispanics.[21]

The *creativity argument* suggests that organizations with diverse and multicultural workforces are generally more creative and innovative than other organizations. If an organization is dominated by one population segment, it follows that its members will generally adhere to norms and ways of thinking that reflect that segment. Moreover, they have little insight or stimulus for new ideas that might be derived from different perspectives. The diverse and multicultural organization, in contrast, is characterized by multiple perspectives and ways of thinking and is therefore more likely to generate new ideas and ways of doing things.[22]

Related to the creativity argument is the *problem-solving argument*. Diversity and multiculturalism are accompanied by an increased pool of information. In virtually any organization, there is some information that everyone has and other information that is unique to each individual. In an organization with little diversity, the larger pool of information is common and the smaller pool is unique. But in a more diverse organization, the pool of unique information is larger. Thus, because more information can be brought to bear on a problem, there is a higher probability that better solutions can be identified.[23]

Finally, the *systems flexibility argument* suggests that organizations must become more flexible as a way of managing a diverse and multicultural workforce. As a direct consequence, the overall organizational system also becomes more flexible. As we discuss in Chapters 3 and 13, organizational flexibility enables the organization to respond better to changes in its environment. Thus, by effectively managing diversity and multiculturalism within its workforce, an organization simultaneously becomes better equipped to address its environment.

Multiculturalism and Conflict

Unfortunately, diversity and multiculturalism in an organization can also create conflict. This conflict can arise for a variety of reasons.[24] One potential avenue for conflict is when an individual thinks that someone has been hired, promoted, or fired because of her or his diversity status. For example, suppose that a male executive loses a promotion to a female executive. If he believes that she was promoted because the organization simply wanted to have more female managers rather than because she was the better candidate for the job, he will likely feel resentful toward both her and the organization itself.

Table 6.1

America's Best Companies for Minorities

Rank 2000 (1999) Company 1999 revenues (millions)	No. of Minorities			Percentages that Are Minorities		Minorities as a Percentage of New Hires
	Board of Directors	Top Fifty Paid	Officials and Managers	Total Workforce	Asian, Black, Hispanic, Native American	
1 (6) **Advantica** Spartanburg, S.C. $1,735	4 of 11	8	33.4%	49.9%	4.3% 10.6% 34.7% 0.3%	69%
2 (*) **Levi Strauss & Co.** San Francisco $6,000	2 of 12	7	35.3%	58%	6.9% 9.2% 41.6% 0.3%	51%
3 (2) **Fannie Mae** Washington D.C. $36,969	N.A.	8	27.6%	40.2%	9.6% 26.3% 4.0% 0.2%	46%
4 (4) **Sempra Energy** San Diego $5,435	5 of 16	6	27.9%	47.1%	7.7% 11.0% 27.7% 0.7%	45%
5 (*) **Dole Food** Westlake Village, CA $5,061	1 of 7	17	36.6%	55.6%	38.9% 1.6% 14.7% 0.4%	71%
6 (1) **Union Bank of California** San Francisco $2,749	4 of 14	6	35.7%	54%	25.9% 8.4% 19.3% 0.4%	61%
7 (3) **Public Service Co. of N.M.** Albuquerque $1,158	3 of 9	9	32.1%	47.1%	0.6% 1.7% 40.7% 4.2%	51%
8 (*) **Avis Rent A Car** Garden City, N.Y. $3,333	2 of 11	5	25%	48%	6.0% 25.9% 15.5% 0.6%	63%
9 (*) **U.S. Postal Service** Washington, D.C. $62,726	2 of 11	11	30%	35.7%	6.4% 21.5% 7.2% 0.5%	50%
10 (7) **SBC Communications** San Antonio $49,489	4 of 24	4	26.1%	34.4%	3.7% 18.4% 11.7% 0.7%	52%
11 (20) **Xerox** Stamford, Conn. $19,228	2 of 16	10	23.4%	28.7%	5.2% 15.4% 7.4% 0.7%	40%

N.A. Not Available

*Not on last year's list.

Source: *Fortune*, July 10, 2000, pp. 190–193. © Time Inc. All rights reserved.

Another source of conflict stemming from diversity or multiculturalism is through misunderstood, misinterpreted, or inappropriate interactions between people of different groups.[25] For example, suppose that a male executive tells a sexually explicit joke to a new female executive. He may intentionally be trying to embarrass her, he may be clumsily trying to show her that he treats everyone the same, or he may think he is making her feel like part of the team. Regardless of his intent, however, if she finds the joke offensive, she will justifiably feel anger and hostility. These feelings may be directed at only the offending individual or more generally toward the entire organization if she believes that its culture facilitates such behaviors. And, of course, sexual harassment itself is both unethical and illegal.

Conflict can also arise as a result of other elements of multiculturalism. For example, when a U.S. manager publicly praises the work of a Japanese employee for his outstanding work, the action stems from the dominant cultural belief in the United States that such recognition is important and rewarding. But because the Japanese culture places a much higher premium on group loyalty and identity than on individual accomplishment, the employee will likely feel ashamed and embarrassed. Thus, a well-intentioned action may backfire and result in unhappiness. A joint venture among IBM (a U.S. company), Siemens (a German company), and Toshiba (a Japanese company) had difficulties attributed to cultural differences in work hours, working styles, interpersonal relations, and conflict.[26]

Conflict may also arise as a result of fear, distrust, or individual prejudice. Members of the dominant group in an organization may worry that newcomers from other groups pose a personal threat to their own position in the organization. For example, when U.S. firms have been taken over by Japanese firms, U.S. managers have sometimes been resentful or hostile to Japanese managers assigned to work with them. People may also be unwilling to accept people who are different from themselves. And personal bias and prejudices are still very real among some people today and can lead to potentially harmful conflict.

Several high-profile problems involving diversity and multiculturalism focused attention on the potential for conflict and how important it is that managers respond appropriately when problems occur. Shoney's Inc., a southern restaurant chain, was charged with racism throughout its managerial ranks. Denny's, another restaurant business, was charged with similar practices. At Texaco, senior executives used racial slurs on a tape subsequently released to the public. And a class-action lawsuit against the financial brokerage giant Smith Barney alleged widespread hostilities and discrimination toward women throughout the firm.[27] In each of these cases, fortunately, the organizations involved have undertaken major programs designed to eliminate such problems in the future.

MANAGEMENT IMPLICATIONS All managers need to know the effects of diversity and multiculturalism in organizations. In particular, they need to appreciate how multiculturalism can provide a basis for competitive advantage. They must also understand how multiculturalism can result in conflict.

■ *Managing Diversity and Multiculturalism in Organizations*

Because of the tremendous potential that diversity and multiculturalism hold for competitive advantage, as well as the possible consequences of associated conflict, much attention has been focused in recent years on how individuals and organizations can manage diversity and multiculturalism better. In the sections that follow, we first discuss individual strategies for dealing with diversity and multiculturalism and then summarize organizational approaches to managing both.

Individual Strategies

One important element of managing diversity and multiculturalism in an organization consists of what individuals themselves can do. The four basic attitudes that individuals can strive for are understanding, empathy, tolerance, and willingness to communicate.

Understanding   The first of these is understanding the nature and meaning of diversity and multiculturalism. Some managers, for example, have taken the basic concepts of equal employment opportunity to an unnecessary extreme. They know that, by law, they cannot discriminate against people on the basis of sex, race, and so forth. Thus, in following this mandate they come to believe that they must treat everyone the same.

But this belief can cause problems when translated into workplace behaviors among people after they have been hired because people are not the same. Although people need to be treated fairly and equitably, managers must understand that differences among people do, in fact, exist. Thus, any effort to treat everyone the same, without regard to their fundamental human differences, will only lead to problems. Managers must understand that cultural factors cause people to behave in different ways and that these differences should be accepted.

Empathy   Related to understanding is empathy. People in an organization should try to understand the perspective of others. For example, suppose a woman joins a group that has traditionally been comprised of white men. Each man may be a little self-conscious about how to act toward the new member and may be interested in making her feel comfortable and welcome. But they may be able to do this even more effectively by empathizing with how she may feel. For example, she may feel disappointed or elated about her new assignment, she may be confident or nervous about her position in the group, and she may be experienced or inexperienced in working with male colleagues. By learning more about her feelings, the group members can further facilitate their ability to work together effectively.

Tolerance   A third related individual approach to dealing with diversity and multiculturalism is tolerance. Even though people learn to understand others, and even though they may try to empathize with others, the fact remains that they may still not accept or enjoy some aspect of their behavior. For example, one organization reported that it had experienced considerable conflict among its U.S. and Israeli employees. The Israeli employees always seemed to want to argue about every issue that arose. The U.S. managers preferred to conduct business more harmoniously and became uncomfortable with the conflict. Finally, after considerable discussion it was learned that many of the Israeli employees simply enjoyed arguing and saw it as part of getting work done. The firm's U.S. employees do not enjoy the arguing, but they are more willing to tolerate it as a fundamental cultural difference between themselves and their colleagues from Israel.[28]

Willingness to Communicate   A final individual approach to dealing with diversity and multiculturalism is communication. Problems often get magnified over these issues because people are afraid or otherwise unwilling to discuss openly issues that relate to diversity or multiculturalism. For example, suppose that a young employee has a habit of making jokes about the age of an elderly colleague. Perhaps the young colleague means no harm and is just engaging in what she sees as good-natured kidding. But the older employee may find the jokes offensive. If the two do not communicate, the jokes will continue and the resentment will grow. Eventually, what started as a minor problem may erupt into a much bigger one.

For communication to work, it must be two-way. If a person wonders if a certain behavior on her or his part is offensive to someone else, the curious individual should just ask. Similarly, if someone is offended by the behavior of another person, he or she should explain to the offending individual how the behavior is perceived and request that it stop. As long as such exchanges are friendly, low key, and nonthreatening, they will generally have a positive outcome. Of course, if the same message is presented in an overly combative manner or if a person continues to engage in offensive behavior after having been asked to stop, problems will only escalate. At this point, third parties within the organization may have to intervene. And in fact, most organizations today have one or more systems in place to address questions and problems that arise as a result of diversity. We now turn our attention to various ways that organizations can indeed better manage diversity.

Organizational Approaches

Whereas individuals are important in managing diversity and multiculturalism, the organization itself must play a fundamental role.[29] Through its various policies and practices, people in the organization come to understand what behaviors are and are not appropriate. Diversity and multicultural training is an even more direct method for managing diversity. And the organization's culture is the ultimate context from which diversity and multiculturalism must be addressed.

Organizational Policies   The starting point in managing diversity and multiculturalism is the policies that an organization adopts to affect, directly or indirectly, how people are treated. Obviously, for instance, the extent to which an organization embraces the premise of equal employment opportunity will determine to a large extent the potential diversity within an organization. But the organization that follows the law to the letter and practices only passive discrimination differs from the organization that actively seeks a diverse and varied workforce.

Another aspect of organizational policies that affects diversity and multiculturalism is how the organization addresses and responds to problems that arise from differences among people. Consider the example of a manager charged with sexual harassment. If the organization's policies put an excessive burden of proof on the individual being harassed and invoke only minor sanctions against the guilty party, it is sending a clear signal about the importance of such matters. But the organization that has a balanced set of policies for addressing questions like sexual harassment sends its employees a message that diversity and individual rights and privileges are important.

Indeed, perhaps the major policy through which an organization can reflect its stance on diversity and multiculturalism is its mission statement. If the organization's mission statement articulates a clear and direct commitment to differences among people, it follows that everyone who comes into contact with that mission statement will grow to understand and accept the importance of diversity and multiculturalism, at least to that particular organization.

Organizational Practices   Organizations can also help manage diversity and multiculturalism through a variety of ongoing practices and procedures. Avon's creation of networks for various groups represents one example of an organizational practice that fosters diversity. In general, the idea is that, because diversity and multiculturalism are characterized by differences among people, organizations can manage that diversity more effectively by following practices and procedures that are based on flexibility rather than rigidity.

Benefits packages, for example, can be structured to accommodate individual situations better. An employee who is part of a dual-career couple and who has no children may require relatively little insurance (perhaps because his spouse's employer provides more complete coverage) and would like to be able to schedule vacations to coincide with those of his spouse. An employee who is a single parent may need a broad spectrum of insurance coverage and may prefer to schedule his vacation time to coincide with school holidays.

Flexible working hours are also a useful organizational practice for accommodating diversity. Differences in family arrangements, religious holidays, cultural events, and so forth, may each dictate that employees have some degree of flexibility in the times when they work. For example, a single parent may need to leave the office every day at 4:30 to pick up the children from their day-care center. An organization that truly values diversity will make every reasonable attempt to accommodate such a need.

Organizations can also facilitate diversity and multiculturalism by making sure that its important committees and executive teams are diverse. Even if diversity exists within the broader organizational context, an organization that does not reflect diversity in groups like committees and teams implies that diversity is not a fully ingrained element of its culture. In contrast, if all major groups and related work assignments reflect diversity, the message is quite a different one. *Today's Management Issues* discusses organizational practices related to gays in the workforce.

Diversity and Multicultural Training   Many organizations are finding that diversity and multicultural training is an effective means for managing diversity and minimizing its associated conflict. More specifically, **diversity and multicultural training** is training that is specifically designed to enable members of an organization to function better in a diverse and multicultural workplace.[30] This training can take a variety of forms. For example, many organizations find it useful to help people learn more about their similarities to and differences from others. Men and women can be taught to work together more effectively and can gain insights into how their own behaviors affect and are interpreted by others. In one organization, a diversity training program helped male managers gain

diversity and multicultural training   Training that is specifically designed to enable members of an organization to function better in a diverse and multicultural workplace

---

T O D A Y ' S   M A N A G E M E N T   I S S U E S

DIVERSITY STRATEGIES FOR GAY-FRIENDLY COMPANIES

Managing diversity is a critical strategy in today's tight labor market, where employers are fighting to keep their employees satisfied while continuing to recruit talented applicants from every possible source. Increasingly, top companies are developing specific strategies for attracting and retaining gay job applicants and employees. Pressure for gay-friendly policies is also coming from within many companies, where gay and lesbian managers and employees have formed formal and informal groups to network, provide support, and push for a more welcoming internal environment.

As a foundation, companies such as J.P. Morgan and IBM, among others, are ensuring that sexual orientation is covered within their corporatewide nondiscrimination policies. Like a growing number of companies, both J.P. Morgan and IBM also offer the same benefits to their employees' domestic partners, regardless of gender. Nearly three thousand U.S. companies follow this practice.

Establishing these kinds of policies and practices is only a start, however. Gay-friendly companies are going beyond the basics to communicate their emphasis on workforce diversity. Xerox, for example, advertises in gay and lesbian publications,

putting the spotlight on the company's diversity and benefits. In addition, more companies are arranging recruiting programs targeted for gay and lesbian job applicants. For example, among the financial services firms that have underwritten recruiting dinners for gay business school students are J.P. Morgan, American Express, and Goldman Sachs. Kodak is one of the sponsors for the Gay Games, a sports event; McKinsey sponsors conferences for gay business students. These kinds of initiatives show the gay community—and everyone else—that the companies value diversity based on sexual orientation as well as gender, age, ethnicity, and other dimensions of diversity.

> *It's getting the message out that Xerox is a gay-friendly company.*
>
> *—Christa Carone, spokesperson, Xerox**

Reference: Stephanie Armour, "Companies Work to Be More Gay-Friendly," *USA Today,* February 28, 2000, p. 1B (*quote on p. 1B).

Diversity training is one strategy for helping to manage diversity in organizations. While some experts question its effectiveness, many businesses nevertheless encourage or require their employees to participate in such training. It is especially common in settings that have recently experienced diversity problems or issues, in part perhaps because it is a tangible action that the organization can point to as part of a campaign to overcome bad press and a damaged corporate reputation that can follow a diversity-related controversy. While 3M already has an exemplary record in the area of diversity, these engineers are participating in what the company calls the "Diversity Training Advantage" to help them gain new insights into how they can more effectively work with others.

insights into how various remarks they made to one another could be interpreted by others as being sexist. In the same organization, female managers learned how to point out their discomfort with those remarks without appearing overly hostile.[31]

Similarly, white and African-American managers may need training to understand each other better. Managers at Mobil Corporation noticed that four African-American colleagues never seemed to eat lunch together. After a diversity training program, they came to realize that the African-American managers felt that if they ate together, their white colleagues would be overly curious about what they might be talking about. Thus, they avoided close associations with one another because they feared calling attention to themselves.[32]

Some organizations even go so far as to provide language training for their employees as a vehicle for managing diversity and multiculturalism. Motorola, for example, provides English language training for its foreign employees on assignment in the United States. At Pace Foods in San Antonio, with a total payroll of over four hundred employees, staff meetings and employee handbooks are translated into Spanish for the benefit of the company's two hundred or so Hispanic employees.

Organizational Culture   The ultimate test of an organization's commitment to managing diversity and multiculturalism, as discussed earlier in this chapter, is its culture.[33] Regardless of what managers say or put in writing, unless there is a basic and fundamental belief that diversity and multiculturalism are valued, it can never become truly an integral part of an organization. An organization that really wants to promote diversity and multiculturalism must shape its culture so that it clearly underscores top management commitment to and support of diversity and multiculturalism in all of its forms throughout every part of the organization. With top management support, however, and reinforced with a clear and consistent set of organizational policies and practices, diversity and multiculturalism can become a basic and fundamental part of an organization.[34]

MANAGEMENT IMPLICATIONS   Managers need to appreciate the fact that diversity and multiculturalism can be managed. They should understand, for example, that such individual strategies as understanding, empathy, tolerance, and a willingness to communicate can help promote diversity. Similarly, managers should also be quite familiar with such organizational strategies as organizational policies and practices, training, and organizational culture.

Toward the Multicultural Organization

multicultural organization An organization that has achieved high levels of diversity, is able to capitalize fully on the advantages of diversity, and has few diversity-related problems

Many organizations today are grappling with cultural diversity. We noted in Chapter 5 that, whereas many organizations are becoming increasingly global, no truly global organization exists. In similar fashion, although organizations are becoming ever more diverse, few are truly multicultural. The **multicultural organization** has achieved high levels of diversity, is able to capitalize fully on the advantages of diversity, and has few diversity-related problems. One recent article described the six basic characteristics of such an organization.[35] These characteristics are illustrated in Figure 6.5.

Figure 6.5

The Multicultural Organization
Few, if any, organizations have become truly multicultural. At the same time, more and more organizations are moving in this direction. When an organization becomes multicultural, it reflects the six basic characteristics shown here.

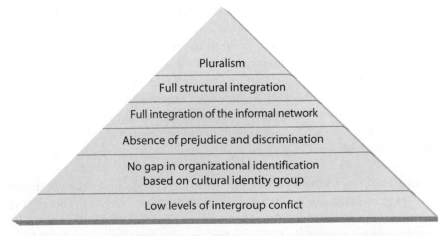

Source: Based on Taylor H. Cox, "The Multicultural Organization," *Academy of Management Executive*, May 1991, pp. 34–47. Reprinted with permission.

First, the multicultural organization is characterized by *pluralism*: every group represented in an organization works to understand every other group. Thus, African-American employees try to understand white employees, and white employees try just as hard to understand their African-American colleagues. In addition, every group represented within an organization has the potential to influence the organization's culture and its fundamental norms.

Second, the multicultural organization achieves *full structural integration*. Full structural integration suggests that the diversity within an organization is a complete and accurate reflection of the organization's external labor market. If around half of the labor market is female, then about half of the organization's employees are female. Moreover, this same proportion is reflected at all levels of the organization. There are no glass ceilings or other subtle forms of discrimination.

Third, the multicultural organization achieves *full integration of the informal network*. This characteristic suggests that there are no barriers to entry and participation in any organizational activity. For example, people enter and exit lunch groups, social networks, communication grapevines, and other informal aspects of organizational activity without regard to age, gender, ethnicity, or other dimension of diversity.

Fourth, the multicultural organization is characterized by an *absence of prejudice and discrimination*. No traces of bias exist, and prejudice is eliminated. Discrimination is not practiced in any shape, form, or fashion. And discrimination is nonexistent, not because it is illegal but because of the lack of prejudice and bias. People are valued, accepted, and rewarded purely on the basis of their skills and what they contribute to the organization.

Fifth, in the multicultural organization there is *no gap in organizational identification based on cultural identity group*. In many organizations today people tend to make presumptions about organizational roles based on group identity. For example, many people walking into an office and seeing a man and woman conversing tend to assume that the woman is the secretary and the man is the manager. No such tendencies exist in the multicultural organization. People recognize that men and women are equally likely to be managers and secretaries.

Finally, there are *low levels of intergroup conflict* in the multicultural organization. We noted earlier that conflict is a likely outcome of increased diversity. The multicultural organization has evolved beyond this point to a state of virtually no conflict among people who differ. People within the organization fully understand, empathize with, have tolerance for, and openly communicate with everyone else. Values, premises, motives, attitudes, and perceptions are so well understood by everyone that any conflict that does arise is over meaningful and work-related issues as opposed to differences in age, gender, ethnicity, or other dimensions of diversity.

MANAGEMENT IMPLICATIONS Managers should be aware of the fact that no truly multicultural organization yet exists. At the same time, though, they should be familiar with the qualities and characteristics that would typify such an organization.

Summary of Key Points

Organization culture is the set of values, beliefs, behaviors, customs, and attitudes that helps the members of the organization understand what it stands for, how it does things, and what it considers important. When the people comprising an organization represent different cultures, their differences in values, beliefs, behaviors, customs, and attitudes reflect multiculturalism. Diversity exists in a community of people when its members differ from one another along one or more important dimensions.

Organization culture is an important environmental concern for managers. Managers must understand that culture is an important determinant of how well their organization will perform. Culture can be determined and managed in several different ways.

Diversity and multiculturalism are increasing in organizations today because of changing demographics, the desire by organizations to improve their workforce, legal pressures, and increased globalization. There are several important dimensions of diversity, including age, gender, and ethnicity. The overall age of the workforce is increasing. More women are also entering the workplace, although there is still a glass ceiling in many settings. In the United

States, more Hispanics are also entering the workplace and the percentage of whites is gradually declining.

Diversity and multiculturalism can affect an organization in a number of different ways. For example, they can be sources of competitive advantage (i.e., cost, resource acquisition, marketing, creativity, problem solving, and systems flexibility arguments). On the other hand, diversity and multiculturalism can also be sources of conflict in an organization.

Managing diversity and multiculturalism in organizations can be done by both individuals and the organization itself. Individual approaches include understanding, empathy, tolerance, and willingness to communicate. Major organizational approaches are through policies, practices, diversity training, and culture.

Few, if any, organizations have become truly multicultural. The major dimensions that characterize organizations as they eventually achieve this state are pluralism, full structural integration, full integration of the informal network, an absence of prejudice and discrimination, no gap in organizational identification based on cultural identity group, and low levels of intergroup conflict attributable to diversity.

Discussion Questions

Questions for Review

1. How is organization culture usually created?
2. Why is diversity and multiculturalism increasing in many organizations today?
3. Summarize the basic impact of diversity and multiculturalism on organizations.
4. Discuss the four basic individual approaches and the four basic organizational approaches to diversity and multiculturalism.

Questions for Analysis

5. Compare and contrast organization culture and the culture of a country.
6. The text outlines many different advantages of diversity and multiculturalism in organizations. Can you think of any disadvantages?
7. What are the basic dimensions of diversity that most affect you personally?

Questions for Application

8. Visit the registrar's office or admissions office at your college or university. Using its enrollment statistics, determine the relative diversity on your campus. Is the student population more or less diverse than the faculty?
9. Assume that you are starting a new organization that is likely to grow rapidly. Develop a plan for becoming a multicultural organization.
10. Assume that you work for a large multinational organization. You have just learned that you are being transferred to India. You also know that you will be the first person of your ethnicity to work there. What steps might you take before you go to minimize problems that your presence might cause?

BUILDING EFFECTIVE *technical* SKILLS

Exercise Overview

Technical skills are the skills necessary to accomplish or understand the specific kind of work being done in an organization. This exercise will enable you to develop Internet skills as they relate to dealing with multicultural issues.

Exercise Background

One of the most important multicultural challenges facing managers today involves language skills. Assume you are the human resource manager for a large domestic company. Your firm has recently decided to enter into a joint venture with three foreign companies, one each from France, Germany, and Korea.

The terms of this joint venture involve your three partners each sending a team of managers to your corporate headquarters for a period of two years. You must make sure that your own top management team has the basic language skills in each of the three languages represented among your partners.

Exercise Task

With the background information above as context, do the following:

1. Use the Internet to obtain information about language training programs and methods.
2. Obtain information about one or more of each such program or method and make a decision about how you should proceed.

BUILDING EFFECTIVE *diagnostic* SKILLS

Exercise Overview

Diagnostic skills are the skills that enable a manager to visualize the most appropriate response to a situation. This exercise will enable you to practice your diagnostic skills as they relate to organization culture and multicultural issues and challenges.

Exercise Background

Your firm has recently undergone a significant increase in its workforce. Many of the new workers you have hired are immigrants from Eastern Europe and Asia. Several do not speak English very well, but all are hard workers who appear to be trying very hard to be successful and to fit in with their coworkers.

Recently, however, some problems have come to your attention. For one thing, several of your female workers have begun to complain about an increase in sexual harassment. For another, your supervisors have noticed an increase in tardiness and absenteeism among all of your workers.

You have decided that some action is clearly needed. However, you are unsure how to proceed. Consequently, you have decided to spend a few days thinking about what to do.

Exercise Task

With the background information above as context, do the following:

1. Think of as many causes as you can to explain each of the two problems you are facing.
2. Determine how you might address each problem, given the potential array of factors that might have contributed to them.
3. What role might organization culture be playing in this situation, apart from issues of multiculturalism?
4. What role might multiculturalism be playing in this situation, apart from issues of organization culture?

BUILDING EFFECTIVE *decision-making* SKILLS

Exercise Overview

Decision-making skills refer to the manager's ability to recognize and define problems and opportunities correctly and then to select an appropriate course of action for solving problems and capitalizing on opportunities. This exercise focuses on decision making about issues related to diversity and multiculturalism.

Exercise Background

For years your firm had relatively little diversity. The one-thousand-member workforce was almost exclusively white and male. But in recent years you have succeeded in increasing diversity substantially. Almost one-third of your employees are now female, while over 40 percent are Hispanic or African American.

Unfortunately, your firm has recently met with some unfortunate financial setbacks. You feel that you have no choice but to lay off about three hundred employees for a period of at least six months. If everything goes well, you also expect to be able to bring them back after six months.

Exercise Task

With the background information above as context, do the following:

1. Develop a layoff plan that will not substantially reduce your firm's diversity.
2. Decide how you will communicate your decision to the workforce.
3. What obstacles do you foresee in implementing your decision?

A WORLD OF DIVERSITY AT IBM

In the mid-1990s, CEO Louis V. Gerstner made two decisions that changed the course of IBM. Big Blue (IBM's popular nickname) was struggling to redefine itself as more than a manufacturer of giant mainframe computers, and its profits were sagging. Gerstner's first major decision was to keep the company intact, despite intense pressure to slim it down by selling selected units. He believed that, with proper management and focus, IBM's many parts could collaborate effectively for more profitable synergy.

Gerstner's second major decision was to make the Internet the focal point of every part of the business. Many technology firms were eyeing the Internet but taking one step at a time, racing to build better web browsers or faster search engines. In contrast, the IBM CEO was looking a few steps beyond, seeing the Internet as an innovative way of expediting transactions and serving customers in every business area. Based on this view of the future, Gerstner decided to invest hundreds of millions of dollars to move IBM onto the Internet. But he realized that reshaping IBM into an Internet-savvy organization required a shift away from the company's traditional straight-laced, buttoned-down culture.

To become a thoroughly Internet-driven company, IBM needed to attract, motivate, and retain the best and brightest talent around the world. Management therefore developed a three-pronged approach to workforce diversity: equal opportunity programs ensure nondiscrimination, affirmative action programs eliminate barriers to opportunities and promote equality among employees, and work/life programs help employees balance their professional and personal responsibilities.

As part of this cultural shift, IBM created a series of task forces to examine relations with specific employee groups, including African-American, Hispanic, gay and lesbian, female, and Native-American employees. Ted Childs, IBM's vice president for global workforce diversity, recalls, "We asked [the task forces] to look at IBM through their constituency and answer, 'What was required for your group to feel welcome and valued

throughout IBM?' and 'What could we do in partnership to maximize your productivity?'" These task forces were so valuable that IBM went on to form local diversity network groups and councils to encourage communication among employees with similar concerns and characteristics. There are currently eighty such network groups, including seventeen for African-American employees.

Grooming managers from all backgrounds for higher-level management positions became another priority. IBM began providing mentors and growth opportunities to fast-track managers through its Executive Resource Program and its Mentoring and Employee Development Program. Women infotech (IT) managers find such programs particularly helpful, according to Diane Hill, a manager at IBM Learning Services. "IT customers are typically male, and sometimes they second-guess women," she explains. "It's important for women to have positive role models in leadership positions."

IBM is also remaking its culture by aggressively recruiting creative tech types to work in special web design centers. Located in hip areas such as near the MTV studio in Los Angeles, the web design centers seem more like dot-com start-ups than IBM outposts. The design centers sport billiard and Ping-Pong tables, and employees are encouraged to bring their dogs (or iguanas) to work. Even employees' business cards look different, with titles such as "concept architect and paradoxiologist" (meaning that the employee works on complex Internet strategies).

As part of a decade-long global effort to attract and keep skilled employees at all levels, IBM has invested $150 million in dependent-care programs, establishing and expanding child-care and elder-care facilities in Canada, the United States, Mexico, Germany, Ireland, and other countries. The goal is to help employees and managers care for children and parents by establishing camps, day-care centers, elder-care programs, and nurseries on or near IBM offices and plants.

IBM's diversity programs are making a difference. Its management ranks are more diverse than ever, and the company has become a recognized leader in Internet activities. But Gerstner and his management team are still feeling pressure. Amid slower revenue growth and more intense competition, some analysts are again calling for plans to refocus or sell parts of the business. So, despite its past successes, Big Blue must prove itself—again.

Case Questions

1. From a cultural standpoint, why would IBM maintain web design centers separate from other non-Internet facilities?

2. Which specific dimensions of diversity are being addressed by IBM's dependent-care programs?

3. What organizational culture and/or multicultural challenges might IBM have to face in the future?

Case References:

"IBM Announces $50 Million Global Dependent Care Fund," *IBM Press Release*, July 12, 2000, http://www.ibm.com/press/prnews (July 18, 2000); David Rocks, "Is Big Blue Thinking Big Enough?" *Business Week*, May 22, 2000, p. 132; Talila Baron, "IT Talent Shortage Renews Interest in Mentoring," *Information Week*, April 24, 2000, pp. 166–169; Robert J. Grossman, "Is Diversity Working?" *HR Magazine*, March 2000, pp. 47–51; Ira Sager, "Gerstner on IBM and the Internet," *Business Week*, December 13, 1999, p. EB40; "Inside IBM: Internet Business Machines," *Business Week*, December 13, 1999, pp. EB20–EB22; "Valuing Diversity: An Ongoing Commitment," *IBM Diversity Programs* (n.d.), http://www-3.ibm.com/employment/us/diverse/program.html (July 18, 2000).

CHAPTER NOTES

1. *Hoover's Handbook of American Business 2000* (Austin, Texas: Hoover's Business Press, pp. 646–647; "A Savvy Captain for Old Navy," *Business Week*, November 8, 1999, pp. 133–134 (quote on p. 134).

2. Terrence E. Deal and Allan A. Kennedy, *Corporate Cultures: The Rights and Rituals of Corporate Life* (Reading, Mass.: Addison-Wesley, 1982).

3. Sue Zesinger, "Ford's Hip Transplant," *Fortune*, May 10, 1999, pp. 82–92.

4. Jay B. Barney, "Organizational Culture: Can It Be a Source of Sustained Competitive Advantage?" *Academy of Management Review*, July 1986, pp. 656–665.

5. For example, see Carol J. Loomis, "Sam Would Be Proud," *Fortune*, April 17, 2000, pp. 131–144.

6. "Why Wells Fargo Is Circling the Wagons," *The Wall Street Journal*, June 9, 1997, pp. 92–93.

7. See Timothy Galpin, "Connecting Culture to Organizational Change," *HRMagazine*, March 1996, pp. 84–94.

8. Gail Robinson and Kathleen Dechant, "Building a Business Case for Diversity, *The Academy of Management Executive*, August 1997, pp. 21–31; see also Orlando C. Richard, "Racial Diversity, Business Strategy, and Firm Performance: A Resource-Based View," *Academy of Management Journal*, 2000, Vol. 43, No. 2, pp. 164–177.

9. "The Coming Job Bottleneck," *Business Week*, March 24, 1997, pp. 184–185; Linda Thornburg, "The Age Wave Hits," *HRMagazine*, February 1995, pp. 40–45.

10. Gary Powell and D. Anthony Butterfield, "Investigating the 'Glass Ceiling' Phenomenon: An Empirical Study of Actual Promotions to Top Management," *Academy of Management Journal*, 1994, Vol. 37, No. 1, pp. 68–86.

11. Karen S. Lyness and Donna E. Thompson, "Above the Glass Ceiling? A Comparison of Matched Samples of Female and Male Executives," *Journal of Applied Psychology*, 1997, Vol. 82, No. 3, pp. 359–375.

12. "What Glass Ceiling?" *USA Today*, July 20, 1999, pp. 1B, 2B.

13. *Occupational Outlook Handbook* (Washington, D.C.: U.S. Bureau of Labor Statistics, 1990–1991).

14. Roy S. Johnson, "The New Black Power," *Fortune*, August 4, 1997, pp. 46–47.

15. "In a Factory Schedule, Where Does Religion Fit In?" *The Wall Street Journal*, March 4, 1999, pp. B1, B12. See also Marc Adams, "Showing Good Faith Toward Muslims," *HRMagazine*, November 2000, pp. 52–65.

16. Jane Easter Bahls, "Make Room for Diverse Beliefs," *HRMagazine*, August 1997, pp. 89–95.

17. "Immigration Is On the Rise, Again," *USA Today*, February 28, 1997, p. 7A.

18. Based on Taylor H. Cox and Stacy Blake, "Managing Cultural Diversity: Implications for Organizational Competitiveness," *The Academy of Management Executive*, August 1991, pp. 45–56. See also Jacqueline A. Gilbert and John M. Ivancevich, "Valuing Diversity: A Tale of Two Organizations," *Academy of Management Executive*, 2000, Vol. 14., No. 1, pp. 93–103.

19. Michelle Neely Martinez, "Work-Life Programs Reap Business Benefits," *HRMagazine*, June 1997, pp. 110–119. See also Cox and Taylor, "Managing Cultural Diversity: Implications for Organizational Competitiveness."

20. For an example, see "A Female Executive Tells Furniture Maker What Women Want," *The Wall Street Journal*, June 25, 1999, pp. A1, A11.

21. "Target Makes a Play for Minority Group Sears Has Cultivated," *The Wall Street Journal*, April 12, 1999, pp. A1, A8.

22. For example, see Tony Simons, Lisa Hope Pelled, and Ken A. Smith, "Making Use of Difference: Diversity, Debate, and Decision Comprehensiveness in Top Management Teams," *Academy of Management Journal*, 2000, Vol. 42, No. 6, pp. 662–673.

23. C. Marlene Fiol, "Consensus, Diversity, and Learning in Organizations," *Organization Science*, August 1994, pp. 403–415.
24. Patricia L. Nemetz and Sandra L. Christensen, "The Challenge of Cultural Diversity: Harnessing a Diversity of Views to Understand Multiculturalism," *Academy of Management Review*, 1996, Vol. 21, No. 2, pp. 434–462. See also "Generational Warfare," *Forbes*, March 22, 1999, pp. 62–66.
25. Christine M. Riordan and Lynn McFarlane Shores, "Demographic Diversity and Employee Attitudes: An Empirical Examination of Relational Demography Within Work Units," *Journal of Applied Psychology*, 1997, Vol. 82, No. 3, pp. 342–358.
26. "Computer Chip Project Brings Rivals Together, but the Cultures Clash," *The Wall Street Journal*, May 3, 1994, pp. A1, A8.
27. "How Shoney's, Belted by a Lawsuit, Found the Path to Diversity," *The Wall Street Journal*, April 16, 1996, pp. A1, A6; Fay Rice, "Denny's Changes Its Spots," *Fortune*, May 13, 1996, pp. 133–142; "The Ugly Talk on the Texaco Tape," *Business Week*, November 18, 1996, p. 58; "Smith Barney's Woman Problem," *Business Week*, June 3, 1996, pp. 102–106.
28. "Firms Address Workers' Cultural Variety," *Wall Street Journal*, February 10, 1989, p. B1.
29. Sara Rynes and Benson Rosen, "What Makes Diversity Programs Work?" *HRMagazine*, October 1994, pp. 67–75.
30. Karen Hildebrand, "Use Leadership Training to Increase Diversity," *HRMagazine*, August 1996, pp. 53–59.
31. "Learning to Accept Cultural Diversity," *Wall Street Journal*, September 12, 1990, pp. B1, B9.
32. "Firms Address Workers' Cultural Variety," *Wall Street Journal*, February 10, 1989, p. B1.
33. Anthony Carneville and Susan Stone, "Diversity—Beyond the Golden Rule," *Training and Development*, October 1994, pp. 22–27.
34. Janice R. W. Joplin and Catherine S. Daus, "Challenges of Leading a Diverse Workforce," *The Academy of Management Executive*, August 1997, pp. 32–47.
35. This discussion derives heavily from Taylor H. Cox, "The Multicultural Organization," *The Academy of Management Executive*, May 1991, pp. 34–47.

PART THREE

Planning and Decision Making

PART FOUR

Basic Elements of Planning and Decision Making

7 Basic Elements of Planning and Decision Making

For decades Procter & Gamble has been seen as one of the preeminent marketing companies in the world. Popular P&G brands such as Tide laundry detergent, Crisco shortening, Ivory soap, Crest toothpaste, and Pampers disposable diapers, for example, long ruled their respective markets. And P&G seemed like an unstoppable juggernaut as its flagship products and brands became increasingly entrenched as icons around the world.

One key to P&G's heritage of success has been a finely tuned set of procedures for developing new products, getting them to market, and then promoting them with relentless efficiency. All told, the firm sells more than three hundred brands in 140 countries. And there is at least one P&G product tucked away in virtually every kitchen cabinet or under every bathroom sink in the United States. Its annual revenues—about $37 billion—are four times those of Colgate-Palmolive and three times those of Kimberly-Clark, its nearest domestic rivals.

Indeed, P&G executives were so bullish in 1997 that they promised investors the firm would double its annual revenues from that year's $35 billion to a stunning $70 billion by the year 2006. And when that goal was announced, Wall Street analysts responded by encouraging investors to buy the firm's stock, and the business press lauded the company for its aggressive and forward-looking leadership. But almost before the ink had dried, observers began to identify chinks in the P&G armor and, within a short time, the firm's growth seemed to grind to a halt.

How could such a well-oiled marketing machine lose its momentum so quickly? As it turns out, P&G's problems had actually started years before but had simply not become apparent until much more recently. In a nutshell, what had been a major advantage for the firm had become a major liability—it had stopped innovating and was taking far too long to make changes and get new products to market. And its long-standing internal policies and procedures were to blame.

Perhaps most symptomatic of the firm's adherence to the "P&G way" is its internal system for writing memos. All internal memos have to follow a precise format. Managers are taught to follow this format, and they are encouraged to return any they receive that don't follow it. One former P&G manager indicated that the average memo had been revised or changed fifteen times before it was ever seen by a brand manager. Another exaggerated that "there's a P&G way for using the bathroom." And this rigid adherence to formula and procedure caused the firm to

"Colgate'll give you a project—and in a week it's out the door. . . . a P&G project can take years."

—unidentified packing supplier for Colgate-Palmolive and Procter & Gamble

After studying this chapter, you should be able to:

- Summarize the function of decision making and the planning process.

- Discuss the purposes of organizational goals, identify different kinds of goals, discuss who sets goals, and describe how to manage multiple goals.

- Identify different kinds of organizational plans, note the time frames for planning, discuss who plans, and describe contingency planning.

- Discuss how tactical plans are developed and executed.

- Describe the basic types of operational plans used by organizations.

- Identify the major barriers to goal setting and planning, how organizations overcome those barriers, and how to use goals to implement plans.

become increasingly less responsive to shifts in its market.

Whereas competitors like Colgate were busily creating new products and nimbly getting them in the hands of consumers, P&G stuck with its tried-and-true approach to simply reformulating existing products and relaunching them as "improved." Tide, for instance, has undergone more than sixty product upgrades since its initial launch. Because the firm had enjoyed such a long period of sustained dominance, the company's culture acquired a pervasive and unerring adherence to precedent. Managers had come to believe they had to do things the way they had always been done, and individuals were criticized or even fired when they tried something new or different.

Looking back over the last decade, P&G's decline becomes more apparent. Its Ivory soap lost the market leadership position in 1991 to Unilever's Dove, and today has less than 5 percent of the market. Pampers disposable diapers have experienced a 50 percent drop in market share and lost the market leadership position to Kimberly-Clark's Huggies in 1993. And Crest toothpaste, perhaps P&G's most entrenched product, was passed by a new Colgate toothpaste in 1998. While Crest was still focusing on cavities—its hallmark since being introduced in 1955—Colgate and other competitors had started stressing not only cavity prevention but also fighting tartar, plaque, bad breath, and gingivitis. And because of these and other setbacks, P&G's hopes of reaching its lofty revenue goal seem increasingly remote.[1]

195

Procter & Gamble's managers have set an ambitious target for the firm's future revenue growth. One risk that they now face, though, is the criticism they can expect and the sense of disappointment that will result if this goal is not met. No matter how well the company performs otherwise, many observers will say the company failed to reach its goal. At the same time, however, the goal focuses attention on what the firm anticipates doing and provides guidance and direction to managers throughout the firm, with clear indicators of how they should manage their operations. In addition, the firm's plans for achieving its goal should help guide day-to-day activities toward growth and expansion.

As we noted in Chapter 1, planning and decision making comprise the first managerial function that organizations must address. This chapter is the first of four that explore the planning process in detail. We begin by briefly relating decision making and planning and then explaining the planning process that most organizations follow. We then discuss the nature of organizational goals and introduce the basic concepts of planning. Next we discuss tactical and operational planning more fully. We conclude with a discussion of how to manage the goal-setting and planning processes.

Decision Making and the Planning Process

Decision making is the cornerstone of planning. Consider, for example, Procter & Gamble's goal of doubling its revenues. The firm's top managers could have adopted an array of alternative options, including increasing revenues by only 25 percent or increasing revenues threefold. The time frame included for the projected revenue growth could also have been somewhat shorter or longer than the ten-year period that was actually specified. Alternatively, the goal could have included diversifying into new markets, cutting costs, or buying competing businesses. Thus, P&G's exact mix of goals and plans for growth rate and time frame reflect choices from among a variety of alternatives.

Clearly, then, decision making is the catalyst that drives the planning process. An organization's goals follow from decisions made by various managers. Likewise, deciding on the best plan for achieving particular goals also reflects a decision to adopt one course of action as opposed to others. We discuss decision making per se in Chapter 9. Our focus here is on the planning process itself. As we discuss goal setting and planning, however, keep in mind that decision making underlies every aspect of setting goals and formulating plans.[2]

The planning process itself can best be thought of as a generic activity. All organizations engage in planning activities, but no two organizations plan in exactly the same fashion. Figure 7.1 is a general representation of the planning process that many organizations attempt to follow. Although most firms follow this general framework, each also has its own nuances and variations.[3]

As Figure 7.1 shows, all planning occurs within an environmental context. If managers do not understand this context, they are unable to develop effective plans. Thus, understanding the environment is essentially the first step in planning. The four previous chapters cover many of the basic environmental issues that affect organizations and how they plan. With this understanding as a foundation, managers must then establish the organization's mission. The mission outlines the organization's purpose, premises, values, and directions. Flowing from the mission are parallel streams of goals and plans. Directly following the mission are strategic goals. These goals and the mission help determine strategic plans. Strategic goals and plans are primary inputs for developing tactical goals. Tactical goals and the original strategic plans help shape tactical plans. Tactical plans, in turn, combine with the tactical goals to shape operational goals. These goals and the appropriate tactical plans determine operational plans. Finally, goals and plans at each level can also be used as input for future activities at all levels. This chapter discusses goals and tactical and operational plans. Chapter 8 covers strategic plans.

MANAGEMENT Managers should recognize
IMPLICATIONS that decision making is the cornerstone of planning. They should also understand that, while all organizations engage in planning activities, no two organizations plan in exactly the same fashion. Consequently, every manager must understand the environmental context that provides the framework for planning within the unique organizational setting.

Figure 7.1

The Planning Process

The planning process takes place within an environmental context. Managers must develop a complete and thorough understanding of this context to determine the organization's mission and to develop its strategic, tactical, and operational goals and plans.

Organizational Goals

Goals are critical to organizational effectiveness, and they serve a number of purposes. Organizations can have several different kinds of goals, all of which must be appropriately managed. And several different kinds of managers must be involved in setting goals.

Purposes of Goals

Goals serve four important purposes.[4] First, they provide guidance and a unified direction for people in the organization. Goals can help everyone understand where the organization is going and why getting there is important.[5] Several years ago Jack Welch, CEO of General Electric Co., set a goal that every business owned by the firm will be either number one or number two in its industry. This goal still helps set the tone for decisions made by GE managers as the company competes with other firms like Whirlpool and Electrolux.[6] Likewise, the goal set for P&G of doubling revenues by the year 2006 helps everyone in the firm recognize the strong emphasis on growth and expansion that is driving the firm.

Second, goal-setting practices strongly affect other aspects of planning. Effective goal setting promotes good planning, and good planning facilitates future goal setting. For example, the ambitious revenue goal set for P&G demonstrates how setting goals and developing plans to reach them should be seen as complementary activities. The strong growth goal should encourage managers to plan for expansion by looking for new market opportunities, for example. Similarly, they must also always be alert for competitive threats and new ideas that will help facilitate future expansion.

Third, goals can serve as sources of motivation to employees of the organization. Goals that are specific and moderately difficult can motivate people to work harder, especially if attaining the goal is likely to result in rewards.[7] The Italian furniture manufacturer Industrie Natuzzi SpA uses goals to motivate its workers. Each craftsperson has a goal for how long it should take to perform her or his job, such as sewing leather sheets together to make a sofa cushion or building wooden frames for chair arms. At the completion of assigned tasks, workers enter their ID numbers and job numbers into the firm's computer system. If they get a job done faster than their goal, a bonus is automatically added to their paycheck.[8]

Finally, goals provide an effective mechanism for evaluation and control. This means that performance can be assessed in the future in terms of how successfully today's goals are accomplished. For example, suppose that officials of the United Way of America set a goal of collecting $250,000 from a particular community. If midway through the campaign they have raised only $50,000, they know that they need to change or intensify their efforts. If they raise only $100,000 by the end of their drive, they will need to study carefully why they did not reach their goal and what they need to do differently next year. On the other hand, if they succeed in raising $265,000, evaluations of their efforts will take on an entirely different character.

Kinds of Goals

Organizations establish many different kinds of goals. In general, these goals vary by level, area, and time frame. Figure 7.2 provides examples of each type of goal for a fast-food chain.

mission A statement of an organization's fundamental purpose

strategic goal A goal set by and for top management of the organization

tactical goal A goal set by and for middle managers of the organization

Level Goals are set for and by different levels within an organization. As we noted earlier, the four basic levels of goals are the mission and strategic, tactical, and operational goals. An organization's **mission** is a statement of its "fundamental, unique purpose that sets a business apart from other firms of its type and identifies the scope of the business's operations in product and market terms."[9] For example, the CEO of Monsanto is attempting to reshape his firm's mission by transforming it into what he calls a "life sciences" firm.[10]

Strategic goals are goals set by and for top management of the organization. They focus on broad, general issues. For example, Procter & Gamble's goal of doubling sales revenues is a strategic goal. **Tactical goals** are set by and for middle managers. Their focus is on how to operationalize actions necessary to achieve

Figure 7.2

Kinds of Organizational Goals for a Regional Fast-Food Chain

Organizations develop many different types of goals. A regional fast-food chain, for example, might develop goals at several different levels and for several different areas.

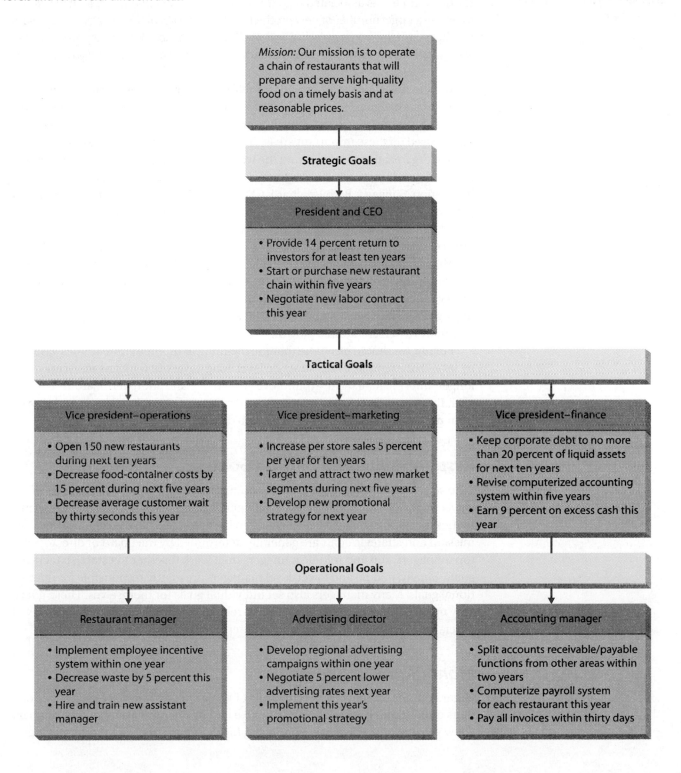

Mission: Our mission is to operate a chain of restaurants that will prepare and serve high-quality food on a timely basis and at reasonable prices.

Strategic Goals

President and CEO
- Provide 14 percent return to investors for at least ten years
- Start or purchase new restaurant chain within five years
- Negotiate new labor contract this year

Tactical Goals

Vice president–operations
- Open 150 new restaurants during next ten years
- Decrease food-container costs by 15 percent during next five years
- Decrease average customer wait by thirty seconds this year

Vice president–marketing
- Increase per store sales 5 percent per year for ten years
- Target and attract two new market segments during next five years
- Develop new promotional strategy for next year

Vice president–finance
- Keep corporate debt to no more than 20 percent of liquid assets for next ten years
- Revise computerized accounting system within five years
- Earn 9 percent on excess cash this year

Operational Goals

Restaurant manager
- Implement employee incentive system within one year
- Decrease waste by 5 percent this year
- Hire and train new assistant manager

Advertising director
- Develop regional advertising campaigns within one year
- Negotiate 5 percent lower advertising rates next year
- Implement this year's promotional strategy

Accounting manager
- Split accounts receivable/payable functions from other areas within two years
- Computerize payroll system for each restaurant this year
- Pay all invoices within thirty days

operational goal A goal set by and for lower-level managers of the organization

the strategic goals. Tactical goals at P&G might center around which new products to launch, which existing products to revise, and so forth.

Operational goals are set by and for lower-level managers. Their concern is with shorter-term issues associated with the tactical goals. An operational goal for P&G might be a target number of new products to launch each of the next five years. (Some managers use the words *objective* and *goal* interchangeably. When they are differentiated, however, the term *objective* is usually used instead of *operational goal*.)

Area   Organizations also set goals for different areas. The restaurant chain shown in Figure 7.2 has goals for operations, marketing, and finance. Hewlett-Packard routinely sets production goals for quality, productivity, and so forth. By keeping activities focused on these important areas, H-P has managed to remain competitive against organizations from around the world. Human resource goals might be set for employee turnover and absenteeism. 3M and Rubbermaid set goals for product innovation. Similarly, Beth Pritchard, CEO of Bath & Body works, has a goal that 30 percent of the products sold in the retail outlets each year will be new.[11]

Time Frame   Organizations also set goals across different time frames. In Figure 7.2, three goals are listed at the strategic, tactical, and operational levels. The first is a long-term goal, the second an intermediate-term goal, and the third a short-term goal. Some goals have an explicit time frame (i.e., open 150 new restaurants during the next ten years) and others have an open-ended time horizon (i.e., maintain 10 percent annual growth).

Finally, we should also note that the meaning of different time frames varies by level. For example, at the strategic level, long-term often means ten years or longer; intermediate term, around five years or so; and short-term, around one year. But two or three years may be long-term at the operational level, and short-term may mean a matter of weeks or even days.

Responsibilities for Setting Goals

Who sets goals? The answer is actually quite simple: all managers should be involved in the goal-setting process. Each manager, however, generally has responsibilities for setting goals that correspond to his or her level in the organization. The mission and strategic goals are generally determined by the board of directors and top managers. Top and middle managers then work together to establish tactical goals. Finally, middle and lower-level managers are jointly responsible for operational goals. Many managers also set individual goals for themselves. These goals may involve career paths, informal work-related goals outside the normal array of official goals, or just about anything of interest or concern to the manager.

Managing Multiple Goals

Organizations set many different kinds of goals and sometimes experience conflicts or contradictions among goals. Nike had problems with inconsistent goals a few years ago. The firm was producing high-quality shoes (a manufacturing goal), but they were not particularly stylish (a marketing goal). As a result, the company lost substantial market share when Reebok International started making shoes that were both high quality and fashionable. When Nike management recognized and corrected the inconsistencies, Nike regained its industry standing.

To address such problems, managers must understand the concept of optimizing. **Optimizing** involves balancing and reconciling possible conflicts among goals. Because goals may conflict with one another, the manager must look for inconsistencies and decide whether to pursue one goal to the exclusion of another or to find a midrange target between the extremes. For example, The Home Depot has achieved dramatic success in the retailing industry by offering do-it-yourselfers high-quality home improvement products at low prices and with good service. The firm has recently announced a goal of doubling its revenues from professional contractors. Among its plans are to set up separate checkout areas and to provide special products for contractors. The challenge, however, will be to keep loyal individual customers while also satisfying professional contractors.[12]

optimizing Balancing and reconciling possible conflicts among goals

MANAGEMENT Managers need to appreciate the various purposes that goals **IMPLICATIONS** play in an organization. They should also appreciate the various kinds of goals that exist. No manager can avoid the goal-setting process because all managers share responsibility for this activity. Finally, managers should also understand that, because some goals may be in conflict with one another, they must be carefully optimized to serve the best overall interests of the organization.

Organizational Planning

Given the clear link between organizational goals and plans, we now turn our attention to various concepts and issues associated with planning itself. In particular, this section identifies kinds of plans, time frames for planning, who is responsible for planning, and contingency planning.

Kinds of Organizational Plans

Organizations establish many different kinds of plans. At a general level, these include strategic, tactical, and operational plans.

Strategic Plans   Strategic plans are the plans developed to achieve strategic goals. More precisely, a **strategic plan** is a general plan outlining decisions of resource allocation, priorities, and action steps necessary to reach strategic goals.[13] These plans are set by the board of directors and top management; generally have an extended time horizon; and address questions of scope, resource deployment, competitive advantage, and synergy. We discuss strategic planning further in Chapter 8.

strategic plan A general plan outlining decisions of resource allocation, priorities, and action steps necessary to reach strategic goals

The processes of setting goals and developing plans involve ongoing and sustained efforts by a variety of managers. Take Intel, for example. Each of the firm's 40,000 employees is equipped with a laptop computer, pager, and cell phone, plus a home PC. Using this technology, Intel employees like these can work together on group projects from anywhere in the world. Hence, they are continuously involved in identifying and developing new business opportunities, seeking new solutions, and enhancing the firm's abilities to compete in an ever-changing world.

tactical plan A plan aimed at achieving tactical goals and developed to implement specific parts of a strategic plan

Tactical Plans   A **tactical plan**, aimed at achieving tactical goals, is developed to implement specific parts of a strategic plan. Tactical plans typically involve upper and middle management and, compared with strategic plans, have a somewhat shorter time horizon and a more specific and concrete focus. Thus, tactical plans are concerned more with actually accomplishing tasks than with deciding what to do. Tactical planning is covered in detail in a later section.

operational plan A plan that focuses on carrying out tactical plans to achieve operational goals

Operational Plans   An **operational plan** focuses on carrying out tactical plans to achieve operational goals. Developed by middle and lower-level managers, operational plans have a short-term focus and are relatively narrow in scope. Each one deals with a fairly small set of activities. We cover operational planning in more detail later.

Time Frames for Planning

As we previously noted, strategic plans tend to have a long-term focus; tactical plans an intermediate-term focus; and operational plans, a short-term focus. The sections that follow address these time frames in more detail. Of course, we should also remember that time frames vary widely from industry to industry, as discussed more fully in *Working with Diversity*.

long-range plan A plan that covers many years, perhaps even decades; common long-range plans are for five years or more

Long-Range Plans   A **long-range plan** covers many years, perhaps even decades. The founder of Matsushita Electric (maker of Panasonic and JVC electronic products), Konosuke Matsushita, once wrote a 250-year plan for his company.[14] Today, however, most managers recognize that environmental change makes it unfeasible to plan too far ahead, but large firms like General Motors and Exxon still routinely develop plans for ten- to twenty-year intervals. GM executives, for example, have a pretty good idea today about new car models that they plan to introduce for at least a decade in advance. The time span for long-range planning

PLANNING AND DECISION MAKING AT INTERNET SPEED

Managers who move from traditional companies to Internet companies must learn how to develop plans and make decisions faster than ever before—working with a mixed management team of web veterans and newcomers. That's what Barbara Hyder found out when she made the transition from international regional president at Mary Kay Cosmetics to CEO of Gloss.com. Although both companies sell cosmetics and personal-care products, Gloss.com's approach to planning and decision making is markedly different, as is the composition of its management team.

When Hyder was at Mary Kay, making a decision to alter a multimillion-dollar advertising campaign would have taken many weeks of discussion and analysis as the issue worked its way through the hierarchy in a series of meetings. In contrast, after Hyder spent five minutes huddling with Gloss.com's president and vice president of marketing, the group agreed to change the company's $20 million advertising plan entirely. Another major decision Hyder faced was whether to launch a new version of the firm's web site, despite some glitches and missing features, or postpone the launch until everything was ready. After listening to both sides during an impromptu twenty-minute management meeting, the CEO decided to go ahead with the launch, citing the highly competitive environment and the opportunity to gain additional consumer feedback.

Although Hyder had years of management and decision-making experience at Mary Kay and earlier at Maybelline, she had no experience with e-commerce before joining Gloss.com. Now she heads a team with managers who are, in some cases, more than a decade younger. She also has to learn their language, the lingo of Internet business that is sprinkled with phrases such as "click-through rates," referring to how many people click on banner advertisements. Just as important, she is bringing with her the language of traditional business that is sprinkled with phrases such as "P&L," referring to profit and loss statements. After all, profitability is the ultimate goal for Gloss.com and its management team.

> *You have to act quickly; speed is of the essence.*
> —*Barbara Hyder,*
> *CEO, Gloss.com**

Reference: Melanie Warner, "Getting Up to Internet Speed," *Fortune,* January 10, 2000, pp. 185–186 (*quote on p. 185).

---

varies from one organization to another. For our purposes, we regard any plan that extends beyond five years as long-range. Managers of organizations in complex, volatile environments face a special dilemma. These organizations probably need a longer time horizon than do organizations in less dynamic environments, yet the complexity of their environment makes long-range planning difficult. Managers at these companies therefore develop long-range plans but must also constantly monitor their environment for possible changes.

Intermediate Plans   An **intermediate plan** is somewhat less tentative and subject to change than is a long-range plan. Intermediate plans usually cover periods from one to five years and are especially important for middle and first-line managers. Thus, they generally parallel tactical plans. For many organizations intermediate planning has become the central focus of planning activities. Nissan, for example, has fallen far behind its domestic rivals Toyota and Honda in areas like profitability and productivity. To turn things around, the firm has developed

intermediate plan A plan that usually covers periods from one to five years

several plans ranging in duration from two to four years, each intended to improve some part of the company's operations. One plan (three years in duration) involves updating the manufacturing technology used in each Nissan assembly factory. Another (four years in duration) calls for shifting more production to foreign plants to lower labor costs.[15]

short-range plan A plan that generally covers a span of one year or less

action plan A plan used to operationalize any other kind of plan

reaction plan A plan designed to allow the company to react to an unforeseen circumstance

Short-Range Plans   A manager also develops a short-range plan, which has a time frame of one year or less. **Short-range plans** greatly affect the manager's day-to-day activities. There are two basic kinds of short-range plans. An **action plan** operationalizes any other kind of plan. When a specific Nissan plant is ready to have its technology overhauled, its managers focus their attention on replacing the existing equipment with new equipment as quickly and as efficiently as possible to minimize lost production time. In most cases this can be done in a matter of a few months, with actual production being halted only for a few weeks. An action plan thus coordinates the actual changes at a given factory. A **reaction plan**, in turn, is a plan designed to allow the company to react to an unforeseen circumstance. At one Nissan factory the new equipment arrived earlier than expected and plant managers had to shut down production more quickly than expected. These managers thus had to react to events beyond their control in ways that still allowed their goals to be achieved. In fact, reacting to any form of environmental turbulence, as described in Chapter 3, is a form of reaction planning.

Responsibilities for Planning

We earlier noted briefly who is responsible for setting goals. We can now expand that initial perspective a bit and examine more fully how different parts of the organization participate in the overall planning process. All managers engage in planning to some degree. Marketing sales managers develop plans for target markets, market penetration, and sales increases. Operations managers plan cost-cutting programs and better inventory control methods. As a general rule, however, the larger an organization becomes, the more the primary planning activities become associated with groups of managers rather than with individual managers.

Planning Staff   Some large organizations develop a professional planning staff. Tenneco, General Motors, Disney, Caterpillar, Raytheon, NCR, Ford, and Boeing all have planning staffs.[16] And although the planning staff was pioneered in the United States, foreign firms like Nippon Telegraph & Telephone have also started using them. Organizations might use a planning staff for a variety of reasons. In particular, a planning staff can reduce the workload of individual managers, help coordinate the planning activities of individual managers, bring to a particular problem many different tools and techniques, take a broader view than individual managers, and go beyond pet projects and particular departments.

Planning Task Force   Organizations sometimes use a planning task force to help develop plans. Such a task force often comprises line managers with a special interest in the relevant area of planning. The task force may also have members from the planning staff if the organization has one. A planning task force is most often created when the organization wants to address a special circumstance. For example, when Electronic Data Systems (EDS) decided to expand its information management services to Europe, managers knew that the firm's normal planning approach would not suffice, and top management created a special planning task force. The task force included representatives from each of the major units within the company, the corporate planning staff, and the management team that would run the European operation. Once the plan for entering the European market was formulated and implemented, the task force was eliminated.[17]

Board of Directors   Among its other responsibilities, the board of directors establishes the corporate mission and strategy. In some companies the board takes an active role in the planning process. At CBS, for example, the board of directors has traditionally played a major role in planning. In other companies the board selects a competent chief executive and delegates planning to that individual.

Chief Executive Officer   The chief executive officer (CEO) is usually the president or the chair of the board of directors. The CEO is probably the single most important individual in any organization's planning process. The CEO plays a major role in the complete planning process and is responsible for implementing the strategy. The board and CEO, then, assume direct roles in planning. The other organizational components involved in the planning process have more of an advisory or consulting role.

Executive Committee   The executive committee is usually composed of the top executives in the organization working together as a group. Committee members usually meet regularly to provide input to the CEO on the proposals that affect their own units and to review the various strategic plans that develop from this input. Members of the executive committee are frequently assigned to various staff committees, subcommittees, and task forces to concentrate on specific projects or problems that might confront the entire organization at some time in the future.

Line Management   The final component of most organizations' planning activities is line management. Line managers are those persons with formal authority and responsibility for the management of the organization. They play an important role in an organization's planning process for two reasons. First, they are a valuable source of inside information for other managers as plans are formulated and implemented. Second, the line managers at the middle and lower levels of the organization usually must execute the plans developed by top management. Line management identifies, analyzes, and recommends program alternatives, develops budgets and submits them for approval, and finally sets the plans in motion.

Contingency Planning

Another important type of planning is **contingency planning**, or the determination of alternative courses of action to be taken if an intended plan of action is

contingency planning The determination of alternative courses of action to be taken if an intended plan of action is unexpectedly disrupted or rendered inappropriate

unexpectedly disrupted or rendered inappropriate.[18] An excellent example of contingency planning is what was for a while called the Y2K problem. Concerns about the impact of technical glitches in computers stemming from their internal clocks changing from 1999 to 2000 resulted in contingency planning for most organizations. Many banks and hospitals, for example, had extra staff available; some organizations created backup computer systems; and some even stockpiled inventory in case they couldn't purchase new products or materials.[19]

The mechanics of contingency planning are shown in Figure 7.3. In relation to an organization's other plans, contingency planning comes into play at four action points. At action point 1, management develops the basic plans of the organization. These may include strategic, tactical, and operational plans. As part of this development process, managers usually consider various contingency events. Some management groups even assign someone the role of devil's advocate to ask, "But what if . . ." about each course of action. A variety of contingencies are usually considered.

At action point 2, the plan that management chooses is put into effect. The most important contingency events are also defined. Only the events that are likely to occur and whose effects will have a substantial impact on the organization are used in the contingency-planning process. Next, at action point 3, the company specifies certain indicators or signs that suggest that a contingency event is about to take place. A bank might decide that a 2-percent drop in interest rates should be considered a contingency event. An indicator might be two consecutive months with a drop of 0.5 percent in each. As indicators of contingency events are being defined, the contingency plans themselves should also be developed. Examples of contingency plans for various situations are delaying plant construction, developing a new manufacturing process, and cutting prices.

After this stage, the managers of the organization monitor the indicators identified at action point 3. If the situation dictates, a contingency plan is implemented.

Figure 7.3

Contingency Planning

Most organizations develop contingency plans. These plans specify alternative courses of action to be taken if an intended plan is unexpectedly disrupted or rendered inappropriate.

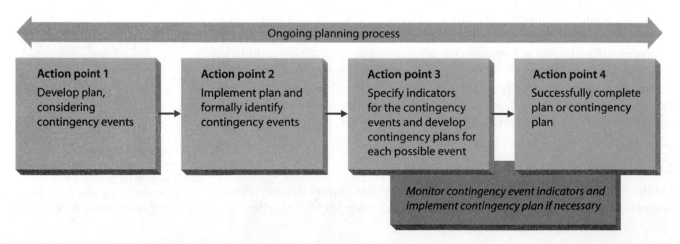

Otherwise the primary plan of action continues in force. Finally, action point 4 marks the successful completion of either the original or a contingency plan.

Contingency planning is becoming increasingly important for most organizations and especially for those operating in particularly complex or dynamic environments. Few managers have such an accurate view of the future that they can anticipate and plan for everything. Contingency planning is a useful technique for helping managers cope with uncertainty and change.

MANAGEMENT IMPLICATIONS Managers should understand that organizations rely on several different kinds of plans that span different levels and different time frames. Similarly, they should also recognize that different managers are responsible for different kinds of planning activities, and they should be ready and prepared to play an appropriate role. In addition, all managers should understand that the potential for unexpected events makes it important to develop contingency plans.

Tactical Planning

As we noted earlier, tactical plans are developed to implement specific parts of a strategic plan. You have probably heard the saying about winning the battle but losing the war. Tactical plans are to battles what strategy is to a war: an organized sequence of steps designed to execute strategic plans. Strategy focuses on resources, environment, and mission, whereas tactics focus primarily on people and action.[20] Figure 7.4 identifies the major elements in developing and executing tactical plans.

Developing Tactical Plans

Although effective tactical planning depends on many factors that vary from one situation to another, we can identify some basic guidelines. First, the manager needs to recognize that tactical planning must address a number of tactical goals derived from a broader strategic goal.[21] An occasional situation may call for a stand-alone tactical plan, but most of the time tactical plans flow from and must be consistent with a strategic plan.

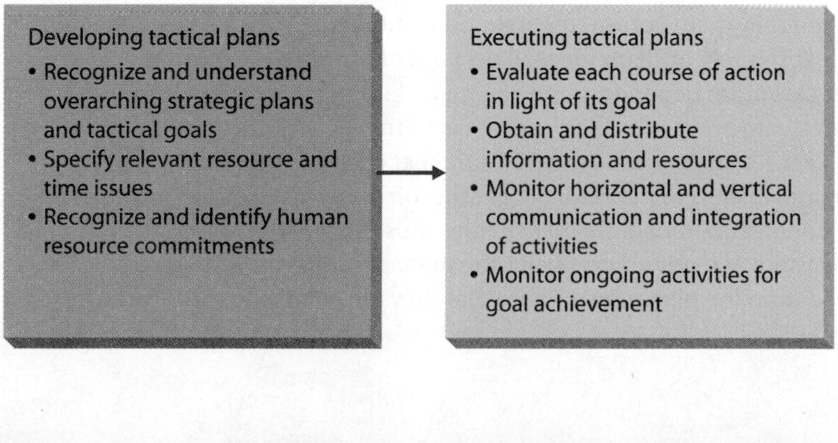

Developing tactical plans
- Recognize and understand overarching strategic plans and tactical goals
- Specify relevant resource and time issues
- Recognize and identify human resource commitments

Executing tactical plans
- Evaluate each course of action in light of its goal
- Obtain and distribute information and resources
- Monitor horizontal and vertical communication and integration of activities
- Monitor ongoing activities for goal achievement

Figure 7.4

Developing and Executing Tactical Plans

Tactical plans are used to accomplish specific parts of a strategic plan. Each strategic plan is generally implemented through several tactical plans. Effective tactical planning involves both development and execution.

For example, a few years ago top managers at Coca-Cola developed a strategic plan for maintaining the firm's dominance of the soft-drink industry. As part of developing the plan, they identified a critical environmental threat—considerable unrest and uncertainty among the independent bottlers who packaged and distributed Coca-Cola's products. To counter this threat and strengthen the company's position simultaneously, Coca-Cola bought several large independent bottlers and combined them into one new organization called Coca-Cola Enterprises. Selling half of the new company's stock reaped millions in profits while still effectively keeping control of the enterprise in Coca-Cola's hands. Thus, the creation of the new business was a tactical plan developed to contribute to the achievement of an overarching strategic goal.[22]

Second, although strategies are often stated in general terms, tactics must specify resources and time frames. A strategy can call for being number one in a particular market or industry, but a tactical plan must specify precisely what activities will be undertaken to achieve that goal. Consider the Coca-Cola example again. Another element of its strategic plan involves increased worldwide market share. To facilitate additional sales in Europe, managers developed tactical plans for building a new plant in the south of France to make soft-drink concentrate and for building another canning plant in Dunkirk. Building these plants represents a concrete action involving measurable resources (i.e., funds to build the plants) and a clear time horizon (i.e., a target date for completion).

Finally, tactical planning requires the use of human resources. Managers involved in tactical planning spend a great deal of time working with other people. They must be in a position to receive information from others in and outside the organization, process that information in the most effective way, and then pass it on to others who might make use of it. Coca-Cola executives have been intensively involved in planning the new plants, setting up the new bottling venture noted earlier, and exploring a joint venture with Cadbury Schweppes in the United Kingdom. Each activity has required considerable time and effort from dozens of managers. One manager, for example, crossed the Atlantic twelve times while negotiating the Cadbury deal.

Executing Tactical Plans

Regardless of how well a tactical plan is formulated, its ultimate success depends on the way it is carried out. Successful implementation, in turn, depends on the astute use of resources, effective decision making, and insightful steps to ensure that the right things are done at the right time and in the right ways. A manager can see an absolutely brilliant idea fail because of improper execution.

Proper execution depends on several important factors. First, the manager needs to evaluate every possible course of action in light of the goal it is intended to reach. Next, he or she needs to make sure that each decision maker has the information and resources necessary to get the job done. Vertical and horizontal communication and integration of activities must be present to minimize conflict and inconsistent activities. And finally, the manager must monitor ongoing activities derived from the plan to make sure that they are achieving the desired results.

This monitoring typically takes place within the context of the organization's ongoing control systems.

For example, managers at The Walt Disney Company recently developed a new strategic plan aimed at spurring growth and profits from foreign markets. One tactical plan developed to stimulate growth involves expanding the cable Disney Channel into more and more foreign markets; another involves building a new theme park near Hong Kong. Although expanding cable television and building a new theme park are big undertakings in their own right, they are still tactical plans within the overall strategic plan focusing on international growth.[23]

MANAGEMENT IMPLICATIONS While strategic planning is, of course, critical to the success of any organization, tactical planning often makes the difference in how well strategies actually work. Thus, tactical plans should be developed and executed with as much care as the organization devotes to other kinds of planning.

Operational Planning

Another critical element in effective organizational planning is the development and implementation of operational plans. Operational plans are derived from tactical plans and are aimed at achieving operational goals. Thus, operational plans tend to be narrowly focused, have relatively short time horizons, and involve lower-level managers. The two most basic forms of operational plans and specific types of each are summarized in Table 7.1.

Table 7.1

Types of Operational Plans

Organizations develop various operational plans to help achieve operational goals. In general, there are two types of single-use plans and three types of standing plans.

Plan	Description
Single-use plan	Developed to carry out a course of action not likely to be repeated in the future
Program	Single-use plan for a large set of activities
Project	Single-use plan of less scope and complexity than a program
Standing plan	Developed for activities that recur regularly over a period of time
Policy	Standing plan specifying the organization's general response to a designated problem or situation
Standard operating procedure	Standing plan outlining steps to be followed in particular circumstances
Rules and regulations	Standing plans describing exactly how specific activities are to be carried out

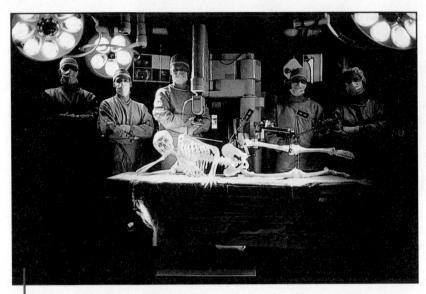

Many surgeons rely heavily on standard operating procedures. For example, these doctors specialize in hip replacement surgeries. A modified industrial robot, shown above the skeleton, is used to drill a precise hole in a femur so that the implant can be fitted exactly as the doctors want it. A clearly defined set of procedures guides the team through every surgery it conducts. At the same time, however, the doctors are also prepared to deviate from established procedures as circumstances warrant.

Single-Use Plans

A **single-use plan** is developed to carry out a course of action that is not likely to be repeated in the future. As Disney proceeds with its new theme park in Hong Kong, it will develop numerous single-use plans for individual rides, attractions, and hotels. The two most common forms of single-use plans are programs and projects.

Programs   A **program** is a single-use plan for a large set of activities. It might consist of identifying procedures for introducing a new product line, opening a new facility, or changing the organization's mission. As part of its own strategic plans for growth, Black & Decker bought General Electric's small-appliance business. The deal involved the largest brand-name switch in history: 150 products were converted from GE to the Black & Decker label. Each product was carefully studied, redesigned, and reintroduced with an extended warranty. A total of 140 steps were used for each product. It took three years to convert all 150 products over to Black & Decker. The total conversion of the product line was a program.

Projects   A **project** is similar to a program but is generally of less scope and complexity. A project may be part of a broader program, or it may be a self-contained single-use plan. For Black & Decker, the conversion of each of the 150 products was a separate project in its own right. Each product had its own manager, its own schedule, and so forth. Projects are also used to introduce a new product within an existing product line or to add a new benefit option to an existing salary package.

single-use plan Developed to carry out a course of action that is not likely to be repeated in the future

program A single-use plan for a large set of activities

project A single-use plan of less scope and complexity than a program

Standing Plans

Whereas single-use plans are developed for nonrecurring situations, a **standing plan** is developed for activities that recur regularly over a period of time. Standing plans can greatly enhance efficiency by routinizing decision making. Policies, standard operating procedures, and rules and regulations are three kinds of standing plans.

standing plan Developed for activities that recur regularly over a period of time

Policies   As a general guide for action, a policy is the most general form of standing plan. A **policy** specifies the organization's general response to a designated problem or situation. For example, McDonald's has a policy that it will not grant a franchise to an individual who already owns another fast-food restaurant. Similarly, Starbucks' has a policy that it will not franchise at all, instead, retaining own-

policy A standing plan that specifies the organization's general response to a designated problem or situation

BEETLE BAILEY By Mort Walker

ership of all Starbucks' coffee shops. Likewise, a university admissions office might establish a policy that admission will be granted only to applicants with a minimum SAT score of 1,000 and a ranking in the top quarter of their high-school classes. Admissions officers may routinely deny admission to applicants who fail to reach these minimum requirements. A policy is also likely to describe how exceptions are to be handled. The university's policy statement, for example, might create an admissions appeals committee to evaluate applicants who do not meet minimum requirements but may warrant special consideration.

Standard Operating Procedures Another type of standing plan is the **standard operating procedure**, or **SOP**. An SOP is more specific than a policy because it outlines the steps to be followed in particular circumstances. The admissions clerk at the university, for example, might be told that when an application is received, he or she should (1) set up a file for the applicant; (2) add test-score records, transcripts, and letters of reference to the file as they are received; and (3) give the file to the appropriate admissions director when it is complete. Gallo Vineyards in California has a three-hundred-page manual of standard operating procedures. This planning manual is credited with making Gallo one of the most efficient wine operations in the United States. McDonald's has SOPs explaining exactly how Big Macs are to be cooked, how long they can stay in the warming rack, and so forth.

Rules and Regulations The narrowest of the standing plans, **rules and regulations** describe exactly how specific activities are to be carried out. Rather than guiding decision making, rules and regulations actually take the place of decision making in various situations. Each McDonald's restaurant has a rule prohibiting customers from using its telephones, for example. The university admissions office might have a rule stipulating that if an applicant's file is not complete two months before the beginning of a semester, the student cannot be admitted until the next semester. Of course, in most organizations a manager at a higher level can suspend or bend the rules. If the high-school transcript of the child of a prominent university alumnus and donor arrives a few days late, the director of admissions might waive the two-month rule. Rules and regulations can become problematic if they are excessive or enforced too rigidly.

Standard operating procedures, rules, and regulations can all be useful methods for saving time, improving efficiency, and streamlining decision making and planning. But it is also helpful to review SOPs, rules, and regulations periodically to ensure that they remain useful. For example, as shown in this cartoon, an SOP for regularly ordering parts and supplies may become less effective if the demand for those parts and supplies changes or disappears.

standard operating procedure (SOP) A standing plan that outlines the steps to be followed in particular circumstances

rules and regulations Describe exactly how specific activities are to be carried out

Rules and regulations and SOPs are similar in many ways. They are both relatively narrow in scope, and each can serve as a substitute for decision making. An SOP typically describes a sequence of activities, whereas rules and regulations focus on one activity. Recall our examples: the admissions-office SOP consisted of three activities, whereas the two-month rule related to one activity only. In an industrial setting, the SOP for orienting a new employee could involve enrolling the person in various benefit options, introducing him or her to coworkers and supervisors, and providing a tour of the facilities. A pertinent rule for the new employee might involve the starting time for work each day.

MANAGEMENT IMPLICATIONS Managers need to understand the various kinds of operating plans that organizations use. This understanding should enable them to assess when to use operating plans. At the same time, managers should be flexible about how they use operating plans.

Managing Goal-Setting and Planning Processes

Obviously, all the elements of goal setting and planning discussed to this point involve managing these processes in some way or another. In addition, however, because major barriers sometimes impede effective goal setting and planning, knowing how to overcome some of the barriers is important.

Barriers to Goal Setting and Planning

Several circumstances can serve as barriers to effective goal setting and planning; the more common ones are listed in Table 7.2. The *World of Management* also discusses barriers to goal setting and planning.

Table 7.2

Barriers to Goal Setting and Planning
As part of managing the goal-setting and planning processes, managers must understand the barriers that can disrupt them. Managers must also know how to overcome the barriers.

Major barriers	Inappropriate goals
	Improper reward system
	Dynamic and complex environment
	Reluctance to establish goals
	Resistance to change
	Constraints
Overcoming the barriers	Understanding the purposes of goals and planning
	Communication and participation
	Consistency, revision, and updating
	Effective reward systems

WORLD OF MANAGEMENT

PLANNING FOR OPEN COMPETITION IN CHINA

As the date approaches for China to open its doors to international competition, managers of many local companies are worried about their ability to fight off foreign rivals. Not Tsingtao Brewery. After years of battling U.S., German, and other beer brands that have targeted internal Chinese markets, Tsingtao's top managers have become seasoned veterans in developing plans for managing the beer business at home and abroad.

Tsingtao's planning process was less formal in the days before foreign competition. Domestic beer consumption was on the rise, so management mostly cranked up production in response to orders that came in from distributors around the country. The company was also exporting to the United States, where its beer is sold in Chinese restaurants. Once experienced global giants such as Anheuser-Busch and Heineken began selling their beers in China, however, Tsingtao was forced to tighten its planning procedures. Even so, sales and profits plummeted during the first few years of all-out competition. Then new management came in, bringing new ideas and a more disciplined approach to setting and meeting goals for matching production to demand. In this way, Tsingtao could lower its inventory costs and keep fresh beer on store shelves.

Thanks to better planning and implementation, Tsingtao's output, sales, and profits have risen dramatically in recent years. At the same time, the company is planning for future growth by buying up struggling breweries all over China. Now the once-robust domestic beer market is showing signs of going flat, which means Tsingtao's managers will have to sharpen their planning skills yet again to stay ahead of non-Chinese beer makers.

> *Some industries are afraid of foreign competition. Competing with foreign brands, we learned how markets worked.*
>
> *—Peng Zuo Yi, CEO, Tsingtao Brewery**

Reference: Paul Wiseman, "Chinese Beer Barrels Up to the World's Bar," *USA Today*, January 18, 2000, pp. 1B, 2B (*quote on p. 1B).

Inappropriate Goals Inappropriate goals come in many forms. Paying a large dividend to stockholders may be inappropriate if it comes at the expense of research and development. Goals may also be inappropriate if they are unattainable. If Kmart were to set a goal of having more revenues than Wal-Mart next year, employees at the company would probably be embarrassed because achieving such a goal would be impossible. Goals may also be inappropriate if they place too much emphasis on either quantitative or qualitative measures of success. Some goals, especially those relating to financial areas, are quantifiable, objective, and verifiable. Other goals, such as employee satisfaction and development, are difficult if not impossible to quantify. Organizations are asking for trouble if they put too much emphasis on one type of goal to the exclusion of the other.

Improper Reward System In some settings, an improper reward system acts as a barrier to goal setting and planning. For example, people may inadvertently be rewarded for poor goal-setting behavior or be unrewarded or even punished for proper goal-setting behavior. Suppose that a manager sets a goal of decreasing turnover next year. If turnover is decreased by even a fraction, the manager can claim success and perhaps be rewarded for the accomplishment. In contrast, a

A dynamic and complex environment is one of the most challenging barriers to effective goal-setting and planning. Consider, for example, the situation faced by Salim Teja, co-founder and chief strategist of Accompany, a Silicon Valley-based online buying club. He took Accompany from an abstract concept to a going concern in less than three months. Teja has had to shift his firm's strategy several times, sometimes within a matter of hours, because of environmental shifts and changes. He uses e-mail to communicate these shifts to Accompany workers immediately, in part so they can better perform their jobs and in part so that they feel more invested in the outcome.

manager who attempts to decrease turnover by 5 percent but actually achieves a decrease of only 4 percent may receive a smaller reward because of her or his failure to reach the established goal. And if an organization places too much emphasis on short-term performance and results, managers may ignore longer-term issues as they set goals and formulate plans to achieve higher profits in the short-term.

Dynamic and Complex Environment   The nature of an organization's environment is also a barrier to effective goal setting and planning. Rapid change, technological innovation, and intense competition can each increase the difficulty of an organization accurately assessing future opportunities and threats. For example, when an electronics firm like IBM develops a long-range plan, it tries to take into account how much technological innovation is likely to occur during that interval. But forecasting such events is extremely difficult. During the early boom years of personal computers, data were stored primarily on floppy disks. Because these disks had a limited storage capacity, hard disks were developed. Whereas the typical floppy disk can hold hundreds of pages of information, a hard disk can store thousands of pages. Today computers increasingly store information on optical disks that hold millions of pages. The manager attempting to set goals and plan in this rapidly changing environment faces a truly formidable task. *Management InfoTech* presents several pertinent examples illustrating how hard it is to predict the future, especially where technology is concerned!

Reluctance to Establish Goals   Another barrier to effective planning is the reluctance of some managers to establish goals for themselves and their units of responsibility. The reason for this reluctance may be lack of confidence or fear of failure. If a manager sets a goal that is specific, concise, and time related, then whether he or she attains it is obvious. Managers who consciously or unconsciously try to avoid this degree of accountability are likely to hinder the organization's planning efforts. Pfizer, a large pharmaceutical company, ran into problems because its managers did not set goals for research and development. Consequently, the organization fell further and further behind because managers had no way of knowing how effective their R&D efforts actually were.

Resistance to Change   Another barrier to goal setting and planning is resistance to change. Planning essentially involves changing something about the organization. As we will see in Chapter 13, people tend to resist change. Avon Products almost drove itself into bankruptcy several years ago because it insisted on contin-

A FEW POORLY CHOSEN WORDS FROM THE PAST

Today is full of blind spots. So was yesterday, the year before, the century before that, the millennium before that. The future is perpetually around the corner, invisible to mere mortals, no matter how wise.

To wit, these pratfalls (culled from the Internet, various media, and Herb London, publisher of *American Outlook* magazine):

"Drill for oil? You mean drill into the ground to try and find oil? You're crazy."

—*Workers to railroad conductor Edwin Drake before he drilled the first successful U.S. oil, 1859*

"Well-informed people know it is impossible to transmit the voice over wires and that were it possible to do so, the thing would be of no practical value."

—Boston Post, *1865*

"Heavier-than-air flying machines are impossible."

—**Lord Kelvin** *of the British Royal Society, one of the nineteenth century's top experts on thermodynamics, 1890s*

"The world is coming to an end in 1950."

—*Historian* **Henry Adams**, *1903*

"There is no likelihood man can ever tap the power of the atom."

—*Nobel Prize–winning physicist* **Robert Milliken**, *1923*

"Who the hell wants to hear actors talk?"

—**H. M. Warner**, *Warner Bros., 1927*

"A rocket will never be able to leave the earth's atmosphere."

—The New York Times, *1936*

"I think there is a world market for maybe five computers."

—*IBM's* **Thomas Watson**, *1943*

"Television won't last because people will soon get tired of staring at a plywood box every night."

—*Producer* **Darryl Zanuck**, *20th Century Fox, 1946*

"If excessive smoking actually plays a role in the production of lung cancer, it seems to be a minor one."

—**W. C. Heuper**, *National Cancer Institute, 1954*

"You ain't going nowhere, son. You ought to go back to driving a truck."

—*The Grand Ole Opry's* **Jim Dunny** *to* **Elvis Presley**, *1954*

Everything that can be invented has been invented.

—*Charles Duell, director of the U.S. patent office, 1899*

"By 2000, politics will simply fade away. We will not see any political parties."

—*Visionary and inventor* **R. Buckminster Fuller**, *1966*

"There is no need for any individual to have a computer in their home."

—**Ken Olson**, *president of Digital Equipment Corp., 1977*

"640K ought to be enough for anybody."

—*Microsoft's* **Bill Gates**, *1981, whose computers now offer more than five hundred times that much memory*

Reference: USA Today, *Tuesday, November 23, 1999, p. 5D. Copyright 1999, USA Today. Reprinted with permission.*

uing a policy of large dividend payments to its stockholders. When profits started to fall, managers resisted cutting the dividends and started borrowing to pay them. The company's debt grew from $3 million to $1.1 billion in eight years. Eventually, managers were forced to confront the problem and cut dividends.

Constraints Constraints that limit what an organization can do are another major obstacle. Common constraints include a lack of resources, government restrictions, and strong competition. For example, Owens-Corning Fiberglass Corp. took on an enormous debt burden as part of its fight to avoid a takeover by Wickes Companies. The company then had such a large debt that it was forced to cut back on capital expenditures and research and development. Those cutbacks greatly constrained what the firm can plan for the future. Time constraints are also a factor. It's easy to say, "I'm too busy to plan today; I'll do it tomorrow." Effective planning takes time, energy, and an unwavering belief in its importance.

Overcoming the Barriers

Fortunately, there are several guidelines for making goal setting and planning effective. Some of the guidelines are also listed in Table 7.2.

Understand the Purposes of Goals and Plans One of the best ways to facilitate goal-setting and planning processes is to recognize their basic purposes. Managers should also recognize that there are limits to the effectiveness of setting goals and making plans. Planning is not a panacea that will solve all of an organization's problems, nor is it an iron-clad set of procedures to be followed at any cost. And effective goals and planning do not necessarily ensure success; adjustments and exceptions are to be expected over time. For example, Coca-Cola once followed a logical and rational approach to setting goals and planning a few years ago when it introduced a new formula to combat Pepsi's increasing market share. But all the plans proved to be wrong as consumers rejected the new version of Coca-Cola. Managers quickly reversed the decision and reintroduced the old formula as Coca-Cola Classic. And it has a larger market share today than before. Even though careful planning resulted in a big mistake, the company came out ahead in the long run.

Communication and Participation Although goals and plans may be initiated at high levels, they must also be communicated to others in the organization. Everyone involved in the planning process should know what the overriding organizational strategy is, what the various functional strategies are, and how they are all to be integrated and coordinated. People responsible for achieving goals and implementing plans must have a voice in developing them from the outset. These individuals almost always have valuable information to contribute, and because they will be implementing the plans, their involvement is critical: people are usually more committed to plans that they have helped shape. Even when an organization is

Establishing goals and then working to achieve them play very important roles in organizational success. Some managers, however, have difficulty in setting meaningful goals. To enhance their abilities to set and achieve goals, some managers are starting to rely on executive coaches—essentially personal consultants who help them function more effectively. When Cheryl Weir started working with Charles Cleary at AT&T, she was unimpressed with his vague goal for his unit of "being number 1" or achieving what she saw as unambitious growth of 5 percent. She led him to set a growth goal of 16 percent and develop a plan for achieving it; and when they met this goal, Cleary's unit was among the top three in the company.

somewhat centralized or uses a planning staff, managers from a variety of levels in the organization should be involved in the planning process. When Compaq Computer set a strategic goal of moving from the number five to the number three position in the computer industry, it developed a detailed brochure explaining the goal and how it was to be achieved and distributed it to every employee in the company.

Consistency, Revision, and Updating   Goals should be consistent both horizontally and vertically. Horizontal consistency means that goals should be consistent across the organization, from one department to the next. Vertical consistency means that goals should be consistent up and down the organization: strategic, tactical, and operational goals must agree with one another. Because goal setting and planning are dynamic processes, they must also be revised and updated regularly. Many organizations are seeing the need to revise and update on an increasingly frequent basis. Citicorp, for example, once used a three-year planning horizon for developing and providing new financial services. That cycle has been cut to two years, and the bank hopes to reduce it to one year very soon.

Effective Reward Systems   In general, people should be rewarded both for establishing effective goals and plans and for successfully achieving them. Because failure sometimes results from factors outside the manager's control, however, people should also be assured that failure to reach a goal will not necessarily bring punitive consequences. Frederick Smith, founder and CEO of Federal Express, has a stated goal of encouraging risk. Thus, when Federal Express lost $233 million on an unsuccessful new service called ZapMail, no one was punished. Smith believed that the original idea was a good one but was unsuccessful for reasons beyond the company's control.

Using Goals to Implement Plans

Goals are often used to implement plans. Formal goal-setting programs represent one widely used method for managing the goal-setting and planning processes concurrently to ensure that both are done effectively. Some firms call this approach *management by objectives*, or *MBO*. We should also note, however, that while many firms use this basic approach, they frequently tailor it to their own special circumstances and use a special term or name for it.[24] For example, Tenneco uses an MBO-type system but calls it the Performance Agreement System, or PAS.

The Nature and Purpose of Formal Goal Setting   The purpose of formal goal setting is generally to give subordinates a voice in the goal-setting and planning processes and to clarify for them exactly what they are expected to accomplish in a given time span. Thus, formal goal setting is often concerned with goal setting and planning for individual managers and their units or work groups.

The Formal Goal-Setting Process   The basic mechanics of the formal goal-setting process are shown in Figure 7.5. This process is described here from an

Figure 7.5

The Formal Goal-Setting Process

Formal goal-setting is an effective technique for integrating goal setting and planning. This figure portrays the general steps that most organizations use when they adopt formal goal-setting. Of course, most organizations adapt this general process to fit their own unique needs and circumstances.

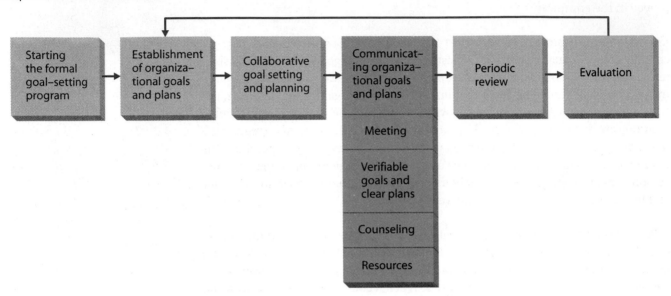

ideal perspective. In any given organization, the steps of the process are likely to vary in importance and may even take a different sequence. As a starting point, however, most managers believe that if a formal goal-setting program is to be successful, it must start at the top of the organization. Top managers must communicate why they have adopted the program, what they think it will do, and that they have accepted and are committed to formal goal setting. Employees must also be educated about what goal setting is and what their role in it will be. Having committed to formal goal setting, managers must implement it in a way that is consistent with overall organizational goals and plans. The idea is that goals set at the top will systematically cascade down throughout the organization.

Although establishing the organization's basic goals and plans is extremely important, collaborative goal setting and planning are the essence of formal goal setting. The collaboration involves a series of distinct steps. First, managers tell their subordinates what organizational and unit goals and plans top management has established. Then managers meet with their subordinates on a one-to-one basis to arrive at a set of goals and plans for each subordinate that both the subordinate and the manager have helped develop and to which both are committed. Next the goals are refined to be as verifiable (quantitative) as possible and to specify a time frame for their accomplishment. They should also be written. Further, the plans developed to achieve the goals need to be stated as clearly as possible and must relate directly to each goal. Managers must play the role of counselors in the goal-setting and planning meeting. For example, they must ensure that the subordinate's goals and plans are attainable and workable and that they will facilitate both the unit's and the organization's goals and plans. Finally, the meeting should spell out the resources that the subordinate will need to implement his or her plans and work effectively toward goal attainment.

Conducting periodic reviews as subordinates are working toward their goals is advisable. If the goals and plans are for a one-year period, meeting quarterly to discuss progress may be a good idea. At the end of the period, the manager meets with each subordinate again to review the degree of goal attainment. They discuss which goals were met and which were not met in the context of the original plans. The reasons for both success and failure are explored, and the employee is rewarded on the basis of goal attainment. In an ongoing goal setting program, the evaluation meeting may also serve as the collaborative goal-setting and planning meeting for the next time period.

The Effectiveness of Formal Goal Setting   Many organizations, including Cypress Semiconductor, Alcoa, Tenneco, Du Pont, General Motors, Boeing, Caterpillar, Westinghouse Electric, and Black & Decker, all use some form of goal setting. As might be expected, goal setting has both strengths and weaknesses. A primary benefit of goal setting is improved employee motivation. By clarifying exactly what is expected, by allowing the employee a voice in determining expectations, and by basing rewards on the achievement of those expectations, organizations create a powerful motivational system for their employees.

Communication is also enhanced through the process of discussion and collaboration. And performance appraisals may be done more objectively, with less reliance on arbitrary or subjective assessment. Goal setting focuses attention on appropriate goals and plans, helps identify superior managerial talent for future promotion, and provides a systematic management philosophy that can have a positive effect on the overall organization. Goal setting also facilitates control. The periodic development and subsequent evaluation of individual goals and plans helps keep the organization on course toward its own long-run goals and plans.

On the other hand, goal setting occasionally fails because of poor implementation. Perhaps the major problem that can derail a goal-setting program is lack of top-management support. Some organizations decide to use goal setting, but then its implementation is delegated to lower management. This approach limits the program's effectiveness because the goals and plans cascading throughout the organization may not actually be the goals and plans of top management and because others in the organization are not motivated to accept and become committed to them. Another problem with goal setting is that some firms overemphasize quantitative goals and plans and burden their systems with too much paperwork and record keeping. Some managers will not or cannot sit down and work out goals and plans with their subordinates. Rather, they "suggest" or even "assign" goals and plans to people. The result is resentment and a lack of commitment to the goal-setting program.[25]

MANAGEMENT Managers need to understand that various barriers to effective
IMPLICATIONS goal setting and planning can exist in any organization. They
should also, of course, know how to overcome these barriers. Finally, they should
recognize that goals can be used to implement plans, especially through a comprehensive goal-setting system.

Summary of Key Points

The planning process is the first basic managerial function that organizations must address. With an understanding of the environmental context, managers develop several different types of goals and plans. Decision making is the underlying framework of all planning because every step of the planning process involves a decision.

Goals serve four basic purposes: to provide guidance and direction, to facilitate planning, to inspire motivation and commitment, and to promote evaluation and control. Goals can be differentiated by level, area, and time frame. All managers within an organization need to be involved in the goal-setting process. Managers need to pay special attention to the importance of managing multiple goals through optimizing and other approaches.

Goals are closely related to planning. The major types of plans are strategic, tactical, and operational. Plans are developed across a variety of time horizons, including long-range, intermediate, and short-range time frames. Essential people in an organization responsible for effective planning are the planning staff, planning task forces, the board of directors, the CEO, the executive committee, and line management. Contingency planning helps managers anticipate and plan for unexpected changes.

After plans have been developed, the manager must address how they will be achieved. This implementation often involves tactical and operational plans. Tactical plans occur at the middle of the organization and have an intermediate time horizon and moderate scope. Tactical plans are developed to implement specific parts of a strategic plan. They must flow from strategy, specify resource and time issues, and commit human resources. Tactical plans must be effectively executed.

Operational plans occur at the lower levels of the organization, have a shorter time horizon, and are narrower in scope. Operational plans are derived from a tactical plan and are aimed at achieving one or more operational goals. Two major types of operational plans are single-use and standing plans. Single-use plans are designed to carry out a course of action that is not likely to be repeated in the future. Programs and projects are examples of single-use plans. Standing plans are designed to carry out a course of action that is likely to be repeated several times. Policies, standard operating procedures, and rules and regulations are all standing plans.

Several barriers exist to effective goal setting and planning. These barriers include inappropriate goals, an improper reward system, a dynamic and complex environment, reluctance to establish goals, resistance to change, and various constraints. Methods for overcoming these barriers include understanding the purposes of goals and plans; communication and participation; consistency, revision, and updating; and an effective reward system. One particularly useful technique for managing goal setting and planning is formal goal setting, a process of collaborative goal setting and planning.

Discussion Questions

Questions for Review

1. Describe the nature of organizational goals. Be certain to include both the purposes and kinds of goals.
2. What is contingency planning? Is being flexible about your plans the same as contingency planning? Why or why not?
3. What is tactical planning? What is operational planning? What are the similarities and differences between them?
4. What are the barriers to goal setting and planning? How can they be overcome? Can you think of any ways to overcome the barriers other than the ways identified in the text?

Questions for Analysis

5. Almost by definition, organizations cannot accomplish all of their goals. Why?
6. Which kind of plan—tactical or operational—should an organization develop first? Why? Does the order of development really make a difference as long as plans of both types are made?
7. Think of examples of each type of operational plan you have used at work, in your school work, or even in your personal life.

Questions for Application

8. Interview the head of the department in which your major exists. What kinds of goals exist for the department and for the members of the department? Share your findings with the rest of the class.
9. Interview a local small-business manager about the time frames for planning that he or she uses. How do your results compare with what you might have expected from the presentation in the textbook?
10. Interview a college or university official to determine the use of single-use and standing plans at your institution. How were these plans developed?

BUILDING EFFECTIVE *conceptual* SKILLS

Exercise Overview

Conceptual skills refer to a person's abilities to think in the abstract. This exercise will help you develop your conceptual skills by relating your own personal goals and plans across different time frames.

Exercise Background

Most people have a general idea of what they want their future to be like. However, few people actually take the time to formulate specific goals and plans for their future. To do so might provide a useful blueprint for achieving those goals while simultaneously helping people better understand the likelihood of various goals actually coming to fruition.

Exercise Task

With the background information above as context, do the following:

1. List ten goals that you would like to have achieved in ten years. These goals might relate to work, family, or anything else you see as important.
2. Next, outline a five-year plan of the goals that you think are necessary to be at the halfway point in achieving your long-term goals.

3. Now do the same thing for each one of the next five years.
4. Evaluate the likelihood of actually being able to achieve each one-year goal, the five-year goals, and the ten-year goals.
5. How might this process be similar to and different from a manager doing the same thing for business goals?

BUILDING EFFECTIVE *time-management* SKILLS

Exercise Overview

Time-management skills refer to the manager's ability to prioritize work, to work efficiently, and to delegate appropriately. This exercise will help you develop your time-management skills by relating them to the process of goal optimization.

Exercise Background

All managers face a myriad of goals, challenges, opportunities, and demands on their time. Juggling all requires a clear understanding of priorities, time availability, and related factors. Assume that you are planning to open your own business, a retail store in a local shopping mall. You are starting from scratch, with no prior business connections. You do, however, have a strong and impressive business plan that you know will work.

In planning your business, you know that you need to meet with the following parties:

1. The mall manager, to negotiate a lease.
2. A local banker, to arrange partial financing.
3. An attorney, to incorporate your business.
4. An accountant, to set up a bookkeeping system.
5. Suppliers, to arrange credit terms and delivery schedules.
6. An advertising agency, to start promoting your business.
7. A staffing agency, to hire employees.
8. A design firm, to plan the physical layout of the store.

Exercise Task

With the background information above as context, do the following:

1. Develop a schedule listing the sequence in which you need to meet with the eight parties noted above. Your schedule should be developed to minimize backtracking (i.e., seeing one party and then having to see her or him again after seeing someone else).
2. Compare your schedule with that of a classmate and discuss differences.
3. Are there different schedules that are equally valid?

BUILDING EFFECTIVE *communication* SKILLS

Exercise Overview

Communication skills refer to the manager's abilities both to convey ideas and information to others effectively and to receive ideas and information effectively from others. Communicating goals is an important part of management and requires strong communication skills.

Exercise Background

Assume that you are the CEO of a large discount retailing company. You have decided that your firm needs to change its strategy to survive. Specifically, you want the firm to move away from discount retailing and move more into specialty retailing.

To do this, you know that you will need to close four hundred of your twelve hundred discount stores within the next year. You also need both to increase the expansion rate of your two existing specialty chains and to launch one new chain. Your tentative plans call for opening three hundred new specialty stores in one business and 150 in the other next year. You also want the basic concept for the new chain to be finalized and to have ten stores open next year as well. Finally, while you will be able to transfer some discounting employees to specialty retail jobs, there will still be a few hundred people put out of work.

Exercise Task

With the background information above as context, do the following:

1. Develop a press release that outlines these goals.
2. Determine the best way to communicate the goals to your employees.
3. Develop a contingency plan for dealing with problems.

CHAPTER CLOSING CASE

Royal Caribbean Plans the Largest Luxury Liner

Top management at Royal Caribbean did not actually set out to create the largest passenger ship in the world. But by the time *Voyager of the Seas* set sail, it had become by far the largest ship in Royal Caribbean's seventeen-ship fleet—triple the size of the fabled *Titanic* and one-quarter larger than any competing ship. At a cost of $700 million, *Voyager* is not just another luxury liner—it represents a huge step toward the future by opening an entirely new portion of the vacation market. It also represents a long-term investment, because cruise ships generally stay in service for at least twenty-five years.

CEO Richard Fain and his managers started planning this ship more than three years before the anticipated launch. Their first step was establishing a challenging mission: to attract vacationers who have never taken a cruise. Because a mere 11 percent of U.S. vacationers have ever taken a cruise, this was a huge potential market as well as a huge gamble. But Fain and his team knew they were planning not for the next year or two but for the next decade, when lifestyles and vacations could be vastly different. For this reason, Royal Caribbean commissioned extensive research into consumer attitudes toward vacation activities. These attitudes became the basis for many of the special features built into *Voyager*, such as a state-of-the-art nightclub and a wedding chapel. Fain and his team also envisioned facilities for other activities not normally found on cruise ships, such as in-line skating, rock climbing, and ice skating.

With this broad outline of features in hand, Royal Caribbean managers began hiring companies to design and build everything, from the chandeliers above, to the dance floors below. Rather than hire only architects and designers with experience working on cruise ships, Fain and his managers invited some proposals from talented designers who had never worked on ships. Although other cruise lines keep costs low and simplify the planning process by hiring the same designer for all ships, Royal Caribbean was more interested in innovation than in saving money. As a result, different parts of the ship were individually designed and often constructed in different parts of the world, then assembled in the shipyard in Turku, Finland. For example, the huge saltwater aquarium tanks were made in Colorado, while the fish came from Florida;

the English pub was designed by a Rhode Island firm; and the Egyptian-theme dance lounge was designed by a British firm.

Planning and coordinating the construction of such a huge ship required careful attention to detail. So Fain created a steering committee of key managers to oversee the entire process. In regular one- to two-day sessions, the committee listened to progress reports and considered ideas for overcoming potential pitfalls. The CEO, known for his sharp memory, frequently asked hard questions that resulted in small and large changes, from moving some light fixtures (to improve the look of the room) to widening the ten-story atrium (to enhance the feeling of spaciousness). Fain and other committee members made numerous trips to Finland to examine the ship under construction and make on-the-spot decisions where necessary, knowing that details such as the noise level in the dining room can make or break the cruise experience for passengers.

Before the launch date, *Voyager* sailed a series of trial runs so managers could check that everything operated properly. Although nearly all of the 1,186 crew members were drawn from other Royal Caribbean ships, they each received ninety-two hours of training about the intricacies of the ship and its equipment. By the time *Voyager* was officially launched, it was more than the world's largest and most expensive passenger ship—it was a major part of Royal Caribbean's future.

Case Questions

1. What kind of operational plan did Royal Caribbean create for the building of *Voyager of the Seas*?

2. What kinds of problems might Royal Caribbean encounter when working on the design and construction of a unique ship such as *Voyager*? What role would contingency planning play in this situation?

3. What constraints might Royal Caribbean have faced when designing and building *Voyager*?

Case Reference

Charles Fishman, "Fantastic Voyage," *Fast Company*, March 2000, pp. 170–200.

CHAPTER NOTES

1. "Rallying the Troops at P&G," *The Wall Street Journal*, August 31, 2000, pp. B1, B4; "P&G: How New and Improved?" *Business Week*, June 21, 1999, p. 36; Katrina Brooker, "Can Procter & Gamble Change Its Culture, Protect Its Market Share, and Find the Next Tide?" *Fortune*, April 26, 1999, pp. 146–152 (quote on p. 150).

2. Patrick R. Rogers, Alex Miller, and William Q. Judge, "Using Information-Processing Theory to Understand Planning/Performance Relationships in the Context of Strategy," *Strategic Management Journal*, 1999, Vol. 20, pp. 567–577.

3. See Peter J. Brews and Michelle R. Hunt, "Learning to Plan and Planning to Learn: Resolving the Planning School/Learning School Debate," *Strategic Management Journal*, 1999, Vol. 20, pp. 889–913.

4. Max D. Richards, *Setting Strategic Goals and Objectives*, 2nd Edition (St. Paul, Minn.: West, 1986).

5. Jim Collins, "Turning Goals into Results: The Power of Catalytic Mechanisms," *Harvard Business Review*, July–August 1999, pp. 71–81.

6. "GE, No. 2 in Appliances, Is Agitating to Grab Share from Whirlpool," *The Wall Street Journal*, July 2, 1997, pp. A1, A6.

7. Kenneth R. Thompson, Wayne A. Hochwarter, and Nicholas J. Mathys, "Stretch Targets: What Makes Them Effective?" *The Academy of Management Executive*, August 1997, pp. 48–58.

8. "A Methodical Man," *Forbes*, August 11, 1997, pp. 70–72.

9. John A. Pearce II and Fred David, "Corporate Mission Statements: The Bottom Line," *The Academy of Management Executive*, May 1987, p. 109.

10. "Monsanto Boss's Vision of 'Life Sciences' Firm Now Confronts Reality," *The Wall Street Journal*, December 21, 1999, pp. A1, A10.

11. "'The McDonald's of Toiletries'," *Business Week*, August 4, 1997, pp. 79–80.

12. "Home Depot: Beyond Do-It-Yourselfers," *Business Week*, June 30, 1997, pp. 86–88.

13. See Charles Hill and Gareth Jones, *Strategic Management*, 5th Edition (Boston: Houghton Mifflin, 2001).

14. *Hoover's Handbook of World Business 2000* (Austin, Texas: Hoover's Business Press, 2000), p. 330.

15. "Nissan's Slow U-Turn," *Business Week*, May 12, 1997, pp. 54–55.

16. Peter Lorange and Balaji S. Chakravarthy, *Strategic Planning Systems*, 2nd Edition (Englewood Cliffs, N.J.: Prentice-Hall, 1989).

17. Richard I. Kirkland, Jr., "Outsider's Guide to Europe in 1992," *Fortune*, October 24, 1988, pp. 121–127.

18. K. A. Froot, D. S. Scharfstein, and J. C. Stein, "A Framework for Risk Management," *Harvard Business Review*, November–December 1994, pp. 91–102.

19. "How the Fixers Fended Off Big Disasters," *The Wall Street Journal*, December 23, 1999, pp. B1, B4.

20. James Brian Quinn, Henry Mintzberg, and Robert M. James, *The Strategy Process* (Englewood Cliffs, N.J.: Prentice-Hall, 1988).

21. Vasudevan Ramanujam and N. Venkatraman, "Planning System Characteristics and Planning Effectiveness," *Strategic Management Journal*, Vol. 8, No. 2, 1987, pp. 453–468.

22. Coca-Cola May Need to Slash Its Growth Targets," *The Wall Street Journal*, January 28, 2000, p. B2.

23. "Disney, Revisited," *USA Today*, December 14, 1999, pp. 1B, 2B.

24. Andrew Campbell, "Tailored, Not Benchmarked," *Harvard Business Review*, March–April 1999, pp. 41–48.

25. See Jack N. Kondrasuk, "Studies in MBO Effectiveness," *Academy of Management Review*, July 1981, pp. 419–430, for a review of the strengths and weaknesses of MBO.

Managing Strategy and Strategic Planning

January 2000 brought with it global celebrations of the new millennium. It also marked one of the most significant mergers in the history of business—the joining of America Online (AOL) and Time Warner into a new enterprise that some observers predicted would rewrite the rules of business for years to come. AOL launched nationwide service in 1989 and went public in 1992. It grew rapidly over the rest of the decade, attracting millions of subscribers and swallowing rival CompuServe and premier Internet portal Netscape along the way.

Time Warner, on the other hand, is an old-line company tracing its roots back almost one hundred years. Time, Inc. was founded in 1922 with the launch of its name-sake magazine *Time*. Over the decades Time also began publication of such periodicals as *Fortune, Sports Illustrated*, and *People*, and

created the cable television network HBO. Warner Brothers was born alongside the Hollywood movie industry when it produced such classics as *Little Caesar* and *Casablanca*. Warner eventually grew to encompass a movie studio, television studios, cable television operations, and a publishing business headlined by such properties as *Superman* comics and *Mad* magazine. These two firms merged in 1989 to create Time Warner; the combined firm subsequently acquired TBS (consisting of CNN and other cable networks), launched numerous new magazines, and started a new broadcast television network.

As the 1990s drew to a close, managers at both AOL and Time Warner realized that their firms had some major strategic weaknesses. AOL, for example, lacked two key competitive assets. For one thing, most of its services were carried by

and delivered through telephone wire; many experts, though, were predicting that the future of this industry rests on so-called broadband technology such as cable television. And for another, AOL itself had precious little "content" to deliver— it simply connected information sources with users who wanted access to that information.

Time Warner, meanwhile, had both of the things AOL desperately needed. Time Warner cable, for example, has over thirteen million subscribers. And information content—magazines, books, music, movies, and television programming—was the very thing Time Warner was based on. But the venerable media company, like so

"This is a merger of equals."

—*Stephen Case, CEO of AOL, and Gerald Levin, CEO of Time Warner*

LEARNING OBJECTIVES

After studying this chapter, you should be able to:

- Discuss the components of strategy, types of strategic alternatives, and the distinction between strategy formulation and strategy implementation.

- Describe how to use SWOT analysis in formulating strategy.

- Identify and describe various alternative approaches to business-level strategy formulation.

- Describe how business-level strategies are implemented.

- Identify and describe various alternative approaches to corporate-level strategy formulation.

- Describe how corporate-level strategies are implemented.

many of its old-line brethren, had failed to figure out for itself how to make the transformation to the e-world. At the time the merger was announced, Time Warner had already made a commitment of $500 million to develop a digital division, but most observers were unenthusiastic or downright skeptical about its ability to become a player.

The idea for a partnership was hatched in September 1999 at an international meeting of high-level CEOs in Paris; the players kept talking and met again two weeks later in Shanghai at a similar event. In October, a merger was formally proposed. Serious negotiations began in November. Two key AOL executives traveled to New York to meet with a senior vice president from Time Warner. The three managers locked themselves in a conference room and used poster-sized sheets of paper to sketch how a combined firm might look. These sheets were then taken back to AOL headquarters for further examination. Finally, all the details were worked out, and a final accord was reached in January 2000. When the deal was announced, the business community was stunned. One observer went so far as to call it the most transformational event in his career. And indeed, the merger was so intriguing that many experts were simply at a loss to figure out what it truly means.[1]

The actions taken by AOL and Time Warner reflect one of the most critical functions that managers perform for their businesses: strategy and strategic planning. Executives at each firm recognized that their respective firms had both significant strengths and worrisome weaknesses. They also saw that by combining their firms they could use the strengths of each firm to offset the weaknesses of the other. And they further recognized that a combined firm would be well positioned to capitalize on the emerging commercial potential of the Internet. Hence, the merger of the two firms represents a significant strategic decision by managers at the two firms.

This chapter discusses how organizations manage strategy and strategic planning. We begin by examining the nature of strategic management, including its components and alternatives. We then describe the kinds of analyses needed for firms to formulate their strategies. Next we examine how organizations first formulate and then implement business-level strategies, followed by a parallel discussion at the corporate level.

The Nature of Strategic Management

strategy A comprehensive plan for accomplishing an organization's goals

strategic management A comprehensive and ongoing management process aimed at formulating and implementing effective strategies; it is a way of approaching business opportunities and challenges

effective strategy A strategy that promotes a superior alignment between the organization and its environment and between the organization and the achievement of its strategic goals

distinctive competence An organizational strength possessed by only a small number of competing firms

scope When applied to *strategy*, it specifies the range of markets in which an organization will compete

resource deployment How an organization will distribute its resources across the areas in which it competes

A **strategy** is a comprehensive plan for accomplishing an organization's goals. **Strategic management**, in turn, is a way of approaching business opportunities and challenges—it is a comprehensive and ongoing management process aimed at formulating and implementing effective strategies. Finally, **effective strategies** are those that promote a superior alignment between the organization and its environment and the achievement of its strategic goals.[2]

The Components of Strategy

In general, a well-conceived strategy addresses three areas: distinctive competence, scope, and resource deployment. A **distinctive competence** is something the organization does exceptionally well. (We discuss distinctive competencies more fully later.) A distinctive competence of The Limited is speed in moving inventory. It tracks consumer preferences daily with point-of-sale computers, transmits orders to suppliers in Hong Kong electronically, charters 747s to fly products to the United States, and has products in stores forty-eight hours later. Because other retailers take weeks or sometimes months to accomplish the same things, The Limited relies on this distinctive competence to stay ahead of its competition.[3]

The **scope** of a strategy specifies the range of markets in which an organization will compete. Hershey Foods has essentially restricted its scope to the confectionery business, with a few related activities in other food-processing areas. In contrast, its biggest competitor, Mars, has adopted a broader scope by competing in the pet-food business and the electronics industry, among others. Some organizations, called *conglomerates*, compete in dozens or even hundreds of markets.

A strategy should also include an outline of the organization's projected **resource deployment**—how it will distribute its resources across the areas in which it competes. General Electric, for example, has been using profits from its highly successful U.S. operations to invest heavily in new businesses in Europe and Asia. Alternatively, the firm might have chosen to invest in different industries in its domestic market and/or to invest more heavily in Latin America. The choices it made about where and how much to invest reflect issues of resource deployment.[4]

Types of Strategic Alternatives

Most businesses today also develop strategies at two distinct levels. These levels provide a rich combination of strategic alternatives for organizations. The two general levels are business strategies and corporate strategies. **Business-level strategy** is the set of strategic alternatives that an organization chooses from as it conducts business in a particular industry or a particular market. Such alternatives help the organization focus its competitive efforts for each industry or market in a targeted manner.

    Corporate-level strategy is the set of strategic alternatives that an organization chooses from as it manages its operations simultaneously across several industries and several markets.[5] As we discuss later, most large companies today compete in a variety of industries and markets. Although they develop business-level strategies for each industry or market, they also develop an overall strategy that helps define the mix of industries and markets that are of interest to the firm.

Effective business strategies generally spell out such things as distinctive competencies, resource deployment, and scope. Consider, for instance, the success currently being enjoyed by Seth Goldman, owner and "Tea-EO" of Honest Tea. The distinctive competence of Honest Tea is its brewing technology: it uses real tea leaves and spring water and adds only a minimum amount of sweetener. It invests heavily in building strong relations with key partners such as socially conscious suppliers and retailers. And it limits operations to packaged tea beverages. Honest Tea has more than doubled its revenues each of the last three years and seems headed toward long-term "prosperi tea."

Strategy Formulation and Implementation

Drawing a distinction between strategy formulation and strategy implementation is also instructive. **Strategy formulation** is the set of processes involved in creating or determining the strategies of the organization, whereas **strategy implementation** is the methods by which strategies are operationalized or executed within the organization. The primary distinction is along the lines of content versus process: the formulation stage determines what the strategy is, and the implementation stage focuses on how the strategy is achieved.

    Sometimes the process of formulating and implementing strategies is rational, systematic, and planned and is often referred to as a **deliberate strategy**—a plan chosen and implemented to support specific goals.[6] Texas Instruments (TI) excels at formulating and implementing deliberate strategies. TI uses a planning

business-level strategy The set of strategic alternatives that an organization chooses from as it conducts business in a particular industry or a particular market

corporate-level strategy The set of strategic alternatives that an organization chooses from as it manages its operations simultaneously across several industries and several markets

strategy formulation The set of processes involved in creating or determining the strategies of the organization; it focuses on the content of strategies

strategy implementation The methods by which strategies are operationalized or executed within the organization; it focuses on the processes through which strategies are achieved

deliberate strategy A plan chosen and implemented to support specific goals

process that assigns most senior managers two distinct responsibilities: an operational, short-term responsibility and a strategic, long-term responsibility. Thus, one manager may be responsible for both increasing the efficiency of semiconductor operations over the next year (operational, short-term) and investigating new materials for semiconductor manufacture in the twenty-first century (strategic, long-term). TI's objective is to help managers make short-term operational decisions while keeping in mind longer-term goals and objectives.

emergent strategy A pattern of action that develops over time in an organization in the absence of missions and goals, or despite missions and goals

Other times, however, organizations use an **emergent strategy**—a pattern of action that develops over time in an organization in the absence of missions and goals, or despite missions and goals.[7] Implementing emergent strategies involves allocating resources even though an organization has not explicitly chosen its strategies. 3M has at times benefited from emergent strategies. The invention of invisible tape, for instance, provides a good example. Entrepreneurial engineers working independently took the invention to their boss, who concluded that it did not have major market potential because it was not part of an approved research and development plan. Only when the product was evaluated at the highest levels in the organization was it accepted and made part of 3M's product mix. Of course, 3M's Scotch tape became a major success, despite the fact that it arose outside the firm's established practices. 3M now counts on emergent strategies to help expand its numerous businesses.

MANAGEMENT IMPLICATIONS   Managers need to appreciate the importance of strategy and strategic management in directing their organization through its competitive environment. Part of this appreciation rests on knowing the difference between business- and corporate-level strategy, and part rests on knowing the difference between deliberate and emergent strategy.

Using SWOT Analysis to Formulate Strategy

SWOT An acronym that stands for strengths, weaknesses, opportunities, and threats

The starting point in formulating strategy is usually SWOT analysis. **SWOT** is an acronym that stands for strengths, weaknesses, opportunities, and threats. As shown in Figure 8.1, SWOT analysis is a careful evaluation of an organization's internal strengths and weaknesses as well as its environmental opportunities and threats. In SWOT analysis, the best strategies accomplish an organization's mission by (1) exploiting an organization's opportunities and strengths while (2) neutralizing its threats and (3) avoiding (or correcting) its weaknesses.

Evaluating an Organization's Strengths

organizational strength A skill or capability that enables an organization to conceive of and implement its strategies

Organizational strengths are skills and capabilities that enable an organization to conceive of and implement its strategies. Sears, for example, has a nationwide network of trained service employees who repair Sears appliances. Jane Thompson, a Sears executive, conceived of a plan to consolidate repair and home-improvement services nationwide under the well-known Sears brand name and to promote it as a general repair operation for all appliances, not just those purchased from Sears. Thus, the firm is capitalizing on existing capabilities and the strength of its name to launch a new operation.[8] Different strategies call on different skills and capabilities. For example, Matsushita Electric has demonstrated strengths in manufacturing and selling consumer electronics under the brand name Panasonic. Matsushita's strength in electronics does not ensure success, however, if the firm expands into insurance, swimming-pool manufacture, or retail. Different strategies such as these require different organizational strengths. SWOT analysis divides organizational strengths into two categories: common strengths and distinctive competencies. *Working with Diversity* also describes how some firms effectively use diversity to build organizational strength.

Common Organizational Strengths

A **common strength** is an organizational capability possessed by numerous competing firms. For example, all the major Hollywood film studios possess common strengths in lighting, sound recording, set and costume design, and makeup. *Competitive parity* exists when large numbers of competing firms can implement the same strategy. In this situation organizations generally attain only average levels of performance. Thus, a film company that exploits only its common strengths in choosing and implementing strategies is not likely to go beyond average performance.

Distinctive Competencies

A distinctive competency is a strength possessed by only a small number of competing firms. Distinctive competencies are rare among a set of competitors. George Lucas's Industrial Light and Magic (ILM), for example, has brought the cinematic art of special effects to new heights. Some of ILM's special effects can be produced by no other organization; these rare special effects are thus ILM's distinctive competencies. Organizations that exploit their distinctive competencies often obtain a *competitive advantage* and attain above-normal economic performance.[9] Indeed, a main purpose of SWOT analysis is to discover an organization's distinctive competencies so that the organization can choose and implement strategies that exploit its unique organizational strengths.

Imitation of Distinctive Competencies

An organization that possesses distinctive competencies and exploits them in the strategies it chooses can expect to obtain a competitive advantage and above-normal economic performance. However, its success will lead other organizations to duplicate these advantages. **Strategic imitation** is the practice of duplicating another firm's distinctive competency and thereby

Figure 8.1

SWOT Analysis

SWOT analysis is one of the most important steps in formulating strategy. Using the organization's mission as a context, managers assess internal strengths (distinctive competencies) and weaknesses as well as external opportunities and threats. The goal is then to develop good strategies that exploit opportunities and strengths, neutralize threats, and avoid weaknesses.

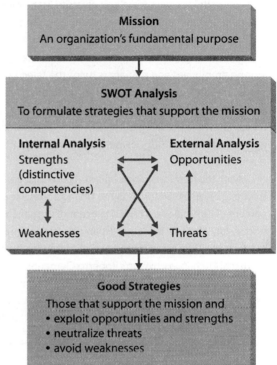

common strength An organizational capability possessed by numerous competing firms

strategic imitation The practice of duplicating another organization's distinctive competency and thereby implementing a valuable strategy

DIVERSITY AS A COMPETITIVE ADVANTAGE

When leading organizations such as SBC Communications, Hyatt, and Public Service Company of New Mexico conduct a SWOT analysis, they can count diversity among their competitive strengths. In today's multicultural environment, a diverse workforce and diversity in the ranks of management and the board of directors can help companies attract talented employees and better serve all kinds of customers.

At Texas-based SBC Communications, for example, diversity among employees and managers helps the telecommunications company understand and respond to the needs of its multicultural customer base. Representatives at SBC's call center speak twenty languages. The company also donates to programs that help minority-owned suppliers obtain financing for business operations.

Hyatt, the hotel chain headquartered in Chicago, has one of the most diverse workforces in the United States. More than 60 percent of its employees and 35 percent of its managers come from Asian, African American, Hispanic, or Native American backgrounds. Hyatt is so committed to diversity that it built a full-size industrial kitchen in Chicago's Roberto Clemente High School to encourage the mainly Latino student body to consider cooking as a career. Already, one Clemente graduate has risen through the ranks to become head banquet chef at a Hyatt hotel.

Diversity is also a priority at the Public Service Company of New Mexico, where Hispanic employees make up more than 40 percent of the workforce. The company goes out of its way to nurture talent through an innovative program in which promising managers serve for four months as the chairman's executive assistant. In addition to arranging the chairman's schedule, the assistants accompany him to a variety of meetings—including sessions with state regulators and corporate directors. Along the way, the assistants soak up valuable knowledge while showing what they can do. So far, three assistants have used the program as a springboard to higher management, adding to the diversity at senior levels and expanding the organization's strengths through their insights and experience.

> *This is a way to find young, talented people in the middle ranks—particularly women and minorities.*
>
> —*Benjamin Montoya, chairman, Public Service Company of New Mexico**

Reference: Christine Y. Chen and Jonathan Hickman, "America's 50 Best Companies for Minorities," *Fortune,* July 10, 2000, pp. 190–200 (*quote on p. 200).

---

implementing a valuable strategy. Although some distinctive competencies can be imitated, others cannot. When a distinctive competency cannot be imitated, strategies that exploit these competencies generate sustained competitive advantages. A **sustained competitive advantage** is a competitive advantage that exists after all attempts at strategic imitation have ceased.[10]

A distinctive competency might not be imitated for three reasons. First, the acquisition or development of the distinctive competency may depend on unique historical circumstances that other organizations cannot replicate. Caterpillar, for example, obtained a sustained competitive advantage when the U.S. Army granted it a long-term contract during World War II. The Army felt obligated to offer this contract because of the acute international construction requirements necessary to meet the army's needs. Caterpillar's current competitors, including Komatsu and Deere & Company, cannot re-create these circumstances.

sustained competitive advantage A competitive advantage that exists after all attempts at strategic imitation have ceased

Second, a distinctive competency might be difficult to imitate because its nature and character might not be known or understood by competing firms. Procter & Gamble, for example, considers that its sustained competitive advantage is based on its manufacturing practices. Large sections of Procter & Gamble's plants are screened off to keep this information secure. Industrial Light & Magic also refuses to disclose how it creates some of its special effects.

Finally, a distinctive competency can be difficult to imitate if it is based on complex social phenomena, like organizational teamwork or culture. Competing organizations may know, for example, that a firm's success is directly traceable to the teamwork among its managers but may not be able to imitate this distinctive competency because teamwork is a difficult thing to create.

Evaluating an Organization's Weaknesses

Organizational weaknesses are skills and capabilities that do not enable an organization to choose and implement strategies that support its mission. An organization has essentially two ways of addressing weaknesses. First, it may need to make investments to obtain the strengths required to implement strategies that support its mission. Second, it may need to modify its mission so that it can be accomplished with the skills and capabilities that the organization already possesses.

In practice, organizations have a difficult time focusing on weaknesses, in part because organization members are often reluctant to admit that they do not possess all the skills and capabilities needed. Evaluating weaknesses also calls into question the judgment of managers who chose the organization's mission in the first place and who failed to invest in the skills and capabilities needed to accomplish it.

Organizations that fail either to recognize or overcome their weaknesses are likely to suffer from competitive disadvantages. An organization has a **competitive disadvantage** when it is not implementing valuable strategies that are being implemented by competing organizations. Organizations with a competitive disadvantage can expect to attain below-average levels of performance.

> **organizational weakness** A skill or capability that does not enable an organization to choose and implement strategies that support its mission

> **competitive disadvantage** A situation in which an organization is not implementing valuable strategies that are being implemented by competing organizations

Evaluating an Organization's Opportunities and Threats

Whereas evaluating strengths and weaknesses focuses attention on the internal workings of an organization, evaluating opportunities and threats requires analyzing an organization's environment. **Organizational opportunities** are areas that may generate higher performance. **Organizational threats** are areas that increase the difficulty of an organization performing at a high level. Porter's five forces model of the competitive environment, as discussed in Chapter 3, can be used to characterize the extent of opportunity and threat in an organization's environment.

Recall that Porter's five forces are level of rivalry, power of suppliers, power of customers, threat of substitutes, and threat of new entrants. In general, when the level of rivalry, the power of suppliers and customers, and the threat of substitutes and new entrants are all high, an industry has relatively few opportunities and

> **organizational opportunity** An area in the environment that, if exploited, may generate higher performance

> **organizational threat** An area in the environment that increases the difficulty of an organization performing at a high level

numerous threats. Firms in these types of industries typically have the potential to achieve only normal economic performance. On the other hand, when the level of rivalry, the power of suppliers and customers, and the threat of substitutes and new entrants are all low, then an industry has numerous opportunities and relatively few threats. These industries hold the potential for above-normal performance for member organizations.[11]

MANAGEMENT   Managers need to understand how to perform a SWOT analy-
IMPLICATIONS   sis. Understanding the differences between common organizational strengths and distinctive competencies can help managers avoid competitive parity and achieve a competitive advantage. Assessing organizational strengths and weaknesses is also a difficult—but very important—part of this process.

Formulating Business-Level Strategies

Several frameworks have been developed for identifying the major strategic alternatives that organizations should consider when choosing their business-level strategies. Three important classification schemes are Porter's generic strategies, the Miles and Snow typology, and strategies based on the product life cycle.

Porter's Generic Strategies

According to Michael Porter, organizations may pursue a differentiation, overall cost leadership, or focus strategy at the business level.[12] Table 8.1 summarizes each of these strategies. An organization that pursues a **differentiation strategy** seeks to distinguish itself from competitors through the quality of its products or services. Firms that successfully implement a differentiation strategy can charge more than competitors because customers are willing to pay more to obtain the extra value they perceive.[13] Rolex pursues a differentiation strategy. Rolex watches are hand made of gold and stainless steel and are subjected to strenuous tests of quality and reliability. The firm's reputation enables it to charge thousands of dollars for its watches. Other firms that use differentiation strategies are Lexus, Nikon, Cross, and Ralph Lauren.

An organization implementing an **overall cost leadership strategy** attempts to gain a competitive advantage by reducing its costs below the costs of competing firms. By keeping costs low, the organization can sell its products at low prices and still make a profit. Timex uses an overall cost leadership strategy. For decades, this firm has specialized in manufacturing relatively simple, low-cost watches for the mass market. The price of Timex watches, starting around $39.95, is low because of the company's efficient high-volume manufacturing capacity. Other firms that implement overall cost leadership strategies are Hyundai, Eastman Kodak, and Bic.

A firm pursuing a **focus strategy** concentrates on a specific regional market, product line, or group of buyers. This strategy may have either a differentiation focus, whereby the firm differentiates its products in the focus market, or an overall

differentiation strategy A strategy in which an organization seeks to distinguish itself from competitors through the quality of its products or services

overall cost leadership strategy A strategy in which an organization attempts to gain a competitive advantage by reducing its costs below the costs of competing firms

focus strategy A strategy in which an organization concentrates on a specific regional market, product line, or group of buyers

Strategy Type	Definition	Examples
Differentiation	Distinguish products or services	Rolex (watches) Mercedes-Benz (automobiles) Nikon (cameras) Cross (writing instruments) Hewlett-Packard (handheld calculators)
Overall cost leadership	Reduce manufacturing and other costs	Timex Hyundai Kodak Bic Texas Instruments
Focus	Concentrate on specific regional market, product market, or group of buyers	Tag Heuer Fiat, Alpha Romeo Polaroid Waterman Pens Fisher Price

Table 8.1

Porter's Generic Strategies
Michael Porter has proposed three generic strategies. These strategies, called differentiation, overall cost leadership, and focus, are each presumed to be widely applicable to many different competitive situations.

cost leadership focus, whereby the firm manufactures and sells its products at low cost in the focus market. In the watch industry, Tag Heuer follows a focus differentiation strategy by selling only rugged waterproof watches to active consumers. Fiat follows a focus cost leadership strategy by selling its automobiles only in Italy and in selected regions of Europe; Alpha Romeo uses focus differentiation to sell its high-performance cars in these same markets. Fisher-Price uses focus differentiation to sell electronic calculators with large, brightly colored buttons to the parents of preschoolers; stockbroker Edward Jones focuses on small town settings. General Mills is focusing new product development on consumers who eat meals while driving—their slogan is, "Can we make it 'one-handed'?" so that drivers can eat or drink it safely.[14]

The Miles and Snow Typology

A second classification of strategic options was developed by Raymond Miles and Charles Snow.[15] These authors suggested that business-level strategies generally fall into one of four categories: prospector, defender, analyzer, and reactor. Table 8.2 summarizes each of these strategies. Of course, different businesses within the same company might pursue different strategies.

A firm that follows a **prospector strategy** is a highly innovative firm that is constantly seeking new markets and new opportunities and is oriented toward growth and risk taking. Over the years, 3M has prided itself on being one of the most innovative major corporations in the world. Employees at 3M are constantly encouraged to develop new products and ideas in a creative and entrepreneurial way. This focus on innovation has led 3M to develop a wide range of new products and markets, including invisible tape and antistain fabric treatments. Amazon.com is also following a prospector strategy because it constantly seeks new market opportunities for selling different kinds of products through its web sites.

prospector strategy A strategy in which the firm is constantly seeking new markets and new opportunities and is oriented toward growth and risk taking

Table 8.2

The Miles and Snow Typology

The Miles and Snow typology identifies four strategic types of organizations. Three of these—the prospector, the defender, and the analyzer—can each be effective in certain circumstances. The fourth type—the reactor—represents an ineffective approach to strategy.

Strategy Type	Definition	Examples
Prospector	Is innovative and growth oriented, searches for new markets and new growth opportunities, encourages risk taking	Amazon.com 3M Rubbermaid
Defender	Protects current markets, maintains stable growth, serves current customers	Bic eBay.com Mrs. Fields
Analyzer	Maintains current markets and current customer satisfaction with moderate emphasis on innovation	DuPont IBM Yahoo!
Reactor	No clear strategy, reacts to changes in the environment, drifts with events	International Harvester in the 1960s and 1970s, Joseph Schlitz Brewing Co., W. T. Grant

defender strategy A strategy in which the firm concentrates on protecting its current markets, maintaining stable growth, and serving current customers

analyzer strategy A strategy in which the firm attempts to maintain its current businesses and to create new market opportunities

reactor strategy A strategy in which a firm has no consistent approach to strategy

The *World of Management* provides a bit more detail about Amazon.com's strategy in Europe.

Rather than seeking new growth opportunities and innovation, a company that follows a **defender strategy** concentrates on protecting its current markets, maintaining stable growth, and serving current customers. With the maturity of the market for writing instruments, Bic has used this approach—it has adopted a less aggressive, less entrepreneurial style of management and has chosen to defend its substantial market share in the industry. It emphasizes efficient manufacturing and customer satisfaction. While eBay is expanding aggressively into foreign markets, the on-line auctioneer is still pursuing what amounts to a defender strategy because it is keeping its focus primarily on the auction business. Thus, while it is prospecting for new markets, its defending its core business focus.[16]

A business that uses an **analyzer strategy** combines elements of prospectors and defenders. Most large companies use this approach because they want both to protect their base of operations and to create new market opportunities. IBM uses analyzer strategies. DuPont is currently using an analyzer strategy. The firm is relying heavily on its existing chemical and fiber operations to fuel its earnings for the foreseeable future. At the same time, though, DuPont is also moving systematically into new business areas such as biotech agriculture and pharmaceuticals. Yahoo! is also using this strategy by keeping its primary focus on its role as an Internet portal while simultaneously seeking to extend that portal into more and more applications.[17]

Finally, a business that follows a **reactor strategy** has no consistent strategic approach; it drifts with environmental events, reacting to but failing to anticipate or influence those events. Not surprisingly, these firms usually do not perform as well as organizations that implement other strategies. Although most organizations would deny using reactor strategies, during the 1970s International Harvester Co. (IH) clearly was a reactor. At a time when IH's market for trucks, construction equipment, and agricultural equipment was booming, IH failed to keep pace with

U.S. E-businesses Prospect for Growth in Europe

U.S. Internet innovators are seeking aggressive growth by building on their successful domestic strategies to enter global markets. Leading e-tailer Amazon.com, for example, used its innovative web technology to fuel an invasion of the British market. Much of the content on Amazon's British site (http://www.amazon.co.uk) is local—CDs by local artists, books by local authors—and is supported by the U.S. parent's on-line shopping technology and marketing expertise. The company used the same strategy to expand in France with a mix of local and global content supported by back-office technology imported from the U.S. parent. In addition, Amazon expanded by buying locally operated Internet bookstores. Despite competition from European e-businesses, Amazon's on-line cash registers have been ringing: its European sales have already outdistanced those of Bertelsmann's BOL, its closest European rival, by 500 percent.

On-line auction innovator eBay has also pursued growth by crossing the Atlantic to open country-specific web sites in Germany (http://www.ebay.de), Great Britain, and France. By initially concentrating on just three new markets, eBay sought to establish a strong customer base and to build economies of scale for higher profitability and future expansion. Despite intense competition, eBay attracted far more users than QXL, its largest European rival, in less than a year.

Taking risks to support aggressive growth and to ensure long-term viability is what helps U.S. e-businesses such as Vaca-tionSpot.com, which lists foreign vacation home rentals, compete more effectively against European rivals such as Belgium's Rent-a-Holiday. Although Rent-a-Holiday had a nine-month head start, VacationSpot (http://vacationspot.com) went beyond merely listing rental properties to allow customers to finalize and pay for rental arrangements on-line. VacationSpot also took financial risks, such as arranging expensive promotion deals with Expedia, Travelocity, and other popular travel web sites to gain wider exposure and to increase market share. Rent-a-Holiday was soon bought by VacationSpot. Then the combined company merged with Expedia, gaining more financial backing and building the on-line clout to become an even more formidable force in the growing market for on-line vacation home rentals.

> *You're not going to get scale by being number one in Norway.*
>
> —*Michael van Swaaij, European managing director for eBay**

References: William Echikson, "American E-tailers Take Europe by Storm," *Business Week*, August 7, 2000, pp. 54–55 (*quote on p. 55); William Echikson, "Home Field Disadvantage," *Business Week*, December 13, 1999, pp. EB72–EB74; "Rough Crossing for eBay," *Business Week*, February 7, 2000, p. EB48.

---

its competitors. By the time a recession cut demand for its products, it was too late for IH to respond, and the company lost millions of dollars. The firm was forced to sell off virtually all of its businesses except its truck-manufacturing business. IH, now renamed Navistar, moved from being a dominant firm in trucking, agriculture, and construction to a medium-size truck manufacturer because it failed to anticipate changes in its environment.

Strategies Based on the Product Life Cycle

The **product life cycle** is a model that shows how sales volume changes over the life of products. Understanding the four stages in the product life cycle helps managers recognize that strategies need to evolve over time. As Figure 8.2 shows, the

product life cycle A model that shows how sales volume changes over the life of products

Figure 8.2

The Product Life Cycle

Managers can use the framework of the product life cycle—introduction, growth, maturity, and decline—to plot strategy. For example, management may decide on a differentiation strategy for a product in the introduction stage and a prospector approach for a product in the growth stage. By understanding this cycle and where a particular product falls within it, managers can develop more effective strategies for extending product life.

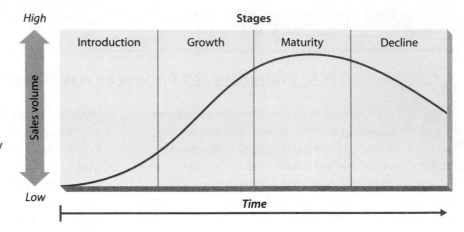

cycle begins when a new product or technology is first introduced. In this *introduction stage*, demand may be very high and sometimes outpaces the firm's ability to supply the product. Managers need to focus their efforts on getting product out the door without sacrificing quality. Managing growth by hiring new employees and managing inventories and cash flow are also concerns during this stage.

During the *growth stage*, more firms begin producing the product, and sales continue to grow. Important management issues include ensuring quality and delivery and beginning to differentiate an organization's product from competitors' products. Entry into the industry during the growth stage may threaten an organization's competitive advantages; thus, strategies to slow the entry of competitors are important.

After a period of growth, products enter a third phase. During this *mature stage*, overall demand growth for a product begins to slow down and the number of new firms producing the product begins to decline. The number of established firms producing the product may also begin to decline. This period of maturity is essential if an organization is going to survive in the long run. Product differentiation concerns are still important during this stage, but keeping costs low and beginning the search for new products or services are also important strategic considerations.

In the *decline stage*, demand for the product or technology decreases, the number of organizations producing the product drops, and total sales drop. Demand often declines because all those who were interested in purchasing a particular product have already done so. Organizations that fail to anticipate the decline stage in earlier stages of the life cycle may go out of business. Those that differentiate their product, keep their costs low, or develop new products or services may do well during this stage.

MANAGEMENT IMPLICATIONS Managers who formulate business-level strategies can adopt one of three competitive strategies advocated by Porter or one of the three strategies described by Miles and Snow. However, they should avoid using a reactor strategy. Managers can also use product life cycles as part of their strategy formulation process.

Firms can sometimes extend the life cycle of their products so as to continue to generate new revenues. Introducing existing products to new consumers or modernizing existing products are common methods for doing this. For example, the venerable Monopoly board game, owned and distributed by the Parker Brothers game company, is one of the most successful game products of all time. But today's game players might not relate to such properties as the Reading Railroad and Water Works or to such institutions as the Community Chest. So, Parker Brothers recently launched a new-economy version of Monopoly in which players buy properties like eBay, Lycos, and Nokia and receive "good news" and "bad news" e-mails.

Implementing Business-Level Strategies

As noted earlier, after business strategies are formulated, they must then be implemented. To do implement business strategies effectively, managers must integrate the activities of several different functions. *Marketing* and *sales*, for example, are used to promote products or services and the overall public image of the organization (often through various types of advertising), price products or services, contact customers directly, and make sales. *Accounting* and *finance* control the flow of money both within the organization and from outside sources to the organization, and *manufacturing* creates the organization's products or services. Organizational *culture*, as discussed in Chapter 6, also helps firms implement their strategies.

Implementing Porter's Generic Strategies

Differentation and cost leadership can each be implemented via these basic organizational functions. (Focus is implemented via the same approaches, depending on which one it is based.)

Differentiation Strategy   In general, to support differentiation, marketing and sales must emphasize the high-quality, high-value image of the organization's products or services. Neiman-Marcus, a department store for financially secure consumers, has excelled at using marketing to support its differentiation strategy. People do not go to Neiman-Marcus just to buy clothes or to shop for home electronics. Instead, a trip to Neiman-Marcus is advertised as a "total shopping experience." Customers who want to shop for $3,000 pet houses, $50,000 mink coats, and $7,000 exercise machines recognize that the store caters to their needs. Other organizations that have used their marketing function to implement a differentiation strategy include Chanel, Calvin Klein, and Bloomingdale's.

Implementing business-level strategy can be complicated, especially when it's necessary to make a change. A few years ago, Jeffrey Bezos launched Amazon.com, an Internet-based book retailer. Amazon.com built its business using a differentiation strategy, billing itself as "Earth's biggest bookstore," offering a huge selection of books, stressing ease-of-use, and relying on mail delivery service. But as other big firms, like Barnes & Noble and Amazon.com's own wholesaler, have launched Internet book selling operations themselves, Bezos has found it necessary to shift to a cost leadership strategy to protect his marketshare and fend off these new competitors.

The function of accounting and finance in a business that is implementing a differentiation strategy is to control the flow of funds without discouraging the creativity needed to develop new products and services constantly to meet customer needs. If keeping track of and controlling the flow of money become more important than determining how money and resources are best spent to meet customer needs, then no organization, whether high-technology firm or fashion designer, will be able to implement a differentiation strategy effectively. In manufacturing, a firm implementing a differentiation strategy must emphasize quality and meeting specific customer needs rather than simply reducing costs. Manufacturing may sometimes have to keep inventory on hand so that customers will have access to products when they want them. Manufacturing may also have to engage in costly customization to meet customer needs.

The culture of a firm implementing a differentiation strategy, like the firm's other functions, must also emphasize creativity, innovation, and response to customer needs. Lands' End's culture puts the needs of customers ahead of all other considerations. This firm, which sells men's and women's leisure clothes through a catalog service, offers a complete guarantee on merchandise. Dissatisfied customers may return clothes for a full refund or exchange, no questions asked. Lands' End takes orders twenty-four hours a day and will ship most orders within twenty-four hours. Lost buttons and broken zippers are replaced immediately. The priority given to customer needs is typical of an organization that is successfully implementing a differentiation strategy.

Overall Cost Leadership Strategy   To support cost leadership, marketing and sales are likely to focus on simple product attributes and how these product attributes meet customer needs in a low-cost and effective manner. These organizations are very likely to engage in advertising. Throughout this effort, however, emphasis is on the value that an organization's products provide for the price, rather than on the special features of the product or service. Advertising for Bic pens ("Writes first time, every time"), Timex watches ("Takes a licking and keeps on ticking"), and Wal-Mart stores ("Always low prices—always") helps these firms implement cost leadership strategies.

Proper emphasis in accounting and finance is also pivotal. Because the success of the organization depends on having costs lower than the competitors', management must take care to reduce costs wherever possible. Tight financial and accounting controls at Wal-Mart, Costco, and MCI have helped these organizations implement cost leadership strategies. Manufacturing typically helps with large runs of highly standardized products. Products are designed both to meet customer needs and to be manufactured easily. Manufacturing emphasizes increased volume of production to reduce the per-unit costs of manufacturing. Organizations such as Toshiba (a Japanese semiconductor firm) and Texas Instruments have used this type of manufacturing to implement cost leadership strategies.

The culture of organizations implementing cost leadership strategies tends to focus on improving the efficiency of manufacturing, sales, and other business functions. Managers in these organizations are almost fanatical about keeping their costs low. Wal-Mart appeals to its customers to leave shopping carts in its parking lot with signs that read "Please—help us keep *your* costs low." Fujitsu Electronics, in its Tokyo manufacturing facilities, operates in plain, unpainted cinderblock and cement facilities to keep its costs as low as possible.

Implementing Miles and Snow's Strategies

Similarly, various issues must be considered when implementing any of Miles and Snow's strategic options. (Of course, no organization would purposefully choose to implement a reactor strategy.)

Prospector Strategy   An organization implementing a prospector strategy is innovative, seeks new market opportunities, and takes numerous risks. To implement this strategy, organizations need to encourage creativity and flexibility. Creativity helps an organization perceive, or even create, new opportunities in its environment; flexibility enables it to change quickly to take advantage of these new opportunities. Organizations often increase creativity and flexibility by adopting a decentralized organization structure. An organization is decentralized when major decision-making responsibility is delegated to middle- and lower-level managers. Johnson & Johnson links decentralization with a prospector strategy. Each of the firm's different businesses is organized into a separate unit, and the managers of these units hold full decision-making responsibility and authority. Often these businesses develop new products for new markets. As the new products develop and sales grow, Johnson & Johnson reorganizes so that each new product is managed in a separate unit.

Defender Strategy   An organization implementing a defender strategy attempts to protect its market from new competitors. It tends to downplay creativity and innovation in bringing out new products or services and focus its efforts instead on lowering costs or improving the performance of current products. Often a firm implementing a prospector strategy will switch to a defender strategy. This happens when the firm successfully creates a new market or business and then attempts to protect its market from competition. A good example is Mrs. Fields. One of the first firms to introduce high-quality, high-priced cookies, Mrs. Fields sold its product in special cookie stores and grew very rapidly. This success, however, encouraged numerous other companies to enter the market. Increased competition, plus reduced demand for high-priced cookies, has threatened Mrs. Fields's market position. To maintain its profitability, the firm has slowed its growth and is now focusing on making its current operation more profitable. This behavior is consistent with the defender strategy.

Analyzer Strategy   An organization implementing an analyzer strategy attempts to maintain its current business and to be somewhat innovative in new businesses. Because the analyzer strategy falls somewhere between prospector strategy (with a focus on innovation) and defender strategy (with a focus on maintaining and improving current businesses), the attributes of organizations implementing the analyzer strategy tend to be similar to both of these other types of organizations. They have tight accounting and financial controls, high flexibility, efficient production and customized products, and high creativity and low costs. Organizations maintain these multiple and contradictory processes with difficulty.

Starbucks is implementing an analyzer strategy. While the firm is growing rapidly, its fundamental business is still coffee. At the same time, however, the firm is cautiously branching out into music and ice cream and other food products, and is experimenting with restaurants with more comprehensive menu selections. This approach is allowing Starbucks to remain focused on its core coffee business but still explore new business opportunities at the same time.

MANAGEMENT IMPLICATIONS   Managers should understand the basic concepts inherent in marketing and sales, accounting and finance, manufacturing, and organization culture. Each function or characteristic plays an important role in implementing any of the business-level strategies.

Formulating Corporate-Level Strategies

Most large organizations are engaged in several businesses, industries, and markets. Each business or set of businesses within such an organization is frequently referred to as a *strategic business unit*, or *SBU*. An organization such as General Electric Co. operates hundreds of different businesses, making and selling products as diverse as jet engines, nuclear power plants, and light bulbs. GE organizes these businesses into approximately twenty SBUs. Even organizations that sell only one product may operate in several distinct markets.

Decisions about which businesses, industries, and markets an organization will enter, and how to manage these different businesses, are based on an organization's corporate strategy. The most important strategic issue at the corporate level concerns the extent and nature of organizational diversification. **Diversification** describes the number of different businesses that an organization is engaged in and the extent to which these businesses are related to one another. There are three types of diversification strategies: single-product strategy, related diversification, and unrelated diversification.[18]

diversification The number of different businesses that an organization is engaged in and the extent to which these businesses are related to one another

Single-Product Strategy

An organization that pursues a **single-product strategy** manufactures just one product or service and sells it in a single geographic market. The WD-40 Company, for example, manufactures only a single product, WD-40 spray lubricant, and sells it in just one market, North America. WD-40 has considered broadening its market to Europe and Asia, but it continues to center all manufacturing, sales, and marketing efforts on one product.

The single-product strategy has one major strength and one major weakness. By concentrating its efforts so completely on one product and market, a firm is likely to be very successful in manufacturing and marketing the product. Because it has staked its survival on a single product, the organization works very hard to make sure that the product is a success. Of course, if the product is not accepted by the market or is replaced by a new one, the firm will suffer. This happened to slide-rule manufacturers when electronic calculators became widely available and to companies that manufactured only black-and-white televisions when low-priced color televisions were first mass-marketed. Similarly, Wrigley has long practiced what amounts to a single-product strategy with its line of chewing gums. But because younger consumers are buying less gum than earlier generations, Wrigley is facing declining revenues and lower profits.[19]

single-product strategy
A strategy in which an organization manufactures just one product or service and sells it in a single geographic market

Related Diversification

Given the disadvantage of the single-product strategy, most large businesses today operate in several different businesses, industries, or markets.[20] If the businesses are somehow linked, that organization is implementing a strategy of **related diversification**. Virtually all larger businesses in the United States use related diversification. *Managing in an E-business World* discusses how Cisco is using this strategy.

related diversification A strategy in which an organization operates in several different businesses, industries, or markets that are somehow linked

Formulating corporate strategy often involves making decisions about diversification. Alcoa's senior managers recently decided the firm needed to begin diversifying if it is to meet the CEO's goal of becoming a $40 billion enterprise by 2004. In recent months, then, the firm has bought Cordant Technologies (a firm that builds engines for the Space Shuttle), Reynolds Metals (a competing aluminum company), and two small aluminum companies in Britain. But since additional acquisitions in the aluminum industry might raise antitrust concerns, Alcoa is now considering additional acquisitions in other industries.

MANAGING IN AN *e*-BUSINESS WORLD

CISCO USES ACQUISITIONS TO STRENGTHEN ITS E-BUSINESS BACKBONE

Making acquisitions work is an important strength in the e-business world, where companies often grow by following a strategy of related diversification. But few companies have the acquisitions expertise or experience of Cisco Systems, which acquired fifty-one firms in six and a half years to add the latest web-related connection products and reshape its strategic direction. Cisco's sophisticated routers and networking equipment serve as the e-business backbone for many Internet companies—a strength the company enhances by buying smaller firms with complementary technology.

Consider Cisco's acquisition of Cerent, which makes fiber-optic equipment. A year before the acquisition, Cisco bought a 9 percent stake in Cerent so it could learn more about the firm and its products. As Cisco's CEO got to know the company better, he saw two key reasons why it would be a good acquisition. First, acquiring Cerent would give Cisco access to the fast-growing market for fiber optics and to Cerent's burgeoning customer base. Second, Cerent's hard-driving, frugal organization culture was similar to Cisco's. Once the decision was made, Cisco negotiated the $6.3 billion acquisition in just two and a half hours spread over three days.

Next, Cisco's integration team stepped in to plan the details before the public announcement. In the two weeks following the agreement, the Cisco team met with Cerent's management to work out differences between the companies' personnel practices and to prepare a package of transition information. Only then did Cerent's CEO announce the acquisition to his employees. Cisco staffers immediately gave every Cerent employee the transition package showing how Cerent's benefits compared with Cisco's benefits. In many cases, Cisco raised salaries and boosted benefits to bring compensation in line with Cisco's compensation. Most important, Cerent's 266 employees were assured that they could never be fired or reassigned without their CEO's permission.

> *You must get on the Net and find new ways to add value.*
>
> —*John Chambers, CEO, Cisco Systems**

Thanks to Cisco's advance planning, the acquisition went smoothly, and Cerent's employees were able to focus on their jobs rather than being distracted by uncertainty. E-business is humming, so Cisco will be relying on its acquisition expertise again and again as it aims for as many as twenty-five acquisitions per year.

References: Scott Thurm, "Joining the Fold: Under Cisco's System, Mergers Usually Work; That Defies the Odds," *Wall Street Journal*, March 1, 2000, pp. A1, A12; Andy Serwer, "There's Something About Cisco," *Fortune*, May 15, 2000, pp. 114–138 (*quote on p. 138).

Bases of Relatedness   Organizations link their different businesses, industries, or markets in different ways. Table 8.3 gives some typical bases of relatedness. In companies such as Philips, a European consumer electronics company, a similar type of electronics technology underlies all the businesses. A common technology in aircraft design links Boeing's commercial and military aircraft divisions, and a common computer design technology links Compaq's various computer products and peripherals.

Organizations such as Philip Morris, RJR Nabisco, and Procter & Gamble operate multiple businesses related by a common distribution network (grocery stores) and common marketing skills (advertising). Disney and Universal rely on strong brand names and reputations to link their diverse businesses, which include movie studios and theme parks. Pharmaceutical firms such as Merck sell numerous products to a single set of customers: hospitals, doctors, patients, and drug-

Table 8.3

Bases of Relatedness in Implementing Related Diversification

Firms that implement related diversification can do so using any number of bases of relatedness. Four frequently used bases of related uses for diversification are similar technology, common distribution and marketing skills, common brand name and reputation, and common customers.

Basis of Relatedness	Examples
Similar technology	Philips, Boeing, Westinghouse, Compaq
Common distribution and marketing skills	RJR Nabisco, Philip Morris, Procter & Gamble
Common brand name and reputation	Disney, Universal
Common customers	Merck, IBM, AMF-Head

stores. Similarly, AMF-Head sells snow skis, tennis rackets, and sportswear to active, athletic customers.

Advantages of Related Diversification   Pursuing a strategy of related diversification has three primary advantages. First, it reduces an organization's dependence on any one of its business activities and thus reduces economic risk. Even if one or two of a firm's businesses lose money, the organization as a whole may still survive because the healthy businesses will generate enough cash to support the others.[21] At The Limited, sales declines at Lerners of New York may be offset by sales increases at Express.

Second, by managing several businesses at the same time, an organization can reduce the overhead costs associated with managing any one business. In other words, if the normal administrative costs required to operate any business, such as legal services and accounting, can be spread over a large number of businesses, then the overhead costs *per business* will be lower than they would be if each business had to absorb all costs itself. Thus, the overhead costs of businesses in a related, diversified firm are usually lower than those of similar businesses that are not part of a larger corporation.[22]

Third, related diversification allows an organization to exploit its strengths and capabilities in more than one business. When organizations do this successfully, they capitalize on synergies, which are complementary effects that exist among their businesses. *Synergy* exists among a set of businesses when the businesses' economic value together is greater than their economic value separately. McDonald's is using synergy as it diversifies into other restaurant and food businesses. For example, its McCafé premium coffee stands in some McDonald's restaurants and its acquisitions of Donatos Pizza, Chipotle Mexican Grill, and Boston Market allow the firm to create new revenue opportunities while utilizing the firm's existing strengths in food-products purchasing and distribution.[23]

Unrelated Diversification

Firms that implement a strategy of **unrelated diversification** operate multiple businesses that are not logically associated with one another. At one time, for example,

unrelated diversification A strategy in which an organization operates multiple businesses that are not logically associated with one another

Quaker Oats owned clothing chains, toy companies, and a restaurant business. Unrelated diversification was a very popular strategy in the 1970s. During this time, several conglomerates like ITT and Transamerica grew by acquiring literally hundreds of other organizations and then running these numerous businesses as independent entities. Even if there are important potential synergies between their different businesses, organizations implementing a strategy of unrelated diversification do not attempt to exploit them.

In theory, unrelated diversification has two advantages. First, a business that uses this strategy should have stable performance over time. During any given period, if some businesses owned by the organization are in a cycle of decline, others may be in a cycle of growth. Unrelated diversification is also thought to have resource allocation advantages. Every year, when a corporation allocates capital, people, and other resources among its various businesses, it must evaluate information about the future of those businesses so that it can place its resources where they have the highest return potential. Given that it owns the businesses in question and thus has full access to information about the future of those businesses, a firm implementing unrelated diversification should be able to allocate capital to maximize corporate performance.

Despite these presumed advantages, research suggests that unrelated diversification usually does not lead to high performance. First, corporate-level managers in such a company usually do not know enough about the unrelated businesses to provide helpful strategic guidance or to allocate capital appropriately. To make strategic decisions, managers must have complete and subtle understanding of a business and its environment. Because corporate managers often have difficulty fully evaluating the economic importance of investments for all the businesses under their wing, they tend to concentrate only on a business's current performance. This narrow attention at the expense of broader planning eventually hobbles the entire organization. Many of International Harvester's problems noted earlier grew from an emphasis on current performance at the expense of investments for the future success of the firm.

Second, because organizations that implement unrelated diversification fail to exploit important synergies, they are at a competitive disadvantage compared to organizations that use related diversification. Universal Studios has been at a competitive disadvantage relative to Disney because its theme parks, movie studios, and licensing divisions are less integrated and therefore achieve less synergy.

For these reasons, almost all organizations have abandoned unrelated diversification as a corporate-level strategy. Transamerica has sold off numerous businesses and now concentrates on a core set of related businesses and markets. Large corporations that have not concentrated on a core set of businesses eventually have been acquired by other companies and then broken up. Research suggests that these organizations are actually worth more when broken up into smaller pieces than they are when joined.[24]

MANAGEMENT
IMPLICATIONS   Managers should understand the various kinds of corporate strategies that can be adopted from the perspective of strategic business units, or SBUs. Although diversification is a very common corporate-level

strategy, managers should have a clear understanding of whether they should use related or unrelated diversification. Appreciating the bases for relatedness is also important.

Implementing Corporate-Level Strategies

In implementing a diversification strategy, organizations face two important questions. First, how will the organization move from a single-product strategy to some form of diversification? Second, once the organization diversifies, how will it manage diversification effectively?

Becoming a Diversified Firm

Most organizations do not start out completely diversified. Rather, they begin operations in a single business, pursuing a particular business-level strategy. Success in this strategy then creates resources and strengths that the organization can use in related businesses.

Internal Development of New Products Some firms diversify by developing their own new products and services within the boundaries of their traditional business operations. Honda followed this path to diversification. Relying on its traditional strength in the motorcycle market, over the years Honda learned how to make fuel-efficient, highly reliable small engines. Honda began to apply its strengths in a new business: manufacturing small, fuel-efficient cars for the Japanese domestic market. These vehicles were first sold in the United States in the late 1960s. Honda's success in U.S. exports led the company to increase the size and improve the performance of its cars. Over the years, Honda has introduced automobiles of increasing quality, culminating in the Acura line of luxury cars. While diversifying into the market for automobiles, Honda also applied its engine-building strengths to produce a line of all-terrain vehicles, portable electric generators, and lawn mowers. In each case, Honda was able to parlay its strengths and resources into successful new businesses.

Replacement of Suppliers and Customers Firms can also become diversified by replacing their former suppliers and customers. A company that stops buying supplies (either manufactured goods or raw materials) from other companies and begins to provide its own supplies has diversified through **backward vertical integration**. Campbell Soup once bought soup cans from several different manufacturers but later began manufacturing its own cans. In fact, Campbell is currently one of the largest can-manufacturing companies in the world, although almost all the cans it makes are used in its soup operations.

An organization that stops selling to one customer and sells instead to that customer's customers has diversified through **forward vertical integration**. G.H. Bass used forward vertical integration to diversify its operations. Bass once sold its

backward vertical integration
An organization's beginning the business activities formerly conducted by its suppliers

forward vertical integration An organization stops selling to one customer and sells instead to that customer's customers

shoes and other products only to retail outlets. More recently, however, Bass opened numerous factory outlet stores, which now sell products directly to consumers. Nevertheless, Bass has not abandoned its former customers, retail outlets. Many firms are also employing forward vertical integration today when they use the Internet to market their products and services directly to consumers.

Mergers and Acquisitions   Another common way for businesses to diversify is through mergers and acquisitions—that is, through purchasing another organization. Such a purchase is called a **merger** when the two organizations being combined are approximately the same size. It is called an **acquisition** when one of the organizations involved is considerably larger than the other. Organizations engage in mergers and acquisitions to diversify through vertical integration by acquiring former suppliers or former customers. Mergers and acquisitions are also becoming more common in other countries such as Germany and China.[25]

Most organizations use mergers and acquisitions to acquire complementary products or complementary services, which are products or services linked by a common technology and common customers. The objective of most mergers and acquisitions is the creation or exploitation of synergies.[26] Synergy can reduce the combined organizations' costs of doing business, it can increase revenues, and it may open the way to entirely new businesses for the organization to enter. For example, in early 2000 MGM Grand paid $4.4 billion for its largest competitor in the gambling industry, Mirage Resorts. The deal will allow MGM Grand to compete with other firms more efficiently while eliminating a major rival.[27] The cartoon illustrates another interesting perspective on mergers and acquisitions.

merger The purchase of one firm by another firm of approximately the same size

acquisition The purchase of a firm by another firm that is considerably larger

Mergers and acquisitions are becoming an increasingly popular way to implement corporate-level strategies. Of course, as illustrated in this cartoon, there is at least theoretically a limit to the extent to which mergers and acquisitions can occur. For example, in recent years the U.S. government has blocked the merger of Staples and Office Depot and fought the merger of American Online and Time Warner. The reasons in each case have involved concerns about reduced competition that might, in turn, lead to higher consumer prices.

"OH, WHY DOESN'T EVERYBODY JUST MERGE WITH EVERYBODY ELSE AND GET IT OVER WITH?"

Managing Diversification

However an organization implements diversification—whether through internal development, vertical integration, or mergers and acquisitions—it must monitor and manage its strategy. The two major tools for managing diversification are (1) organization structure and (2) portfolio management techniques. How organization structure can be used to manage a diversification strategy is discussed in detail in Chapter 12.[28] **Portfolio management techniques** are methods that diversified organizations use to make decisions about what businesses to engage in and how to manage these multiple businesses to maximize corporate performance. Two important portfolio management techniques are the BCG matrix and the GE Business Screen.

BCG Matrix   The **BCG** (for Boston Consulting Group) **matrix** provides a framework for evaluating the relative performance of businesses in which a diversified organization operates. It also prescribes the preferred distribution of cash and other resources among these businesses.[29] The BCG matrix uses two factors to evaluate an organization's set of businesses: the growth rate of a particular market and the organization's share of that market. The matrix suggests that fast-growing markets in which an organization has the highest market share are more attractive business opportunities than slow-growing markets in which an organization has small market share. Dividing market growth and market share into two categories (low and high) creates the simple matrix shown in Figure 8.3.

The matrix classifies the types of businesses that a diversified organization can engage in as dogs, cash cows, question marks, and stars. *Dogs* are businesses that have a very small share of a market that is not expected to grow. Because these businesses do not hold much economic promise, the BCG matrix suggests that organizations either should not invest in them or should consider selling them as soon as possible. *Cash cows* are businesses that have a large share of a market that is not expected to grow substantially. These businesses characteristically generate high profits that the organization should use to support question marks and stars. (Cash cows are "milked" for cash to support businesses in markets that have greater growth potential.) *Question marks* are businesses that have only a small share of a quickly growing market. The future performance of these businesses is uncertain. A question mark that can capture increasing amounts of this growing market may be very profitable. On the other hand, a question mark unable to keep up with market growth is likely to have low profits. The BCG matrix suggests that organizations should carefully invest in question marks. If their performance does not live up to expectations, question marks should be reclassified as dogs and divested. *Stars* are businesses that have the largest share of a rapidly

portfolio management technique A method that diversified organizations use to make decisions about what businesses to engage in and how to manage these multiple businesses to maximize corporate performance

BCG matrix A method of evaluating businesses relative to the growth rate of their market and the organization's share of the market

Figure 8.3

The BCG Matrix

The BCG matrix helps managers develop a better understanding of how different strategic business units contribute to the overall organization. By assessing each SBU on the basis of its market growth rate and relative market share, managers can make decisions about whether to commit further financial resources to the SBU or to sell or liquidate it.

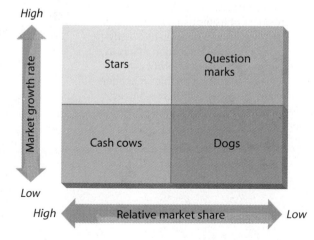

Source: Perspectives, No. 66, "The Product Portfolio." Adapted by permission from The Boston Consulting Group, Inc., 1970.

growing market. Cash generated by cash cows should be invested in stars to ensure their pre-eminent position. For example, when BMW bought Rover a few years ago, experts thought its products would help the German auto maker reach new consumers. But the company was not able to capitalize on this opportunity, so it ended up selling Rover's car business to a British firm and Land Rover to Ford.[30]

GE Business Screen   Because the BCG matrix is relatively narrow and overly simplistic, General Electric (GE) developed the **GE Business Screen**, a more sophisticated approach to managing diversified business units. The Business Screen is a portfolio management technique that can also be represented in the form of a matrix. Rather than focusing solely on market growth and market share, however, the GE Business Screen considers industry attractiveness and competitive position. These two factors are divided into three categories to make the nine-cell matrix shown in Figure 8.4.[31] These cells, in turn, classify business units as winners, losers, question marks, average businesses, or profit producers.

As Figure 8.4 shows, both market growth and market share appear in a broad list of factors that determine the overall attractiveness of an industry and the overall quality of a firm's competitive position. Other determinants of an industry's attractiveness (in addition to market growth) include market size, capital requirements, and competitive intensity. In general, the greater the market growth, the larger the market, the smaller the capital requirements, and the less the competitive intensity, the more attractive an industry will be. Other determinants of an

GE Business Screen A method of evaluating businesses along two dimensions: (1) industry attractiveness and (2) competitive position; in general, the more attractive the industry and the more competitive the position, the more an organization should invest in a business

Figure 8.4

The GE Business Screen

The GE Business Screen is a more sophisticated approach to portfolio management than the BCG matrix. As shown here, several factors combine to determine a business's competitive position and the attractiveness of its industry. These two dimensions, in turn, can be used to classify businesses as winners, question marks, average businesses, losers, or profit producers. Such a classification enables managers to allocate the organization's resources more effectively across various business opportunities.

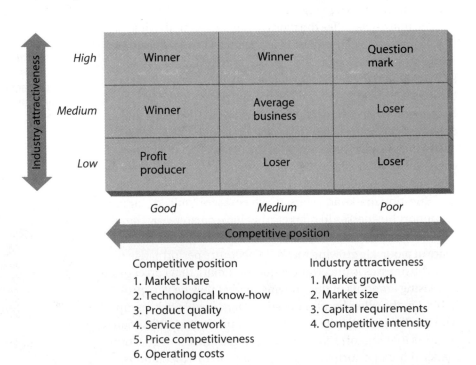

Competitive position
1. Market share
2. Technological know-how
3. Product quality
4. Service network
5. Price competitiveness
6. Operating costs

Industry attractiveness
1. Market growth
2. Market size
3. Capital requirements
4. Competitive intensity

organization's competitive position in an industry (besides market share) include technological know-how, product quality, service network, price competitiveness, and operating costs. In general, businesses with large market share, technological know-how, high product quality, a quality service network, competitive prices, and low operating costs are in a favorable competitive position.

Think of the GE Business Screen as a way of applying SWOT analysis to the implementation and management of a diversification strategy. The determinants of industry attractiveness are similar to the environmental opportunities and threats in SWOT analysis, and the determinants of competitive position are similar to organizational strengths and weaknesses. By conducting this type of SWOT analysis across several businesses, a diversified organization can decide how to invest its resources to maximize corporate performance. In general, organizations should invest in winners and in question marks (where industry attractiveness and competitive position are both favorable), should maintain the market position of average businesses and profit producers (where industry attractiveness and competitive position are average), and should sell losers. For example, Unilever recently assessed its business portfolio using a similar framework and, as a result, decided to sell off several specialty chemical units that were not contributing to the firm's profitability as much as other businesses. The firm then used the revenues from these divestitures and bought more related businesses such as Ben & Jerry's Homemade and Slim-Fast.[32]

MANAGEMENT IMPLICATIONS   Diversification can be achieved through the internal development of new products, replacement of suppliers and customers, and mergers and acquisitions. Managers who are pursuing a diversification strategy should know the advantages and disadvantages of each type of diversification. In addition, they should understand how to manage multiple business units by using such frameworks as the BCG matrix or the GE Business Screen.

Summary of Key Points

A strategy is a comprehensive plan for accomplishing the organization's goals. Strategic management is a comprehensive and ongoing process aimed at formulating and implementing effective strategies. Effective strategies address three organizational issues: distinctive competency, scope, and resource deployment. Most large companies have both business-level and corporate-level strategies. Strategy formulation is the set of processes involved in creating or determining the strategies of an organization. Strategy implementation is the process of executing strategies.

SWOT analysis considers an organization's strengths, weaknesses, opportunities, and threats. Using SWOT analysis, an organization chooses strategies that support its mission and (1) exploit its opportunities and strengths, (2) neutralize its threats, and (3) avoid its weaknesses. Common strengths cannot be ignored, but distinctive competencies hold the greatest promise for superior performance.

A business-level strategy is the plan an organization uses to conduct business in a particular industry or market. Porter suggests that businesses may formulate a differentiation strategy, an overall cost leadership strategy, or a focus strategy at this level. According to Miles and Snow, organizations may choose one of four business-level strategies: prospector, defender, analyzer, or reactor. Business-level strategies may also take into account the stages in the product life cycle.

Strategy implementation at the business level takes place in the areas of marketing, sales, accounting and finance, and manufacturing. Organization culture also influences strategy implementation. Implementation of Porter's generic strategies requires different emphases in each of these organizational areas. Implementation of Miles and Snow's strategies affects organization structure and practices.

A corporate-level strategy is the plan an organization uses to manage its operations across several businesses. A firm that does not diversify is implementing a single-product strategy. An organization pursues a strategy of related diversification when it operates a set of businesses that are somehow linked. Related diversification reduces the financial risk associated with any particular product, reduces the overhead costs of each business, and enables the organization to create and exploit synergy. An organization pursues a strategy of unrelated diversification when it operates a set of businesses that are not logically associated with one another.

Strategy implementation at the corporate level addresses two issues: how the organization will go about its diversification and the way that an organization is managed once it has diversified. Businesses accomplish strategy implementation in three ways: developing new products internally, replacing suppliers (backward vertical integration) or customers (forward vertical integration), and engaging in mergers and acquisitions. Organizations manage diversification through the organization structure that they adopt and through portfolio management techniques. The BCG matrix classifies an organization's diversified businesses as dogs, cash cows, question marks, or stars according to market share and market growth rate. The GE Business Screen classifies businesses as winners, losers, question marks, average businesses, or profit producers according to industry attractiveness and competitive position.

Discussion Questions

Questions for Review

1. What are the two main types of strategic alternatives available to an organization?
2. How does a deliberate strategy differ from an emergent strategy?
3. List and describe Porter's generic strategies and the Miles and Snow typology of strategies.
4. What are the differences among a single-product strategy, a related diversification strategy, and an unrelated diversification strategy?

Questions for Analysis

5. Common strengths among firms cannot give one firm a competitive advantage. Does this mean that an organization should ignore its common strengths in choosing and implementing its strategies? Why or why not?

6. Suppose that an organization does not have any distinctive competencies. If the organization can acquire some distinctive competencies, how long are these strengths likely to remain distinctive competencies? Why?
7. Suppose that an organization moves from a single-product strategy to a strategy of related diversification. How might the organization use SWOT analysis to select attributes of its current business to serve as bases of relatedness among its newly acquired businesses?
8. For decades, Ivory Soap advertised that it is 99 percent pure. Ivory refused to add deodorants, facial creams, or colors to its soap. It also packages its soap in plain paper wrappers—no foil or fancy printing. Is Ivory implementing a product differentiation, low cost, or focus strategy, or some combination of the three? Explain your answer.

Questions for Application

9. Interview a manager and categorize the business- and corporate-level strategies of his or her organization according to Porter's generic strategies, the Miles and Snow typology, and extent of diversification.
10. Will implementing a differentiation strategy always improve an organization's performance? Give three real-world examples in which differentiation did not seem to improve an organization's performance, and describe why it did not. What do these "errors" have in common?

BUILDING EFFECTIVE *decision-making* SKILLS

Exercise Overview

Decision-making skills refer to the manager's ability to recognize and define problems and opportunities correctly and then to select an appropriate course of action to solve problems and capitalize on opportunities. As noted in the chapter, many organizations use SWOT analysis as part of the process of strategy formulation. This exercise will help you better understand how managers obtain the information they need to perform such an analysis and use it as a framework for making decisions.

Exercise Background

SWOT is an acronym for strengths, weaknesses, opportunities, and threats. Good strategies are those that exploit an organization's opportunities and strengths while neutralizing threats and avoiding or correcting weaknesses.

Assume that you have just been hired to run a medium-size manufacturing company. The firm has been manufacturing electric motors, circuit breakers, and similar electronic components for industrial use. In recent years, the firm's financial performance has gradually eroded. You have been hired to turn things around.

Meetings with both current and former top managers of the firm have led you to believe that a new strategy is needed. In earlier times the firm was successful in part because its products were of top quality, which allowed the company to charge premium prices for them. Recently, however, various cost-cutting measures have resulted in a decrease in quality. Competition has also increased. As a result, your firm no longer has a reputation for top quality products, but your manufacturing costs are still relatively high. The next thing you want to do now is to conduct a SWOT analysis.

Exercise Task

With the situation described above as context, do the following:

1. List the sources you will use to obtain information about the firm's strengths, weaknesses, opportunities, and threats.
2. Rate each source in terms of its probable reliability.
3. Rate each source in terms of how easy or difficult it will be to access.
4. How confident should you be in making decisions based on the information obtained?

BUILDING EFFECTIVE *conceptual* SKILLS

Exercise Overview

Conceptual skills refer to the manager's ability to think in the abstract. This exercise gives you some experience in using your conceptual skills on real business opportunities and potential.

Exercise Background

Many successful managers have had at one time or another an idea for using an existing product for new purposes or in new markets. For example, Arm & Hammer baking soda (a food product used in cooking) is now also widely used to absorb odors in refrigerators. Commercials advise consumers simply to open a box of Arm & Hammer and place it in their refrigerators. This has led to a big increase in the sales of the baking soda.

In other situations, managers have extended product life cycles by taking the products into new markets. The most common example today involves products that are becoming obsolete in more industrialized countries but are being introduced in less industrialized countries.

Exercise Task

Apply your conceptual skills by doing each of the following:

1. List ten simple products that have relatively straightforward purposes (i.e., a pencil, which is used for writing).
2. Next, try to identify two or three alternative uses for each product (i.e., a pencil can be used as a splint for a broken finger in an emergency).
3. Evaluate the market potential for each alternative product use as high, moderate, or low (i.e., the market potential for pencils used as splints is low).
4. Form small groups of two or three members and pool your ideas. Each group should choose two or three ideas to present to the class.

BUILDING EFFECTIVE *technical* SKILLS

Exercise Overview

Technical skills are necessary for the manager to accomplish or understand the specific kind of work being done in an organization. This exercise will enable you to sharpen your technical skills with regard to using the Internet and to see how the Internet can facilitate strategic planning.

Exercise Background

Select a company in which you have some interest. It might be a firm that you would like to work for, one where someone you know works, or a firm that is simply in the news a lot. Next, identify the two or three firms that you see as being the firm's biggest competitors. Visit the web sites of the company you originally selected and the competitors you subsequently identified.

Exercise Task

With the preceding background information as context, do the following:

1. Analyze the business and corporate strategies being used by the firm you originally selected.

2. Analyze the business and corporate strategies being used by its competitors.

3. Evaluate the effectiveness of each firm's strategies.

PEPSI'S NEW STRATEGIC FORMULA

The high-stakes rivalry between Pepsi-Cola and Coca-Cola is being played out in supermarkets, restaurants, and convenience stores all over the world. Pepsi-Cola has worked for years, with limited success, to catch up to market-leader Coca-Cola, trying strategy after strategy to regain ground in the United States and abroad. In 1965, Pepsi sought growth through diversification by acquiring Frito-Lay, which makes popular snacks such as Lay's Potato Chips and Doritos. This diversification proved so lucrative that the company, renamed PepsiCo, decided to diversify into fast-food restaurants—thought to be good outlets for soft drinks and snacks—through the purchase of Pizza Hut, Taco Bell, and Kentucky Fried Chicken.

By the mid-1990s, however, snack sales were increasing but growth in the fast-food business had slowed, as had growth in soft drinks. So in 1997, PepsiCo changed its strategy, spinning off the restaurants as a separate business to concentrate on exploiting the synergy between its snacks and its soft drinks. By now, snacks had become PepsiCo's main source of profits—a complete reversal from the early days of diversification, when profits from soft drinks had dwarfed profits from snacks.

Next, PepsiCo introduced its "Power of One" strategy to boost both beverage and snack sales in U.S. supermarkets. Visiting with the CEOs of the twenty-five top chains, PepsiCo's CEO compared the stores' 9 percent profit margins on PepsiCo products with the typical 2 percent margins earned on other items. He stressed that the stores could increase sales and profits by giving PepsiCo products more shelf space and displaying PepsiCo drinks with Frito-Lay snacks. "Power of One" paid off, giving Frito-Lay and Pepsi-Cola more domestic market share. It also gave PepsiCo drinks a huge sales boost in smaller grocery stores throughout Mexico. There, Frito-Lay's Sabritas brand is the runaway market leader, thanks to a low-cost strategy that keeps retail prices as low as sixteen cents per snack.

PepsiCo continued to diversify by buying Tropicana, the leading orange juice brand, and Cracker Jack, a perennial favorite that had lost profitability. By adding more peanuts and offering a four-ounce bag in addition to smaller single-serving and larger family-size packages, PepsiCo returned Cracker Jack to profitability within a year. In addition, through aggressive marketing, the company made best-sellers of its bottled waters and bottled teas. Now PepsiCo's Lipton Iced Tea holds a commanding lead over Coca-Cola's Nestea bottled teas. Pepsi-Cola's sales still lag Coca-Cola's sales in the United States, but PepsiCo's Mountain Dew recently pulled ahead of Diet Coke to become the country's third-largest-selling soda.

Outside the United States, PepsiCo's new soft-drink strategy is to focus on building sales and share in developing countries such as India, where Coca-Cola is not yet the undisputed market leader. This strategy reverses PepsiCo's previous strategy of doggedly battling Coca-Cola in every market. Populous Asian nations such as China and Japan are particular targets for PepsiCo's snack business. Although Frito-Lay holds just a tiny share of the snack market in those countries today, PepsiCo's CEO sees them as the cornerstone of future growth.

Case Questions

1. Where in the Miles and Snow typology does the "Power of One" strategy fit?

2. Which of Porter's generic strategies is Frito-Lay's Sabritas brand pursuing in Mexico? Which is PepsiCo pursuing with its soft-drink strategy?

3. What should PepsiCo consider before implementing its "Power of One" strategy around the world?

Case References

John A. Byrne, "PepsiCo's New Formula," *Business Week*, April 10, 2000, pp. 172–184; John A. Byrne, "Today, Mexico. Tomorrow . . ." *Business Week*, April 10, 2000, p. 184.

CHAPTER NOTES

1. "Happily Ever After?" *Time*, January 24, 2000, pp. 38–43 (quote on p. 39); "Welcome to the 21st Century," *Business Week*, January 24, 2000, pp. 36–44; "You've Got Time Warner," *Wall Street Journal*, January 11, 2000, pp. B1, B12; "Deal Ignites Tech, Media Stocks," *USA Today*, January 11, 2000, pp. 1B, 2B.

2. For early discussions of strategic management, see Kenneth Andrews, *The Concept of Corporate Strategy*, Revised Edition (Homewood, Ill.: Dow Jones-Irwin, 1980); and Igor Ansoff, *Corporate Strategy* (New York: McGraw-Hill, 1965). For more recent perspectives, see Michael E. Porter, "What Is Strategy?" *Harvard Business Review*, November–December 1996, pp. 61–78; and Kathleen M. Eisenhardt, "Strategy as Strategic Decision Making," *Sloan Management Review*, Spring 1999, pp. 65–74.

3. *Hoover's Handbook of American Business 2000* (Austin, Texas: Hoover's Business Press, 2000), pp. 872–873.

4. Jim Rohwer, "GE Digs Into Asia," *Fortune*, October 2, 2000, pp. 164–178.

5. For a discussion of the distinction between business- and corporate-level strategies, see Charles Hill and Gareth Jones, *Strategic Management: An Integrated Approach*, 5th Edition (Boston: Houghton Mifflin, 2001).

6. See Gary Hamel, "Strategy as Revolution," *Harvard Business Review*, July–August 1996, pp. 69–82.

7. See Henry Mintzberg, "Patterns in Strategy Formulation," *Management Science*, October 1978, pp. 934–948; Henry Mintzberg, "Strategy Making in Three Modes," *California Management Review*, 1973, pp. 44–53.

8. "If It's on the Fritz, Take It to Jane," *Business Week*, January 27, 1997, pp. 74–75.

9. Jay Barney, "Firm Resources and Sustained Competitive Advantage," *Journal of Management*, June 1991, pp. 99–120.

10. Jay Barney, "Strategic Factor Markets," *Management Science*, December 1986, pp. 1231–1241; see also Constantinos C. Markides, "A Dynamic View of Strategy," *Sloan Management Review*, Spring 1999, pp. 55–64.

11. See Michael Porter, *Competitive Strategy* (New York: Free Press, 1980).

12. Porter, *Competitive Strategy*. See also Colin Campbell-Hunt, "What Have We Learned About Generic Competitive Strategy? A Meta-Analysis," *Strategic Management Journal*, Vol. 21, 2000, pp. 127–154.

13. Ian C. MacMillan and Rita Gunther McGrath, "Discovering New Points of Differentiation," *Harvard Business Review*, July–August 1997, pp. 133–136.

14. "General Mills Intends to Reshape Doughboy in Its Own Image," *The Wall Street Journal*, July 18, 2000, pp. A1, A8.

15. Raymond E. Miles and Charles C. Snow, *Organizational Strategy, Structure, and Process* (New York: McGraw-Hill, 1978).

16. "Rough Crossing for eBay," *Business Week*, February 7, 2000, p. EB48.

17. See Eric D. Beinhocker, "Robust Adaptive Strategies," *Sloan Management Review*, Spring 1999, pp. 95–105.

18. Alfred Chandler, *Strategy and Structure: Chapters in the History of the American Industrial Enterprise* (Cambridge, Mass.: MIT Press, 1962); Richard Rumelt, *Strategy, Structure, and Economic Performance* (Cambridge, Mass.: Division of Research, Graduate School of Business Administration, Harvard University, 1974); and Oliver Williamson, *Markets and Hierarchies* (New York: Free Press, 1975).

19. "Not the Flavor of the Month," *Business Week*, March 20, 2000, p. 128.

20. K. L. Stimpert and Irene M. Duhaime, "Seeing the Big Picture: The Influence of Industry, Diversification, and Business Strategy on Performance," *Academy of Management Journal*, Vol. 40, No. 3, 1997, pp. 560–583.

21. See Chandler, *Strategy and Structure*, and Yakov Amihud and Baruch Lev, "Risk Reduction as a Managerial Motive for Conglomerate Mergers," *Bell Journal of Economics*, 1981, pp. 605–617.

22. Chandler, *Strategy and Structure*, and Williamson, *Markets and Hierarchies*.

23. "Did Somebody Say McBurrito?" *Business Week*, April 10, 2000, pp. 166–170.

24. See Jay Barney and William G. Ouchi, *Organizational Economics* (San Francisco: Jossey-Bass, 1986), for a discussion of the limitations of unrelated diversification.

25. "Latest Merger Boom Is Happening in China, and Bears Watching," *The Wall Street Journal*, July 30, 1997, pp. A1, A9; "A Breakthrough in Bavaria," *Business Week*, August 4, 1997, p. 54.

26. Kathleen M. Eisenhardt and D. Charles Galunic, "Co-evolving—At Last. A Way to Make Synergies Work," *Harvard Business Review*, January–February 2000, pp. 91–100.

27. "MGM Grand Pays $4.4 Billion for Mirage," *USA Today*, March 7, 2000, p. 1B.

28. See Constantinoes C. Markides and Peter J. Williamson, "Corporate Diversification and Organizational Structure: A Resource-Based View," *Academy of Management Journal*, April 1996, pp. 340–367.

29. See Barry Hedley, "A Fundamental Approach to Strategy Development," *Long Range Planning*, December 1976, pp. 2–11; and Bruce Henderson, "The Experience Curve Reviewed. IV: The Growth Share Matrix of the Product Portfolio," *Perspectives*, No. 135 (Boston: Boston Consulting Group, 1973).

30. "BMW: Unloading Rover May Not Win the Race," *Business Week*, April 3, 2000, p. 59.

31. Michael G. Allen, "Diagramming G.E.'s Planning for What's WATT," in Robert J. Allio and Malcolm W. Pennington (Eds.), *Corporate Planning: Techniques and Applications* (New York: AMACOM, 1979). Limits of this approach are discussed in R. A. Bettis and W. K. Hall, "The Business Portfolio Approach: Where It Falls Down in Practice," *Long Range Planning*, March 1983, pp. 95–105.

32. "Unilever to Sell Specialty-Chemical Unit to ICI of the U.K. for About $8 Billion," *The Wall Street Journal*, May 7, 1997, pp. A3, A12; "For Unilever, It's Sweetness and Light," *The Wall Street Journal*, April 13, 2000, pp. B1, B4.

Managing Decision Making and Problem Solving

Starbucks Corporation has arguably become the highest profile and fastest growing food and beverage company in the United States. Starbucks was started in Seattle in 1971 by three coffee aficionados. Their primary business at the time was buying premium coffee beans, roasting them, and then selling the coffee by the pound. The business performed modestly well and soon grew to nine stores, all in the Seattle area. The three partners sold Starbucks to a former employee, Howard Schultz, in 1987. Schultz promptly reoriented the business away from bulk coffee mail-order sales and emphasized retail coffee sales through the firm's coffee bars. Today, Starbucks is not only the largest coffee importer and roaster of specialty beans, but it is also the largest specialty coffee bean retailer in the United States. In addition, the firm is aggressively moving into several different foreign markets as well.

What is the key to Starbucks' phenomenal growth and success? One important ingredient is its well-conceived and implemented strategy. While Starbucks is opening a new coffee shop somewhere almost every day, this growth is planned and coordinated at each step of the way through careful site selection. And through its astute promotional campaigns and commitment to quality, the firm has elevated the coffee drinking taste of millions of consumers and fueled a significant increase in demand. Another key to Starbucks' success is its near-fanatical emphasis on quality control. For example, milk must be heated to precise temperatures between 150 and 170 degrees, and every espresso shot must be pulled within twenty-three seconds or else it is discarded. And no coffee is allowed to sit on a hot plate for more than twenty minutes. Schultz also refuses to franchise his Starbucks stores, fearing a loss of control and a potential deterioration of quality.

But even a firm as well managed as Starbucks can still make mistakes. Consider what happened, for example, when the firm opened its first store in New York City. Market research showed that New Yorkers strongly preferred drip coffees over the more exotic espresso-style coffees that were Starbucks mainstays in the West. Accordingly, the first Starbucks in New York was opened with more drip coffeemakers and fewer espresso machines than in other stores. But the drip coffees were largely ignored and the line for espresso crept out the door and

"Our management team is 100 percent focused on growing our core business without distraction or dilution from any other initiative."

—*Howard Schultz, CEO of Starbucks*

LEARNING OBJECTIVES

After studying this chapter, you should be able to:

- Define decision making and discuss types of decisions and decision-making conditions.

- Discuss rational perspectives on decision making, including the steps in decision making.

- Describe the behavioral nature of decision making.

- Discuss group and team decision making, including its advantages and disadvantages, and how it can be managed more effectively.

down the block. Thus, a hasty renovation was necessary within the first month the store was open so that it could provide more espresso and less drip coffee.

More recently, Starbucks stumbled again when Schultz announced to a group of investors that he and his management team were focusing their attention on diversification and were busily crafting a grand-scale Internet plan for Starbucks. According to Schultz, the plan would turn the company's web site into a "lifestyle portal" by partnering with various gourmet food vendors and home-decorating businesses. The investors, meanwhile, apparently decided that Schultz was getting too distracted by this plan and that he should remain focused on Starbucks' core businesses. They let him know their feelings by unloading the firm's stock so aggressively that its value plummeted by 28 percent the next day!

Of course, Schultz is a smart executive and he quickly got the message. While not totally abandoning his Internet strategy, he nevertheless began to refocus his attention on Starbucks' core businesses. For example, he stepped up expansion again, which had slowed, and began moving even more aggressively into foreign markets. He also began testing various new concepts for Starbucks coffee shops, such as an expanded lunch menu and a wider assortment of products such as CDs and chocolates. And how did the disgruntled investors take this about-face? They sent the stock price back up by over 30 percent within just a few months.[1]

anagers at Starbucks make decisions every day, and most of these decisions are good ones. Since no one can be right all the time, however, even a skilled executive like Howard Schultz can occasionally make a mistake. But an important key to organizational effectiveness can be a manager's ability to recognize when a bad decision has been made and to respond quickly to mistakes. Indeed, some experts believe that decision making is the most basic and fundamental of all managerial activities.[2] Thus, we discuss it here in the context of the first management function, planning. Keep in mind, however, that although decision making is perhaps most closely linked to the planning function, it is also part of organizing, leading, and controlling.

We begin our discussion by exploring the nature of decision making. We then describe rational perspectives on decision making. Behavioral aspects of decision making are then introduced and described. We conclude with a discussion of group and team decision making.

The Nature of Decision Making

Managers at Ford recently made the decision to buy Land Rover from BMW for nearly $3 billion.[3] At about the same time, the general manager of the Ford dealership in Bryan, Texas, made a decision to sponsor a local youth soccer team for $200. Each of these examples includes a decision, but the decisions differ in many ways. Thus, as a starting point in understanding decision making, we must first explore the meaning of decision making as well as types of decisions and the conditions under which decisions are made.[4]

Decision Making Defined

decision making The act of choosing one alternative from among a set of alternatives

Decision making can refer to either a specific act or a general process. **Decision making** per se is the act of choosing one alternative from among a set of alternatives. The decision-making process, however, is much more than this. One step of the process, for example, is that the person making the decision must recognize that a decision is necessary and identify the set of feasible alternatives before selecting one. Hence, the **decision-making process** includes recognizing and defining the nature of a decision situation, identifying alternatives, choosing the "best" alternative, and putting it into practice.[5]

decision-making process Recognizing and defining the nature of a decision situation, identifying alternatives, choosing the "best" alternative, and putting it into practice

The word *best*, of course, implies effectiveness. Effective decision making requires that the decision maker understand the situation driving the decision. Most people would consider an effective decision to be one that optimizes some set of factors such as profits, sales, employee welfare, and market share. In some situations, though, an effective decision may be one that minimizes loss, expenses, or employee turnover. It may even mean selecting the best method for going out of business, laying off employees, or terminating a contract.

We should also note that managers make decisions about both problems and opportunities. For example, making decisions about how to cut costs by 10 percent

Reprinted with special permission by King Features Syndicate, Inc.

reflects a problem—an undesired situation that requires a solution. But decisions are also necessary in situations of opportunity. Learning that the firm is earning higher-than-projected profits, for example, requires a subsequent decision. Should the extra funds be used to increase shareholder dividends, reinvest in current operations, or expand into new markets?

Of course, it may take a long time before a manager can know if the right decision was made. For example, when George Fisher took over as CEO of Kodak, he made several major decisions that will affect the company for decades. Among other things, for example, he sold off several chemical- and health-related businesses, reduced the firm's debt by $7 billion in the process, launched a major new line of advanced cameras and film called Advantix, and made major new investments in emerging technology such as digital photography. But analysts believe that the payoffs from these decisions will not be know for at least ten years.[6]

Decision making is a pervasive part of most managerial activities. Virtually everything that happens in a company involves making a decision or implementing a decision that has been made. While some decisions are grand and significant in scope, others, such as the ones shown in the center panel of this cartoon, involve more routine, day-to-day activities. And still others, illustrated in the right panel, deal with what to have for lunch or when to take a break. Regardless of their goals, however, the people making the decisions need to take them seriously and do what they believe to be best for the company.

Types of Decisions

Managers must make many different types of decisions. In general, however, most decisions fall into one of two categories: programmed and nonprogrammed.[7] A **programmed decision** is one that is fairly structured or recurs with some frequency (or both). Starbucks uses programmed decisions to purchase new supplies of coffee beans, cups, and napkins, and Starbucks employees are trained in exact procedures for brewing coffee. Likewise, the Bryan Ford dealer made a decision that he will sponsor a youth soccer team each year. Thus, when the soccer club president calls, the dealer already knows what he will do. Many decisions regarding basic operating systems and procedures and standard organizational transactions are of this variety and can therefore be programmed.[8]

Nonprogrammed decisions, on the other hand, are relatively unstructured and occur much less often. Starbucks' decision to focus its Internet strategy on lifestyles and then retreating from that plan are both nonprogrammed decisions. Likewise, Ford's decision to buy Land Rover was also a nonprogrammed decision. Managers faced with such decisions must treat each one as unique, requiring enormous amounts of time, energy, and resources for exploring the situation from all perspectives. Intuition and experience are major factors in nonprogrammed decisions. Most

programmed decision A decision that is fairly structured or recurs with some frequency (or both)

nonprogrammed decision A decision that is relatively unstructured and occurs much less often than a programmed decision

Most important decisions made in organizations are non-programmed in nature. Consider, for example, just a few of the decisions made by the coaches of the U.S and Costa Rican national soccer teams, shown here in a 2000 Gold Cup match. Before tournament play starts, each coach must decide who would be on the team. In preparing for a match or tournament the coach must decide on a training and practice regime. As a match approaches the coach must decide who will play. And after the match begins the coach must determine how substitutions would be made and which plays to run. While there may be "conventional wisdom" to guide some of these decisions, most coaches will apply their intuition and judgment.

of the decisions made by top managers involving strategy (including mergers, acquisitions, and takeovers) and organization design are nonprogrammed. So are decisions about new facilities, new products, labor contracts, and legal issues.

Figure 9.1

Decision-Making Conditions

Most major decisions in organizations today are made under a state of uncertainty. Managers making decisions in these circumstances must be sure to learn as much as possible about the situation and approach the decision from a logical and rational perspective.

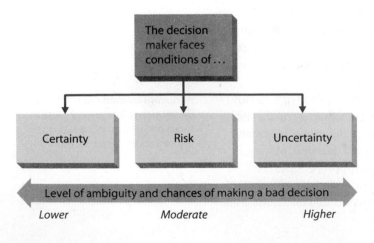

Decision-Making Conditions

Just as there are different kinds of decisions, there are also different conditions in which decisions must be made. Managers sometimes have an almost perfect understanding of conditions surrounding a decision, but at other times they have few clues about those conditions. In general, as shown in Figure 9.1, the circumstances that exist for the decision maker are conditions of certainty, risk, or uncertainty.[9]

Decision Making Under Certainty When the decision maker knows with reasonable certainty what the alternatives are and what conditions are associated with each alternative, a **state of certainty** exists. Suppose, for example, that managers at Singapore Airlines make a decision to buy five new jumbo jets. Their next decision is from whom to buy them. Since there are only two companies in the world who make jumbo jets, Boeing and Airbus, Singapore Airlines knows exactly its options. Each has proven products and will guarantee prices and delivery dates. The airline thus knows the alternative conditions associated with each. There is little ambiguity and relatively low chance of making a bad decision.

Few organizational decisions are made under conditions of true certainty. The complexity and turbulence of the contemporary business world make such situations rare. Even the airplane purchase decision we just considered has less certainty than it appears. The aircraft companies may not be able to guarantee delivery dates, so they may write cost-increase or inflation clauses into contracts. Thus, the airline may be only partially certain of the conditions surrounding each alternative.

Decision Making Under Risk

A more common decision-making condition is a state of risk. Under a **state of risk**, the availability of each alternative and its potential payoffs and costs are all associated with probability estimates. Suppose, for example, that a labor contract negotiator for a company receives a "final" offer from the union right before a strike deadline. The negotiator has two alternatives: to accept or to reject the offer. The risk centers on whether the union representatives are bluffing. If the company negotiator accepts the offer, she avoids a strike but commits to a costly labor contract. If she rejects the contract, she may get a more favorable one if the union is bluffing; she may provoke a strike if it is not.

On the basis of past experiences, relevant information, the advice of others, and her own judgment, she may conclude that there is about a 75 percent chance that union representatives are bluffing and about a 25 percent chance that they will back up their threats. Thus, she can base a calculated decision on the two alternatives (accept or reject the contract demands) and the probable consequences of each. When making decisions under a state of risk, managers must accurately determine the probabilities associated with each alternative. For example, if the union negotiators are committed to a strike if their demands are not met, and the company negotiator rejects their demands because she guesses they will not strike, her

state of certainty A condition in which the decision maker knows with reasonable certainty what the alternatives are and what conditions are associated with each alternative

state of risk A condition in which the availability of each alternative and its potential payoffs and costs are all associated with probability estimates

Decision makers usually face conditions of risk and/or uncertainty. Both conditions were clearly present during the aftermath of the 2000 presidential election. At one level, for example, the individual officials involved in the various recounts in Florida were often trying to decide a voter's intent from looking at a ballot that had not been initially counted for one reason or another. At a different level, political strategists for the two candidates also had to make decisions about which lawsuits to file, which to oppose, and/or which to appeal based on the most likely impact the outcomes of such actions might have on their candidate.

miscalculation will prove costly. As indicated in Figure 9.1, decision making under conditions of risk is accompanied by moderate ambiguity and chances of a bad decision.[10] Ford's decision to buy Land Rover was made under a condition of risk.

Decision Making Under Uncertainty   Most of the major decision making in contemporary organizations is done under a **state of uncertainty**. The decision maker does not know all the alternatives, the risks associated with each, or the likely consequences of each alternative. This uncertainty stems from the complexity and dynamism of contemporary organizations and their environments. Starbucks' initial decision to move more aggressively into lifestyle businesses was made under a state of uncertainty, as was its reversal of that decision. Indeed, the emergence of the Internet as a significant force in today's competitive environment has served to increase uncertainty for most managers. The *World of Manage-*

state of uncertainty A condition in which the decision maker does not know all the alternatives, the risks associated with each, or the likely consequences of each alternative

---

WORLD OF MANAGEMENT

UNCERTAINTY UNDERSCORES ENTREPRENEURIAL DECISIONS IN JAPAN

Uncertainty is a constant for Yasumitsu Shigeta, founder of Japan's Hikari Tsushin, a leading distributor of cell phones and Internet services in Japan. Since founding the company in 1988, when he was in his twenties, Shigeta has ridden wave after wave of new technology to build his business. In 1994, mobile phone service was in its infancy in Japan, with start-ups challenging NTT, the country's long-established telephone service provider. Despite the uncertainty, Shigeta jumped in early to sell phones and service from NTT competitors through a national chain of franchised "Hit Stores." Shigeta's bold decision paid off as mobile phone service—cheaper than traditional phone service because of the competition—became wildly popular.

In 1999, Shigeta again faced a decision under uncertainty. More Japanese were buying personal computers and logging onto the Internet for business and pleasure. The entrepreneur was among the first to see opportunity in helping small businesses access the Internet and set up home pages without hefty investments. He decided to meet this need by providing a "Hit Mail" service with e-mail and web site hosting capabilities for small businesses. He also created a venture capital subsidiary to fund emerging Internet enterprises. Quick decisions were the norm here. As one example, the managing director of this subsidiary moved at Internet speed when he decided on a

$16 million investment in a U.S. dot-com after just ten minutes of investigation.

Then things started to go wrong. More consumers began using NTT's mobile phones because it offered web access. Shigeta's Hit Stores didn't sell NTT phones, so sales leveled off. Next, a Japanese magazine criticized the company's aggressive sales techniques, and rumors circulated about the founder's ethnic background. Shigeta called a news conference to defend himself, but he failed to mention that sales were not growing as expected. Within months, however, the entrepreneur publicly admitted that his company would report a loss for the year. This announcement sent Hikari Tsushin's stock tumbling. Shigeta still believes in his Internet initiatives, and his Hit Mail service continues to grow, but the company's future direction is far from certain.

> *The slightest delay in judgment or decision making will outdate the idea itself, right then and there.*
>
> —*Posted on web site of Hikari Tsushin venture-capital business.*

Reference: Peter Landers and Yumiko Ono, "Without a Net: A Japanese Web Star Takes a Wild Stumble; Can He Rise Again?" *Wall Street Journal*, April 28, 2000, pp. A1, A6 (*quote on p. A6).

ment provides another example of decision making under conditions of uncertainty at NTT, Japan's largest telephone service provider.

To make effective decisions in these circumstances, managers must acquire as much relevant information as possible and approach the situation from a logical and rational perspective. Intuition, judgment, and experience always play major roles in the decision-making process under conditions of uncertainty. Even so, uncertainty is the most ambiguous condition for managers and the one most prone to error.[11] Indeed, many of the problems associated with the massive recall of tires by Firestone and Ford in 2000 were attributed to Firestone's apparent difficulties in responding to ambiguous and uncertain decision parameters regarding the firm's moral, ethical, and legal responsibilities.[12]

MANAGEMENT Managers should remember that decision making is the foun-
IMPLICATIONS dation of much of their work. It is also important to understand the distinction between programmed and nonprogrammed decisions and the different conditions—certainty, risk, and uncertainty—that surround decision-making situations.

Rational Perspectives on Decision Making

Most managers like to think of themselves as rational decision makers. And indeed, many experts argue that managers should try to be as rational as possible in making decisions.[13]

The Classical Model of Decision Making

The **classical decision model** is a prescriptive approach to decision making that tells managers how they should make decisions. It rests on the assumptions that managers are logical and rational and that they make decisions that are in the best interests of the organization. Figure 9.2 shows how the classical model views the decision-making process: (1) decision makers have complete information about the decision situation and possible alternatives, (2) they can effectively eliminate

classical decision model A prescriptive approach to decision making that tells managers how they should make decisions. It assumes that managers are logical and rational and that they make decisions that are in the best interests of the organization

Figure 9.2

The Classical Model of Decision Making
The classical model of decision making assumes that managers are rational and logical. It attempts to prescribe how managers should approach decision situations.

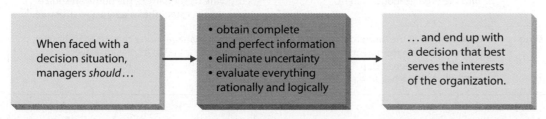

uncertainty to achieve a decision condition of certainty, and (3) they evaluate all aspects of the decision situation logically and rationally. As we see later, these conditions rarely, if ever, actually exist.

Steps in Rational Decision Making

A manager who really wants to approach a decision rationally and logically should try to follow the **steps in rational decision making** listed in Table 9.1. These steps in rational decision making help keep the decision maker focused on facts and logic and help guard against inappropriate assumptions and pitfalls.

steps in rational decision making
Recognize and define the decision situation; identify alternatives; evaluate each alternative in terms of its feasibility, satisfactoriness, and consequences; select the best alternative; implement the chosen alternative; follow up and evaluate the results of the chosen alternative

Recognizing and Defining the Decision Situation   The first step in rational decision making is recognizing that a decision is necessary—that is, there must be some stimulus or spark to initiate the process. For many decisions and problem situations, the stimulus may occur without any prior warning. When equipment malfunctions, the manager must decide whether to repair or replace it. Or when a major crisis erupts, as described in Chapter 3, the manager must quickly decide how to deal with it. As we already noted, the stimulus for a decision may be either

Table 9.1

Steps in the Rational Decision-Making Process

Although the presumptions of the classical decision model rarely exist, managers can approach decision making with rationality. By following the steps of rational decision making, managers ensure that they are learning as much as possible about the decision situation and its alternatives.

Step	Detail	Example
1. Recognizing and defining the decision situation	Some stimulus indicates that a decision must be made. The stimulus may be positive or negative.	A plant manager sees that employee turnover has increased by 5 percent.
2. Identifying alternatives	Both obvious and creative alternatives are desired. In general, the more important the decision, the more alternatives should be generated.	The plant manager can increase wages, increase benefits, or change hiring standards.
3. Evaluating alternatives	Each alternative is evaluated to determine its feasibility, its satisfactoriness, and its consequences.	Increasing benefits may not be feasible. Increasing wages and changing hiring standards may satisfy all conditions.
4. Selecting the best alternative	Consider all situational factors, and choose the alternative that best fits the manager's situation.	Changing hiring standards will take an extended period of time to cut turnover, so increase wages.
5. Implementing the chosen alternative	The chosen alternative is implemented into the organizational system.	The plant manager may need permission from corporate headquarters. The human resource department establishes a new wage structure.
6. Following up and evaluating the results	At some time in the future, the manager should ascertain the extent to which the alternative chosen in step 4 and implemented in step 5 has worked.	The plant manager notes that, six months later, turnover dropped to its previous level.

positive or negative. A manager who must decide how to invest surplus funds, for example, faces a positive decision situation. A negative financial stimulus could involve having to trim budgets because of cost overruns. *Management InfoTech* illustrates how managers at SAP recently recognized and defined a decision situation.

Inherent in problem recognition is the need to define precisely what the problem is. The manager must develop a complete understanding of the problem, its causes, and its relationship to other factors. This understanding comes from careful analysis and thoughtful consideration of the situation. Consider the situation currently being faced in the air travel industry. Because of the growth of international travel related to business, education, and tourism, global carriers like Singapore Airlines, KLM, JAL, British Airways, American Airlines, and others need to increase their capacity for

MANAGEMENT INFOTECH

SAP PLAYS CATCH-UP ON THE INTERNET

The Internet revolution started without SAP. This German software firm made its name developing sophisticated software for managing key operations such as purchasing, production, and customer transactions. But year after year of rapid sales growth during the 1990s gave way to slower growth and lower profits when SAP's top management failed to recognize how the Internet was changing the way companies do business.

Even as SAP continued to introduce complex stand-alone programs, its corporate customers were demanding software capable of web-based connections with customers and suppliers. Competitors such as Ariba and Siebel were already offering such software, but not SAP. From the vantage point of company headquarters in Walldorf, Germany, top managers were not in a hurry to adapt to the Internet and e-commerce. But when U.S. competitor Oracle began touting its e-commerce expertise in a high-profile advertising campaign, one of SAP's founders recognized that the firm needed an Internet strategy.

Two SAP programmers assigned to the task came up with the concept of enhancing the company's existing software with new programs designed to link suppliers and customers via the Internet. Dubbed mySAP.com, this enhancement worked only with SAP programs, a problem for businesses that use software purchased from different sources. Timing was also an issue: General Motors, for example, selected a rival's e-commerce software rather than risk delays in getting mySAP.com up and running.

SAP faced yet another Internet-related decision. While U.S. competitors were using stock options to attract, retain, and reward talented employees, SAP resisted requests by managers of SAP America for a similar plan. Finally, after SAP America's CEO and president left to join rival firms—amid dozens of other management defections from the United States and from international divisions—SAP devised a stock-option plan.

Now mySAP.com is catching up with Hewlett-Packard and other major customers. To speed up software development and keep a closer eye on U.S. Internet trends, SAP has outsourced some work to a Boston-based firm (which was formerly based in Germany). The company has also decided to follow the lead of its U.S. rivals in more aggressively promoting new products and enhancements—even before they are introduced.

> *We made a decision two years ago and there has been a massive paradigm shift to the Internet.*
>
> —*Hasso Plattner, co-founder and co-CEO, SAP**

References: Neal E. Boudette, "How a Software Titan Missed the Internet Revolution," *Wall Street Journal,* January 18, 2000, pp. B1, B4 (*quote on p. B4); "Software Engineering Isn't All, SAP Decides; Image Matters, Too," *Wall Street Journal,* September 26, 2000, pp. A1, A11.

international travel. Since most major international airports are operating at or near capacity already, adding a significant number of new flights to existing schedules is not feasible. As a result, the most logical alternative is to increase capacity on existing flights. Thus, Boeing and Airbus, the world's only manufacturers of large commercial aircraft, have recognized an important opportunity and have defined their decision situation as how to respond best to the need for increased global travel capacity.[14]

Identifying Alternatives   Once the decision situation has been recognized and defined, the second step is to identify alternative courses of effective action. Developing both obvious, standard alternatives and creative, innovative alternatives is generally useful. In general, the more important the decision, the more attention is directed to developing alternatives. If the decision involves a multimillion-dollar relocation, a great deal of time and expertise will be devoted to identifying the best locations. J.C. Penney Company spent two years searching before selecting the Dallas–Fort Worth area for its new corporate headquarters. If the problem is to choose a color for the company softball team uniforms, less time and expertise will be brought to bear.

Although managers should seek creative solutions, they must also recognize that various constraints often limit their alternatives. Common constraints include legal restrictions; moral and ethical norms; authority constraints; or constraints imposed by the power and authority of the manager, available technology, economic considerations, and unofficial social norms. Boeing and Airbus each identified three different alternatives to address the decision situation of increasing international airline travel capacity: they could independently develop new large planes, they could collaborate in a joint venture to create a single new large plane, or they could modify their largest existing planes and thus increase their capacity.

Evaluating Alternatives   The third step in the decision-making process is evaluating each of the alternatives. Figure 9.3 presents a decision tree that can be used to judge different alternatives. The figure suggests that each alternative be evalu-

Figure 9.3

Evaluating Alternatives in the Decision-Making Process

Managers must thoroughly evaluate all the alternatives, which increases the chances that the alternative finally chosen will be successful. Failure to evaluate an alternative's feasibility, satisfactoriness, and consequences can lead to a wrong decision.

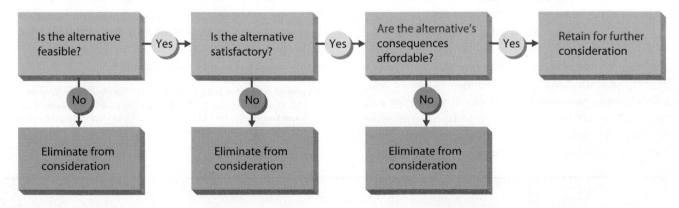

ated in terms of its *feasibility*, its *satisfactoriness*, and its *consequences*. The first question to ask is whether an alternative is feasible. Is it within the realm of probability and practicality? For a small, struggling firm, an alternative requiring a huge financial outlay is probably out of the question. Other alternatives may not be feasible because of legal barriers. And limited human, material, and information resources may make other alternatives impractical.

When an alternative has passed the test of feasibility, it must next be examined to see how well it satisfies the conditions of the decision situation. For example, a manager searching for ways to double production capacity might consider purchasing an existing plant from another company. If closer examination reveals that the new plant would increase production capacity by only 35 percent, this alternative may not be satisfactory.

Finally, when an alternative has proven both feasible and satisfactory, its probable consequences must still be assessed. To what extent will a particular alternative influence other parts of the organization? What financial and nonfinancial costs will be associated with such influences? For example, a plan to boost sales by cutting prices may disrupt cash flows, need a new advertising program, and alter the behavior of sales representatives because it requires a different commission structure. The manager, then, must put "price tags" on the consequences of each alternative. Even an alternative that is both feasible and satisfactory must be eliminated if its consequences are too expensive for the total system. Airbus felt it would be at a disadvantage if it tried simply to enlarge its existing planes, since the Boeing 747 is already the largest aircraft being made and could be expanded to remain the largest. Boeing, meanwhile, was seriously concerned about the risk inherent in building a new and even larger plane, even if it shared the risk with Airbus as a joint venture.

Selecting the Best Alternative Even though many alternatives fail to pass the triple tests of feasibility, satisfactoriness, and affordable consequences, two or more alternatives may remain. Choosing the best of these is the real crux of decision making. One approach is to choose the alternative with the highest combined level of feasibility, satisfactoriness, and affordable consequences. Even though most situations do not lend themselves to objective, mathematical analysis, the manager can often develop subjective estimates and weights for choosing an alternative.

Optimization is also a frequent goal. Because a decision is likely to affect several individuals or units, any feasible alternative will probably not maximize all of the relevant goals. Suppose that the manager of the Kansas City Royals needs to select a new outfielder for the upcoming baseball season. Bill hits .350 but is barely able to catch a fly ball; Joe hits only .175 but is outstanding in the field; and Sam hits .290 and is a solid but not outstanding fielder. The manager would probably select Sam because of the optimal balance of hitting and fielding. Decision makers should also remember that finding multiple acceptable alternatives may be possible—selecting just one alternative and rejecting all the others might not be necessary. For example, the Royals' manager might decide that Sam will start each game,

Managers generally attempt to follow a logical and rational approach to making decisions. This is especially true of individuals in positions like H. Carl McCall, the sole trustee of the Common Retirement Fund for the state of New York. McCall is responsible for managing a portfolio recently valued at $122 billion. The public trust vested in his position makes it especially important that he rationally consider various investment options and then select the ones that will provide the optimal blend of risk and return for the hundreds of thousands of retired state employees who depend on the fund.

Bill will be retained as a pinch hitter, and Joe will be retained as a defensive substitute. In many hiring decisions, the candidates remaining after evaluation are ranked. If the top candidate rejects the offer, it may be automatically extended to the number two candidate, and, if necessary, to the remaining candidates in order. For the reasons noted earlier, Airbus proposed a joint venture with Boeing. Boeing meanwhile decided its best course of action was to modify its existing 747 to increase its capacity. As a result, Airbus then decided to proceed on its own to develop and manufacture a new jumbo jet.

Implementing the Chosen Alternative   After an alternative has been selected, the manager must put it into effect. In some decision situations, implementation is fairly easy; in others, it is more difficult. In the case of an acquisition, for example, managers must decide how to integrate all the activities of the new business, including purchasing, human resource practices, and distribution, into an ongoing organizational framework. For example, when America Online and Time Warner announced their merger, they also acknowledged that it would take at least a year to integrate the two firms into a single entity. Operational plans, which we discussed in Chapter 7, are useful in implementing alternatives.

Managers must also consider people's resistance to change when implementing decisions. The reasons for such resistance include insecurity, inconvenience, and fear of the unknown. When Penney's decided to move its headquarters from New York to Texas, many employees resigned rather than relocate. Managers should anticipate potential resistance at various stages of the implementation process. (Resistance to change is covered in Chapter 13.) Managers should also recognize that, even when all alternatives have been evaluated as precisely as possible and the consequences of each alternative have been weighed, unanticipated consequences are still likely. Any number of things—unexpected cost increases, a less-than-perfect fit with existing organizational subsystems, or unpredicted effects on cash flow or operating expenses, for example—could develop after implementation has begun. Boeing has set its engineers to work expanding the capacity of its 747 from today's 416 passengers to as many as 520 passengers by adding thirty feet to the plane's body. Airbus engineers, meanwhile, are developing design concepts for a new jumbo jet equipped with escalators and elevators and capable of carrying 655 passengers. Airbus's development costs alone are estimated to be more than $12 billion.

Following Up and Evaluating the Results   The final step in the decision-making process requires that managers evaluate the effectiveness of their decision—that is, they should make sure that the chosen alternative has served its original purpose. If an implemented alternative appears not to be working, the manager can respond in several ways. Another previously identified alternative (the second or third choice) could be adopted. Or the manager might recognize that the situation was not correctly defined to start with and begin the process all over again. Finally, the manager might decide that the original alternative is in fact appropriate but has not yet had time to work or should be implemented in a different way.

Failure to evaluate decision effectiveness may have serious consequences. The Pentagon spent $1.8 billion and eight years developing the Sergeant York antiaircraft gun. From the beginning, tests revealed major problems with the weapon system, but not until it was in its final stages, when it was demonstrated to be completely ineffective, was the project scrapped.[15] The examples in the chapter opening incident illustrate a much more effective approach to evaluating decision effectiveness. When New Yorkers expressed their preferences for espresso over drip coffees, Starbucks quickly revamped its cafés. And when investors let Howard Schultz know that they disapproved of his Internet strategy, he quickly changed it. Meanwhile, experts agree that it will be several years before the outcomes of decisions by Boeing and Airbus can be assessed.

MANAGEMENT IMPLICATIONS   Whenever possible managers should strive to apply rationality and logic to the decisions they make. By following the logical sequence of steps that comprise the classical model, managers can lessen risk and reduce uncertainty in many decision-making situations. Of course, at the same time managers should also recognize the "prescriptive" nature of this approach and not adhere to it so rigidly that they fail to consider their own experience and intuition. Finally, they should also know that even using the classical model effectively does not guarantee success.

Behavioral Aspects of Decision Making

If all decision situations were approached as logically as described in the previous section, more decisions would prove to be successful. Yet decisions are often made with little consideration for logic and rationality. Some experts have estimated that U.S. companies use rational decision-making techniques less than 20 percent of the time.[16] And even when organizations try to be logical, they sometimes fail. For example, Starbucks' original decision to emphasis drip over espresso coffee in New York was based on marketing research, taste tests, and rational deliberation—but the decision was still wrong. On the other hand, sometimes when a decision is made with little regard for logic, it can still turn out to be correct.[17] An important ingredient in how these forces work is the behavioral aspect of decision making. The administrative model better reflects these subjective considerations. Other behavioral aspects include political forces, intuition and escalation of commitment, risk propensity, and ethics.

The Administrative Model

Herbert A. Simon was one of the first experts to recognize that decisions are not always made with rationality and logic.[18] Simon was subsequently awarded the Nobel Prize in economics. Rather than prescribing how decisions should be made, his view of decision making, now called the **administrative model**, describes how decisions are often actually made. As illustrated in Figure 9.4, the model holds that managers (1) have incomplete and imperfect information, (2) are constrained by bounded rationality, and (3) tend to satisfice when making decisions.

   Bounded rationality suggests that decision makers are limited by their values and unconscious reflexes, skills, and habits. They are also limited by less than

administrative model A decision-making model showing that managers (1) have incomplete and imperfect information, (2) are constrained by bounded rationality, and (3) tend to satisfice when making decisions

bounded rationality A concept suggesting that decision makers are limited by their values and unconscious reflexes, skills, and habits

Figure 9.4

The Administrative Model of Decision Making

The administrative model is based on behavioral processes that affect how managers make decisions. Rather than prescribing how decisions should be made, it focuses more on describing how they are made.

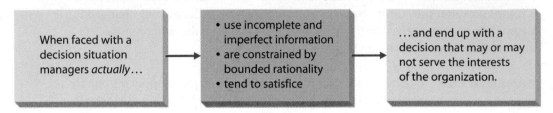

| When faced with a decision situation managers *actually*... | • use incomplete and imperfect information
• are constrained by bounded rationality
• tend to satisfice | ...and end up with a decision that may or may not serve the interests of the organization. |

satisficing The tendency to search for alternatives only until one is found that meets some minimum standard of sufficiency

complete information and knowledge. Bounded rationality partially explains how U.S. auto executives allowed Japanese auto makers to get such a strong foothold in their domestic market. For years, executives at GM, Ford, and Chrysler compared their companies' performance only to one another and ignored foreign imports. The foreign "threat" wasn't acknowledged until the domestic auto market had been changed forever. If managers had gathered complete information from the beginning, they might have been better able to thwart foreign competitors. Essentially, then, the concept of bounded rationality suggests that, although people try to be rational decision makers, their rationality has limits.

Another important part of the administrative model is **satisficing**. This concept suggests that rather than conducting an exhaustive search for the best possible alternative, decision makers tend to search only until they identify an alternative that meets some minimum standard of sufficiency. A manager looking for a site for a new plant, for example, may select the first site she finds that meets basic requirements for transportation, utilities, and price, even though further searching might yield a better location. People satisfice for a variety of reasons. Managers may simply ignore their own motives (such as reluctance to spend time making a decision) and therefore not continue searching after a minimally acceptable alternative is identified. The decision maker may be unable to weigh and evaluate large numbers of alternatives and criteria. Also, subjective and personal considerations often intervene in decision situations.

Because of the inherent imperfection of information, bounded rationality, and satisficing, the decisions made by a manager may or may not actually be in the best interests of the organization. A manager may choose a particular location for the new plant because it offers the lowest price and best availability of utilities and transportation. Or she may choose the location because it's in a community in which she wants to live.

In summary, then, the classical and administrative models paint quite different pictures of decision making. Which is more correct? Actually, each can be used to understand how managers make decisions. The classical model is prescriptive: it explains how managers can at least attempt to be more rational and logical in their approach to decisions. The administrative model can be used by managers to develop a better understanding of their inherent biases and limitations.[19] In the following sections, we describe more fully other behavioral forces that can influence decisions.

Political Forces in Decision Making

Political forces are another major element that contributes to the behavioral nature of decision making. Organizational politics is covered in Chapter 17, but one major element of politics, coalitions, is especially relevant to decision making. A **coalition** is an informal alliance of individuals or groups formed to achieve a common goal. This common goal is often a preferred decision alternative. For example, coalitions of stockholders frequently band together to force a board of directors to make a certain decision.

coalition An informal alliance of individuals or groups formed to achieve a common goal

Coalitions led to the formation of Unisys Corporation, a large computer firm. Sperry was once one of the United States' computer giants, but a series of poor decisions put the company on the edge of bankruptcy. Two major executives waged battle for three years over what to do. One wanted to get out of the computer business altogether, and the other wanted to stay in. Finally, the manager who wanted to remain in the computer business garnered enough support to earn promotion to the corporation's presidency. The other manager took early retirement. Shortly thereafter, Sperry agreed to be acquired by Burroughs Wellcome Co. The resulting combined company was called Unisys.

The impact of coalitions can be either positive or negative. They can help astute managers get the organization on a path toward effectiveness and profitability, or they can strangle well-conceived strategies and decisions. Managers must recognize when to use coalitions, how to assess whether coalitions are acting in the best interests of the organization, and how to constrain their dysfunctional effects.[20]

Intuition and Escalation of Commitment

Two other important decision processes that go beyond logic and rationality are intuition and escalation of commitment to a chosen course of action.

Intuition **Intuition** is an innate belief about something without conscious consideration. Managers sometimes decide to do something because it "feels right" or they have a hunch. This feeling is usually not arbitrary, however. Rather, it is based on years of experience and practice in making decisions in similar situations. An inner sense may help managers make an occasional decision without going through a full-blown rational sequence of steps. For example, a few years ago the New York Yankees called three major sneaker manufacturers, Nike, Reebok, and Adidas, and informed them that they were looking to make a sponsorship deal. While Nike and Reebok were carefully and rationally assessing the possibilities, managers at Adidas quickly realized that a partnership with the Yankees made a lot of sense for them. They responded very quickly to the idea and ended up hammering out a contract while the competitors were still analyzing details.[21] Of course, all managers, but most especially inexperienced ones, should be careful not to rely on intuition too heavily. If rationality and logic are continually flaunted for what "feels right," the odds are that disaster will strike one day.

intuition An innate belief about something without conscious consideration

escalation of commitment A decision maker's staying with a decision even when it appears to be wrong

Escalation of Commitment   Another important behavioral process that influences decision making is **escalation of commitment** to a chosen course of action. In particular, decision makers sometimes make decisions and then become so committed to the course of action suggested by that decision that they stay with it, even when it appears to be wrong.[22] For example, when people buy stock in a company, they sometimes refuse to sell it even after repeated drops in price. They chose a course of action—buying the stock in anticipation of making a profit—and then stay with it even in the face of increasing losses.

For years Pan American World Airways (Pan Am) ruled the skies and used its profits to diversify into real estate and other businesses. But with the advent of deregulation, Pan Am began to struggle and lose market share to other carriers. When Pan Am managers finally realized how ineffective the airline operations had become, the "rational" decision would have been to sell off the remaining airline operations and concentrate on the firm's more profitable businesses, as experts today point out. But because they still saw the company as being first and foremost an airline, they instead began slowly to sell off the firm's profitable holdings to keep the airline flying. Eventually, the company was left with nothing but an ineffective and inefficient airline, and then it had to sell off its more profitable routes before eventually being taken over by Delta. Had Pan Am managers made the more rational decision years earlier, chances are the firm could still be a profitable enterprise today, albeit one with no involvement in the airline industry.[23]

Thus, decision makers must walk a fine line. On the one hand, they must guard against sticking with an incorrect decision too long. To do so can bring about financial decline. On the other hand, managers should not bail out of a seemingly incorrect decision too soon, as did Adidas several years ago. Adidas once dominated the market for professional athletic shoes. It subsequently entered the market for amateur sports shoes and did well there also. But managers interpreted a sales slowdown as a sign that the boom in athletic shoes was over. They thought that they had made the wrong decision and ordered drastic cutbacks. The market took off again with Nike at the head of the pack, and Adidas never recovered. Fortunately, a new management team has changed the way Adidas makes decisions and, as illustrated earlier, the firm is again on its way to becoming a force in the athletic shoe and apparel markets.

Risk Propensity and Decision Making

risk propensity The extent to which a decision maker is willing to gamble when making a decision

The behavioral element of **risk propensity** is the extent to which a decision maker is willing to gamble when making a decision. Some managers are cautious about every decision they make. They try to adhere to the rational model and are extremely conservative in what they do. Such managers are more likely to avoid mistakes, and they infrequently make decisions that lead to big losses. Other managers are extremely aggressive in making decisions and are willing to take risks.[24] They rely heavily on intuition, reach decisions quickly, and often risk big investments on their decisions. As in gambling, these managers are more likely than their conservative counterparts to achieve big successes with their decisions; they are also more likely to incur greater losses.[25] The organization's culture is a prime ingredient in fostering different levels of risk propensity.

Ethics and Decision Making

As we introduced in Chapter 4, individual ethics are personal beliefs about right and wrong behavior. Ethics are clearly related to decision making in a number of ways. For example, suppose after careful analysis a manager realizes that her company could save money by closing her department and subcontracting with a supplier for the same services. But to recommend this course of action would result in the loss of several jobs, including her own. Her own ethical standards will clearly shape how she proceeds.[26] Indeed, each component of managerial ethics (relationships of the firm to its employees, of employees to the firm, and of the firm to other economic agents) involves a wide variety of decisions, all of which are likely to have an ethical component. A manager must remember, then, that just as behavioral processes such as politics and risk propensity affect the decisions she makes, so too do her ethical beliefs. *Today's Management Issues* highlights an ethical situation faced by decision makers at Coca-Cola.

TODAY'S MANAGEMENT ISSUES

LEARNING TO BALANCE MULTIPLE GOALS

Successful companies sometimes see little incentive to change, even when they have difficulty balancing important financial and ethical goals. Coca-Cola is a case in point. For years, Coca-Cola's managers were focused on keeping sales and profits soaring. Behind the scenes, however, African-American employees were raising concerns about possible discrimination in the organization. Finding company officials unresponsive, the employees eventually filed suit, saying that Coca-Cola discriminated in internal decisions over promotions, appraisals, terminations, and compensation.

Initially, Coca-Cola mounted a forceful defense, which caused one former company human resources manager—who was not involved in the lawsuit—to plan a boycott and call for a $200 million settlement. Then the company demoted Carl Ware, its highest ranking African-American executive. Four years before, Ware had sent a memo to Coca-Cola colleagues with suggestions for improving diversity by helping African-American managers move up in the company. Most of Ware's suggestions were never implemented, however, and he decided to retire a few days after he was demoted.

Coca-Cola continued to dispute the charges of discrimination, but now its sales and profits were stalled, and mounting pressure caused a change in top management. When Doug Daft took over as CEO, he asked Carl Ware to return as executive vice president for global public affairs. In addition, Daft implemented two of Ware's recommendations for improving diversity. First, Daft began communicating that diversity was one of the company's key goals. Second, the CEO set up a new compensation system linking pay to progress in achieving diversity goals.

Although the company reached a tentative settlement with the original eight plaintiffs, a new discrimination lawsuit was quickly filed by four more African-American employees. As the legal wrangles continue, Coca-Cola's management team is working hard to maintain an appropriate balance between the organization's diversity goals and its financial goals.

> *They ignored me, ignored me, ignored me to the point where I felt I had no other recourse.*
>
> *—Greg Clark, plaintiff in class-action lawsuit against Coca-Cola**

Reference: Ann Harrington, "Coke Denied … Prevention Is the Best Defense," *Fortune*, July 10, 2000, p. 188 (*quote on p. 188).

MANAGEMENT Managers must understand that various behavioral processes
IMPLICATIONS affect how decisions are made. Their own bounded rationality
and satisficing tendencies, for example, should be acknowledged. Managers
should be on the alert for political forces as they relate to decision making, and
they should also be aware of the role of intuition, escalation of commitment, risk
propensity, and ethics.

Group and Team Decision Making in Organizations

In more and more organizations today, important decisions are made by groups
and teams rather than by individuals. Examples include the executive committee
of General Motors, product design teams at Texas Instruments, and marketing
planning groups at Compaq Computer. Managers can typically choose whether to
have individuals or groups and teams make a particular decision. Thus, knowing
about forms of group and team decision making and their advantages and disadvantages is important.[27]

Forms of Group and Team Decision Making

The most common methods of group and team decision making are interacting
groups, Delphi groups, and nominal groups. Increasingly, these methods of group
decision making are being conducted on-line.

interacting group or team A
decision-making group or team
in which members openly discuss,
argue about, and agree on the best
alternative

Interacting Groups or Teams **Interacting groups or teams** are the most common form of decision-making groups. The format is simple—either an existing or
a newly designated group or team is asked to make a decision. Existing groups or
teams might be functional departments, regular work teams, or standing committees. Newly designated groups or teams can be ad hoc committees, task forces, or
newly constituted work teams. The group or team members talk among themselves, argue, agree, argue some more, form internal coalitions, and so forth. Finally, after some period of deliberation, the group or team makes its decision. An
advantage of this method is that the interactions between people often spark new
ideas and promote understanding. A major disadvantage, though, is that political
processes can play too big a role.

Delphi group A form of group decision making in which a group solicits input from a panel of experts
who contribute individually; their
opinions are combined and, in effect, averaged

Delphi Groups A **Delphi group** is sometimes used for developing a consensus of expert opinion. Developed by the Rand Corporation, the Delphi procedure
solicits input from a panel of experts who contribute individually. Their opinions
are combined and, in effect, averaged. Assume, for example, that the problem is
to establish an expected date for a major technological breakthrough in converting coal into usable energy. The first step in using the Delphi procedure is to obtain the cooperation of a panel of experts. For this situation, experts might

include various research scientists, university researchers, and executives in a relevant energy industry. At first, the experts are asked to predict anonymously a time frame for the expected breakthrough. The persons coordinating the Delphi group collect the responses, average them, and ask the experts for another prediction. In this round, the experts who provided unusual or extreme predictions may be asked to justify them. These explanations may then be relayed to the other experts. When the predictions stabilize, the average prediction is taken to represent the decision of the group of experts. The time, expense, and logistics of the Delphi technique rule out its use for routine, everyday decisions, but it has been successfully used for forecasting technological breakthroughs at Boeing, market potential for new products at General Motors, research and development patterns at Eli Lilly, and future economic conditions by the U.S. government.[28]

More and more often these days, businesses are relying on groups and teams to make critical decisions. Hewlett-Packard recently announced an ambitious program to dramatically improve customer satisfaction with its products. HP assigned the program to two managers, Mei-Lin Cheng and Julie Anderson, and their team. But HP left all the details and major decisions associated with meeting its customer satisfaction goals in the hands of the team.

Nominal Groups Another useful group and team decision-making technique occasionally used is the **nominal group**. Unlike the Delphi method, where group members do not see one another, nominal group members are brought together. The members represent a group in name only, however; they do not talk to one another freely like the members of interacting groups. Nominal groups are used most often to generate creative and innovative alternatives or ideas. To begin, the manager assembles a group of knowledgeable people and outlines the problem to them. The group members are then asked individually to write down as many alternatives as they can think of. The members then take turns stating their ideas, which are recorded on a flip chart or blackboard at the front of the room. Discussion is limited to simple clarification. After all alternatives have been listed, more open discussion takes place. Group members then vote, usually by rank-ordering the various alternatives. The highest ranking alternative represents the decision of the group. Of course, the manager in charge may retain the authority to accept or reject the group decision.

nominal group A structured technique used most often to generate creative and innovative alternatives or ideas

Advantages of Group and Team Decision Making

The advantages and disadvantages of group and team decision making relative to individual decision making are summarized in Table 9.2. One advantage is simply that more information is available in a group or team setting—as suggested by the old axiom, "Two heads are better than one." A group or team represents a broader range of education, experience, and perspective. Partly as a result of this increased information, groups and teams typically can identify and evaluate more alternatives than can one person.[29] The people involved in a group or team decision understand the logic and rationale behind it, are more likely to accept it, and are equipped to communicate the decision to their work groups or departments.[30] Finally, research evidence suggests that groups may make better decisions than do individuals.[31]

Disadvantages of Group and Team Decision Making

Perhaps the biggest drawback of group and team decision making is the additional time and (hence) the greater expense entailed. The increased time stems from interaction and discussion among group or team members. If a given manager's time is worth $50 an hour, and if the manager spends two hours making a decision, the decision "costs" the organization $100. For the same decision, a group of five managers might require three hours of time. At the same $50-an-hour rate, the decision "costs" the organization $750. Assuming the group or team decision is better, the additional expense may be justified, but the fact remains that group and team decision making is more costly.

Group or team decisions may also represent undesirable compromises.[32] For example, hiring a compromise top manager may be a bad decision in the long run because he or she may not be able to respond adequately to various subunits in

Table 9.2

**Advantages and Disadvantages
of Group and Team Decision Making**
To increase the chances that a group or team decision will be successful, managers must learn how to manage the process of group and team decision making. Westinghouse, Federal Express, and IBM are increasingly using groups and teams in the decision-making process.

Advantages	Disadvantages
1. More information and knowledge are available.	1. The process takes longer than individual decision making, so it is costlier.
2. More alternatives are likely to be generated.	2. Compromise decisions resulting from indecisiveness may emerge.
3. More acceptance of the final decision is likely.	3. One person may dominate the group.
4. Enhanced communication of the decision may result.	4. Groupthink may occur.
5. Better decisions generally emerge.	

the organization or have everyone's complete support. Sometimes one individual dominates the group process to the point where others cannot make a full contribution. This dominance may stem from a desire for power or from a naturally dominant personality. The problem is that what appears to emerge as a group decision may actually be the decision of one person.

Finally, a group or team may succumb to a phenomenon known as groupthink. **Groupthink** occurs when the desire for consensus and cohesiveness overwhelms the goal of reaching the best possible decision.[33] Under the influence of groupthink, the group may arrive at decisions that are not in the best interest of either the group or the organization, but the members are more concerned about avoiding conflict among themselves. One of the clearest documented examples of groupthink involved the space shuttle *Challenger* disaster. As NASA was preparing to launch the shuttle, numerous problems and questions arose. At each step of the way, however, decision makers argued that there was no reason to delay and that everything would be fine. Shortly after the launch in January 1986, the shuttle exploded, killing all seven crew members.

groupthink A situation that occurs when a group or team's desire for consensus and cohesiveness overwhelms the goal of reaching the best possible decision

Managing Group and Team Decision-Making Processes

Managers can do several things to help promote the effectiveness of group and team decision making. One is simply being aware at the beginning of the pros and cons of having a group or team make a decision. Time and cost can be managed by setting a deadline by which the decision must be made final. Dominance can be at least partially avoided if a special group is formed just to make the decision. An astute manager, for example, should know who in the organization may try to dominate and can either avoid putting that person in the group or put several strong-willed people together.

To avoid groupthink, each member of the group or team should critically evaluate all alternatives. So that members present divergent viewpoints, the leader should not make his or her own position known too early. At least one member of the group or team might be assigned the role of devil's advocate. And, after reaching a preliminary decision, the group or team should hold a follow-up meeting wherein divergent viewpoints can be raised again if any group members wish to do so.[34] Gould Paper Company used these methods by assigning managers to two different teams. The teams then spent an entire day in a structured debate presenting the pros and cons of each side of an issue to ensure the best possible decision. Sun Microsystems makes most of its major decisions using this same approach.

MANAGEMENT IMPLICATIONS Managers usually have the option of having a decision made by an individual or by a group or team. They should therefore assess the relative advantages and disadvantages of each when deciding how to make a particular decision, as well as the different methods by which groups or teams can be used. If groups or teams are being used, the managers should also take appropriate steps to manage the decision-making process to enhance its effectiveness.

Summary of Key Points

Decisions are an integral part of all managerial activities, but they are perhaps most central to the planning process. Decision making is the act of choosing one alternative from among a set of alternatives. The decision-making process includes recognizing and defining the nature of a decision situation, identifying alternatives, choosing the best alternative, and putting it into practice. Two common types of decisions are programmed and nonprogrammed. Decisions may be made under states of certainty, risk, or uncertainty.

Rational perspectives on decision making rest on the classical model. This model assumes that managers have complete information and that they will behave rationally. The primary steps in rational decision making are (1) recognizing and defining the decision situation, (2) identifying alternatives, (3) evaluating alternatives, (4) selecting the best alternative, (5) implementing the chosen alternative, and (6) following up and evaluating the results of the alternative after it is implemented.

Behavioral aspects of decision making rely on the administrative model. This model recognizes that managers will have incomplete information and that they will not always behave rationally. The administrative model also recognizes the concepts of bounded rationality and satisficing. Political activities by coalitions, managerial intuition, and the tendency to become increasingly committed to a chosen course of action are all important. Risk propensity is another important behavioral perspective on decision making. Finally, ethics also affect how managers make decisions.

To help enhance decision-making effectiveness, managers often use interacting, Delphi, or nominal groups or teams. Group and team decision making in general has several advantages as well as disadvantages relative to individual decision making. Managers can adopt several strategies to help groups and teams make better decisions.

Discussion Questions

Questions for Review

1. Describe the nature of decision making.
2. What are the main features of the classical model of the decision-making process? What are the main features of the administrative model?
3. What are the steps in rational decision making? Which step do you think is the most difficult to carry out? Why?
4. Describe the behavioral nature of decision making. Be certain to provide some detail about political forces, risk propensity, ethics, and commitment in your description.

Questions for Analysis

5. Was your decision about what college or university to attend a rational decision? Did you go through each step in rational decision making? If not, why not?
6. Can any decision be purely rational, or are all decisions at least partially behavioral in nature? Defend your answer against alternatives.
7. Under what conditions would you expect group or team decision making to be preferable to individual decision making, and vice versa? Why?

Questions for Application

8. Interview a local business manager about a major decision that he or she made recently. Try to determine if the manager used each of the steps in rational decision making. If not, which were omitted? Why might the manager have omitted those steps?

9. Interview a local business manager about a major decision that he or she made re-

cently. Try to determine if aspects of the behavioral nature of decision making were involved. If so, which were involved? Why?

10. Interview a department head at your college or university to determine if group or team decision making is used at all. If it is, for what types of decisions is it used?

BUILDING EFFECTIVE *decision-making* AND *communication* SKILLS

Exercise Overview

Decision-making skills refer to the manager's ability to recognize and define problems and opportunities correctly and then to select an appropriate course of action for solving problems and capitalizing on opportunities. Communication skills refer to the manager's abilities both to convey ideas and information to others effectively and to receive ideas and information effectively from others. Not surprisingly, these skills can be highly interrelated. This exercise will give you insights into some of those interrelations.

Exercise Background

Identify a decision that you will need to make sometime in the near future. If you work in a managerial position, you might select a real problem or issue to address. For example, you might use the selection or termination of an employee, the allocation of pay raises, or the selection of someone for a promotion.

If you do not work in a managerial position, you might instead select an upcoming decision related to your academic work. Example decisions might include: what major to select, whether to attend summer school or to work, which job to select, whether to live on or off campus next year, etc. Be sure to select a decision that has not yet been made.

Exercise Task

Using the decision situation you have identified, do each of the following:

1. On a sheet of paper, list the kinds of information that you will most likely use in making your decision. Beside each one, make notes about where you can obtain the information, what form the information will be presented in, the reliability of the information, and other characteristics of the information that you deem to be relevant.

2. Next, assume that you have used the information obtained above and have now made the decision. (It might be helpful at this point to select a hypothetical decision or choice to frame your answers.) On the other side of the paper, list the various communication consequences that come with your decision. For example, if your choice involves an academic major, you may need to inform your advisor and your family. List as many of these communication consequences as you can. Beside each one, make notes about how you would communicate with each party, the timeliness of your communication, and whatever factors that seem to be relevant.

3. What behavioral forces might play a role in your decision?

BUILDING EFFECTIVE *interpersonal* SKILLS

Exercise Overview

Interpersonal skills refer to the manager's ability to understand and motivate individuals and groups. This exercise will allow you to practice your interpersonal skills in a role-playing exercise.

Exercise Background

You supervise a group of six employees who work in an indoor facility in a relatively isolated location. The company you work for has recently adopted an ambiguous policy regarding smoking. Essentially, the policy states that all company work sites are to be smoke free unless the employees at a specific site choose differently and at the discretion of the site supervisor.

Four members of the work group you supervise are smokers. They have come to you with the argument that since they constitute the majority, they should be allowed to smoke at work. The other two members of the group, both nonsmokers, have also discussed the situation with you. They argue that the health-related consequences of secondary smoke should outweigh the preferences of the majority.

To compound the problem, your boss wrote the new policy and is quite defensive about it—numerous individuals have already criticized the policy. You know that your boss will get very angry with you if you also raise concerns about the policy. Finally, you are personally indifferent toward the issue. You do not smoke yourself, but your spouse does smoke. Secondary smoke does not bother you, and you do not have strong opinions about it. Still, you have to make a decision about what to do. You see that your choices are to (1) mandate a smoke-free environment, (2) allow smoking in the facility, or (3) ask your boss to clarify the policy.

Exercise Task

Based on this background information, place yourself in the supervisor's role and do the following:

1. Assume that you have chose option 1. Write down an outline that you will use to announce your decision to the four smokers.
2. Assume that you have chosen option 2. Write down an outline that you will use to announce your decision to the two non-smokers.
3. Assume that you have chosen option 3. Write down an outline that you will use when you meet with your boss.
4. Are there other alternatives?
5. What would you do if you were actually the group supervisor?

BUILDING EFFECTIVE *technical* SKILLS

Exercise Overview

Technical skills are the skills necessary to accomplish or understand the specific kind of work being done in an organization. This exercise will enable you to practice technical skills using the Internet to obtain information for making a decision.

Exercise Background

Assume that you are a business owner seeking a location for a new factory. Your company makes products that are relatively "clean"—that is, they do not pollute the environment, nor will your factory produce any dangerous waste products. Thus, most communities would welcome your plant.

You are seeking a place that has a stable and well-educated workforce, a good quality of life, good health care, and a good educational system. You have narrowed your choice to the towns listed below:

1. Columbia, Missouri
2. Madison, Wisconsin
3. Manhattan, Kansas
4. College Station, Texas
5. Baton Rouge, Louisiana
6. Athens, Georgia

Exercise Task

With this background information as context, do the following:

1. Use the Internet and research each of these cities.
2. Rank-order each city on the basis of the criteria noted.
3. Select the best city for your new factory.

CHAPTER CLOSING CASE

FIRST AID FOR AETNA

Aetna had been offering life insurance and property insurance for more than 140 years when Richard Huber became vice chairman and set in motion major decisions that took the company into an entirely new business. In 1996, Huber foresaw a rosy and profitable future for managed health care, in contrast to the increased competition and interest-rate pressures ahead for Aetna's financial services offerings. So he sold the company's U.S. property and life operations and plunked down $8 billion to buy U.S. Healthcare plus $2 billion to buy Prudential Health. With these purchases, Huber was able to say that Aetna insured one in every ten Americans who have insurance.

In retrospect, however, the price tag for entering the health-care insurance field seems high. Aetna paid the equivalent of $2,800 per member for U.S. Healthcare, compared with a typical price of $600 per managed-care member just four years after Aetna's purchase. The downward direction of these per-member prices reflects the downward direction of profits in the managed health-care business during the late 1990s.

Once Aetna entered the ever-changing world of managed health care, it was subjected to risks and decisions it never faced in the insurance industry. First, it was difficult to project the size of the medical bills Aetna's health-care units might have to pay on behalf of sick or injured members. Second, the units might be sued if they didn't pay for some medical treatments. Third, half of Aetna's health-care members were in managed-care plans. Such plans generally attract older and less healthy members, so costs were on the rise—but by how much was impossible to predict. As a result, Aetna's profit margins became narrower and narrower. According to one analyst, the company's managed-care profit margin was about 7.5 percent when it entered the business but had fallen to just 3.3 percent within four years.

In 1999, Aetna's stock price was battered by two pieces of bad news. The company disclosed that its Prudential health-care unit was losing more money than analysts expected. Only days later, lawyers announced their intention to file charges against Aetna and other managed-care companies over the issue of whether doctors were being forced to restrict member care. Still, Aetna had some strengths that Huber, now CEO, wanted to build on. But as Aetna's share price dropped to its lowest point in more than seven years, Huber submitted his resignation and Bill Donaldson was brought in as CEO.

As one of the founders of investment bank Donaldson, Lufkin and Jenrette, Donaldson was a knowledgeable deal maker. He decided to sell off Aetna's insurance and financial units so the company could concentrate on turning around its health-care operations, which now formed the core of the corporation. After several months of negotiation, Donaldson arranged for Internationale Nederlanden Groep, a Dutch banking and insurance company, to buy the insurance and financial units for $5 billion. Although this relieved some of the pressure, Donaldson was still looking for someone to take the top slot at the company's health-care business because that CEO had retired several months earlier. More tough decisions were ahead for Donaldson and Aetna.

Case Questions

1. How would you describe Richard Huber's risk propensity?

2. Under what conditions did Donaldson make the decision to sell off Aetna's insurance and financial units? Did Huber confront the same conditions when he decided to buy into the health-care business?

3. Before deciding to sell the financial and insurance units, what other options do you think Donaldson considered? How would you evaluate those other options?

Case References

Bill Rigby, "Aetna's Donaldson Does Easy Part, Now Faces Tougher Task," *Reuters*, July 20, 2000, http://www.hoovers.com (July 27, 2000); John Graham, "Train Wreck in Hartford," *Forbes*, March 6, 2000, pp. 70–71.

CHAPTER NOTES

1. "Now, Starbucks Uses Its Bean," *Business Week*, February 14, 2000, pp. 92–93 (quote on p. 92); Vijay Vishwanath and David Harding, "The Starbucks Effect," *Harvard Business Review*, March–April 2000, pp. 17–18; "Smell the Beans," *Forbes*, September 4, 2000, p. 56.

2. Richard Priem, "Executive Judgment, Organizational Congruence, and Firm Performance," *Organization Science*, August 1994, pp. 421–432.

3. "Ford Grabs Big Prize as Steep Losses Force BMW to Sell Rover," *Wall Street Journal*, March 17, 2000, pp. A1, A8.

4. Paul Nutt, "The Formulation Processes and Tactics Used in Organizational Decision Making," *Organization Science*, May 1993, pp. 226–240.

5. For a recent review of decision making, see E. Frank Harrison, *The Managerial Decision Making Process*, 5th Edition (Boston: Houghton Mifflin, 1999).

6. "Kodak Moment Came Early for CEO Fisher, Who Takes a Stumble," *Wall Street Journal*, July 25, 1997, pp. A1, A6.

7. George P. Huber, *Managerial Decision Making* (Glenview, Ill.: Scott, Foresman, 1980).

8. See Paul D. Collins, Lori V. Ryan, and Sharon F. Matusik, "Programmable Automation and the Locus of Decision-Making Power," *Journal of Management*, Vol. 25, 1999, pp. 29–53, for an example.

9. Huber, *Managerial Decision Making*. See also David W. Miller and Martin K. Starr, *The Structure of Human Decisions* (Englewood Cliffs, N.J.: Prentice-Hall, 1976); and Alvar Elbing, *Behavioral Decisions in Organizations*, 2nd Edition (Glenview, Ill.: Scott, Foresman, 1978).

10. "Taking the Angst Out of Taking a Gamble," *Business Week*, July 14, 1997, pp. 52–53.

11. Gerard P. Hodgkinson, Nicola J. Bown, A. John Maule, Keith W. Glaister, and Alan D. Pearman, "Breaking the Frame: An Analysis of Strategic Cognition and Decision Making Under Uncertainty," *Strategic Management Journal*, Vol. 20, 1999, pp. 977–985.

12. "Tension Between Ford and Firestone Mounts Amid Recall Efforts," *Wall Street Journal*, August 28, 2000, pp. A1, A8; "Bridgestone Boss Has Toughness, But Is That What Crisis Demands?" *Wall Street Journal*, September 12, 2000, pp. A1, A18.

13. Glen Whyte, "Decision Failures: Why They Occur and How to Prevent Them," *The Academy of Management Executive*, August 1991, pp. 23–31.

14. Jerry Useem, "Boeing vs. Boeing," *Fortune*, October 2, 2000, pp. 148–160; "Airbus Prepares to 'Bet the Company' as It Builds a Huge New Jet," *Wall Street Journal*, November 3, 1999, pp. A1, A10.

15. Kenneth Labich, "Coups and Catastrophes," *Fortune*, December 23, 1985, p. 125.

16. "The Wisdom of Solomon," *Newsweek*, August 17, 1987, pp. 62–63.

17. "Making Decisions in Real Time," *Fortune*, June 26, 2000, pp. 332–334.

18. Herbert A. Simon, *Administrative Behavior* (New York: Free Press, 1945). Simon's ideas have been refined and updated in Herbert A. Simon, *Administrative Behavior*, 3rd Edition (New York: Free Press, 1976); and Herbert A. Simon, "Making Management Decisions: The Role of Intuition and Emotion," *The Academy of Management Executive*, February 1987, pp. 57–63.

19. Patricia Corner, Angelo Kinicki, and Barbara Keats, "Integrating Organizational and Individual Information Processing Perspectives on Choice," *Organization Science*, August 1994, pp. 294–302.

20. Kimberly D. Elsbach and Greg Elofson, "How the Packaging of Decision Explanations Affects Perceptions of Trustworthi-

ness," *Academy of Management Journal*, Vol. 43, 2000, pp. 80–89.

21. Charles P. Wallace, "Adidas—Back in the Game," *Fortune*, August 18, 1997, pp. 176–182.

22. Barry M. Staw and Jerry Ross, "Good Money After Bad," *Psychology Today*, February 1988, pp. 30–33; and D. Ramona Bobocel and John Meyer, "Escalating Commitment to a Failing Course of Action: Separating the Roles of Choice and Justification," *Journal of Applied Psychology*, Vol. 79, 1994, pp. 360–363.

23. Mark Keil and Ramiro Montealegre, "Cutting Your Losses: Extricating Your Organization When a Big Project Goes Awry," *Sloan Management Review*, Spring 2000, pp. 55–64.

24. Gerry McNamara and Philip Bromiley, "Risk and Return in Organizational Decision Making," *Academy of Management Journal*, Vol. 42, 1999, pp. 330–339.

25. See Brian O'Reilly, "What It Takes to Start a Startup," *Fortune*, June 7, 1999, pp. 135–140, for an example.

26. Martha I. Finney, "The Catbert Dilemma—The Human Side of Tough Decisions," *HRMagazine*, February 1997, pp. 70–78.

27. Edwin A. Locke, David M. Schweiger, and Gary P. Latham, "Participation in Decision Making: When Should It Be Used?" *Organizational Dynamics*, Winter 1986, pp. 65–79; and Nicholas Baloff and Elizabeth M. Doherty, "Potential Pitfalls in Employee Participation," *Organizational Dynamics*, Winter 1989, pp. 51–62.

28. Andre L. Delbecq, Andrew H. Van de Ven, and David H. Gustafson, *Group Techniques for Program Planning* (Glenview, Ill.: Scott, Foresman, 1975); Michael J. Prietula and Herbert A. Simon, "The Experts in Your Midst," *Harvard Business Review*, January–February 1989, pp. 120–124.

29. Norman P. R. Maier, "Assets and Liabilities in Group Problem Solving: The Need for an Integrative Function," in J. Richard Hackman, Edward E. Lawler III, and Lyman W. Porter, eds., *Perspectives on Business in Organizations*, 2nd Edition (New York: McGraw-Hill, 1983), pp. 385–392.

30. Anthony L. Iaquinto and James W. Fredrickson, "Top Management Team Agreement About the Strategic Decision Process: A Test of Some of Its Determinants and Consequences," *Strategic Management Journal*, Vol. 18, 1997, pp. 63–75.

31. Tony Simons, Lisa Hope Pelled, and Ken A. Smith, "Making Use of Difference: Diversity, Debate, and Decision Comprehensiveness in Top Management Teams," *Academy of Management Journal*, Vol. 42, 1999, pp. 662–673.

32. Richard A. Cosier and Charles R. Schwenk, "Agreement and Thinking Alike: Ingredients for Poor Decisions," *The Academy of Management Executive*, February 1990, pp. 69–78.

33. Irving L. Janis, *Groupthink*, 2nd Edition (Boston: Houghton Mifflin, 1982).

34. Janis, *Groupthink*.

Managing New Venture Formation and Entrepreneurship

Just a few years ago James Koch was a high-flying management consultant pulling in over $250,000 a year. To the surprise of his family and friends, however, he quit this job and invested his life's savings in starting a new business from scratch and going head to head with international competitors in a market that had not had a truly successful specialty product in decades. And to their bigger surprise, he succeeded!

The company Koch founded is Boston Beer Co., and its flagship product is a premium beer called Samuel Adams. Koch's family had actually been brewing beer for generations, and he started with a recipe developed by his great-great-grandfather, who had sold the beer in St. Louis in the 1870s under the name Louis Koch Lager. To fund his operation, he used $100,000 in personal savings and another $300,000 invested by his friends.

He set up shop in an old warehouse in Boston, bought some surplus brewing equipment from a large brewery, and started operations. Because his beer used only the highest quality ingredients, he needed to price it at about $1 more per case than such premium imports as Heineken. Boston-area distributors, meanwhile, doubted that consumers would pay $6 per six-pack for an American beer, and most refused to carry it. Thus, Koch himself began selling the beer directly to retailers and bars himself.

But his big break came when he entered Samuel Adams Lager in the Great American Beer Festival, where it won the consumer preference poll—the industry's equivalent of the Oscar. Koch then used this victory as his advertising mantra, proclaiming Samuel Adams as "The Best Beer in America." Sales began to take off, and national distribu-

tors began calling for the beer. To meet surging demand, Koch contracted part of the brewing to a near-deserted Stroh's brewery in Pittsburgh.

During the early 1990s sales of Samuel Adams products grew at an annual rate of over 57 percent and today exceed $250 million per year. Boston Beer also exports Samuel Adams to Germany, where the beer has also become quite popular. Koch, meanwhile, has retained controlling interests in the business and still oversees the day-to-day brewing operations. Indeed, he claims that he has sampled at least one of the firm's products every day since the business started, primarily as a way of monitoring quality.

But Koch's success has not gone unnoticed, especially by industry

> "You don't create a whole new national market in the beer business by being frightened."
>
> —James Koch, founder and owner, Boston Beer Co.

After studying this chapter, you should be able to:

- Discuss the nature of entrepreneurship.

- Describe the roles of entrepreneurs in society.

- Understand the major issues involved in choosing strategies for small firms and the role of international management in entrepreneurship.

- Discuss the structural challenges unique to entrepreneurial firms.

- Understand the determinants of the performance of small firms.

giant Anheuser Busch. Anheuser and other national brewers have recently seen their sales take a hit from so-called microbreweries, small regional or local companies that sell esoteric brews made in small quantities and deriving cachet from their very scarcity. The Boston Beer Co. was the first of these to make it big, and most others are trying to follow in its footsteps. Obviously, therefore, Anheuser Busch has a vested interest in not letting these smaller start-ups gain too much market share, most of which would come at its own expense.

Recently, for example, Koch learned that Anheuser had made inquiries about buying the entire crop from a German hops farmer who has an exclusive arrangement with Boston Beer. Had Anheuser succeeded, Koch says, he would have been put out of business. Anheuser has also complained that the labeling on Samuel Adams is misleading, hiding the fact

that the beer made in Pittsburgh is actually being brewed under contract by Stroh's, not Boston Beer. And the industry giant has even tried to convince wholesalers, who are highly dependent on Anheuser products like Budweiser, to stop selling specialty beers like Samuel Adams. Koch, meanwhile, simply sees all this attention as a clear sign that he has made it.[1]

Just like James Koch, thousands of people all over the world start new businesses each year. And like the Boston Beer Co., some of these businesses succeed while, unfortunately, many others fail. Some of the people who fail in a new business try again, and sometimes it takes two or more failures before a successful business gets under way. Henry Ford, for example, went bankrupt twice before succeeding with the Ford Motor Co.

This process of starting a new business, sometimes failing and sometimes succeeding, is part of what is called entrepreneurship, the subject of this chapter. We begin by exploring the nature of entrepreneurship. We then examine the role of entrepreneurship in the business world and discuss strategies for entrepreneurial organizations. We then describe the structure and performance of entrepreneurial organizations.

The Nature of Entrepreneurship

entrepreneurship The process of planning, organizing, operating, and assuming the risk of a business venture

entrepreneur Someone who engages in entrepreneurship

Entrepreneurship is the process of planning, organizing, operating, and assuming the risk of a business venture. An **entrepreneur**, in turn, is someone who engages in entrepreneurship. James Koch, as highlighted in the chapter opening incident, fits this description. He put his own resources on the line and took a personal stake in the success or failure of his budding enterprise. Business owners who hire professional managers to run their businesses and then turn their attention to other interests are not entrepreneurs. Although they are assuming the risk of the venture, they are not actively involved in organizing or operating it. Likewise, professional managers whose job is running someone else's business are not entrepreneurs because they assume less-than-total personal risk for the success or failure of the business.

Entrepreneurs find new business through many different approaches. For example, take Dineh Mohajer. A few years ago, when she was studying pre-med at USC, she wanted some blue nail polish to wear to a party but couldn't find just the right shade, so she made it herself. She subsequently decided there is a market among Generation X-ers like herself for new approaches to cosmetics and toiletries. So, she dropped out of school and founded Hard Candy and started marketing nail polish with names like Pimp and Porno. Mohajer's firm now has 25 employees and sales of over $10 million a year.

Entrepreneurs start new businesses. We define a **small business** as one that is privately owned by one individual or a small group of individuals and has sales and assets that are not large enough to influence its environment. A small two-person software development company with annual sales of $100,000 would clearly be a small business, whereas Microsoft Corporation is just as clearly a large business. But the boundaries are not always this clear-cut. For example, a regional retailing chain with twenty stores and annual revenues of $30 million may sound large, but it is really very small when compared to such giants as Wal-Mart and Sears.

small business A business that is privately owned by one individual or a small group of individuals; it has sales and assets that are not large enough to influence its environment

MANAGEMENT IMPLICATIONS Managers should understand the nature and meaning of entrepreneurship and the differentiating factors between it and management.

The Role of Entrepreneurship in Society

The history of entrepreneurship and of the development of new businesses is in many ways the history of great wealth and of great failure. Some entrepreneurs have been very successful and have accumulated vast fortunes from their entrepreneurial efforts. For example, when Microsoft Corp. sold its stock to the public in 1986, Bill Gates, then just thirty years old, received $350 million for his share of Microsoft.[2] Today, his holdings—valued at $63 billion—make him the richest person in the United States and one of the richest in the world.[3] Many more entrepreneurs, however, have lost a great deal of money. Research suggests that the majority of new businesses fail within the first few years of founding.[4] Many that last longer do so only because the entrepreneurs themselves work long hours for very little income.

As Figure 10.1 shows, most U.S. businesses employ fewer than one hundred people, and most U.S. workers are employed by small firms. For example, Figure 10.1(a) shows that 86.70 percent of all U.S. businesses employ twenty or fewer people; another 11 percent employ between twenty and ninety-nine people. In contrast, only about one-tenth of 1 percent employ one thousand or more workers. Figure 10.1(b) shows that 25.60 percent of all U.S. workers are employed by firms with fewer than twenty people; another 29.10 percent work in firms that employ between twenty and ninety-nine people. The vast majority of these companies are owner operated.[5] Figure 10.1(b) also shows that 12.70 percent of U.S. workers are employed by firms with one thousand or more total employees.

On the basis of numbers alone, then, small business is a strong presence in the economy, which is true in virtually all the world's mature economies. In Germany, for example, companies with fewer than five hundred employees produce two-thirds of the nation's gross national product, train nine of ten apprentices, and employ four of every five workers. Small businesses also play major roles in the economies of Italy, France, and Brazil. In addition, experts agree that small businesses will be quite important in the emerging economies of countries such as Russia and Vietnam. The contribution of small businesses can be measured in

Figure 10.1

The Importance of Small Business in the United States

Over 86 percent of all U.S. businesses have no more than twenty employees. The total number of people employed by these small businesses is approximately one-fourth of the entire U.S. workforce. Another 29 percent work for companies with fewer than one hundred employees.

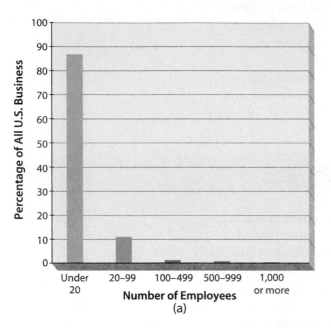 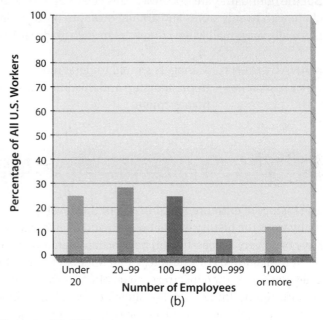

Source: U.S. Census Bureau, *Statistical Abstract of the United States: 1999* (119th Edition), Washington, D.C., 1999.

terms of their effects on key aspects of an economic system. In the United States, these aspects include job creation, innovation, and importance to big business.

Job Creation

In the early 1980s, a widely cited study proposed that small businesses create eight of every ten new jobs in the United States. This contention touched off considerable interest in the fostering of small business as a matter of public policy. As we will see, relative job growth among businesses of different sizes is not easy to determine. It is clear, however, that small businesses—especially in certain industries—are an important source of new (and often well-paid) jobs in this country. According to the Small Business Administration, for example, seven of the ten industries that added the most new jobs in 1998 were in sectors dominated by small businesses. Moreover, small businesses currently account for 38 percent of all jobs in high-technology sectors of the economy.[6]

Note that new jobs are also being created by small firms specializing in international business. For example, Bob Knosp operates a small business in Bellevue, Washington, that makes computerized sign-making systems. Knosp gets over half his sales from abroad and has dedicated almost 75 percent of his workforce to handling international sales. Indeed, according to the SBA, small businesses account for 96 percent of all U.S. exporters.[7]

Although small businesses certainly create many new jobs each year, the importance of entrepreneurial big businesses in job creation should also not be overlooked. While big businesses cut thousands of jobs in the late 1980s and early 1990s, the booming U.S. economy resulted in large-scale job creation in many larger businesses beginning in the mid-1990s. Figure 10.2 details the changes in the number of jobs at sixteen large U.S. companies during the ten-year period between 1990 and 1999. As you can see, General Motors eliminated 181,100 jobs and General Mills and Kmart eliminated over 86,000 jobs each. Wal-Mart alone, however, created 639,000 new jobs during the same period and Dayton Hudson, an additional 100,000.

But even these data have to be interpreted with care. PepsiCo, for example, "officially" eliminated 116,000 jobs. But most of those losses came in 1997, when the firm sold its restaurant chains (KFC, Pizza Hut, and Taco Bell) to Tricon. In reality, therefore, many of the jobs weren't actually eliminated but simply transferred to another employer. Likewise, while most of Wal-Mart's 639,000 new jobs are indeed "new," some came when the company acquired other businesses and thus were not net new jobs.

Figure 10.2

Representative Jobs Created and Lost by Big Business, 1990–1999

All businesses create and eliminate jobs. Because of their size, the magnitude of job creation and elimination is especially pronounced in bigger businesses. This figure provides several representative examples of job creation and elimination at many big U.S. businesses during the 1990s. For example, while General Motors cut 181,100 jobs, Wal-Mart created 639,000 during this decade.

JOB LOSSES

Toys "Я" Us	−3,400
Quaker Oats	−16,340
National Semi-Conductor	−21,100
Kmart	−86,475
General Mills	−86,578
IBM	−92,153
PepsiCo	−116,000
General Motors	−181,100

JOB GAINS

Wal-Mart	+ 639,000
Dayton Hudson	+100,000
Albertson's	+45,000
Circuit City	+36,270
Barnes and Noble	+29,000
Dell Corporation	+22,900
Conagra	+21,631
America Online	+12,100

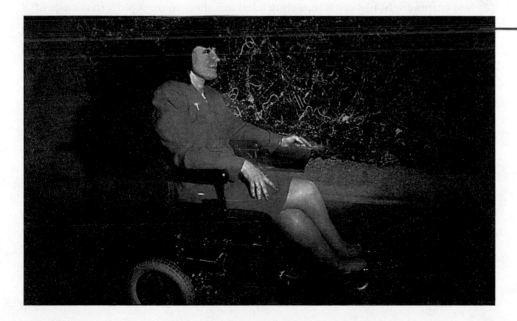

One important economic role played by small business start-ups is the creation of new jobs. For example, Susan Webb owns and manages Webb Transitions, a private employment agency that contracts with public agencies and private companies to help disabled employees return to work. Webb Transitions employs six people, and Ms. Webb forecasts a 10 percent annual revenue growth rate for each of the next several years. And as her business grows, she will continue to add new jobs as well.

At least one message is clear: entrepreneurial business success, more than business size, accounts for most new job creation. Whereas successful retailers such as Wal-Mart and Dayton Hudson have been growing and adding thousands of new jobs, struggling chains such as Kmart have been eliminating thousands. At the same time, flourishing high-tech giants such as Dell, Intel, and Microsoft continue to add jobs at a constant pace. It is also essential to take a long-term view when analyzing job growth. Figure 10.2, for example, shows that IBM has eliminated 92,153 jobs. But the firm actually cut a total of 163,381 jobs between 1990 and 1994. Since 1995, it has created 71,228 new jobs while the company has recovered from an economic slump that caused the original job cuts to be so severe.

The reality, then, is that jobs are created by entrepreneurial companies of all sizes, all of which hire workers and all of which lay them off. Although small firms often hire at a faster rate than large ones, they are also likely to eliminate jobs at a far higher rate. Small firms are also the first to hire in times of economic recovery, large firms the last. Conversely, however, big companies are also the last to lay off workers during economic downswings. In 1999, almost 35 percent of all small businesses had job openings, and almost 20 percent were planning to hire new employees.

Innovation

History has shown that major innovations are as likely to come from small businesses (or individuals) as from big businesses. For example, small firms and individuals invented the personal computer and the stainless-steel razor blade, the transistor radio and the photocopying machine, the jet engine and the self-developing photograph. They also gave us the helicopter and power steering, automatic transmissions and air conditioning, cellophane, and the nineteen-cent ballpoint pen. Today, says the SBA, small businesses supply 55 percent of all "innovations" introduced into the American marketplace.[8]

Not surprisingly, history is repeating itself infinitely more rapidly in the age of computers and high-tech communication. For example, much of today's most innovative software is being written at new start-up companies such as Trilogy Software Inc., an Austin-based company started by Stanford dropout Joe Liemandt. Trilogy's products help optimize and streamline complicated sales and marketing processes for big-business customers such as IBM and Whirlpool.[9] Yahoo! and Netscape brought the Internet into the average American living room, and on-line companies such as Amazon.com are using it to redefine our shopping habits. Each of these firms started out as a small business. So did Alain Rossmann's Phone.com, a new but growing enterprise that helps big companies provide wireless access to the Internet. Similarly, eToys, Inc., another dot.com start-up, is making major inroads in the toy-retailing business.

Of course, not all successful new start-ups are leading-edge dot.com enterprises. Drywall installer Jerry Free, for example, was frustrated by conventional methods of joining angled wallboards. In his spare time, he developed a simple, handheld device that makes it easier and faster to perform this common task. He eventually licensed his invention to United States Gypsum, and it is now widely used throughout the construction industry. As for Free, the experience convinced him that "the cliché about invention being 1 percent inspiration and 99 percent perspiration is true."[10] Popular fashion designer Kate Spade has made it big by introducing a line of stylish purses and handbags sold through such exclusive retailers as Neiman Marcus. Rory Stear and Christopher Staines have succeeded with Freeplay Energy Group, a firm making environmentally friendly wind-up radios that don't need batteries or electricity.[11] Eric Ludewig presides over fast-growing East of Chicago Pizza, a chain he founded when he was twenty-two years old and just out of college.[12]

Importance to Large Businesses

Most of the products made by large manufacturers are sold to consumers by small businesses. For example, the majority of dealerships selling Fords, Chevrolets, Toyotas, and Volvos are independently owned and operated. Moreover, small businesses provide large businesses with many of the services, supplies, and raw materials they need. As we noted, for example, Trilogy Software has become an important supplier to large businesses. Likewise, Microsoft relies heavily on small businesses in the course of its routine business operations. For example, the software giant outsources much of its routine code-writing functions to hundreds of sole proprietorships and other small firms. It also outsources much of its packaging, delivery, and distribution to smaller companies. Dell Computer (www.dell.com) uses this same strategy, buying most of the parts and components used in its computers from small suppliers around the world.

MANAGEMENT IMPLICATIONS All managers, regardless of the size of their organizations, should recognize the important roles played by entrepreneurs in the areas of job creation, innovation, and supporting large businesses.

Strategy for Entrepreneurial Organizations

One of the most basic challenges facing an entrepreneurial organization is choosing a strategy. The three strategic challenges facing small firms, in turn, are choosing an industry in which to compete, emphasizing distinctive competencies, and writing a business plan.[13]

Choosing an Industry

Not surprisingly, small businesses are more common in some industries than in others. The major industry groups that include successful new ventures and small businesses are services, retailing, construction, financial and insurance, wholesaling, transportation, and manufacturing. Obviously, each group differs in its requirements for employees, money, materials, and machines. In general, the more resources an industry requires, the harder it is to start a business and the less likely

Figure 10.3

Small Businesses (Businesses with Less Than Twenty Employees) by Industry

Small businesses are especially strong in certain industries such as retailing and services. On the other hand, there are relatively fewer small businesses in industries such as transportation and manufacturing. The differences are affected primarily by factors such as the investment costs necessary to enter markets in these industries. For example, starting a new airline would require the purchase of large passenger aircraft and airport gates and hiring an expensive set of employees.

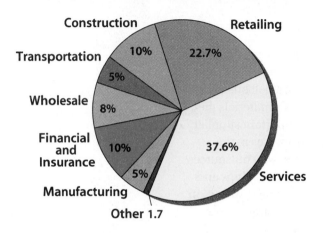

Source: U.S. Census Bureau, *Statistical Abstract of the United States: 1999* (119th Edition), Washington, D.C., 1999.

that the industry is dominated by small firms. Remember, too, that *small* is a relative term: the criteria (number of employees and total annual sales) differ from industry to industry and are often meaningful only when compared with businesses that are truly large. Figure 10.3 shows the distribution of all U.S. businesses employing fewer than twenty people across industry groups.

Services Primarily because they require few resources, service businesses are the fastest growing segment of small-business enterprise. In addition, no other industry group offers a higher return on time invested. Finally, services appeal to the talent for innovation typified by many small enterprises. As Figure 10.3 shows, 37.6 percent of all businesses with fewer than twenty employees are services businesses.

Small-business services range from shoeshine parlors to car rental agencies, from marriage counseling to computer software, from accounting and management consulting to professional dog walking. In Dallas, for example, Jani-King has prospered by selling commercial cleaning services to local companies. In Virginia Beach, Virginia, Jackson Hewitt Tax

Would-be entrepreneurs can increase their chances for success by identifying a niche or potential market that no other business is serving. Consider, for instance, the success enjoyed by Boston entrepreneur Chris Murphy. He knew that some dog owners felt that they faced the same day-care problems experienced by parents of small children. In response, he started The Common Dog, a service that picks dogs up on a school bus, takes them to a day-kennel while their owners work, and drops them off at the end of the day. The service costs the dog owners $325 a month. At the kennel, the dogs enjoy their own small swimming pool, several lounging couches, and frequent walks. They do, however, have to bring their own lunches!

Service has found a profitable niche in providing computerized tax preparation and electronic tax-filing services. Great Clips Inc. is a fast growing, family-run chain of hair salons headquartered in Minneapolis.

David Flanary, Richard Sorenson, and Michael Holloway recently established an Internet-based long-distance telephone service in Austin, Texas, called PointOne Telecommunications. The basic idea was hatched during a tennis match. Recalls Sorenson: "We started getting excited, volleying at the net, and then finally we put the rackets down and went to the side to talk." The firm is off to a great start. Currently, it acts as a wholesale voice carrier, but as soon as its network is completed, PointOne will start signing up its own commercial customers. Investors agree that the company will soon be a major force in telecommunications.[14]

Retailing A retail business sells products manufactured by other firms directly to consumers. There are hundreds of different kinds of retailers, ranging from wig shops and frozen yogurt stands to automobile dealerships and department stores. Usually, however, people who start small businesses favor specialty shops—for example, big men's clothing or gourmet coffees—that let them focus limited resources on narrow market segments. Retailing accounts for 22.7 percent of all businesses with fewer than twenty employees.

John Mackey, for example, launched Whole Foods out of his own frustration at being unable to find a full range of natural foods at other stores. He soon found, however, that he had tapped a lucrative market and started an ambitious expansion program. Today, with ninety outlets in twenty states and Washington, D.C., Whole Foods is the largest natural-foods retailer in the United States, three times larger than its biggest competitor.[15] Likewise, when Olga Tereshko found it difficult to locate just the right cloth diapers and breast-feeding supplies for her newborn son, she decided to start selling them herself. Instead of taking the conventional retailing route, however, Tereshko set up shop on the Internet. Her business, called Little Koala, has continued to expand at a rate of about 10 percent a month, and she has established a customer base of eight thousand to nine thousand loyal customers.[16]

Construction About 10 percent of businesses with fewer than twenty employees are involved in construction. Because many construction jobs are relatively small local projects, local construction firms are often ideally suited as contractors. Many such firms are begun by skilled craftspeople who start by working for someone else and subsequently decide to work for themselves. Common examples of small construction firms include home builders; wood finishers; roofers; painters; and plumbing, electrical, and roofing contractors.

Early business failures

As noted in the text, successful entrepreneurs must choose an industry, emphasize their distinctive competencies, and develop an effective business plan. Unfortunately, entrepreneurs frequently misjudge or do not effectively implement one or more of these activities. As illustrated in this cartoon, for example, providing a product that people do not really want is almost certain to result in failure. Chocolate confections, sausages, and corn-on-the-cob are often popular treats served on sticks at athletic events, fairs, festivals, and carnivals—but cucumbers, peaches, and porcupines are not as well received!

For example, Marek Brothers Construction in College Station, Texas, was started by two brothers, Pat and Joe Marek. They originally worked for other contractors but started their own partnership in 1980. Their only employee is a receptionist. They manage various construction projects, including new-home construction and remodeling, subcontracting out the actual work to other businesses and/or individual craftspersons. Marek Brothers has an annual gross income of about $5 million.

Finance and Insurance   Financial and insurance businesses comprise about 10 percent of all firms with less than twenty employees. In most cases, these businesses either are affiliates of and/or sell products provided by larger national firms. Although the deregulation of the banking industry has reduced the number of small local banks, other businesses in this sector are still doing quite well.

Typically, for example, local State Farm Mutual offices are small businesses. State Farm itself is a major insurance company, but its local offices are run by 16,500 independent agents. In turn, agents hire their own staffs, run their own offices as independent businesses, and so forth. They sell various State Farm insurance products and earn commissions from the premiums paid by their clients. Some local savings and loan operations, mortgage companies, and pawn shops also fall into this category.

Wholesaling   Small-business owners often do very well in wholesaling, too; about 8 percent of businesses with fewer than twenty employees are wholesalers. A wholesale business buys products from manufacturers or other producers and then sells them to retailers. Wholesalers usually buy goods in bulk and store them in quantities at locations that are convenient for retailers. For a given volume of business, therefore, they need fewer employees than manufacturers, retailers, or service providers.

They also serve fewer customers—usually those who repeatedly order large volumes of goods—than other providers. Wholesalers in the grocery industry, for instance, buy packaged food in bulk from companies such as Del Monte and Campbell's and then sell it to both large grocery chains and smaller independent grocers. Luis Espinoza has found a promising niche for Inca Quality Foods, a midwestern wholesaler that imports and distributes Hispanic foods for consumers from Mexico, the Caribbean, and Central America. Partnered with the large grocery-store chain Kroger, Espinoza's firm continues to grow steadily.[17]

Transportation   Some small firms—about 5 percent of all companies with fewer than twenty employees—do well in transportation and transportation-related businesses. Such firms include local taxi and limousine companies, charter airplane services, and tour operators. In addition, in many smaller markets, bus companies and regional airlines subcontract local equipment maintenance to small businesses.

Consider, for example, some of the transportation-related small businesses at a ski resort like Steamboat Springs, Colorado. Most visitors fly to the town of Hayden, about fifteen miles from Steamboat. While some visitors rent vehicles, many others use the services of Alpine Taxi, a small local operation, to transport them to their destinations in Steamboat. While on vacation, they rely on the local bus service, which is subcontracted by the town to another small business, to get to and from the ski slopes each day. Other small businesses offer van tours of the region, hot-air balloon rides, and helicopter lifts to remote areas for extreme skiers. Still others provide maintenance support at Hayden for Continental, American, and United aircraft that serve the area during ski season.

Manufacturing More than any other industry, manufacturing lends itself to big business—and for good reason. Because of the investment normally required in equipment, energy, and raw materials, a good deal of money is usually needed to start a manufacturing business. Automobile manufacturing, for example, calls for billions of dollars of investment and thousands of workers before the first automobile rolls off the assembly line. Obviously, such requirements shut out most individuals. Although Henry Ford began with $28,000, it has been a long time since anyone started a new U.S. car company from scratch.

Research has shown that manufacturing costs often fall as the number of units produced by an organization increases. This relationship between cost and production is called an *economy of scale.*[18] Small organizations usually cannot compete effectively on the basis of economies of scale. As depicted in Figure 10.4(a), organizations with higher levels of production have a major cost advantage over those with lower levels of production. Given the cost positions of small and large firms when there are strong economies of scale in manufacturing, it is not surprising that small manufacturing organizations generally do not do as well as large ones.

Figure 10.4

Economies of Scale in Small Business Organizations
Small businesses sometimes find it difficult to compete in manufacturing-related industries because of the economies of scale associated with plant, equipment, and technology. As shown in (a), firms that produce a large number of units (that is, larger businesses) can do so at a lower per-unit cost. At the same time, however, new forms of technology occasionally cause the economies-of-scale curve to shift, as illustrated in (b). In this case, smaller firms may be able to compete more effectively with larger ones because of the drop in per-unit manufacturing cost.

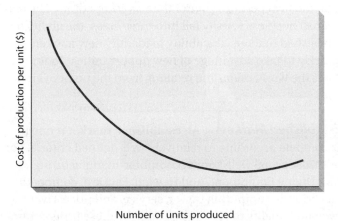

(a) Standard economies-of-scale curve

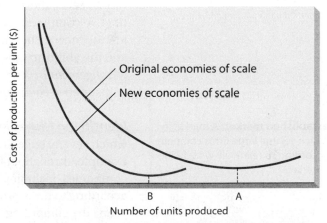

(b) Change in technology that shifts economies of scale and may make small business production possible

Interestingly, when technology in an industry changes, it often shifts the economies-of-scale curve, thereby creating opportunities for smaller organizations. For example, steel manufacturing was historically dominated by a few large companies that owned several huge facilities. With the development of mini-mill technology, however, extracting economies of scale at a much smaller level of production became possible. This type of shift is depicted in Figure 10.4(b). Point A in this figure is the low-cost point with the original economies of scale. Point B is the low-cost point with the economies of scale brought on by the new technology. Notice that the number of units needed for low cost is considerably lower for the new technology. This shift has allowed the entry of numerous smaller firms into the steel industry. Such entry would not have been possible with the older technology.

This example is not meant to suggest that there are no small-business owners who do well in manufacturing—about 5 percent of businesses with fewer than twenty employees are involved in some aspect of manufacturing. Indeed, it is not uncommon for small manufacturers to outperform large businesses in such innovation-driven industries as chemistry, electronics, toys, and computer software. Some small manufacturers prosper by locating profitable niches. For example, brothers Dave and Dan Hanlon and Dave's wife Jennie recently started a new motorcycle-manufacturing business called Excelsior-Henderson. (Excelsior and Henderson are actually names of classic motorcycles from the early years of the twentieth century; the Hanlons acquired the rights to these brand names because of the images they evoke among motorcycle enthusiasts.) The Hanlons started by building four thousand bikes in 1999 and expect to increase slowly to annual production of twenty thousand per year. So far, Excelsior-Henderson motorcycles have been well received (the top-end Excelsior-Henderson Super X sells for about $18,000), and many Harley-Davidson dealers have started to sell them as a means of diversifying their product lines.[19]

Emphasizing Distinctive Competencies

As we defined them in Chapter 8, an organization's distinctive competencies are the aspects of business that the firm performs better than its competitors. The distinctive competencies of small business usually fall into three areas: the ability to identify new niches in established markets, the ability to identify new markets, and the ability to move quickly to take advantage of new opportunities. *Today's Management Issues* explores the world of on-line retailing from the point of view of distinctive competencies.

established market A market in which several large firms compete according to relatively well-defined criteria

Identifying Niches in Established Markets An **established market** is one in which several large firms compete according to relatively well-defined criteria. For example, throughout the 1970s several well-known computer-manufacturing companies, including IBM, Digital Equipment, and Hewlett-Packard, competed according to three product criteria: computing power, service, and price. Over the years, the computing power and quality of service delivered by these firms continued to improve, while prices (especially relative to computing power) continued to drop.

On-Line Start-Ups Challenge Store Retailers

Ever since Jeff Bezos pioneered the idea of an on-line bookstore by launching Amazon.com, the Internet has become a hotbed of entrepreneurial activity as more people open web sites to challenge traditional store retailers. According to Shop.org, a trade association, more than thirty thousand web sites are devoted to on-line retailing. This number includes sites operated by traditional chains such as Wal-Mart as well as web-only giants such as Amazon. Still, the vast majority of on-line retailers sell less than $500,000 worth of merchandise in a year, so traditional retailing is far from dead. But can the on-line start-ups successfully challenge their store counterparts?

With Amazon.com (http://www.amazon.com), Bezos seized the first-mover advantage in books. By the time the Barnes and Noble retail chain recognized the danger and opened its web site (http://www.bn.com), Amazon's discount pricing and user-friendly features had created a loyal and lucrative customer following. Although Barnes and Noble's site now ranks among the Internet's most visited, Amazon attracts many more visitors and completes more sales. Barnes and Noble continues to expand its chain and increase store sales, even though Amazon is siphoning off some of its overall market share.

In toys, web-only eToys (http://www.etoys.com) sought first-mover advantage over its counterparts in store retailing. During its first year-end holiday selling season, eToys' electronic wish lists and other novel features drew widespread media at-tention and helped the company ring up $20 million in sales. By the time eToy's second Christmas rolled around, however, the Toys 'R' Us chain had become a "clicks and mortar" retailer by opening a flashy web site (http://www.toysrus.com) amid much fanfare. Then the Toys 'R' Us site had difficulty handling the onslaught of visitors and fulfilling orders as promised, while eToys' sales soared. But mounting expenses, continuing losses, and intense on-line competition have given eToys headaches of its own and pushed its stock price down.

Given the high cost of sustaining their first-mover advantage, most on-line retailers are struggling with profitability. Well-established on-line pioneers such as Amazon have the best chance of survival, but many smaller sites are headed for a shakeout as more entrepreneurs and more traditional retailers flock to the Internet.

> *It won't be about clicks versus mortar but coming up with a combination where a customer can do a transaction anytime, anywhere.*
>
> —*Elaine Rubin, chairperson of Shop.org**

References: Herb Greenberg, "Dead Mall Walking," *Fortune*, May 1, 2000, p. 304; William Bulkeley and Jim Carlton, "Reality Bites: E-Tail Gets Derailed: How Web Upstarts Misjudged the Game," *Wall Street Journal*, April 5, 2000, pp. A1, A6 (*quote on p. A6); Karl Taro Greenfeld, "Clicks and Bricks," *Time*, December 27, 1999, pp. 88 ff.

Enter Apple Computer and the personal computer. For Apple, user friendliness, not computing power, service, and price, was to be the basis of competition. Apple targeted every manager, every student, and every home as the owner of a personal computer. The major entrepreneurial act of Apple was not to invent a new technology (indeed, the first Apple computers used all standard parts taken from other computers) but to recognize a new kind of computer and a new way to compete in the computer industry.

Apple's approach to competition was to identify a new niche in an established market. A **niche** is simply a segment of a market that is not currently being exploited. In general, small entrepreneurial businesses are better at discovering these niches than are larger organizations. Large organizations usually have so

niche A segment of a market that is not currently being exploited

many resources committed to older, established business practices that they may be unaware of new opportunities. Entrepreneurs can see these opportunities and move quickly to take advantage of them.[20]

Identifying New Markets   Successful entrepreneurs also excel at discovering whole new markets. Discovery can happen in at least two ways. First, an entrepreneur can transfer a product or service that is well established in one geographic market to a second market. This is what Marcel Bich did with ballpoint pens, which occupied a well-established market in Europe before Bich introduced them to this country. Bich's company, Bic Corp., eventually came to dominate the U.S. market.

Second, entrepreneurs can sometimes create entire industries. Entrepreneurial inventions of the dry-paper copying process and the semiconductor have created vast new industries. Not only have the first companies in these markets (Xerox and National Semiconductor, respectively) been very successful, but their entrepreneurial activity has spawned the development of hundreds of thousands of other companies and hundreds of thousands of jobs. Again, because entrepreneurs are not encumbered with a history of doing business in a particular way, they are usually better at discovering new markets than are larger, more mature organizations.

first-mover advantage Any advantage that comes to a firm because it exploits an opportunity before any other firm does

First-Mover Advantages   A **first-mover advantage** is any advantage that comes to a firm because it exploits an opportunity before any other firm does. Sometimes large firms discover niches within existing markets or new markets at just about the same time as small entrepreneurial firms do but are not able to move as quickly as small companies to take advantage of these opportunities.

There are numerous reasons for this difference. For example, many large organizations make decisions slowly because each of their many layers of hierarchy has to approve an action before it can be implemented. Also, large organizations may sometimes put a great deal of their assets at risk when they take advantage of new opportunities. Every time Boeing decides to build a new model of a commercial jet, it is making a decision that could literally bankrupt the company if it does not turn out well. The size of the risk may make large organizations cautious. The dollar value of the assets at risk in a small organization, in contrast, is quite small. Managers may be willing to "bet the company" when the value of the company is only $100,000. They might be unwilling to "bet the company" when the value of the company is $1 billion.

Writing a Business Plan

business plan A document that summarizes the business strategy and how that strategy is to be implemented

Once an entrepreneur has chosen an industry to compete in and determined which distinctive competencies to emphasize, these choices are usually included in a document called a business plan. In a **business plan** the entrepreneur summarizes the business strategy and how that strategy is to be implemented. The very act of preparing a business plan forces prospective entrepreneurs to crystallize their thinking about what they must do to launch their business successfully and obliges them to develop their business on paper before investing time and money in it. The idea of a business plan is not new. What is new is the growing use of specialized business plans by entrepreneurs, mostly because creditors and investors demand them for use in deciding whether to help finance a small business.

The plan should describe the match between the entrepreneur's abilities and the requirements for producing and marketing a particular product or service. It should define strategies for production and marketing, legal aspects and organization, and accounting and finance. In particular, it should answer three questions: (1) What are the entrepreneur's goals and objectives? (2) What strategies will the entrepreneur use to obtain these goals and objectives? and (3) How will the entrepreneur implement these strategies?

Business plans should also account for the sequential nature of much strategic decision making in small businesses. For example, entrepreneurs cannot forecast sales revenues without first researching markets. The sales forecast itself is one of the most important elements in the business plan. Without such forecasts, it is all but impossible to estimate intelligently the size of a plant, store, or office or to determine how much inventory to carry or how many employees to hire.

Another important component of the overall business plan is financial planning, which translates all other activities into dollars. Generally, the financial plan is made up of a cash budget, an income statement, balance sheets, and a breakeven chart. The most important of these statements is the cash budget because it tells entrepreneurs how much money they need before they open for business and how much money they need to keep the business operating.

Entrepreneurship and International Management

Finally, while many people associate international management with large businesses, many smaller companies are also finding expansion and growth opportunities in foreign countries. For example, Fuci Metals, a small but growing enterprise, buys metal from remote locations in areas such as Siberia and Africa and then sells it to big auto makers like Ford and Toyota. Similarly, California-based Gold's Gym is expanding into foreign countries and has been especially successful in Russia.[21] While such ventures are accompanied by considerable risks, they also give entrepreneurs new opportunities and can be a real catalyst for success. The *World of Management* explores some related issues in entrepreneurship and international business.

MANAGEMENT IMPLICATIONS Entrepreneurs should exercise caution when selecting an industry, recognizing that some are easier and others more difficult for a small business. By emphasizing distinctive competencies and relying on a well-formulated business plan, they increase their chances for success. International opportunities should also be given full consideration by small businesses.

WORLD OF MANAGEMENT

EUROPE'S IMMIGRANT ENTREPRENEURS

Even as European Union nations look for ways to limit immigration, the newcomers are bringing drive and innovation to their adopted countries. Many Europeans are concerned about legal and illegal immigrants taking jobs away from local workers and swelling welfare rolls. Despite these concerns, one U.N. study indicates that the region's workforce will dwindle unless the countries admit forty million immigrants by 2025. Clearly, immigration is a key element in economic growth, especially since the newcomers open businesses at a far greater rate than native-born entrepreneurs—creating new jobs and paying taxes to their newly adopted lands.

Consider the experience of Chin Thach, whose Chinese family fled Cambodia for France in 1976. Thach started learning the language at night while working in an automobile factory by day. Within a decade, he had earned enough to join two other immigrant friends in launching a computer assembly firm. Thanks to the entrepreneurs' hard work and dedication, the company's annual sales are now $275 million with a payroll of four hundred employees.

But opening a new venture is not always easy for immigrants. Germany, for example, does not allow foreigners to open new businesses until they have resided in the country for at least four years. Under that law, Polish-born Marek Suida would not have been able to start a moving company in Germany—except that his native-born wife, who is also his business partner, was able to register the company.

On the other hand, Kemal Sahin, who came to Germany from Turkey to complete an engineering degree at Aachen University in 1982, lacked the formal paperwork to take a job but was told he could stay in the country if he opened a business. Sahin arranged to open a store in Aachen and sell T-shirts imported from his homeland. Over the years, Sahin did well enough to buy eighteen textile plants in Turkey and manufacture clothing for export all over the European Union and the United States. His retail chain has grown to more than three hundred stores in Germany; the entire business has nearly ten thousand employees, with annual sales of more than $900 million. Now Sahin's success as an immigrant entrepreneur is inspiring other people to leave Turkey and open new ventures in Germany.

> *My family owned a factory producing soy sauce in Cambodia, and I always wanted my own business.*
>
> —*Chin Thach, co-founder, Abacus Equipement Éléctronique**

Reference: William Echikson, "Unsung Heroes," *Business Week*, March 6, 2000, pp. 92–100 (*quote on p. 92).

■ *Structure of Entrepreneurial Organizations*

With a strategy in place and a business plan in hand, the entrepreneur can then proceed to devise a structure that turns the vision of the business plan into a reality. Many of the same concerns in structuring any business, which are described in the next five chapters of this book, are also relevant to small businesses. For example, entrepreneurs need to consider organization design and to develop job descriptions, organization charts, and management control systems.

The Internet, of course, is rewriting virtually all of the rules for starting and operating a small business. Getting into business is easier and faster than ever before, there are many more potential opportunities than at any time in history, and the ability to gather and assimilate information is at an all-time high. Even so, however, would-be entrepreneurs must still make the right decisions when they start. They must decide, for example, precisely how to get into business. Should they buy an existing business or build from the ground up? In addition, would-be entrepreneurs must find appropriate sources of financing and decide when and how to seek the advice of experts.

Starting the New Business

An old Chinese proverb suggests that a journey of a thousand miles begins with a single step. This is also true of a new business. The first step is the individual's commitment to becoming a business owner. Next comes choosing the goods or services to be offered—a process that means investigating one's chosen industry and market. Making this choice also requires would-be entrepreneurs to assess not only industry trends but also their own skills. Like the managers of existing businesses, new business owners must also be sure that they understand the true nature of their enterprises in which they are engaged.

Buying an Existing Business   After choosing a product and making sure that the choice fits their own skills and interests, entrepreneurs must decide whether to buy an existing business or to start from scratch. Consultants often recommend the first approach. Quite simply, the odds are better: if successful, an existing business has already proved its ability to draw customers at a profit. It has also established working relationships with lenders, suppliers, and the community. Moreover, the track record of an existing business gives potential buyers a much clearer picture of what to expect than any estimate of a new business's prospects. Around 30 percent of the new businesses started in the past decade were bought from someone else. The McDonald's empire, for example, was started when Ray Kroc bought an existing hamburger business and then turned it into a global phenomenon. Likewise, Starbucks was a struggling mail-order business when Howard Schultz bought it and turned his attention to retail expansion.

Starting from Scratch   Some people, however, prefer the satisfaction that comes from planting an idea, nurturing it, and making it grow into a strong and sturdy business. There are also practical reasons to start a business from scratch. A new business does not suffer from the ill effects of a prior owner's errors. The start-up owner is also free to choose lenders, equipment, inventories, locations, suppliers, and workers, unbound by a predecessor's commitments and policies. Of the new businesses begun in the past decade, 64 percent were started from scratch.

Not surprisingly, though, the risks of starting a business from scratch are greater than those of buying an existing firm. Founders of new businesses can only make predictions and projections about their prospects. Success or failure thus depends heavily on identifying a genuine business opportunity—for example, a product for which many customers will pay well but which is currently unavailable to them. To find openings, entrepreneurs must study markets and answer the following questions: (1) Who are my customers? (2) Where are they? (3) At what price will they buy my product? (4) In what quantities will they buy? (5) Who are my competitors? and (6) How will my product differ from those of my competitors?

Finding answers to these questions is a difficult task even for large, well-established firms. But where can the new business owner get the necessary information? Other sources of assistance are discussed later in this chapter, but we briefly describe three of the most accessible here. For example, the best way to gain knowledge about a market is to work in it before going into business in it. For example, if you once worked in a bookstore and now plan to open one of your own, you probably already have some idea about the kinds of books people request and buy. Second, a quick scan of the local Yellow Pages or an Internet search will reveal many potential competitors, as will advertisements in trade journals. Personal visits to these establishments and web sites can give you insights into their strengths and weaknesses. And third, studying magazines, books, and web sites aimed specifically at small businesses can also be of help, as can hiring professionals to survey the market for you.

Financing the New Business

Although the choice of how to start a business is obviously important, it is meaningless unless a new business owner can obtain the money to set up shop. Among the more common sources for funding are family and friends, personal savings, banks and similar lending institutions, investors, and governmental agencies. Lending institutions are more likely to help finance the purchase of an existing business than a new business because the risks are better understood. Individuals starting up new businesses, on the other hand, are more likely to have to rely on their personal resources.

Personal Resources According to a study by the National Federation of Independent Business, an owner's personal resources, not loans, are the most important source of money. Including money borrowed from friends and relatives, personal resources account for over two-thirds of all money invested in new small businesses and one-half of that invested in the purchase of existing businesses. When Michael Dorf and his friends decided to launch a New York nightclub dubbed the Knitting Factory, he started with $30,000 of his own money. Within four months of opening, Dorf asked his father to co-sign the first of four consecutive Milwaukee bank loans (for $70,000, $200,000, $300,000, and, to move to a new facility, $500,000, respectively). Dorf and his partners also engaged in creative bartering, such as putting a sound system company's logo on all its advertising in exchange for free equipment. Finally, because the Knitting Factory has become so successful, other investors are now stepping forward to provide funds—$650,000 from one investor and $4.2 million from another.[22]

Strategic Alliances Strategic alliances are also becoming a popular method for financing business growth. When Steven and Andrew Grundy decided to launch a CD-exchange Internet business called Spun.com, they had very little capital and so made extensive use of alliances with other firms. They partnered, for example, with wholesaler Alliance Entertainment Corp. as a CD supplier. Orders to Spun.com actually go to Alliance, which ships products to customers and bills Spun.com directly. This setup has allowed Spun.com to promote a vast inventory of labels without actually having to buy inventory. All told, the firm has created an alliance network that has provided the equivalent of $40 million in capital.[23]

Lenders   Although banks, independent investors, and government loans all provide much smaller portions of start-up funds than the personal resources of owners, they are important in many cases. Getting money from these sources, however, requires some extra effort. Banks and private investors usually want to see formal business plans—detailed outlines of proposed businesses and markets, owners' backgrounds, and other sources of funding. Government loans have strict eligibility guidelines.

Venture Capital Companies   **Venture capital companies** are groups of small investors seeking to make profits on companies with rapid growth potential. Most of these firms do not lend money; they invest it, supplying capital in return for stock. The venture capital company may also demand a representative on the board of directors. In some cases, managers may even need approval from the venture capital company before making major decisions. Of all venture capital currently committed in the United States, 29 percent comes from true venture capital firms.[24]

venture capital company A group of small investors seeking to make profits on companies with rapid growth potential

For example, Dr. Drew Pinsky, cohost of MTV's Loveline, recently got venture capital funding to extend his program to the Internet from a group of investors collectively known as Garage.com. Garage.com is comprised of several individuals and other investors who specialize in financing Internet start-ups.[25] Similarly, Softbank Inc. is a venture capital firm that has provided funds to over three hundred web companies, including Yahoo! and E*trade. As founder Masayoshi Son puts it, "We're a strategic holding company, investing in companies that are very important in the digital information industry—in e-commerce, financial services, and media."

Small-Business Investment Companies   Taking a more balanced approach in their choices than venture capital companies, small-business investment companies (SBICs) seek profits by investing in companies with potential for rapid growth. Created by the Small Business Investment Act of 1958, SBICs are federally licensed to borrow money from the SBA and to invest it in or lend it to small businesses. They are themselves investments for their shareholders. Past beneficiaries of SBIC capital include Apple Computer, Intel, and Federal Express. In addition, the government has recently begun to sponsor minority enterprise small-business investment companies (MESBICs). As the name suggests, MESBICs specialize in financing businesses that are owned and operated by minorities.

SBA Financial Programs   Since its founding in 1953, the SBA has offered more than twenty financing programs to small businesses that meet standards in size and independence. Eligible firms must also be unable to get private financing at reasonable terms. Because of these and other restrictions, SBA loans have never been a major source of small-business financing. In addition, budget cutbacks at the SBA have reduced the number of firms benefiting from loans. Nevertheless, several SBA programs currently offer funds to qualified applicants.

For example, under the SBA's guaranteed loans program, small businesses can borrow from commercial lenders. The SBA guarantees to repay 75 to 85 percent of the loan amount, not to exceed $750,000. Under a related program, companies engaged in international trade can borrow up to $1.25 million. Such loans may be made for as long as fifteen years. Most SBA lending activity flows through this program.

Sometimes, however, both the desired bank and SBA-guaranteed loans are unavailable (perhaps because the business cannot meet stringent requirements). In such cases, the SBA may help finance the entrepreneur through its immediate participation loans program. Under this arrangement, the SBA and the bank each put up a share of the money, with the SBA's share not to exceed $150,000. Under the local development companies (LDCs) program, the SBA works with a corporation (either for-profit or nonprofit) founded by local citizens who want to boost the local economy. The SBA can lend up to $500,000 for each small business to be helped by an LDC.

Spurred in large part by the boom in Internet businesses, both venture capital and loans are becoming easier to obtain. Most small businesses, for example, report that it has generally gotten increasingly easier to obtain loans over the last ten years. Indeed, some technology companies are being offered so much venture capital that they are turning down part of it to keep from diluting their ownership unnecessarily.

Sources of Management Advice

Financing is not the only area in which small businesses need help. Until World War II, for example, the business world involved few regulations, few taxes, few records, few big competitors, and no computers. Since then, simplicity has given way to complexity. Today, few entrepreneurs are equipped with all the business skills they need to survive. Small-business owners can no longer be their own troubleshooters, lawyers, bookkeepers, financiers, and tax experts. For these jobs, they rely on professional help. To survive and grow, however, small businesses also need advice regarding management. This advice is usually available from four sources: advisory boards, management consultants, the SBA, and a process called networking.

Advisory Boards All companies, even those that do not legally need a board of directors, can benefit from the problem-solving abilities of advisory boards. Thus, some small businesses create boards to provide advice and assistance. For example, an advisory board might help an entrepreneur determine the best way to finance a plant expansion or to start exporting products to foreign markets.

Management Consultants Opinions vary widely about the value of management consultants—experts who charge fees to help managers solve problems. They often specialize in one area, such as international business, small business,

The famous phrase "no man is an island" relates especially well to would-be entrepreneurs and owners of small business start-ups. Regardless of their talents, women and men running their own businesses need all the advice and information they can get. Fortunately, as noted in the text, there are a variety of sources of advice that are available. One very specialized information source is Kanwal Rekhi, shown here in the middle. He started a successful Silicon Valley software firm several years ago and then sold it to Novell for $210 million. He then founded The Indus Entrepreneurs, a networking group for Indians in the Valley. Today Mr. Rekhi spends his time offering advice and assistance to other Indians in the area who are interested in launching their own enterprises.

or manufacturing. Thus, they can bring an objective and trained outlook to problems and provide logical recommendations. They can be quite expensive, however, because some consultants charge $1,000 or more for a day of assistance.

Like other professionals, consultants should be chosen with care. They can be found through major corporations who have used their services and who can provide references and reports on their work. Not surprisingly, they are most effective when the client helps (for instance, by providing schedules and written proposals for work to be done).

The Small Business Administration   Even more important than its financing role is the SBA's role in helping small-business owners improve their management skills. It is easy for entrepreneurs to spend money; SBA programs are designed to show them how to spend it wisely. The SBA offers small businesses four major management counseling programs at virtually no cost.

A small-business owner who needs help in starting a new business can get it free through the Service Corps of Retired Executives (SCORE). All SCORE members are retired executives, and all are volunteers. Under this program, the SBA tries to match the expert to the need. For example, if a small-business owner needs help putting together a marketing plan, the SBA will send a SCORE counselor with marketing expertise.

Like SCORE, the Active Corps of Executives (ACE) program is designed to help small businesses that cannot afford consultants. The SBA recruits ACE volunteers from virtually every industry. All ACE volunteers are currently involved in successful activities, mostly as small-business owners themselves. Together, SCORE and ACE have more than twelve thousand counselors working out of 350 chapters throughout the United States. They provide assistance to some 140,000 small businesses each year.

The talents and skills of students and instructors at colleges and universities are fundamental to the Small Business Institute (SBI). Under the guidance of seasoned professors of business administration, students seeking advanced degrees work closely with small-business owners to help solve specific problems, such as sagging sales or rising costs. Students earn credit toward their degrees, with their grades depending on how well they handle a client's problems. Several hundred colleges and universities counsel thousands of small-business owners through this program every year.

Finally, the newest of the SBA's management counseling projects is its Small Business Development Center (SBDC) program. Begun in 1976, SBDCs are designed to consolidate information from various disciplines and institutions, including technical and professional schools. Then they make this knowledge available to new and existing small businesses. In 1995, universities in forty-five states took part in the program.

Networking   More and more, small-business owners are discovering the value of networking—meeting regularly with one another to discuss common problems and opportunities and, perhaps most important, pool resources. Businesspeople have long joined organizations such as the local chamber of commerce and the National Federation of Independent Businesses (NFIB) to make such contacts.

Today, organizations are springing up all over the United States to facilitate small-business networking. One such organization, the Council of Smaller Enterprises of Cleveland, boasts a total membership of more than ten thousand small-business owners, the largest number in the country. This organization offers its members not only networking possibilities but also educational programs and services tailored to their needs. In a typical year, its eighty-five educational programs draw more than 8,500 small-business owners.

In particular, women and minorities have found networking to be an effective problem-solving tool. The National Association of Women Business Owners (NAWBO) (www.nawbo.org), for example, provides a variety of networking forums. The NAWBO also has chapters in most major cities where its members can meet regularly. Increasingly, women are relying more on other women to help locate venture capital, establish relationships with customers, and provide such essential services as accounting and legal advice. According to Patty Abramson of the Women's Growth Capital Fund, all of these tasks have traditionally been harder for women because, until now, they've never had friends in the right places. "I wouldn't say this is about discrimination," adds Abramson. "It's about not having the relationships, and business is about relationships."

Franchising

The next time you drive or walk around town, be on the alert for a McDonald's, Taco Bell, Subway, Denny's, or KFC restaurant; a 7-Eleven or Circle K convenience store; a RE/Max or Coldwell Banker real estate office; a Super 8 or Ramada motel; a

Blockbuster video store; a Sylvan Learning Center educational center; an Express Oil Change or Precision Auto Wash car-service center; or a Supercuts hair salon. What do these businesses have in common? In most cases, they will be franchised operations, operating under licenses issued by parent companies to local entrepreneurs who own and manage them. These licenses are generally called **franchising agreements**.

As many would-be businesspeople have discovered, franchising agreements are an accessible doorway to entrepreneurship. A franchise is an arrangement that permits the franchisee (buyer) to sell the product of the franchiser (seller, or parent company). Franchisees can thus benefit from the selling corporation's experience and expertise. They can also consult the franchiser for managerial and financial help.

For example, the franchiser may supply financing. It may pick the store location, negotiate the lease, design the store, and purchase necessary equipment. It may train the first set of employees and managers and provide standardized policies and procedures. Once the business is open, the franchiser may offer savings by allowing the business to purchase from a central location. Marketing strategy (especially advertising) may also be handled by the franchiser. Finally, franchisees may benefit from continued management counseling. In short, franchisees receive—that is, invest in—not only their own ready made businesses but also receive expert help in running them.

Franchises offer many advantages to both sellers and buyers. For example, franchisers benefit from the ability to grow rapidly by using the investment money provided by franchisees. This strategy has enabled giant franchisers such as McDonald's and Baskin Robbins to mushroom into billion-dollar concerns in a brief time.

For the franchisee, the arrangement combines the incentive of owning a business with the advantage of access to large-business management skills. Unlike the person who starts from scratch, the franchisee does not have to build a business step by step. Instead, the business is established virtually overnight. Moreover, because each franchise outlet is probably a carbon copy of every other outlet, the chances of failure are reduced. McDonald's, for example, is a model of consistency—Big Macs taste the same everywhere.

Of course, owning a franchise also involves certain disadvantages. Perhaps the most significant is the start-up cost. Franchise prices vary widely. Fantastic Sam's (www.fantasticsams.com) hair salon franchise fees are $30,000, but a Gingiss Formalwear (www.gingiss.com) franchise can run as high as $125,000. Extremely profitable or hard-to-get franchises are even more expensive. A McDonald's franchise costs at least $650,000 to $750,000, and a professional sports team can cost several hundred million dollars. Franchisees may also have continued obligations to contribute percentages of sales to parent corporations.

Buying a franchise also entails intangible costs. For one thing, the small-business owner sacrifices some independence. A McDonald's franchisee cannot change the way hamburgers or milk shakes are made. Nor can franchisees create individual identities in their communities; for all practical purposes, the McDonald's owner is anonymous. In addition, many franchise agreements are difficult to terminate.

Finally, although franchises minimize risks, they do not guarantee success. Many franchisees have seen their investments—and their dreams—disappear

franchising agreement Operation by an entrepreneur (the *franchisee*) under a license issued by a parent company (the *franchiser*); the entrepreneur pays the parent company for the use of trademarks, products, formulas, and business plans

because of poor locations, rising costs, or lack of continued franchiser commitment. Moreover, figures on failure rates are artificially low because they do not include failing franchisees bought out by their franchising parent companies. An additional risk is that the chain itself could collapse. In any given year, dozens—sometimes hundreds—of franchisers close shop or stop selling franchises.

MANAGEMENT IMPLICATIONS   Entrepreneurs should carefully weigh the advantages and disadvantages of different forms of starting a new business, such as buying an existing one or starting from scratch. They should also have a clear plan for financing their business and take advantage of various sources of information and advice. Those considering franchising should be sure they understand its opportunities, advantages, and disadvantages.

The Performance of Entrepreneurial Organizations

The formulation and implementation of an effective strategy plays a major role in determining the overall performance of an entrepreneurial organization. This section examines how entrepreneurial firms evolve over time and the attributes of these firms that enhance their chance for success. For every Henry Ford, Walt Disney, Mary Kay Ash, or Bill Gates—people who transformed small businesses into major corporations—there are many small-business owners and entrepreneurs who fail.

Figure 10.5 illustrates recent trends in new business start-ups and failures. As you can see, over the last ten years new business start-ups have generally run between around 150,000 and 190,000 per year, with 155,141 new businesses being launched in 1998. Over this same period, business failures have generally run between 50,000 and 100,000, with a total of 71,857 failing in 1998. In this section, we look first at a few key trends in small-business start-ups. Then we examine some of the main reasons for success and failure in small-business undertakings.

Trends in New Business Start-Ups

Thousands of new businesses are started in the United States every year. Several factors account for this trend, and in this section we focus on four of them.

Emergence of E-commerce   Clearly, the most significant recent trend in small-business start-ups is the rapid emergence of electronic commerce. Because the Internet has provided fundamentally new ways of doing business, savvy entrepreneurs have been able to create and expand new businesses faster and easier than ever before. Such leading-edge firms as America Online, Amazon.com, Garden.com, and eBay, for example, owe their very existence to the Internet. Figure 10.6 amplifies this point by summarizing the tremendous growth in on-line commerce from 1997 through 2001. In addition, one recent study reported that in 1999, the Internet economy grew overall by 62 percent over the previous year and provided jobs for 2.5 million people.[26]

Figure 10.5

Business Start-Up Successes and Failures

Over the most recent ten-year period for which data are available, new business start-ups numbered between 150,000 and 190,000 per year. Business failures during this same period, meanwhile, ranged from about 50,000 to nearly 100,000 per year.

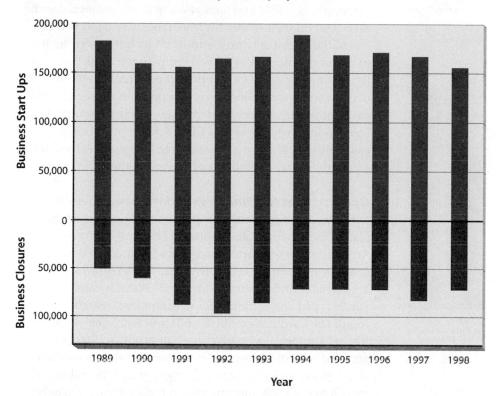

Source: U.S. Census Bureau, *Statistical Abstract of the United States: 1999* (119th Edition), Washington, D.C., 1999.

Indeed, it seems as if new ideas emerge virtually every day. Andrew Beebe, for example, is scoring big with BigStep.com, a web business that essentially creates, hosts, and maintains web sites for other small businesses. So far, BigStep.com has signed up seventy-five thousand small-business clients. Beebe actually provides his basic services for free but earns money by charging for so-called premium services such as customer billing. Karl Jacob's Keen.com is a web business that matches people looking for advice with experts who have the answers. Keen got the idea when he and his father were struggling to fix a boat motor and didn't know where to turn for help. Keen.com attracted one hundred thousand subscribers in just three months.[27]

Crossovers from Large Businesses It is interesting to note that increasingly more businesses are being started by people who have opted to leave large corporations and put their experience and know-how to work for themselves. In some cases, these individuals see great new ideas they want to develop. Often, they get

Figure 10.6

The Growth of On-Line Commerce

On-line commerce is becoming an increasingly important part of the U.S. economy. As shown here, for example, on-line commerce has grown from about $2.5 trillion in 1997 to an estimated $17.4 trillion by 2001. And most indicators suggest that this trend will continue.

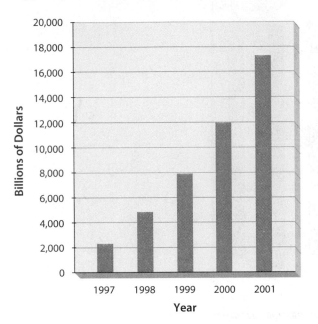

Source: U.S. Census Bureau, *Statistical Abstract of the United States: 1999* (119th Edition), Washington, D.C., 1999.

burned out working for a large corporation. Sometimes they have lost their jobs, only to discover that working for themselves was a better idea anyway.

Cisco Systems CEO John Chambers is acknowledged as one of the best entrepreneurs. But he spent several years working first at IBM and then at Wang Laboratories before he set out on his own. Under his leadership, Cisco has become one of the largest and most important technology companies in the world. Indeed, for a few days in March 2000, Cisco had the world's highest market capitalization, and it remains one of the world's most valuable companies.[28] In a more unusual case, Gilman Louie recently left an executive position at Hasbro's on-line group to head a CIA-backed venture capital firm called In-Q-It. The firm's mission is to help nurture high-tech companies making products of interest to the nation's spies.[29]

Opportunities for Minorities and Women   In addition to big-business expatriates, more small businesses are being started by minorities and women. For example, the number of African-American-owned businesses has increased by 46 percent during the most recent five-year period for which data are available and now totals about 620,000. Chicago's Gardner family is just one of thousands of examples illustrating this trend. The Gardners are the founders of Soft Sheen Products Inc., a firm specializing in ethnic hair products. Soft Sheen attained sales of $80 million in the year before the Gardners sold it to France's L'Oréal S.A. for more than $160 million. The emergence of such opportunities is hardly surprising, either to African-American entrepreneurs or to the corporate marketers who have taken an interest in their companies. African-American purchasing power topped $530 billion in 1999. Up from just over $300 billion in 1990, that increase of 73 percent far outstrips the 57 percent increase experienced by all Americans.[30]

Hispanic-owned businesses have grown at an even faster rate of 76 percent and now number about 862,000. Other ethnic groups are also making their presence felt among U.S. business owners. Business ownership among Asian and Pacific Islanders has increased 56 percent, to over 600,000. Although the number of businesses owned by Native Americans and Alaska Natives is still somewhat small, at slightly over 100,000, the total nevertheless represents a five-year increase of 93 percent.[31]

The number of women entrepreneurs is also growing rapidly. Celeste Johnson, for example, left a management position at Pitney Bowes to launch Obex Inc., which makes gardening and landscaping products from mixed recycled plastics. Katrina Garnett gave up a lucrative job at Oracle to start her own software company, Crossworlds Software Inc. Laila Rubenstein closed her management-consulting practice to create Greeting Cards.com Inc., an Internet-based business selling customizable electronic greetings. "Women-owned business," says Teresa

Cavanaugh, director of the Women Entrepreneur's Connection at BankBoston, "is the largest emerging segment of the small-business market. Women-owned businesses are an economic force that no bank can afford to overlook."[32]

Likewise, the number of women-owned businesses is also growing rapidly. There are now 9.1 million businesses owned by women—about 40 percent of all businesses in the United States. Combined, they generate nearly $4 trillion in revenue a year—an increase of 132 percent since 1992. The number of people employed nationwide at women-owned businesses since 1992 has grown to around 27.5 million—an increase of 108 percent.[33] Figure 10.7 summarizes the corporate backgrounds of women entrepreneurs and provides some insight into what they like about running their own businesses. Corporate positions in general management (25 percent), sales (21 percent), and accounting and finance (18 percent) account for almost two-thirds of the women who start their own businesses. Once in charge of their own businesses, women also report that they like being their own bosses, setting their own hours, controlling their own destinies, relating to customers, making decisions, and achieving goals. *Working with Diversity* provides more information about women as entrepreneurs.

Better Survival Rates Finally, more people are encouraged to test their skills as entrepreneurs because the failure rate among small businesses has been declining in recent years. During the 1960s and 1970s, for example, less than half of all new start-ups survived more than eighteen months; only one in five lasted ten years. Now, however, new businesses have a better chance of surviving. Of new businesses started in the 1980s, for instance, over 77 percent remained in operation for at least three years. Today, the SBA estimates that at least 40 percent of all new businesses can expect to survive for six years. For the reasons discussed in the

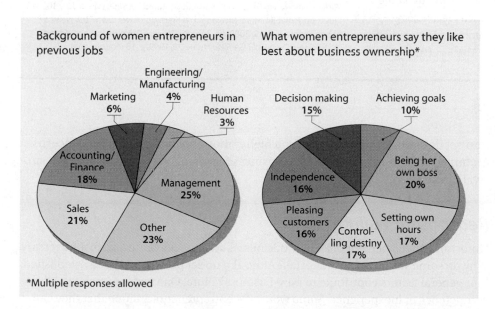

*Multiple responses allowed

Figure 10.7

Where Women Entrepreneurs Come From and What They Like About Their Work
Women entrepreneurs come from all sectors of large businesses, although management and sales are especially well represented. Women entrepreneurs indicate that they really like being their own boss, being independent, setting their own hours, and controlling their own destiny.

Source: From "Women Entrepreneurs," *The Wall Street Journal*, May 24, 1999, p. R12. Reprinted by permission.

WORKING WITH DIVERSITY

SHE'S THE BOSS—AND THE OWNER

More U.S. women are flexing their entrepreneurial muscles, starting businesses at a record rate, boosting the economy, and providing jobs. Nearly four out of every ten U.S. businesses—more than nine million businesses—are owned by women. Their total annual sales top $3.6 trillion, and together they employ twenty-seven million people. From manufacturing and construction to wholesaling and e-commerce, women are starting companies in nearly every type of industry.

Obtaining business financing is still a problem for many women, however. Studies indicate that women have access to smaller credit lines than men and receive less of the venture capital being invested in high-tech start-ups. To address this issue, a growing number of women are founding venture capital firms and searching out suitable investment opportunities among start-ups run by women. The Three Guineas Fund, started by a woman who was formerly a vice president of Cisco Systems, provides funding for women with promising business ideas. It also sponsors a series of venture fairs to allow women entrepreneurs to pitch their ideas to top venture capitalists.

From Silicon Valley in California to Silicon Alley in New York, business incubators are popping up in many areas to help entrepreneurs run high-tech start-ups. Building on this trend, the Three Guineas Fund has financed the Women's Technology Cluster in San Francisco as the first incubator working only with women-owned and -operated businesses. This incubator gives office space to as many as thirteen start-ups at one time and offers both expert advice and networking opportunities to help entrepreneurs guide their businesses through the life cycle. In exchange, the incubator receives 2 percent of the company's equity, which goes toward supporting other start-ups.

Once a company expands beyond thirty employees, it must leave the incubator and operate on its own. LevelEdge.com is one of the businesses that outgrew the Women's Technology Cluster. Founded by Lisa Henderson, LevelEdge (http://www.leveledge.com/) serves as a web-based matchmaker between high school athletes and college recruiters. Just fifteen months after founding LevelEdge, Henderson had garnered enough funding and participation from athletes and colleges to move her fast-growing business out of the incubator and make room for another start-up.

> *Women have been starting businesses for a decade, but these numbers tell us their companies are playing a much more significant role in the health of the economy.*
>
> —*Sharon Hadary, executive director, National Foundation for Women Business Owners**

References: Kevin Ferguson, "Nothing Ventured," *Business Week*, July 10, 2000, pp. F28–F34; Marci McDonald, "A Start-Up of Her Own," *U.S. News & World Report*, May 15, 2000, pp. 34+; Bill Meyers, "Women Increase Standing As Business Owners," *USA Today*, June 29, 1999, p. 1B (*quote on p. 1B).

---

next section, small businesses suffer a higher mortality rate than larger concerns. Among those that manage to stay in business for six to ten years, however, the survival rate levels off.

Reasons for Failure

Unfortunately, 63 percent of all new businesses will not celebrate a sixth anniversary. Why do some succeed and others fail? Although no set pattern has been established, four general factors contribute to new-business failure. One factor is managerial incompetence or inexperience. Some would-be entrepreneurs assume that they can succeed through common sense, overestimate their own managerial acumen, or think that hard work alone will lead to success. But if managers do not know how to make basic business decisions or do not understand the basic concepts and principles of management, they are unlikely to be successful in the long run.

Neglect can also contribute to failure. Some entrepreneurs try either to launch their ventures in their spare time or to devote only a limited amount of time to a new business. But starting a new business requires an overwhelming time commitment. Entrepreneurs who are not willing to put in the time and effort that a business requires are unlikely to survive.

Third, weak control systems can lead to serious problems. Effective control systems are needed to keep a business on track and to help alert entrepreneurs to potential trouble. If control systems do not signal impending problems, managers may be in serious trouble before more visible difficulties alert them.

Finally, insufficient capital can contribute to new business failure. Some entrepreneurs are overly optimistic about how soon they will start earning profits. In most cases, however, it takes months or years before a business is likely to start turning a profit. Amazon.com, for example, has still not earned a profit. Most experts say that a new business should have enough capital to operate at least six months without earning a profit; some recommend enough to last a year.[34]

Reasons for Success

Similarly, four basic factors are typically cited to explain new business success. One set of factors is hard work, drive, and dedication. New-business owners must be committed to succeeding and be willing to put in the time and effort to make it happen. Gladys Edmunds, a single teen-age mother in Pittsburgh, washed laundry, made chicken dinners to sell to cab drivers, and sold fire extinguishers and Bibles door-to-door to earn money to launch her own business. Today, Edmunds Travel Consultants employs eight people and earns about $6 million in annual revenue.[35]

Careful analysis of market conditions can help new-business owners assess the probable reception of their products in the marketplace. This analysis will provide insights about market demand for proposed products and services. Whereas attempts to expand local restaurants specializing in baked potatoes, muffins, and gelato have been largely unsuccessful, hamburger and pizza chains continue to have an easier time expanding into new markets.

Managerial competence also contributes to success. Successful new business owners may acquire competence through training or experience or by using the expertise of others. Few successful entrepreneurs succeed alone or straight out of college. Most spend time working in successful companies and/or partner with others to bring more expertise to a new business.

Finally, luck also plays a role in the success of some firms. For example, after Alan McKim started Clean Harbors (www.cleanharbors.com), an environmental cleanup firm based in New England, he struggled to keep his business afloat. Then the U.S. government committed $1.6 billion to toxic waste cleanup—McKim's specialty. He was able to get several large government contracts and put his business on solid financial footing. Had the government fund not been created at just the right time, McKim may well have failed.

MANAGEMENT Entrepreneurs should keep abreast of trends in new-business
IMPLICATIONS start-ups. They should also have a clear understanding of the
reasons for business failure and success.

Summary of Key Points

Entrepreneurship is the process of planning, organizing, operating, and assuming the risk of a business venture. An entrepreneur is someone who engages in entrepreneurship. In general, entrepreneurs start small businesses. Small businesses are an important source of innovation, create numerous jobs, and contribute to the success of large businesses.

In choosing strategies, entrepreneurs have to consider the characteristics of the industry in which they are going to conduct business. A small business must also emphasize its distinctive competencies. Small businesses generally have several distinctive competencies that they should exploit in choosing their strategy. Small businesses are usually skilled at identifying niches in established markets, identifying new markets, and acting quickly to obtain first-mover advantages. Small businesses are usually not skilled at exploiting economies of scale. Once an entrepreneur has chosen a strategy, the strategy is normally written down in a business

plan. Writing a business plan forces an entrepreneur to plan thoroughly and to anticipate problems that might occur.

With a strategy and business plan in place, entrepreneurs must choose a structure to implement them. All of the structural issues summarized in the next five chapters of this book are relevant to the entrepreneur. In addition, the entrepreneur has some unique structural choices to make. For example, the entrepreneur can buy an existing business or start a new one. In determining financial structure, an entrepreneur has to decide how much personal capital to invest in an organization, how much bank and government support to obtain, and whether to encourage venture capital firms to invest. Entrepreneurs can also rely on various sources of advice.

Several interesting trends characterize new-business start-ups today. There are several reasons why some new businesses fail and others succeed.

Discussion Questions

Questions for Review

1. Why are entrepreneurs and small businesses important to society?
2. In which types of industries do small firms often excel? In which types of industries do small firms struggle?
3. List the financing options available to entrepreneurs. What are the advantages and disadvantages of each?
4. What are the elements of success for small businesses?

Questions for Analysis

5. Entrepreneurs and small businesses play a variety of important roles in society. If these roles are so important, do you think that the government should do more to encourage the development of small business? Why or why not?
6. Franchising agreements seem to be particularly popular ways of starting a new business in industries in which retail outlets are widely spread geographically and where the quality

of goods or services purchased can be evaluated only after the purchase has occurred. For example, a hamburger may look tasty, but you know for sure that it is well made only after you buy it and eat it. By going to a McDonald's, you know exactly the kind and quality of hamburger you will receive, even before you walk in the door. What is it about franchise arrangements that makes them so popular under these conditions?

7. If employing family members can cause problems in a small organization, why is this practice so common?

8. What steps might an entrepreneur take before deciding to expand into a foreign market?

Questions for Application

9. Interview the owner of a small business in your town. Evaluate how successful this small business has been. Using the criteria presented in this chapter, explain its success (or lack of success).

10. Using the information about managing a small business presented in this chapter, analyze whether you would like to work in a small business—either as an employee or as a founder. Given your personality, background, and experience, does working in or starting a new business appeal to you? What are the reasons for your opinion?

BUILDING EFFECTIVE *communication* SKILLS

Exercise Overview

Communication skills refer to the manager's abilities both to convey ideas and information effectively to others and to receive ideas and information from others effectively. While communication skills are important to all organizations, some entrepreneurs argue that they are even more important in smaller organizations. This exercise will help you understand some of the complexities in communicating in smaller businesses.

Exercise Background

Assume that you are the owner/manager of a small retail chain. Your company sells moderately priced apparel for professional men and women. You have ten stores located in the Midwest. Each store has a general manager responsible for the overall management of that specific store. Each store also has one assistant manager.

In addition, your corporate office is staffed by a human resource manager, an advertising specialist, and two buyers. In the past, each store was managed at the total discretion of its local manager. As a result, each store had a different layout, a different culture, and different policies and procedures.

You have decided that you want to begin opening more stores at a rapid pace. To expedite this process, however, you also want to standardize your stores. Unfortunately, however, you realize that many of your current managers will be unhappy with this decision. They will see it as a loss of authority and managerial discretion. Nevertheless, you believe it is important that you make changes to achieve standardization in all areas.

Your plans are to remodel all of your stores to fit a standard layout. You also intend to develop a policy and operations manual for each store. This manual will specify exactly how each store will be managed. You plan to inform your managers of this plan first in a memo and then in a follow-up meeting to discuss questions and concerns.

Exercise Task

With the information described above as context, please do the following:

1. Draft a memo that explains your intentions to the store managers.

2. List the primary objections you anticipate.

3. Outline an agenda for the meeting in which you plan to address the managers' questions and concerns.

4. Do you personally agree with this communication strategy? Why or why not?

BUILDING EFFECTIVE *technical* SKILLS

Exercise Overview

Technical skills are the skills necessary to accomplish or understand the specific work being done in an organization. This exercise will allow you to gain insights into your own technical skills and the relative importance of technical skills in different kinds of organizations.

Exercise Background

Some entrepreneurs have the technical skills that they need to open and run their business successfully. For example, a hair stylist who opens a hair salon, an architect who starts a residential design firm, and a chef who launches a new restaurant all have the technical skills needed to do the work of the organization (hair styling, blueprint rendering, and cooking, respectively).

In other cases, the entrepreneur who starts the organization may have general management skills but may essentially "buy" required technical skills in the labor market. For example, an entrepreneur might start a new restaurant without knowing how to cook by hiring a professional chef to perform this function.

Exercise Task

With the background information provided above as a context, do the following:

1. Listed below are examples of ten small businesses that an individual entrepreneur might conceivably launch. Spend a few minutes thinking about each business. (*Hint*: try to conceptualize an existing local business that might generally fit the description.)
   a. Clothing retail store
   b. Computer clone assembly business
   c. Tavern
   d. Sports-card retail store
   e. Aluminum recycling operation
   f. Used compact disc retail store
   g. Drop-in health-care clinic
   h. Gourmet coffee bean shop
   i. Business services operation
   j. Appliance repair shop
2. Make notes about the specific technical skills required for each business.
3. For each business, decide whether it is especially important that the entrepreneur him- or herself possess the technical skills or whether it is feasible to consider hiring others who possess the skills.
4. What are some major factors that determine the viability of buying technical skills in the labor market?

BUILDING EFFECTIVE *conceptual* SKILLS

Exercise Overview

Conceptual skills refer to the manager's ability to think in the abstract. This exercise will help you relate conceptual skills to entrepreneurship.

Exercise Background

Assume that you have made the decision to open a small business in the local business community when you graduate (the community where you are attending college, not your home). Assume that you have funds to start a business without having to worry about finding other investors.

Without regard to market potential, profitability, or similar considerations, list five businesses that you might want to open and operate based solely on your personal interests. For example, if you enjoy bicycling, you might enjoy opening a shop that caters to cyclists.

Next, without regard to personal attractiveness or interests, list five businesses that you might want to open and operate based solely on market opportunities. Evaluate the prospects for success of each of the ten businesses.

Exercise Task

With this background information as context, do the following:

1. Form a small group with three or four classmates and discuss your respective lists.

Look for instances of where the same type of business appears on either the same or alternative lists. Also look for cases where the same business appears with similar or dissimilar prospects for success.

2. How important is personal interest in small-business success?

3. How important is market potential in small-business success

---

CHAPTER CLOSING CASE

CLEAR CHANNEL FOR ENTREPRENEURIAL SUCCESS

When L. Lowry Mays co-founded Clear Channel Communications in 1972, radio was already an old and unglamorous medium. Although he started with one money-losing country-western radio station in San Antonio, Texas, Mays was an entrepreneur with an eagerness to learn the business and a long-term plan. Watching and waiting, he was ready to act when federal regulations governing ownership of electronic media were relaxed in 1984. Then he began buying small, weak radio stations and low-priced television stations. When the Fox network started looking for affiliates, Mays signed up his stations. That decision paid off as Fox's ratings climbed and it became a major network player in broadcast television.

Mays expanded his media empire in 1999 by acquiring AMFM Inc. This $23.5 billion purchase positioned Clear Channel as the largest operator of radio stations in the United States, with 830 stations broadcasting to ninety-six million listeners in 187 markets. The nearest competitor, Infinity Broadcasting, had only 160 U.S. stations but reached fifty-four million listeners because its stations were in larger metropolitan areas. Because of duplication and federal oversight of the AMFM acquisition, Mays had to sell more than one hundred radio stations, but radio still contributed more than three-quarters of Clear Channel's revenues, while television contributed less than 5 percent of revenues.

Billboards, another decidedly dowdy medium, provided the remainder of Clear Channel's revenues. Mays added this part of his business in the late 1990s. Now Clear Channel offered advertisers a choice of 425,000 billboards in forty-seven U.S. cities as well as radio and television broadcast options for reaching audiences. In fact, the combination of billboards and radio was particularly attractive because television advertising was becoming more expensive and more fragmented as the number of channels multiplied. Mays reasoned that billboards would allow advertisers to reach a large audience and radio would give advertisers a way to repeat their messages over and over—a desirable combination for a reasonable fee.

Will the Internet, today's most glamorous and talked-about medium, threaten Clear Channel Communications? Decades ago, some observers believed that television would bury radio, but Mays—who clearly believes in the power of radio—does not see the Internet displacing the other electronic media. Instead, he has carved a profitable niche selling radio ad time and billboard space to dot-com businesses, many of which have only a shoestring budget on which to build their brands.

In addition, Clear Channel has teamed up with SamsDirect Internet to promote a new domain name alternative for individuals and businesses seeking new Internet addresses. The partners are encouraging people to register for on-line addresses that end in dot-cc (.cc) rather than dot-com (.com), which opens up new opportunities to claim unique or descriptive web addresses. Clear Channel radio stations and billboards in Houston were among the first to carry advertising for the dot-cc domain name registration service. In a dot-com address, the "com" stands for "commercial," to distinguish businesses from nonprofit organizations that use the dot-org (.org) designation. In a dot-cc address, the "cc" stands for CoCos Islands, which are located near Australia, but Clear Channel and SamsDirect see dot-cc as a good alternative for North American businesses that have missed the chance to specific dot-com names. This is yet another example of how Mays has turned innovation to his advantage in the ever-changing world of media.

Case Questions

1. What distinctive competencies has Mays exploited to build Clear Channel Communications?

2. What role has economy of scale played in helping Mays build his business?

3. What else can Mays do to increase synergy among his various businesses?

Case References

Nancy Sarnoff, "New Domain Gives Local Market Second Shot At Filling in the Dots," *Houston Business Journal*, January 29, 2000, pp. 9–15; Brett Pulley, "America's Best Big Companies: Entertainment," *Forbes*, January 10, 2000, pp. 126–127; Stephanie Anderson Forest, "The Biggest Media Mogul You Never Heard Of," *Business Week*, October 18, 1999, p. 56.

CHAPTER NOTES

1. Gary Hamel, "Driving Grassroots Growth," *Fortune*, September 4, 2000, pp. 173–187; "Fortune's 100 Fastest-Growing Companies," *Fortune*, September 4, 2000, pp. 142–160; Ronald B. Lieber, "Beating the Odds," *Fortune*, March 31, 1997, pp. 82–90 (quote on p. 85).
2. Bro Uttal, "Inside the Deal That Made Bill Gates $350,000,000," *Fortune*, July 21, 1986, pp. 23–33.
3. "The 400 Richest People in America," *Forbes*, October 9, 2000, p. 118.
4. Murray B. Low and Ian MacMillan, "Entrepreneurship: Past Research and Future Challenges," *Journal of Management*, June 1988, pp. 139–159.
5. U.S. Department of Commerce, *Statistical Abstract of the United States: 1999* (Washington, D.C.: Bureau of the Census, 1999).
6. "Small Business 'Vital Statistics.'" Accessed May 24, 2000. On-line: http://www.sba.gov/aboutsba/.
7. "Small Business 'Vital Statistics.'"
8. "Small Business 'Vital Statistics.'"
9. Chuck Salter, "Insanity, Inc.," *Fast Company*, January 1999, pp. 100–108.
10. "A Five-Year Journey to a Better Mousetrap," *New York Times*, May 24, 1998, p. 8.
11. "The Top Entrepreneurs," *Business Week*, January 10, 2000, pp. 80–82.
12. "New Entrepreneur, Old Economy," *Wall Street Journal*, May 22, 2000, p. R10.
13. Amar Bhide, "How Entrepreneurs Craft Strategies That Work," *Harvard Business Review*, March–April 1994, pp. 150–163.
14. "Three Men and a Baby Bell," *Forbes*, March 6, 2000, pp. 134–135.
15. *Hoover's Handbook of American Business 2000* (Austin, Texas: Hoover's Business Press, 2000), pp. 1540–1541; Wendy Zellner, "Peace, Love, and the Bottom Line," *Business Week*, December 7, 1998, pp. 79–82.
16. "Giving Birth to a Web Business," *New York Times*, October 15, 1998, p. G5.
17. Nancy J. Lyons, "Moonlight over Indiana," *Inc.*, January 2000, pp. 71–74.
18. F. M. Scherer, *Industrial Market Structure and Economic Performance*, 2nd Edition (Boston: Houghton Mifflin, 1980).
19. "Three Biker-Entrepreneurs Take on Mighty Harley," *New York Times*, August 20, 1999, p. F1.
20. The importance of discovering niches is emphasized in Charles Hill and Gareth Jones, *Strategic Management: An Integrative Approach*, 5th Edition (Boston: Houghton Mifflin, 2001).
21. Gregory Patterson, "An American in . . . Siberia?" *Fortune*, August 4, 1997, p. 63, and "Crazy for Crunchies," *Newsweek*, April 28, 1997, p. 49.
22. Thea Singer, "Brandapalooza," *Inc.* 500, 1999, pp. 69–72.
23. "Cheap Tricks," *Forbes*, February 21, 2000, p. 116.
24. U.S. Department of Commerce, *Statistical Abstract of the United States: 1999* (Washington, D.C.: Bureau of the Census, 1999).
25. Susan Greco, "get$$$now.com," *Inc.*, September 1999, pp. 35–38.
26. "Internet Industry Surges 'Startling' 62%," *USA Today*, June 6, 2000, p. 1B.
27. "Up-and-Comers," *Business Week*, May 15, 2000, pp. EB70–EB72.
28. Andy Serwer, "There's Something About Cisco," *Fortune*, May 15, 2000, pp. 114–138.
29. "High-Tech Advances Push C.I.A. into New Company," *New York Times*, September 29, 1999, p. A14.

30. "The Courtship of Black Consumers," *New York Times*, August 16, 1998, pp. D1, D5.

31. See *The Wall Street Journal Almanac 1999*, pp. 179, 182.

32. "Women Entrepreneurs Attract New Financing," *New York Times*, July 26, 1998, p. 10.

33. "Women Increase Standing as Business Owners," *USA Today*, June 29, 1999, p. 1B.

34. Norman M. Scarborough and Thomas W. Zimmerer, *Effective Small Business Management: An Entrepreneurial Approach*, 6th Edition (Upper Saddle River, N.J.: Prentice Hall, 2000), pp. 412–413.

35. "Expert Entrepreneur Got Her Show on the Road at an Early Age," *USA Today*, May 24, 2000, p. 5B.

The Organizing Process

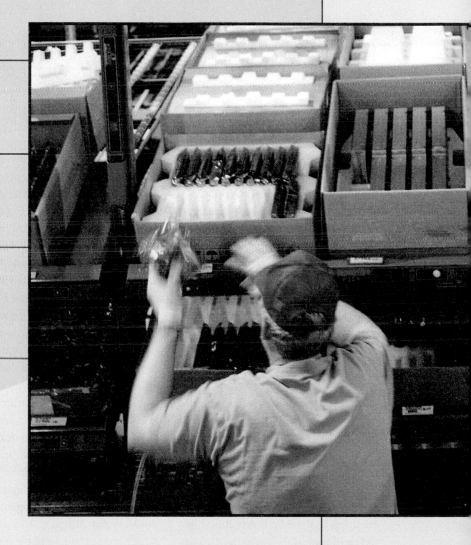

11 Basic Elements of Organizing

Construction has always been a job that encourages specialization. Very different kinds of skills and expertise are needed, for example, to create a foundation from concrete; erect walls from brick, wood, or steel; create networks of pipes for plumbing and wire for electricity; fabricate a weatherproof roof; and finish off an interior with a high-quality appearance. There are even craft specialists within these jobs, though—building walls from steel and building a roof from shingles are far different jobs from building walls from wood and building a roof from metal.

Putting all these pieces together, then, can be a big and complicated job. Thus, someone has to organize and coordinate the overall process, ensuring to the extent possible that the right materials in the right quantities and the right people are at the job site just as they are needed, but not before or after. Until recently, organizing most building projects relied on paper—blueprints were drawn by architects, schedules were created by contractors, and paperwork between contractors and subcontractors flowed back and forth as materials were requested and ordered, work completed and billed, and so forth. But a simple change, such as a redesigned doorway, or one delay, such as an order of materials coming in late, can have a domino effect across dozens of other subcontractors. And, of course, someone had to monitor the project continually, make scheduling and delivery adjustments, and notify suppliers and subcontractors.

Slowly but surely, though, Internet technology is creeping into the construction industry. And as it does so, it's revolutionizing how contractors and subcontractors work and how they interact with one another.

It's also showing signs of enormous potential for lowering costs, shortening construction times, and improving overall efficiency. Indeed, big construction firms like the Turner Corporation and the Bechtel Group have started partnering with e-commerce companies to use web technology for communicating with suppliers and subcontractors.

Now, for example, a project's blueprints can all be provided online; each supplier and each subcontractor can review their part of the project, including scheduling details, on-line. E-mails can be sent to everyone affected, work schedules can be posted, and bid requests can be sent to potential suppliers, all with the push of a button or the click of a mouse. The advent of the newer

> *"Construction has always been a very fragmented industry because it's so local."*
>
> —Kent Allen, Boston e-commerce consultant

LEARNING OBJECTIVES

After studying this chapter, you should be able to:

- Identify the basic elements of organizations.

- Describe alternative approaches to designing jobs.

- Discuss the rationale and the most common bases for grouping jobs into departments.

- Describe the basic elements involved in establishing reporting relationships.

- Discuss how authority is distributed in organizations.

- Discuss the basic coordinating activities undertaken by organizations.

- Describe basic ways in which positions within an organization can be differentiated.

handheld computers like Palms is also accelerating this change because contractors, subcontractors, supervisors, and workers can more readily access information they need at—or even inside—the construction project.

Indeed, Cephren and Bidcom are at the forefront of applying web technology to construction projects. Cephren, for example, has created a software network that serves as a communication system for contractors and subcontractors on a project. Each part of the construction team receives passwords allowing them access to the part of the project relevant to them. For instance, a middle manager working at the construction site might need access to blueprints but not to the minutes of the senior management team's last meeting. Bidcom, meanwhile, deals more with linking contractors and suppliers. Using the Bidcom system, for example, a contractor can put out a call for bids on, say, one hundred steel doors or five hundred windows, with corresponding specifications and delivery details. Suppliers, meanwhile, can review the call and submit bids directly to the contractor. This overall improvement in efficiency can potentially save thousands of dollars on a big construction project.[1]

325

The construction industry has a long and well-established way of getting tasks done, and this system has served it well. But key organizations are boldly exploring new approaches to designing work, linking jobs, and coordinating activities. And these new approaches, in turn, are fundamentally changing the way jobs, businesses, and relationships between businesses are structured. As you will see in this chapter, managing the basic frameworks that organizations use to get their work done—structure—is a fundamental part of the management process.

This chapter discusses many of the critical elements of organization structure that managers can control and is the first of five devoted to organizing, the second basic managerial function identified in Chapter 1. In Part 3, we describe managerial planning—deciding what to do. Organizing, the subject of Part 4, focuses on how to do it. We first elaborate on the meaning of organization structure. Subsequent sections explore the basic elements that managers use to create an organization.

The Elements of Organizing

Imagine asking a child to build a castle with a set of building blocks. She selects a few small blocks and other larger ones. She uses some square ones, some round ones, and some triangular ones. When she finishes, she has her own castle, unlike any other. Another child, presented with the same task, constructs a different castle. He will select different blocks, for example, and combine them in different ways. The children's activities—choosing certain combinations of blocks and then putting them together in unique ways—are analogous to the manager's job of organizing.[2]

organizing Deciding how best to group organizational activities and resources

Organizing is deciding how best to group organizational activities and resources.[3] Just as children select different kinds of building blocks, managers can choose a variety of structural possibilities. And just as the children can assemble the blocks in any number of ways, so too can managers put the organization together in many different ways. Understanding the nature of these building blocks and the different ways in which they can be configured can have a powerful impact on a firm's competitiveness.[4] In this chapter, our focus is on the building blocks themselves—**organization structure**. In Chapter 12 we focus on how the blocks can be put together—organization design.

organization structure The set of elements that can be used to configure an organization

There are six basic building blocks that managers can use in constructing an organization: designing jobs, grouping jobs, establishing reporting relationships between jobs, distributing authority among jobs, coordinating activities between jobs, and differentiating between positions. The logical starting point is the first building block—designing jobs for people within the organization.

MANAGEMENT IMPLICATIONS Managers should understand the basic building blocks of organization structure and recognize that part of the organizing function is knowing how best to assemble these building blocks into an efficient overall structure for the firm.

Designing Jobs

The first building block of organization structure is job design. **Job design** is the determination of an individual's work-related responsibilities.[5] For a machinist at Caterpillar, job design might specify what machines are to be operated, how they are to be operated, and what performance standards are expected. For a manager at Caterpillar, job design might involve defining areas of decision-making responsibility, identifying goals and expectations, and establishing appropriate indicators of success. The natural starting point for designing jobs is determining the level of desired specialization.

job design The determination of an individual's work-related responsibilities

job specialization The degree to which the overall task of the organization is broken down and divided into smaller component parts

Job Specialization

Job specialization is the degree to which the overall task of the organization is broken down and divided into smaller component parts. Job specialization evolved from the concept of *division of labor*. Adam Smith, an eighteenth-century economist, described how a pin factory used division of labor to improve productivity.[6] One man drew the wire, another straightened it, a third cut it, a fourth ground the point, and so on. Smith claimed that ten men working in this fashion were able to produce forty-eight thousand pins in a day, whereas each man working alone could produce only twenty pins per day.

More recently, the best example of the impact of specialization is the automobile assembly line pioneered by Henry Ford and his contemporaries. Mass-production capabilities stemming from job specialization techniques have had a profound impact throughout the world. High levels of low-cost production transformed U.S. society during the last century into one of the strongest economies in the history of the world.[7]

Job specialization is a normal extension of organizational growth. For example, when Walt Disney started his company, he did everything himself—wrote cartoons, drew them, and then marketed them to theaters. As the business grew, he eventually hired others to perform many of these same functions. As growth continued, so too did specialization. For example, as animation artists work on Disney movies today, they may specialize in drawing only a single character. And today, The Walt Disney Company has thousands of different specialized jobs. Clearly, no one person could perform them all.

Designing jobs is a fundamental cornerstone of organizing. Most organizations today rely on a blend of job specialization and such alternatives to specialization as job enrichment and work teams. Take this Cessna factory in Independence, Kansas, for example. All of its assembly employees are expected to have a base specialization. But each is also expected to continuously learn new skills while simultaneously working as part of a team that has a lot to say about how its work gets done.

Benefits and Limitations of Specialization

Job specialization provides four benefits to organizations.[8] First, workers performing small, simple tasks will become very proficient at that task. Second, transfer time between tasks decreases. If employees perform several different tasks, some time is lost as they stop doing the first task and start doing the next. Third, the more narrowly defined a job is, the easier it is to develop specialized equipment to assist with that job. Fourth, when an employee who performs a highly specialized job is absent or resigns, the manager is able to train someone new at relatively low cost. Although specialization is generally thought of in terms of operating jobs, many organizations have extended the basic elements of specialization to managerial and professional levels as well.[9]

On the other hand, job specialization can have negative consequences. The foremost criticism is that workers who perform highly specialized jobs may become bored and dissatisfied. The job may be so specialized that it offers no challenge or stimulation. Boredom and monotony set in, absenteeism rises, and the quality of the work may suffer. Furthermore, the anticipated benefits of specialization do not always occur. For example, a study conducted at Maytag found that the time spent moving work-in-process from one worker to another was greater than the time needed for the same individual to change from job to job.[10] Thus, although some degree of specialization is necessary, it should not be carried to extremes because of the possible negative consequences. Managers must be sensitive to situations in which extreme specialization should be avoided. And indeed, several alternative approaches to designing jobs have been developed in recent years.

Alternatives to Specialization

To counter the problems associated with specialization, managers have sought other approaches to job design that achieve a better balance between organizational demands for efficiency and productivity and individual needs for creativity and autonomy. Five alternative approaches are job rotation, job enlargement, job enrichment, the job characteristics approach, and work teams.[11] In addition to these structural techniques, *Today's Management Issues* describes how firms such as Sempra Energy Information Solutions are using workplace design environments to achieve some of the same benefits.

job rotation An alternative to job specialization that involves systematically moving employees from one job to another

Job Rotation   **Job rotation** involves systematically moving employees from one job to another. A worker in a warehouse might unload trucks on Monday, carry incoming inventory to storage on Tuesday, verify invoices on Wednesday, pull outgoing inventory from storage on Thursday, and load trucks on Friday. Thus, the jobs do not change but, instead, workers move from job to job. Unfortunately, for this very reason, job rotation has not been very successful in enhancing employee motivation or satisfaction. Jobs that are amenable to rotation tend to be relatively standard and routine. Workers who are rotated to a "new" job may be more satisfied at first, but satisfaction soon wanes. Although many companies (among them American Cyanamid, Bethlehem Steel, Ford, Prudential Insurance, TRW, and West-

TODAY'S MANAGEMENT ISSUES

DESIGNING WORKPLACES FOR INDIVIDUAL WORK *AND* TEAMWORK

When Sempra Energy Information Solutions went looking for new office furniture, it rejected the stereotypical cubicles ridiculed by Dilbert and his comic-strip colleagues. Sempra wanted its workplace to reflect the company's innovative approach to helping corporate clients manage their energy costs. The goal was to give its employees some privacy and flexibility while allowing them to stay connected to each other. After months of searching, Sempra settled on a new office setup from Herman Miller.

Unlike cubicles, which are often seen as depersonalizing and isolating, Sempra's office furniture has humanizing touches such as built-in flower vases and slits between workstations to encourage spontaneous communication. The workstations can be arranged in a variety of cluster patterns so employees can work individually yet easily consult with nearby coworkers about problems and projects. Employees can raise or lower work tables and rearrange cabinets and other furniture to suit their own preferences. They can also personalize their work areas by adding photos, team logos, or other decorations to the fabric screens that separate the workstations.

When Sempra first installed the Herman Miller furniture, its employees were taken aback by the openness of the workstations, compared to the more closed-in appearance of their cubicles. On the other hand, by fitting one hundred workstations into an office that previously housed eighty cubicles, Sempra was able to carve out a handful of rooms for team meetings. Despite the open space, noise has not been a problem, and internal communication has been enhanced. In fact, some employees say that they are getting acquainted with coworkers they hardly knew before, which can only improve internal connections.

> *To create new value, companies today have to solve more and more complex problems. It takes people working together to arrive at solutions, and you can't wait for a meeting to make that happen.*
>
> —*Jim Long, lead researcher for Resolve products, Herman Miller**

Reference: Chuck Salter, "Designed to Work," *Fast Company,* April 2000, pp. 255–268 (*quote on p. 260).

---

ern Electric) have tried job rotation, it is most often used today as a training device to improve worker skills and flexibility.

Job Enlargement   On the assumption that doing the same basic task over and over is the primary cause of worker dissatisfaction, **job enlargement** was developed to increase the total number of tasks workers perform. As a result, all workers perform a wide variety of tasks, which presumably reduces the level of job dissatisfaction. Many organizations have used job enlargement, including IBM, Detroit Edison, AT&T, the U.S. Civil Service, and Maytag. At Maytag, for example, the assembly line for producing washing-machine water pumps was systematically changed so that work that had originally been performed by six workers, who passed the work sequentially from one person to another, was performed by four workers, each of whom assembled a complete pump.[12] Unfortunately, although job enlargement does have some positive consequences, they are often offset by several disadvantages: (1) training costs usually rise, (2) unions have argued that pay should increase because the worker is doing more tasks, and (3) in many cases the work remains boring and routine even after job enlargement.

job enlargement An alternative to job specialization that involves increasing the total number of tasks workers perform

job enrichment An alternative to job specialization that involves increasing both the number of tasks the worker does and the control the worker has over the job

Job Enrichment   A more comprehensive approach, **job enrichment**, assumes that increasing the range and variety of tasks is not sufficient by itself to improve employee motivation.[13] Thus, job enrichment attempts to increase both the number of tasks a worker does and the control the worker has over the job. To implement job enrichment, managers remove some controls from the job, delegate more authority to employees, and structure the work in complete, natural units. These changes increase subordinates' sense of responsibility. Another part of job enrichment is to assign new and challenging tasks continually, thereby increasing employees' opportunity for growth and advancement.

AT&T was one of the first companies to try job enrichment. In one experiment, eight typists in a service unit prepared customer service orders. Faced with low output and high turnover, management determined that the typists felt little responsibility to clients and received little feedback. The unit was changed to create a typing team. Typists were matched with designated service representatives, the task was changed from ten specific steps to three more general steps, and job titles were upgraded. As a result, the frequency of order processing increased from 27 to 90 percent, the need for messenger service was eliminated, accuracy improved, and turnover became practically nil.[14] Other organizations that have tried job enrichment include Texas Instruments, IBM, and General Foods. This approach, however, also has disadvantages. For example, work systems should be analyzed before enrichment but this analysis seldom happens, and managers rarely ask for employee preferences when enriching jobs.

job characteristics approach An alternative to job specialization that suggests that jobs should be diagnosed and improved along five core dimensions, taking into account both the work system and employee preferences

Job Characteristics Approach   The **job characteristics approach** is an alternative to job specialization that does take into account the work system and employee preferences.[15] As illustrated in Figure 11.1, the job characteristics approach suggests that jobs should be diagnosed and improved along five core dimensions:

1. *Skill variety:* the number of tasks a person does in a job
2. *Task identity:* the extent to which the worker does a complete or identifiable portion of the total job
3. *Task significance:* the perceived importance of the task
4. *Autonomy:* the degree of control the worker has over how the work is performed
5. *Feedback:* the extent to which the worker knows how well the job is being performed

The higher a job rates on those dimensions, the more employees will experience various psychological states. Experiencing these states, in turn, presumably leads to high motivation, high-quality performance, high satisfaction, and low absenteeism and turnover. Finally, a variable called *growth-need strength* is presumed to affect how the model works for different people. People with a strong desire to grow, develop, and expand their capabilities (indicative of high growth-need strength) are expected to respond strongly to the presence or absence of the basic job characteristics; individuals with low growth-need strength are expected not to respond as strongly or consistently.

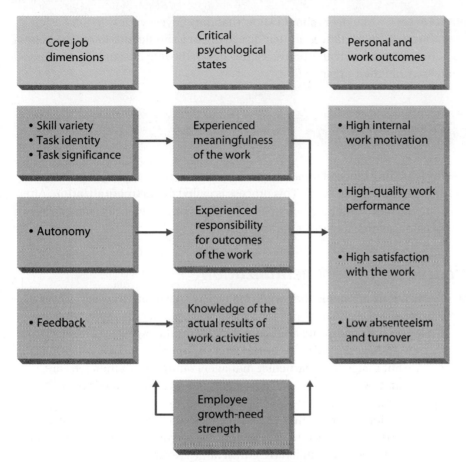

Source: J. R. Hackman and G. R. Oldham, "Motivation Through the Design of Work: Test of a Theory," *Organizational Behavior and Human Performance*, Vol. 16 (1976), pp. 250–279. Copyright © Academic Press, Inc. Reprinted by permission of Academic Press and the authors.

Figure 11.1

The Job Characteristics Approach
The job characteristics approach to job design provides a viable alternative to job specialization. Five core job dimensions may lead to critical psychological states that, in turn, may enhance motivation, performance, and satisfaction while also reducing absenteeism and turnover.

A large number of studies have been conducted to test the usefulness of the job characteristics approach. The Southwestern Division of Prudential Insurance, for example, used this approach in its claims division. Results included moderate declines in turnover and a small but measurable improvement in work quality. Other research findings have not supported this approach as strongly. Thus, although the job characteristics approach is one of the most promising alternatives to job specialization, it is probably not the final answer.

Work Teams   Another alternative to job specialization is **work teams**. Under this arrangement, a group is given responsibility for designing the work system to be used in performing an interrelated set of jobs. In the typical assembly-line system, the work flows from one worker to the next, and each worker has a specified job to perform. In a work team, however, the group itself decides how jobs will be allocated. For example, the work team assigns specific tasks to members, monitors and controls its own performance, and has autonomy over work scheduling.[16] We discuss work teams more fully in Chapter 19.

work team An alternative to job specialization that allows an entire group to design the work system it will use to perform an interrelated set of tasks

MANAGEMENT   Managers should know that they have a variety of job design
IMPLICATIONS   alternatives at their disposal. They should also know the benefits and limitations of each alternative as they decide how to design jobs most appropriately within their organization.

Grouping Jobs: Departmentalization

departmentalization The process
of grouping jobs according to
some logical arrangement

The second building block of organization structure is the grouping of jobs according to some logical arrangement. This process is called **departmentalization**. After
establishing the basic rationale for departmentalization, we identify some common bases along which departments are created.[17]

Rationale for Departmentalization

When organizations are small, the owner-manager can personally oversee everyone who works there. As an organization grows, however, personally supervising
all the employees becomes more and more difficult for the owner-manager. Consequently, new managerial positions are created to supervise the work of others.
Employees are not assigned to particular managers randomly. Rather, jobs are
grouped according to some plan. The logic embodied in such a plan is the basis
for all departmentalization.[18]

Lucent Technologies, the world's largest telephone equipment maker, recently
created four new departments intended to improve its competitiveness. These departments represent activities that have grown large enough within the existing
departmental arrangements that they now warrant separate units. One department will focus on optical networking, one will focus on wireless communication,
one will be responsible for semiconductor operations, and one will handle Lucent's e-business initiatives. The firm's managers believe that these new departments will sharpen the company's focus on these four high-growth areas.[19]

Common Bases for Departmentalization

Figure 11.2 presents a partial organizational chart for Apex Computers, a hypothetical firm that manufactures and sells computers and software. The chart shows
that Apex uses each of the four most common bases for departmentalization:
function, product, customer, and location.

functional departmentalization
Grouping jobs involving the same
or similar activities

Functional Departmentalization   The most common base for departmentalization, especially among smaller organizations, is by function. **Functional departmentalization** groups together those jobs involving the same or similar activities.
(The word *function* is used here to mean organizational functions such as finance
and production rather than the basic managerial functions such as planning or
controlling.) The computer department at Apex has manufacturing, finance, and
marketing departments.

Figure 11.2

Bases for Departmentalization: Apex Computers

Organizations group jobs into departments. Apex—a hypothetical organization—uses all four of the primary bases of departmentalization—function, product, customer, and location. Like Apex, most large organizations use more than one type of departmentalization.

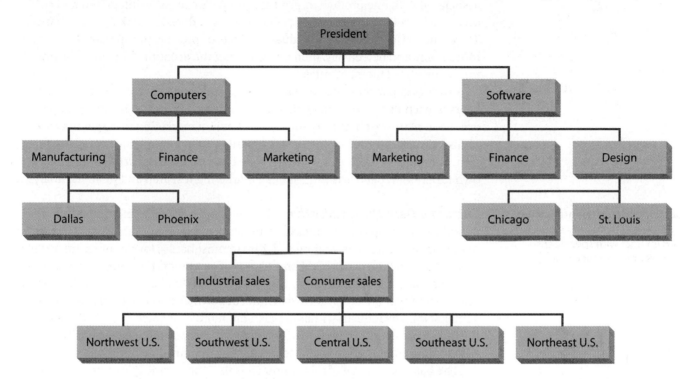

This approach, which is most common in smaller organizations, has three primary advantages. First, each department can be staffed by experts in that functional area. Marketing experts can be hired to run the marketing function, for example. Second, supervision is also facilitated because an individual manager needs to be familiar with only a relatively narrow set of skills. And third, coordinating activities inside each department is easier.

On the other hand, as an organization begins to grow in size, several disadvantages of this approach may emerge. For one, decision making tends to become slower and more bureaucratic. Employees may also begin to concentrate too narrowly on their own units and lose sight of the total organizational system. Finally, accountability and performance become increasingly difficult to monitor. For example, determining whether a new product fails because of production deficiencies or a poor marketing campaign may not be possible.

Product Departmentalization **Product departmentalization**, a second common approach, involves grouping activities around products or product groups. Apex Computers has two product-based departments at the highest level of the firm. One is responsible for all activities associated with Apex's personal computer

product departmentalization
Grouping activities around products or product groups

business, and the other handles the software business. Most larger businesses adopt this form of departmentalization for grouping activities at the business or corporate level.

Product departmentalization has three major advantages. First, all activities associated with one product or product group can be easily integrated and co-ordinated. Second, the speed and effectiveness of decision making are enhanced. Third, the performance of individual products or product groups can be assessed more easily and objectively, thereby improving the accountability of departments for the results of their activities.

Product departmentalization also has two major disadvantages. For one, managers in each department may focus on their own product or product group to the exclusion of the rest of the organization. That is, a marketing manager may see her or his primary duty as helping the group rather than helping the overall organization. For another, administrative costs rise because each department must have its own functional specialists for tasks like marketing research and financial analysis.

customer departmentalization
Grouping activities to respond to and interact with specific customers or customer groups

Customer Departmentalization   Under **customer departmentalization**, the organization groups its activities to respond to and interact with specific customers or customer groups. The lending activities in most banks, for example, are usually tailored to meet the needs of different kinds of customers (i.e., business, consumer, mortgage, and agricultural loans). Figure 11.2 shows that the marketing branch of Apex's computer business has two distinct departments—industrial sales and consumer sales. The industrial sales department handles marketing activities aimed at business customers, whereas the consumer sales department is responsible for wholesaling computers to retail stores catering to individual purchasers.

The basic advantage of this approach is that the organization can use skilled specialists to deal with unique customers or customer groups. It takes one set of skills to evaluate a balance sheet and lend a business $50,000 for operating capital and a different set of skills to evaluate an individual's creditworthiness and lend $10,000 for a new car. However, a fairly large administrative staff is required to integrate the activities of the various departments. In banks, for example, coordination is necessary to make sure that the organization does not overcommit itself in any one area and to handle collections on delinquent accounts from a diverse set of customers.

location departmentalization
Grouping jobs on the basis of defined geographic sites or areas

Location Departmentalization   **Location departmentalization** groups jobs on the basis of defined geographic sites or areas. The defined sites or areas may range in size from a hemisphere to only a few blocks of a large city. The manufacturing branch of Apex's computer business has two plants—one in Dallas and another in Phoenix. Similarly, the design division of its software design unit has two labs—one in Chicago and the other in St. Louis. Apex's consumer sales group has five sales territories corresponding to different regions of the United States. Transportation companies, police departments (precincts represent geographic areas of a city), and the Federal Reserve Bank all use location departmentalization.

The primary advantage of location departmentalization is that it enables the organization to respond easily to unique customer and environmental characteristics in the various regions. On the negative side, a larger administrative staff may be required if the organization must keep track of units in scattered locations.

Other Forms of Departmentalization   Although most organizations are departmentalized by function, product, location, or customer, other forms are occasionally used. Some organizations group certain activities by time. One of the machine shops of Baker Hughes in Houston, for example, operates on three shifts. Each shift has a superintendent who reports to the plant manager, and each shift has its own functional departments. Time is thus the framework for many organizational activities. Other organizations that use time as a basis for grouping jobs include some hospitals and many airlines. In other situations, departmentalization by sequence is appropriate. Many college students, for instance, must register in sequence: seniors on Monday, juniors on Tuesday, and so on. Other areas that may be organized in sequence include credit departments (specific employees run credit checks according to customer name) and insurance claims divisions (by policy number).

Other Considerations   Two final points about job grouping remain to be made. First, departments are often called something entirely different—divisions, units, sections, and bureaus are all common synonyms. The higher we look in an organization, the more likely we are to find departments referred to as divisions. H.J. Heinz, for example, is organized into five major divisions. Nevertheless, the underlying logic behind all the labels is the same: they represent groups of jobs that have been yoked together according to some unifying principle. Second, almost any organization is likely to employ multiple bases of departmentalization, depending on level. Although Apex Computer is a hypothetical firm we created to explain departmentalization, it is quite similar to many real organizations because it uses a variety of bases of departmentalization for different levels and different sets of activities.

MANAGEMENT   Managers need to understand thoroughly the strengths and
IMPLICATIONS   weaknesses of each common method or approach to departmentalization. This understanding will enable them to select the best approach to departmentalization for their own unique circumstances.

■ *Establishing Reporting Relationships*

The third basic element of organizing is the establishment of reporting relationships among positions. Suppose, for example, that the owner-manager of a small business has just hired two new employees, one to handle marketing and one to handle production. Will the marketing manager report to the production manager? Will the production manager report to the marketing manager? Or will each report directly to the owner-manager? These questions reflect the basic issues involved in establishing reporting relationships: clarifying the chain of command and the span of management.

chain of command Clear and distinct lines of authority among all positions in an organization

Chain of Command

Chain of command is an old concept, first popularized in the early years of the twentieth century. For example, early writers about the **chain of command** argued that clear and distinct lines of authority need to be established among all positions in the organization. The chain of command actually has two components. The first, called *unity of command*, suggests that each person within an organization must have a clear reporting relationship to one and only one boss (as we see in this chapter, newer models of organization design successfully violate this premise). The second, called the *scalar principle*, suggests that there must be a clear and unbroken line of authority that extends from the lowest to the highest position in the organization. The popular saying "The buck stops here" is derived from this idea—someone in the organization must ultimately be responsible for every decision. *Working with Diversity* introduces a novel twist on diversity—family and nonfamily management at J. Crew—in the chain of command.

Clear and precise reporting relationships are important in organizations. Police officers need formally defined reporting relationships so that they know who is in charge during a hostage crisis, a burglary investigation, or a drug bust.

span of management The number of people who report to each manager

Narrow Versus Wide Spans

Another part of establishing reporting relationships is determining how many people will report to each manager, which defines the **span of management** (sometimes called the *span of control*). For years managers and researchers sought to determine the optimal span of management. For example, should it be relatively narrow (with few subordinates per manager) or relatively wide (with many subordinates)? One early writer, A. V. Graicunas, went so far as to quantify span of management issues.[20] Graicunas noted that a manager must deal with three kinds of interactions with and among subordinates: direct (the manager's one-to-one relationship with each subordinate), cross (among the subordinates themselves), and group (between groups of subordinates). The number of possible interactions of all types between a manager and subordinates can be determined by the following formula:

$$I = N(2^N/2 + N - 1)$$

where I is the total number of interactions with and among subordinates and N is the number of subordinates.

If a manager has only two subordinates, six potential interactions exist. If the number of subordinates increases to three, the possible interactions total eigh-

MIXING FAMILY AND NONFAMILY MANAGEMENT

Apparel retailing became the family business when Arthur Cinader and his daughter, Emily Woods, co-founded J. Crew in 1983. J. Crew sells stylish casual clothing—such as chino pants—for men and women through catalogs, retail stores, and the Internet. Over the years, the increasing popularity of casual wear for everyday and work occasions allowed the company to expand through new ventures such as Clifford & Wills and Popular Club Plan.

As the 1990s progressed, however, J. Crew faced more intense competition from Gap, Banana Republic, Abercrombie & Fitch, and other casual-clothing chains. Sales were going up but financial pressures were also increasing. With catalog costs rising, the company wanted to switch more customers to its web site and enlarge its chain of retail stores. In 1998, family ownership gave way to a mixture of family, management, and outside ownership through a leveraged buyout arrangement. Texas Pacific Group, an investment firm, became majority owner, while co-founder Woods retained about 20 percent ownership, and a group of J. Crew managers held about 10 percent ownership.

After operating at a loss in 1998, J. Crew sold off Popular Club Plan and closed Clifford & Wills. These changes helped the company reduce its 1999 losses to $6.6 million on sales of $716 million as part of a turnaround strategy. Woods, serving as chairperson, was still juggling apparel design and other top-management responsibilities, such as supervising a new television advertising campaign. Below her, however, the CEO position was in transition. One nonfamily CEO left after only a year. Again reaching outside for a CEO, the company brought in Mark Sarvary, formerly head of Nestlé's frozen foods division, to supervise the firm's finance and operations functions. Within months, Savary was also given control of the design, merchandising, and marketing functions. This change freed Woods to concentrate on building the J. Crew brand—essential to the retail and Internet growth strategy—without the distractions of watching over day-to-day business details.

> *This allows me to focus on near- and long-term strategy and brand development.*
>
> *—Emily Woods, chairperson of J. Crew**

References: Thomas J. Ryan, "J. Crew and Old Navy Measure Success By the Square Foot," *Women's Wear Daily,* June 8, 2000, p.1; Rebecca Quick, "J. Crew CEO Sarvary Broadens Control As Chairman Curbs Day-to-Day Role," *Wall Street Journal,* February 1, 2000, p. B7 (*quote on p. B7); Anne D'Innocenzio, "Megabrands Keep a Firm Grip on the Top 10," *Women's Wear Daily,* January 24, 2000, p. 82S; Thomas J. Ryan, "J. Crew Group Narrows Losses to $6.6 M in Year," *Daily News Record,* April 26, 2000, p. 10.

teen. With five subordinates there are one hundred possible interactions. Although Graicunas offers no prescription for what *N* should be, his ideas demonstrate how complex the relationships become when more subordinates are added. The important point is that each additional subordinate adds more complexity than the previous one did. Going from nine to ten subordinates is very different than going from three to four.

Another early writer, Ralph C. Davis, described two kinds of spans: an operative span for lower-level managers and an executive span for middle and top managers. He argued that operative spans could approach thirty subordinates, whereas executive spans should be limited to between three and nine (depending on the nature of the managers' jobs, the growth rate of the company, and similar factors). Lyndall F. Urwick suggested that an executive span should never exceed six subordinates, and General Ian Hamilton reached the same conclusion.[21] Today we recognize that the span of management is a crucial factor in structuring organizations

Dilbert by Scott Adams © 1997 United Feature Syndicate, Inc.

Distributing authority is a key building block in creating an effective organization. Unfortunately, some managers prefer to avoid accountability for decisions and work to ensure that someone else can always be held responsible for mistakes and errors. This Dilbert cartoon, for instance, illustrates a whimsical view of a manager teaching others how to avoid accountability and pass the buck on to others.

but that there are no universal, cut-and-dried prescriptions for an ideal or optimal span.[22] Later we summarize some important variables that influence the appropriate span of management in a particular situation. First, however, we describe how the span of management affects the overall structure of an organization.

Tall Versus Flat Organizations

Imagine an organization with thirty-one managers and a narrow span of management. As shown in Figure 11.3, the result is a relatively tall organization with five layers of management. With a somewhat wider span of control, however, the flat organization shown in Figure 11.3 emerges. This configuration has only three layers of management.

What difference does it make whether the organization is tall or flat? One early study at Sears Roebuck and Co. found that a flat structure led to higher levels of employee morale and productivity.[23] Researchers have also argued that a tall structure is more expensive (because of the larger number of managers involved) and that it fosters more communication problems (because of the increased number of people through whom information must pass). On the other hand, a wide span of management in a flat organization may result in a manager's having more administrative responsibility (because there are fewer managers) and more supervisory responsibility (because there are more subordinates reporting to each manager). If these additional responsibilities become excessive, the flat organization may suffer.[24]

Many experts agree that businesses can function effectively with fewer layers of organization than they currently have. The Franklin Mint, for example, reduced its number of management layers from six to four. At the same time, CEO Stewart Resnick increased his span of management from six to twelve. In similar fashion, IBM has eliminated several layers of management. One additional reason for this trend is that improved organizational communication networks allow managers to stay in touch with a larger number of subordinates than was possible even just a few years ago.[25]

Figure 11.3

Tall Versus Flat Organizations

Wide spans of management result in flat organizations, which may lead to improved employee morale and productivity as well as increased managerial responsibility. Many organizations today, including IBM and General Electric, are moving toward flat structures to improve communication and flexibility.

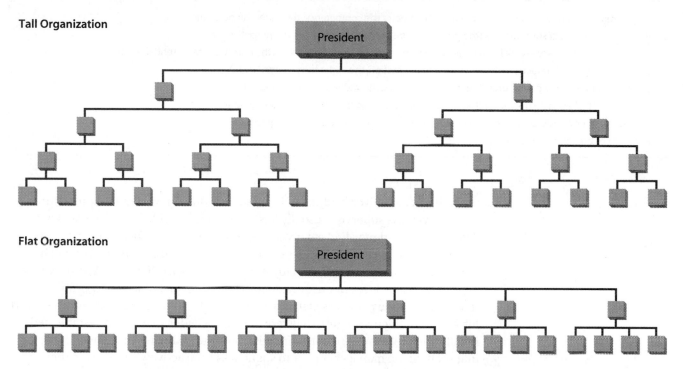

Determining the Appropriate Span

Of course, the initial question remains: How do managers determine the appropriate span for their unique situations? Although no perfect formula exists, researchers have identified a set of factors that influence the span for a particular circumstance.[26] Some of these factors are listed in Table 11.1. For example, if the manager and subordinates are competent and well trained, a wide span may be effective. Physical dispersion is also important. The more widely subordinates are scattered, the narrower the span should be. On the other hand, if all the subordinates are in one location, the span can be somewhat wider. The amount of nonsupervisory work expected of the manager is also important. Some managers, especially at the lower levels of an organization, spend most or all of their time supervising subordinates. Other managers spend a lot of time doing paperwork, planning, and engaging in other managerial activities. Thus, these managers may need a narrower span.

Some job situations also require a great deal of interaction between supervisor and subordinates. In general, the more interaction that is required, the narrower the span should be. Similarly, if there is a fairly comprehensive set of standard

Table 11.1

Factors Influencing the Span of Management
Although researchers have found advantages to the flat organization (less expensive, fewer communication problems than a tall organization, for example), a number of factors may favor a tall organization.

1. Competence of supervisor and subordinates (the greater the competence, the wider the potential span)
2. Physical dispersion of subordinates (the greater the dispersion, the narrower the potential span)
3. Extent of nonsupervisory work in manager's job (the more nonsupervisory work, the narrower the potential span)
4. Degree of required interaction (the less required interaction, the wider the potential span)
5. Extent of standardized procedures (the more procedures, the wider the potential span)
6. Similarity of tasks being supervised (the more similar the tasks, the wider the potential span)
7. Frequency of new problems (the higher the frequency, the narrower the potential span)
8. Preferences of supervisors and subordinates

procedures, a relatively wide span is possible. If only a few standard procedures exist, however, the supervisor usually has to play a larger role in overseeing day-to-day activities and may find a narrower span more efficient. Task similarity is also important. If most of the jobs being supervised are similar, a supervisor can handle a wider span. When each employee is performing a different task, more of the supervisor's time is spent on individual supervision. Likewise, if new problems that require supervisory assistance arise frequently, a narrower span may be called for. If new problems are relatively rare, though, a wider span can be established. Finally, the preferences of both supervisor and subordinates may affect the optimal span. Some managers prefer to spend less time actively supervising their employees, and many employees prefer to be more self-directed in their jobs. A wider span may be possible in these situations.

For example, the Case Corporation factory in Racine, Wisconsin, makes farm tractors exclusively to order in five to six weeks. Farmers can select from among a wide array of options, including engines, tires, power train, and even a CD player. A wide assortment of machines and processes are used to construct each tractor. Workers are highly skilled operators of their particular machines, and each machine is different. In this kind of setup, the complexities of each machine and the advanced skills needed by each operator mean that one supervisor can oversee only a small number of employees.[27]

In some organizational settings, other factors may influence the optimal span of management. The relative importance of each factor also varies in different settings. It is unlikely that all eight factors will suggest the same span; some may suggest a wider span, and others may indicate a need for a narrow span. Hence, managers must assess the relative weight of each factor or set of factors when deciding what the optimal span of management is for their unique situation.

MANAGEMENT IMPLICATIONS Managers should understand the various circumstances that affect the appropriate span of management. They should also be aware of how the span of management specifically results in a relatively taller or flatter organization, as well as the implications of these effects.

Distributing Authority

Another important building block in structuring organizations is the determination of how authority is to be distributed among positions. **Authority** is power that has been legitimized by the organization.[28] Distributing authority is another normal outgrowth of increasing organizational size. For example, when an owner-manager hires a sales representative to market his products, he needs to give the new employee appropriate authority to make decisions about delivery dates, discounts, and so forth. If every decision requires the approval of the owner-manager, he is no better off than he was before he hired the sales representative. The power given to the sales representative to make certain kinds of decisions, then, represents the establishment of a pattern of authority—the sales representative can make some decisions alone and others in consultation with coworkers, and the sales representative must defer some decisions to the boss. Two specific issues that managers must address when distributing authority are delegation and decentralization.[29]

authority Power that has been legitimized by the organization

The Delegation Process

Delegation is the establishment of a pattern of authority between a superior and one or more subordinates. Specifically, **delegation** is the process by which managers assign a portion of their total workload to others.[30]

delegation The process by which managers assign a portion of their total workload to others

Reasons for Delegation The primary reason for delegation is to enable the manager to get more work done. Subordinates help ease the manager's burden by doing major portions of the organization's work. In some instances, a subordinate may have more expertise in addressing a particular problem than the manager does. For example, the subordinate may have had special training in developing

Distributing authority in an organization begins with delegation. At Yahoo!, the big Internet portal, extreme delegation is a fundamental management philosophy. When the firm hired Isabelle Bordry (left) and Clothilde de Mersan to launch and run Yahoo France, U.S. managers were initially concerned about their ability to transfer its management style to the notoriously centralized and rigid French economy. But Bordry and de Mersan have enthusiastically embraced the notion of delegation and are aggressively working to encourage their employees to make their own decisions.

Figure 11.4

Steps in the Delegation Process

Good communication skills can help a manager successfully delegate responsibility to subordinates. A manager must not be reluctant to delegate, nor must he or she fear that the subordinate will do the job so well that the manager's advancement is threatened.

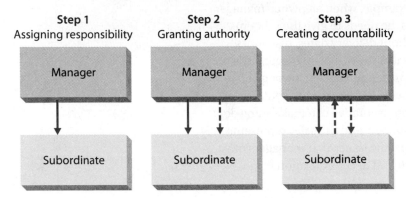

information systems or may be more familiar with a particular product line or geographic area. Delegation also helps develop subordinates. By participating in decision making and problem solving, subordinates learn about overall operations and improve their managerial skills.

Parts of the Delegation Process   In theory, as shown in Figure 11.4, the delegation process involves three steps. First, the manager assigns responsibility, or gives the subordinate a job to do. The assignment of responsibility might range from telling a subordinate to prepare a report to placing the person in charge of a task force. Along with the assignment, the individual is also given the authority to do the job. The manager may give the subordinate the power to requisition needed information from confidential files or to direct a group of other workers. Finally, the manager establishes the subordinate's accountability—that is, the subordinate accepts an obligation to carry out the task assigned by the manager.

These three steps do not occur mechanically, however. Indeed, when a manager and a subordinate have developed a good working relationship, the major parts of the process may be implied rather than stated. The manager may simply mention that a particular job must be done. A perceptive subordinate may realize that the manager is actually assigning the job to her. From past experience with the boss, she may also know, without being told, that she has the necessary authority to do the job and that she is accountable to the boss for finishing the job as "agreed."

Problems in Delegation   Unfortunately, problems often arise in the delegation process. For example, a manager may be reluctant to delegate. Some managers are so disorganized that they are unable to plan work in advance and, as a result, cannot delegate appropriately. Similarly, some managers may worry that subordinates will do too well and pose a threat to their own advancement. And finally, managers may not trust the subordinate to do the job well. Similarly, some subordinates are reluctant to accept delegation. They may be afraid that failure will result in a reprimand. They may also perceive that there are no rewards for accepting additional responsibility. Or they may simply prefer to avoid risk and, therefore, want their boss to take all responsibility.

Norm Brodsky, a small-business owner who built six successful companies, learned firsthand what happens when the CEO cannot effectively delegate. It took Brodsky seven years to build a messenger service into a $120 million operation—and just fourteen months to go from $120 million into bankruptcy. "Where did I go wrong?" he asks rhetorically and provides his own answer: "The company needed management, stability, and structure, and I kept it from getting them. I was so desperate to sustain the head rush of start-up chaos that I made all the final decisions and didn't let the managers do their jobs. In the end I paid a steep price."[31]

There are no quick fixes for these problems. The basic issue is communication. Subordinates must understand their own responsibility, authority, and accountability, and the manager must come to recognize the value of effective delegation. With the passage of time, subordinates should develop their skills and abilities to the point where they can make substantial contributions to the organization. At the same time, managers should recognize that a subordinate's satisfactory performance is not a threat to their own career but an accomplishment by both the subordinate who did the job and the manager who trained the subordinate and was astute enough to entrust the subordinate with the project. Ultimate responsibility for the outcome, however, continues to reside with the manager.

Decentralization and Centralization

Just as authority can be delegated from one individual to another, organizations also develop patterns of authority across a wide variety of positions and departments. **Decentralization** is the process of systematically delegating power and authority throughout the organization to middle and lower-level managers. It is important to remember that decentralization is actually one end of a continuum anchored at the other end by **centralization**, the process of systematically retaining power and authority in the hands of higher-level managers. Hence, a decentralized organization is one in which decision-making power and authority are delegated as far down the chain of command as possible. Conversely, in a centralized organization, decision-making power and authority are retained at the higher levels of management. When H. Ross Perot ran EDS he practiced centralization; his successors have used decentralization. No organization is ever completely decentralized or completely centralized: some firms position themselves toward one end of the continuum, and some lean the other way.[32]

What factors determine an organization's position on the decentralization-centralization continuum? One common determinant is the organization's external environment. Usually, the greater the complexity and uncertainty of the environment, the greater is the tendency to decentralize. Another crucial factor is the history of the organization. Firms have a tendency to do what they have done in the past, so there is likely to be some relationship between what an organization did in its early history and what it chooses to do today in terms of centralization or decentralization. The nature of the decisions being made is also considered. The costlier and riskier the decision, the more pressure there is to centralize. Organizations also consider the abilities of lower-level managers. If lower-level managers do not have the ability to make high-quality decisions, there is likely to be a high level of centralization. If lower-level managers are well qualified, top management can take advantage of their talents by decentralizing; in fact, if top management doesn't, talented lower-level managers may leave the organization.[33]

decentralization The process of systematically delegating power and authority throughout the organization to middle and lower-level managers

centralization The process of systematically retaining power and authority in the hands of higher-level managers

A manager has no clear-cut guidelines for determining whether to centralize or decentralize. Many successful organizations such as Sears and General Electric are quite decentralized. Equally successful firms such as McDonald's and Wal-Mart have remained centralized. IBM has recently undergone a transformation from using a highly centralized approach to a much more decentralized approach to managing its operations. A great deal of decision-making authority was passed from the hands of a select group of top executives down to six product and marketing groups. The reason for the move was to speed the company's ability to make decisions, introduce new products, and respond to customers. For years, most Japanese firms have been highly centralized. Recently, though, many leading Japanese firms have moved toward decentralization.

MANAGEMENT IMPLICATIONS All managers should know the steps in the delegation process. In addition, they should also be aware of problems that can occur as a result of ineffective delegation. Finally, they should also know how the distribution of authority results in centralization or decentralization and the factors that affect each.

Coordinating Activities

A fifth major element of organizing is coordination. As we discussed earlier, job specialization and departmentalization involve breaking jobs down into small units and then combining those jobs into departments. Once this organization has been accomplished, the activities of the departments must be linked—systems must be put into place to keep the activities of each department focused on the attainment of organizational goals. This focus is accomplished by **coordination**—the process of linking the activities of the various departments of the organization.[34]

coordination The process of linking the activities of the various departments of the organization

The Need for Coordination

The primary reason for coordination is that departments and work groups are interdependent—they depend on each other for information and resources to perform their respective activities. The greater the interdependence between departments, the more coordination the organization requires if departments are to be able to perform effectively. There are three major forms of interdependence: pooled, sequential, and reciprocal.[35]

pooled interdependence When units operate with little interaction; their output is simply pooled at the organizational level

Pooled interdependence represents the lowest level of interdependence. Units with pooled interdependence operate with little interaction—the output of the units is pooled at the organizational level. The Gap clothing stores operate with pooled interdependence. Each store is considered a department by the parent corporation. Each has its own operating budget, staff, and so forth. The profits or losses from each store are "added together" at the organizational level. The stores are interdependent to the extent that the final success or failure of one store affects the others, but they do not generally interact on a day-to-day basis.

In **sequential interdependence**, the output of one unit becomes the input for another in a sequential fashion. This arrangement creates a moderate level of interdependence. At Nissan, for example, one plant assembles engines and then ships them to a final assembly site at another plant where the cars are completed. The plants are interdependent because the final assembly plant must have the engines from engine assembly before it can perform its primary function of producing finished automobiles. But the level of interdependence is generally one-way—the engine plant is not necessarily dependent on the final assembly plant.

Reciprocal interdependence exists when activities flow both ways between units. This form is clearly the most complex. Within a Marriott Hotel, for example, the reservations department, front-desk check-in, and housekeeping are all reciprocally interdependent. The reservations department has to provide front-desk employees with information about how many guests to expect each day, and housekeeping needs to know which rooms require priority cleaning. If any of the three units does not do its job properly, the others will all be affected.

sequential interdependence
When the output of one unit becomes the input of another in a sequential fashion

reciprocal interdependence
When activities flow both ways between units

Structural Coordination Techniques

Because of the obvious coordination requirements that characterize most organizations, many techniques for achieving coordination have been developed. Some of the most useful devices for maintaining coordination among interdependent units are the managerial hierarchy, rules and procedures, liaison roles, task forces, and integrating departments.[36] *Managing in an E-business World* illustrates how the international publishing giant Bertlesmann uses structural coordination techniques.

The Managerial Hierarchy   Organizations that use the hierarchy to achieve coordination place one manager in charge of interdependent departments or units. In Kmart distribution centers, major activities include receiving and unloading bulk shipments from railroad cars and loading other shipments onto trucks for distribution to retail outlets. The two groups (receiving and shipping) are interdependent because they share the loading docks and some equipment. To ensure coordination and to minimize conflict, one manager is in charge of the whole operation.

Rules and Procedures   Routine coordination activities can be handled via rules and standard procedures. In the Kmart distribution center, an outgoing truck shipment has priority over an incoming rail shipment. Thus, when trucks are to be loaded, the shipping unit is given access to all of the center's auxiliary forklifts. This priority is specifically stated in a rule. But as useful as rules and procedures often are in routine situations, they are not particularly effective when coordination problems are complex or unusual.

Liaison Roles   We introduced the liaison role of management in Chapter 1. As a device for coordination, a manager in a liaison role coordinates interdependent units by acting as a common point of contact. This individual may not have any

MANAGING IN AN *e*-BUSINESS WORLD

BERTELSMANN ORGANIZES FOR GLOBAL E-COMMERCE

Germany's Bertelsmann AG is the largest book publisher and second largest music distributor in the world, as well as the European leader in television and magazines. Now the company is using its vast content empire to launch an aggressive expansion into cyberspace. Bertelsmann's CEO, Thomas Middelhoff, got an early start in e-commerce by buying a stake in America Online and arranging to deliver content through an AOL partnership. He tried to negotiate a merger with AOL, but Steve Case, AOL's CEO, chose rival media group Time Warner for his merger partner. So Middelhoff retained the content partnership but divested his holdings in AOL Europe and AOL Australia to rethink the company's on-line activities.

After evaluating Bertelsmann's existing Internet businesses, Middelhoff decided that the company's future should be linked to on-line sales of media content rather than Internet access. As a result of this decision, he sold off Bertelsmann's Internet service provider units and pursued an alliance to participate in a European portal for wireless Internet users. Next, he created a new division, the Bertelsmann E-Commerce Group, as an umbrella for five Internet-related units. These include the e-commerce unit, covering the company's stake in on-line book-retailer barnesandnoble.com and bol.com, its European counterpart; the m-commerce unit, covering wireless web and communications activities; the b-commerce unit, covering broadband and other television activities; BECG Ventures, providing venture capital to new technologies; and the strategic alliances unit, covering partnerships with AOL and other Internet companies.

Finally, Middelhoff addressed the critical management issue of coordination. Traditionally, Bertelsmann's divisions had been given a great deal of independence to encourage initiative and innovation. Realizing that Bertelsmann's plans for on-line growth required closer coordination, he created the new position of chief creative officer, charged with identifying internal opportunities for synergy among the diverse global businesses.

> *In Internet time, three months is a year. Make a bad decision or two and you are in trouble. That makes me worried.*
>
> —*Thomas Middelhoff, CEO of Bertelsmann**

References: "Bertelsmann Creates Global E-Commerce Group," *Publishers Weekly*, June 19, 2000, p. 17; "Bertelsmann: Under E-Construction," *The Economist*, June 10, 2000, pp. 69–73 (*quote on p. 70); Deborah Cole, "Powerhouse Cyber Services Make 'Net Gain," *Variety*, May 29, 2000, p. 50.

---

formal authority over the groups but instead simply facilitates the flow of information between units. Two engineering groups working on component systems for a large project might interact through a liaison. The liaison maintains familiarity with each group as well as with the overall project. She can answer questions and otherwise serve to integrate the activities of all the groups.

Task Forces   A task force may be created when the need for coordination is acute. When interdependence is complex and several units are involved, a single liaison person may not be sufficient. Instead, a task force might be assembled by drawing one representative from each group. The coordination function is thus spread across several individuals, each of whom has special information about one of the groups involved. When the project is completed, task force members return to their original positions. For example, a college overhauling its degree requirements might establish a task force made up of representatives from each department affected by the change. Each person retains her or his regular departmental affiliation and duties but also serves on the special task force. After the new requirements are agreed on, the task force is dissolved.

Integrating Departments   Integrating departments are occasionally used for coordination. These are somewhat similar to task forces but are more permanent. An integrating department generally has some permanent members as well as members who are assigned temporarily from units that are particularly in need of coordination. One study found that successful firms in the plastics industry, which is characterized by complex and dynamic environments, used integrating departments to maintain internal integration and coordination.[37] An integrating department usually has more authority than a task force and may even be given some budgetary control by the organization.

In general, the greater the degree of interdependence, the more attention the organization must devote to coordination. When interdependence is pooled or simply sequential, the managerial hierarchy or rules and procedures are often sufficient. When more complex forms of sequential interdependence or simpler forms of reciprocal interdependence exist, liaisons or task forces may be more useful. When reciprocal interdependence is complex, task forces or integrating departments are needed. Of course, the manager must also rely on her or his own experience and insights when choosing coordination techniques for the organization.

MANAGEMENT IMPLICATIONS   Managers need to understand how varying degrees of interdependence determine the need for coordination within their organization. In addition, they also need to know how various structural techniques can be used to facilitate coordination.

Differentiating Between Positions

The last building block of organization structure is differentiating between line and staff positions in the organization. A **line position** is a position in the direct chain of command that is responsible for the achievement of an organization's goals. A **staff position** is intended to provide expertise, advice, and support for line positions.

line position A position in the direct chain of command that is responsible for the achievement of an organization's goals

staff position A position intended to provide expertise, advice, and support for line positions

Differences Between Line and Staff

The most obvious difference between line and staff is purpose—line managers work directly toward organizational goals, whereas staff managers advise and assist. But other distinctions exist as well. One important difference is authority. Line

Some organizations still find it necessary to differentiate between positions along such dimensions as line versus staff. But more and more organizations are finding such differentiation not only unnecessary but also counterproductive. SEI Investments is a good example. All employees in the firm's headquarters in Oaks, Pennsylvania, know how to perform virtually every job in the company. Computer hook-ups are even set up so that they drop down from the ceiling allowing employees to do their work regardless of where in the building they may be.

authority is generally thought of as the formal or legitimate authority created by the organizational hierarchy. Staff authority is less concrete and may take a variety of forms. One form is the authority to advise. In this instance, the line manager can choose whether to seek or to avoid input from the staff; even when advice is sought, the manager might still choose to ignore it.

Another form of staff authority is called compulsory advice. In this case the line manager must listen to the advice but can choose to heed it or ignore it. For example, the pope is expected to listen to the advice of the sacred college of cardinals when dealing with church doctrine, but he may follow his own beliefs when making decisions. Perhaps the most important form of staff authority is called functional authority—formal or legitimate authority over activities related to the staff member's specialty. For example, a human resource staff manager may have functional authority when there is a question of discrimination in hiring. Conferring functional authority is probably the most effective way to use staff positions because the organization can take advantage of specialized expertise while also maintaining a chain of command.

Administrative Intensity

administrative intensity The degree to which managerial positions are concentrated in staff positions

Organizations sometimes attempt to balance their emphasis on line versus staff positions in terms of administrative intensity. **Administrative intensity** is the degree to which managerial positions are concentrated in staff positions. An organization with a high administrative intensity is one with many staff positions relative to the number of line positions; low administrative intensity reflects relatively more line positions. Although staff positions are important in many different areas, they tend to proliferate unnecessarily. All else being equal, organizations would like to devote most of their human resource investment on line managers because, by definition, they contribute to the organization's basic goals. A surplus of staff positions represents a drain on an organization's cash and an inefficient use of resources.

Many organizations have taken steps over the past few years to reduce their administrative intensity by eliminating staff positions. CBS has cut hundreds of staff positions at its New York headquarters, and IBM has cut its corporate staff workforce from seven thousand to 2,300. Burlington Northern generates almost $7 billion in annual sales and manages a workforce of forty-three thousand with a corporate staff of only seventy-seven managers!

MANAGEMENT
IMPLICATIONS
All managers need to understand the fundamental differences that exist between line positions and staff positions in organizations in general and their organization in particular. Managers should also understand the meaning of administrative intensity and how it can be managed most effectively.

Summary of Key Points

Organizations are made up of a series of elements. The most common of these elements involve designing jobs, grouping jobs, establishing reporting relationships, distributing authority, coordinating activities, and differentiating between positions.

Job design is the determination of an individual's work-related responsibilities. The most common form is job specialization. Because of various drawbacks to job specialization, managers have experimented with job rotation, job enlargement, job enrichment, the job characteristics approach, and work teams as alternatives.

After jobs are designed, they are grouped into departments. The most common bases for departmentalization are function, product, customer, and location. Each has its own unique advantages and disadvantages. Large organizations employ multiple bases of departmentalization at different levels.

Establishing reporting relationships starts with clarifying the chain of command. The span of management partially dictates whether the organization is relatively tall or flat. In recent years there has been a trend toward flatter organizations. Several situational factors influence the ideal span.

Distributing authority starts with delegation. Delegation is the process by which the manager assigns a portion of his or her total workload to others. Systematic delegation throughout the organization is decentralization. Centralization involves keeping power and authority at the top of the organization. Several factors influence the appropriate degree of decentralization.

Coordination is the process of linking the activities of the various departments of the organization. Pooled, sequential, or reciprocal interdependence among departments is a primary reason for coordination. Managers can draw on several techniques to help achieve coordination.

A line position is a position in the direct chain of command that is responsible for the achievement of an organization's goals. In contrast, a staff position provides expertise, advice, and support for line positions. Administrative intensity is the degree to which managerial positions are concentrated in staff positions.

Discussion Questions

Questions for Review

1. What is job specialization? What are its advantages and disadvantages?
2. What is meant by departmentalization? Why and how is departmentalization carried out?
3. In what general ways can organizations be shaped? What implications does each of these ways have with regard to the distribution of authority within the organization?

4. How are positions differentiated in organizations? What are the advantages and disadvantages of such differentiation?

Questions for Analysis

5. Seeing how specialization can be utilized in manufacturing organizations is easy. How can it be used by other types of organizations such as hospitals, churches, schools, and restaurants? Should those organizations use specialization? Why or why not?
6. Try to develop a different way to departmentalize your college or university, a local fast-food restaurant, a manufacturing firm, or some other organization. What might be the advantages of your form of organization?
7. Which type of position (line, staff, administrative) is most important to an organization? Why? Could an organization function without any of them? Why or why not?

Questions for Application

8. Go to the library and locate organization charts for ten different organizations. Look for similarities and differences among them and try to account for what you find.
9. Contact two very different local organizations (retailing firm, manufacturing firm, church, civic club, etc.) and interview top managers to develop organization charts for each organization. How do you account for the similarities and differences between them?
10. How many people does the head of your academic department supervise? The dean of your college? The president of your university or college? Why do different spans of management exist for these officials? How might you find out if the spans are appropriate in size?

BUILDING EFFECTIVE *time-management* SKILLS

Exercise Overview

Time-management skills refer to the manager's ability to prioritize work, to work efficiently, and to delegate appropriately. As noted in this chapter, various situational factors affect the appropriate span of management that is optimal for a particular situation. This exercise relates time-management issues with the appropriate span of management.

Exercise Background

Several different factors affect the appropriate span of management for a particular situation. These factors are noted and summarized in Table 11.1 on page 340. The span of management has a direct relationship to the efficient use of the manager's time; that is, a less-than-optimal span of management is likely to result in an inefficient use of time. If the span is too narrow, the manager may have too little work to do, but if the span is too wide, the manager's other work may be neglected.

Exercise Task

Considering the various factors that influence an optimal span of management, respond to the following:

1. Describe how a span inappropriately matched with each factor will result in inefficiencies for both managers and subordinates.
2. If situational factors and the existing span of management are inappropriately matched, it might be possible to change one or the other to achieve a better fit. Examine each factor and decide whether it would be easier to change the factor or the span of management to improve fit.
3. Now assume that you are a manager. Assess the relative importance that you would place on each situational factor to define your own span of management.

BUILDING EFFECTIVE *diagnostic* SKILLS

Exercise Overview

Diagnostic skills are the skills that enable a manager to visualize the most appropriate response to a situation. This exercise will enable you to develop your diagnostic skills as they relate to issues of centralization and decentralization in an organization.

Exercise Background

Managers often find it necessary to change the degree of centralization or decentralization in their organization. Begin this exercise by reflecting on two very different scenarios. In scenario A, assume that you are the top manager in a large organization. The organization has a long and well-known history of being very centralized. For valid reasons beyond the scope of this exercise, assume that you have decided to make the firm much more decentralized. For scenario B, assume the exact opposite situation; that is, assume that you are the top manager of a firm that has always used decentralization but has now decided to become much more centralized.

Exercise Task

With the background information above as context, do the following:

1. List the major barriers you see to implementing decentralization in scenario A.
2. List the major barriers you see to implementing centralization in scenario B.
3. Which scenario do you think would be easiest to implement in reality? That is, is it likely to be easier to move from centralization to decentralization, or from decentralization to centralization? Why?
4. Given a choice of starting your own career in a firm that is either highly centralized or highly decentralized, which do you think you would prefer? Why?

BUILDING EFFECTIVE *conceptual* SKILLS

Exercise Overview

Conceptual skills refer to a person's abilities to think in the abstract. This exercise will help you develop your conceptual skills as they relate to designing jobs.

Exercise Background

Begin by thinking of three different jobs, one that appears to have virtually no enrichment, one that appears to have moderate enrichment, and one that appears to have a great deal of enrichment. These jobs might be positions that you have personally held or positions that you have observed and about which you can make some educated or informed judgments.

Evaluate each job along the five dimensions described in the job characteristics theory. Now see if you can identify ways to improve each of the five dimensions for each job. That is, see if you can determine how to enrich the jobs using the job characteristics theory as a framework.

Finally, meet with a classmate and share your results. See if you can improve your job enrichment strategy based on the critique offered by your classmate.

Exercise Task

With the background information above as context, do the following:

1. What job qualities make some jobs easier to enrich than others?
2. Can all jobs be enriched?
3. Even if a particular job can be enriched, does that always mean that it should be enriched?
4. Under what circumstances might an individual prefer to have a routine and unenriched job?

HEINZ LOOKS BEYOND KETCHUP FOR GROWTH

Heinz's ketchup may flow slowly but its sales are growing quickly. Ketchup is the brightest star among the four thousand products marketed by global food giant H.J. Heinz, which is based in Pittsburgh. Backed by extensive advertising and the introduction of new variations, Heinz ketchup has boosted its U.S. market share from 48 percent to 54 percent in recent years.

However, other Heinz products have lagged behind ketchup's stellar sales performance. Star-Kist tuna, the world's top-selling tuna brand, is faltering because of declining tuna prices and changing consumer tastes. Sales of canned pet foods, such as Heinz's 9-Lives brand, are taking a back seat to sales of dry pet foods, where competitors such as Ralston Purina are stronger. Heinz's Weight Watchers business has felt increased pressure from ConAgra's Healthy Choice and other frozen-food rivals.

To reverse these sales trends and strengthen its global position, Heinz executives have decided to reorganize the company into seven product categories. The largest is the category covering the flagship ketchup brand as well as condiments and sauces such as Heinz 57 steak sauce. This category contributes a bit less than one-third of Heinz's overall sales. The next largest category is frozen foods such as Ore-Ida potato products. The remaining five categories are pet products; soups, beans, and pastas; tuna foods; baby foods; and an "other" category, which covered Weight Watchers until Heinz management decided to sell it.

In the past, local operations managers were in charge of handling Heinz's products in each country. Now Heinz has brought management of all its brands under headquarters control to reduce duplication and improve coordination. Along with job cuts, factory closings, and other changes that enabled the company to focus its resources on fewer products, Heinz was able to shave $200 million off its yearly costs.

The company has also been working on a strategy to grow through acquisitions—although not all its plans have worked out. For example, Heinz wanted to buy the Beech-Nut Nutrition product line to combine with its existing baby foods for more competitive power against Gerber, which holds a 70 percent market share. But the Federal Trade Commission did not allow the purchase because it would have reduced competition in the U.S. market from three strong players to just two. Other acquisitions, such as the purchase of Yoshida brand Asian sauces, have helped Heinz diversify into complementary product areas.

In another change, Heinz has begun investing more to promote current products and launch promising new products. Licensing the Boston Market brand, Heinz has introduced a line of frozen Boston Market Home Style Meals and a line of Boston Market jarred gravies to expand its sales. At the same time, management is carefully nurturing its market-leading products to keep sales on the upswing. One recent innovation is the introduction of green ketchup, enriched with vitamin C, in squeezable containers. The unconventional coloring and easy-grip bottles were designed specifically for children, who make up the largest group of ketchup consumers. Heinz is also starting to package Star-Kist tuna in an easy-open pouch, backing this introduction with a $20 million ad campaign. Ketchup may still be the star of its corporate sales, but Heinz is working hard to give other products a brighter glow.

Case Questions

1. Is Heinz moving toward centralization or decentralization? How is this move likely to affect the balance between line and staff positions?

2. What type of departmentalization is Heinz using? Why is this departmentalization appropriate for the company?

3. How do acquisitions, such as the purchase of Yoshida brand Asian sauces, affect Heinz's organization structure?

Case References

"The FTC Nixes a Pablum Purchase," *Business Week*, July 24, 2000, p. 44; Stephanie Thompson, "EZ Being Green: Kids Line Is Latest Heinz Innovation," *Advertising Age*, July 10, 2000, p. 3; Greg Farrell, "Heinz Puts Focus on Fewer Products," *USA Today*, February 18, 1999, p. 3B; Robert Berner and Kevin Helliker, "Heinz's Worry: 4,000 Products, Only One Star," *USA Today*, September 17, 1999, pp. B1, B4.

CHAPTER NOTES

1. "Construction Heads into the Internet Age," *New York Times*, February 21, 2000, pp. C1, C9; Melanie Warner, "Bidcom," *Fortune*, July 5, 1999, pp. 100–104; "Despite the Hype, B2B Marketplaces Struggle," *USA Today*, May 10, 2000, pp. 1B, 2B.

2. See Kathleen M. Eisenhardt and Shona L. Brown, "Patching—Restitching Business Portfolios in Dynamic Markets," *Harvard Business Review*, May–June 1999, pp. 145–154, for a related discussion.

3. Gareth Jones, *Organization Theory*, 3rd Edition (Upper Saddle River, N.J.: Prentice-Hall, 2000).

4. David A. Nadler and Michael L. Tushman, *Competing by Design—The Power of Organizational Architecture* (New York: Oxford University Press, 1997).

5. Ricky W. Griffin and Gary McMahan, "Motivation Through Job Design," in Jerald Greenberg (ed.), *Organizational Behavior—The State of the Science* (Hillsdale, N.J.: Lawrance Erlbaum Associates, 1994), pp. 23–44.

6. Adam Smith, *Wealth of Nations* (New York: Modern Library, 1937; originally published in 1776).

7. Andrea Gabor, *The Capitalist Philosophers* (New York: Times Business, 2000).

8. Ricky W. Griffin, *Task Design* (Glenview, Ill.: Scott, Foresman, 1982).

9. Anne S. Miner, "Idiosyncratic Jobs in Formal Organizations," *Administrative Science Quarterly*, September 1987, pp. 327–351.

10. M. D. Kilbridge, "Reduced Costs Through Job Enlargement: A Case," *Journal of Business*, Vol. 33, 1960, pp. 357–362.

11. Griffin and McMahan, "Motivation Through Job Enrichment."

12. Kilbridge, "Reduced Costs Through Job Enrichment: A Case."

13. Frederick Herzberg, *Work and the Nature of Man* (Cleveland: World Press, 1966).

14. Robert Ford, "Job Enrichment Lessons from AT&T," *Harvard Business Review*, January–February 1973, pp. 96–106.

15. J. Richard Hackman and Greg R. Oldham, *Work Redesign* (Reading, Mass.: Addison-Wesley, 1980).

16. "Some Plants Tear Out Long Assembly Lines, Switch to Craft Work," *Wall Street Journal*, October 24, 1994, pp. A1, A4.

17. See Étiènne C. Wenger and William M. Snyder, "Communities of Practice: The Organizational Frontier," *Harvard Business Review*, January–February 2000, pp. 139–148, for a related discussion.

18. Richard L. Daft, *Organization Theory and Design*, 7th Edition (Cincinnati: South-Western, 2001).

19. "Lucent to Break Up into Four Divisions," Associated Press news story reported in *The Houston Chronicle*, October 27, 1999, p. B2.

20. A. V. Graicunas, "Relationships in Organizations," *Bulletin of the International Management Institute*, March 7, 1933, pp. 39–42.

21. Ralph C. Davis, *Fundamentals of Top Management* (New York: Harper & Row, 1951); Lyndall F. Urwick, *Scientific Principles and Organization* (New York: American Management Association, 1938), p. 8; and Ian Hamilton, *The Soul and Body of an Army* (London: Edward Arnold, 1921), pp. 229–230.

22. David D. Van Fleet and Arthur G. Bedeian, "A History of the Span of Management," *Academy of Management Review*, 1977, pp. 356–372.

23. James C. Worthy, "Factors Influencing Employee Morale," *Harvard Business Review*, January 1950, pp. 61–73.

24. Dan R. Dalton, William D. Todor, Michael J. Spendolini, Gordon J. Fielding, and Lyman W. Porter, "Organization Structure and Performance: A Critical Review," *Academy of Management Review*, January 1980, pp. 49–64.

25. See Jerry Useem, "Welcome to the New Company Town," *Fortune*, January 10, 2000, pp. 62–70, for a related discussion.

26. David Van Fleet, "Span of Management Research and Issues," *Academy of Management Journal*, September 1983, pp. 546–552.

27. Philip Siekman, "Where 'Build to Order' Works Best," *Fortune*, April 26, 1999, pp. 160C–160V.

28. See Daft, *Organization Theory and Design*.

29. William Kahn and Kathy Kram, "Authority at Work: Internal Models and Their Organizational Consequences," *Academy of Management Review*, 1994, Vol. 19, No. 1, pp. 17–50.

30. Carrie R. Leana, "Predictors and Consequences of Delegation," *Academy of Management Journal*, December 1986, pp. 754–774.

31. Norm Brodsky, "Necessary Losses," *Inc.*, December 1997, pp. 116–119.

32. "Remote Control," *HRMagazine*, August 1997, pp. 82–90.

33. "Toppling the Pyramids," *Canadian Business*, May 1993, pp. 61–65.

34. Kevin Crowston, "A Coordination Theory Approach to Organizational Process Design," *Organization Science*, March–April 1997, pp. 157–166.

35. James Thompson, *Organizations in Action* (New York: McGraw-Hill, 1967). For a recent discussion, see Bart Victor and Richard S. Blackburn, "Interdependence: An Alternative Conceptualization," *Academy of Management Review*, July 1987, pp. 486–498.

36. Jay R. Galbraith, *Designing Complex Organizations* (Reading, Mass.: Addison-Wesley, 1973), and Jay R. Galbraith, *Organizational Design* (Reading, Mass.: Addison-Wesley, 1977).

37. Paul R. Lawrence and Jay W. Lorsch, "Differentiation and Integration in Complex Organizations," *Administrative Science Quarterly*, March 1967, pp. 1–47.

CHAPTER

12 Managing Organization Design

Siemens AG, the large German conglomerate, can trace its roots back over 150 years to when its founder, Werner von Siemens, began making telegraph equipment. And since those early days, communication technology and equipment has been at the core of Siemens's global business enterprises. But as the firm grew, it also diversified into other businesses as well. By the beginning of the 1990s, Siemens was making everything from streetcars to satellites and elevators to electron microscopes.

Siemens has always had engineering at the core of its operations—essentially it designed and made the best products possible but paid little attention to what other firms were doing. So focused on product quality were Siemens's engineers that the firm designed and made its own screws because they assumed that other manufacturers could not meet their exacting standards. At one time, television com-

mercials for Siemens's telephones showed a harried user throwing the receiver against a wall, picking it up, and still having to listen to his boss yell at him. Lost on Siemens at the time, however, was the fact that while the telephone featured in the commercials was tough, it was also heavy and unattractive. And this was just about the time that weight and appearance were becoming increasingly important to customers.

Thus, perhaps it should not have really come as a surprise when Siemens began to struggle about ten years ago. Its biggest global competitors—firms like General Electric, Nokia, ABB, and Philips—had all taken steps both to integrate their various business operations more effectively with one another and to become more nimble and responsive to consumers. Siemens, meanwhile, had remained insular in its thinking and bureaucratic in its operations. But about that same time a new CEO, Heinrich von Pierer, came

on board and quickly recognized that he needed to get the lumbering behemoth back on track if it was to remain competitive.

Beginning in 1992, von Pierer cut Siemens's workforce by 17 percent and sold off several unrelated businesses for $2 billion. He also stripped out several layers of middle management and tried to change the firm's culture to promote and reward innovation better. And he began to move autonomous but related operations into the same business groups. By 1995, his changes started to pay off with increased revenues, lower operating costs, and increased share in several key markets. Unfortunately, however, the firm's turnaround stalled almost as quickly as it had started.

"In Germany, competition was like a wind. Now, it's like a storm. And it will become a hurricane. You have to move fast or lose."

—*Heinrich von Pierer, CEO of Siemens*

LEARNING OBJECTIVES

After studying this chapter, you should be able to:

- Describe the basic nature of organization design.

- Identify and explain the two basic universal perspectives on organization design.

- Identify and explain several situational influences on organization design.

- Discuss how an organization's strategy and its design are interrelated.

- Describe the basic forms of organization design that characterize many organizations.

- Describe emerging issues in organization design.

Closer analysis revealed to von Pierer that while Siemens had indeed taken a big step in the right direction, its competitors had taken even bigger steps toward being agile and nimble players in the rapidly changing market for telecommunications technology and equipment. Undaunted, von Pierer redoubled his efforts to reinvent the firm. Among other things, he decided to continue selling off business units that did not contribute to the firm's telecommunications core enterprises. He also went on an acquisitions binge, buying up viable telecommunications businesses around the world. In addition, he totally overhauled the firm's structure by assigning all of its far-flung operations to one of fourteen core business units. And he also decided to make it clear to the engineers running most Siemens operations that he expected them to perform better.

Now, he holds quarterly meetings with the heads of Siemens's fourteen business units and grills them on their performance. About 60 percent of the pay of those business unit heads is now tied directly to their performance. He also reluctantly cut more jobs, including about one-fifth of all top management jobs in the company. And von Pierer continues to sell off businesses that are either underperforming and/or are not central to telecommunications initiatives. So far, at least, his moves seem to be paying off. Siemens has once again established itself as a leader in its chosen markets, and investors have pushed its valuation to an all-time high. Of course, in the volatile world of high technology, the footing can be slippery and one misstep can again lead to a big fall.[1]

O ne of the major ingredients in managing any business is the creation of an organization design to link the various elements that comprise the organization. There is a wide array of alternatives that managers in any given organization might select for its design. Heinrich von Pierer and his executive team at Siemens are remaking one of the largest major corporations in the world. The basis for this makeover is the firm's organization design; the reasons behind the change involve the firm's environment and its strategy.

In Chapter 11, we identified the basic elements that go into creating an organization. In this chapter, we explore how those elements can be combined to create an overall design for the organization. We first discuss the nature of organization design. We then describe early approaches aimed at identifying universal models of organization design. Situational factors, such as technology, environment, size, and life cycle, are then introduced. Next we discuss the relationship between an organization's strategy and its structure. Basic forms of organization design are described next. We conclude by presenting four emerging issues in organization design.

organization design The overall set of structural elements and the relationships among those elements used to manage the total organization

The Nature of Organization Design

Organization design is a complex and an ever changing process. Take what might appear to be a simple organization—the Atlanta Braves baseball team. The Braves' management team must create a structure that works best for the team itself. They must also include stadium management systems, minor league operations, media contract functions, a licensing group, and a variety of other activities. The design they use is different from all other sports teams, as well as from all other organizations in general.

What is organization design? In Chapter 11, we noted that job specialization and span of management are among the common elements of organization structure. We also described how the appropriate degree of specialization can vary, as can the appropriate span of management. Not really addressed, however, were questions of how specialization and span might be related to one another. For example, should a high level of specialization be matched with a certain span? And will different combinations of each work best with different bases of departmentalization? These and related issues are associated with questions of organization design.[2]

Organization design is the overall set of structural elements and the relationships among those elements used to manage the total organization. Thus, organization design is a means to implement strategies and plans to achieve organizational goals. As we discuss organization design, keep in mind two important points. First, organizations are not designed and then left intact. Most organizations change almost continuously as a result of factors such as situations and people. (The processes of organization change are discussed in Chapter 13.) Second, organization design for larger organizations is extremely complex and has so many nuances and variations that descriptions of them cannot be a full and complete explanation.

MANAGEMENT
IMPLICATIONS Managers should know that designing an organization is an ongoing process that is never really finished. They should recognize that organization design for larger organizations is extremely complex.

Universal Perspectives on Organization Design

In Chapter 2, we made the distinction between contingency and universal approaches to solving management problems. Recall, for example, that universal perspectives try to identify the "one best way" to manage organizations, and contingency perspectives suggest that appropriate managerial behavior in a given situation depends on, or is contingent on, unique elements in that situation. The foundation of contemporary thinking about organization design can be traced back to two early universal perspectives: the bureaucratic model and the behavioral model.

Bureaucratic Model

We also noted in Chapter 2 that Max Weber, an influential German sociologist, was a pioneer of classical organization theory. At the core of Weber's writings was the bureaucratic model of organizations.[3] The Weberian perspective suggests that a **bureaucracy** is a model of organization design based on a legitimate and formal system of authority. Many people associate bureaucracy with "red tape," rigidity, and passing the buck. For example, how many times have you heard people refer disparagingly to "the federal bureaucracy"? And many U.S. managers believe that bureaucracy in the Japanese government is a major impediment to U.S. firms' ability to do business there.

bureaucracy A model of organization design based on a legitimate and formal system of authority

Weber viewed the bureaucratic form of organization as logical, rational, and efficient. He offered the model as a framework to which all organizations should aspire: the "one best way" of doing things. According to Weber, the ideal bureaucracy exhibits five basic characteristics:

1. The organization should adopt a distinct division of labor, and each position should be filled by an expert.
2. The organization should develop a consistent set of rules to ensure that task performance is uniform.
3. The organization should establish a hierarchy of positions or offices that creates a chain of command from the top of the organization to the bottom.
4. Managers should conduct business in an impersonal way and maintain an appropriate social distance between themselves and their subordinates.
5. Employment and advancement in the organization should be based on technical expertise, and employees should be protected from arbitrary dismissal.

Perhaps the best examples of bureaucracies today are government agencies and universities. Consider, for example, the steps you must go through and the forms you must fill out to apply for admission to college, request housing, register each semester, change majors, submit a degree plan, substitute a course, and file for graduation. The reason these procedures are necessary is that universities deal with large numbers of people who must be treated equally and fairly. Hence rules, regulations, and standard operating procedures are needed. Large labor unions are also usually organized as bureaucracies.[4] Some bureaucracies, such as the U.S. Postal Service, are trying to portray themselves as less mechanistic and impersonal. The

The bureaucratic model of organization design relies on logical, rational, and efficient rules and procedures. Many organizations attempt to standardize these rules and procedures by creating forms for people to use when initiating action or requesting approval. Unfortunately, this standardization can lead to such a proliferation of forms that, in turn, people quickly come to see it all as nothing more than "red tape." This point is obviously brought home by Beetle Bailey's request for time off to visit his dentist!

strategy of the postal service is to become more service-oriented as a way to fight back against competitors like Federal Express and UPS. The cartoon illustrates how a bureaucratic organization might operate.

A primary strength of the bureaucratic model is that several of its elements (such as reliance on rules and employment based on expertise) do, in fact, often improve efficiency. Bureaucracies also help prevent favoritism (because everyone must follow the rules) and make procedures and practices very clear to everyone. Unfortunately, however, this approach also has several disadvantages. One major disadvantage is that the bureaucratic model results in inflexibility and rigidity. Once rules are created and put into place, making exceptions or changing them is often difficult. In addition, the bureaucracy often results in the neglect of human and social processes within the organization.

Behavioral Model

behavioral model A model of organization design consistent with the human relations movement and stressing attention to developing work groups and concern about interpersonal processes

Another important universal model of organization design was the **behavioral model**, which paralleled the emergence of the human relations school of management thought. Rensis Likert, a management researcher, studied several large organizations to determine what made some more effective than others.[5] He found that the organizations in his sample that used the bureaucratic model of design tended to be less effective than those that used a more behaviorally oriented model consistent with the emerging human relations movement—in other words, organizations that paid more attention to developing work groups and were more concerned about interpersonal processes.

Likert developed a framework that characterized organizations in terms of eight important processes: leadership, motivation, communication, interactions, decision making, goal setting, control, and performance goals. Likert believed that all organizations could be measured and categorized along a continuum associated with each of these dimensions. He argued that the basic bureaucratic form of organization, which he called a **System 1 design**, anchored one end of each dimension. The characteristics of the System 1 organization in Likert's framework are summarized in Table 12.1.

System 1 design Organization design similar to the bureaucratic model

Table 12.1

System 1 and System 4 Organizations

The behavioral model identifies two extreme types of organization design called System 1 and System 4. The two designs vary in eight fundamental processes. The System 1 design is considered to be somewhat rigid and inflexible.

System 1 Organization	System 4 Organization
1. Leadership process includes no perceived confidence and trust. Subordinates do not feel free to discuss job problems with their superiors, who in turn do not solicit their ideas and opinions.	1. Leadership process includes perceived confidence and trust between superiors and subordinates in all matters. Subordinates feel free to discuss job problems with their superiors, who in turn solicit their ideas and opinions.
2. Motivational process taps only physical, security, and economic motives through the use of fear and sanctions. Unfavorable attitudes toward the organization prevail among employees.	2. Motivational process taps a full range of motives through participatory methods. Attitudes are favorable toward the organization and its goals.
3. Communication process is such that information flows downward and tends to be distorted, inaccurate, and viewed with suspicion by subordinates.	3. Communication process is such that information flows freely throughout the organization—upward, downward, and laterally. The information is accurate and undistorted.
4. Interaction process is closed and restricted. Subordinates have little effect on departmental goals, methods, and activities.	4. Interaction process is open and extensive. Both superiors and subordinates are able to affect departmental goals, methods, and activities.
5. Decision process occurs only at the top of the organization; it is relatively centralized.	5. Decision process occurs at all levels through group processes; it is relatively decentralized.
6. Goal-setting process is located at the top of the organization; discourages group participation.	6. Goal-setting process encourages group participation in setting high, realistic objectives.
7. Control process is centralized and emphasizes fixing of blame for mistakes.	7. Control process is dispersed throughout the organization and emphasizes self-control and problem solving.
8. Performance goals are low and passively sought by managers who make no commitment to developing the human resources of the organization.	8. Performance goals are high and actively sought by superiors who recognize the necessity for making a full commitment to developing, through training, the human resources of the organization.

Source: Adapted from Rensis Likert, *The Human Organization.* Copyright © 1967 by The McGraw-Hill Companies. Reprinted by permission of The McGraw-Hill Companies.

Also summarized in this table are characteristics of Likert's other extreme form of organization design, called **System 4 design**, which was based on the behavioral model. For example, a System 4 organization uses a wide array of motivational processes, and its interaction processes are open and extensive. Other distinctions between System 1 and System 4 organizations are equally obvious. Between the System 1 and System 4 extremes lie the System 2 and System 3 organizations. Likert argued that System 4 should be adopted by all organizations. He suggested that managers should emphasize supportive relationships, establish high performance goals, and practice group decision making to achieve a System 4 organization. Many organizations attempted to adopt the System 4 design during its period of peak popularity. Several years ago, for example, General Motors converted a plant in the Atlanta area from a System 2 to a System 4 organization. Over a period of three years, direct and indirect labor efficiency improved, as did tool-breakage rates, scrap costs, and quality.[6]

Like the bureaucratic model, the behavioral approach has both strengths and weaknesses. Its major strength is that it emphasizes human behavior by stressing

System 4 design Organization design similar to the behavioral model

the value of an organization's employees. Likert and his associates thus paved the way for a more humanistic approach to designing organizations. Unfortunately, the behavioral approach also argues that there is one best way to design organizations—as a System 4. As we see, however, evidence is strong that there is no one best approach to organization design.[7] What works for one organization may not work for another, and what works for one organization may change as that organization's situation changes. Hence, universal models like bureaucracy and System 4 have been largely supplanted by newer models that take contingency factors into account. In the next section, we identify several factors that help determine the best organization design for a particular situation.

situational view of organization design Based on the assumption that the optimal design for any given organization depends on a set of relevant situational factors

MANAGEMENT IMPLICATIONS   Managers should understand the basic concepts inherent in the bureaucratic and behavioral models of organization design. While appreciating their strengths and weaknesses, they should also remember that universal models such as these are not truly applicable to today's organization.

■ *Situational Influences on Organization Design*

An organization's technology can influence its design in a variety of ways. For example, a recent innovation at some Levi Strauss Stores is new technology aimed at helping customers achieve a "perfect fit." As shown here, this sometimes means having the customers sit in a container of water wearing their new "shrink-to-fit" jeans. But this relatively minor technological innovation carries with it a host of organization design implications, such as who will be trained to use, how it will be maintained, and how the firm can limit any potential legal liability.

The **situational view of organization design** is based on the assumption that the optimal design for any given organization depends on a set of relevant situational factors. That is, situational factors play a role in determining the best organization design for any particular circumstance. *The World of Management* describes how situational factors have affected organization design at DaimlerChrysler. Four basic situational factors—core technology, environment, organizational size, and organizational life cycle—are discussed here. Another, strategy is described in the next section.

Core Technology

Technology is the conversion processes used to transform inputs (such as materials or information) into outputs (such as products or services). Most organizations use multiple technologies, but an organization's most important one is called its *core technology*. Although most people visualize assembly lines and machinery when they think of technology,

WORLD OF MANAGEMENT

DaimlerChrysler Steers into a New Organization

When Jürgen Schrempp and Robert Eaton planned the merger of Daimler-Benz and Chrysler, they sought to bring the German and U.S. car manufacturers together in one seamless transnational organization. Daimler was interested in Chrysler's experience in vehicle development and expertise in cost-effective production methods; Chrysler wanted to build on Daimler's core technology and reputation in making upscale vehicles. By merging, the two companies could broaden their market reach and reduce dependence on the highly competitive U.S. market. The combined company would also be in a better position to expand its sales of smaller cars in Europe and in developing countries.

Schrempp and Eaton became co-CEOs of DaimlerChrysler and set up teams to oversee the details of the merger. Although the deal was conceived as a merger of equals, some Chrysler managers soon grumbled that the Daimler side was dominating key positions within the new organization. Chrysler's president was named head of DaimlerChrysler's North American operations, but he left less than a year after the merger, part of a wave of management changes affecting former Chrysler officials. Cultural differences also surfaced, with cost-conscious Chrysler managers aghast at Daimler managers' freer spending.

To smooth the way toward the merger, Schrempp has allowed Chrysler and Mercedes to operate as separate businesses, although they are combining their research and development functions for certain projects. As part of the merger, Mercedes also began manufacturing selected vehicles in Chrysler plants. Although Schrempp says that DaimlerChrysler is now one company, analysts say that the organization won't be able to achieve multibillion-dollar cost-efficiencies without removing more redundancies and sharing more functions throughout the merged organization.

> *We have a structure where we are now able to cover the world, and we have the whole spectrum of products, and we are the most technologically intensive car company in the world.*
>
> —Jürgen E. Schrempp, CEO of DaimlerChrysler*

References: Christine Tierney, Matt Karnitschnig, and Joann Muller, "Defiant Daimler," *Business Week,* August 7, 2000, pp. 90–94 (*quote on p. 94); Jeffrey Ball and Scott Miller, "Full Speed Ahead: Stuttgart's Control Grows with Shakeup at DaimlerChrysler," *Wall Street Journal,* September 24, 1999, pp. A1, A8.

---

the term can also be applied to service organizations. For example, a brokerage firm like Dean Witter uses technology to transform investment dollars into income in much the same way that Union Carbide uses natural resources to manufacture chemical products.

The link between technology and organization design was first recognized by Joan Woodward.[8] Woodward studied one hundred manufacturing firms in southern England. She collected information about such things as the history of each organization, its manufacturing processes, its forms and procedures, and its financial performance. Woodward expected to find a relationship between the size of an organization and its design, but no such relationship emerged. As a result, she began to seek other explanations for differences. Close scrutiny of the firms in her sample led her to recognize a potential relationship between technology and organization design. This follow-up analysis led Woodward first to classify the

technology Conversion processes used to transform inputs into outputs

organizations according to their technology. Three basic forms of technology were identified by Woodward:

1. *Unit or small-batch technology*. The product is custom-made to customer specifications or else it is produced in small quantities. Organizations using this form of technology include a tailor shop like Brooks Brothers (custom suits), a printing shop like Kinko's (business cards, company stationery), and a photography studio.

2. *Large-batch or mass-production technology*. The product is manufactured in assembly-line fashion by combining component parts into another part or finished product. Examples include automobile manufacturers like Subaru, appliance makers like Whirlpool Corporation, and electronics firms like Philips.

3. *Continuous-process technology*. Raw materials are transformed into a finished product by a series of machine or process transformations. The composition of the materials themselves is changed. Examples include petroleum refineries like Exxon and Shell and chemical refineries like Dow Chemical and Hoescht Celanese.

These forms of technology are listed in order of their assumed levels of complexity; that is, unit or small-batch technology is presumed to be the least complex and continuous-process technology the most complex. Woodward found that different configurations of organization design were associated with each technology.

As technology became more complex in Woodward's sample, the number of levels of management increased (that is, the organization was taller). The executive span of management also increased, as did the relative size of its staff component. The supervisory span of management, however, first increased and then decreased as technology became more complex, primarily because much of the work in continuous-process technologies is automated. Fewer workers are needed, but the skills necessary to do the job increase. These findings are consistent with the discussion of the span of management in Chapter 11—the more complex the job, the narrower the span should be.

At a more general level of analysis, Woodward found that the two extremes (unit or small-batch and continuous-process) tended to be very similar to Likert's System 4 organization, whereas the middle-range organizations (large-batch or mass-production) were much more like bureaucracies or System 1. The large-batch and mass-production organizations also had a higher level of specialization.[9] Finally, she found that organizational success was related to the extent to which organizations followed the typical pattern. For example, successful continuous-process organizations tended to be more like System 4 organizations, whereas less successful firms with the same technology were less like System 4 organizations.

Thus, technology appears to play an important role in determining organization design. As future technologies become even more diverse and complex, managers will have to be even more aware of technologies' impact on the design of organizations. For example, the increased use of robotics may necessitate alterations in organization design to accommodate different assembly methods better. Likewise, increased use of new forms of information technology will almost certainly cause organizations to redefine the nature of work and the reporting relationships among individuals.[10]

Environment

In addition to the various relationships described in Chapter 3, environmental elements and organization design are specifically linked in a number of ways. The first widely recognized analysis of environment–organization design linkages was provided by Tom Burns and G. M. Stalker.[11] Like Woodward, Burns and Stalker worked in England. Their first step was identifying two extreme forms of organizational environment: stable (one that remains relatively constant over time) and unstable (subject to uncertainty and rapid change). Next they studied the designs of organizations in each type of environment. Not surprisingly, they found that organizations in stable environments tended to have a different kind of design from organizations in unstable environments. The two kinds of design that emerged were called mechanistic and organic organization.

A **mechanistic organization**, quite similar to the bureaucratic or System 1 model, was most frequently found in stable environments. Free from uncertainty, organizations structured their activities in rather predictable ways by means of rules, specialized jobs, and centralized authority. Mechanistic organizations are also quite similar in nature to bureaucracies. Although no environment is completely stable, Kmart and Wendy's use mechanistic designs. Each Kmart store, for example, has prescribed methods for store design and merchandise-ordering processes. No deviations are allowed from these methods. An **organic organization**, on the other hand, was most often found in unstable and unpredictable environments, in which constant change and uncertainty usually dictate a much higher level of fluidity and flexibility. Motorola (facing rapid technological change) and The Limited (facing constant change in consumer tastes) each use organic designs. A manager at Motorola, for example, has considerable discretion over how work is performed and how problems can be solved.

These ideas were extended in the United States by Paul R. Lawrence and Jay W. Lorsch.[12] They agreed that environmental factors influence organization design but believed that this influence varies between different units of the same organization. In fact, they predicted that each organizational unit has its own unique environment and responds by developing unique attributes. Lawrence and Lorsch suggested that organizations could be characterized along two primary dimensions.

One of these dimensions, **differentiation**, is the extent to which the organization is broken down into subunits. A firm with many subunits is highly differentiated; one with few subunits has a low level of differentiation. The second dimension, **integration**, is the degree to which the various subunits must work together in a coordinated fashion. For example, if each unit competes in a different market and has its own production facilities, it may need little integration with other units. Lawrence and Lorsch reasoned that the degree of differentiation and integration needed by an organization depends on the stability of the environments that its subunits faced.

mechanistic organization Similar to the bureaucratic or System 1 model; most frequently found in stable environments

organic organization Very flexible and informal model of organization design; most often found in unstable and unpredictable environments

differentiation The extent to which the organization is broken down into subunits

integration The degree to which the various subunits must work together in a coordinated fashion

Organizational Size

organizational size The total number of full-time or full-time-equivalent employees

The size of an organization is yet another factor that affects its design.[13] Although several definitions of size exist, we define **organizational size** as the total number of full-time or full-time-equivalent employees. A team of researchers at the University of Aston in Birmingham, England, believed that Woodward had failed to find a size-structure relationship (which was her original expectation) because almost all the organizations she studied were relatively small (three-fourths had fewer than five hundred employees).[14] Thus, they decided to undertake a study of a wider array of organizations to determine how size and technology both individually and jointly affect an organization's design.

Their primary finding was that technology did in fact influence structural variables in small firms, probably because all their activities tended to be centered around their core technology. In large firms, however, the strong technology-design link broke down, most likely because technology is not as central to ongoing activities in large organizations. The Aston studies yielded a number of basic generalizations: when compared to small organizations, large organizations tend to be characterized by higher levels of job specialization, more standard operating procedures, more rules, more regulations, and a greater degree of decentralization.

Organizational Life Cycle

Of course, size is not constant. As we noted in Chapter 10, for example, some small businesses are formed but soon disappear. Others remain as small, independently operated enterprises as long as their owner-managers live. A few, like Compaq Computer, Dell Computer, Liz Claiborne, and Reebok, skyrocket to become organizational giants. And occasionally large organizations reduce their size through layoffs or divestitures. For example, Navistar is today far smaller than was its previous incarnation as International Harvester Co.

organizational life cycle Progression through which organizations evolve as they grow and mature; consists of four stages: birth, youth, midlife, and maturity

Although no consistent pattern always explains changes in size, many organizations progress through a four-stage **organizational life cycle**.[15] The first stage is the *birth* of the organization. The second stage, *youth*, is characterized by growth and the expansion of organizational resources. *Midlife* is a period of gradual growth evolving eventually into stability. Finally, *maturity* is a period of stability, perhaps eventually evolving into decline. Montgomery Ward is an example of a mature organization—it is experiencing little or no growth and appears to be falling behind the rest of the retailing industry today.

Managers must confront a number of organization design issues as the organization progresses through these stages. In general, as an organization passes from one stage to the next, it becomes bigger, more mechanistic, and more decentralized. It also becomes more specialized, devotes more attention to planning, and takes on an increasingly large staff component. Finally, coordination demands increase, formalization increases, organizational units become geographically more dispersed, and control systems become more extensive. Thus, an organization's size and design are clearly linked, and this link is dynamic because of the organizational life cycle.[16]

MANAGEMENT Managers should remember that organization design is nei-
IMPLICATIONS ther static nor universal. It is therefore important that they also
understand how situational factors such as environment, technology, organizational size, and organizational life cycle should be considered when designing an organization.

Strategy and Organization Design

Another important determinant of an organization's design is the strategy adopted by its top managers.[17] In general, corporate and business strategies both affect organization design. Basic organizational functions such as finance and marketing can also affect organization design in some cases.[18]

Corporate-Level Strategy

As we noted in Chapter 8, an organization can adopt a variety of corporate-level strategies. Its choice will partially determine what type of design will be most effective. For example, a firm that pursues a single-product strategy likely relies on functional departmentalization and can use a mechanistic design. If either unrelated or related diversification is used to spur growth, managers need to decide how to arrange the various units within the organizational umbrella. For example, if the firm is using related diversification, there needs to be a high level of coordination among the various units to capitalize on the presumed synergistic opportunities inherent in this strategy. On the other hand, firms using unrelated diversification more likely rely on a strong hierarchical reporting system so that corporate managers can better monitor the performance of individual units within the firm.

An organization that adopts the portfolio approach to implement its corporate-level strategies must also ensure that its design fits its strategy. For example, each strategic business unit may remain a relatively autonomous unit within the organization. But managers at the corporate level need to decide how much decision-making latitude to give the heads of each unit (a question of decentralization); how many corporate-level executives are needed to oversee the operations of various units (a question of span of management); and what information, if any, is shared among the units (a question of coordination).[19]

An organization's strategies can have a major impact on its design. Lawrence Montoya, shown here, is the governor of the Pueblo of Santa Ana tribe of Native Americans near Albuquerque, New Mexico. He leads a thriving set of corporate initiatives on behalf of the tribe, including a hotel and resort, a conference center, and a casino. But each business has its own unique design, and the businesses are linked only very loosely at the corporate level under Montoya's watchful eye.

Business-Level Strategy

Business-level strategies affect the design of individual businesses within the organization as well as the overall organization itself. An organization pursuing a defender strategy, for example, is likely to be somewhat tall and centralized, have narrow spans of management, and perhaps take a functional approach to departmentalization. Thus, it may generally follow the bureaucratic approach to organization design.

In contrast, a prospecting type of organization is more likely to be flatter and decentralized. With wider spans of management, it tries to be very flexible and adaptable in its approach to doing business. A business that uses an analyzer strategy is likely to have an organization design somewhere between these two extremes (perhaps as a System 2 or System 3 organization). Given that a reactor is essentially a strategic failure, its presumed strategy is probably not logically connected to its design.

Generic competitive strategies can also affect organization design. A firm using a differentiation strategy, for example, may structure departments around whatever it is using as a basis for differentiating its products (i.e., marketing in the case of image, manufacturing in the case of quality). A cost leadership strategy necessitates a strong commitment to efficiency and control. Thus, such a firm is more centralized as it attempts to control costs. And a firm using a focus strategy may design itself around the direction of its focus (i.e., location departmentalization if its focus is geographic region, customer departmentalization if its focus is customer groups).

Organizational Functions

The relationship between an organization's functional strategies and its design is less obvious and may be subsumed under corporate- or business-level concerns. If the firm's marketing strategy calls for aggressive marketing and promotion, separate departments may be needed for advertising, direct sales, and promotion. If its financial strategy calls for low debt, it may need only a small finance department. If production strategy calls for manufacturing in diverse locations, organization design arrangements need to account for this geographic dispersion. Human resource strategy may call for greater or lesser degrees of decentralization as a way to develop the skills of new managers at lower levels in the organization. And research and development strategy may dictate various designs for managing the R&D function itself. A heavy commitment to R&D, for example, may require a separate unit with a vice president in charge. A lessor commitment to R&D may be achieved with a director and a small staff.

MANAGEMENT IMPLICATIONS Strategy is also an important factor in determining the best design for a particular organization. Thus, managers should clearly understand both their corporate, business, and functional strategies and how those strategies impinge upon the organization design that is best for the situation.

▪ *Basic Forms of Organization Design*

Because technology, environment, organizational size, organizational life cycle, and strategy can all influence organization design, it should come as no surprise that organizations adopt many different kinds of designs. Most designs, however, fall into one of four basic categories. Others are hybrids based on two or more of the basic forms.

Functional (U-Form) Design

The **functional design** is an organizational arrangement based on the functional approach to departmentalization as detailed in Chapter 11. This design has been termed the **U-form** (for unitary) by the noted economist Oliver E. Williamson.[20] Under the U-form arrangement, the members and units in the organization are grouped into functional departments such as marketing and production.

For the organization to operate efficiently in this design, there must be considerable coordination across departments. This integration and coordination are most commonly the responsibility of the CEO and members of senior management. Figure 12.1 shows the U-form design as applied to the corporate level of a small manufacturing company. In a U-form organization, none of the functional areas can survive without the others. Marketing, for example, needs products from

U-form or **functional design** An organizational arrangement based on the functional approach to departmentalization

Figure 12.1

Functional or U-Form Design for a Small Manufacturing Company
The U-form design is based on functional departmentalization. This small manufacturing firm uses managers at the vice presidential level to coordinate activities within each functional area of the organization. Note that each functional area is dependent on the others.

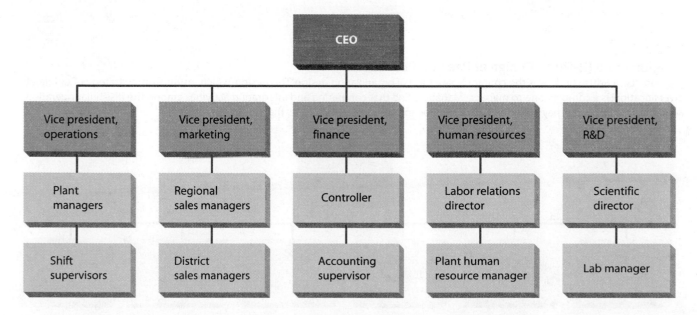

operations to sell and funds from finance to pay for advertising. The WD-40 Company, which makes a popular lubricating oil, and the McIlhenny Company, which makes Tabasco sauce, are both examples of firms that use the U-form design.

In general, this approach shares the basic advantages and disadvantages of functional departmentalization. Thus, it allows the organization to staff all important positions with functional experts and facilitates coordination and integration. On the other hand, it also promotes a functional rather than an organizational focus and tends to promote centralization. And as we noted in Chapter 11, functionally based designs are most commonly used in small organizations because an individual CEO can easily oversee and coordinate the entire organization. As an organization grows, the CEO finds staying on top of all functional areas increasingly difficult.

Conglomerate (H-Form) Design

H-form or conglomerate design
An arrangement used by an organization made up of a set of unrelated businesses

Another common form of organization design is the conglomerate, or H-form, approach.[21] The **conglomerate** design is used by an organization made up of a set of unrelated businesses. Thus, the **H-form design** is essentially a holding company that results from unrelated diversification. (The *H* in this term stands for "holding.")

This approach is based loosely on the product form of departmentalization (see Chapter 11). Each business or set of businesses is operated by a general manager who is responsible for its profits or losses, and each general manager functions independently of the others. Pearson PLC, a British firm, uses the H-form design. As illustrated in Figure 12.2, Pearson consists of six business groups. Although its periodicals and publishing operations are related to one another, all of its other businesses are clearly unrelated. Other firms that use the H-form design include General Electric (aircraft engines, appliances, broadcasting, financial services, lighting products, plastics, and other unrelated businesses) and Tenneco (pipelines, auto parts, shipbuilding, financial services, and other unrelated busi-

Figure 12.2

Conglomerate (H-Form) Design at Pearson PLC

Pearson PLC, a British firm, uses the conglomerate form of organization design. This design, which results from a strategy of unrelated diversification, is a complex one to manage. Managers find that comparing and integrating activities among the dissimilar operations are difficult. Companies may abandon this design for another approach, such as the M-form design.

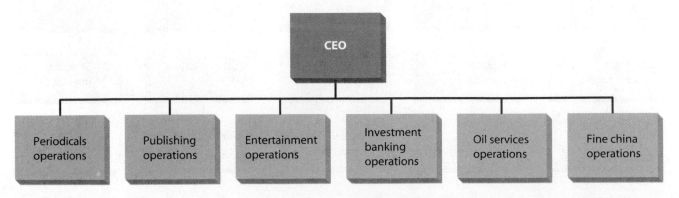

nesses). *Today's Management Issues* describes how Johnson & Johnson is using this approach.

In an H-form organization, a corporate staff usually evaluates the performance of each business, allocates corporate resources across companies, and shapes decisions about buying and selling businesses. The basic shortcoming of the H-form design is the complexity associated with holding diverse and unrelated businesses. Managers usually find comparing and integrating activities across a large number of diverse operations difficult. Research by Michael Porter suggests that many organizations following this approach achieve only average to weak financial performance.[22] Thus, although some U.S. firms are still using the H-form design, many have also abandoned it for other approaches.

TODAY'S MANAGEMENT ISSUES

JOHNSON & JOHNSON STAYS ON THE CONGLOMERATE PATH

Can Johnson & Johnson effectively manage all three of its distinctly different divisions? Its professional business makes medical devices such as surgical products, coronary stents, and wound closures; its pharmaceuticals business makes drugs such as Procrit for anemia and Levaquin for infections; its consumer products business makes baby products, Band-Aids, and Neutrogena skin-care products. This diverse combination of operations generates more than $27 billion in annual sales—with pharmaceuticals, the largest division, bringing in most of the recent sales growth.

CEO Ralph Larsen believes that having three separate divisions under one corporate umbrella gives Johnson & Johnson financial balance in case of a downturn in one division. He also says that this decentralized organization design encourages entrepreneurial spirit within each division. In fact, some parts of this diverse conglomerate are doing quite well—while others are plodding along, causing some concern about the company's diversification strategy.

In the pharmaceuticals division, for example, Johnson & Johnson had to withdraw a heartburn drug from the U.S. market after learning of serious side effects. Another setback occurred when federal regulators refused to approve a diabetes drug that the company spent $20 million to license from its maker. Despite these problems, pharmaceutical products to treat all kinds of medical conditions are in growing demand in both domestic and global markets, so this division remains a particular focus within Johnson & Johnson.

At the same time, other divisions are seeing slower growth. The consumer products division is not growing as quickly as the other two divisions, in part because of declines in international sales. The professional division has suffered because competitors offering improved coronary stents are siphoning off most of Johnson & Johnson's sales of this product. To prevent similar problems in the future, the company is now planning for improvements even before it introduces its first version of a new product. With tighter controls and better planning, Larsen is sticking to his organization design rather than breaking the company into three separate businesses.

> *Twenty years from now, you can tell me whether I am right or wrong. But I am convinced that the future belongs to those companies that are broadly based.*
>
> —*Ralph Larsen, CEO of Johnson & Johnson**

References: Jeff May, "Strong First Quarter Relieves Johnson & Johnson's Pain," *The Star-Ledger (Newark)*, April 18, 2000; "Johnson & Johnson 1999 EPS Rose 13.8% on Sales Increase of 14.5%," *PR Newswire*, January 25, 2000, http://www.jnj.com; Robert Langreth and Ron Winslow, "At J&J, A Venerable Strategy Faces Questions," *Wall Street Journal*, March 5, 1999, pp. B1, B4 (*quote on p. B1).

Divisional (M-Form) Design

M-Form or **divisional design** An organizational arrangement based on multiple businesses in related areas operating within a larger organizational framework

In the divisional design, which is becoming increasingly popular, a product form of organization is also used; in contrast to the H-form design, however, the divisions are related. Thus, the **divisional design**, or **M-form** (for "multidivisional"), is based on multiple businesses in related areas operating within a larger organizational framework. This design results from a strategy of related diversification.

Some activities are extremely decentralized down to the divisional level; others are centralized at the corporate level.[23] As shown in Figure 12.3, The Limited uses this approach. Each of its divisions is headed by a general manager and operates with reasonable autonomy, but the divisions also coordinate their activities as is appropriate. Other firms that use this approach are The Walt Disney Company (theme parks, movies, and merchandising units, all interrelated) and Hewlett-Packard (computers, printers, scanners, electronic medical equipment, and other electronic instrumentation).

The opportunities for coordination and shared resources represent one of the biggest advantages of the M-form design. The Limited's marketing research and purchasing departments are centralized. Thus, a buyer can inspect a manufacturer's entire product line, buy some designs for The Limited chain, others for Express, and still others for Lerner New York. The M-form design's basic objective is to optimize internal competition and cooperation. Healthy competition among divisions for resources can enhance effectiveness, but cooperation should also be promoted. Research suggests that the M-form organization that can achieve and maintain this balance will outperform large U-form and all H-form organizations.[24]

Matrix Design

matrix design An organizational design based on two overlapping bases of departmentalization

The **matrix design**, another common approach to organization design, is based on two overlapping bases of departmentalization.[25] The foundation of a matrix is a set

Figure 12.3

Multidivisional (M-Form) Design at The Limited, Inc.

The Limited, Inc., uses the multidivisional approach to organization design. Although each unit operates with relative autonomy, all units function in the same general market. This design resulted from a strategy of related diversification. Other firms that use M-form designs include PepsiCo and Woolworth Corporation.

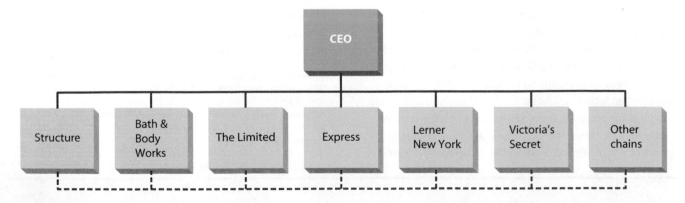

of functional departments. A set of product groups, or temporary departments, is then superimposed across the functional departments. Employees in a matrix are simultaneously members of a functional department (such as engineering) and of a project team.

Figure 12.4 shows a basic matrix design. At the top of the organization are functional units headed by vice presidents of engineering, production, finance, and marketing. Each of these managers has several subordinates. Along the side of the organization are a number of positions called *project manager*. Each project manager heads a project group composed of representatives or workers from the functional departments. Note from the figure that a matrix reflects a *multiple-command structure*—any given individual reports to both a functional superior and one or more project managers.

The project groups, or teams, are assigned to designated projects or programs. For example, the company might be developing a new product. Representatives are chosen from each functional area to work as a team on the new product. They also retain membership in the original functional group. At any given time, a person

Figure 12.4

A Matrix Organization

A matrix organization design is created by superimposing a product form of departmentalization onto an existing functional organization. Project managers coordinate teams of employees drawn from different functional departments. Thus, a matrix relies on a multiple-command structure.

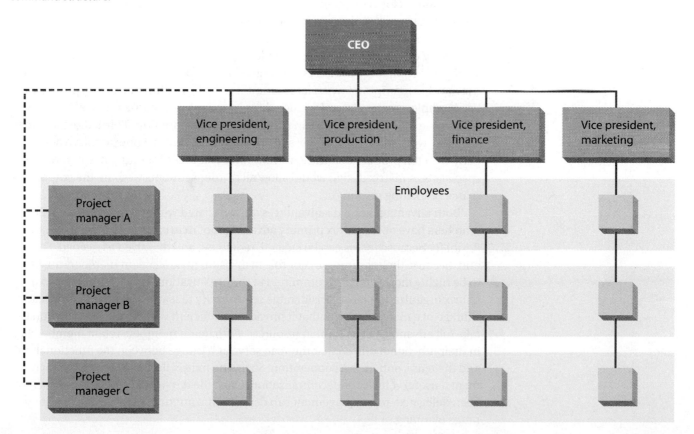

may be a member of several teams as well as a member of a functional group. Ford used this approach in creating its popular Focus automobile. It formed a group called "Team Focus" made up of designers, engineers, production specialists, marketing specialists, and other experts from different areas of the company. This group facilitated getting a very successful product to the market at least a year earlier than would have been possible using Ford's previous approaches.

Martha Stewart has also created a matrix organization for her burgeoning lifestyle business. The company was first organized broadly into media and merchandising groups, each of which has specific product and product groups. Layered on top of this structure are teams of lifestyle experts organized into groups such as cooking, crafts, weddings, and so forth. Each of these groups is targeted toward specific customer needs, but they work as necessary across all of the product groups. For example, a wedding expert might contribute to an article on wedding planning for a Martha Stewart magazine, contribute a story idea for a cable television program, and supply content for a Martha Stewart web site. This same individual might also help select fabrics suitable for wedding gowns for retailing.[26]

Many other organizations have also used the matrix design. Notable among them are American Cyanamid, Monsanto Company, NCR, The Chase Manhattan Bank, Prudential, General Motors, Compaq Computer, and several state and federal government agencies. Some organizations, however, such as Citibank and the Dutch firm Philips, adopted and then dropped the matrix design. Thus, it is important to recognize that a matrix design is not always appropriate.

The matrix form of organization design is most often used in one of three situations.[27] First, a matrix may work when there is strong pressure from the environment. For example, intense external competition may dictate the sort of strong marketing thrust that is best spearheaded by a functional department, but the diversity of a company's products may argue for product departments. Second, a matrix may be appropriate when large amounts of information need to be processed. For example, creating lateral relationships by means of a matrix is one effective way to increase the organization's capacity to process information. Third, the matrix design may work when there is pressure for shared resources. For example, a company with ten product departments may have resources for only three marketing specialists. A matrix design would allow all the departments to share the company's scarce marketing resources.

Both advantages and disadvantages are associated with the matrix design. Researchers have observed six primary advantages of matrix designs. First, it enhances flexibility because teams can be created, redefined, and dissolved as needed. Second, because they assume a major role in decision making, team members are likely to be highly motivated and committed to the organization. Third, employees in a matrix organization have considerable opportunity to learn new skills. A fourth advantage of a matrix design is that it provides an efficient way for the organization to take full advantage of its human resources. Fifth, team members retain membership in their functional unit so that they can serve as a bridge between the functional unit and the team, enhancing cooperation. Sixth, the matrix design gives top management a useful vehicle for decentralization. Once the day-to-day operations have been delegated, top management can devote more attention to areas such as long-range planning.

On the other hand, the matrix design also has some major disadvantages. Employees may be uncertain about reporting relationships, especially if they are simultaneously assigned to a functional manager and to several project managers. To complicate matters, some managers see the matrix as a form of anarchy in which they have unlimited freedom. Another set of problems is associated with the dynamics of group behavior. Groups take longer than individuals to make decisions, may be dominated by one individual, and may compromise too much. They may also get bogged down in discussion and not focus on their primary objectives. Finally, in a matrix, more time may be required for coordinating task-related activities.[28]

Hybrid Designs

Some organizations use a design that represents a hybrid of two or more of the common forms of organization design.[29] For example, an organization may have five related divisions and one unrelated division, making its design a cross between an M-form and an H-form. Indeed, few companies use a design in its pure form: most firms have one basic organization design as a foundation to managing the business but maintain sufficient flexibility so that temporary or permanent modifications can be made for strategic purposes. Ford, for example, used the matrix approach to design the Taurus and the Mustang, but the company is basically a U-form organization showing signs of moving to an M-form design. As we noted earlier, any combination of factors may dictate the appropriate form of design for any particular company.

MANAGEMENT IMPLICATIONS Managers need to understand the various basic forms of organization design, as well as the strengths and weaknesses of each. In addition, it is especially important that key decision makers know the best circumstances for using each approach. Further, they should not follow any given approach too rigidly. Instead, consistent with the hybrid model, managers should pick and choose the best of each model of organization design that fits their own unique needs.

■ Emerging Issues in Organization Design

Finally, in today's complex and ever-changing environment, it should come as no surprise that managers continue to explore and experiment with new forms of organization design. As discussed in *Managing in an E-business World*, for example, Schwab is doing just that. Many organizations today are creating designs for themselves that maximize their ability to adapt to changing circumstances and to a changing environment. They try to accomplish this adaptability by not becoming too compartmentalized or too rigid. As we noted earlier, bureaucratic organizations are hard to change, slow, and inflexible. To avoid these problems, then, organizations can try to be as different from bureaucracies as possible—relatively few rules, general job descriptions, and so forth. This final section highlights some of the more important emerging issues.[30]

THE WEB'S INFLUENCE ON ORGANIZATION DESIGN

No organization design lasts forever, but e-businesses have to be especially attentive to design as they evolve and adapt to the dynamic Internet environment. The number of Internet users continues to rise every day, as does the number of companies opening web-based businesses. Because the Internet offers many choices and allows convenient comparisons between competing products and services, buyers have more power than ever before. As a result, e-businesses stand to lose customers if they fail to adjust to emerging needs and trends.

The Web is also erasing geographic and time boundaries separating companies and consumers, business units and industrial suppliers. With a click of the mouse, customers can quickly find, price, and buy the best products for their requirements—regardless of location or time of day. These changes can spell disaster for bureaucratic organizations unprepared to respond quickly to shifts in customer buying patterns.

Charles Schwab, one of the largest U.S. discount brokerage firms, confronted these issues when management realized that the Internet was changing the way investors buy and sell stocks and bonds. At first, the company set up a separate e-business to offer basic brokerage services with lower fees for web-only transactions. Soon its Internet customers were clamoring for the same service and choices as non-Internet customers. Meantime, non-Internet customers were asking for on-line trading privileges with the same low fees paid by Internet customers. In response, Schwab merged its Internet and non-Internet businesses to create one brokerage firm with multiple access choices for customers and the low fee structure offered by the Internet unit. Now nearly 70 percent of all customer transactions move through the company's web site—making Schwab the leading broker on the Internet.

> *We used to reinvent the company about every ten years. Now it seems like we have to reinvent our company every two years.*
>
> —*David P. Pottruck, president of Charles Schwab**

References: Fred Andrews, "Rock-Solid Values at Reinvention's Core," *New York Times,* April 30, 2000, sec. 3, p. 7 (*quote on p. 7); Megan Barnett, "Schwab's MVP," *Industry Standard,* May 1, 2000, p. 270; Gary Hamel and Jeff Sampler, "The E-Corporation," *Fortune,* December 7, 1998, pp. 80–92.

The Team Organization

team organization An approach to organization design that relies almost exclusively on project-type teams, with little or no underlying functional hierarchy

Some organizations today are using the **team organization**, an approach to organization design that relies almost exclusively on project-type teams, with little or no underlying functional hierarchy. Within such an organization people float from project to project as necessitated by their skills and the demands of those projects. At Cypress Semiconductor, T. J. Rodgers refuses to allow the organization to grow so large that it can't function this way. Whenever a unit or group starts getting too large, he simply splits it into smaller units. Consequently, all units within the organization are small. This approach allows them to change direction, explore new ideas, and try new methods without a rigid bureaucratic organizational context. Although few organizations have actually reached this level of adaptability, Apple Computer and Xerox are among those moving toward it.[31]

The Virtual Organization

Closely related to the team organization is the virtual organization. A **virtual organization** is one that has little or no formal structure. Such an organization typically has only a handful of permanent employees and a very small staff and administrative headquarters facility. As the needs of the organization change, its managers bring in temporary workers, lease facilities, and outsource basic support services to meet the demands of each unique situation. As the situation changes, the temporary workforce changes in parallel, with some people leaving the organization and others entering. Facilities and the services subcontracted to others change as well. Thus, the organization exists only in response to its needs. And increasingly, virtual organizations are conducting most—if not all—of their business on-line.[32]

For example, Global Research Consortium is a virtual organization. GRC offers research and consulting services to firms doing business in Asia. As clients request various services, GRC's staff of three permanent employees subcontract the work to an appropriate set of several dozen independent consultants and/or researchers with whom it has relationships. At any given time, therefore, GRC may have several projects underway and twenty or thirty people working on projects. As the projects change, so too does the composition of the organization.

virtual organization One that has little or no formal structure

The Learning Organization

Another recent approach to organization design is the so-called learning organization. Organizations that adopt this approach work to integrate continuous improvement with continuous employee learning and development. Specifically, a **learning organization** is one that works to facilitate the lifelong learning and personal development of all of its employees while continually transforming itself to respond to changing demands and needs.[33]

While managers might approach the concept of a learning organization from a variety of perspectives, improved quality, continuous improvement, and performance measurement are frequent goals. The idea is that the most consistent and logical strategy for achieving continuous improvement is by constantly upgrading employee talent, skill, and knowledge. For example, if each employee in an organization learns one new thing each day and can translate that knowledge into work-related practice, continuous improvement will logically follow. Indeed, organizations that wholeheartedly embrace this approach believe that only constant learning by employees can make continuous improvement really occur.

In recent years many different organizations have implemented this approach. For example, the Shell Oil Company recently purchased an executive conference center north of its headquarters in Houston. The center boosts state-of-the-art classrooms and instructional technology, lodging facilities, a restaurant, and recreational amenities such as a golf course, swimming pool, and tennis courts. Line managers at the firm rotate through the Shell Learning Center, as the facility has been renamed, and serve as teaching faculty. Such teaching assignments last anywhere from a few days to several months. At the same time, all

learning organization One that works to facilitate the lifelong learning and personal development of all of its employees while continually transforming itself to respond to changing demands and needs

Firms that want to expand internationally often find it necessary to alter their organization design as they grow. For example, Invacare is a growing manufacturer of wheelchairs and other equipment for disabled workers. But because of different working conditions and government regulations in different countries, Invacare has different units for designing and constructing its wheelchairs bound for such countries as Germany, England, and France.

Shell employees routinely attend training programs, seminars, and related activities, all the while learning the latest information they need to contribute more effectively to the firm. Recent seminar topics have ranged from time management to implications of the Americans with Disabilities Act, to balancing work and family demands, to international trade theory.

Issues in International Organization Design

Another emerging issue in organization design is the trend toward the internationalization of business. As we discussed in Chapter 5, most businesses today interact with suppliers, customers, or competitors (or all three) from other countries. The relevant issue for organization design is how to design the firm to deal most effectively with international forces and to compete in global markets. For example, consider a moderate-size company that has just decided to go international. Should it set up an international division? Should it retain its current structure and establish an international operating group? Or should it make its international operations an autonomous subunit?[34]

Figure 12.5 illustrates four of the most common approaches to organization design used for international purposes. The design shown in A is the simplest, relying on a separate international division. Levi Strauss & Co. uses this approach. The design shown in B, used by Ford Motor Co., is an extension of location departmentalization to international settings. An extension of product departmentalization, with each product manager being responsible for all product-related activities regardless of location, is shown in C. Finally, the design shown in D, most typical of larger multinational corporations, is an extension of the multidivisional structure

Figure 12.5

Common Organization Designs for International Organizations

Companies that compete in international markets must create an organization design that fits their own unique circumstances. These four general designs are representative of what many international organizations use. Each is derived from one of the basic forms of organization design.

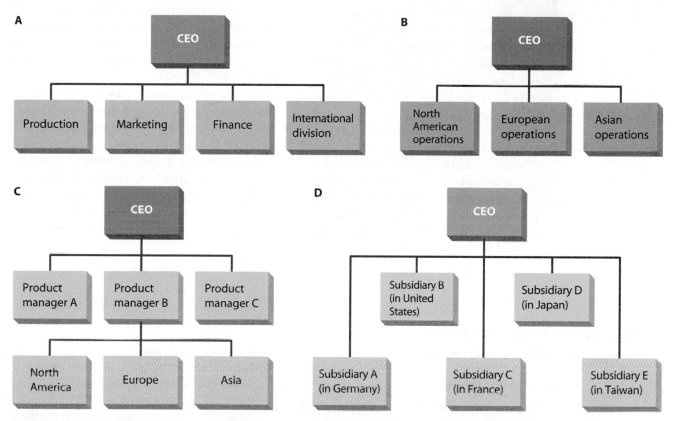

with branches located in various foreign markets. Nestlé and Unilever use this type of design.

MANAGEMENT Managers should be aware of emerging issues in organization
IMPLICATIONS design. They need to be prepared to capitalize on the newest
thinking and breakthroughs regarding organization design to keep pace with their
competitors. Of course, they should also be wary of jumping on any bandwagon
too quickly and falling victim to an ineffective fad.

Summary of Key Points

Organization design is the overall set of structural elements and the relationships among those elements used to manage the total organization. Two early universal models of organization design were the bureaucratic model and the behavioral model. These models attempted to prescribe how all organizations should be designed.

The situational view of organization design is based on the assumption that the optimal organization design is a function of situational factors. Four important situational factors are technology, environment, organizational size, and organizational life cycle. Each of these factors plays a role in determining how an organization should be designed.

An organization's strategy also helps shape its design. In various ways, corporate- and business-level strategies both affect organization design. Basic organizational functions like marketing and finance also play a role in shaping design.

Many organizations today adopt one of four basic organization designs: functional (U-form), conglomerate (H-form), divisional (M-form), or matrix. Other organizations use a hybrid design derived from two or more of these basic designs.

Four emerging issues in organization design are the team organization, the virtual organization, the learning organization, and how international businesses should be designed.

Discussion Questions

Questions for Review

1. Compare and contrast the bureaucratic and behavioral models of organization design. What are the advantages and disadvantages of each?
2. What are the basic situational factors that affect an organization's design?
3. How are an organization's strategy and its structure related?
4. Describe the basic forms of organization design. Outline the advantages and disadvantages of each.

Questions for Analysis

5. Can bureaucratic organizations avoid the problems usually associated with bureaucracies? If so, how? If not, why not? Do you think bureaucracies are still necessary? Why or why not? Is retaining the desirable aspects of bureaucracy and eliminating the undesirable ones possible? Why or why not?
6. The matrix organization design is complex and difficult to implement successfully. Why then do so many organizations use it?
7. Identify common and unique problems in organization design confronted by international businesses when compared with domestic businesses.

Questions for Application

8. What form of organization does your university or college use? What form does your city or town government use? What form do other organizations with which you are familiar use? What similarities and differences do you see? Why?
9. A question in Chapter 8 asks you to interview the manager of a local small business to determine how (or if) he or she formu-

lates strategy. Interview that same manager again to obtain a description of his or her organization design. Can you identify any links between the manager's strategy and the structure of his or her organization? Share your findings with the class.

10. Interview members of a local organization (fast-food chain, department store, bookstore, bank, church, home and school association, etc.) to ascertain how adaptable they perceive their organization to be.

BUILDING EFFECTIVE *communication* SKILLS

Exercise Overview

Communication skills refer to the manager's abilities both to convey ideas and information effectively to others and to receive ideas and information effectively from others. This exercise will enable you to see how communication works in different kinds of organization design.

Exercise Background

This chapter introduces you to several kinds of organization design that a business might use to structure itself. Given that organization design defines, at least in part, the interrelationships among different jobs and positions within the organization, it stands to reason that organization design and communication patterns will be interrelated. Using a sheet of paper, sketch basic organization designs based on the bureaucratic, U-form, M-form, H-form, and matrix designs. Each design should be several levels high and several positions wide.

Exercise Task

With the background information above as context, do the following:

1. Identify a single position toward the middle of each of the organization designs you have drawn and assume that you are holding that position in the organization.
2. Think of a circumstance in which you might need to communicate with four other individuals in the organization. Each should be in a different area and in a different level from your own.
3. Describe the processes you might need to follow for each communication; that is, consider issues such as chain of command, reporting relationships, and so forth.
4. Decide which forms of organization design are most conducive to communication and which are least conducive.
5. Does the content of the message matter? In what ways?

BUILDING EFFECTIVE *conceptual* SKILLS

Exercise Overview

Conceptual skills include a manager's ability to think in the abstract. This exercise will encourage you to apply your conceptual skills to the concepts associated with the situational influences on organization design.

Exercise Background

As noted in this chapter, several factors affect the appropriate design of an organization. The key factors discussed in the text are core technology, the organization's environment, its size, and its life cycle. The chapter does not provide detail, however, about how the situational factors working together in different combinations might affect organization design. For example, how might a particular form of technology and certain environmental forces together influence organization design?

The text also notes several basic forms of organization design, such as the functional, conglomerate, divisional, and matrix approaches. Some implications are also drawn about how situational factors relate to each design.

Exercise Task

With these ideas in mind, do the following:
1. Identify a firm for each of the four basic forms of organization design. Assess the

technology, environment, organizational size, and organizational life cycle for the four firms.
2. Now relate each situational factor to the design used by each firm.
3. Form an opinion about the actual relationship between each factor and the design used by each firm. That is, do you think that each firm's design is directly determined by its environment, or is the relationship you observe coincidental?
4. Can you prioritize the relative importance of the situational factors across the firms? Does the rank-order importance of the factors vary in any systematic way?

BUILDING EFFECTIVE *decision-making* SKILLS

Exercise Overview

Decision-making skills refer to the manager's ability to recognize and define problems and opportunities correctly and then to select an appropriate course of action to solve problems and capitalize on opportunities. The purpose of this exercise is to give you insights into how managers must make decisions within the context of creating an organization design.

Exercise Background

Assume that you have decided to open a casual sportswear business in your local community. Your products will be athletic caps, shirts, shorts, and sweats emblazoned with the logos of your college and local high schools. You are a talented designer and have developed some ideas that will make your products unique and very popular. You have also inherited enough money to get your business up and running and to cover about one year of living expenses (i.e., you do not need to pay yourself a salary).

You intend to buy sportswear in various sizes and styles from other suppliers. Your firm will then use silkscreen processes to add the logos and other decorative touches to the prod-

ucts. Local clothing store owners have seen samples of your products and have indicated a keen interest in selling them. You know, however, that you will still need to service accounts and keep your customers happy.

At the present time, you are trying to determine how many people you need to get your business going and how to group them most effectively into an organization. You realize that you can start out quite small and then expand as sales warrant. However, you also worry that if you are continually adding people and rearranging your organization that confusion and inefficiency will result.

Exercise Task

Step One: Under each of the scenarios below, decide how best to design your organization. Sketch a basic organization chart to show your thoughts.

Scenario 1—You will sell the products yourself, and you intend to start with a workforce of five people.
Scenario 2—You intend to oversee production yourself and to start with a workforce of nine people.

Scenario 3—You do not intend to handle any one function yourself but will instead oversee the entire operation, and you intend to start with a workforce of fifteen people.

Step Two: Form small groups of four to five people each. Compare your various organization charts, focusing on similarities and differences.

Step Three: Working in the same group, assume that five years have passed and that your business has been a big success. You have a large plant for making your products, and you are shipping them to fifteen states. You employ al-

most five hundred people. Create an organization design that you think fits this organization best.

Follow-up Questions

1. How clear or ambiguous were the decisions about organization design?
2. What are your thoughts about starting out too large to maintain stability as opposed to starting small and then growing?
3. What basic factors did you consider in choosing a design?

CHAPTER CLOSING CASE

MANAGING THE GOLDEN ARCHES AROUND THE WORLD

From Boston to Beijing and beyond, the golden arches of McDonald's look out on highways and streets in nearly every country around the world. The Illinois-based fast food chain is working toward higher sales and is defending its market leadership in partnership with the five thousand franchise owners who operate twenty-seven thousand restaurants in the United States and abroad. Although a variety of hamburgers and fish sandwiches built the chain into a powerhouse, McDonald's has not had a large-scale, new-product hit for some years. Therefore, in addition to boosting sales in franchised restaurants, a good portion of McDonald's future growth may have to come from its stakes in nonburger chains, including Donatos Pizza, Chipotle Mexican Grill, and Boston Market.

For years, managers at McDonald's Illinois headquarters tightly controlled prices, product development, and other key functions to ensure chainwide consistency and quality. However, franchisees objected to some corporate decisions. For example, many U.S. franchisees refused to follow the corporation's strategy of cutting prices on Big Macs and breakfast items in 1997. Following that clash between franchisees and corporate management, McDonald's reversed course to decentralize pricing, among other operational details.

Now the specially priced Happy Meal is the only discount that headquarters supports with national advertising, leaving other pricing to the discretion of local franchisees.

McDonald's has also divided its global business into five regional zones and delegated decision-making authority to the managers overseeing each of these regions. This structure put the focus on each region's opportunities and challenges to encourage faster and more responsive reaction to emerging changes and trends. On the local level, franchisees have the freedom to tailor their restaurants and menus to each local market. Customers at one McDonald's in Burleson, Texas, can play computer games while they sip their soft drinks; at a store in Plano, Texas, they sit on richly stained chairs beneath chandeliers. Halfway around the world, customers who visit McDonald's in Hong Kong can order tea and lounge around reading or bring their children to meet Uncle McDonald (the local counterpart of chain mascot Ronald McDonald).

Although the golden arches are clearly a symbol of American culture, franchisees carefully blend the corporation's efficient operating methods with locally influenced food and decor. They also follow McDonald's time-tested practice of promoting from within to build the ranks of local management. Behind the scenes, the fast-food giant searches out local suppliers for international restaurants rather than relying on long-distance shipments of potatoes and other ingredients from a few central suppliers. These details matter because McDonald's has all but saturated the U.S. market, so management is keenly interested in international expansion.

With even more attention to detail, the company is improving its operational expertise by introducing a sophisticated cooking system to speed food preparation and keep menu items hot. Meanwhile, back in the kitchens at McDonald's Illinois headquarters, new-product experts are cooking up new offerings to supplement the chain's traditional menu selections. Did somebody say higher sales?

Case Questions

1. Which organization design is McDonald's using internationally? How is this design appropriate for the company's international situation?

2. How does McDonald's working relationship with franchisees make it a learning organization?

3. Where in the organizational life cycle would you position McDonald's? How does this affect the company's organization design?

Case References

Worth Wren Jr., "McDonald's Reinvents Itself to Recoup Lost Market Share," *Fort Worth Star-Telegram*, July 27, 2000; James L. Watson, "China's Big Mac Attack," *Foreign Affairs*, May–June 2000, pp. 120ff.; Bruce Horovitz, "Restoring the Golden-Arch Shine," *USA Today*, June 16, 1999, p. 3B.

CHAPTER NOTES

1. "Siemens Climbs Back," *Business Week*, June 5, 2000, pp. 79–82 (quote on p. 82); *Hoover's Handbook of World Business 2001* (Austin: Hoover's Business Press, 2001), pp. 548–549.

2. See Gareth Jones, *Organization Theory*, 3rd Edition (Upper Saddle River, N.J.: Prentice-Hall, 2001).

3. Max Weber, *Theory of Social and Economic Organizations*, trans. by T. Parsons (New York: Free Press, 1947).

4. Paul Jarley, Jack Fiorito, and John Thomas Delany, "A Structural Contingency Approach to Bureaucracy and Democracy in U.S. National Unions," *Academy of Management Journal*, 1997, Vol. 40, No. 4, pp. 831–861.

5. Rensis Likert, *New Patterns in Management* (New York: McGraw-Hill, 1961), and Rensis Likert, *The Human Organization* (New York: McGraw-Hill, 1967).

6. William F. Dowling, "At General Motors: System 4 Builds Performance and Profits," *Organizational Dynamics*, Winter 1975, pp. 23–28.

7. Jones, *Organization Theory*. See also "The Great Transformation," *Business Week*, August 28, 2000, pp. 84–99.

8. Joan Woodward, *Industrial Organization: Theory and Practice* (London: Oxford University Press, 1965).

9. Joan Woodward, *Management and Technology, Problems of Progress Industry*, No. 3 (London: Her Majesty's Stationery Office, 1958).

10. William Bridges, "The End of the Job," *Fortune*, September 19, 1994, pp. 62–74.

11. Tom Burns and G. M. Stalker, *The Management of Innovation* (London: Tavistock, 1961).

12. Paul R. Lawrence and Jay W. Lorsch, *Organization and Environment* (Homewood, Ill.: Irwin, 1967).

13. Edward E. Lawler III, "Rethinking Organization Size," *Organizational Dynamics*, Autumn 1997, pp. 24–33; see also Tom Brown, "How Big Is Too Big?" *Across the Board*, July–August 1999, pp. 14–20.

14. Derek S. Pugh and David J. Hickson, *Organization Structure in Its Context: The Aston Program I* (Lexington, Mass.: D.C. Heath, 1976).

15. Robert H. Miles and Associates, *The Organizational Life Cycle* (San Francisco: Jossey-Bass, 1980). See also "Is Your Company Too Big?" *Business Week*, March 27, 1989, pp. 84–94.

16. Douglas Baker and John Cullen, "Administrative Reorganization and Configurational Context: The Contingent Effects of Age, Size, and Change in Size," *Academy of Management Journal*, 1993, Vol. 36, No. 6, pp. 1251–1277. See also Kevin Crowston, "A Coordination Theory Approach to Organizational Process Design," *Organization Science*, March–April 1997, pp. 157–168.

17. See Charles W. L. Hill and Gareth Jones, *Strategic Management: An Analytic Approach*, 5th Edition (Boston: Houghton Mifflin Co., 2001).

18. See "The Corporate Ecosystem," *Business Week*, August 28, 2000, pp. 166–197.

19. Richard D'Aveni and David Ravenscraft, "Economies of Integration Versus Bureaucrat Costs: Does Vertical Integration Improve Performance?" *Academy of Management Journal*, 1994, Vol. 37, No. 5, pp. 1167–1206.

20. Oliver E. Williamson, *Markets and Hierarchies* (New York: Free Press, 1975).

21. Williamson, *Markets and Hierarchies*.

22. Michael E. Porter, "From Competitive Advantage to Corporate Strategy," *Harvard Business Review*, May–June 1987, pp. 43–59.

23. Williamson, *Markets and Hierarchies*.

24. Jay B. Barney and William G. Ouchi (Eds.), *Organizational Economics* (San Francisco: Jossey-Bass, 1986), and Robert E. Hoskisson, "Multidivisional Structure and Performance: The Contingency of Diversification Strategy," *Academy of Management Journal*, December 1987, pp. 625–644. See also Bruce Lamont, Robert Williams, and James Hoffman, "Performance During 'M-Form' Reorganization and Recovery Time: The Effects of Prior Strategy and Implementation Speed," *Academy of Management Journal*, 1994, Vol. 37, No. 1, pp. 153–166.

25. Stanley M. Davis and Paul R. Lawrence, *Matrix* (Reading, Mass.: Addison-Wesley, 1977).

26. "Martha, Inc.," *Business Week*, January 17, 2000, pp. 63–72.

27. Davis and Lawrence, *Matrix*.

28. See Lawton Burns and Douglas Wholey, "Adoption and Abandonment of Matrix Management Programs: Effects of Organizational Characteristics and Interorganizational Networks," *Academy of Management Journal*, Vol. 36, No. 1, pp. 106–138.

29. See Michael Hammer and Steven Stanton, "How Process Enterprises *Really* Work," *Harvard Business Review*, November–December 1999, pp. 108–118.

30. Raymond E. Miles, Charles C. Snow, John A. Mathews, Grant Miles, and Henry J. Coleman, Jr., "Organizing in the Knowledge Age: Anticipating the Cellular Form," *The Academy of Management Executive*, November 1997, pp. 7–24.

31. "The Horizontal Corporation," *Business Week*, December 20, 1993, pp. 76–81; and Shawn Tully, "The Modular Corporation," *Fortune*, February 8, 1993, pp. 106–114.

32. "Management by Web," *Business Week*, August 28, 2000, pp. 84–96.

33. Peter Senge, *The Fifth Discipline* (New York: The Free Press, 1993). See also David Lei, John W. Slocum, and Robert A. Pitts, "Designing Organizations for Competitive Advantage: The Power of Unlearning and Learning," *Organizational Dynamics*, Winter 1999, pp. 24–35.

34. See William G. Egelhoff, "Strategy and Structure in Multinational Corporations: A Revision of the Stopford and Wells Model," *Strategic Management Journal*, Vol. 9, 1988, pp. 1–14, for a recent discussion of these issues. See also Ricky W. Griffin and Michael Pustay, *International Business—A Managerial Perspective*, 3rd Edition (Upper Saddle River, N.J.: Prentice-Hall, 2002).

13 Managing Organization Change and Innovation

Nike, of course, is the world's pre-eminent athletic show company. In 1996, Nike was earning about $4 billion a year from its footwear business and another $2 billion from sports apparel and equipment. That same year the firm's founder and CEO Philip Knight stunned investors and competitors alike when he announced a goal of doubling the firm's annual revenues to a staggering $12 billion by the year 2001. But Nike has recently encountered a series of setbacks that have compelled Knight to embark on a major overhaul of the firm.

Things started coming apart for Nike in the late 1990s. The retirement of Michael Jordan, Nike icon and arguably the world's best-known professional athlete, deprived the firm of its best spokesperson. There was also an unexpected major shift among teen-agers away from athletic shoes to hiking boots and casual leather shoes. Third, a series of

reports involving substandard wages and working conditions at foreign Nike production facilities resulted in a public-relations nightmare and caused some consumers to avoid the company's products. And finally, Nike's brash in-your-face reputation was beginning to get tiresome to many consumers. By 1998, Knight had been forced to back off his bold forecasts from the recent past and Nike was posting lower-than-expected earnings reports virtually every quarter.

This dramatic and unexpected series of events caused Knight to recognize that some big changes were necessary. And it didn't really take him too long to figure out what had happened—the brash upstart had turned into the very establishment that Nike had long deplored; that is, as it had grown, the firm had also been transformed from a nimble and free-form organization

into a traditional bureaucratic behemoth. In addition, market conditions had also changed so completely that Nike's traditional way of doing business would simply no longer work.

Knight was quick to take up the challenge and has set about trying to restore the firm's lost luster. For one thing, he has totally revamped Nike's top management team, and today nine of Nike's forty-one vice presidents have been with the firm less than two years. He has also created a new sense of urgency about costs—in the old days revenues grew so fast that costs almost didn't matter, but

> **"I'm sure Nike's looking for fresh perspective, and newcomers bring a fresh perspective."**
>
> —Paul Heffernan, executive at Nike rival New Balance

LEARNING OBJECTIVES

After studying this chapter, you should be able to:

- Describe the nature of organization change, including forces for change and planned versus reactive change.

- Discuss the steps in organization change and how to manage resistance to change.

- Identify and describe major areas of organization change.

- Discuss the assumptions, techniques, and effectiveness of organization development.

- Describe the innovation process, forms of innovation, the failure to innovate, and how organizations can promote innovation.

today they are continuously scrutinized. Knight also has Nike focusing on new, emerging, and/or growing markets such as women's sports, extreme sports, and international markets. And he is paying much closer attention to foreign factories and production facilities.

Beyond these specific areas, however, Knight is also working to remake the very fabric of Nike. He wants to transform the company into one that incorporates the best of both worlds—an enterprise with the entrepreneurial spark and vision that fueled Nike in its early years combined with a more reasoned and structured business model. Toward this end, he has taken a more hands-on approach to business, spending more time at the company, being an active participant in key meetings, and voicing his opinion more strongly than he has in the past.

Knight has even acknowledged that Nike may have overdosed with its

familiar "swoosh" logo by plastering it so prominently across all its various products and on so many different sporting venues. As a result, the swoosh emblem is being made smaller for some products. And other products are being launched with totally new logos. In a lot of ways, then, it seems that Nike is taking its own message to heart—the firm needed to "just do it," so it is![1]

Philip Knight has had to grapple with something all managers must eventually confront: the need for change. He first perceived that Nike needed to make certain changes because of its growth and because of changes in the marketplace. He then had to figure out how to make those changes. And now that most of them are completed, it will be some time before he and the rest of his managers know whether or not the changes they have made are having the intended effects.

Understanding when and how to implement change is a vital part of management. This chapter describes how organizations manage change. We first examine the nature of organization change and identify the basic issues of managing change. We then identify and described major areas of change, including reengineering, a major type of change undertaken by many firms recently. We examine organization development and conclude by discussing a related area, organizational innovation.

The Nature of Organization Change

organization change Any substantive modification to some part of the organization

Organization change is any substantive modification to some part of the organization.[2] Thus, change can involve almost any aspect of an organization: work schedules, bases for departmentalization, span of management, machinery, organization design, people themselves, and so on. It is important to keep in mind that any change in an organization may have effects extending beyond the actual area where the change is implemented. For example, when Northrup Grumman recently installed a new automated production system at one of its plants, employees were trained to operate new equipment, the compensation system was adjusted to reflect new skill levels, the span of management of supervisors was altered, and several related jobs were redesigned. Selection criteria for new employees were also changed, and a new quality control system was installed.[3] In addition, it is quite common for multiple organization change activities to be going on simultaneously.[4]

Forces for Change

Why do organizations find change necessary? The basic reason is that something relevant to the organization either has changed or is going to change. The organization consequently has little choice but to change as well. Indeed, a primary reason for the problems that organizations often face is failure to anticipate or respond properly to changing circumstances. Forces for change may be external or internal to the organization.[5]

External Forces　　External forces for change derive from the organization's general and task environments. For example, two energy crises, an aggressive Japanese automobile industry, floating currency exchange rates, and floating international interest rates—all manifestations of the international dimension of the general environment—profoundly influenced U.S. automobile companies. New rules of production and competition forced them to alter dramatically the way they do business. In the political area, new laws, court decisions, and regulations affect organizations. The technological dimension may yield new production techniques that the organization needs to explore. The economic dimension is affected by inflation, the cost of living, and money supplies. The sociocultural dimension, reflecting societal values, determines what kinds of products or services will be accepted in the market.

Because of its proximity to the organization, the task environment is an even more powerful force for change. Competitors influence an organization through their price structures and product lines. When Compaq lowers the prices it charges for computers, Dell and Gateway have little choice but to follow suit. Because consumers, as a group, often determine what products can be sold at what prices, organizations must be concerned with consumer tastes and preferences. Suppliers affect organizations by raising or lowering prices or changing product lines. Regulators can have dramatic effects on an organization. For example, if OSHA rules that a particular production process is dangerous to workers, it can force a firm to close a plant until it meets higher safety standards. Unions can force change when they negotiate for higher wages or when their members strike.[6]

Internal Forces   A variety of forces inside the organization may cause change. If top management revises the organization's strategy, organization change is likely to result. A decision by an electronics company to enter the home computer market or a decision to increase a ten-year product sales goal by 3 percent would occasion many organization changes. Other internal forces for change may be reflections of external forces. As sociocultural values shift, for example, workers' attitudes toward their jobs may also shift—and workers may demand a change in working hours or working conditions. In such a case, even though the force is rooted in the external environment, the organization must respond directly to the internal pressure generated.[7]

A variety of forces, some internal and some external, can be important forces for change. Enron Corporation, for example, has become one of the most successful companies in the world by looking for opportunities for change. In simple terms, Enron buys and sells gas and electricity and earns profits on the margin between what it pays and what it earns. Enron managers were among the first, however, to see energy as a commodity that can be traded. These Enron traders in Europe play a major role in determining Europe's gas and power production rates by influencing the prices that buyers will pay. Enron is now branching out into other areas of trading, such as excess capacity on fiber-optic networks.

Planned Versus Reactive Change

Some change is planned well in advance; other change is a reaction to unexpected events. **Planned change** is change that is designed and implemented in an orderly and timely fashion in anticipation of future events. **Reactive change** is a piecemeal response to events as they occur. Because reactive change may be hurried, the potential for poorly conceived and executed change is increased. Planned change is almost always preferable to reactive change.[8]

Georgia-Pacific, a large forest-products business, is an excellent example of a firm that went through a planned and well-managed change process. When A. D. Correll became CEO, he quickly became alarmed at the firm's high accident rate—

planned change Change that is designed and implemented in an orderly and timely fashion in anticipation of future events

reactive change A piecemeal response to events as they occur

nine serious injuries per one hundred employees each year, and twenty-six deaths during the most recent five-year period. While the forest-products business is inherently dangerous, Correll believed that the accident rate was far too high and started a major change effort for improvement. He and other top managers developed a multistage change program intended to educate workers about safety, improve safety equipment in the plant, and eliminate a long-standing part of the firm's culture that made injuries almost a badge of courage. And today, Georgia-Pacific has the best safety record in the industry, with relatively few injuries.[9]

On the other hand, a few years ago Caterpillar was caught flat-footed by a worldwide recession in the construction industry, suffered enormous losses, and took several years to recover. Had managers at Caterpillar anticipated the need for change earlier, they might have been able to respond more quickly. Similarly, Kodak recently announced plans to cut ten thousand jobs, a reaction to sluggish sales and profits. Again, anticipation might have forestalled these job cuts. The importance of approaching change from a planned perspective is reinforced by the frequency of organization change. Most companies or divisions of large companies implement some form of moderate change at least every year and one or more major changes every four to five years.[10] Managers who sit back and respond only when they have to are likely to spend a lot of time hastily changing and rechanging things. A more effective approach is to anticipate forces urging change and plan ahead to deal with them.[11]

MANAGEMENT Managers should understand the meaning and pervasiveness
IMPLICATIONS of change, as well as its potential impact throughout their organization. They should also realize that change seldom stops and that multiple changes may be necessary simultaneously. Managers must also recognize that the need for change can be induced by either external or internal forces. Moreover, they should also value the importance of planned versus reactive change. Their goal should be to plan for change whenever possible.

Managing Change in Organizations

Organization change is a complex phenomenon. A manager cannot simply wave a wand and implement a planned change like magic. Instead, any change must be systematic and logical to have a realistic opportunity to succeed. To implement planning for change, the manager needs to understand the steps of effective change and how to counter employee resistance to change.[12]

Steps in the Change Process

Over the years, researchers have developed a number of models or frameworks outlining steps for change.[13] The Lewin model was one of the first, although a more comprehensive approach is usually more useful.

The Lewin Model   Kurt Lewin, a noted organizational theorist, suggested that every change requires three steps.[14] The first step is *unfreezing*—individuals who will be affected by the impending change must be led to recognize why the change is necessary. Next, the *change itself* is implemented. Finally, *refreezing* involves reinforcing and supporting the change so that it becomes part of the system. For example, one of the changes Caterpillar faced in response to the recession noted earlier involved a massive workforce reduction. The first step (unfreezing) was convincing the United Auto Workers to support the reduction because of its importance to long-term effectiveness. After this unfreezing was accomplished, thirty thousand jobs were eliminated (implementation). Then Caterpillar worked to improve its damaged relationship with its workers (refreezing) by guaranteeing future pay hikes and promising no more cutbacks. As interesting as Lewin's model is, it unfortunately lacks operational specificity. Thus, a more comprehensive perspective is often needed.

A Comprehensive Approach to Change   The comprehensive approach to change takes a systems view and delineates a series of specific steps that often lead to successful change. This expanded model is illustrated in Figure 13.1. The first step is recognizing the need for change. Reactive change might be triggered by employee complaints, declines in productivity, or turnover; court injunctions; sales slumps; or labor strikes. Recognition may simply be managers' awareness that change in a certain area is inevitable. For example, managers may be aware of the general frequency of organizational change undertaken by most organizations and recognize that their organization should probably follow the same pattern. The immediate stimulus might be the result of a forecast indicating new market potential, the accumulation of cash surplus for possible investment, or an opportunity to achieve and capitalize on a major technological breakthrough. Managers might also initiate change today because indicators suggest that it will be necessary in the near future.

Managers must next set goals for the change. To increase market share, to enter new markets, to restore employee morale, to settle a strike, and to identify investment opportunities all might be goals for change. Third, managers must diagnose what brought on the need for change. Turnover, for example, might be caused by low pay, poor working conditions, poor supervisors, or employee dissatisfaction. Thus, although turnover may be the immediate stimulus for change, managers must understand its causes to make the right changes.

The next step is to select a change technique that will accomplish the intended goals. If turnover is caused by low pay, a new reward system may be needed. If the cause is poor supervision, interpersonal skills training may be called for. (Various change techniques are summarized later in this chapter.) After the appropriate

Figure 13.1

Steps in the Change Process

Managers must understand how and why to implement change. A manager who, when implementing change, follows a logical and orderly sequence such as the one shown here is more likely to succeed than a manager whose change process is haphazard and poorly conceived.

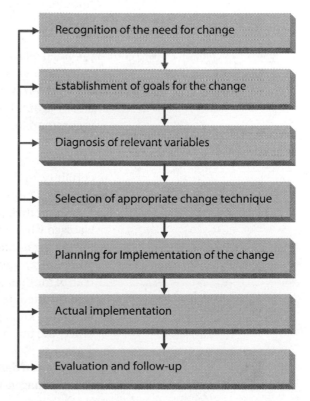

Change is a common event in most organizations today. And while much of this change is necessary and beneficial, managers sometimes engage in change activities that are either unnecessary or poorly conceived. When this happens, it increases the chances that employees will resist the change—they will experience uncertainty, threatened self-interests, different perceptions, and/or feelings of loss. Indeed, as shown in this cartoon, change can be so poorly managed that employees sense it before it even occurs and develop resistance without even knowing the details.

DILBERT by Scott Adams reprinted by permission of United Feature Syndicate.

technique has been chosen, its implementation must be planned. Issues to consider include the costs of the change, its effects on other areas of the organization, and the degree of employee participation ap-propriate for the situation. If the change is implemented as planned, the results should then be evaluated. If the change was intended to reduce turnover, managers must check turnover after the change has been in effect for a specified amount of time. If turnover is still too high, other changes may be necessary.[15]

Understanding Resistance to Change

Another element in the effective management of change is understanding the resistance that often accompanies change.[16] Managers need to know why people resist change and what can be done about their resistance. When Westinghouse first provided all its managers with personal computers, most people responded favorably. One manager, however, resisted the change to the point where he began leaving work every day at noon. It was some time before he began staying in the office all day again. This same phenomenon is illustrated in the cartoon. Such resistance is common for a variety of reasons.

Uncertainty   Perhaps the biggest cause of employee resistance to change is uncertainty. In the face of impending change, employees may become anxious and nervous. They may worry about their ability to meet new job demands, they may think that their job security is threatened, or they may simply dislike ambiguity. Nabisco was once the target of an extended and confusing takeover battle, and during the entire time employees were nervous about the impending change. The *Wall Street Journal* described them this way: "Many are angry at their leaders and fearful for their jobs. They are swapping rumors and spinning scenarios for the ultimate outcome of the battle for the tobacco and food giant. Headquarters staffers in Atlanta know so little about what's happening in New York that some call their office 'the mushroom complex,' where they are kept in the dark."[17]

Threatened Self-Interests   Many impending changes threaten the self-interests of some managers within the organization. A change might potentially diminish their power or influence within the company, so they fight it. Managers at Sears, Roebuck and Co. recently developed a plan calling for a new type of store. The new stores would be somewhat smaller than typical Sears stores and would not be located in large shopping malls. Instead, they would be located in smaller strip centers. They would carry clothes and other "soft goods" but not hardware, appliances, furniture, or automotive products. When executives in charge of the excluded product lines heard about the plan, they raised such strong objections that the plan was put on hold.

Different Perceptions   A third reason that people resist change is due to different perceptions. A manager may make a decision and recommend a plan for change on the basis of her own assessment of a situation. Others in the organization may resist the change because they do not agree with the manager's assessment or perceive the situation differently.[18] Executives at 7-Eleven are currently battling this problem as they attempt to enact a major organizational change. The corporation wants to take its convenience stores a bit upscale and begin selling fancy fresh foods to go, the newest hardcover novels, and some gourmet products. But many franchisees are balking because they see this move as taking the firm away from its core blue-collar customers.[19]

Feelings of Loss   Many changes involve altering work arrangements in ways that disrupt existing social networks. Because social relationships are important, most people resist any change that might adversely affect those relationships. Other intangibles threatened by change include power, status, security, familiarity with existing procedures, and self-confidence.

Overcoming Resistance to Change

Of course, a manager should not give up in the face of resistance to change. Although there are no surefire cures, several techniques have at least the potential to overcome resistance.[20]

Participation   Participation is often the most effective technique for overcoming resistance to change. Employees who participate in planning and implementing a change are better able to understand the reasons for the change. Uncertainty is reduced, and self-interests and social relationships are less threatened. Having had an opportunity to express their ideas and assume the perspectives of others, employees are more likely to accept the change gracefully. A classic study of participation monitored the introduction of a change in production methods among four groups in a Virginia

People in organizations often resist change for a number of different reasons. Today's breathtaking technological advancements in areas such as biotechnology and information processing seem especially troubling to some people. Harvard business professor Clayton Christensen has helped managers in many firms overcome their fear of technological change through his path-breaking work on what he calls disruptive technology. He argues, for instance, that making change a fundamental part of an organization's culture can dramatically reduce resistance to change on the part of people who are members of that organization.

pajama factory.[21] The two groups that were allowed to participate fully in planning and implementing the change improved their productivity and satisfaction significantly relative to the two groups that did not participate. 3M Company recently attributed $10 million in cost savings to employee participation in several organization change activities.[22]

Education and Communication   Educating employees about the need for and the expected results of an impending change should reduce their resistance. If open communication is established and maintained during the change process, uncertainty can be minimized. Caterpillar used these methods to reduce resistance during many of its cutbacks. First, it educated United Auto Worker (UAW) representatives about the need for and potential value of the planned changes. Then management told all employees what was happening, when it would happen, and how it would affect them individually.

Facilitation   Several facilitation procedures are also advisable. For instance, making only necessary changes, announcing those changes well in advance, and allowing time for people to adjust to new ways of doing things can help reduce resistance to change.[23] One manager at a Prudential regional office spent several months systematically planning a change in work procedures and job design. He then became too hurried, coming in over the weekend with a work crew and rearranging the office layout. When employees walked in on Monday morning, they were hostile, anxious, and resentful. What was a promising change became a disaster, and the manager had to scrap the entire plan.

Force-Field Analysis   Although force-field analysis may sound like something out of a Star Trek movie, it can help overcome resistance to change. In almost any change situation, forces are acting for and against the change. To facilitate the change, managers start by listing each set of forces and then trying to tip the balance so that the forces facilitating the change outweigh those hindering the change.

Figure 13.2

Force-Field Analysis for Plant Closing at General Motors

A force-field analysis can help a manager facilitate change. A manager able to identify forces acting both for and against a change can see where to focus efforts to remove barriers to change (such as offering training and relocation to displaced workers). Removing the forces against the change can at least partially overcome resistance.

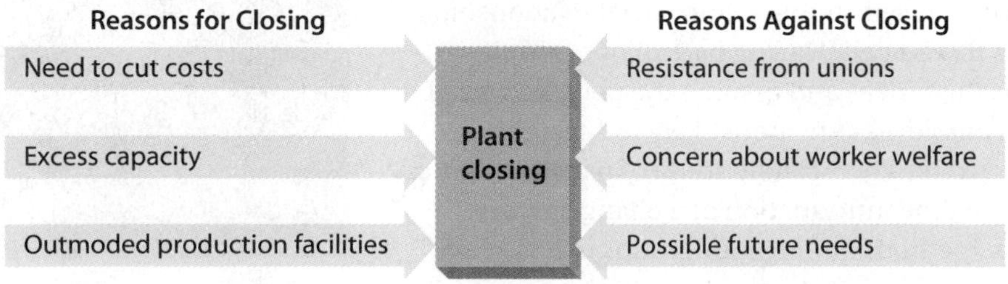

Reasons for Closing	Plant closing	Reasons Against Closing
Need to cut costs		Resistance from unions
Excess capacity		Concern about worker welfare
Outmoded production facilities		Possible future needs

It is especially important to try to remove or at least minimize some of the forces acting against the change. Suppose, for example, that General Motors is considering a plant closing as part of a change. As shown in Figure 13.2, three factors are reinforcing the change: GM needs to cut costs, it has excess capacity, and the plant has outmoded production facilities. At the same time, there is resistance from the UAW, concern for workers losing their jobs, and a feeling that the plant might be needed again in the future. GM might start by convincing the UAW that the closing is necessary with profit and loss figures. It could then offer relocation and retraining to displaced workers. And it might shut down the plant and put it in "moth balls" so that it could be renovated later. The three major factors hindering the change are thus eliminated or reduced in importance.

MANAGEMENT Managers should approach change from a logical and rational
IMPLICATIONS perspective and understand that they should proceed through a progression of events as they enact change. They should also understand that some people are likely to resist change, but that certain techniques can be used to overcome this resistance at least partially.

■ *Areas of Organization Change*

We noted earlier that change can involve virtually any part of an organization. In general, however, most change interventions involve organization structure and design, technology and operations, or people. The most common areas of change within each of these broad categories are listed in Table 13.1.

Table 13.1

Areas of Organization Change

Organization change can affect any part, area, or component of an organization. Most change, however, fits into one of three general areas: organization structure and design, technology and operations, and people.

Organization Structure and Design	Technology and Operations	People
Job design	Information technologies	Abilities and skills
Departmentalization	Equipment	Performance
Reporting relationships	Work processes	Perceptions
Authority distribution	Work sequences	Expectations
Coordination mechanisms	Control systems	Attitudes
Line-staff structure		Values
Overall design		
Culture		
Human resource management		

Changing Structure and Design

Organization change might be focused on any of the basic components of organization structure or on the organization's overall design. Thus, the organization might change the way it designs its jobs or its bases of departmentalization. Likewise, it might change reporting relationships or the distribution of authority. For example, we noted in Chapter 11 the trend toward flatter organizations. Coordination mechanisms and line and staff configurations are also subject to change. On a larger scale, the organization might change its overall design. For example, a growing business could decide to drop its functional design and adopt a divisional design. Or it might transform itself into a matrix. Finally, the organization might change any part of its human resource management system, such as its selection criteria, its performance appraisal methods, or its compensation package.[24] Toyota has been undergoing a significant series of changes in its organization structure and design that are intended to make it a flatter and more decentralized enterprise and thus more responsive to its external environment.[25]

Changing Technology and Operations

Technology is the conversion process used by an organization to transform inputs into outputs. Because of the rapid rate of all technological innovation, technological changes are becoming increasingly important to many organizations. Table 13.1 lists several areas where technological change is likely to be experienced. One important area of change today revolves around information technology. The adoption and institutionalization of information technology innovations is almost con-

Change can take place in a variety of areas in an organization. Technological change is an especially important area of change today. United Parcel Service, for example, is always on the alert for new technology that can improve its efficiency and effectiveness. One of its newest innovations is the wrist-mounted bar-code reader. Users can simply point their hand in the direction of a box, package, or other parcel and the bar-code reader registers the vital information needed to keep the shipment on-track. And users no longer have to stop and look for their reader, since it's strapped to their wrist!

stant in most firms today. Sun Microsystems, for example, has adopted a very short-range planning cycle to be prepared for environmental changes.[26] Another important form of technological change involves equipment. To keep pace with competitors, firms find that replacing existing machinery and equipment periodically with newer models is necessary.

A change in work processes or work activities may be necessary if new equipment is introduced or new products are manufactured. In manufacturing industries, the major reason for changing a work process is to accommodate a change in the materials used to produce a finished product. Consider a firm that manufactures battery-operated flashlights. For many years flashlights were made of metal, but now most are made of plastic. A firm might decide to move from metal to plastic flashlights because of consumer preferences, raw materials costs, or other reasons. Whatever the reason, the technology necessary to make flashlights from plastic differs significantly from that used to make flashlights from metal. Work process changes may occur in service organizations as well as in manufacturing firms. As traditional barber shops and beauty parlors are replaced by hair salons catering to both sexes, for example, the hybrid organizations have to develop new methods for handling appointments and setting prices.

A change in work sequence may or may not accompany a change in equipment or a change in work processes. Making a change in work sequence means altering the order or sequence of the workstations involved in a particular manufacturing process. For example, a manufacturer might have two parallel assembly lines producing two similar sets of machine parts. The lines might converge at one central quality control unit where tolerances are verified by inspectors. The manager, however, might decide to change to periodic rather than final inspection. Under this arrangement, one or more inspections are established farther up the line. Work sequence changes can also be made in service organizations. The processing of insurance claims, for example, could be changed. The sequence of logging and verifying claims, requesting checks, getting countersignatures, and mailing checks could be altered in several ways, such as combining the first two steps or routing the claims through one person while another handles checks. Organizational control systems may also be targets of change.[27]

Changing People

A third area of organization change has to do with human resources. For example, an organization might decide to change the skill level of its workforce. This change might be prompted by changes in technology or by a general desire to upgrade the quality of the workforce. Thus, training programs and new selection criteria might be needed. The organization might also decide to improve its workers' performance level. In this instance, a new incentive system or performance-based training might be in order. Reader's Digest has been attempting to implement significant changes in its workforce. For example, the firm has eliminated 17 percent of its employees, reduced retirement benefits, and taken away many of the perks they once enjoyed. Part of the reason for the changes was to instill in the remaining employees a sense of urgency and the need to adopt a new perspective on how they did their jobs.[28]

Perceptions and expectations are also a common focus of organization change. Workers in an organization might believe that their wages and benefits are not as high as they should be. Management, however, might have evidence that the firm is paying a competitive wage and providing a superior benefit package. The change, then, would be centered on informing and educating the workforce about the comparative value of its compensation package. A common way to do this is to publish a statement that places an actual dollar value on each benefit provided and compares that amount to what other local organizations are providing their workers. Change might also be directed at employee attitudes and values. In many organizations today, managers are trying to eliminate adversarial relationships with workers and adopt a more collaborative relationship. In many ways, changing attitudes and values is perhaps the hardest task to do. *Today's Management Issues* provides a good case in point.

TODAY'S MANAGEMENT ISSUES

NEW LEADERS, NEW MANAGEMENT?

Does new leadership at the top automatically mean change in upper-management appointments? Often, a new CEO or top business manager prefers to replace the existing layer of senior management with hand-picked choices who are more familiar to the leader or more in tune with the leader's planned change in strategy or focus. Sometimes, however, a new leader believes that leaving the current managers in place will ensure stability during the changeover at the top.

At Andersen Consulting (now named Accenture), for example, Joe W. Forehand became global managing partner and CEO following the resignation of the previous CEO, who left to join an Internet company. Within a few months, Forehand had made his own selection of thirteen managers to serve on the twenty-member executive committee governing this international technology consulting company. Four of the new members were from other countries, part of Forehand's strategy to become the leading consulting firm around the world. (The managers who were replaced stayed with Andersen, but in different positions.)

In addition, the CEO established the new position of international chairman and appointed an Andersen veteran to oversee the company's growth in global markets. Forehand's expansion strategy extends to e-commerce, where he is planning to attract consulting contracts from more Internet-based busi-

nesses. In a unique twist, Andersen has also set aside $1 billion to invest in promising Internet businesses, with the investments to be recouped if and when the firms go public and begin to sell shares.

Despite the change at the top, Andersen does not want to encourage turnover within the organization. In fact, management is reaching out to employees who recently left, encouraging them to consider returning and thus take advantage of elements of organizational change such as increased benefits, improved career opportunities, and more web-related assignments. Clearly, the one thing that never changes is an organization's need for talented people at all levels.

> *We are realigning Andersen Consulting's leadership to reflect our strong global presence.*
> —Joe W. Forehand, CEO of Andersen Consulting*

References: Joanne Gordon, "Humbled Giant," *Forbes,* July 24, 2000, http://www.forbes.com/forbes/00/0724/6517060a.htm (August 4, 2000); Larry Greenemeier, "Andersen Plans for E-Business Growth," *Information Week,* April 24, 2000, p. 40; Elizabeth MacDonald, "Andersen Consulting's New Leader Overhauls Firm's Top Management," *Wall Street Journal,* January 20, 2000, p. B18 (*quote on p. B18).

Reengineering in Organizations

Many organizations today have also gone through a massive and comprehensive change program involving all aspects of organization design, technology, and people. Although various terms are used, the term currently in vogue for these changes is *reengineering*. Specifically, **reengineering** is the radical redesign of all aspects of a business to achieve major gains in cost, service, or time.[29] Corning, for example, has undergone a major reengineering over the last few years. Whereas the 150-year-old business once manufactured cookware and other durable consumer goods, it has transformed itself into a high-tech powerhouse making such items as the ultra-thin screens used in products like Palm Pilots and laptop computers.[30]

> **reengineering** The radical redesign of all aspects of a business to achieve major gains in cost, service, or time

The Need for Reengineering

Why are so many organizations finding it necessary to reengineer themselves? We noted in Chapter 2 that all systems, including organizations, are subject to entropy—a normal process leading to system decline. An organization is behaving most typically when it maintains the status quo, doesn't change in synch with its environment, and starts consuming its own resources to survive. In a sense, that is what happened to Kmart. In the early and mid-1970s Kmart was in such a high-flying growth mode that it passed first J.C. Penney and then Sears to become the world's largest retailer. But then the firm's managers grew complacent and assumed that the discount retailer's prosperity would continue and that they need not worry about environmental shifts, the growth of Wal-Mart, and so forth—and entropy set in. The key is to recognize the beginning of the decline and to move immediately toward reengineering. Major problems occur when managers either don't recognize the onset of entropy until it is well advanced or else are complacent in taking steps to correct it.

Approaches to Reengineering

Figure 13.3 shows general steps in reengineering. The first step is setting goals and developing a strategy for reengineering. The organization must know in advance what reengineering is supposed to accomplish and how those accomplishments will be achieved. Next, top managers must begin and direct the reengineering effort. If a CEO simply announces that reengineering is to occur but does nothing else, the program is unlikely to be successful. But if the CEO is constantly involved in the process, underscoring its importance and taking the lead, reengineering stands a much better chance of success.

Most experts also agree that successful reengineering is usually accompanied by a sense of urgency. People in the organization must see the clear and present need for the changes being implemented and appreciate their importance. In addition, most successful reengineering efforts start with a new, clean slate; that is, rather than assuming that the existing organization is a starting point and then trying to modify it, reengineering usually starts by asking questions such as, How are customers best served and competitors best neutralized? New approaches and systems are then created and imposed in place of existing ones.

Figure 13.3

The Reengineering Process

Reengineering is a major redesign of all areas of an organization. To be successful, reengineering requires a systematic and comprehensive assessment of the entire organization. Goals, top management support, and a sense of urgency help the organization re-create itself and blend both top-level and bottom-up perspectives.

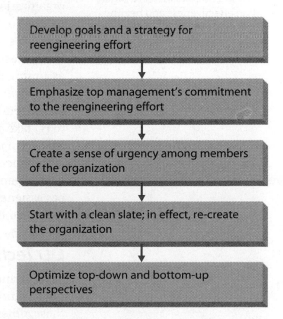

Develop goals and a strategy for reengineering effort

Emphasize top management's commitment to the reengineering effort

Create a sense of urgency among members of the organization

Start with a clean slate; in effect, re-create the organization

Optimize top-down and bottom-up perspectives

Finally, reengineering requires a careful blend of top-down and bottom-up involvement. On the one hand, strong leadership is necessary, but too much involvement by top management can make the changes seem autocratic. Similarly, employee participation is important, but too little involvement by leaders can undermine the program's importance and create a sense that top managers don't care. Thus, care must be taken to balance these two countervailing forces carefully.

MANAGEMENT IMPLICATIONS Managers need to understand the breadth of areas in which organization change can be necessary. They should also note the potential areas of interdependence among areas of change. For example, a change in technology may also necessitate a change in organization structure and people. Finally, managers should understand reengineering, a relatively recent perspective on change that involves massive and total change throughout an organization spanning all three of the traditional change areas of organization design, technology, and people.

Organization Development (OD)

We noted in several places the importance of people and change. A special area of interest that focuses almost exclusively on people is organization development.

OD Assumptions

organization development A planned effort that is organization-wide and managed from the top, and is intended to increase organization effectiveness and health through planned interventions in the organization's process using behavioral science knowledge

Organization development is concerned with changing attitudes, perceptions, behaviors, and expectations. More precisely, **organization development** is a planned effort that is organizationwide and managed from the top, and is intended to increase organization effectiveness and health through planned interventions in the organization's 'process' using behavioral science knowledge.[31] The theory and practice of OD are based on several very important assumptions. The first is that employees have a desire to grow and develop. Another is that employees have a strong need to be accepted by others within the organization. Still another critical assumption of OD is that the total organization and the way it is designed will influence the way individuals and groups within the organization behave. Thus, some form of collaboration between managers and their employees is necessary to (1) take advantage of the skills and abilities of the employees and (2) eliminate aspects of the organization that retard employee growth, development, and group acceptance. Because of the intense personal nature of many OD activities, many large organizations rely on one or more OD consultants (either full-time employees assigned to this function or outside experts hired specifically for OD purposes) to implement and manage their OD program.[32]

OD Techniques

Several kinds of interventions or activities are generally considered to be part of organization development.[33] Some OD programs may use only one or a few of these; other programs use several of them at once.

Diagnostic Activities Just as a physician examines patients to diagnose their current condition, an OD diagnosis analyzes the current condition of an organization. To carry out this diagnosis, managers use questionnaires, opinion or attitude surveys, interviews, archival data, and meetings to assess various characteristics of the organization. The results from this diagnosis may generate profiles of the organization's activities, which can then be used to identify problem areas in need of correction.

Team Building Team-building activities are intended to enhance the effectiveness and satisfaction of individuals who work in groups or teams and to promote overall group effectiveness. Given the widespread use of teams today, these activities have taken on increased importance. An OD consultant might interview team members to determine how they feel about the group; then an off-site meeting could be held to discuss the issues that surfaced and to iron out any problem areas or member concerns. Caterpillar used team building as one method for changing the working relationships between workers and supervisors from confrontational to cooperative. An interesting new approach to team building involves having executive teams participate in group cooking classes to teach them the importance of interdependence and coordination.[34]

Survey Feedback In survey feedback, each employee responds to a questionnaire intended to measure perceptions and attitudes (for example, satisfaction and supervisory style). Everyone involved, including the supervisor, receives the results of the survey. The aim of this approach is usually to change the behavior of supervisors by showing them how their subordinates viewed them. After the feedback has been provided, workshops may be conducted to evaluate results and suggest constructive changes.

Education Educational activities focus on classroom training. Although such activities can be used for technical or skill-related purposes, an OD educational activity typically focuses on "sensitivity skills"—that is, it teaches people to be more considerate and understanding of the people they work with. Participants often go through a series of experiential or role-playing exercises to understand better how others in the organization feel.

Intergroup Activities The focus of intergroup activities is on improving the relationships between two or more groups. We noted in Chapter 11 that, as group interdependence increases, so do coordination difficulties. Intergroup OD activities are designed to promote cooperation or resolve conflicts that arose as a result of interdependence. Experiential or role-playing activities are often used to achieve these goals.

Third-Party Peacemaking Another approach to OD is through third-party peacemaking, which is used most often when substantial conflict exists within the organization. Third-party peacemaking can be appropriate at the individual, group, or organization level. The third party, usually an OD consultant, uses a variety of mediation or negotiation techniques to resolve any problems or conflicts between individuals or groups.

Technostructural Activities   Technostructural activities are concerned with the design of the organization, the technology of the organization, and the interrelationship of design and technology with people on the job. A structural change such as an increase in decentralization, a job design change such as an increase in the use of automation, and a technological change involving a modification in work flow all qualify as technostructural OD activities if their objective is to improve group and interpersonal relationships within the organization.

Process Consultation   In process consultation, an OD consultant observes groups in the organization to develop an understanding of their communication patterns, decision-making and leadership processes, and methods of cooperation and conflict resolution. The consultant then provides feedback to the involved parties about the processes he or she has observed. The goal of this form of intervention is to improve the observed processes. A leader who is presented with feedback outlining deficiencies in his or her leadership style, for example, might be expected to change to overcome them.

Life and Career Planning   Life and career planning helps employees formulate their personal goals and evaluate strategies for integrating their goals with the goals of the organization. Such activities might include specification of training needs and plotting a career map. General Electric has a reputation for doing an outstanding job in this area.

Coaching and Counseling   Coaching and counseling provide nonevaluative feedback to individuals. The purpose is to help people both develop a better sense of how others see them and learn behaviors that will assist others in achieving their work-related goals. The focus is not on how the individual is performing today; instead, it is on how the person can perform better in the future.

Planning and Goal Setting   More pragmatically oriented than many other interventions are activities designed to help managers improve their planning and goal setting. Emphasis still falls on the individual, however, because the intent is to help individuals and groups integrate themselves into the overall planning process. The OD consultant might use the same approach as in process consultation, but the focus is more technically oriented on the mechanics of planning and goal setting.

The Effectiveness of OD

Given the diversity of activities encompassed by OD, it is not surprising that managers report mixed results from various OD interventions. Organizations that actively practice some form of OD include American Airlines, Texas Instruments, Procter & Gamble, Polaroid, and B.F. Goodrich. Goodrich, for example, has trained sixty persons in OD processes and techniques. These trained experts have subsequently become internal OD consultants to assist other managers in applying the techniques.[35] Many other managers, in contrast, report that they have tried OD but discarded it.[36]

OD will probably remain an important part of management theory and practice. Of course, there are no guarantees when dealing with social systems such as organizations, and the effectiveness of many OD techniques is difficult to evaluate. Because all organizations are open systems interacting with their environments, an improvement in an organization after an OD intervention may be attributable to the intervention, but it may also be attributable to changes in economic conditions, luck, or other factors.[37]

MANAGEMENT IMPLICATIONS Organization development is an important form of organization change that focuses on process issues. Managers should recognize the nature of OD before attempting to use any given OD technique. Top management support is necessary for OD to be successful, but managers need to realize also that no matter how well planned it is, OD may still not always work in every situation or for every organization.

■ *Organizational Innovation*

A final element of organization change that we address is innovation. **Innovation** is the managed effort of an organization to develop new products or services or new uses for existing products or services. Innovation is clearly important because, without new products or services, any organization will fall behind its competition.[38]

innovation The managed effort of an organization to develop new products or services or new uses for existing products or services

The Innovation Process

The organizational innovation process consists of developing, applying, launching, growing, and managing the maturity and decline of creative ideas.[39] This process is depicted in Figure 13.4.

Figure 13.4

The Innovation Process

Organizations actively seek to manage the innovation process. These steps illustrate the general life cycle that characterizes most innovations. Of course, as with creativity, the innovation process will suffer if it is approached too mechanically and rigidly.

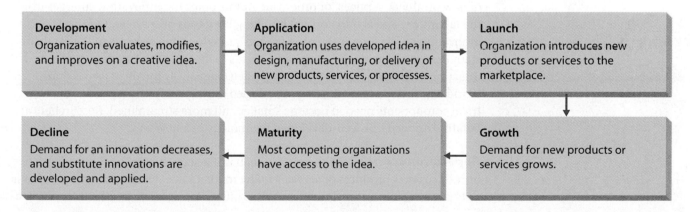

Development
Organization evaluates, modifies, and improves on a creative idea.

Application
Organization uses developed idea in design, manufacturing, or delivery of new products, services, or processes.

Launch
Organization introduces new products or services to the marketplace.

Decline
Demand for an innovation decreases, and substitute innovations are developed and applied.

Maturity
Most competing organizations have access to the idea.

Growth
Demand for new products or services grows.

Innovation comes in a variety of forms. Take this new product, for example—it's a low-flow washing machine that pet owners can use to bathe their dogs and cats. This represents an incremental innovation, since it is derived from existing washing machine technology. It is also a technical rather than a managerial innovation and a product rather than a process innovation.

Innovation Development Innovation development involves the evaluation, modification, and improvement of creative ideas. Innovation development can transform a product or service with only modest potential into a product or service with significant potential. Parker Brothers, for example, decided during innovation development not to market an indoor volleyball game but instead sell separately the appealing little foam ball designed for the game. The firm will never know how well the volleyball game would have sold, but the Nerf ball and numerous related products generated millions of dollars in revenues for Parker Brothers.

Innovation Application Innovation application is the stage in which an organization takes a developed idea and uses it in the design, manufacturing, or delivery of new products, services, or processes. At this point the innovation emerges from the laboratory and is transformed into tangible goods or services. One example of innovation application is the use of radar-based focusing systems in Polaroid's instant cameras. The idea of using radio waves to discover the location, speed, and direction of moving objects was first applied extensively by Allied forces during World War II. As radar technology developed during the following years, the electrical components needed became smaller and more streamlined. Researchers at Polaroid applied this well-developed technology in a new way.[40]

Application Launch Application launch is the stage in which an organization introduces new products or services to the marketplace. The important question is not "Does the innovation work?" but "Will customers want to purchase the innovative product or service?" History is full of creative ideas that did not generate enough interest among customers to be successful. Some notable innovation failures include Sony's seat warmer, the Edsel automobile, and Polaroid's SX-70 instant camera (which cost $3 billion to develop but never sold more than one hundred thousand units in a year).[41] Thus, despite development and application, new products and services can still possibly fail at the launch phase.

Application Growth   Once an innovation has been successfully launched, it then enters the stage of application growth. This period is one of high economic performance for an organization because demand for the product or service is often greater than the supply. Organizations that fail to anticipate this stage may unintentionally limit their growth, as Gillette did by not anticipating demand for its Mach III razor blades. At the same time, overestimating demand for a new product can be just as detrimental to performance. Unsold products can sit in warehouses for years.

Innovation Maturity   After a period of growing demand, an innovative product or service often enters a period of maturity. Innovation maturity is the stage in which most organizations in an industry have access to an innovation and are applying it in approximately the same way. The technological application of an innovation during this stage of the innovation process can be very sophisticated. Because most firms have access to the innovation, either as a result of developing the innovation on their own or copying the innovation of others, however, it does not provide competitive advantage to any one of them. The time that elapses between innovation development and innovation maturity varies notably, depending on the particular product or service. Whenever an innovation involves the use of complex skills (such as a complicated manufacturing process or highly sophisticated teamwork), moving from the growth phase to the maturity phase will take longer. In addition, if the skills needed to implement these innovations are rare and difficult to imitate, then strategic imitation may be delayed and the organization may enjoy a period of sustained competitive advantage.

Innovation Decline   Every successful innovation bears its own seeds of decline. Because an organization does not gain a competitive advantage from an innovation at maturity, it must encourage its creative scientists, engineers, and managers to begin looking for new innovations. This continued search for competitive advantage usually leads new products and services to move from the creative process through innovation maturity and finally to innovation decline. Innovation decline is the stage during which demand for an innovation decreases and substitute innovations are developed and applied.

Forms of Innovation

Each creative idea that an organization develops poses a different challenge for the innovation process. Innovations can be radical or incremental, technical or managerial, and product or process. *Management InfoTech* summarizes how Lucent is pursuing multiple forms of innovation simultaneously.

MANAGEMENT INFOTECH

LUCENT'S BELL LABS RESEARCHERS LOOK AHEAD

Bell Labs is Lucent's secret weapon for innovation. With annual sales topping $40 billion, Lucent—spun off from AT&T in 1996—is the world's leading manufacturer of sophisticated telecommunications equipment such as fiber-optic-network switches. With the spin-off, Lucent gained Bell Labs, the world-renowned research center responsible for such radical innovations as the transistor (which replaced vacuum tubes in midcentury electronic equipment) and cellular telephone technology. Now Bell Labs, which has nurtured eleven Nobel Prize winners and receives four patent approvals every business day, is continuing its quest under the Lucent banner for innovations of the future.

The largest group of researchers is investigating near-term product and process innovations designed to be marketable within five years. This approach is a break from the past, when Bell Labs researchers pursued promising lines of scientific inquiry without having to consider the potential commercial implications. Researchers at today's Bell Labs are much more geared toward studies with real-world applications. From such research has come PathStar, a Lucent product for allowing voice signals to be transmitted along Internet networks, and the Lambda-Router, a large-scale all-optical switching device.

Despite the emphasis on products and processes that have more immediate commercial application, about 20 percent of Bell Labs researchers doing basic research are looking for breakthroughs that might lead to radical innovations in the distant future. In addition, Bell Labs maintains a venture capital unit to fund internal research into diverse projects, such as fingerprint identification technology. Even as product-oriented incremental research and development continues in other parts of Lucent, Bell Labs keeps its researchers pointed toward the innovations of tomorrow—and beyond.

> *The world's smartest people still work here, and everyone is expected to change the landscape.*
>
> —*David Bishop, head of micromechanics research, Bell Labs**

References: Stephanie N. Mehta, "Lucent's New Spin," *Fortune,* August 14, 2000, pp. 30–31; Neil Weinberg and Nikhil Hutheesing, "Wired and Restless," *Forbes,* February 7, 2000, pp. 90–96; Nikhil Hutheesing, "Lucent's Labs," *Forbes,* February 7, 2000, p. 93 (*quote on p. 93).

---

radical innovation A new product, service, or technology developed by an organization that completely replaces the existing product, service, or technology in an industry

incremental innovation A new product, service, or technology that modifies an existing one

Radical Versus Incremental Innovations   **Radical innovations** are new products, services, or technologies developed by an organization that completely replace the existing products, services, or technologies in an industry.[42] **Incremental innovations** are new products, services, or technologies that modify existing ones. Firms that implement radical innovations fundamentally shift the nature of competition and the interaction of firms within their environments. Firms that implement incremental innovations alter, but do not fundamentally change, competitive interaction in an industry.

Over the last several years, organizations have introduced many radical innovations. For example, compact disk technology has virtually replaced long-playing vinyl records in the recording industry, and high-definition television seems likely to replace regular television technology (both black-and-white and color) in the near future. Whereas radical innovations like these tend to be very visible and public, incremental innovations actually are more numerous. One example is Ford's sports utility vehicle, the Explorer. Although other companies had similar products, Ford combined more effectively the styling and engineering that resulted in increased demand for all sports utility vehicles.

Technical Versus Managerial Innovations   **Technical innovations** are changes in the physical appearance or performance of a product or service, or the physical processes through which a product or service is manufactured. Many of the most important innovations over the last fifty years have been technical. For example, the serial replacement of the vacuum tube with the transistor, the transistor with the integrated circuit, and the integrated circuit with the microchip has greatly enhanced the power, ease of use, and speed of operation of a wide variety of electronic products. Not all innovations developed by organizations are technical, however. **Managerial innovations** are changes in the management process by which products and services are conceived, built, and delivered to customers. Managerial innovations do not necessarily affect the physical appearance or performance of products or services directly. In effect, reengineering represents a managerial innovation, as we discussed earlier.

Product Versus Process Innovations   Perhaps the two most important types of technical innovations are product innovations and process innovations. **Product innovations** are changes in the physical characteristics or performance of existing products or services or the creation of brand-new products or services. **Process innovations** are changes in the way products or services are manufactured, created, or distributed. Whereas managerial innovations generally affect the broader context of development, process innovations directly affect manufacturing.

The implementation of robotics, as we discussed earlier, is a process innovation. As Figure 13.5 shows, the effect of product and process innovations on economic return depends on the stage of the innovation process that a new product

technical innovation A change in the physical appearance or performance of a product or service, or the physical processes through which a product or service is manufactured

managerial innovation A change in the management process by which products and services are conceived, built, and delivered to customers

product innovation A change in the physical characteristics or performance of existing products or services or the creation of brand-new products or services

process innovation A change in the way a product or service is manufactured, created, or distributed

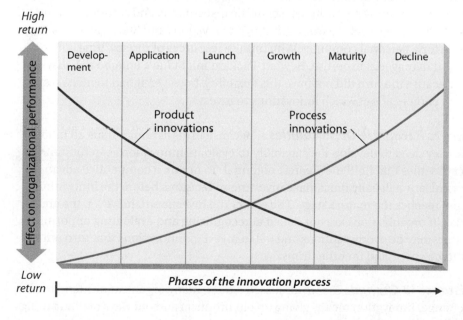

Figure 13.5

Effects of Product and Process Innovation on Economic Return
As the innovation process moves from development to decline, the economic return from product innovations gradually declines. In contrast, the economic return from process innovations increases during this same process.

or service occupies. At first, during development, application, and launch, the physical attributes and capabilities of an innovation most affect organizational performance. Thus, product innovations are particularly important during these beginning phases. Later, as an innovation enters the phases of growth, maturity, and decline, an organization's ability to develop process innovations such as fine-tuning manufacturing, increasing product quality, and improving product distribution becomes important to maintaining economic return.

Japanese organizations have often excelled at process innovation. The market for 35mm cameras was dominated by German and other European manufacturers when, in the early 1960s, Japanese organizations such as Canon and Nikon began making cameras. Some of these early Japanese products were not very successful, but these companies continued to invest in their process technology and eventually were able to increase quality and decrease manufacturing costs. Now these Japanese organizations dominate the worldwide market for 35mm cameras, and the German companies, because they were not able to maintain the same pace of process innovation, are struggling to maintain market share and profitability.

The Failure to Innovate

To remain competitive in today's economy, organizations must be innovative. And yet many organizations that should be innovative are not successful at bringing out new products or services, or do so only after innovations created by others are very mature. Organizations may fail to innovate for at least three reasons.

Lack of Resources   Innovation is expensive in terms of dollars, time, and energy. If a firm does not have sufficient money to fund a program of innovation or does not currently employ the kinds of employees it needs to be innovative, it may lag behind in innovation. Even highly innovative organizations cannot become involved in every new product or service its employees think of. For example, numerous other commitments in the electronic instruments and computer industry forestalled Hewlett-Packard from investing in Steve Jobs and Steve Wozniak's original idea for a personal computer. With infinite resources of money, time, and technical and managerial expertise, Hewlett-Packard might have entered this market early. Because the firm did not have this flexibility, however, it had to make some difficult choices about which innovations to invest in.

Failure to Recognize Opportunities   Because firms cannot pursue all innovations, they need to develop the capability to evaluate innovations carefully and to select the ones that hold the greatest potential. To obtain a competitive advantage, an organization usually must make investment decisions before the innovation process reaches the mature stage. The earlier the investment, however, the greater the risk. If organizations are not skilled at recognizing and evaluating opportunities, they may be overly cautious and fail to invest in innovations that turn out later to be successful for other firms.

Resistance to Change   As we discussed earlier, many organizations tend to resist change. Innovation means giving up old products and old ways of doing things in favor of new products and new ways of doing things. These kinds of changes can be personally difficult for managers and other members of an organization. Thus, resistance to change can slow the innovation process.

Promoting Innovation in Organizations

A wide variety of ideas for promoting innovation in organizations has been developed over the years. *The World of Management* describes how Microsoft is trying to stimulate innovation. Three specific ways for promoting innovation are through the reward system, the organizational culture, and a process called intrapreneurship.[43]

The Reward System   A firm's reward system is the means by which it encourages and discourages certain behaviors by employees. Major components of the reward system include salaries, bonuses, and perquisites. Using the reward system

WORLD OF MANAGEMENT

NEW PRODUCTS LEAD MICROSOFT'S DRIVE INTO ASIA

Microsoft, the worldwide heavyweight in software products, wants to move beyond computers to become a powerful player in new arenas, including Internet access via mobile phones and televisions. Following through on this goal, the company has created a broadband strategy for high-speed delivery of telecommunications, information, and entertainment content to tech-hungry customers in China, Japan, and other Asian countries. Computers are not as prevalent as mobile phones and televisions in Asia, so Microsoft has had to develop an entire array of new products—and work hard to grab market leadership so it can have more influence in shaping the regional broadband industry.

Intrapreneurship is a way of life within Microsoft, where new ideas bubble up all the time from many organizational levels and niches. One of Microsoft's ideas for new broadband products in Asia came from an engineer in the company's Beijing research center. He saw a child trying to surf the Web with an English-language browser, which is cumbersome to use because of the effort in picking out the keyboard equivalents of thousands of Chinese characters.

Based on this observation, the engineer and his colleagues set out to create an easy-to-use Internet-access device, dubbed Venus, that attaches to televisions. Instead of typing in commands, Venus users move around the Web using arrow keys on a remote control. Consumers with keyboards can also use Venus for basic word processing, although games such as chess work well with only the remote. Many more Chinese families have televisions than computers, and Venus costs less than half the price of a locally produced computer, which broadens its appeal.

Because Microsoft's management believes that local companies are best equipped to analyze and respond to local trends and needs, they have forged alliances with Asian giants such as China's Legend. They are also seeking out more companies to provide additional content suitable for access through Venus. The stakes are high, and Microsoft's hard-driving culture is a definite asset in its quest for market leadership. However, consumers are a vital and unknown part of the equation. Will they embrace these new products? Microsoft hopes the answer is yes.

> *Venus plays into our strategic intent in Asia. And that is to promulgate broadband.*
>
> —*Pieter Knook, Microsoft vice president for Asia**

Reference: Neel Chowdhury, "Gates & Co. Attack Asia," *Fortune,* April 17, 2000, pp. 197–208 (*quote on p. 198).

to promote innovation is a fairly mechanical but nevertheless effective management technique. The idea is to provide financial and nonfinancial rewards to people and groups that develop innovative ideas. Once the members of an organization understand that they will be rewarded for such activities, they are more likely to work creatively. With this end in mind, Monsanto Company gives a $50,000 award each year to the scientist or group of scientists that develops the biggest commercial breakthrough.

It is important for organizations to reward creative behavior, but it is vital to avoid punishing creativity when it does not result in highly successful innovations. It is the nature of the creative and innovative processes that many new product ideas will simply not work in the marketplace. Each process is fraught with too many uncertainties to generate positive results every time. An individual may have prepared herself to be creative, but an insight may not be forthcoming. Or managers may attempt to apply a developed innovation, only to recognize that it does not work. Indeed, some organizations operate according to the assumption that if all their innovative efforts succeed, then they are probably not taking enough risks in research and development. At 3M, nearly 60 percent of the creative ideas suggested each year do not succeed in the marketplace.

Managers need to be very careful in responding to innovative failure. If innovative failure is due to incompetence, systematic errors, or managerial sloppiness, then a firm should respond appropriately, for example, by withholding raises or reducing promotion opportunities. People who act in good faith to develop an innovation that simply does not work out, however, should not be punished for failure. If they are, they will probably not be creative in the future. A punitive reward system will discourage people from taking risks and therefore reduce the organization's ability to obtain competitive advantages.

Organizational Culture   As we discussed in Chapter 3, an organization's culture is the set of values, beliefs, and symbols that help guide behavior. A strong, appropriately focused organizational culture can be used to support innovative activity. A well-managed culture can communicate a sense that innovation is valued and will be rewarded and that occasional failure in the pursuit of new ideas is not only acceptable but even expected. In addition to reward systems and intrapreneurial activities, firms such as 3M, Corning, Monsanto, Procter & Gamble, Texas Instruments, Johnson & Johnson, and Merck are all known to have strong, innovation-oriented cultures that value individual creativity, risk taking, and inventiveness.[44]

Intrapreneurship in Larger Organizations   In recent years, many large businesses have realized that the entrepreneurial spirit that propelled their growth becomes stagnant after they transform themselves from a small but growing concern into a larger one. To help revitalize this spirit, some firms today encourage what they call intrapreneurship. **Intrapreneurs** are similar to entrepreneurs except that they develop a new business in the context of a large organization. There are three intrapreneurial roles in large organizations.[45] To use intrapreneurship successfully for encouraging creativity and innovation, the organization must find one or more individuals to perform these roles.

intrapreneurs Similar to entrepreneurs except that they develop a new business in the context of a large organization

The *inventor* is the person who actually conceives of and develops the new idea, product, or service by means of the creative process. Because the inventor may lack the expertise or motivation to oversee the transformation of the product or service from an idea into a marketable entity, however, a second role comes into play. A *product champion* is usually a middle manager who learns about the project and becomes committed to it. He or she helps overcome organizational resistance and convinces others to take the innovation seriously. The product champion may have only limited understanding of the technological aspects of the innovation. Nevertheless, product champions are skilled at knowing how the organization works, whose support is needed to push the project forward, and where to go to secure the resources necessary for successful development. A *sponsor* is a top-level manager who approves of and supports a project. This person may fight for the budget needed to develop an idea, overcome arguments against a project, and use organizational politics to ensure the project's survival. With a sponsor in place, the inventor's idea has a much better chance of being successfully developed.

Several firms have embraced intrapreneurship as a way to encourage creativity and innovation. Colgate-Palmolive has created a separate unit, Colgate Venture Company, staffed with intrapreneurs who develop new products. General Foods developed Culinova Group as a unit to which employees can take their ideas for possible development. S.C. Johnson & Sons established a $250,000 fund to support new product ideas, and Texas Instruments refuses to approve a new innovative project unless it has an acknowledged inventor, champion, and sponsor.

MANAGEMENT IMPLICATIONS   Managers need to realize that innovation is the life-blood of most organizations. Innovation is a process that can be successfully managed, but this management requires managers to understand the various forms of innovation that can exist, why some organizations fail to innovate, and some of the specific activities for promoting innovation.

Summary of Key Points

Organization change is any substantive modification to some part of the organization. Change may be prompted by forces internal or external to the organization. In general, planned change is preferable to reactive change.

Managing the change process is very important. The Lewin model provides a general perspective on the steps involved in change, although a comprehensive model is usually more effective. People tend to resist change because of uncertainty, threatened self-interests, different perceptions, and feelings of loss. Participation, education and communication, facilitation, and force-field analysis are methods for overcoming this resistance.

Many different change techniques or interventions are used. The most common involve changing organizational structure and design, technology, and people. There are several specific areas of change within each of these broad categories. Reengineering is the radical redesign of all aspects of a business to achieve major gains in cost, service, or time. It is occasionally needed to offset entropy. The basic steps are developing goals and strategies, conveying the involvement of top management, creating a sense of urgency, starting with a clean slate, and balancing top-down and bottom-up perspectives.

Organization development is concerned with changing attitudes, perceptions, behaviors, and expectations. Its effective use relies on an important set of assumptions. There are conflicting opinions about the effectiveness of several OD techniques.

The innovation process has six steps: development, application, launch, growth, maturity,

and decline. Basic categories of innovation include radical, incremental, technical, managerial, product, and process. Despite the importance of innovation, many organizations fail to innovate because they lack the required creative individuals, or they are committed to too many other creative activities, fail to recognize opportunities, or resist the change that innovation requires. Organizations can use various tools for overcoming these problems, including the reward system, organizational culture, and intrapreneurship.

Discussion Questions

Questions for Review

1. What forces or kinds of events lead to organization change? Identify each force or event as a planned or reactive change.
2. How is each step in the process of organization change implemented? Are some of the steps likely to meet with more resistance than others? Why or why not?
3. What are the various areas of organization change? How are they similar and how do they differ?
4. What are the steps in the innovation process?

Questions for Analysis

5. Could reactive change of the type identified in question 1 have been planned for ahead of time? Why or why not? Should all organization change be planned? Why or why not?
6. A company has recently purchased equipment that, when installed, will do the work of one hundred employees. The workforce of the company is very concerned and is threatening to take some kind of action. If

you were the human resource manager, what would you try to do to satisfy all parties concerned? Why?

7. Think of several relatively new products or services that you use. What form of innovation is represented by each?

Questions for Application

8. Some people resist change, while others welcome it enthusiastically. To deal with the first group, one needs to overcome resistance to change; to deal with the second, one needs to overcome resistance to stability. What advice can you give a manager facing the latter situation?
9. Can a change made in one area of an organization—in technology, for instance—not lead to change in other areas? Why or why not?
10. Find out more about one of the techniques for organization development presented in this chapter. What are the advantages and disadvantages of that technique relative to other techniques?

BUILDING EFFECTIVE *time-management* SKILLS

Exercise Overview

Time-management skills refer to the manager's ability to prioritize work, to work efficiently, and to delegate appropriately. Using time-management skills wisely can change how a person works.

Exercise Background

Almost every task we perform can theoretically be performed more efficiently. The next time you work on a particular task, such as studying for a test, writing a paper, or working on a project, note your work habits. You might even consider videotaping yourself while you work and reviewing the tape later.

Take special note of what you do that appears not to contribute to task performance. Examples might include going to the refrigerator and getting food, watching television while you

are working, daydreaming, making an unnecessary telephone call, and so forth. Next, estimate how much of the total "work" time was actually spent on activities besides working.

Exercise Task

With the background information above as context, do the following:

1. Assess the extent to which each nonwork activity was wasted effort or contributed in some way to task performance.
2. Describe how the work might have been completed had you not done any of the nonwork activities.
3. Assuming that you might want to change your work habits and thus use your time more efficiently, describe a change approach to do just that.

BUILDING EFFECTIVE *interpersonal* SKILLS

Exercise Overview

A manager's interpersonal skills include her or his abilities to understand and to motivate individuals and groups. These abilities are especially important during a period of change. This exercise will help you understand how to apply your interpersonal skills to a change situation.

Exercise Background

Assume that you are the manager of a retail store in a local shopping mall. Your staff consists of seven full-time and ten part-time employees. The full-time employees have worked together as a team for three years. The part-timers are all local college students; while a couple of them have worked in the store for over a year, there tends to be a lot of turnover among this group.

Your boss, the regional manager, has just informed you that the national chain that owns

your store is planning to open a second store in the same mall. She has also informed you that you must plan and implement the following changes:

1. You will serve as manager of both stores until the sales volume of the new store warrants its own full-time manager.
2. You are to designate one of the full-time employees in your present store as the assistant manager because you will be in the store less often now.
3. To have experienced workers in the new store, you are to select three of your current full-time workers to move to the new store; one of them should also be appointed as assistant manager of that store.
4. You can hire three new people to replace those transferred from your present store and three new people to work at the new store.

5. You can decide for yourself how to deploy your part-timers, but you will need a total of ten in the present store and eight at the new store.

You realize that many of your employees will be unhappy with these changes. They all know each other and work well together. However, the new store will be in a new expansion of the mall and will be a very nice place to work.

Exercise Task

With this background information in mind, do the following:

1. Determine the likely reasons for resistance to this change from your workers.

2. Determine how you will make decisions about promotions and transfers. Make whatever assumptions that you think are warranted.

3. Outline how you will inform your employees about what is going to happen.

4. An alternative strategy that could be adopted would involve keeping the existing staff intact and hiring new employees for the new store. Outline a persuasion strategy for trying to convince your boss that you want to implement this alternative strategy.

BUILDING EFFECTIVE *diagnostic* SKILLS

Exercise Overview

Diagnostic skills help a manager visualize the most appropriate response to a situation. These skills are especially important during a period of organization change.

Exercise Background

Assume that you are the general manager of a hotel located on a tropical island. The hotel is situated along a beautiful stretch of beach and is one of six large resorts in the area. The hotel is owned by a group of foreign investors and is one of the oldest on the island. For several years, the hotel has been operated as a franchise unit of a large international hotel chain, as are all of the others on the island.

For the last few years, the hotel's owners have been taking most of the profits earned for themselves and putting relatively little back into the hotel. They have also let you know that their business is not in good financial health; the money earned from your hotel is being used to offset losses they are incurring elsewhere. In contrast, most of the other hotels around you have recently been refurbished, and plans have

just been announced to build two new ones in the near future.

A team of executives from franchise headquarters has just visited your hotel. They expressed considerable disappointment in the property. They feel that it has not kept pace with the other resorts on the island. They also informed you that if the property is not brought up to their standards, the franchise agreement, up for review in a year, will be revoked. You see this move as potentially disastrous because you would lose their "brand name," access to their reservation system, and so forth.

Sitting alone in your office, you have identified several alternatives that seem viable:

1. Try to convince the owners to remodel the hotel. You estimate that it will take $5 million to meet the franchisor's minimum standards and another $5 million to bring the hotel up to the standards of the top resort on the island.

2. Try to convince the franchisor to give you more time and more options for upgrading the facility.

3. Allow the franchise agreement to terminate and try to succeed as an independent hotel.

4. Assume that the hotel will fail and start looking for another job. You have a good reputation, although you might have to start at a lower level (i.e., as an assistant manager) with another firm.

Exercise Task

With the background information presented above, do the following:

1. Rank-order the four alternatives in terms of their potential success. Make assumptions as appropriate.
2. Identify other alternatives not noted above.
3. Can any alternatives be pursued simultaneously?
4. Develop an overall strategy for trying to save the hotel while also protecting your own interests.

CHAPTER CLOSING CASE

GENERAL ELECTRIC'S GLOBAL CULTURE OF CHANGE

Jack Welch, the long-time CEO of General Electric (GE), was well aware that large organizations can be unwieldy and complacent, even though they need to be streamlined and speedy. This predicament is why Welch and his successor worked out various strategies for managing change and innovation to take advantage of GE's size rather than being tripped up by it. Over the years, GE has been successfully transformed from a largely U.S.-focused company into a truly global, boundaryless business—one of the world's most profitable.

General Electric has long had a few joint ventures in Europe, but for years, its main international business activity was exporting. This situation changed in 1987, when the company exchanged its consumer electronics business for ownership of a French-based medical equipment manufacturer. Within two years, GE made another European acquisition, this time buying a Hungarian lighting manufacturer. Since then, GE has bought more than 133 European firms in industries ranging from insurance to energy equipment, swelling its European payroll to ninety thousand and generating more than $20 billion in annual revenue from the area.

After so many years, GE has worked out a pattern for effectively managing change during and after an acquisition. Even before management has finished negotiating a deal, experts from finance and human resources are drafting a plan to set change in motion immediately after the contract is signed. The first change that occurs after a deal has been completed is that GE's finance expert shows up and starts converting the firm's financial systems to the accepted GE format. GE also sends in an integration manager to supervise the unification effort, while the overall manager of the acquired company concentrates on operations and profitability issues.

Within one hundred days or less, GE has the basic change plan well underway, covering activities ranging from cost-cutting measures to plans for switching from matrix or geographical departmentalization (where it exists) to a functional organization. By this time, GE's experts will have identified and taken steps to remove people who seem to be blocking change within the acquired firm. They will also have identified which personnel should be retained; these people are offered key roles within the integrated organization.

Next, GE introduces its special brand of management tools, including highly effective quality management programs and other best-practices tools that have proven to boost profit margins significantly in other acquired firms. One tool, known as Work-Out, encourages employees to get together and think of a plan for solving any problem in the business, then to present it to management for immediate approval or rejection. This seemingly informal, no-nonsense team tool brings about needed change more quickly and with more grass-roots support than the traditional method of passing the problem up and down the hierarchy in the course of debating and making a decision. In fact, teams are commonplace in every GE unit around the world, moving information through the organization at lightning speed and allowing employees to get the job done without intense management supervision.

The Internet is a powerful catalyst for overall change within GE because top management sees the Web as redefining relationships with customers, employees, and suppliers. To get the corporation ready to take advantage of emerging web-related opportunities, management called for a three-month Work-Out procedure held entirely on-line. Participants shared ideas for breaking down bureaucratic blocks and moving more quickly to implement e-commerce strategies that represent GE's future. GE has also invited web-savvy executives such as Sun Microsystem's Scott McNealy to join its board of directors and prod management about key technology issues. GE knows that with the advent of the Internet, no country is isolated, so it plans to continue

its winning ways by bringing systematic change to every unit around the world.

Case Questions

1. Does Work-Out represent planned or reactive change? Explain your answer.

2. Identify some of the most important internal and external forces for change affecting GE.

3. In what areas does GE intervene to make change after an acquisition? Why does GE concentrate on these areas?

Case References

Brent Schlender, "The Odd Couple," *Fortune*, May 1, 2000, pp. 106–126; Thomas A. Stewart, "See Jack Run. See Jack Run Europe." *Fortune*, September 27, 1999, pp. 124–136.

CHAPTER NOTES

1. "Can Nike Still Do It?" *Business Week*, February 21, 2000. pp. 120–128 (quote on p. 122); *Hoover's Handbook of American Business 2001* (Austin, Texas: Hoover's Business Press, 2001), pp. 1044–1045.

2. For an excellent review of this area, see Achilles A. Armenakis and Arthur G. Bedeian, "Organizational Change: A Review of Theory and Research in the 1990s," *Journal of Management*, 1999, Vol. 25, No. 3, pp. 293–315.

3. For additional insights into how technological change affects other parts of the organization, see P. Robert Duimering, Frank Safayeni, and Lyn Purdy, "Integrated Manufacturing: Redesign the Organization Before Implementing Flexible Technology," *Sloan Management Review*, Summer 1993, pp. 47–56.

4. Joel Cutcher-Gershenfeld, Ellen Ernst Kossek, and Heidi Sandling, "Managing Concurrent Change Initiatives," *Organizational Dynamics*, Winter 1997, pp. 21–38.

5. Michael A. Hitt, "The New Frontier: Transformation of Management for the New Millennium," *Organizational Dynamics*, Winter 2000, pp. 7–15. See also Michael Beer and Nitin Nohria, "Cracking the Code of Change," *Harvard Business Review*, May–June 2000, pp. 133–144.

6. See Warren Boeker, "Strategic Change: The Influence of Managerial Characteristics and Organizational Growth," *Academy of Management Journal*, 1997, Vol. 40, No. 1, pp. 152–170.

7. Alan L. Frohman, "Igniting Organizational Change from Below: The Power of Personal Initiative," *Organizational Dynamics*, Winter 1997, pp. 39–53.

8. Nandini Rajagopalan and Gretchen M. Spreitzer, "Toward a Theory of Strategic Change: A Multi-Lens Perspective and Integrative Framework," *Academy of Management Review*, 1997, Vol. 22, No. 1, pp. 48–79.

9. Anne Fisher, "Danger Zone," *Fortune*, September 8, 1997, pp. 165–167.

10. John P. Kotter and Leonard A. Schlesinger, "Choosing Strategies for Change," *Harvard Business Review*, March–April 1979, p. 106.

11. Clayton M. Christensen and Michael Overdorf, "Meeting the Challenge of Disruptive Change," *Harvard Business Review*, March–April 2000, pp. 67–77.

12. See Eric Abrahamson, "Change Without Pain," *Harvard Business Review*, July–August 2000, pp. 75–85. See also Gib Akin and Ian Palmer, "Putting Metaphors to Work for Change in Organizations," *Organizational Dynamics*, Winter 2000, pp. 67–76.

13. Erik Brynjolfsson, Amy Austin Renshaw, and Marshall Van Alstyne, "The Matrix of Change," *Sloan Management Review*, Winter 1997, pp. 37–54.

14. Kurt Lewin, "Frontiers in Group Dynamics: Concept, Method, and Reality in Social Science," *Human Relations*, June 1947, pp. 5–41.

15. See Connie J. G. Gersick, "Revolutionary Change Theories: A Multilevel Exploration of the Punctuated Equilibrium Paradigm," *Academy of Management Review*, January 1991, pp. 10–36.

16. See Gerald Andrews, "Mistrust, the Hidden Obstacle to Empowerment, *HR Magazine*, November 1994, pp. 66–74, for a good illustration of how resistance emerges.

17. "RJR Employees Fight Distraction Amid Buyout Talks," *Wall Street Journal*, November 1, 1988, p. A8.

18. Arnon E. Reichers, John P. Wanous, and James T. Austin, "Understanding and Managing Cynicism About Organizational

Change," *Academy of Management Executive*, February 1997, pp. 48–59.

19. "How Classy Can 7-Eleven Get?" *Business Week*, September 1, 1997, pp. 74–75.

20. See Paul R. Lawrence, "How to Deal with Resistance to Change," *Harvard Business Review*, January–February 1969, pp. 4–12, 166–176, for a classic discussion.

21. Lester Coch and John R. P. French, Jr., "Overcoming Resistance to Change," *Human Relations*, August 1948, pp. 512–532.

22. Eric von Hippel, Stefan Thomke, and Mary Sonnack, "Creating Breakthroughs at 3M," *Harvard Business Review*, September–October 1999, pp. 47–54.

23. Benjamin Schneider, Arthur P. Brief, and Richard A. Guzzo, "Creating a Climate and Culture for Sustainable Organizational Change," *Organizational Dynamics*, Spring 1996, pp. 7–19.

24. Paul Bate, Raza Khan, and Annie Pye, "Towards a Culturally Sensitive Approach to Organization Structuring: Where Organization Design Meets Organization Development," *Organization Science*, March–April 2000, pp. 197–211.

25. "Founding Clan Vies with Outside 'Radical' for the Soul of Toyota," *Wall Street Journal*, May 5, 2000, pp. A1, A12.

26. David Kirkpatrick, "The New Player," *Fortune*, April 17, 2000, pp. 162–168.

27. Jeffrey A. Alexander, "Adaptive Change in Corporate Control Practices," *Academy of Management Journal*, March 1991, pp. 162–193.

28. "Mr. Ryder Rewrites the Musty Old Book at Reader's Digest," *Wall Street Journal*, April 18, 2000, pp. A1, A10.

29. Thomas A. Stewart, "Reengineering—The Hot New Managing Tool," *Fortune*, August 23, 1993, pp. 41–48.

30. "Old Company Learns New Tricks," *USA Today*, April 10, 2000, pp. 1B, 2B.

31. Richard Beckhard, *Organization Development: Strategies and Models* (Reading, Mass.: Addison-Wesley, 1969), p. 9.

32. W. Warner Burke, "The New Agenda for Organization Development," *Organizational Dynamics*, Summer 1997, pp. 7–20.

33. Wendell L. French and Cecil H. Bell, Jr., *Organization Development: Behavioral Science Interventions for Organization Improvement*, 2nd Edition (Englewood Cliffs, N.J.: Prentice-Hall, 1978).

34. "Memo to the Team: This Needs Salt!" *Wall Street Journal*, April 4, 2000, pp. B1, B14.

35. Roger J. Hower, Mark G. Mindell, and Donna L. Simmons, "Introducing Innovation Through OD," *Management Review*, February 1978, pp. 52–56.

36. "Is Organization Development Catching On? A Personnel Symposium," *Personnel*, November–December 1977, pp. 10–22.

37. For a recent discussion on the effectiveness of various OD techniques in different organizations, see John M. Nicholas, "The Comparative Impact of Organization Development Interventions on Hard Criteria Measures," *Academy of Management Review*, October 1982, pp. 531–542.

38. Constantinos Markides, "Strategic Innovation," *Sloan Management Review*, Spring 1997, pp. 9–24. See also James Brian Quinn, "Outsourcing Innovation: The New Engine of Growth," *Sloan Management Review*, Summer 2000, pp. 13–21.

39. L. B. Mohr, "Determinants of Innovation in Organizations," *American Political Science Review*, 1969, pp. 111–126; G. A. Steiner, *The Creative Organization* (Chicago: University of Chicago Press, 1965); R. Duncan and A. Weiss, "Organizational Learning: Implications for Organizational Design," in B. M. Staw (Ed.), *Research in Organizational Behavior*, Vol. 1 (Greenwich, Conn.: JAI Press, 1979), pp. 75–123; and J. E. Ettlie, "Adequacy of Stage Models for Decisions on Adoption of Innovation," *Psychological Reports*, 1980, pp. 991–995.

40. See Alan Patz, "Managing Innovation in High Technology Industries," *New Management*, September 1986, pp. 54–59.

41. "Flops," *Business Week*, August 16, 1993, pp. 76–82.

42. See Willow A. Sheremata, "Centrifugal and Centripetal Forces in Radical New Product Development Under Time Pressure," *Academy of Management Review*, 2000, Vol. 25, No. 2, pp. 389–408.

43. Dorothy Leonard and Jeffrey F. Rayport, "Spark Innovation Through Empathic Design," *Harvard Business Review*, November–December 1997, pp. 102–115.

44. See Steven P. Feldman, "How Organizational Culture Can Affect Innovation," *Organizational Dynamics*, Summer 1988, pp. 57–68.

45. See Gifford Pinchot III, *Intrapreneuring* (New York: Harper & Row, 1985).

CHAPTER

14 Managing Human Resources in Organizations

SAS Institute Inc., based in rural North Carolina, is perhaps the least-known major software company in the world today. SAS creates software that helps big companies better manage and analyze especially large quantities of data and information. For example, Marriott Hotels uses SAS software to manage its frequent-visitor program; the U.S. government uses SAS software to compute the consumer price index and other complex measures; and pharmaceutical companies like Pfizer and Merck use SAS software to compare near-infinite combinations of elements as they develop new drugs.

Because SAS is a private firm, the general public knows little about its revenues and profits. A few details are illuminating, however. The firm's founder and leader, Jim Goodnight, with a net worth of $3 billion, is listed by *Forbes* as the forty-third richest individual in the United States. (This rank is based on his two-thirds ownership of the company; the other one-third is owned by senior vice president John Sall, who still spends much of his time writing code.) SAS also hires several hundred new employees each year, a clear indicator that the firm is consistently growing at a strong pace. And the firm also continues to invest in impressive—and clearly expensive—buildings and related facilities.

But SAS is even more impressive under the surface. For example, even though it pays salaries that are merely competitive for the industry, the firm's employees are almost fanatical in their devotion to SAS in general and to Jim Goodnight in particular. As a result, annual turnover at SAS is less than 4 percent, far below that of other firms in the industry, and employees are constantly coming up with new and better ways of doing things for the company. And both insiders and outside experts agree that the key to all this is how Goodnight treats his employees.

For example, all SAS employees get unlimited sick days, and they can use sick days to stay home and care for sick family members. To keep work from interfering with employees' families, SAS operates the largest child-care facility in the state. And company cafeterias have baby seats and high chairs so employees can eat with their children. SAS has also adopted a seven-hour workday; the company switchboard shuts down at 5:00 each day, and the front

> *"Jim's idea is that if you hire adults and treat them like adults, then they'll behave like adults."*
>
> —*David Russo, head of human resources at SAS)*

After studying this chapter, you should be able to:

- Describe the environmental context of human resource management, including its strategic importance and its relationship with legal and social factors.

- Discuss how organizations attract human resources, including human resource planning, recruiting, and selecting.

- Describe how organizations develop human resources, including training and development, performance appraisal, and performance feedback.

- Discuss how organizations maintain human resources, including the determination of compensation and benefits and career planning.

- Discuss labor relations, including how employees form unions and the mechanics of collective bargaining.

- Describe the issues associated with managing knowledge, contingent, and temporary workers.

gate is locked at 6:00. Unlike many high-tech firms in other parts of the country, Goodnight doesn't want his employees to work late or to come back to the office on the weekend.

If they want, however, they can come in early—to work out in a lavish 36,000-square-foot gym and health center. The center also offers massages several times a week, as well as classes in golf, tennis, tai chi, and African dance. And center staff even launder dirty workout clothes at the end of the day and return them clean and neatly folded. SAS provides unlimited free soda, coffee, tea, and juice, and has live piano music in the cafeteria. The company shuts down for the week between Christmas and New Year's Day each year, but everyone still gets paid. An on-site health clinic has two full-time physicians and six nurses; health insurance is free for everyone. And all this comes from Jim Goodnight's most fundamental philosophy: if you treat people with dignity and respect and reward them for their contributions, they will treat you the same in return. And when this relationship can be established and maintained within the context of a business, everyone can win.[1]

S AS is one of the most successful businesses around these days. And human resources are clearly an integral part of its success. From its earliest days, Jim Goodnight made a strategic commitment to identify, hire, and retain the best and brightest people available. The firm has been able to maintain this strategy and today is still the employer of choice for many talented people in a highly volatile industry.

This chapter is about how organizations manage the people that comprise them. This set of processes is called human resource management, or HRM. We start by describing the environmental context of HRM. We then discuss how organizations attract human resources. Next we describe how organizations seek to develop the capacities of their human resources. We also examine how high-quality human resources are maintained by organizations. We conclude by discussing labor relations.

The Environmental Context of Human Resource Management

human resource management (HRM) The set of organizational activities directed at attracting, developing, and maintaining an effective workforce

Human resource management (HRM) is the set of organizational activities directed at attracting, developing, and maintaining an effective workforce.[2] Human resource management takes place within a complex and ever-changing environmental context. Three particularly vital components of this context are HRM's strategic importance and the legal and social environment of HRM.

The Strategic Importance of HRM

Human resources are critical for effective organizational functioning. HRM (or personnel, as it is sometimes called) was once relegated to second-class status in many organizations, but its importance has grown dramatically in the last two decades. Its new importance stems from increased legal complexities, the recognition that human resources are a valuable means for improving productivity, and the awareness today of the costs associated with poor human resource management.[3]

Indeed, managers now realize that the effectiveness of their HR function has a substantial impact on the bottom-line performance of the firm. Poor human resource planning can result in spurts of hiring followed by layoffs—costly in terms of unemployment compensation payments, training expenses, and morale. Haphazard compensation systems do not attract, keep, and motivate good employees, and outmoded recruitment practices can expose the firm to expensive and embarrassing discrimination lawsuits. Consequently, the chief human resource executive of most large businesses is a vice president directly accountable to the CEO, and many firms are developing strategic HR plans and integrating those plans with other strategic planning activities.[4]

Even organizations with as few as two hundred employees usually have a human resource manager and a human resource department charged with overseeing these activities. Responsibility for HR activities, however, is shared between the HR department and line managers. The HR department may recruit and initially screen candidates, but the final selection is usually made by managers in the department where the new employee will work. Similarly, although the HR department may establish performance appraisal policies and procedures, the actual evaluating and coaching of employees is done by their immediate superiors.

The Legal Environment of HRM

A number of laws regulate various aspects of employee-employer relations, especially in the areas of equal employment opportunity, compensation and benefits, labor relations, and occupational safety and health. Several major laws are summarized in Table 14.1.

Table 14.1

The Legal Environment of Human Resource Management

As much as any area of management, HRM is subject to wide-ranging laws and court decisions. These laws and decisions affect the human resource function in many areas. For example, AT&T was once fined several million dollars for violating Title VII of the Civil Rights Act of 1964.

Equal Employment Opportunity

Title VII of the Civil Rights Act of 1964 (as amended by the *Equal Employment Opportunity Act of 1972*): forbids discrimination in all areas of the employment relationship

Age Discrimination in Employment Act: outlaws discrimination against people older than forty years

Various executive orders, especially *Executive Order 11246* in 1965: requires employers with government contracts to engage in affirmative action

Pregnancy Discrimination Act: specifically outlaws discrimination on the basis of pregnancy

Vietnam Era Veterans Readjustment Assistance Act: extends affirmative action mandate to military veterans who served during the Vietnam War

Americans with Disabilities Act: specifically outlaws discrimination against disabled persons

Civil Rights Act of 1991: makes it easier for employees to sue an organization for discrimination but limits punitive damage awards if they win

Compensation and Benefits

Fair Labor Standards Act: establishes minimum wage and mandated overtime pay for work in excess of forty hours per week

Equal Pay Act: requires that men and women be paid the same amount for doing the same jobs

Employee Retirement Income Security Act: regulates how organizations manage their pension funds

Family and Medical Leave Act of 1993: requires employers to provide up to twelve weeks of unpaid leave for family and medical emergencies

Labor Relations

National Labor Relations Act: spells out procedures by which employees can establish labor unions and requires organizations to bargain collectively with legally formed unions; also known as the *Wagner Act*

Labor-Management Relations Act: limits union power and specifies management rights during a union-organizing campaign; also known as the *Taft-Hartley Act*

Health and Safety

Occupational Safety and Health Act: mandates the provision of safe working conditions

Title VII of the Civil Rights Act of 1964 Forbids discrimination on the basis of gender, race, color, religion, or national origin in all areas of the employment relationship

adverse impact When minority group members pass a selection standard at a rate less than 80 percent of the rate of majority group members

Equal Employment Opportunity Commission Charged with enforcing Title VII of the Civil Rights Act of 1964, as well as several other employment-related laws

Age Discrimination in Employment Act Outlaws discrimination against people older than forty years; passed in 1967, amended in 1978 and 1986

affirmative action Intentionally seeking and hiring employees from groups that are underrepresented in the organization

Americans with Disabilities Act Forbids discrimination on the basis of disabilities and requires employers to provide reasonable accommodations for disabled employees

Civil Rights Act of 1991 Amends the original Civil Rights Act, making it easier to bring discrimination lawsuits while also limiting punitive damages that can be awarded in those lawsuits

Fair Labor Standards Act Sets a minimum wage and requires overtime pay for work in excess of forty hours per week; passed in 1938 and amended frequently since then

Equal Employment Opportunity   Title VII of the Civil Rights Act of 1964 forbids discrimination on the basis of gender, race, skin color, religion, or national origin in all areas of the employment relationship. The intent of Title VII is to ensure that employment decisions are made on the basis of an individual's qualifications rather than personal biases. The law has reduced direct forms of discrimination (refusing to promote blacks into management, failing to hire men as flight attendants, refusing to hire women as construction workers) as well as indirect forms of discrimination (using employment tests that whites pass at a higher rate than blacks).

Employment requirements such as test scores or other qualifications are legally defined as having an **adverse impact** on minorities and women when such individuals meet or pass the requirement at a rate less than 80 percent of the rate of majority group members. Criteria that have an adverse impact on protected groups can be used only when there is solid evidence that they effectively identify individuals who are better able than others to do the job. The **Equal Employment Opportunity Commission** is charged with enforcing Title VII as well as several other employment-related laws.

The **Age Discrimination in Employment Act**, passed in 1967, amended in 1978, and amended again in 1986, is an attempt to prevent organizations from discriminating against older workers. In its current form, it outlaws discrimination against people older than forty years. Both the Age Discrimination Act and Title VII require passive nondiscrimination, or equal employment opportunity. Employers are not required to seek out and hire minorities but they must treat fairly all who apply.

Several executive orders require that employers holding government contracts engage in **affirmative action**—intentionally seeking and hiring employees from groups that are underrepresented in the organization. These organizations must have a written affirmative action plan that spells out employment goals for underutilized groups and how those goals will be met. These employers are also required to act affirmatively in hiring Vietnam-era veterans and qualified disabled individuals.

In 1990, Congress passed the **Americans with Disabilities Act,** which forbids discrimination on the basis of disabilities and requires employers to provide reasonable accommodations for disabled employees. More recently, the **Civil Rights Act of 1991** amended the original Civil Rights Act, as well as other related laws, by both making it easier to bring discrimination lawsuits (which partially explains the aforementioned backlog of cases) while simultaneously limiting the amount of punitive damages that can be awarded in those lawsuits.

Compensation and Benefits   Laws also regulate compensation and benefits. The **Fair Labor Standards Act**, passed in 1938 and amended frequently since then, sets a minimum wage and requires the payment of overtime rates for work in excess of forty hours per week. Salaried professional, executive, and administrative employees are exempt from the minimum hourly wage and overtime provisions. The **Equal Pay Act of 1963** requires that men and women be paid the same amount for doing the same jobs. Attempts to circumvent the law by having different job titles and pay rates for men and women who perform the same work are also illegal. Basing an employee's pay on seniority or performance is legal, however, even if it means that a man and a woman are paid different amounts for doing the same job.

The provision of benefits is also regulated in some ways by state and federal laws. Certain benefits are mandatory—for example, worker's compensation insurance for employees who are injured on the job. Employers who provide a pension plan for their employees are regulated by the **Employee Retirement Income Security Act of 1974 (ERISA)**. The purpose of this act is to help ensure the financial security of pension funds by regulating how they can be invested. The **Family and Medical Leave Act of 1993** requires employers to provide up to twelve weeks of unpaid leave for family and medical emergencies.

Labor Relations   Union activities and management's behavior toward unions constitute another heavily regulated area. The **National Labor Relations Act** (also known as the Wagner Act), passed in 1935, sets up a procedure for employees of a firm to vote whether to have a union. If they vote for a union, management is required to bargain collectively with the union. The **National Labor Relations Board** was established by the Wagner Act to enforce its provisions. Following a series of severe strikes in 1946, the **Labor-Management Relations Act** (also known as the *Taft-Hartley Act*) was passed in 1947 to limit union power. The law increases management's rights during an organizing campaign. The Taft-Hartley Act also contains the *National Emergency Strike* provision, which allows the president of the United States to prevent or end a strike that endangers national security. Taken together, those laws balance union and management power. Employees can be represented by a legally created and managed union, but the business can make non-employee-related business decisions without interference.

Equal Pay Act of 1963 Requires that men and women be paid the same amount for doing the same jobs

Employee Retirement Income Security Act of 1974 (ERISA) Sets standards for pension plan management and provides federal insurance if pension funds go bankrupt

Family and Medical Leave Act of 1993 Requires employers to provide up to twelve weeks of unpaid leave for family and medical emergencies

National Labor Relations Act Passed in 1935 to set up procedures for employees to vote whether to have a union; also known as the Wagner Act

National Labor Relations Board Established by the Wagner Act to enforce its provisions

Labor-Management Relations Act Passed in 1947 to limit union power; also known as the Taft-Hartley Act

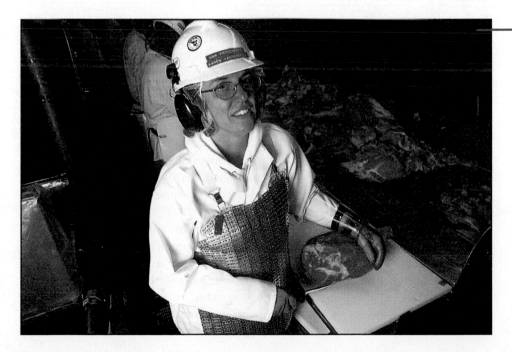

Employee safety and health have become major issues for organizations and their human resource managers. For example, Karen Vanderstoep's job at Hormel requires that she lift heavy pieces of meat and operate dangerous equipment. Note that she is wearing a hard hat, ear protectors, and a heavy apron and gloves. She also stands on a springy rubber mat to reduce fatigue and strain on her knees. These and myriad other improvements have dramatically reduced injuries at the Hormel facility.

Occupational Safety and Health Act of 1970 (OSHA) Directly mandates the provision of safe working conditions

Health and Safety The **Occupational Safety and Health Act of 1970 (OSHA)** directly mandates the provision of safe working conditions. It requires that employers (1) provide a place of employment that is free from hazards that may cause death or serious physical harm and (2) obey the safety and health standards established by the Department of Labor. Safety standards are intended to prevent accidents, whereas occupational health standards are concerned with preventing occupational disease. For example, standards limit the concentration of cotton dust in the air because this contaminant has been associated with lung disease in textile workers. The standards are enforced by OSHA inspections, which are conducted when an employee files a complaint of unsafe conditions or when a serious accident occurs. Spot inspections of plants in especially hazardous industries such as mining and chemicals are also made. Employers who fail to meet OSHA standards may be fined.

Emerging Legal Issues Several other areas of legal concern have emerged during the past few years. One is sexual harassment. Although sexual harassment is forbidden under Title VII, it has received additional attention in the courts recently as more and more victims have decided to confront the problem publicly. Another emerging human resource management issue is alcohol and drug abuse. Both alcoholism and drug dependence are major problems today. Recent court rulings have tended to define alcoholics and drug addicts as disabled, protecting them under the same laws that protect other disabled people. Finally, AIDS has emerged as an important legal issue as well. AIDS victims too are most often protected under various laws protecting the disabled.

Change and HRM

Beyond the objective legal context of HRM, various social changes are also affecting how organizations interact with their employees. First, many organizations are using more and more temporary workers today. This trend, discussed more fully later in the chapter, allows organizations to add workers as necessary without the risk that they may have to eliminate their jobs in the future.

Second, dual-career families are much more common today than just a few years ago. Organizations are finding that they must make accommodations for employees who are dual-career partners. These accommodations may include delaying transfers, offering employment to the spouses of current employees to retain them, and providing more flexible work schedules and benefits packages. A related aspect of social change and HRM, workforce diversity, was covered more fully in Chapter 6.

employment-at-will A traditional view of the workplace in which organizations can fire their employees for any reason; recent court judgments are limiting employment-at-will

Employment-at-will is also becoming an important issue. Although employment-at-will has legal implications, its emergence as an issue is socially driven. **Employment-at-will** is a traditional view of the workplace in which organizations can fire an employee for any reason. Increasingly, however, people are arguing that organizations should be able to fire only people who are poor performers or who violate rules and, conversely, not be able to fire people who report safety violations to OSHA or who refuse to perform unethical activities.

Several court cases in recent years have upheld this latter emerging view and have limited many organizations' ability to terminate employees to those cases where there is clear and just cause or as part of an organizationwide cutback.

MANAGEMENT Managers need to understand and appreciate the value of hu-
IMPLICATIONS man resources as perhaps the most important determinant of an organization's success. Taking a strategic orientation to human resource management is also becoming more popular. In addition, managers must be familiar with the various laws and related regulations that govern human resource practices. The role of change and HRM must also be carefully acknowledged.

Attracting Human Resources

With an understanding of the environmental context of human resource management as a foundation, we are now ready to address its first substantive concern—attracting qualified people who are interested in employment with the organization.

Human Resource Planning

The starting point in attracting qualified human resources is planning. HR planning, in turn, involves job analysis and forecasting the demand and supply of labor.

Job Analysis **Job analysis** is a systematic analysis of jobs within an organization. A job analysis is made up of two parts. The *job description* lists the duties of a job; the job's working conditions; and the tools, materials, and equipment used to perform it. The *job specification* lists the skills, abilities, and other credentials needed to do the job. Job analysis information is used in many human resource activities. For instance, knowing about job content and job requirements is necessary to develop appropriate selection methods and job-relevant performance appraisal systems and to set equitable compensation rates.

job analysis A systematic analysis of jobs within an organization

Forecasting Human Resource Demand and Supply After managers fully understand the jobs to be performed within the organization, they can start planning for the organization's future human resource needs. Figure 14.1 summarizes the steps most often followed. The manager starts by assessing trends in past human resources usage, future organizational plans, and general economic trends. A good sales forecast is often the foundation, especially for smaller organizations. Historical ratios can then be used to predict demand for employees such as operating employees and sales representatives. Of course, large organizations use much more complicated models to predict their future human resource needs.

Forecasting the supply of labor is really two tasks: forecasting the internal supply (the number and type of employees who will be in the firm at some future date) and forecasting the external supply (the number and type of people who will

Figure 14.1

Human Resource Planning

Attracting human resources cannot be left to chance if an organization expects to function at peak efficiency. Human resource planning involves assessing trends, forecasting supply and demand of labor, and then developing appropriate strategies for addressing any differences.

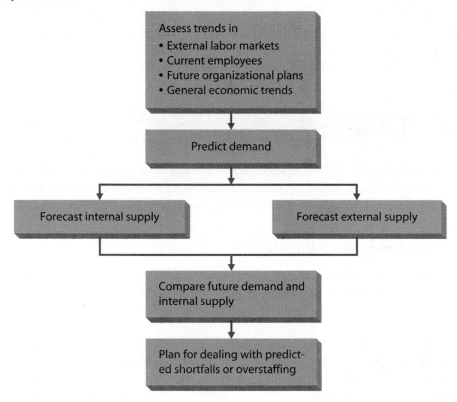

be available for hiring in the labor market at large). The simplest approach merely adjusts present staffing levels for anticipated turnover and promotions. Again, though, large organizations use extremely sophisticated models to make these forecasts.

Union Oil Company of California, for example, has a complex forecasting system for keeping track of the present and future distributions of professionals and managers. The Union Oil system can spot areas where there will eventually be too many qualified professionals competing for too few promotions or, conversely, too few competent people available to fill important positions.[5]

At higher levels of the organization, managers plan for specific people and positions. The technique most commonly used is the **replacement chart**, which lists each important managerial position, who occupies it, how long he or she will probably stay in it before moving on, and who (by name) is now qualified or soon will be qualified to move into the position. This technique allows ample time to plan developmental experiences for persons identified as potential successors to critical man-

replacement chart Lists each important managerial position in the organization, who occupies it, how long he or she will probably stay in it before moving on, and who is or will be a qualified replacement

agerial jobs. Charles Knight, CEO of Emerson Electric Co., has an entire room dedicated to posting the credentials of his top seven hundred executives.[6]

To facilitate both planning and identifying persons for current transfer or promotion, some organizations also have an **employee information system**, or **skills inventory**. Such systems are usually computerized and contain information on each employee's education, skills, work experience, and career aspirations. Such a system can quickly locate all the employees in the organization who are qualified to fill a position requiring, for instance, a degree in chemical engineering, three years of experience in an oil refinery, and fluency in Spanish.

Forecasting the external supply of labor is a different problem altogether. How does a manager, for example, predict how many electrical engineers will be seeking work in Georgia three years from now? To get an idea of the future availability of labor, planners must rely on information from outside sources such as state employment commissions, government reports, and figures supplied by colleges on the number of students in major fields.

employee information system (skills inventory) Contains information on each employee's education, skills, work experience, and career aspirations; usually computerized

recruiting The process of attracting qualified persons to apply for jobs that are open

Matching Human Resource Supply and Demand

After comparing future demand and internal supply, managers can make plans to manage predicted shortfalls or overstaffing. If a shortfall is predicted, new employees can be hired, present employees can be retrained and transferred into the understaffed area, individuals approaching retirement can be convinced to stay on, or labor-saving or productivity-enhancing systems can be installed.

If the organization needs to hire, the external labor supply forecast helps managers plan how to recruit, based on whether the type of person needed is readily available or scarce in the labor market. As we noted earlier, the trend in hiring temporary workers also helps managers in staffing by affording them extra flexibility. If overstaffing is expected to be a problem, the main options are transferring the extra employees, not replacing individuals who quit, encouraging early retirement, and laying people off.

Recruiting Human Resources

Once an organization has an idea of its future human resource needs, the next phase is usually recruiting new employees. **Recruiting** is the process of attracting qualified persons to apply for the jobs that are open. Where do recruits come from? Some recruits are found internally; others come from outside the organization. *Management InfoTech* describes how some firms are using the Internet to recruit new employees.

Bertha Freeman was Detroit's first black female tool-and-die maker. A die is a form carved out of a block of steel to create a reverse version of, say, a car door. It's then installed in a machine that stamps out thousands of car doors. Ms. Freeman got her opportunity when General Motors first opened its apprenticeship program to women in the early 1970s. At the time, GM was doing a lot of internal recruiting; Ms. Freeman was working on one of the company's assembly lines, but was looking for better opportunities. She took the required tests and was the only woman to pass. After a rigorous four-year apprenticeship, she emerged as one of the company's top tool-and-die makers. Today she is with Focus: HOPE, a private nonprofit organization that trains mostly black inner-city kids to become precision machinists.

ATTRACTING APPLICANTS WITH HIGH-TECH TOOLS

DVCi Technologies, which specializes in e-commerce, is one of a growing number of organizations boosting their recruiting efforts by giving job-seekers a high-tech, behind-the-scenes view of the work environment. DVCi aims cameras at employees working in its New York office and posts the images on its web site so potential applicants can get a sense of the workplace and the daily rhythm of activities. This virtual, realistic job preview sets DVCi apart from other Internet firms that are recruiting for similar jobs, and it is a proven recruiting tool: Marta Sant, now senior art director, applied for the job after she spent time looking at the images on the DVCi site.

The U.S. Army takes another approach to on-line recruiting by offering a virtual visit to a typical barracks facility. Potential enlistees can click their way through views of the sleeping quarters, laundry rooms, and other areas. They can also use on-line chat mode to converse with army recruiters or click to download a video clip of a tank. In this way, military recruiters can attract web-savvy recruits who might otherwise have little knowledge of army living arrangements and career opportunities.

Telecommunications giant Sprint invites e-mail inquiries about job openings from people who browse its web site. If no appropriate positions are open, the company retains the inquiries and, through an automated system, e-mails the applicants when suitable jobs become available. Sprint's human resources experts see e-mail as a good way to build relationships with job-seekers and to encourage them to keep the company in mind as a potential employer.

Cisco Systems, which makes systems that power Internet activities, also uses e-mail in its recruiting process. Knowing that applicants are keenly interested in an insider's view of the company, Cisco offers to have employees answer questions by e-mail. This program, dubbed "Make Friends at Cisco," helps job-seekers learn more about actual working conditions from the people who are in the best position to know. At the same time, it ensures that newly hired employees know at least one colleague when they join Cisco.

> *Every company is looking at ways to maximize the Internet as a recruiting tool.*
>
> —*Sonja Ambur, national staffing director for Sprint**

Reference: Stephanie Armour, "Companies Put Web to Work as Recruiter," *USA Today,* January 25, 2000, p. 1B (*quote on p. 1B).

---

internal recruiting Considering present employees as candidates for openings

Internal recruiting means considering present employees as candidates for openings. Promotion from within can help build morale and keep high-quality employees from leaving the firm. In unionized firms, the procedures for notifying employees of internal job change opportunities are usually spelled out in the union contract. For higher-level positions, a skills inventory system may be used to identify internal candidates, or managers may be asked to recommend individuals who should be considered. One disadvantage of internal recruiting is its "ripple effect." When an employee moves to a different job, someone else must be found to take his or her old job. In one organization, 454 job movements were necessary as a result of filling 195 initial openings!

external recruiting Attracting persons outside the organization to apply for jobs

External recruiting involves attracting persons outside the organization to apply for jobs. External recruiting methods include advertising, campus interviews, employment agencies or executive search firms, union hiring halls, referrals by present employees, and hiring "walk-ins" or "gate-hires" (people who show up without being solicited). Of course, a manager must select the most appropriate methods, using the state employment service to find maintenance workers but not a nuclear physicist, for example. Private employment agencies can be a good source of clerical and technical employees, and executive search firms specialize in locating top-management talent. Newspaper ads are often used because they reach a wide audience and thus allow minorities "equal opportunity" to find out about and apply for job openings.

The organization must also keep in mind that recruiting decisions often go both ways—the organization is recruiting an employee, but the prospective employee is also selecting a job.[7] Indeed, recruiters have faced a difficult job in recent years as unemployment has continued to drop. By early two thousand unemployment had dropped to a twenty-five-year low of 4.3 percent. As a result, recruiters at firms such as Sprint, PeopleSoft, and Cognex had started to stress how much "fun" it is to work for them, reinforcing this message with ice cream socials, karaoke contests, softball leagues, and free movie nights.[8] Thus, the organization wants to put its best foot forward, treat all applicants with dignity, and strive for a good person-job fit. Recent estimates suggest that hiring the "wrong" operating employee—one who flops and either quits or must be fired—generally costs the organization at least $5,000 in lost productivity and training. Hiring the wrong manager can cost the organization far more.[9]

One generally successful method for facilitating a good person-job fit is through the so-called **realistic job preview (RJP)**. As the term suggests, the RJP involves providing the applicant with a real picture of what performing the job that the organization is trying to fill would be like.[10]

realistic job preview (RJP) Provides the applicant with a real picture of what performing the job that the organization is trying to fill would be like

Selecting Human Resources

Once the recruiting process has attracted a pool of applicants, the next step is to select whom to hire. The intent of the selection process is to gather from applicants information that will predict their job success and then to hire the candidates likely to be most successful. Of course, the organization can gather information only about factors that are predictive of future performance. The process of determining the predictive value of information is called **validation**.

Two basic approaches to validation are predictive validation and content validation. *Predictive validation* involves collecting the scores of employees or applicants on the device to be validated and correlating their scores with actual job performance. A significant correlation means that the selection device is a valid predictor of job performance. *Content validation* uses logic and job analysis data to establish that the selection device measures the exact skills needed for successful job performance. The most critical part of content validation is a careful job analysis showing exactly what duties are to be performed. The test is then developed to measure the applicant's ability to perform those duties.

validation Determining the extent to which a selection device is predictive of future job performance

Application Blanks   The first step in selection usually is asking the candidate to fill out an application blank. Application blanks are an efficient method of gathering information about the applicant's previous work history, educational background, and other job-related demographic data. They should not contain questions about areas unrelated to the job such as gender, religion, or national origin. Application blank data are generally used informally to decide whether a candidate merits further evaluation, and interviewers use application blanks to familiarize themselves with candidates before interviewing them.

Tests   Tests of ability, skill, aptitude, or knowledge that is relevant to the particular job are usually the best predictors of job success, although tests of general intelligence or personality are occasionally useful as well. In addition to being validated, tests should be administered and scored consistently. All candidates should be given the same directions, should be allowed the same amount of time, and should experience the same testing environment (temperature, lighting, distractions).[11]

Interviews   Although a popular selection device, an interview is sometimes a poor predictor of job success. For example, biases inherent in the way people perceive and judge others on first meeting affect subsequent evaluations by the interviewer. Interview validity can be improved by training interviewers to be aware of potential biases and by increasing the structure of the interview. In a structured interview, questions are written in advance and all interviewers follow the same question list with each candidate they interview. This procedure introduces consistency into the interview procedure and allows the organization to validate the content of the questions to be asked.[12]

For interviewing managerial or professional candidates, a somewhat less structured approach can be used. Question areas and information-gathering objectives are still planned in advance, but the specific questions vary with the candidates' backgrounds. Trammell Crow Real Estate Investors uses a novel approach in hiring managers. Each applicant is interviewed not only by two or three other managers but also by a secretary or young leasing agent. This technique provides information about how the prospective manager relates to nonmanagers.

Assessment Centers   Assessment centers are popular methods used to select managers and are particularly good for selecting current employees for promotion. The assessment center assessment is a content-valid simulation of major parts of the managerial job. A typical center lasts two to three days, with groups of six to twelve persons participating in a variety of managerial exercises. Centers may also include interviews, public speaking, and standardized ability tests. Candidates are assessed by several trained observers, usually managers several levels above the job for which the candidates are being considered. Assessment centers are quite valid if they are properly designed and are fair to members of minority groups and women.[13] For some firms, the assessment center is a permanent facility created for these activities. For other firms, the assessment activities are performed in a multipurpose location such as a conference room. AT&T pioneered the assessment center concept. For years the firm has used assessment centers to make virtually all of its selection decisions for management positions.

Other Techniques Organizations also use other selection techniques depending on the circumstances. Polygraph tests, once popular, are declining in popularity. On the other hand, more and more organizations are requiring that applicants in whom they are interested take physical exams. Organizations are also increasingly using drug tests, especially in situations in which drug-related performance problems could create serious safety hazards. For example, applicants for jobs in a nuclear power plant would likely be tested for drug use. And some organizations today even run credit checks on prospective employees. *Today's Management Issues* describes some additional new high-tech methods that are being used.

MANAGEMENT IMPLICATIONS Managers need to remember that attracting the best possible human resources is an important part of organizational effectiveness. Planning is the first step so that they know how many people the

---

TODAY'S MANAGEMENT ISSUES

TOOLS FOR SCREENING JOB CANDIDATES

Reach out and screen someone? Procter & Gamble is doing it, and Office Depot is doing it, Metokote is doing it. These companies are using a sophisticated interactive voice response (IVR) system to screen out inappropriate job candidates via telephone.

Procter & Gamble used IVR to manage the large number of applications received during a national recruiting campaign seeking skilled production technicians. The recruiting ad included a special phone number and job code. When potential applicants called, they first listened to a taped message about the job specification. This initial step allowed job-seekers to screen themselves out if they lacked the proper qualifications. The IVR system then helped callers schedule local appointments to fill out applications with P&G recruiters. After the application process, recruiters asked candidates to call the IVR system to find out whether they were selected to take a skills test. Those who took the skills test were asked to call the IVR system one more time to find out whether they passed; those who passed used the system to schedule interviews with P&G human resources personnel. This telephone-based system helped P&G screen out inappropriate applicants much earlier in the selection process, thus saving time and money.

Computerized candidate profiling is a screening tool used by Texas New Mexico Power, Optio Software, and Apex Capital to assist in the selection process for salespeople. After screening for suitable credentials, Texas New Mexico Power asks each remaining candidate to take a computerized test designed to profile his or her personality and thinking structure. The system compares each candidate's traits to the traits for success on the job and then generates a report about how well the candidate matches the ideal profile. The system even suggests specific questions for the company's interviewers to ask, along with guidelines for evaluating candidates' answers. This technique helps the interviewers customize their questions for individual candidates and probe more deeply about specific traits and tendencies so they can screen out candidates who are not good matches for the job or the company.

> *People are more honest when interacting with interactive voice response than with a human being.*
>
> —*Linda S. Prince, human resources administrator for Procter & Gamble*[*]

References: Ruth E. Thaler-Carter, "Reach Out and Hire Someone: Automated Response Systems Can Speed Large-Scale Hiring," *HR Magazine,* May 1999, pp. S8–S11 (*quote on p. S11); Elana Harris, "Reduce the Recruiting Risks," *Sales & Marketing Management,* May 2000, p. 18.

organization will need in the future and the array of skills those people will need to possess. Recruiting a pool of qualified applicants and then using the optimal combination of selection techniques to hire the best applicants can be of significant importance to the success of the organization.

■ Developing Human Resources

Regardless of how effective a selection system is, however, most employees need additional training if they are to grow and develop in their jobs. Evaluating their performance and providing feedback are also necessary.

Training and Development

training Teaching operational or technical employees how to do the job for which they were hired

development Teaching managers and professionals the skills needed for both present and future jobs

In HRM, **training** usually refers to teaching operational or technical employees how to do the job for which they were hired. **Development** refers to teaching managers and professionals the skills needed for both present and future jobs. Most organizations provide regular training and development programs for managers and employees. For example, IBM spends more than $700 million annually on programs and has a vice president in charge of employee education. U.S. businesses spend more than $30 billion annually on training and development programs away from the workplace. And this figure doesn't include wages and benefits paid to employees while they are participating in such programs. *The World of Management* discusses how two firms are using the Internet to train employees in different parts of the world.

Training and developing people is an important part of human resource management. Canon, for example, invests heavily in training its employees as part of its goal to remain a leading manufacturer of photography equipment. One of its biggest problems has been trying to balance the trend toward moving production to cheaper labor markets while maintaining high performance levels. One tactic Canon uses is to send its newly hired Malaysian workers to one of its plants in Japan for training. After these workers have gained proficiency, they are sent back to Malaysia to work in Canon's factory there.

WORLD OF MANAGEMENT

Bridging the Distance Through Internet Training

Lockheed Martin and SAP are just two of the rapidly growing number of companies using the Internet to deliver training courses to employees separated by hundreds or thousands of miles. Because travel expenses make up nearly half the cost of classroom training, Internet-based training is far less expensive and can reach many more employees than traditional in-person training. Employees learn at their own speed without leaving their desks, so they remain productive throughout the training period. Finally, employees are actively involved in absorbing and reviewing on-line material, searching out additional details, asking questions, and completing assignments, all of which boosts retention and makes Internet-based training more enjoyable than more passive training methods.

Employees who work for Maryland-based Lockheed Martin are spread across more than fifty nations. To keep employee skills current and to provide specialized training for new hires, the company is piloting a number of Internet-based training programs. Although the defense contractor still offers classroom training, it sees the Internet as a way to avoid the scheduling headaches and travel expenses of bringing employees together for training at central sites. In one of the Lockheed Martin pilot programs, the company is integrating audio and graphics to facilitate on-line interaction among students and instructors. The company has also created a computerized learning library for employees who want to study on their own.

SAP, a software company based in Pennsylvania, is taking a slightly different approach. It uses the Internet to beam live audio and video coverage of instructors' training presentations, accompanied by written notes, to employees around the world. Students can ask questions or make comments by speaking into their computers' built-in microphones. They can also click to view live demonstrations of the software being discussed. Through this kind of Internet-based training, SAP keeps its global workforce updated on the latest software products and techniques.

> *Trying to get workers and managers to carve out time for five days of training off the job site is like extracting teeth without an anesthetic.*
>
> *—Robert Vicek, project manager of Enterprise Information Systems University for Lockheed Martin**

References: Ronald W. Berman, "Internet Training Works for SAP," *Business Week*, May 29, 2000, p. 6; Judith N. Mottle, "Learn at a Distance: Online Learning Is Poised to Become the New Standard," *Information Week*, January 3, 2000, p. 75+ (*quote on p. 75); Jack Wilson, "Internet Training: The Time Is Now," *HR Focus*, March 1999, p. 6.

Assessing Training Needs   The first step in developing a training plan is to determine what needs exist. For example, if employees do not know how to operate the machinery necessary to do their jobs, a training program on how to operate the machinery is clearly needed. On the other hand, when a group of office workers is performing poorly, training may not be the answer. The problem could be motivation, aging equipment, poor supervision, inefficient work design, or a deficiency of skills and knowledge. Only the last could be remedied by training. As training programs are being developed, the manager should set specific and measurable goals specifying what participants are to learn. Managers should also plan to evaluate the training program after employees complete it. The training process from start to finish is diagrammed in Figure 14.2.

Figure 14.2

The Training Process

Managing the training process can go a long way toward enhancing its effectiveness. If training programs are well conceived and well executed, both the organization and its employees benefit. Following a comprehensive process helps managers meet the objectives of the training program.

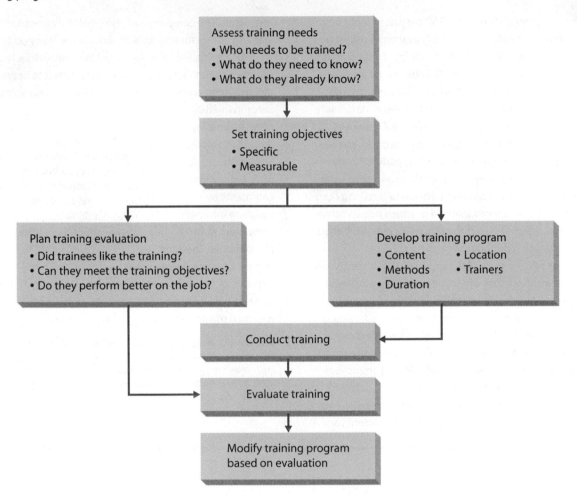

Common Training Methods Many different training and development methods are available. Selection of methods depends on many considerations, but perhaps the most important is training content. When the training content is factual material (such as company rules or explanations of how to fill out forms), assigned reading, programmed learning, and lecture methods work well. When the content is interpersonal relations or group decision-making, however, firms must use a method that allows interpersonal contact such as role-playing or case-discussion groups. When employees must learn a physical skill, methods allowing practice and the actual use of tools and material are needed, as in on-the-job training or vestibule training. (Vestibule training enables participants to focus on safety, learning, and feedback rather than productivity.) CD-rom and Internet-based training are also becoming popular. Xerox, Massachusetts Mutual Life Insurance, and Ford have all reported tremendous success with these methods. Most training programs rely on a mix of methods. Boeing, for example, sends managers to an intensive two-week training seminar involving tests, simulations, role-playing exercises, and CD-ROM flight-simulation exercises.[14]

Evaluation of Training   Training and development programs should always be evaluated. Typical evaluation approaches include measuring one or more relevant criteria (such as attitudes or performance) before and after the training and determining whether the criteria changed. Evaluation measures collected at the end of training are easy to obtain, but actual performance measures collected when the trainee is on the job are more important. Trainees may say that they enjoyed the training and learned a lot, but the true test is whether their job performance improves after their training.

Performance Appraisal

When employees are trained and settled into their jobs, one of management's next concerns is performance appraisal. **Performance appraisal** is a formal assessment of how well employees are doing their job. Employees' performance should be evaluated regularly for many reasons. One reason is that performance appraisal may be necessary for validating selection devices or assessing the impact of training programs. A second reason is administrative—to aid in making decisions about pay raises, promotions, and training. Still another reason is to provide feedback to employees to help them improve their present performance and plan future careers.

performance appraisal A formal assessment of how well an employee is doing his or her job

Because performance evaluations often help determine wages and promotions, they must be fair and nondiscriminatory. In the case of appraisals, content validation is used to show that the appraisal system accurately measures performance on important job elements and does not measure traits or behavior that are irrelevant to job performance.

Common Appraisal Methods   Two basic categories of appraisal methods commonly used in organizations are objective methods and judgmental methods. *Objective measures of performance* include actual output (that is, number of units produced), scrap rate, dollar volume of sales, and number of claims processed. Objective performance measures may be contaminated by "opportunity bias" if some persons have a better chance to perform than others. For example, a sales representative selling snow blowers in Michigan has a greater opportunity than does a colleague selling the same product in Arkansas. Fortunately, adjusting raw performance figures for the effect of opportunity bias and thereby arriving at figures that accurately represent each individual's performance is often possible.

Another type of objective measure, the special performance test, is a method in which each employee is assessed under standardized conditions. This kind of appraisal also eliminates opportunity bias. For example, GTE Southwest Inc. has a series of prerecorded calls that operators in a test booth answer. The operators are graded on speed, accuracy, and courtesy in handling the calls. Performance tests measure ability but do not measure the extent to which one is motivated to use that ability on a daily basis. (A high-ability person may be a lazy performer except when being tested.) Special performance tests must therefore be supplemented by other appraisal methods to provide a complete picture of performance.

Judgmental methods, including ranking and rating techniques, are the most common way to measure performance. Ranking compares employees directly with each other and orders them from best to worst. Ranking has a number of drawbacks. Ranking is difficult for large groups because the persons in the middle of the distribution may be hard to distinguish from one another accurately. Comparisons of people in different work groups are also difficult. For example, an employee ranked third in a strong group may be more valuable than an employee ranked first in a weak group. Another criticism of ranking is that the manager must rank people on the basis of overall performance, although each person likely has both strengths and weaknesses. Furthermore, rankings do not provide useful information for feedback. To be told that one is ranked third is not nearly so helpful as to be told that the quality of one's work is outstanding, its quantity is satisfactory, one's punctuality could use improvement, and one's paperwork is seriously deficient.

Rating differs from ranking because it compares each employee with a fixed standard rather than with other employees. A rating scale provides the standard. Figure 14.3 gives examples of three graphic rating scales for a bank teller. Each

Figure 14.3

Graphic Rating Scales for a Bank Teller

Graphic rating scales are very common methods for evaluating employee performance. The manager who is doing the rating circles the point on each scale that best reflects her or his assessment of the employee on that scale. Graphic rating scales are widely used for many different kinds of jobs.

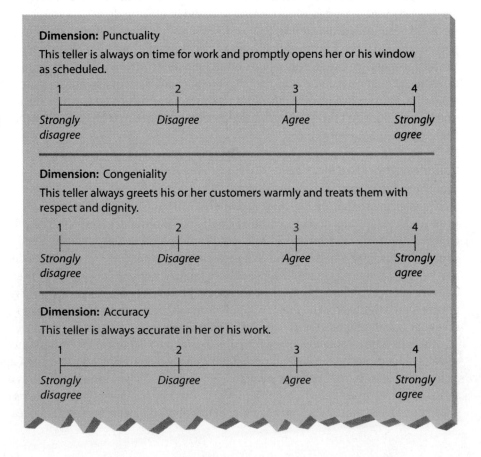

consists of a performance dimension to be rated (punctuality, congeniality, and accuracy) followed by a scale on which to make the rating. In constructing graphic rating scales, performance dimensions relevant to job performance must be selected. In particular, they should focus on job behaviors and results rather than on personality traits or attitudes.

The **behaviorally anchored rating scale (BARS)** is a sophisticated and useful rating method. Supervisors construct rating scales with associated behavioral anchors. They first identify relevant performance dimensions and then generate anchors—specific, observable behaviors typical of each performance level. Figure 14.4 shows an example of a behaviorally anchored rating scale for the dimension "inventory control."

The other scales in this set, developed for the job of department manager in a chain of specialty stores, include "handling customer complaints," "planning special promotions," "following company procedures," "supervising sales personnel," and "diagnosing and solving special problems." BARS can be effective because it requires that management take proper care in constructing the scales and it provides useful anchors for supervisors to use in evaluating people. It is costly, however, because outside expertise is usually needed and because scales must be developed for each job within the organization.

Errors in Performance Appraisal   Errors or biases can occur in any kind of rating or ranking system. One common problem is recency error—the tendency to base judgments on the subordinate's most recent performance because it is most easily recalled. Often a rating or ranking is intended to evaluate performance over an entire time period, such as six months or a year, so the recency error does introduce error into the judgment. Other errors include overuse of one part of the scale—being too lenient, being too severe, or giving everyone a rating of "average."

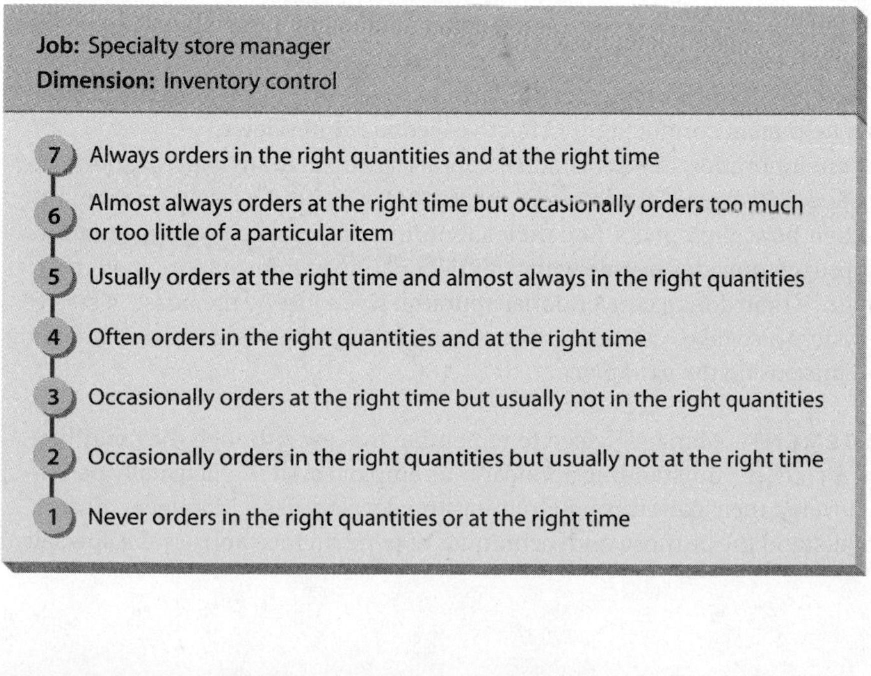

> **behaviorally anchored rating scale (BARS)** A sophisticated rating method in which supervisors construct a rating scale associated with behavioral anchors

Job: Specialty store manager
Dimension: Inventory control

7 — Always orders in the right quantities and at the right time

6 — Almost always orders at the right time but occasionally orders too much or too little of a particular item

5 — Usually orders at the right time and almost always in the right quantities

4 — Often orders in the right quantities and at the right time

3 — Occasionally orders at the right time but usually not in the right quantities

2 — Occasionally orders in the right quantities but usually not at the right time

1 — Never orders in the right quantities or at the right time

Figure 14.4

Behaviorally Anchored Rating Scale

Behaviorally anchored rating scales help overcome some of the limitations of standard rating scales. Each point on the scale is accompanied by a behavioral anchor—a summary of an employee behavior that fits that spot on the scale.

Reprinted with special permission of King Features Syndicate.

Providing performance feedback is a difficult process for many managers. For example, they may have a hard time giving negative feedback or simply feel uncomfortable with the process. And in some cases, as illustrated here, a manager may feel that it is only his or her opinion that counts. The employee, of course, is likely to figure out what is going on and thus the information value of the performance feedback process can be completely lost.

Halo error is allowing the assessment of an employee on one dimension to "spread" to ratings of that employee on other dimensions. For instance, if an employee is outstanding on quality of output, a rater might tend to give her or him higher marks than deserved on other dimensions. Errors can also occur because of race, gender, or age discrimination, intentionally or unintentionally. The best way to offset these errors is to ensure that a valid rating system is developed at the outset and then to train managers in how to use it.

Performance Feedback

The last step in most performance appraisal systems is giving feedback to subordinates about their performance. This step is usually done in a private meeting between the person being evaluated and his or her boss. The discussion should generally be focused on the facts—the assessed level of performance, how and why that assessment was made, and how it can be improved in the future. Feedback interviews are not easy to conduct. Many managers are uncomfortable with the task, especially if feedback is negative and subordinates are disappointed by what they hear. These points are amplified in the cartoon. Properly training managers, however, can help them conduct more effective feedback interviews.[15]

A recent innovation in performance appraisal used in many organizations today is called "360 degree" feedback: managers are evaluated by everyone around them—their boss, their peers, and their subordinates. Such a complete and thorough approach provides people with a far richer array of information about their performance than does a conventional appraisal given just by the boss. Of course, such a system also takes considerable time and must be handled to avoid breeding fear and mistrust in the workplace.[16]

MANAGEMENT IMPLICATIONS Managers need to remember that even though they may hire outstanding applicants as employees, it is still usually necessary to develop their skills through training and development. Managers must also understand the purpose and techniques of performance appraisal. Especially important, in addition, is providing performance feedback to employees after appraisals have been conducted.

Maintaining Human Resources

After organizations have attracted and developed an effective workforce, they must also make every effort to maintain that workforce. To do so requires effective compensation and benefits as well as career planning.

Determining Compensation

Compensation is the financial remuneration given by the organization to its employees in exchange for their work. There are three basic forms of compensation. *Wages* are the hourly compensation paid to operating employees. The current federal minimum hourly wage is $5.15. *Salary* refers to compensation paid for total contributions, as opposed to being based on hours worked. For example, managers earn an annual salary, usually paid monthly. They receive the salary regardless of the number of hours they work. Some firms have started paying all their employees a salary instead of hourly wages. For example, all employees at Chaparral Steel Company earn a salary, starting at $20,000 a year for entry-level operating employees. Finally, *incentives* represent special compensation opportunities that are usually tied to performance. Sales commissions and bonuses are among the most common incentives.

compensation The financial remuneration given by the organization to its employees in exchange for their work

The acute shortage of qualified high-tech employees has led many employers to seek new and unusual ways to attract and retain knowledge workers. Etensity is a web-consulting and services firm. Among a wide array of other benefits, Etensity offers its employees a program it calls Hot Wheels. Essentially, employees can buy the car of their dreams and the company will make half of their car payments for them—as long as the individual remains with the firm. Another Etensity program called Raise the Roof makes interest-free loans of up to $10,000 to help employees buy a home; the loan will then be forgiven if the employees remain with the company for a specified period of time.

Compensation is an important and complex part of the organization-employee relationship. Basic compensation is necessary to provide employees with the means to maintain a reasonable standard of living. Beyond this point, however, compensation also provides a tangible measure of the value of the individual to the organization. If employees do not earn enough to meet their basic economic goals, they will seek employment elsewhere. Likewise, if they believe that their contributions are undervalued by the organization, they may leave or exhibit poor work habits, low morale, and little commitment to the organization. Thus, designing an effective compensation system is clearly in the organization's best interests.[17]

A good compensation system can help attract qualified applicants, retain present employees, and stimulate high performance at a cost reasonable for one's industry and geographic area. To set up a successful system, management must make decisions about wage levels, the wage structure, and the individual wage determination system.

Wage-Level Decision   The wage-level decision is a management policy decision about whether the firm wants to pay above, at, or below the going rate for labor in the industry or the geographic area. Most firms choose to pay near the average, while those that cannot afford more pay below average. Large, successful firms may like to cultivate the image of being "wage leaders" by intentionally paying more than average and thus attracting and keeping high-quality employees. IBM, for example, pays top dollar to get the new employees it wants. McDonald's, on the other hand, often pays close to the minimum wage. The level of unemployment in the labor force also affects wage levels. Pay declines when labor is plentiful and increases when labor is scarce.

Once managers make the wage-level decision, they need information to help set actual wage rates. Managers need to know what the maximum, minimum, and average wages are for particular jobs in the appropriate labor market. This information is collected by means of a wage survey. Area wage surveys can be conducted by individual firms or by local HR or business associations. Professional and industry associations often conduct surveys and make the results available to employers.

Wage-Structure Decision   Wage structures are usually set up through a procedure called **job evaluation**—an attempt to assess the worth of each job relative to other jobs. At Ben & Jerry's Homemade, company policy once dictated that the highest-paid employee in the firm could not make more than seven times what the lowest-paid employee earns. But this policy had to be modified when the company found that it was simply unable to hire a new CEO without paying more than this amount. The simplest method for creating a wage structure is to rank jobs from those that should be paid the most (for example, the president) to those that should be paid the least (for example, a mail clerk or a janitor).

In a smaller firm with few jobs (like Ben & Jerry's, for example), this method is quick and practical, but larger firms with many job titles require more sophisticated methods. The next step is setting actual wage rates on the basis of a combination of survey data and the wage structure that results from job evaluation. Jobs of equal value are often grouped into wage grades for ease of administration.

job evaluation An attempt to assess the worth of each job relative to other jobs

Individual Wage Decisions After wage-level and wage-structure decisions are made, the individual wage decision must be addressed. This decision concerns how much to pay each employee in a particular job. Although the easiest decision is to pay a single rate for each job, a range of pay rates is more typically associated with each job. For example, the pay range for an individual job might be $5.85 to $6.39 per hour, with different employees earning different rates within the range.

A system is then needed for setting individual rates. This determination may be done on the basis of seniority (enter the job at $6.85, for example, and increase ten cents per hour every six months on the job), initial qualifications (inexperienced people start at $6.85, more experienced people start at a higher rate), or merit (raises above the entering rate are given for good performance). Combinations of these bases may also be used.

Because of today's tight labor market, many job seekers are finding it possible to demand higher salaries than ever before. The Internet is also playing a key role in this trend, because job seekers and current employees can more easily get a sense of what their true market value is. If they can document the claim that their value is higher than what their current employer now pays or is offering, they are in a position to demand higher salaries. Consider the case of one compensation executive who met recently with a subordinate to discuss her raise. He was surprised when she produced data from five different web sites supporting her claim for a bigger raise than he had intended to offer.[18]

Determining Benefits

Benefits are things of value other than compensation that the organization provides to its workers. The average company spends an amount equal to more than one-third of its cash payroll on employee benefits. Thus, an average employee who is paid $18,000 per year averages about $6,588 more per year in benefits.

Benefits come in several forms. Pay for time not worked includes sick leave, vacation, holidays, and unemployment compensation. Insurance benefits often include life and health insurance for employees and their dependents. Workers' compensation is a legally required insurance benefit that provides medical care and disability income for employees injured on the job. Social security is a government pension plan to which both employers and employees contribute. Many employers also provide a private pension plan to which they and their employees contribute. Employee service benefits can include tuition reimbursement and recreational opportunities.

Some organizations have instituted "cafeteria benefit plans," whereby basic coverage is provided for all employees but employees are then allowed to choose which additional benefits they want (up to a cost limit based on salary). An employee with five children might choose medical and dental coverage for dependents, a single employee might prefer more vacation time, and an older employee might elect increased pension benefits. Flexible systems are expected to encourage people to stay in the organization and even help the company attract new employees.[19]

In recent years, companies have also started offering even more innovative benefits as a way of accommodating different needs and to deal with a very tight

benefits Things of value other than compensation that an organization provides to its workers

labor market. On-site childcare, mortgage assistance, and generous paid-leave programs are becoming popular.[20] A good benefits plan may encourage people to join and stay with an organization, but it seldom stimulates high performance because benefits are tied more to membership in the organization than to performance. To manage their benefits programs effectively, companies should shop carefully, avoid redundant coverage, and provide only those benefits that employees want. Benefits programs should also be explained to employees in clear and straightforward language so that they can use the benefits appropriately and appreciate what the company is providing.

Career Planning

A final aspect of maintaining human resources is career planning. Few people work in the same jobs their entire career. Some people change jobs within one organization, others change organizations, and many do both. When these movements are haphazard and poorly conceived, both the individual and the organization suffer. Thus, planning career progressions in advance is in everyone's best interest. Of course, planing a thirty-year career for a newcomer just joining the organization is difficult. But planning can help map out what areas the individual is most interested in and help the person see what opportunities are available within the organization.[21]

MANAGEMENT IMPLICATIONS Managers should recognize the critical importance of compensation and benefits. On the one hand, these represent significant costs for the organization and should therefore be carefully monitored and controlled. On the other hand, compensation and benefits are also tangible indicators to the employee of his or her value to the organization and so should be fair and equitable. Career planning is also something all managers should consider for both themselves and their employees.

Managing Labor Relations

labor relations The process of dealing with employees when they are represented by a union

Labor relations is the process of dealing with employees when they are represented by a union.[22] Managing labor relations is an important part of HRM.

How Employees Form Unions

For employees to form a new local union, several events must occur. First, employees must become interested in having a union. Nonemployees who are professional organizers employed by a national union (such as the Teamsters or United Auto Workers) may generate interest by making speeches and distributing literature outside the workplace. Inside, employees who want a union try to convince other workers of the benefits of a union.

The second step is to collect employees' signatures on authorization cards. These cards state that the signer wishes to vote to determine if the union will represent him or her. Thirty percent of the employees in the potential bargaining unit must sign these cards to show the National Labor Relations Board (NLRB) that interest is sufficient to justify holding an election. Before an election can be held, however, the bargaining unit must be defined. The bargaining unit consists of all employees who will be eligible to vote in the election and to join and be represented by the union if one is formed.

The election is supervised by an NLRB representative (or, if both parties agree, the American Arbitration Association—a professional association of arbitrators) and is conducted by secret ballot. If a simple majority of those voting (not of all those eligible to vote) votes for the union, then the union becomes certified as the official representative of the bargaining unit.[23] The new union then organizes itself by officially signing up members and electing officers; it will soon be ready to negotiate the first contract. The union-organizing process is diagrammed in Figure 14.5. If workers become disgruntled with their union, or if management presents strong evidence that the union is not representing workers appropriately, the NLRB can arrange a decertification election. The results of such an election determine whether the union remains certified.

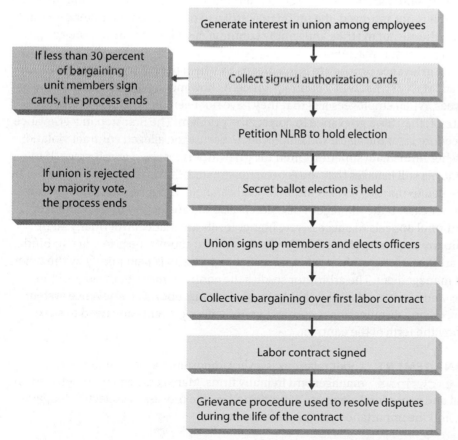

Figure 14.5

The Union-Organizing Process

If employees of an organization want to form a union, the law prescribes a specific set of procedures that both employees and the organization must follow. Assuming that these procedures are followed and the union is approved, the organization must engage in collective bargaining with the new union.

Organizations usually prefer that employees not be unionized because unions limit management's freedom in many areas. Management may thus wage its own campaign to convince employees to vote against the union. "Unfair labor practices" are often committed at this point. For instance, it is an unfair labor practice for management to promise to give employees a raise (or any other benefit) if the union is defeated. Experts agree that the best way to avoid unionization is to practice good employee relations all the time—not just when threatened by a union election. Providing absolutely fair treatment with clear standards in the areas of pay, promotion, layoffs, and discipline; having a complaint or appeal system for persons who feel unfairly treated; and avoiding any kind of favoritism will help make employees feel that a union is unnecessary.

Collective Bargaining

collective bargaining The process of agreeing on a satisfactory labor contract between management and a union

The intent of **collective bargaining** is to agree on a satisfactory labor contract between management and the union. The contract contains agreements about issues such as wages, hours, conditions of employment promotion, layoffs, discipline, benefits, methods of allocating overtime, vacations, rest periods, and the grievance procedure. The process of bargaining may go on for weeks, months, or longer, with representatives of management and the union meeting to make proposals and counterproposals. The resulting agreement must be ratified by the union membership. If it is not approved, the union may strike to put pressure on management, or it may choose not to strike and simply continue negotiating until a more acceptable agreement is reached.

grievance procedure The means by which a labor contract is enforced

The **grievance procedure** is the means by which the labor contract is enforced. Most of what is in a contract concerns how management will treat employees. When employees feel that they have not been treated fairly under the contract, they file a grievance to correct the problem. The first step in a grievance procedure is for the aggrieved employee to discuss the alleged contract violation with her immediate superior. Often the grievance is resolved at this stage. If the employee still believes that she is being mistreated, however, the grievance can be appealed to the next level. A union official can help an aggrieved employee present her case. If the manager's decision is also unsatisfactory to the employee, additional appeals to successively higher levels are made, until finally all in-company steps are exhausted. The final step is to submit the grievance to binding arbitration. An arbitrator is a labor-law expert who is paid jointly by the union and management. The arbitrator studies the contract, hears both sides of the case, and renders a decision that both parties must obey. The grievance system for resolving disputes about contract enforcement prevents any need to strike during the term of the contract.

MANAGEMENT IMPLICATIONS Labor relations is a very important part of human resource management in many firms. Managers need to understand the legal and procedural elements of unionization, the process of collective bargaining, and the importance of a grievance system.

New Challenges in the Changing Workplace

As we have seen throughout this chapter, human resource managers face several ongoing challenges in their efforts to keep their organizations staffed with effective workforces. To complicate matters, new challenges arise as the economic and social environments of business change. We conclude this chapter with a look at two of the most important human resource management issues facing business today.

Managing Knowledge Workers

Employees traditionally added value to organizations because of what they did or because of their experience. In the "information age," however, many employees add value because of what they know.[24]

The Nature of Knowledge Work

Employees whose contributions to an organization are based on what they know are usually called **knowledge workers,** and the skill with which they are managed is a major factor in determining which firms will be successful in the future. Knowledge workers, including computer scientists, engineers, and physical scientists, provide special challenges for the HR manager. They tend to work in high-technology firms and are usually experts in some abstract knowledge base. They often like to work independently and tend to identify more strongly with their professions than with any organization—even to the extent of defining performance in terms recognized by other members of their professions.

As the importance of information-driven jobs grows, the need for knowledge workers continues to grow as well. But these employees require extensive and highly specialized training, and not every organization is willing to make the human capital investments necessary to take advantage of these jobs. In fact, even after knowledge workers are on the job, retraining and training updates are critical to prevent their skills from becoming obsolete. It has been suggested, for example, that the "half-life" of a technical education in engineering is about three years. The failure to update such skills will not only result in the loss of competitive advantage but will also increase the likelihood that the knowledge workers will go to another firm that is more committed to keeping them updated in their field.

Knowledge Worker Management and Labor Markets

In recent years, the demand for knowledge workers has been growing at a dramatic rate. As a result, organizations that need these workers must introduce regular market adjustments (upward) to pay them enough to keep them. This point is especially critical in areas in which demand is growing because even entry-level salaries for these employees are skyrocketing. Once an employee accepts a job with a firm, the employer faces yet another dilemma. Once hired, workers are more subject to the company's internal labor market, which is not likely to be growing as quickly as the external market for knowledge workers as a whole. Consequently, the longer an

knowledge workers Employees whose contributions to an organization are based on what they know

employee remains with a firm, the further behind the market his or her pay falls—unless, of course, it is regularly adjusted (upward).

Not surprisingly, the growing demand for these workers has inspired some fairly extreme measures for attracting them in the first place.[25] High starting salaries and sign-on bonuses are common. British Petroleum Exploration was recently paying starting petroleum engineers with undersea platform-drilling knowledge—not experience, just knowledge—salaries in the six figures, plus sign-on bonuses of over $50,000 and immediate profit sharing. Even with these incentives, HR managers complain that in the Gulf Coast region, they cannot retain specialists because young engineers soon leave to accept sign-on bonuses with competitors. Laments one HR executive: "We wind up six months after we hire an engineer having to fight off offers for that same engineer for more money."[26]

Contingent and Temporary Workers

A final contemporary HR issue of note involves the use of contingent and/or temporary workers. Indeed, recent years have seen an explosion in the use of such workers by organizations.

Trends in Contingent and Temporary Employment In recent years, the number of contingent workers in the workforce has increased dramatically. A contingent worker is a person who works for an organization on something other than a permanent or full-time basis. Categories of contingent workers include independent contractors, on-call workers, temporary employees (usually hired through outside agencies), and contract and leased employees. Another category is part-time workers. The financial-services giant Citigroup, for example, makes extensive use of part-time sales agents to pursue new clients. About 10 percent of the U.S. workforce currently uses one of these alternative forms of employment relationships. Experts suggest, however, that this percentage is increasing at a consistent pace.

Managing Contingent and Temporary Workers Given the widespread use of contingent and temporary workers, HR managers must understand how to use such employees most effectively; that is, they need to understand how to manage contingent and temporary workers.

One key is careful planning. Even though one of the presumed benefits of using contingent workers is flexibility, it is still important to integrate such workers in a coordinated fashion. Rather than having to call in workers sporadically and with no prior notice, organizations try to bring in specified numbers of workers for well-defined periods of time. The ability to do so comes from careful planning.

A second key is understanding contingent workers and acknowledging both their advantages and disadvantages; that is, the organization must recognize what it can and can't achieve from the use of contingent and temporary workers. Expecting too much from such workers, for example, is a mistake that managers should avoid.

Third, managers must carefully assess the real cost of using contingent workers. We noted above, for example, that many firms adopt this course of action to save labor costs. The organization should be able to document precisely its labor-cost savings. How much would it be paying people in wages and benefits if they were on permanent staff? How does this cost compare with the amount spent on contingent workers? This difference, however, could be misleading. We also noted, for instance, that contingent workers might be less effective performers than permanent and full-time employees. Comparing employee for employee on a direct-cost basis, therefore, is not necessarily valid. Organizations must learn to adjust the direct differences in labor costs to account for differences in productivity and performance.

Finally, managers must fully understand their own strategies and decide in advance how they intend to manage temporary workers, specifically focusing on how to integrate them into the organization. On a very simplistic level, for example, an organization with a large contingent workforce must make some decisions about the treatment of contingent workers relative to the treatment of permanent, full-time workers. Should contingent workers be invited to the company holiday party? Should they have the same access to such employee benefits as counseling services and child care? There are no right or wrong answers to such questions. Managers must understand that they need to develop a strategy for integrating contingent workers according to some sound logic and then follow that strategy consistently over time.[27]

MANAGEMENT IMPLICATIONS Managers should stay abreast of changing workplace conditions and situations. At present, these key issues include the management of knowledge workers and the use of contingent and temporary workers.

Summary of Key Points

Human resource management is concerned with attracting, developing, and maintaining the human resources an organization needs. Its environmental context consists of its strategic importance and the legal and social environments that affect human resource management.

Attracting human resources is an important part of the HRM function. Human resource planning starts with job analysis and then focuses on forecasting the organization's future need for employees, forecasting the availability of employees both within and outside the organization, and planning programs to ensure that the proper number and type of employees are available when needed. Recruitment and selection are the processes by which job applicants are attracted, assessed, and hired. Methods for selecting applicants include application blanks, tests, interviews, and assessment centers. Any method used for selection should be properly validated.

Organizations must also work to develop their human resources. Training and development enable employees to perform their present jobs effectively and to prepare for future jobs. Performance appraisals are important for validating selection devices, assessing the impact of training programs, deciding pay raises and promotions, and determining training needs. Both objective and judgmental methods of appraisal can be applied, and a good system usually includes several methods. The validity of appraisal information is always a concern because it is difficult to evaluate accurately the many aspects of a person's job performance.

Maintaining human resources is also important. Compensation rates must be fair compared with rates for other jobs within the organization and with rates for the same or similar jobs in other organizations in the labor market. Properly designed incentive or merit pay systems can encourage high performance, and a good benefits program can help attract and re-

tain employees. Career planning is also a major aspect of human resource management.

If the majority of a company's nonmanagement employees so desire, they have the right to be represented by a union. Management must engage in collective bargaining with the union in an effort to agree on a contract. While the contract is in effect, the grievance system is used to settle disputes with management.

Two important new challenges in the workplace include the management of knowledge workers and issues associated with the use of contingent and temporary workers.

Discussion Questions

Questions for Review

1. What is job analysis and how is it related to human resource planning?
2. Describe recruiting and selection. What are the major sources for recruits? What are the common selection methods?
3. What is the role of compensation and benefits in organizations? How should the amount of compensation and benefits be determined?
4. What are the basic steps that employees can follow if they wish to unionize?

Questions for Analysis

5. What are the advantages and disadvantages of internal and external recruiting? Which do you feel is best in the long term? Why? Be sure to think about this issue from the standpoint of both the organization and individuals (whether inside or outside the organization) who might be considered for positions.
6. How do you know if a selection device is valid? What are the possible consequences of using invalid selection methods? How can an organization ensure that its selection methods are valid?

7. Are benefits more important than compensation to an organization? To an individual? Why?

Questions for Application

8. Write a description and specifications for a job that you have held (office worker, checkout clerk, salesperson, lifeguard). Then contact a company with such a job and obtain an actual description and specifications from that firm. How are your description and specifications like theirs? How are they different?
9. Contact a local organization to determine how that organization evaluates the performance of employees in complex jobs such as middle or higher-level manager, scientist, lawyer, or market researcher. What problems with performance appraisal can you note?
10. Interview someone who is or has been a member of a union to determine his or her reasons for joining. Would you join a union? Why or why not?

BUILDING EFFECTIVE *technical* SKILLS

Exercise Overview

Technical skills refer to the manager's abilities to accomplish or understand work done in an organization. Many managers must have technical skills to be able to hire appropriate people to work in the organization. This exercise will help you use technical skills as part of the selection process.

Exercise Background

Variation One: If you currently work full-time or have worked full-time in the past, select two jobs with which you have some familiarity. Select one job that is relatively low in skill level, responsibility, required education, and pay and one job that is relatively high in the same categories. It will make the exercise more useful to you if you use real jobs that you can relate to at a personal level.

Variation Two: If you have never worked full-time or if you are not personally familiar with an array of jobs, assume that you are a manager for a small manufacturing facility. You need to hire individuals to fill two jobs. One job is for the po-

sition of plant custodian. This individual will sweep floors, clean bathrooms, empty trash cans, and so forth. The other person will be office manager. This individual will supervise a staff of three clerks and secretaries, administer the plant payroll, and coordinate the administrative operations of the plant.

Exercise Task

With the information above as background, do the following:

1. Identify the most basic skills that you think are necessary for someone to perform each job effectively.
2. Identify the general indicators or predictors of whether or not a given individual can perform each job.
3. Develop a brief set of interview questions that you might use to determine whether or not an applicant has the qualifications to perform each job.
4. How important is it that a manager hiring employees to perform a job have the technical skills to do that job him or herself?

BUILDING EFFECTIVE *communication* SKILLS

Exercise Overview

All managers must be able to communicate effectively with others in the organization. Communication is especially important in the human resource area because people are the domain of human resource management.

Exercise Background

Many companies provide various benefits to their workers. These benefits may include pay for time not worked, insurance coverage, pension plans, and so forth. These benefits are often very costly to the organization. As noted in the

text, for example, benefits often equal about one-third of what employees are paid in wages and salaries. In some countries, such as Germany, the figures are even higher.

Yet many employees often fail to appreciate the actual value of the benefits their employers provide to them. For example, they frequently underestimate the dollar value of their benefits. And when comparing their income to that of others or when comparing alternative job offers, many people focus almost entirely on direct compensation—wages and salaries paid directly to the individual.

For example, consider a college graduate who has two offers. One job offer is for $20,000 a year and the other is for $22,000. The individual is likely to see the second offer as being more attractive, even if the first offer has sufficiently more attractive benefits to make the total compensation packages equivalent to one another.

Exercise Task

With this information as context, respond to the following:

1. Why do you think most people focus on pay when assessing their compensation?

2. If you were the human resource manager for a firm, how would you communicate the value of benefits to your employees?

3. Suppose an employee comes to you and says that he is thinking about leaving for a "better job." You then learn that he is defining "better" only in terms of higher pay. How might you help him compare total compensation (including benefits)?

4. Some firms today are cutting their benefits. How would you communicate a benefit cut to your employees?

BUILDING EFFECTIVE *decision-making* SKILLS

Exercise Overview

Decision-making skills include the manager's ability to recognize and define problems and opportunities correctly and then to select an appropriate course of action to solve problems and capitalize on opportunities. This exercise will help you develop decision-making skills by applying them to a human resource problem. Managers must frequently select one or more employees from a pool of employees for termination, layoffs, special recognition, training, or promotion. Each such selection represents a decision.

Exercise Task*

Your company recently developed a plan to identify and train top hourly employees for promotion to first-line supervisor. As part of this program, your boss has requested a ranking of the six hourly employees who report to you with respect to their promotion potential. Given their biographical data, rank them in the order in which you would select them for promotion to first-line supervisor; that is, the person ranked number one would be first in line for promotion. Repeat this process in a group with three or four of your classmates.

Biographical Data

1. *Sam Nelson:* White male, age forty-five, married, with four children. Sam has been with the company for five years, and his performance evaluations have been average to above average. He is well liked by the other employees in the department. He devotes his spare time to farming and plans to farm after retirement.

2. *Ruth Hornsby:* White female, age thirty-two, married, with no children; husband has a management-level job with a power company. Ruth has been with the company for two years and has received above-average performance evaluations. She is very quiet and keeps to herself at work. She says that she is working to save for a down payment on a new house.

3. *Joe Washington:* Black male, age twenty-six, single. Joe has been with the company for three years and has received high performance evaluations. He is always willing to take on new assignments and to work overtime. He is attending college in the evenings and someday wants to start his own business. He is well liked by the other employees in the department.

4. *Ronald Smith:* White male, age thirty-five, recently divorced, with one child, age four. Ronald has received excellent performance evaluations during his two years with the company. He seems to like his present job but has removed himself from the line of progression. He seems to have personality conflicts with some of the employees in the department.

5. *Betty Norris:* Black female, age forty-four, married, with one grown child. Betty has been with the company for ten years and is well liked by fellow employees. Her performance evaluations have been average to below-average, and her advancement has been limited by a lack of formal education. She has participated in a number of technical training programs conducted by the company.

6. *Roy Davis:* White male, age thirty-six, married, with two teen-age children. Roy has been with the company for ten years and has received excellent performance evaluations until last year. His most recent evaluation was average. He is friendly and well liked by his fellow employees. One of his children has had a serious illness for over a year, resulting in a number of large medical expenses. Roy is working a second job on weekends to help with these expenses. He has expressed a serious interest in promotion to first-line supervisor.

Source: From *Supervisory Management: The Art of Working With and Through People*, 3rd Edition, by Donald C. Mosley, Leon C. Megginson, and Paul H. Pietri, Jr. © 1993. Reprinted with permission of South-Western College Publishing, a division of Thomson Learning. Fax 800-730-2215.

CHAPTER CLOSING CASE

HOW THE MOST ADMIRED COMPANIES MANAGE HUMAN RESOURCES

The most admired companies in America have at least one thing in common: they all pay careful attention to the management of that most precious asset, their employees. General Electric, which appears at the top of many "best-managed" lists, has made training and development one of its top priorities. Through ongoing training, assignment rotation, and performance evaluation, GE gives promising managers the skills and seasoning they need to move up and to handle increased responsibilities. The company has also created a unique mentoring program that pairs tech-savvy younger employees with tech-wary senior managers. As the younger employees teach the senior managers how to navigate the Internet, both benefit from the sharing of ideas and expertise. Given GE's intense focus on human resources, it's not surprising that the company attracts twenty applicants for every job opening.

Another company widely admired for its management of human resources is Southwest Airlines. Consistently profitable in a notoriously competitive industry, Southwest hires a mere 4 percent of the ninety thousand people who apply for jobs every year. The airline uses personality tests to identify applicants with the right mix of can-do attitude, communication skills, decision-making skills, and team spirit. New hires are immersed in intensive training at the company's University for People before they start their jobs. When internal conflicts occasionally erupt between employees who handle different jobs, Southwest has the employees switch jobs for a day so they can see the issue from the other side—a tactic that generally diffuses the tension.

Wal-Mart, a perennial on most-admired lists, calls its human resources management group the People Division as a reflection of the firm's no-nonsense approach. Wal-Mart, like other retailing firms, has been plagued by turnover that can run as high as 70 percent among hourly store workers. As many as four hundred thousand employees leave and must be replaced every year. Factoring in new store openings, Wal-Mart winds up hiring some 550,000 employees annually. Now the company is aiming to slash this turnover rate by being more selective in hiring, training, and communicating more effectively, and offering recognition and pay for performance. The effort is already paying off: turnover is dropping, which means Wal-Mart is well on its way toward saving a huge chunk of its recruiting and training budget. The retailer is also known for promoting from within, which attracts ambitious people who are looking for opportunity and who are willing to be held accountable for their decisions—another Wal-Mart hallmark.

Chip-maker Intel, much admired for its management excellence, is always on the lookout for new employees with potential. Competition for applicants with high-tech skills is so fierce that Intel has set up an internship program to attract college students before they are in the market for full-time jobs. Every year, one thousand college interns rotate through different departments, moving from service operations to procurement and other groups to get hands-on, practical experience in the work world. The interns also get immersed in Intel's culture and form relationships that come in handy if they continue working at Intel after graduation—which 70 percent do. Intel invites interns to par-ticipate in benefits such as the stock purchase plan and counts their internship period toward vacation time once they sign on as full-time employees. These college internships help Intel tap a fresh pool of talented employees every year.

Case Questions

1. What recruiting techniques are being used by the companies in this chapter closing case? Why are these techniques effective?

2. Why would Southwest and other companies go beyond the use of applications and interviews when selecting new employees?

3. How do training and development programs help companies reduce turnover?

Case References

Brent Schlender, "The Odd Couple," *Fortune*, May 1, 2000, pp. 106ff; Talila Baron, "Need IT Talent? Cultivate Your Own," *Information Week*, April 24, 2000, p. 170; Matt Murray, "Can the House That Jack Built Stand When He Goes? Sure, Welch Says," *Wall Street Journal*, April 13, 2000, pp. A1, A10; Carol J. Loomis, "Sam Would Be Proud," *Fortune*, April 17, 2000, pp. 130–144; Katrina Brooker, "Can Anyone Replace Herb?" *Fortune*, April 17, 2000, pp. 186–192; "Raising the Bar," *Fortune*, February 21, 2000, pp. 115–116; Geoffrey Colvin, "America's Most Admired Companies," *Fortune*, February 21, 2000, pp. 108ff. Robert Levering and Milton Moskowitz, "The 100 Best Companies to Work For," *Fortune*, January 8, 2001, pp. 148–168.

CHAPTER NOTES

1. "Dr. Goodnight's Company Town," *Business Week*, June 19, 2000, pp. 192-202; Charles Fishman, "Sanity Inc.," *Fast Company*, January 1999, pp. 84–96 (quote on p. 89); Jerry Useem, "Welcome to the New Company Town," *Fortune*, January 10, 2000, pp. 62–70.
2. For a complete review of human resource management, see Angelo S. DeNisi and Ricky W. Griffin, *Human Resource Management* (Boston: Houghton Mifflin, 2001).
3. Patrick Wright and Gary McMahan, "Strategic Human Resources Management: A Review of the Literature," *Journal of Management*, June 1992, pp. 280–319.
4. Augustine Lado and Mary Wilson, "Human Resource Systems and Sustained Competitive Advantage: A Competency-Based Perspective," *Academy of Management Review*, 1994, Vol. 19, No. 4, pp. 699–727.
5. "The New Workforce," *Business Week*, March 20, 2000, pp. 64–70.
6. John Beeson, "Succession Planning," *Across the Board*, February 2000, pp. 38–41.
7. Robert Gatewood, Mary Gowan, and Gary Lautenschlager, "Corporate Image, Recruitment Image, and Initial Job Choice Decisions," *Academy of Management Journal*, 1993, Vol. 36, No. 2, pp. 414–427.
8. "Firms Cook Up New Ways to Keep Workers," *USA Today*, January 18, 2000, p. 1B.
9. Claudio Fernandez-Araoz, "Hiring Without Firing," *Harvard Business Review*, July–August 1999, pp. 109–118.
10. James A. Breaugh and Mary Starke, "Research on Employee Recruiting: So Many Studies, So Many Remaining Questions," *Journal of Management*, 2000, Vol. 26, No. 3, pp. 405–434.
11. Frank L. Schmidt and John E. Hunter, "Employment Testing: Old Theories and New Research Findings," *American Psychologist*, October 1981, 1128–1137.

12. Robert Liden, Christopher Martin, and Charles Parsons, "Interviewer and Applicant Behaviors in Employment Interviews," *Academy of Management Journal*, 1993, Vol. 36, No. 2, pp. 372–386.

13. Paul R. Sackett, "Assessment Centers and Content Validity: Some Neglected Issues," *Personnel Psychology*, Vol. 40, 1987, pp. 13–25.

14. "'Boeing U': Flying by the Book," *USA Today*, October 6, 1997, pp. 1B, 2B.

15. Barry R. Nathan, Allan Mohrman, and John Milliman, "Interpersonal Relations as a Context for the Effects of Appraisal Interviews on Performance and Satisfaction: A Longitudinal Study," *Academy of Management Journal*, June 1991, pp. 352–369.

16. See Angelo S. DeNisi and Avraham N. Kluger, "Feedback Effectiveness: Can 360-Degree Appraisals Be Improved?" *Academy of Management Executive*, 2000, Vol. 14, No. 1, pp. 129–139.

17. Jaclyn Fierman, "The Perilous New World of Fair Pay," *Fortune*, June 13, 1994, pp. 57–64.

18. Stephanie Armour, "Show Me the Money, More Workers Say," *USA Today*, June 6, 2000, p. 1B.

19. "To Each According to His Needs: Flexible Benefits Plans Gain Favor," *Wall Street Journal*, September 16, 1986, p. 29.

20. "The Future Look of Employee Benefits," *Wall Street Journal*, September 7, 1988, p. 21.

21. See Sherry E. Sullivan, "The Changing Nature of Careers: A Review and Research Agenda," *Journal of Management*, 1999, Vol. 25, No. 3, pp. 457–484.

22. Barbara Presley Nobel, "Reinventing Labor," *Harvard Business Review*, July–August 1993, pp. 115–125.

23. John A. Fossum, "Labor Relations: Research and Practice in Transition," *Journal of Management*, Summer 1987, pp. 281–300.

24. Max Boisot, *Knowledge Assets* (Oxford: Oxford University Press, 1998).

25. Thomas Stewart, "In Search of Elusive Tech Workers," *Fortune*, February 16, 1998, pp. 171–172.

26. "Need for Computer Experts Is Making Recruiters Frantic," *New York Times*, December 18, 1999, p. C1.

27. "When Is a Temp Not a Temp?" *Business Week*, December 7, 1998, pp. 90–92.

PART FIVE

The Leading Process

Basic Elements of Individual Behavior in Organizations

15 Basic Elements of Individual Behavior in Organizations

Levi Strauss & Co. and the ubiquitous denim blue jeans it sells around the world have been virtual icons for as long as baby-boomers can remember. Levi's real growth started in the late 1950s when its denim jeans became a virtual uniform for the youth of the United States. The momentum continued into the 1960s as denim took its place alongside incense, tie-died T-shirts, peace signs, and long hair as symbols of a rebellious youth. And as the baby-boomers of the 1950s and 1960s grew into adulthood, Levi's jeans became a fashion staple. Indeed, even the name Levi's became almost synonymous with blue jeans. During the 1970s through the 1990s, Levi's also expanded rapidly overseas and today sells its products in more than seventy countries.

Over the decades, Levi's also forged an innovative relationship with its employees. High levels of job security, an innovative reward structure, and an open and participative approach to management had created a loyal and dedicated workforce that helped keep the organization at the top of its industry. Indeed, when experts first began ranking "best places to work," Levi Strauss was always near the top of the list. Many employees spent their entire careers at Levi, seeing it almost like family and defending it against any and all critics.

But as the decade of the 1990s grew to a close, Levi Strauss seemed to hit a wall. And as a result, the firm found it necessary to re-examine every aspect of its business operations while simultaneously redefining its relationship with its workforce. The catalyst for change was a relatively sudden drop in market share. For example, in 1990 Levi held about one-third of the jeans market in the United States. But by the end of the decade, that figure had been cut in half. Especially disturbing was the fact that today's young consumers particularly had seemed to lose interest in Levi's products.

As a result of this alarming trend, company executives faced an intense and detailed period of introspection to find out what was happening to the company. Their conclusion was that they had been so successful with their core baby-boomer consumers that they had essentially neglected younger consumers. As a result, top-end designers like Tommy Hilfilger and Ralph Lauren and discounted store brands sold at Sears and J.C. Penney had seized significant market share from Levi. In addition, the firm's cost structure was out of line with other clothing manufacturers who had already moved most of their production to lower-cost facilities in other

> *"You can stretch denim over a wide butt, but you can't stretch it over too many generations. The problem is, your parents wore Levi's, and kids want to wear something different."*
>
> —Al Ries, Atlanta-based marketing consultant*

countries. In contrast, Levi had tried to maintain most of its production inside the United States, even though labor costs in this country are higher than at many other locations.

Once they saw their problem, Levi managers took quick action along several fronts. Most painfully, in 1997 the firm announced that it was closing eleven U.S. factories and laying off one-third of its North American workforce—its first layoff in history. In 1999, another twenty-two plants were shuttered and almost six thousand more workers released. Needless to say, these steps dramatically and unalterably changed the firm's relationship with its workforce. Its previously loyal workers quickly became disenchanted and embittered, for example, and went from being the company's staunchest defenders to its biggest critics.

The company also acknowledged that it needed to alter the composition of its executive team to boost creativity and market knowl-

edge. Too many company officials, executives said, had come up through the ranks and knew only one way of doing things—the old tried-and-true Levi's way. Thus, one goal now is to fill 30 percent of all new management jobs with outsiders. Experts agree that it will take the firm a while to get its act together again, but they also acknowledge that the changes seem to fit the situation as well as a pair of the firm's jeans fit after a long day at the office.[1]

Levi Strauss and Co. and its employees are in the process of redefining their relationship with one another. To do so, they are each having to assess how well their respective needs and capabilities now match the other. And different and unique characteristics of each and every employee affect how they feel about these changes and how they will alter their future attitudes about the firm and how they perform their jobs. These characteristics reflect the basic elements of individual behavior in organizations.

This chapter describes several of these basic elements and is the first of several chapters designed to develop a more complete perspective on the leading function of management. In the next section we investigate the psychological nature of individuals in organizations. The next section introduces the concept of personality and discusses several important personality attributes that can influence behavior in organizations. We then examine individual attitudes and their role in organizations. The role of stress in the workplace is then discussed, followed by a discussion of individual creativity. Finally, we describe several basic individual behaviors that are important to organizations.

Understanding Individuals in Organizations

As a starting point in understanding human behavior in the workplace, we must consider the basic nature of the relationship between individuals and organizations. We must also gain an appreciation of the nature of individual differences.

The Psychological Contract

Most people have a basic understanding of a contract. Whenever we buy a car or sell a house, for example, both buyer and seller sign a contract that specifies the terms of the agreement. A psychological contract is similar in some ways to a standard legal contract but is less formal and well defined. In particular, a **psychological contract** is the overall set of expectations held by an individual with respect to what he or she will contribute to the organization and what the organization will provide in return.[2] Thus, a psychological contract is not written on paper nor are all of its terms explicitly negotiated.

The essential nature of a psychological contract is illustrated in Figure 15.1. The individual makes a variety of **contributions**—effort, skills, ability, time, loyalty, and so forth—to the organization. These contributions presumably satisfy various needs and requirements of the organization; that is, because the organization may have hired the person because of her skills, it is reasonable for the organization to expect that she will subsequently display those skills in the performance of her job.

Figure 15.1

The Psychological Contract
Psychological contracts are the basic assumptions that individuals have about their relationships with their organization. Such contracts are defined in terms of contributions by the individual relative to inducements from the organization.

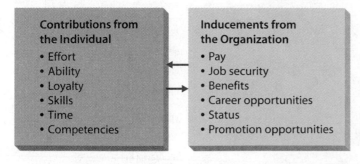

In return for these contributions, the organization provides **inducements** to the individual. Some inducements, like pay and career opportunities, are tangible rewards. Others, like job security and status, are more intangible. Just as the contributions available from the individual must satisfy the needs of the organization, the inducements offered by the organization must serve the needs of the individual; that is, if a person accepts employment with an organization because he thinks he will earn an attractive salary and have an opportunity to advance, he will subsequently expect that those rewards will be forthcoming.

If both the individual and organization perceive that the psychological contract is fair and equitable, they will be satisfied with the relationship and will likely continue it. On the other hand, if either party sees an imbalance or inequity in the contract, that perception may initiate a change. For example, the individual may request a pay raise or promotion, decrease her contributed effort, or look for a better job elsewhere. The organization can also initiate change by requesting that the individual improve his skills through training, transfer the person to another job, or terminate the person's employment altogether.

A basic challenge faced by the organization, then, is to manage psychological contracts. The organization must insure that it is getting value from its employees. At the same time, it must also be sure that it is providing employees with appropriate inducements. If the organization is underpaying its employees for their contributions, for example, they may perform poorly or leave for better jobs elsewhere. On the other hand, if they are being overpaid relative to their contributions, the organization is incurring unnecessary costs.[3]

The Person-Job Fit

One specific aspect of managing psychological contracts is managing the person-job fit. **Person-job fit** is the extent to which the contributions made by the individual match the inducements offered by the organization. In theory, each employee has a specific set of needs that he wants fulfilled and a set of job-related behaviors and abilities to contribute. Thus, if the organization can take perfect advantage of those behaviors and abilities and exactly fulfill his needs, it will have achieved a perfect person-job fit. *Management InfoTech* explains how some organizations are using technology in an effort to improve person-job fit.

Of course, such a precise level of person-job fit is seldom achieved, for several reasons. For one thing, organizational selection procedures are imperfect. Organizations can make approximations of employee skill levels when making hiring decisions and can improve them through training. But even simple performance dimensions are hard to measure objectively and validly. The cartoon provides a humorous example of poor person-job fit.

psychological contract The overall set of expectations held by an individual with respect to what he or she will contribute to the organization and what the organization will provide to the individual

contributions What the individual provides to the organization

inducements What the organization provides to the individual

The person-job fit is an important relationship in any organizational setting. For example, many people would balk at the idea of cleaning the outside windows on the top of a skyscraper, of cutting logs in harsh weather, or, as shown here, trying to train a white tiger. But for Gregg Lee, the animal trainer at Marine World Africa USA in California, it's just all in a day's work!

MANAGEMENT INFOTECH

USING TECHNOLOGY TO GET THE RIGHT PERSON-JOB FIT

In today's high-speed, highly competitive business environment, knowledge is power. Opportunities and challenges can pop up without warning, so companies need people with the right mix of expertise and skills for each situation. The ability to tap employee knowledge effectively is particularly important when companies organize work activities as a series of cross-functional or problem-solving projects rather than as ongoing functional tasks. In this dynamic work environment, how can companies be sure that the right people are working on the right tasks?

For a growing number of firms, the answer is to use technology to identify and catalogue the talents and capabilities of each employee systematically. For example, KPMG, a multinational accounting and consulting firm, uses software from Tacit Knowledge Systems to examine employees' e-mail messages. Based on the content of these messages, the system builds a profile of each employee's areas of expertise. After the employee reviews and edits the personal profile, it is stored in a database. Then, when a KPMG employee needs help with a specific problem or project, he or she queries the system. The software searches the database to identify the expert with the right set of skills and, with the expert's permission, makes the connection with the employee who needs help. This system is only part of the $100 million worth of tech projects KPMG has mounted to capture and share its employees' knowledge.

At Monitor Group, a Boston-based consulting firm, a chief knowledge officer (CKO) is responsible for sharing information about employees' expertise and removing organizational barriers that can slow access to knowledge and experts. Monitor uses the Internet, among other technology tools, to match the right person to the right job—again and again. Jobs, titles, and tasks are constantly in flux as the firm groups and regroups people into teams to tackle a wide variety of projects for clients. And once a project is over, that team's experts are ready to put their knowledge to work on new assignments.

> *Like nomads, we pitch tents and fight battles, then fold up the tents and move on.*
>
> —*Alan Kantrow, chief knowledge officer, Monitor Group**

Reference: Neil Gross, "Mining a Company's Mother Lode of Talent," *Business Week,* August 28, 2000, pp. 135, 137 (*quote on p.137).

---

person-job fit The extent to which the contributions made by the individual match the inducements offered by the organization

Another reason for an imprecise person-job fit is that both people and organizations change. An individual who finds a new job stimulating and exciting may find the same job boring and monotonous after a few years of performing it. And when the organization adopts new technology, it has changed the skills it needs from its employees. Still another reason for imprecision in the person-job fit is that each individual is unique. Measuring skills and performance is difficult enough. Assessing needs, attitudes, and personality is far more complex. Each of these individual differences serves to make matching individuals with jobs a difficult and complex process.

The Nature of Individual Differences

individual differences Personal attributes that vary from one person to another

Individual differences are personal attributes that vary from one person to another. Individual differences may be physical, psychological, and emotional. Taken together, all of the individual differences that characterize any specific person serve to make that individual unique from everyone else. Much of the remainder of this chapter is devoted to individual differences. Before proceeding, however, we must also note the importance of the situation in assessing the behavior of individuals.

Are specific differences that characterize a given individual good or bad? Do they contribute to or detract from performance? The answer, of course, depends on the circumstances. One person may be very dissatisfied, withdrawn, and negative in one job setting but very satisfied, outgoing, and positive in another. Working conditions, coworkers, and leadership are all important ingredients.

Thus, whenever an organization attempts to assess or account for individual differences among its employees, it must also be sure to consider the situation in which behavior occurs. Individuals who are satisfied or productive workers in one context may prove to be dissatisfied or unproductive workers in another. Attempting to consider both individual differences and contributions in relation to inducements and contexts, then, is a major challenge for organizations as they attempt to establish effective psychological contracts with their employees and achieve an optimal fit between people and jobs.

"I'M PUTTING YOU ON THE CHINA SHOP ACCOUNT. DO YOU THINK YOU CAN HANDLE IT?"

P. C. Vey

Person-job fit is a very important construct in organizations. A good person-job fit benefits both the employee and the organization. But a poor person-job fit can result in a dissatisfied and low-performing employee. In the example portrayed here, for example, the manager is literally picking a "bull" to work in a "china shop." And the result is likely to be chaos!

MANAGEMENT IMPLICATIONS Managers should understand the psychological contracts they establish with their employees and take care to be fair and equitable. They also need to realize that people may not be precisely matched with their jobs but still attempt to do as good a job as possible in optimizing this relationship. Finally, managers should also recognize and appreciate the fact that every individual is unique.

Personality and Individual Behavior

Personality traits represent some of the most fundamental sets of individual differences in organizations. **Personality** is the relatively stable set of psychological and behavioral attributes that distinguish one person from another.[4] Managers should strive to understand basic personality attributes and the ways they can affect people's behavior in organizational situations, not to mention their perceptions of and attitudes toward the organization.

personality The relatively stable set of psychological and behavioral attributes that distinguish one person from another

The "Big Five" Personality Traits

Psychologists have identified literally thousands of personality traits and dimensions that differentiate one person from another. But in recent years, researchers have identified five fundamental personality traits that are especially relevant to organizations. Because these five traits are so important and because they are currently the subject of so much attention, they are commonly referred to now as the **"big five" personality traits**.[5] Figure 15.2 illustrates the "big five" traits.

Agreeableness refers to a person's ability to get along with others. Agreeableness causes some people to be gentle, cooperative, forgiving, understanding, and good-natured in their dealings with others. But it results in others being irritable, short-tempered, uncooperative, and generally antagonistic toward other people. While research has not yet fully investigated the effects of agreeableness, it would seem likely that highly agreeable people will be better able to develop good working relationships with coworkers, subordinates, and higher-level managers, whereas less agreeable people will not have particularly good working relationships. This same pattern might also extend to relationships with customers, suppliers, and other key organizational constituents.

Conscientiousness refers to the number of goals on which a person focuses. People who focus on relatively few goals at one time are likely to be organized, systematic, careful, thorough, responsible, and self-disciplined as they work to pursue those goals. Others, however, tend to take on a wider array of goals and, as a result, to be more disorganized, careless, and irresponsible, as well as less thorough and self-disciplined. Research has found that more conscientious people tend to be higher performers than less conscientious people across a variety of different jobs. This pattern seems logical, of course, because more conscientious people will take their jobs seriously and will approach the performance of their jobs in a highly responsible fashion.

"big five" personality traits A popular personality framework based on five key traits that are especially relevant to organizations

agreeableness A person's ability to get along with others

conscientiousness The number of goals on which a person focuses

Figure 15.2

The "Big Five" Model of Personality

The "big five" personality model represents an increasingly accepted framework for understanding personality traits in organizational settings. In general, experts tend to agree that personality traits toward the left end of each dimension, as illustrated in this figure, are more positive in organizational settings, whereas traits closer to the right are less positive.

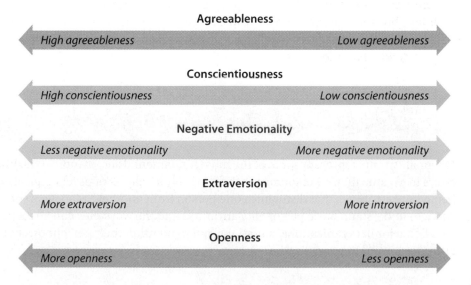

Agreeableness
High agreeableness — Low agreeableness

Conscientiousness
High conscientiousness — Low conscientiousness

Negative Emotionality
Less negative emotionality — More negative emotionality

Extraversion
More extraversion — More introversion

Openness
More openness — Less openness

The third of the "big five" personality dimensions is **negative emotionality**. People with less negative emotionality will be relatively poised, calm, resilient, and secure. But people with more negative emotionality will be more excitable, insecure, reactive, and subject to extreme mood swings. People with less negative emotionality might be expected to handle job stress, pressure, and tension better. Their stability might also lead them to be seen as more reliable than their less stable counterparts.

negative emotionality The extent to which a person is poised, calm, resilient, and secure

Extraversion refers to a person's comfort level with relationships. People who are called extraverts are sociable, talkative, assertive, and open to establishing new relationships. But introverts are much less sociable, talkative, and assertive, and not as open to establishing new relationships. Research suggests that extraverts tend to be higher overall job performers than introverts, and that they are also more likely to be attracted to jobs based on personal relationships like sales and marketing positions.

extraversion A person's comfort level with relationships

Finally, **openness** refers to a person's rigidity of beliefs and range of interests. People with high levels of openness are willing to listen to new ideas and to change their own ideas, beliefs, and attitudes as a result of new information. They also tend to have broad interests and to be curious, imaginative, and creative. On the other hand, people with low levels of openness tend to be less receptive to new ideas and less willing to change their minds. They also tend to have fewer and narrower interests and to be less curious and creative. People with more openness might be expected to be better performers, owing to their flexibility and the likelihood that they will be better accepted by others in the organization. Openness may also encompass an individual's willingness to accept change. For example, people with high levels of openness may be more receptive to change, whereas people with low levels of openness may be more likely to resist change.

openness A person's rigidity of beliefs and range of interests

The "big five" framework continues to attract the attention of both researchers and managers. The potential value of this framework is that it encompasses an integrated set of traits that appear to be valid predictors of certain behaviors in certain situations. Thus, managers who can develop both an understanding of the framework and the ability to assess these traits in their employees will be in a good position to understand how and why they behave as they do.[6] On the other hand, managers must also be careful not to overestimate their ability to assess the "big five" traits in others. Even assessment using the most rigorous and valid measures, for instance, is still likely to be somewhat imprecise. Another limitation of the "big five" framework is that it is based primarily on research conducted in the United States. Thus, there are unanswered questions about its generalizability to other cultures. And even within the United States, a variety of other factors and traits are also likely to affect behavior in organizations.

Other Personality Traits at Work

Besides the "big five," there are also several other personality traits that influence behavior in organizations. Among the most important are locus of control, self-efficacy, authoritarianism, Machiavellianism, self-esteem, and risk propensity. *Managing in an e-Business World* discusses the role that some of these traits played in the formation of Internet Capital Group.

MANAGING IN AN *e*-BUSINESS WORLD

FOUNDERS FUEL E-COMMERCE WITH PERSONALITY

Entrepreneurs Walter W. Buckley III and Kenneth A. Fox share a passion for e-commerce—among other traits. The two worked together scouting deals for a technology investment firm before teaming up in 1996 to found Internet Capital Group (ICG), a company that invests in e-commerce companies. Although other investment firms hold stakes in on-line businesses, ICG's founders were among the first to confine their investments solely to e-commerce start-ups, such as Computerjobs.com, Deja.com, and VerticalNet.

Both Buckley and Fox have a strong entrepreneurial drive that comes from an internal locus of control. Buckley once operated a cleaning service; as the boss, he routinely washed windows and handled whatever tasks needed to be done. When Fox was in high school, he pooled his money with a buddy to buy a snowblower and start a business clearing snow from residential driveways.

In addition, both have high self-efficacy in their roles at ICG. As CEO, Buckley manages overall activities while Fox is managing director of West Coast operations. Given the company's $300 million investment in more than three dozen fast-growing start-ups, the co-founders also have the high risk propensity they need to do business in the volatile e-commerce world. Just as important, they are highly agreeable individuals who know

how to establish and strengthen connections with all kinds of people. This trait is especially critical for recruiting talented employees, forging partnerships, and negotiating investments.

At the same time, the entrepreneurs have clearly capitalized on their differences. Buckley, who is ten years older, is expert at nurturing relationships and building synergy among the various firms in which ICG has invested. One example: Deja.com has set up a special career discussion area on its site with a link to Computerjobs.com. Extroverted and conscientious Fox, on the other hand, is a determined deal-maker who pursues potential investments with great tenacity. Between the two, ICG is well positioned to take advantage of e-commerce opportunities now and in the future.

> *Ken is more outwardly aggressive. But inwardly, Walter is just as bad.*
>
> —*Warren V. Musser, CEO of Safeguard Scientifics**

Reference: Amy Barrett, "Internet Capital's Young Turks," *Business Week,* November 1, 1999, pp. EB64–EB70 (*quote on p. EB70).

---

locus of control The extent to which people believe that their behavior has a real effect on what happens to them

Locus of control is the extent to which people believe that their behavior has a real effect on what happens to them.[7] Some people believe, for example, that if they work hard they will succeed. They may also believe that people who fail do so because they lack ability or motivation. People who believe that individuals are in control of their lives are said to have an *internal locus of control*. Other people think that fate, chance, luck, or other people's behavior determines what happens to them. For example, an employee who fails to get a promotion may attribute that failure to a politically motivated boss or just bad luck rather than to her or his own lack of skills or poor performance record. People who think that forces beyond their control dictate what happens to them are said to have an *external locus of control*.

self-efficacy A person's beliefs about her or his capabilities to perform a task

Self-efficacy is a related but subtly different personality characteristic. **Self-efficacy** is a person's beliefs about his or her capabilities to perform a task.[8] People with high self-efficacy believe that they can perform well on a specific task, while people with low self-efficacy tend to doubt their ability to perform a specific task. While self-assessments of ability contribute to self-efficacy, so too does the individual's personality. Some people simply have more self-confidence than others do. This belief in their ability to perform a task effectively results in them being more self-assured and more able to focus their attention on performance.

Another important personality characteristic is **authoritarianism**, the extent to which an individual believes that power and status differences are appropriate within hierarchical social systems like organizations.[9] For example, a person who is highly authoritarian may accept directives or orders from someone with more authority purely because the other person is "the boss." On the other hand, while a person who is not highly authoritarian may still carry out appropriate and reasonable directives from the boss, he or she is also more likely to question things, express disagreement with the boss, and even to refuse to carry out orders if they are objectionable for some reason. A highly authoritarian manager may be autocratic and demanding, and highly authoritarian subordinates will be more likely to accept this behavior from their leader. On the other hand, a less authoritarian manager may allow subordinates a bigger role in making decisions, and less authoritarian subordinates will respond positively to this behavior.

Machiavellianism is another important personality trait. This concept is named after Niccolo Machiavelli, a sixteenth-century author. In his book entitled *The Prince*, Machiavelli explained how the nobility could more easily gain and use power. **Machiavellianism** is now used to describe behavior directed at gaining power and controlling the behavior of others. Research suggests that Machiavellianism is a personality trait that varies from person to person. More Machiavellian individuals tend to be rational and nonemotional, may be willing to lie to attain their personal goals, put little weight on loyalty and friendship, and enjoy manipulating others' behavior. Less Machiavellian individuals are more emotional, less willing to lie to succeed, value loyalty and friendship highly, and get little personal pleasure from manipulating others.

Self-esteem is the extent to which a person believes that he or she is a worthwhile and deserving individual.[10] A person with high self-esteem is more likely to seek higher status jobs, be more confident in his ability to achieve higher levels of performance, and derive greater intrinsic satisfaction from his accomplishments. In contrast, a person with less self-esteem may be more content to remain in a lower-level job, be less confident of her ability, and focus more on extrinsic rewards. Among the major personality dimensions, self-esteem is the one that has been most widely studied in other countries. While more research is clearly needed, the published evidence suggests that self-esteem as a personality trait does indeed exist in a variety of countries and that its role in organizations is reasonably important across different cultures.[11]

Risk propensity is the degree to which an individual is willing to take chances and make risky decisions. A manager with a high risk propensity, for example, might be expected to experiment with new ideas and gamble on new products. She might also lead the organization in new and different directions. This manager might also be a catalyst for innovation. On the other hand, the same individual might also jeopardize the continued well-being of the organization if the risky decisions prove to be bad ones. A manager with low risk propensity might lead to a

Locus of control is the degree to which an individual believes that behavior has a direct impact on the consequences of that behavior. Most professional athletes, for instance, are very self-confident and assume that they can defeat their opponent. Venus Williams, for instance, shown here winning the Wimbledon title, expects to win every time she steps on the tennis court. Thus, she clearly has an internal locus of control.

authoritarianism The extent to which an individual believes that power and status differences are appropriate within hierarchical social systems like organizations

Machiavellianism Behavior directed at gaining power and controlling the behavior of others

self-esteem The extent to which a person believes that he or she is a worthwhile and deserving individual

risk propensity The degree to which an individual is willing to take chances and make risky decisions

stagnant and overly conservative organization, or help the organization successfully weather turbulent and unpredictable times by maintaining stability and calm. Thus, the potential consequences of risk propensity to an organization are heavily dependent on that organization's environment.

MANAGEMENT IMPLICATIONS   Managers need to realize that people vary along a wide array of personality traits. The "big five" and other traits provide useful frameworks for understanding how and why people differ. At the same time, managers should also realize that myriad other traits exist and that assessing and understanding precisely how a given trait affects behavior is difficult, at best.

■ Attitudes and Individual Behavior

attitudes Complexes of beliefs and feelings that people have about specific ideas, situations, or other people

Another important element of individual behavior in organizations is attitudes. **Attitudes** as complexes of beliefs and feelings that people have about specific ideas, situations, or other people. Attitudes are important because they are the mechanism through which most people express their feelings. An employee's statement that he feels underpaid by the organization reflects his feelings about his pay. Similarly, when a manager says that she likes the new advertising campaign, she is expressing her feelings about the organization's marketing efforts. *Working with Diversity* focuses on the role of diverse attitudes in companies.

Attitudes have three components. The *affective component* of an attitude reflects feelings and emotions an individual has toward a situation. The *cognitive component* of an attitude is derived from knowledge an individual has about a situation. It is important to note that cognition is subject to individual perceptions (something we discuss more fully later). Thus, one person might "know" that a certain political candidate is better than another, while someone else may "know" just the opposite. Finally, the *intentional component* of an attitude reflects how an individual expects to behave toward or in the situation.

To illustrate these three components, consider the case of a manager who places an order for some supplies for his organization from a new office supply firm. Suppose many of the items he orders are out of stock, others are overpriced, and still others arrive damaged. When he calls someone at the supply firm for assistance, he is treated rudely and gets disconnected before his claim is resolved. When asked how he feels about the new office supply firm, he might respond, "I don't like that company (affective component). They are the worst office supply firm I've ever dealt with (cognitive component). I'll never do business with them again (intentional component)."

cognitive dissonance The conflict individuals experience among their own attitudes

People try to maintain consistency among the three components of their attitudes as well as among all their attitudes. However, circumstances sometimes arise that lead to conflicts. The conflict individuals experience among their own attitudes is called **cognitive dissonance**.[12] Say, for example, that an individual who has vowed never to work for a big, impersonal corporation intends instead to open her own business and be her own boss. Unfortunately, a series of financial setbacks leaves

WORKING WITH DIVERSITY

WANTED—EMPLOYEES WITH ECLECTIC BACKGROUNDS

Just as the gray flannel suit is no longer the stereotypical corporate uniform, the "just follow orders" attitude is no longer valued by organizations. With every part of the environment subject to change, companies are looking for employees with an appetite for new opportunities and challenges—people who aren't afraid to take risks and possibly fail. At iXL Enterprises, for example, CEO Bill Nussey likes hiring people with an entrepreneurial background. He even hopes new employees will experience a washout early in their tenure so they don't let fear of failure stand in the way of trying new ideas.

Companies are also searching for employees with the speed and flexibility needed to be effective in today's fast-paced, dynamic work environment. What worked yesterday may not work today or tomorrow, so managers are hungry for employees who also view rapid, constant change in a positive light.

Willingness to get involved is another attitude valued by corporate leaders. Daniel A. Carp, Kodak's CEO, encourages employees at all levels to e-mail him with suggestions or updates. Of course, the flip side of this practice is that managers on the receiving end of these e-mails must have a positive attitude toward comments and feedback from peers and subordinates.

Given the increasing diversity of the workforce in many countries, companies such as Omnicom Group, an advertising conglomerate, want to hire employees with positive attitudes toward cultural differences. They also want employees who can look below the surface to gain a better understanding of coworkers, managers, and subordinates. Finally, leaders such as John J. Dooner, Jr., president of the New York–based advertising giant Interpublic Group, want employees with a sense of humor—a prized quality that can help employees in any organization cope with the unexpected.

> *The glorification of the individual is over.*
>
> —*Bruce A. Pasternick, managing partner for Booz Allen & Hamilton's Organization and Strategic Leadership Center**

Reference: Diane Brady, "Wanted: Eclectic Visionary with a Sense of Humor," *Business Week,* August 28, 2000, pp. 143–144 (*quote on p. 144).

---

her with no choice but to take a job with a large company and work for someone else. Thus, cognitive dissonance occurs: the affective and cognitive components of the individual's attitude conflict with intended behavior. To reduce cognitive dissonance, which is usually an uncomfortable experience for most people, the individual described above might tell herself the situation is only temporary and that she can go back on her own in the near future. Or she might revise her cognitions and decide that working for a large company is more pleasant than she had ever expected.

Work-Related Attitudes

People in organizations form attitudes about many different things. For example, employees are likely to have attitudes about their salary, promotion possibilities, boss, employee benefits, the food in the company cafeteria, and the color of the company softball team uniforms. Of course, some of these attitudes are more important than others. Especially important attitudes are job satisfaction or dissatisfaction and organizational commitment.[13]

job satisfaction or **dissatisfaction** An attitude that reflects the extent to which an individual is gratified by or fulfilled in his or her work

Job Satisfaction or Dissatisfaction.   **Job satisfaction** or **dissatisfaction** is an attitude that reflects the extent to which an individual is gratified by or fulfilled in his or her work. Extensive research conducted on job satisfaction has indicated that personal factors such as an individual's needs and aspirations determine this attitude, along with group and organizational factors such as relationships with coworkers and supervisors and working conditions, work policies, and compensation.[14]

A satisfied employee also tends to be absent less often, to make positive contributions, and to stay with the organization.[15] In contrast, a dissatisfied employee may be absent more often, may experience stress that disrupts coworkers, and may be continually looking for another job. Contrary to what a lot of managers believe, however, high levels of job satisfaction do not necessarily lead to higher levels of performance. One survey has also indicated that contrary to popular opinion, Japanese workers are less satisfied with their jobs than their counterparts in the United States.[16]

organizational commitment An attitude that reflects an individual's identification with and attachment to the organization itself

Organizational Commitment   **Organizational commitment** is an attitude that reflects an individual's identification with and attachment to the organization itself. A person with a high level of commitment is likely to see herself as a true member of the organization (for example, referring to the organization in personal terms like, "We make high-quality products"), to overlook minor sources of dissatisfaction with the organization, and to see herself remaining a member of the organization. In contrast, a person with less organizational commitment is more likely to see himself as an outsider (for example, referring to the organization in less personal terms like, "They don't pay their employees very well"), to express more dissatisfaction about conditions, and not to see himself as a long-term member of the organization. Research suggests that Japanese workers may be more committed to their organizations than are U.S. workers.[17]

Research suggests that commitment strengthens with an individual's age, years with the organization, sense of job security, and participation in decision making.[18] Employees who feel committed to an organization have highly reliable habits, plan a long tenure with the organization, and muster more effort in performance. While there are few definitive guidelines that organizations can follow to promote commitment, there are a few specific guidelines available. For one thing, if the organization treats its employees fairly and provides reasonable rewards and job security, those employees will more likely be satisfied and committed. Allowing employees to have a say in how things are done can also promote all three attitudes.

Affect and Mood in Organizations

Researchers have recently started to focus renewed interest on the affective component of attitudes. Recall from our discussion above that the affect component of an attitude reflects feelings and emotions. While managers once believed that emotions and feelings varied among people from day to day, research now suggests that while some short-term fluctuation does indeed occur, there are also underlying stable predispositions toward fairly constant and predictable moods and emotional states.[19]

Some people, for example, tend to have a higher degree of **positive affectivity**. They are relatively upbeat and optimistic, they have an overall sense of well-being, and they usually see things in a positive light. Thus, they always seem to be in a good mood. Other people, those with more **negative affectivity**, are just the opposite. They are generally downbeat and pessimistic and they usually see things in a negative way. They seem to be in a bad mood most of the time.

Of course, as noted above, there can be short-term variations among even the most extreme types. People with a lot of positive affectivity, for example, may be in a bad mood if they have just received some bad news—being passed over for a promotion, getting extremely negative performance feedback, or being laid off or fired, for instance. Similarly, those with negative affectivity may be in a good mood—at least for a short time—if they have just been promoted, received very positive performance feedback, or had other good things befall them. After the initial impact of these events wears off, however, those with positive affectivity will generally return to their normal positive mood, whereas those with negative affectivity will gravitate back to their normal bad mood.

MANAGEMENT IMPLICATIONS All managers should appreciate the importance of attitudes in organizations. They should be especially concerned with such job-related attitudes as job satisfaction and dissastisfaction and organizational commitment. It is also helpful to understand the causes and consequences of these attitudes.

> **positive affectivity** A tendency to be relatively upbeat and optimistic, have an overall sense of well-being, see things in a positive light, and seem to be in a good mood
>
> **negative affectivity** A tendency to be generally downbeat and pessimistic, see things in a negative way, and seem to be in a bad mood

Perception and Individual Behavior

As noted earlier, an important element of an attitude is the individual's perception of the object about which the attitude is formed. Since perception plays a role in a variety of other workplace behaviors, managers need to have a general understanding of basic perceptual processes.[20] The role of attributions is also important.

Basic Perceptual Processes

Perception is the set of processes by which an individual becomes aware of and interprets information about the environment. As shown in Figure 15.3, basic perceptual processes that are particularly relevant to organizations are selective perception and stereotyping.

> **perception** The set of processes by which an individual becomes aware of and interprets information about the environment

Selective Perception **Selective perception** is the process of screening out information that we are uncomfortable with or that contradicts our beliefs. For example, suppose a manager is exceptionally fond of a particular worker. The manager has a very positive attitude about the worker and thinks he is a top performer. One day the manager notices that the worker seems to be goofing off. Selective perception may cause the manager to forget quickly what he observed. Similarly, suppose

> **selective perception** The process of screening out information that we are uncomfortable with or that contradicts our beliefs

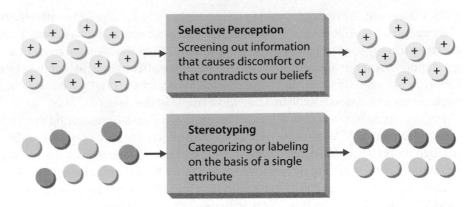

Figure 15.3

Perceptual Processes

Two of the most basic perceptual processes are selective perception and stereotyping. As shown here, selective perception occurs when we screen out information (represented by the – symbols) that causes us discomfort or that contradicts our beliefs. Stereotyping occurs when we categorize or label people on the basis of a single attribute, illustrated here by color.

a manager has formed a very negative image of a particular worker. She thinks this worker is a poor performer and never does a good job. When she happens to observe an example of high performance from the worker, she, too, may not remember it for very long. In one sense, selective perception is beneficial because it allows us to disregard minor bits of information. Of course, this holds true only if our basic perception is accurate. If selective perception causes us to ignore important information, however, it can become quite detrimental.

stereotyping The process of categorizing or labeling people on the basis of a single attribute

Stereotyping **Stereotyping** is the process of categorizing or labeling people on the basis of a single attribute. Common attributes from which people often stereotype are race and gender. Of course, stereotypes along these lines are inaccurate and can be harmful. For example, suppose a manager forms the stereotype that women can perform only certain tasks and that men are best suited for other tasks. To the extent that this affects the manager's hiring practices, the manager is (1) costing the organization valuable talent for both sets of jobs, (2) violating federal law, and (3) behaving unethically. On the other hand, certain forms of stereotyping can be useful and efficient. Suppose, for example, that a manager believes that communication skills are important for a particular job and that speech communication majors tend to have exceptionally good communication skills. As a result, whenever he interviews candidates for jobs, he pays especially close attention to speech communication majors. To the extent that communication skills truly predict job performance and that majoring in speech communication does indeed provide those skills, this form of stereotyping can be beneficial.

Perception and Attribution

attribution A mechanism through which we observe behavior and then attribute causes to it

Perception is also closely linked with another process called attribution. **Attribution** is a mechanism through which we observe behavior and then attribute causes to it.[21] The behavior that is observed may be our own or that of others. For example, suppose someone realizes one day that she is working fewer hours than before, that she talks less about her work, and that she calls in sick more frequently. She might conclude from this realization that she must have become disenchanted with her job and subsequently decide to quit. Thus, she observed her own behavior, attributed a cause to it, and developed what she thought was a consistent response.

More common is attributing cause to the behavior of others. For example, if the manager of the individual described above has observed the same behavior, he might form exactly the same attribution. On the other hand, he might instead decide that she has a serious illness, that he is driving her too hard, that she is experiencing too much stress, that she has a drug problem, or that she is having family problems.

The basic framework around which we form attributions is *consensus* (the extent to which other people in the same situation behave the same way), *consistency* (the extent to which the same person behaves in the same way at different times), and *distinctiveness* (the extent to which the same person behaves in the same way in other situations). For example, suppose a manager observes that an employee is late for a meeting. The manager might further realize that he is the only one who is late (low consensus), recall that he is often late for other meetings (high consistency), and subsequently realize that the same employee is sometimes late for work and returning from lunch (low distinctiveness). This pattern of attributions might cause the manager to decide that the individual's behavior is something that should be changed. As a result, the manager might meet with the subordinate and establish some punitive consequences for future tardiness.

MANAGEMENT IMPLICATIONS Managers need to recognize the role of perception in organizational behavior. Specifically, they should know how selective perception and stereotyping affects not only the behavior of others, but their own behavior as well. Understanding the attribution process is also helpful.

■ Stress and Individual Behavior

Another important element of behavior in organizations is stress. **Stress** is an individual's response to a strong stimulus.[22] This stimulus is called a *stressor*. Stress generally follows a cycle referred to as the **general adaptation syndrome**, or GAS,[23] shown in Figure 15.4. According to this view, when an individual first encounters a stressor, the GAS is initiated and the first stage, alarm, is activated. He may feel panic, wonder how to cope, and feel helpless. For example, suppose a manager is told to prepare a detailed evaluation of a plan by his firm to buy one of its competitors. His first reaction may be, "How will I ever get this done by tomorrow?"

If the stressor is too intense, the individual may feel unable to cope and never really try to respond to its demands. In most cases, however, after a short period of alarm, the individual gathers some strength and starts to resist the negative effects of the stressor. For example, the manager with the evaluation to write may calm down, call home to say that he's working late, role up his sleeves, order coffee, and get to work. Thus, at stage 2 of the GAS, the person is resisting the effects of the stressor.

In many cases, the resistance phase may end the GAS. If the manager can complete the evaluation earlier than expected, he may drop it in his briefcase, smile to himself, and head home tired but satisfied. On the other hand, prolonged

stress An individual's response to a strong stimulus, which is called a **stressor**

general adaptation syndrome General cycle of the stress process

Figure 15.4

The General Adaptation Syndrome
The general adaptation syndrome represents the normal process by which we react to stressful events. At stage 1—alarm—we feel panic and alarm and our level of resistance to stress drops. Stage 2—resistance—represents our efforts to confront and control the stressful circumstance. If we fail, we may eventually reach stage 3—exhaustion—and just give up or quit.

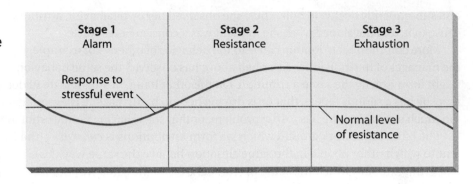

exposure to a stressor without resolution may bring on stage 3 of the GAS—exhaustion. At this stage, the individual literally gives up and can no longer resist the stressor. The manager, for example, might fall asleep at his desk at 3 A.M. and never finish the evaluation.

We should note that stress is not all bad. In the absence of stress, we may experience lethargy and stagnation. An optimal level of stress, on the other hand, can result in motivation and excitement. Too much stress, however, can have negative consequences. It is also important to understand that stress can be caused by "good" as well as "bad" events. Excessive pressure, unreasonable demands on our time, and bad news can all cause stress. But receiving a bonus and then having to decide what to do with the money can be stressful. So, too, can receiving a promotion, gaining recognition, and similar "good" occurrences.

One important line of thinking about stress focuses on Type A and Type B personalities.[24] **Type A** individuals are extremely competitive, are very devoted to work, and have a strong sense of time urgency. They are likely to be aggressive, impatient, and very work-oriented. They have a lot of drive and want to accomplish as much as possible as quickly as possible. **Type B** individuals are less competitive, are less devoted to work, and have a weaker sense of time urgency. Such individuals are less likely to experience conflict with other people and more likely to have a balanced, relaxed approach to life. They can work at a constant pace without time urgency. Type B people are not necessarily more or less successful than Type A people, but they are less likely to experience stress.

type A Individuals who are extremely competitive, are very devoted to work, and have a strong sense of time urgency

type B Individuals who are less competitive, are less devoted to work, and have a weaker sense of time urgency

Causes and Consequences of Stress

Stress is obviously not a simple phenomenon. As depicted in Figure 15.5, several different events can cause stress. Note that this list includes only work-related conditions. We should keep in mind that stress can also be the result of personal circumstances as well.[25]

Causes of Stress   Work-related stressors fall into one of four categories—task, physical, role, and interpersonal demands. *Task demands* are associated with the task itself. Some occupations are inherently more stressful than others. Having to

Figure 15.5

Causes of Work Stress

There are several causes of work stress in organizations. Four general sets of organizational stressors are task demands, physical demands, role demands, and interpersonal demands.

make fast decisions, decisions with less than complete information, or decisions that have relatively serious consequences are some of the situations that can make some jobs stressful. The jobs of surgeon, airline pilot, and stockbroker are relatively more stressful than the jobs of dentist, airplane baggage loader, and office receptionist. While a dentist makes important decisions, he is also likely to have time to make a considered diagnosis and fully explore several different treatments. But during surgery, the surgeon must make decisions quickly, all the while realizing that the wrong one may endanger her patient's life.

Physical demands are stressors associated with the job setting. Working outdoors in extremely hot or cold temperatures, or even in an improperly heated or cooled office, can lead to stress. A poorly designed office that makes it difficult for people to have privacy or promotes too little social interaction can result in stress, as can poor lighting and inadequate work surfaces. Even more severe are actual threats to health. Examples include jobs like coal mining, poultry processing, and toxic waste handling.

Role demands can also cause stress. (Roles are discussed more fully in Chapter 18.) A role is a set of expected behaviors associated with a position in a group or organization. Stress can result from either role ambiguity or role conflict that people can experience in groups. For example, an employee who is feeling pressure from her boss to work longer hours or to travel more while also being asked by her family for more time at home will almost certainly experience stress.[26] Similarly, a new employee experiencing role ambiguity because of poor orientation and training practices by the organization will suffer from stress.

Interpersonal demands are stressors associated with relationships that confront people in organizations. For example, group pressures regarding restriction of output and norm conformity can lead to stress. Leadership style may also cause stress. An employee who feels a strong need to participate in decision making may feel stress if his boss refuses to allow participation. And individuals with conflicting personalities may experience stress if they are required to work too closely together. A person with an internal locus of control might be frustrated when working with someone who prefers to wait and see what happens.

Consequences of Stress   As noted earlier, the results of stress may be positive or negative. The negative consequences may be behavioral, psychological, or medical. Behaviorally, for example, stress may lead to detrimental or harmful actions, such as smoking, alcoholism, overeating, and drug abuse. Other stress-induced behaviors are accidents, violence toward oneself or others, and appetite disorders.

Psychological consequences of stress interfere with an individual's mental health and well-being. These outcomes include sleep disturbances, depression, family problems, and sexual dysfunction. Managers are especially prone to sleep disturbances when they experience stress at work.[27] Medical consequences of stress affect an individual's physiological well-being. Heart disease and stroke have been linked to stress, as have headaches, backaches, ulcers and related disorders, and skin conditions such as acne and hives.

Individual stress also has direct consequences for businesses. For an operating employee, stress may translate into poor quality work and lower productivity. For a manager, it may mean faulty decision making and disruptions in working relationships. Withdrawal behaviors can also result from stress. People who are having difficulties with stress in their jobs are more likely to call in sick or to leave the organization. More subtle forms of withdrawal may also occur. A manager may start missing deadlines, for example, or taking longer lunch breaks. Employees may also withdraw by developing feelings of indifference. The irritation displayed by people under great stress can make them difficult to get along with. Job satisfaction, morale, and commitment can all suffer as a result of excessive levels of stress. So, too, can motivation to perform.

Another consequence of stress is **burnout**—a feeling of exhaustion that may develop when someone experiences too much stress for an extended period of time. Burnout results in constant fatigue, frustration, and helplessness. Increased rigidity follows, as does a loss of self-confidence and psychological withdrawal. The individual dreads going to work, often puts in longer hours but accomplishes less than before, and exhibits mental and physical exhaustion. Because of the damaging effects of burnout, some firms are taking steps to help avoid it. For example, British Airways provides all of its employees with training designed to help them recognize the symptoms of burnout and develop strategies for avoiding it.

burnout A feeling of exhaustion that may develop when someone experiences too much stress for an extended period of time

Managing Stress

Given the potential consequences of stress, it follows that both people and organizations should be concerned about how to limit its more damaging effects. Numerous ideas and approaches have been developed to help manage stress. Some are strategies for individuals, while others are strategies for organizations.[28]

One way people manage stress is through exercise. People who exercise regularly feel less tension and stress, are more self-confident, and are more optimistic. Their better physical condition also makes them less susceptible to many common illnesses. People who don't exercise regularly, on the other hand, tend to feel more stress and are more likely to be depressed. They are also more likely to have heart attacks. And because of their physical condition, they are more likely to contract illnesses.

Another method people use to manage stress is relaxation. Relaxation allows individuals to adapt to, and therefore better deal with, their stress. Relaxation comes in many forms, such as taking regular vacations. A recent study found that people's attitudes toward a variety of workplace characteristics improved significantly following a vacation. People can also learn to relax while on their jobs. For example, some experts recommend that people take regular rest breaks during their normal workday.

People can also use time management to control stress. The idea behind time management is that many daily pressures can be reduced or eliminated if individuals do a better job of managing time. One approach to time management is to write a list every morning of the tasks to be done that day. The items on the list are then grouped into three categories: critical activities that must be performed, important activities that should be performed, and optional or trivial activities that can be delegated or postponed. The individual performs the items on the list in their order of importance.

Finally, people can manage stress through support groups. A support group can be as simple as a group of family members or friends to enjoy leisure time with. Going out after work with a couple of coworkers to a basketball game or a movie, for example, can help relieve stress built up during the day. Family and friends can help people cope with stress on an ongoing basis and during times of crisis. For example, an employee who has just learned that she did not get the promotion she has been working toward for months may find it helpful to have a good friend to lean on, to talk to, or to vent frustration with. People also may make use of more elaborate and formal support groups. Community centers or churches, for example, may sponsor support groups for people who have recently gone through a divorce, the death of a loved one, or some other tragedy.

Organizations are also beginning to realize that they should be involved in helping employees cope with stress. One argument for this trend is that, because the business is at least partially responsible for stress, it should also help relieve it. Another is that stress-related insurance claims by employees can cost the organization considerable sums of money. Still another is that workers experiencing lower levels of detrimental stress will be able to function more effectively. AT&T has initiated a series of seminars and workshops to help its employees cope with the stress they face in their jobs. The firm was prompted to develop these seminars for all three of the reasons noted above.

A wellness/stress management program is a special part of the organization specifically created to help deal with stress. Organizations have adopted stress management programs, health promotion programs, and other kinds of programs for this purpose. The AT&T seminar program noted earlier is similar to this idea, but true wellness programs are ongoing activities that have several different components. They commonly include exercise-related activities as well as classroom instruction programs dealing with smoking cessation, weight reduction, and general stress management.

Some companies are developing their own programs or using existing programs of this type. Johns-Manville, for example, has a gym at its corporate headquarters. Other firms negotiate discounted health club membership rates with local establishments. For the instructional part of the program, the organization can again either sponsor its own training or perhaps jointly sponsor seminars with a local YMCA, civic organization, or church. Organization-based fitness programs facilitate employee exercise, a very positive consideration, but such programs are also quite costly. Still, more and more companies are developing fitness programs for employees.

MANAGEMENT Managers should know the processes through which stress af-
IMPLICATIONS fects people. Being able to assess and deal with the causes and consequences of stress is especially important. Knowing if people are more prone toward Type A or Type B behavior is also of value to managers. Finally, managers need to recognize that they have the capacity to help themselves and others cope with stress more effectively.

■ *Creativity in Organizations*

Organizations frequently look for new ways to make their employees more creative and to promote innovation and entrepreneurial activity. Second City, the improvisational comedy troupe that launched the careers of Bill Murray and John Belushi, has developed a lucrative business by using comedy to help businesses promote creativity. Rob Nickerson, a Canadian comic working for Second City, is helping this room full of Nortel accountants think more creatively. People who attend the sessions swear by them; Second City, meanwhile, charges between $2,500 and $8,500 for a day-long program.

Creativity is yet another important component of individual behavior in organizations. *Today's Management Issues* explores the potential role of workspace in creativity. **Creativity** is the ability of an individual to generate new ideas or to conceive of new perspectives on existing ideas. What makes a person creative? How do people become creative? How does the creative process work? Although psychologists have not yet discovered complete answers to these questions, examining a few general patterns can help us understand the sources of individual creativity within organizations.[29]

The Creative Individual

Numerous researchers have focused their efforts on attempting to describe the common attributes of creative individuals. These attributes generally fall into three categories: background experiences, personal traits, and cognitive abilities.

Background Experiences and Creativity   Researchers have observed that many creative individuals were raised in an environment in which creativity was nurtured. Mozart was raised in a family of musicians and began composing and performing music at age six. Pierre and Marie Curie, great scientists in their own right, also raised a daughter, Irene, who won the Nobel Prize in chem-

TODAY'S MANAGEMENT ISSUES

CAN THE WORKSPACE IMPROVE CREATIVITY?

Although today's employees can share ideas with the click of a mouse or the beep of a cell phone, architects Charles Rose and Maryann Thompson believe that the design of an organization's workspace is equally important for enhancing creativity. These architects are designing technology-free spaces within the office or on the grounds where employees can retreat (alone or in small groups) to think through problems and brainstorm new ideas. They are also designing spaces such as gardens where employees can come together and collaborate in a quiet, contemplative setting.

More companies are designing workspaces with an eye toward fostering interaction and spontaneous discussion of issues and challenges. At Deloitte Consulting in Pittsburgh, for example, consultants often bring their laptops to the office cybercafé, where they can sip a free cappuccino and exchange thoughts about current projects. The office also boasts several "touchdown areas" where coworkers can relax in comfortable chairs while sharing ideas.

How can companies design workspaces to accommodate the idea-storming needs of teams? Sapient, an e-commerce consulting firm, has set aside separate team rooms for engineers working on particular projects. Each team has exclusive use of its room for the duration of its project, which can last for ten weeks or as long as eighteen months. Teams are encouraged to personalize their rooms, making the space more welcoming and more stimulating.

Sometimes the best way to spark creativity is to leave the office altogether. Stephen Zades, CEO of Long Haymes Carr, a North Carolina advertising agency, takes his employees and selected clients on an annual "creative odyssey." On this yearly four-day tour around New York City, the group attends avant-garde theater performances, ogles way-out art, and visits hip boutiques and night spots. During the trip, Zades makes time for participants to talk about the places they've visited and the trends they've spotted. These new experiences give rise to new ways of viewing the world and new ideas for all kinds of client projects.

Where do idea companies get their ideas? How do they tap into something that's on its way in, rather than already passed?

—*Stephen Zades, CEO of advertising agency Long Haymes Carr**

References: Bruce Nussbaum, "Architectural Visions: Designs for the Future," *Business Week*, August 28, 2000, pp. 153–164; Curtis Sittenfeld, "The Creative Odyssey," *Fast Company*, October 1999, pp. 54–56 (*quote on p. 54); Daintry Duffy, "Cube Stakes," *CIO Enterprise*, April 15, 1999, http://www.cio.com/archive/enterprise/041599_wksp_content.html (September 12, 2000).

---

istry. Thomas Edison's creativity was nurtured by his mother. However, people with background experiences very different from those just mentioned have also been creative. The African-American abolitionist and writer Frederick Douglass was born into slavery in Tuckahoe, Maryland, and had very limited opportunities for education. Nonetheless, his powerful oratory and creative thinking helped lead to the Emancipation Proclamation, which outlawed slavery in the United States.

creativity The ability of an individual to generate new ideas or to conceive of new perspectives on existing ideas

Personal Traits and Creativity Certain personal traits have also been linked to creativity in individuals. The traits shared by most creative people are openness, an attraction to complexity, high levels of energy, independence and autonomy, strong self-confidence, and a strong belief that one is, in fact, creative. Individuals who possess these traits are more likely to be creative than are those who do not have them.

Cognitive Abilities and Creativity   Cognitive abilities are an individual's power to think intelligently and to analyze situations and data effectively. Intelligence may be a precondition for individual creativity—although most creative people are highly intelligent, not all intelligent people necessarily are creative. Creativity is also linked with the ability to think divergently and convergently. *Divergent thinking* is a skill that allows people to see differences between situations, phenomena, or events. *Convergent thinking* is a skill that allows people to see similarities between situations, phenomena, or events. Creative people are generally very skilled at both divergent and convergent thinking.

Japanese managers have recently questioned their own creative ability. The concern is that their emphasis on group harmony has perhaps stifled individual initiative and hampered the development of individual creativity. As a result, many Japanese firms, including Omron Corporation, Fuji Photo, and Shimizu Corporation, have launched employee training programs intended to boost the creativity of their employees.[30]

The Creative Process

Although creative people often report that ideas seem to come to them "in a flash," individual creative activity actually tends to progress through a series of stages. Not all creative activity has to follow these four stages, but much of it does.

Preparation   The creative process normally begins with a period of *preparation*. Formal education and training are usually the most efficient ways of becoming familiar with this vast amount of research and knowledge. To make a creative contribution to business management or business services, individuals must usually receive formal training and education in business. This foundation is one reason for the strong demand for undergraduate and master's level business education. Formal business education can be an effective way for an individual to get "up to speed" and begin making creative contributions quickly. Experiences that managers have on the job after their formal training is finished can also contribute to the creative process. In an important sense, the education and training of creative people never really ends. It continues as long as they remain interested in the world and curious about the way things work.

Incubation   The second phase of the creative process is *incubation*—a period of less intense conscious concentration during which the knowledge and ideas acquired during preparation mature and develop. A curious aspect of incubation is that it is often helped along by pauses in concentrated rational thought. Some creative people rely on physical activity such as jogging or swimming to provide a "break" from thinking. Others may read or listen to music. Sometimes sleep may even supply the needed pause.

Insight   Usually occurring after preparation and incubation, insight is a spontaneous breakthrough in which the creative person achieves a new understanding of some problem or situation. *Insight* represents a coming together of all the scattered thoughts and ideas that were maturing during incubation. It may occur suddenly or develop slowly over time. Insight can be triggered by some external event, such as a new experience or an encounter with new data that forces the individual to think about old issues and problems in new ways, or it can be a completely internal event in which patterns of thought finally coalesce in ways that generate new understanding. One manager's key insight led to a complete restructuring of Citibank's back room operations. "Back room operations" refers to the enormous avalanche of paperwork that a bank must process to serve its customers—listing checks and deposits, updating accounts, and preparing bank statements. Historically, back room operations at Citibank had been managed as if they were part of the regular banking operation. But a new executive realized that back room operations had less to do with banking and more to do with manufacturing. The insight, then, was that back room operations could be managed as a paper-manufacturing process. On the basis of this insight, he hired former manufacturing managers from Ford and other automobile companies. By reconceptualizing the nature of back room operations, the executive was able to reduce substantially the costs of these operations for Citibank.

Verification   Once an insight has occurred, *verification* determines the validity or truthfulness of the insight. For many creative ideas, verification includes scientific experiments to determine whether or not the insight actually leads to the results expected. Verification may also include the development of a product or service prototype. A prototype is one product or a very small number of products built just to see if the ideas behind this new product actually work. Product prototypes are rarely sold to the public but are very valuable in verifying the insights developed in the creative process. Once the new product or service is developed, verification in the marketplace is the ultimate test of the creative idea behind it.

Enhancing Creativity in Organizations

Managers who wish to enhance and promote creativity in their organizations can do so in several ways.[31] One important method for enhancing creativity is to make it part of the organization's culture, often through explicit goals. Firms that truly want to stress creativity, like 3M and Rubbermaid, for example, state goals that some percentage of future revenues are to be gained from new products. This goal clearly communicates that creativity and innovation are valued.

Another important part of enhancing creativity is to reward creative successes while being careful not to punish creative failures. Many ideas that seem worthwhile on paper fail to pan out in reality. If the first person to come up with an idea that fails is fired or otherwise punished, others in the organization will become more cautious in their own work. And as a result, fewer creative ideas will emerge.

MANAGEMENT   Managers need to understand the creative process. The ability to
IMPLICATIONS   recognize and nurture creativity in others can be especially valuable, as can creating an environment in which creativity is more likely to emerge.

Types of Workplace Behavior

workplace behavior A pattern of action by the members of an organization that directly or indirectly influences organizational effectiveness

Now that we have looked closely at how individual differences can influence behavior in organizations, let's turn our attention to what we mean by workplace behavior. **Workplace behavior** is a pattern of action by the members of an organization that directly or indirectly influences organizational effectiveness. Important workplace behaviors include performance and productivity, absenteeism and turnover, and organizational citizenship.

Performance Behaviors

performance behaviors The total set of work-related behaviors that the organization expects the individual to display

Performance behaviors are the total set of work-related behaviors that the organization expects the individual to display. Thus, they derive from the psychological contract. For some jobs, performance behaviors can be narrowly defined and easily measured. For example, an assembly line worker who sits by a moving conveyor and attaches parts to a product as it passes by has relatively few performance behaviors. He or she is expected to remain at the workstation and attach the parts correctly. Performance can often be assessed quantitatively by counting the percentage of parts correctly attached.

For many other jobs, however, performance behaviors are more diverse and much more difficult to assess. For example, consider the case of a research and development scientist at Merck. The scientist works in a lab trying to find new scientific breakthroughs that have commercial potential. The scientist must apply knowledge learned in graduate school with experience gained from previous research. Intuition and creativity are also important elements. And the desired breakthrough may take months or even years to accomplish. As we discussed in Chapter 14, organizations rely on a number of different methods for evaluating performance. The key, of course, is to match the evaluation mechanism with the job being performed.

Withdrawal Behavior

absenteeism When an individual does not show up for work

Another important type of work-related behavior is that which results in withdrawal—absenteeism and turnover. **Absenteeism** occurs when an individual does not show up for work. The cause may be legitimate (illness, jury duty, death in the family, etc.) or feigned (reported as legitimate but actually just an excuse to stay home). When an employee is absent, her or his work does not get done at all or a substitute must be hired to do it. In either case, the quantity or quality of actual output is likely to suffer. Obviously, some absenteeism is expected. The key concern of organizations is to minimize feigned absenteeism and reduce legitimate absences as much as possible. High absenteeism may be a symptom of other problems as well, such as job dissatisfaction and low morale.

turnover When people quit their jobs

Turnover occurs when people quit their jobs. An organization usually incurs costs in replacing individuals who have quit, but if turnover involves especially productive people, it is even more costly. Turnover seems to result from several factors, including aspects of the job, the organization, the individual, the labor market, and family influences. In general, a poor person-job fit is also a likely cause of turnover. The current labor shortage is also resulting in higher turnover in many companies due to the abundance of more attractive alternative jobs available to highly qualified individuals.[32]

Efforts to manage turnover directly are frequently fraught with difficulty, even in organizations that concentrate on rewarding good performers. Of course, some turnover is inevitable and in some cases it may even be desirable. For example, if the organization is trying to cut costs by reducing its staff, having people voluntarily choose to leave is preferable to having to terminate them. And if the people who choose to leave are low performers or express high levels of job dissatisfaction, the organization may also benefit from turnover.

organizational citizenship The behavior of individuals that makes a positive overall contribution to the organization

Organizational Citizenship

Organizational citizenship refers to the behavior of individuals that makes a positive overall contribution to the organization.[33] Consider, for example, an employee who does work that is acceptable in terms of both quantity and quality. However, she refuses to work overtime, she won't help newcomers learn the ropes, and she is generally unwilling to make any contribution to the organization beyond the strict performance of her job. While this person may be seen as a good performer, she is not likely to be seen as a good organizational citizen.

Another employee may exhibit a comparable level of performance. In addition, however, he will always work late when the boss asks him to, he takes time to help newcomers learn their way around, and he is perceived as being helpful and committed to the organization's success. While his level of performance may be seen as equal to that of the first worker, he is also likely to be seen as a better organizational citizen.

The determinant of organizational citizenship behaviors is likely to be a complex mosaic of individual, social, and organizational variables. For example, the personality, attitudes, and needs of the individual will have to be consistent with citizenship behaviors. Similarly, the social context, or work group, in which the individual works will need to facilitate and promote such behaviors (we discuss group dynamics in Chapter 18). And the organization itself, especially its culture, must be capable of promoting, recognizing, and rewarding these types of behaviors if they are to be maintained. While the study of organizational citizenship is still in its infancy, preliminary research suggests that it may play a powerful role in organizational effectiveness.[34]

MANAGEMENT IMPLICATIONS   Managers should realize that employees can exhibit a wide array of workplace behaviors. They should try to determine which behaviors are most important and seek ways of encouraging those behaviors instead of alternative behaviors.

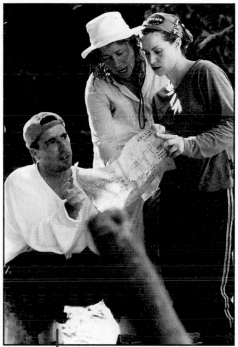

Organizational citizenship refers to the behavior of individuals that makes a positive overall contribution to the organization. The recent spate of so-called "reality programs" on television often rely on citizenship behaviors. These three people, for example, were part of the original *Survivor* television show. People worked together in various games and competitive activities, but the group then voted individuals out of the group one-by-one. In most cases, participants who displayed good citizenship behaviors were among the final contestants vying for the big prize.

Summary of Key Points

Understanding individuals in organizations is an important consideration for all managers. A basic framework that can be used to facilitate this understanding is the psychological contract—the set of expectations held by people with respect to what they will contribute to the organization and what they expect to get in return. Organizations strive to achieve an optimal person-job fit, but this process is complicated by the existence of individual differences.

Personality is the relatively stable set of psychological and behavioral attributes that distinguish one person from another. The "big five" personality traits are agreeableness, conscientiousness, negative emotionality, extraversion, and openness. Other important traits are locus of control, self-efficacy, authoritariansim, Machiavellianism, self-esteem, and risk propensity.

Attitudes are based on emotion, knowledge, and intended behavior. Whereas personality is relatively stable, some attitudes can be formed and changed easily. Others are more constant. Job satisfaction or dissatisfaction and organizational commitment are important work-related attitudes.

Perception is the set of processes by which an individual becomes aware of and interprets information about the environment. Basic perceptual processes include selective perception and stereotyping. Perception and attribution are also closely related.

Stress is an individual's response to a strong stimulus. The general adaption syndrome outlines the basic stress process. Stress can be caused by task, physical, role, and interpersonal demands. Consequences of stress include organizational and individual outcomes, as well as burnout. Several steps can be taken to manage stress.

Creativity is the capacity to generate new ideas. Creative people tend to have certain profiles of background experiences, personal traits, and cognitive abilities. The creative process itself includes preparation, incubation, insight, and verification.

Workplace behavior is a pattern of action by the members of an organization that directly or indirectly influences organizational effectiveness. Performance behaviors are the set of work-related behaviors the organization expects the individual to display and thus fulfill the psychological contract. Basic withdrawal behaviors are absenteeism and turnover. Organizational citizenship refers to behavior that makes a positive overall contribution to the organization.

Discussion Questions

Questions for Review

1. What is a psychological contract? Why is it important?
2. Identify and describe five basic personality attributes.
3. Identify and discuss the steps in the creative process.
4. Identify and describe several important workplace behaviors.

Questions for Analysis

5. An individual was heard to describe someone else as having "no personality." What is wrong with this statement? What did the individual actually mean?
6. Describe a circumstance in which you formed a new attitude about something.
7. As a manager, how would you try to make someone a better organizational citizen?

Questions for Application

8. Write the psychological contract you have in this class. That is, what do you contribute, and what inducements are available? Compare your contract with those of some of your classmates. In what ways are they similar, and in what ways is yours unique?

9. Assume that you are going to hire three new employees for the department store you manage. One will sell shoes, one will manage the toy department, and one will work in the stockroom. Identify the basic characteristics you want in each of the people to achieve a good person-job fit.

10. List the things that cause stress for the typical college student. Now list the ways that college students manage stress. Discuss your lists with those of three of your classmates.

BUILDING EFFECTIVE *conceptual* AND *diagnostic* SKILLS

Exercise Overview

Conceptual skills refer to a manager's ability to think in the abstract, while diagnostic skills focus on responses to situations. These skills must frequently be used together to understand the behavior of others in the organization, as illustrated by this exercise.

Exercise Background

Human behavior is a complex phenomenon in any setting but especially so in organizations. Understanding how and why people choose to diplay particular behaviors can be difficult and frustrating, but quite important. Consider, for example, the following scenario.

Sandra Buckley has worked in your department for several years. Until recently, she has been a model employee. She was always on time or early for work and stayed late whenever necessary to get her work done. She was upbeat and cheerful, and she worked very hard. She frequently said that the company was the best place she had ever worked and that you were the perfect boss.

About six months ago, however, you began to see changes in Sandra's behavior. She began to come in late occasionally, and you cannot remember the last time she agreed to work past 5:00. She also complains a lot. Other workers have started to avoid her because she is so negative all the time. You also suspect that she may be looking for a new job.

Exercise Task

Using the scenario described above as background, do the following:

1. Assume that you have done some background work to find out what has happened. Write a brief case with more information that explains why Sandra's behavior has changed (i.e., your case might include the fact that you recently promoted someone else when Sandra might have expected to get the job). Make the case as descriptive as possible.

2. Relate elements of your case to the various behavioral concepts discussed in this chapter.

3. Decide whether or not you might be about to resolve the situation with Sandra to overcome any issues that have arisen.

4. Which behavioral process or concept discussed in this chapter is easiest to change? Which is the most difficult to change?

BUILDING EFFECTIVE *time-management* SKILLS

Exercise Overview

Time-management skills help people prioritize work, work more efficiently, and delegate appropriately. Poor time-management skills, in turn, may result in stress. This exercise will help you relate time-management skills to stress reduction.

Exercise Background

List several of the major events or expectations that cause stress for you. Stressors might involve school (i.e., hard classes, too many exams, etc.), work (i.e., financial pressures, demanding work schedule), and/or personal circumstances (i.e., friends, romance, family, etc.). Try to be as specific as possible. Also try to identify at least ten different stressors.

Exercise Task

Using the list that you developed, do each of the following:

1. Evaluate the extent to which poor time-management skills on your part play a role in how each stressor affects you. For example, do exams cause stress because you delay studying?
2. Develop a strategy for using time more efficiently in relation to each stressor that relates to time.
3. Note interrelationships among different kinds of stressors and time. For example, financial pressures may cause you to work, but work may interfere with school. Can any of these interrelationships be managed more effectively vis-à-vis time?
4. How do you manage the stress in your life? Is it possible to manage stress in a more time-effective manner?

BUILDING EFFECTIVE *interpersonal* SKILLS

Exercise Overview

Interpersonal skills refer to the ability to communicate with, understand, and motivate individuals and groups. Implicit in this definition is the notion that a manager should try to understand the important characteristics of others, including their personalities. This exercise will give you insights into both the importance of personality in the workplace as well as some of the difficulties associated with assessing personality traits.

Exercise Background

You will first try to determine which personality traits are most relevant for different jobs. You will then write a series of questions that you think may help assess or measure those traits in prospective employees. First, read each of the job descriptions below.

1. *Sales representative:* This position involves calling on existing customers to ensure that they remain happy with your firm's products. It also requires that the sales representatives work to get customers to increase the quantity of your products that they are buying and to attract new customers. It is also important that a sales representative be aggressive but not pushy.
2. *Office manager:* The office manager oversees the work of a staff of twenty secretaries, receptionists, and clerks. The manager hires them, trains them, evaluates their performance, and sets their pay. The manager also schedules working hours and, when necessary, disciplines or fires workers.

3. *Warehouse worker:* Warehouse workers unload trucks and carry shipments to shelves for storage. They also pull customer orders from shelves and take products for packing. The job requires that workers follow orders precisely, and there is little room for autonomy or interaction with others during work.

Exercise Task

Working alone, think of a single personality trait that you think is especially important for a person to perform each of these three jobs effectively. Next, write five questions that, when answered by a job applicant, will help you assess how that applicant scores on that particular trait. These questions should be of the type that can be answered on five-point scales (i.e., strongly agree, agree, neither agree nor disagree, disagree, strongly disagree).

After you have completed writing your questions, exchange them with those of one of your classmates. Pretend you are a job applicant. Provide honest and truthful answers to each question. After each of you has finished answering each other's questions, discuss the traits each of you identified for each position and how well you think your classmate's questions actually measure those traits.

Conclude by addressing the following questions:

1. How easy is it to measure personality?
2. How important do you believe it is for organizations to consider personality in hiring decisions?
3. Do perceptions and attitudes affect how people answer personality questions?

CHAPTER CLOSING CASE

THE RISE OF FREE AGENTS

The sports tradition of free agents is taking hold in the business world. Free agents—self-employed individuals who contract for organizational work on a project basis—already make up more than one-quarter of the U.S. workforce. Within a decade, as many as four in ten workers are likely to be free agents, going from project to project and company to company as their talents are needed.

Several factors are fueling this trend. First, companies that downsized in earlier years find they sometimes need specialists with particular skills to handle certain projects, technologies, or clients. Second, companies can avoid the expense and hassles of constant hiring-and-firing cycles by selectively contracting with free agents to supplement their full-time, permanent workforce during peak sales, planning, or production periods. And third, companies now have the technology to transcend organizational and geographical boundaries by connecting free agents outside the organization with employees inside for effective teamwork and collaboration.

For their part, free agents gain more flexibility in choosing among clients and projects, learning and applying new skills, managing time and other resources, balancing work and family obligations, and negotiating compensation. Free agents can work solo or come together as needed for specific projects. For example, web site designer Andrew Keeler often establishes temporary teams to work with him on projects for Adobe Systems, Hewlett-Packard, and other clients. Keeler has had face-to-face contact with only a few of his free-agent colleagues; in most cases, he uses e-mail to assemble a team, coordinate all work, and complete the project—quickly.

Keeler's experience illustrates one of the downsides to being a free agent: lack of personal interaction. E-mailing a joke adorned with a smiley face just isn't the same as sharing a laugh with a colleague while standing around the proverbial water cooler. Also, free agents can't always find as much work as they'd like, nor do they always get paid on time. Still, free agents in high-demand fields such as e-commerce technology can earn significantly more as independents than as employees, even though they have to arrange for their own health insurance and fund their own retirement accounts instead of receiving those items as corporate benefits.

Companies are increasingly using free agents to keep their organizations flat and lean. When the Finnish telecommunications giant Nokia began selling computer displays in the United States, it hired only five permanent employees to staff the new office. The company relied on a network of free agents and outside suppliers to manage a wide range of activities, from marketing and sales to shipping and technical support.

But how do companies and free agents find each other? In addition to word of mouth communication, more matches are being made on the Internet. Monster Talent Market (http://www.talentmarket.monster.com) allows free agents to post information about their skills, schedules, and prices so companies can bid for their services. FreeAgent.com (http://www.freeagent.com) stores free agents' résumés for review by prospective clients and lists projects open for free agents' bids; similarly, eLance (http://www.elance.com) displays résumés

and projects for which companies are seeking free agents. Free-agents in search of community can visit Guru.com (http://www.guru.com), a site that goes beyond project and free-agent listings to offer articles and advice about working independently. Watch for even more web sites as the free-agent movement gathers momentum outside high-tech industries.

Case Questions

1. How is the free-agent movement likely to influence workplace behaviors?

2. What work-related attitudes are more important for employees than for free agents?

3. Which personality traits do free agents need to be effective?

Case References

Michelle Conlin, "And Now, the Just-in-Time Employee," *Business Week*, August 28, 2000, pp. 169–170; Katherine Mieszkowski, "Report from the Future: The E-Lance Economy," *Fast Company*, November 1999, pp. 66–68; Alan Cohen, "Sites for Free Agents," *PC Magazine*, October 13, 1999, http://www.zdnet.com/pcmag/stories/trends/0,7607,2352981,00.html (September 12, 2000); Rick Overton, "Shift for Brains," *Business 2.0*, October 1, 1999, http://www.business2.com/content/magazine/ebusiness/1999/10/01/16824 (September 12, 2000).

CHAPTER NOTES

1. "Company Cuts Jobs, Closes Plants as Sales Shrink, Popularity Fades, *USA Today*, February 23, 1999, pp. 1B, 2B (quote on p. 2B); "Its Share Shrinking, Levi Strauss Lays Off 6,395," *Wall Street Journal*, November 4, 1997, pp. B1, B8; *Hoover's Handbook of American Business 2001* (Austin, Texas: Hoover's Business Press, 2001), pp. 866–867.

2. Lynn McGarlane Shore and Lois Tetrick, "The Psychological Contract as an Explanatory Framework in the Employment Relationship," in C. L. Cooper and D. M. Rousseau (eds.), *Trends in Organizational Behavior* (London: John Wiley & Sons Ltd., 1994), pp. 80–96.

3. Elizabeth Wolfe Morrison and Sandra L. Robinson, "When Employees Feel Betrayed: A Model of How Psychological Contract Violation Develops," *Academy of Management Review*, January 1997, pp. 226–256.

4. Lawrence Pervin, "Personality" in Mark Rosenzweig and Lyman Porter, eds., *Annual Review of Psychology*, Vol. 36 (Palo Alto, Calif.: Annual Reviews, 1985), pp. 83–114; and S. R. Maddi, *Personality Theories: A Comparative Analysis*, 4th Edition (Homewood, Ill.: Dorsey, 1980).

5. L. R. Goldberg, "An Alternative 'Description of Personality': The Big Five Factor Structure," *Journal of Personality and Social Psychology*, Vol. 59, 1990, pp. 1216–1229.

6. Michael K. Mount, Murray R. Barrick, and J. Perkins Strauss, "Validity of Observer Ratings of the Big Five Personality Factors," *Journal of Applied Psychology*, Vol. 79, No. 2, 1994, pp. 272–280; Timothy A. Judge, Joseph J. Martocchio, and Carl J. Thoreson, "Five-Factor Model of Personality and Employee Absence," *Journal of Applied Psychology*, Vol. 82, No. 5, 1997, pp. 745–755.

7. J. B. Rotter, "Generalized Expectancies for Internal vs. External Control of Reinforcement," *Psychological Monographs*, Vol. 80, 1966, pp. 1–28; see also Simon S. K. Lam and John Schaubroeck, "The Role of Locus of Control in Reactions to Being Promoted and to Being Passed Over: A Quasi-Experiment," *Academy of Management Journal*, 2000, Vol. 43, No. 1, pp. 66–78.

8. Marilyn E. Gist and Terence R. Mitchell, "Self-Efficacy: A Theoretical Analysis of Its Determinants and Malleability," *Academy of Management Review*, April 1992, pp. 183–211.

9. T. W. Adorno, E. Frenkel-Brunswick, D. J. Levinson, and R. N. Sanford, *The Authoritarian Personality* (New York: Harper & Row, 1950).

10. Jon L. Pierce, Donald G. Gardner, and Larry L. Cummings, "Organization-Based Self-Esteem: Construct Definition, Measurement, and Validation," *Academy of Management Journal*, Vol. 32, 1989, pp. 622–648.

11. Michael Harris Bond and Peter B. Smith, "Cross-Cultural Social and Organizational Psychology," in Janet Spence, ed., *Annual Review of Psychology*, Vol. 47 (Palo Alto, Calif.: Annual Reviews, 1996), pp. 205–235.

12. Leon Festinger, *A Theory of Cognitive Dissonance* (Palo Alto, Calif.: Stanford University Press, 1957).

13. See John J. Clancy, "Is Loyalty Really Dead?" *Across the Board*, June 1999, pp. 15–19.

14. Patricia C. Smith, L. M. Kendall, and Charles Hulin, *The Measurement of Satisfaction in Work and Behavior* (Chicago: Rand-McNally, 1969).

15. "Companies Are Finding Real Payoffs in Aiding Employee Satisfaction," *Wall Street Journal*, October 11, 2000, p. B1.

16. James R. Lincoln, "Employee Work Attitudes and Management Practice in the U.S. and Japan: Evidence from a Large Comparative Study," *California Management Review*, Fall 1989, pp. 89–106.

17. Lincoln, "Employee Work Attitudes and Management Practice in the U.S. and Japan: Evidence from a Large Comparative Study."

18. Richard M. Steers, "Antecedents and Outcomes of Organizational Commitment," *Administrative Science Quarterly*, Vol. 22, 1977, pp. 46–56.

19. For research work in this area, see Jennifer M. George and Gareth R. Jones, "The Experience of Mood and Turnover Intentions: Interactive Effects of Value Attainment, Job Satisfaction, and Positive Mood," *Journal of Applied Psychology*, Vol. 81, No. 3, 1996, pp. 318–325; Larry J. Williams, Mark B. Gavin, and Margaret Williams, "Measurement and Nonmeasurement Processes with Negative Affectivity and Employee Attitudes," *Journal of Applied Psychology*, Vol. 81, No. 1, 1996, pp. 88–101.

20. Kathleen Sutcliffe, "What Executives Notice: Accurate Perceptions in Top Management Teams," *Academy of Management Journal*, 1994, Vol. 37, No. 5, pp. 1360–1378.

21. See H. H. Kelley, *Attribution in Social Interaction* (Morristown, N.J.: General Learning Press, 1971) for a classic treatment of attribution.

22. For a recent overview of the stress literature, see Frank Landy, James Campbell Quick, and Stanislav Kasl, "Work, Stress, and Well-Being," *International Journal of Stress Management*, 1994, Vol. 1, No. 1, pp. 33–73.

23. Hans Selye, *The Stress of Life* (New York: McGraw-Hill, 1976).

24. M. Friedman and R. H. Rosenman, *Type A Behavior and Your Heart* (New York: Alfred A. Knopf, 1974).

25. "Work & Family," *Business Week*, June 28, 1993, pp. 80–88.

26. Richard S. DeFrank, Robert Konopaske, and John M. Ivancevich, "Executive Travel Stress: Perils of the Road Warrior," *Academy of Management Executive*, 2000, Vol. 14, No. 2, pp. 58–67.

27. "Breaking Point," *Newsweek*, March 6, 1995, pp. 56–62.

28. John M. Kelly, "Get a Grip on Stress," *HRMagazine*, February 1997, pp. 51–58.

29. See Richard W. Woodman, John E. Sawyer, and Ricky W. Griffin, "Toward a Theory of Organizational Creativity," *Academy of Management Review*, April 1993, pp. 293–321.

30. Emily Thornton, "Japan's Struggle to Be Creative," *Fortune*, April 19, 1993, pp. 129–134.

31. Christina E. Shalley, Lucy L. Gilson, and Terry C. Blum, "Matching Creativity Requirements and the Work Environment: Effects on Satisfaction and Intentions to Leave," *Academy of Management Journal*, 2000, Vol. 43, No. 2, pp. 215–223. See also Filiz Tabak, "Employee Creative Performance: What Makes It Happen?" *The Academy of Management Executive*, Vol. 11, No. 1, 1997, pp. 119–122.

32. "That's It, I'm Outa Here," *Business Week*, October 3, 2000, pp. 96–98.

33. See Philip M. Podsakoff, Scott B. MacKenzie, Julie Beth Paine, and Daniel G. G. Bacharah, "Organizational Citizenship Behaviors: A Critical Review of the Theoretical and Empirical Literature and Suggestions for Future Research," *Journal of Management*, 2000, Vol. 26, No. 3, pp. 513–563, for recent findings regarding this behavior.

34. Dennis W. Organ, "Personality and Organizational Citizenship Behavior," *Journal of Management*, 1994, Vol. 20, No. 2, pp. 465–478; Mary Konovsky and S. Douglas Pugh, "Citizenship Behavior and Social Exchange," *Academy of Management Journal*, 1994, Vol. 37, No. 3, pp. 656–669.

Managing Employee Motivation and Performance

For years Continental Airlines was a company going nowhere. The firm was wallowing in red ink and had perhaps the poorest reputation of any carrier in the airline industry. For example, the company lost $2.4 billion in 1990 alone, and many business travelers routinely refused to fly Continental. The airline also went through two bankruptcies and a succession of ineffective senior leaders. Continental's pilots and rank-and-file workers endured layoffs, wage cuts, poor benefits, and broken promises by management. Indeed, many were frequently embarrassed to tell people where they worked and few were motivated to work any harder than was necessary.

But in late 1994, the situation began to change. The key to what would eventually become one of the biggest turnarounds in the history of U.S. business was the appointment of a new CEO, Gordon Bethune. Bethune, a former fighter pilot in the Navy and chief engineer at Boeing, had a repu-

tation for making tough but effective decisions. He was also known to be fair and open with employees. The board of directors told him to do whatever needed to be done to make Continental competitive again.

One area that needed immediate attention was operations. Bethune frantically cut unprofitable routes and added new and more profitable ones in their places. He also overhauled the firm's ticketing and baggage-handling operations, improved marketing, and updated the firm's fleet of aircraft. He also overhauled Continental's cash management system. But Bethune knew that operations alone were not the only problem areas—he also knew that employee motivation was at the root of many of the company's problems.

One of the biggest problems Bethune had to overcome was the legacy of his predecessors. Employees at Continental had endured ten CEOs in fifteen years. Many of these CEOs, in turn, had at least been per-

ceived as being ineffective and as exhibiting little concern for the company's employees. As a result, many of those same employees had developed a deep-seated mistrust of top managers and few were motivated to follow their lead.

One thing Bethune noticed immediately was that the primary variable-pay component in how the firm paid its pilots was based on fuel-cost savings. As soon as he changed this system to pay instead for on-time performance, Continental moved quickly from last in the industry in on-time performance to the middle of the industry.

Bethune then calculated that this increase in performance was saving the firm millions of dollars, because when planes are late, an airline must often pay for passengers' meals and hotel rooms and for rebooking them

". . . I've never heard of a successful company that didn't have people who liked working there."

—*Gordon Bethune, CEO of Continental Airlines**

After studying this chapter, you should be able to:

- Characterize the nature of motivation, including its importance and basic historical perspectives.

- Identify and describe the major content perspectives on motivation.

- Identify and describe the major process perspectives on motivation.

- Describe reinforcement perspectives on motivation.

- Identify and describe popular motivational strategies.

- Describe the role of organizational reward systems in motivation.

onto other airlines. He divided the total savings by the number of employees and sent each of them a check for that amount—$65 per employee. While not a big sum, this action served as an important demonstration that he was willing to share success with everyone. He also announced that, henceforth, each employee would receive a check for $65 every month that Continental was in the top five in on-time performance and a check for $100 when it was in the top three.

Bethune also wanted to improve communication throughout Continental. He set up a toll-free number for employees to call with complaints and problems. He created a committee to respond to every call within forty-eight hours. He also gave employees his own personal voice mail number, and he returns many of these calls himself. Today, he is careful to refer to Continental's employees as his "coworkers."

Bethune also began to restore wages to employees that had been previously cut. And again, Continental's employees have responded in dramatic fashion. Once the joke of the airline industry, Continental is now among the most profitable carriers in the world, and its reputation among business travelers has soared near the top of the ratings. Indeed, the firm won the J. D. Powers customer satisfaction award as the best long-haul carrier in the United States several times in the last few years, and Continental was recently listed as one of the 100 best companies to work for by *Fortune* magazine.[1]

everal different factors have contributed to the remarkable turnaround at Continental. Enhanced employee motivation, moreover, is clearly one of the most significant. Almost any organization is capable of developing and maintaining a motivated workforce. The trick is figuring how to create a system in which employees can receive rewards that they genuinely want by performing in ways that fit the organization's goals and objectives.

In most settings, people can choose how hard they work and how much effort they expend. Thus, managers need to understand how and why employees make different choices regarding their own performance. The key ingredient behind this choice is motivation, the subject of this chapter. We first examine the nature of employee motivation and then explore the major perspectives on motivation. Newly emerging approaches are then discussed. We conclude with a description of rewards and their role in motivation.

The Nature of Motivation

motivation The set of forces that cause people to behave in certain ways

Motivation is the set of forces that cause people to behave in certain ways.[2] On any given day, an employee may choose to work as hard as possible at a job, to work just hard enough to avoid a reprimand, or to do as little as possible. The goal for the manager is to maximize the likelihood of the first behavior and to minimize the likelihood of the last. This goal becomes all the more important when we understand how critical motivation is in the workplace.

The Importance of Motivation in the Workplace

Individual performance is generally determined by three things: motivation (the desire to do the job), ability (the capability to do the job), and the work environment (the resources needed to do the job). If an employee lacks ability, the manager can provide training or replace the worker. If there is a resource problem, the manager can correct it. But if motivation is the problem, the task for the manager is more challenging. Individual behavior is a complex phenomenon, and the manager may be hard-pressed to figure out the precise nature of the problem and how to solve it. Thus, motivation is important because of its significance as a determinant of performance and because of its intangible character.[3]

The motivation framework in Figure 16.1 is a good starting point for understanding how motivated behavior occurs. The motivation process begins with a need deficiency. For example, when a worker feels that she is underpaid, she experiences a need for more income. In response, the worker searches for ways to satisfy the need, such as working harder to try to earn a raise or seeking a new job. Next, she chooses an option to pursue. After carrying out the chosen option—working harder and putting in more hours for a reasonable period of time, for example—she then evaluates her success. If her hard work resulted in a pay raise, she probably feels good about her situation and will continue to work hard. But if no raise has been provided, she is likely to try another option.

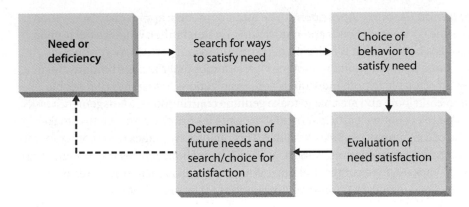

Figure 16.1

The Motivation Framework
The motivation process progresses through a series of discrete steps. Content, process, and reinforcement perspectives on motivation address different parts of this process.

Historical Perspectives on Motivation

To appreciate what we know about employee motivation, it is helpful to review earlier approaches. The traditional, human relations, and human resource approaches have each shed partial light on motivation.[4]

The Traditional Approach   The traditional approach is represented best by the work of Frederick W. Taylor.[5] As noted in Chapter 2, Taylor advocated an incentive pay system. He believed that managers knew more about the jobs being performed than did workers, and he assumed that economic gain was the primary thing that motivated everyone. Other assumptions of the traditional approach are that work is inherently unpleasant for most people and that the money they earn is more important to employees than the nature of the job they are performing. Hence, people could be expected to perform any kind of job if they were paid enough. Although the role of money as a motivating factor cannot be dismissed, proponents of the traditional approach took too narrow a view of the role of monetary compensation and also failed to consider other motivational factors.

The Human Relations Approach   The human relations approach was also summarized in Chapter 2.[6] The human relationists emphasized the role of social processes in the workplace. Their basic assumptions were that employees want to feel useful and important, that employees have strong social needs, and that these needs are more important than money in motivating employees. Advocates of the human relations approach advised managers to make workers feel important and allow them a modicum of self-direction and self-control in carrying out routine activities. The illusion of involvement and importance were expected to satisfy workers' basic social needs and result in higher motivation to perform. For example, a manager might allow a work group to participate in making a decision, even though he or she had already determined what the decision would be. The symbolic gesture of seeming to allow participation was expected to enhance motivation, even though no real participation took place.

The Human Resource Approach   The human resource approach to motivation carries the concepts of needs and motivation one step farther. Whereas the human relationists believed that the illusion of contribution and participation would enhance motivation, the human resource view assumes that the contributions themselves are valuable to both individuals and organizations. It assumes that people want to contribute and are able to make genuine contributions. Management's tasks, then, are to encourage participation and to create a work environment that makes full use of the human resources available. This philosophy guides most contemporary thinking about employee motivation. At Ford, Westinghouse, Texas Instruments, and Hewlett-Packard, for example, work teams are being called on to solve a variety of problems and to make substantive contributions to the organization.

MANAGEMENT IMPLICATIONS   Managers should understand the central role that motivation plays in determining employee job performance. They should also be familiar with traditional approaches to motivation.

Content Perspectives on Motivation

content perspectives Approaches to motivation that try to answer the question, "What factors in the workplace motivate people?"

Content perspectives on motivation deal with the first part of the motivation process—needs and need deficiencies. More specifically, **content perspectives** address the question, "What factors in the workplace motivate people?" Labor leaders often argue that workers can be motivated by more pay, shorter working hours, and improved working conditions. Meanwhile, some experts suggest that motivation can be enhanced more effectively by providing employees with more autonomy and greater responsibility.[7] Both of these views represent content views of motivation. The former asserts that motivation is a function of pay, working hours, and working conditions; the latter suggests that autonomy and responsibility are the causes of motivation. Two widely known content perspectives on motivation are the need hierarchy and the two-factor theory.

The Need Hierarchy Approach

The need hierarchy approach has been advanced by many theorists. Need hierarchies assume that people have different needs that can be arranged in a hierarchy of importance. The two best known are Maslow's hierarchy of needs and the ERG theory.

Maslow's hierarchy of needs
Suggests that people must satisfy five groups of needs in the following order—physiological, security, belongingness, esteem, and self-actualization

Maslow's Hierarchy of Needs   Abraham Maslow, a human relationist, argued that people are motivated to satisfy five need levels.[8] **Maslow's hierarchy of needs** is shown in Figure 16.2. At the bottom of the hierarchy are the *physiological needs*—things like food, sex, and air that represent basic issues of survival and biological function. In organizations, these needs are generally satisfied by adequate wages and the work environment itself, which provides restrooms, adequate lighting, comfortable temperatures, and ventilation.

Next are the *security needs* for a secure physical and emotional environment. Examples include the desire for housing and clothing and the need to be free from

NEEDS

General Examples   Organizational Examples

Achievement — Self-actualization — Challenging job

Status — Esteem — Job title

Friendship — Belongingness — Friends at work

Stability — Security — Pension plan

Food — Physiology — Base salary

Source: Adapted from Abraham H. Maslow, *"A Theory of Human Motivation," Psychology Review,* 1943, Vol. 50, pp. 370–396.

Figure 16.2

Maslow's Hierarchy of Needs

Maslow's hierarchy suggests that human needs can be classified into five categories and that these categories can be arranged in a hierarchy of importance. A manager should understand that an employee may not be satisfied with only a salary and benefits; he or she may also need challenging job opportunities to experience self-growth and satisfaction.

worry about money and job security. These needs can be satisfied in the workplace by job continuity (no layoffs), a grievance system (to protect against arbitrary supervisory actions), and an adequate insurance and retirement benefits package (for security against illness and for the provision of income in later life). Even today, however, depressed industries and economic decline can put people out of work and restore the primacy of security needs.

Belongingness needs relate to social processes. They include the need for love and affection and the need to be accepted by one's peers. These needs are satisfied for most people by family and community relationships outside work and friendships on the job. A manager can help satisfy these needs by allowing social interaction and by making employees feel like part of a team or work group.

Esteem needs actually comprise two different sets of needs: the need for a positive self-image and self-respect and the need for recognition and respect from others. A manager can help address these needs by providing a variety of extrinsic symbols of accomplishment such as job titles, comfortable offices, and similar rewards as appropriate. At a more intrinsic level, the manager can provide challenging job assignments and opportunities for the employee to feel a sense of accomplishment.

At the top of the hierarchy are the *self-actualization* needs. These needs involve realizing one's potential for continued growth and individual development. The self-actualization needs are perhaps the most difficult for a manager to address. In fact, it can be argued that these needs must be met entirely from within the individual. But a manager can help by promoting a culture wherein self-actualization is possible. For instance, a manager could give employees a chance to participate in making decisions about their work and the opportunity to learn and use new information, skills, and capabilities.

Maslow suggests that the five need categories constitute a hierarchy. An individual is motivated first and foremost to satisfy physiological needs. As long as they remain unsatisfied, the individual is motivated only to fulfill them. When satisfaction of physiological needs is achieved, they cease to act as primary motivational factors and the individual moves "up" the hierarchy and becomes concerned with security needs. This process continues until the individual reaches the self-actualization level. Maslow's concept of the need hierarchy has a certain intuitive logic and has been accepted by many managers. But research has revealed certain shortcomings and defects in the theory. Some research has found that the five levels of need are not always present and that the order of the levels is not always the same as postulated by Maslow.[9] In addition, people from different cultures are likely to have different need categories and hierarchies.

ERG theory of motivation
Suggests that people's needs are grouped into three possibly overlapping categories—existence, relatedness, and growth

The ERG Theory   In response to these and similar criticisms, an alternative hierarchy of needs called the **ERG theory of motivation** was developed.[10] This theory collapses the need hierarchy developed by Maslow into three levels. *Existence needs* correspond to the physiological and security needs. *Relatedness needs* focus on how people relate to their social environment. In Maslow's hierarchy, they would encompass both the need to belong and the need to earn the esteem of others. *Growth needs*, the highest level in the ERG schema, include the needs for self-esteem and self-actualization.

Although the ERG theory assumes that motivated behavior follows a hierarchy in somewhat the same fashion as suggested by Maslow, there are two important differences. First, the ERG theory suggests that more than one level of need can cause motivation at the same time. For example, it suggests that people can be motivated by a desire for money (existence), friendship (relatedness), and the opportunity to learn new skills (growth) all at once. Second, the ERG theory has what has been called a *frustration-regression* element. Thus, if needs remain unsatisfied, the individual will become frustrated, regress to a lower level, and begin to pursue

Both Maslow's hierarchy of needs and the ERG theory of motivation suggest that people will be motivated by opportunities for personal growth and development. Take Darien Dash, for example, the first African American to take a dot-com public. Throughout his life he has been motivated to learn new skills, develop new competencies, and explore new opportunities. And now that he has achieved success, he is working just as hard to help others succeed by providing computers, computer training, and Internet access to urban youth who otherwise might not be able to afford them.

those needs again. For example, a worker previously motivated by money (existence needs) may have just been awarded a pay raise sufficient to satisfy those needs. Suppose that he then attempts to establish more friendships to satisfy relatedness needs. If, for some reason, he finds that it is impossible to become better friends with others in the workplace, he eventually gets frustrated and regresses to being motivated to earn even more money.

The Two-Factor Theory

Another popular content perspective is the **two-factor theory of motivation**.[11] Frederick Herzberg developed his theory by interviewing 200 accountants and engineers. He asked them to recall occasions when they had been satisfied and motivated and occasions when they had been dissatisfied and unmotivated. Surprisingly, he found that different sets of factors were associated with satisfaction and with dissatisfaction—that is, a person might identify "low pay" as causing dissatisfaction but would not necessarily mention "high pay" as a cause of satisfaction. Instead, different factors—such as recognition or accomplishment—were cited as causing satisfaction and motivation.

This finding led Herzberg to conclude that the traditional view of job satisfaction was incomplete. That view assumed that satisfaction and dissatisfaction are at opposite ends of a single continuum. People might be satisfied, dissatisfied, or somewhere in between. But Herzberg's interviews had identified two different dimensions altogether: one ranging from satisfaction to no satisfaction and the other ranging from dissatisfaction to no dissatisfaction. This perspective, along with several examples of factors that affect each continuum, is shown in Figure 16.3. Note that the factors influencing the satisfaction continuum—called motivation factors—are related specifically to the work content. The factors presumed to cause dissatisfaction—called hygiene factors—are related to the work environment.

two-factor theory of motivation
Suggests that people's satisfaction and dissatisfaction are influenced by two independent sets of factors—motivation factors and hygiene factors

Figure 16.3

The Two-Factor Theory of Motivation

The two-factor theory suggests that job satisfaction has two dimensions. A manager who tries to motivate an employee using only hygiene factors such as pay and good working conditions will likely not succeed. To motivate employees and produce a high level of satisfaction, managers must also offer factors such as responsibility and the opportunity for advancement (motivation factors).

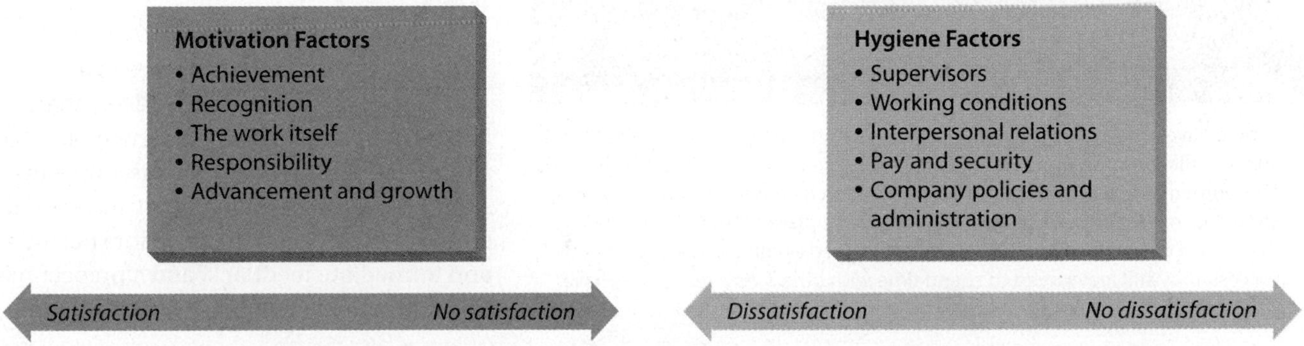

Motivation Factors
- Achievement
- Recognition
- The work itself
- Responsibility
- Advancement and growth

Satisfaction ←——————→ *No satisfaction*

Hygiene Factors
- Supervisors
- Working conditions
- Interpersonal relations
- Pay and security
- Company policies and administration

Dissatisfaction ←——————→ *No dissatisfaction*

Based on these findings, Herzberg argues that there are two stages in the process of motivating employees. First, managers must ensure that the hygiene factors are not deficient. Pay and security must be appropriate, working conditions must be safe, technical supervision must be acceptable, and so on. By providing hygiene factors at an appropriate level, managers do not stimulate motivation but merely ensure that employees are "not dissatisfied." Employees whom managers attempt to "satisfy" through hygiene factors alone will usually do just enough to get by. Thus, managers should proceed to stage two—giving employees the opportunity to experience motivation factors such as achievement and recognition. The result is predicted to be a high level of satisfaction and motivation. Herzberg also goes a step farther than most theorists and describes exactly how to use the two-factor theory in the workplace. Specifically, he recommends job enrichment, as discussed in Chapter 11. He argues that jobs should be redesigned to provide higher levels of the motivation factors.

Although widely accepted by many managers, Herzberg's two-factor theory is not without its critics. One criticism is that the findings in Herzberg's initial interviews are subject to different explanations. Another charge is that his sample was not representative of the general population and that subsequent research often failed to uphold the theory.[12] At the present time, Herzberg's theory is not held in high esteem by researchers in the field. The theory has had a major impact on managers, however, and has played a key role in increasing their awareness of motivation and its importance in the workplace.

Individual Human Needs

In addition to these theories, research has also focused on specific individual human needs that are important in organizations. *Managing in an e-Business World* summarizes how some dot.com businesses are finding Los Angeles to be an especially attractive location for helping employees meet diverse needs. The three most important individual needs are achievement, affiliation, and power.[13]

The **need for achievement**, the best known of the three, is the desire to accomplish a goal or task more effectively than in the past. People with a high need for achievement have a desire to assume personal responsibility, a tendency to set moderately difficult goals, a desire for specific and immediate feedback, and a preoccupation with their task. David C. McClelland,

People have a variety of individual needs, including the needs for achievement and for affiliation. This group of women, for example, clearly reflects both needs. The women are successful venture capitalists in California's Silicon Valley. Their individual needs for achievement have no doubt played a significant role in their climb to success. But while each has attained a high degree of personal success, they still feel a need to spend time with others. As a result, they have started a weekly poker match just to get together and have fun.

MANAGING IN AN *e*-BUSINESS WORLD

LOS ANGELES CULTURE MOTIVATES DOT-COM START-UPS

Although California's Silicon Valley has built a global reputation as an e-business epicenter, Los Angeles is fast becoming a hot location for dot-coms interested in attracting and motivating top industry talent. Why Los Angeles? E-business entrepreneurs and employees clearly want more than a good pay package, stock options, and a pleasant workspace; many are motivated by higher-order needs such as belongingness, esteem, and self-actualization. Los Angeles offers more opportunities to feel part of a vibrant entertainment culture, rub shoulders with Hollywood people, and party or surf with tech types from some of the best-known start-ups on the Web.

A growing number of e-businesses have sprung up in and around Los Angeles, including eToys, Stamps.com, and idealab! Stuart Levy, founder of Mixx Entertainment, chose Los Angeles because of the stimulation provided by its unique blend of multimedia and high-tech activities. And when Los Angeles–based film and television executives get the urge to run an e-business, they stay in the area to benefit from the creativity of its entertainment culture. For example, Chuck Davis quit Walt Disney to take the helm at BizRate.com, while Bill Keenan left e! Entertainment to head up Swap.com (now Spun.com)—both are located in Los Angeles, where they can tap the content talents of local writers and designers and stay in touch with their studio buddies.

Personal contact is high on the list of priorities for e-commerce entrepreneurs as well as employees who spend hour after hour in front of their keyboards. Los Angeles boasts numerous grassroots networking groups where web-savvy employees can mingle, share stories, and troll for new projects and job opportunities. Would-be Internet moguls gather at events such as Venice Interactive.com to hear advice from knowledgeable speakers and to trade business cards. For these e-business participants, Los Angeles is definitely the place to be.

> *For me, content and entertainment are so much a part of what I'm about, and there's no other city, perhaps with the exception of New York, where you can get this combination of multimedia and the Internet.*
>
> *—Stuart Levy, founder of Mixx Entertainment**

Reference: Peter Gumbel and Rick Wartzman, "E-covery: Los Angeles Gets Back Its Groove As the Web Discovers Hollywood," *Wall Street Journal,* January 5, 2000, pp. A1, A12 (*quote on p. A1).

---

the psychologist who first identified this need, argues that only about 10 percent of the U.S. population has a high need for achievement. In contrast, almost 25 percent of the workers in Japan have a high need for achievement.

The **need for affiliation** is less well understood. Like Maslow's belongingness need, the need for affiliation is a desire for human companionship and acceptance. People with a strong need for affiliation are likely to prefer (and perform better in) a job that entails a lot of social interaction and offers opportunities to make friends. The need for power has also received considerable attention as an important ingredient in managerial success.

The **need for power** is the desire to be influential in a group and to control one's environment. Research has shown that people with a strong need for power are likely to be superior performers, have good attendance records, and occupy supervisory positions. One study found that managers as a group tend to have a stronger power motive than the general population and that successful managers tend to have stronger power motives than less successful managers.[14]

need for achievement The desire to accomplish a goal or task more effectively than in the past

need for affiliation The desire for human companionship and acceptance

need for power The desire to be influential in a group and to control one's environment

MANAGEMENT Managers should remember that Maslow's need hierarchy; the
IMPLICATIONS ERG theory; the two-factor theory; and the needs for achievement, affiliation, and power all provide useful insights into factors that cause motivation. What they do not do is shed much light on the process of motivation. They do not explain why people might be motivated by one factor rather than by another at a given level or how people might go about trying to satisfy the different needs. These questions involve behaviors or actions, goals, and feelings of satisfaction—concepts that are addressed by various process perspectives on motivation.

Process Perspectives on Motivation

process perspectives Approaches to motivation that focus on why people choose certain behavioral options to satisfy their needs and how they evaluate their satisfaction after they have attained these goals

Process perspectives are concerned with how motivation occurs. Rather than attempting to identify motivational stimuli, **process perspectives** focus on why people choose certain behavioral options to satisfy their needs and how they evaluate their satisfaction after they have attained these goals. Three useful process perspectives on motivation are the expectancy, equity, and goal-setting theories.

Expectancy Theory

expectancy theory Suggests that motivation depends on two things—how much we want something and how likely we think we are to get it

Expectancy theory suggests that motivation depends on two things—how much we want something and how likely we think we are to get it.[15] Assume that you are approaching graduation and looking for a job. You see in the want ads that General Motors is seeking a new vice president with a starting salary of $500,000 per year. Even though you might want the job, you will not apply because you realize that you have little chance of getting it. The next ad you see is for someone to scrape bubble gum from underneath theater seats for a starting salary of $6 an hour. Even though you could probably get this job, you do not apply because you do not want it. Then you see an ad for a management trainee at a big company with a starting salary of $35,000. You will probably apply for this job because you want it and because you think you have a reasonable chance of getting it.

Expectancy theory rests on four basic assumptions. First, it assumes that behavior is determined by a combination of forces in the individual and in the environment; second, that people make decisions about their own behavior in organizations; third, that different people have different types of needs, desires, and goals; and fourth, that people make choices from among alternative plans of behavior based on their perceptions of the extent to which a given behavior will lead to desired outcomes.

Figure 16.4 summarizes the basic expectancy model. The model suggests that motivation leads to effort and that effort, combined with employee ability and environmental factors, results in performance. Performance, in turn, leads to various outcomes, each of which has an associated value called its valence. The most important parts of the expectancy model cannot be shown in the figure, however. These important parts are the individual's expectation that effort will lead to high

Figure 16.4

The Expectancy Model of Motivation

The expectancy model of motivation is a complex but relatively accurate portrayal of how motivation occurs. According to this model, a manager must understand what employees want (such as pay, promotions, or status) to begin to motivate them.

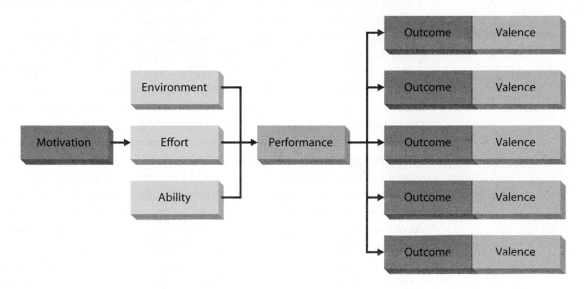

performance, that performance will lead to outcomes, and that each outcome will have some kind of value.

Effort-to-Performance Expectancy The **effort-to-performance expectancy** is the individual's perception of the probability that his or her effort will lead to high performance. When the individual believes that effort will lead directly to high performance, expectancy will be quite strong (a probability close to 1.00). When the individual believes that effort and performance are unrelated, the effort-to-performance expectancy is very weak (a probability close to 0.00). The belief that effort is somewhat but not strongly related to performance carries with it a moderate expectancy (a probability somewhere between 0.00 and 1.00).

Performance-to-Outcome Expectancy The **performance-to-outcome expectancy** is the individual's perception that her or his performance will lead to a specific outcome. For example, if the individual believes that high performance will result in a pay raise, the performance-to-outcome expectancy is high (a probability approaching 1.00). The individual who believes that high performance may lead to a pay raise has a moderate expectancy (a probability between 1.00 and 0.00). The individual who believes that performance has no relationship with rewards has a low performance-to-outcome expectancy (a probability close to 0.00).

Outcomes and Valences Expectancy theory recognizes that an individual's behavior results in a variety of **outcomes**, or consequences, in an organizational setting. A high performer, for example, may get bigger pay raises, faster promotions,

effort-to-performance expectancy The individual's perception of the probability that his or her effort will lead to high performance

performance-to-outcome expectancy The individual's perception that her or his performance will lead to a specific outcome

outcomes Consequences of behaviors in an organizational setting, usually rewards

valence An index of how much an individual values a particular outcome; it is the attractiveness of the outcome to the individual

and more praise from the boss. On the other hand, she may also be subject to more stress and incur resentment from coworkers. Each of these outcomes also has an associated value, or **valence**—an index of how much an individual values a particular outcome. If the individual wants the outcome, its valence is positive; if the individual does not want the outcome, its valence is negative; and if the individual is indifferent to the outcome, its valence is zero.

This part of expectancy theory goes beyond the content perspectives on motivation. Different people have different needs, and they will try to satisfy these needs in different ways. For an employee who has a high need for achievement and a low need for affiliation, the pay raise and promotions cited above as outcomes of high performance might have positive valences, the praise and resentment might have zero valences, and the stress might have a negative valence. For a different employee with a low need for achievement and a high need for affiliation, the pay raise, promotions, and praise might all have positive valences, whereas both resentment and stress could have negative valences.

For motivated behavior to occur, three conditions must be met. First, the effort-to-performance expectancy must be greater than zero (the individual must believe that if effort is expended, high performance will result). The performance-to-outcome expectancy must also be greater than zero (the individual must believe that if high performance is achieved, certain outcomes will follow). And the sum of the valences for the outcomes must be greater than zero. One or more outcomes may have negative valences, but they are offset by the greater absolute value of the positive valences of other outcomes. For example, the attractiveness of a pay raise, a promotion, and praise from the boss may outweigh the unattractiveness of more stress and resentment from coworkers. Expectancy theory suggests that when these conditions are met, the individual is motivated to expend effort.

Starbucks credits its unique stock ownership program with maintaining a dedicated and motivated workforce. Based on the fundamental concepts of expectancy theory, Starbucks employees earn stock as a function of their seniority and performance. Thus, their hard work helps them earn shares of ownership in the company.[16] *Today's Management Issues* explores the role of executive stock options from an expectancy theory perspective.

The Porter-Lawler Extension An interesting extension of expectancy theory has been proposed by Porter and Lawler.[17] Recall from Chapter 2 that the human relationists assumed that employee satisfaction causes high performance. We also noted that research has not supported such a relationship. Porter and Lawler suggest that there may indeed be a relationship between satisfaction and performance, but that it goes in the opposite direction—that is, high performance may lead to high satisfaction. Figure 16.5 summarizes Porter and Lawler's logic. Performance results in rewards for an individual. Some of these are extrinsic (such as pay and promotions); others are intrinsic (such as self-esteem and accomplishment). The individual evaluates the equity, or fairness, of the rewards relative to the effort expended and the level of performance attained. If the rewards are perceived to be equitable, the individual is satisfied.

Equity Theory

After needs have stimulated the motivation process and the individual has chosen an action that is expected to satisfy those needs, the individual assesses the fairness, or equity, of the resultant outcome. **Equity theory** contends that people are motivated to seek social equity in the rewards they receive for performance.[18] Equity is an individual's belief that the treatment he or she receives is fair relative to the treatment received by others. According to equity theory, outcomes from a job include pay, recognition, promotions, social relationships, and intrinsic rewards. To get these rewards, the individual gives inputs to the job, such as time, experience, effort, education, and loyalty. The theory suggests that people view their outcomes and inputs as a ratio and then compare it to the ratio of someone else. This other "person" may be someone in the work group or some sort of group average or composite. The process of comparison looks like this:

$$\frac{\text{outcomes (self)}}{\text{inputs (self)}} = \frac{\text{outcomes (other)}}{\text{inputs (other)}}$$

Both the formulation of the ratios and the comparisons between them are very subjective and are based on individual perceptions. As a result of comparisons, three conditions may result: the individual may feel equitably rewarded, underrewarded, or overrewarded. A feeling of equity will result when the two ratios are equal. This situation may occur even though the other person's outcomes are greater than the individual's own outcomes—provided that the other's inputs are also proportionately greater. Suppose that Mark has a high school education and earns $30,000. He may still feel equitably treated relative to Susan, who earns $35,000, because she has a college degree.

People who feel underrewarded try to reduce the inequity. Such individuals might decrease their inputs by exerting less effort, increasing their outcomes by asking for a raise, distorting the original ratios by rationalizing, trying to get the other person to change her or his outcomes or inputs, leaving the situation, or changing the object of comparison. An individual may also feel overrewarded relative to another person. This situation is not likely to be terribly disturbing to

equity theory Suggests that people are motivated to seek social equity in the rewards they receive for performance

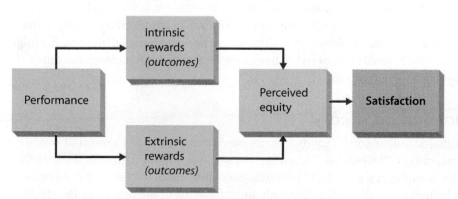

Figure 16.5

The Porter-Lawler Extension of Expectancy Theory

The Porter-Lawler extension of expectancy theory suggests that if performance results in equitable rewards, people will be more satisfied. Thus, performance can lead to satisfaction. Managers must therefore be sure that any system of motivation includes rewards that are fair, or equitable, for all.

Source: Edward E. Lawler III and Lyman W. Porter, "The Effect of Performance on Job Satisfaction," *Industrial Relations,* October 1967, p. 23. Used with permission of the University of California.

TODAY'S MANAGEMENT ISSUES

USING OPTIONS TO REWARD PERFORMANCE AT THE TOP

Managerial performance is measured in many ways against many goals. At publicly traded companies, the long-term trend of the stock price is a key bottom-line measure of top management's performance. As a result, many companies reward CEOs and senior managers with stock options: the right to buy a certain number of shares at a discount after the stock has reached or exceeded a target price. Once the stock price rises to the target level, these managers can buy shares at the discounted price and sell them for an immediate profit. During a bull market, when share prices are generally on the rise, top managers have a higher expectation that their efforts will result in high performance, as reflected in higher stock prices.

Now some executive pay experts are calling for a switch to indexed stock options as a way of linking rewards for top management performance to a more specific outcome standard. The purpose of indexed stock options is to reward performance relative to the performance of a specific industry group or a particular market index. For example, a company might grant options that the CEO can exercise if the stock price moves higher than the Dow Jones Industrial Average or a specific industry grouping within that average. If the company's stock doesn't beat that index, the CEO can't profit from the options.

Proponents say indexed stock options offer top managers sizable rewards for solid performance as reflected in stock prices that exceed a preset target. Even in a bear market, when share prices are generally on the decline, top managers can still expect to profit if their company's share price remains above that of its peers. At the same time, underperforming CEOs will feel the financial pinch if they don't boost performance in a way that is ultimately reflected in the stock price. On the other hand, indexed stock options require complicated accounting measures and entail greater risk, which is why few firms use them. Still, shareholder groups and pension funds are pushing for indexed stock options—and CEOs may embrace them if the stock market swoons, making traditional options valueless.

> *Indexed options hold the executive to a higher standard.*
>
> —*Robin A. Ferracone, chairman, SCA Consulting**

Reference: Jennifer Reingold, "An Options Plan Your CEO Hates," *Business Week*, February 28, 2000, pp. 82–88 (*quote on p. 82).

---

most people, but research suggests that some people who experience inequity under these conditions are somewhat motivated to reduce it. Under such a circumstance, the person might increase his inputs by exerting more effort, reducing his outcomes by producing fewer units (if paid on a per-unit basis), distorting the original ratios by rationalizing, or trying to reduce the inputs or to increase the outcomes of the other person.

Goal-Setting Theory

The goal-setting theory of motivation assumes that behavior is a result of conscious goals and intentions.[19] Therefore, by setting goals for people in the organization, a manager should be able to influence their behavior. Given this premise, the challenge is to develop a thorough understanding of the processes by which people set goals and then work to reach them. In the original version of goal-setting theory, two specific goal characteristics—goal difficulty and goal specificity—were expected to shape performance.

Goal Difficulty   *Goal difficulty* is the extent to which a goal is challenging and requires effort. If people work to achieve goals, it is reasonable to assume they will work harder to achieve more difficult goals. But a goal must not be so difficult that it is unattainable. If a new manager asks her sales force to increase sales by 300 percent, the group may become disillusioned. A more realistic but still difficult goal—perhaps a 30 percent increase—would be a better incentive. A substantial body of research supports the importance of goal difficulty. In one study, for example, managers at Weyerhauser set difficult goals for truck drivers hauling loads of timber from cutting sites to wood yards. Over a nine-month period, the drivers increased the quantity of wood they delivered by an amount that would have required $250,000 worth of new trucks at the previous per-truck average load.[20]

Goal Specificity   *Goal specificity* is the clarity and precision of the goal. A goal of "increasing productivity" is not very specific; a goal of "increasing productivity by 3 percent in the next six months" is quite specific. Some goals, such as those involving costs, output, profitability, and growth, are readily amenable to specificity. Other goals, however, such as improving employee job satisfaction, morale, company image and reputation, ethics, and socially responsible behavior, may be much harder to state in specific terms. Like difficulty, specificity has also been shown to be consistently related to performance. The study of timber truck drivers mentioned above, for example, also examined goal specificity. The initial loads the truck drivers were carrying were found to be 60 percent of the maximum weight each truck could haul. The managers set a new goal for drivers of 94 percent, which the drivers were soon able to reach. Thus, the goal was both specific and difficult.

Because the theory attracted so much widespread interest and research support from researchers and managers alike, an expanded model of the goal-setting process was eventually proposed. The expanded model, shown in Figure 16.6, attempts to capture more fully the complexities of goal setting in organizations.

Figure 16.6

The Expanded Goal-Setting Theory of Motivation

One of the most important emerging theories of motivation is goal-setting theory. This theory suggests that goal difficulty, specificity, acceptance, and commitment combine to determine an individual's goal-directed effort. This effort, when complemented by appropriate organizational support and individual abilities and traits, results in performance. Finally, performance is seen as leading to intrinsic and extrinsic rewards that, in turn, result in employee satisfaction.

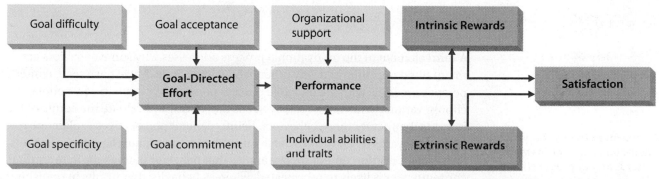

Source: Reprinted, from *Organizational Dynamics*, Autumn 1979, Gary P. Latham and Edwin A. Locke, "A Motivational Technique That Works," p. 79, copyright © 1979 with permission from Elsevier Science.

The expanded theory argues that goal-directed effort is a function of four goal attributes: difficulty and specificity, as already discussed, and acceptance and commitment. *Goal acceptance* is the extent to which a person accepts a goal as his or her own. *Goal commitment* is the extent to which she or he is personally interested in reaching the goal. The manager who vows to take whatever steps are necessary to cut costs by 10 percent has made a commitment to achieve the goal. Factors that can foster goal acceptance and commitment include participating in the goal-setting process, making goals challenging but realistic, and believing that goal achievement will lead to valued rewards.

The interaction of goal-directed effort, organizational support, and individual abilities and traits determine actual performance. Organizational support is whatever the organization does to help or hinder performance. Positive support might mean making available adequate personnel and a sufficient supply of raw materials; negative support might mean failing to fix damaged equipment. Individual abilities and traits are the skills and other personal characteristics necessary for doing a job. As a result of performance, a person receives various intrinsic and extrinsic rewards, which in turn influence satisfaction. Note that the latter stages of this model are quite similar to the Porter and Lawler expectancy model discussed earlier.

MANAGEMENT IMPLICATIONS Expectancy theory can be useful for managers who are trying to improve the motivation of their subordinates. A series of steps can be followed to implement the basic ideas of the theory. First, figure out the outcomes each employee is likely to want. Second, decide what kinds and levels of performance are needed to meet organizational goals. Then make sure that the desired levels of performance are attainable. Also make sure that desired outcomes and desired performance are linked. Next, analyze the complete situation for conflicting expectancies, and ensure that the rewards are large enough. Finally, make sure the total system is equitable (fair to all). The single most important idea for managers to remember from equity theory is that if rewards are to motivate employees, they must be perceived as being equitable and fair. A second implication that managers need to consider is the nature of the "other" to whom the employee is comparing her- or himself. Goal-setting theory can be used to implement both expectancy and equity theory concepts.

Reinforcement Perspectives on Motivation

A third element of the motivational process addresses why some behaviors are maintained over time and why other behaviors change. As we have seen, content perspectives deal with needs, while process perspectives explain why people choose various behaviors to satisfy needs and how they evaluate the equity of the rewards they get for those behaviors. Reinforcement perspectives explain the role of those rewards as they cause behavior to change or remain the same over time. Specifically, **reinforcement theory** argues that behavior that results in rewarding consequences is likely to be repeated, whereas behavior that results in punishing consequences is less likely to be repeated.[21]

reinforcement theory Approach to motivation that explains the role of rewards as they cause behavior to change or remain the same over time

Kinds of Reinforcement in Organizations

There are four basic kinds of reinforcement that can result from behavior—positive reinforcement, avoidance, punishment, and extinction.[22] These four concepts are summarized in Table 16.1. Two kinds of reinforcement strengthen or maintain behavior, whereas the other two weaken or decrease behavior.

Positive reinforcement, a method of strengthening behavior, is a reward or a positive outcome after a desired behavior is performed. When a manager observes an employee doing an especially good job and offers praise, the praise serves as a positive way to reinforce the behavior of good work. Other positive reinforcers in organizations include pay raises, promotions, and awards. Employees who work at General Electric's customer service center receive clothing, sporting goods, and even trips to Disney World as rewards for outstanding performance. The other method of strengthening desired behavior is through **avoidance**. An employee may come to work on time to avoid a reprimand. In this instance, the employee is motivated to perform the behavior of punctuality to avoid an unpleasant consequence that is likely to follow tardiness.

Punishment is used by some managers to weaken undesired behaviors. When an employee is loafing, coming to work late, doing poor work, or interfering with the work of others, the manager might resort to reprimands, discipline, or fines. The logic is that the unpleasant consequence will reduce the likelihood that the employee will choose that particular behavior again. Given the counterproductive side effects of punishment (such as resentment and hostility), it is often advisable to use the other kinds of reinforcement if at all possible. **Extinction** can also be used to weaken behavior, especially behavior that has previously been rewarded. When an employee tells an off-color joke and the boss laughs, the laughter reinforces the behavior and the employee may continue to tell off-color jokes. By

positive reinforcement A method of strengthening behavior with rewards or positive outcomes after a desired behavior is performed

avoidance Used to strengthen behavior by avoiding unpleasant consequences that would result if the behavior were not performed

punishment Used to weaken undesired behaviors by using negative outcomes or unpleasant consequences when the behavior is performed

extinction Used to weaken undesired behaviors by simply ignoring or not reinforcing that behavior

Table 16.1
Elements of Reinforcement Theory
A manager who wants the best chance of reinforcing a behavior would likely offer the employee a positive reinforcement after a variable number of behaviors (variable-ratio reinforcement). For example, the manager could praise the employee after the third credit card application was received. Additional praise might be offered after the next five applications, then again after the next three, the next seven, the next four, and so on.

Arrangement of the Reinforcement Contingencies	
1. **Positive reinforcement.** Strengthens behavior by providing a desirable consequence.	3. **Punishment.** Weakens behavior by providing an undesirable consequence.
2. **Avoidance.** Strengthens behavior by allowing escape from an undesirable consequence.	4. **Extinction.** Weakens behavior by not providing a desirable consequence.
Schedules for Applying Reinforcement	
1. **Fixed Interval.** Reinforcement applied at fixed time intervals, regardless of behavior.	3. **Fixed Ratio.** Reinforcement applied after a fixed number of behaviors, regardless of time.
2. **Variable interval.** Reinforcement applied at variable time intervals.	4. **Variable ratio.** Reinforcement applied after a variable number of behaviors.

simply ignoring this behavior and not reinforcing it, the boss can cause the behavior to subside and eventually become "extinct."

Providing Reinforcement in Organizations

Not only is the kind of reinforcement important, but so is when or how often it occurs. Various strategies are possible for providing reinforcement. These strategies are also listed in Table 16.1. The **fixed-interval schedule** provides reinforcement at fixed intervals of time, regardless of behavior. A good example of this schedule is the weekly or monthly paycheck. This method provides the least incentive for good work because employees know they will be paid regularly regardless of their effort. A **variable-interval schedule** also uses time as the basis for reinforcement, but the time interval varies from one reinforcement to the next. This schedule is appropriate for praise or other rewards based on visits or inspections. When employees do not know when the boss will drop by, they tend to maintain a reasonably high level of effort all the time.

A **fixed-ratio schedule** gives reinforcement after a fixed number of behaviors, regardless of the time that elapses between behaviors. This kind of reinforcement results in an even higher level of effort. For example, when Sears is recruiting new credit-card customers, salespersons get a small bonus for every fifth application returned from their department. Under this arrangement, motivation will be high because each application gets the person closer to the next bonus. The **variable-ratio schedule**, the most powerful schedule in terms of maintaining desired behaviors, varies the number of behaviors needed for each reinforcement. A supervisor who praises an employee for her second order, the seventh order after that, the ninth after that, then the fifth, and then the third is using a variable-ratio schedule. The employee is motivated to increase the frequency of the desired behavior because each performance increases the probability of receiving a reward. Of course, a variable-ratio schedule is difficult (if not impossible) to use for formal rewards such as pay because it would be too complicated to keep track of who was rewarded when.

Managers wanting to use reinforcement theory explicitly to motivate their employees generally do so with a technique called **behavior modification**, or **OB Mod**.[23] An OB Mod program starts by specifying behaviors to be increased (such as producing more units) or decreased (such as coming to work late). These target behaviors are then tied to specific forms of reinforcement. Although many organizations (such as Procter & Gamble and Ford) have used OB Mod, the best-known application was at Emery Air Freight. Management felt that the containers used to consolidate small shipments into fewer, larger shipments were not being packed efficiently. Through a system of self-monitored feedback and rewards, Emery increased container usage from 45 percent to 95 percent and saved over $3 million during the first three years of the program.[24]

MANAGEMENT IMPLICATIONS Managers should be familiar with the role of reinforcement in motivation. Specifically, they should understand how various forms of reinforcement affect behavior and the different schedules that can be used to provide reinforcement.

---

fixed-interval schedules Provide reinforcement at fixed intervals of time, such as regular weekly pay checks

variable-interval schedules Provide reinforcement at varying intervals of time, such as occasional visits by the supervisor

fixed-ratio schedules Provide reinforcement after a fixed number of behaviors, regardless of the time that elapses between behaviors, such as a bonus for every fifth sale

variable-ratio schedules Provide reinforcement after varying numbers of behaviors are performed, such as the use of compliments by a supervisor on an irregular basis

behavior modification or **OB Mod** Method for applying the basic elements of reinforcement theory in an organizational setting

■ *Popular Motivational Strategies*

While these theories provide a solid explanation for motivation, managers must use various techniques and strategies to apply them. Among the most popular motivational strategies today are empowerment and participation and alternative forms of work arrangements.

Empowerment and Participation

Empowerment and participation represent important methods that managers can use to enhance employee motivation. **Empowerment** is the process of enabling workers to set their own work goals, make decisions, and solve problems within their sphere of responsibility and authority. **Participation** is the process of giving employees a voice in making decisions about their own work. Thus, empowerment is a somewhat broader concept that promotes participation in a wide variety of areas, including but not limited to work itself, work context, and work environment.[25]

The role of participation and empowerment in motivation can be expressed in terms of both the content perspectives and the expectancy theory. Employees who participate in decision making may be more committed to executing decisions properly. Furthermore, the successful process of making a decision, executing it, and then seeing the positive consequences can help satisfy one's need for achievement, provide recognition and responsibility, and enhance self-esteem. Simply being asked to participate in organizational decision making may also enhance an employee's self-esteem. In addition, participation should help clarify expectancies; that is, by participating in decision making, employees may better understand the link between their performance and the rewards they want most.

empowerment The process of enabling workers to set their own work goals, make decisions, and solve problems within their sphere of responsibility and authority

participation The process of giving employees a voice in making decisions about their own work

Areas of Participation At one level, employees can participate in addressing questions and making decisions about their own jobs. Instead of just telling them how to do their jobs, for example, managers can ask employees to make their own decisions about how to do them. Based on their own expertise and experience with their tasks, workers might be able to improve their own productivity. In many situations, they might also be well qualified to make decisions about what materials to use, what tools to use, and so forth.

It might also be helpful to let workers make decisions about administrative matters, such as work schedules. If jobs are relatively independent of one another, employees might decide when to change shifts, take breaks, go to lunch, and so forth. A work group or team might also be able to schedule vacations and days off for all its members. Furthermore, employees are getting more opportunities to participate in broader issues of product quality. Such participation has become a hallmark of successful Japanese and other international firms, and many U.S. companies have followed suit.

Techniques and Issues in Empowerment In recent years many organizations have actively sought ways to extend participation beyond the traditional areas. Simple techniques such as suggestion boxes and question-and-answer meetings allow a certain degree of participation, for example. The basic motive has been to capitalize to a larger extent on the assets and capabilities inherent in all employees. Thus, many managers today prefer the term *empowerment* to *participation* because of its more comprehensive character.

One method used to empower workers is the use of work teams. Such teams are collections of employees empowered to plan, organize, direct, and control their own work. Rather than being a traditional "boss," their supervisor plays more the role of a coach. The other method for empowerment is to change their overall method of organizing. The basic pattern is for an organization to eliminate layers from its hierarchy, thereby becoming much more decentralized. Power, responsibility, and authority are delegated as far down the organization as possible, placing the control over work squarely in the hands of those who actually do it.[26]

Regardless of the specific technique or method used, empowerment will enhance organizational effectiveness only if certain conditions exist. First of all, the organization must be sincere in its efforts to spread power and autonomy to lower levels of the organization. Token efforts to promote participation in only a few areas are not likely to succeed. Second, the organization must be committed to maintaining participation and empowerment. Workers will be resentful if they are given more control, only to later have it reduced or taken away altogether. Third, the organization must be systematic and patient in its efforts to empower workers. Turning over too much control too quickly can spell disaster. And finally, the organization must be prepared to increase its commitment to training. Employees being given more freedom in how they work will quite likely need additional training to help them exercise that freedom most effectively.[27]

New Forms of Working Arrangements

Many organizations today are also experimenting with several alternative work arrangements. These alternative arrangements are generally intended to enhance employee motivation and performance by providing them with greater flexibility in how and when they work. Among the more popular alternative work arrangements are variable work schedules, flexible work schedules, job sharing, and telecommuting.[28]

Variable Work Schedules While there are many exceptions, of course, the traditional work schedule starts at 8:00 or 9:00 in the morning and ends at 5:00 in the evening, five days a week. (Of course, many managers work many additional hours outside these times.) Unfortunately, this schedule makes it difficult to attend to routine personal business—going to the bank, seeing a doctor or a dentist for a routine checkup, attending a parent-teacher conference, getting an automobile serviced, and so forth. At a surface level, then, employees locked into this sort of an arrangement may find it necessary to take a sick or vacation day to handle these activities. At a more unconscious level, some people may also feel so powerless and constrained by their job schedule as to grow resentful and frustrated.

To help counter these problems, some businesses have adopted a **compressed work schedule**, working a full forty-hour week in fewer than the traditional five days.[29] One approach involves working ten hours a day for four days, leaving an extra day off. Another alternative is for employees to work slightly less than ten hours a day but to complete the forty hours by lunchtime on Friday. And a few firms have tried allowing employees to work twelve hours a day for three days, followed by four days off. Organizations that have used these forms of compressed workweeks include John Hancock, BP Amoco, and Philip Morris.

Flexible work schedules can be a powerful motivational strategy. Consider, for example, Tina Willford and her employer, First Tennessee Bank. The bank allows Willford to leave work early each day so that she can spend time with her young children. She makes up the time after her children are in bed. First Tennessee considers Willford to be a rising star and is interested in doing whatever it can to both motivate her and keep her satisfied.

One problem with this schedule is that when employees put in too much time in a single day, they tend to get tired and perform at a lower level later in the day.

A schedule that some organizations today are beginning to use is called a "nine-eighty" schedule. Under this arrangement, an employee works a traditional schedule one week and a compressed schedule the next, getting every other Friday off. That is, they work eighty hours (the equivalent of two weeks of full-time work) in nine days. By alternating the regular and compressed schedules across half its workforce, the organization can be fully staffed at all times while still giving employees two full days off each month. Shell Oil and Amoco Chemicals are two of the firms that currently use this schedule.

Flexible Work Schedules   Another promising alternative work arrangement is **flexible work schedules**, sometimes called **flextime**. Flextime gives employees more personal control over the times they work. The workday is broken down into two categories, flexible time and core time. All employees must be at their workstations during core time, but they can choose their own schedules during flexible time. Thus, one employee may choose to start work early in the morning and leave in midafternoon; another to start in the late morning and work until late afternoon; and still another to start early in the morning, take a long lunch break, and work until late afternoon. Organizations that have used the flexible work schedule method for arranging work include Hewlett-Packard, Compaq Computer, Microsoft, and Texas Instruments.

compressed work schedule
Working a full forty-hour week in fewer than the traditional five days
flexible work schedules or **flextime**   Allowing employees to select, within broad parameters, the hours they work

Job Sharing   Yet another potentially useful alternative work arrangement is job sharing. In **job sharing**, two part-time employees share one full-time job. One person may perform the job from 8:00 A.M. to noon and the other from 1:00 P.M. to 5:00 P.M. Job sharing may be desirable for people who want to work only part-time or

job sharing   When two part-time employees share one full-time job

when job markets are tight. For its part, the organization can accommodate the preferences of a broader range of employees and may benefit from the talents of more people.

telecommuting Allowing employees to spend part of their time working off-site, usually at home, by using e-mail, the Internet, and other forms of information technology

Telecommuting   A relatively new approach to alternative work arrangements is **telecommuting**—allowing employees to spend part of their time working off-site, usually at home. By using e-mail, the Internet, and other forms of information technology, many employees can maintain close contact with their organization and get just as much work done at home as they can at the office. The increased power and sophistication of modern communication technology is making telecommuting easier and easier.

MANAGEMENT
IMPLICATIONS   Managers need to be familiar with various motivation strategies and techniques that can be used to improve performance. Empowerment, participation, and various alternative work arrangements should each be understood by managers interested in enhancing the motivation of their subordinates.

■ *Using Reward Systems to Motivate Performance*

"I think I should warn you that the flip side of our generous bonus-incentive program is capital punishment."

Organizations provide rewards and incentives that can serve as positive reinforcement to desired behavior. Similarly, most also have various forms of punishment that can be used to weaken or eliminate undesired behaviors. While not as extreme as the humorous example shown here, positive reinforcement and punishment that are clearly linked to desired and undesired behaviors, respectively, can play a major role in boosting employee performance and organizational effectiveness.

Aside from these types of motivational strategies, an organization's reward system is its most basic tool for managing employee motivation. An organizational **reward system** is the formal and informal mechanisms by which employee performance is defined, evaluated, and rewarded. *The World of Management* discusses how managers today can use the Internet to learn more about rewards that their peers are using around the world.

Effects of Organizational Rewards

Organizational rewards can affect attitudes, behaviors, and motivation. Thus, it is important for managers to understand and appreciate clearly their importance.[30]

Effect of Rewards on Attitudes   Although employee attitudes such as satisfaction are not a major determinant of job performance, they are nonetheless important. They contribute to (or discourage) absenteeism and affect turnover, and they help establish the culture of the organization. We can draw four major generalizations about employee atti-

SEARCHING OUT SALARIES AROUND THE WORLD

How can job-seekers, employees, and human resource professionals find the general salary range for a particular position in Harrisburg or Hong Kong? More and more salary information is migrating to the Internet, where it is available to anyone, anywhere in the world. With just a few keystrokes, employees and job candidates can read advice about negotiating salaries and see how pay packages in e-businesses compare with pay packages in traditional industries. Meanwhile, managers can log on and scroll through local, national, and international surveys of salaries in different fields.

Salary.com (http://www.salary.com), for example, presents news about salary trends, offers expert advice about pay and promotion, and allows users to look up salary ranges for job categories in dozens of U.S. metropolitan areas. Monster.com (http://www.monster.com) offers salary comparison data, negotiating tips, and other information on its various country-specific sites. Visitors to the U.K. Monster site (http://salary.monster.co.uk/salary.monster.co.uk) can click to see what a particular position typically pays (in euros, pounds, and other currencies) in different European countries.

Other sites display the results of salary surveys in specific functional areas. *Industry Week* (http://www.industryweek.com), for instance, regularly reports on national and international salary trends in manufacturing positions. Similarly, *Advertising Age* (http://www.adage.com) displays the results of its salary surveys among marketing and advertising specialists.

Easy Internet availability of salary data is helping job candidates negotiate better starting salaries. It's also helping employees support requests for raises at review time. On the company side, on-line salary data helps managers stay abreast of the latest salary trends for all business locations so they can offer competitive pay packages to attract and retain skilled employees. Now managers, applicants, and employees in nearly any country can support discussions about salary issues with objective, up-to-date information gleaned from on-line sources.

> *The information age is so real time, and [employees] keep one eye on where everyone is.*
>
> —*Mike Caggiano, president of FutureNext**

Reference: Stephanie Armour, "Show Me the Money, More Workers Say," *USA Today*, June 6, 2000, p. 1B (*quote on p. 1B).

---

tudes and rewards.[31] First, employee satisfaction is influenced by how much is received and how much the individual thinks should be received. Second, employee satisfaction is affected by comparisons with what happens to others. Third, employees often misperceive the rewards of others. When an employee believes that someone else is making more money than that person really makes, the potential for dissatisfaction increases. Fourth, overall job satisfaction is affected by how satisfied employees are with both the extrinsic and the intrinsic rewards they derive from their jobs. Drawing from the content theories and expectancy theory, this conclusion suggests that several needs may cause behavior and that behavior may be channeled toward various goals.

reward system The formal and informal mechanisms by which employee performance is defined, evaluated, and rewarded

Effect of Rewards on Behaviors An organization's primary purpose in giving rewards is to influence employee behavior. Extrinsic rewards affect employee satisfaction, which, in turn, plays a major role in determining whether an employee

Managers sometimes resort to unusual rewards as a way to retain valuable employees. Mercer Management, a consulting firm, was having trouble holding on to its best consultants, who were beginning to feel a bit restless. Mercer found that some of them were leaving to help implement strategies they had developed for Mercer clients. So, the firm now allows its consultants to take a leave of absence of up to one year to work for other companies. Mercer consultant Gregg Dixon, for example, helped Binney & Smith develop a new strategy for its popular Crayola crayons. He then went to work for Binney & Smith to help implement the strategy. After he has finished, he will return to his old job at Mercer Management.

merit system   A reward system whereby people get different pay raises at the end of the year depending on their overall job performance

will remain on the job or seek a new job. Reward systems also influence patterns of attendance and absenteeism; if rewards are based on actual performance, employees tend to work harder to earn those rewards.

Effect of Rewards on Motivation   Reward systems are clearly related to the expectancy theory of motivation. The effort-to-performance expectancy is strongly influenced by the performance appraisal that is often part of the reward system. An employee is likely to expend extra effort if he or she knows that performance will be measured, evaluated, and rewarded. The performance-to-outcome expectancy is affected by the extent to which the employee believes that performance will be followed by rewards. Finally, as expectancy theory predicts, each reward or potential reward has a somewhat different value for each individual. One person may want a promotion more than benefits; someone else may want just the opposite.

Designing Effective Reward Systems

What are the elements of an effective reward system? Experts agree that they have four major characteristics.[32] First, the reward system must meet the needs of the individual for basic necessities. Next, the rewards should compare favorably with those offered by other organizations. Unfavorable comparisons with people in other settings could result in feelings of inequity. Third, the distribution of rewards within the organization must be fair. And fourth, the reward system must recognize that different people have different needs and choose different paths to satisfy those needs. Both content theories and expectancy theory contribute to this conclusion. Insofar as possible, various rewards and different methods for achieving them should be made available to employees.

Popular Approaches to Rewarding Employees

Organizational reward systems have traditionally been one of two kinds: a fixed hourly or monthly rate or an incentive system. Fixed-rate systems are familiar to most people. Hourly employees are paid a specific wage (based on job demands, experience, or other factors) for each hour they work. Salaried employees receive a fixed sum of money on a weekly or monthly basis. Although some reductions may be made for absences, the salary amount is usually the same regardless of whether the individual works less than or more than a normal amount of time.[33]

From a motivational perspective, such rewards can be tied more directly to performance through merit pay raises. A **merit system** is one whereby people get different pay raises at the end of the year depending on their overall job performance.[34] When the organization's performance appraisal system is appropriately designed, merit pay is an effective system for maintaining long-term performance. Increasingly, however, organizations are experimenting with various kinds of incentive systems. **Incentive systems** attempt to reward employees in proportion to what they do. A piece-rate pay plan is a good example of an incentive system. In a factory manufacturing luggage, for example, each worker may be paid fifty cents for each handle and set of locks installed on a piece of luggage. Hence, there is incentive for the employee to work hard: the more units produced, the higher the pay. Four increasingly popular incentive systems are profit sharing, gain sharing, lump-sum bonuses, and pay-for-knowledge.

Profit sharing provides a varying annual bonus to employees based on corporate profits. This system unites workers and management toward the same goal—higher profits. Ford, Continental Airlines, USX, and Alcoa all have profit-sharing plans. Gain sharing is a group-based incentive system in which group members all get bonuses when predetermined performance levels are exceeded. The lump-sum bonus plan gives each employee a one-time cash bonus, rather than a base salary increase. Finally, pay-for-knowledge systems focus on paying the individual rather than the job.

incentive system A reward system whereby people get different pay amounts at each pay period in proportion to what they do

MANAGEMENT IMPLICATIONS Managers need to know how rewards affect employee attitudes, behaviors, and motivation. In addition, they should know how to design reward systems and be familiar with new approaches to rewarding employees.

Summary of Key Points

Motivation is the set of forces that cause people to behave in certain ways. Motivation is an important consideration for managers because it, along with ability and environmental factors, determines individual performance. Thinking about motivation has evolved from the traditional view through the human relations approach to the human resource view.

Content perspectives on motivation are concerned with what factor or factors cause motivation. Popular content theories include Maslow's need hierarchy, the ERG theory, and Herzberg's two-factor theory. Other important needs are the needs for achievement, affiliation, and power.

Process perspectives on motivation deal with how motivation occurs. Expectancy theory suggests that people are motivated to perform if they believe that their effort will result in high performance, that this performance will lead to

rewards, and that the positive aspects of the outcomes outweigh the negative aspects. Equity theory is based on the premise that people are motivated to achieve and maintain social equity. Attribution theory is a new process theory. Goal-setting theory assumes that behavior is a result of conscious goals and intentions.

The reinforcement perspective focuses on how motivation is maintained. Its basic assumption is that behavior resulting in positive consequences is likely to be repeated, whereas behavior resulting in negative consequences is less likely to be repeated. Reinforcement contingencies can be arranged in the form of positive reinforcement, avoidance, punishment, and extinction, and they can be provided on fixed-interval, variable-interval, fixed-ratio, or variable-ratio schedules.

Two of the most popular motivational strategies today are empowerment and participation and alternative forms of work arrangements. Empowerment is the process of enabling workers to set their own work goals, make decisions, and solve problems within their sphere of responsibility and authority. Participation is the process of giving employees a voice in making decisions about their own work. Common alternative work arrangements include variable work schedules, flexible work schedules, job sharing, and telecommuting.

Organizational reward systems are the primary mechanisms managers have for managing motivation. Properly designed systems can improve attitudes, motivation, and behaviors. Effective reward systems must provide sufficient rewards on an equitable basis at the individual level. Contemporary reward systems include merit systems and various kinds of incentive systems.

Discussion Questions

Questions for Review

1. What were the basic historical perspectives on motivation?
2. Compare and contrast content, process, and reinforcement perspectives on motivation.
3. How are the emerging perspectives on motivation like the content, process, and reinforcement perspectives? How are they different?
4. What are the similarities and differences among the motivational strategies described in this chapter?

Questions for Analysis

5. Compare and contrast the different content theories. Can you think of any ways in which the theories are contradictory?
6. Expectancy theory seems to make a great deal of sense, but it is complicated. Some people argue that its complexity reduces its value to practicing managers. Do you agree or disagree?
7. Offer examples other than those from this chapter to illustrate positive reinforcement, avoidance, punishment, and extinction.

Questions for Application

8. Think about the worst job you have held. What approach to motivation was used in that organization? Now think about the best job you have held. What approach to motivation was used there? Can you base any conclusions on this limited information? If so, what are they?
9. Interview both managers and workers (or administrators and faculty) from a local organization. What views of or approaches to motivation seem to be in use in that organization?
10. Can you find any local organizations that have implemented or are implementing any of the motivational strategies discussed in this chapter? If so, interview a manager and a worker to obtain their views on the program.

BUILDING EFFECTIVE *interpersonal* SKILLS

Exercise Overview

Interpersonal skills—the ability to understand and motivate individuals and groups—are especially critical when managers attempt to deal with issues associated with equity and justice in the workplace. This exercise will provide you with insights into how these skills may be used.

Exercise Background

You are the manager of a group of professional employees in the electronics industry. One of your employees, David Brown, has asked to meet with you. You think you know what David wants to discuss, and you are unsure about how to proceed.

You hired David about ten years ago. During his time in your group, he has been a solid, but not outstanding, employee. His performance, for example, has been satisfactory in every respect, but seldom outstanding. As a result, he has consistently received average performance evaluations, pay increases, and so forth. Indeed, he actually makes somewhat less today than do a couple of people with less tenure in the group but with stronger performance records.

The company has just announced an opening for a team leader position in your group, and you know that David wants the job. He feels that he has earned the opportunity to have the job on the basis of his consistent efforts. Unfortunately, you see his situation a bit differently. You really want to appoint another individual, Becky Thomas, to the job. Becky has worked for the firm for only six years, but she is your top performer. You want to reward her performance and think that she will do an excellent job. On the other hand, you do not want to lose David because he is a solid member of the group.

Exercise Task

Using the information above, respond to the following:
1. Using equity theory as a framework, how are David and Becky likely to see the situation?
2. Outline a conversation with David in which you will convey your decision to him.
3. What advice might you offer Becky, in her new job, about interacting with David?
4. What other rewards might you offer David to keep him motivated?

BUILDING EFFECTIVE *decision-making* SKILLS

Exercise Overview

Decision-making skills include the manager's ability to recognize and define situations correctly and to select courses of action. This exercise will allow you to use expectancy theory as part of a hypothetical decision-making situation.

Exercise Background

Assume that you are about to graduate from college and have received three job offers, as summarized below:
1. Offer number one is an entry-level position in a large company. The salary offer is for

$30,000, and you will begin work in a very attractive location. However, you also see promotion prospects as being relatively limited, and you know that you are likely to have to move frequently.
2. Offer number two is a position with a new start-up company. The salary offer is $25,000. You know that you will have to work especially long hours. If the company survives for a year, however, opportunities there are unlimited. You may need to move occasionally, but not for a few years.
3. Offer number three is a position in a family-owned business. The salary is $35,000, and

you start as a middle manager. You know that you can control your own transfers, but you also know that some people in the company may resent you because of your family ties.

Exercise Task

Using the three job offers as a framework, do the following:

1. Using expectancy theory as a framework, assess your own personal valence for each outcome in selecting a job.

2. Evaluate the three jobs in terms of their outcomes and associated valences.
3. Which job would you select from among these three?
4. What other outcomes will be important to you in selecting a job?

BUILDING EFFECTIVE *conceptual* SKILLS

Exercise Overview

Conceptual skills refer to the manager's ability to think in the abstract. This exercise will enable you to develop your conceptual skills by relating theory to reality in a personal way.

Exercise Background

First, you will develop a list of things you want from life. Then you will categorize them according to one of the theories in the chapter. Next, you will discuss your results with a small group of classmates.

Exercise Task

1. Prepare a list of approximately fifteen things you want from life. These can be very specific (such as a new car) or very general (such as a feeling of accomplishment in school). Try to include some things you want right now and others you want later in life. Next, choose the one motivational theory discussed in this chapter that best fits your set of needs. Classify each item from your "wish list" in terms of the need or needs it might satisfy.

2. Your instructor will then divide the class into groups of three. Spend a few minutes in the group discussing each person's list and its classification according to needs.
3. After the small-group discussions, your instructor will reconvene the entire class. Discussion should center on the extent to which each theory can serve as a useful framework for classifying individual needs. Students who found that their needs could be neatly categorized or those who found little correlation between their needs and the theories are especially encouraged to share their results.
4. As a result of this exercise, do you now place more or less trust in the need theories as viable management tools?
5. Could a manager use some form of this exercise in an organizational setting to enhance employee motivation?

A LEGEND IN ITS OWN TIME

Living up to its name, Legend Holdings has become the most successful computer maker in China. A group of engineers from the Chinese Academy of Sciences founded Legend in 1984 as a computer trading firm. Originally, the company sold Hewlett-Packard printers and other computer-related products and assembled PCs for a U.S. company. Over time, however, the company evolved into a manufacturer. First, the company developed a new computer system to accommodate Chinese characters; then it was ready to design and produce PCs specifically for the Chinese market.

Thanks to a combination of low labor costs, local sources for parts, a just-in-time manufacturing system, and economies of scale, Legend eventually reduced its production costs and passed the savings on to customers in the form of lower prices. With PCs priced as much as 25 percent below competing models, Legend saw its sales soar in the late 1990s. The sales momentum has made Legend the top-selling PC maker in China, easily surpassing global computer powerhouses such as IBM.

Sales to government agencies and businesses account for a large chunk of Legend's revenues. For example, journalists in the Beijing bureau of Reuters use Legend computers to file their news reports. But the company has also built a solid regional reputation selling and servicing PCs for home use. One of its most popular consumer products is the Conet, a snazzy PC featuring one-button access to the Internet. Another promising product, developed in conjunction with Microsoft, is a set-top device that plugs into a television to enable viewers to browse the Internet.

Behind the scenes, Legend's successful performance has been driven by the vision of chairman Liu Chuanzhi and the hard work of a motivated group of managers and employees. Legend is a publicly traded company listed on the Hong Kong stock exchange, and its reward structure is unusual for China. More than two dozen of the founding employees, including the chairman, have been given shares in the company; their combined stakes are worth more than $800 million. The company offers generous pay packages and grants stock options. Small wonder that managers act like owners when making decisions. The availability of options also helps Legend recruit and retain skilled employees, an especially difficult challenge now that China's economy is expanding at a rapid pace and foreign firms entering the market want to hire local talent.

However, financial rewards are not the chairman's only motivation. Consider Liu's reaction to a comment made by a local computer executive in Taiwan. Showing off a new palm-size PC, the executive told Liu that Legend couldn't create such a product without outside help. The chairman quickly rose to the challenge. On his return to Beijing, the chairman rallied a team of Legend engineers to work together toward the goal of developing a world-class palm-size PC. Within four months, Legend launched the Tianji as the first palm-size PC made by a Chinese manufacturer for the Chinese market—and its less-expensive, full-featured version became an instant hit. Sales were so strong that Legend formed an alliance with a foreign company to adapt the Tianji for the European market.

With demand for PCs swelling throughout China and Asia, Legend wants to expand into other computer-related products and other markets. It is already acquiring computer firms and developing new Internet access products for home and business use. This expansion is part of Liu's plan to reach an aggressive goal of $10 billion in annual sales by 2005. The chairman believes his managers and employees have the attitudes, behaviors, and motivation to make that goal a reality.

Case Questions

1. Which theory or theories seem to explain Liu Chuanzhi's motivation?

2. Under equity theory, how would you expect employees at other Chinese computer companies to react to Legend's stock options and pay packages?

3. How is Liu Chuanzhi applying goal-setting theory at Legend?

Case References

Justin Doebele, "Who Needs an M.B.A.?" *Forbes*, January 24, 2000, p. 80 (quote on p. 80); "Earnings Double for China PC Maker," *CNet*

News.com, July 25, 2000, http://news.cnet.com/news/0-1006-200-2344281.html?tag=st.ne.1002.srchres.ni (September 13, 2000); Lynne Curry, "Legend in the Making," *CFO Asia*, May 1999, http://www.cfoasia.com/archives/9905-22.htm (September 13, 2000).

CHAPTER NOTES

1. "Fliers Give Continental Sky-High Marks," *USA Today*, May 10, 2000, p. 3B; "Continental Delivers Goods," *USA Today*, May 10, 2000, p. 3B; Brian O'Reilly, "The Mechanic Who Fixed Continental," *Fortune*, December 20, 1999, pp. 176–186; Sheila Puffer (Interviewer), "Continental Airlines' CEO Gordon Bethune on Teams and New Product Development," *Academy of Management Executive*, August 1999, Vol. 13, No. 3, pp. 28–35 (quote on p. 32).

2. Richard M. Steers, Gregory A. Bigley, and Lyman W. Porter, *Motivation and Leadership at Work*, 6th Edition (New York: McGraw-Hill, 1996). See also Maureen L. Ambrose and Carol T. Kulik, "Old Friends, New Faces: Motivation Research in the 1990s," *Journal of Management*, 1999, Vol. 25, No. 3, pp. 231–292.

3. See Jeffrey Pfeffer, *The Human Equation* (Boston: Harvard Business School Press, 1998).

4. See Craig Pinder, *Work Motivation in Organizational Behavior* (Upper Saddle River, N.J.: Prentice-Hall, 1998).

5. Frederick W. Taylor, *Principles of Scientific Management* (New York: Harper and Brothers, 1911).

6. Elton Mayo, *The Social Problems of an Industrial Civilization* (Boston: Harvard University Press, 1945); Fritz J. Rothlisberger and W. J. Dickson, *Management and the Worker* (Boston: Harvard University Press, 1939).

7. See Eryn Brown, "So Rich So Young—But Are They Really Happy?" *Fortune*, September 18, 2000, pp. 99–110, for a recent discussion of these questions.

8. Abraham H. Maslow, "A Theory of Human Motivation," *Psychological Review*, Vol. 50, 1943, pp. 370–396; Abraham H. Maslow, *Motivation and Personality* (New York: Harper & Row, 1954); Maslow's most recent work is Abraham H, Maslow and Richard Lowry, *Toward a Psychology of Being* (New York: John Wiley & Sons, 1999).

9. For a review, see Pinder, *Work Motivation in Organizational Behavior*.

10. Clayton P. Alderfer, *Existence, Relatedness, and Growth* (New York: Free Press, 1972).

11. Frederick Herzberg, Bernard Mausner, and Barbara Snyderman, *The Motivation to Work* (New York: Wiley, 1959); Frederick Herzberg, "One More Time: How Do You Motivate Employees?" *Harvard Business Review*, January–February 1987, pp. 109–120.

12. Robert J. House and Lawrence A. Wigdor, "Herzberg's Dual-Factor Theory of Job Satisfaction and Motivation: A Review of the Evidence and a Criticism," *Personnel Psychology*, Winter 1967, pp. 369–389; Victor H. Vroom, *Work and Motivation* (New York: Wiley, 1964). See also Pinder, *Work Motivation in Organizational Behavior*.

13. David C. McClelland, *The Achieving Society* (Princeton, N.J.: Van Nostrand, 1961); David C. McClelland, *Power: The Inner Experience* (New York: Irvington, 1975).

14. David McClelland and David H. Burnham, "Power Is the Great Motivator," *Harvard Business Review*, March–April 1976, pp. 100–110.

15. Victor H. Vroom, *Work and Motivation* (New York: Wiley, 1964).

16. "Starbucks' Secret Weapon," *Fortune*, September 29, 1997, p. 268.

17. Lyman W. Porter and Edward E. Lawler III, *Managerial Attitudes and Performance* (Homewood, Ill.: Dorsey Press, 1968).

18. J. Stacy Adams, "Towards an Understanding of Inequity," *Journal of Abnormal and Social Psychology*, November 1963, pp. 422–436.

19. See Edwin A. Locke, "Toward a Theory of Task Performance and Incentives," *Organizational Behavior and Human Performance*, Vol. 3, 1968, pp. 157–189.

20. Gary P. Latham and J. J. Baldes, "The Practical Significance of Locke's Theory of Goal Setting," *Journal of Applied Psychology*, Vol. 60, 1975, pp. 187–191.

21. B. F. Skinner, *Beyond Freedom and Dignity* (New York: Knopf, 1971).

22. Fred Luthans and Robert Kreitner, *Organizational Behavior Modification and Beyond: An Operant and Social Learning Approach* (Glenview, Ill.: Scott, Foresman, 1985).

23. Luthans and Kreitner, *Organizational Behavior Modification and Beyond*; W. Clay Hamner and Ellen P. Hamner, "Behavior Modification on the Bottom Line," *Organizational Dynamics*, Spring 1976, pp. 2–21.

24. "At Emery Air Freight: Positive Reinforcement Boosts Performance," *Organizational Dynamics*, Winter 1973, pp. 41–50; for a recent update, see Alexander D. Stajkovic and Fred Luthans, "A Meta-Analysis of the Effects of Organizational Behavior Modification on Task Performance, 1975–95," *Academy of Management Journal*, Vol. 40, No. 5, 1997, pp. 1122–1149.

25. David J. Glew, Anne M. O'Leary-Kelly, Ricky W. Griffin, and David D. Van Fleet, "Participation in Organizations: A Preview of the Issues and Proposed Framework for Future Analysis," *Journal of Management*, 1995, Vol. 21, No. 3, pp. 395–421.

26. Robert E. Quinn and Gretchen M. Spreitzer, "The Road to Empowerment: Seven Questions Every Leader Should Consider," *Organizational Dynamics*, Autumn 1997, pp. 37–47.

27. Russ Forrester, "Empowerment: Rejuvenating a Potent Idea," *Academy of Management Executive*, 2000, Vol. 14, No. 3, pp. 67–77.

28. Baxter W. Graham, "The Business Argument for Flexibility, *HRMagazine*, May 1996, pp. 104–110.

29. A. R. Cohen and H. Gadon, *Alternative Work Schedules: Integrating Individual and Organizational Needs* (Reading, Mass.: Addison-Wesley, 1978).

30. Michelle Neely Martinez, "Rewards Given the Right Way," *HRMagazine*, May 1997, pp. 109–118. See also Angelo S. DeNisi and Ricky W. Griffin, *Human Resource Management* (Boston: Houghton Mifflin, 2001).

31. Edward E. Lawler III, *Pay and Organizational Development* (Reading, Mass.: Addison-Wesley, 1981). See also Edward E. Lawler III, *Pay and Organizational Effectiveness: A Psychological View* (New York: McGraw-Hill, 1971).

32. Lawler, *Pay and Organizational Development*.

33. Bill Leonard, "New Ways to Pay Employees," *HRMagazine*, February 1994, pp. 61–69.

34. "Grading 'Merit Pay,'" *Newsweek*, November 14, 1988, pp. 45–46; Frederick S. Hills, K. Dow Scott, Steven E. Markham, and Michael J. Vest, "Merit Pay: Just or Unjust Desserts," *Personnel Administrator*, September 1987, pp. 53–59. See also DeNisi and Griffin, *Human Resource Management*.

CHAPTER

17 Managing Leadership and Influence Processes

In many ways Jacques Nasser may be the quintessential business leader for the twenty-first century. He was born in Lebanon but grew up in Australia. He joined Ford's Australian operation more than thirty years ago as a financial analyst. As Nasser worked his way up the company's hierarchy, he subsequently held increasingly important jobs, first in Latin America and then in Europe. He moved to the United States after being promoted to the key position of president of Ford Automotive Operations. Finally, in 1999 he became Ford's CEO.

Almost from the day he arrived in Detroit, Nasser began to shake things up. For decades the firm had been a stable, hierarchical company that efficiently made cars and, in recent years at least, earned solid profits. But Nasser had a new vision for Ford, one that will, in his opinion, take the company to the very forefront of its industry and transform it into a nimble, flexible organization better attuned to the international automobile industry he sees emerging.

And indeed, the forefront of the industry is exactly where Nasser has set his sights, even though he downplays that goal publicly. After all, General Motors has held the crown as the world's largest automobile company for decades. But while GM's global market share has slowly declined to around 16 percent, Ford's has surged to about 13 percent—clearly putting Ford within striking distance. To help him achieve his ambitions, Nasser has also brought in dozens of senior managers from outside the staid Ford ranks.

Nasser has also made several major changes in Ford's organization structure. Most significantly, he decided to group newly acquired Volvo with Jaguar and Aston Martin, English properties Ford had acquired years earlier, with its own Lincoln division, creating a new unit called the Premier Automotive Group. This new unit is headed by Wolfgang Reitzle, a recruit from BMW, and headquartered in Europe. Nasser also overhauled the structure of Ford's new car design operation and mandated that all senior executives move into the same building to promote interaction and stimulate new ways of thinking.

Nasser's own approach to running Ford is also a bit unique. He is seldom in his office; instead he visits Ford facilities around the world. Indeed, he keeps a calendar marked with national holidays from around the world to coordinate his travel schedule better. For example, he recently took advantage of the

"You've got to earn [a promotion]. The days of entitlement at Ford Motor Co. are gone forever."

—Jacques Nasser, CEO of Ford Motor Company

518

After studying this chapter, you should be able to:

- Describe the nature of leadership and distinguish leadership from management.

- Discuss and evaluate the trait approach to leadership.

- Discuss and evaluate models of leadership, focusing on behaviors.

- Identify and describe the major situational approaches to leadership.

- Identify and describe three related perspectives on leadership.

- Discuss political behavior in organizations and how it can be managed.

Thanksgiving lull in the United States to visit Australia. Nasser also communicates with Ford employees regularly. For instance, every week he writes a chatty e-mail updating employees on what's going on, sending it to more than 89,000 employee mailboxes around the world. He is also stressing the importance of motivation and hard work. For example, he has tied executive compensation to stock performance for the first time since Ford went public in the 1950s. And a recurring message he takes to all Ford employees—who own about 20 percent of the firm's stock—is how their individual contributions add to shareholder value.

Finally, Nasser also won rave reviews for his handling of the recent crisis involving the recall of thousands of sets of Firestone tires on Ford Explorers. Nasser assumed personal responsibility for helping address the problem and routinely met with representatives from the media, the government, and Firestone to ensure that consumers received new tires as quickly as possible. He also did an excellent job of simultaneously acknowledging Ford's role in solving the problem while protecting the corporate reputation by keeping it framed as an issue with Firestone's tires.[1]

acques Nasser has a relatively rare combination of skills that sets him apart from many others: he is both an astute leader and a fine manager, and he recognizes many of the challenges necessary to play both roles. He knows when to make tough decisions, when to lead and encourage his employees, and when to stand back and let them do their jobs. And thus far, Ford is reaping big payoffs from his efforts.

This chapter examines people like Jacques Nasser more carefully by focusing on leadership and its role in management. We characterize the nature of leadership and trace the three major approaches to studying leadership—traits, behaviors, and situations. After examining other perspectives on leadership, we conclude by describing another approach to influencing others—political behavior in organizations.

■ The Nature of Leadership

In Chapter 16, we described various models and perspectives on employee motivation. From the manager's standpoint, trying to motivate people is an attempt to influence their behavior. In many ways, leadership too is an attempt to influence the behavior of others. In this section, we first define leadership, then differentiate it from management, and conclude by relating it to power.

The Meaning of Leadership

leadership As a process, the use of noncoercive influence to shape the group's or organization's goals, motivate behavior toward the achievement of those goals, and help define group or organization culture; as a property, the set of characteristics attributed to individuals who are perceived to be leaders

leaders People who can influence the behaviors of others without having to rely on force; those accepted by others as leaders

Leadership is both a process and a property.[2] As a process—focusing on what leaders actually do—leadership is the use of noncoercive influence to shape the group's or organization's goals, motivate behavior toward the achievement of those goals, and help define group or organization culture.[3] As a property, leadership is the set of characteristics attributed to individuals who are perceived to be leaders. Thus, **leaders** are people who can influence the behaviors of others without having to rely on force; leaders are people whom others accept as leaders.

Leadership Versus Management

From these definitions, it should be clear that leadership and management are related, but they are not the same. A person can be a manager, a leader, both, or neither.[4] Some of the basic distinctions between the two are summarized in Table 17.1. At the left side of the table are four elements that differentiate leadership from management. The two columns show how each element differs when considered from a management and a leadership point of view. For example, when executing plans, managers focus on monitoring results, comparing them with goals, and correcting deviations. In contrast, the leader focuses on energizing people to overcome bureaucratic hurdles to help reach goals. Thus, when Jacques Nasser

Table 17.1

Distinctions Between Management and Leadership

Management and leadership are related, but distinct, constructs. Managers and leaders differ in how they create an agenda, develop a rationale for achieving the agenda, and execute plans, and in the types of outcomes they achieve.

Activity	Management	Leadership
Creating an agenda	**Planning and budgeting.** Establishing detailed steps and timetables for achieving needed results; allocating the resources necessary to make those needed results happen.	**Establishing direction.** Developing a vision of the future, often the distant future, and strategies for producing the changes needed to achieve that vision.
Developing a human network for achieving the agenda	**Organizing and staffing.** Establishing some structure for accomplishing plan requirements, staffing that structure with individuals, delegating responsibility and authority for carrying out the plan, providing policies and procedures to help guide people, and creating methods or systems to monitor implementation.	**Aligning people.** Communicating the direction by words and deeds to everyone whose cooperation may be needed to influence the creation of teams and coalitions that understand the vision and strategies and accept their validity.
Executing plans	**Controlling and problem solving.** Monitoring results versus planning in some detail, identifying deviations, and then planning and organizing to solve these problems.	**Motivating and inspiring.** Energizing people to overcome major political, bureaucratic, and resource barriers by satisfying very basic, but often unfulfilled, human needs.
Outcomes	Produces a degree of predictability and order and has the potential to produce consistently major results expected by various stakeholders (for example, for customers, always being on time; for stockholders, being on budget).	Produces change, often to a dramatic degree, and has the potential to produce extremely useful change (for example, new products that customers want, new approaches to labor relations that help make a firm more competitive).

Source: Reprinted with permission of The Free Press, a division of Simon & Schuster Inc. from *A Force for Change: How Leadership Differs from Management* by John P. Kotter. Copyright © 1990 by John P. Kotter, Inc.

monitors the performance of his employees, he is playing the role of manager. But when he inspires them to work harder at achieving their goals, he is a leader.

Organizations need both management and leadership if they are to be effective. Leadership is necessary to create change, and management is necessary to achieve orderly results. Management in conjunction with leadership can produce orderly change, and leadership in conjunction with management can keep the organization properly aligned with its environment. *Management Infotech* describes Selina Lo, an individual who is clearly both a manager and a leader.

Power and Leadership

To understand leadership fully, it is necessary to understand power. **Power** is the ability to affect the behavior of others. One can have power without actually using it. For example, a football coach has the power to bench a player who is not performing up to par. The coach seldom has to use this power because players recognize that the power exists and work hard to keep their starting positions. In organizational settings, there are usually five kinds of power: legitimate, reward, coercive, referent, and expert.[5]

power The ability to affect the behavior of others

MANAGEMENT INFOTECH

HARD-DRIVING MANAGEMENT IN THE HIGH-TECH ARENA

Managers in high-tech industries have to race the clock as well as the competition, as Selina Y. Lo well knows. Lo is the vice president of product management and marketing for Alteon WebSystems, a young, fast-growing company that makes sophisticated networking systems for web-based businesses such as Ticketmaster Online and Yahoo! Competing against well-established, fleet-footed rivals such as Cisco Systems, Lo uses her considerable power to speed product innovation, spur higher performance, and meet customers' needs.

One reason the CEO of Alteon hired Lo was for her keen sense of cutting-edge technology and her understanding of customer needs, developed during a rising-star background in a series of well-regarded information technology firms. She started with Hewlett-Packard after college, moved to Network Equipment Technologies, and then co-founded Centillion Networks, where she was part of the team that invented an innovative new data-switching device. Small wonder that employees and customers alike respect Lo's judgment and pay close attention when she talks about products and features.

Lo supervises product development for Alteon, a critical function in an industry where a product's life can be measured in months. She spends most of her day in the field, sniffing out customer problems. When she comes back to the office to hammer out design changes with development engineers, her aggressive management style— sometimes pounding the table, sometimes raising her voice—makes it hard for engineers to say no. Although Lo is known as a tough manager, she's also known for her habit of giving away trips and other valuable rewards to recognize performance. After fifteen years in the networking industry, Lo is anything but shy about using her hard-driving approach to overpower the competition and push Alteon to the top of a crowded but lucrative market.

> *I've left a few dead bodies behind me.*
>
> —*Selina Y. Lo, vice president of marketing for Alteon WebSystems**

Reference: Andy Reinhardt,"'I've Left a Few Dead Bodies,'" *Business Week,* January 31, 2000, pp. 69–70 (*quote on p. 69).

---

legitimate power Power granted through the organizational hierarchy; it is the power accorded people occupying particular positions as defined by the organization

reward power The power to give or withhold rewards, such as salary increases, bonuses, promotion recommendations, praise, recognition, and interesting job assignments

Legitimate Power

Legitimate power is power granted through the organizational hierarchy; it is the power accorded people occupying particular positions as defined by the organization. A manager can assign tasks to a subordinate, and a subordinate who refuses to do them can be reprimanded or even fired. Such outcomes stem from the manager's legitimate power as defined and vested in her or him by the organization. Legitimate power, then, is authority. All managers have legitimate power over their subordinates. The mere possession of legitimate power, however, does not by itself make someone a leader. Some subordinates follow only orders that are strictly within the letter of organizational rules and policies. If asked to do something not in their job description, they refuse or do a poor job. The manager of such employees is exercising authority but not leadership.

Reward Power

Reward power is the power to give or withhold rewards. Rewards that a manager may control include salary increases, bonuses, promotion recommendations, praise, recognition, and interesting job assignments. In general, the greater the number of rewards a manager controls and the more important the rewards are to subordinates, the greater is the manager's reward power. If the subordinate sees as valuable only the formal organizational rewards provided by the manager, then he or she is not a leader. If the subordinate also wants and appreciates the manager's informal rewards like praise, gratitude, and recognition, however, then the manager is also exercising leadership.

Coercive Power   **Coercive power** is the power to force compliance by means of psychological, emotional, or physical threat. In the past physical coercion in organizations was relatively common. In most organizations today, however, coercion is limited to verbal and written reprimands, disciplinary layoffs, fines, demotion, and termination. Some managers occasionally go so far as to use verbal abuse, humiliation, and psychological coercion in an attempt to manipulate subordinates. (Of course, most people would agree that these managerial behaviors are not appropriate.) James Dutt, former CEO of Beatrice Company, once told a subordinate that if his wife and family got in the way of his working a twenty-four-hour day seven days a week, he should get rid of them.[6] The more punitive the elements under a manager's control and the more important they are to subordinates, the more coercive power the manager possesses. On the other hand, the more a manager uses coercive power, the more likely he is to provoke resentment and hostility and the less likely he is to be seen as a leader.[7]

Referent Power   Compared with legitimate, reward, and coercive power, which are relatively concrete and grounded in objective facets of organizational life, **referent power** is abstract. It is based on identification, imitation, loyalty, or charisma. Followers may react favorably because they identify in some way with a leader, who may be like them in personality, background, or attitudes. In other situations, followers might choose to imitate a leader with referent power by wearing the same kinds of clothes, working the same hours, or espousing the same management philosophy. Referent power may also take the form of charisma, an intangible attribute of the leader that inspires loyalty and enthusiasm. Thus, a manager might have referent power, but it is more likely to be associated with leadership.

Expert Power   **Expert power** is derived from information or expertise. A manager who knows how to interact with an eccentric but important customer, a scientist who is capable of achieving an important technical breakthrough that no other company has dreamed of, and a secretary who knows how to unravel bureaucratic red tape all have expert power over anyone who needs that information. The more important the information and the fewer the people who have access to it, the greater is the degree of expert power possessed by any one individual. In general, people who are both leaders and managers tend to have a lot of expert power.

Expert power is often an important ingredient in the success of many people. Dr. Susan Love, for example, is a world-renowned expert on women's health in general and breast cancer in particular. Her work is widely recognized and cited, giving her the power to influence public opinion, government health policy, and the daily health habits of millions of women.

coercive power The power to force compliance by means of psychological, emotional, or physical threat

referent power The personal power that accrues to someone based on identification, imitation, loyalty, or charisma

expert power The personal power that accrues to someone based on the information or expertise that they possess

Using Power   How does a manager or leader use power? Several methods have been identified.[8] One method is the *legitimate request,* which is based on legitimate power. The manager requests that the subordinate comply because the subordinate recognizes that the organization has given the manager the right to make the request. Most day-to-day interactions between manager and subordinate are of this type. Another use of power is *instrumental compliance,* which is based on the reinforcement theory of motivation. In this form of exchange, a subordinate complies to get the reward the manager controls. Suppose that a manager asks a subordinate to do something outside the range of the subordinate's normal duties, such as working extra hours on the weekend, terminating a relationship with a long-standing buyer, or delivering bad news. The subordinate complies and, as a direct result, reaps praise and a bonus from the manager. The next time the subordinate is asked to perform a similar activity, that subordinate will recognize that compliance will be instrumental in her getting more rewards. Hence, the basis of instrumental compliance is clarifying important performance-reward contingencies.

A manager is using *coercion* when she suggests or implies that the subordinate will be punished, fired, or reprimanded if he does not do something. *Rational persuasion* occurs when the manager can convince the subordinate that compliance is in the subordinate's best interest. For example, a manager might argue that the subordinate should accept a transfer because it would be good for the subordinate's career. In some ways, rational persuasion is like reward power except that the manager does not really control the reward.

Still another way a manager can use power is through *personal identification.* A manager who recognizes that she has referent power over a subordinate can shape the behavior of that subordinate by engaging in desired behaviors: the manager consciously becomes a model for the subordinate and exploits personal identification. Sometimes a manager can induce a subordinate to do something consistent with a set of higher ideals or values through *inspirational appeal.* For example, a plea for loyalty represents an inspirational appeal. Referent power plays a role in determining the extent to which an inspirational appeal is successful because its effectiveness depends at least in part on the persuasive abilities of the leader.

A dubious method of using power is through *information distortion.* The manager withholds or distorts information to influence subordinates' behavior. For example, if a manager has agreed to allow everyone to participate in choosing a new group member but subsequently finds one individual whom she really prefers, she might withhold some of the credentials of other qualified applicants so that the desired member is selected. This use of power is dangerous. It may be unethical, and if subordinates find out that the manager has deliberately misled them, they will lose their confidence and trust in that manager's leadership.[9]

MANAGEMENT IMPLICATIONS   Managers need to recognize the distinctions between leadership as a process and as a property. They should also appreciate the differences between leadership and management. And finally, managers need to know the most common bases of power and how to use those bases most effectively.

The Search for Leadership Traits

The first organized approach to studying leadership analyzed the personal, psychological, and physical traits of strong leaders. The trait approach assumed that some basic trait or set of traits differentiated leaders from nonleaders. If those traits could be defined, potential leaders could be identified. Researchers thought that leadership traits might include intelligence, assertiveness, above-average height, good vocabulary, attractiveness, self-confidence, and similar attributes.[10]

During the first several decades of this century, hundreds of studies were conducted in an attempt to identify important leadership traits. For the most part, the results of the studies were disappointing. For every set of leaders who possessed a common trait, a long list of exceptions was also found, and the list of suggested traits soon grew so long that it had little practical value. Alternative explanations usually existed even for relations between traits and leadership that initially appeared valid. For example, it was observed that many leaders have good communication skills and are assertive. Rather than those traits being the cause of leadership, however, successful leaders may begin to display those traits after they have achieved leadership positions.

Although most researchers gave up trying to identify traits as predictors of leadership ability, many people still explicitly or implicitly adopt a trait orientation.[11] For example, politicians are all too often elected on the basis of personal appearance, speaking ability, or an aura of self-confidence. In addition, traits like honesty and integrity may very well be fundamental leadership traits that serve an important purpose. *The World of Management* discusses leadership traits as they apply to the CEO of Goodyear.

MANAGEMENT Managers need to understand the concept of leadership traits, **IMPLICATIONS** but they should pay most attention to avoiding the pitfalls of relying on or making inferences about a person's leadership ability based on various traits.

Leadership Behaviors

Spurred on by their lack of success in identifying useful leadership traits, researchers soon began to investigate other variables, especially the behaviors or actions of leaders. The new hypothesis was that effective leaders somehow behaved differently than less-effective leaders. Thus, the goal was to develop a more complete understanding of leadership behaviors.

WORLD OF MANAGEMENT

GLOBAL VIEW FROM THE TOP

Good leaders must be agile, adaptable, and open to new opportunities—qualities that Sam Gibara developed through years of moving from country to country. Born in Egypt and raised in France, Gibara moved to Massachusetts to earn his MBA from Harvard and then returned to France as a management trainee with Goodyear Tire & Rubber. During his tenure with the Ohio-based tire company, he was moved through various management positions in Europe, Morocco, and Canada before settling in Akron, Ohio, as CEO.

Stanley Gault, the previous CEO, handpicked and groomed Gibara for the top slot precisely because of this varied background. Gault saw in Gibara more than a capable manager: he believed that Gibara's fluency in multiple languages and his experience living and working in diverse cultures provided a well-rounded background for presiding over a global enterprise.

In fact, Gibara's adaptability and understanding of global differences have proven quite valuable. For example, Goodyear had once tried and failed to buy Japan's Sumitomo Rubber Industries. Years later, when Gibara became CEO, he made another overture to Sumitomo, despite the advice of colleagues who were convinced the attempt would fail again. Instead of acting pushy and talking bluntly, Gibara took an entirely different approach, based on his personal knowledge of other cultures. He began by humbly apologizing for the earlier buyout attempt, then waited patiently for Sumitomo's managers to open the door to new discussions. After a long series of negotiation meetings, Sumitomo finally agreed to a global alliance that gave Goodyear control over the Japanese operations it wanted.

Under Gibara's leadership, management at Goodyear has become more diverse: foreign-born professionals have been hired to fill more than 25 percent of the company's open positions in the past few years. A more global perspective helps Gibara and his team effectively manage Goodyear's far-flung operations and customer base—yet Gibara is also direct and decisive, qualities typically exhibited by U.S. managers. At Goodyear, good leadership at the top taps the best characteristics of managers around the world.

> *Americans move around in the U.S. more than Germans do in Germany or French in France. And every time you move, it broadens you, it gives you new opportunities.*
>
> —*Sam Gibara, CEO of Goodyear**

Reference: Timothy Aeppel, "American Way: From Egypt to Europe to Ohio, a CEO Finds a Place to Call Home," *Wall Street Journal*, December 22, 1999, pp. A1, A6 (*quote on p. A1).

Michigan Studies

job-centered leader behavior The behavior of leaders who pay close attention to an employee's job and work procedures involved with that job

employee-centered leader behavior The behavior of leaders who develop cohesive work groups and ensure employee satisfaction

Researchers at the University of Michigan, led by Rensis Likert, began studying leadership in the late 1940s.[12] Based on extensive interviews with both leaders (managers) and followers (subordinates), this research identified two basic forms of leader behavior: job centered and employee centered. Managers using **job-centered leader behavior** pay close attention to subordinates' work, explain work procedures, and are keenly interested in performance. Managers using **employee-centered leader behavior** are interested in developing a cohesive work group and ensuring that employees are satisfied with their jobs. Their primary concern is the welfare of subordinates.

The two styles of leader behavior were presumed to be at the ends of a single continuum. Although this assumption suggests that leaders may be extremely job-centered, extremely employee-centered, or somewhere between, Likert studied only the two end styles for contrast. He argued that employee-centered leader behavior generally tended to be more effective. We should also note the similarities between Likert's leadership research and his Systems 1 through 4 organization design (discussed in Chapter 12). Job-centered leader behavior is consistent with the System 1 design (rigid and bureaucratic), whereas employee-centered leader behavior is consistent with the System 4 design (organic and flexible). When Likert advocates moving organizations from System 1 to System 4, he is also advocating a transition from job-centered to employee-centered leader behavior.

Ohio State Studies

At about the same time that Likert was beginning his leadership studies at the University of Michigan, a group of researchers at Ohio State also began studying leadership.[13] The extensive questionnaire surveys conducted during the Ohio State studies also suggested that there are two basic leader behaviors or styles: initiating-structure behavior and consideration behavior. When using **initiating-structure behavior,** the leader clearly defines the leader-subordinate role so that everyone knows what is expected, establishes formal lines of communication, and determines how tasks will be performed. Leaders using **consideration behavior** show concern for subordinates and attempt to establish a friendly and supportive climate. The behaviors identified at Ohio State are similar to those described at Michigan, but there are important differences. One major difference is that the Ohio State researchers did not interpret leader behavior as being one-dimensional: each behavior was assumed to be independent of the other. Presumably, then, a leader could exhibit varying levels of initiating structure and at the same time varying levels of consideration.

At first, the Ohio State researchers thought that leaders who exhibit high levels of both behaviors would be more effective than other leaders. A study at International Harvester Co. (now Navistar International Corp.), however, suggested a more complicated pattern.[14] The researchers found that employees of supervisors who ranked high on initiating structure were high performers but expressed low levels of satisfaction and had a higher absentee rate. Conversely, employees of supervisors who ranked high on consideration had low performance ratings but high levels of satisfaction and few absences from work. Later research isolated other variables that make consistent prediction difficult and determined that situational influences also occurred. (This body of research is discussed in the section on situational approaches to leadership.)

Two common leader behaviors are those that focus on the job and those that focus on people. Take Nobuyuki Idei, CEO of Sony, for example. Mr Idei is totally focused on insuring that Sony retains its preeminence among the world's consumer products giants. To help keep the firm on track, he is constantly setting new goals, developing new strategies, and pushing the firm into new markets. But at the same time, his colleagues report that he is a sensitive and caring leader who is always concerned for the well-being of others.

initiating-structure behavior The behavior of leaders who define the leader-subordinate role so that everyone knows what is expected, establish formal lines of communication, and determine how tasks will be performed

consideration behavior The behavior of leaders who show concern for subordinates and attempt to establish a friendly and supportive climate

Managerial Grid

Yet another behavioral approach to leadership is the Managerial Grid.[15] The Managerial Grid provides a means for evaluating leadership styles and then training managers to move toward an ideal style of behavior. The Managerial Grid is shown in Figure 17.1. The horizontal axis represents **concern for production** (similar to job-centered and initiating-structure behaviors), and the vertical axis represents **concern for people** (similar to employee-centered and consideration behavior). Note the five extremes of managerial behavior: the 1,1 manager (impoverished management), who exhibits minimal concern for both production and people; the 9,1 manager (authority-obedience), who is highly concerned about production but exhibits little concern for people; the 1,9 manager (country club management), who has the exact opposite concerns from the 9,1 manager; the 5,5 manager (organization management), who maintains adequate concern for both people and

concern for production That part of the Managerial Grid that deals with the job and production aspects of leader behavior

concern for people That part of the Managerial Grid that deals with the people aspects of leader behavior

Figure 17.1

The Leadership Grid®

The Leadership Grid® is a method of evaluating leadership styles. The overall objective of an organization using the Grid® is to train its managers using OD techniques so that they are simultaneously more concerned for both people and production (9, 9 style on the Grid®).

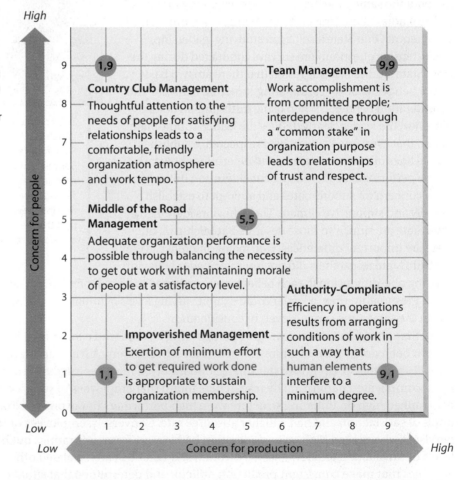

Source: The Leadership Grid Figure for *Leadership Dilemmas—Grid Solutions* by Robert R. Blake and Anne Adams McCanse. (Formerly the Managerial Grid by Robert R. Blake and Jane S. Mouton.) Houston: Gulf Publishing Company, p. 29. Copyright © 1997 by Grid International, Inc. Reproduced by permission of the owners.

production; and the 9,9 manager (team management), who exhibits maximum concern for both people and production.

According to this approach, the ideal style of managerial behavior is 9,9. Thus, there is a six-phase program to assist managers in achieving this style of behavior. A. G. Edwards, Westinghouse, FAA, Equicor, and other companies have used the Managerial Grid with reasonable success. However, there is little published scientific evidence regarding its true effectiveness.

The leader-behavior theories have played an important role in the development of contemporary thinking about leadership. In particular, they urge us not to be preoccupied with what leaders are (the trait approach) but to concentrate on what leaders do (their behaviors). Unfortunately, these theories also make universal prescriptions about what constitutes effective leadership. When we are dealing with complex social systems composed of complex individuals, few if any relationships are consistently predictable, and certainly no formulas for success are infallible. Yet the behavior theorists tried to identify consistent relationships between leader behaviors and employee responses in the hope of finding a dependable prescription for effective leadership. As we might expect, they often failed. Other approaches to understanding leadership were therefore needed. The catalyst for these new approaches was the realization that, although interpersonal and task-oriented dimensions might be useful to describe the behavior of leaders, they were not useful for predicting or prescribing it. The next step in the evolution of leadership theory was the creation of situational models.

MANAGEMENT Managers should appreciate the importance of leadership
IMPLICATIONS behaviors, as well as be familiar with the basic kinds of leadership behaviors most well understood. At the same time, however, managers should also recognize that universal or "one best way" models of leadership are of dubious value.

■ *Situational Approaches to Leadership*

Situational models assume that appropriate leader behavior varies from one situation to another. The goal of a situational theory, then, is to identify key situational factors and to specify how they interact to determine appropriate leader behavior. *Working with Diversity* discusses how Carly Fiorina uses a situational approach to leadership at Hewlett-Packard.

Before discussing the major situational theories, we should first discuss an important early model that laid the foundation for subsequent developments. In a 1958 study of the decision-making process, Robert Tannenbaum and Warren H. Schmidt proposed a continuum of leadership behavior. Their model is much like the original Michigan framework.[16] Besides purely job-centered behavior (or "boss-centered" behavior, as they termed it) and employee-centered ("subordinate-centered") behavior, however, they identified several intermediate behaviors that

WORKING WITH DIVERSITY

BLENDING OUTSIDERS AND INSIDERS TO REACH CORPORATE GOALS

Sometimes it takes an outsider like Carly Fiorina to bring out the best in an organization. Plucked from a division presidency at Lucent Technologies, Fiorina was the first outsider to serve as CEO of Hewlett-Packard. The company, based in Palo Alto, California, had a global reputation for quality computers, printers, and scientific products. However, the combination of a conservative culture and an unwieldy structure was slowing the company down. Fiorina was recruited to use her leadership skills to shake up the organization and put it back on track toward faster growth.

Within months, the new CEO proposed a reorganization to streamline Hewlett-Packard's bloated structure by collapsing eighty-three separate business units into twelve, then aligning these into four divisional groups. Although long-tenured insiders advised her that employees need more time and preparation to adapt to the structure, Fiorina directed its implementation in just ninety days.

Despite their misgivings, the insiders found that the new organization was a big improvement. Now, design teams for different divisions work together to develop products such as laser printers and inkjet printers that are completely compatible. Even more important, Fiorina's new structure enabled managers to reach across divisional lines and pull together a complete package of products and services for customers such as Amazon.com. Previously, the managers of each autonomous business didn't always cooperate with those outside their own unit, even when corporatewide goals were at stake.

Seeing Hewlett-Packard employees as high achievers, Fiorina scrapped the company's previous profit-sharing program and substituted a new performance-based incentive plan. Then she provided both financial and moral support to boost employees' efforts in achieving growth goals. For example, Fiorina began touring the research laboratories on a monthly basis to find out what was new and to encourage innovation. When she heard that one promising project was about to lose its funding, she quickly restored its budget. In addition, Fiorina called meetings frequently to inspire employees and celebrate good results. As time goes on, this CEO's leadership will continue to be a critical factor in Hewlett-Packard's ability to combat competitors and achieve faster growth.

> *The feeling was, here was Carly, who wasn't a long time in the H-P culture, who doesn't understand our business and the H-P Way, and doesn't understand our strengths, particularly in businesses that were viewed as so successful for so long.*
>
> —*Neal Martini, an executive in Hewlett-Packard's printer division**

Reference: David P. Hamilton, "Soul Saver: Inside Hewlett-Packard, Carly Fiorina Combines Discipline, New-Age Talk," *Wall Street Journal*, August 22, 2000, pp. A1, A18 (*quote on p. A18).

---

a manager might consider. These behaviors are shown on the leadership continuum in Figure 17.2.

This continuum of behavior moves from the one extreme of having the manager make the decision alone to the other extreme of having the employees make the decision with minimal guidance. Each point on the continuum is influenced by characteristics of the manager, subordinates, and the situation. Managerial characteristics include the manager's value system, confidence in subordinates, personal inclinations, and feelings of security. Subordinate characteristics include the subordinates' need for independence, readiness to assume responsibility, tolerance for ambiguity, interest in the problem, understanding of goals, knowledge, experience, and expectations. Situational characteristics that affect decision mak-

Figure 17.2

Tannenbaum and Schmidt's Leadership Continuum

The Tannenbaum and Schmidt leadership continuum was an important precursor to modern situational approaches to leadership. The continuum identifies seven levels of leadership that range between the extremes of boss-centered and subordinate-centered leadership.

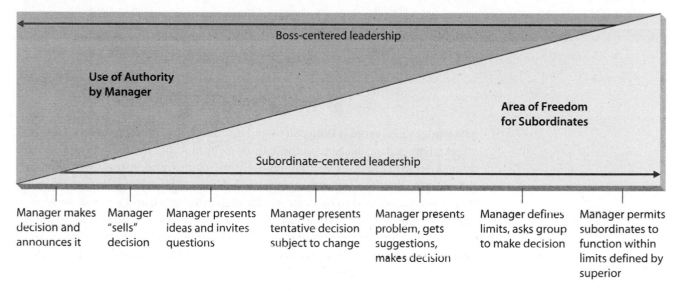

Boss-centered leadership

Use of Authority by Manager

Area of Freedom for Subordinates

Subordinate-centered leadership

| Manager makes decision and announces it | Manager "sells" decision | Manager presents ideas and invites questions | Manager presents tentative decision subject to change | Manager presents problem, gets suggestions, makes decision | Manager defines limits, asks group to make decision | Manager permits subordinates to function within limits defined by superior |

Source: Reprinted by permission of the *Harvard Business Review*. An exhibit from "How to Choose a Leadership Pattern" by Robert Tannenbaum and Warren Schmidt (May–June 1973). Copyright © 1973 by the President and Fellows of Harvard College; all rights reserved.

ing include the type of organization, group effectiveness, the problem itself, and time pressures. Although this framework pointed out the importance of situational factors, it was only speculative. It remained for others to develop more comprehensive and integrated theories. In the following sections, we describe four of the most important and widely accepted situational theories of leadership: the LPC theory, the path-goal theory, Vroom's decision tree approach, and the leader-member exchange approach.

LPC Theory

The **LPC theory**, developed by Fred Fiedler, was the first true situational theory of leadership.[17] (As we will discuss below, LPC stands for "least preferred coworker.") Beginning with a combined trait and behavior approach, Fiedler identified two styles of leadership: task-oriented (analogous to job-centered and initiating-structure behavior) and relationship-oriented (similar to employee-centered and consideration behavior). He went beyond the earlier behavioral approaches by arguing that the style of behavior is a reflection of the leader's personality, and that most personalities fall into one of his two categories, task-oriented or relationship-oriented by nature. Fiedler measures leader style by means of a controversial questionnaire called the **least preferred coworker** (**LPC**) measure. To use the measure,

LPC theory A theory of leadership that suggests that the appropriate style of leadership varies with situational favorableness

least preferred coworker (LPC) The measuring scale that asks leaders to describe the person with whom he or she is able to work least well

a manager or leader is asked to describe the specific person with whom he or she is able to work least well—the LPC—by filling in a set of sixteen scales anchored at each end by a positive or negative adjective. For example, three of the sixteen scales are:

Helpful	__ __ __ __ __ __ __ __	Frustrating
	8 7 6 5 4 3 2 1	
Tense	__ __ __ __ __ __ __ __	Relaxed
	1 2 3 4 5 6 7 8	
Boring	__ __ __ __ __ __ __ __	Interesting
	1 2 3 4 5 6 7 8	

The leader's LPC score is then calculated by adding the numbers below the line checked on each scale. Note in these three examples that the higher numbers are associated with the positive qualities (helpful, relaxed, and interesting), whereas the negative qualities (frustrating, tense, and boring) have low point values. A high total score is assumed to reflect a relationship orientation and a low score is assumed to reflect a task orientation on the part of the leader. The LPC measure is controversial because researchers disagree about its validity. Some question exactly what an LPC measure reflects and whether the score is an index of behavior, personality, or some other factor.[18]

Favorableness of the Situation   The underlying assumption of situational models of leadership is that appropriate leader behavior varies from one situation to another. According to Fiedler, the key situational factor is the favorableness of the situation from the leader's point of view. This factor is determined by leader-member relations, task structure, and position power. *Leader-member relations* refer to the nature of the relationship between the leader and the work group. If the leader and the group have a high degree of mutual trust, respect, and confidence, and if they like one another, relations are assumed to be good. If there is little trust, respect, or confidence, and if they do not like each other, relations are poor. Naturally, good relations are more favorable.

Task structure is the degree to which the group's task is well defined. The task is structured when it is routine, easily understood, and unambiguous and when the group has standard procedures and precedents to rely on. An unstructured task is nonroutine, ambiguous, complex, and with no standard procedures or precedents. You can see that high structure is more favorable for the leader, whereas low structure is less favorable. For example, if the task is unstructured, the group will not know what to do and the leader will have to play a major role in guiding and directing its activities. If the task is structured, the leader will not have to get so involved and can devote time to nonsupervisory activities.

Position power is the power vested in the leader's position. If the leader has the power to assign work and to reward and punish employees, position power is assumed to be strong. But if the leader must get job assignments approved by someone else and does not administer rewards and punishment, position power is weak and it is more difficult to accomplish goals. From the leader's point of view, strong position power is clearly preferable to weak position power. However, position power is not as important as task structure and leader-member relations.

Favorableness and Leader Style   Fiedler and his associates conducted numerous studies linking the favorableness of various situations to leader style and the effectiveness of the group.[19] The results of these studies—and the overall framework of the theory—are shown in Figure 17.3. To interpret the model, look first at the situational factors at the top of the figure: good or bad leader-member relations, high or low task structure, and strong or weak position power can be combined to yield eight unique situations. For example, good leader-member relations, high task structure, and strong position power (at the far left) are presumed to define the most favorable situation; bad leader-member relations, low task structure, and weak position power (at the far right) are the least favorable. The other combinations reflect intermediate levels of favorableness.

Below each set of situations is shown the degree of favorableness and the form of leader behavior found to be most strongly associated with effective group performance for those situations. When the situation is most and least favorable, Fiedler has found that a task-oriented leader is most effective. When the situation is only moderately favorable, however, a relationship-oriented leader is predicted to be most effective.

Figure 17.3

The Least-Preferred Coworker Theory of Leadership

Fiedler's LPC theory of leadership suggests that appropriate leader behavior varies as a function of the favorableness of the situation. Favorableness, in turn, is defined by task structure, leader-member relations, and the leader's position power. According to LPC theory, the most and least favorable situations call for task-oriented leadership, whereas moderately favorable situations suggest the need for relationship-oriented leadership.

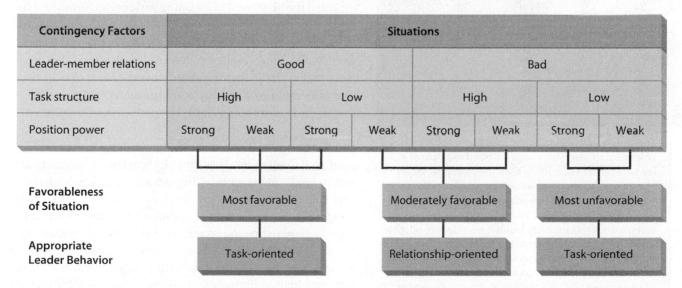

Flexibility of Leader Style   Fiedler argued that, for any given individual, leader style is essentially fixed and cannot be changed: leaders cannot change their behavior to fit a particular situation because it is linked to their particular personality traits. Thus, when a leader's style and the situation do not match, Fiedler argued that the situation should be changed to fit the leader's style. When leader-member relations are good, task structure is low, and position power is weak, the leader style most likely to be effective is relationship-oriented. If the leader is task-oriented, a mismatch exists. According to Fiedler, the leader can make the elements of the situation more congruent by structuring the task (by developing guidelines and procedures, for instance) and increasing power (by requesting additional authority or by other means).

Fiedler's contingency theory has been attacked on the grounds that it is not always supported by research, that his findings are subject to other interpretations, that the LPC measure lacks validity, and that his assumptions about the inflexibility of leader behavior are unrealistic.[20] However, Fiedler's theory was one of the first to adopt a situational perspective on leadership. It has helped many managers recognize the important situational factors they must contend with, and it has fostered additional thinking about the situational nature of leadership. In recent years Fiedler has attempted to address some of the concerns about his theory by revising it and adding additional elements such as cognitive resources.

Path-Goal Theory

The path-goal theory of leadership—associated most closely with Martin Evans and Robert House—is a direct extension of the expectancy theory of motivation discussed in Chapter 14.[21] Recall that the primary components of expectancy theory included the likelihood of attaining various outcomes and the value associated with those outcomes. The **path-goal theory** of leadership suggests that the primary functions of a leader are to make valued or desired rewards available in the workplace and to clarify for the subordinate the kinds of behavior that will lead to goal accomplishment and valued rewards—that is, the leader should clarify the paths to goal attainment.

The path-goal theory is an important situational model of leadership. Mari Matsunaga is a good example of a leader who has successfully used the path-goal theory. She designed I-mode, an astonishingly successful mobile-phone Internet service provided by NTT and which is today among the world's largest mobile-phone companies. Ms. Matsunaga found it necessary to adopt a variety of leadership styles as she dealt with old-line technical engineers, modern consumers, and government bureaucrats, and she had to constantly account for a variety of environmental characteristics as she developed her new enterprise.

Leader Behavior   The most fully developed version of path-goal theory identifies four kinds of leader behavior. *Directive leader behavior* is letting subordinates know what is expected of them, giving guidance and direction, and scheduling work. *Supportive leader behavior* is being friendly and approachable, showing concern for subordinate welfare, and treating subordinates as equals. *Participative leader behavior* is consulting subordinates, soliciting suggestions, and allowing participation in decision making. *Achievement-oriented leader behavior* is setting challenging goals, expecting subordinates to perform at high levels, encouraging subordinates, and showing confidence in subordinates' abilities.

In contrast to Fiedler's theory, path-goal theory assumes that leaders can change their style or behavior to meet the demands of a particular situation. For example, when encountering a new group of subordinates and a new project, the leader may be directive in establishing work procedures and in outlining what needs to be done. Next, the leader may adopt supportive behavior to foster group cohesiveness and a positive climate. As the group becomes familiar with the task and as new problems are encountered, the leader may exhibit participative behavior to enhance group members' motivation. Finally, achievement-oriented behavior may be used to encourage continued high performance.

Situational Factors   Like other situational theories of leadership, path-goal theory suggests that appropriate leader style depends on situational factors. Path-goal theory focuses on the situational factors of the personal characteristics of subordinates and environmental characteristics of the workplace.

Important personal characteristics include the subordinates' perception of their own ability and their locus of control. If people perceive that they are lacking in ability, they may prefer directive leadership to help them understand path-goal relationships better. If they perceive themselves to have a lot of ability, however, employees may resent directive leadership. Locus of control is a personality trait. People who have an internal locus of control believe that what happens to them is a function of their own efforts and behavior. Those who have an external locus of control assume that fate, luck, or "the system" determines what happens to them. A person with an internal locus of control may prefer participative leadership, whereas a person with an external locus of control may prefer directive leadership. Managers can do little or nothing to influence the personal characteristics of subordinates, but they can shape the environment to take advantage of these personal characteristics by providing rewards and structuring tasks, for example.

Environmental characteristics include factors outside the subordinate's control. Task structure is one such factor. When structure is high, directive leadership is less

path-goal theory A theory of leadership suggesting that the primary functions of a leader are to make valued or desired rewards available in the workplace and to clarify for the subordinate the kinds of behavior that will lead to goal accomplishment and valued rewards

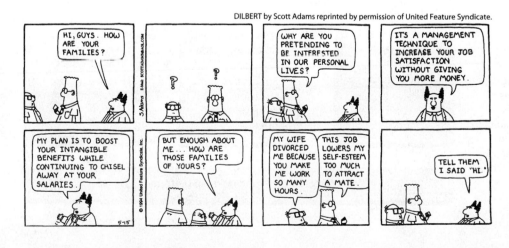

DILBERT by Scott Adams reprinted by permission of United Feature Syndicate.

Most effective leaders demonstrate sincere interest in the personal welfare of their followers. This interest can extend to concern about their families and personal lives as well. When the interest is real, employees may feel more valued and appreciated by their leader and develop stronger job satisfaction and dedication. But if the leader's interest is superficial and is an obvious ploy to show interest, employees will likely see what's going on and come to resent and to lose respect for the leader.

effective than when structure is low. Subordinates do not usually need their boss to tell them continually how to do an extremely routine job. The formal authority system is another important environmental characteristic. Again, the higher the degree of formality, the less directive is the leader behavior that will be accepted by subordinates. The nature of the work group also affects appropriate leader behavior. When the work group provides the employee with social support and satisfaction, supportive leader behavior is less critical. When social support and satisfaction cannot be derived from the group, the worker may look to the leader for this support.

The basic path-goal framework as illustrated in Figure 17.4 shows that different leader behaviors affect subordinate's motivation to perform. Personal and environmental characteristics are seen as defining which behaviors lead to which outcomes. The path-goal theory of leadership is a dynamic and incomplete model. The original intent was to state the theory in general terms so that future research could explore a variety of interrelationships and modify the theory. Research that has been done suggests that the path-goal theory is a reasonably good description of the leadership process and that future investigations along these lines should enable us to discover more about the link between leadership and motivation.[22]

Vroom's Decision Tree Approach

Vroom's decision tree approach
Predicts what kinds of situations call for what degrees of group participation

The third major contemporary approach to leadership is **Vroom's decision tree approach**. The earliest version of this model was proposed by Victor Vroom and Philip Yetton and later revised and expanded by Vroom and Arthur Jago.[23] Most recently, Vroom has developed yet another refinement of the original model.[24] Like the path-goal theory, this approach attempts to prescribe a leadership style appropriate to a given situation. It also assumes that the same leader may display different leadership styles. But Vroom's approach concerns itself with only a single aspect of leader behavior: subordinate participation in decision making.

Basic Premises   Vroom's decision tree approach assumes that the degree to which subordinates should be encouraged to participate in decision making depends on the characteristics of the situation. In other words, no one decision-

Figure 17.4

The Path-Goal Framework
The path-goal theory of leadership suggests that managers can use four types of leader behavior to clarify subordinates' paths to goal attainment. Personal characteristics of the subordinate and environmental characteristics within the organization both must be taken into account when determining which style of leadership will work best for a particular situation.

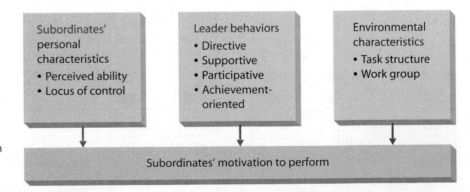

making process is best for all situations. After evaluating different problem attributes (characteristics of the problem or decision), the leader determines an appropriate decision style that specifies the amount of subordinate participation.

Vroom's current formulation suggests that managers use one of two different decision trees.[25] The manager first assesses the situation in terms of several factors. This assessment involves determining whether the given factor is "high" or "low" for the decision to be made. For instance, the first factor is decision significance. If the decision is extremely important and may have a major impact on the organization (i.e., choosing a location for a new plant), its significance is high. But if the decision is routine and its consequences are not terribly important (i.e., selecting a color for the firm's softball team uniforms), its significance is low. This assessment guides the manager through the paths of the decision tree to a recommended course of action. One decision tree is to be used when the manager is primarily interested in making the decision on the most timely basis possible; the other is to be used when time is less critical and the manager is interested in helping subordinates to improve and develop their own decision-making skills.

The two decision trees are shown in Figures 17.5 and 17.6. The problem attributes (situational factors) are arranged along the top of the decision tree. To use the model, the decision maker starts at the left side of the diagram and assesses the first problem attribute (decision significance). The answer determines the path to the second node on the decision tree, where the next attribute (importance of commitment) is assessed. This process continues until a terminal node is reached. In this way, the manager identifies an effective decision-making style for the situation.

Decision-Making Styles The various decision styles reflected at the ends of the tree branches represent different levels of subordinate participation that the manager should attempt to adopt in a given situation. The five styles are defined as follows:

Decide: The manager makes the decision alone and then announces or "sells" it to the group.

Consult (individually): The manager presents the program to group members individually, obtains their suggestions, and then makes the decision.

Consult (group): The manager presents the problem to group members at a meeting, gets their suggestions, and then makes the decision.

Facilitate: The manager presents the problem to the group at a meeting, defines the problem and its boundaries, and then facilitates group member discussion as they make the decision.

Delegate: The manager allows the group to define for itself the exact nature and parameters of the problem and then to develop a solution.

Vroom's decision tree approach represents a very focused but quite complex perspective on leadership. To compensate for this difficulty, Vroom has developed elaborate expert system software to help managers assess a situation accurately and quickly and then to make an appropriate decision regarding employee participation.[26] Many firms, including Halliburton Company, Litton Industries, and Borland International, have provided their managers with training in using the various versions of this model.

Figure 17.5

Vroom's Time-Driven Decision Tree

This matrix is recommended for situations where time is of the highest importance in making a decision. The matrix operates like a funnel. You start at the left with a specific decision problem in mind. The column headings denote situational factors that may or may not be present in that problem. You progress by selecting High or Low (H or L) for each relevant situational factor. Proceed down the funnel, judging only those situational factors for which a judgment is called for, until you reach the recommended process.

Decision Significance	Importance of Commitment	Leader Expertise	Likelihood of Commitment	Group Support	Group Expertise	Team Competence	
H	H	H	H	—	—	—	Decide
			L	H	H	H	Delegate
						L	Consult (group)
					L	—	
				L	—	—	
H	H	L	H	H	H	H	Facilitate
						L	Consult (individually)
					L	—	
				L	—	—	
H	H	L	L	H	H	H	Facilitate
						L	Consult (group)
					L	—	
				L	—	—	
H	L	H	—	—	—	—	Decide
H	L	L		H	H	—	Facilitate
					L		Consult (individually)
				L	—		
L	H	—	H	—	—	—	Decide
L	H	—	L	—	H	—	Delegate
			L	—	L	—	Facilitate
L	L	—	—	—	—	—	Decide

(Left vertical label: PROBLEM STATEMENT)

Source: Adapted and reprinted from *Leadership and Decision-Making* by Victor H. Vroom and Philip W. Yetton, by permission of the University of Pittsburgh Press. © 1973 by University of Pittsburgh Press.

Evaluation and Implications   Because Vroom's current approach is relatively new, it has not been fully and scientifically tested. The original model and its subsequent refinement, however, attracted a great deal of attention and generally was supported by research.[27] For example, there is some support for the idea that individuals who make decisions consistent with the predictions of the model are more effective than those who make decisions inconsistent with it. The model therefore appears to be a tool that managers can apply with some confidence in deciding how much subordinates should participate in the decision-making process.

The Leader-Member Exchange Approach

Because leadership is such an important area, managers and researchers continue to study it. As a result, new ideas, theories, and perspectives are continuously being developed. The **leader-member exchange** (**LMX**) **model** of leadership, conceived by George Graen and Fred Dansereau, stresses the importance of variable relationships between supervisors and each of their subordinates.[28] Each supervisor-

leader-member exchange (LMX) model Stresses the importance of variable relationships between supervisors and each of their subordinates

Decision Significance	Importance of Commitment	Leader Expertise	Likelihood of Commitment	Group Support	Group Expertise	Team Competence	
P R O B L E M S T A T E M E N T H	H	—	H	H	H	H	**Decide**
						L	**Facilitate**
					L	—	**Consult (group)**
				L	—	—	
			L	H	H	H	**Delegate**
						L	**Facilitate**
					L	—	
				L	—	—	**Consult (group)**
	L	—	—	H	H	H	**Delegate**
						L	**Facilitate**
					L	—	**Consult (group)**
				L	—	—	
L	H	—	H	—	—	—	**Decide**
			L	—	—	—	**Delegate**
	L	—	—	—	—	—	**Decide**

Figure 17.6
Vroom's Development-Driven Decision Tree
This matrix is to be used when the leader is more interested in developing employees than in making the decision as quickly as possible. Just as with the time-driven tree shown in Figure 17.5, the leader assesses up to seven situational factors. These factors, in turn, funnel the leader to a recommended process for making the decision.

Source: Adapted and reprinted from *Leadership and Decision-Making*, by Victor H. Vroom and Phillip W. Yetton, by permission of the University of Pittsburgh Press. © 1973 by University of Pittsburgh Press.

subordinate pair is referred to as a "vertical dyad." The model differs from earlier approaches because it focuses on the differential relationship leaders often establish with different subordinates. Figure 17.7 shows the basic concepts of the leader-member exchange theory.

The model suggests that supervisors establish a special relationship with a small number of trusted subordinates referred to as the in-group. The in-group usually receives special duties requiring responsibility and autonomy; they may also receive special privileges. Subordinates who are not part of this group are called the out-group, and they receive less of the supervisor's time and attention. Note in the figure that the leader has a dyadic, or one-to-one, relationship with each of the five subordinates.

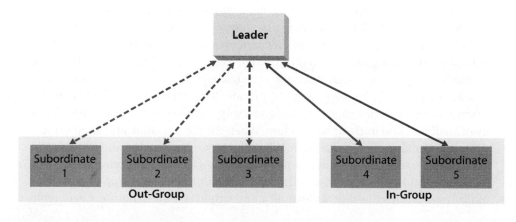

Figure 17.7
The Leader-Member Exchange (LMX) Model
The LMX model suggests that leaders form unique independent relationships with each of their subordinates. As illustrated here, a key factor in the nature of this relationship is whether the individual subordinate is in the leader's out-group or in-group.

Early in his or her interaction with a given subordinate, the supervisor initiates either an in-group or out-group relationship. It is not clear how a leader selects members of the in-group, but the decision may be based on personal compatibility and subordinates' competence. Research has confirmed the existence of in-groups and out-groups. In addition, studies generally have found that in-group members have a higher level of performance and satisfaction than out-group members.[29]

MANAGEMENT IMPLICATIONS The most important thing for managers to remember about the situational theories is their underlying assumption that appropriate leadership behavior depends on elements of the situation. The LPC theory points to some of these situational factors. The path-goal theory stresses that leaders can change their behaviors to match the situation best. Vroom's decision tree approach provides guidance about employee participation in decision making. The LMX approach underscores the importance of in-groups and out-groups as well as the importance of individual relationships between leaders and followers.

■ Related Perspectives on Leadership

Because of its importance to organizational effectiveness, leadership continues to be the focus of a great deal of research and theory building. New approaches that have attracted much attention are the concepts of substitutes for leadership and transformational leadership.

Substitutes for Leadership

substitutes for leadership A concept that identifies situations in which leader behaviors are neutralized or replaced by characteristics of subordinates, the task, and the organization

The concept of **substitutes for leadership** was developed because existing leadership models and theories do not account for situations in which leadership is not needed.[30] They simply try to specify what kind of leader behavior is appropriate. The substitute concepts, however, identify situations in which leader behaviors are neutralized or replaced by characteristics of the subordinate, the task, and the organization. For example, when a patient is delivered to a hospital emergency room, the professionals on duty do not wait to be told what to do by a leader. Nurses, doctors, and attendants all go into action without waiting for directive or supportive leader behavior from the emergency-room supervisor.

Characteristics of the subordinate that may serve to neutralize leader behavior include ability, experience, need for independence, professional orientation, and indifference toward organizational rewards. For example, employees with a high level of ability and experience may not need to be told what to do. Similarly, a subordinate's strong need for independence may render leader behavior ineffective. Task characteristics that may substitute for leadership include routineness, the availability of feedback, and intrinsic satisfaction. When the job is routine and simple, the subordinate may not need direction. When the task is challenging and intrinsically satisfying, the subordinate may not need or want social support from a leader.

Organizational characteristics that may substitute for leadership include formalization, group cohesion, inflexibility, and a rigid reward structure. Leadership may not be necessary when policies and practices are formal and inflexible, for example. Similarly, a rigid reward system may rob the leader of reward power and thereby decrease the importance of the role. Preliminary research has provided support for the concept of substitutes for leadership.[31]

Charismatic Leadership

The concept of **charismatic leadership**, like trait theories, assumes that charisma is an individual characteristic of the leader. **Charisma** is a form of interpersonal attraction that inspires support and acceptance. All else being equal, then, someone with charisma is more likely to be able to influence others than is someone without charisma. For example, a highly charismatic supervisor will be more successful in influencing subordinate behavior than a supervisor who lacks charisma. Thus, influence is again a fundamental element of this perspective.

Robert House first proposed a theory of charismatic leadership in 1977 based on research findings from various social science disciplines.[32] His theory suggests that charismatic leaders are likely to have a lot of self-confidence, a firm conviction in their beliefs and ideals, and a strong need to influence people. They also tend to communicate high expectations about follower performance and express confidence in followers. Donald Trump is an excellent example of a charismatic leader. Even though he has made his share of mistakes and generally is perceived as only an "average" manager, many people view him as larger than life.[33]

There are three elements of charismatic leadership in organizations that most experts acknowledge today.[34] First, the leader needs to be able to envision the future, to set high expectations, and to model behaviors consistent with meeting those expectations. Next, the charismatic leader must be able to energize others

charismatic leadership Assumes that charisma is an individual characteristic of the leader

charisma A form of interpersonal attraction that inspires support and acceptance

Phil Jackson is considered to be one of the top coaches in the National Basketball Association, having won world championships first with the Chicago Bulls and more recently with the Los Angeles Lakers. One key to his success is his personal charisma. Jackson is able to simultaneously command both the respect and the affection of his players. This rare combination allows him to channel and direct the energies of players toward the singular goal of winning basketball games, putting aside personal goals and petty differences of opinion.

through a demonstration of personal excitement, personal confidence, and patterns of success. And finally, the charismatic leader enables others by supporting them, by empathizing with them, and by expressing confidence in them.

Charismatic leadership ideas are quite popular among managers today and are the subject of numerous books and articles. Unfortunately, few studies have specifically attempted to test the meaning and impact of charismatic leadership. There are also lingering ethical issues about charismatic leadership, however, that trouble some people. For example, several notorious historical leaders were no doubt very charismatic individuals. To the extent that a charismatic leader is followed due solely to his or her personal attractiveness, those followers may engage in behaviors that they might have otherwise rejected. *Managing in an e-Business World* describes the role of charisma at two Internet start-up companies.

MANAGING IN AN *e*-BUSINESS WORLD

CHARISMATIC INTERNET LEADERSHIP

Ola Ahlvarsson and Jay Chiat may head Internet companies thousands of miles apart, but they have one important leadership quality in common: charisma. Ahlvarsson, a world champion kickboxer, is the founder of Result Venture Knowledge International in Sweden, a company devoted to generating ideas for new Internet businesses. Guided by his far-reaching vision of Europe as an Internet business center—and fueled by his boundless personal enthusiasm—Ahlvarsson has had a hand in establishing more than twenty web companies.

Ahlvarsson comes up with a seemingly endless stream of web business ideas that he pushes to market as quickly as possible. His company develops detailed business plans for each, secures financial backing, works on the web site and operational launch, and retains a piece of the business as it matures and becomes independent. Thanks to Ahlvarsson's foresight and drive, these fledgling e-businesses often have a head start over aggressive U.S. web firms seeking to expand in Europe. Despite increased competition, Ahlvarsson is confident that his knowledge of local markets gives his companies the edge they need to thrive.

Across the Atlantic Ocean, Jay Chiat, another charismatic leader, built and then sold a hugely successful advertising agency before heading ScreamingMedia (http://www.screamingmedia.com), a broker of Internet content. Chiat's company acts as an intermediary between news organizations and web sites hungry for timely content. As a leader, Chiat is as interested in forging a creative, inspirational internal climate as he is in bringing a good product to the company's one-thousand-plus business customers.

Every time an employee closes a deal, the entire office celebrates at the sounding of a gong. Good enough is never enough for this work-hard, play-hard leader, who expects—and gets—the best from his staff, every day. When Chiat felt tension developing between different departments within ScreamingMedia, his solution was to throw everyone together at a party and encourage lots of informal mixing and mingling. As e-commerce grows and Internet competition becomes even more intense, both Chiat and Ahlvarsson will be out in front, leading their employees to even higher performance.

> *He has a mysterious capacity to make people want to do their best work.*
>
> —*Designer Milton Glaser, talking about Jay Chiat**

References: William Echikson, "Europe's Top E.Business Leaders," *Business Week*, February 7, 2000, pp. EB58–EB59; Warren Berger, "The Cool Thing About Aggregation," *Wired*, October 2000, pp. 186–200 (*quote on p. 196); "The E Gang," *Forbes*, July 24, 2000, pp. 145–172.

Transformational Leadership

Another new perspective on leadership has been called by several labels: charismatic leadership, inspirational leadership, symbolic leadership, and transformational leadership. We use the term **transformational leadership** and define it as leadership that goes beyond ordinary expectations by transmitting a sense of mission, stimulating learning experiences, and inspiring new ways of thinking.[35] Because of rapid change and turbulent environments, transformational leaders are increasingly being seen as vital to the success of business.

A recent popular-press article identified seven keys to successful leadership: trusting one's subordinates, developing a vision, keeping cool, encouraging risk, being an expert, inviting dissent, and simplifying things.[36] Although this list was the result of a simplistic survey of the leadership literature, it is nevertheless consistent with the premises underlying transformational leadership. So, too, are recent examples cited as effective leadership. Take, for example, the case of General Electric. When Jack Welch assumed the position of CEO, GE was a lethargic behemoth composed of more than one hundred businesses. Decision making was slow, and bureaucracy stifled individual initiative. Welch stripped away the bureaucracy, streamlined the entire organization, sold dozens of businesses, and bought many new ones. Indeed, Welch's most recent change at GE was his acquisition of Honeywell in late 2000 for $44 billion.[37] He literally re-created the organization, and today GE is one of the most admired and profitable firms in the world. Transformational leadership was the basis for all of Welch's changes.

MANAGEMENT IMPLICATIONS Managers should understand and appreciate the basic nature of charisma in organizations. In addition, they should also be fully aware of the distinctions between transformational leadership and what experts call transactional leadership—routine and administrative activities generally associated with management.

transformational leadership Leadership that goes beyond ordinary expectations by transmitting a sense of mission, stimulating learning experiences, and inspiring new ways of thinking

■ *Political Behavior in Organizations*

Another common influence on behavior is politics and political behavior. **Political behavior** describes activities carried out for the specific purpose of acquiring, developing, and using power and other resources to obtain one's preferred outcomes.[38] Political behavior may be undertaken by managers dealing with their subordinates, subordinates dealing with their managers, and managers and subordinates dealing with others at the same level. In other words, it may be directed upward, downward, or laterally. Decisions ranging from where to locate a manufacturing plant to where to put the company coffeepot are subject to political action. In any situation, individuals may engage in political behavior to further their own ends, to protect themselves from others, to further goals they sincerely believe to be in the organization's best interest, or simply to acquire and exercise power. And power may be sought by individuals, by groups of individuals, or by groups of groups.[39]

political behavior The activities carried out for the specific purpose of acquiring, developing, and using power and other resources to obtain one's preferred outcomes

While political behavior is difficult to study because of its sensitive nature, one early survey found that many managers believed that politics influenced salary and hiring decisions in their firms. Many also believed that the incidence of political behavior was greater at the upper levels of their organizations and less at the lower levels. More than one-half of the respondents felt that organizational politics was bad, unfair, unhealthy, and irrational, but most suggested that successful executives have to be good politicians and be political to "get ahead."[40]

Common Political Behaviors

Research has identified four basic forms of political behavior widely practiced in organizations.[41] One form is *inducement*, which occurs when a manager offers to give something to someone else in return for that individual's support. For example, a product manager might suggest to another product manager that she will put in a good word with his boss if he supports a new marketing plan that she has developed. A second tactic is *persuasion*, which relies on both emotion and logic. An operations manager wanting to construct a new plant on a certain site might persuade others to support his goal on grounds that are objective and logical (the site is less expensive and taxes are lower) as well as subjective and personal.

A third political behavior involves the *creation of an obligation*. For example, one manager might support a recommendation made by another manager for a new advertising campaign. Although he may really have no opinion on the new campaign, he may think that by going along he is incurring a debt from the other manager and will be able to "call in" that debt when he wants to get something done and needs additional support. *Coercion* is the use of force to get one's way. For example, a manager may threaten to withhold support, rewards, or other resources as a way to influence someone else.

Impression management is a subtle form of political behavior that deserves special mention. **Impression management** is a direct and intentional effort by someone to enhance his or her image in the eyes of others. People engage in impression management for a variety of reasons. They may do so to further their own career. By making themselves look good, they think they are more likely to receive rewards, to be given attractive job assignments, and to receive promotions. They may also engage in impression management to boost their own self-esteem. When people have a solid image in an organization, others make them aware of it through compliments, respect, and so forth. Still another reason people use impression management is in an effort to acquire more power, and hence more control.

People attempt to manage how others perceive them through various mechanisms. Appearance is one of the first things people think of. Hence, a person motived by impression management will pay close attention to choice of attire, selection of language, and the use of manners and body posture. People interested in impression management are also likely to jockey to be associated only with successful projects. By being assigned to high-profile projects led by highly successful managers, a person can begin to link their own name with such projects in the minds of others.

Sometimes people too strongly motivated by impression management become obsessed by it and may resort to dishonest and/or unethical means. For example,

impression management A direct and intentional effort by someone to enhance his or her image in the eyes of others

some people have been known to take credit for others' work in an effort to make themselves look better. People have also been known to exaggerate or even falsify their personal accomplishments in an effort to build an enhanced image.[42]

Managing Political Behavior

By its very nature, political behavior is tricky to approach in a rational and systematic way. But managers can handle political behavior so that it does not do excessive damage. First, managers should be aware that even if their actions are not politically motivated, others may assume that they are. Second, by providing subordinates with autonomy, responsibility, challenge, and feedback, managers reduce the likelihood of political behavior by subordinates. Third, managers should avoid using power if they want to avoid charges of political motivation. Fourth, managers should get disagreements out in the open so that subordinates will have less opportunity for political behavior, using conflict for their own purposes. Finally, managers should avoid covert activities. Behind-the-scene activities give the impression of political intent even if none really exists.[43] Other guidelines include clearly communicating the bases and processes for performance evaluations, tying rewards directly to performance, and minimizing competition among managers for resources.[44]

Of course, those guidelines are a lot easier to list than they are to implement. The well-informed manager should not assume that political behavior does not exist or, worse yet, attempt to eliminate it by issuing orders or commands. Instead, the manager must recognize that political behavior exists in virtually all organizations and that it cannot be ignored or stamped out. It can, however, be managed in such a way that it will seldom inflict serious damage on the organization. It may even play a useful role in some situations.[45] For example, a manager may be able to use his or her political influence to stimulate a greater sense of social responsibility or to heighten awareness of the ethical implications of a decision.

MANAGEMENT IMPLICATIONS Managers need to understand the dynamics of political behavior in organizations. In particular, they should know the more common political behaviors, including impression management, as well as methods for managing political behavior.

Summary of Key Points

As a process, leadership is the use of noncoercive influence to shape the group's or organization's goals, motivate behavior toward the achievement of those goals, and help define group or organization culture. As a property, leadership is the set of characteristics attributed to those who are perceived to be leaders. Leadership and management are often related but are also different. Managers and leaders use legitimate, reward, coercive, referent, and expert power.

The trait approach to leadership assumed that some basic trait or set of traits differentiated leaders from nonleaders. The leadership-behavior approach assumed that the behavior of effective leaders was somehow different from the behavior of nonleaders. Research at the University of Michigan and Ohio State identified two basic forms of leadership behavior—one concentrating on work and performance and the other concentrating on employee welfare and support. The Managerial Grid attempts to train managers to exhibit high levels of both forms of behavior.

Situational approaches to leadership recognize that appropriate forms of leadership behavior are not universally applicable and attempt to specify situations in which various behaviors are appropriate. The LPC theory suggests that a leader's behaviors should be either task-oriented or relationship-oriented depending on the favorableness of the situation. The path-goal theory suggests that directive, supportive, participative, or achievement-oriented leader behaviors may be appropriate, depending on the personal characteristics of subordi-

nates and the environment. Vroom's decision tree approach maintains that leaders should vary the extent to which they allow subordinates to participate in making decisions as a function of problem attributes. The leader-member exchange model focuses on individual relationships between leaders and followers and on in-group versus out-group considerations.

Related leadership perspectives are the concepts of substitutes for leadership, charismatic leadership, and the role of transformational leadership in organizations.

Political behavior is another influence process frequently used in organizations. Impression management, one especially important form of political behavior, is a direct and intentional effort by someone to enhance his or her image in the eyes of others. Managers can take steps to limit the effects of political behavior.

Discussion Questions

Questions for Review

1. Could someone be a manager but not a leader? A leader but not a manager? Both a leader and a manager? Explain.
2. What were the major findings of the Michigan and Ohio State studies of leadership behaviors? Briefly describe each group of studies and compare and contrast their findings.
3. What are the situational approaches to leadership? Briefly describe each and compare and contrast their findings.
4. Describe charismatic and transformation perspectives on leadership. How can they be integrated with existing approaches to leadership?

Questions for Analysis

5. How is it possible for a leader to be task-oriented and employee-oriented at the same time? Can you think of other forms of leader behavior that would be important

to a manager? If so, share your thoughts with the class.
6. When all or most of the leadership substitutes are present, does the follower no longer need a leader? Why or why not?
7. Why should members of an organization be aware that political behavior may be going on within the organization? What might occur if they were not aware of it?

Questions for Application

8. What traits seem best to describe student leaders? Military leaders? Business leaders? Political leaders? Religious leaders? What might account for the similarities and differences in your lists of traits?
9. Think about a decision that would affect you as a student. Use Vroom's decision tree approach to decide whether the administrator making that decision should involve students in the decision. Which parts of the

model seem most important in making that decision? Why?

10. How do you know if transformational leadership is present in a group or organization?

Could transformational leadership ever lead to dysfunctional outcomes for individuals or organizations? If so, why? If not, why not?

BUILDING EFFECTIVE *diagnostic* SKILLS

Exercise Overview

Diagnostic skills help a manager visualize appropriate responses to a situation. One situation managers often face is whether to use power to solve a problem. This exercise will help you develop your diagnostic skills as they relate to using different types of power in different situations.

Exercise Background

Several methods have been identified for using power:

1. In a legitimate request, the manager requests that the subordinate comply because the subordinate recognizes that the organization has given the manager the right to make the request. Most day-to-day interactions between manager and subordinate are of this type.

2. In instrumental compliance, a subordinate complies to get the reward the manager controls. Suppose that a manager asks a subordinate to do something outside the range of the subordinate's normal duties, such as working extra hours on the weekend, terminating a relationship with a long-standing buyer, or delivering bad news. The subordinate complies and, as a direct result, reaps praise and a bonus from the manager. The next time the subordinate is asked to perform a similar activity, that subordinate will recognize that compliance will be instrumental in her getting more rewards. Hence, the basis of instrumental compliance is clarifying important performance-reward contingencies.

3. Coercion is used when the manager suggests or implies that the subordinate will be punished, fired, or reprimanded if he does not do something.

4. Rational persuasion occurs when the manager can convince the subordinate that compliance is in the subordinate's best interest. For example, a manager might argue that the subordinate should accept a transfer because it would be good for the subordinate's career. In some ways, rational persuasion is like reward power except that the manager does not really control the reward.

5. Personal identification occurs when a manager recognizes that she has referent power over a subordinate and can shape the behavior of that subordinate by engaging in desired behaviors. The manager consciously becomes a model for the subordinate and exploits personal identification.

6. Inspirational appeal occurs when a manager can induce a subordinate to do something consistent with a set of higher ideals or values. For example, a plea for loyalty represents an inspirational appeal.

Exercise Task

With these ideas in mind, do the following:

1. Relate each of the uses of power listed above to the five types of power identified in the chapter. That is, indicate which type(s) of power is most closely associated with each use of power, which type(s) may be related to each use of power, and which type(s) is unrelated to each use of power.

2. Is a manager more likely to be using multiple forms of power at the same time or to be using a single type of power?

3. Identify other methods and approaches to using power.

4. What are some of the dangers and pitfalls associated with using power?

BUILDING EFFECTIVE *decision-making* SKILLS

Exercise Overview

Vroom's decision tree approach to leadership is an effective method for determining how much participation a manager might allow his or her subordinates in making a decision. This exercise will enable you to refine your decision-making skills by applying Vroom's approach to a hypothetical situation.

Exercise Background

Assume that you are the branch manager of the west coast region of the United States for an international manufacturing and sales company. The company is making a major effort to control costs and boost efficiency. As part of this effort, the firm recently installed a networked computer system linking sales representatives, customer service employees, and other sales support staff. The goal of this network was to increase sales while simultaneously cutting sales expenses.

Unfortunately, just the opposite has resulted—sales are down slightly, while expenses are increasing. You have looked into this problem and believe that the computer hardware that people are using is fine. You also believe, however, that the software used to run the system is flawed: it is too hard to use and it provides less than complete information.

Your employees disagree with your assessment, however. They believe that the entire system is fine. They attribute the problems to poor training in using the system and a lack of incentive for using it to solve many problems that they already know how to handle using other methods. Some of them also think that their colleagues are just resisting change.

Your boss has just called and instructed you to "solve the problem." She indicated that she has complete faith in your ability to do so, that decisions about how to proceed will be left to you, and that she wants a report suggesting a course of action in five days.

Exercise Task

Using the information presented above, do the following:

1. Using your own personal preferences and intuition, describe how you think you would proceed.
2. Now use Vroom's approach to determine a course of action.
3. Compare and contrast your initial approach and the approach suggested by Vroom's approach.

BUILDING EFFECTIVE *conceptual* SKILLS

Exercise Overview

Conceptual skills refer to the manager's ability to think in the abstract. This exercise will enable you to apply your conceptual skills to the identification of leadership qualities in others.

Exercise Task

1. Working alone, list the names of ten people you think of as leaders. Note that the names should not necessarily be confined to

"good" leaders but instead should identify "strong" leaders.
2. Form small groups with three or four classmates and compare lists. Focus on common and unique examples, as well as the kinds of individuals listed (i.e., male versus female, contemporary versus historical, business versus nonbusiness, etc.).
3. From all the lists, choose two leaders whom most people in the group consider to be the most successful and least successful.

4. Identify similarities and differences between the two successful leaders and between the two less successful leaders.

5. Relate the successes and failures to at least one theory or perspective discussed in the chapter.

6. Select one group member to report your findings to the rest of the class.

CHAPTER CLOSING CASE

HOW SOUTHWEST AIRLINES SOARS

Southwest Airlines has been profitable since 1973—an enviable record no other U.S. airline can match, let alone beat. Much of the credit for the airline's enduring success goes to CEO Herb Kelleher, an affable, hard-driving leader whose fun-loving personality pervades the entire organization, top to bottom. After all, how many airlines have the ticker symbol LUV or paint Seaworld's "Shamu the Whale" on a jetliner?

The history of Southwest reflects its CEO's tenacity. Kelleher had a law practice in San Antonio when a client suggested starting a discount airline to link three Texas cities. After five years of legal battles due to competitors' objections—before deregulation opened the skies to anything-goes competition and pricing—Southwest finally got off the ground in 1971. To keep airfares low, the start-up avoided extras such as meal service and got planes in and out of the gate in twenty minutes or less. The airline now serves dozens of cities across the United States using the original formula of low prices, low costs, and high productivity to keep profits high. In fact, Southwest's operating margins are now three times higher than the industry average.

Kelleher knows that other airlines can buy the same planes and fly the same routes, even set the same prices. What they can't imitate, he pointedly notes, is Southwest's legendary team spirit. The workforce of 30,000 is fiercely loyal to Kelleher and the company, pitching in to get things done on time and within budget. Consider the reaction when Kelleher wrote a memo warning employees that rising fuel prices threatened the airline's profitability and asking every employee to find a way to save $5 per day. Within six weeks, employees had dreamed up enough cost-cutting measures to save more than $2 million—and ideas were still coming in.

Under Kelleher, Southwest has made flying fun for employees and passengers alike. Flight attendants set the tone by weaving in humorous remarks along with their regular in-flight announcements; gate agents lighten up by wearing offbeat hats and bantering with passengers getting on and off planes. Southwest employees really let loose on Halloween, wearing wacky costumes, decorating gate areas, and munching on trick-or-treat snacks.

Keeping this spirit alive as the airline expands is a major challenge. Southwest uses personality testing to identify job applicants who will fit in with the airline's unique approach to business because they are cheerful, optimistic, team-oriented, good communicators, and they can take initiative and make decisions. New hires are then sent to the airline's University for People to hone their interpersonal and technical skills and to learn about the airline's traditions. In the field, local culture committees are charged with perpetuating the culture at each airport and outpost through meetings, games, and parties.

When trouble erupts within the organization, the solution generally comes out of Southwest's own culture. For example, flight attendants once complained about the work schedules devised by the scheduling department; the schedulers, meanwhile, said the flight attendants were uncooperative. In typical Southwest style, management successfully defused the situation by having the two groups switch jobs to learn firsthand about the pressures each group faced.

What would Southwest be like under another CEO? Management is already thinking ahead to the time, not so long from now, when Kelleher steps down and a new CEO takes over. Although Kelleher is always ready with a funny line, even on formal occasions, he turns serious when speaking about leaving a legacy that will keep Southwest soaring for the long term. Until he relinquishes the CEO position, however, Kelleher will keep pushing to bring the Southwest spirit to new destinations, keep costs down, keep profits high, and—above all—put the fun back in flying.

Case Questions

1. What leadership theories and concepts have contributed to Herb Kelleher's success at Southwest?

2. Do you consider Kelleher to be a manager, a leader, or both? Why?

3. What should Southwest look for in a CEO who will succeed Kelleher?

Case Reference

Katrina Brooker, "Can Anyone Replace Herb?" *Fortune*, April 17, 2000, pp. 186–192.

CHAPTER NOTES

1. "Making Bold Strokes, Fine Points, Nasser Puts His Mark on Ford," *Wall Street Journal*, April 7, 1999, pp. A1, A8; Sue Zesiger, "Ford's Hip Transplant," *Fortune*, May 10, 1999, pp. 82–92; "Driving Change: An Interview with Ford Motor Company's Jacques Nasser," *Harvard Business Review*, March–April 1999, pp. 76–88; "Remaking Ford," *Business Week*, October 11, 1999, pp. 132–142 (quote on pp. 132–133); Alex Taylor III, "Jac Nasser's Biggest Test," *Fortune*, September 18, 2000, pp. 123–128.

2. See Ronald A. Heifetz and Donald L. Laurie, "The Work of Leadership," *Harvard Business Review*, January–February 1997, pp. 124–134. See also Arthur G. Jago, "Leadership: Perspectives in Theory and Research," *Management Science*, March 1982, pp. 315–336; "The New Leadership," *Business Week*, August 28, 2000, pp. 100–187; and Jim Collins, "Level 5 Leadership: The Triumph of Humility and Fierce Resolve," *Harvard Business Review*, January 2001, pp. 66–78.

3. Gary A. Yukl, *Leadership in Organizations*, 3rd Edition (Englewood Cliffs, N.J.: Prentice-Hall, 1994), p. 5; see also Gregory G. Dess and Joseph C. Pickens, "Changing Roles: Leadership in the 21st Century," *Organizational Dynamics*, Winter 2000, pp. 18–28.

4. John P. Kotter, "What Leaders Really Do," *Harvard Business Review*, May–June 1990, pp. 103–111. See also Daniel Goleman, "Leadership That Gets Results," *Harvard Business Review*, March–April 2000, pp. 78–88, and Keith Grints, *The Arts of Leadership* (Oxford: Oxford University Press, 2000).

5. John R. P. French and Bertram Raven, "The Bases of Social Power," in Dorwin Cartwright, ed., *Studies in Social Power* (Ann Arbor, Mich.: University of Michigan Press, 1959), pp. 150–167.

6. Hugh D. Menzies, "The Ten Toughest Bosses," *Fortune*, April 21, 1980, pp. 62–73.

7. Bennett J. Tepper, "Consequences of Abusive Supervision," *Academy of Management Journal*, 2000, Vol. 43, No. 2, pp. 178–190.

8. Thomas A. Stewart, "Get with the New Power Game," *Fortune*, January 13, 1997, pp. 58–62.

9. For more information on the bases and uses of power, see Philip M. Podsakoff and Chester A. Schriesheim, "Field Studies of French and Raven's Bases of Power: Critique, Reanalysis, and Suggestions for Future Research," *Psychological Bulletin*, Vol. 97, 1985, pp. 387–411; Robert C. Benfari, Harry E. Wilkinson, and Charles D. Orth, "The Effective Use of Power," *Business Horizons*, May–June 1986, pp. 12–16; and Yukl, *Leadership in Organizations*.

10. Bernard M. Bass, *Bass & Stogdill's Handbook of Leadership*, 3rd Edition (Riverside, N.J.: Free Press, 1990).

11. Shelley A. Kirkpatrick and Edwin A. Locke, "Leadership: Do Traits Matter?" *The Academy of Management Executive*, May 1991, pp. 48–60; see also Robert J. Sternberg, "Managerial Intelligence: Why IQ Isn't Enough," *Journal of Management*, Vol. 23, No. 3, 1997, pp. 475–493.

12. Rensis Likert, *New Patterns of Management* (New York: McGraw-Hill, 1961); Rensis Likert, *The Human Organization* (New York: McGraw-Hill, 1967).

13. The Ohio State studies stimulated many articles, monographs, and books. A good overall reference is Ralph M. Stogdill and A. E. Coons, eds., *Leader Behavior: Its Description and Measurement* (Columbus, Ohio: Bureau of Business Research, Ohio State University, 1957).

14. Edwin A. Fleishman, E. F. Harris, and H. E. Burt, *Leadership and Supervision in Industry* (Columbus, Ohio: Bureau of Business Research, Ohio State University, 1955).

15. Robert R. Blake and Jane S. Mouton, *The Managerial Grid* (Houston: Gulf Publishing, 1964); Robert R. Blake and Jane S. Mouton, *The Versatile Manager: A Grid Profile* (Homewood, Ill.: Dow Jones-Irwin, 1981).

16. Robert Tannenbaum and Warren H. Schmidt, "How to Choose a Leadership Pattern," *Harvard Business Review*, March–April 1958, pp. 95–101.

17. Fred E. Fiedler, *A Theory of Leadership Effectiveness* (New York: McGraw-Hill, 1967).

18. Chester A. Schriesheim, Bennett J. Tepper, and Linda A. Tetrault, "Least Preferred Co-Worker Score, Situational Control, and Leadership Effectiveness: A Meta-Analysis of Contingency Model Performance Predictions," *Journal of Applied Psychology*, 1994, Vol. 79, No. 4, pp. 561–573.

19. Fiedler, *A Theory of Leadership Effectiveness*; Fred E. Fiedler and M. M. Chemers, *Leadership and Effective Management* (Glenview, Ill.: Scott, Foresman, 1974).

20. For recent reviews and updates, see Lawrence H. Peters, Darrell D. Hartke, and John T. Pohlmann, "Fiedler's Contingency Theory of Leadership: An Application of the Meta-Analysis Procedures of Schmidt and Hunter," *Psychological Bulletin*, Vol. 97, pp. 274–285; and Fred E. Fiedler, "When to Lead, When to Stand Back," *Psychology Today*, September 1987, pp. 26–27.

21. Martin G. Evans, "The Effects of Supervisory Behavior on the Path-Goal Relationship," *Organizational Behavior and Human Performance*, May 1970, pp. 277–298; Robert J. House and Terence R. Mitchell, "Path-Goal Theory of Leadership," *Journal of Contemporary Business*, Autumn 1974, pp. 81–98. See also Yukl, *Leadership in Organizations*.

22. For a recent review, see J. C. Wofford and Laurie Z. Liska, "Path-Gaol Theories of Leadership: A Meta-Analysis," *Journal of Management*, 1993, Vol. 19, No. 4, pp. 857–876.

23. See Victor H. Vroom and Philip H. Yetton, *Leadership and Decision Making* (Pittsburgh: University of Pittsburgh Press, 1973); Victor H. Vroom and Arthur G. Jago, *The New Leadership* (Englewood Cliffs, N.J.: Prentice-Hall, 1988).

24. Victor Vroom, "Leadership and the Decision-Making Process," *Organizational Dynamics*, 2000, Vol. 28, No. 4, pp. 82–94.

25. Vroom and Jago, *The New Leadership*.

26. Vroom and Jago, *The New Leadership*.

27. See Madeline E. Heilman, Harvey A. Hornstein, Jack H. Cage, and Judith K. Herschlag, "Reaction to Prescribed Leader Behavior as a Function of Role Perspective: The Case of the Vroom-Yetton Model," *Journal of Applied Psychology*, February 1984, pp. 50–60; R. H. George Field, "A Test of the Vroom-Yetton Normative Model of Leadership," *Journal of Applied Psychology*, February 1982, pp. 523–532.

28. George Graen and J. F. Cashman, "A Role-Making Model of Leadership in Formal Organizations: A Developmental Approach," in J. G. Hunt and L. L. Larson (eds.), *Leadership Frontiers* (Kent, Ohio: Kent State University Press, 1975), pp. 143–165; Fred Dansereau, George Graen, and W. J. Haga, "A Vertical Dyad Linkage Approach to Leadership Within Formal Organizations: A Longitudinal Investigation of the Role-Making Process," *Organizational Behavior and Human Performance*, Vol. 15, 1975, pp. 46–78.

29. See Charlotte R. Gerstner and David V. Day, "Meta-Analytic Review of Leader-Member Exchange Theory: Correlates and Construct Issues," *Journal of Applied Psychology*, 1997, Vol. 82, No. 6, pp. 827–844; Chester A. Schriesheim, Linda L. Neider, and Terri A. Scandura, "Delegation and Leader-Member Exchange: Main Effects, Moderators, and Measurement Issues," *Academy of Management Journal*, 1999, Vol. 41, No. 3, pp. 298–318.

30. Steven Kerr and John M. Jermier, "Substitutes for Leadership: Their Meaning and Measurement," *Organizational Behavior and Human Performance*, December 1978, pp. 375–403.

31. See Charles C. Manz and Henry P. Sims, Jr., "Leading Workers to Lead Themselves: The External Leadership of Self-Managing Work Teams," *Administrative Science Quarterly*, March 1987, pp. 106–129. See also "Living Without a Leader," *Fortune*, March 20, 2000, pp. 218–219.

32. See Robert J. House, "A 1976 Theory of Charismatic Leadership," in J. G. Hunt and L. L. Larson, eds., *Leadership: The Cutting Edge* (Carbondale, Ill.: Southern Illinois University Press, 1977), pp. 189–207. See also Jay A. Conger and Rabindra N. Kanungo, "Toward a Behavioral Theory of Charismatic Leadership in Organizational Settings," *Academy of Management Review*, October 1987, pp. 637–647.

33. Stratford P. Sherman, "Donald Trump Just Won't Die," *Fortune*, August 13, 1990, pp. 75–79.

34. David A. Nadler and Michael L. Tushman, "Beyond the Charismatic Leader: Leadership and Organizational Change," *California Management Review*, Winter 1990, pp. 77–97.

35. James MacGregor Burns, *Leadership* (New York: Harper & Row, 1978). See also Rajnandini Pillai, Chester A. Schriesheim, and Eric J. Williams, "Fairness Perceptions and Trust as Mediators for Transformational and Transactional Leadership: A Two-Sample Study," *Journal of Management*, 1999, Vol. 25, No. 6, pp. 897–933.

36. Labich, "The Seven Keys to Business Leadership."

37. "On Eve of Retirement, Jack Welch Decides to Stick Around a Bit," *Wall Street Journal*, October 23, 2000, pp. A1, A32.

38. Jeffrey Pfeffer, *Power in Organizations* (Marshfield, Mass.: Pitman Publishing, 1981), p. 7.

39. Timothy Judge and Robert Bretz, "Political Influence Behavior and Career Success," *Journal of Management*, 1994, Vol. 20, No. 1, pp. 43–65.

40. Victor Murray and Jeffrey Gandz, "Games Executives Play: Politics at Work," *Business Horizons*, December 1980, pp. 11–23; Jeffrey Gandz and Victor Murray, "The Experience of Workplace Politics," *Academy of Management Journal*, June 1980, pp. 237–251.

41. Don R. Beeman and Thomas W. Sharkey, "The Use and Abuse of Corporate Power," *Business Horizons*, March–April 1987, pp. 26–30.

42. See William L. Gardner, "Lessons in Organizational Dramaturgy: The Art of Impression Management," *Organizational Dynamics*, Summer 1992, pp. 51–63; Elizabeth Wolf Morrison and Robert J. Bies, "Impression Management in the Feedback-Seeking Process: A Literature Review and Research Agenda," *Academy of Management Review*, July 1991, pp. 522–541.

43. Murray and Gandz, "Games Executives Play."

44. Beeman and Sharkey, "The Use and Abuse of Corporate Power."

45. Stefanie Ann Lenway and Kathleen Rehbein, "Leaders, Followers, and Free Riders," An Empirical Test of Variation in Corporate Political Involvement," *Academy of Management Journal*, December 1991, pp. 893–905.

18 Managing Interpersonal Relations and Communication

While few people may have heard of Chaparral Steel Corp., the company enjoys a strong reputation as one of the most effective firms in the steel industry. Chaparral was founded as a subsidiary of Texas Industries about thirty years ago and today enjoys annual sales of over $800 million. In earlier times, most steel companies were large, bureaucratic operations like U.S. Steel (now USX) and Bethlehem Steel. However, increased competition from low-cost foreign steel firms—especially those in Japan and Korea—caused major problems for these manufacturers with their high overhead costs and inflexible modes of operation.

These competitive pressures, in turn, led to the formation of so-called mini-mills like Chaparral and Nucor. Because of their size, technology, and flexibility, these firms can maintain much lower production costs and respond more quickly to customer requests. And today, Chaparral is recognized as one of the best of this new breed of steel companies. For example, while most mills produce an average of one ton of steel for every three to five labor-hours, Chaparral produces a ton with less than 1.2 labor-hours.

Since its inception, Chaparral has been led by Gordon Forward. Forward knew that if Chaparral was going to succeed, it would need to be managed in new and different ways. One of the first things he decided to do was to break down the traditional barriers that often exist between management and labor. Thus, he mandated that there would be no reserved parking spaces and no separate dining area for managers. He also insisted that all employees be paid on a salary basis—no time clocks or time sheets for anyone. He also pioneered a concept called "open book manage-

ment"—any employee can access any document, record, or other piece of information at any time.

Moreover, Forward himself maintains an open-door policy. Any employee can drop by his office at any time, with or without an appointment, and discuss issues or ask questions about what is going on in the company. Forward also believes in trusting everyone in the organization. When the firm recently needed a new rolling mill lathe, it budgeted $1 million for its purchase, then put the purchase decision in the hands of an operating machinist. That machinist, in turn, investigated various

> *"We encourage people at all organizational levels to have face-to-face dialogues."*
>
> *—Dennis Beach, Chaparral Executive Vice President*

After studying this chapter, you should be able to:

- Describe the interpersonal nature of organizations.

- Describe the role and importance of communication in the manager's job.

- Identify the basic forms of communication in organizations.

- Discuss informal communication, including its various forms and types.

- Describe how the communication process can be managed to recognize and overcome barriers.

options, visited other mills in Japan and Europe, and then recommended an alternative piece of machinery costing less than half of the budgeted amount.

Forward also recognizes the importance of investing in and rewarding people. Continuous education is an integral part of Chaparral's culture, with a variety of classes being offered all the time. Everyone also participates in the good—and the bad—times. For example, workers have a guaranteed base salary that is adequate, but below the standard market rate. In addition, however, each employee gets a pay-for-performance bonus based on his or her individual achievements. Finally, there are also companywide bonuses paid to everyone on a quarterly basis. These bonuses are tied to overall company performance.[1]

Gordon Forward seems to have what is a surprisingly rare combination of communication skills and managerial acumen. Communication is a vital part of managerial work. Indeed, managers around the world agree that communication is one of their most important tasks. It is important for them to communicate with others and thus to convey their vision and goals for the organization. And it is important for others to communicate with them so that they will better understand what's going on in their environment and how they and their organizations can become more effective.

This chapter is the first of two that focuses on interpersonal processes in organizations. We first establish the interpersonal nature of organizations and then discuss communication, one of the most basic forms of interaction among people. We begin by examining communication in the context of the manager's job. We then identify and discuss forms of interpersonal, group, and organizational communication. After discussing informal types of communication, we describe how organizational communication can be effectively managed. In the next chapter, we discuss other elements of interpersonal relations, group and team processes, and conflict.

The Interpersonal Nature of Organizations

In Chapter 1, we noted how much of a manager's job involves scheduled and unscheduled meetings, telephone calls, and related activities. Indeed, a great deal of what all managers do involves interacting with other people, both inside and outside the organization. The schedule that follows is a typical day for the president of a Houston-based company, part of a larger firm headquartered in California. He kept a log of his activities for several different days so you could better appreciate the nature of managerial work.

7:45–8:15 A.M. Arrive at work; review hard-copy mail sorted by assistant.

8:15–8:30 A.M. Scan *Wall Street Journal*; read and respond to incoming e-mail.

8:30–9:00 A.M. Meet with labor officials and plant manager to resolve minor labor disputes.

9:00–9:30 A.M. Review internal report; read and respond to incoming e-mail.

9:30–10:00 A.M. Meet with two marketing executives to review advertising campaign; instruct them to fax approvals to advertising agency.

10:00–11:30 A.M. Meet with company executive committee to discuss strategy, budgetary issues, and competition (this committee meets weekly).

11:30–12:00 noon. Send new e-mail; read and respond to incoming e-mails.

12:00–1:15 P.M. Lunch with the financial vice president and two executives from another subsidiary of the parent corporation. Primary topic of discussion is the Houston Rockets basketball team. Place three calls from cellular phone en-route to lunch, and receive one call en-route back to office.

1:15–1:45 P.M. Meet with human resource director and assistant about a recent OSHA inspection; establish a task force to investigate the problems identified and to suggest solutions.

1:45–2:00 P.M. Read and respond to incoming e-mail.

2:00–2:30 P.M. Conference call with four other company presidents.

2:30–3:00 P.M. Meet with financial vice president about a confidential issue that came up at lunch (unscheduled).

3:00–3:30 P.M. Work alone in office; read and respond to incoming e-mail; send new e-mail.

3:30–4:15 P.M. Meet with a group of sales representatives and the company purchasing agent.

4:15–5:30 P.M. Work alone in office.

5:30–7:00 P.M. Play racquetball at nearby athletic club with marketing vice president.

How did this manager spend his time? He spent most of it working, communicating, and interacting with other people. And this compressed daily schedule does not include several other brief telephone calls, brief conversations with his assistant, and brief conversations with other managers. Clearly, interpersonal relations, communication, and group processes are a pervasive part of all organizations and a vital part of all managerial activities.[2]

Interpersonal Dynamics

The nature of interpersonal relations in an organization is as varied as the individual members themselves. At one extreme, interpersonal relations can be personal and positive. This situation occurs when the two parties know each other, have mutual respect and affection, and enjoy interacting with one another. Two managers who have known each other for years, play golf together on weekends, and are close personal friends will likely interact at work in a positive fashion. At the other extreme, interpersonal dynamics can be personal but negative. This situation is most likely when the parties dislike one another, do not have mutual respect, and do not enjoy interacting with one another. Suppose a manager has fought openly for years to block the promotion of another manager within the organization. Over the objections of the first manager, however, the other manager eventually gets promoted to the same rank. When the two of them must interact, it will most likely be in a negative manner.

Interpersonal dynamics are a major part of organizational life. Much of the work people do involves interacting with others—sometimes in positive ways, sometimes in negative ways. These executives are attending a company party at the Boston Children's Museum. While they are obviously enjoying themselves, their interactions will also affect their working relationships after the party has ended.

Most interactions fall between these two extremes because members of the organization interact in a professional way focused primarily on goal accomplishment. The interaction deals with the job at hand, is relatively formal and structured, and is task-directed. Two managers may respect each other's work and recognize the professional competence that each brings to the job. However, they may also have few common interests and little to talk about besides the job they are doing. These different types of interaction may occur between individuals, between groups, or between individuals and groups, and they can change over time. The two managers in the second scenario, for example, might decide to bury the hatchet and adopt a detached, professional manner. The two managers in the third example could find more common ground than they anticipated and evolve toward a personal and positive interaction.

Outcomes of Interpersonal Behaviors

Several events can happen as a result of interpersonal behaviors. Recall from Chapter 16, for example, that numerous perspectives on motivation suggest that people have social needs. Interpersonal relations in organizations can be a primary source of need satisfaction for many people. For people with a strong need for affiliation, high-quality interpersonal relations can be an important positive element in the workplace. However, when this same person is confronted with poor-quality working relationships, the effect can be just as great in the opposite direction.

Interpersonal relations also serve as a solid basis for social support. Suppose that an employee receives a poor performance evaluation or is denied a promotion. Others in the organization can lend support because they share a common frame of reference—an understanding of the causes and consequences of what happened. Good interpersonal relations throughout an organization can also be a source of synergy. People who support one another and who work well together can accomplish much more than people who do not support one another and who do not work well together. Another outcome, implied earlier, is conflict—people may leave an interpersonal exchange feeling angry or hostile. But a common thread is woven throughout all these outcomes—communication between people in the organization.[3]

MANAGEMENT IMPLICATIONS Managers need to remember that interpersonal dynamics form the crux of most managerial work. Moreover, they should be aware that the outcomes of interpersonal behaviors and interactions can take different forms.

Communication and the Manager's Job

As evidenced by the daily log presented earlier, a typical day for a manager includes doing desk work, attending scheduled meetings, placing and receiving telephone calls, reading correspondence, answering correspondence, attending unscheduled meetings, and tours.[4] Most of these activities involve communication. In fact, managers usually spend over half their time on some form of communication. Communication always involves two or more people, so other behavioral processes such as motivation, leadership, and group and team processes all come into play. Top executives must handle communication effectively if they are to be true leaders.

A Definition of Communication

Imagine three managers working in an office building. The first is all alone but is nevertheless yelling for a subordinate to come help. No one appears, but he con-

tinues to yell. The second is talking on the telephone to a subordinate, but static on the line causes the subordinate to misunderstand some important numbers being provided by the manager. As a result, the subordinate sends fifteen hundred crates of eggs to 150 Fifth Street, when he should have sent 150 crates of eggs to 1500 Fifteenth Street. The third manager is talking in her office with a subordinate who clearly hears and understands what is being said. Each of these managers is attempting to communicate but with different results.

Communication is the process of transmitting information from one person to another. Did any of our three managers communicate? The last did and the first did not. How about the second? In fact, she did communicate. She transmitted information and information was received. The problem was that the message transmitted and the message received were not the same. The words spoken by the manager were distorted by static and noise. **Effective communication**, then, is the process of sending a message in such a way that the message received is as close in meaning as possible to the message intended. Although the second manager engaged in communication, it was not effective.

Our definition of effective communication is based on the ideas of meaning and consistency of meaning. Meaning is the idea that the individual who initiates the communication exchange wishes to convey. In effective communication, the meaning is transmitted in such a way that the receiving person understands it. For example, consider the following messages:

1. The high today will be only 40 degrees.
2. It will be cold today.
3. Ceteris paribus
4. Xn1gp bo5cz4ik ab19

communication The process of transmitting information from one person to another

effective communication The process of sending a message in such a way that the message received is as close in meaning as possible to the message intended

You probably understand the meaning of the first statement. The second statement may seem clear at first, but it is somewhat less clear than the first statement because cold is a relative condition and the word can mean different things to different people. Fewer still understand the third statement because it is written in Latin. None of you understands the last statement because it is written in a secret code that your author developed as a child.

The Role of Communication in Management

We noted earlier the variety of activities that fill a manager's day. Meetings, telephone calls, and correspondence are all necessary parts of every manager's job—and all clearly involve communication. On a typical Monday, Nolan Archibald, CEO of Black & Decker, attended five scheduled meetings and two unscheduled meetings; had fifteen telephone conversations; received and/or sent over one hundred e-mails plus twenty-nine letters, memos, and reports; and dictated ten letters.

To understand better the link between communication and management, recall the variety of roles that managers must fill. Each of the ten basic managerial roles discussed in Chapter 1 (see Table 1.2) would be impossible to fill without communication.[5] Interpersonal roles involve interacting with supervisors, subordinates, peers, and others outside the organization. Decisional roles require managers to seek out information to use in making decisions and then to communicate those decisions to others. Informational roles focus specifically on the acquiring and disseminating of information.

Communication also relates directly to the basic management functions of planning, organizing, leading, and controlling. Environmental scanning, integrating planning-time horizons, and decision making, for example, all necessitate communication. Delegation, coordination, and organization change and development also entail communication. Developing reward systems and interacting with subordinates as part of the leading function would be impossible without some form of communication. And communication is essential to establishing standards, monitoring performance, and taking corrective actions as part of control. Clearly, then, communication is a pervasive part of almost all managerial activities.[6]

The Communication Process

Figure 18.1 illustrates how communication generally takes place between people. The process of communication begins when one person (the sender) wants to transmit a fact, idea, opinion, or other information to someone else (the receiver). This fact, idea, or opinion has meaning to the sender, whether it be simple and concrete, or complex and abstract. For example, Linda Porter, a marketing representative at Canon, recently landed a new account and wanted to tell her boss about it. This fact and her motivation to tell her boss represented meaning.

The next step is to encode the meaning into a form appropriate to the situation. The encoding might take the form of words, facial expressions, gestures, or even artistic expressions and physical actions. For example, the Canon representative might have said, "I just landed the Acme account," "We just got some good

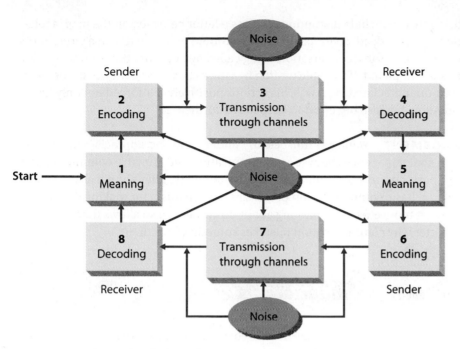

Figure 18.1

The Communication Process
As the figure shows, noise can disrupt the communication process at any step. Managers must therefore understand that a conversation in the next office, a fax machine out of paper, and the receiver's worries may all thwart the manager's best attempts to communicate.

The numbers indicate the sequence in which steps take place.

news from Acme," "I just spoiled Xerox's day," "Acme just made the right decision," or any number of other things. She actually chose the second message. Clearly, the encoding process is influenced by the content of the message, the familiarity of sender and receiver, and other situational factors.

After the message has been encoded, it is transmitted through the appropriate channel or medium. The channel by which the present encoded message is being transmitted to you is the printed page. Common channels in organizations include meetings, e-mail, memos, letters, reports, and telephone calls. Linda Porter might have written her boss a note, sent him an e-mail, called him on the telephone, or dropped by his office to convey the news. Because both she and her boss were out of the office when she got the news, she called and left a message for him on his voice mail.

After the message is received, it is decoded back into a form that has meaning for the receiver. As noted earlier, the consistency of this meaning can vary dramatically. Upon hearing about the Acme deal, the sales manager at Canon might have thought, "This'll mean a big promotion for both of us," "This is great news for the company," or "She's blowing her own horn too much again." His actual feelings were closest to the second statement. In many cases, the meaning prompts a response, and the cycle is continued when a new message is sent by the same steps back to the original sender. The manager might have called the sales representative to offer congratulations, written her a personal note of praise, offered praise in an e-mail, or sent a formal letter of acknowledgment. Linda's boss wrote her a personal note.

"Noise" may disrupt communication anywhere along the way. Noise can be the sound of someone coughing, a truck driving by, or two people talking close at hand. It can also include disruptions such as a letter being lost in the mail, a telephone line going dead, an e-mail getting misrouted or infected with a virus, or one of the participants in a conversation being called away before the communication process is completed. If the note written by Linda's boss had gotten lost, she might have felt unappreciated. As it was, his actions positively reinforced not only her efforts at Acme but also her effort to keep him informed.

MANAGEMENT IMPLICATIONS Managers must clearly understand and appreciate the differences between communication and effective communication and the pervasive role of communication in their work. They should also be familiar with the basic communication process as a mechanism for making their communication more effective. Learning about this process also allows them to understand better why communication mistakes sometimes occur.

Forms of Communication in Organizations

Managers need to understand several kinds of communication that are common in organizations today. These include interpersonal communication, communication in networks and teams, organizational communication, and electronic communication.

Interpersonal Communication

Interpersonal communication generally takes one of two forms, oral and written. As we will see, each has clear strengths and weaknesses.

oral communication Face-to-face conversations, group discussions, telephone calls, and other situations in which the spoken word is used to express meaning

Oral Communication **Oral communication** takes place in face-to-face conversations, group discussions, telephone calls, and other situations in which the spoken word is used to express meaning. Henry Mintzberg demonstrated the importance of oral communication when he found that most managers spend between 50 and 90 percent of their time talking to people.[7] Oral communication is so prevalent for several reasons. The primary advantage of oral communication is that it promotes prompt feedback and interchange in the form of verbal questions or agreement, facial expressions, and gestures. Oral communication is also easy (all the sender needs to do is talk), and it can be done with little preparation (though careful preparation is advisable in certain situations). The sender does not need pencil and paper, keyboard, or other equipment. In one survey, 55 percent of the executives sampled felt that their own written communication skills were fair or poor, so they chose oral communication to avoid embarrassment![8]

However, oral communication also has drawbacks. It may suffer from problems of inaccuracy if the speaker chooses the wrong words to convey meaning or leaves out pertinent details, if noise disrupts the process, or if the receiver forgets part of the message. In a two-way discussion, there is seldom time for a thoughtful, considered response or for introducing many new facts, and there is no permanent record of what has been said. In addition, although most managers are comfortable talking to people individually or in small groups, fewer enjoy speaking to larger audiences.[9]

Written Communication "Putting it in writing" in a letter, report, memorandum, hand-written note, or e-mail can solve many of the problems inherent in oral communication. Nevertheless, and perhaps surprisingly, **written communication** is not as common as one might imagine, nor is it a mode of communication much respected by managers. One sample of managers indicated that only 13 percent of the mail they received was of immediate use to them.[10] Over 80 percent of the managers who responded to another survey indicated that the written communication they received was of fair or poor quality.[11]

The biggest single drawback of traditional forms of written communication is that it inhibits feedback and interchange. When one manager sends another manager a letter, it must be written or dictated, typed, mailed, received, routed, opened, and read. If there is a misunderstanding, it may take several days for it to be recognized, let alone rectified. While the use of e-mail is, of course, much faster, both sender and receiver must still have access to a computer and the receiver must open and read the message for it to actually be received. A phone call could settle the whole matter in just a few minutes. Thus, written communication often inhibits feedback and interchange and is usually more difficult and time consuming than oral communication.

Of course, written communication offers some advantages. It is often quite accurate and provides a permanent record of the exchange. The sender can take the time to collect and assimilate the information and can draft and revise it before it is transmitted. The receiver can take the time to read it carefully and can refer to it repeatedly, as needed. For these reasons, written communication is generally preferable when important details are involved. At times it is important to one or both parties to have a written record available as evidence of exactly what took place. Julie Regan, founder of Toucan-Do, an importing company based in Honolulu, relies heavily on formal business letters in establishing contacts and buying merchandise from vendors in Southeast Asia. She believes that such letters give her an opportunity to think carefully about what she wants to say, to tailor her message to each individual, and to avoid misunderstandings later.

Choosing the Right Form Which form of interpersonal communication should the manager use? The best medium will be determined by the situation. Oral communication or e-mail is often preferred when the message is personal, nonroutine, and brief. More formal written communication is usually best when the message is more impersonal, routine, and longer. The manager can also combine media to capitalize on the advantages of each. For example, a quick telephone call to set up

People communicate with one another in a variety of ways and in many different settings. Consider this team of Netscape employees. They are using oral communication as they talk while they eat lunch. They are also using written communication from the papers stacked on the table and electronic communication in the form of e-mail. Moreover, they are using nonverbal communication with their body language and facial expressions.

written communication Memos, letters, reports, notes, and other methods in which the written word is used to transmit meaning

a meeting is easy and gets an immediate response. Following up the call with a reminder e-mail or handwritten note helps ensure that the recipient will remember the meeting, and it provides a record of the meeting having been called. Electronic communication, discussed more fully later, blurs the differences between oral and written communication and can help each be more effective.

Communication in Networks and Work Teams

communication network
The pattern through which the members of a group or team communicate

While communication among team members in an organization is clearly interpersonal in nature, substantial research also focuses specifically on how people in networks and work teams communicate with one another. A **communication network** is the pattern through which the members of a group or team communicate. Researchers studying group dynamics have discovered several typical networks in groups and teams consisting of three, four, and five members. Representative networks among members of five-member teams are shown in Figure 18.2.[12]

In the wheel pattern, all communication flows through one central person who is probably the group's leader. In a sense the wheel is the most centralized network because one person receives and disseminates all information. The Y pattern is slightly less centralized—two persons are close to the center. The chain offers a more even flow of information among members, although two people (those at each end) interact with only one other person. This path is closed in the circle pattern. Finally, the all-channel network, the most decentralized, allows a free flow of information among all group members. Everyone participates equally, and the group's leader, if there is one, is not likely to have excessive power.

Research conducted on networks suggests some interesting connections between the type of network and group performance. For example, when the group's task is relatively simple and routine, centralized networks tend to perform with greatest efficiency and accuracy. The dominant leader facilitates performance by coordinating the flow of information. When a group of accounting clerks is logging incoming invoices and distributing them for payment, for example, one centralized leader can coordinate tasks efficiently. When the task is complex and nonroutine, such as making a major decision about organizational strategy, decentralized networks tend to be most effective because open channels of communication per-

Figure 18.2

Types of Communication Networks
Research on communication networks has identified five basic networks for five-person groups. These networks vary in terms of information flow, position of the leader, and effectiveness for different types of tasks. Managers might strive to create centralized networks when group tasks are simple and routine. Alternatively, managers can foster decentralized groups when group tasks are complex and nonroutine.

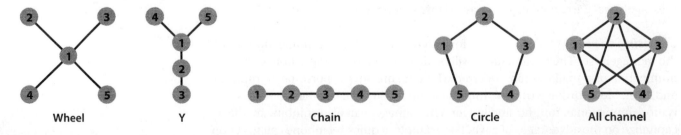

DILBERT by Scott Adams reprinted by permission of United Feature Syndicate, Inc.

Vertical communication is communication that flows up and down the organizational hierarchy, usually along formal reporting channels involving supervisors and subordinates. In some organizational settings, generally those characterized by trust and openness, anyone can feel free to talk to others several levels higher or lower in the organization. But in other cases, such as the one shown here, individuals who bypass the formal chain of command can create serious problems for themselves. This result usually relates to a feeling of insecurity and/or strong needs for power and control on the part of those who may feel bypassed.

mit more interaction and a more efficient sharing of relevant information. Managers should recognize the effects of communication networks on group and organizational performance and should try to structure networks appropriately.

Organizational Communication

Still other forms of communication in organizations is that which flows among and between organizational units or groups. Each of these involves oral or written communication, but each also extends to broad patterns of communication across the organization.[13] As shown in Figure 18.3, two of these forms of communication follow vertical and horizontal links in the organization. As discussed in *Working with Diversity*, organizational communication is increasingly spanning international boundaries.

Vertical Communication   **Vertical communication** is communication that flows up and down the organization, usually along formal reporting lines—that is, it is the communication that takes place between managers and their superiors

vertical communication Communication that flows up and down the organization, usually along formal reporting lines; it takes place between managers and their subordinates and may involve several different levels of the organization

Figure 18.3

Formal Communication in Organizations

Formal communication in organizations follows official reporting relationships and/or prescribed channels. For example, vertical communication, shown here with dashed lines, flows between levels in the organization and involves subordinates and their managers. Horizontal communication flows between people at the same level and is usually used to facilitate coordination.

← ——— Vertical communication

←- - - - Horizontal communication

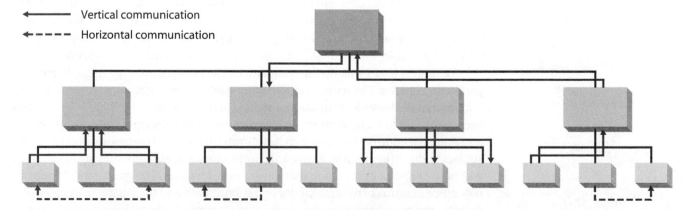

WORKING WITH DIVERSITY

SHARING THE WORKLOAD WITH COLLEAGUES IN OTHER COUNTRIES

When employees in Caltex Petroleum's Singapore headquarters work with colleagues in accounting or web site management, they have to stop and think whether to call Manila, where the accounting department is located, or South Africa, where web development is located. Caltex, a joint venture between Texaco and Chevron, operates a chain of gasoline stations across Southeast Asia and Africa and in countries between. The company was once based in Dallas but moved the main office to Singapore to be closer to its main markets. Thanks to telecommunications technology, Caltex can open an office wherever it finds an expert workforce and keep employees linked horizontally and vertically by phone, fax, and—most frequently—e-mail.

Caltex is in the vanguard of a movement to move selected positions out of higher-cost countries (such as the United States and some European countries) and into lower-cost nations (such as Ireland, Jamaica, India, and the Philippines). By hiring skilled, English-speaking employees for software development, customer service support, clerical activities, and other jobs, employers can save 30 percent or more on labor costs, gain access to a larger labor pool, and take advantage of time differences to keep work flowing virtually around the clock.

Citigroup and Microsoft are just two of a growing number of global firms that have opened software outposts in Ireland,

Motorola and Bell Labs both operate research centers in Bangalore, and General Electric Capital has a customer service call center in India employing one thousand representatives. General Electric is so happy with the integration of this workforce that it is opening more offices in India to handle payroll and other functions.

In this Internet age, countries must have a strong telecommunications infrastructure to attract the interest of multinational companies. U.S.-based companies such as Brigade are flocking to ready-wired high-tech office parks in India, where they can set up shop quickly and hire computer-savvy locals to work on customer service projects for Compaq and other clients. As these firms recognize, e-mail shrinks the time and distance between employees in far-flung offices while facilitating communication in every direction.

> *As technology and communication improve, we are scattering centers of excellence around the world.*
>
> *—William Pfluger, general manager of Caltex's accounting division in Manila**

Reference: Mark Clifford and Manjeet Kripalani, "Different Countries, Adjoining Cubicles," *Business Week,* August 28, 2000, pp. 182–184 (*quote on p.182).

and subordinates. Vertical communication may involve only two people, or it may flow through several different organizational levels. A common perspective on vertical communication that exists in some organizations is illustrated in the cartoon.

Upward communication consists of messages from subordinates to superiors. This flow is usually from subordinates to their direct superior, then to that person's direct superior, and so on, up the hierarchy. Occasionally, a message might bypass a particular superior. The typical content of upward communication is requests, information that the lower-level manager thinks is of importance to the higher-level manager, responses to requests from the higher-level manager, suggestions, complaints, and financial information. Research has shown that upward communication is more subject to distortion than is downward communication. Subordinates are likely to withhold or distort information that makes them look bad. The greater the degree of difference in status between superior and subordinate and the greater the degree of distrust, the more likely the subordinate is to suppress or distort information.[14] For example, subordinates might choose to withhold information about problems from their boss if they thought the news would make him angry and if they thought they could solve the problem themselves without his ever knowing about it.

Downward communication occurs when information flows down the hierarchy from superiors to subordinates. The typical content of these messages is directives on how something is to be done, the assignment of new responsibilities, performance feedback, and general information that the higher-level manager thinks will be of value to the lower-level manager. Vertical communication can, and usually should, be two-way in nature; that is, give-and-take communication with active feedback is generally likely to be more effective than one-way communication.[15]

Horizontal Communication Whereas vertical communication involves a superior and a subordinate, **horizontal communication** involves colleagues and peers at the same level of the organization. For example, an operations manager might communicate to a marketing manager that inventory levels are running low and that projected delivery dates should be extended by two weeks. Horizontal communication probably occurs more among managers than among nonmanagers.

This type of communication serves several purposes.[16] It facilitates coordination among interdependent units. For example, a manager at Motorola was once researching the strategies of Japanese semiconductor firms in Europe. He found a great deal of information that was relevant to his assignment. He also uncovered some additional information that was potentially important to another department, so he passed it along to a colleague in that department, who used it to improve his own operations. Horizontal communication can also be used for joint problem solving, as when two plant managers at Northrup Grumman got together to work out a new method to improve productivity. Finally, horizontal communication plays a major role in work teams with members drawn from several departments.

> **horizontal communication**
> Communication that flows laterally within the organization; it involves colleagues and peers at the same level of the organization and may involve individuals from several different organizational units

Electronic Communication

Finally, electronic communication has recently taken on much greater importance in organizations. Both formal information systems and personal information technology have reshaped how managers communicate with one another. *Managing in an e-Business World* clearly amplifies this point.

Formal Information Systems Another increasingly important method of organizational communication is information systems. This method is accomplished by a managerial approach or an operational approach. The managerial approach involves the creation of a position usually called the chief information officer, or CIO. General Mills, Xerox, and Burlington Industries have all created such a position. The CIO is responsible for determining the information-processing needs and requirements of the organization and then putting in place systems that facilitate smooth and efficient organizational communication.

The operational approach, often part of the CIO's efforts, involves the creation of one or more formal information systems linking all relevant managers, departments, and facilities in the organization. In the absence of such a system, a marketing manager, for example, may need to call a warehouse manager to find out

MANAGING IN AN *e*-BUSINESS WORLD

CISCO CASTS ITS COMMUNICATIONS NET WIDER

Many companies use their web sites to communicate with customers. However, Cisco Systems casts its communications net even wider, using the Internet to facilitate speedy communication among employees, suppliers, distributors, and other business partners as well as with customers. Using the Web for internal and external communication is a natural step for a company that makes switchers and other electronic equipment to power the Internet.

Cisco employees log onto the company's internal web site an average of thirty times every day to tap on-line training programs, read announcements, upload expense reports, and check or change benefits plans. Managers do all that and more via the Web: they file employee performance reviews, check the latest departmental sales figures, and search for competitive data.

Suppliers and distributors benefit from easy access to the latest details about Cisco orders, sales, and specifications. Singapore-based supplier Flextronics International, for example, can instantly find out what it should gear up to manufacture by looking at a special section of Cisco's web site. Based on information Cisco posts about orders just received, Flextronics can quickly build and ship the needed products. Everybody benefits: Flextronics knows exactly what to produce and when, customers receive speedy delivery of ordered products, and Cisco keeps costs low while satisfying customers.

Customer service gets a big boost from Cisco's web-based communication. Many big commercial customers, such as the Hannaford Brothers grocery chain, like the convenience of checking the technical support part of Cisco's site to diagnose their network problems or locate technical update details. In fact, 85 percent of customers seeking technical support for Cisco products go to the web site for answers instead of calling the company—a big savings for Cisco. Still, Cisco's technical experts receive e-mail alerts about any problem a customer hasn't been able to fix after an hour of looking for information on the web site. At that point, Cisco's experts resort to non-Internet technology: they pick up the phone and call to see what they can do to help the customer solve the problem.

> *I can't remember the last time I called Cisco.*
>
> —*Ed Taggart, network manager for Cisco client Hannaford Brothers**

Reference: Scott Thurm, "Eating Their Own Dog Food," *Wall Street Journal,* April 19, 2000, pp. B1, B4 (*quote on p. B4).

---

how much of a particular product is in stock before promising shipping dates to a customer. An effective formal information system allows the marketing manager to get the information more quickly, and probably more accurately, by plugging directly into a computerized information system. Because of the increased emphasis and importance of these kinds of information systems, we cover them in detail in Chapter 22.

Personal Electronic Technology   In recent years, the nature of organizational communication has changed dramatically, mainly because of breakthroughs in personal electronic communication technology, and the future promises even more change. Electronic typewriters and photocopying machines were early breakthroughs. The photocopier, for example, makes it possible for a manager to have a typed report distributed to large numbers of other people in an extremely short time. Personal computers have accelerated the process even more. E-mail networks, the

Internet, and corporate intranets promise to carry communication technology even further in the years to come.

It is now possible to have teleconferences in which managers stay at their own locations (such as offices in different cities) but are seen on television or computer monitors as they "meet." A manager in New York can keyboard a letter or memorandum at her personal computer, point and click with a mouse, and have it delivered to hundreds or even thousands of colleagues around the world in a matter of seconds. Highly detailed information can be retrieved with ease from large electronic databanks. This technology has given rise to a new version of an old work arrangement—telecommuting is the label given to a new electronic cottage industry. In a cottage industry, people work at home (in their "cottages") and periodically bring the product of their labor to the company. In telecommuting, people work at home on their computers and transmit their work to the company by means of telephone or cable modems.

Electronic communication technology is profoundly changing the way people work and live. For example, Paul Webster was recently traveling to Phoenix on business. Anticipating travel delays, he used his cell phone to call www.travel.com and get an update on both weather and traffic conditions. After learning that the exit he had planned to take was closed, he was quickly able to obtain step-by-step directions for an alternative route.

Cellular phones and fax machines have made it even easier for managers to communicate with one another. Many now use cellular phones to make calls while commuting to and from work and carry them in briefcases so they can receive calls while at lunch. Fax machines make it easy for people to use written communication media and get rapid feedback. And new personal computing devices such as Palm Pilots are further revolutionizing how people communicate with one another.

Psychologists, however, are beginning to associate some problems with these communication advances. For one thing, managers who are seldom in their "real" offices are likely to fall behind in their fields and to be victimized by organizational politics because they are not present to keep in touch with what's going on and to protect themselves. They drop out of the organizational grapevine and miss much of the informal communication that takes place. The use of electronic communication at the expense of face-to-face meetings and conversations makes it hard to build a strong culture, develop solid working relationships, and create a mutually supportive atmosphere of trust and cooperativeness.[17] Finally, electronic communication is also opening up new avenues for dysfunctional employee behavior such as the passing of lewd or offensive materials to others. For example, the New York Times Company recently fired almost 10 percent of its workers at one of its branch offices for sending inappropriate e-mails at work.[18]

MANAGEMENT IMPLICATIONS   Managers should realize that they have more modes of communication available to them today than at any time in history. Interpersonal, team-based, organizational, and electronic communication channels make it easier than ever before to keep in contact with others and to procure and distribute information. However, managers should also be aware of pitfalls that can occur as a result of using various specific communication methods.

Informal Communication in Organizations

The aforementioned forms of organizational communication all represent planned, formal communication mechanisms. In many cases, however, much of the communication that takes place in an organization transcends these formal channels and instead follows any of several informal methods. Figure 18.4 illustrates numerous examples of informal communication. Common forms of informal communication in organizations include the grapevine, management by wandering around, and nonverbal communication.

The Grapevine

grapevine An informal communication network that can permeate an entire organization

The **grapevine** is an informal communication network that can permeate an entire organization. Grapevines are found in all organizations except the very smallest, but they do not always follow the same patterns as, nor do they necessarily coincide with, formal channels of authority and communication. Research has identified several kinds of grapevines.[19] The two most common are illustrated in Figure 18.5. The gossip chain occurs when one person spreads the message to many other people. Each one, in turn, may either keep the information confidential or pass it on to others. The gossip chain is likely to carry personal information. The other common grapevine is the cluster chain, in which one person passes the information to a selected few individuals. Some of the receivers pass the information to a few other individuals; the rest keep it to themselves.

Figure 18.4

Informal Communication in Organizations

Informal communication in organizations may or may not follow official reporting relationships and/or prescribed channels. It may cross different levels and different departments or work units, and may or may not have anything to do with official organizational business.

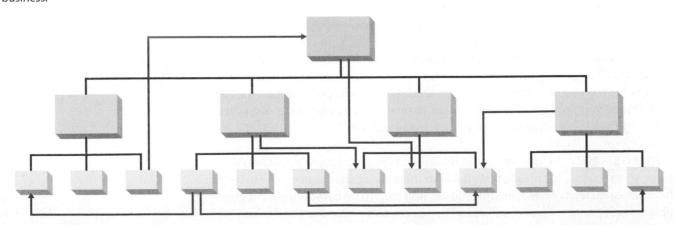

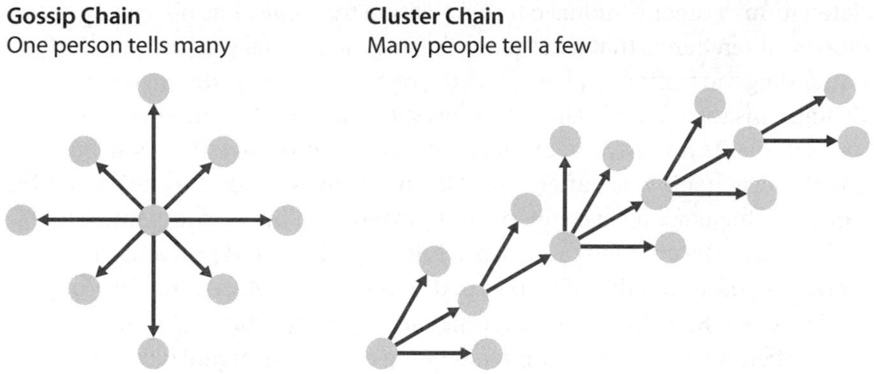

Gossip Chain
One person tells many

Cluster Chain
Many people tell a few

Source: Adapted from *Human Behavior at Work: Organizational Behavior*, Eighth Edition, by Keith Davis and John W. Newstrom. Copyright © 1989 by McGraw-Hill. Reprinted by permission of The McGraw-Hill Companies.

Figure 18.5

Common Grapevine Chains Found in Organizations
The two most common grapevine chains in organizations are the gossip chain (in which one person communicates messages to many others) and the cluster chain (in which many people pass messages to a few others).

There is some disagreement about the accuracy of the information carried by the grapevine, but research is increasingly finding it to be fairly accurate, especially when the information is based on fact rather than speculation. One recent study found that the grapevine may be between 75 percent and 95 percent accurate.[20] That same study also found that informal communication is increasing in many organizations for two basic reasons. One contributing factor is the recent increase in merger, acquisition, and takeover activity. Because such activity can greatly affect the people within an organization, it follows that they may spend more time talking about it.[21] The second contributing factor is that, as more and more corporations move facilities from inner cities to suburbs, employees tend to talk less and less to others outside the organization and more and more to each other.

Attempts to eliminate the grapevine are fruitless, but fortunately the manager does have some control over it. By maintaining open channels of communication and responding vigorously to inaccurate information, the manager can minimize the damage the grapevine can do. The grapevine can actually be an asset. By learning who the key people in the grapevine are, for example, the manager can partially control the information they receive and use the grapevine to sound out employee reactions to new ideas such as a change in human resource policies or benefit packages. The manager can also get valuable information from the grapevine and use it to improve decision making.[22]

Management by Wandering Around

Another increasingly popular form of informal communication is called **management by wandering around**.[23] The basic idea is that some managers keep in touch with what's going on by wandering around and talking with people—immediate subordinates, subordinates far down the organizational hierarchy, delivery people, customers, or anyone else who is involved with the company in some way. Bill Marriott, for example, frequently visits the kitchens, loading docks, and custodial work areas whenever he tours a Marriott hotel. He claims that by talking with employees throughout the hotel, he gets new ideas and has a better feel for the entire company.

management by wandering around An approach to communication that involves the manager literally wandering around and having spontaneous conversations with others who are involved with the company in some way

A related form of organizational communication that really has no specific term is the informal interchange that takes place outside the normal work setting. Employees attending the company picnic, playing on the company softball team, or taking fishing trips together will almost always spend part of their time talking about work. For example, Texas Instruments engineers at the Lewisville, Texas, facility often frequent a local bar in town after work. On any given evening, they talk about the Dallas Cowboys, the newest government contract received by the company, the weather, their boss, the company's stock price, local politics, and problems at work. There is no set agenda, and the key topics of discussion vary from group to group and from day to day. Still, the social gatherings serve an important role. They promote a strong culture and enhance understanding of how the organization works.

Nonverbal Communication

Nonverbal communication is any communication exchange that does not use words or that uses words to carry more meaning than the strict definition of the words themselves. Nonverbal communication is a powerful but little understood form of communication in organizations. It often relies on facial expression, body movements, physical contact, and gestures. One study found that as much as 55 percent of the content of a message is transmitted by facial expression and body posture and that another 38 percent derives from inflection and tone. Words themselves account for only 7 percent of the content of the message.[24]

Research has identified three kinds of nonverbal communication practiced by managers—images, settings, and body language.[25] In the organizational context, images are the kinds of words people elect to use. "Damn the torpedoes, full speed ahead" and "Even though there are some potential hazards, we should proceed with this course of action" may convey the same meaning. Yet the person who uses the first expression may be perceived as a maverick, a courageous hero, an individualist, or a reckless and foolhardy adventurer. The person who uses the second might be described as aggressive, forceful, diligent, or narrow-minded and resistant to change. In short, our choice of words conveys much more than just the strict meaning of the words themselves.

The setting for communication also plays a major role in nonverbal communication. Boundaries, familiarity, the home turf, and other elements of the setting are all important. Much has been written about the symbols of power in organizations. The size and location of an office, the kinds of furniture in the office, and the accessibility of the person in the office all communicate useful information. For example, H. Ross Perot positions his desk so that it is always between him and a visitor. This layout keeps him in charge. When he wants a less formal dialogue, he moves around to the front of the desk and sits beside his visitor. Michael Dell of Dell Computers has his desk facing a side window so that when he turns around to greet a visitor, there is never anything between them.

A third form of nonverbal communication is body language.[26] The distance we stand from someone as we speak has meaning. In the United States, standing very close to someone you are talking to generally signals either familiarity or aggression. The English and Germans stand farther apart than Americans do when talking, whereas the Arabs, Japanese, and Mexicans stand closer together.[27] Eye contact is another effective means of nonverbal communication. For example, prolonged eye contact might suggest either hostility or romantic interest. Other kinds of body language include body and arm movement, pauses in speech, and mode of dress.

The manager should be aware of the importance of nonverbal communication and recognize its potential impact. Giving an employee good news about a reward with the wrong nonverbal cues can destroy the reinforcement value of the reward. Likewise, reprimanding an employee but providing inconsistent nonverbal cues can limit the effectiveness of the sanctions. The tone of the message, where and how the message is delivered, facial expressions, and gestures can all amplify or weaken the message, or change the message altogether.

MANAGEMENT IMPLICATIONS Managers need to appreciate the power and pervasiveness of informal communication. The grapevine, for example, can be a powerful force with which managers must contend. Management by wandering around can be an effective way of learning. And nonverbal communication can frequently convey a great deal of information.

Managing Organizational Communication

In view of the importance and pervasiveness of communication in organizations, it is vital for managers to understand how to manage the communication process.[28] Managers should understand how to maximize the potential benefits of communication and minimize the potential problems. We begin our discussion of communication management by considering the factors that might disrupt effective communication and how to deal with them.

Barriers to Communication

Several factors may disrupt the communication process or serve as barriers to effective communication.[29] As shown in Table 18.1, these barriers may be divided into two classes: individual and organizational.

Individual Barriers Several individual barriers may disrupt effective communication. One common problem is conflicting or inconsistent signals. A manager is

Individual Barriers	Organizational Barriers
Conflicting or inconsistent cues	Semantics
Credibility about the subject	Status or power differences
Reluctance to communicate	Different perceptions
Poor listening skills	Noise
Predispositions about the subject	Overload

Table 18.1

Barriers to Effective Communication
Numerous barriers can disrupt effective communication. Some of these barriers involve individual characteristics and processes. Others are functions of the organizational context in which communication is taking place.

sending conflicting signals when she says on Monday that things should be done one way but then prescribes an entirely different procedure on Wednesday. Inconsistent signals are being sent by a manager who says that he has an open-door policy and wants his subordinates to drop by but keeps his door closed and becomes irritated whenever someone stops in.

Another barrier is lack of credibility. Credibility problems arise when the sender is not considered a reliable source of information. He may not be trusted or may not be perceived as knowledgeable about the subject at hand. When a politician is caught withholding information or when a manager makes a series of bad decisions, the extent to which they will be listened to and believed thereafter diminishes. In extreme cases, people may talk about something they obviously know little or nothing about.

Some people are simply reluctant to initiate a communication exchange. This reluctance may occur for various reasons. A manager may be reluctant to tell subordinates about an impending budget cut because he knows they will be unhappy about it. Likewise, a subordinate may be reluctant to transmit information upward for fear of reprisal or because he or she feels that such an effort would be futile.

Poor listening habits can be a major barrier to effective communication. Some people are simply poor listeners. When someone is talking to them, they may be daydreaming, looking around, reading, or listening to another conversation. Because they are not concentrating on what is being said, they may not comprehend part or all of the message. They may even think that they are really paying attention, only to realize later that they cannot remember parts of the conversation.

Receivers may also bring certain predispositions to the communication process. They may already have their minds made up, firmly set in a certain way. For example, a manager many have heard that his new boss is unpleasant and hard to work with. When she calls him for an introductory meeting, he may go into that meeting predisposed to dislike her and discount what she has to say.

Organizational Barriers Other barriers to effective communication involve the organizational context in which the communication occurs. Semantics problems arise when words have different meanings for different people. Words and phrases such as "profit," "increased output," and "return on investment" may have positive meanings for managers but less positive meanings for labor.

Communication problems may also arise when people of different power or status try to communicate with each other. The company president may discount a suggestion from an operating employee, thinking, "How can someone at that level help me run my business?" Or when the president inspects a new plant, workers may be reluctant to offer suggestions because of their lower status. The marketing vice president may have more power than the human resource vice president and consequently may not pay much attention to a staffing report submitted by the human resource department.

If people perceive a situation differently, they may have difficulty communicating with one another. When two managers observe that a third manager has not spent much time in her office lately, one may believe that she has been to several important meetings while the other may think she is "hiding out." If they need to talk about her in some official capacity, problems may arise because one has a positive impression and the other has a negative impression.

Environmental factors may also disrupt effective communication. As mentioned earlier, noise may affect communication in many ways. Similarly, overload may be a problem when the receiver is being sent more information than he or she can handle effectively. As e-mail becomes increasingly common, many managers report getting so many messages each day that they sometimes feel overwhelmed.[30] And when the manager gives a subordinate many projects on which to work and at the same time the subordinate is being told by family and friends to perform activities outside of work, overload may result and communication effectiveness is diminished.

Finally, as businesses become more and more global, different languages can create problems. To counter these problems, some firms are adopting an "official language." For example, when the German chemical firm Hoechst merged with the French firm Rhone-Poulenc, the new company adopted English as its official language. Indeed, English is increasingly becoming the standard business language around the world.[31] *Management Infotech* discusses an interesting communication barrier that has arisen in the U.S. military.

MANAGEMENT INFOTECH

TONE DOWN THE TECHNOLOGY—AND THAT'S AN ORDER

The U.S. military is going back to communication basics. The chairman of the Joint Chiefs of Staff has ordered military personnel to tone down the technology in their electronic slide presentations because the razzle-dazzle is detracting from the message. From noisy sound effects to eye-popping animation and convoluted diagrams, military presentations are so laden with flashy extras that listeners sometimes have difficulty distilling the main ideas.

Formal slide presentations have a long tradition within the U.S. military, where they have been used to update commanders about troop movements. Now jazzy electronic slide presentations have taken the place of static overheads as up-and-coming officers try to impress their superiors by cramming every possible detail into their presentations. Too often, these presentations wind up as a war of graphics, with presenters adding more electronic bells and whistles so they will stand out.

Listeners complain that these electronic slide shows can be endless and mind-numbing—the last reaction a presenter wants when discussing sensitive defense issues or asking for increased funding. In fact, Navy Secretary Richard Danzig wants his briefings submitted in writing so he won't have to sit through presentation after presentation with electronic slide accompaniment.

Because electronic slides are easy and inexpensive to create, military personnel in other countries are starting to use the technology to enliven presentations to their commanders. Meanwhile, electronic slide shows are not disappearing from military briefings throughout the Pentagon, although they are becoming somewhat simpler in response to the growing backlash from the top. And organizations that work with the U.S. military have adopted electronic slide presentations to show they can speak the same graphics language as their audience.

> *People are not listening to us, because they are spending so much time trying to understand these incredibly complex slides.*
>
> —*Louis Caldera, U.S. Secretary of the Army**

Reference: Greg Jaffe, "What's Your Point, Lieutenant? Just Cut to the Pie Charts," *Wall Street Journal*, April 26, 2000, pp. A1, A6 (*quote on p. A1).

Table 18.2

Overcoming Barriers to Communication

Because communication is so important, managers have developed several methods of overcoming barriers to effective communication. Some of these methods involve individual skills, whereas others are based on organizational skills.

Individual Skills	Organizational Skills
Develop good listening skills	Follow up
Encourage two-way communication	Regulate information flows
Be aware of language and meaning	Understand the richness of media
Maintain credibility	
Be sensitive to receiver's perspective	
Be sensitive to sender's perspective	

Improving Communication Effectiveness

Considering how many factors can disrupt communication, it is fortunate that managers can resort to several techniques for improving communication effectiveness.[32] As shown in Table 18.2, these techniques include both individual and organizational skills.

Individual Skills   The single most important individual skill for improving communication effectiveness is being a good listener.[33] Being a good listener requires that the individual be prepared to listen, not interrupt the speaker, concentrate on both the words and the meaning being conveyed, be patient, and ask questions as appropriate.[34] So important are good listening skills that companies like Delta, IBM, and Boeing conduct programs to train their managers to be better listeners. Figure 18.6 illustrates the characteristics of poor listeners versus good listeners.

In addition to being a good listener, several other individual skills can also promote effective communication. Feedback, one of the most important, is facilitated by two-way communication. Two-way communication allows the receiver to ask questions, request clarification, and express opinions that let the sender know

Figure 18.6

More and Less Effective Listening Skills

Effective listening skills are a vital part of communication in organizations. There are several barriers that can contribute to poor listening skills by individuals in organizations. Fortunately, there are also several practices for improving listening skills.

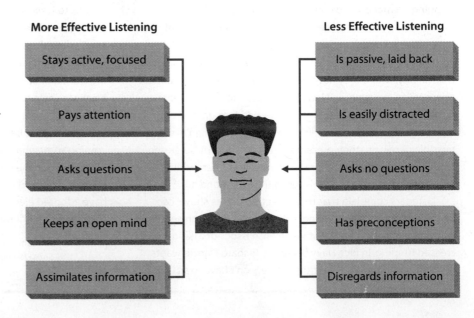

More Effective Listening	Less Effective Listening
Stays active, focused	Is passive, laid back
Pays attention	Is easily distracted
Asks questions	Asks no questions
Keeps an open mind	Has preconceptions
Assimilates information	Disregards information

whether he or she has been understood. In general, the more complicated the message, the more useful is two-way communication. In addition, the sender should be aware of the meanings that different receivers might attach to various words. For example, when addressing stockholders, a manager might use the word "profits" often. When addressing labor leaders, however, she may choose to use "profits" less often.

Furthermore, the sender should try to maintain credibility. Maintaining credibility can be accomplished by not pretending to be an expert when one is not, by "doing one's homework" and checking facts, and by otherwise being as accurate and honest as possible. The sender should also try to be sensitive to the receiver's perspective. A manager who must tell a subordinate that she has not been recommended for a promotion should recognize that the subordinate will be frustrated and unhappy. The content of the message and its method of delivery should be chosen accordingly. The manager should be primed to accept a reasonable degree of hostility and bitterness without getting angry in return.[35] Finally, the receiver should also try to be sensitive to the sender's point of view. Suppose that a manager has just received some bad news—for example, that his position is being eliminated next year. Others should understand that he may be disappointed, angry, or even depressed for a while. Thus, they might make a special effort not to take too much offense if he snaps at them, and they might look for signals that he needs someone to talk to.

Organizational Skills Three useful organizational skills can also enhance communication effectiveness for both the sender and the receiver—following up, regulating information flow, and understanding the richness of different media. Following up simply involves checking at a later time to be sure that a message has been received and understood. After a manager mails a report to a colleague, she might call a few days later to make sure the report has arrived. If it has, the manager might ask whether the colleague has any questions about it. Regulating information flow means that the sender or receiver takes steps to ensure that overload does not occur.

For the sender, avoiding overload could mean not passing too much information through the system at one time. For the receiver, it might mean calling attention to the fact that he is being asked to do too many tasks at once. Many managers limit the influx of information by periodically weeding out the list of journals and routine reports they receive, or they train a secretary to screen phone calls and visitors. Both senders and recievers should also understand the richness associated with different media. When a manager is going to lay off a subordinate temporarily, the message should be delivered in person. A face-to-face channel of communication gives the manager an opportunity to explain the situation and answer questions. When the purpose of the message is to grant a pay increase, written communication may be appropriate because it can be more objective and precise. The manager could then follow up the written notice with personal congratulations.

MANAGEMENT IMPLICATIONS Managers need to be aware of the many forces that can disrupt communication in their organizations. Just as important, they should also be aware of how to overcome those barriers and use these techniques and methods as much as possible.

Summary of Key Points

Communication is the process of transmitting information from one person to another. Effective communication is the process of sending a message so that the message received is as close in meaning as possible to the message intended.

Communication is a pervasive and important part of the manager's world. The communication process consists of a sender encoding meaning and transmitting it to one or more receivers, who receive the message and decode it into meaning. In two-way communication, the process continues with the roles reversed. Noise can disrupt any part of the overall process.

Several forms of organizational communication exist. Interpersonal communication focuses on communication among a small number of people. Two important forms of interpersonal communication, oral and written, offer unique advantages and disadvantages. Thus, the manager should weigh the pros and cons of each when choosing a medium for communication. Communication networks are recurring patterns of communication among members of a group or work team. Vertical communication between superiors and subordinates may flow upward or downward. Horizontal communication involves peers and colleagues at the same level in the organization. Organizations also use information systems to manage communication. Electronic communications is having a profound effect on managerial and organizational communication.

There is also a great deal of informal communication in organizations. The grapevine is the informal communication network among people in an organization. Management by wandering around is also a popular informal method of communication. Nonverbal communication includes facial expressions, body movement, physical contact, gestures, and inflection and tone.

Managing the communication process necessitates recognizing the barriers to effective communication and understanding how to overcome them. Barriers can be identified at both the individual and organizational level. Likewise, both individual and organizational skills can be used to overcome these barriers.

Discussion Questions

Questions for Review

1. Define communication. What are the components of the communication process?
2. Which form of interpersonal communication is best for long-term retention? Why? Which form is best for getting across subtle nuances of meaning? Why?
3. Describe three different communication networks. Which type of network seems to describe the grapevine most accurately? Why?
4. What are the informal methods of communication? Identify five examples of nonverbal communication that you have recently observed.

Questions for Analysis

5. Is it possible for an organization to function without communication? Why or why not?
6. At what points in the communication process can problems occur? Give examples of communication problems and indicate how they might be prevented or alleviated.

7. In terms of the barriers most likely to be encountered, what are the differences between horizontal and vertical communication in an organization? How might a formal information system be designed to reduce such barriers?

Questions for Application

8. What forms of communication have you experienced today? What form of communication is involved in a face-to-face conversation with a friend? A telephone call from a customer? A traffic light or crossing signal? A picture of a cigarette in a circle with a slash across it? An area around machinery defined by a yellow line painted on the floor?

9. Interview a local manager to determine what forms of communication are used in his or her organization. Arrange to observe that manager for a couple of hours. What forms of communication did you observe?

10. How are electronic communication devices likely to affect the communication process in the future? Why? Interview someone from a local organization who uses electronic communications to see if she or he feels as you do.

BUILDING EFFECTIVE *technical* SKILLS

Exercise Overview

Technical skills are the skills necessary to perform the work of the organization. This exercise will help you develop and apply technical skills involving the Internet and its potential for gathering information relevant to making important decisions.

Exercise Task

Assume that you are a manager for a large national retailer. You have been assigned the responsibility for identifying potential locations for the construction of a warehouse and distribution center. The idea behind such a center is that the firm can use its enormous purchasing power to buy many products in bulk quantities at relatively low prices. Individual stores can then order specific quantities they need from the warehouse.

The location will need an abundance of land. The warehouse itself, for example, will occupy more than four square acres of land. In addition, it must be close to railroads and major highways because shipments will be arriving by both rail and trucks, although outbound shipments will be exclusively by truck. Other important variables are that land prices and the cost of living should be relatively low and weather conditions should be mild (to minimize disruptions to shipments).

The firm's general experience is that small to midsize communities work best. Moreover, warehouses are already in place in the western and eastern parts of the United States, so this new one will most likely be in the central or south-central area. Your boss has asked you to identify three or four possible sites.

Exercise Task

With the information above as a framework, do the following:
1. Use the Internet to identify as many as ten possible locations.
2. Using additional information from the Internet, narrow the set of possible locations to three or four.
3. Again using the Internet, find out as much as possible about the potential locations.

BUILDING EFFECTIVE *communication* SKILLS

Exercise Overview

Communication skills refer to a manager's ability to convey ideas and information effectively to others and to receive ideas and information from others effectively. This exercise focuses on the best communication skills needed to convey information best.

Exercise Background

Assume that you are a middle manager for a large electronics firm. People in your organization generally use one of three means for communicating with one another. The most common way is verbal communication, either face to face or by telephone. Electronic mail is also widely used. Finally, a surprisingly large amount of communication is still done with paper, such as memos, reports, or letters.

During the course of a typical day, you receive and send a variety of messages and other communication. You generally use some combination of all the communication methods noted above during the course of any given day. The following is a list of items that you need to communicate today:

1. You must schedule a meeting with five subordinates.
2. You want to congratulate a coworker who just had a baby.
3. You need to reprimand a staff assistant who has been coming in to work late for the last several days.
4. You must inform the warehouse staff that several customers have recently complained because their shipments were not properly packed.
5. You need to schedule a meeting with your boss.
6. You need to announce two promotions.
7. You must fire someone who has been performing poorly for some time.
8. You need to inform several individuals about a set of new government regulations that will soon affect them.
9. You must inform a supplier that your company will soon be cutting back on its purchases because a competing supplier has lowered its prices and you plan to shift more of your business to that supplier.
10. You must resolve a disagreement between two subordinates who both want to take their vacations at the same time.

Exercise Task

Using the information presented above, do the following:

1. Indicate which methods of communication would be appropriate for each situation.
2. Rank-order the methods for each communication situation from best to worst.
3. Compare your rankings with those of a classmate and discuss any differences.

BUILDING EFFECTIVE *time-management* SKILLS

Exercise Overview

Time-management skills refer to the manager's ability to prioritize work, to work efficiently, and to delegate appropriately. This exercise will help you develop your time-management skills as they relate to communication.

Exercise Background

Communication is a vital and necessary part not only of management but our daily lives as well. We benefit when communication takes place in effective ways. But ineffective communication can be a major source of wasted time and energy.

Exercise Task

With this idea as context, do the following:

1. Reflect on your communication for one day. Recall who you talked to, when, for how long, and about what subjects.
2. Do the same for mail you received and mail you sent.
3. Evaluate each communication exchange as being more valuable or less valuable.
4. Estimate how much time you spent on less valuable communication.
5. Decide how you could have either avoided those less valuable communication exchanges or made them more valuable.
6. How much control do we really have over our communication?

CHAPTER CLOSING CASE

COMMUNICATION IS THE REAL THING FOR COCA-COLA

Coca-Cola was in trouble when Douglas Daft became CEO following the brief tenure of M. Douglas Ivester. The previous year, European Union regulators had raided the European offices of Coca-Cola and its bottlers and leveled serious anticompetitive charges against the venerable soft-drink marketer. That same year, the company was hurt by negative publicity when hundreds of people in Belgium complained of headaches and nausea after drinking Coca-Cola beverages. Ultimately, Coca-Cola's products were found to have posed no health threat, but top management's slow response to the scare contributed to the firm's reputation for aggressive, arrogant behavior. This situation so disturbed some company executives that they departed from tradition and submitted a confidential memo criticizing Coca-Cola's actions. To complicate matters, worldwide sales were slowing due to economic woes in some countries, employee morale was lower, and the stock price was lagging.

Clearly, the company had a lot of relationships to repair by the time Daft became CEO. Daft opened a new chapter in Coca-Cola's history by taking a more conciliatory tone in his internal and external communications. Stronger stakeholder relationships, in the CEO's view, would go a long way toward helping polish Coca-Cola's image and protect its 51 percent share of the global market for fizzy soft drinks.

So Daft set out on a goodwill tour designed to improve communication around the world. In Belgium, the CEO met with the regulator who had pursued antitrust charges against Coca-Cola the year before. Daft listened intently as the regulator explained his reasoning and spoke against the company's highly aggressive behavior. Afterward, Daft said that the company had to stop arguing and start listening when competing in other countries. By strengthening relationships with regulators, Daft hoped to get a better understanding of local rules and, at the same time, put Coca-Cola in a better light.

Daft also met with Italy's top antitrust regulator, who had presided over an investigation that resulted in Coca-Cola paying a $16 million fine for anticompetitive practices. Again, the CEO sought to rebuild relations by asking what the company had done wrong and paying close attention as the regulator spoke his mind. Daft also directed the top Coca-Cola executive in Europe to find ways of working more closely with regulators, smoothing the way for business practices that fit both the company's goals and the European Union's competitive guidelines.

The goodwill tour included meetings and meals with local Coca-Cola managers, which afforded opportunities to talk informally about Daft's vision for the company and his strategies for building bridges to numerous constituencies. The CEO also met with the U.S. ambassador to France, several CEOs of French firms, and numerous Coca-Cola executives around Europe. Back home, Daft made it a point to stay in touch with members of the board and the bottlers who make and distribute Coca-Cola's products. By making contact with so many people inside and outside the organization, Daft was developing a more rounded picture of Coca-Cola's strengths and weaknesses.

Since his initial goodwill tour, Daft has returned to Europe several times to meet with managers, bottlers, and regulators. He has also brought some of his senior U.S. and European managers together in Europe to hear reports on regional results and initiatives. In line with Daft's preference for direct communication, oral presentations are shorter, more to the point, and heavier on recommendations. The CEO is also speeding up decision making, allowing Coca-Cola to bring new products to new and existing markets much faster than before. Knowing that 80 percent of the company's profits are derived from sales outside the United States, Daft is stressing decentralization rather than concentrating functions and power in Coca-Cola's Atlanta headquarters. At the same time, he is signaling his determination to keep the lines of communication open so Coca-Cola gains a new reputation for cooperation throughout the world.

Case Questions

1. Where in the communication process would you recommend that Daft concentrate on making changes?

2. Why would Daft bring U.S. and European executives together to make oral presentations about regional results, rather than asking them to share written reports?

3. Which barriers to communication did Daft seem to be addressing during his goodwill tour?

Case References

Betsy McKay, "New Formula" to Fix Coca-Cola, Daft Sets Out to Get Relationships Right," *Wall Street Journal*, June 23, 2000, pp. A1, A12; *Hoover's Handbook of American Business 2001* (Austin, Texas: Hoover's Business Press, 2001), pp. 390–391.

CHAPTER NOTES

1. *Hoover's Handbook of American Business 2000* (Austin, Texas: Hoover's Business Press, 2001), pp. 1070–1071; John Case, "Opening the Books," *Harvard Business Review*, March–April 1997, p. 118–129; Brian Dumaine, "Chaparral Steel: Unleash Workers and Cut Costs," *Fortune*, May 18, 1992, p. 88.

2. See John J. Gabarro, "The Development of Working Relationships," in Jay W. Lorsch, ed., *Handbook of Organizational Behavior* (Englewood Cliffs, N.J.: Prentice-Hall, 1987), pp.

172–189; see also "Team Efforts, Technology, Add New Reasons to Meet," *USA Today*, December 8, 1997, pp. 1A, 2A.

3. See C. Gopinath and Thomas E. Becker, "Communication, Procedural Justice, and Employee Attitudes: Relationships Under Conditions of Divestiture," *Journal of Management*, 2000, Vol. 26, No. 1, pp. 63–83.

4. Henry Mintzberg, *The Nature of Managerial Work* (New York: Harper & Row, 1973).

5. Mintzberg, *The Nature of Managerial Work*.

6. See Batia M. Wiesenfeld, Sumita Raghuram, and Raghu Garud, "Communication Patterns as Determinants of Or-

ganizational Identification in a Virtual Organization," *Organization Science*, 1999, Vol. 10, No. 6, pp. 777–790.

7. Mintzberg, *The Nature of Managerial Work.*

8. Reid Buckley, "When You Have to Put It to Them," *Across the Board*, October 1999, pp. 44–48.

9. "Executives Who Dread Public Speaking Learn to Keep Their Cool in the Spotlight," *Wall Street Journal*, May 4, 1990, pp. B1, B6.

10. Mintzberg, *The Nature of Managerial Work.*

11. Buckley, "When You Have to Put It to Them."

12. A. Vavelas, "Communication Patterns in Task-Oriented Groups," *Journal of the Accoustical Society of America*, Vol. 22, 1950, pp. 725–730; Jerry Wofford, Edwin Gerloff, and Robert Cummins, *Organizational Communication* (New York: McGraw-Hill, 1977).

13. Nelson Phillips and John Brown, "Analyzing Communications in and Around Organizations: A Critical Hermeneutic Approach," *Academy of Management Journal*, 1993, Vol. 36, No. 6, pp. 1547–1576.

14. Walter Kiechel III, "Breaking Bad News to the Boss," *Fortune*, April 9, 1990, pp. 111–112.

15. Mary Young and James Post, "How Leading Companies Communicate with Employees," *Organizational Dynamics*, Summer 1993, pp. 31–43.

16. For one example, see Kimberly D. Elsbach and Greg Elofson, "How the Packaging of Decision Explanations Affects Perceptions of Trustworthiness," *Academy of Management Journal*, 2000, Vol. 43, No. 1, pp. 80–89.

17. Walter Kiechel III, "Hold for the Communicaholic Manager," *Fortune*, January 2, 1989, pp. 107–108.

18. "Those Bawdy E-Mails Were Good for a Laugh—Until the Ax Fell," *Wall Street Journal*, February 4, 2000, pp. A1, A8.

19. Keith Davis, "Management Communication and the Grapevine," *Harvard Business Review*, September–October 1953, pp. 43–49.

20. "Spread the Word: Gossip Is Good," *Wall Street Journal*, October 4, 1988, p. B1.

21. See David M. Schweiger and Angelo S. DeNisi, "Communication with Employees Following a Merger: A Longitudinal Field Experiment," *Academy of Management Journal*, March 1991, pp. 110–135.

22. Nancy B. Kurland and Lisa Hope Pelled, "Passing the Word: Toward a Model of Gossip and Power in the Workplace," *Academy of Management Review*, 2000, Vol. 25, No. 2, pp. 428–438.

23. See Tom Peters and Nancy Austin, *A Passion for Excellence* (New York: Random House, 1985).

24. Albert Mehrabian, *Nonverbal Communication* (Chicago: Aldine, 1972).

25. Michael B. McCaskey, "The Hidden Messages Managers Send," *Harvard Business Review*, November–December 1979, pp. 135–148.

26. David Givens, "What Body Language Can Tell You That Words Cannot," *U.S. News & World Report*, November 19, 1984, p. 100.

27. Edward J. Hall, *The Hidden Dimension* (New York: Doubleday, 1966).

28. For a detailed discussion of improving communication effectiveness, see Courtland L. Bove and John V. Thill, *Business Communication Today*, 3rd Edition (New York: McGraw-Hill, 1992).

29. See Otis W. Baskin and Craig E. Aronoff, *Interpersonal Communication in Organizations* (Glenview, Ill.: Scott, Foresman, 1980).

30. See "You Have (Too Much) E-Mail," *USA Today*, March 12, 1999, p. 3B.

31. Justin Fox, "The Triumph of English," *Fortune*, September 18, 2000, pp. 209–212.

32. Joseph Allen and Bennett P. Lientz, *Effective Business Communication* (Santa Monica, Calif.: Goodyear, 1979).

33. See "Making Silence Your Ally," *Across the Board*, October 1999, p. 11.

34. Boyd A. Vander Houwen, "Less Talking, More Listening," *HRMagazine*, April 1997, pp. 53–58.

35. For a discussion of these and related issues, see Eric M. Eisenberg and Marsha G. Witten, "Reconsidering Openness in Organizational Communication," *Academy of Management Review*, July 1987, pp. 418–426.

19 Managing Work Groups and Teams

Few people have ever heard of a small company called Fastener Supply. The twenty-three-year-old, eighteen-employee company based in Reading, Massachusetts, distributes eighteen thousand different types of metal, rubber, and nylon fasteners—devices used to hold together the parts that comprise everything from automobiles to personal computers to bug zappers. Motorola, Polaroid, and Lucent Technologies are among the company's biggest 350 or so customers.

No one at Fastener Supply believed that the firm had a quality problem. At the same time, however, John Jenkins, the company president, was aware of recent trends and concerns in quality management and knew that his firm needed to be ahead of the industry, not behind it. A small firm like Fastener Supply can really suffer from the loss of only one big customer, so Jenkins decided to be proactive with regard to quality.

An initial quality audit revealed no significant customer complaints. And on a percentage basis, everything seemed to be fine. For example, fewer than 1 percent of the firm's fasteners failed to meet customer standards. But in absolute terms, the numbers didn't look quite as good. Because the firm ships over seventy million products a year, about 112,000 fasteners were returned each year due to a quality problem. Jenkins decided to cut that rate to five hundred per million.

To tackle this problem, Jenkins created a team of three employees, one each from purchasing, sales, and quality control. The group was named the Continuous Improvement Team, or CIT, and given the charge of reducing customer rejection rate by 50 percent. The team members were initially concerned about meeting such an ambitious goal but quickly set to work.

They decided to focus their efforts on three areas: supplier quality, customer feedback, and training. Fastener Supply doesn't actually make fasteners at all but instead buys them from various fastener manufacturers. The CIT instructed each of the firm's suppliers to improve their own quality for production and delivery or risk losing business. Some suppliers did indeed balk, and thirty-seven were dropped from Fastener Supply's supplier network. The remaining 250 or so did meet the new standards and continue to have a strong relationship with the firm.

The CIT also sought feedback about areas where customers were not unhappy but where there was still room for improvement. Almost forty useful suggestions were re-

"Staying still wasn't going to cut it anymore."

—*John Jenkins, president of Fastener Supply*

After studying this chapter, you should be able to:

- Define and identify types of groups and teams in organizations, discuss reasons people join groups and teams, and the stages of group and team development.

- Identify and discuss four essential characteristics of groups and teams.

- Discuss interpersonal and intergroup conflict in organizations.

- Describe how organizations manage conflict.

ceived and implemented. For example, one suggestion was that a Fastener Supply representative inform customers in advance when a shipment was going to be delayed for even a day or two. While the firm had been notifying customers about extended delays, it was easy enough to begin doing it routinely. Finally, the CIT also suggested that all employees at Fastener Supply receive more training in every phase of the operation, ranging from packing and loading boxes to logging inventory in computers. As a result, virtually all phases of the firm's operations improved as well. For example, the year after shipping employees received better training, only two of the seven thousand boxes shipped were returned with parts damaged from bad packing.

By virtually any measure, the CIT has been a big success for Fastener Supply. It actually beat its lofty quality improvement goal by driving defects down to only 216 per million, a phenomenally low level. In addition, the firm's business has been increasing at a rapid pace as word of its quality spreads throughout the industry. But neither the firm nor the CIT are finished. Indeed, the mantra heard throughout Fastener Supply today is achieving the ultimate goal—zero defects. While this ideal may never truly be reached, Fastener Supply's CIT vows to keep working toward it.[1]

John Jenkins at Fastener Supply recognized and took advantage of what many experts are increasingly seeing as a tremendous resource for all organizations—the power of groups and teams. When he needed some changes made at his firm, Jenkins could have just mandated them himself. Or he could have hired an outside consulting firm to tell his employees how to improve. Instead, he created a team of employees and allowed them to figure it out themselves.

This chapter is about processes that lead to and follow from activities like those at Fastener Supply. In the last chapter we established the interpersonal nature of organizations. We extend that discussion here by first introducing basic concepts of group and team dynamics. Subsequent sections explain the characteristics of groups and teams in organizations. We then describe interpersonal and intergroup conflict. Finally, we conclude with a discussion of how conflict can be managed.

Groups and Teams in Organizations

group Two or more people who interact regularly to accomplish a common purpose or goal

Groups are a ubiquitous part of organizational life. They are the basis for much of the work that gets done, and they evolve both inside and outside the normal structural boundaries of the organization. We will define a **group** as two or more people who interact regularly to accomplish a common purpose or goal.[2] The purpose of a group or team may range from preparing a new advertising campaign to sharing information informally, to making important decisions, to fulfilling social needs.

Types of Groups and Teams

In general, three basic kinds of groups are found in organizations—functional groups, task groups and teams, and informal or interest groups.[3] These groups are illustrated in Figure 19.1.

functional group A permanent group created by the organization to accomplish a number of organizational purposes with an indefinite time horizon

Functional Groups   A **functional group** is a permanent group created by the organization to accomplish a number of organizational purposes with an indefinite time horizon. The advertising department at Kmart, the management department at the University of North Texas, and the nursing staff at the Mayo Clinic are functional groups. The advertising department at Kmart, for example, seeks to plan effective advertising campaigns, increase sales, run in-store promotions, and develop a unique identity for the company. It is assumed that the functional group will remain in existence after it attains its current objectives—those objectives will be replaced by new ones.

informal or **interest group** Created by its own members for purposes that may or may not be relevant to organizational goals

Informal or Interest Groups   An **informal** or **interest group** is created by its own members for purposes that may or may not be relevant to organizational goals. It also has an unspecified time horizon. A group of employees who lunch together every day may be discussing how to improve productivity or embezzle money, or they may discuss local politics and sports. As long as the group members enjoy eating together, they will probably continue to do so. When lunches cease to be pleasant, they will seek other company or a different activity.

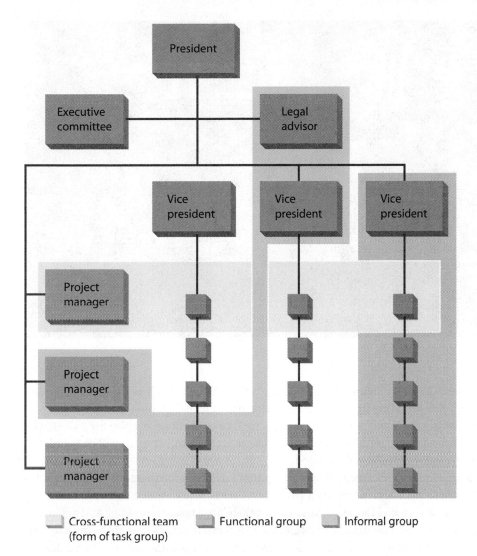

Figure 19.1

Types of Groups in Organizations
Every organization has many different types of groups. In this hypothetical organization, a functional group is shown within the blue area, a cross-functional group within the yellow area, and an informal group within the green area.

☐ Cross-functional team (form of task group)   ☐ Functional group   ☐ Informal group

Informal groups can be a powerful force that managers cannot ignore. One writer described how a group of employees at a furniture factory subverted their boss's efforts to increase production. They tacitly agreed to produce a reasonable amount of work but not to work too hard. One man kept a stockpile of completed work hidden as a backup in case he got too far behind. In another example, auto workers described how they left out gaskets and seals and put soft-drink bottles inside doors.[4] Of course, informal groups can also be a positive force, as demonstrated recently when Continental airline's employees worked together to buy a new motorcycle for Gordon Bethune, the company's CEO, to show their support and gratitude for his excellent leadership.

Task Groups   A **task group** is a group created by the organization to accomplish a relatively narrow range of purposes within a stated or implied time horizon. Most committees and task forces are task groups. The organization specifies group

task group A group created by the organization to accomplish a relatively narrow range of purposes within a stated or implied time horizon

Task groups are created by the organization to accomplish a relatively narrow range of purposes within a stated or implied time horizon. Take this group of software engineers, for example. They work for Trilogy Software, a high-tech firm based in Austin, Texas. The group is working on the development of a new software application program. Once the program is finished, the task group members will return to their previous responsibilities.

team A group of workers who function as a unit, often with little or no supervision, to carry out work-related tasks, functions, and activities

membership and assigns a relatively narrow set of goals, such as developing a new product or evaluating a proposed grievance procedure. The time horizon for accomplishing these purposes is either specified (a committee may be asked to make a recommendation within sixty days) or implied (the project team will disband when the new product is developed).

Teams are a special form of task group that have become increasingly popular.[5] In the sense used here, a **team** is a group of workers who function as a unit, often with little or no supervision, to carry out work-related tasks, functions, and activities. Table 19.1 lists and defines some of the various types of teams that are being used today. Earlier forms of teams included autonomous work groups and quality circles. Today, teams are also sometimes called *self-managed teams*, *cross-functional teams*, or *high-performance teams*. Many firms today are routinely using teams to carry out most of their daily operations.[6]

Organizations create teams for various reasons. For one thing, they give more responsibility for task performance to the workers who are actually performing the tasks. They also empower workers by giving them greater authority and decision-making freedom. In addition, they allow the organization to capitalize on the knowledge and motivation of their workers. Finally, they enable the organization to shed its bureaucracy and to promote flexibility and responsiveness. Ford used a team to design its new compact Focus. General Motors also used a team to develop the newest model of the Chevrolet Blazer.

When an organization decides to use teams, it is essentially implementing a major form of organization change, as discussed in Chapter 13. Thus, it is important to follow a logical and systematic approach to planning and implementing teams in an existing organization design. It is also important to recognize that re-

Table 19.1

Types of Teams

Problem-solving team Most popular type of team; comprises knowledge workers who gather to solve a specific problem and then disband.

Management team Consists mainly of managers from various functions like sales and production; coordinates work among other teams

Work team An increasingly popular type of team, work teams are responsible for the daily work of the organization; when empowered, they are self-managed teams

Virtual team A new type of work team that interacts by computer; members enter and leave the network as needed and may take turns serving as leader

Quality circle Declining in popularity, quality circles, comprising workers and supervisors, meet intermittently to discuss workplace problems

Source: "Types of Teams" adapted from Brian Dumaine, "The Trouble with Teams," *Fortune,* September 5, 1994. Copyright © 1994 Time Inc. All rights reserved.

sistance may be encountered. This resistance is most likely from first-line managers who will be giving up much of their authority to the team. Many organizations find that they must change the whole management philosophy of such managers away from being a supervisor to being a coach or facilitator.[7]

After teams are in place, managers should continue to monitor their contributions and their functioning. In the best circumstance, teams will become very cohesive groups with high performance norms. To achieve this state, the manager can use any or all of the techniques described later in this chapter for enhancing cohesiveness. If implemented properly, and with the support of the workers themselves, performance norms will likely be relatively high. That is, if the change is properly implemented, the team participants will understand the value and potential of teams and the rewards they may expect as a result of their contributions. On the other hand, poorly designed and implemented teams will do a less effective job and may detract from organizational effectiveness.[8]

Why People Join Groups and Teams

People join groups and teams for various reasons. They join functional groups simply by virtue of joining organizations. People accept employment to earn money or to practice their chosen profession. Once inside the organization, they are assigned to jobs and roles and thus become members of functional groups. People in existing functional groups are told or asked or they volunteer to serve on committees, task forces, and teams. People join informal or interest groups for a variety of reasons, most of them quite complex.[9] Indeed, the need to be a team player has grown so strong today that many organizations will actively resist hiring someone who does not want to work with others.[10]

Interpersonal Attraction One reason people choose to form informal or interest groups is that they are attracted to each other. Many different factors contribute to interpersonal attraction. When people see a lot of each other, pure proximity increases the likelihood that interpersonal attraction will develop. Attraction is increased when people have similar attitudes, personality, or economic standing.

Group Activities   Individuals may also be motivated to join a group because the activities of the group appeal to them. Jogging, playing bridge, bowling, discussing poetry, playing war games, and flying model airplanes are all activities that some people enjoy. Many of them are more enjoyable to participate in as a member of a group, and most require more than one person. Many large firms like Shell Oil and Apple Computer have a league of football, softball, or bowling teams. A person may join a bowling team not because of any noticeable attraction to other group members but simply because being a member of the group allows that person to participate in a pleasant activity. Of course, if the level of interpersonal attraction of the group is very low, a person may choose to forgo the activity rather than join the group.

Group Goals   The goals of a group may also motivate people to join. The Sierra Club, which is dedicated to environmental conservation, is a good example of this kind of interest group. Various fund-raising groups are another illustration. Members may or may not be personally attracted to the other fundraisers, and they probably do not enjoy the activity of knocking on doors asking for money, but they join the group because they subscribe to its goal. Workers join unions like the United Auto Workers because they support its goals.

Need Satisfaction   Still another reason for joining a group is to satisfy the need for affiliation. New residents in a community may join the Newcomers Club partially as a way to meet new people and partially just to be around other people. Likewise, newly divorced individuals often join support groups as a way to have companionship.

People join groups for a variety of reasons. These women actually reflect two different reasons for joining a group. First, they individually joined the Delta Sigma Theta sorority for a variety of reasons, including interpersonal attraction, group activities, need satisfaction, and other reasons. Second, they then joined a larger group walking in support of breast cancer survivors because they support its goal.

Instrumental Benefits A final reason people join groups is that membership is sometimes seen as instrumental in providing other benefits to the individual. For example, it is fairly common for college students entering their senior year to join several professional clubs or associations because listing such memberships on a résumé is thought to enhance the chances of getting a good job. Similarly, a manager might join a certain racquet club not because she is attracted to its members (although she might be) and not because of the opportunity to play tennis (although she may enjoy it). The club's goals are not relevant and her affiliation needs may be satisfied in other ways. However, she may feel that being a member of this club will lead to important and useful business contacts. The racquet club membership is instrumental in establishing those contacts. Membership in civic groups such as Junior League and Rotary may be solicited for similar reasons.

Stages of Group and Team Development

Imagine the differences between a collection of five people who have just been brought together to form a group or team and a group or team that has functioned like a well-oiled machine for years. Members of a new group or team are unfamiliar with how they will function together and are tentative in their interactions. In a group or team with considerable experience, members are familiar with one another's strengths and weaknesses and are more secure in their role in the group. The former group or team is generally considered to be immature; the latter, mature. To progress from the immature phase to the mature phase, a group or team must go through certain stages of development, as shown in Figure 19.2.[11]

The first stage of development is called *forming*. The members of the group or team get acquainted and begin to test which interpersonal behaviors are acceptable and which are unacceptable to the other members. The members are very dependent on others at this point to provide cues about what is acceptable. The basic ground rules for the group or team are established and a tentative group structure may emerge. At Reebok, for example, a merchandising team was created to handle its sportswear business. The team leader and his members were barely acquainted and had to spend a few weeks getting to know one another.

The second stage of development, often slow to emerge, is *storming*. During this stage there may be a general lack of unity and uneven interaction patterns. At the same time, some members of the group or team may begin to exert themselves to become recognized as the group leader or at least to play a major role in shaping the group's agenda. In Reebok's team, some members advocated a rapid expansion into the marketplace; others argued for a slower entry. The first faction won, with disastrous results. Because of the rush, product quality was poor and deliveries were late. As a result, the team leader was fired and a new manager placed in charge.

The third stage in the development, called *norming*, usually begins with a burst of activity. During this stage each person begins to recognize and accept her or his role and to understand the roles of others. Members also begin to accept one another and to develop a sense of unity. There may also be temporary regressions to the previous stage. For example, the group or team might begin to accept one

Figure 19.2

Stages of Group Development

As groups mature, they tend to evolve through four distinct stages of development. Managers must understand that group members need time to become acquainted, accept each other, develop a group structure, and become comfortable with their roles in the group before they can begin to work directly to accomplish goals.

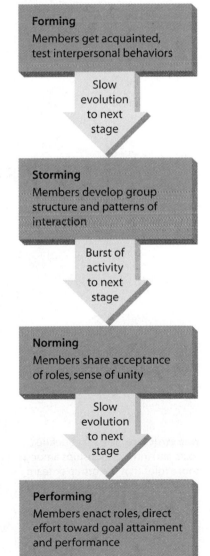

particular member as the leader. If this person later violates important norms and otherwise jeopardizes his or her claim to leadership, conflict might re-emerge as the group rejects this leader and searches for another. Reebok's new leader transferred several people away from the team and set up a new system and structure for managing tasks. The remaining employees accepted his new approach and settled into doing their jobs.

Performing, the final stage of group or team development, is again slow to develop. The team really begins to focus on the problem at hand. The members enact the roles they have accepted, interaction occurs, and the efforts of the group are directed toward goal attainment. The basic structure of the group or team is no longer an issue but has become a mechanism for accomplishing the purpose of the group. Reebok's sportswear business is now growing consistently and has successfully avoided the problems that plagued it at first.

MANAGEMENT   Managers should recognize the variety of groups that can exist **IMPLICATIONS**   in an organization. Knowledge about teams is especially important in many modern organizations. In addition, they should understand and appreciate the various reasons that people join groups and teams. Finally, they should also understand and be able to recognize the stages of group development that a newly created group passes through as it becomes more mature.

Characteristics of Groups and Teams

As groups and teams mature and pass through the four basic stages of development, they begin to take on four important characteristics—a role structure, norms, cohesiveness, and informal leadership.[12] As described in *Today's Management Issues*, some organizations are redefining the role of top managers so that a team approach can be applied to the role of CEO.

Role Structures

role The part an individual plays in helping the group reach its goals

role structure The set of defined roles and interrelationships among those roles that the group or team members define and accept

Each individual in a team has a part—or **role**—to play in helping the group reach its goals. Some people are leaders, some do the work, some interface with other teams, and so on. Indeed, a person may take on a *task-specialist role* (concentrating on getting the group's task accomplished) or a *socioemotional role* (providing social and emotional support to others on the team). A few people, usually the leaders, perform both roles; a few others may do neither. The group's **role structure** is the set of defined roles and interrelationships among those roles that the group or team members define and accept. Each of us belongs to many groups and therefore plays multiple roles—in work groups, classes, families, and social organizations.[13]

Role structures emerge as a result of role episodes, as shown in Figure 19.3. The process begins with the expected role—what other members of the team expect the individual to do. The expected role gets translated into the sent role—the messages and cues that team members use to communicate the expected role to the individual. The perceived role is what the individual perceives the sent role to

TODAY'S MANAGEMENT ISSUES

TEAMS TAKE ON ROLE OF CHIEF OPERATING OFFICER

Not so long ago, the chief operating officer (COO) position was a steppingstone to the coveted chief executive officer (CEO) position at the top of the organizational pyramid. COOs worked closely with the heads of different units within the corporation to implement strategy and keep operations running smoothly. When Robert F. Cotter was COO of Starwood Hotels and Resorts Worldwide, for example, he saw himself as having hands-on responsibility for making the CEO's vision a reality. In many businesses, the difference in the CEO and COO roles came down to focus: the CEO was expected to concentrate on external issues and stakeholder relationships, while the COO looked after nitty-gritty, in-house matters.

These days, however, the COO role is disappearing from many organization charts. This change is due in part to the increased complexity of today's global corporations, which challenges the ability of any one person to monitor, let alone lead and coordinate, the working of diverse and disparate divisions. In addition, the ever-more turbulent business environment demands speedier decision making about a wider range of questions, folding another level of complexity into the COO's already difficult role. Finally, the trend toward flatter and more decentralized structures is causing top management to rethink the need for any position that separates the CEO from the executives in charge of the company's operating units.

Now many companies are doing away with the formal position of COO and dividing the role among a team of senior managers. Reporting to the CEO, such teams are empowered to decide on budgetary allocations, find ways of boosting productivity, and tweak implementation of strategy in response to or anticipation of environmental developments. The title of COO may be vanishing, but companies still need to be sure that someone—or some team—is keeping a close eye on everyday operations.

> *With companies managing a range of different business models, it's difficult to have all that come together in the head of one person.*
>
> —*David A. Nadler, chairman of Mercer Delta Consulting**

Reference: Diane Brady, "An Executive Whose Time Has Gone," *Business Week,* August 28, 2000, p. 125 (*quote on p. 125).

---

mean. Finally, the enacted role is what the individual actually does in the role. The enacted role, in turn, influences future expectations of the team. Of course, role episodes seldom unfold this easily. When major disruptions occur, individuals may experience role ambiguity, conflict, or overload.[14]

Figure 19.3

The Development of a Role

Roles and role structures within a group generally evolve through a series of role episodes. The first two stages of role development are group processes as the group members let individuals know what is expected of them. The other two parts are individual processes as the new group members perceive and enact their roles.

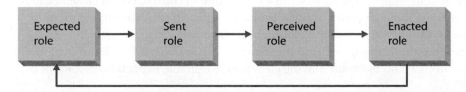

role ambiguity When the sent role is unclear and the individual does not know what is expected of him or her

Role Ambiguity   **Role ambiguity** arises when the sent role is unclear. If your instructor tells you to write a term paper but refuses to provide more information, you will probably experience role ambiguity. You do not know what the topic is, how long the paper should be, what format to use, or when the paper is due. In work settings, role ambiguity can stem from poor job descriptions, vague instructions from a supervisor, or unclear cues from coworkers. The result is likely to be a subordinate who does not know what to do. Role ambiguity can be a significant problem for both the individual who must contend with it and the organization that expects the employee to perform.

role conflict When the messages and cues comprising the sent role are clear but contradictory or mutually exclusive

Role Conflict   **Role conflict** occurs when the messages and cues comprising the sent role are clear but contradictory or mutually exclusive.[15] One common form is *interrole conflict*—conflict between roles. For example, if a person's boss says that to get ahead one must work overtime and on weekends, and the same person's spouse says that more time is needed at home with the family, conflict may result. In a matrix organization, interrole conflict often arises between the roles one plays in different teams as well as between team roles and one's permanent role in a functional group.

  Intrarole conflict may occur when the person gets conflicting demands from different sources within the context of the same role. A manager's boss may tell her that she needs to put more pressure on subordinates to follow new work rules. At the same time, her subordinates may indicate that they expect her to get the rules changed. Thus, the cues are in conflict, and the manager may be unsure about which course to follow. *Intrasender conflict* occurs when a single source sends clear but contradictory messages. This situation might arise if the boss says one morning that there can be no more overtime for the next month but after lunch tells someone to work late that same evening. *Person-role conflict* results from a discrepancy between the role requirements and the individual's personal values, attitudes, and needs. If a person is told to do something unethical or illegal, or if the work is distasteful (for example, firing a close friend), person-role conflict is likely. Role conflict of all varieties is of particular concern to managers. Research has shown that conflict may occur in different situations and lead to various adverse consequences, including stress, poor performance, and rapid turnover.

role overload When expectations for the role exceed the individual's capabilities

Role Overload   A final consequence of a weak role structure is **role overload**, which occurs when expectations for the role exceed the individual's capabilities. When a manager gives an employee several major assignments at once while increasing the person's regular workload, the employee will probably experience role overload. Role overload may also result when an individual takes on too many roles at one time. For example, a person trying to work extra hard at a job, run for election to the school board, serve on a committee in church, coach Little League baseball, maintain an active exercise program, and be a contributing member to her or his family will probably encounter role overload.

  In a functional group or team, the manager can take steps to avoid role ambiguity, conflict, and overload. Having clear and reasonable expectations and sending clear and straightforward cues can eliminate role ambiguity. Consistent expectations that take into account the employee's other roles and personal value system may minimize role conflict. Role overload can be avoided simply by recognizing the individual's capabilities and limits. In friendship and interest groups, role structures are likely to be less formal; hence, the possibility of role ambiguity, conflict, or overload may not be so great. However, if one or more of these problems do occur, they may be difficult to handle. Because roles in friendship and interest groups are less likely to be partially defined by a formal authority structure or written job descriptions, the individual cannot turn to these sources to clarify a role.

Behavioral Norms

Norms are standards of behavior that the group or team accepts for its members. Most committees, for example, develop norms governing their discussions. A person who talks too much is perceived as doing so to make a good impression or to get his or her own way. Other members may not talk much to this person, may not sit nearby, may glare at the person, and may otherwise "punish" the individual for violating the norm. Norms, then, define the boundaries between acceptable and unacceptable behavior.[16] Some groups develop norms that limit the upper bounds of behavior to "make life easier" for the group. In general, these norms are counterproductive—don't make more than two comments in a committee discussion or don't produce any more than you have to. Other groups may develop norms that limit the lower bounds of behavior. These norms tend to reflect motivation, commitment, and high performance—don't come to meetings unless you've read the reports to be discussed, or produce as much as you can. Managers can sometimes use norms for the betterment of the organization. For example, Kodak has successfully used group norms to reduce injuries in some of its plants.[17]

norms Standards of behavior that the group or team accepts for its members

Norm Generalization The norms of one group cannot always be generalized to another group. Some academic departments, for example, have a norm suggesting that faculty members dress professionally on teaching days. People who fail to observe this norm are "punished" by sarcastic remarks or even formal reprimands. In other departments the norm may be casual clothes, and the person unfortunate enough to wear dress clothes may be punished just as vehemently. Even within the same work area, similar groups or teams can develop different norms. One team may strive always to produce above its assigned quota; another may maintain productivity just below its quota. The norm of one team may be to act friendly and cordial to its supervisor; that of another team may be to remain aloof and distant. Some differences are due primarily to the composition of the teams.

Norm Variation In some cases there can also be norm variation within a group or team. A common norm is that the least senior member of a group is expected to perform unpleasant or trivial tasks for the rest of the group. These tasks might be to wait on customers who are known to be small tippers (in a restaurant), to deal with complaining customers (in a department store), or to handle the low commission line of merchandise (in a sales department). Another example is when

Groups and teams are powerful forces in many organizations. People working together in a coordinated and integrated way can often accomplish far more than they could working alone. One problem that can arise, however, is called "free-riding." Free-riding occurs when someone in a group or team fails to carry out his or her responsibilities and lets others do all the work. As illustrated in this cartoon, the Viking in the back of the boat is neglecting his work and letting the rest of the group carry his weight. Thus, he is a free rider!

THE FAR SIDE   By GARY LARSON

certain individuals, especially informal leaders, may violate some norms. If the team is going to meet at 8 o'clock, anyone arriving late will be chastised for holding everyone up. Occasionally, however, the informal leader may arrive a few minutes late. As long as this behavior does not happen too often, the group will probably not do anything.

Norm Conformity Four sets of factors contribute to norm conformity. First, factors associated with the group are important. For example, some groups or teams may exert more pressure for conformity than others. Second, the initial stimulus that prompts behavior can affect conformity. The more ambiguous the stimulus (for example, news that the team is going to be transferred to a new unit), the more pressure there is to conform. Third, individual traits determine the individual's propensity to conform (for example, more intelligent people are often less susceptible to pressure to conform). Finally, situational factors such as team size and unanimity influence conformity. As an individual learns the group's norms, he can do several different things. The most obvious is to adopt the norms. For example, the new male professor who notices that all the other men in the department dress up to teach can also start wearing a suit. A variation is to try to obey the "spirit" of the norm while retaining individuality. The professor may recognize that the norm is actually to wear a tie; thus, he might succeed by wearing a tie with his sport shirt, jeans, and sneakers.

The individual may also ignore the norm. When a person does not conform, several things can happen. At first the group may increase its communication with the deviant individual to try to bring her back in line. If this solution does not work, communication may decline. Over time, the group may begin to exclude the individual from its activities and, in effect, ostracize the person. Finally, we need to consider briefly another aspect of norm conformity—socialization. **Socialization** is generalized norm conformity that occurs as a person makes the transition from being an outsider to being an insider. A newcomer to an organization, for example,

socialization Generalized norm conformity that occurs as a person makes the transition from being an outsider to being an insider in the organization

INFORMALITY CREEPS INTO THE EUROPEAN WORKPLACE

Traditionally, European businesspeople have used formal courtesy titles such as *Herr* (German for "mister") and *Mademoiselle* (French for "miss") when addressing their colleagues. Now the norm of using coworkers' first names, entrenched in London and in other parts of Great Britain—as well as across the Atlantic in the United States—is slowly starting to spread in workplaces throughout the European continent.

One reason for this change is that coworkers from other countries who frequently collaborate with British colleagues are getting used to the first-name convention and carrying over the habit when they work with non-British colleagues. Second, younger employees prefer the informality of first names—especially when working with colleagues who are around the same age. And third, the large number of Americans working in Europe are reinforcing the habit because they are accustomed to calling colleagues by their first names.

Given the increasingly multicultural composition of the workforce in London and other European business centers, shifts like this one are becoming more commonplace. For example, the London branch of the investment banking firm J.P. Morgan employs people from more than fifty countries. In London overall, expatriates from the United States make up the largest proportion of foreign workers; other well-represented groups include employees and managers posted to London from France, Italy, Spain, and Germany.

A growing number of the European expatriates in London welcome the informality of being on a first-name basis with coworkers, in part because it encourages less rigid protocol in business settings. On the other hand, some expatriates who expect to remain in London for only a short time resist using first names because they believe they will have to break the habit when they return to work in their native countries. Despite such resistance, however, the long tradition of using courtesy titles in Europe is slowly but steadily giving way to the first-name norm in work settings.

> *Here in the trading room, the average age is 28, so I would find it difficult to call my colleagues* monsieur.
>
> —*Christian Lengelle, a financial trader in London**

Reference: Astrid Wendlandt, "Formality Gives Way to First Names in City of London's Mix of Manners," *Financial Times,* August 15, 2000, p. 11 (*quote on p. 11).

---

gradually begins to learn the norms about issues such as dress, working hours, and interpersonal relations. As the newcomer adopts these norms, she is being socialized into the organizational culture. Some organizations, like Texas Instruments, work to manage the socialization process; others leave it to happenstance. *The World of Management* discusses how socialization is slowly changing norms in Europe to promote more informality in the workplace.

Cohesiveness

A third important team characteristic is cohesiveness. **Cohesiveness** is the extent to which members are loyal and committed to the group. In a highly cohesive team, the members work well together, support and trust one another, and are generally effective at achieving their chosen goal.[18] In contrast, a team that lacks cohesiveness is not very coordinated, and its members do not necessarily support

cohesiveness The extent to which members are loyal and committed to the group; the degree of mutual attractiveness within the group

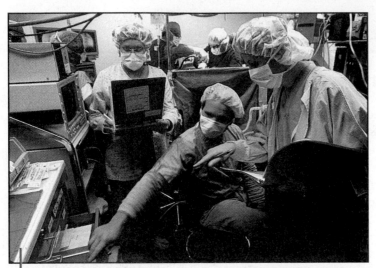

Cohesive teams can be highly effective contributors to the success of any organization. This team, for example, consists of doctors and nurses working together to lower costs at Methodist Healthcare System in San Antonio. The team members share the same performance norms, and their close personal relationships have led the team to become more cohesive as they find new answers and help reach their goal. To date, the overall cost reduction program to which they belong has yielded savings of over $60 million.

one another fully and may have a difficult time reaching goals. Of particular interest are the factors that increase and reduce cohesiveness and the consequences of team cohesiveness. These factors are listed in Table 19.2.

Factors That Increase Cohesiveness   Five factors can increase the level of cohesiveness in a group or team. One of the strongest is intergroup competition. When two or more groups are in direct competition (for example, three sales groups competing for top sales honors or two football teams competing for a conference championship), each group is likely to become more cohesive. Second, just as personal attraction plays a role in causing a group to form, so too does attraction seem to enhance cohesiveness. Third, favorable evaluation of the entire group by outsiders can increase cohesiveness. Thus, a group's winning a sales contest or a conference title or receiving recognition and praise from a superior will tend to increase cohesiveness.

If all the members of the group or team agree on its goals, cohesiveness is likely to increase.[19] And the more frequently members of the group interact with each other, the more likely the group is to become cohesive. A manager who wants to foster a high level of cohesiveness in a team might do well to establish some form of intergroup competition, assign members to the group who are likely to be attracted to one another, provide opportunities for success, establish goals that all members are likely to accept, and allow ample opportunity for interaction.

Factors That Reduce Cohesiveness   Five factors are also known to reduce team cohesiveness. First of all, cohesiveness tends to decline as a group increases in size. Second, when members of a team disagree on what the goals of the group

Table 19.2

Factors That Influence Group Cohesiveness

Several different factors can potentially influence the cohesiveness of a group. For example, a manager can establish intergroup competition, assign compatible members to the group, create opportunities for success, establish acceptable goals, and foster interaction to increase cohesiveness. Other factors can be used to decrease cohesiveness.

Factors That Increase Cohesiveness	Factors That Reduce Cohesiveness
Intergroup competition	Group size
Personal attraction	Disagreement on goals
Favorable evaluation	Intragroup competition
Agreement on goals	Domination
Interaction	Unpleasant experiences

should be, cohesiveness may decrease. For example, when some members believe the group should maximize output and others think output should be restricted, cohesiveness declines. Third, intragroup competition reduces cohesiveness. When members are competing among themselves, they focus more on their own actions and behaviors than on those of the group.

Fourth, domination by one or more persons in the group or team may cause overall cohesiveness to decline. Other members may feel that they are not being given an opportunity to interact and contribute, and they may become less attracted to the group as a consequence. Finally, unpleasant experiences that result from group membership may reduce cohesiveness. A sales group that comes in last in a sales contest, an athletic team that sustains a long losing streak, and a work group reprimanded for poor-quality work may all become less cohesive as a result of their unpleasant experience.

Consequences of Cohesiveness In general, as teams become more cohesive, their members tend to interact more frequently, conform more to norms, and become more satisfied with the team. Cohesiveness may also influence team performance. However, performance is also influenced by the team's performance norms. Figure 19.4 shows how cohesiveness and performance norms interact to help shape team performance.

When both cohesiveness and performance norms are high, high performance should result because the team wants to perform at a high level (norms) and its members are working together toward that end (cohesiveness). When norms are high and cohesiveness is low, performance will be moderate. Although the team wants to perform at a high level, its members are not necessarily working well together. When norms are low, performance will be low, regardless of whether group cohesiveness is high or low. The least desirable situation occurs when low performance norms are combined with high cohesiveness. In this case all team members embrace the standard of restricting performance (because of the low performance norm), and the group is united in its efforts to maintain that standard (because of the high cohesiveness). If cohesiveness were low, the manager might be able to raise performance norms by establishing high goals and rewarding goal attainment or by bringing in new group members who were high performers. But a highly cohesive group is likely to resist these interventions.[20]

Figure 19.4

The Interaction Between Cohesiveness and Performance Norms

Group cohesiveness and performance norms interact to determine group performance. From the manager's perspective, high cohesiveness combined with high performance norms is the best situation, and high cohesiveness with low performance norms is the worst situation. Managers who can influence the level of cohesiveness and performance norms can greatly improve the effectiveness of a work group.

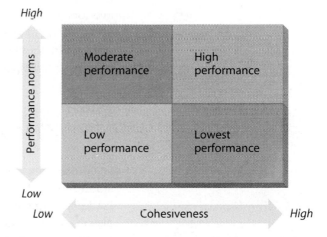

Formal and Informal Leadership

Most functional groups and teams have a formal leader—that is, one appointed by the organization or chosen or elected by the members of the group. Because friendship and interest groups are formed by the members themselves, however, any formal leader must be elected or designated by the members. Although some groups do designate such a leader (a softball team may elect a captain, for example), many do not. Moreover, even when a formal leader is designated, the group or team may also look to others for leadership. An **informal leader** is a person who engages in leadership activities but whose right to do so has not been formally recognized by the organization or group. The formal and the informal leader in any group or team may be the same person, or they may be different people. We noted earlier the distinction between the task-specialist and socioemotional roles within groups. An informal leader is likely to be a person capable of carrying out both roles effectively. If the formal leader can fulfill one role but not the other, an informal leader often emerges to supplement the formal leader's functions. If the formal leader cannot fill either role, one or more informal leaders may emerge to carry out both sets of functions.

> **informal leader** A person who engages in leadership activities but whose right to do so has not been formally recognized by the organization or group

Is informal leadership desirable? In many cases informal leaders are quite powerful because they draw from referent or expert power. When they are working in the best interest of the organization, they can be a tremendous asset. Notable athletes such as Brett Favre and Mia Hamm are classic examples of informal leaders. However, when informal leaders work counter to the goals of the organization, they can cause significant difficulties. Such leaders may lower performance norms, instigate walkouts or wildcat strikes, or otherwise disrupt the organization.

MANAGEMENT IMPLICATIONS   Managers need to understand clearly the four basic characteristics of groups and teams. Specifically, they need to understand and know how to manage role structures to minimize role ambiguity, conflict, and overload. The importance of behavioral norms also cannot be overlooked. Managers should also understand the power of cohesiveness, the factors that can increase and decrease it, and how it interacts with performance norms. Finally, managers should also know the difference between formal and informal leadership and be able to identify their key informal leaders.

Interpersonal and Intergroup Conflict

Of course, when people work together in an organization, things do not always go smoothly. Conflict is an inevitable element of interpersonal relationships in organizations. In this section we will look at how conflict affects overall performance. We also explore the causes of conflict between individuals, between groups, and between an organization and its environment.

The Nature of Conflict

> **conflict** A disagreement between two or more individuals, groups, or organizations

Conflict is a disagreement between two or more individuals, groups, or organizations. This disagreement may be relatively superficial or very strong. It may be short-lived or it can exist for months or even years, and it may be work-related or personal. Conflict may manifest itself in various ways. People may compete with one another, glare at one another, shout, or withdraw. Groups may band together to protect popular members or oust unpopular members. Organizations may seek legal remedy. *Working with Diversity* discusses how casual dress policies are creating conflict in some organizations.

Most people assume that conflict is something to be avoided because it connotes antagonism, hostility, unpleasantness, and dissension. Indeed, managers and management theorists have traditionally viewed conflict as a problem to be avoided.[21] In recent years, however, we have come to recognize that, although conflict can be a major problem, certain kinds of conflict may also be beneficial.[22] For example, when two members of a site selection committee disagree over the best location for a new plant, each may be forced to study and defend his or her preferred alternative more thoroughly. As a result of more systematic analysis and

---

WORKING WITH DIVERSITY

BACK TO BLAZERS AND BUTTON-DOWNS?

Seeking to improve morale and break down hierarchical barriers, many U.S. companies embraced casual dress during the 1990s. The trend started with dress-down Fridays and, at some companies, led to casual wear being accepted at work on almost any day. Now a backlash against overly casual dress is bringing blazers and button-downs back to the workplace.

One problem companies have encountered is conflicting definitions of exactly what constitutes casual dress. After management adopted a casual dress code at Development Counselors International, for example, some employees began wearing workout clothing to the office. The company finally resolved the conflict by forming a committee to establish standards indicating what items of apparel were acceptable. According to surveys, jeans, polo shirts, and sneakers are generally acceptable as casual dress at many companies, while tight-fitting spandex clothing, short shorts, and sweat pants are not.

Another problem is that too-casual attire may conflict with behavior norms, encouraging undesirable—and possibly illegal—behavior. Almost half of the companies responding to a recent survey said that absenteeism increased after casual dress was adopted; 30 percent said they saw an increase in flirtatious behavior as well. Clothing that is too tight or too revealing may provoke attention that, in extreme cases, can escalate to sexual harassment. This situation can also be addressed by establishing specific dress standards so all employees understand what they may and may not wear to work.

To prevent conflict, a growing number of companies are requiring traditional business attire. Korn/Ferry International, a recruiting firm in Chicago, tried a casual dress policy but switched back to business clothing after the one-year experiment. Some larger companies are requiring more professional clothing on a branch-by-branch basis, depending on whether employees meet the public or work in the back office. But the backlash isn't always initiated by management. Consider the situation at Invigo, a California based Internet company that permits nearly every kind of casual dress. Fridays have been different, however, since Invigo's engineers decided on their own to designate it as their department's unofficial dress-up day.

> *This is a business, and business attire is appropriate. If you dress inappropriately, sometimes your business becomes more relaxed. Dressing up means you're more productive.*
>
> —*Lawrence Schwartz, CEO of Service911.com**

Reference: Stephanie Armour, "Companies Rethink Casual Clothes," *USA Today*, June 27, 2000, pp. 1A, 2A (*quote on p. 2A).

Figure 19.5

The Nature of Organizational Conflict

Either too much or too little conflict can be dysfunctional for an organization. In either case performance may be low. However, an optimal level of conflict that sparks motivation, creativity, innovation, and initiative can result in higher levels of performance. T. J. Rodgers, CEO of Cypress Semiconductor, maintains a moderate level of conflict in his organization as a way of keeping people energized and motivated.

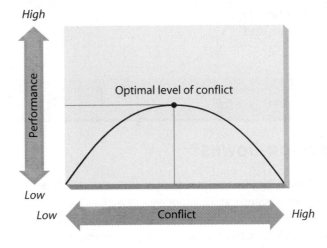

discussion, the committee may make a better decision and be better prepared to justify it to others than if everyone had agreed from the outset and accepted an alternative that was perhaps not well analyzed.

As long as conflict is being handled in a cordial and constructive manner, it is probably serving a useful purpose in the organization. On the other hand, when working relationships are being disrupted and the conflict has reached destructive levels, it has likely become dysfunctional and needs to be addressed.[23] We discuss ways of dealing with such conflict later in this chapter.

Figure 19.5 depicts the general relationship between conflict and performance for a group or organization. If there is absolutely no conflict in the group or organization, its members may become complacent and apathetic. As a result, group or organizational performance and innovation may begin to suffer. A moderate level of conflict among group or organizational members, on the other hand, can spark motivation, creativity, innovation, and initiative and raise performance. Too much conflict, though, can produce undesirable results such as hostility and lack of cooperation, which lower performance. The key for managers is to find and maintain the optimal amount of conflict that fosters performance. Of course, what constitutes optimal conflict varies with both situation and the people involved.[24]

Causes of Conflict

Conflict may arise in both interpersonal and intergroup relationships. Occasionally conflict between individuals and groups may be caused by particular organizational strategies and practices. A third arena for conflict is between an organization and its environment.

Interpersonal Conflict   Conflict between two or more individuals is almost certain to occur in any organization, given the great variety in perceptions, goals, attitudes, and so forth, among its members. William Gates, founder and CEO of Microsoft, and Kazuhiko Nishi, a former business associate from Japan, ended a long-term business relationship because of interpersonal conflict. Nishi accused Gates of becoming too political, while Gates charged that Nishi became to unpredictable and erratic in his behavior.[25]

A frequent source of interpersonal conflict in organizations is what many people call a personality clash—when two people distrust each others' motives, dislike one another, or for some other reason simply can't get along.[26] Conflict may also arise between people who have different beliefs or perceptions about some aspect of their work or their organization. For example, one manager may want the organization to require that all employees use Microsoft Office software to promote standardization. Another manager may believe that different software packages should be allowed to recognize individuality. Similarly, a male manager may disagree with his female colleague over whether the organization is guilty of discriminating against women in promotion decisions.

Conflict can also result from excess competitiveness among individuals. Two people vying for the same job, for example, may resort to political behavior in an effort to gain an advantage. If either competitor sees the other's behavior as inappropriate, accusations are likely to result. Even after the "winner" of the job is determined, such conflict may continue to undermine interpersonal relationships, especially if the reasons given in selecting one candidate are ambiguous or open to alternative explanation. Robert Allen resigned as CEO of Delta Airlines because he disagreed with other key executives over how best to reduce the carrier's costs. After he began looking for a replacement for one of his rivals without the approval of the firm's board of directors, the resultant conflict and controversy left him no choice but to leave.[27]

Intergroup Conflict Conflict between two or more organizational groups is also quite common. For example, the members of a firm's marketing group may disagree with the production group over product quality and delivery schedules. Two sales groups may disagree over how to meet sales goals, and two groups of managers may have different ideas about how best to allocate organizational resources.

Many intergroup conflicts arise more from organizational causes than interpersonal causes. In Chapter 11, we described three forms of group interdependence—pooled, sequential, and reciprocal. Just as increased interdependence makes coordination more difficult, it also increases the potential for conflict. For example, recall that in sequential interdependence, work is passed from one unit to another. Intergroup conflict may arise if the first group turns out too much work (the second group will fall behind), too little work (the second group will not meet its own goals), or poor-quality work.

At a J.C. Penney's department store, conflict recently arose between stockroom employees and sales associates. The sales associates claimed that the stockroom employees were slow in delivering merchandise to the sales floor so that it could be priced and shelved. The stockroom employees, in turn, claimed that the sales associates were not giving them enough lead time to get the merchandise delivered and failed to understand that they had additional duties besides carrying merchandise to the sales floor.

Just like people, different departments often have different goals, and these goals may often be incompatible. A marketing goal of maximizing sales, achieved partially by offering many products in a wide variety of sizes, shapes, colors, and models, probably conflicts with a production goal of minimizing costs, achieved partially by long production runs of a few items. Reebok recently confronted this very situation. One group of managers wanted to introduce a new sportswear line as quickly as possible, while other managers wanted to expand more deliberately and cautiously. Because the two groups were not able to reconcile their differences effectively, conflict between the two factions led to quality problems and delivery delays that plagued the firm for months.

Competition for scarce resources can also lead to intergroup conflict. Most organizations—especially universities, hospitals, government agencies, and businesses in depressed industries—have limited resources. In one New England town, for example, the public works department and the library recently battled over funds from a federal construction grant. The Oldsmobile, Pontiac, and Chevrolet divisions of General Motors have frequently fought over the rights to manufacture various new products developed by the company.

Conflict Between Organization and Environment   Conflict that arises between one organization and another is called interorganizational conflict. A moderate amount of interorganizational conflict resulting from business competition is, of course, expected, but sometimes conflict becomes more extreme. For example, the owners of Jordache Enterprises Inc. and Guess? Inc. battled in court for years over ownership of the Guess label, allegations of design theft, and several other issues.[28] Similarly, General Motors and Volkswagen went to court to resolve a bitter conflict that spanned more than four years. It all started when a key GM executive, Jose Ignacio Lopez de Arriortua, left for a position at Volkswagen. GM claimed that he took with him key secrets that could benefit its German competitor. After the messy departure, dozens of charges and countercharges were made by the two firms, and only a court settlement was able to put the conflict to an end.[29]

Conflict can also arise between an organization and other elements of its environment. For example, an organization may conflict with a consumer group over claims made about its products. McDonald's faced this problem a few years ago when it published nutritional information about its products that omitted details about fat content. A manufacturer might conflict with a governmental agency such

Conflict can arise for a variety of reasons. This Israeli border guard and Palestinian citizen are experiencing conflict due to both religious and political reasons. The Palestinian was seeking to enter a mosque for Friday prayers; however, the Israeli guard was ordered to keep Palestinians from entering this particular part of Jerusalem because of concerns about political tension and unrest.

as OSHA. For example, the firm's management may believe it is in compliance with OSHA regulations, while officials from the agency itself feel that the firm is not in compliance. Or a firm might conflict with a supplier over the quality of raw materials. The firm may think the supplier is providing inferior materials, while the supplier thinks the materials are adequate. Finally, individual managers may obviously have disagreements with groups of workers. For example, a manager may think her workers are doing poor-quality work and that they are unmotivated. The workers, on the other hand, may believe they are doing a good job and that the manager is doing a poor job of leading them.

MANAGEMENT Managers need to have a thorough understanding of conflict.
IMPLICATIONS In particular, they need to understand the nature of conflict and the primary forces that may cause conflict to arise in their organizations.

Managing Conflict in Organizations

How do managers cope with all this potential conflict? Fortunately, as Table 19.3 shows, there are ways to stimulate conflict for constructive ends, to control conflict before it gets out of hand, and to resolve it if it does. Below we look at ways of managing conflict.

Stimulating Conflict

In some situations, an organization may stimulate conflict by placing individual employees or groups in competitive situations. Managers can establish sales contests, incentive plans, bonuses, or other competitive stimuli to spark competition. As long as the ground rules are equitable and all participants perceive the contest as fair, the conflict created by the competition is likely to be constructive because each participant will work hard to win (thereby enhancing some aspect of organizational performance).

Stimulating conflict
  Increase competition among individuals and teams
  Hire outsiders to shake things up
  Change established procedures
Controlling conflict
  Expand resource base
  Enhance coordination of interdependence
  Set supraordinate goals
  Match personalities and work habits of employees
Resolving and eliminating conflict
  Avoid conflict
  Convince conflicting parties to compromise
  Bring conflicting parties together to confront and negotiate conflict

Table 19.3

Methods for Managing Conflict
Conflict is a powerful force in organizations and has both negative and positive consequences. Thus, managers can draw upon several different techniques to stimulate, control, resolve, or eliminate conflict, depending on their unique circumstances.

Another useful method for stimulating conflict is to bring in one or more outsiders who will shake things up and present a new perspective on organizational practices. Outsiders may be new employees, current employees assigned to an existing work group, or consultants or advisers hired on a temporary basis. Of course, this action can also provoke resentment from insiders who feel they were qualified for the position. The Beecham Group, a British company, once hired an executive from the United States for its CEO position expressly to change how the company did business. His arrival brought with it new ways of doing things and a new enthusiasm for competitiveness. Unfortunately, some valued employees also chose to leave Beecham because they resented some of the changes that were made.

Changing established procedures, especially procedures that have outlived their usefulness, can also stimulate conflict. Such actions cause people to reassess how they perform their jobs and whether they perform them correctly. For example, one university president announced that all vacant staff positions could be filled only after written justification had received his approval. Conflict arose between the president and the department heads who felt they were having to do more paperwork than was necessary. Most requests were okayed, but because department heads now had to think through their staffing needs, a few unnecessary positions were appropriately eliminated.

Controlling Conflict

One method of controlling conflict is to expand the resource base. Suppose a top manager receives two budget requests for $100,000 each. If she has only $180,000 to distribute, the stage is set for conflict because each group will feel its proposal is worth funding and will be unhappy if it is not fully funded. If both proposals are indeed worthwhile, it may be possible for her to come up with the extra $20,000 from some other source and thereby avoid difficulty.

As noted earlier, pooled, sequential, and reciprocal interdependence can all result in conflict. If managers use an appropriate technique for enhancing coordination, they can reduce the probability that conflict will arise. Techniques for coordination (described in Chapter 11) include making use of the managerial hierarchy, relying on rules and procedures, enlisting liaison persons, forming task forces, and integrating departments. At the J.C. Penney store mentioned earlier, the conflict was addressed by providing salespeople with clearer forms on which to specify the merchandise they needed and in what sequence. If one coordination technique does not have the desired effect, a manager might shift to another.

Competing goals can also be a potential source of conflict among individuals and groups. Managers can sometimes focus employee attention on higher-level, or superordinate, goals as a way of eliminating lower-level conflict. When labor unions such as the United Auto Workers make wage concessions to ensure survival of the automobile industry, they are responding to a superordinate goal. Their immediate goal may be higher wages for members, but they realize that without the automobile industry, their members would not even have jobs.

Finally, managers should try to match the personalities and work habits of employees to avoid conflict between individuals. For instance, two valuable subordinates, one a chain smoker and the other a vehement nonsmoker, should probably not be required to work together in an enclosed space. If conflict does arise between incompatible individuals, a manager might seek an equitable transfer for one or both of them to other units.

Resolving and Eliminating Conflict

Despite everyone's best intentions, conflict will sometimes flare up. If it is disrupting the workplace, creating too much hostility and tension, or otherwise harming the organization, attempts must be made to resolve it. Some managers who are uncomfortable dealing with conflict choose to avoid the conflict and hope it will go away. Avoidance may sometimes be effective in the short run for some kinds of interpersonal disagreements, but it does little to resolve long-run or chronic conflict. Even more unadvisable, though, is "smoothing"—minimizing the conflict and telling everyone that things will "get better." Often the conflict will only worsen as people continue to brood over it.

Compromise is striking a middle-range position between two extremes. This approach can work if it is used with care, but in most compromise situations someone wins and someone loses. Budget problems are one of the few areas amenable to compromise because of their objective nature. Assume, for example, that additional resources are not available to the manager mentioned earlier. She has $180,000 to divide, and each of two groups claims to need $100,000. If the manager believes that both projects warrant funding, she can allocate $90,000 to each. The fact that the two groups have at least been treated equally may minimize the potential conflict.

The confrontation approach to conflict resolution—also called interpersonal problem solving—consists of bringing the parties together to confront the conflict. The parties discuss the nature of their conflict and attempt to reach an agreement or a solution. Confrontation requires a reasonable degree of maturity on the part of the participants, and the manager must structure the situation carefully. If handled well, this approach can be an effective means of resolving conflict. In recent years, many organizations have experimented with a technique called alternative dispute resolution, using a team of employees to arbitrate conflict in this way.[30]

Regardless of the approach, organizations and their managers must realize that conflict must be addressed if it is to serve constructive purposes and to prevent destructive consequences. Conflict is inevitable in organizations, but its effects can be constrained with proper attention. For example, Union Carbide once sent two hundred of its managers to a three-day workshop on conflict management. The managers engaged in a variety of exercises and discussions to learn with whom they were most likely to come into conflict and how they should try to resolve it. As a result, managers at the firm later reported that hostility and resentment in the organization had been greatly diminished and that people in the firm reported more pleasant working relationships.[31]

> **MANAGEMENT**   Managers need to understand that conflict may need to be
> **IMPLICATIONS**   stimulated, controlled, and/or resolved and eliminated. They
> should thus be familiar with the various techniques available to accomplish
> each of these ends, as well as understanding the benefits and weaknesses of each
> technique.

Summary of Key Points

A group is two or more people who interact regularly to accomplish a common purpose or goal. General kinds of groups in organizations are functional groups, task groups and teams, and informal or interest groups. A team is a group of workers that functions as a unit, often with little or no supervision, to carry out organizational goals.

People join functional groups and teams to pursue a career. Their reasons for joining informal or interest groups include interpersonal attraction, group activities, group goals, need satisfaction, and potential instrumental benefits. The stages of team development include testing and dependence, intragroup conflict and hostility, development of group cohesion, and focusing on the problem at hand.

Four important characteristics of teams are role structures, behavioral norms, cohesiveness, and informal leadership. Role structures define task and socioemotional specialists and may be weakened by role ambiguity, role conflict, or role overload. Norms are standards of behavior for group members. Cohesiveness is the extent to which members are loyal and committed to the team and to one another. Several factors can increase or reduce team cohesiveness. The relationship between performance norms and cohesiveness is especially important. Informal leaders are those people whom the group members themselves choose to follow.

Conflict is a disagreement between two or more people, groups, and/or organizations. Too little or too much conflict may hurt performance, but an optimal level of conflict may improve performance. Interpersonal and intergroup conflict in organizations may be caused by personality differences or by particular organizational strategies and practices.

Organizations may encounter conflict with one another and with various elements of the environment. Three methods of managing conflict are to stimulate it, control it, or resolve and eliminate it.

Discussion Questions

Questions for Review

1. What is a group? Describe the several different types of groups and indicate the similarities and differences between them.
2. Why do people join groups? Do all teams develop through all the stages discussed in this chapter? Why or why not?
3. Describe the characteristics of teams. How might the management of a mature team differ from the management of teams that are not yet mature?
4. Describe the nature and causes of conflict in organizations. Is conflict always bad? Why or why not?

Questions for Analysis

5. Is it possible for a group to be of more than one type at the same time? If so, under what circumstances? If not, why not?
6. Think of several groups of which you have been a member. Why did you join each? Did each group progress through the stages of development discussed in this chapter? If not, why not?
7. Do you think teams are a valuable new management technique that will endure, or are they just a fad that will be replaced with something else in the near future?

Questions for Application

8. Find local organizations that regularly use groups in their operations. What kinds of groups are being used? How are they being used? Is that use effective? Why or why not?
9. Find out if a local business is using teams. If so, talk to a manager or team participant at the company and learn about her or his experiences.
10. Would a manager want to stimulate conflict in his or her organization? Why or why not? Interview several managers of local business organizations to obtain their views on the use of conflict and compare them to your answer to this question.

BUILDING EFFECTIVE *interpersonal* SKILLS

Exercise Overview

A manager's interpersonal skills refer to her or his ability to understand and motivate individuals and groups. Clearly, then, interpersonal skills play a major role in determining how well a manager can interact with others in a group setting. This exercise will allow you to practice your interpersonal skills in relation to just such a setting.

Exercise Background

You have just been transferred to a new position supervising a group of five employees. The business you work for is fairly small and has few rules and regulations. Unfortunately, the lack of rules and regulations is creating a problem that you must now address.

Specifically, two of the group members are nonsmokers. They are becoming increasingly vocal about the fact that two other members of the group smoke at work. These two workers feel that the secondary smoke in the workplace is endangering their health and want to establish a nonsmoking policy like that of many large businesses today.

The two smokers, however, argue that since the firm did not have such a policy when they started working there, it would be unfair to impose such a policy on them now. One of them, in particular, says that he turned down an attractive job with another company because he wanted to work in a place where he could smoke.

The fifth worker is also a nonsmoker but says that she doesn't care if others smoke. Her husband smokes at home anyway, and so she is used to being around smokers. You suspect that if the two vocal nonsmokers are not appeased, they may leave. At the same time, you also think that the two smokers will leave if you mandate a no-smoking policy. All five workers do good work, and you do not want any of them to leave.

Exercise Task

With this information as context, do the following:

1. Explain the nature of the conflict that exists in this work group.
2. Develop a course of action for dealing with the situation.

BUILDING EFFECTIVE *conceptual* SKILLS

Exercise Overview

Groups and teams are becoming ever more important in organizations. This exercise will allow you to practice your conceptual skills as they apply to work teams in organizations.

Exercise Background

Several highly effective groups exist outside the boundaries of typical business organizations. For example, each of the following represents a team:

1. A basketball team
2. An elite military squadron
3. A government policy group such as the presidential cabinet
4. A student planning committee

Exercise Task

1. Identify an example of a real team, such as one of the above. Choose one that (a) is not part of a normal business and (b) you can argue is highly effective.
2. Determine the reasons for the team's effectiveness.
3. Determine how a manager can learn from this particular team and use its success factors in a business setting.

BUILDING EFFECTIVE *time-management* SKILLS

Exercise Overview

Time-management skills refer to the manager's ability to prioritize work, to work efficiently, and to delegate appropriately. This exercise will enable you to develop time-management skills as they relate to running team meetings.

Exercise Background

While teams and team meetings are becoming more and more common, some managers worry that they waste too much time. Listed below are several suggestions that experts have made for being more efficient in a meeting:

1. Have an agenda.
2. Meet only when there is a reason.
3. Set a clear starting and ending time.
4. Put a clock in front of everyone.
5. Take away all the chairs and make people stand.
6. Lock the door at starting time to "punish" late-comers.
7. Give everyone a role in the meeting.
8. Use visual aids.
9. Have a recording secretary to document what transpires.
10. Have a one-day-a-week meeting "holiday"—a day on which no one can schedule a meeting.

Exercise Task

With the information above as context, do the following:

1. Evaluate the likely effectiveness of each of these suggestions.
2. Rank-order the suggestions in terms of their likely value.
3. Identify at least three other suggestions that you think might improve the efficiency of a team meeting.

TOTAL TEAMWORK SPARKS IMAGINATION

Run more like a circus than a traditional company, Imagination Ltd., a London-based design firm, relies on high-performance teams to create museum exhibitions, design cruise ship lighting, develop product packaging, and much more. Its 350 employees are experts in twenty-six wide-ranging disciplines, including architecture, lighting, graphics, web design, and choreography. Despite this diversity, Imagination is anything but hierarchical: only four employees have official titles such as creative director. How does anything get done? Imagination's answer is total teamwork.

When a client consults with Imagination, the company quickly assembles a cross-functional team of in-house experts to help define the project and determine the goals. Once the client and Imagination agree on the scope of the project, the team members come up with a specific goal statement they use to guide their work. For example, when Imagination was hired to create a pleasant waiting area for people lining up for the Skyscape attraction inside London's Millennium Dome, the goal statement called for creating a climate of "uncomplicated joy." The team for this project started with an architect, lighting expert, graphics expert, and film director, then expanded to include a choreographer. As in other Imagination projects, the Skyscape team met weekly to brainstorm, flesh out the best ideas, and then adjourn to bring the ideas to life. Clients don't attend these meetings, but their views are well represented and their feedback is incorporated into team decisions.

Because personnel in other parts of the company are often affected by team actions, everyone is invited to attend each team's weekly project meetings. This tradition keeps the entire workforce informed of problems and progress and allows non–team members to plan ahead for a later role, such as arranging for printing or transportation at the end of the project. In effect, the entire company functions as a team, with employees monitoring projects and staying up to date so they are ready to get involved when their expertise is needed.

Many organizations assemble teams of free agents who are hired to work on particular projects and then leave after their work is complete. However, one of Imagination's strengths is that its experts are all employees, so their talents are available to any team at any time. Another strength is that Imagination's teams have no formal leadership. Instead, every member accepts responsibility for the project's success and acts accordingly, providing input and tackling tasks that bring the entire team closer to its goal.

Imagination's team members have earned reputations as experts in their fields and have developed respect for each other through the course of multiple team experiences. As a result, they are open to each other's ideas and listen carefully when colleagues make suggestions. Such interaction crosses disciplines, as well, with writers offering advice to lighting specialists, for example. The diversity of a team and the free flow of ideas and information stimulates creativity and enhances the team's effectiveness. Nonetheless, team meetings can be noisy and difficult on occasion, as members staunchly defend their creative ideas and argue over different approaches.

Since Imagination was established in 1978, its talented teams have tackled a wide range of design challenges. One team created the lighting design for Disney cruise ships; another created the dinosaur exhibit for the Natural History Museum in London; yet another designed the Millennium Dome Journey Zone building and exhibit content for corporate sponsor Ford Motor. The company has even worked with clients to train the personnel who staff the places it has designed, to ensure that the entire experience lives up to the goals set at the start of the project. Thanks to total teamwork, Imagination continues to build on its rich internal resources to meet clients' goals in new and exciting ways.

Case Questions

1. What role does conflict play in stimulating creativity at Imagination?

2. Why do Imagination's teams function well without formal leadership?

3. What factors appear to be increasing the cohesiveness of Imagination's teams?

Case Reference

Charles Fishman, "Total Teamwork: Imagination Ltd.," *Fast Company,* April 2000, pp. 156–168.

CHAPTER NOTES

1. Bradley L. Kirkman and Benson Rosen, "Powering Up Teams," *Organizational Dynamics,* Winter 2000, pp. 48–58; "Fastener's 3-Prong Plan Yields Perfection," *USA Today,* May 2, 1997, p. 9B. (quote on p. 9B).

2. See Gregory Moorhead and Ricky W. Griffin, *Organizational Behavior,* 6th Edition (Boston: Houghton Mifflin, 2001), for a review of definitions of groups.

3. Dorwin Cartwright and Alvin Zander, eds., *Group Dynamics: Research and Theory,* 3rd Edition (New York: Harper & Row, 1968).

4. Robert Schrank, *Ten Thousand Working Days* (Cambridge, Mass.: MIT Press, 1978); Bill Watson, "Counter Planning on the Shop Floor," in Peter Frost, Vance Mitchell, and Walter Nord, eds., *Organizational Reality,* 2nd Edition (Glenview, Ill.: Scott, Foresman, 1982), pp. 286–294.

5. Bradley L. Kirkman and Benson Rosen, "Powering Up Teams," *Organizational Dynamics,* Winter 2000, pp. 48–58.

6. Brian Dumaine, "Payoff from the New Management," *Fortune,* December 13, 1993, pp. 103–110.

7. "Why Teams Fail," *USA Today,* February 25, 1997, pp. 1B, 2B.

8. Brian Dumaine, "The Trouble with Teams," *Fortune,* September 5, 1994, pp. 86–92. See also Susan G. Cohen and Diane E. Bailey, "What Makes Teams Work: Group Effectiveness Research from the Shop Floor to the Executive Suite," *Journal of Management,* 1997, Vol. 23, No. 3, pp. 239–290.

9. Marvin E. Shaw, *Group Dynamics—The Psychology of Small Group Behavior,* 4th Edition (New York: McGraw-Hill, 1985).

10. "How to Avoid Hiring the Prima Donnas Who Hate Teamwork," *Wall Street Journal,* February 15, 2000, p. B1.

11. See Connie Gersick, "Marking Time: Predictable Transitions in Task Groups," *Academy of Management Journal,* June 1989, pp. 274–309. See also Avan R. Jassawalla and Hemant C. Sashittal, "Building Collaborative Cross-Functional New Product Teams," *Academy of Management Review,* 1999, Vol. 13, No. 3, pp. 50–60.

12. See Michael Campion, Gina Medsker, and A. Catherine Higgs, "Relations Between Work Group Characteristics and Effectiveness: Implications for Designing Effective Work Groups," *Personnel Psychology,* Winter 1993, pp. 823–850, for a review of other team characteristics.

13. David Katz and Robert L. Kahn, *The Social Psychology of Organizations,* 2nd Edition (New York: Wiley, 1978), pp. 187–221. See also Greg L. Stewart and Murray R. Barrick, "Team Structure and Performance: Assessing the Mediating Role of Intrateam Process and the Moderating Role of Task Type," *Academy of Management Journal,* 2000, Vol. 43, No. 2, pp. 135–148, and Michael G. Pratt and Peter O. Foreman, "Classifying Managerial Responses to Multiple Organizational Identities," *Academy of Management Review,* 2000, Vol. 25, No. 1, pp. 18–42.

14. See Travis C. Tubre and Judith M. Collins, "Jackson and Schuler (1985) Revisited: A Meta-Analysis of the Relationships Between Role Ambiguity, Role Conflict, and Job Performance," *Journal of Management,* 2000, Vol. 26, No. 1, pp. 155–169.

15. Robert L. Kahn, D. M. Wolfe, R. P. Quinn, J. D. Snoek, and R. A. Rosenthal, *Organizational Stress: Studies in Role Conflict and Role Ambiguity* (New York: Wiley, 1964).

16. Daniel C. Feldman, "The Development and Enforcement of Group Norms," *Academy of Management Review,* January 1984, pp. 47–53.

17. "Companies Turn to Peer Pressure to Cut Injuries as Psychologists Join the Battle," *Wall Street Journal,* March 29, 1991, pp. B1, B3.

18. James Wallace Bishop and K. Dow Scott, "How Commitment Affects Team Performance," *HRMagazine,* February 1997, pp. 107–115.

19. Anne O'Leary-Kelly, Joseph Martocchio, and Dwight Frink, "A Review of the Influence of Group Goals on Group Performance," *Academy of Management Journal,* 1994, Vol. 37, No. 5, pp. 1285–1301.

20. Philip M. Podsakoff, Michael Ahearne, and Scott B. MacKenzie, "Organizational Citizenship Behavior and the Quantity and Quality of Work Group Performance, *Journal of Applied Psychology,* Vol. 82, No. 2, 1997, pp. 262–270.

21. Suzy Wetlaufer, "Common Sense and Conflict," *Harvard Business Review,* January–February 2000, pp. 115–125.

22. Kathleen M. Eisenhardt, Jean L. Kahwajy, and L. J. Bourgeois III, "How Management Teams Can Have a Good Fight," *Harvard Business Review,* July–August 1997, pp. 77–89.

23. Thomas Bergmann and Roger Volkema, "Issues, Behavioral Responses and Consequences in Interpersonal Conflicts," *Journal of Organizational Behavior,* 1994, Vol. 15, pp. 467–471.

24. Robin Pinkley and Gregory Northcraft, "Conflict Frames of Reference: Implications for Dispute Processes and Outcomes," *Academy of Management Journal*, 1994, Vol. 37, No. 1, pp. 193–205.

25. "How 2 Computer Nuts Transformed Industry Before Messy Breakup," *Wall Street Journal*, August 27, 1996, pp. A1, A10.

26. Bruce Barry and Greg L. Stewart, "Composition, Process, and Performance in Self-Managed Groups: The Role of Personality," *Journal of Applied Psychology*, Vol. 82, No. 1, 1997, pp. 62–78.

27. "Delta CEO Resigns After Clashes with Board," *USA Today*, May 13, 1997, p. B1.

28. "A 'Blood War' in the Jeans Trade," *Business Week*, November 13, 1999, pp. 74–81.

29. Peter Elkind, "Blood Feud," *Fortune*, April 14, 1997, pp. 90–102.

30. "Solving Conflicts in the Workplace Without Making Losers," *Wall Street Journal*, May 27, 1997, p. B1.

31. "Teaching Business How to Cope with Workplace Conflicts," *Business Week*, February 18, 1990, pp. 136, 139.

The Controlling Process

613

20 Basic Elements of Control

Waste Management, started in 1971, is one of the world's largest private waste management companies. The firm does business in the United States, Canada, and Europe and, in 1998, earned more than $12 billion in revenues. The company has an excellent reputation for handling trash disposal efficiently and for effectively managing recycling programs. Unfortunately, however, Waste Management's own operations are currently in such disarray that its managers are having to focus most of their energies on sorting out the firm's own waste.

The company's problems first became public in 1997 when an interim CEO took over company reins. As it turned out, massive accounting problems had overstated the firm's earnings for years and its stock was taking a nosedive. An intensive audit seemed to rectify the situation, however, and in 1998 senior manage-ment at Waste Management agreed to merge with a smaller but fast-growing competitor named USA Waste Services. They also agreed to put USA Waste's respected but inexperienced CEO in charge of the new combined company.

For a while everything seemed to be working out well. The new company, which kept the Waste Management moniker, was attracting new business and reporting optimistic business forecasts for future revenues and profit. But in late 1999 everything came crashing down again. The original problems at Waste Management had not been corrected at all, and as a result of the merger, the situation had quickly gone from bad to worse!

One major problem the firm was experiencing was that, in addition to the big merger between Waste Management and USA Waste, the firm had also acquired literally dozens of other smaller businesses during a short period of time. But the firm did not appoint a senior executive to oversee the integration of these various businesses and, as a result, some operations were being poorly merged, some were being inexplicably shut down, and others remained in competition with one another.

Costs were also not being closely monitored. For example, even though USA Waste had put down a $2 million nonrefundable deposit for a new $30 million corporate jet for the CEO's use, after the merger a new $40 million jet was ordered because the merger would result in even more travel demands for the CEO. And after the firm failed to meet its earning estimates in the second quarter of 1999, no one at

> *"I'm not proud of the fact that, in retrospect, we didn't know what the hell was going on."*
>
> *—Roderick M. Hills, Waste Management board member*

After studying this chapter, you should be able to:

- Explain the purpose of control, identify different types of control, and describe the steps in the control process.

- Identify and explain the three forms of operations control.

- Describe budgets and other tools of financial control.

- Identify and distinguish between two opposing forms of structural control.

- Discuss the relationship between strategy and control, including international strategic control.

- Identify characteristics of effective control, why people resist control, and how managers can overcome this resistance.

the company could adequately explain why!

Finally, just as the true nature of the crisis was becoming obvious, the CEO was diagnosed with a serious brain tumor. But relying on his assurances that he would return to work shortly, Waste Management's board took no action and allowed the firm to continue to drift. Only after it became clear that he would not be able to resume working did the board take any action to reestablish control. So in early 2000 senior members of the board took control of the firm again and set about straightening out what could only be called a big mess. Indeed, so extensive were the problems at Waste Management that when new audits were called for, Arthur Andersen assigned 1,160 auditors to the account.

As the numbers started rolling in, Waste Management executives began to recognize the severity of their problems—$211 million in uncollectible bills, $305 million in unrecorded expenses, and $226 million in miscellaneous costs. All told, accounting irregularities resulted in

$1.76 billion in charges. And finally, Waste Management's board thinks it has identified all the major problems and either corrected them or at least put them on the road to recovery. Of course, it is not the first time they thought they had turned things around, so investors are keeping a wary eye on things.[1]

615

Senior management at Waste Management has failed at one of the most fundamental management responsibilities—control. In general, the CEO did a poor job of monitoring costs and keeping the organization on track, and the board of directors failed to monitor the performance and activities of the CEO and other top managers adequately. Effective control helps managers decide where they want their business to go, point it in that direction, and create systems to keep it on track. Ineffective control, meanwhile, can result in a lack of focus, weak direction, and poor overall performance.

As we discussed in Chapter 1, control is one of the four basic managerial functions that provide the organizing framework for this book. This chapter is the first of three devoted to this important area. In the first section of the chapter, we explain the purpose of control. We then look at types of control and the steps in the control process. The rest of the chapter examines the four levels of control most organizations must employ to remain effective: operations, financial, structural, and strategic control. We conclude by discussing the characteristics of effective control, noting why some people resist control, and describing what organizations can do to overcome this resistance. The remaining two chapters in this part focus on managing operations and managing information.

The Nature of Control in Organizations

control The regulation of organizational activities so that some targeted element of performance remains within acceptable limits

Control is the regulation of organizational activities so that some targeted element of performance remains within acceptable limits. Without this regulation, organizations have no indication of how well they perform in relation to their goals. Like a ship's rudder, control keeps the organization moving in the proper direction. At any point in time, it compares where the organization is in terms of performance (financial, productive, or otherwise) to where it is supposed to be. Control provides an organization with a mechanism for adjusting its course if performance falls outside acceptable boundaries. For example, Federal Express has a performance goal of delivering 99 percent of its packages on time. If on-time deliveries fall to 97 percent, control systems will signal the problem to managers so they can make necessary adjustments in operations to regain the target level of performance. An organization without effective control procedures is not likely to reach its goals—or if it does reach them, to know that it has! *Today's Management Issues* discusses the nature of control in e-businesses.

The Purpose of Control

As Figure 20.1 illustrates, control provides an organization with ways to adapt to environmental change, to limit the accumulation of error, to cope with organizational complexity, and to minimize costs. These four functions of control are worth a closer look.

TODAY'S MANAGEMENT ISSUES

E-BUSINESSES TIGHTEN UP FOR SURVIVAL

What happens when dot-com pandemonium dies down and e-businesses have to face fiscal reality? In the early stages of Internet fever, many e-businesses spent lavishly on advertising, staffing, offices, and other items. Growth potential seemed unlimited, and venture capitalists were happy to fund promising start-ups. As competition increased and profitability continued out of reach, however, more e-businesses felt pressure to impose or tighten controls to survive. For some firms—even those as young as one or two years old—the control measures were too little and too late.

One common way of minimizing costs, for on-line and off-line businesses alike, is to lower payroll expenses. The search portal AltaVista and the toy retail site KBKids are two of many Internet-based businesses that have taken this approach. During one six-month period, e-businesses laid off nearly 5,400 employees, a trend that is expected to continue as the sector matures. Still, layoffs aren't always enough to save companies that compete in the complex and dynamic on-line environment. Look at the short history of eParties, a party-planning web site. The firm opened for business on the Web in December 1999; by June 2000, it had fired its entire workforce of twenty-nine and agreed to be acquired by eToys, an on-line toy retailer.

E-businesses can target other areas for expense control as well. Streamline.com, an on-line grocer, has tried to avoid lay-offs by cutting back spending on facilities, for example. At the same time, the firm has pushed hard to boost sales by bringing its average grocery order up to $120. Pushed to the brink by ongoing financial obligations, however, Streamline.com has publicly said that it needs a major cash infusion to stay afloat. Whether Streamline winds up as a division of a larger company or becomes another dot-com casualty, along with Boo.com, BBQ.com, and other defunct e-businesses, its rocky road emphasizes the critical need for effective control from the very start.

> *Dot-coms are merely taking the next evolutionary step where the companies that do not produce are sorted out. It seems as if this sector may have reached this stage faster than any other in recent memory.*
>
> —*John Challenger, CEO of Challenger, Gray & Christmas**

References: Ken Yamada, "Shop Talk: Layoffs Today Mean Layoffs Tomorrow," *RedHerring,* June 6, 2000, http://www.redherring.com/industries/2000/0606/Indshoptalk060600.html; Keith Regan, "Dealing with Dot-Com Desperation," *E-Commerce Times,* August 25, 2000, http://www.ecommerce-times.com/news/viewpoint2000/view000825-1.shtml; Mick Brady, "The Bright Side of the Dot-Com Shakeout," *E-Commerce Times,* July 6, 2000, http://www.ecommercetimes.com/news/articles2000/000706-2.shtml (*quote from this web site).

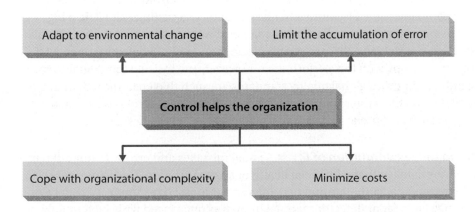

Figure 20.1

The Purpose of Control

Control is one of the four basic management functions in organizations. The control function, in turn, has four basic purposes. Properly designed control systems can fulfill each of these purposes.

Control plays a number of important purposes in organizations. Starbucks, for example, takes pride in the quality of coffees it serves and works to insure that they meet various quality standards for freshness, temperature, taste, and strength. To help uphold these quality standards, coffee tasters like Mary Williams sample as many as 300 cups of coffee a day for Starbucks. This continuous scrutiny helps the firm catch any problems in roasting, grinding, or brewing that may have inadvertently occurred.

Adapting to Environmental Change In today's complex and turbulent business environment, all organizations must contend with change.[2] If managers could establish goals and achieve them instantaneously, control would not be needed. But between the time a goal is established and the time it is reached, many events in the organization and its environment can disrupt movement toward the goal—or even to change the goal itself. A properly designed control system can help managers anticipate, monitor, and respond to changing circumstances.[3] In contrast, an improperly designed system can result in organizational performance that falls far below acceptable levels.

For example, Michigan-based Metalloy, a forty-six-year-old, family-run metal casting company, signed a contract to make engine-seal castings for NOK, a big Japanese auto parts maker. Metalloy was satisfied when its first five-thousand-unit production run yielded 4,985 acceptable castings and only 15 defective ones. NOK was quite unhappy with this performance, however, and insisted that Metalloy raise its standards. In short, global quality standards are such that customers demand near-perfection from their suppliers. A properly designed control system can help managers such as those at Metalloy stay better attuned to rising standards.

Limiting the Accumulation of Error Small mistakes and errors do not often inflict serious damage to the financial health of an organization. Over time, however, small errors may accumulate and become very serious. For example, Whistler Corporation, a large radar detector manufacturer, was once faced with such rapidly escalating demand that it essentially stopped worrying about quality. The defect rate rose from 4 percent to 9 percent to 15 percent, and eventually reached 25 percent. One day, a manager realized that one hundred of the firm's 250 employees were spending all their time fixing defective units and that $2 million worth of inventory was awaiting repair. Had the company adequately controlled quality as it responded to increased demand, the problem would have never reached such proportions. Similarly, Fleetwood Enterprises, a large manufacturer of recreational vehicles, has suffered because its managers did not adequately address several small accounting and production problems years ago. These small problems have now grown into large ones, and the firm is struggling with how to correct them.[4]

Coping with Organizational Complexity   When a firm purchases only one raw material, produces one product, has a simple organization design, and enjoys constant demand for its product, its managers can maintain control with a very basic and simple system. But a business that produces many products from myriad raw materials and has a large market area, a complicated organization design, and many competitors needs a sophisticated system to maintain adequate control. In part, this fact explains what happened at Waste Management—after the firm merged with USA Waste, the new enterprise was so large and complex that the existing control systems were simply inadequate.

Minimizing Costs   When it is practiced effectively, control can also help reduce costs and boost output. For example, Georgia-Pacific Corporation, a large wood products company, learned of a new technology that could be used to make thinner blades for its saws. The firm's control system was used to calculate the amount of wood that could be saved from each cut made by the thinner blades relative to the costs used to replace the existing blades. The results have been impressive—the wood that is saved by the new blades each year fills eight hundred railcars. As Georgia-Pacific discovered, effective control systems can eliminate waste, lower labor costs, and improve output per unit of input. Similarly, the CEO of Travelers' Insurance decided that a $60,000 cost for repairing a broken fountain in front of company headquarters was excessive and instead spent only $20,000 to have it filled and planted with a low-maintenance tree.[5] And Coca-Cola recently announced that it would lay off six thousand workers to reduce its labor costs.[6]

Types of Control

The examples of control given thus far have illustrated the regulation of several organizational activities, from producing quality products to coordinating complex organizations. Organizations practice control in several different areas and at different levels, and the responsibility for managing control is widespread.

Areas of Control   Control can focus on any area of an organization. Most organizations define areas of control in terms of the four basic types of resources they use: physical, human, information, and financial resources.[7] Control of physical resources includes inventory management (stocking neither too few nor too many units in inventory), quality control (maintaining appropriate levels of output quality), and equipment control (supplying the necessary facilities and machinery). Control of human resources includes selection and placement, training and development, performance appraisal, and compensation. Control of information resources includes sales and marketing forecasting, environmental analysis, public relations, production scheduling, and economic forecasting. Financial control involves managing the organization's debt so that it does not become excessive, ensuring that the firm always has enough cash on hand to meet its obligations but that it does not have excess cash in a checking account, and that receivables are collected and bills paid on time.

In many ways, the control of financial resources is the most important area because financial resources are related to the control of all the other resources in an organization: too much inventory leads to storage costs; poor selection of personnel leads to termination and rehiring expenses; inaccurate sales forecasts lead to disruptions in cash flows and other financial effects. Financial issues tend to pervade most control-related activities. Indeed, financial issues form the basic problem faced by Waste Management. Various inefficiencies and operating blunders put the company in a position where it was losing money everywhere but lacked sufficient control to pinpoint specific problems.

Levels of Control   Control can be broken down by area, as Figure 20.2 shows, and it can also be broken down by level within the organizational system. **Operations control** focuses on the processes the organization uses to transform resources into products or services (quality control is one type of operations control).[8] **Financial control** is concerned with the organization's financial resources. Monitoring receivables to make sure customers are paying their bills on time is an example of financial control. **Structural control** is concerned with how the elements of the organization's structure are serving their intended purposes. Monitoring the administrative ratio to make sure staff expenses do not become excessive is an example of structural control. Finally, **strategic control** focuses on how effectively the organization's corporate, business, and functional strategies are succeeding in helping the organization meet its goals. For example, if a corporation has been unsuccessful in implementing its strategy of related diversification, its managers need to identify the reasons and either change the strategy or renew their efforts to implement it. We discuss these four levels of control more fully later in this chapter.

Responsibilities for Control   Traditionally, managers have been responsible for overseeing the wide array of control systems and concerns in organizations. They decide which types of control the organization will use, and they implement control systems and take actions based on the information provided by control systems. Thus, ultimate responsibility for control rests with all managers throughout an organization.

operations control Focuses on the processes the organization uses to transform resources into products or services

financial control Concerned with the organization's financial resources

structural control Concerned with how the elements of the organization's structure are serving their intended purposes

strategic control Focuses on how effectively the organization's corporate, business, and functional strategies are succeeding in helping the organization meet its goals

Figure 20.2

Levels of Control

Managers use control at several different levels. The most basic levels of control in organizations are strategic, structural, operations, and financial control. Each level must be managed properly if control is to be most effective.

Most larger organizations also have one or more specialized managerial positions called controller. A **controller** is responsible for helping line managers with their control activities, for coordinating the organization's overall control system, and for gathering and assimilating relevant information. Many businesses that use an H-form or M-form organization design have several controllers: one for the corporation and one for each division. The job of controller is especially important in organizations where control systems are complex.[9] As part of its turnaround effort, Waste Management has established controller positions at each of its locations—some six hundred in all.

In addition, many organizations are also beginning to use operating employees to help maintain effective control. Indeed, employee participation is often used as a vehicle for allowing operating employees an opportunity to help facilitate organizational effectiveness. For example, Whistler Corporation increased employee participation in an effort to turn its quality problems around. As a starting point, the quality control unit, formerly responsible for checking product quality at the end of the assembly process, was eliminated. Next, all operating employees were encouraged to check their own work and told that they would be responsible for correcting their own errors. As a result, Whistler has eliminated its quality problems and is now highly profitable once again.

Steps in the Control Process

Regardless of the type or levels of control systems an organization needs, there are four fundamental steps in any control process.[10] These steps are illustrated in Figure 20.3.

Establish Standards   The first step in the control process is establishing standards. A **control standard** is a target against which subsequent performance will

controller A position in organizations that helps line managers with their control activities

control standard A target against which subsequent performance will be compared

Figure 20.3

Steps in the Control Process
Having an effective control system can help ensure that an organization achieves its goals. Implementing a control system, however, is a systematic process that generally proceeds through four interrelated steps.

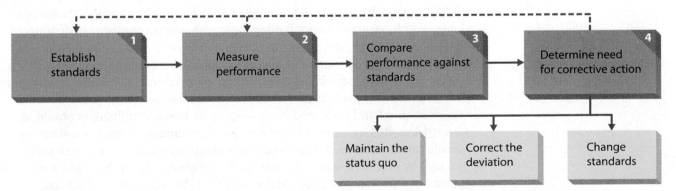

be compared.[11] Employees at Taco Bell fast-food restaurant, for example, work toward the following service standards:

1. A minimum of 95 percent of all customers will be greeted within three minutes of their arrival.
2. Preheated tortilla chips will not sit in the warmer more than thirty minutes before they are served to customers.
3. Empty tables will be cleaned within five minutes after being vacated.

Standards established for control purposes should be expressed in measurable terms. Note that standard 1 above has a time limit of three minutes and an objective target of 95 percent of all customers. In standard 3, the objective target is implied: "all" empty tables.

Control standards should also be consistent with the organization's goals. Taco Bell has organizational goals involving customer service, food quality, and restaurant cleanliness. A control standard for a retailer like Home Depot should be consistent with its goal of increasing its annual sales volume by 25 percent within five years. A hospital trying to shorten the average hospital stay by a patient will have control standards that reflect current averages. A university reaffirming its commitment to academics might adopt a standard of graduating 80 percent of its student athletes within five years of their enrollment. Control standards can be as narrow or as broad as the level of activity to which they apply and must follow logically from organizational goals and objectives.

A final aspect of establishing standards is to identify performance indicators. Performance indicators are measures of performance that provide information directly relevant to what is being controlled. For example, suppose an organization is following a tight schedule in building a new plant. Relevant performance indicators could be buying a site, selecting a building contractor, and ordering equipment. Monthly sales increases are not, however, directly relevant. On the other hand, if control is being focused on revenue, monthly sales increases are relevant, whereas buying land for a new plant is less relevant.

Measure Performance   The second step in the control process is measuring performance. Performance measurement is a constant, ongoing activity for most organizations. For control to be effective, performance measures must be valid. Daily, weekly, and monthly sales figures measure sales performance, and production performance may be expressed in terms of unit cost, product quality, or volume produced. Employee performance is often measured in terms of quality or quantity of output but, for many jobs, measuring performance is not so straightforward.

A research and development scientist at Merck, for example, may spend years working on a single project before achieving a breakthrough. A manager who takes over a business on the brink of failure may need months or even years to turn the failure around. Valid performance measurement, however difficult to obtain, is nevertheless vital in maintaining effective control, and performance indicators usually can be developed. The scientist's progress, for example, may be partially assessed by peer review, and the manager's success may be evaluated by her ability to convince creditors that she will eventually be able to restore profitability.

Compare Performance Against Standards The third step in the control process is comparing measured performance against established standards. Performance may be higher than, lower than, or identical to the standard. In some cases comparison is easy. The goal of each product manager at General Electric is to make the product either number one or number two (on the basis of total sales) in its market. Since this standard is clear and total sales easy to calculate, it is relatively simple to determine whether this standard has been met. Sometimes, however, comparisons are less clear-cut. If performance is lower than expected, the question is, How much deviation from standards can be allowed before taking remedial action? For example, is increasing sales by 7.9 percent when the standard was 8.0 percent close enough?

The timetable for comparing performance to standards depends on various factors, including the importance and complexity of what is being controlled. For longer-run and higher-level standards, comparisons may be appropriate annually. In other circumstances, more frequent comparisons are necessary. For example, a business with a cash shortage may need to monitor its on-hand cash reserves daily.

Determine Need for Corrective Action The final step in the control process is determining the need for corrective action. Decisions regarding corrective actions draw heavily on a manager's analytic and diagnostic skills. After comparing performance against control standards, one of three actions is appropriate: maintain the status quo (do nothing), correct the deviation, or change the standard. Maintaining the status quo is preferable when performance essentially matches the standard, but it is more likely that some action will be needed to correct a deviation from the standard.

Sometimes, performance that is higher than expected may also cause problems for organizations. For example, when Chrysler first introduced its popular PT Cruiser, demand was so strong there were waiting lists and many customers were willing to pay more than the suggested retail price to obtain a car. The company was reluctant to increase production, primarily because it feared demand would eventually drop. At the same time, however, it didn't want to alienate potential customers. Consequently, Chrysler decided to simply reduce its advertising. This curtailed demand a bit and limited customer frustration.

Changing an established standard usually is necessary if it was set too high or too low at the outset. This requirement is apparent if large numbers of employees routinely beat the standard by a wide margin or if no employees ever meet the standard. Also, standards that seemed perfectly appropriate when they were established may need to be adjusted because circumstances have since changed.

MANAGEMENT IMPLICATIONS Managers should understand the various fundamental purposes of control. In addition, they should be familiar with the types of control in organizations, especially those that are most relevant to their own work. Managers should also accept responsibility for their role in the organization's control functions. Finally, they should be thoroughly knowledgeable about the steps in the control process.

Operations Control

Preliminary control focuses on the resources an organization brings in from the environment. Cree, Inc., for instance, is the leading producer of the blue, light-emitting diodes that help backlight car dashboards, cell phone displays, and other electronic devices. This Cree employee is inspecting a new shipment of semiconductors the firm received from one of its suppliers to make sure that they meet the firm's high quality standards.

One of the four levels of control practiced by most organizations, operations control, is concerned with the processes the organization uses to transform resources into products or services. As Figure 20.4 shows, the three forms of operations control—preliminary, screening, and postaction—occur at different points in relation to the transformation processes used by the organization.

Preliminary Control

Preliminary control concentrates on the resources—financial, material, human, and information—that the organization brings in from the environment. Preliminary control attempts to monitor the quality or quantity of these resources before they enter the organization. Firms like PepsiCo and General Mills hire only college graduates for their management training program, and even then only after applicants satisfy several interviewers and selection criteria. In this way, they control the quality of the human resources entering the organization. When Sears orders merchandise to be manufactured under its own brand name, it specifies rigid standards of quality, thereby controlling physical inputs. Organizations also control financial and information resources. For example, privately held companies like UPS and Mars limit the extent to which outsiders can buy their stock, and tele-

preliminary control Attempts to monitor the quality or quantity of financial, material, human, and information resources before they actually become part of the system

Figure 20.4

Forms of Operations Control

Most organizations develop multiple control systems that incorporate all three basic forms of control. For example, the publishing company that produced this book screens inputs by hiring only qualified persons, typesetters, and printers (preliminary control). In addition, quality is checked during the transformation process, such as after the manuscript is typeset (screening control), and the outputs—printed and bound books—are checked before they are shipped from the bindery (postaction control).

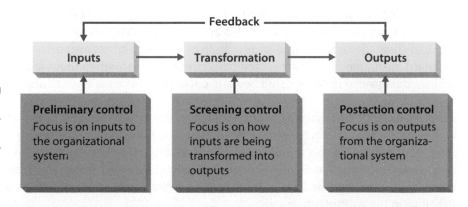

E-PURCHASING KEEPS INPUTS UNDER CONTROL

Buying from other businesses is big business. Every year, companies buy more than $7 trillion worth of parts, supplies, and services from suppliers around the world. Not so long ago, purchasing agents and other buyers had to hunt through mountains of supplier catalogs and make dozens of phone calls to track down stock numbers and quotes before writing purchase orders. Now, by using technology to tighten control of the purchasing function, a company can take much of the time and the hassle out of the process of acquiring inputs—and can expand its scope to scour the globe for the lowest prices or the quickest delivery times.

On the CheMatch.com web site, for example, buyers can see current market prices and availability for chemicals such as benzene and order on-line with a few keystrokes. On the Petrocosm Marketplace site, buyers for energy companies can instantly compare competitive prices on drilling machinery and other supplies, then place orders on-line. On FreeMarkets.com, buyers can arrange reverse auctions in which suppliers bid for the right to provide a particular input.

The savings can be enormous, as the following examples show. John Deere's e-purchasing initiative is expected to shave 5 percent off its annual cost of parts and supplies. Over the course of five years, the farm-equipment manufacturer will save a total of $1 billion, giving its bottom line a healthy boost. What's more, Deere is achieving these impressive results while reducing the size of its purchasing department by 25 percent. United Technologies, an energy company, has slashed its input expenses by almost $800 million. IBM now uses the Web to buy 90 percent of its supplies, streamlining its control of a $45 million supply budget. And on-line reverse auctions have helped the Naval Supply Systems Command save 22 percent on bunk units purchased for U.S. Navy ships. Tighter control, increased efficiency, and lower costs—the combination makes e-purchasing an attractive technique for businesses of any size.

> *With anonymity, you can move in the market without moving the market. It's a lot easier to click a mouse than call around the world.*
>
> —*Carl McCutcheon, CEO of CheMatch.com**

References: Del Jones, "E-Purchasing Saves Businesses Billions," *USA Today*, February 7, 2000, pp. 1B, 2B (*quote on p. 2B); "Contract Awarded in NAVSUP's Second Reverse Auction," *NAVICP*, August 3, 2000, http://www.navicp.navy.mil/news/reverseauction2.htm (read on-line October 2, 2000).

vision networks verify the accuracy of news stories before they are broadcast. *Management Infotech* explains how some businesses today are using electronic purchasing as part of their preliminary control processes.

Screening Control

Screening control focuses on meeting standards for product and/or service quality or quantity during the actual transformation process itself. Screening control relies heavily on feedback processes. For example, in a Compaq Computer factory, computer system components are checked periodically as each unit is being assembled. This checking is done to ensure that all the components assembled up to that point are working properly. The periodic quality checks provide feedback to workers so they know what, if any, corrective actions to take. Because they are useful in identifying the cause of problems, screening controls tend to be used more often than other forms of control.

screening control Relies heavily on feedback processes during the transformation process

More and more companies are adopting screening controls because they are an effective way to promote employee participation and catch problems early in the overall transformation process. For example, Corning adopted screening controls for use in manufacturing television glass. In the past, television screens were inspected only after they were finished. Unfortunately, over 4 percent of them were later returned by customers because of defects. Now the glass screens are inspected at each step in the production process rather than at the end, and the return rate from customers has dropped to .03 percent.

Postaction Control

postaction control Monitors the outputs or results of the organization after the transformation process is complete

Postaction control focuses on the outputs or results of the organization after the transformation process is complete. Corning's old system was postaction control—final inspection after the product is completed. While Corning abandoned its postaction control system, it still may be an effective method of control, primarily if a product can be manufactured in only one or two steps or if the service is fairly simple and routine. Although postaction control alone may not be as effective as preliminary or screening control, it can provide management with information for future planning. For example, if a quality check of finished goods indicates an unacceptably high defective rate, the production manager knows that he or she must identify the causes and take steps to eliminate them. Postaction control also provides a basis for rewarding employees. Recognizing that an employee has exceeded personal sales goals by a wide margin, for example, may alert the manager that a bonus or promotion is in order.

Postaction control focuses on the outputs of an organization after the transformation process is complete. These Ford inspectors, for example, are taking a close look at a freshly minted Mustang that has just rolled off the assembly line. While the car received numerous screening control inspections as it was being built, this final inspection is one last step intended to insure that no major defects or other problems have been missed.

Most organizations use more than one form of operations control. For example, Honda's preliminary control includes hiring only qualified employees and specifying strict quality standards when ordering parts from other manufacturers. Honda uses numerous screening controls in checking the quality of components during assembly of cars. A final inspection and test drive as each car rolls off the assembly line is part of the company's postaction control.[12] Indeed, most successful organizations employ a wide variety of techniques to facilitate operations control.

MANAGEMENT IMPLICATIONS Managers should know the four basic levels of control used in organizations. They should also understand that many organizations use more than one level of control simultaneously.

Financial Control

Financial control is the control of financial resources as they flow into the organization (i.e., revenues, shareholder investments), are held by the organization (i.e., working capital, retained earnings), and flow out of the organization (i.e., payment of expenses). Businesses must manage their finances so that revenues are sufficient to cover expenses and still return a profit to the firm's owners. Not-for-profit organizations such as universities have the same concerns: their revenues (from tax dollars or tuition) must cover operating expenses and overhead. Dickson Poon is a Chinese investor who has profited by relying heavily on financial control. He buys distressed up-scale retailers like Britain's Harvey Nichols and the U.S.'s Barney's, imposes strict financial controls, and begins generating hefty profits.[13] A complete discussion of financial management is beyond the scope of this book, but we will examine the control provided by budgets and other financial control tools.

financial control Control of financial resources as they flow into the organization, are held by the organization, and flow out of the organization

Well-established and monitored financial regulations in most of today's developed economies ensure that financial control systems can be easily followed and readily interpreted and evaluated. But less certainty exists in some of today's developing economies. The Almaty stock exchange in Kazakhstan is subject to few rules and has no operating procedures. Not surprisingly, the exchange has had difficulty in attracting foreign investors. But as these economies mature and continue to develop, new controls will be created and investors can have more faith in the financial information they are given.

Budgetary Control

A **budget** is a plan expressed in numerical terms.[14] Organizations establish budgets for work groups, departments, divisions, and the whole organization. The usual time period for a budget is one year, although breakdowns of budgets by the quarter or month are also common. Budgets are

budget A plan expressed in numerical terms

generally expressed in financial terms, but they may occasionally be expressed in units of output, time, or other quantifiable factors.

Because of their quantitative nature, budgets provide yardsticks for measuring performance and facilitate comparisons across departments, between levels in the organization, and from one time period to another. Budgets serve four primary purposes. They help managers coordinate resources and projects (because they use a common denominator, usually dollars). They help define the established standards for control. They provide guidelines about the organization's resources and expectations. Finally, budgets enable the organization to evaluate the performance of managers and organizational units.

Types of Budgets   Most organizations develop and make use of three different kinds of budgets—financial, operating, and nonmonetary. Table 20.1 summarizes the characteristics of each of these.

A financial budget indicates where the organization expects to get its cash for the coming time period and how it plans to use it. Since financial resources are critically important, the organization needs to know where those resources will be coming from and how they are to be used. The financial budget provides answers to both these questions. Usual sources of cash include sales revenue, short- and long-term loans, the sale of assets, and the issuance of new stock.

For years Exxon Mobil has been very conservative in its capital budgeting. As a result, the firm has amassed a huge financial reserve but has been overtaken in

Table 20.1

Types of Budgets
Organizations use various types of budgets to help manage their control function. The three major categories of budgets are financial, operating, and nonmonetary budgets. There are several different types of budgets in each category. Each budget must be carefully matched with the specific function being controlled to be most effective.

Type of Budget	What Budget Shows
Financial budget	**Sources and uses of cash**
Cash-flow or cash budget	All sources of cash income and cash expenditures in monthly, weekly, or daily periods
Capital expenditures budget	Costs of major assets such as a new plant, machinery, or land
Balance sheet budget	Forecast of the organization's assets and liabilities in the event all other budgets are met
Operating budget	**Planned operations in financial terms**
Sales or revenue budget	Income the organization expects to receive from normal operations
Expense budget	Anticipated expenses for the organization during the coming time period
Profit budget	Anticipated differences between sales or revenues and expenses
Nonmonetary budget	**Planned operations in nonfinancial terms**
Labor budget	Hours of direct labor available for use
Space budget	Square feet or meters of space available for various functions
Production budget	Number of units to be produced during the coming time period

sales by Royal Dutch/Shell. More recently, Exxon Mobil has decided to loosen its purse strings and begin budgeting more for capital expenditures. For example, while Exxon Mobil's capital budget was less than $8 billion in 1994, managers increased this budget to $11 billion in 2000, and plan to increase it to around $14 billion by the year 2002.[15]

An operating budget is concerned with planned operations within the organization. It outlines what quantities of products and/or services the organization intends to create and what resources will be used to create them. IBM creates an operating budget that specifies how many of each model of its personal computer will be produced each quarter.

A nonmonetary budget is simply a budget expressed in nonfinancial terms, such as units of output, hours of direct labor, machine hours, or square-foot allocations. Nonmonetary budgets are most commonly used by managers at the lower levels of an organization. For example, a plant manager can schedule work more effectively knowing that he or she has eight thousand labor hours to allocate in a week, rather than trying to determine how to best spend $76,451 in wages in a week.

Developing Budgets Traditionally, budgets were developed by top management and the controller and then imposed on lower-level managers. Although some organizations still follow this pattern, many contemporary organizations now allow all managers to participate in the budget process. As a starting point, top management generally issues a call for budget requests, accompanied by an indication of overall patterns the budgets may take. For example, if sales are expected to drop in the next year, managers may be told up front to prepare for cuts in operating budgets.

As Figure 20.5 shows, the heads of each operating unit typically submit budget requests to the head of their division. An operating unit head might be a department manager in a manufacturing or wholesaling firm or a program director in a social service agency. The division heads might include plant managers, regional sales managers, or college deans. The division head integrates and consolidates the budget requests from operating unit heads into one overall division budget request. A great deal of interaction among managers usually takes place at this stage, as the division head coordinates the budgetary needs of the various departments.

Division budget requests are then forwarded to a budget committee. The budget committee is usually composed of top managers. The committee reviews budget requests from several divisions and, once again, duplications and inconsistencies are corrected.

Figure 20.5

Developing Budgets in Organizations

Most organizations use the same basic process to develop budgets. Operating units are requested to submit their budget requests to divisions. These divisions, in turn, compile unit budgets and submit their own budgets to the organization. An organizational budget is then compiled for approval by the budget committee, controller, and CEO.

Operating unit budget requests	Division budget requests	Organizational budget
		• Prepared by budget committee • Approved by budget committee, controller, and CEO

Finally, the budget committee, the controller, and the CEO review and agree on the overall budget for the organization as well as specific budgets for each operating unit. These decisions are then communicated back to each manager.

Strengths and Weaknesses of Budgeting Budgets offer numerous advantages, but they also have weaknesses. On the plus side, budgets facilitate effective control. Placing dollar values on operations enables managers to monitor operations better and to pinpoint problem areas. Budgets also facilitate coordination and communication between departments because they express diverse activities in a common denominator (dollars). Budgets help maintain records of organizational performance and are logical complements to planning; that is, as managers develop plans they should simultaneously consider control measures to accompany them. Organizations can use budgets to link plans and control by first developing budgets as part of the plan and then using those budgets as part of control.

On the other hand, some managers apply budgets too rigidly. Budgets are intended to serve as frameworks, but managers sometimes fail to recognize that changing circumstances may warrant budget adjustments. The process of developing budgets can also be very time consuming. Finally, budgets may limit innovation and change. When all available funds are allocated to specific operating budgets, it may be impossible to procure additional funds to take advantage of an unexpected opportunity.

Indeed, for these very reasons, some organizations are working to scale back their budgeting system. While most organizations are likely to continue to use budgets, the goal is to make them less confining and rigid. For example, Xerox, 3M, and Digital Equipment have all cut back on their budgeting systems by reducing the number of budgets they generate and by injecting more flexibility into the budgeting process.[16]

Other Tools of Financial Control

Although budgets are the most common means of financial control, other useful tools are financial statements, ratio analysis, and financial audits. *Managing in an e-Business World* discusses some of the problems that today's businesses, especially e-commerce enterprises, face in accounting for intangible assets.

financial statement A profile of some aspect of an organization's financial circumstances

Financial Statements A **financial statement** is a profile of some aspect of an organization's financial circumstances. There are commonly accepted and required ways that financial statements should be prepared and presented.[17] The two most basic financial statements prepared and used by virtually all organizations are a balance sheet and an income statement.

balance sheet List of assets and liabilities of an organization at a specific point in time, usually the last day of an organization's fiscal year

The **balance sheet** lists the assets and liabilities of the organization at a specific point in time, usually the last day of an organization's fiscal year. For example, the balance sheet may summarize the financial condition of an organization on December 31, 2000. Most balance sheets are divided into current assets (assets that are relatively liquid, or easily convertible into cash), fixed assets (assets that are longer-term in nature and less liquid), current liabilities (debts and other obligations that must be paid in the near future), long-term liabilities (payable over an extended period of time), and stockholders' equity (the owners' claim against the assets).

MANAGING IN AN e-BUSINESS WORLD

ACCOUNTING FOR ACCOUNTING METHODS

When managers talk about the "bottom line" and the "P and L," they are talking about figures on their firms' financial statements. Managers have long used the income statement and other financial statements as essential tools of control, comparing this quarter's "P" (profit) or "L" (loss) to last quarter's results, for example. However, this static, highly regulated method of accounting for financial performance may need updating to reflect the way companies do business in the Internet age.

Professor Baruch Lev of New York University's Stern School of Business says that conventional financial statements make no allowance for valuable but completely intangible assets. Tangible assets like equipment are routinely listed and valued under the assets section of the balance sheet, but not intangibles such as the innovative methods used for new products, the strength of the brand, or the size of the customer base.

A few years ago, America Online (AOL) tried a new approach to account for the way it acquires new customers, a key asset because customers are the source of monthly subscription revenues. Instead of classifying customer acquisition tactics such as the distribution of free trial disks as expenses—the usual accounting method—AOL capitalized some of the costs to write them off over a longer period. Lower expenses made AOL's profitability look better, but financial analysts objected, and AOL was finally forced to expense the full costs on revised financial statements.

MicroStrategy, a software and Internet firm, faced a different accounting dilemma. After clinching a $50 million, multiyear deal covering programs and services, the company decided to show the revenue on its financial statements all at once rather than year by year. However, the U.S. Securities and Exchange Commission doesn't allow companies to account for revenue before it's actually collected, so MicroStrategy had to restate its sales figures—downward.

> *We are using a five-hundred-year-old system to make decisions in a complex business environment in which the essential assets that create value have fundamentally changed.*
>
> —*Professor Baruch Lev of New York University's Stern School of Business**

Professor Lev suggests revamping accounting methods to show the financial value of intangible assets that boost the company's value. This technique would help managers of e-businesses do a better job of controlling those assets and would provide a standard method of presenting financial performance for review by investors and other stakeholders.

References: Alan M. Webber, "New Math for a New Economy," *Fast Company,* January–February 2000, pp. 214–224 (*quote on p. 217); Adam Zagorin, "The E-Numbers Game," *Time,* August 15, 2000, p. 66.

Whereas the balance sheet reflects a snapshot profile of an organization's financial position at a single point in time, the **income statement** summarizes financial performance over a period of time, usually one year. For example, the income statement might be for the period January 1, 2000, through December 31, 2000. The income statement summarizes the firm's revenues less its expenses to report net income (i.e., profit or loss) for the period. Information from the balance sheet and income statement is used in computing important financial ratios.

income statement A summary of financial performance over a period of time, usually one year

Ratio Analysis Financial ratios compare different elements of a balance sheet and/or income statement to one another. **Ratio analysis** is the calculation of one or more financial ratios to assess some aspect of the organization's financial health. Organizations use different financial ratios as part of financial control.

ratio analysis The calculation of one or more financial ratios to assess some aspect of the organization's financial health

For example, *liquidity ratios* indicate how liquid (easily converted into cash) an organization's assets are. *Debt ratios* reflect ability to meet long-term financial obligations. *Return ratios* show managers and investors how much return the organization is generating relative to its assets. *Coverage ratios* help estimate the organization's ability to cover interest expenses on borrowed capital. *Operating ratios* indicate the effectiveness of specific functional areas rather than the total organization. The Walt Disney Company relies heavily on financial ratios to keep its financial operations on track.[18]

audit An independent appraisal of an organization's accounting, financial, and operational systems

Financial Audits   **Audits** are independent appraisals of an organization's accounting, financial, and operational systems. The two major types of financial audit are the external audit and the internal audit.

External audits are financial appraisals conducted by experts who are not employees of the organization.[19] External audits are typically concerned with determining that the organization's accounting procedures and financial statements are compiled in an objective and verifiable fashion. The organization contracts with certified public accountants (CPAs) for this service. The CPA's main objective is to verify for stockholders, the IRS, and other interested parties that the methods by which the organization's financial managers and accountants prepare documents and reports are legal and proper. External audits are so important that publicly held corporations are required by law to have external audits regularly, as assurance to investors that the financial reports are reliable. An external audit at U.S. Shoe Corporation once discovered some significant accounting irregularities in one of the firm's divisions. As a result, the firm was fined and had to revamp its entire accounting system.[20]

Some organizations are also starting to employ external auditors to review other aspects of their financial operations. For example, now there are auditing firms that specialize in checking corporate legal bills. An auditor for the Fireman's Fund Insurance Corporation uncovered several thousands of dollars in legal fee errors. Other auditors are beginning to specialize in real estate, employee benefits, and pension plan investments.[21]

Whereas external audits are conducted by external accountants, an *internal audit* is handled by employees of the organization. Its objective is the same as that of an external audit—to verify the accuracy of financial and accounting procedures used by the organization. Internal audits also examine the efficiency and appropriateness of financial and accounting procedures. Because the staff members who conduct them are permanent employees of the organization, internal audits tend to be more expensive than external audits. But employees, who are more familiar with the organization's practices, may also point out significant aspects of the accounting system besides its technical correctness. Large organizations such as Dresser Industries and Ford have internal auditing staffs that spend all their time conducting audits of different divisions and functional areas of the organizations. Smaller organizations may assign accountants to an internal audit group on a temporary or rotating basis.

MANAGEMENT IMPLICATIONS   Regardless of their area of responsibility, all managers should understand the basics of financial control. In particular, they need to know how budgets are used for control and how budgets are developed, and they must know about other tools of financial control.

Structural Control

Organizations can create designs for themselves that result in very different approaches to control. Two major forms of structural control, bureaucratic control and clan control, represent opposite ends of a continuum, as shown in Figure 20.6.[22] The six dimensions shown in the figure represent perspectives adopted by the two extreme types of structural control; that is, they have different goals, degrees of formality, performance focus, organization designs, reward systems, and levels of participation. Although a few organizations fall precisely at one extreme or the other, most tend toward one end but may have specific characteristics of either.

Bureaucratic Control

Bureaucratic control is an approach to organization design characterized by formal and mechanistic structural arrangements. As the term suggests, It follows the bureaucratic model. The goal of bureaucratic control is employee compliance.

bureaucratic control A form of organizational control characterized by formal and mechanistic structural arrangements

Figure 20.6

Organizational Control
Organizational control generally falls somewhere between the two extremes of bureaucratic and clan control. NBC television uses bureaucratic control, whereas Levi Strauss uses clan control.

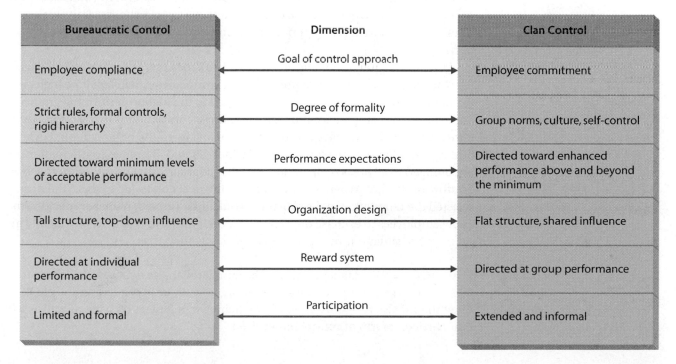

Bureaucratic Control	Dimension	Clan Control
Employee compliance	Goal of control approach	Employee commitment
Strict rules, formal controls, rigid hierarchy	Degree of formality	Group norms, culture, self-control
Directed toward minimum levels of acceptable performance	Performance expectations	Directed toward enhanced performance above and beyond the minimum
Tall structure, top-down influence	Organization design	Flat structure, shared influence
Directed at individual performance	Reward system	Directed at group performance
Limited and formal	Participation	Extended and informal

Organizations that use it rely on strict rules and a rigid hierarchy, insist that employees meet minimally acceptable levels of performance, and often have a tall structure. They focus their rewards on individual performance and allow only limited and formal employee participation.

NBC television applies structural controls that reflect many elements of bureaucracy. The organization relies on numerous rules to regulate employee travel, expense accounts, and other costs. A new performance appraisal system precisely specifies minimally acceptable levels of performance for everyone. The organization's structure is considerably taller than those of the other major networks, and rewards are based on individual contributions. Perhaps most significantly, many NBC employees have argued that they have too small a voice in how the organization is managed.

In another example, a large oil company recently made the decision to allow employees to wear casual attire to work. But a committee then spent weeks developing a twenty-page set of guidelines on what was and was not acceptable. For example, denim pants are not allowed. Similarly, athletic shoes may be worn as long as they are not white. And all shirts must have a collar. Nordstrom, the department store chain, is also moving toward bureaucratic control as it works to centralize all its purchasing in an effort to lower costs.[23]

Clan Control

clan control An approach to organizational control characterized by informal and organic structural arrangements

Clan control, in contrast, is an approach to organizational design characterized by informal and organic structural arrangements. As Figure 20.6 shows, its goal is employee commitment to the organization. Accordingly, it relies heavily on group norms and a strong corporate culture, and gives employees the responsibility for controlling themselves. Employees are encouraged to perform beyond minimally acceptable levels. Organizations using this approach are usually relatively flat. They direct reward at group performance and favor widespread employee participation.

Levi Strauss practices clan control. The firm's managers use groups as the basis for work and have created a culture wherein group norms help facilitate high performance. Rewards are subsequently provided to the higher-performing groups and teams. The company's culture also reinforces contributions to the overall team effort, and employees have a strong sense of loyalty to the organization. Levi Strauss has a flat structure and power is widely shared. Employee participation is encouraged in all areas of operation. Another company that uses this approach is Southwest Airlines. When Southwest made the decision to "go casual," the firm resisted the temptation to develop dress guidelines. Instead, managers decided to allow employees to exercise discretion over their attire, and to deal with clearly inappropriate situations on a case-by-case basis as they arise.

MANAGEMENT IMPLICATIONS   Managers should be familiar with the two basic forms of structural control used by organizations: bureaucratic and clan. They should also recognize which form their own organization uses, as well as why that particular form of control has evolved.

Strategic Control

Given the obvious importance of an organization's strategy, it is also important that the organization assess how effective that strategy is in helping the organization meet its goals.[24] To do so requires that the organization integrate its strategy and control systems. This requirement is especially relevant for the global organization.

Integrating Strategy and Control

Strategic control is aimed at ensuring that the organization is maintaining an effective alignment with its environment and moving toward achieving its strategic goals. Strategic control generally focuses on five aspects of organizations—structure, leadership, technology, human resources, and information and operational control systems. For example, an organization should periodically examine its structure to determine whether or not it is facilitating the attainment of the organization's strategic goals. Suppose a firm using a functional (U-form) design has an established goal of achieving a 20 percent sales growth rate per year. However, performance indicators show it is currently growing only at a rate of 10 percent per year. Detailed analysis might reveal that the current structure is inhibiting growth in some way (for example, by slowing decision making and inhibiting innovation) and that a divisional (M-form) design is more likely to bring about the desired growth (by speeding decision making and promoting innovation).

strategic control Control aimed at ensuring that the organization is maintaining an effective alignment with its environment and moving toward achieving its strategic goals

In this way, strategic control focuses on the extent to which implemented strategy achieves the organization's strategic goals. If, as outlined above, one or more avenues of implementation are inhibiting the attainment of goals, that avenue should be changed. Consequently, the firm might find it necessary to alter its structure, replace key leaders, adopt new technology, modify its human resources, or change its information and operational control systems. For example, Ikea, the Swedish furniture manufacturer, has experienced disappointing performance from its internationalization strategy. As a result, the company has recently announced a major change in how it will manage its international operations.[25] In particular, the firm has closed many of its underperforming outlets and centralized control back to corporate headquarters in Sweden.

Strategic control is critical to the success of many businesses. Take Minnesota-based Fastenal Co. Its CEO, Bob Kierlin, shown here with a team of employees, has made a strategic decision to provide his employees with few perks and no pensions. However, he believes strongly in extreme decentralization. He gives employees tremendous decision-making authority to carry out their jobs. Kierlin thinks that highly motivated employees prefer the power to work with almost total independence over more traditional kinds of rewards like extra vacation time or fitness centers. He ties pay raises and stock ownership to long-term performance and gives employees open access to information, which gives them the opportunity and the motivation to work in the best interests of the firm.

International Strategic Control

Because of both their relatively large size and the increased complexity associated with international business, global organizations must take an especially pronounced strategic view of their control systems. One very basic question that has to be addressed is whether to manage control from a centralized or decentralized perspective.[26] Under a centralized system, each organizational unit around the world is responsible for frequently reporting the results of its performance to headquarters. Managers from the home office often visit foreign branches to observe firsthand how the units are functioning.

BP Amoco, Unilever, Procter & Gamble, and Sony each use this approach. They believe centralized control is effective because it allows the home office to keep better informed of the performance of foreign units and to maintain more control over how decisions are made. For example, BP Amoco discovered that its Australian subsidiary was not billing its customers for charges as quickly as were its competitors. By shortening the billing cycle, BP Amoco now receives customer payments five days faster than before. Managers believe that they discovered this oversight only because of a centralized financial control system.

Organizations that use a decentralized control system require foreign branches to report less frequently and in less detail. For example, each unit may submit summary performance statements on a quarterly basis and provide full statements only once a year. Similarly, visits from the home office are less frequent and less concerned with monitoring and assessing performance. IBM, Ford, and Shell all use this approach. Because Ford practices decentralized control of its design function, European designers have developed several innovative automobile design features. Managers believe that if they had been more centralized, designers would not have had the freedom to develop their new ideas.

MANAGEMENT IMPLICATIONS   Managers need to understand how control and strategy are related. In addition, managers in companies with international operations need to be familiar with the special control issues that they face.

Managing Control in Organizations

Effective control, whether at the operations, financial, structural, or strategic level, successfully regulates and monitors organizational activities. To use the control process, managers must recognize the characteristics of effective control and understand how to identify and overcome occasional resistance to control.[27]

Characteristics of Effective Control

Control systems tend to be most effective when they are integrated with planning and when they are flexible, accurate, timely, and objective.

Integration with Planning   Control should be linked with planning. The more explicit and precise this link, the more effective the control system. The best way to integrate planning and control is to account for control as plans develop. In other words, as goals are set during the planning process, attention should be paid to developing standards that will reflect how well the plan is realized. Managers at Champion Spark Plug Company decided to broaden their product line to include a full range of automotive accessories—a total of twenty-one new products. As part of this plan, managers decided in advance what level of sales they wanted to realize from each product for each of the next five years. They established these sales goals as standards against which actual sales would be compared. Thus, by accounting for their control system as they developed their plan, managers at Champion did an excellent job of integrating planning and control.

Flexiblity   The control system itself must be flexible enough to accommodate change. Consider, for example, an organization whose diverse product line requires seventy-five different raw materials. The company's inventory control system must be able to manage and monitor current levels of inventory for all seventy-five materials. When a change in product line changes the number of raw materials needed, or when the required quantities of the existing materials change, the control system should be flexible enough to handle the revised requirements. The alternative—designing and implementing a new control system—is an avoidable expense. Champion's control system includes a mechanism that automatically shipped products to major customers to keep their inventory at predetermined levels. The firm had to adjust this system when one of its biggest customers decided not to stock the full line of Champion products. Because its control system was flexible, modifying it for the customer was relatively simple.

Accuracy   Managers make a surprisingly large number of decisions based on inaccurate information. Field representatives may hedge their sales estimates to make themselves look better. Production managers may hide costs to meet their targets. Human resource managers may overestimate their minority recruiting prospects to meet affirmative action goals. In each case the information other managers receive is inaccurate, and the results of inaccurate information may be quite dramatic. If sales projections are inflated, a manager might cut advertising (thinking it is no longer needed) or increase advertising (to build momentum). Similarly, a production manager unaware of hidden costs may quote a sales price much lower than desirable. Or a human resources manager may speak out publicly on the effectiveness of the company's minority recruiting, only to find out later that these prospects have been overestimated. In each case, the result of inaccurate information is inappropriate managerial action.

Timeliness   Timeliness does not necessarily mean quickness. Rather, it describes a control system that provides information as often as is necessary. Since Champion has a wealth of historical data on its spark plug sales, it does not need information on spark plugs as frequently as it needs sales feedback for its newer products. Retail organizations usually need sales results daily so that they can manage cash flow and adjust advertising and promotion. In contrast, they may require information about physical inventory only quarterly or annually. In general, the more uncertain and unstable the circumstances, the more frequently measurement is needed.

Objectivity   The control system should provide information that is as objective as possible. To appreciate this detail, imagine the task of a manager responsible for control of his organization's human resources. He asks two plant managers to submit reports. One manager notes that morale at his plant is "okay," that grievances are "about where they should be," and that turnover is "under control." The other reports that absenteeism at her plant is running at 4 percent, that sixteen grievances have been filed this year (compared with twenty-four last year), and that turnover is 12 percent. The second report will almost always be more useful than the first. Of course, managers also need to look beyond the numbers when assessing performance. For example, a plant manager may be boosting productivity and profit margins by putting too much pressure on workers and using poor quality materials. As a result, impressive short-run gains may be overshadowed by longer run increases in employee turnover and customer complaints.

Resistance to Control

Managers may sometimes make the mistake of assuming that the value of an effective control system is self-evident to employees. This assumption is not always accurate, however. Many employees resist control, especially if they feel overcontrolled, if they think control is inappropriately focused or that it rewards inefficiency, or if they are uncomfortable with accountability.

Overcontrol   Occasionally, organizations try to control too many details. This situation becomes especially problematic when the control affects employee behavior directly. An organization that instructs its employees when to come to work, where to park, when to have morning coffee, and when to leave for the day exerts considerable control over people's daily activities. Yet many organizations attempt to control not only these but other aspects of work behavior as well. Of particular relevance in recent years is the effort of some companies to control their employees' access to private e-mail and the Internet during work hours. Some companies have no policies governing these activities, some attempt to limit it, and some attempt to forbid it altogether.[28]

Troubles arise when employees perceive these attempts to limit their behavior as being unreasonable. A company that tells its employees how to dress, how to arrange their desks, and how to wear their hair may meet with more resistance. Employees at Chrysler (now a part of DaimlerChrysler) used to complain because they were forced to park in a distant parking lot if they drove a non-Chrysler vehicle. People felt that these efforts to control their personal behavior (i.e., what kind of car to drive) were excessive. Managers eventually removed these controls and now allow open parking. Some employees at Abercrombie & Fitch argue that the firm is guilty of overcontrol because of its strict dress and grooming requirements—for example, no necklaces or facial hair for men and only natural nail polish and earrings no larger than a dime for women.

Inappropriate Focus   The control system may be too narrow or it may focus too much on quantifiable variables and leave no room for analysis or interpretation. A sales standard that encourages high-pressure tactics to maximize short-run sales may do so at the expense of goodwill from long-term customers. Such a standard is too narrow. A university reward system that encourages faculty members to publish large numbers of articles but fails to consider the quality of the work is also inappropriately focused. Employees resist the intent of the control system by focusing their efforts only at the performance indicators being used. The cartoon features another example of inappropriately focused control.

Rewards for Inefficiency   Imagine two operating departments that are approaching the end of the fiscal year. Department 1 expects to have $5,000 of its budget left over; department 2 is already $3,000 in the red. As a result, department 1 is likely to have its budget cut for the next year ("They had money left, so they obviously got too much to begin with") and department 2 is likely to get a budget increase ("They obviously haven't been getting enough money"). Thus, department 1 is punished for being efficient and department 2 is rewarded for being inefficient. (No wonder departments commonly hasten to deplete their budgets as the end of the year approaches!) As with inappropriate focus, people resist the intent of this control and behave in ways that run counter to the organization's original intent.

"You've got to really wonder just how many more cut-backs this department can absorb!"

Cartoon by Bradford Veley

In recent years, many organizations have sought ways to lower their costs through cost-cutting programs. They have reduced their workforces, eliminated perquisites, and outsourced services that independent contractors can do for a lower price. But some experts worry that many organizations have cut too much, increasing pressure and stress on the employees who are left. While it is doubtful that any organization has gone to the lengths illustrated in this cartoon, many employees nevertheless are feeling the consequences of these cutbacks.

Too Much Accountability   Effective controls allow managers to determine whether or not employees discharge their responsibilities successfully. If standards are properly set and performance accurately measured, managers know when problems arise and which departments and individuals are responsible. People who do not want to be accountable for their mistakes or who do not want to work as hard as their boss therefore might like to resist control. For example, American Express has a system that provides daily information on how many calls each of its customer service representatives handles. If one representative has typically worked at a slower pace and handled fewer calls than other representatives, that individual's deficient performance can now be pinpointed more easily.

Overcoming Resistance to Control

Perhaps the best way to overcome resistance to control is to create effective control to begin with. If control systems are properly integrated with organizational planning and if the controls are flexible, accurate, timely, and objective, the organization will be less likely to overcontrol, to focus on inappropriate standards, or to reward inefficiency. Two other ways to overcome resistance are encouraging participation and developing verification procedures.

Encourage Employee Participation   Chapter 12 notes that participation can help overcome resistance to change. By the same token, when employees are involved with planning and implementing the control system, they are less likely to resist it. For instance, employee participation in planning, decision making, and quality control at the Chevrolet Gear Axle plant in Detroit has resulted in increased employee concern for quality and a greater commitment to meeting standards.

Develop Verification Procedures   Multiple standards and information systems provide checks and balances in control and allow the organization to verify the accuracy of performance indicators. Suppose a production manager argues that she failed to meet a certain cost standard because of increased prices of raw materials. A properly designed inventory control system will either support or contradict her explanation. Suppose that an employee who was fired for excessive absences argues that he was not absent "for a long time." An effective human resource control system should have records that support the termination. Resistance to control declines because these verification procedures protect both employees and management. If the production manager's claim about the rising cost of raw materials is supported by the inventory control records, she will not be held solely accountable for failing to meet the cost standard, and some action will probably be taken to lower the cost of raw materials.

MANAGEMENT   Managers should know the basic characteristics of effective
IMPLICATIONS   control. They should also understand and be familiar with why employees are likely to resist control, as well as techniques that can be used to overcome this resistance.

Summary of Key Points

Control is the regulation of organizational activities so that some targeted element of performance remains within acceptable limits. Control provides ways to adapt to environmental change, to limit the accumulation of errors, to cope with organizational complexity, and to minimize costs. Control can focus on financial, material, information, and human resources and includes operations, financial, structural, and strategic levels. Control is the function of managers, the controller, and increasingly operating employees.

Steps in the control process are (1) establish standards of expected performance, (2) measure actual performance, (3) compare performance to the standards, and (4) evaluate the comparison and take appropriate action.

Operations control focuses on the processes the organization uses to transform resources into products or services. Preliminary control is concerned with the resources that serve as inputs to the system. Screening control is concerned with the transformation processes used by the organization. Postaction control is concerned with the outputs of the organization. Most organizations need multiple control systems because one system alone cannot provide adequate control.

Financial control focuses on controlling the organization's financial resources. The foundation of financial control is the budget, a plan expressed in numerical terms. Most organizations rely on financial, operating, and nonmonetary budgets. Financial statements, various kinds of ratios, and external and internal audits are also important tools organizations use as part of financial control.

Structural control addresses how well an organization's structural elements serve their intended purpose. Two basic forms of structural control are bureaucratic and clan. Bureaucratic control is relatively formal and mechanistic, whereas clan control is informal and organic. Most organizations use a form of organizational control somewhere between these two extremes.

Strategic control focuses on how effectively the organization's strategies are succeeding in helping the organization meet its goals. The integration of strategy and control is generally achieved through organization structure, leadership, technology, human resources, and information and operational control systems. International strategic control is also important for multinational organizations. The basic issue of international strategic control is whether to practice centralized or decentralized control.

One way to increase the effectiveness of control is to integrate planning and control fully. The control system should also be flexible, accurate, timely, and as objective as possible. Employees may resist organizational controls because of overcontrol, inappropriate focus, rewards for inefficiency, and a desire to avoid accountability. Managers can overcome this resistance by improving the effectiveness of controls, allowing employee participation, and developing verification procedures.

Discussion Questions

Questions for Review

1. What is the purpose of organizational control? Why is it important?
2. What are the steps in the control process? Which step is likely to be the most difficult to perform? Why?
3. What are the similarities and differences between the various forms of operations control? What are the costs and benefits of each form?
4. How can a manager understand and overcome resistance and make control effective?

Questions for Analysis

5. How is the controlling process related to the functions of planning, organizing, and leading?
6. Are the differences in bureaucratic control and clan control related to differences in organization structure? If so, how? If not, why not? (The terms do sound similar to those used to discuss the organizing process.)
7. Do you use a budget for your personal finances? Relate your experiences with budgeting to the discussion in the chapter.

Questions for Application

8. Does your college or university have a controller? If so, find out how the position fits into the organization's design. If not, why do you think such a position has not been created?

9. Interview several local managers to determine which form of operations control—preliminary, screening, postaction, or multiple—is most frequently used by them. How might you account for what you found?

10. Ask managers from different parts of the same organization or from different organizations what makes controls effective. How do their views compare with those presented in this chapter? Why might differences exist?

BUILDING EFFECTIVE *time-management* SKILLS

Exercise Overview

Time-management skills—a manager's abilities to prioritize work, to work efficiently, and to delegate appropriately—play a major role in the control function; that is, a manager can use time-management skills to control his or her own work more effectively. This exercise will help demonstrate the relationship between time-management skills and control.

Exercise Background

You are a middle manager in a small manufacturing plant. Today is Monday and you have just returned from a week of vacation. The first thing you discover is that your secretary will not be in today. His aunt died, and he is out of town at the funeral. He did, however, leave you the following note:

Dear Boss:
Sorry about not being here today. I will be back tomorrow. In the meantime, here are some things you need to know:

1. Ms. Glinski [your boss] wants to see you today at 4:00.
2. The shop steward wants to see you as soon as possible about a labor problem.
3. Mr. Bateman [one of your big customers] has a complaint about a recent shipment.
4. Ms. Ferris [one of your major suppliers] wants to discuss a change in the delivery schedule.

5. Mr. Prescott from the Chamber of Commerce wants you to attend a breakfast meeting on Wednesday to discuss our expansion plans.
6. The legal office wants to discuss our upcoming OSHA inspection.
7. Human resources wants to know when you can interview someone for the new supervisor's position.
8. Jack Williams, the machinist you fired last month, has been hanging around the parking lot and his presence is making some employees uncomfortable.

Exercise Task

With the information above as context, do the following:

1. Prioritize the work that needs to be done to address the information above into three categories: very timely, moderately timely, and less timely.
2. Are importance and timeliness the same thing?
3. What additional information must you acquire before you can begin to prioritize this work?
4. How would your approach differ if your secretary were in today?

BUILDING EFFECTIVE *diagnostic* SKILLS

Exercise Overview

Diagnostic skills enable managers to visualize responses to situations. Because control focuses on regulating organizational activities, diagnostic skills are clearly important to the determination of what activities should be regulated, how to assess activities best, and how to respond to deviations. This exercise helps demonstrate the nature of this relationship.

Exercise Background

You are the manager of a popular, locally owned restaurant. Your restaurant competes with such chains as Chili's, Bennegan's, and Applebee's. However, you have been able to maintain your market share in light of increased competition from these outlets by concentrating on providing exceptional service.

Recently, you have become aware of three trends that concern you. First, your costs are in-creasing. Monthly charges for food purchases seem to be growing at an exceptionally rapid pace. Second, customer complaints are also increasing. While the actual number of complaints is still quite small, complaints are nevertheless increasing. And finally, turnover among your employees is also increasing. While turnover in the restaurant business is almost always very high, the recent increases are in marked contrast to your historical patterns of turnover.

Exercise Task

Using the information presented above, do the following:

1. Identify as many potential causes as possible for each of the three problem areas.
2. Group each cause into one of two categories: "more likely" and "less likely."
3. Develop at least one potential action that you might take to address each cause.

BUILDING EFFECTIVE *decision-making* SKILLS

Exercise Overview

Decision-making skills refer to the manager's ability to recognize and define problems and opportunities correctly and then to select an appropriate course of action to solve problems and capitalize on opportunities. This exercise will enable you to practice your decision-making skills in relation to organizational control.

Exercise Background

Assume that you are the top manager of a medium-size manufacturing company. The company is family-owned, and several family members work in various managerial positions. Because of your own special skills and abilities, you have just been brought in from outside to run the company. The company has a long-standing tradition of avoiding debt and owns several smaller businesses in related industries.

Over the last few years the company has lagged in productivity and efficiency and now finds itself in desperate straits. Profits have just about disappeared and one of your bigger competitors may be planning to take over the business. You have hired a consulting firm to help you identify alternatives for turning the situation around. The primary options are:

1. Issue a public stock offering (an Initial Public Offering, or IPO) to raise funds.
2. Borrow money from a bank to finance a turnaround.

3. Sell several of the smaller operations to fund a turnaround.
4. Seek a buyer for the entire firm.

Exercise Task

With the background information above as context, do the following:

1. Evaluate each of the options from a strategic standpoint.
2. How does each option relate to control?
3. Select the one that appeals to you most.
4. Describe the likely barriers you will encounter with the option you have chosen.

CONTROL KEEPS SIEBEL SYSTEMS ON THE FAST TRACK

Control is paying off for Siebel Systems, a fast-growing U.S. company that rings up $1.6 billion in annual sales of sophisticated software to corporations such as British Telecom and Sun Microsystems. Siebel's software helps corporate customers better manage sales and other critical functions, allowing more effective monitoring and control of activities and results. Tom Siebel, the founder and CEO of Siebel, is a strong believer in control. He enforces standards for almost everything in the organization, from employee performance to customer service to service response. This enforcment helps him maintain control over operations, finances, structure, and strategy covering 5,200-plus employees in one hundred offices worldwide.

Siebel needs peak performance day in and day out to fuel the company's torrid rate of growth, which is more than 117 percent a year. So every six months, the company ranks the employees in each department. Those who fall in the lowest 5 percent are terminated, while top performers are rewarded. Still, Siebel's turnover is lower than that of other high-tech firms. This control process will help Siebel maintain high performance while doubling its global workforce to more than ten thousand and adding two million square feet of office space in the coming years.

Operations are another area where Siebel exerts strict control. Too often, software companies announce plans to introduce updated or new programs, then miss the launch date by months or even years. Not Siebel. Customers know that the company can be depended on to release updated versions of its software every spring. They also know they can get speedy, knowledgeable help if they have problems installing or operating some of the complex programs Siebel sells. The CEO and his management team set an example for all employees by spending considerable time working with customers. Seibel, for example, devotes about 60 percent of his working day meeting with customers, learning about their problems, offering advice, and showing how his firm's products can provide solutions.

Wall Street appreciates public companies with strong financial controls, so it's not surprising that investors have flocked to Siebel. The company's habit of beating analysts' expectations every quarter since the company first offered its stock in 1996—and the upward trend of its stock price—has definitely pleased investors. Although some competitors have been caught in accounting scandals through the years, Siebel's tight controls have kept its finances running smoothly, another reason for its investor appeal. Until recently, the CEO was the only manager who could sign off on expenses over $10,000; now two senior managers have been given the authority to approve expenses up to $50,000, with higher amounts going to Siebel's desk for review and approval.

Unlike many high-tech firms, Siebel has an unwritten dress code mandating professional business wear at work. Male employees are expected to appear in suits and ties; female employees are expected to wear skirts or pants suits. This dress code supports the air of professionalism that pervades the entire company. Every Siebel office is decorated in the same way, with blue carpeting and off-white walls, gray desktops, and maple furniture. Every desk is neat, with no empty soda cans or empty pizza cartons (eating at the desk is forbidden). In another departure from Silicon Valley norms, Siebel doesn't allow the basketball games and beer blasts that are so common in many high-tech firms. In short, Siebel is all business, an approach that impresses customers and adds, in a small way, to Siebel's ability to compete against Oracle, PeopleSoft, Baan, and other rivals.

As CEO, Siebel holds tight rein on his company, but he has lately begun sharing some control with other top executives. For example, he appointed a chief operating officer to oversee day-to-day issues in marketing and sales, engineering, and services. Still, he expects managers and employees to move quickly when he asks questions or requests action. After Siebel met with a customer one Friday, he promised a complete proposal by Monday—impossible for many companies but a normal reaction time for the people at Siebel.

Case Questions

1. Identify as many forms of control as possible in this case.

2. What are the advantages and disadvantages of concentrating control in the hands of one top manager?

3. Does Siebel sound like a good working environment for you? Why or why not?

Case Reference

Melanie Warner, "Confessions of a Control Freak," *Fortune*, September 4, 2000, pp. 130–140.

CHAPTER NOTES

1. "Star Rescuers Took on Waste Management—And Ended Up Tarnished," *Wall Street Journal*, February 29, 2000, pp. A1, A8; *Hoover's Handbook of American Business 2001* (Austin, Texas: Hoover's Business Press, 2001), pp. 1542–1543.

2. Thomas A. Stewart, "Welcome to the Revolution," *Fortune*, December 13, 1993, pp. 66–77.

3. William Taylor, "Control in an Age of Chaos," *Harvard Business Review*, November–December 1994, pp. 64–70.

4. "Fleetwood: Not a Happy Camper Company," *Business Week*, October 9, 2000, pp. 88–90.

5. "At Travelers, It's Trim, Trim, Trim," *Business Week*, February 10, 1997, p. 101.

6. "Coke to Lay Off 6,000 Workers," *USA Today*, January 27, 2000, p. 1B.

7. Mark Kroll, Peter Wright, Leslie Toombs, and Hadley Leavell, "Form of Control: A Critical Determinant of Acquisition Performance and CEO Rewards," *Strategic Management Journal*, Vol. 18, No. 2, 1997, pp. 85–96.

8. Sim Sitkin, Kathleen Sutcliffe, and Roger Schroeder, "Distinguishing Control from Learning in Total Quality Management: A Contingency Perspective," *Academy of Management Review*, 1994, Vol. 19, No. 3, pp. 537–564.

9. Robert Lusch and Michael Harvey, "The Case for an Off-Balance-Sheet Controller," *Sloan Management Review*, Winter 1994, pp. 101–110.

10. Edward E. Lawler III and John G. Rhode, *Information and Control in Organizations* (Pacific Palisades, Calif.: Goodyear, 1976).

11. Charles W. L. Hill, "Establishing a Standard: Competitive Strategy and Technological Standards in Winner-Take-All Industries," *The Academy of Management Executive*, Vol. 11, No. 2, 1997, pp. 7–16.

12. "An Efficiency Guru Refits Honda to Fight Auto Giants," *Wall Street Journal*, September 15, 1999, p. B1.

13. "Luxury's Mandarin," *Newsweek*, August 25, 1997, p. 43.

14. See Belverd E. Needles, Jr., Henry R. Anderson, and James C. Caldwell, *Principles of Accounting*, 7th Edition (Boston: Houghton Mifflin, 1999).

15. "The Tiger Is on the Prowl," *Forbes*, April 21, 1997, pp. 42–43.

16. Thomas A. Stewart, "Why Budgets Are Bad for Business," *Fortune*, June 4, 1990, pp. 179–190.

17. Needles, Anderson, and Caldwell, *Principles of Accounting*.

18. "Mickey Mouse, CPA," *Forbes*, March 10, 1997, pp. 42–43.

19. Needles, Anderson, and Caldwell, *Principles of Accounting*.

20. "Questions About U.S. Shoe Corp. Continue to Mount," *Wall Street Journal*, April 5, 1990, p. A4.

21. "Auditors of Corporate Legal Bills Thrive," *Wall Street Journal*, February 13, 1991, p. B1.

22. William G. Ouchi, "The Transmission of Control Through Organizational Hierarchy," *Academy of Management Journal*, June 1978, pp. 173–192; Richard E. Walton, "From Control to Commitment in the Workplace," *Harvard Business Review*, March–April 1985, pp. 76–84.

23. "Nordstrom Cleans Out Its Closets," *Business Week*, May 22, 2000, pp. 105–108.

24. Peter Lorange, Michael F. Scott Morton, and Sumantra Ghoshal, *Strategic Control* (St. Paul, Minn.: West, 1986). See also Joseph C. Picken and Gregory G. Dess, "Out of (Strategic) Control," *Organizational Dynamics*, Summer 1997, pp. 35–45.

25. "Ikea's New Game Plan," *Business Week*, October 6, 1997, pp. 99–102.

26. See Hans Mjoen and Stephen Tallman, "Control and Performance in International Joint Ventures," *Organization Science*, May–June 1997, pp. 257–265.

27. See Diana Robertson and Erin Anderson, "Control System and Task Environment Effects on Ethical Judgment: An Exploratory Study of Industrial Salespeople," *Organization Science*, November 1993, pp. 617–629, for a recent study of effective control.

28. "Workers, Surf at Your Own Risk," *Business Week*, June 12, 2000, pp. 105–106.

21

Managing Operations, Quality, and Productivity

Young Joseph Hartmann immigrated to the United States from Bavaria in 1877. Soon after arriving he started a small trunk-making company and used the skills he had learned in his homeland. Today, Hartmann Luggage, a division of Brown-Forman Corporation and based in Lebanon, Tennessee, is among the most respected names in the luggage industry.

The firm makes a full line of luggage products, ranging from business cases to suitcases to computer cases. Hartmann bags are also among the most expensive in the industry, with even a small bag costing hundreds of dollars. So why are consumers willing to pay such a premium price for a suitcase? One of the reasons is the quality that characterizes Hartmann bags. Hartmann luggage has a lifetime guarantee—the company will repair or replace any damaged product for as long as

it's in the possession of its original owner. It honors warranties even when it's apparent that product damage is attributable to owner neglect, and it has repaired bags as old as forty years.

Why is the firm able to offer such a strong guarantee? In large part it's due to the quality construction used to make the bags and the rigorous testing to which they are subjected before being placed on the market. For example, almost all the work on a Hartmann bag is done by hand by trained workers who excel at their craft. The company also uses only the highest quality materials, ranging from industrial strength belting leather to the strongest cloth and metal hinges. And its manufacturing systems are among the most efficient in the industry.

But it is in the quality control testing lab that Hartmann truly excels. For example, every new case or

bag Hartmann intends to make is first tested for a lifetime of use before being placed into production. And most of this testing is done with special machines that Hartmann managers have conceptualized and constructed and that are a fundamental part of its operations systems.

One of its machines, for example, is call the "tumble tester." This large machine resembles a ferris wheel with a cage. A bag is put inside the cage, and the wheel slowly begins to turn. The bag tumbles like a towel in a clothes dryer, crashing against metal protrusions made to resemble the baggage handling system in an airport. The machine simulates the treatment the bags will receive in just such an airport. Each test run is for seven thousand turns, simulating five years' worth of bouncing.

"We have repaired or refurbished bags that are forty years old."

—*Gail Jamison, Hartmann repair section chief*

After studying this chapter, you should be able to:

- Describe and explain the nature of operations management.

- Identify and discuss the components involved in designing effective operations systems.

- Discuss organizational technologies and their role in operations management.

- Identify and discuss the components involved in implementing operations systems and supply chain management.

- Explain the meaning and importance of managing quality and total quality management.

- Explain the meaning and importance of managing productivity, productivity trends, and ways to improve productivity.

Another machine Hartmann uses lifts a briefcase up and down every few seconds, as many as one hundred thousand times in all. This machine assesses the wear and tear lifting creates on the briefcase handle. If the wear is excessive, stronger leather will be used. Another machine tests the amount of energy or tension needed to pull apart the stitches that hold a bag together. Among the most interesting machines Hartmann uses is a treadmill-like device that simulates asphalt, tile, and carpet—testing how a bag holds up to being dragged or pulled from an airport to a parking lot. Other machines test wheel strength or the durability of shoulder straps, or how well a bag holds up to ultraviolet rays, rain, humidity, heat, and ice.

Given the extensive battery of tests that Hartmann bags must pass, it's little wonder that the firm backs them with such a praiseworthy guarantee. And there's little wonder that consumers who can afford to pay the price are eager to own the firm's products.[1]

Managers at Hartmann Luggage have made quality a hallmark of their company's operations. This quality, in turn, has allowed them to charge premium prices and earn superior profits. But to be successful with this strategy, the firm must also have the confidence that its products can withstand the demands of consumers and hold up to the rigors of daily and business use. And they must use operations management effectively as part of their overall strategy.

In this chapter, we explore operations management, quality, and productivity. We first introduce operations management and discuss its role in general management and organizational strategy. The next three sections discuss designing operations systems, organizational technologies, and implementing operations systems. We then introduce and discuss various issues in managing for total quality. Finally, we discuss productivity, which is closely related to quality.

■ *The Nature of Operations Management*

operations management The set of managerial activities used by an organization to transform resource inputs into products, services, or both

Operations management is at the core of what organizations do as they add value and create products and services. But what exactly are operations? And how are they managed? **Operations management** is the set of managerial activities used by an organization to transform resource inputs into products, services, or both. When Dell Computer buys electronic components, assembles them into PCs, and then ships them to customers, it is engaging in operations management. When a Pizza Hut employee orders food and paper products and then combines dough, cheese, and tomato paste to create a pizza, he or she is engaging in operations management.

The Importance of Operations

Operations is an important functional concern for organizations because efficient and effective management of operations goes a long way toward ensuring competitiveness and overall organizational performance, as well as quality and productivity. Inefficient or ineffective operations management, on the other hand, will almost inevitably lead to poorer performance and lower levels of both quality and productivity. Indeed, *Management Infotech* illustrates how Hershey Foods learned what can happen when operations go awry.

Manufacturing and production are frequently key components of a company's quality management efforts. IGT Corporation makes electronic slot machines that are sold to casinos and other gambling operations around the world. Because of the stringent government regulations that affect this industry, and the potential costs that errors might create, it is extremely important that all machines be of the highest quality. Thus this inspector is closely examining a transparent cover sheet that will announce whether or not the gambler has struck it rich!

MANAGEMENT INFOTECH

MANAGING OPERATIONS MANAGEMENT SYSTEMS

Hershey Foods got quite a scare during one recent Halloween candy-selling season. Over the summer months, Hershey had installed new software and computers to manage its ordering and fulfillment functions. By fall, however, the system was still not running as it should. Stores waited and waited for the Reese's Peanut Butter Cups, Hershey's Kisses, and other varieties of Hershey's 3,300 candies they had ordered for trick or treat. As Halloween approached, Hershey was quoting a twelve-day turnaround on orders—twice as long as its usual fulfillment period—and filling only part of most orders.

Even when shipments moved out of its warehouses, Hershey couldn't find out from the new system what had been shipped or where; sales representatives wound up calling customers to find out what they had received. To fulfill orders placed by larger customers such as Kmart, Hershey sent some shipments by truck and some by air, absorbing the extra cost to get its candies onto store shelves as quickly as possible. Meanwhile, worried retailers began placing extra orders with other candy manufacturers to fill their shelves and meet consumer demand. By the time Halloween arrived, Hershey's sales were $100 million lower than expected and its profits were down by 19 percent.

Hershey's experiences emphasize the challenges of implementing state-of-the-art operations systems. Although detailed planning and exhaustive testing will smooth the way toward successful implementation, software bugs and even the smallest incompatibilities can derail a system. Fear of system slowdowns or breakdowns haunt many organizations. The two computers that process electronic payments between the world's banks at the New York Clearing House, for example, run on software that is as bug-free as possible because a breakdown would disrupt the entire international financial network. Thanks to constant vigilance, the computers have been operational an astounding 99.99 percent of the time. Not every organization requires this level of quality, but because companies are increasingly dependent on automated systems for managing purchasing, inventory, and other key operations, managers must use extra care and allow extra time when upgrading or installing operations systems software.

> *Improvements in some quarters are followed by increased risks in others. And new systems introduce more problems than the systems they replace.*
>
> —*Peter G. Neumann, a computer scientist with SRI International**

References: Peter Galuszka, "Just-in-Time Manufacturing Is Working Overtime," *Business Week,* November 8, 1999, pp. 36–37; Emily Nelson and Evan Ramstad, "Trick or Treat: Hershey's Biggest Dud Has Turned Out to Be New Computer System," *Wall Street Journal,* October 29, 1999, pp. A1, A6; Neil Gross, Marcia Stepanek, and Otis Port, "Software Hell," *Business Week,* December 6, 1999, pp. 87–89 (quote on p. 88).

In an economic sense, operations management creates value and utility of one type or another, depending on the nature of the firm's products or services. If the product is a physical good, such as a Harley-Davidson motorcycle, operations creates value and provides form utility by combining many dissimilar inputs (sheet metal, rubber, paint, combustion engines, and human skills) to make something (e.g., a motorcycle) that is more valuable than the actual cost of the inputs used to create it. The inputs are converted from their incoming forms into a new physical form. This conversion is typical of manufacturing operations and essentially reflects the organization's technology.

In contrast, the operations activities of American Airlines create value and provide time and place utility through its services. The airline transports passengers and freight according to agreed-on departure and arrival places and times. Other service operations, such as a Coors Brothers Beer distributorship or The Gap retail chain, create value and provide place and possession utility by bringing the customer and products made by others together. Although the organizations in these examples produce different kinds of products or services, their operations processes share many important features.[2]

Manufacturing and Production

manufacturing A form of business that combines and transforms resource inputs into tangible outcomes that are then sold to others

Because manufacturing once dominated U.S. industry, the entire area of operations management used to be called production management. **Manufacturing** is a form of business that combines and transforms resource inputs into tangible outcomes that are then sold to others. The Goodyear Tire and Rubber Company is a manufacturer because it combines rubber and chemical compounds and uses blending equipment and molding machines to create tires. Broyhill is a manufacturer because it buys wood and metal components, pads, and fabric and then combines them into furniture.

During the 1970s, manufacturing entered a long period of decline in the United States, primarily because of foreign competition. U.S. firms had grown lax and sluggish, and new foreign competitors came into the market with better equipment and much higher levels of efficiency. For example, steel companies in the Far East were able to produce high-quality steel for much lower prices than were U.S. companies like Bethlehem Steel and U.S. Steel (now USX Corporation). Faced with a battle for survival, many companies underwent a long and difficult period of change by eliminating waste and transforming themselves into leaner and more efficient and responsive entities. They reduced their workforces dramatically, closed antiquated or unnecessary plants, and modernized their remaining plants. In the last decade, their efforts have started to pay dividends because U.S. business has regained its competitive position in many different industries. Although manufacturers from other parts of the world are still formidable competitors and U.S. firms may never again be competitive in some markets, the overall picture is much better than it was just a few years ago. And prospects continue to look bright.[3]

Service Operations

service organization An organization that transforms resources into an intangible output and creates time or place utility for its customers

During the decline of the manufacturing sector, a tremendous growth in the service sector kept the U.S. economy from declining at the same rate. A **service organization** is one that transforms resources into an intangible output and creates time or place utility for its customers. For example, Merrill Lynch makes stock transactions for its customers, Avis leases cars to its customers, and your local hairdresser cuts your hair. In 1947, the service sector was responsible for less than half of the U.S. gross national product (GNP). By 1975, however, this figure reached 65 percent, and by 1999 it was over 75 percent. The service sector has been responsible for almost 90 percent of all new jobs created in the United States during the 1990s. Managers have come to see that many of the tools, techniques, and methods used in a factory are also useful to a service firm. For example, managers of automobile plants and hair salons each have to decide how to design their facility, identify the best location for it, determine optimal capacity, make decisions about inventory storage, set procedures for purchasing raw materials, and set standards for productivity and quality.

The Role of Operations in Organizational Strategy

It should be clear by this point that operations management is very important to organizations. Beyond its direct impact on intangibles such as competitiveness, quality, and productivity, it also directly influences the organization's overall level of effectiveness. For example, the deceptively simple strategic decision about whether to stress high quality regardless of cost, lowest possible cost regardless of quality, or some combination of the two has numerous important implications. A highest possible quality strategy will dictate state-of-the-art technology and rigorous control of product design and materials specifications. A combination strategy might call for lower-grade technology and less concern about product design and materials specifications. Just as strategy affects operations management, so too does operations management affect strategy. Suppose that a firm decides to upgrade the quality of its products or services. The organization's ability to implement the decision depends in part on current production capabilities and other resources. If existing technology will not permit higher-quality work and if the organization lacks the resources to replace its technology, increasing quality to the desired new standards will be difficult.

MANAGEMENT IMPLICATIONS   The importance of operations management should be obvious to all managers. They should also have an understanding of the similarities and differences between manufacturing and service businesses. Finally, managers need to know the role of operations management in their firm's strategy.

Designing Operations Systems

The problems, challenges, and opportunities faced by operations managers revolve around the acquisition and utilization of resources for conversion. Their goals include both efficiency and effectiveness. Several issues and decisions must be addressed as operations systems are designed. The most basic ones are product-service mix, capacity, and facilities.

Determining Product-Service Mix

A natural starting point in designing operations systems is determining the **product-service mix**. This decision flows from corporate, business, and marketing strategies. Managers have to make several decisions about their products and services, starting with how many and what kinds to offer.[4] Procter & Gamble, for

product-service mix How many and what kinds of products or services (or both) to offer

example, makes regular, tartar-control, gel, and various other formulas of Crest toothpaste and packages them in several different sizes of tubes, pumps, and other dispensers. Similarly, workers at Subway sandwich stores can combine different breads, vegetables, meats, and condiments in hundreds of different kinds of sandwiches. Decisions also have to be made regarding the level of quality desired, the optimal cost of each product or service, and exactly how each is to be designed. GE, for example, recently reduced the number of parts in its industrial circuit breakers from 28,000 to 1,275. The whole process was achieved by carefully analyzing product design and production methods.

Capacity Decisions

capacity The amount of products, services, or both that can be produced by an organization

The **capacity** decision involves choosing the amount of products, services, or both that can be produced by the organization. Determining whether to build a factory capable of making five thousand or eight thousand units per day is a capacity decision. So, too, is deciding whether to build a restaurant with one hundred or one hundred fifty seats or a bank with five or ten teller stations. The capacity decision is truly a high-risk one because of the uncertainties of future product demand and the large monetary stakes involved. An organization that builds capacity exceeding its needs may commit resources (capital investment) that will never be recovered. Alternatively, an organization can build a facility with a smaller capacity than expected demand. Doing so may result in lost market opportunities, but it may also free capital resources for use elsewhere in the organization.

A major consideration in determining capacity is demand. A company operating with fairly constant monthly demand might build a plant capable of producing an amount each month roughly equivalent to its demand. But if its market is characterized by seasonal fluctuations, building a smaller plant to meet normal demand and then adding extra shifts staffed with temporary workers and/or paying permanent workers extra to work more hours during peak periods might be the most effective choice. Likewise, a restaurant that needs one hundred fifty seats for Saturday night but never needs more than one hundred at any other time during the week would probably be foolish to expand to one hundred fifty seats. During the rest of the week, it must still pay to light, heat, cool, and clean the excess capacity.

Facilities Decisions

facilities The physical locations where products or services are created, stored, and distributed

Facilities are the physical locations where products or services are created, stored, and distributed. Major decisions pertain to facilities location and facilities layout.

location The physical positioning or geographic site of facilities

Location Location is the physical positioning or geographic site of facilities and must be determined by the needs and requirements of the organization. A company that relies heavily on railroads for transportation needs to be located close to rail facilities. GE decided that it did not need six plants to make circuit breakers, so it invested heavily in automating one plant and closed the other five. Different organizations in the same industry may have different facilities requirements.

Benetton uses only one distribution center for the entire world, whereas Wal-Mart has several distribution centers in the United States alone. A retail business must choose its location very carefully to be convenient for consumers.

Layout   The choice of physical configuration, or the **layout**, of facilities is closely related to other operations decisions. The three entirely different layout alternatives shown in Figure 21.1 help demonstrate the importance of the layout decision. A **product layout** is appropriate when large quantities of a single product are needed. It makes sense to custom design a straight-line flow of work for a product when a specific task is performed at each workstation as each unit flows past. Most assembly lines use this format. For example, Dell's personal computer factories use a product layout.

Process layouts are used in operations settings that create or process a variety of products. Auto repair shops and health-care clinics are good examples. Each car and each person is a separate "product." The needs of each incoming job are diagnosed as it enters the operations system, and the job is routed through the unique sequence of workstations needed to create the desired finished product. In a process layout, each type of conversion task is centralized in a single workstation or department. All welding is done in one designated shop location, and any car that requires welding is moved to that area. This setup is in contrast to the product

layout The physical configuration of facilities, the arrangement of equipment within facilities, or both

product layout A physical configuration of facilities arranged around the product; used when large quantities of a single product are needed

process layout A physical configuration of facilities arranged around the process; used in facilities that create or process a variety of products

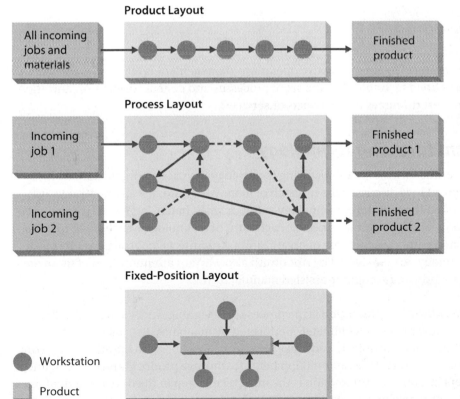

Product Layout

Process Layout

Fixed-Position Layout

● Workstation

▢ Product

Figure 21.1

Approaches to Facilities Layout

When a manufacturer produces large quantities of a product (such as cars or computers), it may arrange its facilities into an assembly line (product layout). In a process layout, the work (such as patients in a hospital or custom pieces of furniture) moves through various workstations. Locomotives and bridges are both manufactured in a fixed-position layout.

layout, in which several different workstations may perform welding operations if the conversion task sequence so dictates. In a hospital, all X-rays are done in one location, all surgeries in another, and all physical therapy in yet another. Patients are moved from location to location to get the services they need.

The **fixed-position layout** is used when the organization is creating a few very large and complex products. Aircraft manufacturers like Boeing and shipbuilders like Newport News use this method. An assembly line capable of moving a 747 would require an enormous plant, so instead the airplane itself remains stationary and people and machines move around it as it is assembled.

The cellular layout is a relatively new approach to facilities design. **Cellular layouts** are used when families of products can follow similar flow paths. A clothing manufacturer, for example, might create a cell, or designated area, dedicated to making a family of pockets, such as pockets for shirts, coats, blouses, and slacks. Although each kind of pocket is unique, the same basic equipment and methods are used to make all of them. Hence, all pockets might be made in the same area and then delivered directly to different product layout assembly areas where the shirts, coats, blouses, and slacks are being assembled.

MANAGEMENT IMPLICATIONS Managers need to be familiar with how the product-service mix, capacity, and facilities decisions and issues all contribute to organizational effectiveness, quality, and productivity.

fixed-position layout A physical configuration of facilities arranged around a single work area; used for the manufacture of large and complex products such as airplanes

cellular layout A physical configuration of facilities used when families of products can follow similar flow paths

Organizational Technologies

One central element of effective operations management is technology. In Chapter 3 we defined **technology** as the set of processes and systems used by organizations to convert resources into products or services.

technology The set of processes and systems used by organizations to convert resources into products or services

Manufacturing Technology

Numerous forms of manufacturing technology are used in organizations. In Chapter 11 we discussed the research of Joan Woodward. Recall that Woodward identified three forms of technology—unit or small batch, large batch or mass production, and continuous process.[5] Each form of technology was thought to be associated with a specific type of organization structure. Of course, newer forms of technology not considered by Woodward also warrant attention. Two of these are automation and computer-assisted manufacturing.

Automation   **Automation** is the process of designing work so that it can be completely or almost completely performed by machines. Because automated machines operate quickly and make few errors, they increase the amount of work that can be done. Thus, automation helps to improve products and services, and it fosters innovation. Automation is the most recent step in the development of machines and machine-controlling devices. Machine-controlling devices have been around since the 1700s. James Watt, a Scottish engineer, invented a mechanical

automation The process of designing work so that it can be completely or almost completely performed by machines

speed control to regulate the speed of steam engines in 1787. The Jacquard loom, developed by a French inventor, was controlled by paper cards with holes punched in them. Early accounting and computing equipment was controlled by similar punched cards.

Automation relies on feedback, information, sensors, and a control mechanism. Feedback is the flow of information from the machine back to the sensor. Sensors are the parts of the system that gather information and compare it to some preset standards. The control mechanism is the device that sends instructions to the automatic machine. Early automatic machines were primitive, and the use of automation was relatively slow to develop. These elements are illustrated by the example in Figure 21.2. A thermostat has sensors that monitor air temperature and compare it to a preset low value. If the air temperature falls below the preset value, the thermostat sends

Manufacturing technology continues to become increasingly sophisticated. Take this DaimlerChrysler automobile factory in Indiana, for instance. The machinist is using traditional assembly-line technology and equipment to perform a basic job. In addition, though, the PC monitor is also providing the machinist with information about how well the job is being performed. This allows the machinist to do both faster and higher-quality work.

an electrical signal to the furnace, turning it on. The furnace heats the air. When the sensors detect that the air temperature has reached a value higher than the low preset value, the thermostat stops the furnace. The last step (shutting off the furnace) is known as feedback, a critical component of any automated operation.

The big move to automate factories began during World War II. The shortage of skilled workers and the development of high-speed computers combined to bring about a tremendous interest in automation. Programmable automation (the use of computers to control machines) was introduced during this era and far outstripped conventional automation (the use of mechanical or electromechanical devices to

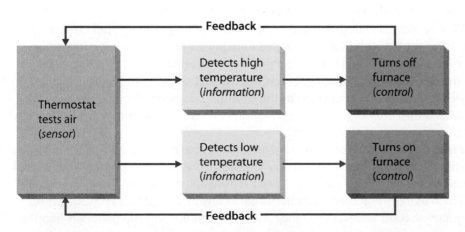

Figure 21.2

A Simple Automatic Control Mechanism

All automation includes feedback, information, sensors, and a control mechanism. A simple thermostat is an example of automation. Another example is Benetton's distribution center in Italy. Orders are received, items pulled from stock and packaged for shipment, and invoices are prepared and transmitted with no human intervention.

control machines). The automobile industry began to use automatic machines for a variety of jobs. In fact, the term *automation* came into use in the 1950s in the automobile industry. The chemical and oil-refining industries also began to use computers to regulate production. During the 1990s automation became a major element in the manufacture of computers and computer components such as electronic chips and circuits. This computerized, or programmable, automation presents the greatest opportunities and challenges for management today.

The impact of automation on people in the workplace is complex. In the short term, people whose jobs are automated may find themselves without jobs. In the long term, however, more jobs are created than are lost. Nevertheless, not all companies are able to help displaced workers find new jobs, so the human costs are sometimes high. In the coal industry, for instance, automation has been used primarily in mining. The output per miner has risen dramatically from the 1950s on. The demand for coal, however, has decreased, and productivity gains resulting from automation have lessened the need for miners. Consequently, a lot of workers have lost their jobs, and the industry has not been able to absorb them. In contrast, in the electronics industry, the rising demand for products has led to increasing employment opportunities despite the use of automation.[6]

computer-assisted manufacturing Technology that relies on computers to design or manufacture products

Computer-Assisted Manufacturing   Current extensions of automation generally revolve around computer-assisted manufacturing. **Computer-assisted manufacturing** is technology that relies on computers to design or manufacture products. One type of computer-assisted manufacturing is *computer-aided design (CAD)*—the use of computers to design parts and complete products and to simulate performance so that prototypes need not be constructed. Boeing uses CAD technology to study hydraulic tubing in its commercial aircraft. Japan's automotive industry uses it to speed up car design. GE used CAD to change the design of circuit breakers, and Benetton uses CAD to design new styles and products. Oneida Ltd., the table flatware firm, used CAD to design a new spoon in only two days.[7] CAD is usually combined with *computer-aided manufacturing (CAM)* to ensure that the design moves smoothly to production. The production computer shares the design computer's information and can have machines with the proper settings ready when production is needed. A CAM system is especially useful when re-orders come in because the computer can quickly produce the desired product, prepare labels and copies of orders, and send the product out.

Closely aligned with this approach is *computer-integrated manufacturing (CIM)*. In CIM, CAD and CAM are linked together and computer networks adjust machine placements and settings automatically to enhance both the complexity and the flexibility of scheduling. In settings that use these technologies, all manufacturing activities are controlled by the computer network. Because the network can access the company's other information systems, CIM is both a powerful and a complex management control tool.

Flexible manufacturing systems (FMS) usually have robotic work units or workstations, assembly lines, and robotic carts or some other form of computer-controlled transport system to move material as needed from one part of the system to another. FMS such as the one at IBM's manufacturing facility in Lexington, Kentucky, rely on computers to coordinate and integrate automated production and materials-handling facilities. And Ford Motor Company recently used FMS to transform an English factory producing Ford Escorts into a Jaguar plant making its new Jaguar X-Type luxury cars. With traditional methods, the plant would have been closed, its workers laid off, and the factory practically rebuilt from the ground up. But by using FMS, Ford was able to keep the plant open and running continuously while new equipment was being installed and its workers were being retrained in small groups.[8]

These systems are not without disadvantages, however. For example, because they represent fundamental change, they also generate resistance. And because of their tremendous complexity, CAD systems are not always reliable. CIM systems are so expensive that they raise the breakeven point for firms using them. This change means that the firm must operate at high levels of production and sales to be able to afford the systems.

robot Any artificial device that can perform functions ordinarily thought to be appropriate for human beings

Robotics   Another trend in manufacturing technology is computerized robotics. A **robot** is any artificial device that can perform functions ordinarily thought to be appropriate for human beings. Robotics refers to the science and technology of the construction, maintenance, and use of robots. The use of industrial robots has steadily increased since 1980 and is expected to continue to increase slowly as more companies recognize the benefits that accrue to users of industrial robots.[9]

Welding was one of the first applications for robots, and it continues to be the area for most applications. In second place and close behind is materials handling. Other applications include machine loading and unloading; painting and finishing; assembly; casting; and machining applications such as cutting, grinding, polishing, drilling, sanding, buffing, and deburring. DaimlerChrysler, for instance, recently replaced about two hundred welders with fifty robots on an assembly line and increased productivity about 20 percent. The use of robots in inspection work is increasing. They can check for cracks and holes, and they can be equipped with vision systems to perform visual inspections.

Robots are also beginning to move from the factory floor to lots of other applications. The Dallas police used a robot to apprehend a suspect who had barricaded himself in an apartment building. The robot smashed a window and reached with its mechanical arm into the building. The suspect panicked and ran outside. At the Long Beach Memorial Hospital in California, brain surgeons are assisted by a robot arm that drills into the patient's skull with excellent precision. Some newer applications involve remote work. For example, the use of robot submersibles controlled from the surface can help divers in remote locations. Surveillance robots fitted with microwave sensors can do what a human guard cannot, such as "seeing" through nonmetallic walls and in the dark. In other applications, automated farming (agrimation) uses robot harvesters to pick fruit from a variety of trees.

Robots are also used by small manufacturers. One robot slices carpeting to fit the inside of custom vans in an upholstery shop. Another stretches balloons flat so that

Organizational technologies are becoming increasingly more complex and complicated, especially as they relate to automation and robotics. Automobile manufacturers, for example, have used robots for years to perform such tasks as welding automotive body parts together. For the most part, though, robots lack the ability to think or to simulate human emotion. Cynthia Breazeal and her colleagues at M.I.T., however, are trying to change that. Dr. Breazeal recently introduced a new robot called Kismet. Kismet has the capacity to simulate human emotion and to change its "facial" expression to match its "mood." If such technology can be perfected, robots may be able to play a greater role in the future as service providers for customers in such settings as restaurants and other retail establishments.

they can be spray-painted with slogans at a novelties company. At a jewelry company, a robot holds class rings while they are engraved by a laser. These robots are lighter, faster, stronger, and more intelligent than those used in heavy manufacturing and are the types that more and more organizations will be using in the future.

Service Technology

Service technology is also changing rapidly, and it is also moving more and more toward automated systems and procedures. In banking, for example, new technological breakthroughs have led to automated teller machines and have made it much easier to move funds between accounts or between different banks. Many people now have their paychecks deposited directly into a checking account, from which many of their bills are then automatically paid. And credit card transactions by Visa customers are recorded and billed electronically. *Today's Management Issues*

TODAY'S MANAGEMENT ISSUES

MANAGING SERVICE QUALITY FROM AFAR

What happens to quality when services are delivered by a loose-knit network of far-flung offices? As U-Haul International has found out, managing service quality from afar is far from easy. Based in Phoenix, Arizona, U-Haul is the original rent-a-truck company targeting do-it-yourself movers. With 15,800 local offices stretching across the United States and Canada, U-Haul maintains a fleet of ninety-three thousand rental trucks that are driven a total of 850 million miles every year, as customers criss-cross the continent with possessions in tow.

Although U-Haul has direct control over service quality in the 1,100 rental locations it owns, it has much less influence over service in the thousands of locations operated by independent dealers. All dealers are required to keep up with truck maintenance every five thousand miles, but that's about the only mandate U-Haul sets. The company does not require independent dealers to maintain standard hours of operation, achieve a minimum cleanliness level, or enforce an employee dress code.

What's more, U-Haul provides little formal training for independent dealers and their employees, apart from explaining how to arrange for truck rentals and returns. Dealers use the company's automated system for logging truck reservations, but a new system—long delayed—will help the corporate office manage the movement of trucks more effectively. The new

system is also expected to streamline the customer registration and payment process, which will cut the time needed to complete each transaction by one-fifth. Without the system, however, U-Haul has no central customer database. So when customers call the main U-Haul number to complain about poor service, the corporate office can only write down the details and forward the information to a regional director or to the dealer involved. Action to resolve complaints sometimes takes months, customers say.

Still, U-Haul continues to outpace competitors, holding a much higher market share than Ryder/Budget, the second largest moving truck rental firm. CEO Edward J. Shoen stresses that the majority of U-Haul's customers are satisfied and that the company works to resolve every problem. Ensuring consistently high service quality is not an easy task, as U-Haul's management knows.

> *We don't insist [independent dealers] answer the phone a standard way.*
>
> —Edward J. Shoen, president of U-Haul International*

References: Joanne Gordon, "U-Hell," *Forbes,* March 20, 2000, pp. 70–72 (*quote on p. 72); *Hoover's Handbook of American Business 2001* (Austin, Texas: Hoover's Business Press, 2001), pp. 126–127.

provides an interesting example of how one firm, U-Haul, uses decentralized service technology to lease its trucks.

Hotels use increasingly sophisticated technology to accept and record room reservations. Universities use new technologies to store and provide access electronically to all manner of books, scientific journals, government reports, and articles. Hospitals and other health-care organizations use new forms of service technology to manage patient records, dispatch ambulances, and monitor vital signs. Restaurants use technology to record and fill customer orders, order food and supplies, and prepare food. Given the increased role that service organizations are playing in today's economy, even more technological innovations are likely to be developed in the years to come.[10]

MANAGEMENT Managers should be knowledgeable about the basic forms and
IMPLICATIONS dimensions of manufacturing technology, both those that their organizations currently use and those their organizations might use in the future. In addition, they should also be familiar with service technology and its relevance to operations management.

Implementing Operations Systems Through Supply Chain Management

After operations systems have been properly designed and technologies developed, they must then be put into use by the organization. Their basic functional purpose is to control transformation processes to ensure that relevant goals are achieved in areas such as quality and costs. Operations management has numerous special

Businesses are continuously looking for new ways to improve their supply chain management technology so as to be more efficient and more competitive. Take Aeroquip, for example. The Ohio firm makes a variety of metal connectors, fittings, adapters, and rubber hoses. Aeroquip has improved its effectiveness dramatically in recent years by changing its whole approach to inventory management and control. This 210,000-square-foot distribution center adjoins Aeroquip's main factory. A combination of human labor and automation can get parts to their needed locations in the factory within just a few minutes of an order being placed. This speed, in turn, allows the plant to supply many high-priority orders to customers within four hours.

purposes within this control framework, including purchasing and inventory management. Indeed, this area of management has become so important in recent years that a new term—supply chain management—has been coined. Specifically, **supply chain management** can be defined as the process of managing operations control, resource acquisition and purchasing, and inventory so as to improve overall efficiency and effectiveness.[11]

supply chain management The process of managing operations control, resource acquisition and purchasing, and inventory so as to improve overall efficiency and effectiveness

Operations Management as Control

One way of using operations management as control is to coordinate it with other functions. Monsanto Company, for example, established a consumer products division that produces and distributes fertilizers and lawn chemicals. To facilitate control, the operations function was organized as an autonomous profit center. Monsanto finds this arrangement effective because its manufacturing division is given the authority to determine not only the costs of creating the product but also the product price and the marketing programs.

In terms of overall organizational control, a division like the one used by Monsanto should be held accountable only for the activities over which it has decision-making authority. It would be inappropriate, of course, to make operations accountable for profitability in an organization that stresses sales and market share over quality and productivity. Misplaced accountability results in ineffective organizational control, to say nothing of hostility and conflict. Depending on the strategic role of operations then, operations managers are accountable for different kinds of results. For example, in an organization using bureaucratic control, accountability will be spelled out in rules and regulations. In a clan system, it is likely to be understood and accepted by everyone.

Within operations, managerial control ensures that resources and activities achieve primary goals such as a high percentage of on-time deliveries, low unit-production cost, or high product reliability. Any control system should focus on the elements that are most crucial to goal attainment. For example, firms in which product quality is a major concern (as it is at Rolex) might adopt a screening control system to monitor the product as it is being created. If quantity is a pressing issue (as it is at Timex), a postaction system might be used to identify defects at the end of the system without disrupting the manufacturing process itself.

Purchasing Management

purchasing management Buying the materials and resources needed to create products and services

Purchasing management is concerned with buying the materials and resources needed to create products and services. In many ways, purchasing is at the very heart of effective supply chain management. The purchasing manager for a retailer like Sears, Roebuck is responsible for buying the merchandise that the store will sell. The purchasing manager for a manufacturer buys raw materials, parts, and machines needed by the organization. Large companies like GE, IBM, and Siemens have large purchasing departments.[12] The manager responsible for purchasing must balance numerous constraints. Buying too much ties up capital and increases storage costs. Buying too little might lead to shortages and high reordering costs. The manager must also make sure that the quality of what is purchased meets the organization's needs, that the supplier is reliable, and that the best financial terms are negotiated.

Many firms have recently changed their approach to purchasing as a means to lower costs and improve quality and productivity. Rather than relying on hundreds or even thousands of suppliers, many companies are reducing their number of suppliers and negotiating special production-delivery arrangements.[13] For example, the Honda plant in Marysville, Ohio, found a local business owner looking for a new opportunity. They negotiated an agreement whereby he would start a new company to mount car stereo speakers into plastic moldings. He delivers finished goods to the plant three times a day, and Honda buys all he can manufacture. Thus, he has a stable sales base, Honda has a local and reliable supplier, and both companies benefit.

Inventory Management

Inventory control, also called materials control, is essential for effective operations management. The four basic kinds of inventories are *raw materials, work-in-process, finished-goods*, and *in-transit* inventories. As shown in Table 21.1, the sources of control over these inventories are as different as their purposes. Work-in-process inventories, for example, are made up of partially completed products that need further processing; they are controlled by the shop-floor system. In contrast, the quantities and costs of finished-goods inventories are under the control of the overall production scheduling system, which is determined by high-level planning decisions. In-transit inventories are controlled by the transportation and distribution systems.

Like most other areas of operations management, inventory management changed notably in recent years. One particularly important breakthrough is the **just-in-time (JIT) method**. First popularized by the Japanese, the JIT system reduces the organization's investment in storage space for raw materials and in the materials themselves. Historically, manufacturers built large storage areas and filled them with materials, parts, and supplies that would be needed days, weeks, and even months in the future. A manager using the JIT approach orders materials

inventory control Managing the organization's raw materials, work-in-process, finished goods, and products in-transit

just-in-time (JIT) method An inventory system that has necessary materials arriving as soon as they are needed (just in time) so that the production process is not interrupted

Table 21.1

Inventory Types, Purposes, and Sources of Control
JIT is a recent breakthrough in inventory management. With JIT inventory systems, materials arrive just as they are needed. JIT therefore helps an organization control its raw materials inventory by reducing the amount of space it must devote to storage.

Type	Purpose	Source of Control
Raw materials	Provide the materials needed to make the product	Purchasing models and systems
Work-in-process	Enables overall production to be divided into stages of manageable size	Shop-floor control systems
Finished goods	Provide ready supply of products on customer demand and enable long, efficient production runs	High-level production scheduling systems in conjunction with marketing
In-transit (pipeline)	Distributes products to customers	Transportation and distribution control systems

and parts more often and in smaller quantities, thereby reducing investment in both storage space and actual inventory. The ideal arrangement is for materials to arrive just as they are needed—or just in time.[14]

Recall our example about the small firm that assembles stereo speakers for Honda. That firm delivers stereo speakers in plastic molding three times a day, making it unnecessary for Honda to carry large quantities of the speakers in inventory. In an even more striking example, Johnson Controls makes automobile seats for DaimlerChrysler and ships them by small truckloads to a DaimlerChrysler plant seventy-five miles away. Each shipment is scheduled to arrive two hours before it is needed. Clearly, the JIT approach requires high levels of coordination and cooperation between the company and its suppliers. If shipments arrive too early, DaimlerChrysler has no place to store them. If they arrive too late, the entire assembly line may have to be shut down, resulting in enormous expense. When properly designed and used, the JIT method controls inventory very effectively.

MANAGEMENT IMPLICATIONS Managers should understand how operations systems can be used to enhance quality. In particular, they should be familiar with the role of operations management as control and the importance of purchasing and inventory management as elements of effective supply chain management.

Managing Total Quality

Quality and productivity have become major determinants of business success or failure today and have become central issues in managing organizations.[15] But as we will see, achieving higher levels of quality is not an easy accomplishment. Simply ordering that quality be improved is about as effective as waving a magic wand.[16] The catalyst for its emergence as a mainstream management concern was foreign business, especially Japanese business. And nowhere was it more visible than in the auto industry. During the energy crisis in the late 1970s, many people bought Toyotas, Hondas, and Nissans because they were more fuel-efficient than U.S. cars. Consumers soon found, however, that not only were the Japanese cars more fuel efficient, they were also of higher quality than U.S. cars. Parts fit together better, the trim work was neater, and the cars were more reliable. Thus, after the energy crisis subsided, Japanese cars remained formidable competitors because of their reputations for quality.

The Meaning of Quality

quality The totality of features and characteristics of a product or service that bear on its ability to satisfy stated or implied needs

The American Society for Quality Control defines **quality** as the totality of features and characteristics of a product or service that bear on its ability to satisfy stated or implied needs.[17] Quality has several different attributes. Table 21.2 lists eight basic dimensions that determine the quality of a particular product or service. For example, a product that has durability and is reliable is of higher quality than a product with less durability and reliability.

Quality is also relative. For example, a Lincoln is a higher-grade car than a Ford Taurus, which in turn is a higher-grade car than a Ford Focus. The difference in quality stems from differences in design and other features. The Focus, however, is considered a high-quality car relative to its engineering specifications and price. Likewise, the Taurus and Lincoln may also be high-quality cars, given their standards and prices. Thus, quality is both an absolute and a relative concept.

Quality is relevant for both products and services. While its importance for products like cars and computers was perhaps recognized first, service firms ranging from airlines to restaurants have also come to see that quality is a vitally important determinant of their success or failure. Service quality, as we will discuss later in this chapter, has thus also become a major competitive issue in U.S. industry today.

The Importance of Quality

To help underscore the importance of quality, the U.S. government created the **Malcolm Baldrige Award**, named after the former secretary of commerce who championed quality in U.S. industry. The award, administered by an agency of the Commerce Department, is given annually to firms that achieve major improvements in the quality of their products or services; that is, the award is based on changes in quality as opposed to absolute quality.

Recent winners of the Baldrige Award include Motorola; the Cadillac Division of General Motors; and

Quality improvement has become a major challenge for most companies today. One interesting area where quality has become especially important is what insiders call "green chemistry"—preventing pollution by better product engineering. 3M, for example, is dedicated to reducing the amount of polluting solvents it uses in its various products. Perhaps surprisingly, however, green chemistry has also helped the firm develop new products, many of which can be produced at lower cost and /or higher quality. This new plastic film, for example, serves as an iridescent reflector in products such as lamps and lights.

---

1. **Performance.** A product's primary operating characteristic. Examples are automobile acceleration and a television's picture clarity.
2. **Features.** Supplements to a product's basic functioning characteristics, such as power windows on a car.
3. **Reliability.** A probability of not malfunctioning during a specified period.
4. **Conformance.** The degree to which a product's design and operating characteristics meet established standards.
5. **Durability.** A measure of product life.
6. **Serviceability.** The speed and ease of repair.
7. **Aesthetics.** How a product looks, feels, tastes, and smells.
8. **Perceived quality.** As seen by a customer.

Table 21.2

Eight Dimensions of Quality
These eight dimensions generally capture the meaning of quality, which is a critically important ingredient to organizational success today. Understanding the basic meaning of quality is a good first step to managing it more effectively.

Source: Adapted and reprinted by permission of *Harvard Business Review,* from "Competing on the Eight Dimensions of Quality," by David A. Garvin, November/December 1987. Copyright © 1987 by Harvard Business School Publishing Corporation.

Malcolm Baldrige Award Named after a former secretary of commerce, this prestigious award is given to firms that achieve major quality improvements

divisions of Texas Instruments, AT&T, Xerox, and Ritz-Carlton. In addition, numerous other quality awards have also been created. For example, The Rochester Institute of Technology and *USA Today* give their Quality Cup award not to entire organizations but to individual teams of workers within organizations. Quality is also an important concern for individual managers and organizations for three very specific reasons: competition, productivity, and costs.[18]

Competition   Quality has become one of the most competitive points in business today. Ford, DaimlerChrysler, General Motors, and Toyota, for example, each argue that its cars and trucks are higher in quality than the cars and trucks of the others. And American, United, and Continental airlines each claim that it provides the best and most reliable service. Indeed, it seems that almost every U.S. business has adopted quality as a major point of competition. Thus, a business that fails to keep pace may find itself falling behind foreign competition *and* other U.S. firms.[19]

Productivity   Managers have also come to recognize that quality and productivity are related. In the past, many managers thought that they could increase output (productivity) only by decreasing quality. Managers today have learned the hard way that such an assumption is almost always wrong. If a firm installs a meaningful quality enhancement program, three events are likely to result. First, the number of defects is likely to decrease, causing fewer returns from customers. Second, because the number of defects goes down, resources (materials and people) dedicated to reworking flawed output will be decreased. Third, because making employees responsible for quality reduces the need for quality inspectors, the organization can produce more units with fewer resources.

Costs   Improved quality also lowers costs. Poor quality results in higher returns from customers, high warranty costs, and lawsuits from customers injured by faulty products. Future sales are lost because of disgruntled customers. An organization with quality problems often has to increase inspection expenses just to catch defective products. We noted in Chapter 20, for example, how Whistler Corporation was using one hundred of its two hundred fifty employees just to fix poorly assembled radar detectors.[20]

Total Quality Management

Once an organization makes a decision to enhance the quality of its products and services, it must then decide how to implement this decision. The most pervasive approach to managing quality has been called **total quality management**, or **TQM**—a real and meaningful effort by an organization to change its whole approach to business and to make quality a guiding factor in everything the organization does.[21] Figure 21.3 highlights the major characteristics of TQM.

total quality management (TQM) A strategic commitment by top management to change its whole approach to business and to make quality a guiding factor in everything the organization does

Strategic Commitment   The starting point for TQM is a strategic commitment by top management. Such commitment is important for several reasons. First, the organizational culture must change to recognize that quality is not just an ideal but is

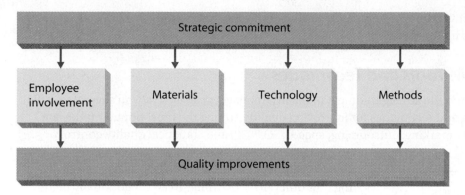

Figure 21.3

Total Quality Management

Quality is one of the most important issues facing organizations today. Total quality management, or TQM, is a comprehensive effort to enhance an organization's product or service quality. TQM involves the five basic dimensions shown here. Each is important and must be addressed effectively if the organization truly expects to increase quality.

instead an objective goal that must be pursued.[22] Second, a decision to pursue the goal of quality carries with it some real costs—for expenditures such as new equipment and facilities. Thus, without a commitment from top management, quality improvement will prove to be just a slogan or gimmick, with little or no real change.

Employee Involvement Employee involvement is another critical ingredient in TQM. Almost all successful quality enhancement programs involve making the person responsible for doing the job responsible for making sure it is done right.[23] By definition, then, employee involvement is a critical component in improving quality. Work teams, discussed in Chapter 19, are common vehicles for increasing employee involvement.

Technology New forms of technology are also useful in TQM programs. Automation and robots, for example, can often make products with higher precision and better consistency than can people. Investing in higher-grade machines capable of doing jobs more precisely and reliably often improves quality. For example, Nokia has achieved notable improvements in product quality by replacing many of its machines with new equipment. Similarly, most U.S. auto and electronics firms have all made significant investments in technology to help boost quality.

Materials Another important part of TQM is improving the quality of the materials that organizations use. Suppose that a company that assembles stereos buys chips and circuits from another company. If the chips have a high failure rate, consumers will return defective stereos to the company whose nameplate appears on them, not to the company that made the chips. The stereo firm then loses in two ways: refunds to customers and a damaged reputation. As a result, many firms have increased the quality requirements they impose on their suppliers as a way of improving the quality of their own products. Recall from our opening incident that Hartmann uses only high-quality materials in its luggage.

Methods Improved methods can improve product and service quality. Methods are operating systems used by the organization during the actual transformation process. For example, American Express Company has found ways to cut its approval time for new credit cards from twenty-two to only five days. This cut results in improved service quality.

TQM Tools and Techniques

Beyond the strategic context of quality, managers can also rely on several specific tools and techniques for improving quality. Among the most popular today are benchmarking, outsourcing, speed, ISO 9000, and statistical quality control.

INSPECTION-ON-A-SHOESTRING

Looks pretty clean!

Seems A-OK to me!

I don't have a problem with it!

Effective total quality management requires major commitments from an organization. Thorough and rigorous quality checks and inspections are often a fundamental part of quality management. But managers who pay only lip service to inspections, such as the managers illustrated here checking water quality, should not be surprised later when they discover major quality problems throughout their organizations. Only by using objective and rigorous statistical quality control measures can the firm be assured of high-quality products and services.

Benchmarking   **Benchmarking** is the process of learning how other firms do things in an exceptionally high-quality manner. Some approaches to benchmarking are simple and straightforward. For example, Xerox routinely buys copiers made by other firms and takes them apart to see how they work. This practice enables the firm to stay abreast of improvements and changes its competitors are using. When Ford was planning the newest version of the Taurus, it identified the four hundred features that customers identified as being most important to them. It then found the competing cars that did the best job on each feature. Ford's goal was to equal or surpass each of its competitors on those four hundred features. Other benchmarking strategies are more indirect. For example, many firms study how L.L.Bean manages its mail-order business, how Disney recruits and trains employees, and how Federal Express tracks packages for applications they can employ in their own businesses.[24]

Outsourcing   Another innovation for improving quality is outsourcing. **Outsourcing** is the process of subcontracting services and operations to other firms that can do them cheaper and/or better. If a business performs each and every one of its own administrative and business services and operations, it is almost certain to be doing at least some of them in an inefficient and/or low-quality manner. If those areas can be identified and outsourced, the firm will save money and realize a higher-quality service or operation.[25] Until recently, for example, Eastman Kodak handled all its own computing operations. Now, however, those operations are subcontracted to IBM, which handles all of Kodak's computing. The result is higher-quality computing systems and operations for Kodak at lower cost than before.

Speed   A third popular TQM technique is speed. **Speed** is the time needed by the organization to get something accomplished, and it can be emphasized in any area, including developing, making, and distributing products or services.[26] A good illustration of the power of speed comes from General Electric. At one point, the firm needed six plants and three weeks to produce and deliver custom-made industrial circuit-breaker boxes. By emphasizing speed, the same product can now

1. Start from scratch (it's usually easier than trying to do what the organization does now faster).
2. Minimize the number of approvals needed to do something (the fewer people who have to approve something, the faster approval will get done).
3. Use work teams as a basis for organization (teamwork and cooperation work better than individual effort and conflict).
4. Develop and adhere to a schedule (a properly designed schedule can greatly increase speed).
5. Don't ignore distribution (making something faster is only part of the battle).
6. Integrate speed into the organization's culture (if everyone understands the importance of speed, things will naturally get done quicker).

Source: Adapted from Brian Dumaine, "How Managers Can Succeed Through Speed," *Fortune*, February 13, 1989, pp. 54–59. © 1989 Time Inc. All rights reserved.

Table 21.3

Guidelines for Increasing the Speed of Operations

Many organizations today are using speed for competitive advantage. Listed in the table are six common guidelines that organizations follow when they want to shorten the time they need to get things accomplished. Although not every manager can do each of these things, most managers can do at least some of them.

be delivered in three days, and only a single plant is involved. Table 21.3 identifies several basic suggestions that have helped companies increase the speed of their operations. For example, GE found it better to start from scratch with a remodeled plant. GE also wiped out the need for approvals by eliminating most managerial positions and set up teams as a basis for organizing work. Stressing the importance of the schedule helped Motorola build a new plant and start production of a new product in only eighteen months.

ISO 9000 Still another useful technique for improving quality is ISO 9000. **ISO 9000** refers to a set of quality standards created by the International Organization for Standardization. Five such standards, numbered 9000 to 9001, cover areas such as product testing, employee training, record keeping, supplier relations, and repair polices and procedures. Firms that want to meet these standards apply for certification and are audited by a firm chosen by the organization's domestic affiliate (in the United States, the American National Standards Institute). These auditors review every aspect of the firm's business operations in relation to the standards. Many firms report that merely preparing for an ISO 9000 audit has been helpful. Many firms today, including General Electric, Du Pont, Eastman Kodak, British Telecom, and Philips Electronics, are urging—or in some cases requiring—that their suppliers achieve ISO 9000 certification.[27]

Statistical Quality Control A final quality control technique is **statistical quality control (SQC)**. As the term suggests, SQC is primarily concerned with managing quality.[28] It is a set of specific statistical techniques that can be used to monitor quality. *Acceptance sampling* involves sampling finished goods to ensure that quality standards have been met. Acceptance sampling is effective only when the correct percentage of products that should be tested (for example, 2, 5, or 25 percent) is determined. This decision is especially important when the test renders the product useless. Flashcubes, wine, and collapsible steering wheels, for example, are consumed or destroyed during testing. Another SQC method is *in-process sampling*. In-process sampling involves evaluating products during production so that

benchmarking The process of learning how other firms do things in an exceptionally high-quality manner

outsourcing The process of subcontracting services and operations to other firms that can do them cheaper and/or better

speed The time needed by the organization to get something accomplished; it can be emphasized in any area, including developing, making, and distributing products or services

ISO 9000 A set of quality standards created by the International Organization for Standardization

statistical quality control (SQC) A set of specific statistical techniques that can be used to monitor quality; includes acceptance sampling and in-process sampling

needed changes can be made. The painting department of a furniture company might periodically check the tint of the paint it is using. The company can then adjust the color as necessary to conform to customer standards. The advantage of in-process sampling is that it allows problems to be detected before they accumulate.

MANAGEMENT All managers today need to understand and appreciate the im-
IMPLICATIONS portance of total quality. Specifically, they need to understand the meaning of quality as well as its importance. The ingredients of total quality management are important in many organizations today. Various TQM tools and techniques are also important.

Managing Productivity

While the current focus on quality by U.S. companies is a relatively recent phenomenon, managers have been aware of the importance of productivity for several years. The stimulus for this attention was a recognition that the gap between productivity in the United States and productivity in other industrialized countries was narrowing. This section describes the meaning of productivity and underscores its importance. After summarizing recent productivity trends, we suggest ways that organizations can increase their productivity.

The Meaning of Productivity

productivity An economic measure of efficiency that summarizes the value of outputs relative to the value of the inputs used to create them

In a general sense, **productivity** is an economic measure of efficiency that summarizes the value of outputs relative to the value of the inputs used to create them.[29] Productivity can be and often is assessed at different levels and in different forms.

Levels of Productivity By level of productivity, we mean the units of analysis used to calculate or define productivity. For example, aggregate productivity is the total level of productivity achieved by a country. Industry productivity is the total productivity achieved by all the firms in a particular industry. Company productivity, as the term suggests, is the level of productivity achieved by an individual company. Unit productivity and individual productivity refer to the productivity achieved by a unit or department within an organization and the level of productivity attained by a single person, respectively.

Forms of Productivity There are many different forms of productivity. Total factor productivity is defined by the following formula:

$$\text{Productivity} = \frac{\text{Outputs}}{\text{Inputs}}$$

Total factor productivity is an overall indicator of how well an organization uses all its resources, such as labor, capital, materials, and energy, to create all its products and services. The biggest problem with total factor productivity is that all the ingredients must be expressed in the same terms—dollars (it is difficult to add hours of labor to the number of units of a raw material in a meaningful way). Total factor productivity also gives little insight into how a situation can be changed to improve productivity. Consequently, most organizations find it more useful to calculate a partial productivity ratio. Such a ratio uses only one category of resource. For example, labor productivity can be calculated by the following simple formula:

$$\text{Labor productivity} = \frac{\text{Outputs}}{\text{Direct labor}}$$

This method has two advantages. First, it is not necessary to transform the units of input into another unit. Second, this method provides managers with specific insights into how changing different resource inputs affects productivity. Suppose that an organization can manufacture one hundred units of a particular product with twenty hours of direct labor. The organization's labor productivity index is 5 (or 5 units per labor hour). Now suppose that worker efficiency is increased (through one of the ways to be discussed later in this chapter) so that the same twenty hours of labor results in the manufacture of 120 units of the product. The labor productivity index increases to 6 (6 units per labor hour), and the firm can see the direct results of a specific managerial action.

The Importance of Productivity

Managers consider it important that their firms maintain high levels of productivity for various reasons. Firm productivity is a primary determinant of an organization's level of profitability and, ultimately, its ability to survive. If one organization is more productive than another, it will have more products to sell at lower prices and have more profits to reinvest in other areas. Productivity also partially determines people's standards of living within a particular country. At an economic level, businesses consume resources and produce goods and services. The goods and services created within a country can be used by that country's citizens or exported for sale in other countries. The more goods and services the businesses within a country can produce, the more goods and services the country's citizens will have. Even goods that are exported result in financial resources flowing back into the home country. Thus, the citizens of a highly productive country are likely to have noticeably higher standards of living than are the citizens of a country with low productivity.

Productivity Trends

The United States has the highest level of productivity in the world. For example, Japanese workers produce only about 76 percent as much as U.S. workers, while German workers produce about 84 percent as much.[30] But in recent years, other countries have been closing the gap.[31] This trend was a primary factor in the decisions made by U.S. businesses to retrench, retool, and become more competitive in the world marketplace. For example, General Electric's dishwasher plant in Louisville has cut its inventory requirements by 50 percent, reduced labor costs from 15 percent to only 10 percent of total manufacturing costs, and cut product development time in half. As a result of these kinds of efforts, productivity trends have now leveled out and U.S. workers are generally maintaining their lead in most industries.[32]

One important factor that has hurt U.S. productivity indices has been the tremendous growth of the service sector in the United States. While this sector grew, its productivity levels did not. One part of this problem relates to measurement. For example, it is fairly easy to calculate the number of tons of steel produced at a Bethlehem Steel mill and divide it by the number of labor hours used; it is more difficult to determine the output of an attorney or a certified public accountant. Still, almost everyone agrees that improving service-sector productivity is the next major hurdle facing U.S. business.[33]

Figure 21.4 shows manufacturing productivity growth since 1960 in terms of annual average percentage of increase. As you can see, that growth slowed during the 1970s but began to rise again in the late 1980s. Some experts believe that productivity both in the United States and abroad will continue to improve at even more impressive rates. Their confidence rests on the potential ability of technology to improve operations. For example, Ford Motor Company has unveiled plans for a comprehensive purchasing network it calls AutoXchange. This system will replace all of its current purchasing arrangements, eliminating the need for personal contracts, paper and telephone ordering, and the like—saving billions of dollars and sharply boosting productivity in the process. Ford projects that this part of its business may well achieve annual productivity growth rates of up to 10 percent.[34]

Figure 21.4

Manufacturing and Service Productivity Growth Trends (1970–2000)

Both manufacturing productivity and service productivity in the United States continue to grow, although manufacturing productivity is growing at a faster pace. Total productivity, therefore, also continues to grow.

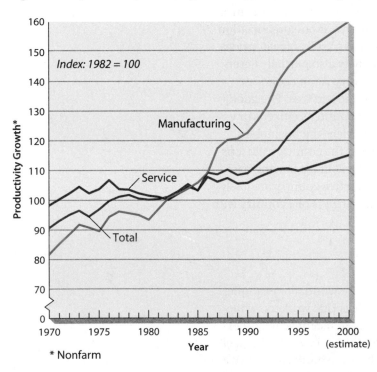

* Nonfarm

Source: U.S. Bureau of Labor Statistics.

Improving Productivity

How does a business or industry improve its productivity? Numerous specific suggestions made by experts generally fall into two broad categories: improving operations and increasing employee involvement.

Improving Operations One way that firms can improve operations is by spending more on research and development (R&D). R&D spending helps identify new products, new uses for existing products, and new methods for making products. Each of these research activities contributes to productivity. For example, Bausch & Lomb almost missed the boat on extended-wear contact lenses because the company had neglected R&D. When it became apparent that its major competitors were almost a year ahead of Bausch & Lomb in developing the new lenses, management made R&D a top priority. As a result, the company made several scientific breakthroughs, shortened the time needed to introduce new products, and greatly enhanced both total sales and profits—and all with a smaller workforce than the company used to employ. Even though other countries are greatly increasing their R&D spending, the United States continues to be the world leader in this area.

Another way firms can boost productivity through operations is by reassessing and revamping their transformation facilities. We noted earlier how one of GE's modernized plants does a better job than six antiquated ones. Just building a new factory is no guarantee of success, but IBM, Ford, Caterpillar, and many other businesses have achieved dramatic productivity gains by revamping their production facilities. Facility refinements are not limited to manufacturers. Most McDonald's restaurants now have drive-through windows, and many have moved soft-drink dispensers out to the restaurant floor so customers can get their own drinks. Each of these moves is an attempt to increase the speed with which customers can be served and thus is an increase in productivity.

Increasing Employee Involvement The other major thrust in productivity enhancement has been toward employee involvement. We noted earlier that participation can enhance quality; it can also boost productivity. Examples of this involvement are an individual worker being given a bigger voice in how she does her job, a formal agreement of cooperation between management and labor, and total involvement throughout the organization. GE eliminated most of the supervisors at its one new circuit-breaker plant and put control in the hands of workers.

Another method popular in the United States is increasing the flexibility of an organization's workforce by training employees to perform several different jobs. Such cross-training allows the firm to function with fewer workers because workers can be transferred easily to areas where they are most needed. For example, the Lechmere department store in Sarasota, Florida, encourages workers to learn numerous jobs within the store. One person in the store can operate a forklift in the stockroom, serve as a cashier, or provide customer service on the sales floor. At one Motorola plant, 397 of 400 employees have learned at least two skills under a similar program. *Working with Diversity* discusses the importance of computer literacy in enhancing productivity in the sawmill business today.

Rewards are essential to making employee involvement work. Firms must reward people for learning new skills and using them proficiently. At Motorola, for example, workers who master a new skill are assigned for five days to a job requiring them to use that skill. If they perform with no errors, they are moved to a higher pay grade and then they move back and forth between jobs as they are needed. If there is a performance problem, they receive more training and practice. This approach is fairly new, but preliminary indicators suggest that it can

WORKING WITH DIVERSITY

COMPUTER-LITERATE WORKERS NEEDED AT THE MILL

Sawmills have come into the computer age, leading to more diversity in their workforces. Although strength was once a primary qualification for mill workers, sawmills like Willamette Industries now put a premium on computer literacy. During the process of sawing giant logs into straight pieces of lumber, sawmills traditionally wasted a lot of wood. These days, however, mills have improved productivity and quality by computerizing many operations and adding technology to assist employees in moving raw materials through the mill. As a result, Oregon-based Willamette and its counterparts around the country are on the lookout for employees who know how to work with computers.

At Willamette, laser sensors analyze the dimensions of each 2,500-pound log and determine how to slice it and thus yield the most saleable lumber with the least waste. If the computer finds that a log is too long to move easily through the saw, it signals employees to cut the log shorter; if the computer detects a curve in the log, it automatically adjusts the saw blade to compensate. The computer can even examine the latest market prices for boards of various sizes and determine which cuts will extract the most profitable sizes and shapes from a particular log. Logs that need finishing touchups move through additional sensors that guide computerized saws to square off ragged ends. Within a few years, the mill may install ultrasound or other advanced technologies for identifying problems such as rot inside logs, which laser equipment can't detect.

Thanks to all these enhancements, Willamette has been able to continue producing the same amount of lumber with 12 percent fewer logs and 20 percent fewer employees. Higher productivity helps the mill cope with another problem. Like so many of its competitors and companies in numerous other industries, Willamette can't always find a large enough pool of qualified job candidates during high-employment periods. Thus, computerizing operations helps the mill operate at full capacity with a smaller workforce—but a workforce that is computer-savvy.

> *I've just been amazed at the technological improvements.*
>
> —*Mark Elston, plant manager for Willamette Industries**

Reference: George Hager, "Sawmill Illustrates the Buzz About Productivity," *USA Today,* March 21, 2000, pp. 1B, 2B (*quote on p. 2B).

increase productivity significantly. Many unions resist such programs because they threaten job security and reduce a person's identification with one skill or craft.

MANAGEMENT IMPLICATIONS Managers should understand the nature and meaning of productivity. They should also appreciate its importance. In addition, they should be familiar with productivity trends and be acquainted with common methods for improving productivity.

Summary of Key Points

Operations management is the set of managerial activities that organizations use in creating their products and services. Operations management is important to both manufacturing and service organizations. It plays an important role in an organization's strategy.

The starting point in using operations management is designing appropriate operations systems. Key decisions that must be made as part of operations systems design relate to product and service mix, capacity, and facilities.

Technology plays an important role in quality. Automation is especially important today. Numerous computer-aided manufacturing techniques are widely practiced. Robotics in particular is a growing area. Technology is as relevant to service organizations as it is to manufacturing organizations.

After an operations system has been designed, it must then be implemented. Major areas of interest during the use of operations systems are purchasing and inventory management.

Quality is a major consideration for all managers today. Quality is important because it affects competition, productivity, and costs. Total quality management is a comprehensive, organization wide effort to enhance quality through various avenues.

Productivity is also a major concern to managers. Productivity is a measure of how efficiently an organization is using its resources to create products or services. The United States still leads the world in individual productivity, but other industrialized nations are catching up.

Discussion Questions

Questions for Review

1. What is the relationship of operations management to overall organizational strategy? Where do productivity and quality fit into that relationship?
2. What are the major components of operations systems? How are they designed?
3. What is quality? Why is it so important today?
4. What is productivity? How can it be increased?

Questions for Analysis

5. Is operations management linked most closely to corporate-level, business-level, or functional strategies? Why or in what way?
6. How might the management functions of planning, organizing, and leading relate to the management of quality and productivity?

7. Some people argue that quality and productivity are inversely related; as one goes up, the other goes down. How can that argument be refuted?

Questions for Application

8. Research information on several different organizations' uses of operations management. What similarities and differences do you find? Why do you think those similarities and differences exist?
9. Interview local managers in different kinds of organizations (business, service, religious) to determine how they deal with quality and productivity.
10. Consider your college or university as an organization. How might it develop a TQM program?

BUILDING EFFECTIVE *conceptual* SKILLS

Exercise Overview

A manager's conceptual skills are her or his ability to think in the abstract. As this exercise will demonstrate, a relationship often exists between the conceptual skills of key managers in an organization and that organization's ability to implement total quality initiatives.

Exercise Background

Conceptual skills may be useful in helping managers see opportunities for improving some aspect of their own operations in observations or experiences gleaned from dealings with other organizations.

To begin this exercise, carefully recall the last time you ate in a restaurant that involved some degree of self-service. Examples might include a fast-food restaurant like McDonald's, a cafeteria, or even a traditional restaurant with a salad bar. Recall as much about the experience as possible and develop some ideas about why the restaurant is organized and laid out as it is.

Now carefully recall the last time you purchased something in a retail outlet. Possible examples might be an article of clothing from a specialty store, a book from a bookstore, or some software from a computer store. Again recall as much about the experience as possible and develop some ideas about why the store is organized and laid out as it is.

Exercise Task

Using the two examples you developed above, do the following:

1. Identify three or four elements of the service received at each location that you think most directly influenced—either positively or negatively—the quality and efficiency of the experience there.
2. Analyze the service elements from one organization and see if they can somehow be used by the other.
3. Now repeat the process for the second organization.

BUILDING EFFECTIVE *diagnostic* SKILLS

Exercise Overview

As noted in the chapter, the quality of a product or service is relative to price and expectations. A manager's diagnostic skills—the ability to visualize responses to a situation—can be useful in helping to position quality relative to price and expectations.

Exercise Background

Think of a recent occasion in which you purchased a tangible product, for example, clothing, electronic equipment, luggage, or professional supplies, that you subsequently came to feel was of especially high quality. Now recall another product that you evaluated as having appropriate or adequate quality, and a third that

you felt had low or poor quality. Next, recall parallel experiences involving purchases of services. Examples might include an airline, train, or bus trip; a meal in a restaurant; a haircut; or an oil change for your car.

Finally, recall three experiences in which both products and services were involved. Examples might include having questions answered by someone about a product you were buying or returning a defective or broken product for a refund or warranty repair. Try to recall instances in which there was an apparent disparity between product and service quality (i.e., a poor-quality product accompanied by outstanding service or a high-quality product accompanied by mediocre service).

Exercise Task

Using the nine examples identified above, do the following:

1. Assess the extent to which the quality you associated with each was a function of price and your expectations.

2. Could the quality of each be improved without greatly affecting price? If so, how?
3. Can high-quality service offset only adequate or even poor product quality? Can outstanding product quality offset only adequate or even poor-quality service?

BUILDING EFFECTIVE *technical* SKILLS

Exercise Overview

Technical skills are the skills necessary to accomplish or understand the specific kind of work being done in an organization. This exercise will help you see how technical skills relate to quality, productivity, and operations management.

Exercise Background

Select a product that you use regularly. Examples might include computers, compact disks, books, or apparel. Next, do some research to learn as much as you can about how the product you chose is designed, produced, and distributed to consumers.

Assume that you have decided to go into business to make the product selected. Create two columns on a sheet of paper. In one column

list all the activities necessary to produce the product that you know how to do (i.e., install software on a computer, sew two pieces of fabric together). Then list in the next column the activities that you do not know how to do.

Exercise Task

With the background information above as context, do the following:

1. Specify where people might learn the skills necessary to perform all the activities for the product you intend to make.
2. Rank-order the importance of the skills regarding the product.
3. Determine how many different people you will likely need to employ and thus have a full skill set available.

CHAPTER CLOSING CASE

BUILDING BETTER CARS IN BRAZIL

Better in Brazil? DaimlerChrysler, Volkswagen, Ford, General Motors, and Toyota are just some of the auto manufacturers that have opened factories in Brazil to turn out cars, vans, and trucks. These auto makers and their suppliers have been pioneering productivity-boosting methods that save money and streamline the assembly process.

One innovation is the combination of just-in-time (JIT) and just-in-sequence (JIS) methods. Here's how DaimlerChrysler and its suppliers are using these methods to make Dakota pickup trucks in a manufacturing center south of São Paulo. Dana Corp., a key supplier, is responsible for procuring 205 parts from sixty-seven suppliers to build chassis subassemblies (complete with fuel tank, brakes, suspension, and wheels). Dana's trucks haul three subassemblies down the road to the Chrysler factory a few miles away every forty-two minutes. The subassemblies arrive in time to be combined with engines and incorporated into the pickup truck cabs rolling down the assembly line at that moment. Thanks to JIT and JIS methods, a new Dakota truck rolls off the end of the line every fourteen minutes. Daimler-Chrysler saves space because the subassemblies are put together in Dana's facility. It also saves time and effort because Dana, not DaimlerChrysler, has to locate and purchase all the parts for the subassemblies.

The Dakota plant is home to another money-saving idea: outsourcing an activity that is still performed on the premises. Supplier PPG Industries provides the paints as well as the employees to prime and paint each Dakota truck within DaimlerChrysler's factory. As a result, DaimlerChrysler doesn't have to invest in raw materials or hire employees for this part of the manufacturing process—and it benefits from PPG's expertise in developing new paints and painting practices.

Even the assembly lines look different. In the newer VW-Audi and Mercedes factories in Brazil, for example, cars move through the first half of the assembly line mounted on large wooden platforms. Workers stand on these platforms and complete their assembly tasks, then dismount and walk back to the car behind to go through the routine again. In contrast, workers in traditional plants generally have to work as they walk to keep up with cars moving down the assembly lines. VW-Audi also tracks vehicles as they progress through the factory by posting a transmitter on each car's roof and monitoring the signals to identify slowdowns and to keep output on schedule.

Suppliers like Dana Corp. play a critical role in maintaining productivity in these plants. Johnson Controls, which makes car seats, instrument panels, and other components, has five production centers in Brazil and is thinking of building additional facilities to give its factory customers what they want, when they want it. Yet suppliers still have to juggle their own purchasing,

inventory, and production functions to achieve productivity goals by minimizing costs while maximizing output. Dana, for example, needs sufficient capacity to keep up with its customers' manufacturing capacity; anticipating future demand, the Dana facility has excess capacity right now, as does the Dakota plant it serves. And locating near a particular plant to provide JIT and JIS benefits effectively ties the supplier to that customer, which can cause problems if the customer reduces output or withdraws from the market.

Competitive pressures also affect what suppliers decide to do in Brazil. After all, no supplier wants to say no to a customer—and then watch as a rival says yes and takes away a significant chunk of business. At the same time, suppliers are making hefty investments in plant, equipment, and personnel to accommodate their automaker customers. Although experts are projecting increased demand for cars and other vehicles, which should translate into higher sales for auto makers and their suppliers, an economic turndown or a currency crisis could hurt. On the other hand, with little increase in demand in the United States, Japan, and Europe, the auto makers are looking toward South American markets for future growth—and advances in productivity.

Case Questions

1. What issues do operations managers for the auto makers and their suppliers face in Brazil?

2. What total quality management tools and techniques are being applied in these Brazilian operations?

3. Which of the three approaches to facilities layout do the auto makers appear to be using in Brazil? Why is this approach appropriate?

Case References

Philip Siekman, "Building 'Em Better in Brazil," *Fortune*, September 6, 1999, pp. 246(c)–246(v); Philip Siekman, "Where 'Build to Order' Works Best," *Fortune*, April 26, 1999, pp. 160(c)–160(v).

CHAPTER NOTES

1. *Hoover's Handbook of American Business 2000* (Austin, Texas: Hoover's Business Press, 2000), pp. 284–285; "The Quest for Quality Is in the Bag(gage)," *USA Today*, September 23, 1997, p. 12E (quote on p. 12E).

2. Paul M. Swamidass, "Empirical Science: New Frontier in Operations Management Research," *Academy of Management Review*, October 1991, pp. 793–814.

3. See Anil Khurana, "Managing Complex Production Processes," *Sloan Management Review*, Winter 1999, pp. 85–98.

4. For an example, see Robin Cooper and Regine Slagmulder, "Develop Profitable New Products with Target Costing," *Sloan Management Review*, Summer 1999, pp. 23–34.

5. Joan Woodward, *Industrial Organization: Theory and Practice* (London: Oxford University Press, 1965).

6. See "Tight Labor? Tech to the Rescue," *Business Week*, March 20, 2000, pp. 36–37.

7. "Computers Speed the Design of More Workaday Products," *Wall Street Journal*, January 18, 1985, p. 25.

8. "New Plant Gets Jaguar in Gear," *USA Today*, November 27, 2000, p. 4B.

9. "Thinking Machines," *Business Week*, August 7, 2000, pp. 78–86.

10. James Brian Quinn and Martin Neil Baily, "Information Technology: Increasing Productivity in Services," *The Academy of Management Executive*, 1994, Vol. 8, No. 3, pp. 28–37.

11. See Charles J. Corbett, Joseph D. Blackburn, and Luk N. Van Wassenhove, "Partnerships to Improve Supply Chains," *Sloan Management Review*, Summer 1999, pp. 71–82, and Jeffrey K. Liker and Yen-Chun Wu, "Japanese Automakers, U.S. Suppliers, and Supply-Chain Superiority," *Sloan Management Review*, Fall 2000, pp. 81–93.

12. See "Siemens Climbs Back," *Business Week*, June 5, 2000, pp. 79–82.

13. See M. Bensaou, "Portfolios of Buyer-Supplier Relationships," *Sloan Management Review*, Summer 1999, pp. 35–44.

14. "Just-in-Time Manufacturing Is Working Overtime," *Business Week*, November 8, 1999, pp. 36–37.

15. "Quality—How to Make It Pay," *Business Week*, August 8, 1994, pp. 54–59.

16. Rhonda Reger, Loren Gustafson, Samuel DeMarie, and John Mullane, "Reframing the Organization: Why Implementing Total Quality Is Easier Said Than Done," *Academy of Management Review*, 1994, Vol. 19, No. 3, pp. 565–584.

17. Ross Johnson and William O. Winchell, *Management and Quality* (Milwaukee: American Society for Quality Control, 1989). See also Carol Reeves and David Bednar, "Defining Quality: Alternatives and Implications," *Academy of Management Review*, 1994, Vol. 19, No. 3, pp. 419–445, and C. K. Prahalad and M. S. Krishnan, "The New Meaning of Quality in the Information Age," *Harvard Business Review*, September–October 1999, pp. 109–120.

18. W. Edwards Deming, *Out of the Crisis* (Cambridge, Mass.: MIT Press, 1986).

19. David Waldman, "The Contributions of Total Quality Management to a Theory of Work Performance," *Academy of Management Review*, 1994, Vol. 19, No. 3, pp. 510–536.

20. Joel Dreyfuss, "Victories in the Quality Crusade," *Fortune*, October 10, 1988, pp. 80–88.

21. Thomas Y. Choi and Orlando C. Behling, "Top Managers and TQM Success: One More Look After All These Years," *The Academy of Management Executive*, Vol. 11, No. 1, 1997, pp. 37–48.

22. James Dean and David Bowen, "Management Theory and Total Quality: Improving Research and Practice Through Theory Development," *Academy of Management Review*, 1994, Vol. 19, No. 3, pp. 392–418.

23. Edward E. Lawler, "Total Quality Management and Employee Involvement: Are They Compatible?" *The Academy of Management Executive*, 1994, Vol. 8, No. 1, pp. 68–79.

24. Jeremy Main, "How to Steal the Best Ideas Around," *Fortune*, October 19, 1992, pp. 102–106.

25. See James Brian Quinn, "Strategic Outsourcing: Leveraging Knowledge Capabilities," *Sloan Management Review*, Summer 1999, pp. 8–22.

26. Thomas Robertson, "How to Reduce Market Penetration Cycle Times," *Sloan Management Review*, Fall 1993, pp. 87–96.

27. Ronald Henkoff, "The Hot New Seal of Quality," *Fortune*, June 28, 1993, pp. 116–120. See also Mustafa V. Uzumeri, "ISO 9000 and Other Metastandards: Principles for Management Practice?" *The Academy of Management Executive*, Vol. 11, No. 1, 1997, pp. 21–28.

28. Paula C. Morrow, "The Measurement of TQM Principles and Work-Related Outcomes," *Journal of Organizational Behavior*, July 1997, pp. 363–376.

29. John W. Kendrick, *Understanding Productivity: An Introduction to the Dynamics of Productivity Change* (Baltimore: Johns Hopkins, 1977).

30. "The Productivity Payoff Arrives," *Fortune*, June 27, 1994, pp. 79–84.

31. "Study: USA Losing Competitive Edge," *USA Today*, April 25, 1997, p. 9D.

32. "Why the Productivity Revolution Will Spread," *Business Week*, February 14, 2000, pp. 112–118.

33. Michael van Biema and Bruce Greenwald, "Managing Our Way to Higher Service-Sector Productivity," *Harvard Business Review*, July–August 1997, pp. 87–98.

34. See "Yank the Supply Chain," *Fortune*, November 15, 2000, pp. 152–159.

22 Managing Information and Information Technology

Highsmith Inc., based in Fort Atkinson, Wisconsin, is one of the largest mail-order suppliers of library and school equipment (book displays, audio-visual equipment), furniture, and supplies (educational software) in the United States. Indeed, its current catalog includes over twenty-five thousand items. One fundamental key to Highsmith's business success has been its strategic approach to managing information.

A central resource in Highsmith's information system is its corporate library. Internal information resources include books, magazines, over seven hundred journals, CD-ROM sources, and support software. Its networked computerized information system also provides electronic links to external information sources such as commercial databases and numerous interlibrary systems. In addition, Highsmith li-brarians maintain an informal network of information providers throughout the country. The library staff itself plays an essential role because of its expertise and experience in identifying and locating information requests from any of Highsmith's activity areas and on business processes ranging from corporate planning to self-improvement.

President and CEO Duncan Highsmith believes that external events—even some that seem remote and unrelated to the business—can create threats and opportunities for companies. He believes that if employees are focused only on internal operations, they won't see the bigger picture, so he encourages a more eclectic approach of information gathering from a broad range of sources. New cultural trends and political forces eventually change the way a society functions, and Highsmith doesn't want to get caught short when they do. He wants to anticipate changes that can reshape the social environment and he wants to be prepared in advance rather than be forced to react after the fact.

Highsmith is also convinced that if the right data is assembled in the right way, information gleaned from various sources—from seemingly eclectic sources—is the only way to get a clear picture of the future. He believes that, with access to the right information, his employees can anticipate changes and then turn them to the company's advantage. However, he does not believe that focusing on the future comes naturally to most people. That approach, he contends, doesn't work when you need to make strategic-level decisions.

"The right information can help create strategic choices for a business."

—Duncan Highsmith, CEO of Highsmith, Inc.

LEARNING OBJECTIVES

After studying this chapter, you should be able to:

■ Describe the role and importance of information in the manager's job and identify the basic building blocks of information technology.

Discuss the basic factors that determine an organization's information technology needs and describe the basic kinds of information systems used by organizations.

■ Discuss how information systems can be managed.

■ Describe how information systems affect organizations

One interesting characteristic of Highsmith's organization chart is that the library is portrayed at the same level as the firm's other important functions, including marketing, human resources, and accounting. And Lisa Gueda Carreño, the firm's senior librarian, plays the role of senior manager. Carreño is also responsible for maintaining the firm's information system so that its usefulness is maximized for everyone in the organization.

The strength of the system is its role as a knowledge-management tool. Specifically, Highsmith's information system allows anyone in the firm to access any information they need in whatever form is most useful to them. And although Carreño relies on the Internet, she also realizes that, as an information source, it isn't always perfect. Indeed, she argues that it's full of potentially misleading hype and promises,

and it's unfamiliar territory to new users. Web-search services—Internet search directories, web browsers, and search engines—often provide spotty information, ranging from full-disclosure sites to sites that offer the truth but not the whole truth. Some web services report information only for sites that pay to be listed and ignore others. Even among those that report on a huge number of companies, some may give preferential treatment—that is, more favorable reports—to business partners.[1]

As the Highsmith experience illustrates, information systems and communication networks can have a dramatic effect on the firm's culture and its performance. Indeed, today's businesses rely on information management in ways that could not have been foreseen as recently as a decade ago. Managers now turn to digital technology as an integral part of organizational resources and as a means of conducting everyday business. Every major firm's business activities—such as designing services, ensuring product delivery and cash flow, evaluating employees, and creating advertising—are linked to information systems. Effective information management requires a commitment of resources to establish, maintain, and upgrade as new technologies emerge.

This chapter is about advances made by organizations in establishing, maintaining, and upgrading information technology. We describe the role and importance of information to managers, the characteristics of useful information, and information management as control, and we identify the basic building blocks of information systems. We discuss the general and specific determinants of information technology needs. We then discuss the primary kinds of information technology used in organizations and describe how this technology is managed.

Information and the Manager

Information has always been an integral part of every manager's job. Its importance and therefore the need to manage it continue to grow at a rapid clip. To appreciate this trend, we need to understand the role of information in the manager's job, the characteristics of useful information, and the nature of information management as control.

Role of Information in the Manager's Job

In Chapters 1 and 18, we highlighted the role of communication in the manager's job. Information is a vital part of communication, so management and information are closely related. Indeed, it is possible to conceptualize management itself as a series of steps involving the reception, processing, and dissemination of information. As illustrated in Figure 22.1, the manager is constantly bombarded with data and information (the difference between the two is noted later).

Suppose that Bob Henderson is an operations manager for a large manufacturing firm. During the course of a normal day, Bob receives many different pieces of information from formal and informal conversations and meetings, telephone calls, personal observations, e-mails, letters, reports, memos, the Internet, and trade publications. He gets a report from a subordinate that explains exactly how to solve a pressing problem, so he calls the subordinate and tells him to put the solution into effect immediately. He scans a copy of a report prepared for another manager, sees that it has no relevance to him, and discards it. He sees a *Wall Street Journal* article that he knows Sara Ferris in marketing should see, so he passes it on to her. He gets an electronic summary of yesterday's production report, but since

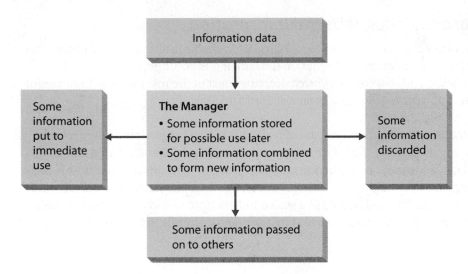

Figure 22.1

Managers as Information Processors

Managers who receive information and data must decide what to do with it. Some is stored for possible later use, and other information is combined to form new information. Subsequently, some is used immediately, some is passed on to others, and some is discarded.

he knows he won't need to analyze it for another week, he stores it. He observes a worker doing a job incorrectly and realizes that the incorrect method is associated with a mysterious quality problem that someone told him about last week.

A key part of information-processing activity is differentiating between data and information. **Data** are raw figures and facts reflecting a single aspect of reality. The facts that a plant has thirty-five machines, that each machine is capable of producing one thousand units of output per day, that current and projected future demand for the units is thirty thousand per day, and that workers sufficiently skilled to run the machines make $20 an hour are data.

Information is data presented in a way or form that has meaning.[2] Thus, combining and summarizing the four pieces of data given above provides information—the plant has excess capacity and is therefore incurring unnecessary costs. Information has meaning to a manager and provides a basis for action. The plant manager might use the information and decide to sell four machines (perhaps keeping one as a backup) and transfer five operators to other jobs.

A related term is **information technology (IT)**. Information technology refers to the resources used by an organization to manage information that it needs to carry out its mission. IT may consist of computers, computer networks, telephones, facsimile machines, and other pieces of hardware. In addition, IT also involves software that facilitates the system's abilities to manage information in a way that is useful for managers.[3]

The grocery industry uses data, information, and information technology to automate inventory and checkout facilities. The average Kroger store, for example, carries over twenty-one thousand items in each of its stores. Computerized scanning machines at the checkout counters can provide daily sales figures for any product. These numbers alone are data and have little meaning in their pure form. But information is created from this data by another computerized system. Using this IT system, managers can identify how any given product or product line is selling in any number of stores over any meaningful period of time.

data Raw figures and facts reflecting a single aspect of reality

information Data presented in a way or form that has meaning

information technology (IT) The resources used by an organization to manage information that it needs to carry out its mission

Characteristics of Useful Information

What factors differentiate between information that is useful and information that is not useful? In general, information is useful if it is accurate, timely, complete, and relevant. *Management Infotech* describes part of the role that less-than-useful information played in recent events at Ford and Firestone.

accurate information Provides a valid and reliable reflection of reality

Accurate   For information to be of real value to a manager, it must be accurate. Accuracy means that the information must provide a valid and reliable reflection of reality. A Japanese construction company once bought information from a consulting firm about a possible building site in London. The Japanese were told that the land, which would be sold in a sealed bid auction, would attract bids of close to $250 million. They were also told that the land currently held an old building

---

MANAGEMENT INFOTECH

DATABASE DECISIONS

The pattern of problems that led to the second-largest tire recall in U.S. history might have been detected earlier if Ford had received and analyzed data about the tires used as original equipment on Explorer vehicles. More than 6.5 million Firestone tires were recalled in 2000 because of unexpected tread separation that, in some cases, led to accidents. Ford got involved because millions of its Explorer sport-utility vehicles rolled out of dealerships equipped with Firestone tires, as did some of its Mercury Mountaineer SUVs and Ford Ranger pickups.

Problems with Firestone tires on Ford Explorers first surfaced in the early 1990s, when attorneys began filing lawsuits over deaths that occurred after tire treads separated and vehicles flipped over. By 1999, Ford was receiving reports from the Persian Gulf and Latin America that some Firestone tires were failing without warning on Ford vehicles. The company replaced tires on nearly forty-seven thousand SUVs in those countries, but managers didn't distinguish these incidents as part of a broader pattern. Ford engineers dissected a sample of used tires from Explorer models and invited Firestone to conduct its own tests, but neither company found any evidence of problems.

Although Ford routinely received complaints about parts under warranty, it did not receive warranty data about the tires on its vehicles. Instead, Firestone, as the manufacturer, was responsible for handling the warranty claims on its tires, so it col-

lected the data when necessary. Without a database of information about problems on various brands and types of tires, Ford couldn't compare the frequency of problems involving Firestone tires on Explorers with problems involving other tires.

As the National Highway Traffic Safety Administration began looking into the issue, Ford undertook an intensive investigation to find out whether other brands of tires had experienced separation problems on its vehicles. It also worked with Firestone to analyze tire warranty data and determine where most of the problems had occurred and which plants had manufactured the problem tires. By the time the tires were recalled, Ford personnel had pored over countless records—and built a database the company planned to share with the tire manufacturers.

> *Taken across the aggregate number of vehicles out there, the incident reports involved a very minuscule number.*
>
> —*Unnamed Ford executive.* *

Reference: Robert L. Simison, Karen Lundegaard, Norihiko Shirouzu, and Jenny Heller, "Blowout: How the Tire Problem Turned into a Crisis for Firestone and Ford," *Wall Street Journal*, August 10, 2000, pp. A1, A12 (*quote on A12).

that could easily be demolished. Thus, the Japanese bid $255 million—which ended up being $90 million more than the next-highest bid. And to make matters worse, a few days later the British government declared the building historic, preempting any thought of demolition. Clearly, the Japanese acted on information that was less than accurate.

Timely Information also needs to be timely. Timeliness does not necessarily mean speediness; it means only that information needs to be available in time for appropriate managerial action. What constitutes timeliness is a function of the situation facing the manager. When Marriott was gathering information for its Fairfield Inn project, managers projected a six-month window for data collection. They felt this amount of time would give them an opportunity to do a good job of getting the information they needed while not delaying the project too much. In contrast, Marriott's computerized reservation and accounting system can provide a manager today with last night's occupancy level at any Marriott facility.[4]

Complete Information must tell a complete story for it to be useful to a manager. If it is less than complete, the manager is likely to get an inaccurate or distorted picture of reality. For example, managers at Kroger used to think that house-brand products were more profitable than national brands because they yielded higher unit profits. On the basis of this information, they gave house brands a lot of shelf space and centered a lot of promotional activities around them. As Kroger's managers became more sophisticated in understanding their information, however, they realized that national brands were actually more profitable over time because they sold many more units than house brands during any given period of time. Hence, while a store might sell ten cans of Kroger coffee in a day with a profit of fifty cents per can (total profit of $5.00), it would also sell fifteen cans of Maxwell House with a profit of forty cents per can (total profit of $6.00) and ten vacuum bags of Starbucks coffee with a profit of $1.00 per bag (total profit of $10.00). With this more complete picture, managers can do a better job of selecting the right mix of Kroger, Maxwell House, and Starbucks coffee to display and promote.

Relevant Finally, information must be relevant if it is to be useful to managers. Relevance, like timeliness, is defined according to the needs and circumstances of a particular manager. Operations managers need information on costs and productivity, human resource managers need information on hiring needs and

Organizations rely on information that needs to be accurate, timely, complete, and relevant. Consider, for example, Sameday.com, an Internet firm based in Southern California. Sameday.com handles inventory and delivery for a roster of web businesses in the Los Angeles area. The firm prides itself on getting shipments to customers as close to "now" as possible. But in order to do this, these Sameday.com drivers must have information that tells them exactly what needs to be delivered, where, when, and in what sequence.

timely information Available in time for appropriate managerial action

complete information Provides the manager with all the information he or she needs

relevant information Assures managers that the information is useful to them in their particular circumstances for their particular needs

turnover rates, and marketing managers need information on sales projections and advertising rates. As Wal-Mart contemplates countries for possible expansion opportunities, it gathers information about local regulations, customs, and so forth. But the information about any given country isn't really relevant until the decision is made to enter that market.

Information Management as Control

The manager also needs to appreciate the role of information in control—indeed, to see information management as a vital part of the control process in the organization.[5] As already noted, managers receive much more data and information than they need or can use. Accordingly, deciding how to handle each piece of data and information involves a form of control.[6]

The control perspective on information management is illustrated in Figure 22.2. Information enters, is used by, and leaves the organization. For example, Marriott took great pains to make sure it got all the information it needed to plan for and enter the economy lodging business. Once this preliminary information was gathered, it was necessary to ensure that the information was made available in the proper form to everyone who needed it. In general, the effort to ensure that information is accurate, timely, complete, and relevant is a form of screening control. Finally, Marriott wanted to make sure that its competitors did not learn about its plans until the last possible minute. It also wanted to time and orchestrate news releases, public announcements, and advertising for maximum benefit. These efforts thus served a postaction control function.

MANAGEMENT
IMPLICATIONS Managers need to understand and appreciate the role of information in their jobs. In addition, they should know the characteristics that typify useful information and understand the control function served by effective information management.

Figure 22.2

Information Management as Control

Information management can be part of the control system via preliminary, screening, and/or postaction control mechanisms. Because information from the environment is just as much a resource as raw materials or finances, it must be monitored and managed to promote its efficient and effective utilization.

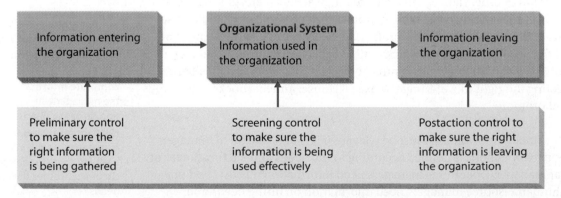

Building Blocks of Information Technology

Information technology is generally of two types—manual or computer-based. All information technology, and the systems that it defines, has five basic parts. Figure 22.3 diagrams these parts for a computer-based information technology system. The *input medium* is the device used to add data and information into the system. For example, the optical scanner at Kroger enters point-of-sale information. Likewise, someone can also enter data through a keyboard, with a mouse, or from other computers or the Internet.

The data entered into the system typically flow first to a processor. The *processor* is the part of the system capable of organizing, manipulating, sorting, or performing calculations or other transformations with the data. Most systems also have one or more *storage devices*—places where data can be stored for later use. Floppy disks, hard drives, CD-ROM disks, magnetic tapes, and optical disks are common forms of storage devices. As data are transformed into useable information, the resultant information must be communicated to the appropriate person by means of an *output medium*. Common ways to display output are video displays, printers, and facsimile machines, as well as by transmission to other computers or web pages.

Finally, the entire information technology system is operated by a *control system*—most often software of one form or another. Simple systems in smaller organizations can use off-the-shelf software. Microsoft Windows and DOS are general operating systems that control other more specialized types of software. Microsoft Word and WordPerfect are popular systems for word processing. Lotus 1-2-3 and Excel are popular spreadsheet programs, and dBase and Access are frequently used for database management. Of course, elaborate systems of the type used by large

Figure 22.3

Building Blocks of a Computer-Based Information System

Computer-based information systems generally have five basic components—an input medium, a processor, an output medium, a storage device, and a control system. Non–computer-based systems use parallel components for the same basic purposes.

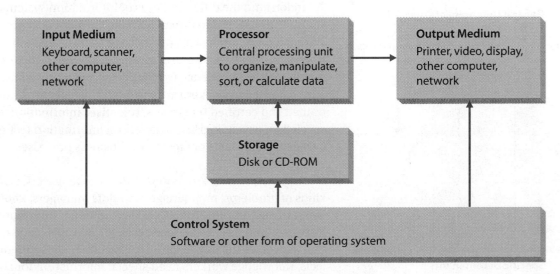

businesses require a special customized operating system. When organizations start to link computers together into a network, the operating system must be even more complex.

As we noted earlier, information technology systems need not be computerized. Many small organizations still function quite well with a manual system using paper documents, routing slips, paper clips, file folders, file cabinets, and a single personal computer. Increasingly, however, even small businesses are abandoning their manual systems for computerized ones. As hardware prices continue to drop and software becomes more and more powerful, computerized information systems will likely be within the reach of any business that wants to have one.

MANAGEMENT IMPLICATIONS Managers should be familiar with the basic components that comprise an information system and how they relate to one another.

Types of Information Systems

In a sense, the phrase *information system* may be a misnomer: it suggests that there is one system when, in fact, a firm's employees will have different interests, job responsibilities, and decision-making requirements. One information system cannot accommodate such a variety of information requirements. Instead, "the information system" is several complex information systems that share information while serving different levels of the organization, different departments, or different operations.

Figure 22.4

Determinants of an Organization's Information-Processing Needs
Information-processing needs are determined by user groups and system requirements and such specific managerial factors as their area and level in the organization.

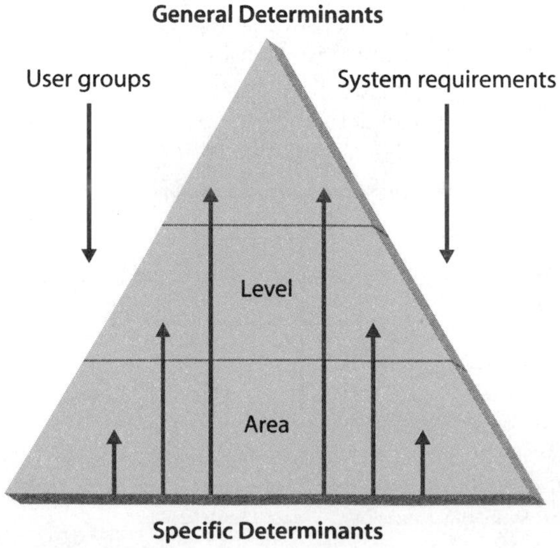

General Determinants

User groups   System requirements

Level

Area

Specific Determinants

User Groups and System Requirements

To understand the different kinds of information systems that organizations use, it is instructive first to consider user groups and system requirements. This perspective is illustrated in Figure 22.4. In general, there are four user groups, each with different system requirements. Knowledge workers represent a special user category. **Knowledge workers** are specialists, usually professionally trained and certified (engineers, scientists, information technology specialists, psychologists), who rely on information technology to design new products or create new business processes.

Managers at Different Levels Because they work on different kinds of problems, top managers, middle managers, knowledge workers, and first-line managers have different information needs. First-line (or operational) managers, for example, need information to oversee the day-to-day details of their departments or projects. Knowledge workers need special information for conducting technical projects. Meanwhile, middle managers need summaries and analyses for setting intermediate and long-range goals for the departments or projects under their supervision. Finally, top management analyzes broader trends in the economy, the business environment, and overall company performance for conducting long-range planning for the entire organization.

Consider the various information needs for a flooring manufacturer. Sales managers (first-level managers) supervise salespeople, assign territories to the sales force, and handle customer service and delivery problems. They need current information on the sales and delivery of products: lists of incoming customer orders and daily delivery schedules to customers in their territories. Regional managers (middle managers) set sales quotas for each sales manager, prepare budgets, and plan staffing needs for the upcoming year. They need information on monthly sales by product and region. Knowledge workers developing new flooring materials need information on the chemical properties of adhesives and compression strengths for floor structures. Finally, top managers need both external and internal information. Internally, they use sales data summarized by product, customer type, and geographic region, along with comparisons to previous years. Equally important is external information on consumer behavior patterns, the competition's performance, and economic forecasts.

Information has become a major component in the work of all managers and the activities of all organizations. Indeed, new and exciting methods and sources for gathering and analyzing information are appearing almost daily. Of course, as shown here in this cartoon, managers must ensure that they are getting the information they truly need and that it is of sufficient quality to meet their needs. Flawed or old information may do more harm than no information at all!

knowledge workers Specialists, usually professionally trained and certified (engineers, scientists, information technology specialists, psychologists), who rely on information technology to design new products or create new business processes

Functional Areas and Business Processes Each business function—marketing, human resources, accounting, operations, finance—has its own information requirements. In addition, many businesses are organized according to various business processes, and these process groups also need special information. Each of these user groups and departments, then, is represented by an information system. When organizations add to these systems the four systems needed by the four levels of users discussed above, the total number of information systems and applications increases significantly. Top-level finance managers, for example, are concerned with long-range planning for capital expenditures on future facilities and equipment and with determining sources of capital funds.

In contrast, a business-process group will include users—both managers and employees—drawn from all organizational levels. The supply chain management group, for instance, may be in the process of trimming back the number of suppliers. The information system supporting this project would contain information ranging across different organization functions and management levels: the group will need information and expert knowledge on marketing, warehousing and distribution, production, communications technology, purchasing, suppliers, and finance. It will also need different perspectives on operational, technical, and managerial issues: determining technical requirements for new suppliers, specifying task responsibilities for participating firms, and determining future financial requirements.

Major Systems by Level

In this section, we discuss different kinds of systems that provide applications at some organizational levels but not at others. For any routine, repetitive, highly structured decision, a specialized application will suffice. System requirements for knowledge workers, however, will probably vary because knowledge workers often face varied and specialized problems. Applications of information systems for middle- or top-level management decisions must also be flexible, although for different reasons. In particular, they will use a broader range of information collected from various sources, both external and internal.

transaction-processing system (TPS) Applications of information processing for basic day-to-day business transactions

Transaction-Processing Systems
Transaction-processing systems (TPS) are applications of information processing for basic day-to-day business transactions. Taking customer orders from on-line retailers, approval of claims at insurance companies, receiving and confirming reservations by airlines, payroll processing and bill payment at almost every company—all are routine business processes. Typically, the TPS for first-level (operational) activities is well defined, with predetermined data requirements, and follows the same steps to complete all transactions in the system.

Systems for Knowledge Workers and Office Applications
Systems for knowledge workers and office applications support the activities of both knowledge workers and employees in clerical positions. They provide assistance for data processing and other office activities, including the creation of communications documents. Like other departments, the information systems (IS) department includes both knowledge workers and data workers.

Many different kinds of information systems exist today. Microsoft is hoping one of its newest, Venus, catches on. Venus is designed for the Chinese market where there are over 20,000 different language characters. The complexity of the Chinese language, meanwhile, makes it difficult to write software for navigating the Internet and communicating with other computers. Venus relies on arrows rather than characters to navigate the Internet; it also works with a television set rather than a PC. Microsoft hopes that Venus will become the standard information system in China, linking together millions of users.

Needless to say, the explosion of new support systems—word processing, document imaging, desktop publishing, computer-aided design, simulation modeling—has increased the productivity of both office and knowledge workers. Desktop publishing combines graphics and word-processing text to produce professional-quality print and web documents. Document-imaging systems can scan paper documents and images, convert them into digital form for storage on disks, retrieve them, and transmit them electronically to workstations throughout the network.

Systems for Operations/Data Workers People who run the company's computer equipment are usually called system operations workers. They make sure that the right programs are run in the correct sequence and they monitor equipment to ensure that it is operating properly. Many organizations also have employees for entering data into the system for processing.

Management Information Systems **Management information systems (MIS)** support an organization's managers by providing daily reports, schedules, plans, and budgets. A simple MIS is shown in Figure 22.5. Each manager's information activities vary according to his or her functional area (say, accounting or marketing) and management level. Whereas middle-level managers focus mostly on internal activities and information, higher-level managers are engaged in both internal and external activities. Middle managers, the largest MIS user group, need networked information to plan such upcoming activities as personnel training, materials movement, and cash flows. They also need to know the current status of the jobs and projects carried out in their departments: What stage is it at now? When will it be finished? Is there an opening so we can start the next job? Many of a firm's management information systems—cash flow, sales, production scheduling, shipping—are indispensable for helping managers find answers to such questions.

management information system (MIS) Supports an organization's managers by providing daily reports, schedules, plans, and budgets

Figure 22.5

A Basic Management Information System

A basic management information system relies on an integrated database. Managers in various functional areas can access the database and get information they need to make decisions. For example, operations managers can access the system to determine sales forecasts by marketing managers, and financial managers can check human resource files to identify possible candidates for promotions into the finance department.

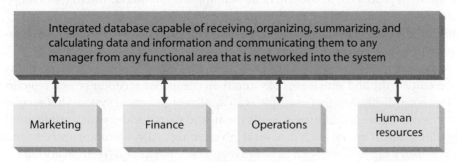

decision support system (DSS)
An interactive system that locates and presents information needed to support the decision-making process

Decision Support Systems Middle-and top-level managers receive decision-making assistance from a **decision support system** (**DSS**): an interactive system that locates and presents information needed to support the decision-making process. Whereas some DSSs are devoted to specific problems, others serve more general purposes, allowing managers to analyze different types of problems. Thus, a firm that often faces decisions on plant capacity, for example, may have a capacity DSS. The manager inputs data on anticipated levels of sales, working capital, and customer-delivery requirements. Then the DSS's built-in transaction processors manipulate the data and make recommendations on the best levels of plant capacity for each future time period. In contrast, a general-purpose system, such as a marketing DSS, might respond to various marketing-related problems. It may be programmed to handle what-if questions such as, "When is the best time to introduce a new product if my main competitor introduces one in three months, our new product has an eighteen-month expected life, demand is seasonal with a peak in the autumn, and my goal is to gain the largest possible market share?" The DSS can assist in decisions for which predetermined solutions are unknown by using sophisticated modeling tools and data analysis.

executive support system (ESS)
A quick-reference, easy-access application of information systems specially designed for instant access by upper-level managers

Executive Support Systems An **executive support system** (**ESS**) is a quick-reference, easy-access application of information systems specially designed for instant access by upper-level managers. ESSs are designed to assist with executive-level decisions and problems, ranging from "What lines of business should we be in five years from now?" to "Based on forecasted developments in electronic technologies, to what extent should our firm be globalized in five years? In ten years?" The ESS also uses a wide range of both internal information and external sources, such as industry reports, global economic forecasts, and reports on competitors' capabilities. Because senior-level managers do not usually possess advanced computer skills, they prefer systems that are easily accessible and adaptable. Accordingly, ESSs are not designed to address only specific, predetermined problems. Instead, they allow the user some flexibility in attacking different problem situations. They are easily accessible by means of simple keyboard strokes or even voice commands.

artificial intelligence (AI) The construction of computer systems, both hardware and software, to imitate human behavior—in other words, systems that perform physical tasks, use thought processes, and learn

Artificial Intelligence and Expert Systems **Artificial intelligence** (**AI**) can be defined as the construction of computer systems, both hardware and software, to imitate human behavior—in other words, systems that perform physical tasks, use thought processes, and learn. In developing AI systems, knowledge workers—business specialists, modelers, information-technology experts—try to design computer-based systems capable of reasoning so that computers, instead of people, can perform certain business activities.

One example is a credit-evaluation system that decides which loan applicants are creditworthy and which are risky and then composes acceptance and rejection letters accordingly. Another example is an applicant-selection system that receives interviewees' job applications, screens them, and then decides which applicants are the best matches for each of several job openings. AI systems are also designed with sensory capabilities, such as lasers that "see," "hear," and "feel." In addition, as machines become more sophisticated in processing natural languages, humans can give instructions and ask questions merely by speaking to a computer.

A special form of AI program, the expert system, is designed to imitate the thought processes of human experts in a particular field. Expert systems incorporate the rules that an expert applies to specific types of problems, such as the judgments that a physician makes for diagnosing illnesses. In effect, expert systems supply everyday users with "instant expertise." General Electric's Socrates Quick Quote, for example, imitates the decisions of a real estate expert and then places a package of recommendations about real estate transactions at the fingertips of real estate dealers on GE's private computer network. A system called MOCA (Maintenance Operations Center Advisor) schedules routine maintenance for American Airlines' entire fleet by imitating the thought processes of a maintenance manager.

The Internet

While not everyone would automatically think of it this way, the Internet is also an information system, and one that is becoming more and more important to business every day. The **Internet** (or the "**Net**," for short)—the largest public data communications network—is a gigantic network of networks serving millions of computers and offers information on business, science, and government and provides communication flows among more than 170,000 separate networks around the world. Originally commissioned by the Pentagon as a communication tool for use during war, the Internet now allows personal computers in almost any location to be linked together. The Net has gained in popularity because it is an efficient tool for information retrieval and makes available an immense store of academic, technical, and business information.

Internet (Net) A gigantic network of networks serving millions of computers and offering information on business, science, and government and providing communication flows among more than 170,000 separate networks around the world

Because it can transmit information fast and at low cost—lower than long-distance phone service, postal delivery, and overnight delivery—the Net has also become the most important e-mail system in the world. For thousands of businesses, therefore, the Net has joined—and is even replacing—the telephone, fax machine, and express mail as a standard means of communication. Although individuals cannot connect directly to the Internet, they can subscribe, for small monthly usage fees, to the Net via an **Internet service provider** (**ISP**) such as Prodigy, America Online, or Earthlink. An ISP is a commercial firm that maintains a permanent connection to the Net and sells temporary connections to subscribers.[7]

Internet service provider (ISP) A commercial firm that maintains a permanent connection to the Net and sells temporary connections to subscribers

The Internet's popularity continues to grow for both business and personal applications. In 2000, more than 302 million Net users were active on links connecting more than 180 countries. In the United States alone, more than fifty million users were on the Net every day. Its power to change the way business is conducted has been amply demonstrated in both large and small firms. Digital Equipment Corp. (DEC), for instance, is a heavy Internet user. With more than thirty-one thousand computers connected to the Net, DEC's monthly e-mail volume has passed the one-million-message mark. DEC also linked its Alpha AXP high-speed business computer to the Internet so that potential buyers and software developers could spend time using and evaluating it. Almost instantly, 2,500 computer users in twenty-seven countries used the Net to explore the Alpha AXP.

The Net has also benefited small companies, especially as a means of expanding market research and improving customer service and as a source of information. In San Leandro, California, for example, TriNet Employer Group subscribes to Ernst & Young's on-line consulting program, called Ernie. For $3,500 a year, TriNet controller Lyle DeWitt sends questions from his computer and gets an answer from an Ernst & Young expert within forty-eight hours. Aiming for small clients who cannot afford big-name consulting advice, Ernie answers questions on health insurance, benefit plans, immigration issues, and payroll taxes.

World Wide Web (WWW) A system with universally accepted standards for storing, retrieving, formatting, and displaying information

The World Wide Web   Thanks to the **World Wide Web** (**WWW**, or simply "the Web"), the Internet is easy to use and allows users around the world to communicate electronically with little effort. The World Wide Web is a system with universally accepted standards for storing, retrieving, formatting, and displaying information.[8] It provides the "common language" that enables us to "surf" the Net and makes the Internet available to a general audience, rather than only to technical users such as computer programmers. To access a web site, for example, the user must specify the uniform resource locator (URL) that points to the resource's unique address on the web.

Servers and Browsers   Each web site opens with a home page—a screen display that welcomes the visitor with a greeting that may include graphics, sound, and visual enhancements introducing the user to the site. Additional pages give details on the sponsor's products and explain how to contact help in using the site. Often, they furnish URLs for related web sites that the user can link to simply by pointing and clicking. The person who is responsible for maintaining an organization's web site is usually called a *webmaster*. Large web sites use dedicated workstations—large computers known as *web servers*—that are customized for managing, maintaining, and supporting web sites.

With hundreds of thousands of new web pages appearing each day, cyberspace is now providing billions of pages of publicly accessible information. Sorting through this maze would be frustrating and inefficient without access to a **web browser**—the software that enables the user to access information on the web. A browser runs on the user's PC and supports the graphics and linking capabilities needed to navigate the Web. Netscape Navigator has enjoyed as much as an 80 percent market share, although its dominance is now being challenged by other browsers, including its own Netscape Communicator and Microsoft's Internet Explorer.

web browser The software that enables the user to access information on the Web

Directories and Search Engines   The web browser offers additional tools—web site directories and search engines—for navigating on the Web. Among the most successful cyberspace enterprises are companies such as Yahoo!, which maintains free-to-use directories of web content. When Yahoo! is notified about new web sites, it classifies them in its directory. The user enters one or two keywords (say, "compact disk") and the directory responds by retrieving from the directory a list of web sites with titles containing those words.

In contrast to a directory, a search engine will search millions of web pages without preclassifying them into a directory. It searches for web pages that contain the same words as the user's search terms. Then it displays addresses for those that come closest to matching, then the next closest to matching, and so on. A search engine, such as AltaVista, Radar, or Lycos, may respond to more than ten million inquiries per day. Thus, it shouldn't be a surprise that both directories and search engines are packed with paid ads.[9] At the beginning of 2000, Yahoo! was the leader in portal sites—sites used by Net surfers as primary home pages—although Lycos was closing fast in the race for most users.

Intranets   The success of the Internet has led some companies to extend the Net's technology internally, for browsing internal web sites containing information throughout the company. These private networks, or **intranets**, are accessible only to employees via entry through electronic firewalls. Firewalls (discussed later) are used to limit access to an intranet. At Compaq Computer, the intranet allows employees to shuffle their retirement savings among various investment funds. Ford's intranet connects 120,000 workstations in Asia, Europe, and the United States to thousands of Ford web sites containing private information on Ford activities in production, engineering, distribution, and marketing. Sharing such information has helped reduce the lead-time for getting car models into production from thirty-six to twenty-four months. Ford's latest project in improving customer service through internal information sharing is called manufacturing on demand. For example, the Mustang that required fifty days' delivery time in 1996 is available in less than two weeks. The savings to Ford, of course, will be billions of dollars in inventory and fixed costs.[10]

> **intranet** A communication network similar to the Internet but operating within the boundaries of a single organization

Extranets   Sometimes firms allow outsiders access to their intranets. These so-called **extranets** allow selectd outsiders limited access to an organization's internal information system, or intranet. The most common application allows buyers to enter the seller's system to see which products are available for sale and delivery, thus providing product-availability information quickly to outside buyers. Industrial suppliers, too, are often linked into their customers' intranets so that they can see planned production schedules and ready supplies as needed for customers' upcoming operations.

> **extranet** A communication network that allows selected outsiders limited access to an organization's internal information system, or intranet

MANAGEMENT IMPLICATIONS   Managers must always understand the importance of matching information systems with the needs and requirements of their users. To do so, of course, they need to have a fundamental understanding of both user groups and system requirements as well as the different kinds of information systems that can be used. And all managers, of course, need to understand the Internet and its role in information and information technology.

◼ *Managing Information Systems*

At this point, the value and importance of information systems should be apparent. There are still important questions to be answered, however. How are such systems developed, and how are they used on a day-to-day basis? This section provides insights into these issues and related areas.

Creating Information Systems

The basic steps involved in creating an information system are outlined in Figure 22.6. The first step is to determine the information needs of the organization and to establish goals for what is to be achieved with the proposed system. It is absolutely imperative that the project have full support and an appropriate financial commitment from top management if it is to be successful. Once the decision has been made to develop and install an information system, a task force is usually assembled to oversee everything. As discussed earlier, target users must be well represented on such a task force.

Next, three tasks can be done simultaneously. One task is to assemble a database. Most organizations already possess the information they need for an information

Figure 22.6

Establishing an Information System

Establishing an information system is a complex procedure. Managers must realize, however, that the organization's information management needs will change over time, and some steps of the process may have to be repeated in the future.

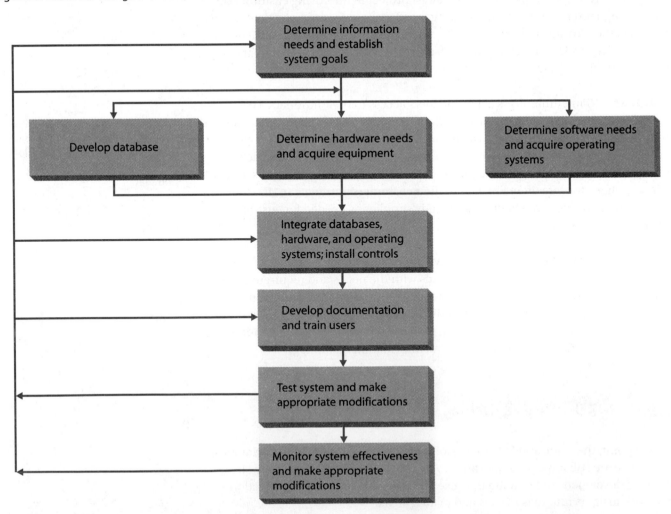

system, but it is often not in the correct form. The Pentagon has spent large sums of money to transform all its paper records into computer records. Many other branches of the government are also working hard to computerize their data.[11]

While the database is being assembled, the organization must also determine its hardware needs and acquire the appropriate equipment. Some systems rely solely on one large mainframe computer; others are increasingly using personal computers. Equipment is usually obtained from large manufacturers like IBM, Compaq, Sun, and Dell. Finally, software requirements must also be determined and an appropriate operating system obtained. Again, off-the-shelf packages will sometimes work, although most companies find it necessary to do some customization to suit their needs.[12]

The actual information system is created by integrating the databases, the hardware, and the software. Obviously, the mechanics of doing this task are beyond the scope of this discussion. The company usually has to rely on the expertise of outside consulting firms along with the vendors who provided the other parts of the system to put it all together. During this phase, the equipment is installed, cables are strung between units, the data are entered into the system, the operating system is installed and tested, and so forth. System controls are also installed at the same time. A control is simply a characteristic of the system that limits certain forms of access or limits what a person can do with the system. For example, top managers may want to limit access to certain sensitive data to a few key people. These people may be given private codes that must be entered before the data is made available. It is important to make sure that data cannot be accidentally erased by someone who happens to press the wrong key.

The next step is to develop documentation of how the system works and train people to use it. Documentation refers to manuals, computerized help programs, diagrams, and instruction sheets. Essentially, it tells people how to use the system for different purposes. Beyond pure documentation, however, training sessions are also common. Such sessions allow people to practice using the system under the watchful eye of experts.

The system must then be tested and appropriate modifications made. Regardless of how well planned an information system is, there will almost certainly be glitches. For example, the system may be unable to generate a report that needs to be made available to certain managers. Or the report may not be in the appropriate format. Or certain people may be unable to access data that they need and thus obtain other information from the system. In most cases, the consultants or internal group that installed the system will be able to make such modifications as the need arises.

The organization must recognize that information management needs will change over time. Even though the glitches are straightened out and the information system is put into normal operation, modifications may still be needed in the future. For example, after Black & Decker acquired General Electric's small-appliance business, it had to overhaul its own information system to accommodate all the new information associated with its new business. Information management is a continuous process. Even if an effective information system can be created and put into use, there is still a good chance that it will need to be modified occasionally to fit changing circumstances.

Integrating Information Systems

In very large and complex organizations, information systems must also be integrated. This integration may involve links between different information systems within the same organization or between different organizations altogether. Within an organization, for example, it is probably necessary for the marketing system and the operations system to be able to communicate with one another.

Linking systems together is not as easy. For example, PepsiCo recently acquired Quaker Oats. In all likelihood, each firm had its own complex and integrated information network. But since each firm's network may have relied on different technologies, hardware, and operating systems, integrating the two firms has been a costly and complex undertaking. Similarly, suppose a firm installs one system in one of its divisions using Dell equipment and Microsoft software, and then installs a different system in another division using Hewlett-Packard equipment and Lotus software. If and when the firm decides to tie its two distinct systems together, it may face considerable difficulties, like PepsiCo and Quaker.

There are two ways of overcoming this problem. One is to develop everything at once. Unfortunately, this alternative is expensive, and sometimes managers simply can't anticipate today exactly what their needs will be tomorrow. The other method is to adopt a standard type of system at the beginning so that subsequent additions fit properly.[13] Even then, however, breakthroughs in information system technology may still make it necessary to change approaches in midstream.

Using Information Systems

The real test of the value of an information system is how it can be used. Ideally, an information system should be simple to use and nontechnical—that is, one should not have to be a computer expert to use the system. In theory, a manager should be able to access a modern information system by turning on a computer and pressing certain keys in response to menu prompts. The manager should also be able to enter appropriate new data or request that certain kinds of information be provided. The requested information might first be displayed on a computer screen or monitor. After the manager is satisfied, the information can then be printed on paper with a standard printer, or the manager can store the information back in the system for possible future use or for use by others.

One implication relates to the span of management and the number of levels of an organization. Innovations in information technology enable a manager to stay in touch with an increasingly large number of managers and subordinates. T. J. Rodgers, CEO of Cypress Semiconductor Corp., uses the firm's information system to check on the progress of each of his employees every week. Using this and related approaches, spans of management are likely to widen and organizational levels decrease. And some organizations are using their information-processing capabilities to network with other companies. Pacific Intermountain Express, a large Western trucking company, gives customers access to its own computer network so they can check the status of their shipments.

The Travelers Corporation has made effective use of its information system by hiring a team of trained nurses to review health-insurance claims. The nurses tap into the company's regular information system and analyze the medical diagnoses provided with each claim. They can use this information to determine whether a second opinion is warranted before a particular surgical procedure is approved. They enter their decision directly into the system. When the claim form is printed, it contains a provision that spells out whether the claimant must seek a second opinion before proceeding with a particular treatment.

Managing Information Security

An increasingly common concern for businesses today is security. Security measures for protection against intrusion are a constant challenge. To gain entry into most systems, users have protected passwords that guard against unauthorized access, but many firms rely on additional protective software for safeguards. To protect against intrusions by unauthorized outsiders, companies use security devices, called electronic firewalls, in their systems. **Firewalls** are software and hardware systems that allow employees access to both the Internet and the company's internal computer network while barring entry by outsiders.

Security for electronic communications is an additional concern. Electronic transmissions can be intercepted, altered, and read by intruders. To prevent unauthorized access, many firms rely on encryption: use of a secret numerical code to scramble the characters in the message so the message is not understandable during transmission. Only personnel with the deciphering codes can read them. Protection for preserving data files and databases is not foolproof and typically involves making backup copies to be stored outside the computer system, usually in a safe. Thus, damaged system files can be replaced by backup.

Finally, the most important security factor is the people in the system. At most firms, personnel are trained in the responsibilities of computer use and warned of the penalties for violating system security. For example, each time the computer boots up, a notice displays the warning that software and data are protected and spells out penalties for unauthorized use. *Today's Management Issues* provides some additional insights into the nature of information security.

Information security is a major issue in business today. As illustrated by this recent magazine cover, individuals and businesses alike are concerned with protecting their information, maintaining confidentiality, and keeping unauthorized users from having access to their information systems.

firewalls Software and hardware systems that allow employees access to both the Internet and the company's internal computer network while barring entry by outsiders

Understanding Information System Limitations

It is also necessary to recognize the limits of information systems. Several are listed in Table 22.1. First of all, as already noted, information systems are expensive and difficult to develop. Thus, organizations may try to cut too many corners or install a system in such a piecemeal fashion that its effectiveness suffers.

Information systems simply are not suitable for some tasks or problems. Complex problems requiring human judgment must still be addressed by humans. Information systems are often a useful tool for managers, but they can seldom

SNIFFING OUT COMPETITIVE DATA

Competitive intelligence is incorporated into the decision-making processes of many companies. Motorola, Apple Computer, and Compaq use it. But where does legitimate competitive intelligence end and questionable corporate spying begin? Employees and consultants have engaged in a wide range of tactics to collect competitive data, from swiping documents out of rivals' dumpsters, to looking up public filings of rivals' patents, to analyzing on-line information about competitors. One study estimated that stolen information cost large U.S. corporations $45 billion in 1999. Although the stakes are high, experts admit that the line separating ethical from unethical tactics is not always clear.

Consider what happened when software giant Oracle Corporation hired an intelligence firm to investigate groups that Oracle suspected were closely tied to Microsoft and its defense against federal antitrust charges. After the *Wall Street Journal* reported that the intelligence firm had offered to buy trash gathered from one of the group's wastebaskets, Oracle issued a statement saying that it had hired the firm but had been repeatedly assured that the activities used were completely legal. Industry specialists disagree on how often intelligence gatherers use questionable techniques, in part because few organizations that fall victim to such tactics are willing to talk publicly about the problem.

With increased globalization, companies are battling more rivals in more countries. The FBI has begun tracking the activities of eight countries it claims are trying to uncover trade secrets to benefit firms based in those countries. Meanwhile, European officials claim that the United States is using global surveillance of electronic communications to funnel data to U.S. firms—a charge U.S. officials deny.

When properly gathered and analyzed, competitive intelligence can be extremely valuable. For example, Motorola maintains intelligence offices around the world to monitor competitors and identify clues to new technologies and organizational changes. Its intelligence experts are invited to high-level business strategy meetings so they can provide input to support executive decision making. Over the years, Motorola has used such data to make decisions about strategic alliances and about reengineering internal operations. For Motorola and for many other companies, legitimate competitive intelligence has become a vital tool.

> *In most cases, people wouldn't have a problem distinguishing what is illegal or unethical conduct versus obtaining information from public sources.*
>
> —Peter Toren, a New York attorney*

References: Neil King, Jr., and Jess Bravin, "Call It Mission Impossible Inc.—Corporate Spying Firms Thrive," *Wall Street Journal*, July 3, 2000, pp. B1, B4 (*quote on p. B4); "Oracle Admits Hiring Investigators Who Sought Trash of Pro-Microsoft Groups," *Tech Law Journal*, June 28, 2000, http://techlawjournal.com/election/20000628.htm (October 5, 2000).

replace managers. Managers may also come to rely too much on information systems. As a consequence, the manager may lose touch with the real-world problems he or she needs to be concerned about. Similarly, access to unlimited information can result in overload, rendering managers less effective than they would be if they had reduced access to information![14]

Information may not be as accurate, timely, complete, or relevant as it appears. People often think that because a computer performed the calculations, the answer must be correct—especially if the answer is calculated to several decimal places. But if the initial information was flawed, all resultant computations using it are likely to be flawed as well. And as discussed in the *World of Management*, information systems linking people who speak different languages can also have limited effectiveness.

Table 22.1

Limitations of Information Systems

Although information systems play a vital role in modern organizations, they are not without their limitations. In particular, information systems have six basic limitations. For example, one major limitation of installing an information system is cost. For a large company, an information system might cost several million dollars.

1. Information systems are expensive and difficult to develop and implement.
2. Information systems are not suitable for all tasks or problems.
3. Managers sometimes rely on information systems too much.
4. Information provided to managers may not be as accurate, timely, complete, or relevant as it first appears.
5. Managers may have unrealistic expectations of what the information system can do.
6. The information system may be subject to sabotage, computer viruses, or downtime.

WORLD OF MANAGEMENT

TOO MUCH LOST IN THE TRANSLATION

Can translation technology help businesses bring their World Wide Web pages to the world? That's what Vladimir Bogdanov, president of Allmusic.com, needed to do when he purchased software to translate his site's text from English into six languages for a global audience interested in music and musicians. Unfortunately, the translations were far from polished; Bogdanov says that international readers actually laughed at the quirky wording. He quickly arranged for traditional translation services, choosing the human touch over the electronic approach.

Numerous web sites offer free, instant translation services for those who want to communicate messages in other languages. At the AltaVista Babel Fish site (http://world.altavista.com), for example, users simply choose the languages being translated to and from, then type in the words, phrases, or sentences to be translated. At a click of the mouse, the site prepares a literal translation. Because translations are basically word for word, single words or phrases often translate more smoothly than sentences.

Even web sites such as Multicity.com (http://www.multicity.com), which specializes in translating conversations to support chat and instant messaging functions in several European languages, have difficulty with the meaning of idioms and slang terms. As a result, chatters fare better when they avoid slang and follow standard grammatical conventions instead. Users seeking to translate just one or two words can find the foreign-language equivalents on Allwords.com and, at a click, hear the correct pronunciations.

People who communicate on-line in languages other than English sometimes face the problem of writing words in a different alphabet or character set, such as Cyrillic or Hindi. WordWalla.com (http://www.WordWalla.com) comes to the rescue with an on-line keyboard that shows the correct characters for the chosen language. Of course, users must be familiar with the language to operate this system.

The machine translation did such a crude job and put words in such odd places.

— Vladimir Bogdanov, president of Allmusic.com*

Researchers are working on artificial intelligence systems capable of identifying and translating the subtle nuances of more sophisticated messages without human intervention. For now, however, many companies are turning to professional translators rather than risk simplistic or laughable electronic translations.

Reference: Silvia Sansoni, "Tongue-Tied," *Forbes,* September 11, 2000, p. 80 (quote on p. 80).

Managers sometimes have unrealistic expectations about what information systems can accomplish. They may believe that the first stage of implementation will result in a full-blown communication network that a child could use. When the manager comes to see the flaws and limits of the system, she or he may become disappointed and, as a result, not use the system effectively. Finally, the information system may be subject to sabotage, computer viruses, or downtime. Disgruntled employees have been known to enter false data deliberately. And a company that relies too much on a computerized information system may find itself totally paralyzed in the event of a simple power outage or a crippling computer virus.

MANAGEMENT IMPLICATIONS   Managers should know the processes involved in establishing an information system. They should know how to integrate and use information systems as they are being created and after they have been implemented. Security issues are a growing concern. Knowing the limitations of information systems is quite important.

The Impact of Information Systems on Organizations

Information systems are clearly an important part of most modern organizations. Their effects are felt in various ways. Indeed, the rapid growth of information technologies has changed the very structure of business organizations.

Leaner Organizations

Information networks are leading to leaner companies with fewer employees and simpler structures. Because today's networked firm can maintain information links between both employees and customers, more work can be accomplished with fewer people. Bank customers, for example, can dial into a twenty-four-hour information system and find out their current balances from a digital voice. In the industrial sector, assembly workers at an IBM plant used to receive instructions from supervisors or special staff. Now instructions are delivered electronically to their workstations.

Widespread reductions in middle-management positions and the elimination of several layers in organizational structure are possible because information networks now provide direct communications between the top managers and workers at lower levels. The operating managers who formerly communicated company policies, procedures, or work instructions to lower-level employees are being replaced by electronic information networks.

More Flexible Operations

Electronic networks allow businesses to offer customers greater variety and faster delivery cycles. Recovery after heart surgery, for example, is expedited by custom-tailored rehabilitation programs designed with integrated information systems.

Each personalized program integrates the patient's history with information from physicians and rehabilitation specialists and then matches the patient with an electronically monitored exercise regimen. Products such as cellular phones, PCs, and audio systems can be custom-ordered, too, with the customer's choice of features and options and next-day delivery. The principle is called mass-customization: although companies produce in large volumes, each unit features the unique variations and options that the customer prefers.

Flexible production and fast delivery depend on an integrated network to coordinate all the transactions, activities, and process flows necessary to make quick adjustments in the production process. The ability to organize and store massive volumes of information is crucial, as are the electronic links among customers, manufacturers, materials suppliers, and shippers.

Increased Collaboration

Collaboration, not only among internal units but with outside firms as well, is on the rise because networked systems make it cheaper and easier to contact everyone, whether they are other employees or outside organizations.[15] Aided by intranets, more companies are learning that complex problems can be solved better by means of collaboration, either in formal teams or through spontaneous interaction. In the new networked organization, decisions that were once the domain of individuals are now shared as both people and departments have become more interdependent. The design of new products, for example, was once an engineering responsibility. Now, it can be a shared responsibility because so much information is accessible for evaluation from various perspectives: marketing, finance, production, engineering, and purchasing can share their different stores of information and determine the best overall design.

Naturally, networked systems are also helpful in *business-to-business* relationships. Increasingly, organizational buyers and suppliers are becoming so closely networked that they sometimes seem to be working for one organization. In the financial services industry, for example, institutional investors are networked with investment bankers, thus allowing efficient buying and selling of initial stock offerings. In manufacturing, Ford's parts suppliers are linked to Ford's extranet. Because they know Ford's current production schedule and upcoming requirements, they can move materials into Ford plants more quickly and more accurately.

A step toward even greater collaboration between companies—the so-called virtual company—has become possible through networking. As we saw in Chapter 12, a virtual company can be a temporary team assembled by a single organization. But a virtual company can also be created when several firms join forces. Each contributes different skills and resources that, collectively, result in a competitive business that would not be feasible for any of the collaborators acting alone. A company with marketing and promotional skills, for example, may team up with firms that are experts in warehousing and distribution, engineering, and production. Networking allows collaborators to exchange ideas, plan daily activities, share customer information, and otherwise coordinate their efforts, even if their respective facilities are far apart.

Advances in information systems are affecting organizations today in a wide variety of ways. One area of change involves more flexible work sites. Take Carla Patterson, for instance. Ms. Patterson is a field representative for Nebraska's Department of Economic Development. She spends about half of her work time in the office, but spends the other half working at home. But because she is so extensively networked into the agency's information systems, most of her colleagues don't know when Ms. Patterson is at home and when she is in her office.

More Flexible Work Sites

Geographic separation of the workplace from company headquarters is more common than ever because of networked organizations. Employees no longer work only at the office or the factory, nor are all of a company's operations performed at one location. The sales manager for an advertising agency may visit the company office in New York once every two weeks, preferring instead to work over the firm's electronic network from her home office in Florida. A medical researcher for the Cleveland Clinic may work at a home office networked into the clinic's system.[16]

A company's activities may also be geographically scattered but highly coordinated thanks to a networked system. Many e-businesses, for example, conduct no activities at one centralized location. When you order products from an Internet storefront—say, a chair, a sofa, a table, and two lamps—the chair may come from a cooperating warehouse in Philadelphia and the lamps from a manufacturer in California, while the sofa and table may be shipped directly from two manufacturers in North Carolina. All these activities are launched instantaneously by the customer's order and coordinated through the network, just as if all were being processed at one location.[17]

Improved Management Processes

Networked systems have changed the very nature of the management process. The activities, methods, and procedures of today's manager differ significantly from those that were common just a few years ago. Once, for example, upper-level managers did not concern themselves with all the detailed information that filtered upward in the workplace because it was expensive to gather, slow in coming, and quickly became out of date. Workplace management was delegated to middle and first-line managers.

With networked systems, however, instantaneous information is accessible in a convenient, useable format. Consequently, more and more upper managers use it routinely for planning, leading, directing, and controlling operations. Today, a top manager can find out the current status of any customer order, inspect productivity statistics for each workstation, and analyze the delivery performance of any driver and vehicle. More important, managers can better coordinate companywide performance. They can identify departments that are working well together and those that are creating bottlenecks. Hershey's networked system, for example, includes SAP—an enterprise-resource-planning model—that identifies the current status of any order and traces its progress from order entry through customer delivery receipt of payment. Progress and delays at intermediate stages—materials ordering, inventory availability, production scheduling, packaging, warehousing, distribution—can be checked continuously to determine which operations should be coordinated more closely with others to improve overall performance.

Changed Employee Behaviors

Information systems also directly affect the behaviors of people in organizations. Some of these effects are positive; others can be negative. On the plus side, information systems usually improve individual efficiency. Some people also enjoy their work more because they have fun using the new technology. As a result of computerized bulletin boards and e-mail, groups can form across organizational boundaries.

On the negative side, information systems can lead to isolation because people have everything they need to do their jobs without interacting with others. Managers can work at home easily, with the possible side effects of making them unavailable to others who need them or removing them from key parts of the social system. Computerized working arrangements also tend to be much less personal than other methods. For example, a computer-transmitted "pat on the back" will likely mean less than a real one. Researchers are just beginning to determine how individual behaviors and attitudes are affected by information systems.[18]

MANAGEMENT IMPLICATIONS Managers should be aware of several different ways in which information technology can affect—and is affecting—their organizations and how they work. They should also be aware of the fact that these effects can be positive or negative.

Summary of Key Points

Information is a vital part of every manager's job. For information to be useful, it must be accurate, timely, complete, and relevant. Information technology is best conceived of as part of the control process. Information technology systems contain five basic components: an input medium, a processor, storage, a control system, and an output medium. While the final form will vary, both manual and computerized information systems have these components.

An organization's information technology needs are determined by several factors, most notably user groups and system requirements. There are several basic kinds of information systems, including transaction-processing systems, basic management information systems, decision support systems, and executive information systems. Each provides certain types of information and is most valuable for specific types of managers. Each should also be matched to the needs of user groups.

Managing information systems involves five basic elements. The first is deciding how to create information systems. Of course, this step actually involves a wide array of specific activities and steps. The systems must then be integrated. Managers must then be able to use them. Information security is also an important consideration in managing information systems. Finally, managers should be aware of the limitations of information systems.

Information systems affect organizations in various ways. Major influences include leaner organizations, more flexible operations, increased collaboration, more flexible work sites, improved management processes, and changed employee behaviors.

Discussion Questions

Questions for Review

1. What are the characteristics of useful information? How can information management aid in organizational control?
2. What are the building blocks of information systems? How are they related to one another?
3. What is a management information system? How can such a system be used to benefit an organization?
4. What is an expert system? Do such systems have any significant potential for use by business organizations? Why or why not?

Questions for Analysis

5. In what ways is a management information system like an inventory control system or a production control system? In what ways is it different?
6. It has been said that the information revolution now occurring is like the industrial revolution in terms of the magnitude of its impact on organizations and society. What leads to such a view? Why might that view be an overstatement?
7. Is it possible for "information experts" in an organization to become too powerful? If so, how might the situation be prevented? If not, why not?

Questions for Application

8. Interview a local business manager about the use of information in his or her organization. How is information managed? Is a computer system used? How well is the information system integrated with other aspects of organizational control?
9. Your college or university library deals in information. What kind of information system is used? Is it computerized? How might the information system be redesigned to be of more value to you?
10. Go to the library and see if you can locate a reference on the use of an expert system in a business firm. If you can, share it with the class. Why might this assignment be difficult?

BUILDING EFFECTIVE *communication* SKILLS

Exercise Overview

Communication skills refer to the manager's abilities both to convey ideas and information effectively to others and to receive ideas and information from others effectively. This exercise will help you see how communication skills relate to information technology.

Exercise Background

Newer forms of information technology like e-mail and cellular telephones are changing the ways that managers communicate with one another. In some ways, these forms of communication are similar to earlier forms, but in other ways they are fundamentally different.

Go to the library and research the business literature from the 1960s. Look specifically for how-to articles dealing with telephone etiquette and letter-writing fundamentals. Find at least one list of dos and don'ts about each form of communication.

Exercise Task

With the background information above as context, do the following:

1. Identify suggestions from each list that seem to be just as applicable to modern forms of information technology.

2. Identify suggestions from each list that do not seem to be applicable to modern forms of information technology.

3. Compile your own how-to list for using modern information technology.

4. Add to your list suggestions for using other forms of information technology, such as facsimiles and voice-mail.

BUILDING EFFECTIVE *interpersonal* SKILLS

Exercise Overview

Interpersonal skills refer to the ability to communicate with, understand, and motivate individuals and groups. Information technology has obvious links with interpersonal skills.

Exercise Background

Your company is at the forefront of modern information technology. All of your managers have voice-mail and e-mail, all are networked, and many have started working at home. They point out that they are more productive at home and don't really need to come into the office every day to get their work done. And indeed, productivity is booming.

But a situation recently arose and has caused you some concern. Specifically, you have two employees who have each worked for you for almost six months and who communicate with one another on a regular basis—but have not met face to face. Because you have always thought of your company as a warm and friendly place to work, you are alarmed that you may be losing these characteristics.

Exercise Task

With the background information above as context, do the following:

1. Decide whether or not face-to-face communication is important today.

2. If it is, develop a plan for enhancing interpersonal relations among your employees without losing the competitive advantage you have gained from information technology.

3. If it is not, develop a rationale that you might use to placate or comfort an employee who complains about the lack of interpersonal relations.

BUILDING EFFECTIVE *time-management* SKILLS

Exercise Overview

Time-management skills refer to the manager's ability to prioritize work, to work efficiently, and to delegate appropriately. This exercise focuses on how time management and information technology relate to one another.

Exercise Background

One of the biggest implied advantages of modern information technology today is time management—modern technology is supposed to make us more productive and more efficient and make it easier to communicate with one another. At the same time, most people acknowledge that information technology can also get out of hand.

Listed below are five forms of information technology:

1. Cellular telephone
2. E-mail
3. Voice-mail
4. Internet
5. Facsimile machine

Start this exercise by thinking of ways that each form can both save and waste time.

Exercise Task

With the background information above as context, do the following:

1. Describe what a manager can do to capitalize on the advantages and minimize the disadvantages of each form of information technology in terms of time management.
2. Some managers have argued that they have become more efficient by turning off one or more of these information technology devices. Critique this idea from a time-management perspective.
3. Identify two other forms of information technology you use and characterize them in terms of time management.

DAIMLERCHRYSLER DRIVES ONTO THE WEB

Should web-based services be built into the dashboard or accessed through portable devices such as cell phones? That's only one of the issues facing DaimlerChrysler in its quest to offer drivers the latest and greatest information technology in vehicles of the future. With the Internet changing every day and competing auto makers moving forward with an array of high-tech initiatives, DaimlerChrysler is revving up its North American research and technology center in Palo Alto, California, to locate and lock up consumer-friendly technology for tomorrow's cars, vans, and trucks. The company also wants to use web-based technology to deliver various services to car buyers, such as information about local traffic and entertainment, as well as to boost operational efficiency.

To start, the auto maker set up a multimillion-dollar venture-capital fund and is buying stakes in outside firms that make promising new technologies. In one recent deal, DaimlerChrysler paid $3.8 million to invest in Iteris, a company that is preparing a device to warn commercial truckers when their vehicles are drifting out of the lane. However, the company will have to step harder on its accelerator pedal to keep up with the speedy pace of deal-making in Silicon Valley, where many technology start-ups are based.

DaimlerChrysler lost an early opportunity to acquire ImpulseSale.com, a start-up that plans to beam advertisements to drivers' cell phones. Despite three meetings and serious negotiations, the acquisition decision had to thread its way through DaimlerChrysler's bureaucracy—not an easy or fast process in an organization with key executives and operations on two continents. In the meantime, a faster-moving firm bought ImpulseSale.com before DaimlerChrysler made its final decision. Now the German headquarters of Daimler-Chrysler has transferred a venture-capital manager to its research and technology office in Palo Alto, a move that should expedite decisions.

Still, DaimlerChrysler is as an automotive manufacturer with relatively little experience evaluating and backing risky high-tech ventures. To implement its Internet strategy, the company must determine when it would be most advantageous to develop a technology internally and when it would be better to use outside sources. It must also weigh the merits of taking a small stake in a start-up versus negotiating to acquire it. For example, the company took a stake in VirtualBank, which is setting up a system to allow customers to handle financial services transactions via their cell phones.

On a broader scale, DaimlerChrysler is using the Internet to improve productivity through more efficient on-line purchasing and other activities. The company joined with General Motors, Ford, Renault, and Nissan to form Covisint, a business-to-business (B2B) on-line marketplace where all of the auto makers can make deals with more than thirty thousand suppliers of parts, components, and services. It also took a stake in The Cobalt Group and hired the company to build 2,100 e-commerce web sites for Chrysler, Jeep, and Dodge dealers. These sites will provide buyers with up-to-date information such as vehicle specifications, rebates, model availability, pricing, and other details.

In all, DaimlerChrysler is ready to invest $100 million in building its Internet initiatives to add dot-com pizzazz to its automotive business. Chairman Jürgen Schrempp sees great potential in web-based technology, and he's putting his executive muscle behind speedier implementation of the company's various strategies. Between the operational savings from higher productivity and the potential revenue from devices and services based on new technology, DaimlerChrysler stands to profit from steering in the direction of the web.

Case Questions

1. Why would DaimlerChrysler want separate web sites for its dealers rather than offering one integrated web-based system shared by all dealers?

2. How might DaimlerChrysler's Internet activities contribute to its ability to improve product and service quality?

3. Identify the new service technologies in which DaimlerChrysler is involved. What other service technology innovations should the company consider investing in?

Case References

Robert Conlin, "DaimlerChrysler to Unveil Internet Division," *E-Commerce Times*, June 21, 2000, http://www.ecommercetimes.com/news/articles2000/000621-7.shtml (October 6, 2000); Ephraim Schwartz, "Go Shopping on the Subway," *InfoWorld*, June 23, 2000, http://www.cnn.com/2000/tech/computing/06/23/mobile.buy.idg (October 6, 2000); Jeffrey Ball, "DaimlerChrysler Hires a Silicon Valley Gadfly to Map Its Web Drive," *Wall Street Journal*, April 27, 2000, pp. B1, B4.

CHAPTER NOTES

1. Leigh Buchana, "The Smartest Little Company in America," *Inc.*, January 1999, pp. 43–54; Chad Abresch and Craig Johnson, "Productivity Plus," *Business and Health*, September 2000, p. 55.

2. See Michael H. Zack, "Managing Codified Knowledge," *Sloan Management Review*, Summer 1999, pp. 45–58.

3. Donald A. Marchand, William J. Kettinger, and John D. Rollins, "Information Orientation: People, Technology, and the Bottom Line," *Sloan Management Review*, Summer 2000, pp. 69–79.

4. Edward W. Desmond, "How Your Data May Soon Seek You Out," *Fortune*, September 13, 1997, pp. 149–154.

5. William J. Bruns, Jr., and F. Warren McFarlin, "Information Technology Puts Power in Control Systems," *Harvard Business Review*, September–October 1987, pp. 89–94.

6. N. Venkatraman, "IT-Enable Business Transformation: From Automation to Business Scope Redefinition," *Sloan Management Review*, Winter 1994, pp. 73–84.

7. Kenneth C. Laudon and Jane P. Laudon, *Essentials of Management Information Systems*, 3rd Edition (Upper Saddle River, NJ: Prentice Hall, 1999), p. 267.

8. Laudon and Laudon, *Essentials of Management Information Systems*, p. 270.

9. See "The Killer Ad Machine," *Forbes*, December 11, 2000, pp. 168–178.

10. Mary Cronin, "Ford's Intranet Success," *Fortune*, March 30, 1998, p. 158.

11. "The Messy Business of Culling Company Files," *Wall Street Journal*, May 22, 1997, pp. B1, B2.

12. "Software That Plows Through Possibilities," *Business Week*, August 7, 2000, p. 84.

13. See "Do One Thing, and Do It Well," *Business Week*, June 19, 2000, pp. 94–100.

14. For example, see "Swamped Workers Switch to 'Unlisted' E-Mails," *USA Today*, September 7, 1999, p. 1A.

15. Robert Kraut, Charles Steinfield, Alice P. Chan, Brian Butler, and Anne Hoag, "Coordination and Virtualization: The Role of Electronic Networks and Personal Relationships," *Organization Science*, Vol. 10, No. 6, 1999, pp. 722–740.

16. See Mahmoud M. Watad and Frank J. DiSanzo, "The Synergism of Telecommuting and Office Automation," *Sloan Management Review*, Winter 2000, pp. 85–96.

17. Manju K. Ahuja and Kathleen M. Carley, "Network Structure in Virtual Organizations," *Organization Science*, Vol. 10, No. 6, 1999, pp. 741–757.

18. "Worksite Face-Off: Techie vs. User," *USA Today*, June 17, 1997, pp. B1, B2.

Tools for Planning and Decision Making

This appendix discusses a number of the basic tools and techniques that managers can use to enhance the efficiency and effectiveness of planning and decision making. We first describe forecasting, an extremely important tool, and then discuss several other planning techniques. Next we discuss several tools that relate more to decision making. We conclude by assessing the strengths and weaknesses of the various tools and techniques.

Forecasting

To plan, managers must make assumptions about future events. But unlike wizards of old, planners cannot simply look into a crystal ball. Instead, they must develop forecasts of probable future circumstances. **Forecasting** is the process of developing assumptions or premises about the future that managers can use in planning or decision making.

forecasting The process of developing assumptions or premises about the future that managers can use in planning or decision making

Sales and Revenue Forecasting

As the term implies, **sales forecasting** is concerned with predicting future sales. Because monetary resources (derived mainly from sales) are necessary to finance both current and future operations, knowledge of future sales is of vital importance. Sales forecasting is something that every business, from Exxon to a neighborhood pizza parlor, must do. Consider, for example, the following questions that a manager might need to answer:

sales forecasting The prediction of future sales

1. How much of each of our products should we produce next week? next month? next year?
2. How much money will we have available to spend on research and development and on new-product test marketing?
3. When and to what degree will we need to expand our existing production facilities?
4. How should we respond to union demands for a 5 percent pay increase?
5. If we borrow money for expansion, when can we pay it back?

None of these questions can be answered adequately without some notion of what future revenues are likely to be. Thus, sales forecasting is generally one of the first steps in planning.

Unfortunately, the term *sales forecasting* suggests that this form of forecasting is appropriate only for organizations that have something to sell. But other kinds of organizations also depend on financial resources, and so they also must forecast. The University of South Carolina, for example, must forecast future state aid before planning course offerings, staff size, and so on. Hospitals must forecast their future income from patient fees, insurance payments, and other sources to assess their ability to expand. Although we will continue to use the conventional term, keep in mind that what is really at issue is **revenue forecasting**.

revenue forecasting The prediction of future revenues from all sources

Several sources of information are used to develop a sales forecast. Previous sales figures and any obvious trends, such as the company's growth or stability, usually serve as the base. General economic indicators, technological improvements, new marketing strategies, and the competition's behavior all may be added together to ensure an accurate forecast. Once projected, the sales (or revenues) forecast becomes a guiding framework for various other activities. Raw-material expenditures, advertising budgets, sales-commission structures, and similar operating costs are all based on projected sales figures.

Organizations often forecast sales across several time horizons. The longer-run forecasts may then be updated and refined as various shorter-run cycles are completed. For obvious reasons, a forecast should be as accurate as possible, and the accuracy of sales forecasting tends to increase as organizations learn from their previous forecasting experience. But the more uncertain and complex future conditions are likely to be, the more difficult it is to develop accurate forecasts. To offset these problems partially, forecasts are more useful to managers if they are expressed as a range rather than as an absolute index or number. If projected sales increases are expected to be in the range of 10 to 12 percent, a manager can consider all the implications for the entire range. A 10 percent increase could dictate one set of activities; a 12 percent increase could call for a different set of activities.

Technological Forecasting

technological forecasting The prediction of what future technologies are likely to emerge and when they are likely to be economically feasible

Technological forecasting is another type of forecasting used by many organizations. It focuses on predicting what future technologies are likely to emerge and when they are likely to be economically feasible. In an era when technological breakthrough and innovation have become the rule rather than the exception, it is important that managers be able to anticipate new developments. If a manager invests heavily in existing technology (such as production processes, equipment, and computer systems) and the technology becomes obsolete in the near future, the company has wasted its resources.

The most striking technological innovations in recent years have been in electronics, especially semiconductors. Home computers, electronic games, and sophisticated communications equipment are all evidence of the electronics explosion. Given the increasing importance of technology and the rapid pace of technological innovation, it follows that managers will grow increasingly concerned with technological forecasting in the years to come.

Other Types of Forecasting

Other types of forecasting are also important to many organizations. Resource forecasting projects the organization's future needs for and the availability of human resources, raw materials, and other resources. General economic conditions are the subject of economic forecasts. For example, some organizations undertake population or market-size forecasting. Some organizations also attempt to forecast future government fiscal policy and various government regulations that might be put into practice. Indeed, almost any component in an organization's environment may be an appropriate area for forecasting.

Forecasting Techniques

To carry out the various kinds of forecasting we have identified, managers use several different techniques.[1] Time-series analysis and causal modeling are two common quantitative techniques.

Time-Series Analysis   The underlying assumption of **time-series analysis** is that the past is a good predictor of the future. This technique is most useful when the manager has a lot of historical data available and when stable trends and patterns are apparent. In a time-series analysis, the variable under consideration (such as sales or enrollment) is plotted across time, and a "best-fit" line is identified.[2] Figure A.1 shows how a time-series analysis might look. The dots represent the number of units sold for each year from 1994 through 2002. The best-fit line has also been drawn in. It is the line around which the dots cluster with the least variability. A manager who wants to know what sales to expect in 2003 simply extends the line. In this case the projection would be around eighty-two hundred units.

Real time-series analysis involves much more than simply plotting sales data and then using a ruler and a pencil to draw and extend the line. Sophisticated mathematical procedures, among other things, are necessary to account for seasonal and cyclical fluctuations and to identify the true best-fit line. In real situations, data seldom follow the neat pattern found in Figure A.1. Indeed, the data points may be so widely dispersed that they mask meaningful trends from all but painstaking, computer-assisted inspection.

time-series analysis A forecasting technique that extends past information into the future through the calculation of a best-fit line

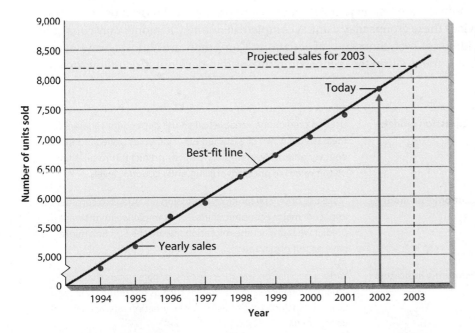

Figure A.1

An Example of Time-Series Analysis

Because time-series analysis assumes that the past is a good predictor of the future, it is most useful when historical data are available, trends are stable, and patterns are apparent. For example, it can be used for projecting estimated sales for products like shampoo, pens, and automobile tires. (Of course, few time-series analyses yield such clear results because there is almost always considerably more fluctuation in data from year to year.)

causal modeling A group of different techniques that determine casual relationships between different variables

regression model An equation that uses one set of variables to predict another variable

Causal Modeling Another useful forecasting technique is **causal modeling**. Actually, the term *causal modeling* represents a group of several techniques. Table A.1 summarizes three of the most useful approaches. **Regression models** are equations created to predict a variable (such as sales volume) that depends on several other variables (such as price and advertising). The variable being predicted is called the *dependent variable*; the variables used to make the prediction are called *independent variables*. A typical regression equation used by a small business might take this form:

$$y = ax_1 + bx_2 + cx_3 + d$$

where

y = the dependent variable (sales in this case)

x_1, x_2, and x_3 = independent variables (advertising budget, price, and commissions)

a, b, and c = weights for the independent variables calculated during development of the regression model

d = a constant

To use the model, a manager can insert various alternatives for advertising budget, price, and commissions into the equation and then compute y. The calculated value of y represents the forecasted level of sales, given various levels of advertising, price, and commissions.[3]

Econometric models employ regression techniques at a much more complex level. **Econometric models** attempt to predict major economic shifts and the potential impact of those shifts on the organization. They might be used to predict various age, ethnic, and economic groups that will characterize different regions of the United States in the year 2010 and also to predict the kinds of products and services these groups may want. A complete econometric model may consist of hundreds or even thousands of equations. Computers are almost always necessary to apply them. Given the complexities involved in developing econometric mod-

econometric model A causal model that predicts major economic shifts and the potential impact of those shifts on the organization

Table A.1

Summary of Causal Modeling Forecasting Techniques

Managers use several different types of causal models in planning and decision making. Three popular models are regression models, econometric models, and economic indicators.

Regression models	Used to predict one variable (called the dependent variable) on the basis of known or assumed other variables (called independent variables). For example, we might predict future sales based on the values of price, advertising, and economic levels.
Econometric models	Make use of several multiple-regression equations to consider the impact of major economic shifts. For example, we might want to predict what impact the migration toward the Sun Belt might have on our organization.
Economic indicators	Various population statistics, indexes, or parameters that predict organizationally relevant variables such as discretionary income. Examples include cost-of-living index, inflation rate, and level of unemployment.

els, many firms that decide to use them rely on outside consultants specializing in this approach.

Economic indicators, another form of causal model, are population statistics or indexes that reflect the economic well-being of a population. Examples of widely used economic indicators include the current rates of national productivity, inflation, and unemployment. In using such indicators, the manager draws on past experiences that have revealed a relationship between a certain indicator and some facet of the company's operations. Pitney Bowes Data Documents Division, for example, can predict future sales of its business forms largely on the basis of current GNP estimates and other economic growth indexes.

Qualitative Forecasting Techniques   Organizations also use several qualitative techniques to develop their forecasts. A **qualitative forecasting technique** relies more on individual or group judgment or opinion rather than on sophisticated mathematical analyses. The Delphi procedure, described in Chapter 9 as a mechanism for managing group decision-making activities, can also be used to develop forecasts. A variation of it—the *jury-of-expert-opinion* approach—involves using the basic Delphi process with members of top management. In this instance, top management serves as a collection of experts asked to make a prediction about something—competitive behavior, trends in product demand, and so forth. Either a pure Delphi or a jury-of-expert-opinion approach might be useful in technological forecasting.

The *sales-force-composition* method of sales forecasting is a pooling of the predictions and opinions of experienced salespeople. Because of their experience, these individuals are often able to forecast quite accurately what various customers will do. Management combines these forecasts and interprets the data to create plans. Textbook publishers use this procedure to project how many copies of a new title they might sell.

The *customer evaluation* technique goes beyond an organization's sales force and collects data from customers of the organization. The customers provide estimates of their own future needs for the goods and services that the organization supplies. Managers must combine, interpret, and act on this information. This approach, however, has two major limitations. Customers may be less interested in taking time to develop accurate predictions than are members of the organization itself, and the method makes no provision for including any new customers that the organization may acquire. Wal-Mart helps its suppliers use this approach by providing them with detailed projections regarding what it intends to buy several months in advance.

Selecting an appropriate forecasting technique can be as important as applying it correctly. Some techniques are appropriate only for specific circumstances. For example, the sales-force-composition technique is good only for sales forecasting. Other techniques, like the Delphi method, are useful in a variety of situations. Some techniques, such as the econometric models, require extensive use of computers, whereas others, such as customer evaluation models, can be used with little mathematical expertise. For the most part, selection of a particular technique depends on the nature of the problem, the experience and preferences of the manager, and available resources.[4]

economic indicator A key population statistic or index that reflects the economic well-being of a population

qualitative forecasting technique One of several techniques that rely on individual or group judgment rather than on mathematical analyses

Other Planning Techniques

Of course, planning involves more than just forecasting. Other tools and techniques that are useful for planning purposes include linear programming, breakeven analysis, and simulations.

Linear Programming

linear programming A planning technique that determines the optimal combination of resources and activities

Linear programming is one of the most widely used quantitative tools for planning. **Linear programming** is a procedure for calculating the optimal combination of resources and activities. It is appropriate when there is some objective to be met (such as a sales quota or a certain production level) within a set of constraints (such as a limited advertising budget or limited production capabilities).

To illustrate how linear programming can be used, assume that a small electronics company produces two basic products—a high-quality cable television tuner and a high-quality receiver for picking up television audio and playing it through a stereo amplifier. Both products go through the same two departments, first production and then inspection and testing. Each product has a known profit margin and a high level of demand. The production manager's job is to produce the optimal combination of tuners (T) and receivers (R) that maximizes profits and uses the time in production (PR) and in inspection and testing (IT) most efficiently. Table A.2 gives the information needed for the use of linear programming to solve this problem.

The *objective function* is an equation that represents what we want to achieve. In technical terms, it is a mathematical representation of the desirability of the consequences of a particular decision. In our example, the objective function can be represented as follows:

$$\text{Maximize profit} = \$30X_T + \$20X_R$$

where

R = the number of receivers to be produced

T = the number of tuners to be produced

The \$30 and \$20 figures are the respective profit margins of the tuner and receiver, as noted in Table A.2. The objective, then, is to maximize profits.

However, this objective must be accomplished within a specific set of constraints. In our example, the constraints are the time required to produce each product in each department and the total amount of time available. These data are also found in Table A.2 and can be used to construct the relevant constraint equations:

$$10T + 6R \leq 150$$

$$4T + 4R \leq 80$$

(that is, we cannot use more capacity than is available), and of course,

$$T \geq 0$$

$$R \geq 0$$

Table A.2

Production Data for Tuners and Receivers

Linear programming can be used to determine the optimal number of tuners and receivers an organization might make. Essential information needed to perform this analysis includes the number of hours each product spends in each department, the production capacity for each department, and the profit margin for each product.

Department	Number of Hours Required per Unit		Production Capacity for Day (in Hours)
	Tuners (T)	Receivers (R)	
Production (PR)	10	6	150
Inspection and testing (IT)	4	4	80
Profit margin	$30	$20	

The set of equations consisting of the objective function and constraints can be solved graphically. To start, we assume that production of each product is maximized when production of the other is at zero. The resultant solutions are then plotted on a coordinate axis. In the PR department, if $T = 0$ then:

$$10T + 6R \leq 150$$

$$10(0) + 6R \leq 150$$

$$R \leq 25$$

In the same department, if $R = 0$ then:

$$10T + 6(R) \leq 150$$

$$10T + 6(0) \leq 150$$

$$T \leq 15$$

Similarly, in the IT department, if no tuners are produced,

$$4T + 4R \leq 80$$

$$4(0) + 4R \leq 80$$

$$R \leq 20$$

and, if no receivers are produced,

$$4T + 4R \leq 80$$

$$4T + 4(0) \leq 80$$

$$T \leq 20$$

The four resulting inequalities are graphed in Figure A.2. The shaded region represents the feasibility space, or production combinations that do not exceed the capacity of either department. The optimal number of products will be defined at one of the four

Figure A.2

The Graphical Solution of a Linear Programming Problem

Finding the graphical solution to a linear programming problem is useful when only two alternatives are being considered. When problems are more complex, computers that can execute hundreds of equations and variables are necessary. Virtually all large firms, such as General Motors, Texaco, and Sears, use linear programming.

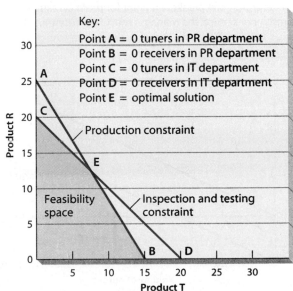

Key:
Point A = 0 tuners in PR department
Point B = 0 receivers in PR department
Point C = 0 tuners in IT department
Point D = 0 receivers in IT department
Point E = optimal solution

corners of the shaded area—that is, the firm should produce twenty receivers only (point C), fifteen tuners only (point B), thirteen receivers and seven tuners (point E), or no products at all. With the constraint that production of both tuners and receivers must be greater than zero, it follows that point E is the optimal solution. That combination requires 148 hours in PR and 80 hours in IT and yields $470 in profit. (Note that if only receivers were produced, the profit would be $400; producing only tuners would mean $450 in profit.)

Unfortunately, only two alternatives can be handled by the graphical method, and our example was extremely simple. When there are other alternatives, a complex algebraic method must be employed. Real-world problems may require several hundred equations and variables. Clearly, computers are necessary to execute such sophisticated analyses. Linear programming is a powerful technique, playing a key role in both planning and decision making. It can be used to schedule production, select an optimal portfolio of investments, allocate sales representatives to territories, or produce an item at some minimum cost.

Breakeven Analysis

Linear programming is called a *normative procedure* because it prescribes the optimal solution to a problem. Breakeven analysis is a *descriptive procedure* because it simply describes relationships among variables; then it is up to the manager to make decisions. We can define **breakeven analysis** as a procedure for identifying the point at which revenues start covering their associated costs. It might be used to analyze the effects on profits of different price and output combinations or various levels of output.

breakeven analysis A procedure for identifying the point at which revenues start covering their associated costs

Figure A.3 represents the key cost variables in breakeven analysis. Creating most products or services includes three types of costs: fixed costs, variable costs, and total costs. *Fixed costs* are costs that are incurred regardless of what volume of output is being generated. They include rent or mortgage payments on the building, managerial salaries, and depreciation of plant and equipment. *Variable costs* vary with the number of units produced, such as the cost of raw materials and direct labor used to make each unit. *Total costs* are fixed costs plus variable costs. Note that because of fixed costs, the line for total costs never begins at zero.

Other important factors in breakeven analysis are revenue and profit. *Revenue*, the total dollar amount of sales, is computed by multiplying the number of units sold by the sales price of each unit. *Profit* is then determined by subtracting total costs from total revenues. When revenues and total costs are plotted on the same axes, the breakeven graph shown in Figure A.4 emerges. The point at which the lines representing total costs and total revenues cross is the breakeven point. If the company represented in Figure A.4

Figure A.3

An Example of Cost Factors for Breakeven Analysis

To determine the breakeven point for profit on sales for a product or service, the manager must first determine both fixed and variable costs. These costs are then combined to show total costs.

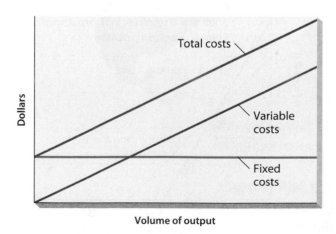

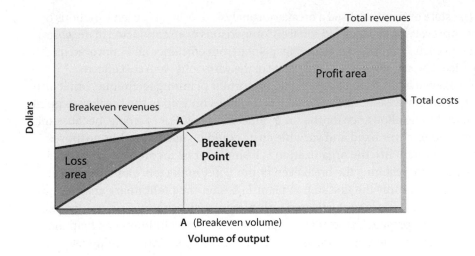

Figure A.4

Breakeven Analysis

After total costs are determined and graphed, the manager then graphs the total revenues that will be earned on different levels of sales. The regions defined by the intersection of the two graphs show loss and profit areas. The intersection itself shows the breakeven point—the level of sales at which all costs are covered but no profits are earned.

sells more units than are represented by point A, it will realize a profit; selling below that level will result in a loss.

Mathematically, the breakeven point (expressed as units of production or volume) is shown by the formula

$$BP = \frac{TFC}{P - VC}$$

where

BP = breakeven point

TFC = total fixed costs

P = price per unit

VC = variable cost per unit

Assume that you are considering the production of a new garden hoe with a curved handle. You have determined that an acceptable selling price will be $20. You have also determined that the variable costs per hoe will be $15, and you have total fixed costs of $400,000 per year. The question is, How many hoes must you sell each year to break even? Using the breakeven model, you find that

$$BP = \frac{TFC}{P - VC}$$

$$BP = \frac{400,000}{20 - 15}$$

BP = 80,000 units

Thus, you must sell eighty thousand hoes to break even. Further analysis would also show that if you could raise your price to $25 per hoe, you would need to sell only forty thousand to break even, and so on.

The state of New York used a breakeven analysis to evaluate seven variations of prior approvals for its Medicaid service. Comparisons were conducted of the costs involved in each variation against savings gained from efficiency and improved quality of service. The state found that only three of the variations were cost effective.[5]

Breakeven analysis is a popular and important planning technique, but it also has noteworthy weaknesses. It considers revenues only up to the breakeven point, and it makes no allowance for the time value of money. For example, because the funds used to cover fixed and variable costs could be used for other purposes (such as investment), the organization is losing interest income by tying up its money prior to reaching the breakeven point. Thus, managers often used breakeven analysis as only the first step in planning. After the preliminary analysis has been completed, more sophisticated techniques (such as rate-of-return analysis or discounted-present-value analysis) are used. Those techniques can help the manager decide whether to proceed or to divert resources into other areas.

Simulations

organizational simulation A model of a real-world situation that can be manipulated to discover how it functions

Another useful planning device is simulation. The word *simulate* means to copy or to represent. An **organizational simulation** is a model of a real-world situation that can be manipulated to discover how it functions. Simulation is a descriptive, rather than a prescriptive, technique. Northern Research & Engineering Corporation is an engineering consulting firm that helps clients plan new factories. By using a sophisticated factory simulation model, the firm recently helped a client cut several machines and operations from a new plant and to save over $750,000.

To consider another example, suppose the city of Houston was going to build a new airport. Issues to be addressed might include the number of runways, the direction of those runways, the number of terminals and gates, the allocation of various carriers among the terminals and gates, and the technology and human resources needed to achieve a target frequency of takeoffs and landings. (Of course, actually planning such an airport would involve many more variables than these.) A model could be constructed to simulate these factors, as well as their interrelationships. The planner could then insert several different values for each factor and observe the probable results.

Simulation problems are in some ways similar to those addressed by linear programming, but simulation is more useful in very complex situations characterized by diverse constraints and opportunities. The development of sophisticated simulation models may require the expertise of outside specialists or consultants, and the complexity of simulation almost always necessitates the use of a computer. For these reasons, simulation is most likely to be used as a technique for planning in large organizations that have the required resources.

PERT

PERT A planning tool that uses a network to plan projects involving numerous activities and their interrelationships

A final planning tool that we will discuss is PERT. **PERT**, an acronym for Program Evaluation and Review Technique, was developed by the U.S. Navy to help coordinate the activities of three thousand contractors during the development of the

Polaris nuclear submarine, and it was credited with saving two years of work on the project. It has subsequently been used by most large companies in different ways. The purpose of PERT is to develop a network of activities and their interrelationships and thus highlight critical time intervals that affect the overall project. PERT follows six basic steps:

1. Identify the activities to be performed and the events that will mark their completion.
2. Develop a network showing the relationships among the activities and events.
3. Calculate the time needed for each event and the time necessary to get from each event to the next.
4. Identify within the network the longest path that leads to completion of the project. This path is called the critical path.
5. Refine the network.
6. Use the network to control the project.

Suppose that a marketing manager wants to use PERT to plan the test marketing and nationwide introduction of a new product. Table A.3 identifies the basic steps involved in carrying out this project. The activities are then arranged in a network like the one shown in Figure A.5. In the figure, each completed event is represented by a number in a circle. The activities are indicated by letters on the lines connecting the events. Notice that some activities are performed independently of one another and that others must be performed in sequence. For example, test production (activity a) and test site location (activity c) can be done at the same time, but test site location has to be done before actual testing (activities f and g) can be done.

Activities		Events	
		1	Origin of project.
a	Produce limited quantity for test marketing.	2	Completion of production for test marketing.
b	Design preliminary package.	3	Completion of design for preliminary package.
c	Locate test market.	4	Test market located.
d	Obtain local merchant cooperation.	5	Local merchant cooperation obtained.
e	Ship product to selected retail outlets.	6	Product for test marketing shipped to retail outlets.
f	Monitor sales and customer reactions.	7	Sales and customer reactions monitored.
g	Survey customers in test-market area.	8	Customers in test-market area surveyed.
h	Make needed product changes.	9	Product changes made.
i	Make needed package changes.	10	Package changes made.
j	Mass-produce the product.	11	Product mass-produced.
k	Begin national advertising.	12	National advertising carried out.
l	Begin national distribution.	13	National distribution completed.

Table A.3

Activities and Events for Introducing a New Product
PERT is used to plan schedules for projects, and it is particularly useful when many activities with critical time intervals must be coordinated. Besides launching a new product, PERT is useful for projects like constructing a new factory or building, remodeling an office, or opening a new store.

Figure A.5

A PERT Network for Introducing a New Product

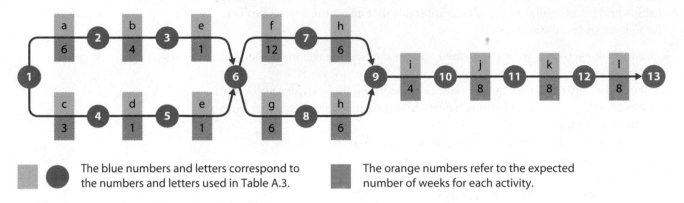

The blue numbers and letters correspond to the numbers and letters used in Table A.3.

The orange numbers refer to the expected number of weeks for each activity.

The time needed to get from one activity to another is then determined. The normal way to calculate the time between each activity is to average the most optimistic, most pessimistic, and most likely times, with the most likely time weighted by 4. Time is usually calculated with the following formula:

$$\text{Expected time} = \frac{a + 4b + c}{6}$$

where

a = optimistic time

b = most likely time

c = pessimistic time

critical path The longest path through a PERT network

The expected number of weeks for each activity in our example is shown in parentheses along each path in Figure A.5. The **critical path**—or the longest path through the PERT network—is then identified. This path is considered critical because it shows the shortest time in which the project can be completed. In our example, the critical path is 1-2-3-6-7-9-10-11-12-13, totaling fifty-seven weeks. PERT thus tells the manager that the project will take fifty-seven weeks to complete.

The first network may be refined. If fifty-seven weeks to completion is too long a time, the manager might decide to begin preliminary package design before the test products are finished. Or the manager might decide that ten weeks rather than twelve is a sufficient time period to monitor sales. The idea is that if the critical path can be shortened, so too can the overall duration of the project. The PERT network serves as an ongoing framework for both planning and control throughout the project. For example, the manager can use it to monitor where the project is relative to where it needs to be. Thus, if an activity on the critical path takes longer than planned, the manager needs to make up the time elsewhere or live with the fact that the entire project will be late.

Decision-Making Tools

Managers can also use a number of tools that relate more specifically to decision making than to planning. Two commonly used decision-making tools are payoff matrices and decision trees.

Payoff Matrices

A **payoff matrix** specifies the probable value of different alternatives, depending on different possible outcomes associated with each. The use of a payoff matrix requires that several alternatives be available, that several different events could occur, and that the consequences depend on which alternative is selected and on which event or set of events occurs. An important concept in understanding the payoff matrix, then, is probability. A **probability** is the likelihood, expressed as a percentage, that a particular event will or will not occur. If we believe that a particular event will occur seventy-five times out of one hundred, we can say that the probability of its occurring is 75 percent, or .75. Probabilities range in value from 0 (no chance of occurrence) to 1.00 (certain occurrence—also referred to as 100 percent). In the business world, there are few probabilities of either 0 or 1.00. Most probabilities that managers use are based on subjective judgment, intuition, and historical data.

The **expected value** of an alternative course of action is the sum of all possible values of outcomes from that action multiplied by their respective probabilities. Suppose, for example, that a venture capitalist is considering investing in a new company. If he believes there is a .40 probability of making $100,000, a .30 probability of making $30,000, and a .30 probability of losing $20,000, the expected value (*EV*) of this alternative is

$$EV = .40(100,000) + .30(30,000) + .30(-20,000)$$

$$EV = 40,000 + 9,000 - 6,000$$

$$EV = \$43,000$$

The investor can then weigh the expected value of this investment against the expected values of other available alternatives. The highest *EV* signals the investment that should most likely be selected.

For example, suppose another venture capitalist wants to invest $20,000 in a new business. She has identified three possible alternatives: a leisure products company, an energy enhancement company, and a food-producing company. Because the expected value of each alternative depends on short-run changes in the economy, especially inflation, she decides to develop a payoff matrix. She estimates that the probability of high inflation is .30 and the probability of low inflation is .70. She then estimates the probable returns for each investment in the event of both high and low inflation. Figure A.6 shows what the payoff matrix

payoff matrix A decision-making tool that specifies the probable value of different alternatives, depending on different possible outcomes associated with each

probability The likelihood, expressed as a percentage, that a particular event will or will not occur

expected value When applied to alternative courses of action, the sum of all possible values of outcomes from that action multiplied by their respective probabilities

Figure A.6

An Example of a Payoff Matrix

A payoff matrix helps the manager determine the expected value of different alternatives. A payoff matrix is effective only if the manager ensures that probability estimates are as accurate as possible.

		High inflation *(probability of .30)*	Low inflation *(probability of .70)*
Investment alternative **1**	Leisure products company	−$10,000	+$50,000
Investment alternative **2**	Energy enhancement company	+$90,000	−$15,000
Investment alternative **3**	Food-processing company	+$30,000	+$25,000

might look like (a minus sign indicates a loss). The expected value of investing in the leisure products company is

$$EV = .30(-10,000) + .70(50,000)$$

$$EV = -3,000 + 35,000$$

$$EV = \$32,000$$

Similarly, the expected value of investing in the energy enhancement company is

$$EV = .30(90,000) + .70(-15,000)$$

$$EV = 27,000 + (-10,500)$$

$$EV = \$16,500$$

And, finally, the expected value of investing in the food-processing company is

$$EV = .30(30,000) + .70(25,000)$$

$$EV = 9,000 + 17,500$$

$$EV = \$26,500$$

Investing in the leisure products company, then, has the highest expected value.

Other potential uses for payoff matrices include determining optimal order quantities, deciding whether to repair or replace broken machinery, and deciding which of several new products to introduce. Of course, the real key to using payoff matrices effectively is making accurate estimates of the relevant probabilities.

Decision Trees

decision tree A planning tool that extends the concept of a payoff matrix through a sequence of decisions

Decision trees are like payoff matrices because they enhance a manager's ability to evaluate alternatives by making use of expected values. However, they are most appropriate when there are several decisions to be made in sequence.

Figure A.7 illustrates a hypothetical decision tree. The small firm represented wants to begin exporting its products to a foreign market, but limited capacity re-

Figure A.7

An Example of a Decision Tree

A decision tree extends the basic concepts of a payoff matrix through multiple decisions. This tree shows the possible outcomes of two levels of decisions. The first decision is whether to expand to China or to France. The second decision, assuming that the company expands to China, is whether to increase shipments to China, build a plant close to China, or initiate shipping to France.

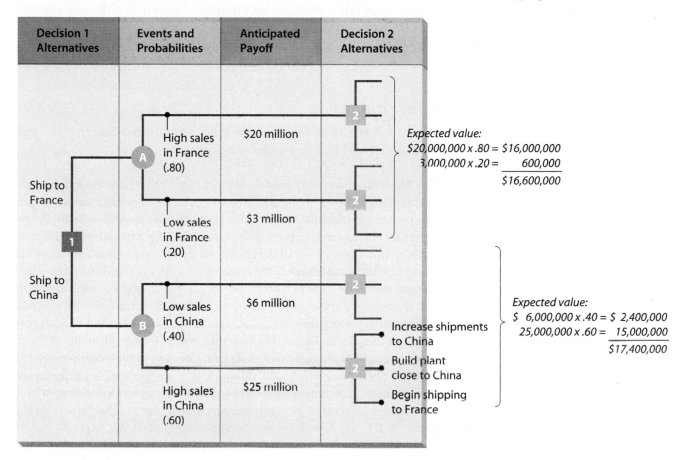

stricts it to only one market at first. Managers feel that either France or China would be the best place to start. Whichever alternative is selected, sales for the product in that country may turn out to be high or low. In France, there is a .80 chance of high sales and a .20 chance of low sales. The anticipated payoffs in these situations are predicted to be $20 million and $3 million, respectively. In China, the probabilities of high versus low sales are .60 and .40, respectively, and the associated payoffs are presumed to be $25 million and $6 million. As shown in Figure A.7, the expected value of shipping to France is $16,600,000, whereas the expected value of shipping to China is $17,400,000.

The astute reader will note that this part of the decision could have been set up as a payoff matrix. However, the value of decision trees is that we can extend the model to include subsequent decisions. Assume, for example, that the company begins shipping to China. If high sales do in fact materialize, the company will soon reach another decision situation. It might use the extra revenues to (1) increase shipments to China, (2) build a plant close to China and thus cut shipping costs, or (3) begin shipping to France. Various outcomes are possible for each decision, and each outcome will also have both a probability and an anticipated payoff. It is therefore possible to compute expected values back through several tiers of decisions all the way to the initial one. As it is with payoff matrices, determining probabilities accurately is the crucial element in the process. Properly used, however, decision trees can provide managers with a useful road map through complex decision situations.

Other Techniques

In addition to payoff matrices and decision trees, several other quantitative methods are also available to facilitate decision making.

inventory model A technique that helps managers decide how much inventory to maintain

Inventory Models   **Inventory models** are techniques that help the manager decide how much inventory to maintain. Target Stores uses inventory models to help determine how much merchandise to order, when to order it, and so forth. Inventory consists of both raw materials (inputs) and finished goods (outputs). Polaroid, for example, maintains a supply of the chemicals that it uses to make film, the cartons it packs film in, and packaged film ready to be shipped. For finished goods, both extremes are bad: excess inventory ties up capital, whereas a small inventory may result in shortages and customer dissatisfaction. The same holds for raw materials: too much inventory ties up capital, but if a company runs out of resources, work stoppages may occur. Finally, because the process of placing an order for raw materials and supplies has associated costs (such as clerical time, shipping expenses, and higher unit costs for small quantities), it is important to minimize the frequency of ordering. Inventory models help the manager make decisions that optimize the size of inventory. New innovations in inventory management such as **just-in-time**, or **JIT**, rely heavily on decision-making models. A JIT system involves scheduling materials to arrive in small batches as they are needed, thereby eliminating the need for a big reserve inventory, warehouse space, and so forth.[6]

just-in-time (JIT) An inventory management technique in which materials are scheduled to arrive in small batches as they are needed, eliminating the need for resources such as big reserves and warehouse space

queuing model A model used to optimize waiting lines in organizations

Queuing Models   **Queuing models** are intended to help organizations manage waiting lines. We are all familiar with such situations: shoppers waiting to pay for groceries at Kroger, drivers waiting to buy gas at an Exxon station, travelers calling American Airlines for reservations, and customers waiting for a teller at Citibank. Take the Kroger example. If a store manager has only one check-out stand in operation, the store's cost for check-out personnel is very low; however, many customers are upset by the long line that frequently develops. To solve the problem, the store manager could decide to keep twenty check-out stands open at all times. Customers would like the short waiting period, but personnel costs would be very high. A queuing model would be appropriate in this case to help the manager determine the optimal number of check-out stands: the number that would balance personnel costs and customer waiting time. Target Stores uses queuing models to determine how many check-out lanes to put in its retail stores.

Distribution Models   A decision facing many marketing managers relates to the distribution of the organization's products. Specifically, the manager must decide where the products should go and how to transport them. Railroads, trucking, and air freight have associated shipping costs, and each mode of transportation follows different schedules and routes. The problem is to identify the combination of routes that optimize distribution effectiveness and distribution costs. **Distribution models** help managers determine this optimal pattern of distribution.

Game Theory   **Game theory** was originally developed to predict the effect of one company's decisions on competitors. Models developed from game theory are intended to predict how a competitor will react to various activities that an organization might undertake, such as price changes, promotional changes, and the introduction of new products. If Wells Fargo Bank were considering raising its prime lending rate by 1 percent, it might use a game theory model to predict whether Citicorp would follow suit. If the model revealed that Citicorp would do so, Wells Fargo would probably proceed; otherwise, it would probably maintain the current interest rates. Unfortunately, game theory is not yet as useful as it was originally expected to be. The complexities of the real world combined with the limitation of the technique itself restrict its applicability. Game theory, however, does provide a useful conceptual framework for analyzing competitive behavior, and its usefulness may be improved in the future.

Artificial Intelligence   A fairly new addition to the manager's quantitative tool kit is **artificial intelligence (AI)**. The most useful form of AI is the expert system.[7] An expert system is essentially a computer program that attempts to duplicate the thought processes of experienced decision makers. For example, Hewlett-Packard has developed an expert system that checks sales orders for new computer systems and then designs preliminary layouts for those new systems. HP can now ship the computer to a customer in components for final assembly on site. This approach has enabled the company to cut back on its own final-assembly facilities.

distribution model A model used to determine the optimal pattern of distribution across different carriers and routes

game theory A planning tool used to predict how competitors will react to various activities that an organization might undertake

artificial intelligence (AI) A computer program that attempts to duplicate the thought processes of experienced decision makers

Strengths and Weaknesses of Planning Tools

Like all issues confronting management, planning tools of the type described here have several strengths and weaknesses.

Weaknesses and Problems

One weakness of the planning and decision-making tools discussed in this appendix is that they may not always adequately reflect reality. Even with the most sophisticated and powerful computer-assisted technique, reality must often be simplified. Many problems are also not amenable to quantitative analysis because important elements of them are intangible or nonquantifiable. Employee morale or satisfaction, for example, is often a major factor in managerial decisions.

The use of these tools and techniques may also be quite costly. For example, only larger companies can afford to develop their own econometric models. Even though the computer explosion has increased the availability of quantitative aids, some expense is still involved and it will take time for many of these techniques to become widely used. Resistance to change also limits the use of planning tools in some settings. If a manager for a retail chain has always based decisions for new locations on personal visits, observations, and intuition, she or he may be less than eager to begin using a computer-based model for evaluating and selecting sites. Finally, problems may arise when managers have to rely on technical specialists to use sophisticated models. Experts trained in the use of complex mathematical procedures may not understand or appreciate other aspects of management.

Strengths and Advantages

On the plus side, planning and decision-making tools offer many advantages. For situations that are amenable to quantification, they can bring sophisticated mathematical processes to bear on planning and decision making. Properly designed models and formulas also help decision makers "see reason." For example, a manager might not be inclined to introduce a new product line simply because she or he doesn't think it will be profitable. After seeing a forecast predicting first-year sales of one hundred thousand units coupled with a breakeven analysis showing profitability after only twenty thousand, however, the manager will probably change her or his mind. Thus, rational planning tools and techniques force the manager to look beyond personal prejudices and predispositions. Finally, the computer explosion is rapidly making sophisticated planning techniques available in a wider range of settings than ever before.

The crucial point to remember is that planning tools and techniques are a means to an end, not an end in themselves. Just as a carpenter uses a hand saw in some situations and an electric saw in others, a manager must recognize that a particular model may be useful in some situations but not in others that may call for a different approach. Knowing the difference is one mark of a good manager.

Summary of Key Points

Managers often use various tools and techniques as they develop plans and make decisions. Forecasting is one widely used method. Forecasting is the process of developing assumptions or premises about the future. Sales or revenue forecasting is especially important. Many organizations also rely heavily on technological forecasting. Time-series analysis and causal modeling are important forecasting techniques. Qualitative techniques are also widely used.

Managers also use other planning tools and techniques in different circumstances. Linear programming helps optimize resources and activities. Breakeven analysis helps identify how many products or services must be sold to cover costs. Simulations model reality. PERT helps plan how much time a project will require.

Other tools and techniques are useful for decision making. Constructing a payoff matrix, for example, helps a manager assess the expected value of different alternatives. Decision trees are used to extend expected values across multiple decisions. Other popular decision-making tools and techniques include inventory models, queuing models, distribution models, game theory, and artificial intelligence.

Various strengths and weaknesses are associated with each of these tools and techniques, as well as with their use by a manager. The key to success is knowing when each should and should not be used and knowing how to use and interpret the results that each provides.

APPENDIX NOTES

1. For a classic review, see John C. Chambers, S. K. Mullick, and D. Smith, "How to Choose the Right Forecasting Technique," *Harvard Business Review*, July–August 1971, pp. 45–74.
2. Charles Ostrom, *Time-Series Analysis: Regression Techniques* (Beverly Hills, Calif.: Sage Publications, 1980).
3. Fred Kerlinger and Elazar Pedhazur, *Multiple Regression in Behavioral Research* (New York: Holt, 1973).
4. Chambers, Mullick, and Smith, "How to Choose the Right Forecasting Technique"; see also J. Scott Armstrong, *Long-Range Forecasting: From Crystal Ball to Computers* (New York: Wiley, 1978).
5. Edward Hannan, Linda Ryan, and Richard Van Orden, "A Cost-Benefit Analysis of Prior Approvals for Medicaid Services in New York State," *Socio-Economic Planning Sciences*, 1984, Vol. 18, pp. 1–14.
6. Ramon L. Alonso and Cline W. Fraser, "JIT Hits Home: A Case Study in Reducing Management Delays," *Sloan Management Review*, Summer 1991, pp. 59–68.
7. Beau Sheil, "Thinking about Artificial Intelligence," *Harvard Business Review*, July–August 1987, pp. 91–97; and Dorothy Leonard-Barton and John J. Sviokla, "Putting Expert Systems to Work," *Harvard Business Review*, March–April 1988, pp. 91–98.

Photo Credits

Part One: pp. 2-3: Jason Fulford; *Chapter 1*: p. 5: ReutersNewMedia Inc./CORBIS; p. 7: Jonathon Saunders; p. 14: Jim Sulley/WirePix/The Image Works; p. 18: Michael Lewis; p. 26: Jean-François Campos/Agence VU. *Chapter 2*: p. 35: Carol Lundeen; p. 36: Susan Van Etten; p. 40: Corbis/Bettmann; p. 45: AT&T Archives; p. 52: Munshi Ahmed; p. 56: Mark Richards. *Part Two*: pp. 66-67: Juliana Thomas; *Chapter 3*: p. 69: Spencer Grant/PhotoEdit; p. 72: Radhika Chalasani/SIPA; p. 82: Olivier Laude; p. 85: AP/Wide World Photos; p. 89: Paxton. *Chapter 4*: p. 101: Galen Rowell/CORBIS; p. 104: Brian Coats; p. 111: AP/Wide World Photos; p. 117: Reuters/Emelio Guzman/Archive Photos; p. 121: Robert Wright. *Chapter 5*: p. 131: Fujifotos/The Image Works; p. 135: Ronnie Kamin/PhotoEdit; p. 141: Christopher Liu/China Stock; p. 145: © Ami Vitale/Newsmakers/Liaison Agency; p. 155: Morad Bouchakour/UNIT Creative Management. *Chapter 6*: p. 163: William Mercer McLeod; p. 165: Mark Richards; p. 166: Girl Ray; p. 172: Fergus Greer/ICON International; p. 183: AP/Wide World Photos. *Part Three*: pp. 192–193: Gail Albert Halaban/SABA; *Chapter 7*: p. 195: Tom Ulman/Liaison Agency; p. 202: Deborah Mesa-Pelly; p. 210: George Steinmetz; p. 214: Gerry Gropp; p. 216: Alex Tehrani. *Chapter 8*: p. 227: Leslie Hugh Stone/The Image Works; p. 229: Evan Kafka; p. 239: AP/Wide World Photos; p. 240: Rex Rystedt; p. 243: Mason Morfit. *Chapter 9*: p. 259: Carol Lundeen; p. 262: AP/Wide World Photos; p. 263: Reuters/Archive Photos; p. 269: Karen Kuehn/Matrix; p. 277: Andy Freeberg. *Chapter 10*: p. 287: David Grahm; p. 288: Lara Jo Regan/SABA Press; p. 291: Chris Usher/Corbis Sygma; p. 294: Republished with permission of Globe Newspaper Company, Inc. from the May 10, 2000 issue of *The Boston Globe* © 2000. Photo by David L. Ryan; p. 307: Gail Albert Halaban/SABA. *Part Four*: pp. 322–323: Robert Wright; *Chapter 11*: p. 325: © 2000 PhotoDisc, Inc. All rights reserved. p. 327: Eli Reichman; p. 336: Michael Newman/PhotoEdit; p. 341: Luc Choquer/Metis Images; p. 348: David Fields. *Chapter 12*: p. 355: AFP/Corbis; p. 356: Thomas Hart Shelby; p. 360: Mark Richards/PhotoEdit; p. 365: Gendolyn Cates; p. 376: Scott Goldsmith. *Chapter 13*: p. 385: Will Hart/PhotoEdit; p. 387: Richard Baker/IPG/Matrix; p. 391: Dana Smith/Black Star; p. 394: Steven Ahlgren; p. 402: AP/Wide World Photos. *Chapter 14*: p. 417: AP/Wide World Photos; p. 421: Steve Woit; p. 425: Erin Patrice O'Brien; p. 430: Greg Girard/Contact Press Images; p. 437: Sarah A. Friedman. *Part Five*: pp. 452–453: Kiho Park/Kistone; *Chapter 15*: p. 455: Mark Richards; p. 457: Michael K. Nichols/National Geographic Image Collection; p. 463: Reuters/Archive Photos; p. 474: Sarah A. Friedman; p. 479: Reuters/HO/Archive Photos. *Chapter 16*: p. 487: Kristine Larsen; p. 492: Andre Lambertson/SABA; p. 494: Mark Richards; p. 507: Kenneth Jarecke/Contact Press Images; p. 510: Pham. *Chapter 17*: p. 519: Mark Wilson/Newsmakers/Liaison Agency; p. 523: Dana Fineman/SYGMA; p. 527: Michael O'Neill/Corbis Outline; p. 534: Makoto Ishida; p. 541: Todd Warshaw/ICON Sports Media. *Chapter 18*: p. 553: © 2000 PhotoDisc, Inc. All rights reserved.; p. 555: Ken Martin/Impact Visuals; p. 557: Steven Ahlgren; p. 561: Olivier Laude/Liaison Agency; p. 567: John Wiltse. *Chapter 19*: p. 583: Courtesy of Fastener Supply Company; p. 586: Phillippe Diederich; p. 588: Liaison/Newsmakers/Online USA; p. 596 Will Panich/Courtesy of Baxter International; p. 602: Reuters NewMedia, Inc./Corbis *Part Six*: pp. 612–613: Chack Savage/CORBIS Stock Market; *Chapter 20*: p. 615: © 2000 PhotoDisc, Inc. All rights reserved; p. 618:

Name Index

Organization and Product Index

Subject Index

Presenting the Latest **Hot Topics**